D1415233

ACCOUNTING
INFORMATION
SYSTEMS

JAMES A. HALL

Department of Business
College of Business and Economics
Lehigh University

South-Western College Publishing
Thomson Learning™

Australia • Canada • Mexico • Singapore • Spain • United Kingdom • United States

3RD
EDITION

Accounting Information Systems, 3e
by James A. Hall

Publisher: Dave Shaut
Acquisitions Editor: Rochelle Kronzek
Developmental Editor: Leslie Kauffman, Litten Editing and Production, Inc.
Marketing Manager: Jennifer Codner
Production Editor: Kara ZumBahlen
Media Production Editor: Lora Craver
Manufacturing Coordinator: Doug Wilke
Internal Design: Kim Rokusek, rokusek design, Quincy, IL
Cover Design: Paul Neff Design, Cincinnati
Cover Image: ©PhotoDisc, Inc.
Production House: Cover to Cover Publishing, Inc.
Compositor: Janet Sprowls, Cover to Cover Publishing, Inc.
Printer: West Group

COPYRIGHT ©2001 by South-Western College Publishing, a division of Thomson Learning. The Thomson Learning logo is a registered trademark used herein under license.

All Rights Reserved. No part of this work covered by the copyright hereon may be reproduced or used in any form or by any means—graphic, electronic, or mechanical, including photocopying, recording, taping, or information storage and retrieval systems—without the written permission of the publisher.

Printed in the United States of America
2 3 4 5   03 02 01

For more information contact South-Western College Publishing, 5101 Madison Road, Cincinnati, Ohio, 45227 or find us on the Internet at
http://www.swcollege.com

For permission to use material from this text or product, contact us by
• **telephone: 1-800-730-2214**
• **fax: 1-800-730-2215**
• **web: http://www.thomsonrights.com**

Library of Congress Cataloging-in-Publication Data

Hall, James A.,
    Accounting information systems / James A. Hall.--3rd ed.
        p. cm.
    Includes index.
    ISBN 0-324-02639-0 (Package, text with booklet)
    ISBN 0-324-07089-6 (Text only)
    ISBN 0-324-07090-X (Booklet only)
      1. Information storage and retrieval systems--Accounting. 2. Accounting--Data processing. I. Title.

    HF5679 .H26 2000
    657'.0285'574--dc21

                                                                00-032200

This book is printed on acid-free paper.

BRIEF TABLE OF CONTENTS

TABLE OF CONTENTS

PREFACE

Among accounting courses, accounting information systems (AIS) courses tend to be the least standardized. Often the objectives, background, and orientation of the instructor, rather than adherence to a standard body of knowledge, determines the direction the AIS course takes. This textbook covers a full range of AIS topics to provide instructors with flexibility in setting the direction and intensity for their courses. At the same time, for those who desire a structured model, the first nine chapters of the text along with the chapters on electronic commerce and computer controls provide what has proven to be a successful template for developing an AIS course.

Earlier editions of this book have been used successfully in introductory, advanced, and graduate-level AIS courses. Throughout the book, AIS topics are presented from the accountant's perspective as an end user, designer, and auditor of information systems. While the book was written primarily to meet the needs of accounting majors about to enter the modern business world, it is an effective text for general business and industrial engineering students who seek a thorough understanding of AIS as part of their professional education.

KEY FEATURES

CONCEPTUAL FRAMEWORK

This book employs a conceptual framework to emphasize the professional and legal responsibility of accountants, auditors, and management for the design, operation, and control of AIS applications. This responsibility pertains to business events that are narrowly defined as financial transactions. Systems that process nonfinancial transactions are not subject to the same standards of design, operation, and control. Supporting the information needs of all users in a modern organization, however, requires systems that integrate both accounting and nonaccounting functions. While providing the organization with unquestioned benefit, a potential consequence of such integration is a loss of control due to the blurring of the lines that traditionally separate AIS from non-AIS functions. The conceptual framework presented in this book distinguishes traditional AIS applications and promotes recognition of this important domain of responsibility.

EVOLUTIONARY APPROACH

Over the past fifty years, accounting information systems have been represented by a number of different approaches or models. Each new model evolved because of the shortcomings and limitations of its predecessor. An interesting feature in this evolution is that older models are not immediately replaced by the newest technique. Thus, at any point in time, various generations of systems exist across different organizations and may even coexist within a single enterprise. The modern accountant needs to be familiar with the operational characteristics of all AIS approaches that he or she is likely to encounter. This book deals extensively with five such models that include both traditional and state-of-the-art systems: manual processes; flat file systems; the database approach; the resources, events, and agents (REA) model; and enterprise resource planning (ERP) systems.

**EMPHASIS ON
INTERNAL
CONTROLS**

The book presents a conceptual model for internal control based on *Statement on Auditing Standards (SAS) No. 78*. This model is used to discuss control issues for both manual processes and computer-based information systems (CBIS). Two chapters are devoted to the control of CBIS. Special emphasis is given to the following areas: computer operating systems, database management systems, electronic data interchange (EDI), electronic commerce systems, ERP systems, the systems development and maintenance process, the organization of the computer function, the security of data processing centers, and computer applications.

**EXPOSURE
TO SYSTEMS
DESIGN AND
DOCUMENTATION
TOOLS**

The book examines various approaches and methodologies used in systems analysis and design, including structured design, computer-aided software engineering, and prototyping. In conjunction with these general approaches, professional systems analysts and programmers use a number of documentation techniques to specify the key features of systems. Accountants and auditors often work closely with systems professionals during systems design and must learn to communicate in their language. The book deals extensively with such documentation techniques as data flow and entity relationship diagrams, as well as systems, program, and document flowcharts. The book contains numerous cases and assignments designed to develop the students' competency with these tools.

SIGNIFICANT CHANGES IN THE THIRD EDITION

**CHANGES TO TEXT
ORGANIZATION**

The third edition incorporates a number of changes to chapter organization. Some material has been expanded upon. To make room for three new chapters, some material has been contracted and some dropped. The main changes are outlined below.

- The treatment of the expenditure cycle has been expanded to two chapters. Chapter 5 deals with procurement and cash disbursement systems. Chapter 6 covers payroll and fixed asset systems.
- Chapter 8 combines both financial reporting and management reporting systems, which had been the topics of two separate chapters in the second edition. This coupling within Chapter 8 permits better integration of material pertaining to discretionary and nondiscretionary reporting issues.
- Chapter 10 is a new chapter that presents the REA model. REA is an alternative accounting framework for modeling an organization's critical resources, events, and agents (REA) and the relationships between them. Once adopted, both accounting and nonaccounting data about these phenomena can be identified, captured, and stored in a centralized database.
- Chapter 11 is another new chapter that deals with enterprise resource planning (ERP) systems. ERP systems are commercial software packages that evolved primarily from traditional manufacturing resource planning (MRP II) systems. The objective of ERP is to integrate key processes of the organization such as order entry, manufacturing, procurement and accounts payable, payroll, human resources, and more. Implementing ERP is an undertaking of massive proportions that raises a number of behavioral, operational, risk, and control issues of importance to accountants.

    Accompanying this text is an instruction booklet that allows the students to gain access to SAP's IDES system. IDES is a Web-based educational application of SAP's R/3 system. R/3 is the leading ERP product on the market. On-line instructions, also provided, guide students as they complete various R/3 assignments that are contained in the end-of-chapter material.

● Chapter 12 is a third new chapter that explores key operational and accounting issues pertaining to electronic commerce. The chapter addresses many diverse topics, including the electronic buying and selling of goods and services, on-line delivery of digital products, electronic data interchange (EDI), electronic funds transfer (EFT), and Internet-based systems including both business-to-consumer and business-to-business systems. The chapter addresses important topics related to the control of electronic commerce, including firewalls, cryptography, digital signatures, and more.

● The appendix containing comprehensive case studies has been removed from the book and placed on the Web site at http://hall.swcollege.com. Two new term project cases have been added to this material. These cases are also repeated in the *Instructor's Manual*.

CHANGES TO CONTENT

The end-of-chapter problems have been significantly revised. All of the internal control cases in the revenue and expenditure cycle chapters have been replaced with new cases.

Chapter 1—The Information System: An Accountant's Perspective
An evolutionary model is introduced that traces systems development through several key stages. This model provides the framework for integrating material in the remaining chapters.

Chapter 2—Introduction to Transaction Processing
Flat file structures that were previously covered in Chapter 9 are now presented in Chapter 2. This move is consistent with the evolutionary model mentioned above and allows a more focused treatment of relational databases covered in Chapter 9.

Chapter 3—Ethics, Fraud, and Internal Control
The discussion of fraud has been updated to include the results of a research study conducted by the Association of Certified Fraud Examiners.

Chapters 4, 5, and 6—The Revenue and Expenditure Cycles
The basic approach to the revenue and expenditure cycle material has remained unchanged. The expenditure cycle treatment, however, has been expanded to Chapters 5 and 6. Chapter 6 now includes the fixed asset system.

Chapter 8—General Ledger, Financial Reporting, and Management Reporting Systems
This chapter combines and integrates material that was previously presented in separate chapters.

Chapter 9—Database Management Systems
This chapter has been revised to emphasize the relational database model. Material pertaining to hierarchical and network models has been moved to the appendix.

Chapter 10—The REA Approach to Business Process Modeling
The discussion of the REA model builds on the database material presented in Chapter 9. REA data modeling is discussed and reconciled with traditional data modeling techniques.

Chapter 11—Enterprise Resource Planning Systems

This new chapter presents a number of issues related to ERP systems, data warehouse systems, and data mining techniques. As mentioned previously, the chapter provides a number of hands-on exercises based on SAP through Internet access to SAP's R/3 IDES site.

Chapter 12—Electronic Commerce Systems

This new chapter deals with a number of e-commerce topics that were outlined above.

Chapters 13 and 14—The Systems Development Process, Parts I and II

Three chapters were devoted to the systems development life cycle in the second edition. This material has been reorganized into two, more streamlined, chapters for the third edition. This was accomplished through careful trimming and by moving certain topics such as database design into earlier chapters.

Chapters 15 and 16—Controlling Computer-Based Information Systems, Parts I and II

These chapters have been revised and updated to deal with a numbers of issues pertaining to operating systems security and control over electronic commerce.

Chapter 17—Information Systems Auditing and Assurance

This chapter has been updated to address issues related to the emerging field of assurance. The treatment of IS auditing has been better reconciled to classical management assertions and the development of audit objectives. Two areas of significant revision are audit procedures related to operating systems and electronic commerce.

ORGANIZATION AND CONTENT

PART 1: OVERVIEW OF ACCOUNTING INFORMATION SYSTEMS

Chapter 1, The Information System: An Accountant's Perspective

This chapter places the subject of accounting information systems in perspective for accountants. It is divided into four major sections, each dealing with a different aspect of information systems. The first section explores the information environment of the firm. It introduces basic systems concepts, identifies the types of information used in business, and describes the flows of information through an enterprise. This section also presents a framework for viewing accounting information systems in relation to other information systems components. The second section of the chapter deals with the impact of organizational structure on AIS. The centralized and distributed models are used to illustrate extreme cases in point. The third section reviews the evolution of information systems models. Accounting information systems have been represented by a number of different approaches or models. Five dominant models are examined: manual processes; flat file systems; the database approach; the resources, events, agents (REA) model; and enterprise resource planning (ERP) systems. The final section discusses the role of accountants as users, designers, and auditors of AIS. The nature of the responsibilities shared by accountants and computer professionals for developing AIS applications are examined.

Chapter 2, Introduction to Transaction Processing

The second chapter expands on the subject of transaction cycles introduced in Chapter 1. While the operational details of specific transaction cycles are covered in subsequent chapters, this chapter presents material that is common to all cycles. Topics covered include the relationship between source documents, journals, ledgers, and financial statements in both manual and computer-based systems; system documentation techniques, such as data flow diagrams, entity relationship (ER) diagrams, document systems, and program flowcharts; and data processing techniques, including batch systems with sequential files, batch systems with direct access files, and real-time systems. The techniques and approaches presented in this chapter are applied to specific business cycle applications in later chapters. The chapter is supported by material located on the Web site that provides a review of basic computer technology.

Chapter 3, Ethics, Fraud, and Internal Control

Chapter 3 deals with the related topics of ethics, fraud, and internal control. The chapter first examines ethical issues related to business and specifically to computer systems. The questions raised are intended to stimulate class discussions.

The chapter then addresses the subject of fraud. There is perhaps no area of greater controversy for accountants than their responsibility to detect fraud. Part of the problem stems from confusion about what constitutes fraud. This section distinguishes between management fraud and employee fraud. The chapter presents techniques for identifying unethical and dishonest management and for assessing the risk of management fraud. Employee fraud can be prevented and detected by a system of internal controls. The section discusses several fraud techniques that have been perpetrated in both manual and computer-based environments. The results of a research study conducted by the Association of Certified Fraud Examiners are presented.

The final section of the chapter describes the internal control structure and control activities specified in SAS 78. The control concepts discussed in this chapter are applied to specific applications in chapters that follow.

PART 2:
TRANSACTION
CYCLES AND
BUSINESS
PROCESSES

Chapters 4, 5, and 6, The Revenue and Expenditure Cycles

The approach taken in all three chapters is similar. First, the business cycle is reviewed conceptually using data flow diagrams to present key features of each major subsystem. Then the subsystems are examined in detail within the context of a manual environment. Taking this approach promotes the students' understanding of key activities, data requirements, and the critical segregation of duties that pertain to the business cycle. Each system is then reexamined using alternative technology assumptions. First, an automated batch system with sequential files is presented; then the changes brought about by using direct access files are examined. Finally, each system is reengineered to incorporate real-time technology.

At each technology juncture, the effects on procedures, operational efficiency, and internal controls are examined. This approach provides the student with a solid understanding of the business tasks in each cycle and an awareness of how different technologies influence changes in the operation and control of the systems.

Chapter 7, The Conversion Cycle

Manufacturing systems represent a dynamic aspect of AIS. Chapter 7 describes several manufacturing environments, including traditional mass production (batch) processing, just-in-time production systems, and computer-integrated manufacturing. These environments are driven by such information technologies as materials requirements planning (MRP) and manufacturing resources planning (MRP II). The chapter addresses the shortcomings of traditional accounting models and the advantages of activity-based accounting (ABC) in assessing value-added business activities.

Chapter 8, General Ledger, Financial Reporting, and Management Reporting Systems

Chapter 8 examines the objectives, operational features, and control issues of three related systems: the general ledger system (GLS), the financial reporting system (FRS), and the management reporting system (MRS). The emphasis is on operational controls and the use of advanced computer technology to enhance efficiency in each of these systems. The chapter distinguishes between the MRS and the FRS in two key respects. First, the general ledger is the primary data source for the FRS. The MRS, on the other hand, draws upon financial and nonfinancial data from operations as well as traditional general ledger data. The second distinction is that the financial reporting performed by the FRS is mandatory, while MRS applications are discretionary. Neither the applications themselves nor the content, timing, or format of the information they produce are mandated by authoritative bodies such as the IRS, SEC, or AICPA. Organization management implements MRS applications at its discretion based on its need for information. The chapter examines a number of factors that influence and shape management information needs. These include the decision-making process, management principles, decision type and management level, problem structure, reports and reporting methods, responsibility reporting, and behavioral issues pertaining to reporting.

PART 3: ADVANCED TECHNOLOGIES IN ACCOUNTING INFORMATION SYSTEMS

Chapter 9, Database Management Systems

Chapter 9 deals with the design and management of an organization's data resources. It begins by demonstrating how problems associated with traditional flat file systems are resolved under the database approach. The second section describes in detail the functions and relationship among four primary elements of the database environment: the users, the database management system (DBMS), the database administrator (DBA), and the physical database. The third section is devoted to an in-depth explanation of the characteristics of the relational model. A number of database design topics are covered, including data modeling, deriving relational tables from ER diagrams, the creation of user views, and data normalization techniques. The fourth section concludes the chapter with a discussion of distributed database issues. It examines three possible database configurations in a distributed environment: centralized, partitioned, and replicated databases.

Chapter 10, The REA Approach to Business Process Modeling

Chapter 10 presents the REA model as a means of specifying and designing accounting information systems that serve the needs of all users within an organization. The chapter is comprised of three major sections. The first introduces the REA approach and describes how it overcomes a number of problems associated with traditional accounting practice. The second section examines traditional database applications and their limitations. Although superior to flat file systems, traditional database systems suffer from serious problems that limit their usefulness. A limitation of particular importance is their almost exclusive support of financial information users and their inadequacy at meeting the growing need for nonfinancial information. A second problem is their inability to respond to noneconomic events that may be of extreme importance to an organization. The third section provides a detailed review of the steps involved in developing an REA model. This approach is then compared to the traditional ER approach to modeling business processes.

Chapter 11, Enterprise Resource Planning Systems

This chapter presents a number of issues related to the implementation of enterprise resource planning (ERP) systems. It is comprised of five major sections. The first outlines the key features of a generic ERP system by comparing the function and data storage techniques of a traditional flat file or database system to that of an ERP. The second section describes various ERP configurations related to servers, databases, and bolt-on software. Data warehousing is the topic of the third section. A data warehouse is a relational or multidimensional database that supports on-line analytical processing (OLAP). A number of issues are discussed, including data modeling, data extraction from operational databases, data cleansing, data transformation, and loading data into the warehouse. The fourth section examines risks associated with ERP implementation. These include "big bang" issues, opposition to change within the organization, choosing the wrong ERP model, choosing the wrong consultant, cost overrun issues, and disruptions to operations. The fifth section reviews several control and auditing issues related to ERPs. The discussion follows the SAS 78 framework. The chapter appendix provides a review of the leading ERP software products including SAP, Oracle, PeopleSoft, J. D. Edwards, and BAAN.

Chapter 12, Electronic Commerce Systems

Driven by the Internet revolution, electronic commerce is dramatically expanding and undergoing radical changes. While electronic commerce promises enormous opportunities for consumers and businesses, its effective implementation and control are urgent challenges facing organization management and accountants. To properly evaluate the potential exposures and risks in this environment, the modern accountant must be familiar with the technologies and techniques that underlie electronic commerce. This chapter deals with three aspects of electronic commerce: (1) the intraorganizational usage of networks to support distributed data processing, (2) traditional business-to-business transactions conducted via EDI systems, and (3) Internet-based commerce including business-to-consumer and business-to-business relationships. The chapter examines the technologies, topologies, and applications of electronic commerce in the three areas. It presents the risks associated with electronic commerce, reviews security and assurance techniques used to reduce risk and promote trust, and concludes with a discussion of electronic commerce's implications for the accounting profession.

PART 4: SYSTEMS DEVELOPMENT ACTIVITIES

Chapters 13 and 14, The Systems Development Process, Parts I and II

These chapters examine the accountant's role in the systems development process. Chapter 13 deals with the tasks of systems planning and systems analysis. It reviews the commercial software and in-house systems development options available to organizations. The chapter examines automated techniques to improve the systems development process such as prototyping and computer-aided software engineering (CASE). It examines conceptual design issues and outlines the basic features of both the structured and object-oriented approaches to systems design. Chapter 14 covers issues related to systems selection, detailed systems design, and systems implementation. Topics include the design of a feasibility study, cost-benefit analysis, the development of structure diagrams from data flow diagrams, and software development. Broader issues pertaining to planning system implementation are also examined.

Several comprehensive cases designed to serve as team-based systems development projects are available from the Web site. These cases have been used effectively by groups of three or four students working as a design team. Each case has sufficient details to allow analysis of user needs, preparation of a conceptual solution, and the development of a detailed design, including user views (input and output), processes, and databases.

PART 5:
COMPUTER
CONTROLS AND
AUDITING

Chapters 15 and 16, Controlling Computer-Based Information Systems, Parts I and II

The introduction of computer technology restructures traditional business processes and requires unique internal control techniques that address new forms of exposures. Computer control issues are raised and discussed conceptually throughout the text. However, due to the need for an integrating framework that incorporates many different aspects of the computer environment, specific computer control techniques and procedures are treated separately after all the relevant technology topics have been examined. The control framework for addressing these exposures identifies ten classes of controls. Chapter 15 discusses controls for operating systems, data management systems, organizational structure of the computer function, systems development activities, systems maintenance procedures, and the operation of the computer center. Chapter 16 deals with Internet and Intranet controls, electronic data interchange controls, personal computer controls, and controlling application programs.

Chapter 17, Information Systems Auditing and Assurance

The proliferation of computer-based information systems has had a tremendous impact on the field of auditing. Computer technology has engendered the need for new auditing techniques for evaluating AIS internal controls and for verifying the accuracy of the data produced by accounting systems. This chapter begins by drawing a distinction between the auditor's traditional attestation function and the emerging field of assurance services, both of which may involve similar audit tests discussed in the chapter. The auditing topics covered build directly on the control material presented in Chapters 15 and 16. The following topics are discussed at length: assessing the control structure of the firm, the components of audit risk, and the relationship between audit objectives and tests of internal controls. The chapter presents five computer-assisted audit tools and techniques (CAATT) approaches for testing application controls: the test data method, base case system evaluation, tracing, integrated test facility, and parallel simulation.

SUPPLEMENTS

SOFTWARE

Integrated Accounting for Accounting Information Systems, by Dale Klooster and Warren Allen, is a completely functioning Windows-based accounting system that performs the following tasks: sales order processing, cash receipts, billing, accounts payable, cash disbursements, payroll, fixed asset accounting, general ledger processing, and financial reporting. The system uses a combination of real-time and batch processing techniques. It has an extensive on-line help feature. *Integrated Accounting for Accounting Information Systems* modules relate specifically to material covered in Chapters 4, 5, 6, and 8, and includes operating instructions and homework problems that test students' knowledge and exposes them to a realistic accounting system.

Building Accounting Systems Using Access 7.0, 2/e, by James Perry and Gary Schneider, leads students through the creation of database tables, forms, queries, and reports for each major transaction cycle. This text and CD-ROM combination help students understand how relational databases are constructed and used in accounting systems.

INTERNET COVERAGE

Additional teaching and learning resources, including PowerPoint slides, student study notes, and cases on internal control and systems development will be available for Internet delivery. Visit the Web site at: http://hall.swcollege.com to access these resources.

INSTRUCTOR'S MANUAL

The instructor's manual, by Margarita Lenk of Colorado State University, was written with the first-time instructor in mind. The manual contains lecture notes for each chapter and also suggests which parts of the chapter to cover in class and which to leave to the students for independent study. The manual also includes a helpful assignment grid indicating subject content and degree of difficulty of each exercise. Additional comprehensive cases are included, as well as two new term project cases. Selected figures from the chapters are provided in the back of the manual as overhead transparency masters.

POWERPOINT SLIDES

The PowerPoint slides, prepared by Patrick Wheeler of University of South Florida, provide colorful lecture outlines of each chapter of the text.

TEST BANK

The test bank, prepared by Helen Savage of Youngstown State University, has been revised and expanded and contains true/false, multiple-choice, short answer, and essay questions. It is available in both print and computerized versions.

SOLUTIONS MANUAL

The solutions manual, written by James A. Hall of Lehigh University, contains solutions to all end-of-chapter problems and cases.

ACKNOWLEDGMENTS

I want to thank the Institute of Internal Auditors, Inc., and the Institute of Certified Management Accountants for permission to use problem materials from past examinations. I am grateful to Dr. Helen Savage for her work on the test bank and student study notes, Professor Margarita Lenk for preparing the instructor's manual, and

Professor Patrick Wheeler for preparing the PowerPoint slides. I would also like to thank Professor Alan Sangster for co-authoring Chapter 10 of this text.

My thanks also to the following people for reviewing the book in various stages of its production and for providing helpful input:

Timothy D. Cairney
Florida Atlantic University

C. Janie Chang
San Jose State University

Bill Cummings
Northern Illinois University

David R. Fordham
James Madison University

Gary G. Johnson
Southeast Missouri State University

Ron Kucic
University of Denver

Leslie R. Porter
University of Southern California

Robin Potson
Michigan State University

Robert E. Rosacker
University of South Dakota

Helen M. Savage
Youngstown State University

Ed Scribner
New Mexico State University

Jerry D. Siebel
University of South Florida

Kenton Walker
University of Wyoming

James A. Hall
Lehigh University

DEDICATION

To my wife Eileen, and my children
Elizabeth and Katie

PART 1

OVERVIEW OF ACCOUNTING INFORMATION SYSTEMS

CHAPTER

1

The Information System:
An Accountant's Perspective

Unlike many other accounting subjects, information systems (IS) does not have a well-defined body of knowledge about which there is general agreement; there are many diverse opinions as to what IS is and what it is not. This book focuses on a specialized subset of information systems—**accounting information systems (AIS)**. AIS applications are distinguished from other information systems applications by the legal and professional obligations they impose on an organization's management and accountants. The proper discharge of these responsibilities requires a precise understanding of the objectives and functions of AIS.

The purpose of this chapter is to place the subject of accounting information systems in perspective for accountants. Toward this end, the chapter is divided into four major sections, each dealing with a different aspect of information systems. The first section explores the information environment of the firm. It introduces basic systems concepts, identifies the types of information used in business, and describes the flows of information through an organization. This section also presents a framework for viewing accounting information systems in relation to other information systems components. The discussion centers on the need for accountants to distinguish clearly between financial and nonfinancial transactions. The second section of the chapter deals with the impact of organizational structure on AIS. Here we examine the business organization as a system of functional areas. The accounting function plays an important role as the purveyor of financial information for the rest of the organization. The third section reviews the evolution of information systems models. Accounting information systems have been represented by a number of different approaches or models. Five models are examined: manual processes, flat-file systems, the database approach, the REA (resources, events, and agents) model, and ERP (enterprise resource planning) systems. The final section discusses the role of accountants as users, designers, and auditors of AIS. In particular, we examine the nature of the responsibilities shared by accountants and computer professionals for developing AIS applications.

LEARNING OBJECTIVES

After studying this chapter, you should:

- Understand the primary information flows within the business environment.
- Understand the difference between accounting information systems and management information systems.
- Understand the difference between a financial transaction and a nonfinancial transaction.
- Be able to distinguish between information and data.
- Know the three fundamental objectives of all information systems.
- Know the principal features of the general model for information systems.
- Be familiar with the functional areas of a business and their principal activities.
- Recognize the need for functional independence between accounting and other business areas.
- Know the basic differences between the centralized and distributed approaches to data processing.
- Understand the stages in the evolution of information systems.
- Understand the relationship between external auditing, internal auditing, and IT auditing.

THE INFORMATION ENVIRONMENT

We begin the study of AIS with the recognition that information is a business resource. Like the other business resources of raw materials, capital, and labor, information is vital to the survival of the contemporary business organization. Every business day, vast quantities of information flow to decision makers and other users to meet a variety of internal needs. In addition, information flows out of the organization to external users, such as customers, suppliers, and stakeholders who have an interest in the firm. Figure 1–1 presents an overview of these internal and external **information flows**.

The pyramid in Figure 1–1 shows the business organization divided horizontally into several levels of activity. Business operations form the base of the pyramid. These activities consist of the product-oriented work of the organization, such as manufacturing, sales, and distribution. Above the base level, the organization is divided into three management tiers: operations management, middle management, and top management. Operations management is directly responsible for controlling day-to-day operations. Middle management is accountable for the short-term planning and coordination of activities necessary to accomplish organizational objectives. Top management is responsible for longer-term planning and setting organizational objectives. Every individual in the organization, from business operations to top management, needs information to accomplish his or her tasks.

Notice in Figure 1–1 how information flows in two directions within the organization: horizontally and vertically. The horizontal flow supports operations-level tasks with highly detailed information about the many business transactions affecting the firm. This includes information on such events as the sale and shipment of goods, the use of labor and materials in the production process, and internal transfers of re-

FIGURE 1–1

Internal and External
Flows of Information

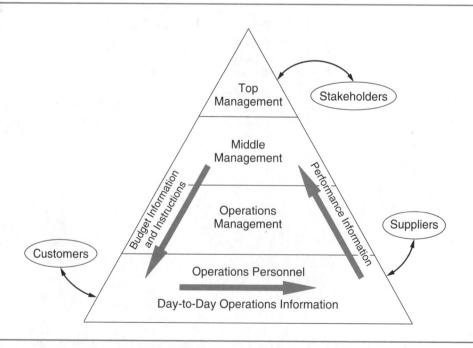

sources from one department to another. The vertical flow distributes summarized information about operations and other activities upward to managers at all levels. Management uses this information to support its various planning and control functions. Information also flows downward from senior managers to junior managers and operations personnel in the form of instructions, quotas, and budgets.

A third flow of information depicted in Figure 1–1 represents exchanges between the organization and users in the external environment. External users fall into two groups: **trading partners** and **stakeholders**. Exchanges with trading partners include customer sales and billing information, purchase information for suppliers, and inventory receipts information. Stakeholders are entities outside (or inside) the organization with a direct or indirect interest in the firm. Stockholders, financial institutions, and government agencies are examples of external stakeholders. Information exchanges with these groups include financial statements, tax returns, and stock transaction information. Inside stakeholders include accountants and internal auditors.

All user groups have unique information requirements. The level of detail and the nature of the information they receive differ considerably. For example, managers cannot use the highly detailed information needed by operations personnel. Management information is more summarized and oriented toward reporting on overall performance and problems rather than routine operations. The information must identify potential problems in time for management to take corrective action. External stakeholders, on the other hand, require information very different from that of management and operations users. Their financial statement information, based on generally accepted accounting principles, is accrual-based and far too aggregated for most internal uses.

WHAT IS A SYSTEM?

For many, the term **system** generates mental images of computers and programming. In fact, the term has much broader applicability. Some systems are naturally occurring, while others are artificial. Natural systems range from the atom—a system of electrons, protons, and neutrons—to the universe—a system of galaxies, stars, and planets. All life forms, plant and animal, are examples of natural systems. Artificial systems are man-made. These systems include everything from clocks to submarines and social systems to information systems.

Elements of a System

Regardless of their origin, all systems possess some common elements. The following definition specifies:

> A system is a group of two or more interrelated components or subsystems that serve a common purpose.

Let's analyze this general definition to gain an understanding of how it applies to businesses and information systems.

Multiple Components. A system must contain more than one part. For example, a yo-yo carved from a single piece of wood and attached to a string is a system. Without the string, it is not a system.

Relatedness. A common purpose relates the multiple parts of the system. Although each part functions independently of the others, all parts serve a common objective. If a particular component does not contribute to the common goal, then it is not part of the system. For instance, a pair of ice skates and a volleyball net are both components. However, they lack a common purpose and thus do not form a system.

System Versus Subsystem. The distinction between the terms *system* and *subsystem* is a matter of perspective. For our purposes, these terms are interchangeable. A system is called a **subsystem** when it is viewed in relation to the larger system of which it is a part. Likewise, a subsystem is called a system when it is the focus of attention. Animals, plants, and other life forms are systems. They are also subsystems of the ecosystem in which they exist. From a different perspective, animals are systems composed of many smaller subsystems, such as the circulatory subsystem and the respiratory subsystem.

Purpose. A system must serve at least one purpose, but it may serve several. Whether a system provides a measure of time, electrical power, or information, serving a purpose is its fundamental justification. When a system ceases to serve a purpose, it should be replaced.

An Example of an Artificial System

An automobile is an example of an artificial system that is familiar to most of us and that satisfies the definition of a system provided above. To simplify matters, let's assume that the automobile system serves only one purpose: providing conveyance. To do so requires the harmonious interaction of hundreds or even thousands of subsystems. For simplicity, Figure 1–2 depicts only a few of these.

FIGURE 1–2

Primary Subsystems of an Automobile

Primary Subsystems of an Automobile

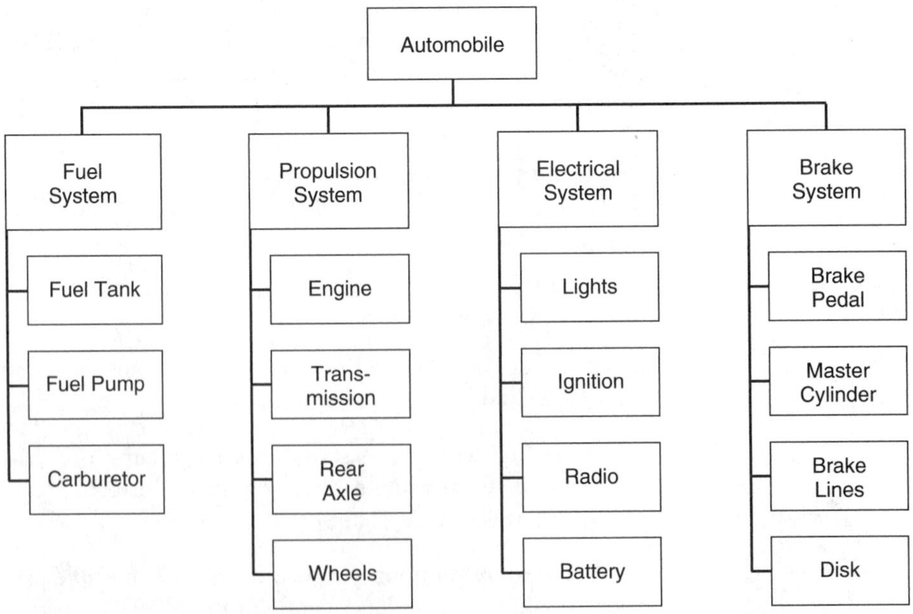

Figure 1–2 illustrates two points of particular importance to the study of information systems: system decomposition and subsystem interdependency.

System Decomposition. Decomposition is the process of dividing the system into smaller subsystem parts. This is a convenient way of representing, viewing, and understanding the relationships among subsystems. By decomposing a system, we can present the overall system as a hierarchy and view the relationships between subordinate and higher-level subsystems. Each subordinate subsystem performs one or more specific functions to help achieve the overall objective of the higher-level system. Figure 1–2 shows an automobile decomposed into four primary subsystems: the fuel subsystem, the propulsion subsystem, the electrical subsystem, and the braking subsystem. Each contributes in a unique way to the system's objective, conveyance. These second-level subsystems are decomposed further into two or more subordinate subsystems at a third level. Each third-level subsystem performs a task in direct support of its second-level system.

Subsystem Interdependency. A system's ability to achieve its goal depends upon the effective functioning and harmonious interaction of its subsystems. If a vital subsystem fails or becomes defective and can no longer meet its specific objective, the overall system will fail to meet its objective. For example, if the fuel pump (a vital subsystem of the fuel system) fails, then the fuel system fails to meet its objective. With the failure of the fuel system (a vital subsystem of the automobile), the entire system fails. On the other hand, when a non-vital system fails, the primary objective can still be met. For instance, if the radio (a subsystem of the electrical system) fails, the automobile can still convey passengers.

Designers of all types of systems must recognize the consequences of subsystem failure and provide the appropriate level of control. For example, a systems designer may provide control by designing a backup (redundant) system that comes into play when the primary system fails. Control should be provided on a cost-benefit basis. It is neither economical nor necessary to back up every subsystem. However, backup is essential when excessive negative consequences result from a subsystem failure. Hence, virtually every modern automobile has a backup braking system, whereas very few have a backup stereo system.

Like automobile designers, information system designers must identify critical subsystems, anticipate the cost of their failure, and design cost-effective control procedures. As we shall see in subsequent chapters, accountants feature very prominently in this task.

A Framework for Information Systems

The **information system** is the set of formal procedures by which data are collected, processed into information, and distributed to users.

Figure 1–3 shows the information system of a manufacturing firm decomposed into its elemental subsystems. Notice that two broad classes of systems emerge from the decomposition: the *accounting information system (AIS)* and the *management information system (MIS)*. We will use this framework to identify the domain of AIS and to distinguish it from that of MIS. It should be stressed that Figure 1–3 is a conceptual view. A physical information system is not likely to be organized into such discrete packages. More often, MIS and AIS applications will be integrated to achieve operational efficiency.

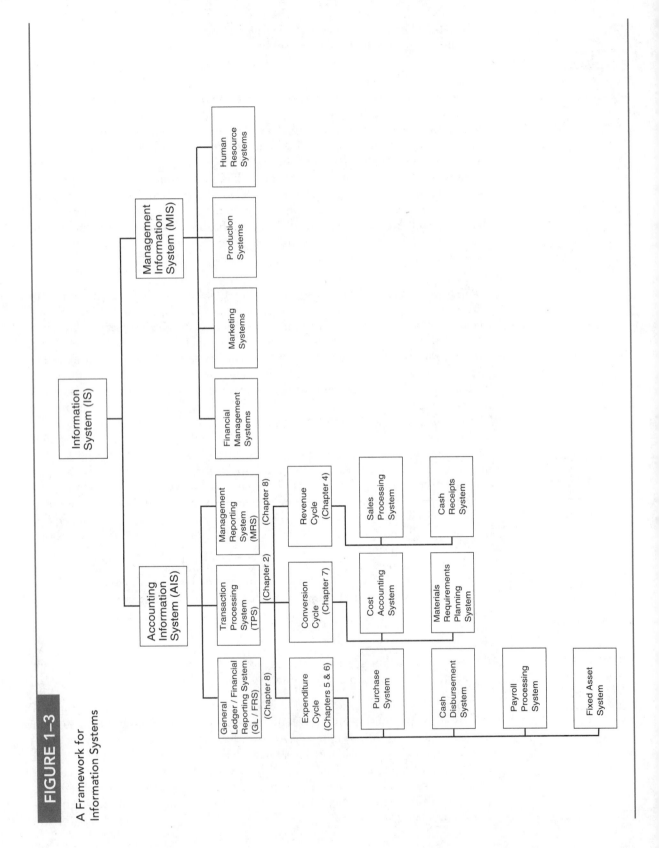

FIGURE 1-3

A Framework for Information Systems

The distinction between AIS and MIS subsystems centers on the concept of a transaction, as illustrated by Figure 1–4. The information system accepts input, called transactions, which are converted through various processes into output information that goes to users. Transactions fall into two classes: *financial transactions* and *nonfinancial transactions*. Before discussing this distinction, let's first broadly define a transaction:

> A **transaction** is an event that affects or is of interest to the organization and that is processed by its information system as a unit of work.

This definition encompasses both financial and nonfinancial events. Since financial transactions are of particular importance to the accountant's understanding of information systems, we need a more precise definition for this class of transaction:

> A **financial transaction** is an economic event that affects the assets and equities of the organization, is reflected in its accounts, and is measured in monetary terms.

Sales of products to customers, purchases of inventory from vendors, and cash disbursements and receipts are all examples of financial transactions. Every business organization is legally bound to process these types of transactions.

Nonfinancial transactions include all events processed by the organization's information system that do not meet the narrow definition of a financial transaction. For example, adding a new supplier of raw materials to the list of valid suppliers is an event that may be processed by the enterprise's information system as a transaction. The result of processing may be a decision to place an order with the new supplier. Important as this information obviously is, it is not a financial transaction, and the firm has no legal obligation to process it correctly—or at all.

Financial transactions and nonfinancial transactions are closely related and are often processed by the same physical system. For example, consider a portfolio management system that collects and tracks stock prices (nonfinancial transactions). When the stocks reach a threshold price, the system places an automatic buy or sell order (financial transaction). There is no law requiring that the company make the optimal decision to buy or sell. However, once the order is placed, the processing of the transaction must comply with legal and professional guidelines. Similarly, a change in a customer's name or address must be processed to keep the customer file current. Although not a financial transaction, this is vital information for processing financial transactions—future sales to the customer.

The Accounting Information System

AIS subsystems process financial transactions and nonfinancial transactions that directly affect the processing of financial transactions. The AIS comprises three major

---

FIGURE 1–4

Transactions
Processed by the
Information System

subsystems: (1) the **transaction processing system (TPS)**, which supports daily business operations with numerous documents and messages for users throughout the organization; (2) the **general ledger/financial reporting system (GL/FRS)**, which produces the traditional financial statements, such as the income statement, balance sheet, statement of cash flows, tax returns, and other reports required by law; and (3) the **management reporting system (MRS)**, which provides internal management with special-purpose financial reports and information needed for decision making, such as budgets, variance reports, and responsibility reports. We examine each of these subsystems later.

The Management Information System

Management often requires information that goes beyond the capability of AIS. As organizations grow in size and complexity, specialized functional areas emerge requiring additional information for production planning and control, sales forecasting, inventory warehouse planning, market research, and so on. The **management information system (MIS)** processes nonfinancial transactions that are not normally processed by traditional AIS. Table 1–1 gives examples of typical MIS applications related to functional areas of a firm.

The Changing Role of Accounting Information

Some management decisions require information that integrates financial and nonfinancial data. For example, a purchasing manager, evaluating the performance of suppliers, wants to know the number and financial value of inventory orders placed with specific vendors during a period of time. In addition, the manager needs to know the number of deliveries that exceeded the normal lead time, and any inventory stockout conditions that resulted from late deliveries.

Such integrated information, if it could be provided at all, would traditionally come from separate AIS and MIS applications functioning independently. The AIS application would supply the cost of purchases data, while the delivery time and

TABLE 1–1	**Examples of MIS Applications in Functional Areas**
Function	**Examples of MIS Applications**
Production	Production Planning and Control Systems Job Scheduling Systems
Finance	Portfolio Management Systems Capital Budgeting Systems
Marketing	Market Analysis New Product Development Product Analysis
Distribution	Warehouse Organization and Scheduling Delivery Scheduling Vehicle Loading and Allocation Models
Personnel	Human Resource Management Systems • Job skill tracking system • Employee benefits system

stockout data (if available) would come from an MIS application. The two sets of data would then need to be integrated and reported to the manager. The task of supplying managers with integrated information is inefficient and expensive when the supporting information systems are not integrated. Also, lack of coordination between financial and nonfinancial systems can produce unreliable information, resulting in poor management decisions.

To improve operational efficiency and gain competitive advantage in the market place, many organizations have reengineered their information systems to include both AIS and MIS features. This has impacted the traditional role of accountants as they assume new responsibility for providing reliable nonfinancial data. In chapters that follow, we will study the characteristics of both traditional and reengineered systems and will examine alternative accounting models such as REA (resource, events, and agents) and ERP (enterprise resource planning) systems that integrate financial and nonfinancial data.

Why Distinguish between AIS and MIS?

Given the changes that are occurring in accounting, is there a need to distinguish between AIS and MIS? The answer to this question is "yes." Publicly held organizations must provide financial reports to interested external parties. The management, accountants, and auditors of public firms have a legal responsibility for the design, operation, control, and audit of AIS applications that impact the financial statements. Naturally, MIS applications are also important to the enterprise, otherwise they should not have been implemented. However, the legal and professional standards that characterize AIS clearly distinguish it from MIS. With the increasing integration of financial and nonfinancial systems, organization management, systems professionals, and accountants need a conceptual model that reflects this important distinction.

AIS SUBSYSTEMS

We devote separate chapters to an in-depth study of each AIS subsystem depicted in Figure 1–3. At this point, we shall briefly outline the role of each subsystem.

Transaction Processing System

The transaction processing system (TPS) is central to the overall function of the information system by:

- Converting economic events into financial transactions.
- Recording financial transactions in the accounting records (journals and ledgers).
- Distributing essential financial information to operations personnel to support their daily operations.

The transaction processing system deals with business events that occur frequently. In a given day, a firm may process thousands of transactions. To deal efficiently with such volume, similar types of transactions are grouped together into *transaction cycles*. The TPS consists of three transaction cycles: the *revenue cycle*, the *expenditure cycle*, and the *conversion cycle*. Each cycle captures and processes different types of financial transactions. Chapter 2 provides an overview of transaction processing. Chapters 4, 5, 6, and 7 deal with the revenue, expenditure, and conversion cycles.

General Ledger/Financial Reporting Systems

The general ledger system (GLS) and the financial reporting system (FRS) are two closely related subsystems. However, because of their operational interdependency, they are generally viewed as a single integrated system—the GL/FRS. The bulk of the input to the GL portion of the system comes from the transaction cycles. Summaries of transaction cycle activity are processed by the GLS to update the general ledger control accounts. Other, less frequent events, such as stock transactions, mergers, and lawsuit settlements, for which there may be no formal processing cycle in place, also enter the GLS through alternate sources.

The financial reporting system measures and reports the status of financial resources and the changes in those resources. The FRS communicates this information primarily to external users. This type of reporting is called *nondiscretionary* because the organization has few or no choices in the information that it provides. Much of this information consists of traditional financial statements, tax returns, and other legal documents.

Management Reporting System

The management reporting system (MRS) provides the internal financial information needed to manage a business. Managers must deal immediately with many day-to-day business problems, as well as plan and control their operations. Managers require different information for the various kinds of decisions they must make. Typical reports produced by the MRS include budgets, variance reports, cost-volume-profit analyses, and reports using current (rather than historical) cost data. This type of reporting is called discretionary reporting because the organization can choose what information to report and how to present it.

A GENERAL MODEL FOR AIS

Figure 1–5 presents the **general model for viewing AIS applications**. This is a general model because it describes all information systems, regardless of their technological architecture. The elements of the general model are end users, data sources,

FIGURE 1–5

General Model
for Accounting
Information Systems

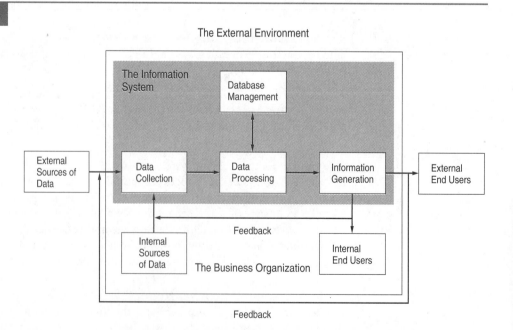

data collection, data processing, database management, information generation, and feedback.

End Users

End users fall into two general groups: *external* and *internal*. External users include creditors, stockholders, potential investors, regulatory agencies, tax authorities, suppliers, and customers. Institutional users such as banks, the SEC, and the IRS receive information in the form of financial statements, tax returns, and other reports that the firm has a legal obligation to produce. Trading partners (customers and suppliers) receive transaction-oriented information including purchase orders, billing statements, and shipping documents.

Internal users include management at every level of the organization, as well as operations personnel. In contrast to external reporting, the organization has a great deal of latitude in the way it meets the needs of internal users. Although there are some well-accepted conventions and practices, internal reporting is governed primarily by what gets the job done. System designers, including accountants, must balance the desires of internal users against legal and economic concerns such as adequate control and security, proper accountability, and the cost of providing alternative forms of information. Thus, internal reporting poses a less structured and generally more difficult challenge than external reporting. On the other hand, it is an open field for experimentation, invention, and innovation.

Data Versus Information.   Before discussing the data sources portion of Figure 1–5, we must make an important distinction between the terms *data* and *information*. **Data** are facts, which may or may not be processed (edited, summarized, or refined) and have no direct effect on the user. By contrast, **information** causes the user to take an *action* that he or she otherwise could not, or would not, have taken. Information is often defined simply as processed data. This is an inadequate definition. Information is determined by the *effect* it has on the user, not by its physical form. For example, a purchasing agent receives a daily report listing raw material inventory items that are at low levels. This report causes the agent to place orders for more inventory. The facts in this report have information content for the purchasing agent. However, this very same report in the hands of the personnel manager is a mere collection of facts, or data, causing no action and having no information content.

We can see from this example that one person's information is another person's data. Thus, information is not just a set of processed facts arranged in a formal report. Information allows users to take action to resolve conflicts, reduce uncertainty, and make decisions. We should note that action does not necessarily mean a physical act. For instance, a purchasing agent who receives a report showing that inventory levels are adequate will respond by ordering nothing. The agent's action to do nothing is a conscious decision, triggered by information and different from doing nothing because of being uninformed.

The distinction between data and information has pervasive implications for the study of information systems. If output from the information system fails to cause users to act, the system serves no purpose and has failed in its primary objective.

Data Sources

Data sources are financial transactions that enter the information system from both internal and external sources. *External financial transactions* are the most common source of data for most organizations. These are economic exchanges with other business entities and individuals outside the firm. Examples include the sale of goods and services, the purchase of inventory, the receipt of cash, and the disbursement of cash (including payroll). *Internal financial transactions* involve the exchange or movement of resources within the organization. Examples include the movement of raw materials into work in process (WIP), the application of labor and overhead to WIP, the transfer of WIP into finished goods inventory, and the depreciation of plant and equipment.

Data Collection

Data collection is the first operational stage in the information system. The objective is to ensure that event data entering the system are valid, complete, and free from material errors. In many respects, this is the most important stage in the system. Should transaction errors pass through data collection undetected, the system may process the errors and generate erroneous and unreliable output. This, in turn, could lead to incorrect actions and poor decisions by the users.

Two rules govern the design of data collection procedures: *relevance* and *efficiency*. The information system should capture only relevant data. A fundamental task of the system designer is to determine what is and what is not relevant. He or she does so by analyzing the user's needs. Only data that ultimately contribute to information (as defined previously) are relevant. The data collection stage should be designed to filter irrelevant facts from the system.

Efficient data collection procedures are designed to collect data only once. These data can then be made available to multiple users. Capturing the same data more than once leads to data redundancy and inconsistency. Information systems have limited collection, processing, and data storage capacity. Data redundancy overloads facilities and reduces the overall efficiency of the system. Inconsistency among redundant data elements can result in inappropriate actions and bad decisions.

Data Processing

Once collected, data usually require processing to produce information. Tasks in the **data processing** stage range from simple to complex. Examples include mathematical algorithms (such as linear programming models) used for production scheduling applications, statistical techniques for sales forecasting, and posting and summarizing procedures used for accounting applications.

Database Management

The organization's **database** is its physical repository for financial and nonfinancial data. We use the term *database* in the generic sense. It can be a filing cabinet or a computer disk. Regardless of the database's physical form, we can represent its contents in a logical hierarchy. The levels in the data hierarchy—*attribute*, *record*, and *file*—are illustrated in Figure 1–6.

Data Attribute. The data attribute is the most elemental piece of potentially useful data in the database. An attribute is a logical and relevant characteristic of an entity about which the firm captures data. The attributes shown in Figure 1–6 are *logical* because they all relate sensibly to a common entity—accounts receivable. Each attribute is also *relevant* because it contributes to the information content of the entire set. As proof of this, the absence of any single relevant attribute reduces or destroys the information content of the set. The addition of irrelevant or illogical data would not enhance the information content of the set.

FIGURE 1–6

The Data Hierarchy

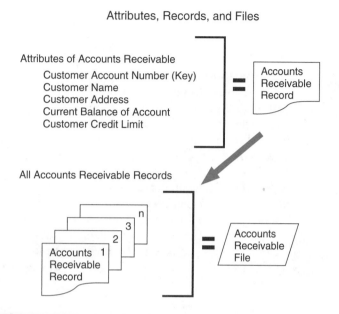

Attributes, Records, and Files

Attributes of Accounts Receivable
   Customer Account Number (Key)
   Customer Name
   Customer Address
   Current Balance of Account
   Customer Credit Limit

= Accounts Receivable Record

All Accounts Receivable Records

Accounts Receivable Record 1 2 3 n

= Accounts Receivable File

Record. A record is a complete set of attributes for a single occurrence within an entity class. For example, a particular customer's name, address, and account balance is one occurrence (or record) within the accounts receivable class. To find a particular record within the database, we must be able to identify it uniquely. Therefore, every record in the database must be unique in at least one attribute.[1] This unique identifier attribute is the *primary key*. Because no natural attribute (such as customer name) can guarantee uniqueness, we typically assign artificial keys to records. The key for the accounts receivable records in Figure 1–6 is the customer account number. This is the only unique identifier in this record class. The other attributes possess values that may also exist in other records. For instance, multiple customers may have the same name, sales amounts, credit limits, and balances. Using any one of these as a key to find a record in a large database would be a difficult task. However, these nonunique attributes are often used as *secondary keys* for categorizing data. For example, the account balance attribute can be used to prepare a list of customers with balances greater than $10,000.

Files. A file is a complete set of records of an identical class. For example, *all* the accounts receivable records of the organization constitute the accounts receivable file. Similarly, files are constructed for other classes of records such as inventory, accounts payable, and payroll. The organization's database is the entire collection of such files.

Database Management Tasks. **Database management** involves three fundamental tasks: *storage*, *retrieval*, and *deletion*. The storage task assigns keys to new records and stores them in their proper location in the database. Retrieval is the task of locating

---

1   When we get into more advanced topics, we will see how a combination of nonunique attributes can be used as a unique identifier.

and extracting an existing record from the database for processing. After processing is complete, the storage task restores the updated record to its place in the database. Deletion is the task of permanently removing obsolete or redundant records from the database.

Information Generation

Information generation is the process of compiling, arranging, formatting, and presenting information to users. Information can be an operational document such as a sales order, a structured report, or a message on a computer screen. Regardless of physical form, useful information has the following characteristics: *relevance*, *timeliness*, *accuracy*, *completeness*, and *summarization*.

Relevance. The contents of a report or document must serve a purpose. This could be to support a manager's decision or a clerk's task. We have established that only data relevant to a user's action have information content. Therefore, the information system should present only relevant data in its reports. Reports containing irrelevancies waste resources and may be counterproductive to the user. Irrelevancies detract attention from the true message of the report and may result in incorrect decisions or actions.

Timeliness. The age of information is a critical factor in determining its usefulness. Information must be no older than the time period of the action it supports. For example, if a manager makes decisions daily to purchase inventory from a supplier based upon an inventory status report, then the information in the report should be no more than a day old.

Accuracy. Information must be free from material errors. However, materiality is a difficult concept to quantify. It has no absolute value; it is a problem-specific concept. This means that, in some cases, information must be perfectly accurate. In other instances, the level of accuracy may be lower. Material error exists when the amount of inaccuracy in information causes the user to make poor decisions or to fail to make necessary decisions. We sometimes must sacrifice absolute accuracy to obtain timely information. Often, perfect information is not available within the user's decision time frame. Therefore, in providing information, system designers seek a balance between information that is as accurate as possible, yet timely enough to be useful.

Completeness. No piece of information essential to a decision or task should be missing. For example, a report should provide all necessary calculations and present its message clearly and unambiguously.

Summarization. Information should be aggregated in accordance with the user's needs. Lower-level managers tend to need information that is highly detailed. As information flows upward through the organization to top management, it becomes more summarized. We shall look more closely at the effects that organizational structure and managerial level have on information reporting later in this chapter.

Feedback

Feedback is a form of output that is sent back to the system as a source of data. Feedback may be *internal* or *external* and is used to initiate or alter a process. For example, an inventory status report signals the inventory control clerk that items of inventory have fallen to, or below, their minimum allowable levels. Internal feedback from this information will *initiate* the inventory ordering process to replenish the inventories. Similarly, external feedback about the level of uncollected customer accounts can be used to *adjust* the organization's credit granting policies.

Information System Objectives

Each organization must tailor its information system to the needs of its users. Therefore, specific information system objectives may differ from firm to firm. However, three fundamental objectives are common to all systems. They are:

1. *To support the stewardship function of management.* Stewardship refers to management's responsibility to properly manage the resources of the firm. The information system provides information about resource utilization to external users via traditional financial statements and other mandated reports. Internally, management receives stewardship information from various responsibility reports.
2. *To support management decision making.* The information system supplies managers with the information they need to carry out their decision-making responsibilities.
3. *To support the firm's day-to-day operations.* The information system provides information to operations personnel to assist them in the efficient and effective discharge of their daily tasks.

ACQUISITION OF INFORMATION SYSTEMS

We conclude this section with a brief discussion of how organizations obtain information systems. Usually, they do so in two ways: (1) they develop customized systems from scratch through in-house systems development activities and (2) they purchase preprogrammed commercial systems from software vendors. Larger organizations with unique and frequently changing needs engage in in-house development. The formal process by which this is accomplished is called the **system development life cycle**. Smaller companies and larger firms that have standardized information needs are the primary market for commercial software. Three basic types of commercial software are turnkey systems, backbone systems, and vendor-supported systems.

Turnkey systems are completely finished and tested systems that are ready for implementation. Typically, they are general-purpose systems or systems customized to a specific industry. In either case, the end user must have standard business practices that permit the use of "canned" or "off-the-shelf" systems. The better turnkey systems, however, have built-in software options that allow the user to customize input, output, and processing through menu choices. However, configuring the systems to meet user needs can be a formidable task. Enterprise resource planning (ERP) systems such as *Oracle, SAP, J.D. Edwards* and *PeopleSoft* are examples of this approach to systems implementation. ERP systems are discussed later in this chapter.

Backbone systems consist of a basic system structure on which to build. The primary processing logic is preprogrammed, and the vendor then designs the user interfaces to suit the client's unique needs. A backbone system is a compromise between a custom system and a turnkey system. This approach can produce very satisfactory results, but customizing the system is costly.

Vendor-supported systems are custom (or customized) systems that client organizations purchase commercially rather than develop in-house. Under this approach, the software vendor designs, implements, and maintains the system for its client. This is a popular option with health-care and legal services organizations that have complex systems requirements but which are not of sufficient magnitude to justify retaining an in-house systems development staff. Indeed, this has become a popular option for many organizations that traditionally have relied on in-house development but have chosen to outsource these activities. In recent years, public accounting firms have expanded their involvement in the vendor-supported market.

ORGANIZATIONAL STRUCTURE

The structure of an organization reflects the distribution of responsibility, authority, and accountability throughout the organization. These flows are illustrated in Figure 1–7. Firms achieve their overall objectives by establishing measurable financial goals for their operational units. For example, budget information flows downward. This is the mechanism by which senior management conveys to their subordinates the standards against which they will be measured for the coming period. The results of the subordinates' actions, in the form of performance information, flow upward to senior management. Understanding the distribution pattern of responsibility, authority, and accountability is essential for assessing the information needs of users.

BUSINESS SEGMENTS

Business organizations consist of functional units or **segments**. Firms organize into segments to promote internal efficiencies through the specialization of labor and cost-effective resource allocations. Managers within a segment can focus their attention on narrow areas of responsibility to achieve higher levels of operating efficiency.

There are several ways to segment a firm. Three of the most common approaches include segmentation by:

1. *Geographic Location.* Many organizations have operations dispersed across the country and around the world. They do this to gain access to resources, markets, or lines of distribution. A convenient way to manage such operations is to organize the management of the firm around each geographic segment as a quasi-autonomous entity.

FIGURE 1–7

The Flows of Responsibility, Authority, and Accountability through the Organization

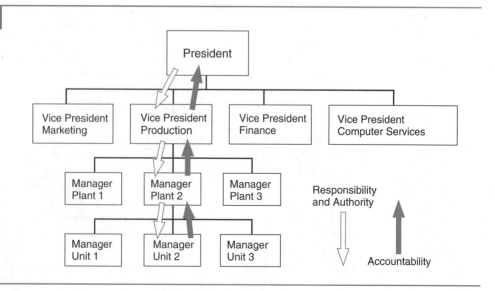

2. *Product Line.* Companies that produce highly diversified products often organize around product lines, creating separate divisions for each. Product segmentation allows the organization to devote specialized management, labor, and resources to segments separately, almost as if they were separate firms.
3. *Business Function.* Functional segmentation divides the organization into areas of specialized responsibility based on tasks. The functional areas are determined according to the flow of primary resources through the firm. Examples of business function segments are marketing, production, finance, and accounting.

Some firms use more than one method of segmentation. For instance, an international conglomerate may segment its operations first geographically, then by product within each geographic region, and then functionally within each product segment.

FUNCTIONAL SEGMENTATION

Segmentation by business function is the most common method of organizing. To illustrate it, we will assume a manufacturing firm that uses these resources: materials, labor, financial capital, and information. Table 1–2 shows the relationship between functional segments and these resources.

The titles of functions and even the functions themselves will vary greatly among organizations, depending upon their size and line of business. A public utility may have little in the way of a marketing function compared to an automobile manufacturer. A service organization may have no formal production function and little in the way of inventory to manage. One firm may call its labor resource *personnel* while another uses the term *human resources*. Keeping in mind these variations, we will briefly discuss the functional areas of the hypothetical firm shown in Figure 1–8. Because of their special importance to the study of information systems, the accounting and computer services functions are given separate and more detailed treatment.

Materials Management

The objective of materials management is to plan and control the materials inventory of the company. A manufacturing firm must have sufficient inventories on hand to meet its production needs and yet avoid excessive inventory levels. Every dollar invested in inventory is a dollar that is not earning a return. Furthermore, idle inventory can become obsolete, lost, or stolen. Ideally, a firm would coordinate

TABLE 1–2

Functions from Resources

Resource	Business Function
Materials	Inventory Management Production Marketing Distribution
Labor	Personnel
Financial Capital	Finance
Information	Accounting Computer Services

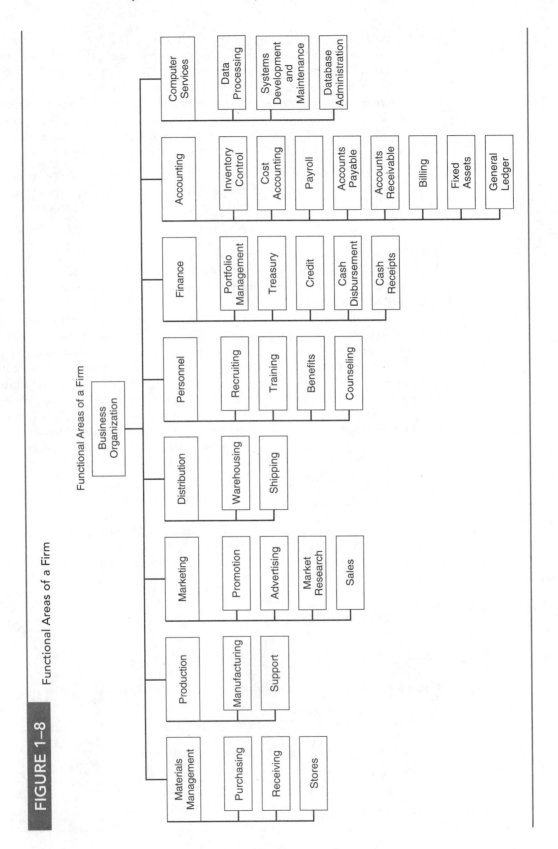

FIGURE 1-8   Functional Areas of a Firm

inventory arrivals from suppliers such that they move directly into the production process. However, as a practical matter, most organizations maintain safety stocks to carry them through the lead time between placing the order for inventory and its arrival. We see from Figure 1–8 that materials management has three subfunctions:

Purchasing is responsible for ordering inventory from vendors when inventory levels fall to their reorder points. The nature of this task varies among organizations. In some cases, purchasing is no more than sending a purchase order to a designated vendor. In other cases, this task involves soliciting bids from a number of competing vendors. The nature of the business and the type of inventory determines the extent of the purchasing function.

Receiving is the task of accepting the inventory previously ordered by purchasing. Receiving activities include counting and checking the physical condition of these items. This is an organization's first, and perhaps only, opportunity to detect incomplete deliveries and damaged merchandise before they move into the production process.

Stores takes physical custody of the inventory received and releases these resources into the production process as needed.

Production

Production activities occur in the conversion cycle where raw materials, labor, and plant assets are used to create finished products. The specific activities are determined by the nature of the products being manufactured. In general they fall into two broad classes: (1) primary manufacturing activities and (2) production support activities. Primary manufacturing activities shape and assemble raw materials into finished products. Production support activities ensure that primary manufacturing activities operate efficiently and effectively. These include, but are not limited to, the following types of activities:

Production planning involves scheduling the flow of materials, labor, and machinery to efficiently meet production needs. This requires information about the status of sales orders, raw materials inventory, finished goods inventory, and machine and labor availability.

Quality control monitors the manufacturing process at various points to ensure that the finished products meet the firm's quality standards. Effective quality control detects problems early to facilitate corrective action. Failure to do so may result in excessive waste of materials and labor.

Maintenance keeps the firm's machinery and other manufacturing facilities in running order. The manufacturing process relies on its plant and equipment and cannot tolerate breakdowns during peak production periods. Therefore, the key to maintenance is prevention—the scheduled removal of equipment from operations for cleaning, servicing, and repairs. Many manufacturers have elaborate preventive maintenance programs. To plan and coordinate these activities, maintenance engineers need extensive information about the history of equipment usage and future scheduled production.

Marketing

The marketplace needs to know about and have access to a firm's products. The marketing function deals with the strategic problems of product promotion, advertising, and market research. On an operational level, marketing performs such daily activities as sales order entry.

Distribution

Distribution is the activity of getting the product to the customer after the sale. This is a critical step. Much can go wrong before the customer takes possession of the product. Excessive lags between the taking and filling of orders, incorrect shipments, or damaged merchandise can result in customer dissatisfaction and lost sales. Ultimately, success depends on filling orders accurately in the warehouse, packaging goods correctly, and shipping them quickly to the customer.

Personnel

Competent and reliable employees are a valuable resource to a business. The objective of the personnel function is to effectively manage this resource. A well-developed personnel function includes recruiting, training, continuing education, counseling, evaluating, labor relations, and compensation administration.

Finance

The finance function manages the financial resources of the firm through banking and treasury activities, portfolio management, credit evaluation, cash disbursements, and cash receipts. Because of the cyclical nature of business, many firms swing between positions of excess funds and cash deficits. In response to these cash flow patterns, financial planners seek lucrative investments in stocks and other assets and low-cost lines of credit from banks. The finance function also administers the daily flow of cash in and out of the firm.

THE ACCOUNTING FUNCTION

The accounting function manages the financial information resource of the firm. In this regard, it plays two important roles in transaction processing. First, accounting captures and records the financial effects of the firm's transactions. These include such events as the movement of raw materials from the warehouse into production, shipments of the finished products to customers, cash flows into the firm and deposits in the bank, the acquisition of inventory, and the discharge of financial obligations.

Second, the accounting function distributes transaction information to operations personnel to coordinate many of their key tasks. Accounting activities that contribute directly to business operations include inventory control, cost accounting, payroll, accounts payable, accounts receivable, billing, fixed asset accounting, and the general ledger. We deal with each of these specifically in later chapters. For the moment, however, we need to maintain a broad view of accounting to understand its functional role in the organization.

The Value of Information

The value of information to a user is determined by its **reliability**. We saw earlier that the purpose of information is to lead the user to a desired action. For this to happen, information must possess certain attributes—relevance, accuracy, completeness, summarization, and timeliness. When these attributes are consistently present, information has reliability and provides value to the user. Unreliable information has no value. At best, it is a waste of resources. A more negative implication of unreliable information is that it can lead to dysfunctional decisions. Consider the following example:

A marketing manager signed a contract with a customer to supply a large quantity of product by a certain deadline. He made this decision based on information about finished goods inventory levels. However, because of faulty record keeping, the information was incorrect. The actual inventory levels of the product are insufficient to meet the order, and the necessary quantities cannot be manufactured by the deadline. Failure to comply with the terms of the contract may result in litigation.

This bad sales decision was a result of flawed information. Effective decisions require information that has a high degree of reliability.

Accounting Independence

The need to ensure the reliability of accounting information places the accounting function in a unique position within the organization. Information reliability rests heavily on the concept of accounting **independence**. Simply stated, accounting activities must be separate and independent of the functional areas that maintain custody of physical resources. For example, accounting monitors and records the movement of raw materials into production and the sale of finished goods to customers. Accounting authorizes purchases of raw materials and the disbursement of cash payments to vendors and employees. Accounting supports these functions with information but does not actively participate in their physical activities. Effective user decisions require that such vital information be supplied by an independent source to ensure its integrity.

THE COMPUTER SERVICES FUNCTION

Returning to Figure 1–8, the final area to be discussed is the computer services function. Like accounting, the computer services function is associated with the information resource. Its activities can be organized in a number of different ways. One extreme structure is the *centralized data processing* approach; at the other extreme is the *distributed data processing* approach. Most organizational structures fall somewhere between these extremes and embody elements of both.

Centralized Data Processing

Under the **centralized data processing** model, all data processing is performed by one or more large computers housed at a central site that serve users throughout the organization. Figure 1–9 illustrates this approach in which computer services activities are consolidated and managed as a shared organization resource. End users compete for these resources on the basis of need. The computer services function is usually treated as a cost center whose operating costs are charged back to the end users. Figure 1–8 illustrates a centralized computer services function. Figure 1-10 shows the computer service areas of operation in more detail. These include database administration, data processing, and systems development and maintenance. The key functions of each of these areas are described next.

Database Administration. Centrally organized companies maintain their data resources in a central location that is shared by all end users. In this shared data arrangement, a special independent group—database administration—headed by the database administrator is responsible for the security and integrity of the database. We explore the database concept and the role of the database administrator in Chapter 9.

FIGURE 1–9

Centralized Data
Processing Approach

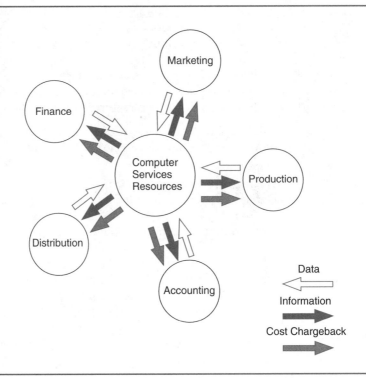

FIGURE 1–10

Organization of
Computer Services
Function in a
Centralized System

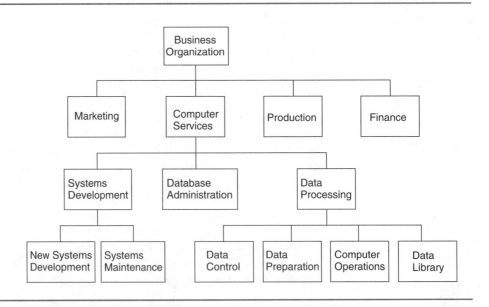

Data Processing. The data processing group manages the computer resources used
to perform the day-to-day processing of transactions. It consists of the following
organizational functions: *data control*, *data conversion*, *computer operations*, and the *data
library*.

Some organizations have a *data control* group as liaison between the end user and data processing. Data control is responsible for receiving batches of transaction documents for processing from end users and then distributing computer output (documents and reports) back to the users. The *data conversion* function transcribes transaction data from paper documents to magnetic media (tape or disk) suitable for computer processing. The original documents are returned to the user. The magnetic transaction files produced in this step are later processed by the central computer, which is managed by the *computer operations group*. Accounting applications are usually run according to a strict schedule that is controlled by the central computer.

The *data library* is a room adjacent to the computer center that provides safe storage for the off-line data files, such as magnetic tapes and removable disk packs. A data librarian who is responsible for the receipt, storage, retrieval, and custody of data files controls access to the library. The librarian issues tapes to computer operators and takes custody of files when processing is completed. The trend in recent years toward real-time processing and the increased use of direct access files (discussed in Chapter 2) has reduced or eliminated the role of the data librarian in many organizations.

Systems Development and Maintenance. The information systems needs of users are met by two related functions: system development and systems maintenance. The former group is responsible for analyzing user needs and for designing new systems to satisfy those needs. The participants in system development include systems professionals, end users, and stakeholders.

Systems professionals include systems analysts, database designers, and programmers who design and build the system. Systems professionals gather facts about the user's problem, analyze the facts, and formulate a solution. The product of their efforts is a new information system.

End users are those for whom the system is built. They are the managers who receive reports from the system and the operations personnel who work directly with the system as part of their daily responsibilities.

Stakeholders are individuals inside or outside the firm who have an interest in the system, but are not end users. They include accountants, internal auditors, external auditors, and others who oversee systems development.

Once a new system has been designed and implemented, the systems maintenance group assumes responsibility for keeping it current with user needs. Over the course of the system's life (often several years), between 80 and 90 percent of its total cost will be attributable to maintenance activities.

Distributed Data Processing

For many years, economies of scale favored large, powerful computers and the centralized processing approach. Recent developments in small, powerful, and inexpensive systems have changed this picture dramatically. An alternative to the centralized model is the concept of **distributed data processing (DDP)**. The topic of DDP is quite broad, touching upon such related topics as end-user computing, commercial software, networking, and office automation. Simply stated, DDP involves reorganizing the computer services function into small *information processing units* (IPUs) that are distributed to end users and placed under their control. The degree to which computer services are distributed will vary depending upon the philosophy and objectives of the organization's management. IPUs may be distributed according to business function, geographic location, or both. Any or all of the computer services activities represented in Figure 1–10 may be distributed. Figure 1–11 shows a possible new organizational structure following the distribution of all data processing tasks to the end-user areas.

Notice that the central computer services function has been eliminated from the organization structure. Individual operational areas now perform this role. In recent years DDP has become an economic and operational feasibility that has revolutionized business operations. DDP is, however, a mixed bag of advantages and disadvantages. Some of the more important of these are discussed next.

Disadvantages of DDP. We should bear in mind that the disadvantages of DDP might also be described as the advantages of a centralized approach. The discussion focuses on important issues that carry control implications that accountants should recognize. The loss of control is one of the most serious disadvantages of DDP. Other potential problems include the inefficient use of resources, the destruction of audit trails, inadequate segregation of duties, an increased potential for programming errors and systems failures, and the lack of standards. Specific problems are examined below.

Mismanagement of organizationwide resources. Some argue that when organizationwide resources exceed a threshold amount, say 5 percent of the total operations budget, they should be controlled and monitored centrally. Information processing services (such as computer operations, programming, data conversion, and database management) represent a significant expenditure for many organizations. Those opposed to DDP argue that distributing responsibility for these resources will inevitably lead to their mismanagement and suboptimal utilization.

FIGURE 1–11

Organizational Structure for a Distributed Processing System

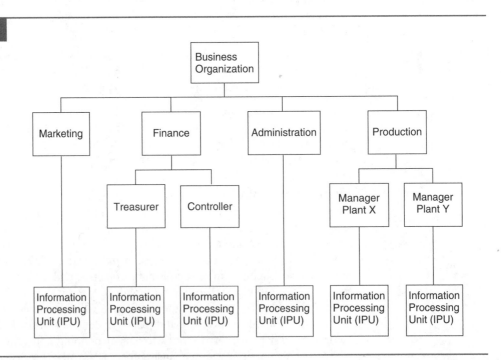

Hardware and software incompatibility. Distributing the responsibility for hardware and software purchases to user management can result in uncoordinated and poorly conceived decisions. Working independently, decision makers may settle on dissimilar and incompatible operating systems, technology platforms, spreadsheet programs, word processors, and database packages. Such hardware and software incompatibilities can degrade and disrupt communications between organizational units.

Redundant tasks. Autonomous systems development activities distributed throughout the firm can result in each user area reinventing the wheel. For example, application programs created by one user, which could be used with little or no change by others, will be redesigned from scratch rather than shared. Likewise, data common to many users may be recreated for each IPU, resulting in a high level of data redundancy. This has implications for data accuracy and consistency.

Consolidating incompatible activities. The distribution of the computer services function to individual user areas results in the creation of many very small units that do not permit the necessary separation of incompatible functions. For example, within a single IPU, the same person may program applications, perform program maintenance, enter transaction data into the computer, and operate the computer equipment. This situation represents a fundamental violation of internal control. However, achieving an adequate segregation of duties may not always be possible in some distributed environments.

Hiring qualified professionals. End-user managers may lack the knowledge to evaluate the technical credentials and relevant experience of candidates applying for a position as a computer professional. Also, if the organizational unit into which a new employee is entering is small, the opportunity for personal growth, continuing education, and promotion may be limited. For these reasons, IPU managers sometimes experience difficulty attracting highly qualified personnel. This problem spills over into the domain of accountants and auditors. The risk of programming errors and system failures increases directly with the level of employee incompetence.

Lack of standards. Because of the distribution of responsibility in the DDP environment, standards for developing and documenting systems, choosing programming languages, acquiring hardware and software, and evaluating performance may be unevenly applied or nonexistent. Opponents of DDP argue that the risks associated with the design and operation of a data processing system are made tolerable only if such standards are consistently applied. This requires that standards be imposed centrally. There is much to be said for this argument. In our examination of information systems auditing and assurance in Chapter 17, we shall see how the application of standards plays an important role in the auditor's evaluation of internal control.

Advantages of DDP. The most commonly cited advantages of DDP are related to cost savings, increased user satisfaction, and improved operational efficiency. Specific issues are discussed below.

Cost reductions. In the past, achieving economies of scale was the principal justification for the centralized approach. The economics of data processing favored large, expensive, powerful computers. The wide variety of needs that such centralized systems had to satisfy called for computers that were highly generalized and employed complex operating systems.

Powerful yet inexpensive microcomputers and minicomputers, which can cost effectively perform specialized functions, have changed the economics of data processing dramatically. In addition, the unit cost of data storage, which was once the justification for consolidating data in a central location, is no longer the prime consideration. Moreover, the move to DDP can reduce costs in two other areas: (1) data can be entered and edited at the IPU, thus eliminating the centralized tasks of data preparation and data control; and (2) application complexity can be reduced, which in turn reduces development and maintenance costs.

Improved cost control responsibility. Managers assume the responsibility for the financial success of their operations. This requires that they be properly empowered with the authority to make decisions about resources that influence their overall success. When managers are precluded from making the decisions necessary to achieve their goals, their performance can be negatively influenced. A less aggressive and less effective management may evolve.

If information processing capability is critical to the success of a business operation, then should not management be given control over these resources? This argument counters the argument presented earlier favoring the centralization of organizationwide resources. Proponents of DDP argue that the benefits from improved management attitudes outweigh the additional costs incurred from distributing these resources.

Improved user satisfaction. Perhaps the most often cited benefit of DDP is improved user satisfaction. This derives from three areas of need that too often go unsatisfied in the centralized approach: (1) as previously stated, users desire to control the resources that influence their profitability; (2) users want systems professionals (analysts, programmers, and computer operators) who are responsive to their specific situation; and (3) users want to become more actively involved in developing and implementing their own systems. Proponents of DDP argue that providing more customized support—feasible only in a distributed environment—has direct benefits for user morale and productivity.

Backup. The final argument in favor of DDP is the ability to back up computing facilities to protect against potential disasters such as fires, floods, sabotage, and earthquakes. One solution is to build excess capacity into each IPU. If a disaster destroys a single site, its transactions can be processed by the other IPUs. This requires close coordination between decision makers to ensure that they do not implement incompatible hardware and software at their sites.

The Need for Careful Analysis

DDP carries a certain leading-edge prestige value that, during an analysis of its pros and cons, may overwhelm important considerations of economic benefit and operational feasibility. Some organizations have made the move to DDP without considering fully whether the distributed organizational structure will better achieve their business objectives. Some DDP initiatives have proven to be ineffective, and even counterproductive, because decision makers saw in these systems virtues that were more symbolic than real. Before taking such an aggressive step, decision makers must assess the true merits of DDP for their organization. Accountants have an opportunity and an obligation to play an important role in this analysis.

THE EVOLUTION OF INFORMATION SYSTEM MODELS

Over the past fifty years, accounting information systems have been represented by a number of different approaches or models. Each new model evolved because of the shortcomings and limitations of its predecessor. An interesting feature in this evolution is that older models are not immediately replaced by the newest technique. Thus, at any point in time, various generations of systems exist across different organizations and may even coexist within a single enterprise. The modern accountant needs to be familiar with the operational features of all AIS approaches that he or she is likely to encounter. This book deals extensively with five such models: manual processes, flat file systems, the database approach, the REA (resources, events, and agents) model, and ERP (enterprise resource planning) systems. Each of these is briefly outlined below.

THE MANUAL PROCESS MODEL

The manual process model is the oldest and most traditional form of accounting systems. Manual systems constitute the physical events, resources, and personnel that characterize many business processes. This includes such tasks as order-taking, warehousing materials, manufacturing goods for sale, shipping goods to customers, and placing orders with vendors. Traditionally, this model also includes the physical task of record keeping. Often, manual record keeping is used to teach the principles of accounting to business students. This approach, however, is simply a training aid. These days manual records are rarely used in practice.

Nevertheless, there is merit in studying the manual process model before mastering computer-based systems. First, learning manual systems helps establish an important link between the AIS course and other accounting courses. The AIS course is often the only accounting course in which students see where data originate, how they are collected, and how and where information is used to support day-to-day operations. By examining information flows, key tasks, and the use of traditional accounting records in transaction processing, the students' bookkeeping focus is transformed into a business processes perspective.

Secondly, the logic of a business process is more easily understood when it is not shrouded by technology. The information needed to trigger and support events such as selling, warehousing, and shipping is fundamental and independent of the technology that underlies the information system. For example, a shipping notice, informing the billing process that a product has been shipped, serves this purpose whether it is produced and processed manually or electronically. Once students understand what tasks need to be performed, they are better equipped to explore different and better ways of performing these tasks through technology.

Finally, manual procedures facilitate understanding internal control activities, including segregation of functions, supervision, independent verification, audit trails, and access controls. Since human nature lies at the heart of many internal control issues, we should not overlook the importance of this aspect of the information system.

THE FLAT FILE MODEL

The flat file approach is most often associated with so-called **legacy systems**. These are large mainframe systems that were implemented in the late 1960s through the 1980s. Organizations today still use these systems extensively. Eventually, they will be replaced by modern database management systems, but in the meantime accountants must continue to deal with legacy system technologies.

The **flat file model** describes an environment in which individual data files are not related to other files. End users in this environment *own* their data files rather than *share* them with other users. Data processing is thus performed by standalone applications rather than integrated systems.

When multiple users need the same data for different purposes, they must obtain separate data sets structured to their specific needs. Figure 1-12 illustrates how customer sales data might be presented to three different users in a durable goods retailing organization. The accounting function needs customer sales data organized by account number and structured to show outstanding balances. This is used for cus-

FIGURE 1–12

Flat File Model

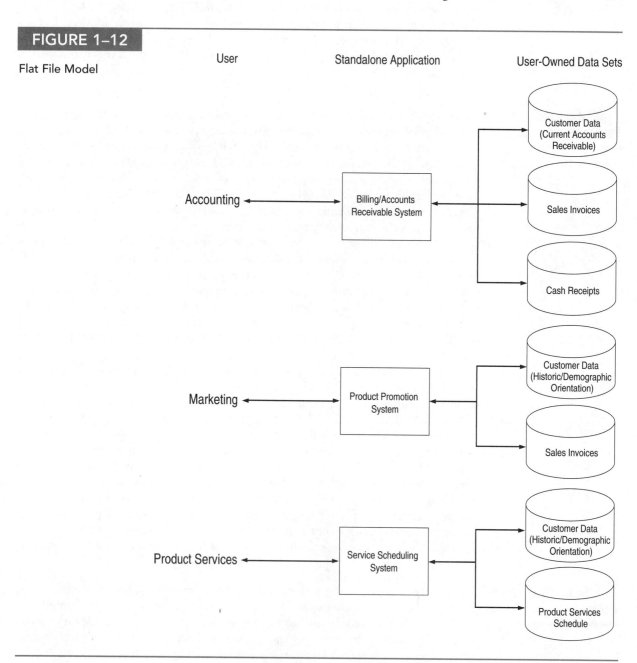

tomer billing, accounts receivable maintenance, and financial statement preparation. Marketing needs customer sales history data organized by demographic keys. They use this for targeting new product promotions and for selling product upgrades. The product services group needs customer sales data organized by products and structured to show scheduled service dates. Such information is used for making after-sales contacts with customers to schedule preventive maintenance and to solicit sales of service agreements.

The data redundancy demonstrated in this example contributes to three significant problems in the flat file environment: **data storage**, **data updating**, and **currency of information**. These and other problems associated with flat files are discussed in following sections.

Data Storage
An efficient information system captures and stores data only once and makes this single source available to all users who need it. In the flat file environment, this is not possible. To meet the private data needs of users, organizations must incur the costs of both multiple collection and multiple storage procedures. Some commonly used data may be duplicated dozens, hundreds, or even thousands of times.

Data Updating
Organizations have a great deal of data stored in files that require periodic updating to reflect changes. For example, a change to a customer's name or address must be reflected in the appropriate master files. When users keep separate files, all changes must be made separately for each user. This adds significantly to the task and the cost of data management.

Currency of Information
In contrast to the problem of performing multiple updates is the problem of failing to update all the user files affected by a change in status. If update information is not properly disseminated, the change will not be reflected in some users' data, resulting in decisions based on outdated information.

Task-Data Dependency
Another problem with the flat file approach is the user's inability to obtain additional information as his or her needs change. This problem is called **task-data dependency**. The user's information set is constrained by the data that he or she possesses and controls. Users act independently rather than as members of a user community. In such an environment, it is very difficult to establish a mechanism for the formal sharing of data. Therefore, new information needs tend to be satisfied by procuring new data files. This takes time, inhibits performance, adds to data redundancy, and drives data management costs even higher.

Flat Files Limit Data Integration
The flat file approach is a single-view model. Files are structured, formatted, and arranged to suit the specific needs of the *owner* or primary user of the data. Such structuring, however, may exclude data attributes that are useful to other users, thus preventing successful integration of data across the organization. For example, since the accounting function is the primary user of accounting data, these data are often captured, formatted, and stored to accommodate financial reporting and GAAP. This

structure, however, may be useless to the organization's other (nonaccounting) users of accounting data, such as the marketing, finance, production, and engineering functions. These users are presented with three options: (1) do not use accounting data to support decisions; (2) manipulate and massage the existing data structure to suit their unique needs; or (3) obtain additional private sets of the data and incur the costs and operational problems associated with data redundancy.

In spite of these inherent limitations, many large organizations still use flat files for their general ledger and other financial systems. Most members of the data processing community assumed that the end of the century would see the end of legacy systems. Instead, corporate America invested billions of dollars making these systems year-2000 (Y2K) compliant. Legacy systems continue to exist because they add value for their users and will not be replaced until they cease to add value. Students who may have to work with these systems in practice should be aware of their key features.

THE DATABASE MODEL

An organization can overcome the problems associated with flat files by implementing the **database model** to data management. Figure 1-13 illustrates how this approach centralizes the organization's data into a common database that is *shared* by other users. With the organization's data in a central location, all users have access to the data they need to achieve their respective objectives. Access to the data resource is controlled by a **database management system (DBMS)**. The DBMS is a special software system that is programmed to know which data elements each user is authorized to access. The user's program sends requests for data to the DBMS, which validates and authorizes access to the database in accordance with the user's level of authority. If the user requests data that he or she is not authorized to access, the request is denied. Clearly, the organization's procedures for assigning user authority are an important control issue for auditors to consider.

The most striking difference between the database model and the flat file model is the pooling of data into a common database that is shared by all organizational users. With access to the full domain of entity data, changes in user information needs

FIGURE 1–13

Database Model

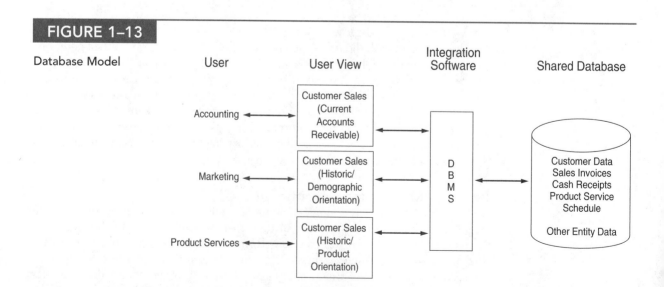

can be satisfied without obtaining additional private data sets. Users are constrained only by the limitations of the data available to the entity and the legitimacy of their need to access it. Through data sharing, the following traditional problems associated with the flat file approach *may* be overcome.

> *Elimination of data redundancy.* Each data element is stored only once, thereby eliminating data redundancy and reducing data collection and storage costs. For example, customer data exists only once, but is shared by accounting, marketing, and product services users. To accomplish this, the data are stored in a generic format that supports multiple users.

> *Single update.* Because each data element exists in only one place, it requires only a single update procedure. This reduces the time and cost of keeping the database current.

> *Current values.* A single change to a database attribute is automatically made available to all users of the attribute. For example, a customer address change entered by the billing clerk is immediately reflected in the marketing and product services views.

Flat file and early database systems are called **traditional systems**. Within this context, the term "traditional" means that the organization's information systems applications (its programs) function independently of each other rather than as an integrated whole. Early database management systems were designed to interface directly with existing flat file programs. Thus, when an organization replaced its flat files with a database it did not have to spend millions of dollars rewriting its existing programs. Indeed, early database applications performed essentially the same independent functions as their flat files counterparts. Another factor that limited integration was the structured database models of the era. These models were inflexible and did not permit the degree of data sharing that is found in modern database systems. While some degree of integration was achieved with this type of database, the primary and immediate advantage to the organization was the reduction in data redundancy.

True integration, however, would not be possible until the arrival of the **relational database model**. This flexible database approach permits the design of integrated systems applications capable of supporting the information needs of multiple users from a common set of integrated **database tables**. We should note, however, that the relational database model merely permits integration to occur; integration is not guaranteed. Poor systems design can occur under any model. In fact, most organizations today that employ a relational database run applications that are traditional in design and which do not make full use of relational technology. The two remaining models to be discussed (REA and ERP) employ relational database technology more effectively.

THE REA MODEL

REA is an accounting framework for modeling an organization's critical *Resources*, *Events*, and *Agents* (REA) and the relationships between them. Once specified, both accounting and nonaccounting data about these phenomena can be identified, captured, and stored in a relational database. From this repository, user views can be constructed that meet the needs of all users in the organization. The availability of multiple views allows flexible use of transaction data and permits the development of accounting information systems that promote, rather than inhibit, integration.

The REA model was proposed in 1982 as a theoretical model for accounting.[2] Advances in database technology have focused renewed attention on REA as a practical alternative to the classical accounting framework. The key elements of the REA model are summarized as follows.

Resources

Economic **resources** are the assets of the organization. They are defined as objects that are both scarce and under the control of the enterprise. This definition departs from the traditional model since it does not include accounts receivable. An account receivable is an artifact record used simply to store and transmit data. Since it is not an essential element of the system, it need not be included in the database. Instead, accounts receivable are derived from the difference between sales to customers and the cash received in payment of sales.

Events

Economic **events** are phenomena that affect changes in resources. They can result from activities such as production, exchange, consumption, and distribution. Economic events are the critical information elements of the accounting system and should be captured in a highly detailed form to provide a rich database.

Agents

Economic **agents** are individuals and departments that participate in an economic event. They are parties both inside and outside the organization with discretionary power to use or dispose of economic resources. Examples of agents include sales clerks, production workers, shipping clerks, customers, and vendors.

The REA model requires that accounting phenomena be characterized in a manner consistent with the development of multiple user views. Business data must not be preformatted or artificially constrained and should reflect all relevant aspects of the underlying economic events. As such, REA procedures and databases are structured around events rather than accounting artifacts such as journals, ledgers, charts of accounts, and double-entry accounting. Under the REA model, business organizations prepare financial statements directly from the event database. The following sales and cash receipts events for a hypothetical retailer can be used to illustrate the inherent differences between classical and REA accounting:

> Sept 1: Sold 5 units of product X21 @ $30 per unit and 10 units of product Y33 @ $20 per unit to customer Smith (Total sale = $350). The unit cost of the inventory is $16 and $12, respectively (Total CGS = $270).

> Sept 30: Received $200 cash from customer Smith on account, check number 451.

In flat file or non-REA database systems the two events would be recorded in a set of classical accounts like those shown in Figure 1-14. This involves summarizing the events to accommodate the account structure. The details of the transactions are, however, not captured under this approach.

---

2   W. E. McCarthy, "The REA Accounting Model: A Generalized Framework for Accounting Systems in a Shared Data Environment." *The Accounting Review* (July 1982): pp. 554–557.

FIGURE 1-14

Classical Accounting Records in a Non-REA System

Account Receivable File

Customer Number	Customer Name	Debit	Credit	Balance
23456	Smith	350	200	150

Cost of Goods Sold File

Acct Number	Debit	Credit
5734	270	

Sales File

Acct Number	Credit
4975	350

An REA accounting system would capture these transactions in a series of relational database tables that emphasize events rather than accounts. This is illustrated in Figure 1-15. Each table deals with a separate aspect of the transaction. Data pertaining to the customer, the invoice, specific items sold, etc., can thus be captured for multiple uses and users. The tables of the database are linked via common attributes called primary keys (PK) and embedded foreign keys (FK) that permit integration. In contrast, the files in the traditional system are independent of each other and thus cannot accommodate such detailed data gathering. As a result, traditional systems must summarize event data at the loss of potentially important facts.

Traditional accounting records including journals, ledgers, and charts of accounts do not exist as physical files or tables under the REA model. For financial reporting purposes, views or images of traditional accounting records are constructed from the event tables. For example, the amount of Smith's account receivable balance is derived from {total sales (Quant sold * Sale Price) less cash received (Amount) = (350 − 200) = 150}. If necessary or desired, journal entries and general ledger amounts can also be derived from these event tables. For example, the cost of goods sold control account balance is (Quant sold * Unit cost) summed for all transactions for the period.

REA is a conceptual model, not a physical system. Many of its tenets, however, are found within advanced database systems. The most notable application of REA philosophy is seen in the proliferation of ERP systems, which are discussed next.

ERP SYSTEMS

Enterprise resource planning (ERP) is an information system model that enables an organization to automate and integrate its key business processes. ERP breaks down traditional functional barriers by facilitating data sharing, information flows, and the introduction of common business practices among all organizational users. The implementation of an ERP system can be a massive undertaking that can span several years. Because of their complexity and size, few organizations are willing or able to commit the necessary financial and physical resources and incur the risk of

FIGURE 1–15

Event Database in an REA System

CUSTOMER Table

(PK)

Cust Num	Name	Address	Tel Num	Credit Limit	Billing Date	Anniver
23456	Smith	125 Elm St., City	610-555-1234	$5000	12	12/9/89

INVOICE Table

(PK) (FK)

Invoice Num	Invoice Date	Ship Date	Terms	Carrier	Cust Num
98765	9/01/97	9/03/97	Net 30	UPS	23456

LINE ITEM Table

(PK) (FK)

Product Num	Invoice Num	Quant Sold
X21	98765	5
Y33	98765	10

PRODUCT Table

(PK)

Product Num	Description	Sale Price	Unit Cost	QOH	Reorder Point
X21	Something or other	$30	$22	200	50
Y33	Something else	$20	$16	159	60

CASH_REC Table

(PK) (FK)

Trans Num	Cust Num	Check Num	Amount	Check Date	Date Posted
77654	23456	451	$200	Sept 28	Sept 30

developing an ERP system in-house. Hence, virtually all ERPs are commercial products. The recognized leaders in the market are SAP, Oracle, Baan, J.D. Edwards & Co., and PeopleSoft Inc.

ERP packages are sold to client organizations in modules that support standard processes. Some common ERP modules include:

Asset Management
Financial Accounting
Human Resources
Industry-Specific Solutions
Plant Maintenance
Production Planning
Quality Management
Sales and Distribution
Inventory Management

One of the problems with standardized modules is that they may not always meet the organization's exact needs. For example, a textile manufacturer in India implemented an ERP package only to discover that extensive, unexpected, and expensive modifications had to be made to the system. The ERP would not allow the user to assign two different prices to the same bolt of cloth. The manufacturer charged one price for domestic consumption, but another (four times higher) for exported products. That particular ERP system, however, provided no way to assign two prices to the same item while maintaining an accurate inventory count.

Organizations that hope to successfully implement an ERP will need to modify their business processes to suit the ERP, modify the ERP to suit their business or, more likely, modify both. Often, additional software applications need to be connected to the ERP to handle unique business functions, particularly industry-specific tasks. These applications, often called bolt-ons, are not always designed to communicate with ERP packages. The process of creating a harmonious whole can be quite complex and sometimes fails, resulting in significant losses to the organization. ERP packages are enormously expensive, but the savings in efficiencies should be significant. Organization management should exercise great care in deciding which, if any, ERP is best for them.

The evolution of information systems models outlined in this section provides a framework for much of the material contained this book. Chapters 2 through 8 deal with business processes, security, fraud, controls, and a variety of other issues related to traditional (manual, flat file, and early database) systems. Chapters 9 through 12 examine advanced database systems, the REA model, ERP, and other emerging technologies.

THE ROLE OF THE ACCOUNTANT

The final section of this chapter deals with the accountant's relationship to the information system. Accountants are primarily involved in three ways: as system *users*, as system *designers*, and as system *auditors*.

ACCOUNTANTS AS USERS

In most organizations, the accounting function is the single largest user of computer services. All systems that process financial transactions impact the accounting function in some way. As end users, accountants must provide a clear picture of their needs to the professionals who design their systems. For example, the accountant must specify accounting rules and techniques to be used, internal control requirements, and special algorithms such as depreciation models. The accountant's participation in systems development should be active rather than passive. The principal cause of design errors that result in system failure is the absence of user involvement.

ACCOUNTANTS AS SYSTEM DESIGNERS

An appreciation of the accountant's responsibility for system design requires a historic perspective that predates the computer as a business information tool. Traditionally, accountants have been responsible for key aspects of the information system, including assessing the information needs of users, defining the content and format of output reports, specifying sources of data, selecting the appropriate accounting rules, and determining the controls necessary to preserve the integrity and efficiency of the information system.

These traditional systems were physical, observable, and unambiguous. The procedures for processing information were manual, and the medium for transmitting and storing data was paper. With the arrival of the computer, manual procedures were replaced by computer programs, and records were stored magnetically. The part to be played by accountants in this new era became the subject of much controversy. Lacking computer skills, accountants were generally uncertain about their status and unwilling to explore this emerging technology.

Many accountants relinquished their traditional responsibilities to the new generation of computer professionals who were emerging in their organizations. Computer programmers, often with no accounting or business training, assumed full responsibility for the design of accounting information systems. As a result, many systems violated accounting principles and lacked necessary controls. Large system failures and computer frauds marked this period in accounting history. By the mid-1970s, in response to these problems, the accounting profession began to reassess the accountant's professional and legal responsibilities for computer-based systems.

Today, we recognize that the responsibility for systems design is divided between accountants and computer professionals as follows: the accounting function is responsible for the *conceptual system*, and the computer function is responsible for the *physical system*. To illustrate the distinction between conceptual and physical systems, consider the following example:

> The credit department of a retail business requires information about delinquent accounts from the accounts receivable department. This information supports decisions made by the credit manager regarding the creditworthiness of customers.

The design of the **conceptual system** involves specifying the criteria for identifying delinquent customers and the information that needs to be reported. The accountant determines the nature of the information required, its sources, its destination, and the accounting rules that need to be applied. The **physical system** is the medium and method for capturing and presenting the information. The computer professionals determine the most economical and effective technology for accomplishing the task. Hence, systems design should be a collaborative effort. Because of the uniqueness of each system and the susceptibility of systems to serious error and even fraud, the accountant's involvement in systems design should be pervasive. In later chapters, we shall see that the active participation of accountants is critical to the system's success.

ACCOUNTANTS AS SYSTEM AUDITORS

Auditing is a form of independent attestation performed by an expert—the auditor—who expresses an opinion about the fairness of a company's financial statements. Public confidence in the reliability of internally produced financial statements rests directly on their being validated by an independent expert auditor. This service is often referred to as the **attest function**. Auditors form their opinions based on a systematic process that will be explained in Chapter 17.

Audits are conducted by both internal and external auditors. External auditing is often called "independent auditing" because it is performed by certified public accounting (CPA) firms that are independent of the client organization's management. External auditors represent the interests of third-party stakeholders in the organization, such as stockholders, creditors, and government agencies.

External Auditing

Historically the external accountant's responsibility as a systems **auditor** was limited to the attest function described previously. In recent years this role has been expanded by the broader concept of assurance.

Assurance. **Assurance services** are professional services, including the attest function, that are designed to improve the quality of information, both financial and nonfinancial, used by decision makers. The domain of assurance services is intentionally unbounded so that it does not inhibit the growth of future services that are currently unforeseen. For example, assurance services may be contracted to provide information about the quality or marketability of a product. Alternatively, a client may need information about the efficiency of a production process or the effectiveness of their network security system. Assurance services are intended to help people make better decisions by improving information. This information may come as a by-product of the attest function, or it may ensue from an independently motivated review.

The evolution of the accounting profession is expected to follow the assurance services model. All of the "Big Five" professional services firms have now renamed their traditional audit functions "Assurance Services." The organizational unit responsible for conducting information technology (IT) audits is named either *IT Risk Management, Information Systems Risk Management*, or *Operational Systems Risk Management (OSRM)* and typically is a division of assurance services.

IT Auditing. **IT auditing** is usually performed as part of broader financial audit. The IT auditor attests to the integrity of elements of the organization's information system that have become complicated by computer technology. Periodically, the auditor must evaluate selected components of the accounting information system to establish their degree of compliance with organizational objectives and internal control standards. Since most organizations' accounting systems are computerized to some extent, the IT audit may be a large portion of the total audit. We examine IT auditing issues and discuss several specific techniques in Chapter 17.

Internal Auditing

Internal auditing is an appraisal function housed within the organization. Internal auditors perform a wide range of activities on behalf of the organization, including conducting financial statement audits, examining an operation's compliance with organizational policies, reviewing the organization's compliance with legal obligations, evaluating operational efficiency, detecting and pursuing fraud within the firm, and conducting IT audits.

As you can see, the tasks performed by external and internal auditors are similar. The feature that most clearly distinguishes the two groups is their respective constituencies. External auditors represent third-party outsiders, while internal auditors represent the interests of management. We shall not attempt to distinguish between these groups by placing arbitrary limits on their respective roles. Rather, in the chapters that follow, we shall refer to internal, external, and IT auditors simply as "auditors" or "accountants."

Summary

The first section of the chapter introduced basic systems concepts and presented a framework for distinguishing between accounting information systems and management information systems. This distinction is related to the types of transactions these systems process. AIS applications process financial transactions, and MIS applications process nonfinancial transactions. The section then presented a general model for accounting information systems. The model comprises four major tasks that exist in all AIS applications: data collection, data processing, database management, and information generation. The distinction between data and information is an important one. Data are facts; information causes the user to take action. The products of information systems must be frequently assessed in terms of their information content. The section presented three fundamental objectives of accounting information systems. The AIS should:

1. Support the stewardship function of management.
2. Support the decision-making processes of managers.
3. Support the day-to-day operations of the firm.

Organizations acquire information systems in two general ways: they develop systems in-house, and they purchase commercial systems from vendors. Three types of commercial software options were discussed.

The second section examined the relationship between organizational structure and the information system. It focused on functional segmentation as the predominant method of structuring a business and examined the functions of a typical manufacturing firm. The section presented two general methods of organizing the computer services function: the centralized approach and the distributed approach. The centralized approach maintains the computer resources of the firm in a central location, which are shared by the other functional areas. The distributed approach places computer resources under the direct control of end users. This trend in organizing the information system involves the extensive use of networks to permit communications among users in various functional areas.

The third section reviewed the evolution of information systems models. Accounting information systems have been represented by a number of different approaches or models. Each new model evolved because of the shortcomings and limitations of its predecessor. As new approaches evolved, however, the predecessor or legacy systems often remained in service. Thus, at any point in time, various generations of systems exist across different organizations and may even coexist within a single enterprise. Five models were examined: manual processes, flat file systems, the database approach, the REA (resources, events, and agents) model, and ERP (enterprise resource planning) systems.

The final section of the chapter examined the accountant's relationship to the information system, which is defined by three roles: users of information systems, designers of information systems, and auditors of information systems.

In most organizations, the accounting function is the single largest user of computer services. As end users of information systems, accountants must provide a clear picture of their needs to the professionals who design their systems. They must specify the accounting techniques to be used, internal control requirements, and special decision rules. The accountant's participation in this role should be active rather than passive.

An important distinction is made between the responsibilities of the computer services function and the accounting function for designing the information system. The computer services function is responsible for the physical system; the accounting function is responsible for the conceptual system.

Finally, the section examined the role of accountants as auditors of the information system. Auditing is an independent attestation performed by the auditor, who expresses an opinion about the fairness of a company's financial statements. Audits are conducted by both internal and external auditors. External auditing is often called "independent auditing" because it is performed by certified public accounting firms on behalf of third-party stakeholders in the organization. Historically the external auditor's responsibility was limited to the attest function. In recent years this role has been expanded by the broader concept of assurance. Assurance services are professional services, including the attest function, which are designed to improve the quality of information used by decision makers. Internal auditing is an appraisal function housed within the organization that performs a range of services for management. One form of auditing conducted by both external and internal auditors is information technology (IT) audits. The IT auditor attests to the integrity of elements of the organization's information system that have become complicated by computer technology.

Key Terms

accounting information systems (AIS)   (2)
agents   (34)
assurance services   (39)
attest function   (39)
auditing   (39)
auditor   (39)
backbone systems   (17)
centralized data processing   (23)
conceptual system   (38)
currency of information   (31)
data   (13)
data collection   (14)
data processing   (14)
data sources   (13)
data storage   (31)
data updating   (31)
database   (14)
database management   (15)
database management system (DBMS)   (32)
database model   (32)
database tables   (33)
distributed data processing (DDP)   (25)

end users   (13)
enterprise resource planning (ERP)   (35)
events   (34)
feedback   (16)
financial transaction   (9)
flat file model   (30)
general ledger/financial reporting system
   (GL/FRS)   (10)
general model for viewing AIS applications   (12)
independence   (23)
information   (13)
information flows   (4)
information generation   (16)
information system   (7)
internal auditing   (39)
IT auditing   (39)
legacy systems   (29)
management information system (MIS)   (10)
management reporting system (MRS)   (10)
nonfinancial transaction   (9)
physical system   (38)
REA   (33)

relational database model   (33)
reliability   (22)
resources   (34)
segments   (18)
stakeholders   (5)
subsystem   (6)
system   (5)
system development life cycle   (17)

task-data dependency   (31)
trading partners   (5)
traditional systems   (33)
transaction   (9)
transaction processing system (TPS)   (10)
turnkey systems   (17)
vendor-supported systems   (17)

Review Questions

1. What are the four levels of activity in the pyramid representing the business organization? Distinguish between horizontal and vertical flows of information.
2. Distinguish between natural and artificial systems.
3. What are the elements of a system?
4. What is system decomposition and subsystem interdependency? How are they are related?
5. What is the relationship among data, information, and an information system?
6. Distinguish between AIS and MIS.
7. What are the three cycles of transaction processing systems?
8. What is discretionary reporting?
9. What are the characteristics of good or useful information?
10. What rules govern data collection?
11. What are the levels of data hierarchy?
12. What are the three fundamental tasks of database management?
13. What is feedback and how is it useful in an information system?
14. What are the fundamental objectives of all information systems?
15. What does stewardship mean and what is its role in an information system?
16. Distinguish between responsibility, authority, and accountability. Which flow upward and which flow downward?
17. Distinguish between turnkey, backbone, and vendor-supported systems.
18. List each of the functional areas and their sub-functions.
19. What are the roles of internal and external auditors?
20. What is the role of a database administrator?
21. Name the three most common ways to segment an organization.
22. What is the role of the accounting function in an organization?
23. Distinguish between the centralized and distributed approaches to organizing the computer services function.
24. What is the role of the data control group?
25. What is distributed data processing?
26. What are the advantages and disadvantages of distributed data processing?
27. What types of tasks become redundant in a distributed data processing system?
28. What is a flat file system?
29. What are the three general problems associated with data redundancy?
30. Define the key elements of the REA model.
31. What is an ERP system?
32. What three roles are played by accountants with respect to the information system?
33. Define the term *attest function*.
34. Define the term *assurance*.
35. What is IT auditing?
36. Distinguish between conceptual and physical systems.

Discussion Questions

1. Discuss the differences between internal and external users of information and their needs and demands on an information system. Historically, which type of user has the firm catered to most?

2. Comment on the level of detail necessary for operations management, middle management, and stockholders.

3. Distinguish between financial and nonfinancial transactions. Give three examples of each.

4. Why have reengineering efforts been made to integrate AIS and MIS?

5. Do you think transaction processing systems differ significantly between service and manufacturing industries? Are they equally important to both sectors?

6. Discuss the difference between the financial reporting system and general ledger system.

7. Examine Figure 1–5 and discuss where and how problems can arise that can cause the resulting information to be "bad" or ineffective.

8. Discuss how the elements of efficiency, effectiveness, and flexibility are crucial to the design of an information system.

9. Discuss what is meant by the statement "The accounting system is a conceptual flow of information that represents the physical flows of personnel, raw materials, machinery, and cash through the organization."

10. Discuss the importance of accounting independence in accounting information systems. Give an example of where this concept is important (use an example other than inventory control).

11. Discuss why it is crucial that internal auditors report solely to the uppermost level of management (either to the chief executive officer or the audit committee of the board of directors) and answer to no other group.

12. Contrast centralized data processing with distributed data processing. How do the roles of systems professionals and end users change? What do you think the trend is today?

13. Discuss how conceptual and physical systems differ and which functions are responsible for each of these systems.

14. If accountants are viewed as providers of information, then why are they consulted as system users in the systems development process?

15. Do you agree with the statement "The term *IT auditor* should be considered obsolete because it implies a distinction between 'regular' auditors and auditors who examine computerized AIS"? Why or why not?

16. What are the primary reasons for segmenting organizations?

17. Why is it important to organizationally separate the accounting function from other functions of the organization?

18. What is the most likely system acquisition method—in-house, turnkey, backbone, or vendor-supported—for each of the following situations?
   - A plumbing supply company with 12 employees that sells standard products to wholesale customers in a local community needs a system to manage its affairs.
   - A major oil company with diverse holdings, complex oil leases, and esoteric accounting practices needs a system that can coordinate its many enterprises.
   - A municipal government needs a system that complies with standard government accounting practices but can be integrated with other existing systems.

19. The REA model is based on the premise that "business data must not be preformatted or artificially constrained and must reflect all relevant aspects of the underlying economic events." What does this mean and how is it applied?

20. ERP systems are comprised of a highly integrated set of standardized modules. Discuss the advantages and potential disadvantages of this approach.

Multiple-Choice Questions

1. CMA 686 5-1
   Accounting systems are designed to
   a. analyze and interpret information.
   b. allow managers to manage by exception.
   c. provide information required to support decisions.
   d. record and report business transactions.
   e. create database management systems.

2. CMA 1287 3-16
   One of the ingredients of the primary quality of relevance is
   a. verifiability.
   b. predictive value.
   c. neutrality.
   d. due process.
   e. representational faithfulness.
3. CMA 1287 3-17
   Accounting information that users can depend on to represent the economic conditions or events that it purports to represent best defines
   a. relevance.
   b. timeliness.
   c. feedback value.
   d. reliability.
   e. verifiability.
4. CMA 1290 2-15
   Accounting information that is capable of making a difference in a decision by helping users to confirm or correct expectations best defines
   a. neutrality.
   b. timeliness.
   c. accuracy.
   d. verifiability.
   e. relevance.
5. CMA 1290 2-16
   One of the ingredients of the primary quality of reliability is
   a. verifiability.
   b. feedback value.
   c. timeliness.
   d. comparability.
   e. consistency.
6. CMA 685 5-29
   A database is
   a. essential for storage of large data sets.
   b. a collection of related files.
   c. a real-time system.
   d. a network of computer terminals.
   e. a task-oriented file system.
7. When viewed from the highest to most elemental level, the data hierarchy is
   a. attribute, record, file.
   b. record, attribute, key.
   c. file, record, attribute.
   d. file, record, key.
   e. key, record, file.
8. Which is NOT an accountant's primary role in information systems?

a. system users
b. system auditors
c. system designers
d. system programmers

9. Which is NOT a primary function of an AIS transaction processing system?
   a. converting economic events into financial transactions
   b. distributing financial information to operations personnel to support their daily operations
   c. monitoring external economic events
   d. recording financial transactions in the accounting records
10. Which of the following best describes the activities of the materials management function?
    a. purchasing, receiving, and inventory control
    b. receiving, sales, distribution, and purchasing
    c. receiving, storage, purchasing, and accounts payable
    d. purchasing, receiving, and storage
    e. purchasing, storage, and distribution
11. Which of the following best describes the activities of the production function?
    a. maintenance, inventory control, and production planning
    b. production planning, quality control, manufacturing, and cost accounting
    c. quality control, production planning, manufacturing, and payroll
    d. maintenance, production planning, storage, and quality control
    e. manufacturing, quality control, and maintenance
12. Which of the following best describes the activities of the accounting function?
    a. inventory control, accounts payable, fixed assets, and payroll
    b. fixed assets, accounts payable, cash disbursements, and cost accounting
    c. purchasing, cash receipts, accounts payable, cash disbursements, and payroll
    d. inventory control, cash receipts, accounts payable, cash disbursements, and payroll
    e. inventory control, cost accounting, accounts payable, cash disbursements, and payroll
13. Which statement best describes the issue of distributed data processing (DDP)?
    a. The centralized and DDP approaches are mutually exclusive, an organization must choose one approach or the other.

b. The philosophy and objective of the organization's management will determine the extent of DDP in the firm.

c. In a minimum DDP arrangement, only data input and output are distributed, leaving the tasks of data control, data conversion, database management, and data processing to be centrally managed.

d. The greatest disadvantage of a totally distributed environment is that the distributed IPU locations are unable to communicate and coordinate their activities.

e. Although hardware (such as computers, database storage, and input/output terminals) can be effectively distributed, the systems development and maintenance tasks must remain centralized for better control and efficiency.

14. CMA (Adapted) 687 5-15
    A major disadvantage of distributed data processing is
    a. the increased time between job request and job completion.
    b. the potential for hardware and software incompatibility among users.
    c. the disruption caused when the mainframe goes down.
    d. that users are not likely to be involved.
    e. that data processing professionals may not be properly involved.

Problems

1. **Users of Information**
   Classify the following users of information as either:
   I—internal user
   T—external user: trading partner
   S—external user: stakeholder
   a. Internal Revenue Service
   b. Inventory control manager
   c. Board of directors
   d. Customers
   e. Lending institutions
   f. Securities and Exchange Commission
   g. Stockholders
   h. Chief executive officer
   i. Suppliers
   j. Bondholders

2. **Subsystems**
   Use the human body system to illustrate the concepts of system decomposition and subsystem interdependency. Draw a hierarchical chart similar to the one in Figure 1–2 and discuss the interdependencies.

3. **AIS Model**
   Examine the following diagram and determine what essential mechanism is missing. Once you have identified the missing element, discuss its importance.

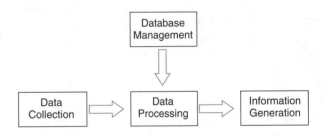

4. **AIS & MIS Features**
   List some AIS and MIS information from which salespeople may benefit. Clearly indicate whether the information item would be an output of a traditional AIS or MIS system. Finally, discuss the benefits of integrating this information.

5. **Information System Categorization**
   Classify the following items as either:
   TPS—transaction processing system
   FRS—financial reporting system
   MRS—management reporting system
   a. Variance reports
   b. Sales order capture
   c. Balance sheet
   d. Budgets
   e. Purchase order preparation
   f. Tax returns
   g. Sales summary by product line
   h. Cash disbursements preparation

i. Annual report preparation

j. Invoice preparation

k. Cost-volume-profit analysis

6. Organizational Chart

Draw an organizational chart for your college or university. What is the "output" for a college or university, and hence what are the "production" departments?

7. Organization Functions

Based on Figure 1–8, draw a diagram of functional segments for an oil company that has the following operations:

a. A head office in New York, New York, responsible for international and national marketing, acquisition of leases and contracts, and corporate reporting.

b. Two autonomous regional facilities in Tulsa, Oklahoma, and New Orleans, Louisiana. These facilities are responsible for oil exploration, drilling, refining, storage, and the distribution of petroleum products to corporate service stations throughout the country and abroad.

8. Organization Functions

Based on Figure 1–8, draw a diagram of functional segments for a manufacturer of diversified products. The general characteristics of the firm are as follows:

a. The organization produces three unrelated products: lawn and garden furniture for sale in home improvement centers and department stores; plastic packaging products for the electronics and medical supply industries; and paper products (e.g., plates, cups, and napkins) for the fast-food industry.

b. Although the manufacturing facilities are located within a single complex, none of the three products share the same suppliers, customers, or physical production lines.

c. The organization's functional activities include design, production, distribution, marketing, finance, human resources, and accounting.

9. Functional Segmentation

The current organization structure of Blue Sky Company, a manufacturer of small sailboats, is presented as follows.

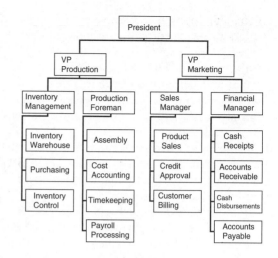

Required:

a. What operational problems (inefficiency, errors, fraud, etc.) do you think Blue Sky could experience because of this structure?

b. Draw a new diagram reflecting an improved structure that solves the problems identified above. If necessary, you may add up to two new positions.

10. Communications

Before the mid-1970s, systems programmers and businesspeople (including accountants) did not communicate well with one another. The programmers were criticized for using too much jargon, and the businesspeople were criticized for not adequately expressing their needs. Efforts have been made to overcome this communication gap, but room for improvement still exists. What problems do you think resulted from this communication gap? What do you think you can do to help close the gap even more when you enter the workforce?

11. Characteristics of Useful Information

All records in a database must be uniquely identifiable in at least one attribute, which is its primary key. Drawing on your general knowledge of accounting, identify the primary key for the following types of accounting records. To illustrate, the first record is done for you.

Record Type	*Primary Key*
Accounts Receivable	Customer Number
Accounts Payable	
Inventory	

Customer Sales Orders
Purchase Orders to vendors
Cash Receipts (checks) from customers
Cash Disbursements (checks) to vendors
Employee Payroll Earnings records

12. Data Attributes

Drawing from your basic accounting knowledge, list the relevant data attributes that constitute the record types below. Identify which attribute is the primary key for the record.

Accounts Payable record
Inventory record
Customer Sales Orders record
Purchase Orders to vendors
Cash Receipts (checks) from customers
Employee Payroll Earnings records

13. CMA (Adapted) 1288-5Y6
Distributed Data Processing

In the last two decades, there has been a transition from a centralized mainframe computer environment to a distributed network where an organization has the ability to share computer processing. One of the fastest-growing segments of the computer industry is the local area network (LAN), which is said to be the wave of the future. LANs permit the transfer of information between microcomputers, word processors, data storage devices, printers, voice devices, and telecommunication devices. Current opinion holds that the flow of organizational communications has been enhanced by the transition from the optimization of computers experienced in the traditional distributed network to the optimization of human resources in the LAN environment.

Required:

a.   Describe the reasons why an organization would choose a distributed network over the traditional centralized computer environment.

b.   Compare and contrast the characteristics of a traditional distributed computer network with those of a local area network as they are related to the:
i.   utilization of computer hardware.
ii.   user interaction and the sharing of electronic information.

c.   Identify and explain three problems that can result from the use of local area networks.

d.   Explain the hardware characteristics associated with a computer modem as they relate to distributed information processing.

CHAPTER

2

Introduction to Transaction Processing

Chapter 1 introduced the transaction processing system (TPS) as an activity consisting of three major subsystems called *cycles*: the revenue cycle, the expenditure cycle, and the conversion cycle. While each cycle performs different specific tasks and supports different objectives, they share common characteristics. For example, all three TPS cycles capture financial transactions, record the effects of transactions in accounting records, and provide information about transactions to users in support of their day-to-day activities. In addition, transaction cycles produce much of the raw data from which management reports and financial statements are derived. Because of their financial impact on the firm, transaction cycles command much of the accountant's professional attention.

The purpose of this chapter is to present some preliminary topics that are common to all three transaction processing cycles. In subsequent chapters, we shall draw heavily from this material as we examine the individual subsystems of each cycle in detail. The chapter is organized into four major sections. The first is an overview of transaction processing. This section defines the broad objective of the three transaction cycles and specifies the roles of their individual subsystems. The second section describes the relationship among accounting records in forming an audit trail in both manual and computer-based systems. The third section examines documentation techniques used to represent systems. This section presents six documentation techniques for manual and computer-based systems. The fourth section of this chapter addresses computer-based systems. Most organizations employ computer technology in some form to process transactions. This section reviews the fundamental effects of alternative technologies on transaction processing.

LEARNING OBJECTIVES

After studying this chapter, you should:

- Understand the broad objectives of transaction cycles.
- Recognize the types of transactions processed by each of the three transaction cycles.
- Know the basic accounting records used in transaction processing systems.
- Understand the relationship between traditional accounting records and their magnetic equivalents in computer-based systems.
- Be familiar with the documentation techniques used for representing manual and computer-based systems.
- Understand the differences between batch and real-time processing and the impact of these technologies on transaction processing.

AN OVERVIEW OF TRANSACTION PROCESSING

TPS applications process financial transactions. A financial transaction was defined in Chapter 1 as:

> An economic event that affects the assets and equities of the firm, is reflected in its accounts, and is measured in monetary terms.

The most common financial transactions are economic exchanges with external parties. These include the sale of goods or services, the purchase of inventory, the discharge of financial obligations, and the receipt of cash on account from customers. Financial transactions also include certain internal events such as the depreciation of fixed assets; the application of labor, raw materials, and overhead to the production process; and the transfer of inventory from one department to another.

Financial transactions are common business events that occur with regularity. For instance, thousands of transactions of a particular type (sales to customers) may occur daily. To deal efficiently with such volume, business firms group similar types of transactions into transaction cycles.

TRANSACTION CYCLES

Three transaction cycles process most of the firm's economic activity: the expenditure cycle, the conversion cycle, and the revenue cycle. These cycles exist in all types of businesses—both profit-seeking and not-for-profit. For instance, every business (1) incurs expenditures in exchange for resources (expenditure cycle), (2) provides value added through its products or services (conversion cycle), and (3) receives revenue from outside sources (revenue cycle). Figure 2–1 shows the relationship of these cycles and the resource flows between them.

THE EXPENDITURE CYCLE

Business activities begin with the acquisition of materials, property, and labor in exchange for cash—the **expenditure cycle**. Figure 2–1 shows the flow of cash from the organization to the various providers of these resources. Most expenditure transactions are based on a credit relationship between the trading parties. The actual disbursement of cash takes place at some point after the receipt of the goods or services. Days or even weeks may pass between these two events. Thus, from a systems perspective, this transaction has two parts: a physical component (the acquisition of the goods) and a financial component (the cash disbursement to the supplier). Each component is processed by a separate subsystem of the cycle. The major subsystems of the expenditure cycle are outlined below. Because of the extent of this body of material, two chapters are devoted to the expenditure cycle. Purchases/accounts payable and cash disbursements systems are the topics of Chapter 5. Payroll and fixed asset systems are examined in Chapter 6.

Purchases/accounts payable system. This system recognizes the need to acquire physical inventory (such as raw materials) and places an order with the vendor. When the goods are received, the purchases system records the event by increasing inventory and establishing an account payable to be paid at a later date.

Cash disbursements system. When the obligation created in the purchases system falls due, the cash disbursement system authorizes the payment, dis-

FIGURE 2–1

Relationship between
Transaction Cycles

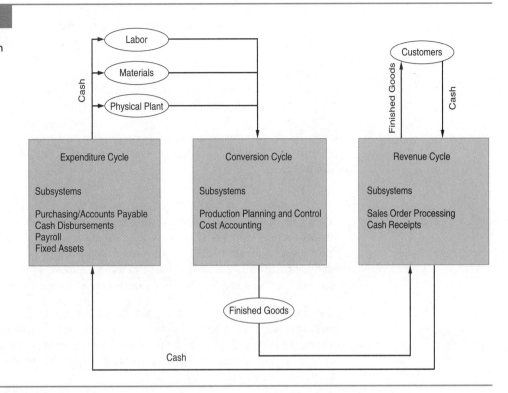

burses the funds to the vendor, and records the transaction by reducing the cash and accounts payable accounts.

Payroll system. The payroll system collects labor usage data for each employee, computes the payroll, and disburses paychecks to the employees. Conceptually, payroll is a special-case purchases and cash disbursements system. Because of accounting complexities associated with payroll, most firms have a separate system for payroll processing.

Fixed asset system. A firm's fixed asset system processes transactions pertaining to the acquisition, maintenance, and disposal of its fixed assets. These are relatively permanent items that collectively often represent the largest financial investment by the organization. Examples of fixed assets include land, buildings, furniture, machinery, and motor vehicles.

THE CONVERSION CYCLE

The **conversion cycle** is comprised of two major subsystems: the production system and the cost accounting system. The production system involves the planning, scheduling, and control of the physical product through the manufacturing process. This includes determining raw materials requirements, authorizing the work to be performed and the release of raw materials into production, and directing the movement of the work in process through its various stages of manufacturing. The cost accounting system monitors the flow of cost information related to production. Information produced by this system is used for inventory valuation, budgeting, cost control, performance reporting, and management decisions, such as "make or buy" decisions. We examine the basic features of these systems in Chapter 7.

Manufacturing firms convert raw materials into finished products through formal conversion cycle operations. The conversion cycle is not usually formal and observable in service and retailing establishments. Nevertheless, these firms still engage in conversion cycle activities that culminate in the development of a salable product or service. These activities include the readying of products and services for market and the allocation of resources such as depreciation, building amortization, and prepaid expenses to the proper accounting period. However, unlike manufacturing firms, merchandising companies do not process these activities through formal conversion cycle subsystems.

THE REVENUE CYCLE

Firms sell their finished goods to customers through the **revenue cycle**, which involves processing cash sales, credit sales, and the receipt of cash following a credit sale. Revenue cycle transactions also have a physical and a financial component, which are processed separately. The primary subsystems of the revenue cycle, which are the topics of Chapter 4, are briefly outlined below.

> *Sales order processing.* The majority of business sales are made on credit and involve such tasks as preparing sales orders, granting credit, shipping products (or rendering of a service) to the customer, billing customers, and recording the transaction in the accounts (accounts receivable, inventory, expenses, and sales).

> *Cash receipts.* For credit sales, some period of time (days or weeks) passes between the point of the sale and the receipt of cash. Cash receipts processing includes collecting cash, depositing cash in the bank, and recording these events in the accounts (accounts receivable and cash).

ACCOUNTING RECORDS

MANUAL SYSTEMS

This section describes the purpose of each type of **accounting record** used in transaction cycles. We begin with traditional records used in manual systems (documents, journals, and ledgers) and then examine their magnetic counterparts in computer-based systems.

Documents

A document provides evidence of an economic event and may be used to initiate transaction processing. Some documents are a result of transaction processing. In this section, we discuss three types of documents: source documents, product documents, and turnaround documents.

Source Documents. Economic events give rise to some documents being created at the beginning (the source) of the transaction. These are called **source documents**. Source documents are used to capture and formalize transaction data needed for processing by the transaction cycle. Figure 2–2 shows the creation of a source document.

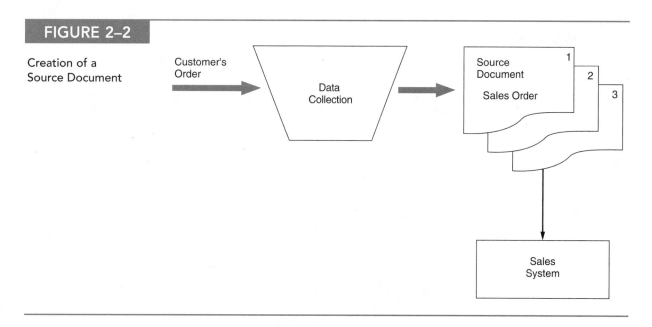

FIGURE 2–2

Creation of a
Source Document

The economic event (the sale) causes the sales clerk to prepare a multipart sales order, which is formal evidence that a sale occurred. Copies of this source document enter the sales system and are used to convey information to various functions, such as billing, shipping, and accounts receivable. The information in the sales order triggers specific activities in each of these departments.

Product Documents. **Product documents** are the result of transaction processing rather than the triggering mechanism for the process. For example, a payroll check to an employee is a product document of the payroll system. Figure 2–3 extends the example in Figure 2–2 to illustrate that the customer's bill is a product document of the sales system. We will study many other examples of product documents in later chapters.

Turnaround Documents. **Turnaround documents** are product documents of one system that become source documents for another system. This is illustrated in Figure 2–4. The customer receives a perforated two-part bill or statement. The top portion of this document is the actual bill, and the bottom portion is the remittance advice. When customers make a payment, they remove the remittance advice and return it to the company along with their check. A turnaround document carries important information about a customer's account to help the cash receipts system process the check. One of the problems faced by designers of cash receipts systems is matching customer payments to the correct customer accounts. By providing this needed information as a product of the sales system, we can be sure of its accuracy when it is received by the cash receipts system.

Journals

A **journal** is a record of chronological entry. At some point in the transaction process, when all relevant facts about the transaction are known, the event is recorded in a journal in chronological order. Documents are the primary source of data for

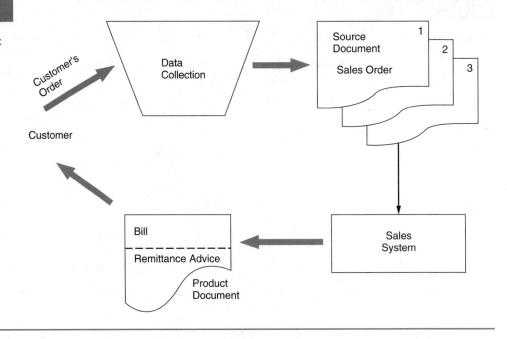

FIGURE 2–3

A Product Document

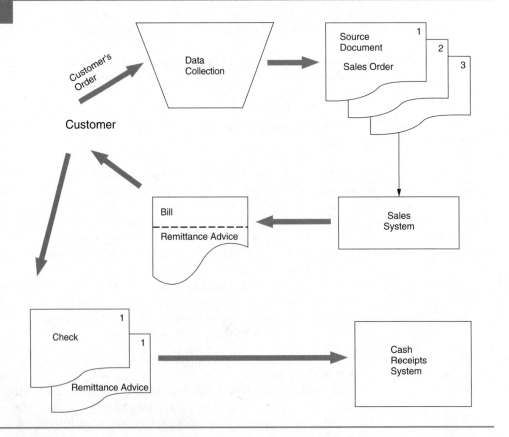

FIGURE 2–4

A Turnaround
Document

journals. Figure 2–5 shows a sales order being recorded in the sales journal (see the discussion of special journals below). Each transaction requires a separate journal entry, reflecting the accounts affected and the amounts to be debited and credited. Often, there is a time lag between initiating a transaction and recording it in the accounts. The journal holds a complete record of transactions processed by the organization and thus provides a means for posting to accounts. There are two primary types of journals: *special journals* and the *general journal*.

Special Journals. Special journals are used to record specific classes of transactions that occur in high volume. Such transactions can be grouped together in a special journal and processed more efficiently than a general journal permits. Figure 2–6 shows a special (sales) journal for recording sales transactions.

As you can see, the sales journal provides a specialized format for recording only sales transactions. At the end of the processing period (month, week, or day), a clerk posts the amounts in the columns to the ledger accounts indicated (see the discussion of ledgers). For example, the total of sales will be posted to account number 401. Most organizations use several other special journals, including the cash receipts journal, cash disbursements journal, purchases journal, and the payroll journal.

FIGURE 2–5

Sales Order Recorded in Sales Journal

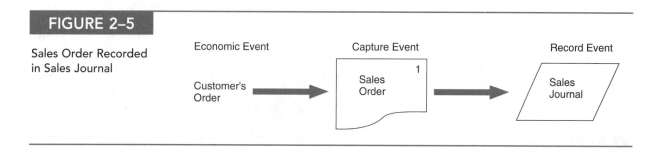

FIGURE 2–6

Sales Journal

Date	Customer	Invoice Num.	Acct. Num.	Post	Debit Acct. Rec. #102	Credit Sales #401
Sept. 1	Hewitt Co.	4523	1120		3300	3300
15	Acme Drilling	8821	1298		6825	6825
Oct. 3	Buell Corp.	22987	1030		4000	4000
10	Check Ltd.	66734	1110		8500	8500

Register. The term *register* denotes certain types of special journals. For example, the payroll journal is often called the *payroll register*. However, we also use the term *register* to denote a log. For example, a receiving register is a log of all receipts of raw materials or merchandise ordered from vendors. Similarly, a shipping register is a log that records all shipments to customers.

General Journal. Firms use the general journal to record nonrecurring, infrequent, and dissimilar transactions. For example, we usually record periodic depreciation and closing entries in the general journal. Figure 2–7 shows one page from a general journal. Note that the columns are nonspecific, allowing any type of transaction to be recorded. The entries are recorded in chronological order.

As a practical matter, most organizations have replaced their general journal with a journal voucher system. A journal voucher is actually a special source document that contains a single journal entry specifying the general ledger accounts that are affected. Journal vouchers are used to record summaries of routine transactions, nonroutine transactions, adjusting entries, and closing entries. The total of journal vouchers processed are equivalent to the general journal. Subsequent chapters discuss the use of this technique in transaction processing.

Ledgers

A **ledger** is a book of financial accounts, which reflect the financial effects of the firm's transactions after they are posted from the various journals. Whereas journals show the chronological effect of business activity, ledgers show activity by account type. A ledger indicates the increases, decreases, and current balance of each account.

FIGURE 2–7

General Journal

GENERAL JOURNAL   PAGE

	DATE	DESCRIPTION	POST. REF.	DEBIT	CREDIT	
1	Sept. 1, 2001	Depreciation expense	520	5 0 0 0		1
2		Accumulated depreciation	210		5 0 0 0	2
3						3
4	Sept. 2, 2001	Insurance expense	525	1 2 0 0		4
5		Prepaid insurance	180		1 2 0 0	5
6						6
7	Sept. 3, 2001	Cash	101	1 1 0 0 0		7
8		Capital stock	310		1 1 0 0 0	8
9						9
10						10
11						11
12						12

Organizations use this financial information to prepare financial statements, support daily operations, and prepare internal reports. Figure 2–8 shows the flow of financial information from the source documents to the journal and into the ledgers.

There are two basic types of ledgers: (1) the *general ledger*, which contains the firm's account information in the form of highly summarized control accounts and (2) *subsidiary ledgers*, which contain the details of the individual accounts that constitute a particular control account.[1]

General Ledger. The general ledger summarizes the activity for each of the organization's accounts. The general ledger department updates these records from journal vouchers prepared from special journals and other sources located throughout the organization. The general ledger presented in Figure 2–9 shows the beginning balances, the changes, and the ending balances as of a particular date for several different accounts.

The general ledger provides a single value for each control account, such as accounts payable, accounts receivable, and inventory. This highly summarized information is sufficient for financial reporting, but it is not useful for supporting daily business operations. For example, for financial reporting purposes, the firm's total accounts receivable value must be presented as a single figure in the balance sheet. This value is obtained from the accounts receivable control account in the general ledger. However, to actually collect the cash represented by this asset, the firm must have certain detailed information about the customers that is not provided by this summary figure. It must know which customers owe money, how much each customer owes, when the customer last made payment, when the next payment is due, and so on. The accounts receivable subsidiary ledger contains these essential details.

Subsidiary Ledger. Subsidiary ledgers are kept in various accounting departments of the firm. These include inventory, accounts payable, payroll, and accounts receivable.

FIGURE 2–8

Flow of Information from the Economic Event to the General Ledger

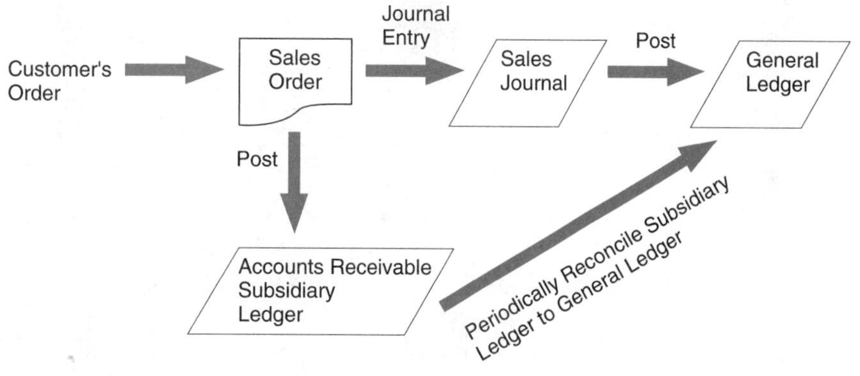

---

1   Not all control accounts in the general ledger have corresponding subsidiary accounts. Accounts such as sales and cash typically have no supporting details in the form of a subsidiary ledger.

FIGURE 2–9   General Ledger

Cash   ACCOUNT NO. 101

DATE		ITEM	POST. REF.	DEBIT	CREDIT	BALANCE DEBIT	BALANCE CREDIT
Sept.	10		S1	3 3 0 0		3 3 0 0	
Sept.	15		S1	6 8 2 5		1 0 1 2 5	
Oct.	3		S1	4 0 0 0		1 4 1 2 5	
Oct.	10		CD1		2 8 0 0	1 1 3 2 5	

Accounts Receivable   ACCOUNT NO. 102

DATE		ITEM	POST. REF.	DEBIT	CREDIT	BALANCE DEBIT	BALANCE CREDIT
Sept.	1		S1	1 4 0 0		1 4 0 0	
Sept.	8		S1	2 6 0 5		4 0 0 5	
Sept.	15		CR1		1 6 5 0	2 3 5 5	

Accounts Payable   ACCOUNT NO. 201

DATE		ITEM	POST. REF.	DEBIT	CREDIT	BALANCE DEBIT	BALANCE CREDIT
Sept.	1		P1		2 0 5 0 0		2 0 5 0 0
Sept.	10		CD1	2 8 0 0			1 7 7 0 0

Purchases   ACCOUNT NO. 502

DATE		ITEM	POST. REF.	DEBIT	CREDIT	BALANCE DEBIT	BALANCE CREDIT
Sept.	1		P1	2 0 5 0 0		2 0 5 0 0	

This separation provides better control and support of operations. Figure 2–10 illustrates that the total of account balances in a subsidiary ledger should equal the balance in the corresponding general ledger control account. Thus, in addition to providing financial statement information, the general ledger is a mechanism for verifying the overall accuracy of accounting data that has been processed by separate sources. Any event incorrectly recorded in a journal or subsidiary ledger will cause an out-of-balance condition that should be detected during the general ledger update. By periodically reconciling summary balances from subsidiary accounts, journals, and control accounts, the completeness and accuracy of transaction processing can be formally assessed.

THE AUDIT TRAIL

The accounting records described previously provide an **audit trail** for tracing transactions from source documents to the financial statements. Of the many purposes

---

FIGURE 2–10

Relationship between the Subsidiary Ledger and the General Ledger

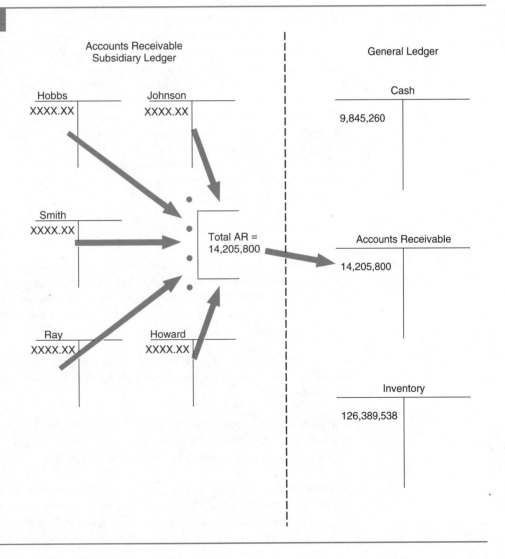

served by the audit trail, most important to accountants is the year-end audit. While the study of financial auditing falls outside the scope of this text, the following thumbnail sketch of the audit process will demonstrate the importance of the audit trail.

The external auditor periodically evaluates the financial statements of publicly-held business organizations on behalf of its stockholders and other interested parties. The auditor's responsibility involves, in part, the review of selected accounts and transactions to determine their validity, accuracy, and completeness. Let's assume an auditor wishes to verify the accuracy of a client's accounts receivable (AR) as published in its annual financial statements. The auditor can trace the AR figure on the balance sheet to the general ledger AR control account. This balance can then be reconciled with the total for the AR subsidiary ledger. Rather than examining every transaction that affected the AR account, the auditor will use a sampling technique to examine a representative subset of transactions. Following this approach, the auditor can select a number of accounts from the AR subsidiary ledger and trace these back to the sales journal. From the sales journal, the auditor can identify the specific source documents that initiated the transactions and pull them from the files to verify their validity and accuracy.

The audit of accounts receivable often includes a procedure called *confirmation*. This involves contacting selected customers to determine if the transactions recorded in the accounts actually took place and that customers agree with the recorded balance. Information contained in source documents and subsidiary accounts enables the auditor to identify and locate customers chosen for confirmation. The results from reconciling the AR subsidiary ledger with the control account and from confirming customers' accounts help the auditor form an opinion about the accuracy of accounts receivable as reported on the balance sheet. The auditor performs similar tests on all of the client firm's major accounts and transactions to arrive at an overall opinion about the fair presentation of the financial statement. The audit trail plays an important role in this process.

COMPUTER-BASED SYSTEMS

Types of Files

While audit trails in computer-based systems are less observable than in traditional manual systems, they still exist. Accounting records in computer-based systems are represented by four different types of magnetic files: master files, transaction files, reference files, and archive files. Figure 2–11 illustrates the relationship of these files in forming an audit trail.

Master File. A **master file** generally contains account data. The general ledger and subsidiary ledgers are examples of master files. Data values in master files are updated from transactions.

Transaction File. A **transaction file** is a temporary file holding transaction records that will be used to change or update data in a master file. Sales orders, inventory receipts, and cash receipts are examples of transaction files.

Reference File. A **reference file** stores data that are used as standards for processing transactions. For example, the payroll program may refer to a tax table to calculate the proper amount of withholding taxes for payroll transactions. Other reference files include price lists used for preparing customer invoices, lists of authorized suppliers,

| FIGURE 2-11 | Accounting Records in a Computer-Based System |

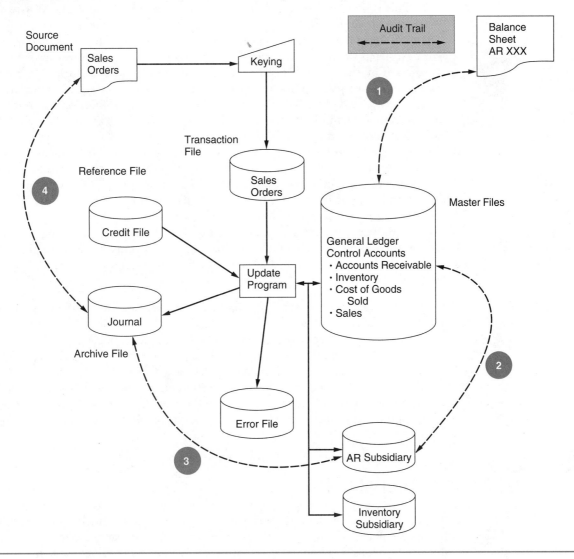

employee rosters, and customer credit files for approving credit sales. The reference file in Figure 2–11 is a credit file.

Archive File. An **archive file** contains records of past transactions that are retained for future reference. These transactions form an important part of the audit trail. Archive files include journals, prior-period payroll information, lists of former employees, records of accounts written off, and prior-period ledgers.

The Magnetic Audit Trail
Let's walk through the system represented in Figure 2–11 to illustrate how computer files provide an audit trail. We begin with the capture of the economic event. In this

example, sales are recorded manually on source documents, just as in the manual system. The next step in this process is to convert the source documents to magnetic form. This is done in the data input stage, where the transactions are edited and a transaction file of sales orders is produced. Some computer systems do not use physical source documents. Instead, transactions are captured directly on magnetic media. The next step is to update the various master file subsidiary and control accounts that are affected by the transaction. During the update procedure, additional editing of transactions takes place. Some transactions may prove to be in error or invalid for such reasons as incorrect account numbers, insufficient quantities on hand, or customer credit problems. In this example, the system determines the available credit for each customer from the credit file before processing the sale. Any records that are rejected for credit problems are transferred to the error file. The remaining good records are used to update the master files. Only these transactions are added to the archive file that serves as the sales journal. By copying the valid transactions to the journal, the original transaction file is not needed for audit trail purposes. This file can now be erased (scratched) in preparation for the next batch of sales orders.

Like the paper trail, this magnetic audit trail allows transaction tracing. Again, an auditor attempting to evaluate the accuracy of the accounts receivable figure published in the balance sheet could do so via the following steps, which are identified in Figure 2–11.

1. Compare the accounts receivable balance in the balance sheet with the master file AR control account balance.
2. Reconcile the AR control figure with the AR subsidiary account total.
3. Select a sample of update entries made to accounts in the AR subsidiary ledger and trace these to transactions in the sales journal (archive file).
4. From these journal entries, identify specific source documents that can be pulled from their files and verified. If necessary, the auditor can confirm the accuracy and propriety of these source documents by contacting the customers in question.

DOCUMENTATION TECHNIQUES

The old saying that a picture is worth a thousand words is extremely applicable when it comes to documenting systems. A written description of a system can be wordy and difficult to follow. Experience has shown that a visual image can convey vital system information more effectively and efficiently than words do. As both systems designers and auditors, accountants use system documentation routinely. The ability to document systems in graphic form is thus an important skill for accountants to master. Six basic documentation techniques are introduced in this section: entity relationship (ER) diagrams, data flow diagrams, document flowcharts, system flowcharts, program flowcharts, and record layout diagrams.

ENTITY RELATIONSHIP DIAGRAM

An **entity relationship (ER) diagram** is a documentation technique used to represent the relationship between entities (resources, events, and agents) in a system. Figure 2–12 shows the symbol set used in an ER diagram. The rectangle symbol represents entities in the system. An **entity** is a resource (an automobile, cash, or inventory), an event (selecting an automobile, ordering goods, receiving cash, or updating

FIGURE 2–12

Entity Relationship
Diagram Symbols

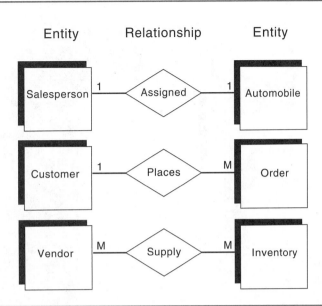

accounting records), or an agent (salesperson, customer, or vendor). The nature of the relationship between two entities is represented by the diamond symbol.

Entity relationships can also be described in terms of **cardinality**. This is the numerical mapping between entity instances. A relationship can be one-to-one (1:1), one-to-many (1:M), or many-to-many (M:M). In the simplest sense, if we think of entities as file of records, cardinality is the maximum number of records in one file that are related to a single record in the other file and vice versa.

Cardinality can reflect organizational policy. For instance, the 1:1 cardinality in the first example in Figure 2–12 suggests that each salesperson in the organization is assigned one automobile. Another organization may decide to assign a single automobile to one or more salespersons who must share it. This policy would be reflected by a 1:M relationship. The M:M relationship between vendor and inventory in Figure 2–12 implies that the organization buys the same type of products from more than one vendor. A company policy to buy similar items from a single vendor would change the cardinality to 1:M.

DATA FLOW DIAGRAMS

The **data flow diagram** (DFD) uses symbols to represent the processes, data sources, data flows, and entities in a system. Figure 2–13 presents the symbol set most commonly used. DFDs are used to represent systems at different levels of detail from very general to highly detailed. Later we will study the construction of multilevel DFDs. At this point, a single-level DFD is sufficient to demonstrate its use as a documentation tool. We see an example of this in Figure 2–14 (page 65).

This partial sales order system is composed of the following major processes:

1. Approve sales.
2. Ship goods.
3. Bill customers.
4. Prepare accounts receivable.

FIGURE 2–13

Data Flow
Diagram
Symbol Set

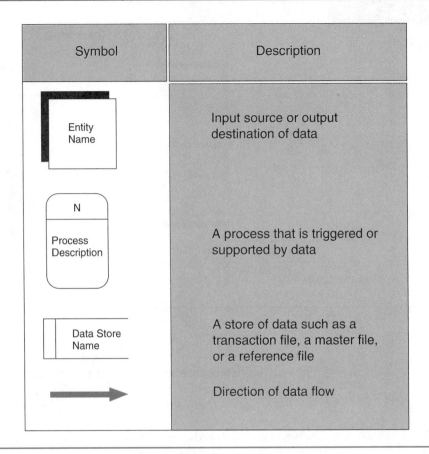

Symbol	Description
Entity Name	Input source or output destination of data
N Process Description	A process that is triggered or supported by data
Data Store Name	A store of data such as a transaction file, a master file, or a reference file
→	Direction of data flow

The accounting records used in each process are represented as data stores, and the data flows between processes are represented by labeled arrows.

DFDs are used extensively by systems analysts to represent the logical elements of the system. However, this technique does not represent the physical system. In other words, DFDs show what logical tasks are being done, but not how they are done or who (or what) is performing them. For example, the DFD does not show whether the sales approval process is separated physically from the billing process in compliance with internal control objectives.

FLOWCHARTS

A flowchart is graphical representation of a system that describes the *physical* relationship between its key entities. Flowcharts can be used to represent manual activities, computer processing activities, or both. A **document flowchart** is used to depict the elements of a *manual system* including accounting records (documents, journals, ledgers, and files), organizational departments involved in the process, and activities (both clerical and physical) that are performed in the departments.

System flowcharts portray the computer aspects of a system. They depict the relationships between input (source) data, transaction files, computer programs, master files, and output reports produced by the system. System flowcharts also describe

FIGURE 2–14   Data Flow Diagram for Sales Order Processing System

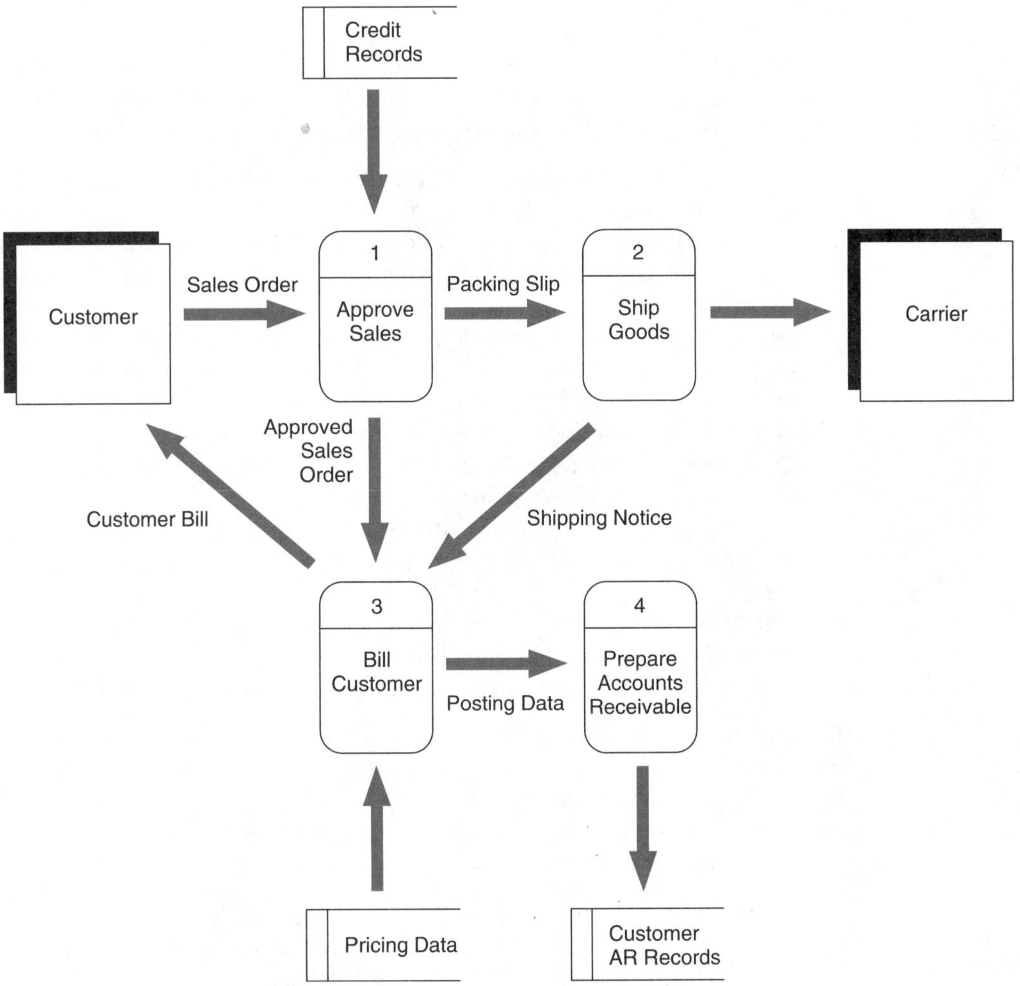

the type of media being used in the system, such as magnetic tape, magnetic disks, and terminals.

The dichotomy between document flowcharts and system flowcharts reflects the dichotomy that traditionally existed between the manual and the computer aspects of an information system. Today, the human–machine interface is far more fluid than it was in the past. For example, transactions may be entered into the system directly by end users, processing often occurs in real time on the user's desktop computer, and output may be delivered to the user via a terminal rather than paper reports. Thus, modern systems are comprised of both manual and computer operations.

The flowcharting examples that follow will illustrate the use of traditional *document flowcharts* to represent manual systems and *system flowcharts* to describe systems that employ both manual and computer operations. *Program flowcharts* that describe the internal logic of computer programs are explained last.

Document Flowcharts

To demonstrate the preparation of a document flowchart, let's assume that an auditor needs to flowchart a sales order system to evaluate its internal controls and procedures. The auditor will begin by interviewing individuals involved in the sales order process to determine what they do. This information will be captured in a set of facts similar to those below. Keep in mind that the purpose here is to demonstrate flowcharting. Thus, for clarity, the system facts are intentionally simplistic.

1. A clerk in the sales department receives customer orders by mail and prepares four copies of a sales order.
2. Copy 1 of the sales order is sent to the credit department for approval. The other three copies and the original customer order are filed temporarily pending credit approval.
3. The credit department clerk validates the customer's order against credit records kept in the credit department. The clerk signs Copy 1 to signify approval and returns it to the sales clerk.
4. When the sales clerk receives credit approval he or she files Copy 1 and the customer order in the department. The clerk sends Copy 2 to the warehouse and Copies 3 and 4 to the shipping department.
5. The warehouse clerk picks the products from the shelves, records the transfer in the stock records, and sends the products and Copy 2 to the shipping department.
6. The shipping department receives Copy 2 and the goods from the warehouse, attaches Copy 2 as a packing slip, and ships the goods to the customer. Finally, the clerk files Copies 3 and 4 in the shipping department.

Based on these facts the auditor can create a flowchart of this partial system. It is important to note that flowcharting is as much an art form as it is a technical skill, giving the flowchart author a great deal of license. Nevertheless, the primary objective should be to provide an unambiguous description of the system. With this in mind, certain rules and conventions need to be observed:

- The flowchart should be labeled to clearly identify the system that it represents.
- The correct symbols should be used to represent the entities in the system.
- All symbols on the flowchart should be labeled.
- Lines should have arrowheads to clearly show the process flow and sequence of events.
- If complex processes need additional explanation for clarity, a text description should be included on the flowchart or in an attached document referenced by the flowchart.

Lay Out the Physical Areas of Activity. Remember that a flowchart reflects the physical system, which is represented as vertical columns of events and actions separated by lines of demarcation. Generally, each of these areas of activity is a separate column with a heading. From the system facts above we see that there are four distinct areas of activity—sales department, credit department, warehouse, and shipping department. The first step in preparing the flowchart is to lay out these areas of activity and label each of them. This step is illustrated in Figure 2–15.

Transcribe the Written Facts into Visual Format. At this point we are ready to start representing the system facts using visual objects. These will be selected from the symbols set presented in Figure 2-16 (page 68). We begin with the first stated fact:

| FIGURE 2–15 | Flowchart Showing Areas of Activity |

Sales Department	Credit Department	Warehouse	Shipping Department

1. *A clerk in the sales department receives customer orders by mail and prepares four copies of a sales order.*

Figure 2–17 (page 69) illustrates how this fact could be represented. The customer is the source of the order but is not part of the system. The oval object is typically used to convey a data source or recipient that is apart from the system being flowcharted. The document symbol entering the sales department signifies the customer order and is labeled accordingly. The bucket-shaped symbol represents a manual process. In this case, the clerk in the sales department prepares four copies of the sales order. Notice that the clerk's task, not the clerk, is depicted. The arrows between the objects show the direction of flow and the sequence of events.

By transcribing each fact in this way a flowchart is systematically constructed. See how the second and third facts restated below add to the flowchart in Figure 2–18 (page 70).

2. *Copy 1 of the sales order is sent to the credit department for approval. The other three copies and the original customer order are filed temporarily pending credit approval.*

FIGURE 2–16

Symbols Set for
Document Flowcharts

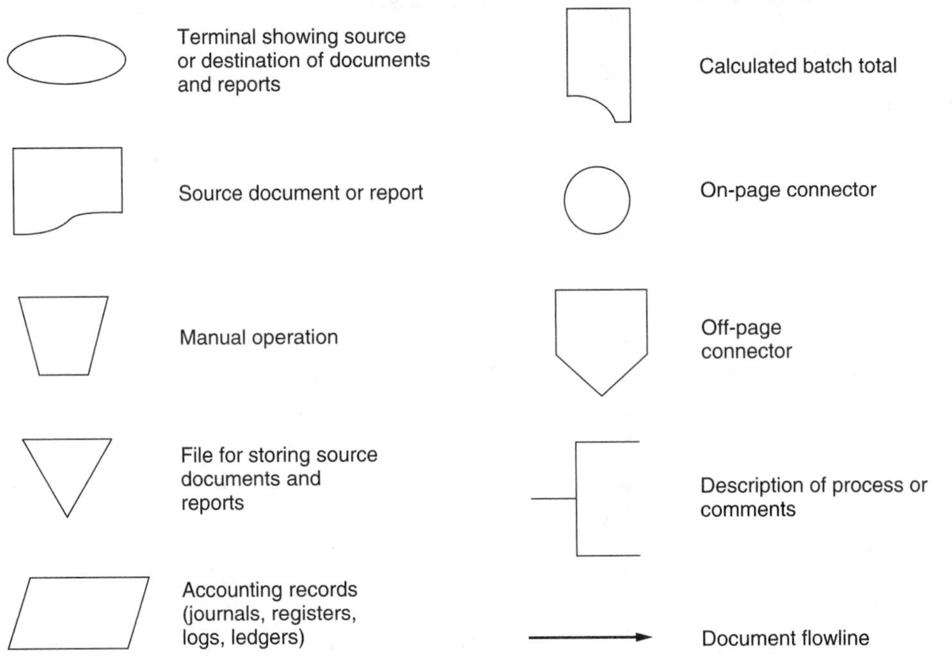

(ellipse)	Terminal showing source or destination of documents and reports
(document symbol)	Source document or report
(trapezoid)	Manual operation
(inverted triangle)	File for storing source documents and reports
(parallelogram)	Accounting records (journals, registers, logs, ledgers)
(torn document)	Calculated batch total
(circle)	On-page connector
(home plate)	Off-page connector
(annotation bracket)	Description of process or comments
(arrow)	Document flowline

3. *The credit department clerk validates the customer's order against credit records kept in the credit department. The clerk signs Copy 1 to signify approval and returns it to the sales clerk.*

Two new symbols are introduced in this figure. First, the upside-down triangle symbol represents the temporary file mentioned in fact 2. This is a physical file of paper documents such as a drawer in a filing cabinet or desk. Such files are typically arranged according to a specified order. To signify the filing system used the file symbol will usually contain an "N" for numeric (invoice number), "C" for chronological (date), or "A" for alphabetical order (customer name). Secondly, the parallelogram shape represents the credit records mentioned in fact 3. This symbol is used to depict many types of accounting records such as journals, subsidiary ledgers, general ledgers, and shipping logs.

Having laid these foundations, let's now complete the flowchart by depicting the remaining facts below.

4. *When the sales clerk receives credit approval he or she files Copy 1 and the customer order in the department. The clerk sends Copy 2 to the warehouse and Copies 3 and 4 to the shipping department.*
5. *The warehouse clerk picks the products from the shelves, records the transfer in the stock records, and sends the products and Copy 2 to the shipping department.*
6. *The shipping department receives Copy 2 and the goods from the warehouse, attaches Copy 2 as a packing slip, and ships the goods to the customer. Finally, the clerk files Copies 3 and 4 in the shipping department.*

The completed flowchart is presented in Figure 2–19 (page 71). Notice the circular symbol labeled "A". This is an on-page connector used to replace flowchart lines that

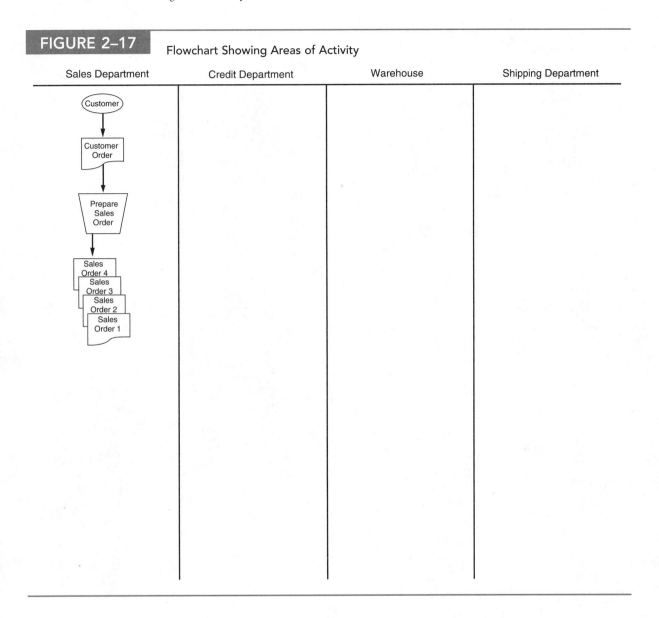

FIGURE 2–17   Flowchart Showing Areas of Activity

otherwise would cause excessive clutter on the page. In this instance, the connector replaces the lines that signify the movement of Copies 3 and 4 from the sales department to the shipping department. Lines should be used whenever possible to promote clarity. Restricted use of connectors, however, can improve the readability of the flowchart. Notice also that the physical products or goods mentioned in facts 4 and 5 are not shown on the flowchart. The document (Copy 2) that accompanies and controls the goods is shown. Some purists argue that a document flowchart should show only the flow of *documents*, not physical assets. On the other hand, if showing the physical asset improves the understandability of the flowchart, then its inclusion adds value.

Finally, for visual clarity, document flowcharts show the processing of a single transaction only. You should keep in mind that transactions usually pass through

FIGURE 2–18   Flowchart Showing Areas of Activity

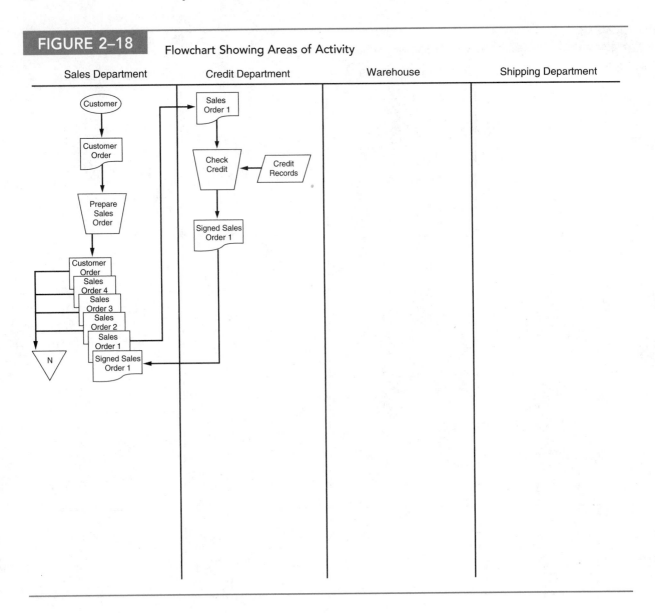

manual procedures in batches (groups). Before moving on to the next documentation technique, we need to examine some important issues related to batch processing.

Batch Processing

Batch processing permits the efficient management of a large volume of transactions. A **batch** is a group of similar transactions (such as sales orders) that are accumulated over time and then processed together. There are two general advantages to batch processing. First, organizations increase efficiency by grouping together large numbers of transactions into batches rather than processing each event separately. Thus, a business can achieve an efficient allocation of its processing resources by employing specialized, cost-effective procedures to deal with these batches. Batch processing is an economical method of high-volume transaction processing.

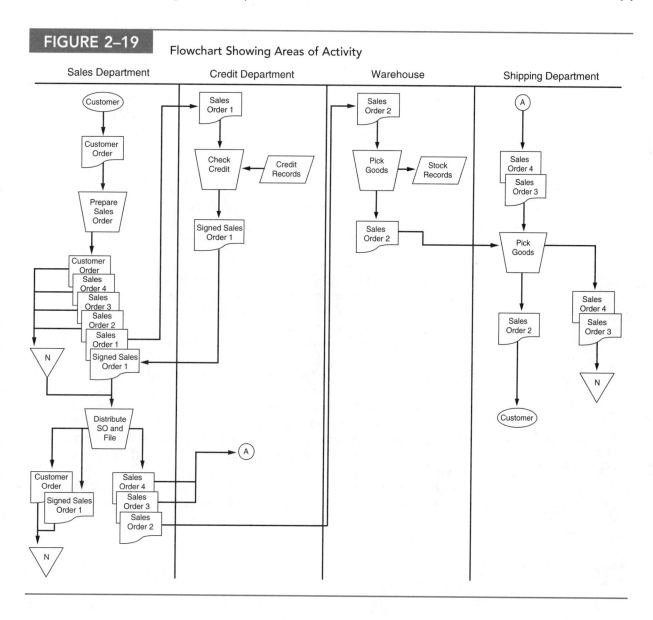

FIGURE 2–19   Flowchart Showing Areas of Activity

Second, batch processing provides control over the transaction process. The accuracy of the process can be established by periodically reconciling the batch against the control figure. For example, assume that the total value of a batch of sales orders is $100,000. This number can be recorded when the batch is first assembled and then recalculated at various points during its processing. If an error occurs during processing (e.g., a sales order is lost), then the recalculated batch total will not equal the original batch total, and the problem will be detected.

Both of these advantages have implications for designing batch systems. The first is that economies are derived by having batches that are as large as possible. The cost of processing each transaction is reduced when the fixed costs of data processing are allocated across a large number of transactions. The second implication is that finding an error in a very large batch may prove difficult. When a batch is small, error identification is much easier. In designing a batch system, the accountant should seek a balance between the economic advantage of large batches and the troubleshooting advantage of small batches. There is no magic number for the size of a batch. This decision is based on a number of operational, business, and economic factors. Among these are the volume of transactions, the competitiveness of the industry, the normal frequency of errors, the financial implications of an undetected error, and the costs of processing. Depending on these factors, a system might process small batches (50 to 100 items) several times a day or an entire day's activity as a single batch.

System Flowcharts

We now examine the use of a system flowchart to represent a system that includes both manual and computer processes. The symbol set used to construct the system flowchart will come from Figure 2–16 and Figure 2–20. Again, our example is based on a sales order system that is described by the following facts.

1. A clerk in the sales department receives customer orders by mail and enters the information into a computer terminal that is attached to a computer program in the computer operations department. The original customer order is filed in the sales department. Facts 2, 3, and 4 below relate to activities that occur in the computer operations department.

2. A computer program edits the transactions, checks the customers' credit by referencing a credit history file, and produces a transaction file of sales orders.

3. The sales order transaction file is then processed by an update program that posts the transactions to the account receivables (AR) and inventory files.

4. Finally, the update program produces three paper copies of the sales order. Copy 1 goes to the warehouse and Copies 2 and 3 go to the shipping department.

5. The warehouse clerk picks the products from the shelves, records the transfer in the stock records, and sends the products and Copy 1 to the shipping department.

6. The shipping department receives Copy 1 and the goods from the warehouse, attaches Copy 1 as a packing slip, and ships the goods to the customer. Finally, the clerk files Copies 2 and 3 in the shipping department.

FIGURE 2–20

Symbols Set for System Flowcharts

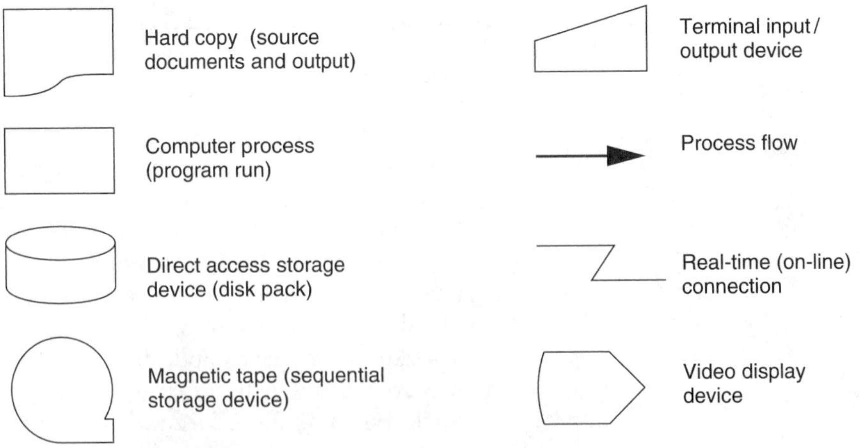

- Hard copy (source documents and output)
- Computer process (program run)
- Direct access storage device (disk pack)
- Magnetic tape (sequential storage device)
- Terminal input/output device
- Process flow
- Real-time (on-line) connection
- Video display device

Lay Out the Physical Areas of Activity. The flowcharting process begins by creating a template that depicts the areas of activity similar to the one in Figure 2–15. The only difference is that this system has a computer operations department and does not have a credit department.

Transcribe the Written Facts into Visual Format. As with the document flowchart, the next step is to systematically transcribe the written facts into visual objects. Figure 2–21 illustrates how facts 1, 2, and 3 above translate visually.

The customer, customer order, and file symbols in this flowchart are the same as in the previous document flowchart example. The sales clerk's activity, however, is now automated and the manual process symbol has been replaced with a computer terminal symbol. Also, since this is a data *input* operation the arrowhead on the

FIGURE 2–21   Flowchart Showing the Translation of Facts 1, 2, and 3 into Visual Symbols

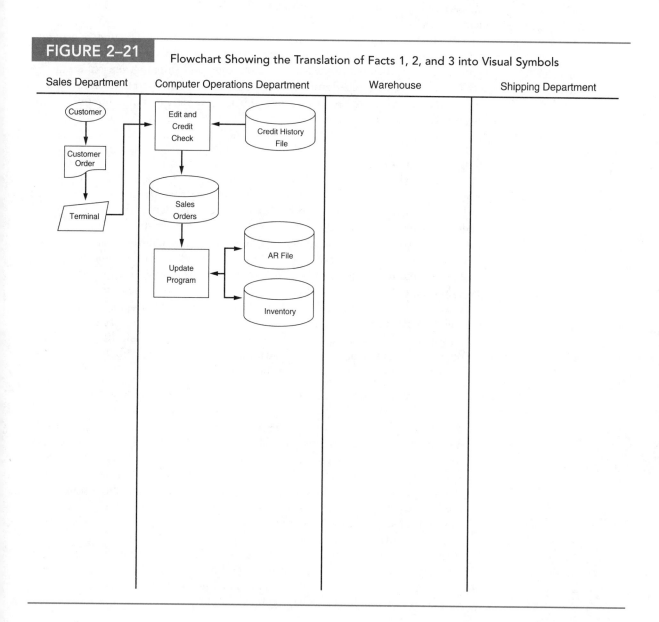

flowchart line points in the direction of the edit and credit check program. If the terminal were also used to receive output (the facts do not specify such an operation), arrowheads would be on both ends of the line.

As with the document flowchart, the emphasis here is on the physical system. For example, the terminal used by the sales clerk to enter customer orders is physically located in the sales department, but the programs that process the transactions and the files that are used, created, and updated by these events are stored in a separate computer operations department.

Notice how the flowchart line points from the credit history file to the edit program. This indicates that the file is read (referenced) but not changed (updated) by the program. In contrast, the interactions between the update program and the AR and inventory files are two-way. Records are read by the program, updated to reflect the transactions, and then written back to the files. The logic of a file update is explained later in the chapter.

Let's now translate the remaining facts into visual symbols. The update program in fact 4 produces three hard-copy documents in the computer operations department, which are then distributed to the warehouse and shipping departments. The activities described by facts 5 and 6 and the symbols that represent them are very similar to those described in the previous document flowchart example. Figure 2–22 illustrates the completed system flowchart.

Program Flowcharts

The system flowchart in Figure 2–22 shows the relationship between two computer programs, the files that they use, and the outputs that they produce. However, this level of documentation does not provide the operational details that are sometimes needed. For example, an auditor wishing to assess the correctness of the edit program's logic cannot do so from the system flowchart. This requires a **program flowchart**. The symbol set used for program flowcharts is presented in Figure 2–23.

Every program represented in a system flowchart should have a supporting program flowchart that describes its logic. Figure 2–24 (page 76) presents the logic of the edit program shown in Figure 2–25 (page 77). Each step of the program's logic is represented by a separate symbol, and each symbol represents one or more lines of computer program code. The flow-lines between the symbols establish the logical order of execution. Tracing the flowchart downward from the start symbol, the program performs the following logical steps in the order listed:

1. The program retrieves a single record from the unedited transaction file and stores it in memory.
2. The first logical test is to see if the program has reached the end-of-file (EOF) condition for the transaction file. Most file structures use a special record or marker to indicate an EOF condition. When EOF is reached, the edit program will terminate and the next program in the system (in this case, the update program) will be executed. As long as there is a record in the unedited transaction file, the result of the EOF test will be "no" and process control is passed to the next logical step in the edit program.
3. Processing involves a series of tests to identify certain clerical and logical errors. Each test, represented by a decision symbol, evaluates the presence or absence of a condition. For example, an edit test could be to detect the presence of alphabetic data in a field that should contain only numeric data. We examine specific edit and validation tests in Chapter 16.

FIGURE 2–22 — Flowchart Showing All Facts Translated Into Visual Symbols

Sales Department	Computer Operations Department	Warehouse	Shipping Department

Sales Department:
- Customer
- Customer Order
- Terminal
- Customer Order
- N

Computer Operations Department:
- Edit and Credit Check
- Credit History File
- Sales Orders
- Update Program
- AR File
- Inventory
- A
- Sales Order 3
- Sales Order 2
- Sales Order 1

Warehouse:
- Sales Order 1
- Pick Goods → Stock Records
- Sales Order 1

Shipping Department:
- A
- Sales Order 3 / Sales Order 2
- Pick Goods
- Sales Order 1
- Sales Order 2 / Sales Order 3
- Customer
- N

FIGURE 2–23

Program Flowchart Symbols

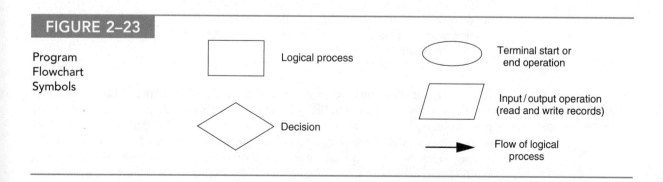

- ▭ Logical process
- ⬦ Decision
- ◯ Terminal start or end operation
- ▱ Input / output operation (read and write records)
- ⟶ Flow of logical process

FIGURE 2–24

Program Flowchart

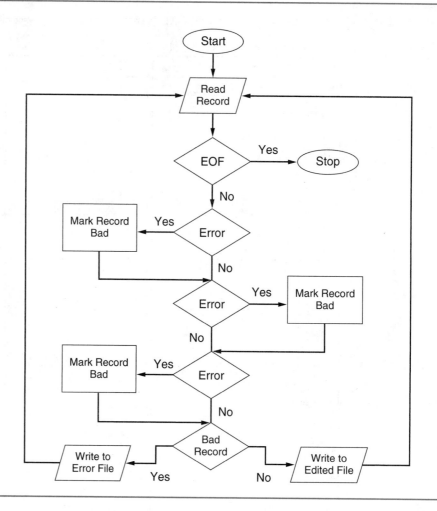

4. Error-free records are sent to the edited transaction file.
5. Records containing errors are sent to the error file.
6. The program loops back to Step 1 and the process is repeated until the EOF condition is reached.

Accountants sometimes use program flowcharts to verify the correctness of program logic. They compare flowcharts to the actual program code to determine whether the program is actually doing what the documentation describes. Program flowcharts provide essential details for conducting information technology (IT) audits, which we examine in Chapter 17.

RECORD LAYOUT DIAGRAMS

Record layout diagrams are used to reveal the internal structure of the records that constitute a file or database table. The layout diagram usually shows the name, data type, and length of each attribute (or field) in the record. Detailed data structure information is needed for such tasks as identifying certain types of system failures, analyzing error reports, and designing tests of computer logic for debugging and auditing purposes. A simpler form of record layout, shown in Figure 2–26, suits our

FIGURE 2–25

System Flowchart

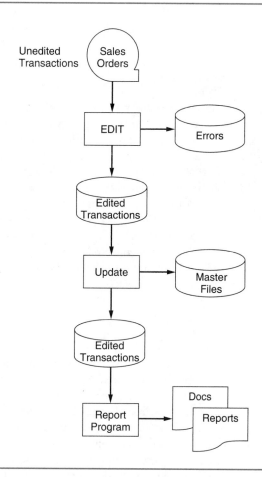

purposes best. This type of layout shows the content of a record. Each data attribute and key field is shown in terms of its name and relative location.

COMPUTER-BASED ACCOUNTING SYSTEMS

The final section in this chapter examines alternative computer-based transaction processing models. Computer-based accounting systems fall into two broad classes: batch systems and real-time systems. A number of alternative configurations exist

FIGURE 2–26

Record Layout Diagram for Customer File

Customer File

Key

Customer Number	Customer Name	Street Address	City	State	Zip Code	Credit Limit

within each of these classes. Systems designers base their configuration choices on a variety of considerations. Table 2–1 summarizes some of the distinguishing characteristics of batch and real-time processing that feature prominently in these decisions.

DIFFERENCES BETWEEN BATCH AND REAL-TIME SYSTEMS

Time Lag

Batch systems assemble transactions into groups for processing. In this approach, there is always a time lag between the point at which an economic event occurs and the point at which it is reflected in the firm's accounts. The amount of lag depends on the frequency of batch processing. Time lags can range from minutes to weeks. Payroll processing is an example of a typical batch system. The economic events—the application of employee labor—occur continuously throughout the pay period. At the end of the period, the paychecks for all employees are prepared together as a batch.

Real-time systems process transactions individually at the moment the economic event occurs. As records are not grouped into batches, there are no time lags between occurrence and recording. An example of real-time processing is an airline reservations system, which processes requests for services from one traveler at a time while he or she waits.

Resources

Generally speaking, batch systems demand fewer organizational resources (such as programming costs, computer time, and user training) than real-time systems. For example, batch systems can use sequential files stored on magnetic tape. Real-time systems must use direct access files that require more expensive storage devices, such as magnetic disks. In practice, however, these cost differentials are disappearing. As a result of declines in storage media costs, many organizations are turning to magnetic disks for both batch and real-time processing.

The most significant resource differentials are in the areas of systems development (programming) and computer operations. As batch systems are generally sim-

TABLE 2–1   Characteristic Differences between Batch and Real-Time Processing

DISTINGUISHING CHARACTERISTIC	DATA PROCESSING METHODS	
	Batch	Real-Time
Information Time Frame	Lag exists between time when the economic event occurs and when it is recorded.	Processing takes place when the economic event occurs.
Resources	Generally, fewer resources (hardware, programming, training) are required.	More resources are required than for batch processing.
Efficiency	Large numbers of transactions are processed with fewer resources committed.	Greater resource commitment is required per unit of output.

pler than their real-time counterparts, they tend to have shorter development periods and are easier for programmers to maintain. On the other hand, as much as 50 percent of the total programming costs for real-time systems are incurred in designing the user interfaces. Real-time systems must be friendly, forgiving, and easy to work with. Pop-up menus, on-line tutorials, and special "help" features require additional programming and add greatly to the cost of the system.

Finally, real-time systems require dedicated processing capacity. Real-time systems must deal with transactions as they occur. Some types of systems must be available 24 hours a day whether they are being used or not. The computer capacity dedicated to such systems cannot be used for other purposes. Thus, implementing a real-time system may require either the purchase of a dedicated computer or an investment in additional computer capacity. In contrast, batch systems use computer capacity only when the program is being run. There is no idle time. When the batch job completes processing, the freed-up capacity can be reallocated to other applications.

Efficiency Versus Effectiveness

Processing more transactions at a lower unit cost makes batch systems more efficient than real-time systems. For this reason, batch processing is very popular in AIS, which is characterized by high-volume transaction processing needs. However, real-time systems may be the only effective way to do a particular job. For instance, an airline reservations system cannot wait until 100 passengers (an efficient batch size) assemble in the travel agent's office before it processes their transactions.

In selecting a data processing mode, the designer must consider the trade-off involved. If immediate access to current information is critical to the user's needs, then real-time processing is the logical choice. When time lags in information have no detrimental effects on the user's performance and scale economies can be achieved by processing large batches, then batch mode processing is probably the superior choice.

With these general characteristics in place, we are almost ready to view the system configurations most commonly used in transaction processing. Before we do, however, we need to briefly review the data structure alternative employed by transaction processing systems.

DATA STRUCTURES

Data structures constitute the physical and logical arrangement of data in files and databases. Understanding how data are organized and accessed is central to understanding transaction processing. Data structures have two fundamental components: organization and access method. **Organization** refers to the way records are physically arranged on the secondary storage device (e.g., a disk). This may be either *sequential* or *random*. The records in sequential files are stored in contiguous locations that occupy a specified area of disk space. Records in random files are stored without regard for their physical relationship to other records of the same file. In fact, random files may have records distributed throughout a disk. The **access method** is the technique used to locate records and to navigate through the database or file.

No single structure is best for all processing tasks, and selecting a structure involves a trade-off between desirable features. The file operation requirements that influence the selection of the data structure are listed in Table 2–2.

In the following section, we examine several data structures that are used in flat file systems. Recall from Chapter 1 that the flat file model describes an environment in which individual data files are not integrated with other files. End users in this

TABLE 2–2	Typical File Processing Operations

1. Retrieve a record from the file based on its primary key value.
2. Insert a record into a file.
3. Update a record in the file.
4. Read a complete file of records.
5. Find the next record in a file.
6. Scan a file for records with common secondary keys.
7. Delete a record from a file.

environment *own* their data files rather than *share* them with other users. Data processing is thus performed by standalone applications rather than integrated systems. The **flat file approach** is a single-view model that characterizes legacy systems in which data files are structured, formatted, and arranged to suit the specific needs of the *owner* or primary user of the system. Such structuring, however, may omit or corrupt data attributes that are essential to other users, thus preventing successful integration of systems across the organization.

Sequential Structure

Figure 2–27 illustrates the **sequential structure**, which is typically called the **sequential access method**. Under this arrangement, for example, the record with key value 1875 is placed in the physical storage space immediately following the record with key value 1874. Thus, all records in the file lie in contiguous storage spaces in a specified sequence (ascending or descending) arranged by their primary key.

Sequential files are simple and easy to process. The application starts at the beginning of the file and processes each record in sequence. Of the file processing operations in Table 2–2, this approach is efficient for Operations 4 and 5, which are,

FIGURE 2–27	Sequential Storage and Access Method

Records Are Read Sequentially

Key 1874 | Other Data   Key 1875 | Other Data   Key 1876 | Other Data

Keys Are in Sequence
(in this case, ascending order)

respectively, reading an entire file and finding the next record in the file. Also, when a large portion of the file (perhaps 20 percent or more) is to be processed in one operation, the sequential structure is efficient for record updating (Operation 3 in Table 2–2). Sequential files are not efficient when the user is interested in locating only one or a few records on a file. A simple analogy can be made with an audio cassette. If you want to listen to only the tenth song on the tape, you must fast-forward to the point where you think the song is located and then press the play button. Some searching is usually required to find the beginning of the song. However, if you are interested in hearing all the songs on the tape, you can simply play it from the beginning. An example of a sequential file application is payroll processing, where 100 percent of the employee records on the payroll file are processed each payroll period. Magnetic tape is a cheap, effective, and commonly used storage medium for sequential files. Sequential files may also be stored on magnetic disks.

The sequential access method does not permit accessing a record directly. Applications that require direct access operations need a different data structure. The techniques described next address this need.

Direct Access Structures

Direct access structures store data at a unique location, known as an address, on a hard disk or floppy disk. The disk address is a numeric value that represents the cylinder, surface, and block location on the disk.[2] The operating system uses this address to store and retrieve the data record. Using our music analogy again, the direct access approach is similar to the way songs are stored on a compact disc. If the listener chooses, he or she can select a specific song directly without searching through all the other songs.

An important part of the direct access approach is in determining the disk address, which is based on the record's primary key. Bank account numbers, social security numbers, credit card numbers, and license plate numbers are examples of primary keys that are translated into addresses to store and retrieve data by different business applications. The techniques described below are examples of data structures that have direct access capability.

Indexed Structure

An **indexed structure** is so named because, in addition to the actual data file, there exists a separate index that is itself a file of record addresses. This index contains the numeric value of the physical disk storage location (cylinder, surface, and record block) for each record in the associated data file. The data file itself may be organized either sequentially or randomly. Figure 2–28 presents an example of an indexed random file.

Records in an **indexed random file** are dispersed throughout a disk without regard for their physical proximity to other related records. In fact, records belonging to the same file may reside on different disks. A record's physical location is unimportant as long as the operating system software can find it when needed. Searching

---

2   For further explanation about disk addresses, see Section A of the chapter appendix entitled *Secondary Storage*.

FIGURE 2–28 Indexed Random File Structure

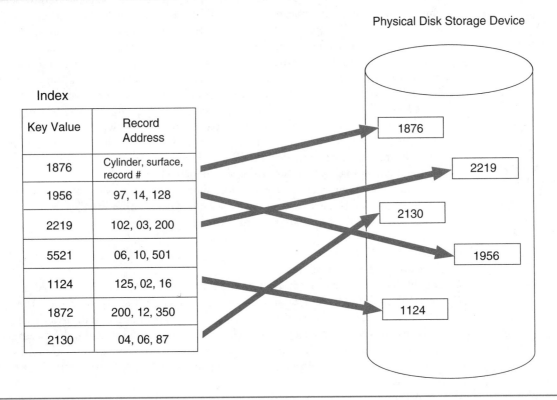

the index for the desired key value, reading the corresponding storage location (address), and then moving the disk read-write head to the address location accomplish this. When a new record is added to the file, the data management software selects a vacant disk location, stores the record, and adds the new address to the index.

The physical organization of the index itself may be either sequential (by key value) or random. Random indexes are easier to maintain, in terms of adding records, because new key records are simply added to the end of the index without regard to their sequence. Indexes in sequential order are more difficult to maintain because new record keys must be inserted between existing keys. One advantage of a sequential index is that it can be searched rapidly. Because of its logical arrangement, algorithms can be used to speed the search through the index to find a key value. This becomes particularly important for large data files with associated large indexes.

The principal advantage of indexed random files is in operations involving the processing of individual records (Operations 1, 2, 3, and 6 in Table 2–2). Another advantage is their efficient use of disk storage. Records may be placed wherever there is space without concern for maintaining contiguous storage locations. However, random files are not efficient structures for operations that involve processing a large portion of a file. A great deal of access time may be required to access an entire file of records that are randomly dispersed throughout the storage device. Sequential files are more efficient for this purpose.

VSAM Structure

The **virtual storage access method (VSAM)** structure is used for very large files that require routine batch processing and a moderate degree of individual record processing. For instance, the customer file of a public utility company will be processed in batch mode for billing purposes and directly accessed in response to individual customer queries. Because of its sequential organization, the VSAM structure can be searched sequentially for efficient batch processing. Figure 2–29 illustrates how VSAM uses indexes to allow direct access processing.

The VSAM structure is used for files that often occupy several cylinders of contiguous storage on a disk. To find a specific record location, the VSAM file uses a number of indexes that describe in summarized form the contents of each cylinder. For example, in Figure 2–29, we are searching for a record with the key value 2546. The access method goes first to the overall file index, which contains only the highest key value for each cylinder in the file, and determines that Record 2546 is somewhere on Cylinder 99. A quick scan of the surface index for Cylinder 99 reveals that the record is on Surface 3 of Cylinder 99. VSAM indexes do not provide an exact physical address for a single record. However, they identify the disk track where the record in question resides. The last step is to search the identified track sequentially to find the record with key value 2546.

FIGURE 2–29   VSAM Used for Direct Access

VSAM—Virtual Storage Access Method

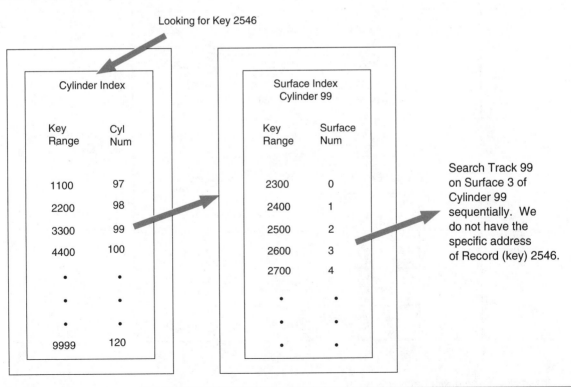

The VSAM structure is moderately effective for Operations 1 and 3 in Table 2–2. Because VSAM must read multiple indexes and search the track sequentially, the average access time for a single record is slower than the indexed sequential or indexed random structures. Direct access speed is sacrificed to achieve very efficient performance in Operations 4, 5, and 6.

The greatest disadvantage with the VSAM structure is that it does not perform record insertion operations (Operation 2) efficiently. Because the VSAM file is organized sequentially, inserting a new record into the file requires the physical relocation of all the records located beyond the point of insertion. The indexes that describe this physical arrangement must, therefore, also be updated with each insertion. This is extremely time-consuming and disruptive to operations. One method of dealing with this problem is to store new records in an overflow area that is physically separate from the other data records in the file. Figure 2–30 shows how this is done.

A VSAM file has three physical components: the indexes, the prime data storage area, and the overflow area. Rather than inserting a new record directly into the prime area, the data management software places it in a randomly selected location in the overflow area. It then records the address of the location in a special field (called a *pointer*) in the prime area. Later, when searching for the record, the indexes direct the access method to the track location where the record *should* reside. The pointer at that location reveals the record's *actual* location in the overflow area. Thus, accessing a record may involve searching the indexes, searching the track in the prime data

FIGURE 2–30 Inserting a Record into a VSAM File

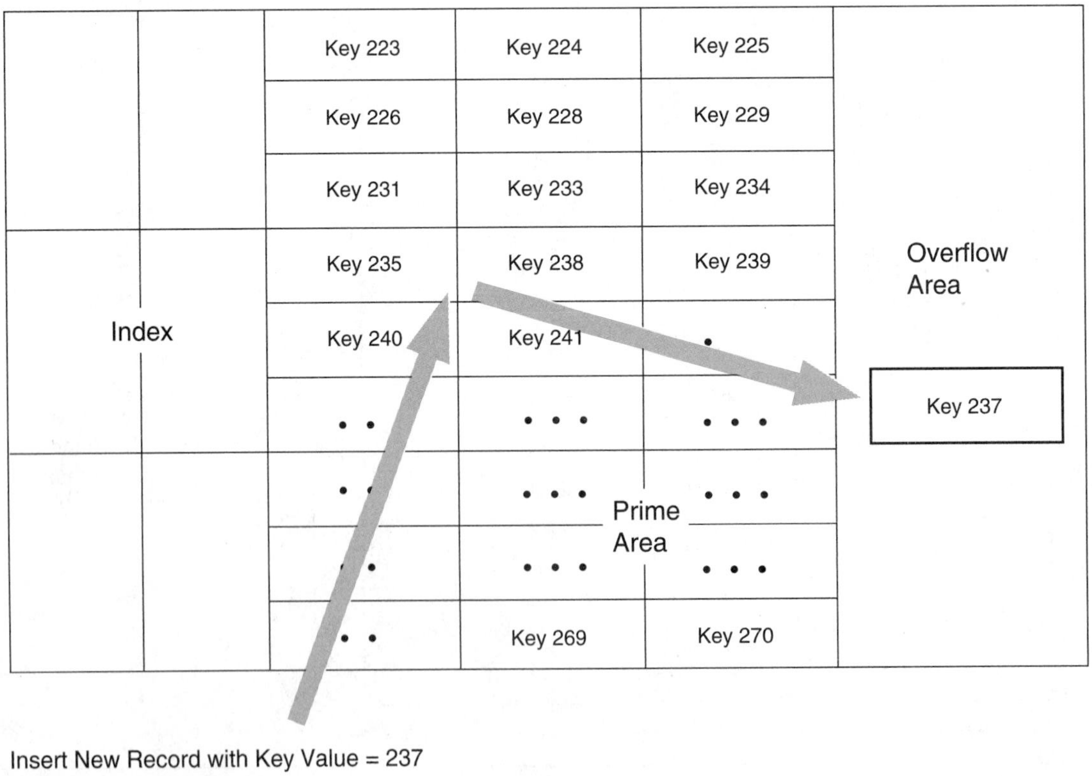

Insert New Record with Key Value = 237

area, and finally searching the overflow area. This slows data access time for both direct access and batch processing.

Periodically, the VSAM file must be reorganized by integrating the overflow records into the prime area and then reconstructing the indexes. This involves time, cost, and disruption to operations. Therefore, when a file is highly volatile (records are added or deleted frequently), the maintenance burden associated with the VSAM approach tends to render it impractical. However, for large, stable files that need both direct access and batch processing, the VSAM structure is a popular option.

Hashing Structure

A **hashing structure** employs an algorithm that converts the primary key of a record directly into a storage address. Hashing eliminates the need for a separate index. By calculating the address, rather than reading it from an index, records can be retrieved more quickly. Figure 2–31 illustrates the hashing approach.

This example assumes an inventory file with 100,000 inventory items. The algorithm divides the inventory number (the primary key) into a prime number. Recall that a prime number is one that can be divided only by itself and 1 without leaving a residual value. Therefore, the calculation will always produce a value that can be translated into a storage location. Hence, the residual 6.27215705 becomes cylinder

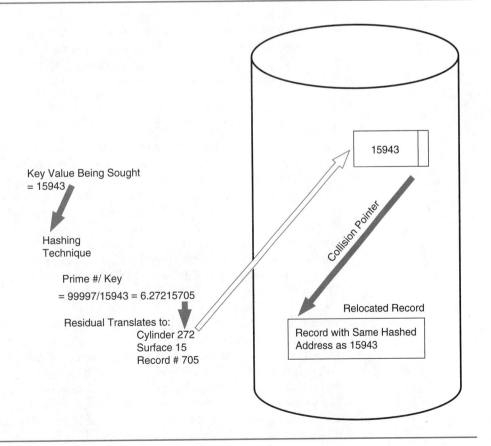

FIGURE 2–31

Hashing Technique with Pointer to Relocate the Collision Record

Key Value Being Sought
= 15943

Hashing Technique

Prime #/ Key
= 99997/15943 = 6.27215705

Residual Translates to:
Cylinder 272
Surface 15
Record # 705

15943

Collision Pointer

Relocated Record

Record with Same Hashed Address as 15943

272, surface 15, and record number 705. The hashing structure uses a random file organization because the process of calculating residuals and converting them into storage locations produces widely dispersed record addresses.

The principal advantage of hashing is access speed. Calculating a record's address is faster than searching for it through an index. This structure is suited to applications that require rapid access to individual records in performing Operations 1, 2, 3, and 6 in Table 2–2.

The hashing structure has two significant disadvantages. First, this technique does not use storage space efficiently. The storage location chosen for a record is a mathematical function of its primary key value. The algorithm will never select some disk locations because they do not correspond to legitimate key values. As much as one-third of the disk pack may be wasted.

The second disadvantage is the reverse of the first. Different record keys may generate the same (or similar) residual, which translates into the same address. This is called a *collision* because two records cannot be stored at the same location. One solution to this problem is to randomly select a location for the second record and place a pointer to it from the first (the calculated) location. The dark arrow in Figure 2–31 represents the use of this technique.

The collision problem slows down access to records. Locating a record displaced in this manner involves first calculating its theoretical address, searching that location, and then determining the actual address from the pointer contained in the record at that location. This has an additional implication for Operation 7 in Table 2–2—deleting a record from a file. If the first record is deleted from the file, the pointer to the second (collision) record will also be deleted and the address of the second record will be lost. This can be dealt with in two ways: (1) After deleting the first record, the collision record can be physically relocated to its calculated address, which is now vacant; or (2) The first record is marked "deleted" but is left in place to preserve the pointer to the collision record.

Pointer Structure

Figure 2–32 presents the **pointer structure**, which in this example is used to create a *linked-list file*. This approach stores in a field of one record the address (pointer) of a related record. The pointers provide connections between the records. In this example, Record 124 points to the location of Record 125, Record 125 points to 126, and so on. As each record is processed, the computer program reads the pointer field to locate the next one. The last record in the list contains an end-of-file marker. The records in this type of file are spread over the entire disk without concern for their physical proximity with other related records. Pointers used in this way make efficient use of disk storage space and are efficient structures for applications that involve Operations 4, 5, and 6 in Table 2–2.

Types of Pointers. Figure 2–33 (page 88), shows three types of pointers: physical address, relative address, and logical key pointers. A **physical address pointer** contains the actual disk storage location (cylinder, surface, and record number) needed by the disk controller. This physical address allows the system to access the record directly without obtaining further information. This method has the advantage of speed, since it does not need to be manipulated further to determine a record's location. However, it also has two disadvantages: First, if the related record is moved from one disk location to another, the pointer must be changed. This is a problem when disks are pe-

FIGURE 2–32

A Linked-List File

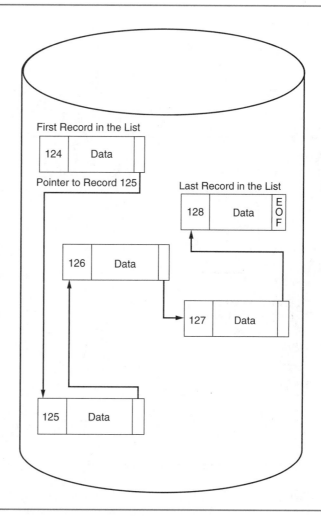

riodically reorganized or copied. Second, the physical pointers bear no logical relationship to the records they identify. If a pointer is lost or destroyed and cannot be recovered, the record it references is also lost.

A **relative address pointer** contains the relative position of a record in the file. For example, the pointer could specify the 135th record in the file. This must be further manipulated to convert it to the actual physical address. The conversion software calculates this by using the physical address of the beginning of the file, the length of each record in the file, and the relative address of the record being sought.

A **logical key pointer** contains the primary key of the related record. This key value is then converted into the record's physical address by a hashing algorithm.

Database Structures

The basic data structures discussed above form the foundation for complex database structures that are examined in Chapter 9. A major advantage of the **database approach** is the degree of process integration and data sharing that can be achieved. Two-dimensional flat files are independent structures that are not linked logically or

FIGURE 2–33   Types of Pointers

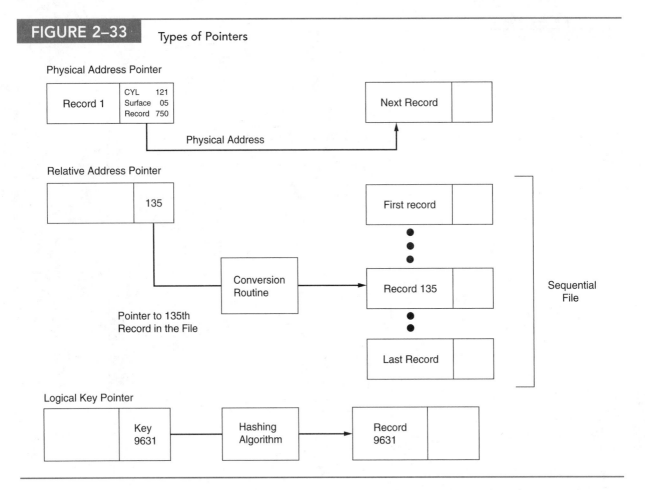

physically to other files. The database model allows the organization to move to new levels of data integration by providing linkages within and between files. Thus, a third (depth) dimension is added to better serve multiple-user needs.

In practice, organizations may employ any of the above approaches in various combinations for storing, accessing, and processing accounting data. In addition, flat-file systems may coexist alongside modern systems that employ the latest database technology.

ALTERNATIVE DATA PROCESSING APPROACHES

In chapters that follow, we will examine many configurations of computer technology used in processing accounting transactions. These systems can be divided into four general data processing approaches: batch processing using sequential files, batch processing using direct access files, batch processing using real-time data collection, and real-time processing. The general features of each model are outlined in the sections that follow.

BATCH PROCESSING USING SEQUENTIAL FILES

The most basic computer-processing configuration is batch mode using sequential file structures. Figure 2–34 illustrates this method.

Each program in a batch system is called a **run**. In this example, there is an edit run, an AR file update run, an inventory file update run, and two intermediate sort

FIGURE 2–34

Batch System Using
Sequential Files

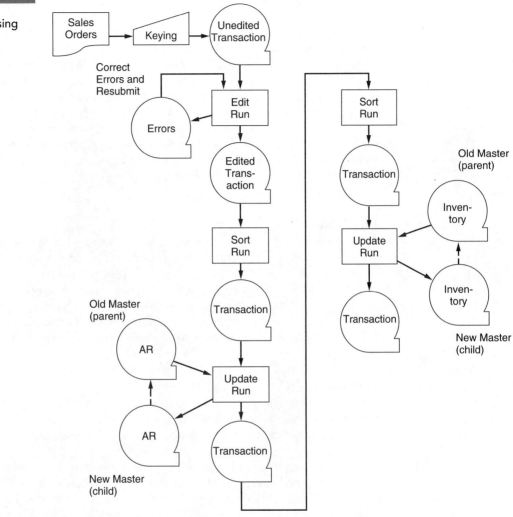

runs. The entire file or batch of records is processed through each run before it moves to the next run. When the last run finishes processing the batch, the session terminates.

A prominent feature of this system is the use of sequential files, which are simple to create and maintain. Although sequential files are still used by organizations for backup purposes, their presence in data processing is declining. This file structure is effective for managing large files, such as those used by federal and state agencies that have a high activity ratio. The activity ratio of a file is defined as the percentage of records on the file that are processed each time the file is accessed. For example, a federal payroll file has an activity ratio of 1:1. Each time the payroll file is accessed (payday), all the records on it are processed because everyone gets a paycheck.

The sequential files in the system shown in Figure 2–34 are represented in the flowchart as tapes, but remember that disks are also a common medium for sequential files. The operational description that follows applies equally to both types of media.

Keystroke

The first step in this process is keystroke. In this example, clerks transcribe source documents (sales orders) to magnetic tape for processing later. The transaction file created in this step contains data about customer sales. These data are used to update the appropriate customer and inventory records. As an internal control measure, the keystroke clerks calculate control totals for the batch based on the total sales amount and total number of inventory items sold. This information will be used by the system to maintain the integrity of the process. After every processing run, control totals are recalculated and compared to the previously calculated value. Thus, if a record is incompletely processed, lost, or processed more than once, the batch totals calculated after the run will not equal the beginning batch totals. Once the system detects an out-of-balance condition, it sends error reports to users and data control personnel. We examine batch control techniques in Chapter 16.

Edit Run

At a predetermined time each day, the data processing department executes this batch system. The edit program is the first to be run. This program identifies clerical errors in the batch and automatically removes these records from the transaction file. Error records go to a separate error file, where an authorized person corrects and resubmits them for processing with the next day's batch. The edit program recalculates the batch total to reflect changes due to the removal of error records. The resulting "clean" transaction file then moves to the next program in the system.

Sort Runs

Before updating a sequential master file, the transaction file must be sorted and placed in the same sequence as the master file. Figure 2–35 presents record structures for the sales order transaction file and two associated master files, accounts receivable and inventory.

Notice that the record structure for the sales order file contains a primary key (PK)—a unique identifier—and two secondary key (SK) fields, ACCOUNT NUMBER and INVENTORY NUMBER. ACCOUNT NUMBER is used to identify the customer account to be updated in the AR master file. INVENTORY NUMBER is the key for locating the inventory record to be updated in the inventory master file. To simplify the example, we assume that each sale is for a single item of inventory. Because the AR update run comes first in the sequence, the sales order file must first be sorted by ACCOUNT NUMBER and then sorted by INVENTORY NUMBER to update inventory.

Update Runs

Updating a master file record involves changing the value of one or more of its variable fields to reflect the effects of a transaction. The system in our example performs two separate update procedures. The AR update program recalculates customer balances by adding the value stored in the INVOICE AMOUNT field of a transaction record to the CURRENT BALANCE field value in the associated AR record. The inventory update program reduces inventory levels by deducting the QUANTITY SOLD value of a transaction record from the QUANTITY ON HAND field value

FIGURE 2–35   Record Structures for Sales, Inventory, and Accounts Receivable Files

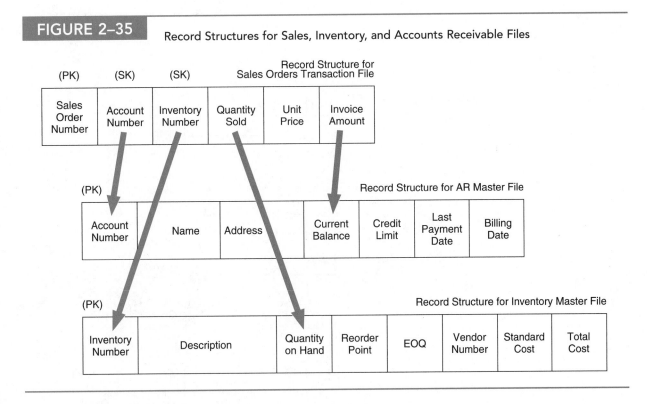

of the associated inventory record. The general logic for a sequential file update is described in Section B of the chapter appendix.

Sequential File Backup Procedures

An important characteristic of the sequential file update process is that it produces a new physical master file. The new file contains all of the records from the original file, including those that were updated by transactions and those that were not updated. The original master continues to exist. This feature provides an automatic backup capability called the *grandparent-parent-child* approach. The parent is the original master file, and the child is the newly created (updated) file. With the next batch of transactions, the child becomes the parent, the original parent becomes the grandparent (the backup), and a new child is created. Should the current master file (the child) become lost, damaged, or corrupted by erroneous data, a new child can be created from the original parent and the corresponding transaction file. We examine this control technique in Chapter 15.

BATCH PROCESSING USING DIRECT ACCESS FILES

Changing the file structures from sequential to direct access greatly simplifies the system. Figure 2–36 shows a system that is functionally equivalent to the one presented in Figure 2–35 but reengineered to use **direct access files**. Notice the use of disk symbols to represent direct access storage device (DASD) media.

The shift to direct access files causes two noteworthy changes to this system. The first is the elimination of the sort programs. A disadvantage of sequential file

FIGURE 2-36

**Batch Processing
Using Direct
Access Files**

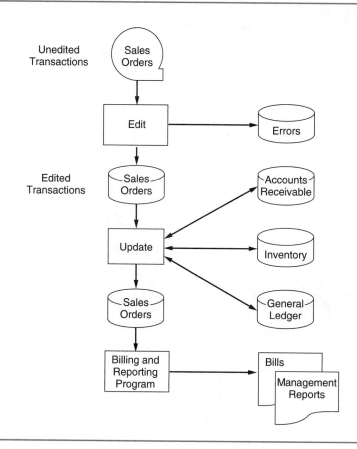

updating is the need to sort the transaction file before each update run. Sorting consumes a good deal of computer time and is error-prone when very large files are involved. Using direct access files eliminates the need to sort transactions into a predetermined sequence.

The second change is the elimination of automatic file backup in this system. Direct access update does not produce a new physical master as a by-product of the process. Instead, changes to field values are made to the original physical file. Providing file backup requires separate procedures.

Updating Direct Access Files

Each record in a direct access file is assigned a unique disk location or *address* that is determined by its key value. Because only a single valid location exists for each record, updating the record must occur in-place. Figure 2–37 shows this technique.

In this example, an account receivable record with a $100 current balance is being updated by a $50 sale transaction. The master file record is permanently stored at a disk address designated Location A. The update program reads both the transaction record and the master file record into memory. The receivable is updated to reflect the new current balance value of $150 and then returned to Location A. The original current balance value of $100 is destroyed when replaced by the new value of $150.

FIGURE 2–37

Destructive
Update
Approach

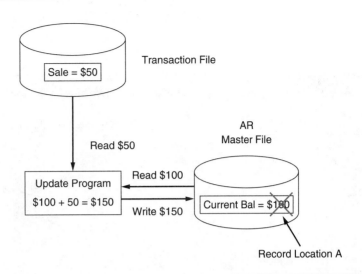

Record Location A

This technique is called *destructive update*. A detailed explanation of the direct access update process is provided in Section C of the chapter appendix.

Direct Access File Backup Procedures

The destructive update approach leaves no backup copy of the original master file. Only the current value is available to the user. If the current master becomes damaged or corrupted in some way, no backup version exists from which to reconstruct the file. To preserve adequate accounting records, special **backup procedures**, such as those shown in Figure 2–38, must be implemented.

Before each update run, the master file being updated is copied to tape (or another disk) to create a backup version of the original file. Should the current master be destroyed after the update process, reconstruction is possible in two stages. First, a special restoration program uses the backup file to create a pre-update version of the master file. Second, the file update process is repeated using the previous batch of transactions to restore the master to its current condition. Because of the potential

FIGURE 2–38

Backup and Recovery
Procedures for Direct
Access Files

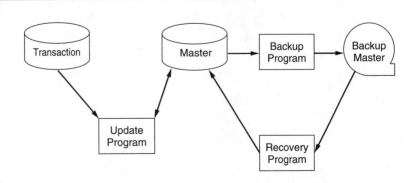

risk to accounting records, accountants are naturally concerned about the adequacy of all backup procedures. In Chapter 15 we examine many issues related to file backup.

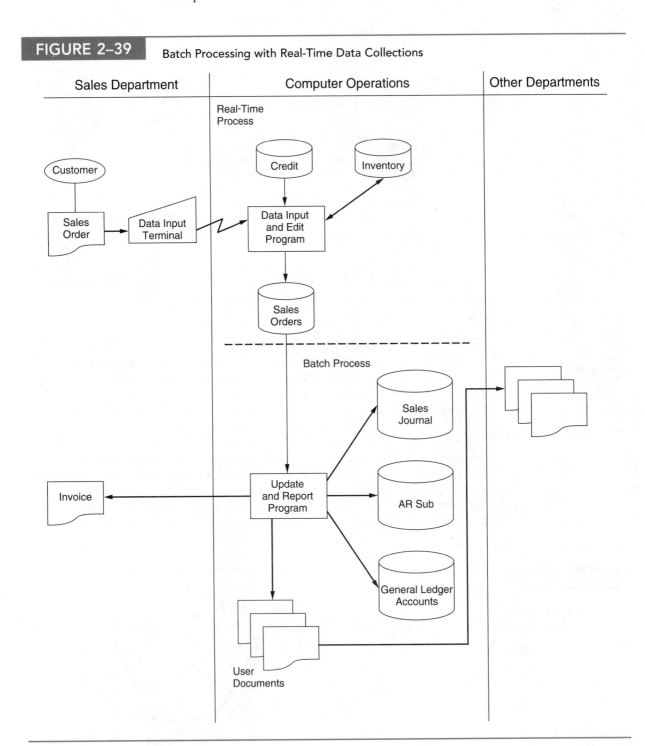

FIGURE 2–39   Batch Processing with Real-Time Data Collections

BATCH PROCESSING
USING REAL-TIME
DATA COLLECTIONS

The systems examined thus far describe a process by which transactions are sent in batches to a central location for conversion to magnetic media. A popular alternative is to capture transaction data at its source in real time. Real-time processing is also called "on-line" because the system, in this case the data collection portion of it, is available to the user at all times. By distributing data input capability to users, certain transaction errors can be prevented or detected and corrected at their source. The result is a transaction file that is free from most of the errors that plague data processing. Figure 2–39 illustrates this approach.

Real-time data collection can be used with both the batch/sequential and the batch/direct access update techniques. In both cases, however, the transaction file produced in the data collection stage must be a direct access structure.

REAL-TIME
PROCESSING

Real-time systems process the entire transaction when it occurs. For example, a sales order processed by the system in Figure 2–40 can be captured, filled, and shipped the same day. Such a system has many potential benefits, including improved productivity, reduced inventory, increased inventory turnover, decreased lags in customer billing, and enhanced customer satisfaction. Since transaction information is transmitted electronically, physical source documents can be eliminated or greatly reduced.

Real-time processing employs exclusive use of direct access files and involves some level of network technology. Terminals at distributed sites throughout the organization are used for receiving, processing, and sending information about current transactions. These must be linked together in a network arrangement so users can communicate. The operational characteristics of networks are examined in Chapter 12.

Summary

This chapter divided the treatment of transaction processing systems into four major sections. The first section provided an overview of transaction processing, showing its vital role as an information provider for financial reporting, internal management reporting, and the support of day-to-day operations. To deal efficiently with large volumes of financial transactions, business organizations group together transactions of similar types into transaction cycles. Three transaction cycles account for most of a firm's economic activity: the revenue cycle, the expenditure cycle, and the conversion cycle. The second section described the relationship among accounting records in both manual and computer-based systems. The third section of the chapter presented an overview of documentation techniques used to describe the key features of systems. Accountants must be proficient in the use of documentation tools to perform their professional duties. Six types of documentation are commonly used for this purpose: entity relationship diagrams, data flow diagrams, document flowcharts, system flowcharts, program flowcharts, and data structure diagrams. Finally, the chapter examined the types of computer technology used for transaction processing. Two broad approaches were discussed: batch processing and real-time processing. This section reviewed four system configurations derived from these approaches: (1) batch processing using sequential files, (2) batch processing using direct access files, (3) batch processing using real-time data collection, and (4) real-time processing. The section

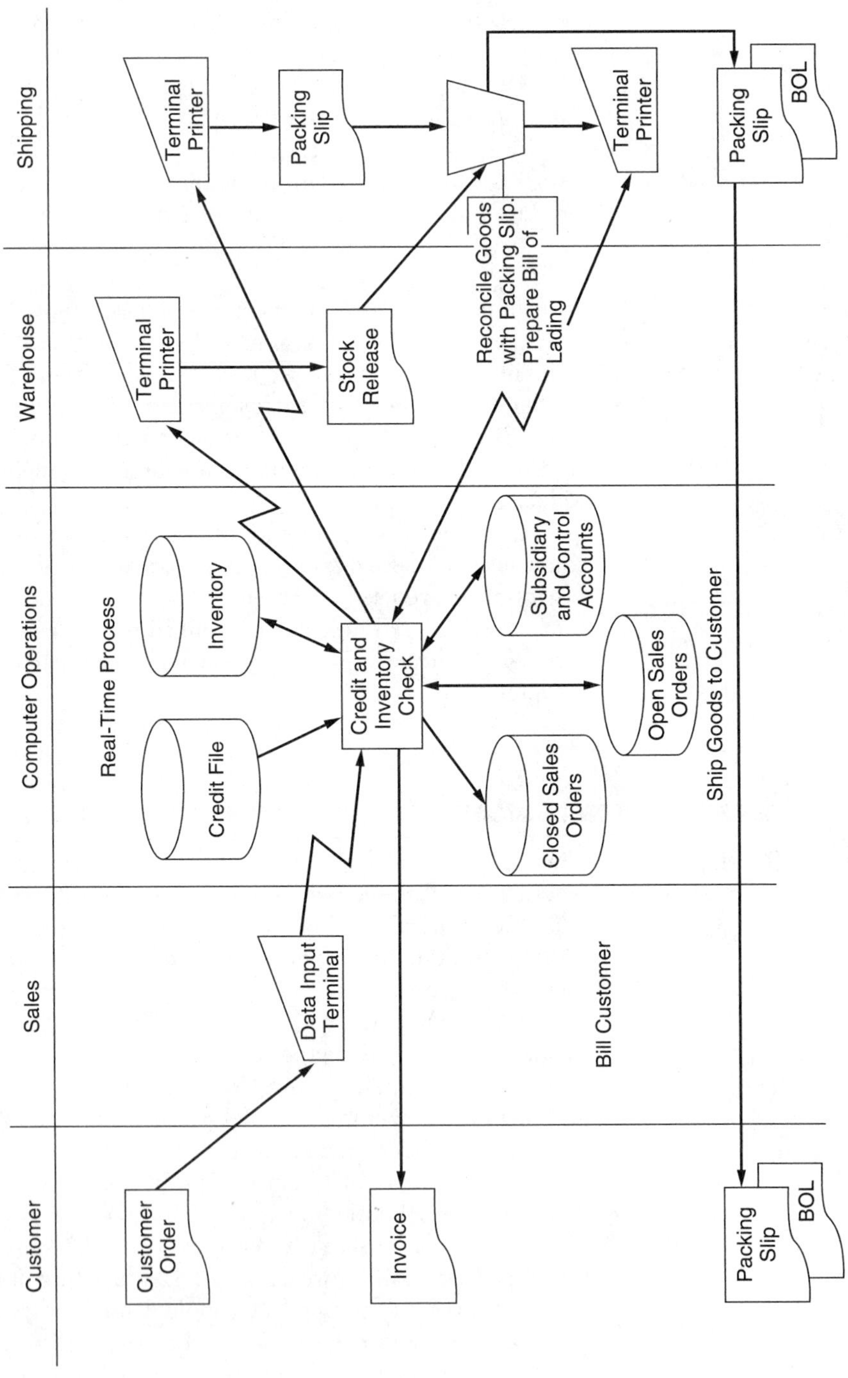

FIGURE 2-40   Real-Time Processing of Sales Orders

also examined several data structures used by the flat file and early (navigational) database models.

Appendix

SECTION A:
SECONDARY
STORAGE

A computer's secondary storage includes devices used to store and retrieve system software, application software, and data on magnetic or optical media, such as magnetic tape, hard or floppy disks, and CD-ROMs.

Magnetic Tape

As a secondary storage medium, magnetic tape has some important advantages. For example, large amounts of data can be stored on magnetic tape at a relatively low cost, and magnetic tape is reusable. The primary disadvantage is that data recorded on magnetic tape use the sequential access method; thus, the retrieval of information from magnetic tape is slower than with other storage media.

Magnetic tapes for mainframes range in width from one-half to one inch and in length from 2,400 to 3,600 feet. A byte of data (representing a character, digit, or special symbols) is recorded on the tape along its width. (One byte equals eight binary digits, or bits. A bit is the smallest possible unit of electronic information, either a 0 or a 1.) A logical sequence of characters makes up a *field*, and several fields make up a *record*. The number of characters that can be recorded on one inch of tape is known as the tape's *density*. The density of magnetic tape ranges from 1,600 to several thousand bytes per inch. One magnetic tape might contain several million characters of data.

A tape drive is used to record bits of data onto magnetic tape. The tape drive reads and writes blocks of data at a time. Each block is separated by an interblock gap, which instructs the tape drive to stop reading or writing the data until another block is requested. Figure 2–41 shows records blocked together on a magnetic tape.

FIGURE 2–41   Records Blocked on a Magnetic Tape

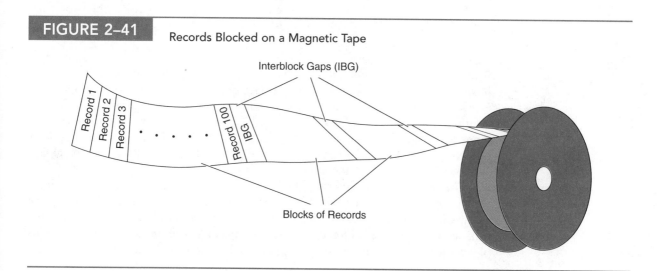

The tape drives used today in conjunction with microcomputers are usually programmed to back up (copy) the data on the hard disk. If the computer "crashes" (that is, if the data on the disk are destroyed), a duplicate of the data will be available.

Magnetic Disks

The data stored on magnetic disks (hard disks or floppy disks) are considered to be nonvolatile. The data will reside in a certain location on the magnetic surface until they are replaced with different data or erased. Data can be recorded to magnetic disks using either of the access methods described earlier.

To get the disk ready to receive data, its surface must be formatted. An operating system utility program formats the disk by dividing it into circular tracks and wedge-shaped sectors, which cut across the tracks. The number of bytes that can be stored at a particular track and sector determines the disk's density.

Disks are known as *direct access storage devices* because a piece of data can be accessed directly on the disk. Database management systems and application software work with the operating system to determine the location of the required data.

A disk has a rotating magnetic surface and a read-write head. The read-write head is on an access arm that moves back and forth over the magnetic surface. The time that elapses from when the operating system requests a piece of data to when it is read into the computer is called *access time*. The access time of a particular hard disk is a function of several factors: (1) the seek time—how fast the read-write head moves into position over a particular track; (2) the switching time—the time needed to activate the read-write head; (3) the rotational delay time— the time it takes to rotate the disk area under the read-write head; and (4) the data transfer time—the time it takes for the data to be transferred from the disk track to primary storage. Most microcomputer hard disks have an access time of 5 to 60 milliseconds.

The *file allocation table* is an area on the disk that keeps track of the name of each file, the number of bytes in the file, the date and time it was created, the type of file, and its location (address) on the disk. A file may be stored in just one place on the disk, or it may be spread across several locations. In the latter case, the disk's read-write head must skip among various addresses to read the entire file into the primary memory.

We have used the term *address* several times to represent a disk storage location. Let's now examine the elements of a disk address.

Disk Address. As we have seen, the surface of a disk is divided into magnetized tracks that form concentric circles of data. The floppy disk for a microcomputer may have 40 or 80 tracks on a surface, while the surface of a mainframe disk could contain several hundred tracks. These tracks are logically divided into smaller blocks or record locations where data records reside. Each location is unique and has an address—a numerical value. Depending upon the disk's size and density, hundreds or thousands of records may be stored on a single track. Figure 2–42 shows data storage on a disk. For illustration purposes, the physical size of the records is greatly exaggerated.

The concept of an address applies to all types of magnetic disks, including individual floppy disks and hard disks used in microcomputers and the larger mainframe disk-packs. A difference lies in the way the disks are physically arranged. Mainframe disks are often stacked on top of one another in a disk-pack arrangement that resembles a stack of phonograph records. Figure 2–43 (page 100) illustrates this technique.

FIGURE 2–42   How Data is Stored on a Disk

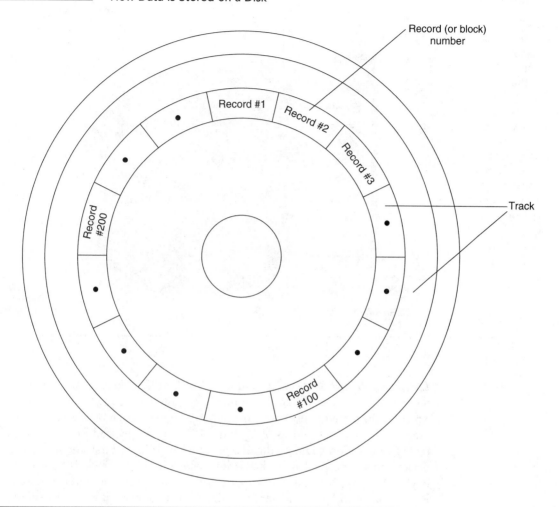

The disks are mounted to a central spindle that rotates at over 3,500 revolutions per minute. Each disk surface is provided with a separate read-write head that is used for storing and retrieving data.

Data Storage on a Disk-pack. Every disk in a disk-pack has two surfaces with the same number of tracks on each surface. Figure 2–43 shows that Track 100 exists on the top and bottom surfaces of each disk in the disk-pack. Therefore, this disk-pack containing 11 disks has 22 occurrences of Track 100. To protect the data from exposure to damage, the very top and bottom surfaces of the disk-pack are not used, yielding 20 data storage surfaces for Track 100.

When viewed collectively, the same track on each surface in the disk-pack is called a *cylinder*. Therefore, in our example, Cylinder 100 contains 20 tracks of data. However, the cylinders on a microcomputer's floppy disk or hard disk contain only two tracks because these disks have only two surfaces.

FIGURE 2–43

A Hard Disk. The access mechanism can position itself to access data from each of the four hundred cylinders. A cylinder is a set of all tracks with the same distance from the axis about which the disk-pack rotates. In this example, there are twenty tracks in each cylinder.

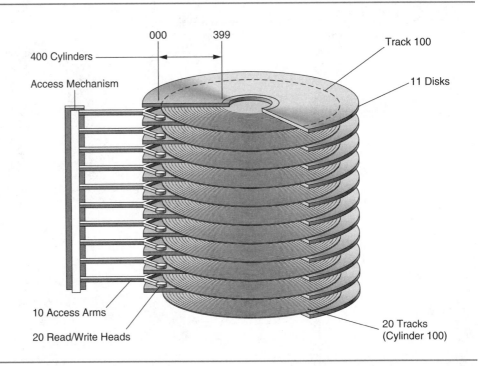

Locating a Record Based on its Address. A disk address consists of three components: the cylinder number, the surface number, and the record (or block) number. To find a record, the system must know the numeric value for each of these components. For example, if a record's address is Cylinder 105, Surface 15, and Record Block 157, the record in question could be directly accessed as follows: First, the disk-pack control device moves the read-write heads into position above Track 105 on each surface (Cylinder 105). Next, it activates the read-write head for Surface 15. Finally, as Record Block 157 passes under the active read-write head, it is either read or written.

The key task in direct access storage and retrieval is ascertaining the record's address. This may be determined from tables or calculations based on its primary key. Several direct access techniques are examined in Chapter 9.

Optical Disks

Optical disks are growing in popularity. The advantage of optical disks is that they can store very large amounts of data. A compact disc, one type of optical disk, is as portable as a floppy disk but can store more than 600 MB of data. There are several types of optical disk storage systems, including CD-ROM, WORM, and erasable optical disks.

A *CD-ROM (compact disc read-only memory)* is a secondary storage device that contains data or programs imprinted by the manufacturer. The CD-ROM is a read-only device; that is, the user cannot write to (alter) the data on the CD. The *write-once, read-many (WORM)* disk is a secondary storage device that allows the user to write to the disk one time. An *erasable optical disk* allows the user to store and modify data on the disk many times.

The logic of a sequential file update procedure is based upon the following assumptions and conditions:

1. The transaction (T) file contains fewer records than the master (M) file. An organization may have thousands of customers listed in its customer (accounts receivable) file, but only a small percentage of these customers actually purchased goods during the period represented by the current batch of transactions.
2. More than one transaction record may correspond to a given master file record. For example, a department store sells its RCA 27-inch TV to several customers during a one-day special offer. All of these transactions are separate records in the batch and must be processed against the same inventory master file record.
3. Both transaction file and master file must be in the same sequential order. For purposes of illustration, we will assume this to be ascending order.
4. The master file is presumed to be correct. Therefore, any sequencing irregularities are presumed to be errors in the transaction file and will cause the update process to terminate abnormally.

With these assumptions in mind, let's walk through the update logic presented in Figure 2–44. This logic is divided into three sections: start-up, update loop, and end procedures.

Start-Up

The process begins by reading the first transaction (T) and the first master (M) record from their respective files into the computer's memory. The T and M records in memory are designated as the *current records*.

Update Loop

The first step in the update loop is to compare the key fields of both records. One of three possible conditions will exist: T = M, T > M, or T < M.

T = M. When the key of T is equal to that of M, the transaction record matches the master record. Having found the correct master, the program updates the master from the transaction. The update program then reads another T record and compares the keys. If they are equal, the master is updated again. This continues until the key values change; recall that under Assumption 2, there may be many Ts for any M record.

T > M. The normal change in the key value relationship is for T to become greater than M. This is so because both T and M are sorted in ascending order (Assumption 3). The T > M relation signifies that processing on the current master record is complete. The updated master (currently stored in computer memory) is then written to a new master file—the child—and a new M record is read from the original (parent) file.

Because the transaction file represents a subset of the master (Assumption 1), there normally will be gaps between the key values of the transaction records. Figure 2–45 (page 103) illustrates this with sample transactions and corresponding master file records. Notice the gap between Key 1 and Key 4 in the transaction file. When Key 4 is read into memory, the condition T > M exists until Master Record 4 is read. Before this, Master Records 2 and 3 are read into memory and then immediately written to the new master without modification.

FIGURE 2–44   Program Flowchart of Sequential File Update Logic

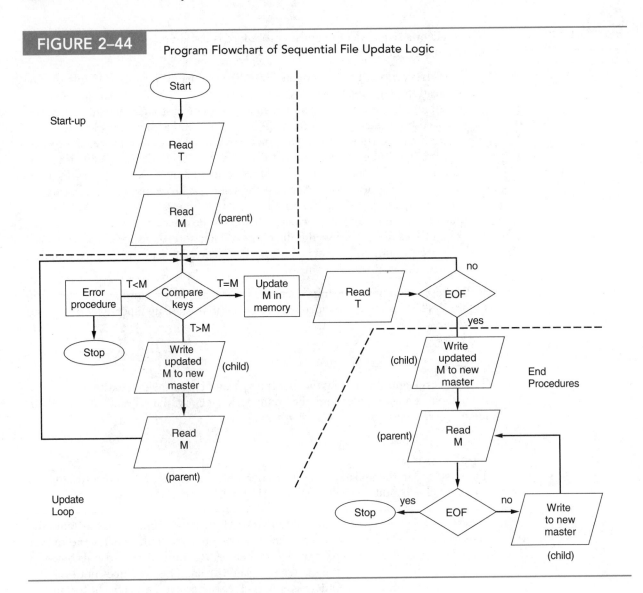

T < M. The T < M key relationship signifies an error condition. The key of the current T record should only be smaller than that of the current M record if a T record is out of sequence (Assumption 4). To illustrate, refer to Figure 2–45. Notice that the record with Key Value 10 in the transaction file is out of sequence. This goes undetected until the next T record (Key 7) is read. At this point, the computer's memory contains M Record 10 (M10), and the previous M records (M6 through M9) have been read and then written, unchanged, to the new master. Reading Record T7 produces the condition T < M. It is now impossible to update Records M7 and M9 from their corresponding T records. The sequential file update process can only move forward through the files. Skipped records cannot be recovered and updated out of sequence. Because of this, the update process will be incomplete, and the data processing department must execute special error procedures to remedy the problem. We examine various error handling techniques in Chapter 16.

FIGURE 2–45

Sample Transactions
and Master File
Records

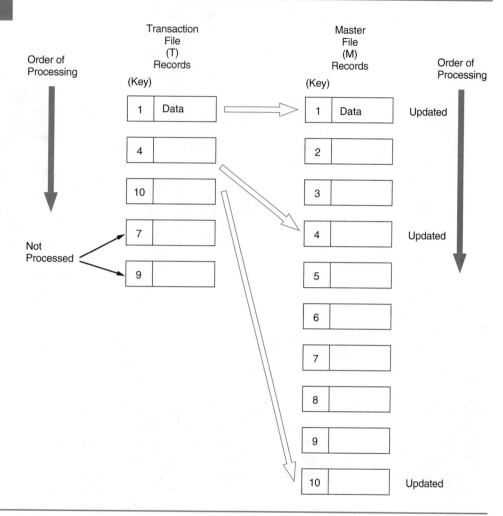

End Procedures

When the last T record is read and processed, the update loop procedure is complete. This is signaled by a special EOF record in the transaction file. At this point, one of two possible conditions will exist:

1.   The M record in memory is the last record on the M file, or;
2.   There are still unprocessed records on the M file.

Assuming the second condition is true, the remaining records on the M file must be copied to the new master file. Some file structures indicate EOF with a record containing high key values (that is, the key field is filled with 9s) to force a permanent T > M condition, in which case all remaining M records will be read and copied to the new file. Other structures use a special EOF marker. The logic in this example assumes the latter approach. When the EOF condition is reached for the master and all the M records are copied, the update procedure is terminated.

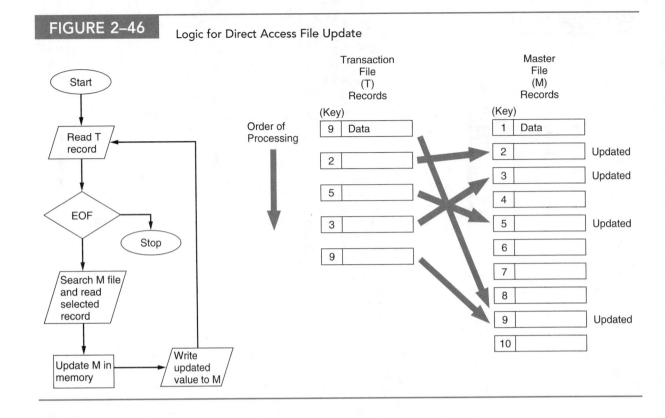

FIGURE 2–46   Logic for Direct Access File Update

SECTION C:
GENERAL LOGIC
FOR DIRECT
ACCESS FILE
UPDATE

Figure 2–46 presents the general logic for updating direct access files. The two sample files of data provided will be used to illustrate this process. Notice that this logic is simpler than that used for sequential files. There are three reasons for this. First, since record sequencing is irrelevant, the logic does not need to consider the relationship between the T and M key values. Consequently, the update program does not need to deal explicitly with the problem of multiple T records for a given M record. Second, unprocessed master records are not copied to a new master file. Third, complex procedures for searching the master file and retrieving the desired M record are performed by the computer's operating system rather than by the update program.

The transaction file in Figure 2–46 is read from top to bottom. Each record is processed as it is encountered and without regard for its key sequence. First, T9 is read into memory. The operating system then searches for and retrieves the corresponding record (M9) from the master file. The current record is updated in memory and immediately written back to its original location on the master file. Records T2, T5, and T3 are all processed in the same manner. Finally, the second T9 transaction is processed just as the first, resulting in M9 being updated twice.

Key Terms

access method   (79)
accounting record   (52)

archive file   (61)
audit trail   (59)

Review Questions

1. What three transaction cycles exist in all businesses?
2. Name the major subsystems of the expenditure cycle.
3. Identify and distinguish between the physical and financial components of the expenditure cycle.
4. Name the major subsystems of the conversion cycle.
5. Name the major subsystems of the revenue cycle.
6. Name the three types of documents.
7. Name the two types of journals.
8. Distinguish between a general journal and journal vouchers.
9. Name the two types of ledgers.
10. What is an audit trail?
11. What is the confirmation process?
12. What are the four types of files typically found in a computer-based system?
13. Distinguish between entity relationship diagrams, data flow diagrams, document flowcharts, and system flowcharts.
14. What is meant by cardinality in entity relationship diagrams?
15. What is a batch? What are the advantages of batch processing?
16. Distinguish between efficiency and effectiveness.
17. Distinguish between batch and real-time processing.
18. Distinguish between the flat file and database approaches to data management.
19. What are the two fundamental components of data structures?
20. What are the criteria that influence the selection of the data structure?
21. What are the advantages and disadvantages of using a sequential data structure? Give an example of each.
22. What are the advantages and disadvantages of using an indexed random file structure? An indexed sequential file structure?
23. What are the three physical components of a VSAM file? Explain how a record is searched through these components.
24. What is a pointer? Discuss the three commonly used types of pointers and their relative merits.
25. What are four different data processing approaches?
26. What is the purpose of the following batch computer programs: edit run, sort run, and update run?

27. What master file backup method is used for sequential file structures?
28. How do backup procedures for files with a direct access structure differ from sequential files?
29. What major changes will occur in a batch update system as a result of changing the master file structure from sequential to direct access?
30. What type of storage medium must be used for the transaction file in a batch system with real-time data collection?

31. Can a batch update system that uses real-time collection also use sequential master files? Explain.
32. What are the advantages of real-time data processing?
33. In general, the resource requirements for real-time systems are greater than for batch systems. Explain this statement.

Discussion Questions

1. Discuss the flow of cash through the transaction cycles. Include in your discussion the relevant subsystems and any time lags that may occur.
2. Explain whether the cost accounting system primarily supports internal or external reporting.
3. Discuss the role of the conversion cycle for service and retailing entities.
4. Can a turnaround document contain information that is subsequently used as a source document? Why or why not?
5. Would the write-down of obsolete inventory be recorded in a special journal or the general journal? Why?
6. Are both registers and special journals necessary?
7. Discuss the relationship between the balance in the accounts payable general ledger control account and what is found in the accounts payable subsidiary ledger.
8. What role does the audit trail play in the task of confirmation?
9. Explain how the magnetic audit trail functions.
10. Are large batch sizes preferable to small batch sizes? Explain.

11. What form can source documents take in a computer-based system?
12. Explain how a hashing structure works and why it's quicker than using an index. Give an example. If it's so much faster, why isn't it used exclusively?
13. Describe a specific accounting application that could make use of a VSAM file.
14. Explain the following three types of pointers: physical address pointer, relative address pointer, and logical key pointer.
15. Should an auditor wishing to assess the adequacy of separation of functions examine a data flow diagram, a document flowchart, or a system flowchart? Why?
16. If transactions are dependent upon one another, should the organization use a batch or real-time system? What if the transactions are independent of one another?
17. Discuss the issues involved in choosing between batch processing using sequential files and batch processing using direct access files. Also discuss the backup procedures for the master file for both of these methods.

Multiple-Choice Questions

1. CMA 1284 5-27
   An advantage of having a computer maintain an automated error log in conjunction with computer edit programs is that
   a. reports can be developed that summarize the errors by type, cause, and person responsible.
   b. less manual work is required to determine how to correct errors.
   c. better editing techniques will result.
   d. the audit trail is maintained.
   e. correction procedures will become highly automated.

2. CMA 685 5-21

A systems tool that depicts the flow of information relating to a particular transaction through an organization is a

a. document flowchart.
b. program flowchart.
c. decision table.
d. work distribution analysis.
e. systems survey.

3. CMA 686 5-9

Devices that are used only to perform sequential file processing will not permit

a. data to be edited on a separate computer run.
b. the use of a database structure.
c. data to be edited in an off-line mode.
d. batch processing to be initiated from a terminal.
e. data to be edited on a real-time basis.

4. CMA 687 5-9

Turnaround documents

a. are generated by the computer and eventually return to it.
b. generally circulate only within the computer center.
c. are only used internally in an organization.
d. are largely restricted to use in a manual system.
e. can be read and processed only by the computer.

5. The production subsystem of the conversion cycle includes all of the following EXCEPT

a. determining raw materials requirements.
b. make or buy decisions of components parts.
c. release of raw materials into production.
d. scheduling the goods to be produced.

6. Which of the following files is a temporary file?

a. transaction file
b. master file
c. reference file
d. none of the above

7. A diagramming tool used to represent the logical elements of a system is a

a. programming flowchart.
b. entity relationship diagram.
c. document flowchart.
d. data flow diagram.

8. Which of the following is NOT an advantage of direct access files over sequential files?

a. shorter record access time
b. elimination of automatic file backup

c. less unnecessary rewriting of unchanged records
d. they are all advantages

9. CIA 586 III-31

The use of pointers can save time when sequentially updating a

a. master file.
b. database management system.
c. batch file.
d. random file.

10. It is appropriate to use a sequential file structure when

a. records are routinely inserted.
b. a large portion of the file will be processed in one operation.
c. records need to be scanned using secondary keys.
d. single records need to be retrieved.

11. Which statement is NOT correct?

a. The sequential file structure is appropriate for payroll records.
b. An advantage of a sequential index is that it can be searched rapidly.
c. The indexed sequential access method performs record insertion operations efficiently.
d. The principal advantage of the hashing structure is speed of access.

12. Which statement is NOT correct?

a. Indexed random files are dispersed throughout the storage device without regard for physical proximity with related records.
b. Indexed random files use disk storage space efficiently.
c. Indexed random files are efficient when processing a large portion of a file at one time.
d. Indexed random files are easy to maintain in terms of adding records.

13. Which statement is NOT correct? The indexed sequential access method

a. is used for very large files that need both direct access and batch processing.
b. may use an overflow area for records.
c. provides an exact physical address for each record.
d. is appropriate for files that require few insertions or deletions.

14. Which statement is true about a hashing structure?

a. The same address could be calculated for two records.

b. Storage space is used efficiently.

c. Records cannot be accessed rapidly.

d. A separate index is required.

15. In a hashing structure,
    a. two records can be stored at the same address.
    b. pointers are used to indicate the location of all records.
    c. pointers are used to indicate location of a record with the same address as another record.
    d. all locations on the disk are used for record storage.

16. Pointers can be used for all the following except
    a. to locate the subschema address of the record.
    b. to locate the physical address of the record.
    c. to locate the relative address of the record.
    d. to locate the logical key of the record.

17. An advantage of a physical address pointer is that
    a. it points directly to the actual disk storage location.

b. it is easily recovered if it is inadvertently lost.

c. it remains unchanged when disks are reorganized.

d. all of the above are advantages of the physical address pointer.

18. Pointers are used to
    a. link records within a file.
    b. link records between files.
    c. identify records stored in overflow.
    d. all of the above.

19. In a hierarchical model,
    a. links between related records are implicit.
    b. the way to access data is by following a predefined data path.
    c. an owner (parent) record may own just one member (child) record.
    d. a member (child) record may have more than one owner (parent).

Problems

1. **Transaction Cycle Identification**

   Categorize each of the following activities into the expenditure, conversion, or revenue cycles and identify the applicable subsystem.
   a. Preparing the weekly payroll for manufacturing personnel
   b. Releasing raw materials for use in the manufacturing cycle
   c. Recording the receipt of payment for goods sold
   d. Recording the order placed by a customer
   e. Ordering raw materials
   f. Determining the amount of raw materials to order

2. **Document Flowchart**

   Figure 2–4 illustrates how a customer order is transformed into a source document, a product document, and a turnaround document. Develop a similar flowchart for the process of paying hourly employees. Assume time sheets are used and the payroll department must total the hours. Each hour worked by any employee must be charged to some account (a cost center). Each week, the manager of each cost center receives a report listing the employee's name and the number of hours charged to this center. The manager

   is required to verify that this information is correct by signing the form and noting any discrepancies, then sending this form back to payroll. Any discrepancies noted must be corrected by the payroll department.

3. **Entity Relationship Diagram**

   Shown on the next page is an ER diagram for an accounts payable system. Describe this system in English terms, indicating whether a one-to-one, one-to-many, or many-to-many relationship exists.

4. **Entity Relationship Diagram**

   Refer to the ER diagram in Problem 3.
   a. Adjust the diagram to deal with the purchases of raw materials for manufacturing purposes (you may wish to refer to Chapter 7).
   b. Adjust the diagram to deal with the purchases of merchandise for resale (you may wish to refer to Chapter 5).

5. **Entity Relationship Diagram**

   Prepare an ER diagram, in good form, for the sales revenue cycle, which consists of both sales processing and cash receipts. Describe the system in English terms, indicating whether a one-to-one, one-to-many, or many-to-many relationship exists. (You may wish to refer to Chapter 4.)

Problem 3: Entity Relationship Diagram

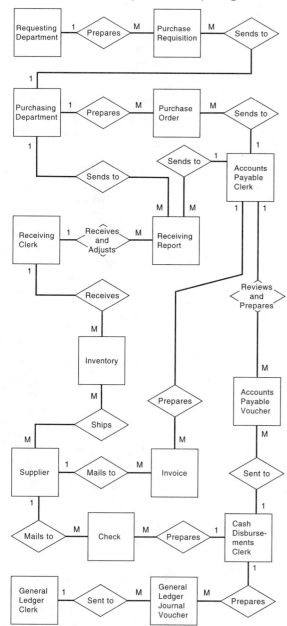

6. File Classification

Determine whether the following types of files for a physician's office would most accurately be classified as master, transaction, reference, or archive files.

a. Patient history file, which contains a list of every diagnosis made for each patient

b. Patient credit file, which contains the patient's year-to-date charges, as well as the current amount due

c. Services file, which is a list of all services performed by the doctor and the applicable charges

d. Insurance file, which contains a list of insurance companies honored

e. Daily visits file, which contains a record for each patient seen by the physician on a given day

f. Diagnosis file, which is a list of the 200 most common diagnoses made by the physician

g. Former patient file, which contains a history of patients who have not made an appointment in the last three years or are deceased

7. Data Flow Diagram

Prepare a data flow diagram depicting the course registration process at your college or university.

8. CMA (Adapted) 686 5-15 to 5-17 System Flowchart

Using the diagram on the next page, answer the following questions:

a. What does Symbol 2 depict?

b. What does the operation by Symbols 3 and 4 depict?

c. What does Symbol 6 depict?

9. System Flowchart

Analyze the system flowchart on the following page and describe in detail the processes that are occurring.

10. System Flowchart and Program Flowchart

From the diagram in Problem 9, identify three types of errors that may cause a payroll record to be placed in the error file. Use a program flowchart to illustrate the edit program.

11. System Flowchart

The flowchart on page 111 presents a batch update system that uses sequential files.

a. Redraw this flowchart to represent a batch system with direct access files.

b. Describe the principal operational changes to the system that result from the new file structure.

c. Illustrate with a flowchart and describe the file backup procedures for this system.

Problem 8: System Flowchart

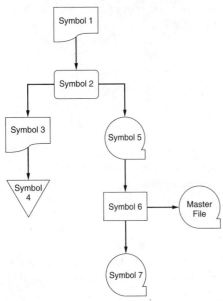

Problem 9: System Flowchart

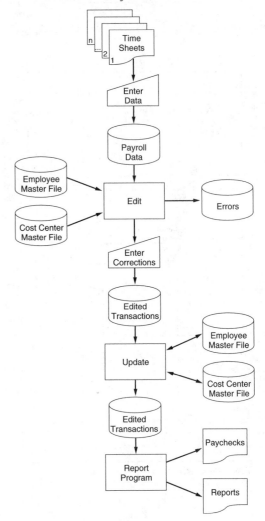

12. System Documentation—Revenue Cycle

The following describes the revenue cycle procedures for a hypothetical company:

Customer orders are received by the sales department and are transcribed by a clerk onto a six-part sales order. Copies of the source document are distributed to various departments.

- Copies 1, 2, and 3 go to the warehouse clerk, who picks the goods from the shelves and ships them to the customer. The clerk sends Copy 1 of the sales order along with the goods to the customer. Copy 2 is sent to the billing department, and Copy 3 is filed in the warehouse.
- Copies 4, 5, and 6 are sent to the billing department, where they are temporarily filed by the billing clerk.
- When the billing clerk receives Copy 2 from the warehouse, she pulls the other copies from the temporary file and completes the documents by adding prices, taxes, and freight charges, which she obtains from reference files. The billing clerk then makes an entry in the sales journal, sends Copy 4 (customer bill) to the customer, and sends Copies 5 and 6 to the accounts receivable (AR) and inventory control (IC) departments, respectively.
- Upon receipt of the documents from the billing clerk, the AR and IC clerks post the transactions to their respective subsidiary ac-

counts. They then file the document in the department.

- On the payment due date, the customer sends a check for the full amount and a copy of the bill (the remittance advice) to the company. These documents are received by the mail room clerk, who distributes them as follows:
  1. The check goes to the cash receipts clerk, who records it in the cash receipts journal and prepares two deposit slips. One deposit slip and the check is sent to the bank; the other deposit slip is filed in the cash receipts department.
  2. The remittance advice is sent to the AR clerk, who posts to the subsidiary accounts and then files the document.

Problem 11: System Flowchart

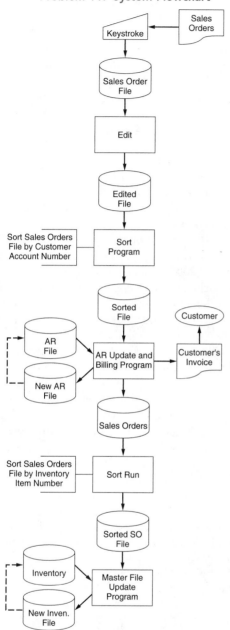

Required:
Prepare a data flow diagram and a document flow-chart of the revenue cycle procedures described above.

13. System Documentation— Expenditure Cycle

The following describes the expenditure cycle procedures for a hypothetical company:

- The inventory control clerk examines the inventory records for items that must be replenished, and prepares a two-part purchase requisition. Copy 1 of the requisition goes to the purchases department, and Copy 2 is filed.

- Upon receipt of the requisition, the purchases clerk selects a supplier from the valid vendor file (reference file) and prepares a three-part purchase order. Copy 1 is sent to the supplier; Copy 2 goes to the accounts payable department, where it is filed temporarily; and Copy 3 is filed in the purchases department.

- A few days after the supplier ships the order, the goods arrive at the receiving department. They are inspected and the receiving clerk prepares a three-part receiving report describing the number and quality of the items received. Copy 1 of the receiving report accompanies the goods to the warehouse, where they are secured and the receiving report is filed. Copy 2 goes to inventory control, where the clerk posts to the inventory records and files the document. Copy 3 goes to the accounts payable department, where it is filed with the purchase order.

- A day or two later, the accounts payable (AP) clerk receives the supplier's invoice (bill) for the items shipped. The clerk pulls the purchase order and receiving report from the temporary file and compares the quantity ordered, quantity received, and the price charged. After reconciling the three documents, the clerk enters the purchase in the purchases journal and posts the amount owed to the accounts payable subsidiary account.

- On the payment due date, the AP clerk posts to the AP subsidiary account to remove the liability and prepares a voucher authorizing payment to the vendor. The voucher is then sent to the cash disbursements clerk.

- Upon receipt of the voucher, the cash disbursements clerk prepares a check and sends it to the supplier. A copy of the check is filed in the department.

Required:
Prepare a data flow diagram and a document flow-chart of the expenditure cycle procedures described above.

14. System Documentation—Payroll

The following describes the payroll procedures for a hypothetical company:

- Every Thursday, the timekeeping clerk sends employee time cards to the payroll department for processing.
- Based on the hours worked as indicated by the time cards, the employee pay-rate and withholding information in the employee file, and the tax-rate reference file, the payroll clerk calculates gross pay, withholdings, and net pay for each employee. The clerk then prepares paychecks for each employee, files copies of the paychecks in the payroll department, and posts the earnings to the employee records. Finally, the clerk prepares a payroll summary and sends it and the paychecks to the cash disbursement (CD) department.
- The CD clerk reconciles the payroll summary with the paychecks and records the transaction in the cash disbursements journal. The clerk then files the payroll summary and sends the paychecks to the treasurer for signing.
- The signed checks are then sent to the paymaster, who distributes them to the employees on Friday morning.

Required:
Prepare a data flow diagram and a document flowchart of the payroll procedures described above.

15. Access Methods

For each of the following file processing operations, indicate whether a sequential file, indexed random file, virtual storage access method (VSAM), hashing, or pointer structure would work best. You may choose as many as you wish for each step. Also indicate which would perform the least optimally.

a. Retrieve a record from the file based upon its primary key value.
b. Update a record in the file.
c. Read a complete file of records.
d. Find the next record in a file.
e. Insert a record into a file.
f. Delete a record from a file.
g. Scan a file for records with secondary keys.

16. File Organization

For the following situations, indicate the most appropriate type of file organization. Explain your choice.

a. A local utility company has 80,000 residential customers and 10,000 commercial customers. The monthly billings are staggered throughout the month and, as a result, the cash receipts are fairly uniform throughout the month. For 99 percent of all accounts, one check per month is received. These receipts are recorded in a batch file, and the customer account records are updated biweekly. In a typical month, customer inquires are received at the rate of about 20 per day.
b. A national credit card agency has 12 million customer accounts. On average, 30 million purchases and 700,000 receipts of payments are processed per day. Additionally, the customer support hot line provides information to approximately 150,000 credit card holders and 30,000 merchants per day.
c. An airline reservations system assumes that the traveler knows the departing city. From that point, fares and flight times are examined based on the destination. Once a flight is identified as being acceptable to the traveler, then the availability is checked and, if necessary, a seat is reserved. The volume of transactions exceeds one-half million per day.
d. A library system stocks over 2 million books and has 30,000 patrons. Each patron is allowed to check out five books. On average, there are 1.3 copies of each title in the library. Over 3,000 books are checked out each day, with approximately the same amount being returned daily. The checked out books are posted immediately, as well as any returns of overdue books by patrons who wish to pay their fines.

17. Virtual Storage Access Method

Using the index provided on the next page, explain, step-by-step, how Key 12987 would be found using the virtual storage access method. Once a surface on a cylinder is located, what is the average number of records that must be searched?

18. Hashing Algorithm

The systems programmer uses a hashing algorithm to determine storage addresses. The hashing structure is 9,997/key. The resulting number is then used to locate the record. The first two digits after the decimal point represent the cylinder number, while the second two digits repre-

CYLINDER INDEX		SURFACE INDEX CYLINDER	
Key Range	*Cylinder Number*	*Key Range*	*Surface Number*
2,000	44	12,250	0
4,000	45	12,500	1
6,000	46	12,750	2
8,000	47	13,000	3
10,000	48	13,250	4
12,000	49	13,500	5
14,000	50	14,750	6
16,000	51	15,000	7
18,000	52		
20,000	53		

sent the surface number. The fifth, sixth, and seventh digits after the decimal point represent the record number. This algorithm results in a unique address 99 percent of the time. What happens the remainder of the time when the results of the algorithm are not unique? Explain in detail the storage process when Key=3 is processed first, Key=2307 at a later date, and shortly thereafter Key=39.

Appendix Problem

Update Process

Examine the diagram, which contains the processing order for a transaction file and a master file for a sequential file update process. Indicate the order in which the transactions are processed. Indicate which master file records are updated and which are read and written, unchanged, into the new master file. Also illustrate the relationship between the transaction file and the master file, that is, T = M, T < M, and T > M, in your answer.

How would the update change if a direct access file is used instead?

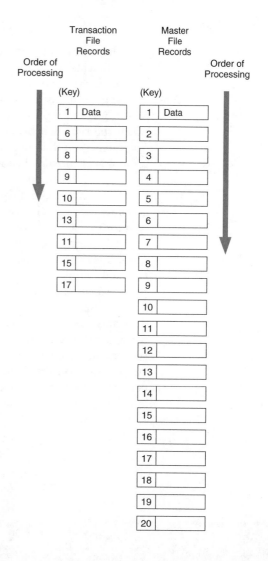

CHAPTER

3

Ethics, Fraud, and Internal Control

This chapter examines three closely related subjects of importance to accountants and other students of information systems: business ethics, fraud, and internal control. We begin the chapter by surveying ethical issues that highlight the organization's conflicting responsibilities to its employees, shareholders, customers, and the general public. Organization managers have an ethical responsibility to seek a balance between the risks and benefits to these constituents that result from their decisions. Management and accountants must recognize the new implications of information technologies for such historic issues as working conditions, the right to privacy, and the potential for fraud.

The second section is devoted to the subject of fraud and its implications for accountants. No major aspect of the independent auditor's role has caused more concern for the public accounting profession than the auditor's responsibility for detecting fraud during an audit. Although the term *fraud* is very familiar in today's financial press, it is not always clear what constitutes fraud. In this section, we discuss the nature and meaning of fraud, differentiate between employee fraud and management fraud, explain fraud-motivating forces, and review some common fraud techniques.

The final section in the chapter examines the subject of internal control. Both managers and accountants are concerned about the adequacy of the organization's internal control structure as a means of deterring fraud and preventing errors. In this section, internal control issues are first presented on a conceptual level. We then discuss internal control within the context of *Statement on Auditing Standards No. 78*, the current authoritative pronouncement on the subject. The chapter concludes by examining the impact of the computer-based information system on the internal control structure.

# LEARNING OBJECTIVES

After studying this chapter, you should:

- Understand the broad issues pertaining to business ethics.
- Know why the subject of ethics is important to the study of accounting information systems.
- Have a basic understanding of ethical issues related to the use of information technology.
- Be able to distinguish between management fraud and employee fraud.
- Be familiar with the common fraud techniques used in both manual systems and computer-based systems.
- Be aware of the gap that exists between the expectations of financial statements users and the ability of auditors to detect fraud.
- Understand the internal control structure defined by *Statement on Auditing Standards No. 78*.
- Recognize the implications of computer technology on the internal control structure.

ETHICAL ISSUES IN BUSINESS

With scandals in the banking industry, stories of computer crimes and viruses, and almost daily charges of impropriety and illegalities by public officials in Washington, one cannot help but wonder about the current state of ethics in America. Such business activities as kickbacks, fraud, consumer deception, conflicts of interest, and the selling of products that are banned in the United States to Third World countries are all too common. Countless journal and newspaper articles, books, television programs, and movies are concerned with ethics or, more precisely, the lack of ethics, in business, politics, education, and everyday life.

Ethical standards are derived from societal mores and deep-rooted personal beliefs about issues of right and wrong that are not universally agreed upon. It is quite possible for two individuals, both of whom consider themselves to be acting ethically, to be on opposite sides of an issue. Often, we confuse ethical issues with legal issues. When the Honorable Gentleman from the state of ————, who is charged with ethical misconduct, stands before Congress and proclaims that he is "guilty of no wrongdoing," is he really saying that he did not break the *law*?

Accreditation bodies, such as the American Assembly of Collegiate Schools of Business and the Association for Computing Machinery, in conjunction with businesspeople, are increasingly incorporating ethical issues into the business curriculum. Although a thorough treatment of ethics is impossible within the space available, the objective of this section is to heighten the reader's awareness of ethical issues relating to business, information systems, and computer technology.

WHAT IS BUSINESS ETHICS?

Ethics pertains to the principles of conduct that individuals use in making choices and guiding their behavior in situations that involve the concepts of right and wrong. More specifically, **business ethics** involves finding the answers to two questions:

1. How do managers decide on what is right in conducting their business?
2. Once managers have recognized what is right, how do they achieve it?

Ethical issues in business can be divided into four areas: equity, rights, honesty, and the exercise of corporate power. Table 3–1 identifies some of the business practices in each of these areas that have ethical implications.

While interest in business ethics has increased significantly over the last decade, the subject has concerned both scholars and the public since the beginnings of the Western economy. Concerns about the moral shortcomings of financiers, bankers, and investors are found in many historical writings. In fact, many contemporary debates about the nature of business ethics are centuries old.[1]

John F. Akers, former chairman of the board and CEO of IBM Corporation, states: "Our ethical standards come out of the past—out of our inheritance as a people: religious, philosophical, historical. And the more we know of that past, the more surefootedly we can inculcate ethical conduct in the future."[2]

Ethical behavior and personal gain are closely related issues. Medieval Catholicism deemed capitalism and money making to be morally wrong: "a Catholic

---

1   D. Vogel, "Business Ethics Past and Present," *Public Interest* (Winter 1991): 49–64.
2   J. F. Akers, "Ethics and Competitiveness—Putting First Things First," *Sloan Management Review* (Winter 1989): 69–71.

TABLE 3–1	**Ethical Issues in Business**	
Equity	Executive Salaries Comparable Worth Product Pricing	
Rights	Corporate Due Process Employee Health Screening Employee Privacy Sexual Harassment Affirmative Action Equal Employment Opportunity Whistle-Blowing	
Honesty	Employee and Management Conflicts of Interest Security of Organization Data and Records Misleading Advertising Questionable Business Practices in Foreign Countries Accurate Reporting of Shareholder Interests	
Exercise of Corporate Power	Political Action Committees Workplace Safety Product Safety Environmental Issues Divestment of Interests Corporate Political Contributions Downsizing and Plant Closures	

SOURCE: Adapted from: The Conference Board, "Defining Corporate Ethics," in P. Madsen and J. Shafritz, *Essentials of Business Ethics* (New York: Meridian, 1990), p. 18.

could no more have been an ethical moneylender six centuries ago than he could be a socially responsible drug dealer today."[3] Many medieval merchants did act unscrupulously by any standards. But if their business was thought to be fundamentally immoral, why should they try to perform it ethically? How could they?

The Protestant Reformation made it possible for the successful businessperson to be an ethical individual as well. Profit and heaven were thus no longer mutually exclusive pursuits. A diligent worker could be rewarded financially as a sign of God's favor. Further, the acquisition of personal wealth could be socially beneficial. Hence, businesspeople were rewarded with profits for fulfilling the needs and expectations of their customers, employees, and investors.

Protestant business ethics has had a significant impact on Western culture. Nineteenth-century Americans were very concerned with the relationship between the moral character of individuals and success in business. Contemporary business ethics shifts the focus away from the individual's character to the organization's actions. In addition, current discussions about business ethics have taken on a secular tone. Nonetheless, we remain preoccupied with the relationship of ethics and profit.

In today's world, many people feel that business ethics is an oxymoron. However, good ethical behavior should also be good for business. This does not mean that firms

---

3   Vogel, "Business Ethics Past and Present."

that act ethically will prosper. Ethical behavior is a necessary but not a sufficient condition for business success. An equally important corollary is that firms that act unethically should be punished.

HOW SOME FIRMS ADDRESS ETHICAL ISSUES

In 1990, the Business Roundtable, composed of the chief executive officers of 200 major corporations, set up a task force that included several ethicists as consultants. The group studied ethics programs at ten companies and made recommendations that would help to ensure ethical practices within organizations. These included greater commitment of top management to improving ethical standards, written codes that clearly communicate management expectations, programs to implement ethical guidelines, and techniques to monitor compliance.[4]

Some very successful companies have long emphasized ethics. For example, Boeing uses line managers to lead ethics training sessions and maintains a toll-free number to enable employees to report violations. General Mills has published guidelines for dealing with vendors, competitors, and customers, and emphasizes open decision making. Johnson & Johnson's "credo" of corporate values is integral to its culture. It holds companywide meetings that challenge the credo tenets and uses surveys to ascertain compliance.[5]

The Role of Management in Maintaining the Ethical Climate
Organization managers must create and maintain an appropriate ethical atmosphere; they must limit the opportunity and temptation for unethical behavior within the firm. It is not enough for managers to rely merely on each individual's conscience. The individual must be made aware of the firm's commitment to ethics above short-term increases in profit and efficiency.[6]

Although top management's attitude toward ethics sets the tone for business practice, in many situations it is up to lower-level managers to uphold a firm's ethical standards. Reported abuses of ethical standards in Wall Street scandals have typically been perpetrated by relatively junior employees. Methods must be developed for including lower-level managers and nonmanagers in the ethics schema of the firm. Managers and nonmanagers alike should be made aware of the firm's code of ethics, be given decision models, and participate in training programs that explore ethical issues.

Ethical Development
Most individuals develop a code of ethics as a result of their family environment, formal education, and personal experiences. Behavioral stage theory suggests that we all go through several stages of moral evolution before settling on one level of ethical reasoning.[7] The levels in the stage theory model are presented in Figure 3–1. Man-

---

4   J. A. Byrne, "Businesses Are Signing up for Ethics 101," *Business Week* (15 February 1988): 56–57.
5   *Ibid.*
6   S. W. Gellerman, "Managing Ethics from the Top Down," *Sloan Management Review* (Winter 1989): 73–79.
7   G. Baxter and C. Rarick, "Education for the Moral Development of Managers: Kohlberg's Stages of Moral Development and Integrative Education," in James A. O'Brien, *Management Information Systems: A Managerial End User Perspective* (Boston: Irwin, 1993): 545.

FIGURE 3–1   Behavioral Stage Theory

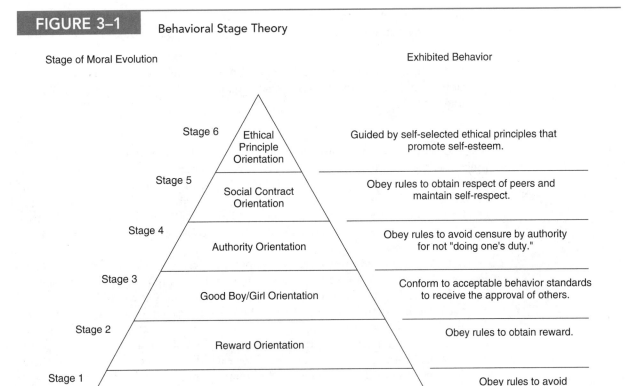

Stage of Moral Evolution

Exhibited Behavior

Stage 6 — Ethical Principle Orientation — Guided by self-selected ethical principles that promote self-esteem.

Stage 5 — Social Contract Orientation — Obey rules to obtain respect of peers and maintain self-respect.

Stage 4 — Authority Orientation — Obey rules to avoid censure by authority for not "doing one's duty."

Stage 3 — Good Boy/Girl Orientation — Conform to acceptable behavior standards to receive the approval of others.

Stage 2 — Reward Orientation — Obey rules to obtain reward.

Stage 1 — Punishment Orientation — Obey rules to avoid punishment.

agers who achieve Stage 6 are guided by self-chosen ethical principles and are not influenced by social pressure, fear, or guilt in their decisions.

Making Ethical Decisions

Business schools can and should be involved in the ethical development of future managers. Business programs can teach students analytical techniques to use in trying to understand and put into perspective a firm's conflicting responsibilities to its employees, shareholders, customers, and the public.

Every ethical decision has both risks and benefits. For example, implementing a new computer-based information system in an organization may cause some employees to lose their jobs, while those who remain enjoy the benefit of improved working conditions. Seeking a balance between these consequences is the managers' **ethical responsibility**. The following ethical principles provide some guidance in the discharge of this responsibility.[8]

Proportionality. The benefit from a decision must outweigh the risks. Furthermore, there must be no alternative decision that provides the same or greater benefit with less risk.

---

8   M. McFarland, "Ethics and the Safety of Computer System," *Computer*, (February 1991).

Justice. The benefits of the decision should be distributed fairly to those who share the risks. Those who do not benefit should not carry the burden of risk.

Minimize risk. Even if judged acceptable by the above principles, the decision should be implemented so as to minimize all of the risks and avoid any unnecessary risks.

WHAT IS COMPUTER ETHICS?

The use of information technology in business has had a major impact on society and thus raises significant ethical issues regarding computer crime, working conditions, privacy, and more. **Computer ethics** is "the analysis of the nature and social impact of computer technology and the corresponding formulation and justification of policies for the ethical use of such technology . . . [This includes] concerns about software as well as hardware and concerns about networks connecting computers as well as computers themselves."[9]

Bynum has defined three levels of computer ethics: pop, para, and theoretical.[10] *Pop* computer ethics is simply the exposure to stories and reports found in the popular media regarding the good or bad ramifications of computer technology. The society at large needs to be aware of such things as computer viruses and computer systems designed to aid handicapped persons. *Para* computer ethics involves taking a real interest in computer ethics cases and acquiring some level of skill and knowledge in the field. All systems professionals need to reach this level of competency so they can do their jobs effectively. Students of accounting information systems should also achieve this level of ethical understanding. The third level, *theoretical* computer ethics, is of interest to multidisciplinary researchers who apply the theories of philosophy, sociology, and psychology to computer science with the goal of bringing some new understanding to the field.

A New Problem or Just a New Twist on an Old Problem?

There are many ethical issues to which students should be exposed. Some will argue that the pertinent issues have already been examined in some other domain. For example, the issue of property rights has been explored and has resulted in copyright, trade secret, and patent laws. Although computer programs are a new type of asset, many feel that they should not be considered as different from other forms of property. So a fundamental question is whether computers represent new ethical problems or just create new twists on old problems. Where the latter is the case, we need only to understand the generic values that are at stake and the principles that should then apply.[11] However, a large contingent vociferously disagrees with the premise that computers are no different than other technology. For example, many reject the notion of intellectual property being the same as real property. There is, as yet, no consensus on this matter.

---

9   J. H. Moor, "What Is Computer Ethics?" *Metaphilosophy* 16 (1985): 266–75.

10   T. W. Bynum, "Human Values and the Computer Science Curriculum" (Working paper for the National Conference on Computing and Values, August 1991).

11   G. Johnson, "A Framework for Thinking about Computer Ethics" in J. Robinette and R. Barquin (eds.), *Computers and Ethics: A Sourcebook for Discussions* (Brooklyn: Polytechnic Press, 1989): 26–31.

Below we have listed several issues of concern for the student of accounting information systems. This listing is not presumed to be exhaustive, and a full discussion of each of the issues is beyond the scope of this chapter. Instead, the issues are very briefly defined, and several trigger questions are provided. It is hoped that these questions will serve as discussion starters in the classroom. To give each of them a label and separate treatment, some overlap between issues is unavoidable.

Privacy

People desire to be in full control of what and how much information about themselves is available to others, and to whom it is available. This is the issue of **privacy**. "[P]rivacy is a matter of the restricted access to persons or information about persons."[12] The creation and maintenance of huge, shared databases makes it necessary to protect people from the potential misuse of data. This raises the issue of **ownership** in the personal information industry.[13] Should the privacy of individuals be protected through policies and systems? No laws currently govern this industry, yet the demand for personal information (for targeted mailing lists, for example) is ever-growing. What information about oneself does the individual "own"? Why can firms that are unrelated to individuals buy and sell information about these individuals without their permission?

Security (Accuracy and Confidentiality)

Computer **security** is an attempt to avoid such undesirable events as a loss of confidentiality or data integrity. Security systems attempt to prevent fraud and other misuse of computer systems; they act to protect and further the legitimate interests of the system's constituencies. The ethical issues involving security arise from the emergence of shared, computerized databases that have the potential to cause irreparable harm to individuals by disseminating inaccurate information to authorized users, such as through incorrect credit reporting.[14] There is a similar danger in disseminating accurate information to persons unauthorized to receive it. However, increasing security can actually cause other problems. For example, security can be used both to protect personal property and to undermine freedom of access to data, which may have a deleterious effect on some individuals. Which is the more important goal? Automated monitoring can be used to detect intruders or other misuse, yet it can also be used to spy on legitimate users, thus diminishing their privacy. Where is the line to be drawn? What is an appropriate use and level of security? Which is most important: security, accuracy, or confidentiality?

Ownership of Property

Laws designed to preserve real property rights have been extended to cover what is referred to as intellectual property, that is, software. The question here becomes,

---

12   J. H. Moor, "The Ethics of Privacy Protection," *Library Trends* 39 (1990): 69–82.

13   W. Ware, "Contemporary Privacy Issues" (Working paper for the National Conference on Computing and Human Values, August 1991).

14   K. C. Laudon, "Data Quality and Due Process in Large Interorganizational Record Systems," *Communications of the ACM* (1986): 4–11.

what can an individual (or organization) own? Ideas? Media? Source code? Object code? A related question is whether or not owners and users should be constrained in their use or access. Copyright laws have been invoked in an attempt to protect those who develop software from having it copied. Unquestionably, the hundreds and thousands of program development hours should be protected from piracy. However, many believe the copyright laws can cause more harm than good. For example, should the "look and feel" of a software package be granted copyright protection? The League for Programming Freedom argues that this flies in the face of the original intent of the law. Whereas the purpose of copyrights is to "promote the progress of science and the useful arts," allowing a user interface the protection of copyright may do just the opposite. The best interest of computer users is served when industry standards emerge; copyright laws work to disallow this. This same group also argues against the use of patents for software. Patents protect the holder against anyone using the same basic process, even if it is independently developed. Since patent searches are very expensive and quite unreliable, programmers may be sued for inadvertently using a process on which someone else holds the patent. Firms exist whose only mission is to obtain patents, then sue software developers for patent infringement. In trying to resolve these issues, social goals (such as preservation and dissemination of information, justice of distribution, and maximum potential of resources) are found to conflict with personal goals (recognition and credit, control, empowerment). Part of the problem lies in the uniqueness of software, its ease of dissemination, and the possibility of exact replication. Does software fit with the current categories and conventions regarding ownership?

Equity in Access

Some barriers to access are intrinsic to the technology of information systems, but some are avoidable through careful system design. Several factors, some of which are not unique to information systems, can limit access to computing technology. The economic status of the individual or the affluence of an organization will determine the ability to obtain information technology. Culture also limits access, for example, where documentation is prepared in only one language or is poorly translated. Safety features, or the lack thereof, have limited access to pregnant women, for example. How can hardware and software be designed with consideration for differences in physical and cognitive skills? What is the cost of providing equity in access? For what groups of society should equity in access become a priority?

Environmental Issues

Computers with high-speed printers allow for the production of printed documents faster than ever before. It is probably easier just to print a document than to consider whether it should be printed and how many copies really need to be made. It may be more efficient or more comforting to have a hard copy in addition to the electronic version. However, paper comes from trees, a precious natural resource, and ends up in landfills if not properly recycled. Should organizations limit nonessential hard copies? Can *nonessential* be defined? Who can and should define it? Should proper recycling be required? How can it be enforced?

Artificial Intelligence

A new set of social and ethical issues has arisen out of the popularity of expert systems. Because of the way these systems have been marketed, that is, as decision makers or replacements for experts, some people rely on them significantly. Therefore, both knowledge engineers (those who write the programs) and domain experts (those who provide the knowledge about the task being automated) must be concerned about their responsibility for faulty decisions, incomplete or inaccurate knowledge bases, and the role given to computers in the decision-making process.[15] Additionally, the proliferation of knowledge-based systems has the potential to cause a displacement of "experts" (most of whom are in middle-management positions) similar to that which occurred to artisans during the Industrial Revolution. Further, since expert systems attempt to clone a manager's decision-making style, an individual's prejudices may implicitly or explicitly be included in the knowledge base. Some of the questions that need to be explored are: Who is responsible for the completeness and appropriateness of the knowledge base? Who is responsible for a decision made by an expert system that causes harm when implemented? Who owns the expertise once it is coded into a knowledge base?

Unemployment and Displacement

Many jobs have been and are being changed as a result of the availability of computer technology. People unable or unprepared to change are displaced and are finding it difficult to obtain new jobs. Should employers be responsible for retraining workers who are displaced as a result of the computerization of their functions? As mentioned above, even white-collar professionals are at risk for displacement. Should there be a concern over the exploitation of experts? How can the good provided by information systems be reconciled with their potential for harm?

Misuse of Computers

Computers can be misused in many ways. Copying proprietary software, using a company's computer for personal benefit, and snooping through other people's files are just a few obvious examples.[16] Although copying proprietary software (except to make a personal backup copy) is clearly illegal, it is commonly done. Why do people feel that it is not necessary to obey this law? Are there any good arguments for trying to change this law? What harm is done to the software developer when people make unauthorized copies? A computer is not an item that deteriorates with use, so is there any harm to the employer if it is used for an employee's personal benefit? Does it matter if the computer is used during company time or outside of work hours? Is there a difference if some profit-making activity takes place rather than, for example, using the computer to write a personal letter? Does it make a difference if a profit-making activity takes place during or outside of working hours? Is it okay to look through paper files that clearly belong to someone else? Is there any difference between paper files and computer files?

Internal Control Responsibility

A business cannot meet its financial obligations or achieve its objectives if its information is unreliable. Therefore, managers must establish and maintain a system of

---

15   R. Dejoie, G. Fowler, and D. Paradice (eds.), *Ethical Issues in Information Systems* (Boston: Boyd & Fraser, 1991).

16   K. A. Forcht, "Assessing the Ethic Standards and Policies in Computer-Based Environments," in R. Dejoie, G. Fowler, and D. Paradice (eds.), *Ethical Issues in Information Systems* (Boston: Boyd & Fraser, 1991).

appropriate internal controls to ensure the integrity and reliability of their data.[17] Because much of the internal control system relates to the transaction processing system, information systems professionals and accountants are central to ensuring control adequacy.

Deadlines for putting new systems into place often become unachievable. For example, cutting corners by omitting audit trails and other controls might be suggested as a way to complete the project on time.[18] What are the ramifications of cutting certain corners? Is it ever appropriate? What is the purpose of an audit trail? What are the consequences for a system without one? How much control is adequate?

Internal control is central to this chapter and to this text. Before we can adequately deal with this topic, however, we need to consider the related topic of fraud.

FRAUD AND ACCOUNTANTS

Perhaps no major aspect of the independent auditor's role has caused more controversy for the public accounting profession than the responsibility for the detection of fraud during an audit. Over the last 20 years, the structure of the U.S. financial reporting system has become the subject of congressional inquiries, and the issue of the auditor's role in detecting fraud has gathered momentum to the point where the public accounting profession today faces a crisis in public confidence in its ability to perform the independent attestation function.

The Securities and Exchange Commission, the courts, and the public, along with Congress, are focusing more and more on business failures and questionable practices by the management of corporations that engage in alleged fraud. The question consistently being asked is, "Where were the auditors?"

Although fraud is a very familiar term in today's financial press, its meaning is not always clear. For example, in cases of bankruptcies and business failures, alleged fraud is more often poor management decisions or adverse business conditions. Under such circumstances, it becomes necessary to clearly define and understand the nature and meaning of fraud.

Fraud denotes a false representation of a material fact made by one party to another party with the intent to deceive and induce the other party to justifiably rely on the fact to his or her detriment. According to common law, a fraudulent act must meet the following five conditions:

1. *False representation.* There must be a false statement or a nondisclosure.
2. *Material fact.* A fact must be a substantial factor in inducing someone to act.
3. *Intent.* There must be the intent to deceive or the knowledge that one's statement is false.
4. *Justifiable reliance.* The misrepresentation must have been a substantial factor on which the injured party relied.
5. *Injury or loss.* The deception must have caused injury or loss to the victim of the fraud.

---

17 All companies registered with the Securities and Exchange Commission are required by law (Foreign Corrupt Practices Act of 1977) to maintain such a system of internal control.

18 E. Cohen and L. Cornwell, "A Question of Ethics: Developing Information Systems Ethics," *Journal of Business Ethics* 8 (1989): 431–37.

Fraud in the business environment has a more specialized meaning. It is an intentional deception, misappropriation of a company's assets, or manipulation of its financial data to the advantage of the perpetrator. In the accounting literature, fraud is also commonly known as "white-collar crime," "defalcation," "embezzlement," and "irregularities." The auditor deals with fraud typically at two levels: employee fraud and management fraud. It is essential to distinguish between these two types of fraud since each has different responsibilities and implications for auditors.

Employee fraud or fraud by nonmanagement employees is generally designed to directly convert cash or other assets to the employee's personal benefit. Typically, the employee circumvents the company's internal control system for personal gain. If a company has an effective system of internal control, defalcations or embezzlements can usually be prevented or detected.

Employee fraud usually involves three steps: (1) stealing something of value (an asset), (2) converting the asset to a usable form (cash), and (3) concealing the crime to avoid detection. The third step is often the most difficult. It may be relatively easy for a storeroom clerk to steal inventories from the employer's warehouse, but altering the inventory records to hide the theft is more of a challenge.

Management fraud is more insidious than employee fraud and often escapes detection until irreparable damage or loss has been suffered by the organization. Usually management fraud does not involve the direct theft of assets. The Treadway Commission on Fraudulent Financial Reporting observes that on a macrolevel, management may engage in fraudulent activities to obtain a higher price from a stock or debt offering or just to meet the expectations of investors. The Commission on Auditors' Responsibilities calls it a "performance fraud" that often uses deceptive practices to inflate earnings or to forestall the recognition of either insolvency or a decline in earnings. Management fraud on a microlevel may typically involve materially misstating financial data and reports to gain additional compensation, to garner a promotion, or to escape the penalty for poor performance. Management fraud typically contains three special characteristics:[19]

1. The fraud is perpetrated at levels of management above the one to which internal control structures generally relate.
2. The fraud frequently involves using the financial statements to create an illusion that an entity is more healthy and prosperous than it actually is.
3. If the fraud involves misappropriation of assets, it frequently is shrouded in a maze of complex business transactions, often involving related third parties.

The preceding characteristics of management fraud suggest that management can often perpetrate irregularities by overriding an otherwise effective internal control structure (that is, an internal control structure that would prevent similar irregularities by other employees). When management uses the financial statements to create an illusion, "the input data usually is manipulated to include false or questionable transactions or to include false or questionable judgment with respect to expense allocations or revenue recognition."[20]

---

19   R. Grinaker, "Discussant's Response to a Look at the Record on Auditor Detection of Management Fraud," *Proceedings of the 1980 Touche Ross University of Kansas Symposium on Auditing Problems* (Kansas City: University of Kansas, 1980).

20   *Ibid.*

FACTORS THAT CONTRIBUTE TO FRAUD

According to one study, people engage in fraudulent activity as a result of an interaction of forces both within an individual's personality and the external environment. These forces are classified into three major categories: (1) *situational pressures*, (2) *opportunities*, and (3) *personal characteristics (integrity)*. Figure 3–2 graphically displays the interplay of these three fraud-motivating forces.[21]

Figure 3–2 suggests that a person with a high level of personal integrity and limited pressure and opportunity to commit fraud is most likely to behave honestly. Similarly, an individual with less personal integrity, when placed in situations with increasing pressure and given the opportunity, is most likely to commit fraud.

While these factors, for the most part, fall outside of the auditors' sphere of influence, auditors can develop a *red-flag* checklist to detect possible fraudulent activity.

FIGURE 3–2   Fraud-Motivating Forces

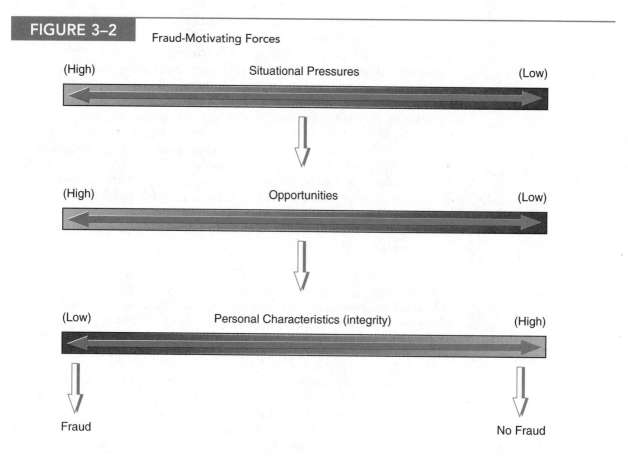

SOURCE: Adapted from W. S. Albrecht and M. B. Romney, "Auditing Implications Derived from a Review of Cases and Articles Relating to Fraud," *Proceedings of the 1980 Touche Ross University of Kansas Symposium on Auditing Problems* (Kansas City: University of Kansas, 1980).

---

21   M. Romney, W. S. Albrecht, and D. J. Cherrington, "Auditors and the Detection of Fraud," *Journal of Accountancy* (May 1980).

To that end, a questionnaire approach could be used to help external auditors uncover motivations for committing fraud. Some of the larger public accounting firms have developed checklists to help uncover fraudulent activity during an audit. Questions for such a checklist might include:[22]

- Do key executives have unusually high personal debt?
- Do key executives appear to be living beyond their means?
- Do key executives engage in habitual gambling?
- Do key executives appear to abuse alcohol or drugs?
- Do any of the key executives appear to lack personal codes of ethics?
- Are economic conditions unfavorable within the company's industry?
- Does the company use several different banks, none of which sees the company's entire financial picture?
- Do any key executives have close associations with suppliers?
- Is the company experiencing a rapid turnover of key employees, either through quitting or being fired?
- Do one or two individuals dominate the company?

A review of some of these questions suggests that the contemporary auditor may use special investigative agencies to run a complete but confidential background check on the key managers of existing and prospective client firms.

FINANCIAL LOSSES FROM FRAUD

A 1996 study by Certified Fraud Examiners (CFE) estimated losses from fraud and abuse to be 6 percent of annual revenues.[23] The actual cost of fraud is difficult to quantify for a number of reasons: (1) not all fraud is detected; (2) of that detected, not all is reported; (3) in many fraud cases, incomplete information is gathered; (4) information is not properly distributed to management or law enforcement authorities; and (5) too often, business organizations decide to take no civil or criminal action against the perpetrator(s) of fraud. In addition to the direct economic loss to the organization, indirect costs including reduced productivity, the cost of legal action, increased unemployment, and business disruption due to investigation of the fraud need to be considered.

The CFE study examined organizations in twelve different industries. The median dollar loss by industry is presented in Table 3–2. The study concluded that organizations with 100 or fewer employees were the most vulnerable to fraud. The education industry suffered the smallest losses, while the real estate financing industry suffered the largest losses. The large losses in the real estate segment reflect the savings and loan debacle of the late 1980s.

THE PERPETRATORS OF FRAUDS

The CFE study examined the personal characteristics of fraud perpetrators. The median financial loss was calculated for the following classifications: position in the organization, gender, age, marital status, and education. The results of the study are presented in the tables that follow.

---

22   *Ibid.*
23   Report to the Nation: Occupational Fraud and Abuse. (Association of Fraud Examiners, 1996): 15.

TABLE 3-2	**Losses from Fraud by Industry**

Industry	Loss from Fraud
Real Estate and Finance	$475,000
Manufacturing	274,000
Banking	200,000
Oil & Gas	173,000
Construction	142,000
Health Care	105,000
Retail	100,000
Service	95,000
Insurance	72,000
Government	50,000
Utility	50,000
Education	32,000

Median Loss by Position within the Organization

The study indicated that 58 percent of the reported fraud cases were committed by nonmanagerial employees, 30 percent by managers, and 12 percent by owner/executives. However, the median fraud perpetrated by nonmanagerial employees was significantly lower than the management and executive frauds. Table 3–3 shows that nonmanagerial employees were responsible for a median loss of $60,000, compared to $250,000 for managers and $1 million for executives.

Median Loss by Gender

Table 3–4 shows that the median loss per case caused by males ($185,000) was nearly four times that caused by females ($48,000).

Median Loss by Age

Table 3–5 indicates that perpetrators 25 years of age or younger cause median losses of about $12,000, while employees 60 and older perpetrated frauds that were on average 28 times larger—$346,000.

TABLE 3-3	**Losses from Fraud by Position**

Position	Percent of Frauds	Dollar Value
Owners	12	$1,000,000
Management	30	250,000
Employees	58	60,000

TABLE 3–4	Losses from Fraud by Gender	
	Gender	**Loss from Fraud**
	Male	$185,000
	Female	48,000

TABLE 3–5	Losses from Fraud by Age	
	Age Range	**Loss**
	< 25	$ 12,000
	26 – 20	50,000
	31 – 35	54,000
	36 – 40	100,000
	41 – 50	196,000
	51 – 60	280,000
	> 60	346,000

Median Loss by Marital Status
Table 3–6 shows that married employees commit the greatest number of frauds with the largest median losses.

Median Loss by Education
Table 3–7 shows a relationship between the perpetrator's educational level and the median loss caused by his or her fraud. The frauds of high school graduates averaged only $50,000, while those with advanced degrees averaged $275,000.

TABLE 3–6	Losses from Fraud by Marital Status	
	Marital Status	**Loss**
	Married	$150,000
	Divorced	80,000
	Single	54,000
	Separated	50,000

TABLE 3–7	Losses from Fraud by Education	
Education Level	**Loss**	
High School	$ 50,000	
College	200,000	
Post Graduate	275,000	

Conclusions to be Drawn

What do these results tell us? On the surface they seem to suggest that an organization can reduce or eliminate fraud by hiring only unmarried, adolescent, female dropouts from high school. A little deeper analysis, however, takes us back to a point that was made earlier. Notwithstanding the importance of personal ethics, *situational pressures* and *opportunity* contribute greatly to fraud.

Situational Pressures

As people age, they tend to marry and assume greater responsibilities. Life creates significant situational pressures that at one time or another will test the ethics and honesty of most people. If we assume that heads of households tend to feel situational pressures more severely than other family members, and recognize that more heads of households (in the economic sense) are men than women, then some of the variance due to gender is explained.

Opportunity

The real culprit responsible for explaining the loss variance presented above is opportunity. Opportunity can be redefined as control over assets or access to assets. Indeed, control and access are essential elements of opportunity. The financial loss differences associated with most of the classifications above are explained by the opportunity factor.

- *Gender*. While the demographic picture is changing, more men than women occupy positions of authority in business organizations, which provide them greater access to assets.
- *Position*. Those in the highest positions have the greatest access to company funds and assets.
- *Age*. Older employees tend to occupy higher-ranking positions and therefore generally have greater access to company assets.
- *Education*. Generally, those with more education occupy higher positions in their organizations and therefore have greater access to company funds and other assets.

FRAUD SCHEMES

Fraud schemes can be classified in a number of different ways. For purposes of discussion, this section presents the classification format derived by the Association of

Certified Fraud Examiners. Three broad categories of fraud schemes are defined: fraudulent statements, corruption, and asset misappropriation.[24]

Fraudulent Statements

Fraudulent statements are associated with management fraud. While all fraud involves some form of financial misstatement, to meet the definition under this class of fraud scheme, the statement itself must bring direct or indirect financial benefit to the perpetrator. In other words, the statement is not simply a vehicle for obscuring or covering a fraudulent act. For example, misstating the cash account balance to cover the theft of cash does not fall under this class of fraud scheme. On the other hand, understating liabilities to present a more favorable financial picture of the organization does qualify. Fraudulent statements account for about 5 percent of the fraud cases covered in the CFE fraud study.

Corruption

Corruption involves an executive, manager, or employee of the organization in collusion with an outsider. The CFE study identifies four principal types of corruption: bribery, illegal gratuities, conflicts of interest, and economic extortion. Corruption accounts for about 10 percent of occupational fraud cases.

Bribery.   **Bribery** involves giving, offering, soliciting, or receiving things of value to influence an official in the performance of his or her lawful duties. Officials may be employed by government (or regulatory) agencies or by private organizations. Bribery defrauds the entity (business organization or government agency) of the right to honest and loyal services from those employed by it. The following is an example of bribery.

> The manager of a meat-packing company offers a U.S. health inspector a cash payment. In return, the inspector suppresses his report of health violations discovered during a routine inspection of the meat-packing facilities. In this situation, the victims are those who rely upon the honest reporting of the inspector. The loss is salary paid to the inspector for work not performed and any damages that result from failure to perform.

Illegal Gratuities.   An **illegal gratuity** involves giving, receiving, offering, or soliciting something of value because of an official act that has been taken. This is similar to a bribe, but the transaction occurs after the fact. The following is an example of an illegal gratuity.

> The plant manager in a large corporation uses his influence to ensure that a request for proposals is written in such a way that only one contractor will be able to submit a satisfactory bid. As a result, the favored contractor's proposal is accepted at a noncompetitive price. In return, the contractor secretly makes a financial payment to the plant manager. The victims in this case are those who expect a competitive procurement process. The loss is the excess

---

24   *Ibid.*: 31–34.

costs incurred by the company because of the noncompetitive pricing of the construction.

Conflicts of Interest. Every employer should expect that his or her employees will conduct their duties in a way that serves the interests of the employer. A **conflict of interest** occurs when an employee acts on behalf of a third party during the discharge of his or her duties or has self-interest in the activity being performed. When the employee's conflict of interest is unknown to the employer and results in financial loss, then fraud has occurred. The preceding examples of bribery and illegal gratuities also constitute conflicts of interest. This type of fraud can exist, however, when bribery and illegal payments are not present, but the employee has an interest in the outcome of the economic event. The following is an example.

> A purchasing agent for a building contractor is also part owner in a plumbing supply company. The agent has sole discretion in selecting vendors for the plumbing supplies needed for buildings under contract. The agent directs a disproportionate number of purchase orders to his company, which charges above-market prices for its products. The agent's financial interest in the supplier is unknown to his employer.

Economic Extortion. **Economic extortion** is the use (or threat) of force (including economic sanctions) by an individual or organization to obtain something of value. The item of value could be a financial or economic asset, information, or cooperation to obtain a favorable decision on some matter under review. The following is an example of economic extortion.

> A contract procurement agent for a state government threatens to blacklist a highway contractor if he does not make a financial payment to the agent. If the contractor fails to cooperate, the blacklisting will effectively eliminate him from consideration for future work. Faced with a threat of economic loss, the contractor makes the payment.

Asset Misappropriation

The most common form of fraud scheme involves some type of asset misappropriation. Eighty-five percent of the frauds included in the CFE study fall into this category. Assets can be misappropriated either directly or indirectly for the perpetrator's benefit. Certain assets are more susceptible than others to misappropriation. Transactions involving cash, checking accounts, inventory, supplies, equipment, and information are the most vulnerable to abuse. Examples of fraud schemes involving asset misappropriation are described below.

Charges to Expense Accounts. The theft of an asset creates an imbalance in the basic accounting equation (assets = equities), which the criminal must adjust if the theft is to go undetected. The most common way to conceal the imbalance is to charge the asset to an expense account and reduce equity by the same amount. For example, the theft of $20,000 cash could be charged to a miscellaneous operating expense account. The loss of the cash reduces the firm's assets by $20,000. To offset this, equity is reduced by $20,000 when the miscellaneous expense account is closed to retained earnings, thus keeping the accounting equation in balance. This technique has the advantage of limiting the criminal's exposure to one period. When the expense account is closed to retained earnings, its balance is reset to zero to begin the new period.

Lapping. **Lapping** involves the use of customer checks, received in payment of their accounts, to conceal cash previously stolen by an employee. For example, the employee first steals and cashes a check for $500 sent by Customer A. To conceal the accounting imbalance caused by the loss of the asset, Customer A's account is not credited. Later (the next billing period), the employee uses a $500 check received from Customer B and applies this to Customer A's account. Funds received in the next period from Customer C are then applied to the account of Customer B, and so on.

Employees involved in this sort of fraud often rationalize that they are simply borrowing the cash and plan to repay it at some future date. This kind of accounting cover-up must continue indefinitely or until the employee returns the funds. Lapping is usually detected when the employee leaves the organization or becomes sick and must take time off work. Unless the fraud is perpetuated, the last customer to have funds diverted from his or her account will be billed again, and the lapping technique will be detected. Employers can deter lapping by periodically rotating employees into different jobs and forcing them to take scheduled vacations.

Transaction Fraud. **Transaction fraud** involves deleting, altering, or adding false transactions to divert assets to the perpetrator. This technique may be used to ship inventories to the perpetrator in response to a fraudulent sales transaction or to disburse cash in payment of a false liability. A common type of transaction fraud involves the distribution of fraudulent paychecks to nonexistent employees. For example, an employee who has left the organization is kept on the payroll by her immediate supervisor. Each week, the supervisor continues to submit time cards to the payroll department just as if the employee was still working for the firm. The fraud works best in organizations that distribute employee paychecks to the supervisor, who then distributes them to the employees. The supervisor forges the ex-employee's signature and then cashes the check. Although the organization has lost cash, the fraud can go undetected because the credit to the cash account is offset by a debit to payroll expense.

Computer Fraud Schemes. Since computers lie at the heart of most organizations' accounting information systems today, the topic of **computer fraud** is of special importance to auditors. While the objectives of the fraud are the same—misappropriation of assets—the techniques used to commit computer fraud vary greatly.

No one knows for sure how much businesses lose each year to computer fraud, but estimates ranging from $500 million to $10 billion per year give some indication of the problem's magnitude. One reason for the discrepancy between these estimates is that computer fraud is not well defined. For example, we saw in the ethics section of this chapter that some people do not view copying commercial computer software to be unethical. On the other side of this issue, software vendors consider this to be a criminal act. Regardless of how narrowly or broadly computer fraud is defined, most agree that it is a rapidly growing phenomenon.

For our purposes, computer fraud includes the following:

- The theft, misuse, or misappropriation of assets by altering computer-readable records and files.
- The theft, misuse, or misappropriation of assets by altering the logic of computer software.

- The theft or illegal use of computer-readable information.
- The theft, corruption, illegal copying, or intentional destruction of computer software.
- The theft, misuse, or misappropriation of computer hardware.

The general model for accounting information systems shown in Figure 3–3 portrays, conceptually, the key stages of an information system. Each stage in the model—data collection, data processing, database management, and information generation—is a potential area of risk for certain types of computer fraud.

Data Collection. **Data collection** is the first operational stage in the information system. The objective is to ensure that event data entering the system are valid, complete, and free from material errors. In many respects, this is the most important stage in the system. Should transaction errors pass through data collection undetected, the organization runs the risk that the system will process the errors and generate erroneous and unreliable output. This, in turn, could lead to incorrect actions and poor decisions by the users.

Two rules govern the design of data collection procedures: relevance and efficiency. The information system should capture only relevant data. A fundamental task

---

FIGURE 3–3   The General Model for Accounting Information Systems

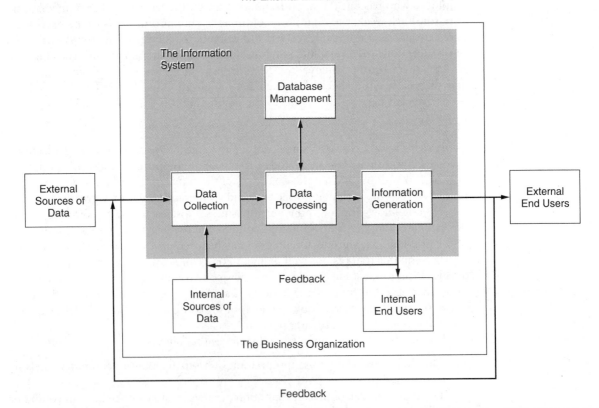

of the system designer is to determine what is and what is not relevant. He or she does so by analyzing the user's needs. Only data that ultimately contribute to information are relevant. The data collection stage should be designed to filter irrelevant facts from the system.

Efficient data collection procedures are designed to collect data only once. These data can then be made available to multiple users. Capturing the same data more than once leads to data redundancy and inconstancy. Information systems have limited collection, processing, and data storage capacity. Data redundancy overloads facilities and reduces the overall efficiency of the system. Inconsistency among data elements can result in inappropriate actions and bad decisions.

The simplest way to perpetrate a computer fraud is at the data collection or data entry stage. This is the computer equivalent of the transaction fraud discussed previously. Frauds of this type require little or no computer skills. The perpetrator need only understand how the system works to enter data that it will process. The fraudulent act involves falsifying data as it enters the system. This can be to delete, alter, or add a transaction. For example, to commit a payroll fraud, the perpetrator may insert a fraudulent payroll transaction along with other legitimate transactions. Unless the insertion is detected by internal controls, the system will generate an additional paycheck for the perpetrator. A variation on this type of fraud is to change the Hours Worked field in an otherwise legitimate payroll transaction to increase the amount of the paycheck.

Still another variant on this fraud is to disburse cash in payment of a false account payable. By entering fraudulent supporting documents (purchase order, receiving report, and supplier invoice) into the data collection stage of the accounts payable system, a perpetrator can fool the system into creating an accounts payable record for a nonexistent purchase. Once the record is created, the system will presume it is legitimate and, on the due date, will disperse funds to the perpetrator in payment of a bogus liability.

The trend toward distributed data processing and networking increasingly exposes organizations to transaction frauds from remote locations. "Masquerading," "piggybacking," and "hacking" are examples of such fraud techniques. Masquerading involves a perpetrator gaining access to the system from a remote site by pretending to be an authorized user. This usually requires first gaining authorized access to a password. Piggybacking is a technique in which the perpetrator at a remote site taps into the telecommunications lines and latches onto an authorized user who is logging into the system. Once in the system, the perpetrator can masquerade as the authorized user. Hacking may involve piggybacking or masquerading techniques. Hackers are distinguished from other computer criminals because their motives are not usually to defraud for financial gain. They are motivated primarily by the challenge of breaking into the system rather than the theft of assets. Nevertheless, hackers have caused extensive damage and loss to organizations. Many believe that the line between hackers and the more classic computer criminals is thin.

Data Processing.   Once collected, data usually require processing to produce information. Tasks in the data processing stage range from simple to complex. Examples include mathematical algorithms (such as linear programming models) used for production scheduling applications, statistical techniques for sales forecasting, and posting and summarizing procedures used for accounting applications.

Data processing frauds fall into two classes: program fraud and operations fraud. **Program fraud** includes the following techniques: (1) creating illegal programs that can access data files to alter, delete, or insert values into accounting records; (2) destroying or corrupting a program's logic using a computer virus; or (3) altering program logic to cause the application to process data incorrectly. For example, the program a bank uses to calculate interest on its customers' accounts will produce rounding errors. This happens because the precision of the interest calculation is greater than the reporting precision. Therefore, interest figures that are calculated to a fraction of one cent must be rounded to whole numbers for reporting purposes. A complex routine in the interest-calculation program keeps track of the rounding errors so that the total interest charge to the bank equals the sum of the individual credits. This involves temporarily holding the fractional amounts left over from each calculation in an internal memory accumulator. When the amount in the accumulator totals one cent (plus or minus), the penny is added to the customer's account that is being processed. In other words, one cent is added to (or deleted from) customer accounts randomly. A type of program fraud called the *salami fraud* involves modifying the rounding logic of the program so it no longer adds the one cent randomly. Instead, the modified program always adds the plus cent to the perpetrator's account but still adds the minus cent randomly. This can divert a considerable amount of cash to the perpetrator, but the accounting records stay in balance to conceal the crime.

Operations fraud is the misuse or theft of the firm's computer resources. This often involves using the computer to conduct personal business. For example, a programmer may use the firm's computer time to write software that he sells commercially. A CPA in the controller's office may use the company's computer to prepare tax returns and financial statements for her private clients. Similarly, a corporate lawyer with a private practice on the side may use the firm's computer to search for court cases and decisions in commercial databases. The cost of accessing the database is charged to the organization and hidden among other legitimate charges.

Database Management. The organization's database is its physical repository for financial and nonfinancial data. Database management involves three fundamental tasks: storage, retrieval, and deletion. The *storage* task assigns keys to new records and stores them in their proper location in the database. *Retrieval* is the task of locating and extracting an existing record from the database for processing. After processing is complete, the storage task restores the updated record to its place in the database. *Deletion* is the task of permanently removing obsolete or redundant records from the database.

Database management fraud includes altering, deleting, corrupting, destroying, or stealing an organization's data. Because access to database files is an essential element of this fraud, it is usually associated with transaction or program fraud. The most common technique is to access the database from a remote site and browse the files for useful information that can be copied and sold to competitors. Disgruntled employees have been known to destroy company data files simply to harm the organization. One method is to insert a destructive routine called a *logic bomb* into a program. At a specified time, or when certain conditions are met, the logic bomb erases the data files that the program accesses. For example, a disgruntled programmer who was contemplating leaving an organization inserted a logic bomb into the payroll system. Weeks later, when the system detected that the programmer's name had been removed from the payroll file, the logic bomb was activated and erased the payroll file.

Information Generation. Information generation is the process of compiling, arranging, formatting, and presenting information to users. Information can be an operational document such as a sales order, a structured report, or a message on a computer screen. Regardless of physical form, useful information has the following characteristics: **relevance**, **timeliness**, **accuracy**, **completeness**, and **summarization**.

- *Relevance.* The contents of a report or document must serve a purpose. This could be to support a manager's decision or a clerk's task. We have established that only data relevant to a user's action have information content. Therefore, the information system should present only relevant data in its reports. Reports containing irrelevancies waste resources and may be counterproductive to the user. Irrelevancies detract attention from the true message of the report and may result in incorrect decisions or actions.
- *Timeliness.* The age of information is a critical factor in determining its usefulness. Information must be no older than the time period of the action it supports. For example, if a manager makes decisions daily to purchase inventory from a supplier based upon an inventory status report, then the information in the report should be no more than a day old.
- *Accuracy.* Information must be free from material errors. However, materiality is a difficult concept to quantify. It has no absolute value; it is a problem-specific concept. This means that in some cases, information must be perfectly accurate. In other instances, the level of accuracy may be lower. Material error exists when the amount of inaccuracy in information causes the user to make poor decisions or to fail to make necessary decisions. We sometimes must sacrifice absolute accuracy to obtain timely information. Often perfect information is not available within the decision time frame of the user. Therefore, in providing information, system designers seek a balance between information that is as accurate as possible, yet timely enough to be useful.
- *Completeness.* No piece of information essential to a decision or task should be missing. For example, a report should provide all necessary calculations and present its message clearly and unambiguously.
- *Summarization.* Information should be aggregated in accordance with a user's needs. Lower-level managers tend to need information that is highly detailed. As information flows upward through the organization to top management, it becomes more summarized. Later in this chapter, we shall look more closely at the effects that organizational structure and managerial level have on information reporting.

A common form of fraud at the information generation stage is to steal, misdirect, or misuse computer output. One simple but effective technique called **scavenging** involves searching through the trash cans of the computer center for discarded output. A perpetrator can often obtain useful information from the carbon sheets removed from multipart reports or from paper reports that were rejected during processing. Sometimes output reports are misaligned on the paper or slightly garbled during printing. When this happens, the output must be reprinted and the original output is often thrown in the trash.

Another form of fraud called **eavesdropping** involves listening to output transmissions over telecommunications lines. Technologies are readily available that enable perpetrators to intercept messages being sent over unprotected telephone lines and microwave channels. Most experts agree that it is practically impossible to prevent a determined perpetrator from accessing data communication channels. Data encryption can, however, render useless any data captured through eavesdropping.

INTERNAL CONTROL CONCEPTS AND PROCEDURES

With the backdrop of ethics and fraud in place, let's now examine internal control techniques for dealing with some of these problems. Organization management is required by law to establish and maintain an adequate system of internal control. Consider the following Securities and Exchange Commission statement on this matter:

> The establishment and maintenance of a system of internal control is an important management obligation. A fundamental aspect of management's stewardship responsibility is to provide shareholders with reasonable assurance that the business is adequately controlled. Additionally, management has a responsibility to furnish shareholders and potential investors with reliable financial information on a timely basis. An adequate system of internal control is necessary to management's discharge of these obligations.[25]

Corporate management has not always lived up to its internal control responsibility. With the discovery that U.S. business executives were using their organizations' funds to bribe foreign officials, internal control issues, formerly of little interest to stockholders, quickly became a matter of public concern. From this scandal came the passage of the **Foreign Corrupt Practices Act of 1977** (FCPA). Among its provisions, the FCPA requires companies registered with the SEC to:

1. Keep records that fairly and reasonably reflect the transactions of the firm and its financial position.
2. Maintain a system of internal control that provides reasonable assurance that the organization's objectives are met.

The FCPA has had a significant impact on organization management. With the knowledge that violation of the FCPA could lead to heavy fines and imprisonment, managers have developed a deeper concern for control adequacy.

Since much of the internal control system relates directly to transaction processing, accountants are key participants in ensuring control adequacy. This section deals first with internal control at a conceptual level. It then presents the control framework defined by SAS 78.

INTERNAL CONTROL IN CONCEPT

The **internal control system** comprises policies, practices, and procedures employed by the organization to achieve four broad objectives:

1. To safeguard assets of the firm.
2. To ensure the accuracy and reliability of accounting records and information.
3. To promote efficiency in the firm's operations.
4. To measure compliance with management's prescribed policies and procedures.[26]

---

25   Securities and Exchange Commission, Securities Release 34-13185 (19 January 1977).
26   American Institute of Certified Public Accountants, *AICPA Professional Standards*, vol. 1 (New York: AICPA, 1987), AU Sec. 320.30-35.

Modifying Assumptions

Inherent in these control objectives are four modifying assumptions that guide designers and auditors of internal control systems.[27]

Management Responsibility. This concept holds that the establishment and maintenance of a system of internal control is a **management responsibility**. The FCPA supports this postulate.

Reasonable Assurance. The internal control system should provide **reasonable assurance** that the four broad objectives of internal control specified above are met. This means that no system of internal control is perfect and the cost of achieving improved control should not outweigh its benefits.

Methods of Data Processing. The internal control system should achieve the four broad objectives regardless of the data processing method used. However, the techniques used to achieve these objectives will vary with different types of technology.

Limitations. Every system of internal control has limitations on its effectiveness. These include (1) the possibility of error—no system is perfect, (2) circumvention—personnel may circumvent the system through collusion or other means, (3) management override—management is in a position to override control procedures by personally distorting transactions or by directing a subordinate to do so, and (4) changing conditions—conditions may change over time so that existing controls may become ineffectual.

Exposures and Risk

Figure 3–4 portrays the internal control system as a shield that protects the firm's assets from numerous undesirable events that bombard the organization. These include attempts at unauthorized access to the firm's assets (including information); fraud perpetrated by persons both in and outside the firm; errors due to employee incompetence, faulty computer programs, and corrupted input data; and mischievous acts, such as unauthorized access by computer hackers and threats from computer viruses that destroy programs and databases.

The absence or weakness of a control is called an **exposure**. Exposures, which are illustrated as holes in the control shield in Figure 3–4, increase the firm's risk to financial loss or injury from undesirable events. A weakness in internal control may expose the firm to one or more of the following types of risks:

1. Destruction of assets (both physical assets and information).
2. Theft of assets.
3. Corruption of information or the information system.
4. Disruption of the information system.

---

27   American Institute of Certified Public Accountants, Committee on Auditing Procedure, Internal
      Control—Elements of a Coordinated System and Its Importance to Management and the
      Independent Public Accountant, *Statement on Auditing Standards No. 1*, Sec. 320 (New York:
      AICPA, 1973).

FIGURE 3–4

Internal Control Shield

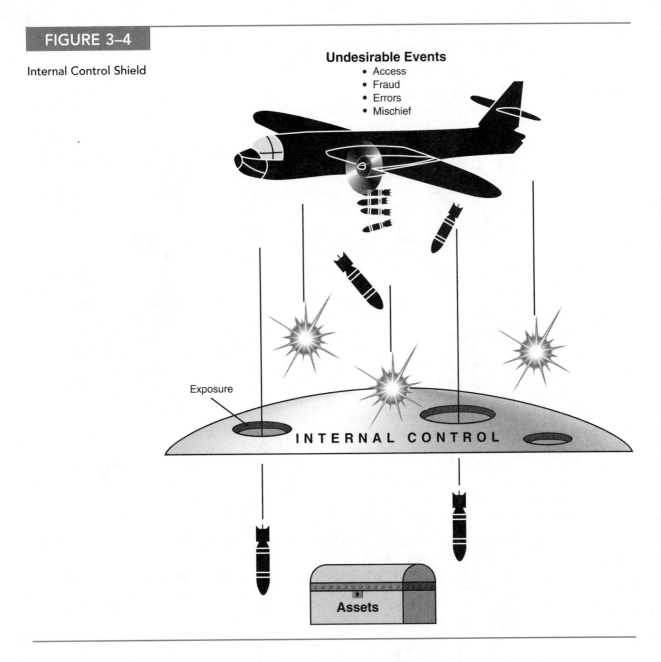

Undesirable Events
- Access
- Fraud
- Errors
- Mischief

Exposure

INTERNAL CONTROL

Assets

The Preventive-Detective-Corrective Internal Control Model

Figure 3–5 illustrates that the internal control shield is comprised of three levels of control: preventive controls, detective controls, and corrective controls. This is the PDC control model.

Preventive Controls. Prevention is the first line of defense in the control structure. **Preventive controls** are passive techniques designed to reduce the frequency of occurrence of undesirable events. Preventive controls force compliance with prescribed or desired actions and thus screen out aberrant events. When designing internal control systems, an ounce of prevention is most certainly worth a pound of cure. Preventing errors and fraud is far more cost-effective than detecting and correcting

| FIGURE 3–5 | Preventive, Detective, and Corrective Controls |

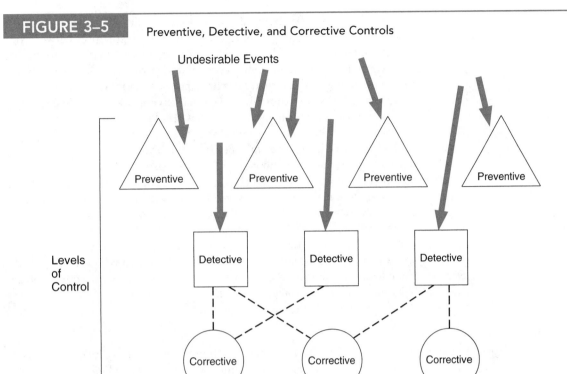

problems after they occur. The vast majority of undesirable events can be blocked at this first level. For example, a well-designed source document is an example of a preventive control. The logical layout of the document into zones that contain specific data, such as customer name, address, items sold, and quantity, forces the clerk to enter the necessary data. The source documents can therefore prevent necessary data from being omitted. However, not all problems can be anticipated and prevented. Some will elude the most comprehensive network of preventive controls.

Detective Controls. **Detective controls** form the second line of defense. These are devices, techniques, and procedures designed to identify and expose undesirable events that elude preventive controls. Detective controls reveal specific types of errors by comparing actual occurrences to preestablished standards. When the detective control identifies a departure from standard, it sounds an alarm to attract attention to the problem. For example, assume a clerk entered the following data on a customer sales order:

Quantity	Price	Total
10	$10	$1,000

Before processing this transaction and posting to the accounts, a detective control should recalculate the total value using the price and quantity. Thus, the error in total price would be detected.

Corrective Controls. **Corrective controls** are actions taken to reverse the effects of errors detected in the previous step. There is an important distinction between detective controls and corrective controls. Detective controls identify undesirable events and draw attention to the problem; corrective controls actually fix the problem. For any detected error, there may be more than one feasible corrective action, but the best course of action may not always be obvious. For example, in viewing the error above, your first inclination may have been to change the total value from $1,000 to $100 to correct the problem. This presumes that the quantity and price values on the document are correct; they may not be. At this point, we cannot determine the real cause of the problem; we know only that one exists.

Linking a corrective action to a detected error, as an automatic response, may result in an incorrect action that causes a worse problem than the original error. For this reason, error correction should be viewed as a separate control step that should be taken cautiously.

The PDC control framework is conceptually pleasing but offers little practical guidance for designing control systems. For this, we need a more precise set of objectives. The current authoritative document for specifying internal control objectives and techniques is the *Statement on Auditing Standards No. 78.*[28] We discuss the elements of this document in the next section.

AUDITING AND AUDITING STANDARDS

In Chapter 1, we defined auditing as an attestation of the client organization's historical financial statements, performed by an independent auditor. The product of the attestation is a formal written report that expresses an opinion about the reliability of the assertions contained in the financial statements. The auditor's report expresses an opinion as to whether the financial statements are in conformity with *generally accepted accounting principles*. External users of financial statements are presumed to rely on the auditor's opinion about the reliability of financial statements in making decisions. To do so, users must be able to place their trust in the auditor's competence, professionalism, integrity, and independence. Auditors are guided in their professional responsibility by the ten *generally accepted auditing standards (GAAS)* presented in Table 3–8.

Auditing standards are divided into three classes: general qualification standards, field work standards, and reporting standards. GAAS establishes a framework for prescribing auditor performance, but it is not sufficiently detailed to provide meaningful guidance in specific circumstances. To provide specific guidance, the American Institute of Certified Public Accountants (AICPA) issues *Statements on Auditing Standards (SASs)* as authoritative interpretations of GAAS. SASs are often referred to as *auditing standards*, or *GAAS*, although they are not the ten generally accepted auditing standards.

Statements on Auditing Standards

The first SAS (SAS 1) was issued by the AICPA in 1972. Since then, more than 80 other SASs have been issued to provide auditors with guidance on a spectrum of topics, including methods of investigating new clients, procedures for collecting information from attorneys regarding contingent liability claims against clients, and techniques for obtaining background information on the client's industry.

---

28   American Institute of Certified Public Accountants, *SAS No. 78—Consideration of Internal Control in a Financial Statement Audit: An Amendment to SAS No. 55* (New York: AICPA, 1995).

TABLE 3–8	**Generally Accepted Auditing Standards**

General Standards	Standards of Field Work	Reporting Standards
1. The auditor must have adequate technical training and proficiency.	1. Audit work must be adequately planned.	1. The auditor must state in the report whether financial statements were prepared in accordance with generally accepted accounting principles.
2. The auditor must have independence of mental attitude.	2. The auditor must gain a sufficient understanding of the internal control structure.	2. The report must identify those circumstances in which generally accepted accounting principles were not applied.
3. The auditor must exercise due professional care in the performance of the audit and the preparation of the report.	3. The auditor must obtain sufficient, competent evidence.	3. The report must identify any items that do not have adequate information disclosures.
		4. The report shall contain an expression of the auditor's opinion on the financial statements as a whole.

Statements on Auditing Standards are regarded as authoritative pronouncements because every member of the profession must follow their recommendations or be able to show why a SAS does not apply in a given situation. The burden of justifying departures from SAS falls upon the individual auditor.

Statement on Auditing Standards No. 78

In this text, we are particularly interested in **Statement on Auditing Standards No. 78** (SAS 78). This document conforms to the recommendations of the Committee of Sponsoring Organizations of the Treadway Commission (COSO). SAS 78 describes the complex relationship between the firm's internal controls, the auditor's assessment of risk, and the planning of audit procedures. Chapter 17 examines the audit process and explains this relationship in detail. Our objective at this point is to understand the components of internal control. In this regard, SAS 78 also provides guidance to systems professionals and accountants who are responsible for designing internal controls. In several chapters that follow, we shall see how the concepts presented here apply in specific systems.

INTERNAL CONTROL COMPONENTS

Internal control as defined in SAS 78 consists of five components: the control environment, risk assessment, information and communication, monitoring, and control activities.

The Control Environment

The **control environment** is the foundation for the other four control components. The control environment sets the tone for the organization and influences the control awareness of its management and employees. Important elements of the control environment are:

- The integrity and ethical values of management.
- The structure of the organization.
- The participation of the organization's board of directors and the audit committee, if one exists.
- Management's philosophy and operating style.
- The procedures for delegating responsibility and authority.
- Management's methods for assessing performance.
- External influences, such as examinations by regulatory agencies.
- The organization's policies and practices for managing its human resources.

SAS 78 requires that auditors obtain sufficient knowledge to assess the attitude and awareness of the organization's management, board of directors, and owners regarding internal control. The following paragraphs provide examples of techniques that may be used to obtain an understanding of the control environment:

1. Auditors should assess the integrity of the organization's management and may use investigative agencies to report on the backgrounds of key managers. Some of the "Big Five" public accounting firms employ ex-FBI agents whose primary responsibility is to perform background checks on existing and prospective clients. If cause for serious reservations comes to light about the integrity of the client, the auditor should withdraw from the audit. The reputation and integrity of the company's managers are critical factors in determining the auditability of the organization. Auditors cannot function properly in an environment in which client management is deemed to be unethical and corrupt.

2. Auditors should be aware of conditions that would predispose the management of an organization to commit fraud. Some of the obvious conditions may be lack of sufficient working capital, adverse industry conditions, bad credit ratings, and the existence of extremely restrictive conditions in bank or indenture agreements. If auditors encounter any such conditions, their examination should give due consideration to the possibility of fraudulent financial reporting. Appropriate measures should be taken, and every attempt should be made to uncover any fraud.

3. Auditors should understand a client's business and industry and should be aware of conditions peculiar to the industry that may affect the audit. Auditors should read industry-related literature and familiarize themselves with the risks that are inherent in the business.

4. Auditors should determine if the board of directors establishes the business policy for the organization and if it monitors management and organization operations. An independent internal audit group that reports to the audit committee of the board of directors is an excellent environmental control.

5. From organizational charts and job descriptions, auditors can assess whether segregation between organizational functions is adequate. In particular, auditors are concerned with the segregation of duties within and between the accounting function and other functional areas. We introduced the importance of accounting independence in the previous chapter. Later in this chapter, we explore this issue further.

Risk Assessment

Organizations must perform a **risk assessment** to identify, analyze, and manage risks relevant to financial reporting. Risks can arise or change from circumstances such as:

- Changes in the operating environment that impose new or changed competitive pressures on the firm.
- New personnel that hold a different or inadequate understanding of internal control.
- New or reengineered information systems that affect transaction processing.
- Significant and rapid growth that strains existing internal controls.
- The implementation of new technology into the production process or information system that impacts transaction processing.
- The introduction of new product lines or activities with which the organization has little experience.
- Organizational restructuring resulting in the reduction and/or reallocation of personnel such that business operations and transaction processing are affected.
- Entering into foreign markets that may impact operations (i.e., the risks associated with foreign currency transactions).
- Adoption of a new accounting principle that impacts the preparation of financial statements.

SAS 78 requires that auditors obtain sufficient knowledge of the organization's risk assessment procedures to understand how management identifies, prioritizes, and manages the risks related to financial reporting.

Information and Communication

The accounting information system consists of the records and methods used to initiate, identify, analyze, classify, and record the organization's transactions and to account for the related assets and liabilities. The quality of information generated by the AIS impacts management's ability to take actions and make decisions in connection with the organization's operations and to prepare reliable financial statements. An effective accounting information system will:

- Identify and record all valid financial transactions.
- Provide timely information about transactions in sufficient detail to permit proper classification and financial reporting.
- Accurately measure the financial value of transactions so their effects can be recorded in financial statements.
- Accurately record transactions in the time period in which they occurred.

SAS 78 requires that auditors obtain sufficient knowledge of the organization's information system to understand:

- The classes of transactions that are material to the financial statements and how those transactions are initiated.
- The accounting records and accounts that are used in the processing of material transactions.
- The transaction processing steps involved from the initiation of a transaction to its inclusion in the financial statements.
- The financial reporting process used to prepare financial statements, disclosures, and accounting estimates.

Monitoring

Management must determine that internal controls are functioning as intended. **Monitoring** is the process by which the quality of internal control design and operation can be assessed. This may be accomplished by separate procedures or by ongoing activities.

An organization's internal auditors may monitor the entity's activities in separate procedures. They gather evidence of control adequacy by testing controls, then communicate control strengths and weaknesses to management. As part of this process, internal auditors make specific recommendations for improvement to controls.

Ongoing monitoring may be achieved by integrating special computer modules into the information system that capture key data and/or permit tests of controls to be conducted as part of routine operations. Imbedded modules thus allow management and auditors to maintain constant surveillance over the functioning of internal controls. In Chapter 17, we examine a number of embedded module techniques.

Another technique for achieving ongoing monitoring is the judicious use of management reports. Timely reports allow managers in functional areas such as sales, purchasing, production, and cash disbursements to oversee and control their operations. By summarizing activities, highlighting trends, and identifying exceptions from normal performance, well-designed management reports provide evidence of internal control function or malfunction. In Chapter 11, we review the management reporting system and examine the characteristics of effective management reports.

Control Activities

Control activities are the policies and procedures used to ensure that appropriate actions are taken to deal with the organization's identified risks. Control activities can be grouped into two distinct categories: *computer controls* and *physical controls*.

Computer Controls. Computer controls constitute a body of material that is of primary concern to us. These controls, which relate specifically to the IT environment and IT auditing, fall into two broad groups: **general controls** and **application controls**. General controls pertain to entity-wide concerns such as controls over the data center, organization databases, systems development, and program maintenance. Application controls ensure the integrity of specific systems such as sales order processing, accounts payable, and payroll applications. In later chapters we examine a framework for viewing general and application controls and the risks to which they relate. However, before pursuing this material further, we need to review more fundamental, but important, physical control issues.

Physical Controls. This class of control activities relates primarily to traditional accounting systems that employ manual procedures. However, an understanding of these control concepts also gives insight to the risks and control concerns associated with the IT environment. Our discussion will address the issues pertaining to six traditional categories of physical control activities: transaction authorization, segregation of duties, supervision, accounting records, access control, and independent verification. For each control category, the IT implications will also be reviewed.

Transaction Authorization. The purpose of **transaction authorization** is to ensure that all material transactions processed by the information system are valid and in accordance with management's objectives. Authorizations may be general or specific.

General authority is granted to operations personnel to perform day-to-day operations. An example of general authorization is the procedure to authorize the purchase of inventories from a designated vendor only when inventory levels fall to their predetermined reorder points. This is called a *programmed procedure* (not necessarily in the computer sense of the word). The decision rules are specified in advance, and no additional approvals are required. On the other hand, specific authorizations deal with case-by-case decisions associated with nonroutine transactions. An example of this is the decision to extend a particular customer's credit limit beyond the normal amount. Specific authority is usually a management responsibility.

In an IT environment, transaction authorization may consist of coded rules embedded within computer programs. For example, a program module in a purchases system will determine when, how much, and from which vendor inventories are ordered. Such transactions may be initiated automatically and without human involvement. Within this setting, it may be difficult for auditors to assess whether these transactions are in compliance with management's objectives. For instance, is the organization buying inventory only when it is needed? Are correct quantities being purchased only from approved vendors? Because automated authorization procedures are unobserved by management, control failure may go unnoticed until the firm experiences some adverse symptoms. In the case of purchases authorization, symptoms of a problem may take the form of an inventory stockout or an excessive buildup of inventory. Unfortunately, by the time the problem is recognized, the firm may have incurred substantial financial losses.

In an IT environment, the responsibility for achieving the control objectives of transaction authorization rests directly on the accuracy and consistency (integrity) of the computer programs that perform these tasks. Later in the text, we explore several control techniques that promote computer program integrity. As we shall see, program integrity bears directly on many control issues.

Segregation of Duties. One of the most important control activities is the segregation of employee duties to minimize incompatible functions. **Segregation of duties** can take many forms, depending upon the specific duties to be controlled. However, the following three objectives provide general guidelines applicable to most organizations. These objectives are illustrated in Figure 3–6.

> *Objective 1.* The segregation of duties should be such that the authorization for a transaction is separate from the processing of the transaction. For example, purchases should not be initiated by the purchasing department until authorized by the inventory control department. This separation of tasks is a control to prevent the purchase of unnecessary inventory by individuals.

> *Objective 2.* Responsibility for the custody of assets should be separate from the record keeping responsibility. For example, the department that has physical custody of finished goods inventory (the warehouse) should not keep the official inventory records. Accounting for finished goods inventory is performed by inventory control, an accounting function. When a single individual or department has responsibility for both asset custody and record keeping, the potential for fraud exists. Assets can be stolen or lost, and the accounting records falsified to hide the event.

> *Objective 3.* The organization should be structured so that a successful fraud requires collusion between two or more individuals with incompatible responsibilities. For example, no individual should have sufficient access to

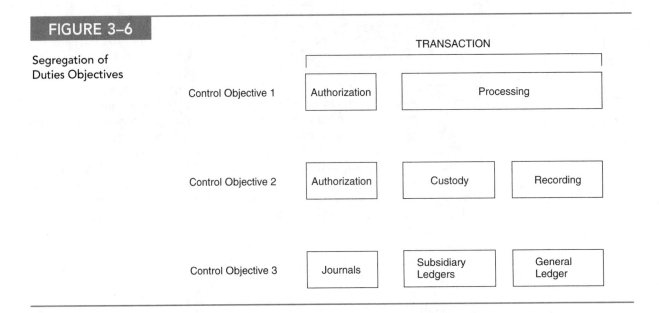

FIGURE 3–6

Segregation of
Duties Objectives

accounting records to perpetrate a fraud. Hence, journals, subsidiary ledgers, and the general ledger are maintained separately. For most people, the thought of approaching another employee with the proposal to collude in a fraud presents an insurmountable psychological barrier. The fear of rejection and subsequent disciplinary action discourages solicitations of this sort. However, when employees with incompatible responsibilities work together daily in close quarters, the resulting familiarity will tend to erode this barrier. For this reason, the segregation of incompatible tasks should be physical as well as organizational. Indeed, concern about personal familiarity on the job is the justification for establishing rules prohibiting nepotism.

In an IT environment, segregation of duties is not identical to that of the manual environment. Computer programs typically perform tasks that are deemed incompatible in a manual system. For example, a program may be solely responsible for authorizing a purchase, processing the purchase order, and recording the account payable. When the supplier's invoice arrives, the computer will also determine the timing and amount of the payment to be made.

There are several reasons why duties that are separated in a manual system need not be separated in an IT environment. It would be inefficient, contrary to the objectives of automation, and operationally futile to separate incompatible tasks among several different programs simply to emulate traditional manual procedures. The reason for segregating duties in a manual environment is to control against some negative aspect of human behavior. Humans make mistakes and occasionally perpetrate frauds. Segregating duties helps to prevent and detect such acts. Computers do not make mistakes and do not perpetrate frauds. Most so-called computer errors are actually programming errors that are, in fact, human errors. Because they possess unimpeachable integrity, no computer has ever perpetrated a fraud unless programmed to do so by a human. Separating computer processing functions, therefore, serves no purpose.

Part 1 Overview of Accounting Information Systems

Segregation of duties still plays a role in the IT environment. However, the IT auditor's attention must be redirected to those activities that threaten application integrity. For example, once the proper functioning of a program is established at system implementation, its integrity must be preserved throughout the application's life cycle. The activities of *program development*, *program operations*, and *program maintenance* are critical IT functions that must be adequately separated.

Supervision. Implementing adequate segregation of duties requires that a firm employ a sufficiently large number of employees. Achieving adequate segregation of duties often presents difficulties for small organizations. Obviously, it is impossible to separate five incompatible tasks among three employees. Therefore, in small organizations or in functional areas that lack sufficient personnel, management must compensate for the absence of segregation controls with close **supervision**. For this reason, supervision is often called a *compensating control*.

An underlying assumption of supervision control is that the firm employs competent and trustworthy personnel. Obviously, no company could function for long on the alternative assumption that its employees are incompetent and dishonest. The "competent and trustworthy employee" assumption promotes supervisory efficiency. Firms can thus establish a managerial span of control whereby a single manager supervises several employees. In manual systems, maintaining a span of control tends to be straightforward because both manager and employees are at the same physical location.

In an IT environment, supervisory control must be more elaborate than in manual systems for three reasons. The first relates to the problem of attracting competent employees. The technology of data processing creates an exceedingly complex environment that demands a unique class of employees. Those who design, program, maintain, and operate the firm's computer system must possess highly specialized skills. These individuals operate in a dynamic setting characterized by a high rate of staff turnover. The task of restaffing is complicated further by rapid changes in technology, which tend to frustrate management's ability to assess the competence of prospective employees.

The second reason reflects management's concern over the trustworthiness of data processing personnel in high-risk areas. Some systems professionals serve in positions of authority that permit direct and unrestricted access to the organization's programs and data. The combination of technical skill and opportunity in the hands of an individual, who may be mischievous or corrupt, represents a significant exposure to the organization.

The third reason is management's inability to adequately observe employees in an IT environment. The activities of employees engaged in data processing are frequently hidden from management's direct observation. For example, data processing personnel may be distributed throughout various areas and perform their functions remotely via telecommunications links. Supervisory controls must, therefore, be designed into the computer system to compensate for the lack of direct supervision.

Accounting Records. The traditional **accounting records** of an organization consist of source documents, journals, and ledgers. These records capture the economic essence of transactions and provide an audit trail of economic events. The audit trail enables the auditor to trace any transaction through all phases of its processing from the initiation of the event to the financial statements. Organizations must maintain audit trails for two reasons. First, this information is needed for conducting day-to-day operations. The audit trail helps employees respond to customer inquiries by showing the current status of transactions in process. Second, the audit trail plays an essential role in the financial audit of the firm. It enables external (and internal) auditors to verify selected transactions by tracing them from the financial statements to the ledger accounts, to the journals, to the source documents, and back to their original source. For reasons of both practical expedience and legal obligation, business organizations must maintain sufficient accounting records to preserve their audit trails.

The obligation to maintain an audit trail exists in an IT environment just as it does in a manual setting. However, automated accounting records and audit trails are very different from those in manual systems. Some computer systems maintain no physical source documents. Journals and ledgers often do not exist in the traditional sense. Instead, records of transactions and other economic events are fragmented across several normalized database tables. Audit trails may take the form of pointers, hashing techniques, indexes, or embedded keys that link record fragments between and among the database tables. To meet their responsibilities, auditors must understand the operational principles of the database management systems in use and the effects on accounting records and audit trails of alternative file structures.

Access Control. The purpose of **access controls** is to ensure that only authorized personnel have access to the firm's assets. Unauthorized access exposes assets to misappropriation, damage, and theft. Therefore, access controls play an important part in safeguarding assets. Access to assets can be direct or indirect. Physical security devices, such as locks, safes, fences, and electronic and infrared alarm systems, control against direct access. Indirect access to assets is achieved by gaining access to the records and documents that control their use, ownership, and disposition. For example, an individual with access to all the relevant accounting records can destroy the audit trail that describes a particular sales transaction. Thus, by removing the records of the transaction, including the account receivable balance, the sale may never be billed and the firm will never receive payment for the items sold. The access controls needed to protect accounting records will depend upon the technological characteristics of the accounting system. In a manual system, accounting records are physical and tend to be distributed among several locations. Indirect access control is accomplished by controlling the use of documents and records and by segregating the duties of those who must access and process these records.

In the IT environment, accounting records are often concentrated within the data processing center on mass storage devices. Data consolidation exposes the organization to two forms of threat: (1) computer fraud and (2) losses from disasters.

> *Fraud.* An individual with the proper skills and unrestricted access to accounting records is in a prime position to perpetrate a fraud. With all the necessary records in one location, the successful perpetrator does not need to gain access to several different places and is thus more likely to achieve his or her objective without detection.

> *Disasters.* Disasters such as fires in Los Angeles caused by civil unrest, earthquakes in southern California, floods in the Midwest, hurricanes in Florida, the bombing of the World Trade Center, and less spectacular events such as computer hardware failures all can destroy an organization's accounting records. A firm unable to recover its essential records may well be unable to continue in business. For example, if the firm's accounts receivable file is de-

stroyed, it may be unable to determine what its customers owe for goods and services previously provided. Access control in the IT environment includes provisions for the physical security of the computer facilities. With all of its eggs in one basket, the firm must protect the basket well.

Another problem unique to the IT environment is controlling access to computer programs. During the development phase, computer applications come under a great deal of scrutiny and testing intended to expose logic errors. However, concern for application integrity should not cease when systems are implemented. Errors and fraud exposures are more likely to occur after implementation in the operational period of the system's life cycle, called the *maintenance phase*. During this period, which may last for years, a typical application may be modified dozens of times. This is an opportunity for errors to be inserted unintentionally in the application and for the computer criminal to perpetrate a fraud by making an illegal program change.

Access control in an IT environment covers many levels of exposure. Controls that address these exposures include techniques designed to limit personnel access authority, restrict access to computer programs, provide physical security for the data processing center, ensure adequate backup for data files, and provide disaster recovery capability. Some access controls are technological procedures and devices, while others are physical barriers implemented through organizational segregation of duties. But underlying all access control techniques is the fundamental principle of "need to know." Individuals should be granted access to data, programs, and restricted areas only when a need in connection with their assigned tasks has been demonstrated. This principle should never be violated.

Independent Verification. **Verification procedures** are independent checks of the accounting system to identify errors and misrepresentations. Verification differs from supervision because it takes place after the fact, by an individual who is not directly involved with the transaction or task being verified. Supervision takes place while the activity is being performed, by a supervisor with direct responsibility for the task. Through independent verification procedures, management can assess (1) the performance of individuals, (2) the integrity of the transaction processing system, and (3) the correctness of data contained in accounting records. Examples of independent verifications include:

- Reconciling batch totals at points during transaction processing.
- Comparing physical assets with accounting records.
- Reconciling subsidiary accounts with control accounts.
- Reviewing management reports (both computer and manually generated) that summarize business activity.

The timing of verification depends upon the technology employed in the accounting system and the task under review. Some verifications occur several times an hour; some are done several times a day; and others are performed daily, weekly, monthly, and annually.

Independent verification control is needed in the manual environment because employees sometimes make mistakes or forget to perform necessary tasks. In an IT environment, computer programs perform many routine tasks. Being precise machines, computers will always do what their programs specify; if these programs are accurate and complete, there is no reason to perform an independent check on their functioning as an ongoing operational procedure. Once again, our concern rests with application integrity. In the IT environment, IT auditors perform an independent verification function by evaluating controls over systems development and maintenance activities and occasionally by reviewing the internal logic of programs.

THE IMPORTANCE OF THE INTERNAL CONTROLS

The five components of internal control—the control environment, risk assessment, information and communication, monitoring, and control activities—provide the auditor with important information about the risks of material misrepresentation in financial statements and fraud. Auditors are therefore required to obtain a sufficient knowledge of the internal controls to plan their audits. For example, the internal controls in place affect how the auditor will assess whether an organization has reported all of its liabilities. The auditor must understand how purchases are initiated, processed, and recorded. The internal control structure provides this information and guides the auditor in the planning of specific tests to determine the likelihood and extent of financial statement misrepresentation.

Summary

This chapter began by examining ethical issues that societies have pondered for centuries. It is increasingly apparent that good ethics is a necessary condition for the long-term profitability of a business. This requires that ethical issues be understood at all levels of the firm, from top management to line workers. Business schools have a responsibility to educate students about the ethical issues in business and those related specifically to each functional area of study. In this section, we identified several ethical issues of direct concern to accountants and other students of information systems.

In the second section, we examined fraud and its relationship to auditing. Fraud falls into two general categories: employee fraud and management fraud. Employee frauds are generally designed to convert cash or other assets directly to the employee's personal benefit. Typically, the employee circumvents the company's internal control structure for personal gain. However, if a company has an effective system of internal control, defalcations or embezzlements can usually be prevented or detected. Management fraud typically involves the material misstatement of financial data and reports to attain additional compensation or promotion or to escape the penalty for poor performance. Managers that perpetrate fraud often do so by overriding the internal control structure. The section examined several well-documented fraud techniques used in both manual and computer-based systems.

The third section examined the subject of internal control. The adequacy of internal control structure is an issue of great importance to both management and accountants. Internal control was examined first using the PDC control model that classifies controls as preventive, detective, and corrective. Next, the authoritative framework specified in SAS 78 was examined. This model of control divides the internal control into the control environment, risk assessment, information and communication, monitoring, and control activities. Control activities include transaction authorization, segregation of duties, supervision, adequate accounting records, access control, and independent verification. The chapter concluded by examining the impact of the computer-based information system on control procedures specified by SAS 78.

Key Terms

access controls   (150)
accounting records   (149)
accuracy   (137)
application controls   (146)
bribery   (131)
business ethics   (116)
completeness   (137)
computer ethics   (120)
computer fraud   (133)
conflict of interest   (132)
control activities   (146)
control environment   (144)
corrective controls   (142)
data collection   (134)
database management fraud   (136)
detective controls   (141)
eavesdropping   (137)
economic extortion   (132)
employee fraud   (125)
ethical responsibility   (119)
ethics   (116)
exposure   (139)
Foreign Corrupt Practices Act of 1977   (138)
fraud   (124)
general controls   (146)

illegal gratuity   (131)
internal control system   (138)
lapping   (133)
management fraud   (125)
management responsibility   (139)
monitoring   (146)
operations fraud   (136)
ownership   (121)
preventive controls   (140)
privacy   (121)
program fraud   (135)
reasonable assurance   (139)
relevance   (137)
risk assessment   (145)
scavenging   (137)
security   (121)
segregation of duties   (147)
Statement on Auditing Standards No. 78   (143)
summarization   (137)
supervision   (149)
timeliness   (137)
transaction authorization   (146)
transaction fraud   (133)
verification procedures   (151)

Review Questions

1. What is ethics?
2. What is business ethics?
3. What are the four areas of ethical business issues?
4. What is a business code of ethics?
5. What are three ethical principles that may provide some guidance for ethical responsibility?
6. What is computer ethics?
7. How do the three levels of computer ethics—pop, para, and theoretical—differ?
8. Are computer ethical issues new problems or just a new twist on old problems?
9. What are the computer ethical issues regarding privacy?
10. What are the computer ethical issues regarding security?
11. What are the computer ethical issues regarding ownership of property?
12. What are the computer ethical issues regarding equity in access?
13. What are the computer ethical issues regarding the environment?
14. What are the computer ethical issues regarding artificial intelligence?
15. What are the computer ethical issues regarding unemployment and displacement?
16. What are the computer ethical issues regarding misuse of computers?
17. What are the computer ethical issues regarding internal control responsibility?
18. What are the five conditions that constitute fraud under common law?
19. What is fraud in the business environment?
20. What is employee fraud?
21. What is management fraud?

22. What are the three forces within an individual's personality and the external environment that interact to promote fraudulent activity?
23. How can external auditors attempt to uncover motivations for committing fraud?
24. What is lapping?
25. What is transaction fraud?
26. What is bribery?
27. What is economic extortion?
28. What is conflict of interest?
29. What is computer fraud and what types of activities does it include?
30. At which stage of the general accounting model is it easiest to commit computer fraud?
31. What are the four broad objectives of internal control?
32. What are the four modifying assumptions that guide designers and auditors of internal control systems?
33. Give an example of a preventive control.
34. Give an example of a detective control.
35. Give an example of a corrective control.
36. What is the objective of SAS 78?
37. What are the five internal control components described in the *Statement on Auditing Standards No. 78*?
38. What are the four broad classes of control activities defined by SAS 78?

Discussion Questions

1. Distinguish between ethical issues and legal issues.
2. Some argue against corporate involvement in socially responsible behavior because the costs incurred by such behavior place the organization at a disadvantage in a competitive market. Discuss the merits and flaws of this argument.
3. Although top management's attitude toward ethics sets the tone for business practice, sometimes it is up to lower-level managers to uphold a firm's ethical standards. John, an operations-level manager, discovers that the company is illegally dumping toxic materials and is in violation of environmental regulations. John's immediate supervisor is involved in the dumping. What action should John take?
4. When a company has a strong internal control structure, stockholders can expect the elimination of fraud. Comment on the soundness of this statement.
5. Distinguish between employee fraud and management fraud.
6. The estimates of losses annually due to computer fraud vary widely. Why do you think obtaining a good estimate of this figure is difficult?
7. How has the Foreign Corrupt Practices Act of 1977 had a significant impact on organization management?
8. Discuss the concept of exposure and explain why firms may tolerate some exposure.
9. If detective controls signal error flags, why shouldn't these types of controls automatically make a correction in the identified error? Why are corrective controls necessary?
10. Most accounting firms allow their employees to marry within the accounting firm; however, they do not allow an employee to remain working for them if he or she marries an employee of one of their auditing clients. Why do you think this policy exists?
11. Discuss whether a firm with fewer employees than there are incompatible tasks should rely more heavily on general authority than specific authority.
12. An organization's internal audit department is usually considered to be an effective control mechanism for evaluating the organization's internal control structure. The Birch Company's internal auditing function reports directly to the controller. Comment on the effectiveness of this organizational structure.
13. According to SAS 78, the proper segregation of functions is an effective internal control procedure. Comment on the exposure (if any) caused by combining the tasks of paycheck preparation and distribution to employees.
14. What are the five conditions necessary for an act to be considered fraudulent?
15. Distinguish between exposure and risk.
16. Explain the characteristics of management fraud.

17. The text identifies a number of personal traits of managers and other employees that might help uncover fraudulent activity. Discuss three.
18. Give two examples of employee fraud and explain how the thefts might occur.
19. Discuss the fraud schemes of bribery, illegal gratuities, and economic extortion.
20. Explain at least three forms of computer fraud.
21. Why are the computer ethics issues of privacy, security, and property ownership of interest to accountants?
22. A profile of fraud perpetrators prepared by the Association of Certified Fraud Examiners revealed that adult married males with advanced degrees commit a disproportionate amount of fraud. Explain these findings.
23. Explain whether authorizations are necessary in a computer environment.

24. Explain how a computer-based information systems environment affects the segregation of functions.
25. Explain how a computer-based information systems environment affects supervision.
26. Explain how a computer-based information systems environment affects the firm's obligation to maintain adequate accounting records.
27. Explain how a computer-based information systems environment affects access control.
28. Explain how a computer-based information systems environment affects independent verification.

Multiple-Choice Questions

1. CMA 1283 3-11

   When an organization has a strong internal control structure, management can expect various benefits. The benefit least likely to occur is
   a. reduced cost of an external audit.
   b. elimination of employee fraud.
   c. availability of reliable data for decision-making purposes.
   d. some assurance of compliance with the Foreign Corrupt Practices Act of 1977.
   e. some assurance that important documents and records are protected.

2. CMA 1288 3-28

   An internal control structure should follow certain basic principles to achieve the objectives of internal control. One of these principles is the segregation of duties. Which of the following examples does not violate the principle of segregation of duties?
   a. The treasurer has the authority to sign checks but gives the signature block to the assistant treasurer to run the check-signing machine.
   b. The warehouse clerk, who has the custodial responsibility over inventory in the warehouse, may authorize disposal of damaged goods.

   c. The sales manager has the responsibility to approve credit and the authority to write off accounts.
   d. The department time clerk is given the undistributed payroll checks to mail to absent employees.
   e. The accounting clerk who shares the record keeping responsibility for the accounts receivable subsidiary ledger performs the monthly reconciliation of the subsidiary ledger and the control account.

3. CMA 1288 3-24

   Internal control objectives are to be accomplished with reasonable assurance. The concept of reasonable assurance recognizes that
   a. the auditor's primary responsibility is the detection of fraud.
   b. employee carelessness can weaken an internal control structure.
   c. the control procedure should not have a significant adverse effect on efficiency or profitability.
   d. judgmentally selected samples cannot meet the criteria for statistical validity.
   e. the precision of an estimate is directly related to reliability (confidence level).

4. To conceal the theft of cash receipts from customers in payment of their accounts, which of the following journal entries should the bookkeeper make?

DR	CR
a. Miscellaneous Expense	Cash
b. Petty Cash	Cash
c. Cash	Accounts Receivable
d. Sales Returns	Accounts Receivable
e. None of the above	

5. Which of the following controls would best prevent the lapping of accounts receivable?
   a. Segregate duties so that the clerk responsible for recording in the accounts receivable subsidiary ledger has no access to the general ledger.
   b. Request that customers review their monthly statements and report any unrecorded cash payments.
   c. Require customers to send payments directly to the company's bank.
   d. Request that customers make the check payable to the company.
6. Providing timely information about transactions in sufficient detail to permit proper classification and financial reporting is an example of
   a. the control environment.
   b. risk assessment.
   c. information and communication.
   d. monitoring.
7. Ensuring that all material transactions processed by the information system are valid and in accordance with management's objectives is an example of
   a. transaction authorization.
   b. supervision.
   c. accounting records.
   d. independent verification.
8. Which of the following is often called a compensating control?
   a. transaction authorization
   b. supervision
   c. accounting records
   d. independent verification
9. Which of the following is NOT a necessary condition under common law to constitute a fraudulent act?
   a. injury or loss
   b. material fact
   c. written documentation
   d. justifiable reliance
10. The fraud scheme that is similar to the "borrowing from Peter to pay Paul" scheme is
    a. expense account fraud.
    b. bribery.
    c. lapping.
    d. transaction fraud.

Problems

1. **Fraud Scheme**
   A purchasing agent for a home improvement center is also part owner in a wholesale lumber company. The agent has sole discretion in selecting vendors for the lumber sold through the center. The agent directs a disproportionate number of purchase orders to his company, which charges above-market prices for its products. The agent's financial interest in the supplier is unknown to his employer.

Required:
What type of fraud is this and what controls can be implemented to prevent or detect the fraud?

2. **Fraud Scheme**
   A procurement agent for a large metropolitan building authority threatens to blacklist a building contractor if he does not make a financial payment to the agent. If the contractor does not cooperate, the contractor will be denied future work. Faced with a threat of economic loss, the contractor makes the payment.

Required:
What type of fraud is this and what controls can be implemented to prevent or detect the fraud?

3. **CMA 1288 3-22**
   Segregation of Function
   An effective system of internal control includes the segregation of incompatible duties. Some of the examples presented represent incompatible duties. Comment on the specific exposures (if any) that are caused by the combination of tasks.

a. The treasurer has the authority to sign checks but gives the signature block to the assistant treasurer to run the check-signing machine.
b. The warehouse clerk, who has custodial responsibility over inventory in the warehouse, may authorize disposal of damaged goods.
c. The sales manager, who works on commission based on gross sales, approves credit and has authority to write off uncollectible accounts.
d. The shop foreman submits time cards and distributes paychecks to employees.
e. The accounting clerk posts to individual accounts receivable subsidiary accounts and performs the reconciliation of the subsidiary ledger and the general ledger control account.

4. **CMA 1288 3-23**
   Segregation of Duties
   Explain why each of the following combinations of tasks should, or should not, be separated to achieve adequate internal control.
   a. Approval of bad debt write-offs and the reconciliation of the accounts receivable subsidiary ledger and the general ledger control account.
   b. Distribution of payroll checks to employees and approval of employee time cards.
   c. Posting of amounts from both the cash receipts and the cash disbursements journals to the general ledger.
   d. Writing checks to vendors and posting to the cash account.
   e. Recording cash receipts in the journal and preparing the bank reconciliation.

5. **Expense Account Fraud**
   While auditing the financial statements of Petty Corporation, the certified public accounting firm of Trueblue and Smith discovered that its client's legal expense account was abnormally high. Further investigation of the records indicated the following:
   • Since the beginning of the year, several disbursements totaling $15,000 had been made to the law firm of Swindle, Fox, and Kreip.
   • Swindle, Fox, and Kreip were not Petty Corporation's attorneys.
   • A review of the canceled checks showed that they had been written and approved by Mary Boghas, the cash disbursements clerk.
   • Boghas's other duties included performing the end-of-month bank reconciliation.

   • Subsequent investigation revealed that Swindle, Fox, and Kreip are representing Mary Boghas in an unrelated embezzlement case in which she is the defendant. The checks had been written in payment of her personal legal fees.

   Required:
   a. What control procedures could Petty Corporation have employed to prevent this unauthorized use of cash? Classify each control procedure in accordance with the SAS 78 framework (authorization, segregation of functions, supervision, and so on).
   b. Comment on the ethical issues in this case.

6. **Tollbooth Fraud**
   Collectors at Tollbooths A and B (see the following figure) have colluded to perpetrate a fraud. Each day, Tollbooth Collector B provides A with a number of toll tickets pre-stamped from Tollbooth B. The price of the toll from Point B to Point A is 35 cents. The fraud works as follows:
   Drivers entering the turnpike at distant points south of B will pay tolls up to $5. When these drivers leave the turnpike at Point A, they pay the full amount of the toll printed on their tickets. However, the tollbooth collector replaces the tickets collected from the drivers with the 35-cent tickets provided by B, thus making it appear that the drivers entered the turnpike at Point B. The difference between the 35-cent tickets submitted as a record of the cash receipts and the actual amounts paid by the drivers is pocketed by Tollbooth Collector A and shared with B at the end of the day. Using this technique, Collectors A and B have stolen over $20,000 in unrecorded tolls this year.

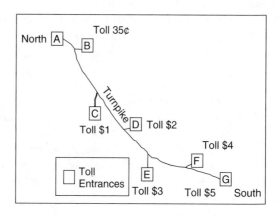

Required:

What control procedures could be implemented to prevent or detect this fraud? Classify the control procedures in accordance with SAS 78.

7. CMA 1289 3-Y6
Causes of Fraud

The studies conducted by the National Commission on Fraudulent Financial Reporting (the Treadway Commission) revealed that fraudulent financial reporting usually occurs as the result of certain environmental, institutional, or individual influences and opportune situations. These influences and opportunities, present to some degree in all companies, add pressures and motivate individuals and companies to engage in fraudulent financial reporting. The effective prevention and detection of fraudulent financial reporting requires an understanding of these influences and opportunities, while evaluating the risk of fraudulent financial reporting that these factors can create in a company. The risk factors to be assessed include not only internal ethical and control factors but also external environmental conditions.

Required:

a. Identify two situational pressures in a public company that would increase the likelihood of fraud.
b. Identify three corporate circumstances (opportune situations) where fraud is easier to commit and detection is less likely.
c. For the purpose of assessing the risk of fraudulent financial reporting, identify the external environmental factors that should be considered in the company's
    i.   industry.
    ii. business environment.
    iii. legal and regulatory environment.
d. List several recommendations that top management should incorporate to reduce the possibility of fraudulent financial reporting.

8. CMA 1289 3-4
Evaluation of Internal Control

Oakdale, Inc. is a subsidiary of Solomon Publishing and specializes in the publication and distribution of reference books. Oakdale's sales for the past year exceeded $18 million, and the company employed an average of 65 employees.

Solomon periodically sends a member of the internal audit department to audit the operations of each of its subsidiaries, and Katherine Ford, Oakdale's treasurer, is currently working with Ralph Johnson of Solomon's internal audit staff. Johnson has just completed a review of Oakdale's investment cycle and prepared the following report.

General

Throughout the year, Oakdale has made both short-term and long-term investments in securities; all securities are registered in the company's name. According to Oakdale's bylaws, long-term investment activity must be approved by its board of directors, while short-term investment activity may be approved by either the president or the treasurer.

Transactions

All purchases and sales of short-term securities were made by the treasurer. The long-term security purchases were approved by the board, while the long-term security sale was approved by the president. Because the treasurer is listed with the broker as the company's contact, all revenue from these investments (dividends and interest) is received by this individual, who then forwards the checks to accounting for processing.

Documentation

Purchase and sale authorizations, along with the broker's advices, are maintained in a file by the treasurer. The certificates for all long-term investments are kept in a safe deposit box at the local bank; only the president of Oakdale has access to this box. An inventory of this box was made, and all certificates were accounted for. Certificates for short-term investments are kept in a locked metal box in the accounting office. Other documents, such as long-term contracts and legal agreements, are also kept in this box. There are three keys to the box held by the president, the treasurer, and the accounting manager. The accounting manager's key is available to all accounting personnel should they require documents kept in this box. Documentation for two of the current short-term investments could not be located in this box; the accounting manager explained that some of the investments are for such short periods of time that formal documentation is not always provided by the broker.

Accounting Records

Deposits of checks for interest and dividends earned on investments are recorded by the accounting department, but these checks could not be traced to the cash receipts journal maintained by the individual who normally opens, stamps, and logs incoming checks. These amounts are journalized monthly in an account for investment revenue. Checks drawn for investment purchases are authorized by the treasurer, and checks in excess of $15,000 must be signed by the treasurer and the president. When securities are sold, the broker deposits the proceeds directly in Oakdale's bank account by an electronic funds transfer.

Each month, the accounting manager and the treasurer prepare the journal entries required to adjust the short-term investment account. There was insufficient backup documentation attached to the journal entries reviewed to trace all transactions; however, the balance in the account at the end of last month closely approximates the amount shown on the statement received from the broker. The amount in the long-term investment account is correct, and the transactions can be clearly traced through the documentation attached to the journal entries. There are no attempts made to adjust either account to the lower of aggregate cost or market.

Required:

To achieve Solomon Publishing's objective of sound internal control, the company believes the following four controls are basic for an effective system of accounting control:

* Authorization of transactions
* Complete and accurate record keeping
* Access control
* Internal verification
  a. For each of the four controls listed above, describe its purpose.
  b. Identify an area in Oakdale's investment procedures that violates each of the four controls listed above.
  c. For each of the violations identified, describe how Oakdale can correct each weakness.

9. Financial Aid Fraud

Harold Jones, the financial aid officer at a small university, manages all aspects of the financial aid program for needy students. Jones receives requests for aid from students, determines whether the students meet the aid criteria, authorizes aid payments, notifies the applicants that their request has been either approved or denied, writes the financial aid checks on the account he controls, and requires that the students come to his office to receive the checks in person. For years, Jones has used his position of authority to perpetrate the following fraud:

Jones encourages students who clearly will not qualify to apply for financial aid. Although the students do not expect aid, they apply on the "off chance" that it will be awarded. Jones modifies the financial information in the students' applications so that it falls within the established guidelines for aid. He then approves aid and writes aid checks payable to the students. The students, however, are informed that aid was denied. Since the students expect no aid, the checks in Jones's office are never collected. Jones forges the students' signatures and cashes the checks.

Required:

Identify the internal control procedures (classified per SAS 78) that could prevent or detect this fraud.

10. Kickback Fraud

The kickback is a form of fraud often associated with purchasing. Most organizations expect their purchasing agents to select the vendor that provides the best products at the lowest price. To influence the purchasing agent in his or her decision, vendors may grant the agent financial favors (cash, presents, football tickets, and so on). This activity can result in orders being placed with vendors that supply inferior products or charge excessive prices.

Required:

Describe the controls that an organization can employ to deal with kickbacks. Classify each control as either preventive, detective, or corrective.

11. Ethics

Discuss your ethical concerns (if any) and what your actions would be if you were confronted with the following situations:
a. You work for a law firm that subscribes to LEXIS/NEXIS. The fees charged to the law firm are based upon usage. You observe that one of your fellow employees (a law clerk attending law school) spends about one hour a

day using this service to search for cases for his law class.

b. Your employer recently bought a laptop computer for your business use. You use a database package extensively in your work on your desktop computer. Your employer does not have a site license for this software and has asked you to install the previously purchased copy (for your desktop computer) onto your laptop.

c. You heard a rumor that top management in your organization has been reading its employees' e-mail messages. You ask your boss, and she confirms the rumor.

Internal Control Cases

1. Bern Fly Rod Company

Bern Fly Rod Company is a small manufacturer of high-quality graphite fly-fishing rods. It sells its products to fly-fishing shops throughout the United States and Canada. Bern began as a small company with four salespeople, all family members of the owner. Due to the high popularity and recent growth in fly-fishing, Bern now employs a sales force of 16, and for the first time employs nonfamily members. The salespeople travel around the country giving fly-casting demos of their new models. Once the sales orders are generated, inventory availability is determined and, if necessary, the salesperson sends the order directly to the manufacturing department for immediate production. Sales staff compensation is tied directly to their sales figures. Bern's financial statements for the December year-end reflect unprecedented sales, 35 percent higher than last year. Further, sales for December account for 40 percent of all sales. Last year, December sales accounted for only 20 percent of all sales.

Required:

Analyze the above situation and assess any potential internal control issues and exposures. Discuss some preventive measures this firm may wish to implement.

2. Breezy Company

(This case was prepared by Elizabeth Morris, Lehigh University)

Breezy Company of Bethlehem, Pennsylvania, is a small wholesale distributor of heating and cooling fans. The company deals with retailing firms that buy small to medium quantities of fans. The president, Chuck Breezy, was very pleased with the marked increase in sales over the past couple of years. Recently, however, the accountant informed Chuck that although net income has increased, the percentage of uncollectibles has tripled. Due to the small size of the business, Chuck fears he may not be able to sustain these increased losses in the future. He asked his accountant to analyze the situation.

Background

In 1998, the sales manager, John Breezy, moved to Alaska, and Chuck hired a young college graduate to take over the position. The company had always been a family business and, therefore, measurements of individual performance had never been a large consideration. The sales levels had been relatively constant because John had been content to sell to certain customers with whom he had been dealing for years. Chuck was leery about hiring outside of the family for this position. To try to keep sales levels up, he established a reward incentive based on net sales. The new sales manager, Bob Sellmore, was eager to set his career in motion and decided he would attempt to increase the sales levels. To do this, he recruited new customers while keeping the old clientele. After one year, Bob had proved himself to Chuck, who decided to introduce an advertising program to further increase sales. This brought in orders from a number of new customers, many of whom Breezy had never done business with before. The influx of orders excited Chuck so much that he instructed Jane Breezy, the finance manager, to raise the initial credit level for new customers. This induced some customers to purchase more.

Existing System

The accountant wrote up a comparative income statement to show changes in revenues and expenses over the last three years, shown in Exhibit A. Currently, Bob is receiving a commission of 2 percent of net

EXHIBIT A
BREEZY COMPANY
COMPARATIVE INCOME STATEMENT
FOR YEARS 1999, 2000, 2001

	1999	2000	2001
Revenues:			
Net Sales	350,000	500,000	600,000
Other Revenue	60,000	60,000	62,000
Total Revenue	410,000	560,000	662,000
Expenses:			
Cost of Goods Sold	140,00	200,000	240,000
Bad Debt Expense	7,000	20,000	36,000
Salaries Expense	200,000	210,000	225,000
Selling Expense	5,000	15,000	20,000
Advertising Expense	0	0	10,000
Other Expenses	20,000	30,000	35,000
Total Expenses	372,000	475,000	566,000
Net Income	30,000	85,000	96,000

sales. Breezy Company uses credit terms of net 30 days. At the end of previous years, bad debt expense amounted to approximately 2 percent of net sales.

As the finance manager, Jane performs credit checks. In previous years, Jane had been familiar with most clients and approved credit on the basis of past behavior. When dealing with new customers, Jane usually approved a low credit amount and increased it after the customer exhibited reliability. With the large increase in sales, Chuck felt that the current policy was restricting a further rise in sales levels. He decided to increase credit limits to eliminate this restriction. This policy, combined with the new advertising program, should attract many new customers.

Future

The new level of sales impresses Chuck and he wishes to expand, but he also wants to keep uncollectibles to a minimum. He believes the amount of uncollectibles should remain relatively constant as a percentage of sales. Chuck is thinking of expanding his production line, but wants to see uncollectibles drop and sales stabilize before he proceeds with this plan.

Required:

Analyze the weaknesses in internal control and suggest improvements.

3. Whodunit?

(This case was prepared by Karen Collins, Lehigh University)

The following facts relate to an actual embezzlement case.

Someone stole more than $40,000 from a small company in less than two months. Your job is to study the following facts, try to figure out who was responsible for the theft and how it was perpetrated, and (most important) suggest ways to prevent something like this from happening again.

Facts

Location of company: a small town on the eastern shore of Maryland. Type of company: crabmeat processor, selling crabmeat to restaurants located in Maryland. Characters in the story (names are made up):

- John Smith, president and stockholder (husband of Susan).
- Susan Smith, vice president and stockholder (wife of John).
- Tommy Smith, shipping manager (son of John and Susan).
- Debbie Jones, office worker. She began working part-time for the company six months before the theft. (At that time, she was a high school senior and was allowed to work afternoons through a school internship program.) Upon graduation from high school (several weeks before the theft was discovered), she began working full time. Although she is not a member of the family, the Smiths have been close friends with Debbie's parents for more than ten years.

Accounting Records

All accounting records are maintained on a microcomputer. The software being used consists of the following modules:

1. A general ledger system, which keeps track of all balances in the general ledger accounts and produces a trial balance at the end of each month.
2. A purchases program, which keeps track of purchases and maintains detailed records of accounts payable.
3. An accounts receivable program, which keeps track of sales and collections on account and maintains individual detailed balances of accounts receivable.
4. A payroll program.

Performance of Key Functions by Individual(s)

John, president
Susan, vice president
Tommy, son and shipping manager
Debbie, office worker

	Individual(s) Performing Task	
	Most of the Time	Sometimes
1. Receiving order from customers	John	All others
2. Overseeing production of crabmeat	John or Tommy	—
3. Handling shipping	Tommy	John
4. Billing customers (entering sales into accounts receivable program)	Debbie	Susan
5. Opening mail	John	All others
6. Preparing bank deposit tickets and making bank deposits	Susan or Debbie	All others
7. Recording receipt of cash and checks (entering collections of accounts receivable into accounts receivable program)	Debbie	Susan
8. Preparing checks (payroll checks and payments of accounts payable)	Susan or Debbie	—
9. Signing checks	John	—
10. Preparing bank reconciliations	John	—
11. Preparing daily sales reports showing sales by type of product	Susan	—
12. Summarizing daily sales reports to obtain monthly sales report by type of product	Susan or Debbie	—
13. Running summaries of AR program, AP program, and payroll program at month end and inputting summaries into GL program	Susan or Debbie	—
14. Analyzing trial balance at month end and analyzing open balances in accounts receivable and accounts payable	Susan	—

The modules are not integrated (that is, data are not transferred automatically between modules). At the end of the accounting period, summary information generated by the purchases, accounts receivable, and payroll programs must be entered into the general ledger program to update the accounts affected by these programs.

Sales

The crabmeat processing industry in this particular town was unusual in that selling prices for crabmeat were set at the beginning of the year and remained unchanged for the entire year. The company's customers, all restaurants located within 100 miles of the plant, ordered the same quantity of crabmeat each week. Because prices for the crabmeat remained the same all year and the quantity ordered was always the same, the weekly invoice to each customer was always for the same dollar amount.

Manual sales invoices were produced when orders were taken, although these manual invoices were not prenumbered. One copy of the manual invoice was attached to the order shipped to the customer. The other copy was used to enter the sales information into the computer.

When the customer received the order, the customer would send a check to the company for the amount of the invoice. Monthly bills were not sent to customers unless the customer was behind in payments (that is, did not make a payment for the invoiced amount each week).

Note: The industry was unique in another way: many of the companies paid their workers with cash each week (rather than by check). It was, therefore, not unusual for companies to request large sums of cash from the local banks.

When Trouble Was Spotted

Shortly after the May 30 trial balance was run, Susan began analyzing the balances in the various accounts. The balance in the cash account agreed with the cash balance she obtained from a reconciliation of the company's bank account.

However, the balance in the accounts receivable control account in the general ledger did not agree with the total of the accounts receivable subsidiary ledger (which shows a detail of the balances owed by each customer). The difference was not very large, but the balances should be in 100 percent agreement.

At this point, Susan asked me if I would help her locate the problem. In reviewing the computerized accounts receivable subsidiary ledger, I noticed the following:

1. The summary totals from this report were not the totals that were entered into the general ledger program at month end. Different amounts had been entered. No one could explain why this had happened.
2. Some sheets in the computer listing had been ripped apart at the bottom. (In other words, the listing of the individual accounts receivable balances was not a continuous list but had been split at several points.)
3. When an adding machine tape of the individual account balances was run, the individual balances

did not add up to the total at the bottom of the report.

Susan concluded that the accounts receivable program was not running properly. My recommendation was that an effort be made to find out why the accounts receivable control account and the summary totals per the accounts receivable subsidiary ledger were not in agreement and why we were finding problems with the accounts receivable listing. Since the accounts receivable subsidiary and accounts receivable control account in the general ledger had been in agreement at the end of April, the effort should begin with the April ending balances for each customer by manually updating all of the accounts. The manually adjusted May 30 balances should then be compared with the computer-generated balances and any differences investigated.

After doing this, Susan and John found several differences. The largest difference was the following:

CUSTOMER ACCOUNT PER MANUAL RECONSTRUCTION			
Dr.		**Cr.**	
Sale #1	5,000	Pmt. #1	5,000
Sale #2	5,000	Pmt. #2	5,000
Sale #3	5,000	Pmt. #3	5,000
Sale #4	5,000	—	—
Ending Balance	5,000		

CUSTOMER ACCOUNT PER MANUAL RECONSTRUCTION			
Dr.		**Cr.**	
Sale #1	5,000	Pmt. #1	5,000
Sale #3	5,000	Pmt. #2	5,000
Sale #3	5,000	Pmt. #3	5,000
Ending Balance	0		

Although they found the manual sales invoice for Sale #2, Susan and John concluded (based on the computer records) that Sale #2 did not take place. I was not sure, so I recommended that they call this customer and ask him the following:

1. Did he receive this order?
2. Did he receive an invoice for it?
3. Did he pay for the order?
4. If so, did he have a copy of his canceled check?

Although John felt that this would be a waste of time, he called the customer. He received an affirmative answer to all of his questions. In addition, he found that the customer's check was stamped on the back not with the normally used "for deposit only" stamp of the company but with an address stamp giving only the company's name and city. When questioned, Debbie said that she sometimes used this stamp.

Right after this question, Debbie, who was sitting nearby at the computer, called Susan to the computer and showed her the customer's account. She said that the payment for $5,000 was in fact recorded in the customer's account. I came over to the computer and looked at the account. The payments were listed like this:

Amount	Date of Payment
$5,000	May 3
$5,000	May 17
$5,000	May 23
$5,000	May 10

I questioned the order of the payments—why was a check supposedly received on May 10 entered in the computer after checks received on May 17 and 23? About 30 seconds later, the computer malfunctioned and the accounts receivable file was lost. Every effort to retrieve the file gave the message "file not found."

About five minutes later, Debbie presented Susan with a copy of a bank deposit ticket dated May 10 with several checks listed on it, including the check that the customer said had been sent to the company. The deposit ticket, however, was not stamped by the bank (which would have verified that the deposit had been received by the bank) and did not add up to the total at the bottom of the ticket (it was off by 20 cents).

At this point, being very suspicious, I gathered all documents I could and left the company to work on the problem at home, away from any potential suspects. I received a call from Susan about four hours later saying that she felt much better. She and Debbie had gone to Radio Shack (the maker of their computer program) and Radio Shack had confirmed Susan's conclusion that the computer program was malfunctioning. She and Debbie were planning to work all weekend reentering transactions into the computer. She said that everything looked fine and not to waste my time working on the problem.

I felt differently. How do you feel?

Required:

a. If you were asked to help this company, could you conclude from the evidence presented that an embezzlement took place? What would you do next?

b. Who do you think was the embezzler?

c. How was the embezzlement accomplished?

d. What improvements would you recommend in internal control to prevent this from happening again? In answering this question, try to identify at least one suggestion from each of the six classes of internal control activities discussed in this chapter (under the section "Control Activities"): transaction authorization, segregation of duties, supervision, accounting records, access control, and independent verification.

e. Would the fact that the records were maintained on a microcomputer aid in this embezzlement scheme?

PART
2
TRANSACTION CYCLES AND BUSINESS PROCESSES

CHAPTER

4

The Revenue Cycle

Economic enterprises, both for-profit and not-for-profit, generate revenues through business processes that constitute their revenue cycle. In its simplest form, the revenue cycle is the direct exchange of finished goods or services for cash in a single transaction between a seller and a buyer. More complex revenue cycles process sales on credit. Many days or weeks may pass between the point of sale and the subsequent receipt of cash. This time lag splits the revenue transaction into two phases: (1) the physical phase, involving the transfer of assets or services from the seller to the buyer; and (2) the financial phase, involving the receipt of cash by the seller in payment of the account receivable. As a matter of processing convenience, most firms treat each phase as a separate transaction. Hence, the revenue cycle actually consists of two major subsystems: (1) the sales order processing subsystem and (2) the cash receipts subsystem. Our study of the revenue cycle describes the procedures for a hypothetical merchandising firm that makes credit sales to its customers. The two subsystems of this process are treated separately.

This chapter is organized into three main sections. The first section provides an overview of revenue cycle activities and the logical tasks, key participants, sources and uses of information, and movement of key documents through the organization. A manual system is used to demonstrate these characteristics. The second section explores computer-based systems in the revenue cycle. The focus is on alternative technologies used to achieve various levels of organizational change from simple automation of a manual process to reengineering the work flow. The final section examines microcomputer systems and the control implications of the continuing trend toward end-user computing.

LEARNING OBJECTIVES

After studying this chapter, you should:

- Recognize the fundamental tasks that must be performed in the revenue cycle, regardless of the level of technology in place.
- Be able to identify the functional departments involved in revenue cycle activities and trace the flow of revenue transactions through the organization.
- Be able to specify the documents, journals, and accounts that provide audit trails, promote the maintenance of historical records, support internal decision making, and sustain financial reporting.
- Understand the risks associated with the revenue cycle and recognize the controls that reduce these risks.
- Be aware of the operational and control implications of technology used to automate and reengineer the revenue cycle.

OVERVIEW OF REVENUE CYCLE ACTIVITIES

To present the logical functions of the revenue cycle, we will study data flow diagrams (DFDs) and document flowcharts depicting a manual environment. Although most organizations employ computer technology in one form or another to perform these tasks, there is merit in studying manual systems before studying computer-based systems. Most organizations have some manual operations, such as selling, warehousing, and shipping functions. The information needed to trigger and support these tasks is fundamentally independent of the technology that underlies the information system. For example, a shipping notice tells the billing process that a product has been shipped to a customer and that a bill should now be prepared. The shipping notice serves this purpose whether it is produced and processed manually or electronically.

Students of AIS are better able to understand the logic of a system when it is not complicated unnecessarily by technology. Once we establish clearly what needs to be done, we will then explore different and better ways of doing it using technology.

The DFD in Figure 4–1 presents an overview of the logical activities that constitute the sales order processing system. These processes are described in the following steps.

1. The sales process begins with a customer contacting the sales department. This initial contact may be by telephone, mail, or in person. The sales department captures the essential details of this event on a sales order. This information triggers a number of tasks.

2. The first step in the sales process is to authorize the transaction by obtaining credit approval for the customer.

3. When credit is approved, the sales information is released to the billing, warehouse, and shipping processes.

4. The next step is to ship the merchandise, which should be done as soon after credit approval as possible. If required to wait too long, the customer may cancel the order and go elsewhere. The shipping process reconciles the products received from the warehouse with the sales information that it received earlier. This reconciliation ensures that the firm sends the correct goods to the customer. If an error has occurred, such as picking the wrong goods or quantities from the warehouse shelves, the problem should be detected at this point. Assuming all is well with the order, the goods will be packaged and shipped via common carrier to the customer. The shipping information is then sent to the billing process.

5. The billing process compiles the relevant facts about the transaction (product prices, handling charges, freight, taxes, and discount terms) and bills the customer. The billing process then transmits this information to the accounts receivable and inventory control processes.

6. Accounts receivable receives the billing information and records this in the customer's account.

7. Likewise, inventory control uses information from billing to adjust the inventory records to reflect a decrease in inventory.

8. Periodically (after each batch, daily, weekly, monthly, or so forth) the billing, accounts receivable, and inventory control processes transmit summarized information to the general ledger process. This includes (1) the total of all sales from billing, (2) the total increases to accounts receivable, and (3) the total decrease in inventory. From this information, the general ledger process posts to the control

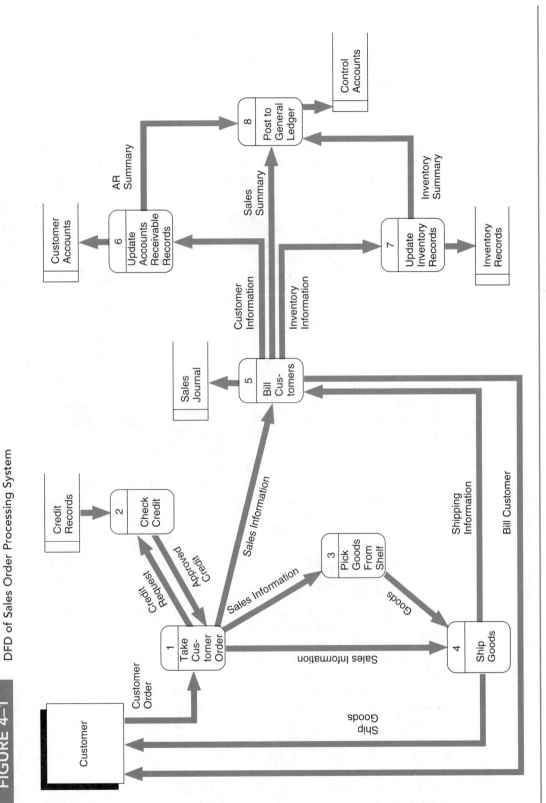

FIGURE 4–1   DFD of Sales Order Processing System

accounts affected by sales transactions during this period. In addition, the general ledger process reconciles these independently compiled summaries to identify record keeping errors. For example, if billing had failed to bill a customer or accounts receivable had recorded an incorrect amount, a discrepancy between their summarized figures would be detected in the general ledger process. However, if the summaries balance, the overall process is assumed to have functioned correctly.

MANUAL PROCEDURES

The document flowchart in Figure 4–2 shows the manual procedures and the documents typically found in a manual sales order system.

The Sequence of Activities

Referring to Figure 4–2, let's trace the sequence of manual activities through the departments affected by the sales process. We will examine the specific documents, journals, and ledgers as they are encountered in each stage of this system.

The Sales Department. The sales process begins in the sales department with the receipt of a **customer order** indicating the type and quantity of merchandise being requested. At this point, the customer order is not in a standard format and may not be a physical document. Orders may arrive by mail, by telephone, or from a field representative who visited the customer's place of business. When the customer is also a business entity, the order is usually a copy of the customer's purchase order. Purchase orders are an expenditure cycle document and are discussed in Chapter 5. If the customer order is not in the standard format needed by the seller's order processing system, it must be transcribed into a formal sales order.

Recall from Chapter 2 that the purpose of a source document is to capture the economic essence of a transaction. The principal source document in the sales order system is the **sales order**, an example of which is presented in Figure 4–3 (page 173).

The sales order captures such vital information as the name and address of the customer; the customer's account number; the name, number, and description of the items sold; the quantities and unit prices of each item sold; and other financial information such as taxes, discounts, and freight charges. Multiple copies of sales orders are produced to serve different purposes. The number of copies created will vary from system to system, depending on the operations to be supported. The hypothetical system in Figure 4–2 uses sales order copies for credit authorizations, packing slips, stock release documents, shipping notices, sales invoices, and ledger posting. In an actual system, the various sales order copies would be numbered or color-coded to signify their purpose and distribution. Copies that are used for more than one purpose, and that go to several locations, sometimes have routing information printed on them.

After preparing the sales order, the sales clerk files one copy of it in the **customer open order file** for future reference. Filling the order and getting the product to the customer may take days or even weeks. Customers frequently contact their suppliers by telephone to check the status of their orders. To facilitate customer inquiries, the open order file is often organized alphabetically by customer name. Although customer name is not an efficient primary key for accessing data, it is used as a secondary key to cross-reference customers' orders since customers do not always know their account numbers and may not have copies of their invoices handy. In these situations,

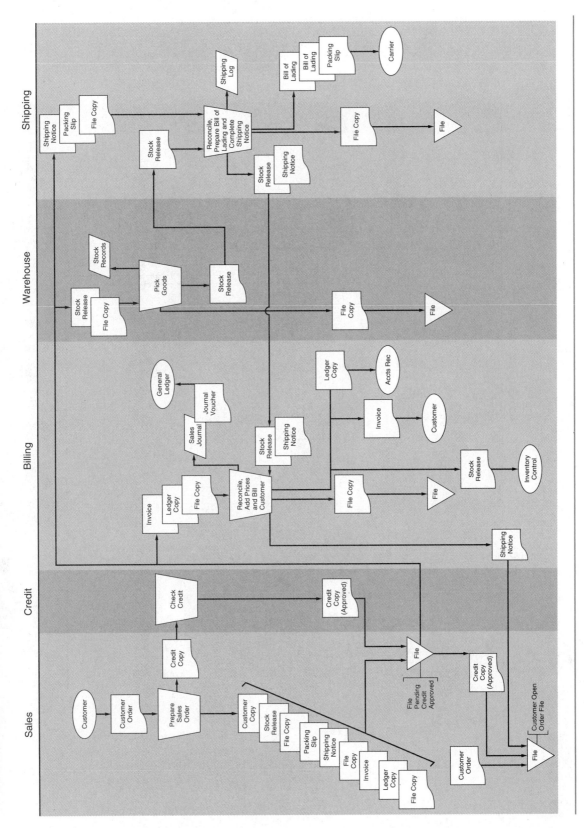

FIGURE 4–2   Manual Sales Order Processing System

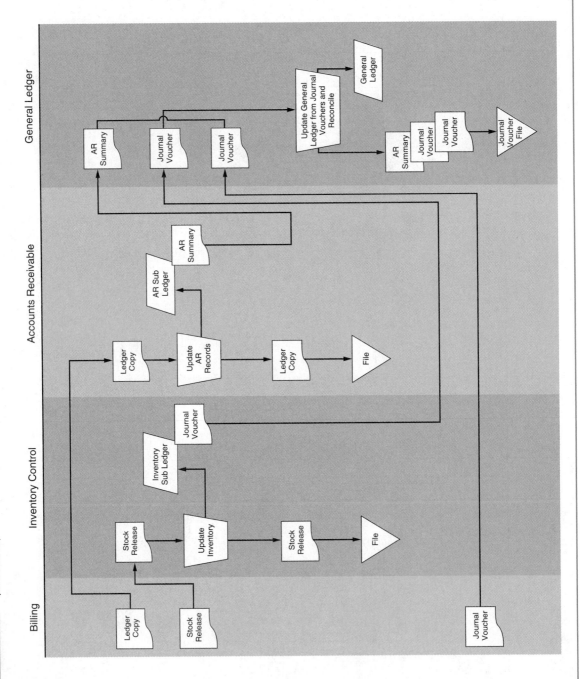

FIGURE 4–2

(continued)

FIGURE 4–3

Sales Order

CHARGE SALE INVOICE

MONTEREY PENINSULA CO-OP
527 River Road
Chicago, IL 60612
(312) 555-0407

INVOICE NUMBER _____

SOLD TO
FIRM NAME _____
ATTENTION OF _____
ADDRESS _____
CITY _____
STATE _____ ZIP _____

INVOICE DATE _____
PREPARED BY _____
CREDIT TERMS _____

CUSTOMER PURCHASE ORDER
NUMBER _____
DATE _____
SIGNED BY _____

SHIPMENT DATE _____
SHIPPED VIA _____
B.O.L. NO. _____

QUANTITY ORDERED	PRODUCT NUMBER	DESCRIPTION	QUANTITY SHIPPED	UNIT PRICE	TOTAL
		TOTAL SALE			
		CUSTOMER ACCT. NO.			
		VERIFICATION			

the customer file enables the clerk to find the sales order and respond to the customer's questions.

The Credit Department. The first step in this department is transaction authorization, which involves verifying the customer's creditworthiness. The circumstances of the sale will determine the nature of the credit check. For example, a seller may perform a full financial investigation on new customers to establish a line of credit.

However, once a credit limit is set, credit checking on subsequent sales may be nothing more than ensuring that the current sale does not exceed the limit.

In our hypothetical system, the **credit authorization** copy of the sales order is sent to the credit department for approval. The returned approval triggers the release of the other sales order copies simultaneously to various departments. The credit copy is filed in the customer open order file until the transaction is completed.

Warehouse Procedures. The sales department sends the **stock release** (also called the *picking ticket*) copy of the sales order to the warehouse. This document identifies the items of inventory that must be located and picked from the warehouse shelves. It also provides formal authorization for the warehouse clerk to release custody of the specified assets. After picking the stock, the clerk initials the stock release copy to indicate that the order is complete and accurate. Any out-of-stock items are noted on the stock release copy. One copy of the stock release travels with the goods to the shipping department, and the other is filed in the warehouse to provide a record of the transaction. The clerk then adjusts the stock records to reflect the reduction in inventory. The stock records are *not* the formal accounting records for these assets. Assigning the warehouse clerk responsibility for asset custody and record keeping would violate internal control. The inventory accounting records are kept in the inventory control department.

Shipping Department. Before the arrival of the goods and the stock release copy, the shipping department receives the **packing slip** and **shipping notice** copies from the sales department. The packing slip travels with the goods to the customer to describe the contents of the order. Packing slips may be placed either inside the shipping container or attached to the outside in a special plastic pouch. The shipping notice informs the billing department that the customer's order has been filled and shipped. This document contains such pertinent facts as the date of shipment, items and quantities shipped, the carrier, and freight charges. In some systems, the shipping notice is a separate document prepared by the shipping clerk.

Upon receiving the goods from the warehouse, the shipping clerk reconciles the physical items with the stock release documents, the packing slip, and the shipping notice to verify the correctness of the order. This is an important step and the last opportunity to detect errors before shipment. The shipping clerk packages the goods, attaches the packing slip to the container, completes the shipping notice, and prepares a **bill of lading**. The bill of lading is a formal contract between the seller and the shipping company (carrier) to transport the goods to the customer. This document establishes legal ownership and responsibility for assets in transit. Figure 4–4 shows a bill of lading.

The shipping clerk transfers custody of the goods, the packing slip, and two copies of the bill of lading to the carrier, then performs the following tasks:

1. Records the shipment in the shipping log.
2. Sends the stock release document and the shipping notice to the billing department as proof of shipment.
3. Files one copy each of the bill of lading and the shipping document.

Billing Department. The billing department plays a central role in the sales order system. It collects information about sales transactions and reconciles, assimilates, and distributes this information to other departments.

FIGURE 4–4

Bill of Lading

UNIFORM STRAIGHT BILL OF LADING — Domestic

Monterey Peninsula Co-op
527 River Road
Chicago, IL 60612
(312) 555-0407

Document No._____

Shipper No._____

Carrier No._____

Date_____

TO:

Consignee _____

Street _____

City/State _____   Zip Code _____

_____
(Name of Carrier)

Route:

Vehicle

No. Shipping Units	Kind of packaging, description of articles, special marks and exceptions	Weight	Rate	Charges

TOTAL CHARGES $

The agreed or declared value of the property is hereby specifically stated by the shipper to be not exceeding: $ _____ per_____	IF WITHOUT RECOURSE: The carrier shall not make delivery of this shipment without payment of freight _____ (Signature of Consignor)
FREIGHT CHARGES Check appropriate box: [ ] Freight prepaid [ ] Collect [ ] Bill to shipper	Signature below signifies that the goods described above are in apparent good order, except as noted. Shipper hereby certifies that he is familiar with all the bill of lading terms and agrees with them.
SHIPPER Monterey Peninsula Co-op	CARRIER
PER	PER DATE

(This bill of lading is to be signed
by the shipper and agent of the
carrier issuing same.)
CONSIGNEE

Figure 4–2 shows that upon credit approval, the billing department receives the invoice, ledger copy, and file copy of the sales order from the sales department. These have been held pending receipt of the shipping notice and the stock release document. The **sales invoice** is the customer's bill, which shows the items and quantities shipped, their unit prices, shipping charges, and the total amount of the charges to the customer. The **ledger copy** and **file copy** contain the same information for internal use.

The shipment of goods marks the completion of the economic event and the point at which the customer should be billed. Billing before shipment occurs can promote inaccuracies in record keeping and inefficiencies in operations. When the sales order is originally prepared, some of the details about the transaction are not known with certainty and are subject to change. For example, there may be insufficient inventories in stock to fill the order. When this happens, the warehouse clerk places these items on **back-order** and adjusts the stock release document to reflect the amounts actually going to the customer. Typically, suppliers do not bill customers for back-orders until they are shipped. Billing for goods not shipped causes confusion, damages relations with customers, and requires additional work to make adjustments to the accounting records.

To prevent such problems, the billing department awaits notification from shipping before it bills. The stock release document and shipping notice describe the products that were actually shipped to the customer. When this information reaches the billing department, the clerk pulls the invoice and ledger copies from the temporary file and performs the following steps:

1. Compares the items and quantities shown on the invoice and ledger copies with the information on the stock release and shipping documents.
2. If necessary, adjusts the invoice and ledger copies to reflect the reality of the transaction.
3. Adds unit prices, taxes, and freight charges to the invoice, ledger, and file copies.
4. Applies terms of the sale, such as quantity and early payment discounts.
5. Sends the invoice to the customer.
6. Sends the shipping document to the sales department to close the open customer file.

In addition, the billing department performs the following record keeping–related tasks:

1. Records the sale in the sales journal.
2. Sends the ledger copy of the sales order to accounts receivable.
3. Sends the stock release document to inventory control.
4. Files a copy of the invoice in the billing department's permanent file.

The **sales journal** is a special journal for recording sales transactions. Each sales invoice is entered in the journal as a separate item. At the end of the period, the clerk summarizes these entries and prepares a **journal voucher** that is sent to the general ledger for posting to the following accounts:

	DR	CR
Accounts Receivable-Control	XXXX.XX	
Sales		XXXX.XX

Figure 4–5 illustrates a journal voucher. Each journal voucher represents a general journal entry and identifies the general ledger accounts affected. Summaries of trans-

FIGURE 4–5

Journal Voucher

Journal Voucher		Number: **JV6-03** Date: _10/7/2001_	
Account Number	Account Name	Amount DR.	CR.
20100	Accounts Receivable	$5,000	
50200	Sales		$5,000
Explanation: _to record total credit sales for 10/7/2001_			
Approved by: _JRM_		Posted by: _MJJ_	

actions, adjusting entries, and closing entries are all entered into the general ledger in this way. When properly approved, journal vouchers are an effective control against unauthorized entries to the general ledger. The journal voucher system eliminates the need for a formal general journal, which is replaced by a **journal voucher file**.

Inventory Control Department. The inventory control department uses the stock release document to update the **inventory subsidiary ledger** accounts. In a perpetual inventory system, every inventory item has its own inventory record in the ledger containing, at a minimum, the data depicted in Figure 4–6. Each stock release document reduces the quantity on hand of one or more inventory accounts. After posting, the stock release document is filed. At the end of the period, the financial value of the total reduction in inventory is summarized in a journal voucher and sent to the general ledger department for posting to the following accounts:

	DR	CR
Cost of Goods Sold	XXX.XX	
Inventory—Control		XXX.XX

FIGURE 4–6

Inventory Subsidiary Ledger

Perpetual Inventory Record – Item # 86329

Item Description	Date	Units Received	Units Sold	Qnty On Hand	Reorder Point	EOQ	Qnty On Order	Purch Order #	Vendor Number	Standard Cost	Total Inven. Cost
3" Pulley	9/15			50	950	200	1,000	—	—	—	2	1,900
	9/18		300	650							1,300
	9/20		100	550							1,100
	9/27		300	250							500
	10/1		100	150	200	1,000	1,000	87310	851	2	300
	10/7	1,000		1,150			—				2,300

Accounts Receivable Department. The **accounts receivable** department posts from the ledger copy of the sales order to the customer accounts in the **accounts receivable subsidiary ledger**. Every customer has a record in the AR subsidiary ledger containing the following pieces of information: customer name; customer address; credit data; transaction dates; invoice numbers; and credits for payments, returns, and allowances. Figure 4–7 shows an example record in an AR subsidiary ledger.

Each ledger copy of the sales order is used to increase a customer's account for the full amount of the sale. After posting, the AR clerk files the ledger copy. Periodically, the clerk summarizes the individual account balances into a single figure and sends this to the general ledger. The purpose for this information is discussed next.

General Ledger Department. By the close of the processing period, the general ledger department has received journal vouchers from the billing and inventory control departments and an account summary from the accounts receivable department. The information serves two purposes:

1. The general ledger uses the journal vouchers to post to the following control accounts:

	DR	CR
Accounts Receivable—Control	XXXX.XX	
Cost of Goods Sold	XXX.XX	
Inventory—Control		XXX.XX
Sales		XXXX.XX

The general ledger contains only control accounts (it provides no supporting detail) and requires only summary posting information.

2. The account summary independently provided by the accounts receivable department is used to verify the internal accuracy of the overall process. By reconciling journal vouchers and account summaries received from operating departments, the general ledger can detect many types of errors. We examine this point more closely in a later section dealing with revenue cycle controls.

Back-Order Procedures

When the quantities of a product on hand are insufficient to fill the customer's order, a back-order document is created. This may be either a new sales order for the out-

FIGURE 4–7

Accounts Receivable Subsidiary Ledger

Name: Howard Supply   Account Number 1435
Address: 121 Maple St.
          Winona, NY 18017

Date	Explanation	Invoice Number	Payment (CR)	Sale (DR)	Account Balance
9/27	3" Pulley (300 Units)	92131		600.00	600.00
10/7			600.00		0.00

standing items or a copy of the current sales order adjusted to reflect the missing products. The back-order is then placed in a special holding file until the inventories arrive from the supplier. Back-orders are satisfied before new sales are processed.

SALES RETURNS

From time to time, customers return the merchandise they have purchased. This occurs for a number of reasons:

- The seller sent the buyer the wrong merchandise.
- The goods were defective.
- The product was damaged in shipment.
- The seller shipped the goods too late or they were delayed in transit, and the buyer refused delivery.

When a return is necessary, the buyer will request the seller to grant a credit allowance for the unwanted products. The flowchart in Figure 4–8 describes the formal procedures for approving and processing returned items.

Sales Return Procedures

Receiving Department. When items are returned, the receiving clerk counts, inspects, and prepares a return slip describing the items. These goods go to the warehouse with a copy of the return slip. The second copy of the return slip goes to the sales department.

Sales Department. Upon receipt of the return slip, the sales clerk prepares a **credit memo**. This document is the authorization for the customer to receive credit for the merchandise returned. Figure 4–9 (page 181) illustrates a credit memo. Note that the credit memo is similar in appearance to a sales order. Some systems actually use a copy of the sales order marked "credit memo."

In cases where *specific* authorization is required (i.e., the amount of the return or circumstances surrounding the return exceed the employee's general authority), the sales clerk sends the credit memo to the credit department for approval. However, if the clerk has sufficient general authority to approve the return, the credit memo will go directly to the billing department.

Credit Department. The credit manager evaluates the circumstances of the return and makes a judgment to grant or disapprove credit. The manager then returns the credit memo to the sales department.

Billing Department. The billing clerk receives the credit memo from the sales department and records the credit in the sales journal as a contra entry. The clerk then sends the credit memo to inventory control for posting. At the end of the period, total sales returns are summarized in a journal voucher and sent to the general ledger department.

Inventory Control and AR Departments. The inventory control clerk adjusts the inventory records and forwards the credit memo to accounts receivable, where the customer's account is adjusted. Both the inventory control and accounts receivable departments send summary information to the general ledger department. Specifically, inventory control sends a journal voucher summarizing the total value of

FIGURE 4–8   Sales Returns Procedures

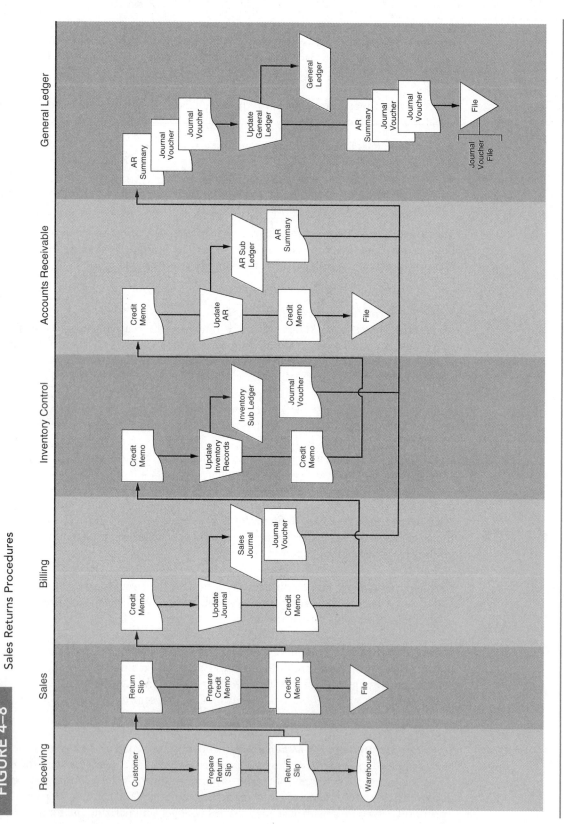

FIGURE 4–9

Credit Memo

Credit Memo

Monterey Peninsula Co-Op   Customer
527 River Road   Invoice # _____
Chicago, IL 60612
(312) 555-0407

Received from _____   Reason for Return

Address _____   _____

City _____   _____

State _____ Zip _____   _____

Product Number	Description	Quantity Returned	Unit Price	Total
Approved By:			Total Credit	

the inventory returns, and accounts receivable sends an account summary of the AR subsidiary ledger.

General Ledger Department. The general ledger clerk receives a journal voucher from billing and inventory control and an account summary from the accounts receivable department. The clerk posts from the journal vouchers to the following control accounts:

	DR	CR
Inventory—Control	XXX.XX	
Sales Returns and Allowances	XXXX.XX	
Cost of Goods Sold		XXX.XX
Accounts Receivable—Control		XXXX.XX

The general ledger clerk reconciles the accounts receivable subsidiary summary with the accounts receivable control account to verify the accuracy of the posting process. The journal vouchers and summaries are then filed.

CASH RECEIPTS SYSTEM

The data flow diagram in Figure 4–10 portrays the receipt of cash in payment of accounts receivable. There are many variants of this process; entities not engaged in retailing or manufacturing, such as banks, insurance companies, and hospitals, may use different methods.

1. The checks and supporting accounting information (customer account number, customer name, amount of the check, and so on) provided on the remittance advice arrive at the mail room, where they are separated. The checks go to the cashier in the cash receipts department, and the remittance advice goes to the accounts receivable department.
2. The checks received by the cashier are recorded in the cash receipts journal and promptly deposited in the bank.
3. The remittance advice received by the accounts receivable department is used to reduce the customer's account balance according to the amount of the payment.

FIGURE 4–10   DFD of Cash Receipts System

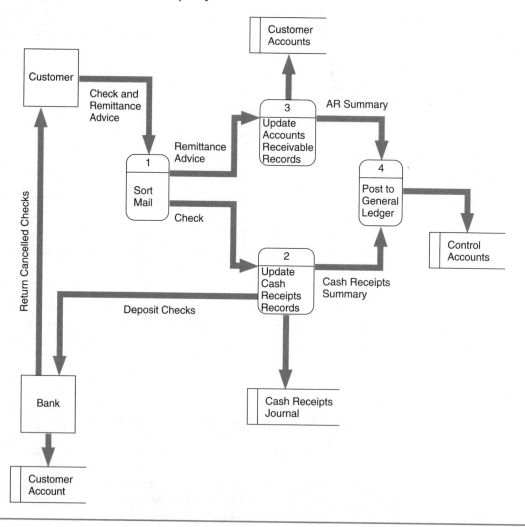

4.   Cash receipts and accounts receivable departments send summary information to the general ledger department. This information is reconciled and used to update the accounts receivable control and cash accounts.

Cash Receipts Procedures

Figure 4–11 presents a document flowchart depicting the cash receipts procedures.

Mail Room Procedures. The mail room receives the customer's check along with a source document called the **remittance advice**. This document contains key information required to service the customer's account. Figure 4–12 shows an example of a remittance advice.

The remittance advice is an example of a turnaround document, as described in Chapter 2. Often, it is a portion of the original invoice used to bill the customer. When payment is made, the customer tears off the remittance advice portion and returns it to the seller with the cash payment. The importance of this document is most apparent in firms that have a large number of customer accounts and process large volumes of cash receipts daily. For example, processing a check from John Smith in payment of his account with no supporting details may require a search of many records to find the correct John Smith. Such searches are time-consuming and costly, but the task is greatly simplified when the customer provides the seller with the necessary account number and posting information. Because of the possibility of transcription errors and omissions, sellers are generally reluctant to ask customers to provide this information directly on their checks. A more efficient method of dealing with this problem is for the seller to provide remittance information to the buyer through the original billing process. Later, when this documentation is returned with the customer's payment, the seller can rely upon its accuracy.

Mail room personnel route the checks and remittance advices to an administrative clerk who endorses the checks "For Deposit Only" and reconciles the amounts on the remittance advice with the check. The clerk then records each check on a form called a **remittance list** (or *cash prelist*). The remittance list is a record of all cash received. In this example, the clerk prepares three copies of the remittance list. The original copy goes to the cashier, along with the checks. The second copy goes to the accounts receivable department with the remittance advices. The third goes to the assistant controller for overall cash reconciliation.

Cash Receipts Department. The cashier verifies the accuracy and completeness of the checks against the prelist. Any checks that get lost or misdirected between the mail room and the cash receipts department should be identified at this point. After reconciling the prelist to the checks, the cashier records the cash receipts in the **cash receipts journal**. All cash receipts transactions, including cash sales, miscellaneous cash receipts, and cash received on account, are recorded in the cash receipts journal. Figure 4–13 (page 186) illustrates this with an example of each type of transaction. Notice that each check received from a customer is listed as a separate line item in the cash receipts journal.

Next, the clerk prepares a bank **deposit slip** in triplicate showing the total amount of the day's receipts and forwards the checks and two copies of the deposit slip to the bank. Upon deposit of the funds, the bank teller validates the deposit slip and returns a copy to the controller. At the end of the day, the cash receipts clerk summarizes the journal entries and prepares a journal voucher with the entry shown on page 186.

FIGURE 4–11   Flowchart of Cash Receipts System

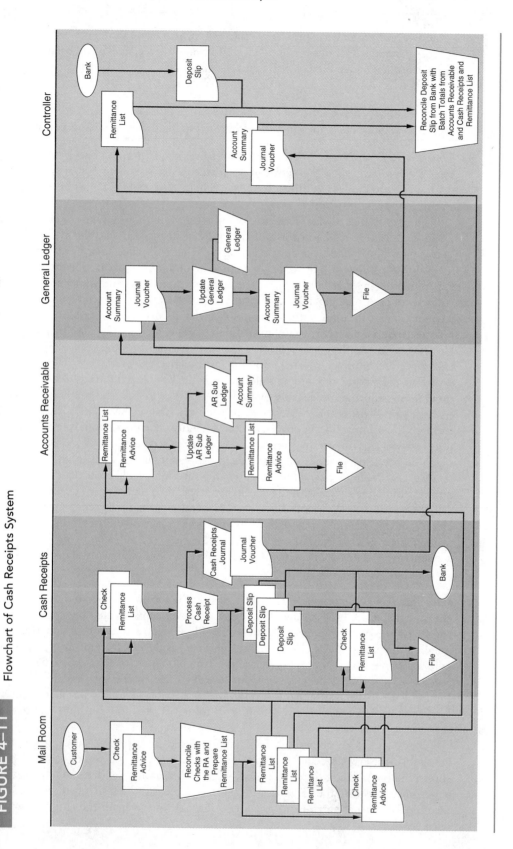

FIGURE 4–12	Remittance Advice

Send To:

Monterey Peninsula Co-Op
527 River Road
Chicago, IL 60612
(312) 555-0407

Page: 1

Remittance Advice:

Date	Customer No.	Amount Pd.	Check No.
10/4/01	811901	125.00	2002

- -

Please return the upper portion with your payment — Thank You

To: John Smith
R.D. #2, Box 312
Prunedale, CA 09278–5704

Due Date	Customer No.	Amount Due
10/10/01	811901	125.00

Date	Invoice Number	Description	Amount Due	
9/28/01	6112115	Cleaning Supplies	125.00	

Thank you for giving Monterey Peninsula the opportunity to serve you

Previous Bal. _____300.00_____
Payments _____300.00_____
Credits _____125.00_____
Late Fees _____—_____
Tax _____—_____
Ending Bal. _____125.00_____

FIGURE 4–13	Cash Receipts Journal

<table>
<tr><td colspan="9" align="center">Cash Receipts Journal</td></tr>
<tr>
<td>Date</td>
<td>Account</td>
<td>Post Ref</td>
<td>Check #</td>
<td>Cash Acct. # 101 (Debit)</td>
<td>Sales Discounts Acct. # 430 (Debit)</td>
<td>Accounts Receivable Acct. # 102</td>
<td>Sales Acct. # 401 Credit</td>
<td>Sundry Accounts Debit (Credit)</td>
</tr>
<tr><td>9/3</td><td>Capital Stock</td><td>301</td><td>2150</td><td>14,000</td><td></td><td></td><td></td><td>14,000</td></tr>
<tr><td>9/5</td><td>Ogment Supply</td><td>✓</td><td>6712</td><td>2,970</td><td>30</td><td>3,000</td><td></td><td></td></tr>
<tr><td>9/9</td><td>Marvin Co.</td><td></td><td>3491</td><td>1,000</td><td></td><td></td><td>1,000</td><td></td></tr>
<tr><td></td><td></td><td></td><td></td><td></td><td></td><td></td><td></td><td></td></tr>
<tr><td></td><td></td><td></td><td></td><td></td><td></td><td></td><td></td><td></td></tr>
</table>

	DR	CR
Cash	XXXX.XX	
Accounts Receivable—Control		XXXX.XX

The clerk transmits the journal voucher to the general ledger department.

Accounts Receivable Department. The accounts receivable clerk posts from the remittance advices to the customers' accounts in the AR subsidiary ledger. After posting, the remittance advices are filed to provide an audit trail. At the end of the day, the AR clerk summarizes the AR subsidiary accounts and forwards the summary to the general ledger department.

General Ledger Department. Periodically, the general ledger department receives a journal voucher from the cash receipts department and an account summary from the accounts receivable department. A clerk posts to the AR and cash control accounts from the journal voucher, reconciles the AR control account with the AR subsidiary account summary, and files the journal voucher.

Controller Department. Periodically (weekly or monthly), a clerk from the office of the **controller** (or an employee not involved with the cash receipts procedures) reconciles cash receipts by comparing the following documents: (1) a copy of the prelist, (2) deposit slips received from the bank, and (3) journal vouchers from the cash receipts and accounts receivable departments.

REVENUE CYCLE CONTROLS

Chapter 3 defined six classes of internal control activities that guide us in designing and evaluating transaction processing controls. They are transaction authorization, segregation of duties, supervision, accounting records, access control, and independent verification. Table 4–1 summarizes the specific control activities used in the revenue cycle.

TABLE 4–1	**Summary of Revenue Cycle Controls**		
		CONTROL POINTS IN THE SYSTEM	
	Control Activity	**Sales Processing**	**Cash Receipts**
	Transaction authorization	Credit check Return policy	Remittance list (cash prelist)
	Segregation of duties	Credits is separate from processing; inventory control is separate from warehouse; AR subsidiary ledger is separate from general ledger	Cash receipts are separate from AR and cash account; AR subsidiary ledger is separate from GL
	Supervision		Mail room
	Accounting records	Sales orders, sales journals, AR subsidiary ledger, AR control (general ledger), inventory subsidiary ledger, inventory control, sales account (GL)	Remittance advices, checks, remittance list, cash receipts journal, AR subsidiary ledger, AR control account, cash account
	Access	Physical access to inventory; access to accounting records above	Physical access to cash; access to accounting records above
	Independent verification	Shipping department, billing department, general ledger	Cash receipts, general ledger, bank reconciliation

Transaction Authorization

Credit Check. The objective of transaction authorization is to ensure that only valid transactions are processed. The credit department is the point of authorization for sales order processing. This department ensures the proper application of the firm's credit policies. The principal concern is the creditworthiness of the customer. In making this judgment, the credit department may employ various techniques and tests. The complexity of credit procedures will vary depending on the organization, its relationship with the customer, and the materiality of the transaction. The specific authorizations required in unique circumstances (such as a first-time customer's request for credit) may take time. However, decisions that fall within an employee's general authority (such as verifying that the current transaction does not exceed the customer's credit limit) can be dealt with very quickly. Once credit is approved, the transaction can then be processed further.

Return Policy. The credit department authorizes the processing of sales returns. This determination is based on the nature of the sale and the circumstances of the return. The concepts of specific and general authority also influence this activity. Most organizations have specific rules for granting cash refunds and credits to customer accounts.

Cash Prelist. The cash prelist provides a means for verifying that customer checks and remittance advices match in amount. The presence of an extra remittance advice in the accounts receivable department or the absence of a customer's check in the cash receipts department would be detected when the batch is reconciled with the prelist. Thus, the prelist *authorizes* the posting of a remittance advice to a customer's account.

Segregation of Duties

Segregating duties ensures that no single individual or department processes a transaction in its entirety. The number of employees and the volume of transactions being processed influence how the segregation is accomplished. Recall from Chapter 3 that three rules guide systems designers in this task:

Rule 1. Transaction authorization should be separate from transaction processing. Within the revenue cycle, the credit department is segregated from the rest of the process, so formal authorization of a transaction is an independent event. The importance of this separation is clear when one considers the potential conflict in objectives between the individual salesperson and the organization. Often, compensation for sales staff is based on their sales levels. To achieve their personal objective of maximizing sales volume, sales personnel may not always consider the creditworthiness of the prospective customer. The credit department, acting as an independent authorization group, detects risky customers and discourages poor and irresponsible sales decisions.

Rule 2. Asset custody should be separate from the task of asset record keeping. In the sales order processing system, the inventory warehouse has custody of the physical assets, and the accounting function (general ledger and inventory control departments) maintains the records.

In the cash receipts system, the cash receipts department takes custody of the physical asset (cash), and the accounting function (general ledger and accounts receivable departments) keeps the accounting records. The cashier reports to the treasurer, who has responsibility for liquid assets. The accounting function is the responsibility of the controller. These two functions should not be commingled.

Rule 3. The organization should be structured so that the perpetration of a fraud requires collusion between two or more individuals. The record keeping functions must be carefully divided. Specifically, the subsidiary ledgers (AR and inventory), the journals (sales and cash receipts), and the general ledger should be separately maintained. An individual with total record keeping responsibility, in collusion with someone with asset custody, is in a position to perpetrate fraud. By separating these tasks, collusion must involve more people, which increases the risk of detection and is, therefore, less likely to occur.

Supervision

Some firms have too few employees to achieve an adequate separation of functions. These firms must rely on supervision as a form of compensating control. By closely supervising employees who perform potentially incompatible functions, a firm can compensate for the exposure inherent in a system.

Supervision can also provide control in systems that are properly segregated. For example, in the cash receipts system, the mail room is a point of exposure for any firm. The individual who opens the mail has access both to cash (the asset) and to the remittance advice (the record of the transaction). A dishonest employee may use this opportunity to steal the check, cash it, and destroy the remittance advice, thus leaving no evidence of the transaction. Ultimately, this sort of fraud will come to light when the customer receives another bill and, in response, produces the canceled check. However, by the time the firm gets to the bottom of this problem, the perpetrator may have committed the crime many times over and left the organization. Detecting crimes after the fact accomplishes little. Prevention is the best solution. The deterrent effect of supervision can provide an effective preventive control.

Accounting Records

Chapter 2 described how a firm's source documents, journals, and ledgers must form an audit trail that allows independent auditors to trace transactions through their various stages of processing. This control is also an important operational feature. Sometimes transactions get lost in the system. By following the audit trail, management can discover where in the system an error occurred. Several specific control techniques contribute to the audit trail.

Prenumbered Source Documents. **Prenumbered source documents** (sales orders, shipping notices, remittance advices, and so on) are sequentially numbered by the printer and allow every transaction to be identified uniquely. This permits the isolation and tracking of a single event (among many thousands) through the accounting system. Without a unique tag, one transaction looks very much like another. Verifying financial data and tracing transactions would be difficult or even impossible without prenumbered source documents.

Special Journals. By grouping similar transactions together into special journals, the system provides a concise record of an entire class of events. For this purpose, revenue cycle systems use the sales journal and the cash receipts journal.

Subsidiary Ledgers. Two subsidiary ledgers are used for capturing transaction event details in the revenue cycle: the inventory and accounts receivable subsidiary ledgers. The sale of products reduces affected inventory subsidiary accounts and increases the customers' accounts receivable subsidiary accounts. The receipt of cash from customers reduces their accounts receivable subsidiary accounts. These subsidiary records provide a link back to journal entries and to the source documents that captured the events.

General Ledger. The general ledger control accounts are the basis for financial statement preparation. Revenue cycle transactions affect the following general ledger accounts: sales, inventory, cost of goods sold, accounts receivable, and cash. Journal vouchers that summarize activity captured in journals and subsidiary ledgers flow into the general ledger to update these accounts. Thus, we have a complete audit trail from the financial statements to the source documents via the general ledger, subsidiary ledgers, and special journals.

Files. The revenue cycle employs several temporary and permanent files that contribute to the audit trail. These files are the physical repositories for various documents. The following are typical examples of revenue cycle files:

- The **open sales order file** is a file of customer orders that have not yet been filled.
- The **price data reference file** is a listing of prices for each type of merchandise. Clerks preparing invoices use this file to obtain the correct price to place on the invoice.
- The **sales history file** is a file of closed sales transactions. The sales history file contains a copy of the invoice sent to the customer, along with a copy of the shipping document.
- The **shipping report file** (or *shipping log*) specifies the items that were shipped during the period.
- The **credit memo file** contains copies of credit memos that have been posted to customer accounts.

Access Controls

Access controls prevent and detect unauthorized and illegal access to the firm's assets. The physical assets of the revenue cycle are inventories and cash. Limiting access to these assets includes:

- Warehouse security, such as fences, alarms, and guards.
- Depositing cash daily in the bank.
- Using a safe or night deposit box for cash.
- Locking cash drawers and safes in the cash receipts department.

Access control over information involves restricting access to documents that control physical assets, that is, source documents, journals, and ledgers. An individual with unrestricted access to records can effectively manipulate the physical assets of the firm. The following are examples of risks associated with the revenue cycle:

1. An individual with access to the AR subsidiary ledger could remove his or her account (or someone else's) from the books. With no record of the account, the firm would not send the customer monthly statements.
2. Access to sales order documents may permit an unauthorized individual to trigger the shipment of a product.
3. An individual with access to both cash and the general ledger cash account could remove cash from the firm and cover the act by adjusting the cash account.

Independent Verification

The objective of independent verification is to promote and verify the accuracy and completeness of procedures performed by others in the system. To be effective, independent verifications must occur at key points in the process where errors can be detected quickly and corrected. Independent verification controls in the revenue cycle exist at the following points:

1. The shipping department verifies that the goods sent from the warehouse are correct in type and quantity. Before the goods are sent to the customer, the stock release document and the packing slip are reconciled.
2. The billing department reconciles the shipping notice with the sales invoice to ensure that customers are billed only for the quantities shipped.
3. The general ledger department also plays an important verification role. General ledger clerks reconcile journal vouchers that were independently prepared in var-

ious departments. The billing department summarizes the sales journal, inventory control summarizes decreases in the inventory subsidiary ledger, the cash receipts department summarizes the cash receipts journal, and accounts receivable summarizes the AR subsidiary ledger. Each of these departments sends its journal vouchers and other summary figures to the general ledger department, where the information is reconciled and posted to the respective control accounts.

The general ledger department can detect certain types of transaction processing errors. For example, the total of all credit sales recorded by billing should equal the total increases posted to the accounts receivable subsidiary accounts. A sales transaction that is entered in the journal but not posted to the customer's account would be detected by the general ledger function. The specific cause of an out-of-balance condition could not be determined at this point, but the error would be noted. Finding the error may require examining all the transactions processed during the period. This could be tedious and time-consuming. For this reason, rather than summarizing an entire day's transactions in a single batch, firms often group transactions into small batches of 50 to 100 items. This facilitates end-of-day balancing procedures by isolating a problem to a specific batch.

COMPUTER-BASED ACCOUNTING SYSTEMS

Now that we have an understanding of the fundamental operational tasks and controls that constitute the revenue cycle, let's examine how they are affected by computer technology. Technology can be a powerful instrument for achieving organizational change. At the low end of the organizational change spectrum is *automation*; at the upper end is *reengineering*. **Automation** involves using technology to improve the efficiency and effectiveness of a task. The automated system simply emulates the traditional manual process. **Reengineering**, on the other hand, involves radically rethinking the business process and the flow of work. The objective of reengineering is to greatly reduce the cost of business by identifying and eliminating nonvalue-added tasks. This involves replacing traditional procedures with procedures that are innovative and sometimes very different from those that previously existed.

In this section we examine the effects of automation on both the sales order processing and cash receipts systems. We then examine methods for reengineering these processes. We also review the key features of point-of-sale (POS) systems, which combine features of both credit and cash sales processes. Finally, we examine electronic data interchange (EDI) and the Internet as alternative techniques of reengineering the revenue cycle. Microcomputer-based accounting systems are discussed in the last section of the chapter.

The file structures used to illustrate the following data processing methods are presented in Figure 4–14. Notice that the transaction file of sales order records has three key fields—Sales Order Number, Account Number, and Inventory Number. Sales Order Number is the primary key (PK) because it is the only field that uniquely identifies each sales order record in the file. This is the preprinted number on the physical source document that is transcribed during the keystoke operation. In systems that do not use physical source documents, this is a unique number that is generated by the computer program. The primary key is critical in preserving the audit trail. It provides the link between magnetic sales order records stored on a computer disk and the physical source documents and business events that they represent.

FIGURE 4–14   File Structures for Sales, Inventory, and Accounts Receivable Files

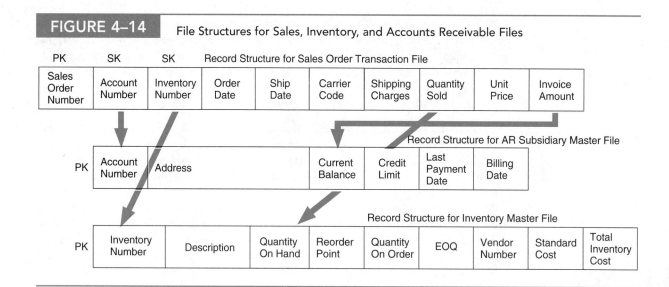

Account Number and Inventory Number are both secondary keys (SK) as neither of these keys can uniquely identify the records in the sales order file. For instance, there could be more than one sales order for a customer. Similarly, the same inventory item type may be sold to more than one customer. Hence, the values for these keys are not unique. The purpose of these keys is to locate the corresponding records in the AR subsidiary and inventory master files.

The file structures presented in Figure 4–14 are characteristic of the "flat file" approach to data management. A simplifying assumption in this hypothetical system is that each sales order record is for a single item of inventory. This one-to-one relationship is unrealistic because one sales order could, in fact, be for many different inventory items. In Chapter 8, we study the database approach to data management. At that point we will examine more complex file structures that permit the representation of "one-to-many" and "many-to-many" relationships that are frequently found in business transactions. However, for our current purposes, the simpler flat file approach can better be used to illustrate the operational features of the following systems.

BATCH PROCESSING USING SEQUENTIAL FILES

Figure 4–15 illustrates an automated sales order system that uses batch processing and sequential files. The most noteworthy departure from the manual system is the absence of accounting functions in day-to-day operations. The traditional accounting procedures of billing, inventory control, accounts receivable, and general ledger are performed by a new function called *data processing*. However, other operational tasks are unaffected by the introduction of this level of technology. Sales order taking, credit checking, warehousing, and shipping are performed just as they were in the manual system. The two principal advantages of this approach are cost savings and error reduction. By automating its accounting function, a firm can reduce its accounting staff and its exposure to clerical errors.

Since this system uses the sequential file structure for its accounting records, either tapes or disks can be employed as the physical storage medium. However, the use of tapes has declined considerably in recent years. For day-to-day operations, tapes

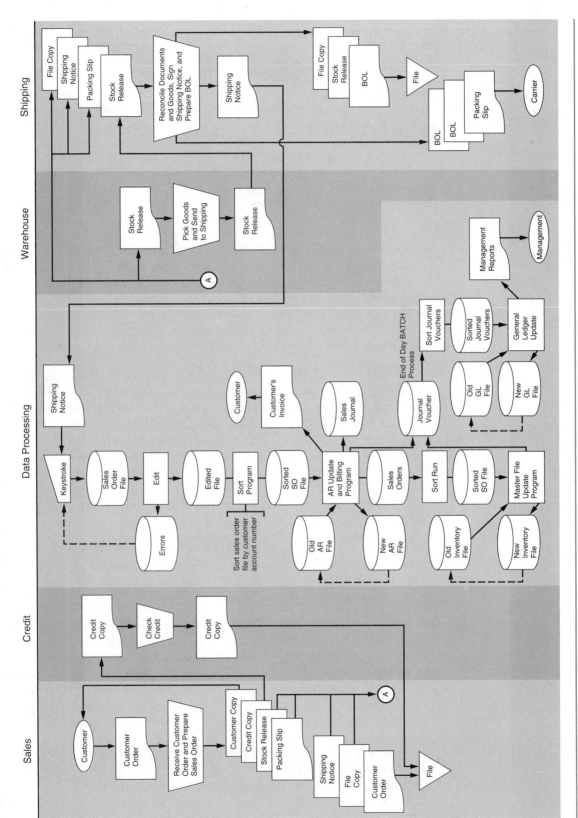

FIGURE 4–15   Batch Processing with Sequential Files

are inefficient because someone must mount them on a tape drive and then dismount the tape when the job ends. This approach is labor intensive and expensive. The constant decline in the per-unit cost of disk storage in recent years has destroyed the economic advantage of using tapes. Typically, an organization using sequential files will now employ disk storage devices. The operational features of sequential files are the same for both tape and disk media, but the disk storage devices can be left on-line for ease of access requiring no human intervention. Today, tapes are used primarily as backup devices and for storing archive data. For these purposes, they are an efficient and effective storage medium.

The computer processing phases of a batch system with sequential files was discussed in detail in Chapter 2. The main points of that discussion are briefly reviewed below.

Keystroke. The process begins with the arrival of batches of shipping notices from the shipping department. These documents are copies of the sales orders that contain accurate information about the number of units shipped and information about the carrier. The keystroke clerk converts the shipping notices to magnetic media to produce a transaction file of sales orders. This is a continuous process. Several times throughout the day, the keystroke clerk receives and converts batches of shipping notices. The resulting transaction file will thus contain many separate batches of sales orders. **Batch control totals** are calculated for each batch on the file.

Edit Run. Periodically, the batch sales order system is executed. In our example, we will assume that this occurs at the end of each business day. The edit program is the first run in the batch process. This program validates transactions by testing each record for the existence of clerical or logical errors. Typical tests include field checks, limit tests, range tests, and price times quantity extensions. Recall from Chapter 2 that detected errors are removed from the batch and copied to a separate error file. Later, these are corrected by an authorized person and resubmitted for processing with the next day's business. The edit program recalculates the batch control totals to reflect changes due to the removal of error records. The "clean" transaction file is then passed to the next run in the process.

Sort Run. At this point, the sales order file is in no useful sequence. Remember from an earlier discussion that a transaction file must be placed in the same sequence as the master file it is updating. The first sort run in this system rearranges the sales order file by order of the secondary key—Account Number.

AR Update and Billing Run. The AR update program posts to accounts receivable by sequentially matching the Account Number key in each sales order record with the corresponding record in the AR subsidiary master file. This procedure creates a new AR subsidiary master file that incorporates all the changes to customer accounts affected by the transaction records. The original AR subsidiary master file remains complete and unchanged by the process. This automatic backup feature is an advantage of sequential file processing. Figure 4–16 illustrates this method with some sample records.

Each sales transaction record processed is added to the sales journal file. At the end of the run, these are summarized and an entry is made to the journal voucher file to reflect total sales and total increases to accounts receivable.

To spread the billing task evenly over the month, some firms employ **cycle billing** of their customers. The update program searches the billing date field in the

FIGURE 4-16 Update of Accounts Receivable from Sales Orders

Sales Order Transaction File

PK	SK								
Order #	Acct Num	Inven Num	Order Date	Ship Date	Carrier Code	Shipping Charges	Qnty Sold	Unit Price	Invoice Amount
3	1	17	12/22	12/24	011	10	25	10	250
1	4	14	12/22	12/24	011	5	10	2	20
2	7	16	12/22	12/24	011	20	100	5	500

Transaction File Sorted by Secondary Key to Primary Key of Master File.

Original Account Receivable Master File

Update Fields

PK		Current	Credit	Last Payment	Billing
ACCT NUM	Address	Balance	Limit	Date	Date
1	123 Elm St., City	350	1000	12/8/01	1
2	35 Main S.	600	1500	12/12/01	1
3	510 Barclay Dr. Beth.	1000	1500	12/5/01	1
4	26 Taylo Rd. Alltn.	100	2000	12/16/01	8
5	4 High St., Naz.	800	1000	12/9/01	1
6	850 1st, Beth	700	2000	12/7/01	8
7	78 Market Alltn.	150	2000	12/17/01	15

New Account Receivable Master File

ACCT NUM	Address	Current Balance	Credit Limit	Last Payment Date	Billing Date
1	123 Elm St., City	600	1000	12/8/01	1
2	35 Main S.	600	1500	12/12/01	1
3	510 Barclay Dr. Beth.	1000	1500	12/5/01	1
4	26 Taylo Rd. Alltn.	120	2000	12/16/01	8
5	4 High St., Naz.	800	1000	12/9/01	1
6	850 1st, Beth	700	2000	12/7/01	8
7	78 Market Alltn.	650	2000	12/17/01	15

AR subsidiary master file for those customers to be billed on a certain day of the month and prepares statements for the selected accounts. The statements are then mailed to the customer.

Sort and Inventory Update Runs. The procedures for the second sort and inventory update runs are similar to those described above. The sort program sorts the sales order file on the secondary key—Inventory Number. The inventory update program reduces the Quantity On Hand field in the affected inventory records by the Quantity Sold field in each sales order record. A new inventory master file is created in the process. Figure 4–17 illustrates the process.

In addition, the program compares values of the Quantity On Hand and the Reorder Point fields to identify inventory items that need to be replenished. This information is sent to the purchasing department. Finally, a journal voucher is prepared to reflect cost of goods sold and the reduction in inventory.

General Ledger Update Run. Under the sequential file approach, the general ledger master file is not updated after each batch of transactions. To do so would result in the recreation of the entire general ledger every time a batch of transactions (such as sales orders, cash receipts, purchases, cash disbursements, and so on) is processed. Firms using sequential files typically employ separate end-of-day procedures to update the general ledger accounts. This technique is depicted in Figure 4–15.

At the end of the day, the general ledger system accesses the journal voucher file. This file contains journal vouchers reflecting all of the day's transactions processed by the organization. The journal vouchers are sorted by general ledger account number and posted to general ledger in a single run, and a new general ledger is created.

The end-of-day procedures will also generate a number of management reports. These may include sales summaries, inventory status reports, transaction listings, journal voucher listings, and budget and performance reports. Quality management reports play a key role in helping management monitor operations to ensure that controls are in place and functioning properly. In Chapter 11, we examine management information needs and management reporting techniques.

BATCH SYSTEM USING DIRECT ACCESS FILES

Figure 4–18 (page 198) shows how the batch processing system depicted in Figure 4–15 is improved by switching to direct access files. Notice, however, that the manual procedures and the keystroke and edit operations are unchanged. The essential difference is the simplified file update process.

Update Procedures

Figure 4–19 (page 199) illustrates the direct access update process using sample data. Starting at the top of the unsorted sales order file, the update program posts the first transaction to the inventory and accounts receivable master files concurrently using the secondary keys (Inventory Number and Account Number) to locate the corresponding records directly. The program then moves to the next transaction record and repeats the process. This continues until all records in the transaction file have been posted. When the program reaches the end of the transaction file, it terminates.

The direct access approach has the following advantages over the sequential file update process:

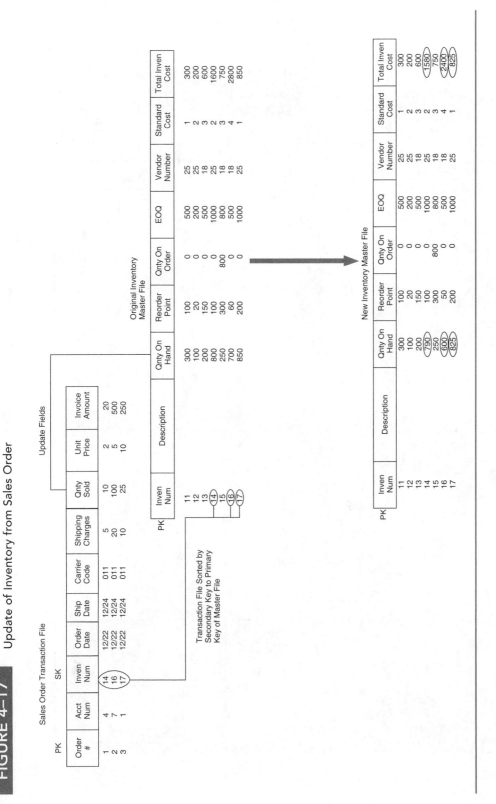

FIGURE 4–17   Update of Inventory from Sales Order

FIGURE 4–18 Batch Sales System with Direct Access Files

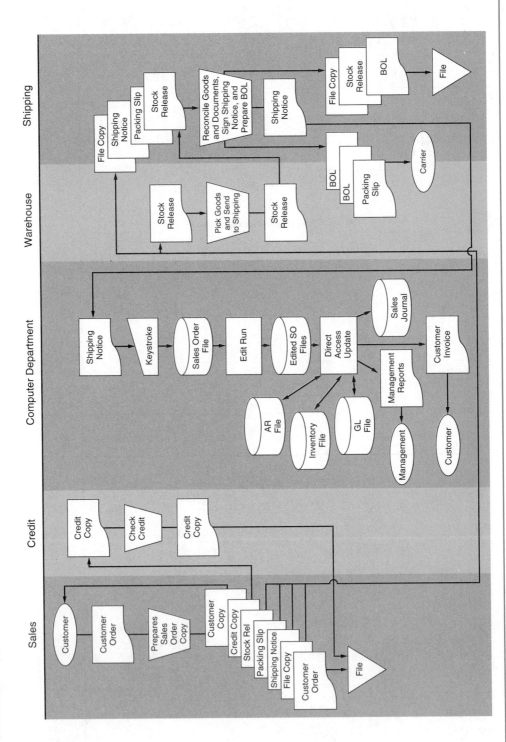

FIGURE 4–19   Direct Access Update of AR and Inventory Files Concurrently

Sales Order Transaction File

PK	SK	SK			
Order #	Acct Num	Inven Num	Qnty Sold	Unit Price	Invoice Amount
1	4	14	10	2	20
2	7	16	100	5	500
3	1	17	25	10	250

Inventory Master File

PK									
Inven Num	Units Received	Units Sold	Qnty on Hand	Reorder Point	Qnty on Order	EOQ	Vendor Number	Standard Cost	Total Inven Cost
11			300	100	0	500	25	1	300
12			100	20	0	200	25	2	400
13			200	150	0	500	18	3	600
14			790	100	0	1000	25	2	1590
15			250	300	800	800	18	3	750
16			600	60	0	500	18	4	2400
17			825	200	0	1000	25	1	825

Master file records are accessed directly and updated in place. This process does not create a new master file.

Accounts Receivable Master

PK					
Acct Num	Address	Current Balance	Credit Limit	Last Payment Date	Billing Date
1	123 Elm St., City	600	1000	12/8/01	1
2	35 Main S.	600	1500	12/12/01	1
3	510 Barclay Dr. Beth.	1000	1500	12/5/01	1
4	26 Taylo Rd. Alltn.	120	2000	12/16/01	8
5	4 High St., Naz.	800	1000	12/9/01	1
6	850 1st, Beth.	700	2000	12/7/01	8
7	78 Market Alltn.	650	2000	12/17/01	15

1. *No sort run.* Since the sequence of transactions is unimportant in direct access procedures, there is no need to sort the transaction file. This saves processing time and computer resources.

2. *Master files are not recreated.* Using the direct access method, the system updates the affected master records in-place. Unlike the sequential approach, this method does not create a new physical master file. There are two advantages to this. First, frequent small batches can be processed efficiently against a large master file. In batch systems with sequential files, the tendency is to process large batches of transactions less frequently to justify the time and cost of recreating the master files. As this is not necessary in direct access systems, processing can be done frequently and files can be kept current. Second, if the general ledger is also a direct access file, it can be updated after each batch, thus providing a more timely reconciliation. With the sequential approach, the general ledger is updated in separate end-of-day procedures.

3. *Greater file versatility.* The direct access files used by one system in batch mode can also be used by other systems in real-time mode. For example, a customer service clerk can use the accounts receivable file to respond to telephone inquiries from customers. Because of the AR file's direct access capability, the clerk can access the file via a real-time inquiry system. The clerk would not be able to retrieve the information directly from a sequential file.

REENGINEERING SALES ORDER PROCESSING WITH REAL-TIME TECHNOLOGY

Figure 4–20 illustrates a reengineered sales order system. Many of the manual procedures and physical documents of the previous system are replaced by interactive computer terminals. This system provides real-time input and output with batch updating of only some master files.

Update Procedures

Sales Procedures. Under real-time processing, sales clerks receiving orders from customers process each transaction separately as it is received. Using a computer terminal connected to an edit/inquiry program, the clerk performs the following tasks in real-time mode:

1. A credit check is performed by directly accessing the customer credit file. This file contains information such as the customer's credit limit, current balance, date of last payment, and current credit status. Based upon programmed criteria, the customer's request for credit is approved or denied.

2. If credit is approved, the clerk then accesses the inventory master file and checks the availability of the inventory. The system reduces inventory by the quantities of items sold to present an accurate and current picture of inventory on hand and available for sale.

3. The system automatically transmits an electronic stock release message to the warehouse and a shipping notice to the shipping department, and records the sale in the open sales order file. The structure of this file includes a CLOSED field that contains either the value N or Y to indicate the status of the order. Closed records (those containing the value Y) have been shipped, so the customer can now be billed. This field is used later to identify closed records to the batch procedure. The default value in this field when the record is created is N. It is changed to Y when the goods are shipped to the customer. The sales clerk can determine the status of an order in response to customer inquires by viewing the records.

FIGURE 4–20   Real-Time Sales Order System

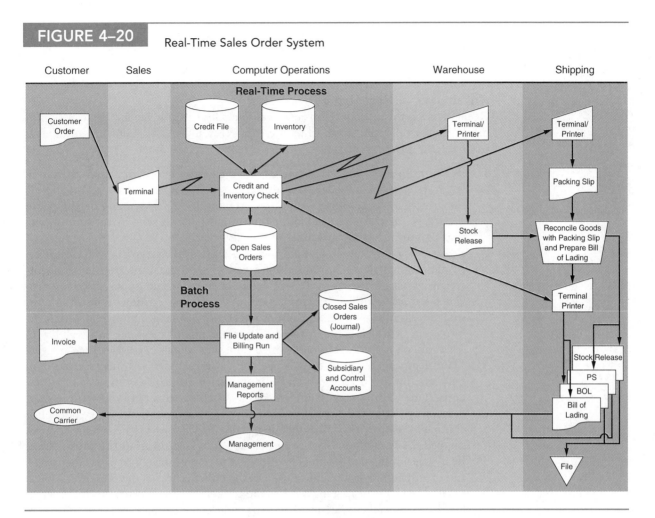

Warehouse Procedures. The warehouse clerk's terminal immediately produces a hard-copy printout of the electronically transmitted stock release document. The clerk then picks the goods and sends them, along with a copy of the stock release document, to the shipping department.

Shipping Department. A shipping clerk reconciles the goods, the stock release document, and the hard-copy packing slip produced on the terminal. The clerk then selects a carrier and prepares the goods for shipment. From the terminal, the clerk transmits to the central computer a shipping notice containing shipping date and freight charges. The shipping clerk updates the open sales order record in real time and places a Y value in the CLOSED field, thus *closing* the sales order.

Master File Update Procedures

At the end of the day, the batch update program searches the open sales order file for records marked closed and updates the following master files: AR-Subsidiary, Inventory-Control, Sales, AR-Control, and Cost of Goods Sold. Recall that the inventory subsidiary file was updated as part of the real-time procedures. The batch program prepares and mails customer bills and transfers the closed sales records to the **closed sales order file**, which is equivalent to the sales journal.

Advantages of Real-Time Processing

Reengineering the sales order processes to include real-time technology can significantly reduce operating costs while increasing revenues. The following advantages make this approach an attractive option for many organizations:

1. Real-time processing greatly shortens the cash cycle of the firm. Lags inherent in batch systems can cause delays of several days between taking an order and billing the customer. A real-time system with remote terminals reduces or eliminates these lags. An order received in the morning may be shipped by early afternoon, thus permitting same-day billing of the customer.

2. Real-time processing can give a firm a competitive advantage in the marketplace. By maintaining current inventory information, sales staff can determine immediately whether the inventories are on hand. In contrast, batch systems do not provide salespeople with current information. As a result, a portion of the order must sometimes be back-ordered, causing uncertainty for the customer. Current information provided through real-time processing enhances the firm's ability to maximize customer satisfaction, which translates to increased sales.

3. Manual procedures tend to produce clerical errors, such as incorrect account numbers, invalid inventory numbers, and price-quantity extension miscalculations. These errors may go undetected in batch systems until the source documents reach data processing, by which time the damage may already be done. For example, the firm may find that it has shipped goods to the wrong address, shipped the wrong goods, or promised goods to a customer at the wrong price. Real-time editing permits the identification of many kinds of errors as they occur and greatly improves the efficiency and the effectiveness of operations.

4. Finally, real-time processing reduces the amount of paper documents in a system. Hard-copy documents are expensive to produce and clutter the system. The permanent storage of these documents can become a financial and operational burden. Documents in electronic form are efficient, effective, and adequate for most audit trail purposes.

BATCH CASH RECEIPTS SYSTEM WITH DIRECT ACCESS FILES

Cash receipts procedures are natural batch systems. Unlike sales transactions, which tend to occur continuously throughout the day, cash receipts are discrete events. Checks and remittance advices arrive from the postal service in batches. Likewise, the deposit of cash receipts in the bank usually happens as a single event at the end of the business day. Because of these characteristics, many firms see no significant benefit from investing in costly real-time cash procedures.

The cash receipts system in Figure 4–21 uses direct access files and batch processing. The technology employed in this example is used to automate traditional procedures. The following discussion outlines the main points of this system.

Update Procedures

Mail Room. The mail room separates the checks and remittance advices and prepares a remittance list. These checks and a copy of the remittance list are sent to the

FIGURE 4-21   Computer-Based Cash Receipts System

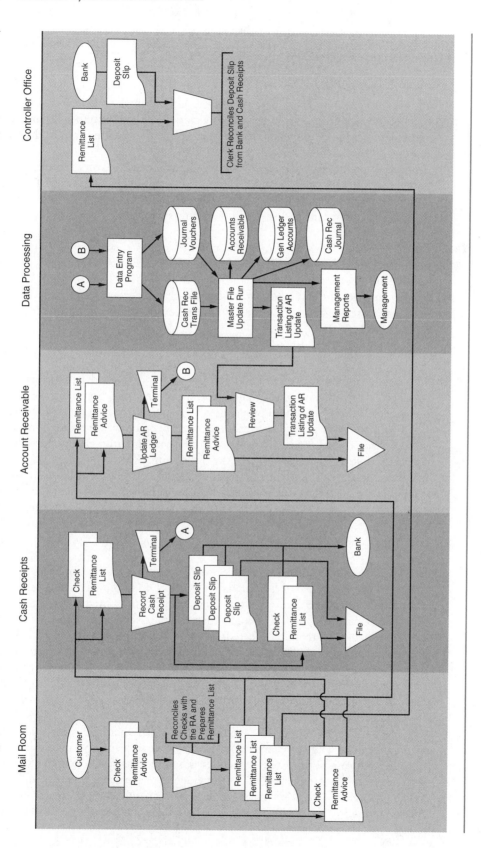

cash receipts department. The remittance advices and a copy of the remittance list go to the accounts receivable department.

Cash Receipts Department. The cash receipts clerk reconciles the checks and the remittance list and prepares the deposit slips. Via terminal, the clerk creates a journal voucher record of total cash received. The clerk files the remittance list and one copy of the deposit slip. At the end of the day, the clerk deposits the cash in the bank.

Accounts Receivable Department. The accounts receivable clerk receives and reconciles the remittance advices and remittance list. Via terminal, the clerk creates the cash receipts transaction file based on the individual remittance advices. The clerk then files the remittance advices and the remittance list.

Data Processing Department. At the end of the day, the batch program reconciles the journal voucher with the transaction file of cash receipts, and updates the AR subsidiary and the general ledger control accounts (AR—Control and Cash). This process employs the direct access method described earlier. Finally, the system produces a transaction listing that the accounts receivable clerk will reconcile against the remittance list.

REENGINEERED CASH RECEIPTS PROCESS

The task of opening envelopes and comparing remittance advices against customer checks is labor intensive, costly, and creates a control risk. Some organizations have reengineered their mail room procedures to effectively reduce the risk and the cost.

The mail room clerk places batches of unopened envelopes into a machine that automatically opens them and separates their contents into remittance advices and checks. Simple logic is used to make the distinction. Since the remittance advice contains the address of the payee organization, it must be placed at the front of the envelope by the customer to be displayed through the window. When the envelope is opened, the machine *knows* that the first document in the envelope is the remittance advice. The second is, therefore, the check. The process is performed internally and, once the envelopes are opened, the documents cannot be accessed by the mail room clerk.

The system uses special transaction validation software that employs artificial intelligence that is capable of reading handwriting. The system scans the remittance advices and the checks to verify that the dollar amounts presented on each are equal and that the checks are signed. Any items that are inconsistent or cannot be interpreted by the validation system are rejected and processed separately by hand. The system prepares a computer-readable file of cash receipts, which is then posted to the appropriate customer and general ledger accounts. Batches of checks are sent to the cash receipts department for deposit in the bank. Transaction listings are sent to management in the accounts receivable, cash receipts, and general ledger departments for review and audit purposes.

The advantages of improved control and reduced operating costs can be achieved by organizations with sufficient transaction volume to justify the investment in hardware and software. The system works best when there is a high degree of consistency between remittance advices and customer checks. Partial payments, multiple payments (a single check covering multiple invoices), and clerical errors on customer checks complicate the process and may cause a high number of rejections that require separate processing.

POINT-OF-SALE (POS) SYSTEMS

The revenue cycle systems that we have examined so far are used by organizations that extend lines of credit to their customers. Obviously, this assumption is not valid for all types of business enterprises. For example, grocery stores do not usually function under this model. They exchange goods directly for cash in a transaction that is consummated at the point of sale.

Point-of-sale (POS) systems like the one shown in Figure 4–22 are used extensively in grocery stores, department stores, and other types of retail organizations. In this example, only cash, checks, and bank credit card sales are valid. The organization maintains no customer accounts receivable. Inventory is kept on the store's shelves, not in a separate warehouse. The customers personally pick the items they wish to buy and carry them to the check-out location, where the transaction begins.

Daily Procedures

First, the check-out clerk scans the **universal product code (UPC)** label on the items being purchased with a laser light scanner. The scanner, which is the primary input device of the POS system, may be hand-held or mounted in the check-out table. The POS system is connected on-line to the inventory file from which it retrieves product price data and displays this on the clerk's terminal. The inventory quantity on hand is reduced in real time to reflect the items sold. As items fall to a minimum levels, they are automatically reordered.

When all the UPCs are scanned, the system automatically calculates taxes, discounts, and the total for the transaction. In the case of credit card transactions, the sales clerk obtains transaction approval from the credit card issuer via an on-line connection. When the approval is returned, the clerk prepares a credit card voucher for the amount of the sale, which the customer signs. The clerk gives the customer one copy of the voucher and secures a second copy in the cash drawer of the register. For cash sales, the customer renders cash for the full amount of the sale, which the clerk secures in the cash drawer.

The clerk enters the transaction into the POS system via the register's keypad and a record of the sale is added to the sales journal in real time. The record contains the following key data: date, time, terminal number, total amount of sale, cash or credit card sale, cost of items sold, sales tax, and discounts taken. The sale is also recorded on a two-part paper tape. One copy is given to the customer as a receipt; the other is secured internally within the register and cannot be accessed by the clerk. This internal tape is later used to close out the register when the clerk's shift is over.

At the end of the clerk's shift, a supervisor unlocks the register and retrieves the internal tape. The cash drawer is removed and replaced with a new cash drawer containing a known amount of start-up cash (float) for the next clerk. The supervisor and the clerk whose shift has ended take the cash drawer to the cash room (treasury), where the contents are reconciled against the internal tape. The cash drawer should contain cash and credit card vouchers equal to the amount recorded on the tape. Very often, small discrepancies will exist due to errors in making change for customers. Organizational policy will specify how cash discrepancies are handled. Some organizations require sales clerks to cover all cash shortages via payroll deductions. Other organizations establish a materiality threshold. Cash shortages within the threshold are recorded but not deducted from the employee's pay. However, excess shortages should be reviewed for possible disciplinary action.

When the contents of the cash drawer have been reconciled, the cash receipts clerk prepares a cash reconciliation form and gives one copy to the sales clerk as a

FIGURE 4–22   Point-of-Sale System

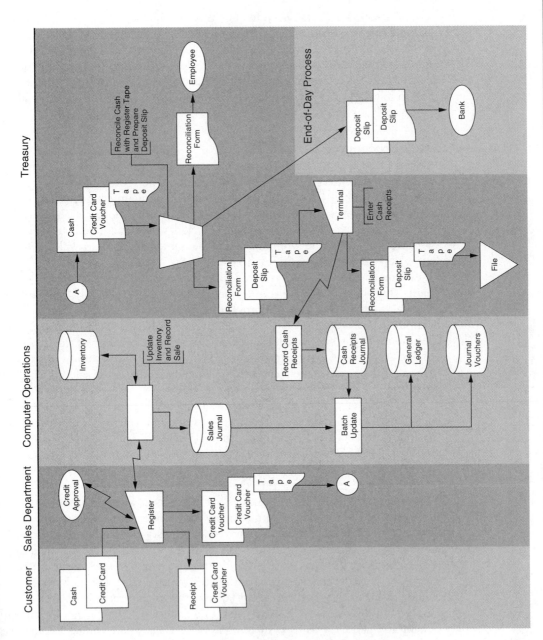

receipt for cash remitted and records cash received and cash short/over in the cash receipts journal. The clerk files the credit card vouchers and secures the cash in the safe for deposit in the bank at the end of the day.

End-of-Day Procedures

At the end of the day, the cash receipts clerk prepares a three-part deposit slip for the total amount of the cash received. One copy is filed and the other two accompany the cash to the bank. Since cash is involved, armed guards are often used to escort the funds to the bank repository.

Finally, a batch program summarizes the sales and cash receipts journals, prepares a journal voucher, and posts to the general ledger accounts as follows:

	DR	CR
Cash	XXXX.XX	
Cash Over/Short	XX.XX	
Account Receivable (credit card)	XXX.XX	
Cost of Goods Sold	XXX.XX	
Sales		XXXX.XX
Inventory		XXX.XX

The accounting entry above may vary among businesses. Some companies will treat credit card sales as cash. Others will maintain an account receivable until the credit card issuer transfers the funds into their account.

REENGINEERING USING EDI

Doing Business via EDI

Many organizations have reengineered their sales order process through **electronic data interchange (EDI)**. EDI technology was devised to expedite routine transactions between manufacturers and wholesalers, and between wholesalers and retailers. The customer's computer is connected directly to the seller's computer via telephone lines. When the customer's computer detects the need to order inventory, it automatically transmits an order to the seller. The seller's system receives the order and processes it automatically. This system requires little or no human involvement.

EDI is more than just a technology. It represents a unique business arrangement between the buyer and seller in which they agree, in advance, to the terms of their relationship. For example, they agree to the selling price, the quantities to be sold, guaranteed delivery times, payment terms, and methods of handling disputes. These terms are binding and codified in a trading partner agreement. Once the agreement is in place, no individual in either the buying or selling company actually authorizes or approves a particular EDI transaction. In its purest form, the exchange is completely automated.

EDI poses unique control problems for an organization. One problem is ensuring that, in the absence of explicit authorization, only valid transactions are processed. Another risk is that a trading partner, or someone masquerading as a trading partner, will access the firm's accounting records in a way that is unauthorized by the trading partner agreement. In Chapter 7, we examine the key features of EDI and its implications for business. Controls over EDI are discussed in Chapter 16.

REENGINEERING USING THE INTERNET

Doing Business on the Internet

Thousands of organizations worldwide are establishing home pages on the Internet to promote their products and solicit sales. By entering the seller's home page address into the Internet communication program from a microcomputer, a potential customer can access the seller's product list, scan the product line, and place an order. Typically, Internet sales are credit card transactions. The customer's order and credit card information is attached to the seller's e-mail file. An employee reviews the order, verifies credit, and enters the transaction into the seller's system for processing in the normal way. Because of the need to review the e-mail file before processing, the turnaround time for processing Internet sales is often longer than for telephone orders. Research is currently underway to develop intelligent agents (software programs) that review and validate Internet orders automatically as they are received.

Unlike EDI, which is a formal business arrangement between trading partners, the Internet connects an organization to the thousands of potential business partners with whom the organization shares no formal agreement. In addition to unprecedented business opportunities, risks for both the seller and the buyer accompany this type of technology. Connecting to the Internet exposes the organization to threats from computer hackers, viruses, and transaction fraud. Many organizations take these threats seriously and implement controls including password techniques, message encryption, and firewalls to minimize their risk. The technology of networks is discussed in Chapter 12. In Chapter 16, we examine techniques for controlling these technologies.

CONTROL CONSIDERATIONS FOR COMPUTER-BASED SYSTEMS

The remainder of this section looks at the relationship between internal controls and alternative processing technologies. We identify the nature of new exposures and gain some insight into their ramifications. Solutions to many of these problems are beyond the level of discussion at this point. Chapters 15 and 16 are devoted to this extensive body of material.

Authorization

The task of transaction authorization in real-time processing systems is automated. Management and accountants should be concerned about the correctness of the computer-programmed decision rules and the quality of the data used in this decision.

In POS systems, the authorization process involves validating credit card charges and establishing that the customer is the valid user of the card. After receiving approval from the credit card company on-line, the clerk should match the customer's signature on the sales voucher with the one on the credit card.

Segregation of Duties

A number of tasks that are normally segregated in manual systems are consolidated in the data processing function of computer-based systems. The computer function now performs inventory control, accounts receivable, billing, and general ledger tasks. As we no longer have task segregation in these areas, our concern focuses on the integrity of the computer programs that perform these tasks. The accountant should seek answers to such questions as: Is the logic of the computer program correct? Has anyone tampered with the application since it was last tested? Have changes been made to the program that could have caused an undisclosed error?

These questions remind the accountant of the need for segregation of duties in the design, maintenance, and operation of computer programs. The programmers who write the original computer programs must not also be responsible for making program changes. Both of these functions must also be separate from the daily task of operating the system.

Supervision

In an earlier discussion, we examined the importance of supervision over cash-handling procedures in the mail room. The individual who opens the mail has access both to cash (the asset) and to the remittance advice (the record of the transaction). A dishonest employee has an opportunity to steal the check and destroy the remittance advice. This risk exists in both manual systems and computer-based systems that use manual mail room procedures.

In a POS system, where both inventory and cash are at risk, supervision is particularly important. Inventory in the POS system can be directly accessed by customers, and the crime of shoplifting is of great concern to management. Supervision in the form of surveillance cameras and shop floor security personnel can reduce the risk. These techniques are also used to observe sales clerks handling cash receipts from customers. In addition, the cash register's internal tape is a form of supervision. The tape contains a record of all sales transactions processed at the register. Only the clerk's supervisor has access to the tape, which is used at the end of the shift to balance the cash drawer.

Access Control

In computerized systems, accounting records are stored on magnetic media that are vulnerable to unauthorized and undetected access. This may take the form of an attempt at fraud, an act of malice by a disgruntled employee, or an honest accident. Additional exposures exist in real-time systems that often maintain accounting records entirely in magnetic form. Without physical source documents for backup, the destruction of magnetic files can leave the firm without adequate accounting records. To preserve the integrity of accounting records, the organization must implement controls that limit file accessibility. Also at risk are the computer programs that make programmed decisions, manipulate accounting records, and permit access to assets. Without proper access controls over programs, a firm can suffer devastating losses to fraud and errors. Adequate access control involves a number of physical and software techniques that we shall cover in depth in Chapter 15.

Since POS systems involve cash transactions, the organization must establish accountability for the cash asset by restricting access to it. One method is to assign each sales clerk to a separate cash register for an entire shift. When the clerk leaves the register to take a break, the cash drawer should be locked to prevent unauthorized access. This can be accomplished with a physical lock and key or by a password lock. If clerks are required to share registers, responsibility for asset custody is split among them and accountability is lost. At the end of the clerk's shift, he or she should remove the cash drawer and immediately deposit the funds in the cash room.

Inventory in the POS system must also be protected from unauthorized access and theft. This can be achieved by both physical restraints and electronic devices. For example, steel cables are often used in clothing stores to secure expensive leather coats to the clothing rack. Locked showcases are used to display jewelry and costly electronic equipment. Magnetic tags can be attached to merchandise, which will sound an alarm when removed from the store.

Accounting Records

Journals. The audit trail is affected in a direct way when key documents such as journals are maintained on magnetic storage devices. Accountants should be skeptical about accepting, on face value, the accuracy of computer-produced hard-copy printouts of these files. The reliability of facsimile documents for auditing and accounting purposes rests directly on the quality of the controls that protect their magnetic sources from unauthorized manipulation.

Ledgers. The organization's ledgers are also in magnetic form. These master files are the basis for financial reporting and many internal decisions. Again, the accountant should be concerned about the quality of controls over the programs that update, manipulate, and produce reports from these files.

Sequential File Backup. The physical loss, destruction, or corruption of accounting records is a concern associated with computer systems. The sequential file update approach provides an effective method for reducing the risk. By providing backup files automatically, a firm can reconstruct a destroyed master file from the latest existing version of the file and its corresponding transaction file.

Direct Access File Backup. A significant control implication of the direct access approach is its effect on file backup. The direct access update method does not recreate the master file. Therefore, file backup requires separate procedures before the update run. This technique was discussed in Chapter 2. Backup activities are performed by the data processing department behind the scenes and may not be shown on the system flowchart. The accountant should verify that such procedures are performed for all subsidiary and general ledger files. Although backup requires significant time and computer resources, these procedures are essential in preserving the integrity of accounting records stored on direct access files.

Independent Verification

The consolidation of accounting tasks under one computer functional area removes some of the independent verification control from the system. Independent verification is restored somewhat by performing batch control balancing after each run and by producing management reports and summaries for end users to review.

MICROCOMPUTER-BASED ACCOUNTING SYSTEMS

There are hundreds of microcomputer accounting systems on the market. In contrast to mainframe systems that are usually custom-designed to meet the specific requirements of their users, microcomputer applications are designed to be general-purpose systems that can serve a wide range of needs. This strategy allows software vendors to mass-produce error-free standard products that retail in the range of $200 to $2,000. Not surprisingly, microcomputer accounting systems are popular with smaller firms that use them to automate their manual systems and become more efficient and competitive. Microcomputer systems have also made inroads with larger companies that have downsized and decentralized their operations. Constantly declining hardware costs and ever-increasing computing power has spurred the recent growth in end-user computing that most certainly will continue.

Most microcomputer systems are modular in design. Typical business modules include sales order processing and accounts receivable, purchases and accounts payable, cash receipts, cash disbursements, general ledger and financial reporting, inventory control, and payroll. Their modular design provides users with some degree of flexibility in tailoring systems to their specific needs. However, many vendors target their products to the unique needs of specific industries, such as health care, transportation, and food services. By so doing, these firms forgo the advantages of flexibility to achieve a market niche. The modular design technique is illustrated in Figure 4–23.

The central control program provides the user interface to the system. From this control point, the user makes menu selections to invoke application modules as needed. By selecting the sales module, for instance, the user can enter customer orders in real time. At the end of the day, in batch mode, the user can enter cash receipts, purchases, and payroll transactions.

Commercial systems usually have fully integrated modules. This means that data transfers between modules occur automatically. For example, an integrated system will ensure that all transactions captured by the various modules have been balanced and posted to subsidiary and general ledger accounts before the general ledger module produces the financial reports.

MICROCOMPUTER CONTROL ISSUES

Microcomputer accounting systems create unique control problems for accountants. The risks arise from weaknesses that are inherent to the microcomputer environment. These are briefly discussed below. Specific control techniques for dealing with these exposures are covered in Chapter 16.

Segregation of Duties

Microcomputer systems tend to have inadequate segregation of duties. An individual may be responsible for entering all transaction data, including sales orders, cash

FIGURE 4–23

Microcomputer
Accounting
System Modules

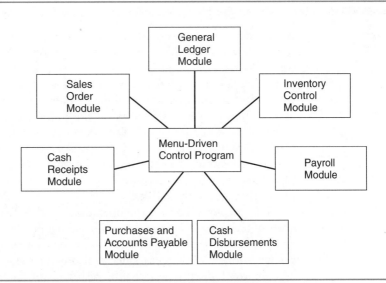

receipts, invoices, and disbursements. In a manual system, this degree of authority would be similar to assigning accounts receivable, accounts payable, cash receipts, and cash disbursement responsibilities to the same person. The exposure is compounded when the individual is also responsible for developing (programming) the application he or she runs.

There may be little that can be done in small companies to avoid these conflicts of duties. Controlling the microcomputer environment requires a high degree of supervision, adequate management reports (such as detailed listings of all transactions), and frequent independent verification. For example, the accountant or a supervisor should reconcile daily transaction details with the affected subsidiary and control accounts.

Access Control

Microcomputer systems generally provide inadequate control over access to data files. While some applications achieve modest security through password control to the files, this control can often be circumvented by accessing the data files directly via the operating system. Solutions for dealing with the problem include data encryption, disk locks, and physical security devices.

Accounting Records

The microcomputer environment is plagued by data losses that threaten accounting records and audit trails. Computer disk failure is the primary cause of data loss. When this happens, recovery of the data stored on the disk may be impossible. Formal procedures for creating backup copies of data files and programs can reduce this threat considerably. In a mainframe environment, backup is provided automatically. However, making backup files in the microcomputer environment requires a conscious action by the users, who often fail to appreciate the importance of the act until it is too late.

Summary

Business enterprises generate revenues through formal activities that constitute their revenue cycle. Most organizations function on a credit basis, whereby some time passes between the point of sale and the receipt of cash. This time lag splits the revenue cycle into two major subsystems: (1) the sales order processing subsystem and (2) the cash receipts subsystem. This chapter examined the revenue cycle of a typical merchandising firm and focused on the following areas: (1) the functional departments of the revenue cycle and the flow of transaction information that links them; (2) the documents, journals, and accounts that provide audit trails, promote the maintenance of historical records, support internal decision making, and support financial reporting; and (3) the exposure to risks in the revenue cycle and the control techniques that reduce these risks.

The chapter examined the operational and control implications of different degrees of technology. First, we examined batch processing techniques. These methods improve record keeping efficiency and effectiveness but have little impact on physical operations. We then examined real-time processing and its effect on operations. This approach greatly shortens the cash cycle of the firm and can provide a competitive advantage by improving operational effectiveness. The current information provided through real-time processing enhances the firm's ability to make sales and promote customer satisfaction. In addition, real-time processing reduces the amount of paper documents in a system.

Next, we turned to control issues in an electronic environment and found that computer processing consolidates many processes, thus removing some traditional segregation of duties. The integrity of the computer programs that now perform these tasks becomes a matter of great concern to the organization. We also saw that magnetic transaction files replace the traditional sales and cash receipts journals in an electronic environment and are an important component of the audit trail. The organization must, therefore, control access to its accounting files and the programs that update and manipulate them. Finally, we examined the important issue of data backup. Sequential file updating techniques create backup files automatically. However, direct access files require separate backup procedures.

The final section in this chapter dealt with the subject of microcomputer accounting systems. The modular design of these systems allows users to tailor the system to their specific needs. This feature has resulted in a tremendous growth in end-user computing that is changing the way many organizations do business. The microcomputer environment poses some unique exposures that accountants must recognize. Three of the most serious exposures are (1) the lack of properly segregated duties; (2) microcomputer operating systems that do not have the sophistication of mainframes, making it particularly difficult to restrict access to data; and (3) computer failures and inadequate backup procedures that rely too heavily on human intervention and thus threaten the security of accounting records.

Key Terms

accounts receivable   (178)
accounts receivable subsidiary ledger   (178)
automation   (191)
back-order   (176)
batch control totals   (194)
bill of lading   (174)
cash receipts journal   (183)
closed sales order file   (202)
controller   (186)
credit authorization   (174)
credit memo   (179)
credit memo file   (190)
customer open order file   (170)
customer order   (170)
cycle billing   (194)
deposit slip   (183)
electronic data interchange (EDI)   (207)
file copy   (176)
inventory subsidiary ledger   (177)

journal voucher   (176)
journal voucher file   (177)
ledger copy   (176)
open sales order file   (190)
packing slip   (174)
point-of-sale (POS) systems   (205)
prenumbered source documents   (189)
price data reference file   (190)
reengineering   (191)
remittance advice   (183)
remittance list   (183)
sales history file   (190)
sales invoice   (176)
sales journal   (176)
sales order   (170)
shipping notice   (174)
shipping report file (shipping log)   (190)
stock release (picking ticket)   (174)
universal product code (UPC)   (205)

Review Questions

1. What document initiates the sales process?
2. Distinguish between a packing slip, shipping notice, and a bill of lading.
3. What function does the receiving department serve in the revenue cycle?
4. The general ledger clerk receives summary data from which departments? What form of summary data?
5. What are three authorization controls?
6. What are the three rules that ensure that no single employee or department processes a transaction in its entirety?
7. At which points in the revenue cycle are independent verification controls necessary?
8. What is automation and why is it used?
9. What is the objective of reengineering?
10. Distinguish between an edit run, sort run, and update run.
11. What are the key features of a point-of-sale system?
12. How is the primary key critical in preserving the audit trail?
13. What are the advantages of real-time processing?
14. Why does billing receive a copy of the sales order when the order is approved but does not bill until the goods are shipped?
15. Why was EDI devised?
16. What types of unique control problems are created by the use of microcomputer accounting systems?

Discussion Questions

1. Why do firms have separate departments for warehousing and shipping? What about warehousing and inventory control? Doesn't this just create more paperwork?
2. Distinguish between the sales order, billing, and accounts receivable departments. Why can't the sales order or accounts receivable departments prepare the bills?
3. Explain the purpose of having mail room procedures.
4. In a manual accounting system, what advantage does the journal voucher system have over the traditional general journal system?
5. How could an employee embezzle funds by issuing an unauthorized sales credit memo if the appropriate segregation of duties and authorization controls were not in place?
6. What task can the accounts receivable department engage in to verify that all checks sent by the customers have been appropriately deposited and recorded?
7. Why is access control over revenue cycle documents just as important as the physical control devices over cash and inventory?
8. How can reengineering of the sales order processing subsystem be accomplished by using the Internet?
9. For a batch processing system using sequential files, describe the intermediate and permanent files that are created after the edit run has successfully been completed when processing the sales order file and updating the accounts receivable and inventory master files.
10. Why has the use of magnetic tapes as a storage medium declined in recent years? What are their primary uses currently?
11. Discuss both the tangible and intangible benefits of real-time processing.
12. Discuss how the nature of the necessary internal control features is affected by switching from a manual system to:
    a. a large-scale computer-based accounting system, or
    b. a microcomputer-based accounting system.
13. Under what circumstances will automated mail room procedures provide the most benefit? The least benefit?
14. What makes point-of-sale systems different from revenue cycles of manufacturing firms?
15. Is a point-of-sale system that uses bar coding and a laser light scanner foolproof against inaccurate updates? Discuss.
16. How is EDI more than technology? What unique control problems may it pose?

Multiple-Choice Questions

1. Which document is NOT prepared by the sales department?
   a. packing slip
   b. shipping notice
   c. bill of lading
   d. stock release
2. Which document triggers the update of the inventory subsidiary ledger?
   a. bill of lading
   b. stock release
   c. sales order
   d. shipping notice
3. Which function should NOT be performed by the billing department?
   a. Record the sales in the sales journal.
   b. Send the ledger copy of the sales order to accounts receivable.
   c. Send the stock release document and the shipping notice to the billing department as proof of shipment.
   d. Send the stock release document to inventory control.
4. When will a credit check approval most likely require specific authorization by the credit department?
   a. when verifying that the current transaction does not exceed the customer's credit limit
   b. when verifying that the current transaction is with a valid customer
   c. when a valid customer places a materially large order
   d. when a valid customer returns goods
5. Which type of control is considered to be a mitigating control?
   a. segregation of duties
   b. access control
   c. supervision
   d. accounting records
6. Which of the following is NOT an independent verification control?
   a. The shipping department verifies that the goods sent from the warehouse are correct in type and quantity.
   b. General ledger clerks reconcile journal vouchers that were independently prepared in various departments.
   c. The use of prenumbered sales orders.

   d. The billing department reconciles the shipping notice with the sales invoice to ensure that customers are billed for only the quantities shipped.
7. CMA Adapted 684 3-29
   Which one of the following poses the biggest threat with respect to potential losses?
   a. The petty cash custodian has the ability to steal petty cash. Documentation for all disbursements from the fund must be submitted with the request for replenishment of the fund.
   b. An inventory control clerk at a manufacturing plant has the ability to steal one completed television set from inventory a year. The theft probably will never be detected.
   c. An accounts receivable clerk, who approves sales returns and allowances, receives customer remittances and deposits them in the bank. Limited supervision is maintained over the employee.
   d. A clerk in the invoice processing department fails to match a vendor's invoice with its related receiving report. Checks are not signed unless all appropriate documents are attached to a voucher.
   e. An accounting clerk has the ability to record unauthorized journal entries. All journal entries are reviewed by an accounting department supervisor each month.
8. CMA 1288 3-26
   In a well-designed internal control structure in which the cashier receives remittances from the mail room, the cashier should not
   a. endorse the checks.
   b. prepare the bank deposit slip.
   c. deposit remittances daily at a local bank.
   d. prepare a list of mail receipts.
   e. post the receipts to the accounts receivable subsidiary ledger.
9. CMA 689 3-15
   Which of the following situations represents an internal control weakness in accounts receivable?
   a. Internal auditors confirm customer accounts periodically.
   b. Delinquent accounts are reviewed only by the sales manager.

c. The cashier is denied access to customers' records and monthly statements.

d. Customers' statements are mailed monthly by the accounts receivable department.

e. Customers' subsidiary records are maintained by someone who has no access to cash.

Problems

1. Systems Description

Describe the procedures, documents, and departments involved when insufficient inventory is available to fill a customer's approved order.

2. Batch Processing

Refer to Figure 4–15 in the chapter and explain where the batch totals come from and which accounts in the general ledger are affected in the end-of-day batch process.

3. CMA Adapted 1287 5-7 through 5-12 Document Flowchart Analysis

Use the flowchart in the next column to answer the following questions:

a. The customer checks accompanied by the control tape (refer to Symbol A) would be forwarded to whom?

b. The appropriate description that should be placed in Symbol B would be what?

c. The next action to take with the customer remittance advices (refer to Symbol C) would be to do what?

d. The appropriate description that should be placed in Symbol D would be what?

e. The appropriate description that should be placed in Symbol E would be what?

f. The flowchart can be best described as representing what type of processing system?

4. CMA Adapted 690 5-1 through 5-5 Document Authorization and Transfer

Marport Company is a manufacturing company that uses forms and documents in its accounting information systems for record keeping and internal control. The departments in Marport's organizational structure and their primary responsibilities are shown in the table on the next page. Using this information, answer the following questions.

Problem 3: Document Flowchart Analysis

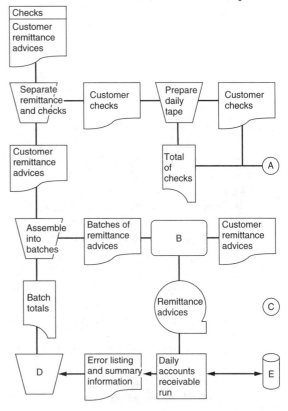

a. The initiation of the purchase of materials and supplies would be the responsibility of what department?

b. The document generated by the department identified in (a) above to initiate the purchasing process would be what?

c. Multiple copies of the purchase order are prepared for record keeping and distribution with one copy sent to the vendor and one retained by the purchasing department. In addition, for proper information flow and internal control purposes, a version of the purchase order

Problem 4: Document Authorization and Transfer

Accounts payable—authorize payments and prepare vouchers	Payroll—compute and prepare the company payroll
Accounts receivable—maintain customer accounts	Personnel—hire employees, as well as maintain records on job positions and employees
Billing—prepare invoices to customers for goods sold	Purchasing—place orders for materials and supplies
Cashier—maintain a record of cash receipts and disbursements	Production—manufacture finished goods
Credit department—verify the credit rating of customers	Production planning—decide the types and quantities of products to be produced
Cost accounting—accumulate manufacturing costs for all goods produced	Receiving—receive all materials and supplies
Finished goods storeroom—maintain the physical inventory and related stock records of finished goods	Sales—accept orders from customers
General accounting—maintain all records for the company's general ledger	Shipping—ship goods to customers
Internal audit—appraise and monitor internal controls, as well as conduct operational and management audits	Stores control—safeguard all materials and supplies until needed for production
Inventory control—maintain perpetual inventory records for all manufacturing materials and supplies	Timekeeping—prepare and control time worked by hourly employees
Mail room—process incoming, outgoing, and interdepartmental mail	

would be distributed to what other departments?

d. What documents must the accounts payable department review before it can properly authorize payment for the purchase of materials and supplies?

e. Which document is used to transfer responsibility for goods between the seller of goods and a common carrier?

5. **CMA Adapted**
Segregation of Functions
Refer to the Marport Company in Problem 4 and determine whether the following situations rep-

resent a proper segregation of functions in the processing of orders from customers.

a. Invoice preparation by the billing department and posting to the customers' accounts by the accounts receivable department.

b. Approval of a sales credit memo because of a product return by the sales department with subsequent posting to the customer's account by the accounts receivable department.

c. Shipping of goods by the shipping department that have been retrieved from stock by the finished goods storeroom department.

d. Posting to the appropriate general ledger accounts by general accounting on the basis of batch totals prepared and verified by the billing department.

6. CMA 688 5-2
Internal Controls

Jem Clothes, Inc. is a 25-store chain, concentrated in the Northeast, that sells ready-to-wear clothes for young men and women. Each store has a full-time manager and an assistant manager, both of whom are paid a salary. The cashiers and sales personnel are typically young people working part-time who are paid an hourly wage plus a commission based on sales volume. The accompanying flowchart on the following page depicts the flow of a sales transaction through the organization of a typical store. The company uses unsophisticated cash registers with four-part sales invoices to record each transaction. These sales invoices are used regardless of the payment type (cash, check, or bank card).

On the sales floor, the salesperson manually records his or her employee number and the transaction (clothes, class, description, quantity, and unit price), totals the sales invoice, calculates the discount when appropriate, calculates the sales tax, and prepares the grand total. The salesperson then gives the sales invoice to the cashier, retaining one copy in the sales book.

The cashier reviews the invoice and inputs the sale. The cash register mechanically validates the invoice by automatically assigning a consecutive number to the transaction. The cashier is also responsible for getting credit approval on charge sales and approving sales paid by check. The cashier gives one copy of the invoice to the customer and retains the second copy as a store copy and the third for a bank card, if deposit is needed. Returns are handled in exactly the reverse manner, with the cashier issuing a return slip.

At the end of each day, the cashier sequentially orders the sales invoices and takes cash register totals for cash, bank card, and check sales, and cash and bank card returns. These totals are reconciled by the assistant manager to the cash register tapes, the total of the consecutively numbered sales invoices, and the return slips. The assistant manager prepares a daily reconciliation report for the store manager's review.

Cash, check, and bank card sales are reviewed by the manager, who then prepares the daily bank deposit (bank card sales invoices are included in the deposit). The manager makes the deposit at the bank and files the validated deposit slip.

The cash register tapes, sales invoices, and return slips are then forwarded daily to the central data processing department at corporate headquarters for processing. The data processing department returns a weekly sales and commission activity report to the manager for review.

a. Identify six strengths in the Jem Clothes system for controlling sales transactions.
b. For each strength identified, explain what problem(s) Jem Clothes has avoided by incorporating the strength in the system for controlling sales transactions.

Use the following format in preparing your answer.

1. *Strength*   2. *Problem(s) Avoided*

7. Stewardship

Identify which department has stewardship over the following journals, ledgers, and files:
a. Customer open order file
b. Sales journal
c. Journal voucher file
d. Cash receipts journal
e. Inventory subsidiary ledger
f. Accounts receivable subsidiary ledger
g. Sales history file
h. Shipping report file
i. Credit memo file
j. Sales order file
k. Closed sales order file

8. Control Weaknesses

For the past 11 years, Elaine Wright has been an employee of the Star-Bright Electrical Supply store. Elaine is a very diligent employee who rarely calls in sick and takes her vacation days staggered throughout the year so that no one else gets bogged down with her tasks for more than one day. Star-Bright is a small store that employs only four people other than the owner. The owner and one of the employees help customers with their electrical needs. One of the employees handles all receiving, stocking, and shipping of merchandise. Another employee handles the purchasing, payroll, general ledger, inventory, and accounts payable functions. Elaine handles all of the point-of-sale cash receipts and prepares the

Problem 6: Internal Controls

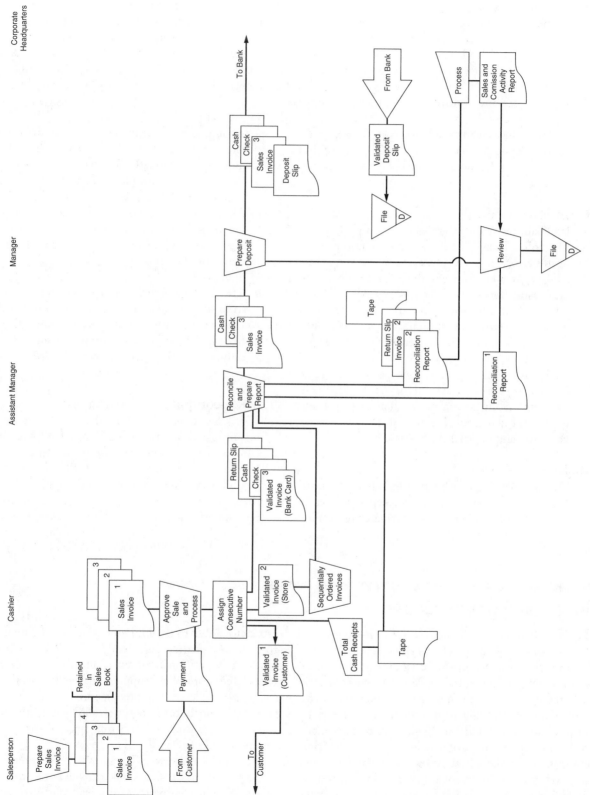

daily deposits for the business. Furthermore, Elaine opens the mail and deposits all cash receipts (about 30 percent of the total daily cash receipts). Elaine also keeps the accounts receivable records and bills the customers who purchase on credit.

a. Point out any control weaknesses you see in the above scenario.

b. List some recommendations to remedy any weaknesses you have found working under the constraint that no additional employees can be hired.

9. Internal Control

Iris Plant owns and operates three floral shops in Magnolia, Texas. The accounting functions have been performed manually. Each of the shops has a manager who oversees the cash receipts and purchasing functions for the shop. All bills are sent to the central shop and are paid by a clerk who also prepares payroll checks and maintains the general journal. Iris is seriously considering switching to a computerized system. With so many information systems packages on the market, Iris is overwhelmed. Advise Iris as to which business modules you think her organization could find beneficial. Discuss advantages, disadvantages, and internal control issues.

10. Internal Control

You are investing your money and opening a fast-food Mexican restaurant that accepts only cash for payments. You plan on periodically issuing

coupons through the mail and in local newspapers. You are particularly interested in access controls over inventory and cash. Design a carefully controlled system and draw a document flowchart to represent it. Identify and discuss the key control issues.

11. Data Processing

The computer processing portion of a sales order system is represented by the flowchart on the following page. Answer the following questions:

a. What type of data processing system is this? Explain, and be specific.

b. The auditor suggests that this system can be greatly simplified by changing to direct access files. Explain the major operational changes that would occur in the system if this were done.

c. The auditor warns of control implications from this change that must be considered. Explain the nature of the control implications.

d. Sketch a flowchart (the computerized portion only) of the proposed new system. Use correct symbols and label the diagram.

12. Microcomputer AIS packages

Visit a microcomputer store that carries accounting information system packages. Examine and compare four packages on cost, capabilities (number of business modules), file constraints, flexibility, built-in controls, and support. Rank these systems and write a report supporting your recommendation.

Internal Control Cases

1. Teddy's Toys Wholesale Distributors
(Prepared by Cheryl Padula, Lehigh University)

Teddy's Toys is a medium-sized wholesale distributor of toys and games, located in Pennsylvania, that distributes throughout the northeastern portion of the United States. An English entrepreneur, Theodore E. Bear, established Teddy's in 1990. His previous experience as vice president of a major toy manufacturing company in England led Ted to take his talents overseas to try to create his own toy distribution center. Teddy's competition is limited to a few other small

distributors, due to the limited region and the type of stores to which they sell. Teddy's size and cost base prevent competition between it and large manufacturers. Ted wanted to supply the smaller localized chains and single-standing retail stores around the region. His distribution center would handle the accounts of these smaller stores that larger distribution centers would not handle.

Ted was a risk-taker. He supplied the common, always popular lines of toys, but also held inventory of some select lines of toys that were relatively unknown.

Problem 11: Data Processing

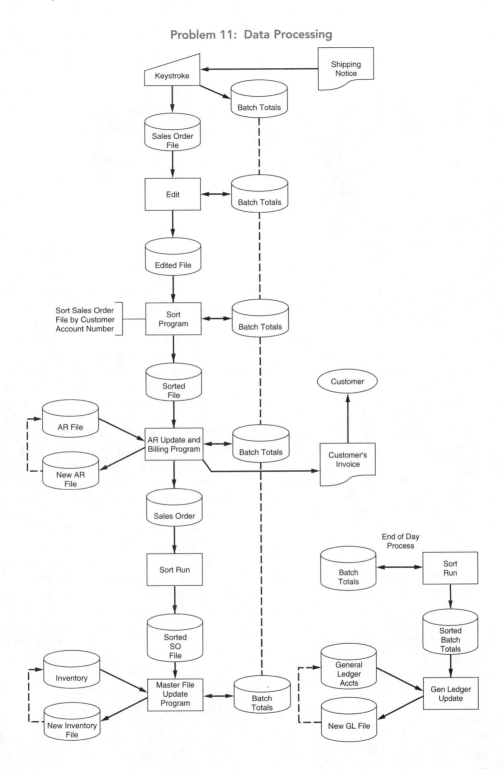

One toy in particular was one that held massive popularity in England due to its widely viewed children's television show. Ted brought a large supply with him to the United States in hopes that the popularity of the toy would make its way overseas. The TV show started to sweep the United States, and toys from the show were in high demand. Since Teddy's was the only distribution center of its size to carry such a large stock of this particular toy, sales skyrocketed, causing the company to grow extremely rapidly.

The company currently employs 150 people full-time with many temporary workers hired for seasonal work. Sales are currently at $28 million and growing. The company does business with 10 large wholesale suppliers and various small suppliers. Teddy's has a large stock investment with ordering lead times of 2–3 days for shipment to their customers on in-stock items and 7–10 days for out-of-stock items.

There are certain supplier problems that plague the company. Seasonal stock outs occur as well as excess inventories of products that don't sell. Because Ted is such a risk-taker by supplying different and unique items, there is an excess of inventory that raises carrying costs and takes up shelf space.

During the rapid expansion of the company, Ted concentrated more on developing a good reputation with a high level of customer satisfaction and creating a fun but stable work environment for his employees. Now that the company is firmly established and growing at a steady pace, Ted has the opportunity to take a step back and evaluate the system as a whole to identify current and potential problems that have surfaced throughout the daily operations.

One evening over dinner with his friend Ernie N. Bertrand, who happens to be a consultant with a large accounting firm, Ted began discussing company problems. Always willing to help a friend, Ernie encouraged Ted to describe the company's revenue cycle so he could determine where the bugs were.

"Okay, here goes. Our excellent sales staff out in the field brings in all the new customers. Each salesperson has his or her own territory to cover, but there still exists a high level of competition between them for new customers and sales quotas. They work on commission, which really motivates a worker. One salesperson in particular does an excellent job, we call him 'Mr. Wizard' because he always seems to be able to conjure up a new customer or a sale whenever he needs one. He is either extremely lucky or magical. He always seems to find the customers with the right credit history as well, since they do all approvals for credit lines themselves.

"All sales orders are taken over the phone by the customer service department. The representatives get calls from the pre-approved customers for inventory checks and to place orders. We have a serious customer satisfaction problem here because of the inventory levels problem we talked about earlier. After checking the inventory and placing the order, they later find out from the warehouse that the inventory they ordered is not on the shelf, even though it is in the records. Or sometimes, the records will have one amount when they are checking the levels and another when they actually place the order. The customer service manager, Sheera, says the representatives are reluctant to call customers back when they find out the inventory is not available. Instead, they allow the order to go through and place what is not available on back-order. The customer doesn't find out until after the shipment is received. Usually this is not a problem, but sometimes I receive calls from angry customers. This happens so infrequently, however, that they just continue to follow this practice. Sheera does not want to force the employees to deal with an irate customer. Once an order is placed, the computer system automatically removes the items from inventory in real time.

"Two times a day, the customer service department generates the picks, which are basically the stock release and packing slip in one. The picks are taken to the warehouse, where the manager, Barbie, takes them to distribute to her workers. Barbie hands the picks to each of her workers to take the inventory off the shelf and pack it accordingly. She has the employees work independently because she feels more work will get done, especially during the busy season when we bring in temporary help. One problem we can't seem to get rid of is inventory disappearing off the shelves, especially during the busy season. A lot of merchandise seems to walk right off the shelves as soon as Christmas hits. It is almost as if the seasonal help feel we are their personal department store. No matter how many supervisors we can spare to put back there, we just can't stop it. Maybe you can help me with that one? Anyway, to continue, Barbie also has Ken's department staff clerk help her when he has slack time in his department. It should be a good use of their idle time, but sometimes the two don't accomplish much when working together.

"Once the items are packed and ready to go, Barbie enters the information for shipping into a terminal to update the records and generate two copies of the bill of lading. One copy of the bill of lading is sent with the packages and the other is filed with the second copy of the packing slip. The shipper collects merchandise twice a day. At the end of each day, a batch run is completed to update the sales journal, and the accounts receivable subsidiary and general ledger control accounts. This process also automatically generates sales invoices for each shipment sent, which are printed and mailed by the cash receipts department."

"Okay, what about the cash receipts system?" said Ernie.

"All checks from the customers are received in our mail room. During the peak season, we bring in temporary workers from the local college to help out, but we have had problems with the theft of checks. This was discovered after large number of customers called to complain that their accounts did not reflect payments they had made.

"Once all the checks are gathered for the day, they are placed inside a bin outside the office of Bill, the supervisor. He has a lot of paperwork each day so he stays in his office most of the time, with the door closed to drown out workers' voices. Bill reconciles the checks to the remittance advices and prepares the remittance list, which he sends with the checks to the accounts receivable department. The accounts receivable clerk, Ritche, records the receipts in the cash receipts journal and the accounts receivable account on his computer before preparing the deposit. He then prepares the deposit slips and takes the checks and slips to the bank before his lunch break. He also files a copy of the checks received and deposit slips in his files along with the remittance advices and list. Again, all posting to the general ledger is done at the end of the day in one batch. One particular problem we have in this department is an unusually high number of bad debts. I'm not sure what causes this, but I really would like to bring that number down.

"Whew! That was a lot of explaining. I hope you get the general picture of what is going on. It is a little difficult to tell someone, rather than show them, your daily operations. Well, what do you think, Ernie?"

Required:
1. Create a data flow diagram of the current system.
2. Create a document flowchart of the existing system.
3. Analyze the internal control weaknesses in the system. Model your response according to the six categories of physical control activities specified in SAS 78.
4. Prepare a system flowchart of a redesigned computer-based system that resolves the control weaknesses that you identified.

2. Get Wet Pool Supply Company
(Prepared by Jana Clark and Amy Hamilton, Lehigh University)

Get Wet Company is currently one of the fastest-growing pool supply companies in the industry. The company is located in Florida, with company headquarters in Tampa and two branch stores in Miami and Panama City. Get Wet employs 50 people at the retail stores and about 100 employees at the headquarters. The retail store employees are hired to perform many of the mundane tasks involved with the business. These individuals are younger and less experienced and, as a result, Get Wet has a high employee turnover rate. Also, due to their rapid growth, the company is always looking to hire new employees.

Get Wet offers its customers a wide variety of products, including flotation devices (rafts and inner tubes), pool toys, pool chemicals, and basic pool-cleaning items. The supply company has a customer base that includes private pool owners and small municipal townships. Due to the wide array of products Get Wet offers its customers, the company relies on numerous vendors to fulfill its needs. These vendors include chemical suppliers, pool-cleaning item suppliers, and pool toy suppliers. Also, Get Wet relies on a general supplier, Speedy, for basic swimming and pool needs. The supplies are delivered to the company headquarters in Tampa and later distributed to the retail stores for storage in their stockrooms.

Get Wet's two branch stores have a history of seasonal sales because of the nature of the pool supply industry. Summer is by far the busiest season, due in part to tourism. In addition to these profits, Get Wet has recently landed a large account from Waterworld USA, one of Florida's largest water parks. Get Wet's president, John Poole, is delighted with the direction his company is headed, but he also feels the company may not be completely ready for this growth. It currently employs both low-level computer technology and manual procedures in its accounting system. John feels the system needs to be revised in order to ensure that the company will be able to handle the new accounts now and in the future.

Revenue Cycle
Corey Chlorine, Get Wet's leading salesperson, contacts customers by phone and captures the details of the customer's order. He then prepares six copies of the sales order, which are sent to the warehouse and billing department.

Wally Water, the warehouse department supervisor, feels that having the warehouse and shipping processes combined into one department is very efficient. He feels that as the supervisor he is better able to control inventory and is constantly aware of what is coming in or going out. From the sales department, Wally receives two copies of the stock release, the packing slip and the shipping notice. A copy of both the stock release and shipping notice are then sent to the billing department, while the other stock release is used to update inventory. The packing slip, along with two copies of the bill of lading, is sent to the carrier. Once inventory has been updated, the journal voucher is sent to the general ledger department.

Greta Billings, the clerk in the billing department, receives the invoice and ledger copy of the sales order from Corey. Once she has received the shipping notice and stock release from the warehouse and shipping department, she sends the invoice to the customer and records the transaction in the sales journal. Then she sends a journal voucher to the general ledger department. The ledger copy of the invoice is sent to accounts receivable for updating the subsidiary ledger.

Yurr Price, the accounts receivable clerk, is responsible for a variety of tasks. In addition to updating customer accounts using the ledger copy he receives from billing, Yurr also has an important role in the cash receipts system. He receives the check and remittance advice from the mail room, which he then uses to update the cash receipts journal. Once this has been completed, Yurr deposits the check in the bank and uses the remittance advice to update customers' accounts. The cash receipts journal voucher and account summary are then sent to the general ledger department.

Required:
1. Create a data flow diagram of the current system.
2. Create a document flowchart of the existing system.
3. Analyze the internal control weaknesses in the system. Model your response according to the six categories of physical control activities specified in SAS 78.
4. Prepare a system flowchart of a redesigned computer-based system that resolves the control weaknesses that you identified.

3. Trenton Net Company, Inc.
(Prepared by Sarah Swift and Jill Holloran, Lehigh University)

Trenton Net Company, Inc. was established in 1953 as a family-run manufacturer of nets, largely supplying the fishing industry. It has two manufacturing plants, one located in Trenton, New Jersey, and the other in Jonesport, Maine. As the fishing industry began to decline in Maine, Trenton Net expanded into different market segments to stay in business. As they diversified their products, the magnitude of their business expanded. Their products still include the original fishing nets but most of their sales now come from sport nets, amusement park nets, debris nets, material-handling nets, and various custom net orders of various uses.

In the Trenton plant, the company receives bulk nylon netting from their supplier, Johnson Netting Co., and manipulate the knotless netting into products for their customers. In the Jonesport factory, the plant staff manufactures knotted netting from nylon rope that they manually tie together to create nets. The nylon rope is supplied by E.I. Dupont. Trenton Net has also started to carry other products besides nets since they have expanded their product line. To complement their nets they sell various hardware pieces that they purchase from various vendors. Trenton Net has also begun to sell accessories that complement their sport nets, such as baseball bats, baseballs, pitching machines, and other sports equipment which they buy from name-brand suppliers.

Trenton Net has incurred many problems in the past with regards to its inventory. A factory worker alerts the purchasing department when they are running low on netting material. At that point it may be too late and the job being manufactured will be delayed. If more orders come in for the same unavailable material these, too, will be delayed and sales may be lost. Trenton Net does not like to carry excess inventory of the sport accessories they offer because this area is still experimental and they are not sure if their customers will want to buy these products. Therefore, if an order is received for baseball bats, they may not be able to fill it on time because they will have to order it from their supplier.

The customers of Trenton Net Company vary greatly due to their large product base. Many universities and secondary schools buy item from Trenton Net for their sports complexes, such as baseball batting cages. Amuse-ment parks use safety nets for their rides and construction workers rely on debris nets for on-site construction. Also, many companies that have warehouse facilities utilize netting in their daily operations and material storage.

As Trenton Net expanded into these new market segments, the CEO decided to gain exposure by advertising in the Thomas Register, an industrial trade advertising book. Trenton Net has also incurred significant advertising expense in trade show participation and various trade magazines. This investment has caused a dramatic increase in sales from $400,000 just five years ago, to just over $1,000,000 today. The physical size of Trenton Net has also expanded to just over 120 employees.

Description of Revenue Cycle Procedures

The sales order process begins when a sales representative takes a customer order over the phone and manually fills out an order form. The sales order is then sent to another member of the sales team who enters the order into the microcomputer and prints multiple copies of the sales order. One copy is stamped as the pending order and placed in the customer open order file in the sales department with the original customer order. The factory order, shipping slip, and packing slip are all sent to the factory. In the factory the employees that make the nets look at the order and pull the material as needed from the warehouse. Once the project is completed, the factory order is marked as finished and placed in a completed factory order file in the factory. The finished net, shipping slip, and packing slip are sent to the shipping department. There a shipping clerk prepares the bill of lading, packs the goods in a box with the packing slip, and gives two copies of the bill of lading to the carrier who will deliver the package to the customer. The shipping slip is marked with the freight information and is sent to the billing department with a copy of the bill of lading.

When the bill of lading and shipping slip with the freight information is received in the billing/accounts receivable department, the clerk looks up the original sales order on a microcomputer and adds the freight prices. Once all relevant information is added to the invoice, the clerk invoices the order and mails two copies of the invoice to the customer. Another copy of the invoice is placed in an open accounts receivable file and one is placed in a completed sales file. When the clerk invoices the order on the computer it automatically updates the sales journal and the accounts receivable subsidiary ledger, which is all part of the commercial accounting software that the company is currently using. The general ledger is also automatically updated when the sales journal and accounts receivable subsidiary ledger are updated. Now the bill of lading and shipping slip are sent to the sales department to close the customer open order file. The pending order and original customer order from the customer open order file are stapled to the shipping slip and bill of lading and sent back to the billing accounts receivable department to be filed in the completed sales file.

If goods are returned to Trenton Net, the receiving department prepares two return slips and sends one to the warehouse with the goods and the other to the sales department. A clerk in the sales department will then prepare a credit memo, which is then be sent to the billing/accounts receivable department. There a clerk will mark the return on the microcomputer, which will update the sales journal and the accounts receivable subsidiary ledger. The credit memo is then filed in this department with the paperwork from the completed sale. The general ledger again is automatically updated when the sales journal and accounts receivable subsidiary ledger are updated.

The office manager, Anne, receives all mail and sends both the checks and remittance advices to the accounts receivable department. There a clerk will pull the invoice copy from the open accounts receivable file and send it along with the checks and remittance advices to the cash receipts department. A clerk in the cash receipts department will process the check and remittance advice by entering the information onto a microcomputer. This will update the cash receipt journal and the accounts receivable subsidiary ledger, which in turn will automatically update the general ledger on the computer. Then the clerk will prepare a deposit slip for the check, which will be taken to the bank by the cash receipts department manager, Jim, on his lunch hour. Copies of the deposit slip, remittance advice, and the deposited check are then filed in the cash receipts department. The invoice copy is marked as paid and sent to the billing/ accounts receivable department to be filed in the completed sale file.

Required:

1. Create a data flow diagram of the current system.

2. Create a document flowchart of the existing system.

3. Analyze the internal control weaknesses in the system. Model your response according to the six categories of physical control activities specified in SAS 78.

4. Prepare a system flowchart of a redesigned computer-based system that resolves the control weaknesses that you identified.

4.   Mom and Pop's Printing Press
(Prepared by Rick LaNeve and Hong Wai Ng, Lehigh University)

Mom and Pop's Printing Press is a former family-owned company that recently incorporated due to an increased need for capital. Mom and Pop's prints and distributes soft-cover books in bulk to a variety of customers, including schools, libraries, and general bookstores. The text materials are acquired on disk; Mom and Pop's then converts them to metal plates to be used in printing the finished books.

Mom and Pop's employs approximately 150 workers. The facility runs 24 hours a day, utilizing three shifts of workers, and caters to large clients. Mom and Pop's appears to be doing very well; just recently they won a major account from a rival printing press, forcing the rival out of business. Because of their incorporation, Mom and Pop's management decided to bring in an auditing team to review the system and look for potential problems.

Competition among Mom and Pop's suppliers is fierce. Management is concerned that the purchasing agent might be involved in a kickback fraud, since the cost of goods sold has risen disproportionately in recent months. Mom and Pop's keeps a very large inventory of paper and ink, since these are the two crucial components of production. If a stockout occurred, the receipt of a vital order would be six weeks late.

The Auditors' Observations of the Revenue Cycle

The book sales process begins in the office that houses the salespeople. Here eight representatives work with the customers. An account executive takes the customer order, and prepares a customer copy, a file copy, and a packing slip. The file copy is filed, the packing slip is sent to the warehouse, and the customer copy is sent to the accounting department.

The warehouse receives the packing slip and picks the goods. The packing slip is then used to update the inventory file and to prepare a journal voucher. After these are prepared, the packing slip is sent to the shipping department.

The packing slip is used to reconcile the goods before being shipped out. It is then used to prepare the bill of lading (3 copies) and complete the shipping notice. The shipping log is then updated. The shipping notice is sent to the accounting department. Two copies of the bill of lading are sent with the carrier, along with the packing slip and the goods. The third copy is filed.

The customer copy of the sales order is reconciled with the shipping notice, then used to update the sales journal and prepare a journal voucher. An invoice is created (3 copies). One copy is filed, the other is sent to the customer as a bill, and the third is used to update the accounts receivable file. The general ledger is updated using the journal voucher for the billing process and the journal voucher from the warehouse. Out of this ledger updating process flows the accounts receivable summary and the journal voucher, which is placed in the journal voucher file.

Cash Receipts

A secretary opens the mail containing customer checks and remittance advices. The checks and remittance advices are then sent to the accounting department. The accounting department first processes the cash receipts. Out of this process comes the deposit slip (2 copies), the checks, the remittance advices, as well as the updating of the cash receipts journal and the production of a journal voucher. The deposit slips and the checks are then taken to the bank for deposit into Mom and Pop's account. The remittance advices are used to update the accounts receivable subsidiary ledger. They are then placed into a file. The account summary that results from this update process is used along with the journal voucher to update the general ledger. The account summary and the journal voucher are then reconciled with the deposit slip from the bank.

Required:

1. Create a data flow diagram of the current system.

2. Create a document flowchart of the existing system.

3. Analyze the internal control weaknesses in the system. Model your response according to the six categories of physical control activities specified in SAS 78.

4. Prepare a system flowchart of a redesigned computer-based system that resolves the control weaknesses that you identified.

5. BSJ Limousine Service, Inc.

(Prepared by Jen Sinelnkov, Lehigh University)

BSJ Limousine Service, Inc. is a luxury transportation service located in New York, New York. Founded in 1980, BSJ has been gaining market share steadily over the last decade. BSJ receives orders from customers to transport them to specified destinations. The company provides top-quality service. The limousines are equipped with a full bar and a comfort leather interior.

The past two years have been extremely profitable for the relatively small company. With only 100 employees, BSJ has been experiencing control issues. Also, the manual transaction processing system, as well as the low-level computer technology the company uses, cannot support the volume of business. Out of the 100 employees, 60 are limousine drivers, 15 are administrative positions, 5 are executive positions, and 20 are maintenance positions. With the recent expansion, BSJ's employees are finding it difficult to carry on daily processes. Also, management is concerned about the possibility of fraudulent activity. For this reason, the company has hired Vinsinades, LLP to assess the organizations' business processes.

On the revenue cycle side, the two main functions are the sales order processing system and the cash receipts system. The sales order processing system consists of many steps beginning with a customer order and ending with the final customer drop off and entry of ride information. The cash receipts system records the inflow of revenue.

BSJ has three classes of customers: (1) hotel customers who have a fixed monthly contract with BSJ to shuttle guests from the airport to their hotel and vice versa; (2) general customers who call on a periodic basis for transportation to social events, airports, etc., and (3) corporate customers who have an account with BSJ to transport executives from their hotels to the office and back again.

The manual transaction processing system is similar for all three types of customers. General customers are required to place their orders over the phone at least seven days in advance. Hotel customers are slightly different. Instead of placing an order, there is a contract that two limousines always shuttle back and forth from that hotel to the local airport.

Corporate customers place regular orders for a car in advance like the general customers. For example, XYZ Company may call on March 5 for a car on March 15 to transport five executives from the hotel to the office. First, the call is received by a receptionist who logs the sales order manually in a notebook. The receptionist records orders throughout the day. At the end of the day, the receptionist gives the notebook to the scheduler. The scheduler compiles and sorts the orders, then creates a schedule for the next day using a basic spreadsheet application. The spreadsheet is sorted by date and printed at the end of each day. From the schedule, monthly invoices are prepared in triplicate. One copy is filed, one is sent to the customer as their bill, and the other is sent to the accounts payable department where it is used to update the accounts receivable records. The information is then posted to the AR subsidiary ledger. The invoice is then filed. Finally, the general ledger is updated and the process is complete.

On the cash receipts side, the customer returns the remittance advice with a check for the amount of the monthly service. Once received, all in one step, a clerk sorts the incoming envelopes and separates the remittance advices from the checks. Once separate, the remittance advice is reconciled with the check. The cash receipt is processed and the accounts receivable subsidiary ledger is updated to the cash receipts journal. A journal voucher is created from the cash receipts journal, while an account summary is created from the AR subsidiary ledger. Three deposit slips are created after the check and remittance advice is reconciled. Two copies of the deposit slip go to the bank, while the third is filed with the check and the remittance advice. Next, the account summary is sent to the controllers' department. The deposit slip from the bank is reconciled with the batch totals from the accounts receivable/ cash receipts department.

Required:
1. Create a data flow diagram of the current system.
2. Create a document flowchart of the existing system.
3. Analyze the internal control weaknesses in the system. Model your response according to the six categories of physical control activities specified in SAS 78.
4. Prepare a system flowchart of a redesigned computer-based system that resolves the control weaknesses that you identified.

6. Symmons Shower Heads

(Prepared by Kevin Shmelzer,
PriceWaterhouseCoopers)

Kevin Symmons founded Symmons Shower Heads Company in 1982. This manufacturing firm started from scratch and has evolved into one of many competitors in the shower head industry. Symmons Shower Heads products can be found throughout the northeast in homes, restaurants, and educational institutions. This family-owned and operated company tries to keep the atmosphere and the relationships it has with its employees, suppliers, and customers close and tight knit. Due to its continued success, Symmons Shower Heads (SSH) has realized its need to evolve and become more up to date in today's technologically advanced business environment. This necessitates SSH automating many of its procedures, including its production process and accounting process, which currently is basically manual. Last year, gross sales were estimated at $150 million, which was an increase of 5 percent from the previous year. SSH employs 320 workers, which includes both its sales force and manufacturing personnel. SSH retains many of its employees because they are paid well and treated with care and respect. The average length of service for employees is 11 years. SSH also fosters interaction among employees through lunches, picnics, and softball games. This allows for cross-functional integration on a social level. It is not uncommon for families to be employed as well. In fact, SSH tries to induce this by providing free day care for employee's children. This is just another example of the close-knit family atmosphere.

Currently, SSH has a supplier base of 250, but actively uses approximately 65 suppliers routinely. The terms with their suppliers vary, including prepaid blanket orders, 2/10 n30, and 5/5 n20. The primary supplies SSH receives are steel, aluminum, valve bodies, sand castings, handles, injection molding, seals, nuts, and bolts.

SSH main products are shower heads (four models), pressure-balancing shower valves, single-lever bathroom and kitchen faucets (five models), and thermostat water control systems (two models). The parts for each of these products are purchased and then each individual product is assembled by both hand and machine. These products are sold to plumbing wholesalers and distributors as well as specialty engineers. Currently, there are 1,500 active accounts, and a total of 3,000–4,000 accounts. There are eight personnel on the sales force. Their responsibility is to service current customers and secure new accounts. Orders are placed through the sales personnel either over the phone or in person when the associate visits the customer. The terms of sales depends on the customer and is either 2/10 n30, 10/5 n20, or prepaid.

Sales Order Process

The sales order process begins with customer contact in the sales department by phone, mail, fax, or in person. The sales department captures the essential detail for the customer order. Then, the sales department performs the credit check and prepares several copies of the sales order. A stock release copy is sent to the warehouse. The billing department receives the invoice copy, the ledger copy, and a file copy. The shipping notice, packing slip, and file copies of the sales order are sent to the shipping department.

The billing department updates the sales journal and prepares a journal voucher, which is sent to the general ledger department. In addition, billing sends the invoice to the customer and the ledger copy to accounts receivable. It files the file copy for its records.

The warehouse receives the stock release copy of the order from the sales department, picks the goods, and sends the stock release to the billing department, where it is forwarded to inventory control. Also in the warehouse, a clerk enters into a computer terminal the items removed from inventory to update the inventory file.

The shipping department prepares two copies of a bill of lading and reviews the shipping notice. One copy of the bill of lading, the packing slip, and the goods are given to the carrier for delivery to the customer. The file copy and a copy of the bill of lading are filed in the shipping department. Also, the clerk uses the shipping notice information to update the shipping log from a computer terminal.

Inventory control receives the stock release, which it uses to update the inventory control account through a computer terminal. The stock release is then filed. Next, the accounts receivable department receives the ledger copy from the billing department. The AR department updates the AR subsidiary ledger and an account summary is sent to the general ledger department. The ledger copy is filed. The general ledger department reconciles the journal voucher from billing and the accounts receivable summary. The general ledger is then adjusted, and the journal vouchers are filed.

Cash Receipts Procedures

The process begins in the mail room where clerks open customer remittance envelopes and reconcile the checks with the remittance advices and prepare a remittance list. The checks, remittance list, and remittance advices are sent to the cash receipts department.

In the cash receipts department, the cash receipts journal is updated and the journal voucher is sent to the general ledger department. Next, two of the deposit slips are sent to the bank, and the check and remittance advice are filed. The cash receipts department also updates the AR subsidiary ledger, files the remittance advice, and sends the account summary to the general ledger department.

Required:

1. Create a data flow diagram of the current system.
2. Create a document flowchart of the existing system.
3. Analyze the internal control weaknesses in the system. Model your response according to the six categories of physical control activities specified in SAS 78.
4. Prepare a system flowchart of a redesigned computer-based system that resolves the control weaknesses that you identified.

7. Mitchell Law Firm

(Prepared by Heather Dillon and Kellie Seaman,
Lehigh University)

Annis Mitchell is a law firm operating from a main office in Tampa, Florida. The satellite offices for the firm are located in Ft. Myers, Naples, and Tallahassee, and there is also an associate office in Germany. The firm's clients include major national and local corporate businesses, as well as local individual clients. The firm employs 133 people: 65 lawyers, 42 secretaries, 10 in word processing, 4 in accounting, 8 in the mail room/ records department, 2 in reception, and 2 in the administrator's office. The annual gross revenues are approximately $12 million, with all excess profits distributed to the shareholders (partners) of the firm.

General Information

The current accounting system is computerized, utilizing a batch approach, with some direct access capabilities. Time entry, receipts and disbursement entries, check processing, and various other functions are processed in batches. Functions such as correction of typographical errors in time entries and generation of bills is done on a direct access basis. The accounting department consists of Karen, Peggy, Heather, and Frankie. Peggy and Heather are primarily responsible for billing and accounts receivable. Frankie enters cash disbursements into the system and processes the checks. Karen oversees all general ledger functions as well as receiving and verifying many of the firm's general bills, such as telephone and insurance. Heather and Karen both assist Frankie by entering disbursements and processing checks when needed.

Sales Order Processing System

The generation of accounts receivable begins with the potential client contacting the firm to have legal work performed. The secretary of the attorney contacted processes a preliminary client by completing a three-part client initiation form and forwarding it to the records department. The records department performs the conflict check. The potential client's information is input into the computer system; a list of all new client information is run daily. This list is distributed to the lawyers of the firm, who review it and determine if the potential clients create any conflicts with existing clients. If a potential client has no major conflicts, then a file is set up in the file room and on the computer system for the new client and a client number is assigned, which becomes the primary key. Part one of the client initiation form is placed in that file, part two is returned to the secretary for the attorney's files, and part three is forwarded to the billing department to be filed there.

Attorneys keep track of their hours by writing down the time spent on each task that day. The time sheet is then input into the computer by the secretary at the end of that day or the beginning of the next. A tight reign is kept on the attorneys to ensure that the time is input into the system as soon as possible after the day is over. At the beginning of each day, the billing department posts the time batches to the accounting system, and distributes the edit runs to the secretaries to look for errors and other corrections. If there are corrections to be made, the edit list is returned to the billing department for correction. If there are no corrections to be made, the list is discarded or filed, depending on the attorney or secretary who input the time. When the batches are posted, the time automatically is posted to the client's billing file.

At the end of each month, pre-bills are run for the billing process. The pre-bill is the listing of all hours incurred for a client in the month. These pre-bills are distributed to the attorneys, who review them and decide exactly how to bill the client. They have the option of writing up or down the hours incurred, not billing the client during that month, or sending the bill as is. Once they have reviewed the pre-bill, it is returned to the billing department to be edited and then the final bill is run. The final bill is returned to the attorney, who approves it and has his or her secretary send it to the client. The secretary then sends a list of all bills sent to clients to the billing department, which updates the client files to show the new accounts receivable.

The billing department consists of two members of the accounting department, Peggy and Heather.

Cash Receipts System

All mail comes into the mail room. There the mail is separated and distributed to the addressees, but not opened. All unspecified mail is forwarded to Debi, who is the secretary to the administrator of the firm. All payments are also forwarded to Debi, no matter who physically receives them. Payments that are sent to the accounting department by clients are automatically forwarded to Debi as well. She receives the payments and any remittance advices that are attached. More often than not, there is no identifying information for the payment except a client number on the check. Corporate clients are more likely to include invoice and client/case numbers on their check attachments. All checks received are placed in a file folder in Debi's drawer until after the morning mail is distributed. At that point, she collects all the payments received and takes them to Cheyenne, the upstairs receptionist. Cheyenne separates the checks from any remittance advices and creates the cash pre-list, which totals the days receipts as well as the month's total to date. Nine copies of the pre-list are made. Six are forwarded to the partners of the firm, one to the administrator, one to the billing department, and one is filed by Cheyenne. The billing copy is filed in a separate folder to be checked at the end of the month, and the other copies are reviewed and either filed or discarded by the recipient.

Cheyenne then forwards the checks to Frankie and any remittance advices to Peggy or Heather. Frankie then creates a two-part deposit ticket. One part of the ticket remains in the ticket book, and the

second part goes with the checks to the bank. Once the ticket is created, Frankie takes the ticket and checks and makes a photocopy of them. The photocopy is given to Heather or Peggy and attached to the remittance advices. The checks are taken to the records department/mail room, which then takes the checks to the bank. The deposit confirmation received from the bank is brought to Frankie, who attaches it to the copy of the deposit ticket in the deposit book.

Peggy or Heather takes the copies of the checks and the remittance advices and posts the amounts to the clients' accounts. Any unknown amounts are left out of the system until the client account they are to be attached to is determined. All amounts must be in the system by the end of the month, when a cash receipts report is run from the accounting system. The monthly to-date total of Cheyenne's pre-list and the month's collections to date on the journal must match. The month cannot be closed out for accounting purposes until those two totals match.

Required:

1. Create a data flow diagram of the current system.
2. Create a document flowchart of the existing system.
3. Analyze the internal control weaknesses in the system. Model your response according to the six categories of physical control activities specified in SAS 78.
4. Make suggestions as to how these weaknesses can be resolved.

8. D & K Supplement Warehouse
(Prepared by Dale Kessler, Lehigh University)

D & K Supplement Warehouse (D&K) is a mail-order company specializing in vitamins, minerals, organic herbs, meal replacements, protein powders, and basic supplements. D&K sells these products mostly to body builders and various health-conscience people in the United States, but also has about a 15 percent customer base located internationally. The company, which is located in an industrial park in Bethlehem, Pennsylvania, has sales clerks taking phone orders 24 hours a day from customers who wish to purchase products from D&K's product lists and catalogs. Customers can find these product lists mainly in body builder and health magazines like *Flex* and *Prevention*, and in gyms and doctors' offices. D&K's catalog, containing their full list of products, is periodically mailed to current and potential customers, and also to anyone requesting it. Once an order is placed it takes five days for the order to reach the customer. D&K outsources their order deliveries to UPS.

D&K was started in 1990 to target those consumers who did not have time to stop at nutritional stores. It did not make a profit until 1993 because consumers had to become accustomed to the idea of ordering their nutritional products by phone. Once the concept caught on, D&K's profits soared. In 1994 and 1995, profits increased 30 percent each year. By 1996, the market became saturated and profits dropped 5 percent. The competition had also caught on to the concept. In 1997, profits were down 8 percent and from all reasonable indicators D&K should end 1998 with a 12 percent drop in profit. At this point in time, D&K's president knows they have a serious problem on their hands. The president found out that the competition is able to get their orders to customers in two days, three days less than D&K. D&K just assumed their longer lead time was due to their highly manual system which they are planning to redesign in early 1999 with a highly computerized system. Despite the initial installation, purchase, and setup costs, the benefits of the redesigned system outweigh its costs and profits are to be generated within 1fi to 2 years. Also, D&K realized that their competitors were benefiting from D&K's initial market research and their organizational processes and strategies. Competitors were building off D&K's foundation, allowing them to have lower overhead costs and thus lower prices.

To get to the root of their problems, D&K has hired a local consulting firm to analyze their organization. The consultants are here today to begin reviewing D&K's operations. They will start by examining the revenue cycle procedures because the they suspect that internal control problems exist.

Sales Department
Customer orders for supplements are received via phone, fax, or e-mail. Sales are documented either by the actual sales orders mailed or faxed to the company, or are transcribed by a sales representative when taking orders over the phone. Sales order copies are sent to the credit department.

Customers sales are on credit, usually through an existing account. In the case of a new customer, an account must be established. The customer account record includes a customer's name, address, age,

phone number, gender, history with company, and a unique customer number provided by D&K.

Once credit is approved, three copies of sales order are sent to billing. The sales department is notified and the sales order clerk, Fred, updates the sales journal. The approved sales order is filed in the sales department and three copies of the sales order are sent to the warehouse.

Billing Department
The billing department uses the information from the sales department which is reconciled and used to bill the customer. A copy of the sales order is filed and the ledger copy is sent to accounts receivable.

Warehousing Department
John in the warehouse has been with the company since its inception. He knows his job well and is a big supplement buff. He prepares the packing slips and collects the supplements from inventory; he also updates the inventory records due to his great abilities and knowledge of inventory processes. The inventory records are updated via a computer terminal with a commercial inventory software package. Allowing John to perform a variety of tasks allows D&K to simplify its inventory warehouse procedures. The merchandise is then sent with two copies of the sales order and the packing slips to Ralph in the shipping department. He takes one copy of sales order and files it.

Accounts Receivable Department
When Leroy in the accounts receivable department receives the ledger copy from the billing department he posts the information to customer accounts via a computer terminal, which automatically updates affected general ledger accounts. After this posting is achieved, Leroy takes the ledger copy and files it.

Cash Receipts Department
At the end of each day the cash receipt's clerk, Ladon, prepares a three-part deposit slip for the total amount of cash received. One copy is filed and the other two copies accompany the cash to the bank. Credit card sales are processed directly by electronic transfers of funds. Checks received in payment of an account go to Frank in the mail room. He makes sure he is the only one receiving the checks that come in through the mail. Ladon, in the cash receipts, is Frank's cousin. Ladon records checks received as well as takes

the remittance advice because he performs the accounts receivable duties as well. Even though large amounts of cash are involved, Ladon takes the cash receipts to the bank alone.

A remittance advice is used to reduce customers' account balances according to the amount of payment. The cash receipts department automatically updates the account records by a terminal with the appropriate software package. The cash receipts department sends summary information about customer accounts and cash deposited to the accounts receivable department. The information is reconciled and used to update the general ledger accounts in the accounts receivable department.

Required:
1. Create a data flow diagram of the current system.
2. Create a document flowchart of the existing system.
3. Analyze the internal control weaknesses in the system. Model your response according to the six categories of physical control activities specified in SAS 78.
4. Prepare a system flowchart of a redesigned computer-based system that resolves the control weaknesses that you identified.

9. Kidswear Inc.
(Prepared by Nate Soron, Paul Troiano, and Alexis Yap, Lehigh University)

Kidswear, Inc. is a mail-order wholesaler of high-quality children's casual clothes. The company, which is located in Chicago, Illinois, carries a variety of manufacturer brands. Their warehouse and office are located on the same site. Kidswear employs 150 employees, mainly in their warehouse and sales order processing department. Gross sales for 1997 totaled ten million dollars.

Kidswear has long-standing relationships with fifteen major suppliers. All products are received FOB destination point to the warehouse. The company has agreements with all suppliers that standard ordering lead time is one week, however, recently Kidswear has been experiencing stockouts.

Kidswear customers are department stores and clothing stores. Orders are placed directly over the phone via the company's toll-free number. Currently Kidswear can process and ship via ground transportation in five days. Customers can expect to receive their orders in eight to ten business days. Customers pay on credit terms and are billed when their order is shipped. Kidswear is considering doing business over the Internet to increase their customer base.

This year Kidswear is expecting a decrease in sales revenue. A survey revealed that customers are unhappy with the back-orders and long delivery lead time.

Revenue Cycle
A customer places an order by calling Kidswear's toll-free number. A sales representative approves the sale, creates the formal sales order and stock release, and sends the documents to the warehouse (shipping) department.

A warehouse clerk receives the sales order and stock release, picks the goods, and arranges for the goods to be shipped. The clerk then updates the inventory subsidiary ledger. Warehouse employees work very well together and help each other out when they are busy. To reduce processing time, access to the warehouse is open, thus permitting any employee to transport goods out of the warehouse to the delivery trucks.

The warehouse clerk then prepares the shipping notice and gives the shipping company the shipping notice and the goods to be shipped. After the goods are on their way to the customer, the employee sends the sales order, the stock release, and a copy of the shipping notice to the accounting department.

An accounting department employee prepares and mails a copy of the invoice to the customer. The employee then files the original invoice, sales order, shipping notice, and stock release and uses the invoice to update the accounts receivable ledger, general ledger, and the sales journal.

Cash Receipts Process
The mail room clerk receives the customer check and the remittance advice. The clerk forwards the check and advice to the cash receipts department. Recently a number of mail room employees resigned. Because of the staff shortage, the mail room supervisor is very busy with increased administrative responsibilities. She spends all day in her office and does not oversee the opening of the mail.

The cash receipts clerk uses the advice to update the accounts receivable ledger and stores the check in a locked drawer in his desk until the end of the week. Each Friday the clerk prepares the bank deposit slip and deposits the checks for the week into the firm's account. Upon returning from the bank, the clerk uses the deposit slip to update the general ledger and the cash receipts journal.

Required:

1. Create a data flow diagram of the current system.
2. Create a document flowchart of the existing system.
3. Analyze the internal control weaknesses in the system. Model your response according to the six categories of physical control activities specified in SAS 78.
4. Prepare a system flowchart of a redesigned computer-based system that resolves the control weaknesses that you identified.

10. D&F Music Club

(Prepared by Katie Daley and Gail Freeston, Lehigh University)

D&F is a distributor of CDs and cassettes that offers benefits such as discount prices and an introductory offer of 10 CDs or cassettes for a penny (not including the shipping and handling costs). Its primary target customers are college students; its main marketing strategy is constant deals to club members. The company's main competitors in the industry are BMG and Columbia House, which both offer similar promotions. D&F started in 1993 with an office in Harrisburg, Pennsylvania, initially targeting college students in the surrounding area. They realized there was a high demand for discounted music merchandise and the convenience of delivery by mail within universities. After their second year, with a constant increase in customer orders, D&F relocated to Philadelphia because it was located near more colleges and universities. The move has had a positive effect on net profits and demand, supporting their decision to continue the growth of the company. D&F recently expanded their facility to be able to fulfill a higher demand for their services. Their customer base ranges from areas as close as Villanova University to as far as Boston College. As of 1998, there were 103 employees. Their prior year's gross sales were $125 million.

D&F's market share is on the rise, but is not yet comparable to the magnitude of BMG and Columbia House. However, the corporation's goals for the upcoming years include establishing itself as an industry player through increased customer satisfaction and loyalty. D&F is also considering the installation of a new information processing system. This system will reengineer their current business functions by reducing loopholes in their internal control problems.

D&F receives CDs and cassettes from various wholesale suppliers and music store chains, totaling 32 suppliers nationwide. The office has its own warehouse, stores its own merchandise, and is responsible for replenishing the inventory. D&F has had no substantial problems in the past with their suppliers. On the other hand, they have encountered problems with excess inventory, stockouts, and discrepancies with inventory records.

Revenue Cycle

When an individual is interested in becoming a member of D&F Music Club, they can call the toll-free number and speak with a sales representative, who will establish a new account for him/her. A customer's account record contains his or her name, address, phone number, previous orders he/she made with the company, and a randomly assigned unique customer account number. D&F Music Club feels that a check on a customer's financial history is not necessary.

If an existing customer wants to place an order, he/she can call the same toll-free number and place an order with a sales representative. A sales clerk then prepares a sales order, packing slip, and shipping notice. The sales order is sent to Bill in the credit department. The packing slip and shipping notice are sent to the billing department.

Bill's responsibility is to run a background check on the customer's history with the company to verify that no delinquent accounts exist. If the sales order is approved, Bill prepares a stock release that is sent to the warehouse, and the customer's order can continue to be processed.

John, an employee in the billing department, receives the approved sales order, shipping notice, and packing slip. After he reconciles them to verify that all the information on each source document is correct, he prepares the invoice, makes a copy of it, and sends it to the customer. A copy of the sales order, shipping notice, and packing slip is sent to the warehouse department as well, to plan for the shipment of goods. Every Monday morning, John updates the sales journal to record the sales from the week before.

Chris, a warehouse employee, receives the stock release from Bill in the credit department, and then verifies the information with the sales order, shipping notice, and packing slip. Chris then picks the goods and calls Federal Express. He proceeds to update the inventory subsidiary ledger for the CDs and/or cassettes he is shipping to the customer. The security in the warehouse is well designed—a key is given to all authorized personnel for entrance into the warehouse. However, once inside, it is easy for an employee to steal inventory without anyone else noticing. Chris then prepares the bill of lading before 2:00 p.m., when Federal Express arrives. After the goods are shipped, the sales order, shipping notice, and packing slip are sent to Sandy, the accounts receivable clerk.

Sandy files the documents that Chris sent her and updates the accounts receivable and general ledgers for the customer's account. On a weekly basis, Sandy reviews each customer's account to make sure the customer is not overdue. If he/she is late on a payment, Sandy immediately sends a letter to the customer, stating the amount owed D&F Music Club.

When customers makes a payment on their account to the company, they are required to send both the remittance advice that was attached to the invoice and a check with their account number on it. Scott, a mail room clerk, handles all the payments D&F receives. It is his responsibility to separate the check and remittance advice and prepare the remittance list. The remittance list is sent, along with the checks, to the cash receipts department.

Laura, the cash receipts clerk and Scott's mother, reconciles the checks with the remittance advice before preparing the deposit slip. Each Wednesday, Laura makes a point to deposit the checks at Summit Bank. Until that time, she keeps them locked in a safe in her office. Once she has a bank receipt, verifying the dollar amount of checks deposited, she sends it to Sandy in the accounting department.

Upon obtaining the bank receipt, Sandy files it and updates the cash receipts journal to record the amount deposited. She also updates the general ledger and accounts receivable for the customer's account. There are times when many transactions must be recorded, especially right after the Christmas season, and it is possible to overlook a customer's payment. For this reason, Sandy asks their internal auditor, Jim, to reconcile the general ledger each month, to make sure a payment on account is not omitted. However, this has not been caught in time in the past and customers have been sent overdue letters in the mail, claiming they are delinquent on their accounts.

Upon the receipt of the CDs or cassettes ordered, the customer has a 15-day trial period. If, at the end of that period, he/she sends a payment, it is understood that the goods have been accepted. If, on the other hand, the customer is dissatisfied with the product for any reason, he/she can return it to D&F Music Club at no charge. However, the customer must call the company to obtain an authorization number in order to return the CD or cassette. When the goods arrive, Chris prepares the return slip, makes a copy of it, sends it to billing, and files his copy. He then proceeds to update the inventory subsidiary ledger.

After John receives the return slip, he prepares two credit memos. One is sent to the accounts receivable department and the other is filed. Once this is completed, John updates the sales journal.

Sandy updates the accounts receivable and general ledgers based upon the credit memo received from John. The credit memo authorizes that the customer not be billed for the goods. Once this occurs, the customer should no longer be charged for the purchase.

Required:

1. Create a data flow diagram of the current system.
2. Create a document flowchart of the existing system.
3. Analyze the internal control weaknesses in the system. Model your response according to the six categories of physical control activities specified in SAS 78.

11. The Right Fit Company

(Prepared by Jonathan Wowak, Lehigh University)

The Right Fit Company consists of five stores in the Tri-State area that are in the sneaker retail business. The main store, located in Manhattan, is where the headquarters resides. The Right Fit Company is in business of selling high-quality sneakers at low prices. The vision statement for Right Fit is: The Right Fit Company's future depends upon the purchase of sneakers and related items at wholesale that will satisfy the customers in the Tri-State area.

The Right Fit Company buys directly from wholesalers and deals mainly with credit purchases. Right Fit's main customers consist of children and young adults, therefore, the sales are mostly cash sales (about 80 percent). Credit sales consist of sales made in which the local stores cannot meet the required inventory needed to complete the sale; most of the credit sales are made in bulk to local high school, college, and professional athletic teams. The sales to athletic teams are mostly made in batches. The gross sales figures for previous years are as follows:

	Gross Sales
1993	$ 750,000
1994	875,000
1995	935,000
1996	1,100,000

The Right Fit Company has seen a 47 percent increase in gross profit since 1993. In 1996, credit sales amounted to $220,000. The credit sales mostly consist of sales made on The Right Fit credit card. As of December 31, 1996, Right Fit had a total of 120 employees: 80 salespeople; 40 executives and their staff.

The Right Fit Company has had many problems with suppliers in the past. By being a small organization it is hard for Right Fit to purchase directly from Nike, Reebok, or any of the other large sneaker manufacturers. Right Fit mainly deals mainly with 5 wholesalers in the Tri-State area. In the sneaker industry, one major problem that Right Fit must face is excess inventory. The Right Fit Company must find a way to limit inventory levels while maintaining customer satisfaction. The lead times from its current wholesalers is too great to keep up with sneaker technology. Sneaker technology, as defined by Right Fit, is the changing styles of sneakers as new stars come upon the professional athlete horizon. It is almost impossible to carry every size of every shoe, so Right Fit must find a way to eliminate lead time, but lower inventory levels.

The president of the company, George Busch, focused the problem on the revenue and expenditure cycles. Right Fit has implemented low-level technology into its revenue cycle. Mr. Busch feels that it would benefit the company if they use computer technology only in the revenue cycle as a test run or evaluation period. Mr. Busch assigned his two closest friends, Dan Peacock and Cathy Powers, to review the cycles and eliminate the major problems. The major problems include lowering inventory levels while still satisfying the customer's demand, fulfilling sales orders with only one warehouse in Manhattan, keeping up with sneaker technology, and maintaining its status as the third-leading sneaker retailer in the Tri-State area behind Foot Locker and Kmart.

Revenue Cycle

The revenue cycle concentrates on two areas: point-of-sale transactions and credit sales. The point-of-sale (POS) transactions are mostly cash sales made directly at the stores. The POS transactions occur at the terminals located in each of the stores. The inventory kept at each store is considered part of the whole company. The POS transaction initiates upon a cash or credit card transaction. Each of the terminals will check the store's inventory for the goods and then prepare a credit card voucher or cash receipt. Each of the stores then electronically sends the data to the Manhattan store.

The cash receipts department processes the cash received, the credit vouchers, and the terminal's tapes. Bill Wagner, the point-of-sale cash clerk, enters the data into his terminal and prepares a deposit slip that will be sent with the cash to the bank by Bill himself. One copy of the deposit slip is then filed. After receiving the information in the computer department, Jill Dunn immediately updates the inventory and sales journal files on her computer. At the end of the day, the cash receipts and general ledger files are updated. The cash sales are processed immediately at the stores, while the credit sales are processed through the Manhattan office.

The credit sales are either sales made in which the local stores do not have the inventory needed or bulk sales made to the local high school, college, and professional athletic teams. These athletic teams' purchases trigger the sales order processing system. When a customer makes a purchase at one of the five stores (sales department), a clerk immediately enters the customer order into a terminal that is connected to the shipping department located in the Manhattan office. Ryan Crawford receives the customer's order at the Manhattan shipping department terminal. Ryan prepares a stock request and a packing slip from the customer order at the terminal and gives them to Brad Simon, one of his best friends and also in the shipping department.

Brad and four other employees then go to the inventory, which is located in the shipping department, and finds the items. Brad prepares a shipping notice and two copies of the bill of lading. Phillip Ford takes the goods, the packing slip, and one copy of the bill of lading to the loading dock. At the loading dock the goods and the paperwork are put on a truck and shipped directly to the customer. The other copy of the bill of lading and the stock release are filed in the shipping department.

Additionally, Brad sends the shipping notice to Nancy Anderson or one of the three employees in the computer department, which acts as the general ledger. Nancy enters the shipping data into her computer. She performs an edit run on the sales order files and then proceeds to update the accounts. Since The Right Fit Company's credit sales are made in bulk, Nancy updates the sales journal, the accounts receivable files, the general ledger files, and the inventory files all at once. After the update, Nancy prepares the customer invoice and remittance advice from the shipping notice and sends it to the customer.

After receiving the checks and the remittance advices from the customers, Paul Sinclair, the mail room clerk, sends the checks to the cash receipts department and the remittance advice, along with a batch total for the day, to the accounts receivable department. Ralph Bretz of the accounts receivable department takes the batch total and the remittance advices in order to update the accounts receivable subsidiary accounts. The batch total and the remittance advice are filed. Upon posting to the AR subsidiary accounts, Ralph enters the summary data into his computer. The batch total from Ralph's computer is electronically sent to Charlie Bauers in the computer department.

Clara Fishman, of the cash receipts department, receives the checks from the mail room. Clara processes the cash receipts and prepares two copies of a deposit slip. In addition to the deposit slips, Clara enters the data into her computer, which is then sent to Charlie in the computer department. Mike Stark then takes one copy of the deposit slip and the checks to the bank for deposit. The second copy of the deposit slip is filed in the cash receipts department.

In the computer department, or the general ledger department, Charlie uses a data entry program to create a batch total file and a cash receipts transaction file. Since the cash receipts are totaled at the end of the day, an update is made on the master files from the cash receipts transaction file and the batch total file. The update includes the accounts receivable file, the general ledger files, and the cash receipts journal.

Required:
1. Create a data flow diagram of the current system.
2. Create a document flowchart of the existing system.
3. Analyze the internal control weaknesses in the system. Model your response according to the six categories of physical control activities specified in SAS 78.

12. Grand Slam Company
(Prepared by Erin Kerler and Matt Ristau, Lehigh University)
Grand Slam Company is a top-of-the-line baseball equipment manufacturer that specializes in fielder's gloves but which also produces bats, balls, and other baseball accessories. The gloves made by Grand Slam are known in the industry to be one of the best gloves available on the market and are used by a large number of Major League Baseball players. Grand Slam is located in Dallas, Texas, and sells nationwide, concentrating heavily on the southern U.S. and California. It sells its product mainly to specialty sporting goods stores that focus on and are known for baseball equipment. Grand Slam has about 250 employees, with the majority in Dallas and the others located throughout the country on sales assignments.

Given the superior quality of the products manufactured by Grand Slam, the suppliers must provide them with the highest quality raw materials. Grand Slam has run into some problems finding a supplier that can provide them with the top-quality leather hides that it needs to make their gloves. They have tried various suppliers, and have had problems finding one that will send small shipments more frequently. The ones that can do this have problems with providing consistent quality.

Another factor that Grand Slam deals with is that the baseball equipment market is very much a seasonal market. This is a major reason for the concentration in the southern states—in this region baseball is played all year, as opposed to in the north where the weather doesn't allow for year-round baseball. However, the overall market still peaks around the first of March, and slowly declines throughout the rest of the year. Another market factor that Grand Slam recognizes is that baseball is becoming less popular with children. Basketball and soccer are gaining in popularity every year, and baseball is losing a large number of kids to these sports.

Grand Slam also has some internal problems that need to be addressed. The firm's revenue and expenditure cycles have various internal control weaknesses that should be looked into by the company's management. The company may be losing significant amounts of money through fraud or inefficiencies, and the company cannot afford to allow these potential problems to go unchecked.

The Revenue Cycle
When Grand Slam Company receives the customer's order, the sales department prepares three documents; the customer copy, the packing slip, and the file copy. The original customer order is filed in the sales department. The customer copy is sent back to the customer, while the packing slip and the file copy are sent to the shipping department.

The shipping department takes the packing slip and picks the goods out of inventory and prepares the shipping notice along with two copies of a bill of lading. The packing slip and one copy of the bill of lading are sent with the carrier. The file copy of the sales order and the other copy of the bill of lading are filed by date in the shipping department. The shipping notice is sent to the computer department for processing.

The computer department receives the shipping notice and data entry personnel key the information into the computer. This data is stored in the sales order files. Then, through the direct access method, the accounts receivable, inventory, and general ledger files are updated. The sales journal is also updated at this time. As a result of this process a customer invoice is created, which is then sent to the customer.

After customers receive an invoice, they send their checks to the mail room. Here the checks are gathered and a check summary is created. The mail room then forwards the checks and a copy of the check summary to the cash receipts department. The accounts receivable department is sent the other copy of the check summary.

In the cash receipts department, the checks are reconciled to the check summary and entered into the cash receipts journal, producing a cash receipts summary. This summary is sent to the general ledger department. A deposit slip is created from this process and is given to the bank along with the checks for deposit.

The accounts receivable department takes the check summary and updates the accounts receivable subsidiary ledger, then files the check summary. An accounts receivable summary is produced from this updating process, and is sent to the general ledger department. The general ledger department reconciles the accounts receivable summary and the cash receipts summary, then posts the information to the general ledger. A copy of the accounts receivable summary and the cash receipts summary are then filed in the general ledger department. Finally the controller is given copies of the accounts receivable summary, check summary, and cash receipts summary and reconciles the totals with the general ledger.

Required:
1. Create a data flow diagram of the current system.
2. Create a document flowchart of the existing system.
3. Analyze the internal control weaknesses in the system. Model your response according to the six categories of physical control activities specified in SAS 78.
4. Prepare a system flowchart of a redesigned computer-based system that resolves the control weaknesses that you identified.

5

The Expenditure Cycle Part I: Purchases and Cash Disbursements Procedures

The objective of the expenditure cycle is to convert the organization's cash into the physical materials and the human resources it needs to conduct business. In this chapter we concentrate on systems and procedures for acquiring raw materials and finished goods from suppliers. The following chapter examines payroll and fixed asset systems.

Most business entities operate on a credit basis and do not pay for resources until after acquiring them. The time lag between these events splits the procurement process into two phases: (1) the physical phase, involving the acquisition of the resource, and (2) the financial phase, involving the disbursement of cash. As a practical matter, these are treated as independent transactions that are processed through separate subsystems.

This chapter examines the principal features of the two major subsystems that constitute the expenditure cycle: (1) the purchases processing subsystem and (2) the cash disbursements subsystem. The chapter is organized into two main sections. The first section provides an overview of the purchases and cash disbursements process, the logical tasks, the key entities, the sources and uses of information, and the flow of key documents through an organization. We illustrate these features with a manual system. The second section explores computer-based systems, focusing on the operational and control implications of alternative data processing methods.

LEARNING OBJECTIVES

After studying this chapter, you should:

- Recognize the fundamental tasks that constitute the purchases and cash disbursements process.
- Be able to identify the functional departments involved in purchases and cash disbursements activities and trace the flow of these transactions through the organization.
- Be able to specify the documents, journals, and accounts that provide audit trails, promote the maintenance of historical records, and support internal decision making and financial reporting.
- Understand the exposures associated with purchases and cash disbursements activities and recognize the controls that reduce these risks.
- Be aware of the operational features and the control implications of technology used in purchases and cash disbursements systems.

OVERVIEW OF PURCHASES AND CASH DISBURSEMENTS ACTIVITIES

PURCHASES PROCESSING SYSTEM

The data flow diagram in Figure 5–1 presents an overview of the logical activities that constitute the purchases processing system. These processes are described in the following steps.

1. The purchase function begins by recognizing the need to restock inventories through the observation of inventory records. Inventory levels decline through

---

FIGURE 5–1   DFD for Purchases System

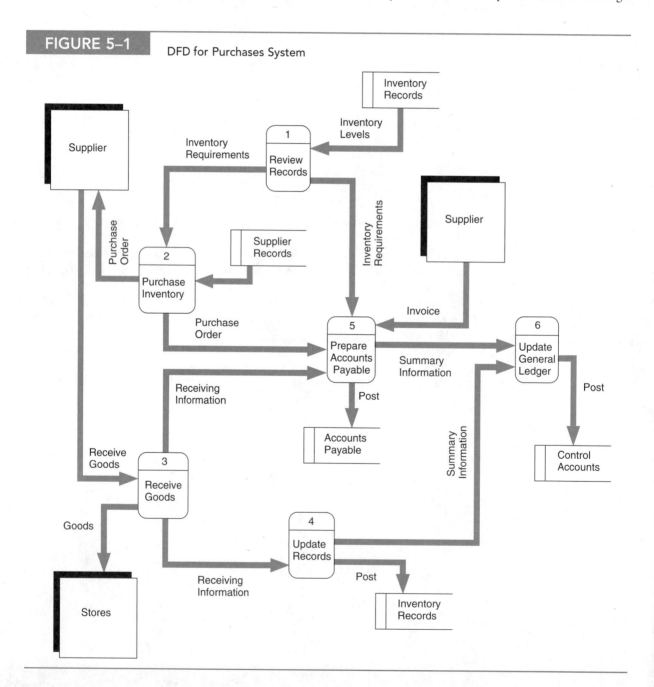

either direct sales to customers (a revenue cycle activity) or transfers into the manufacturing process (conversion cycle activities). Inventory requirement information is sent to both the purchasing and accounts payable (AP) processes.

2. The purchasing process determines the quantity to order, selects a supplier, and prepares a purchase order. The information is sent to both the supplier and the AP process.

3. After a period of time, the firm receives the inventory items from the supplier. Goods received are inspected for quality and quantity and sent to the stores or warehouse.

4. Information about the receipt of inventory is used to update the inventory records.

5. The AP process receives the invoice from the supplier. AP reconciles this with the other information it has compiled for the transaction and records an obligation to pay at some future date, depending on the terms of trade with the supplier. Usually, payment will occur on the last possible day to take full advantage of interest earned and discounts offered.

6. The general ledger receives summary information from accounts payable (total increases in liabilities) and inventory control (total increases in inventory). This information is reconciled for accuracy and posted to the accounts payable and inventory control accounts.

A MANUAL SYSTEM

Figure 5–2 presents a document flowchart of the manual purchases system. In general, the procedures described below apply to both manufacturing and retailing firms. A major difference lies in the way transactions are authorized. Manufacturing firms purchase raw materials for production. Their purchasing decisions are authorized by the production planning and control function that is described in Chapter 7. Merchandising firms purchase finished goods for resale. The inventory control function provides the purchase authorization for this type of firm.

Inventory Control

Firms deplete their inventories by transferring raw materials into the production process (the conversion cycle) and by selling finished goods to customers (revenue cycle). Our illustration assumes the latter case, in which inventory control monitors and records finished goods inventory levels. When inventories drop to a predetermined reorder point, the clerk prepares a **purchase requisition**. Figure 5–3 (page 243) presents an example of a purchase requisition. One copy of the purchase requisition goes to the purchasing department, and one copy goes to accounts payable, where the AP clerk files it in the **accounts payable pending file**. The inventory control clerk files the last copy in the **open purchase requisition file**.

Depending on the method used to identify inventory requirements, either a separate purchase requisition will be prepared for each item or, alternatively, a single requisition can contain multiple items. For example, if the inventory control clerk recalculates inventory on hand after each sale is processed, a separate purchase requisition will be prepared for each item as the need is recognized. This can result in multiple purchase requisitions for a given vendor. Later in the purchases process, these purchase requisitions must be combined into a single purchase order (discussed next) that goes to the vendor. In this type of system, each purchase order will be associated with one or more purchase requisitions.

FIGURE 5-2 Manual Purchases System

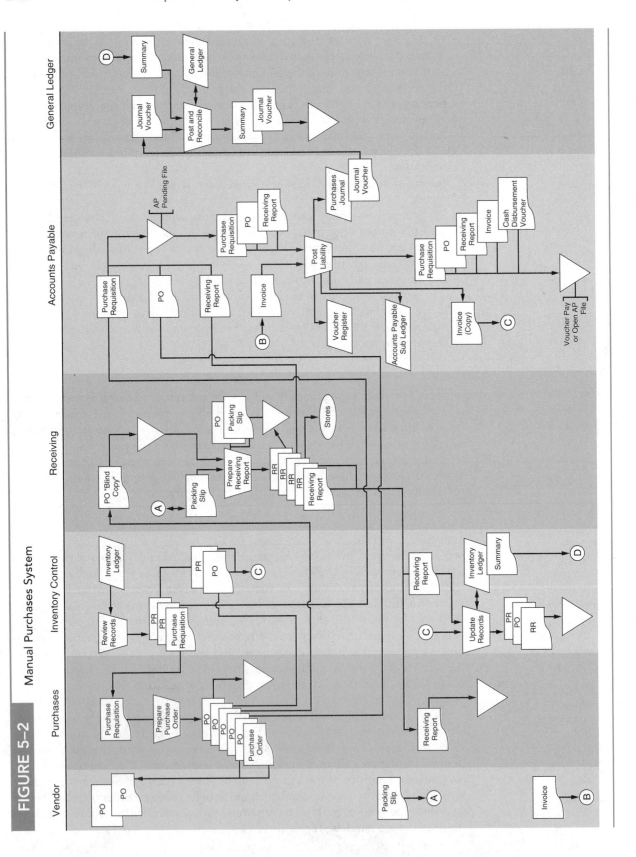

FIGURE 5–3	Purchase Requisition

<table>
<tr><td colspan="3" style="text-align:center">Hampshire Supply Co.
Purchase Requisition</td><td>No. 89631</td></tr>
</table>

Hampshire Supply Co.
Purchase Requisition
No. **89631**

Suggested Vendor   _Jones and Harper Co._
                   1620 North Main St.
                   Bethlehem PA 18017

Date Prepared		Date Needed
8/15/01		*9/1/01*

Part No.	Quantity	Description	Unit Price	Extended Price
86329	*200*	*Engine Block Core Plug*	*$1.10*	*$220*

Prepared By: *RBJ*	Approved By: *THJ*	Total Amount *$220.00*	Vendor Account *4001*

If, however, the inventory control clerk searches for inventory deficiencies periodically as a batch task (the end of the day), inventory requirements can be grouped on a single purchase requisition for each vendor. In this case, each purchase order will be supported by a single purchase requisition.

Purchasing Department

The purchasing department receives the purchase requisitions, sorts them by vendor if necessary, and prepares a multi-part **purchase order** (PO) for each vendor, as illustrated in Figure 5–4. One copy of the PO goes to inventory control, where the clerk files it with the open purchase requisition. One copy of the PO goes to AP for filing in the AP pending file. One copy (the *blind copy*) goes to the receiving department, where it is filed until the inventories arrive. Two copies of the PO go to the vendor. The purchases clerk files the last copy along with the purchase requisition in the **open purchase order file**.

Inventory control can supply much of the ordering information needed by the purchasing department directly from the inventory records. This information includes the name and address of the primary supplier, the economic order quantity (EOQ)[1] of the item, and the standard or expected unit cost of the item. Providing the purchasing department with this information on the purchase requisition greatly facilitates the purchasing process. For many firms, 80 to 90 percent of their inventory

---

[1]   The economic order quantity model and other inventory models are covered in Chapter 7.

FIGURE 5–4   Purchase Order

		Hampshire Supply Co. Purchase Order			No. **23591**
To :	Jones and Harper Co. 1620 North Main St. Bethlehem PA 18017				Please show the above number on all shipping documents and invoices

Vendor Number	Date Ordered		Date Needed	Purchasing Agent	Terms
4001		8/15/01	9/1/01	J. Buell	2/10, n/30

Purchase Req. No.	Part No.	Quantity	Description	Unit Price	Extended Price
89631	86329	200	Engine Block Core Plug	$1.10	$220.00
89834	20671	100	Brake Shoes	9.50	950.00
89851	45218	10	Spring Compressors	33.00	330.00

Prepared By :	BKG	Approved By :	RMS	Total Amount	$1,500.00

needs may be dealt with routinely in this way. This allows the purchasing department to devote its efforts to solving problems dealing with scarce, expensive, or unusual inventory. Obtaining these special items often consumes a disproportionate amount of time and effort. To obtain the best prices and terms for the firm, the purchasing department may need to prepare detailed product specifications and request bids from competing vendors.

Receiving

Most firms encounter a time lag (sometimes a significant one) between placing the order and receiving the inventory. During this time, the copies of the PO reside in temporary files in various departments. Note that no economic event has yet occurred. At this point, the firm has received no inventories and incurred no financial obligation. Hence, there is no basis for making a formal entry into any accounting record. However, firms often make memo entries of pending inventory receipts and obligations.

Receipt of Inventories. The next event in the expenditure cycle is the receipt of the inventory. Goods arriving from the vendor are reconciled with the blind copy of the PO. The **blind copy**, illustrated in Figure 5–5, contains no quantity or price information about the products being received. The purpose of the blind copy is to force the receiving clerk to count and inspect inventories to complete the receiving report. At times, receiving docks are very busy and the receiving staff is under pressure to unload the delivery trucks and sign the bill of lading so the truck drivers can go on their

FIGURE 5–5 Blind Copy Purchase Order

		Hampshire Supply Co. Purchase Order			No. **23591**
To :	Jones and Harper Co. 1620 North Main St. Bethlehem PA 18017				Please show the above number on all shipping documents and invoices

Vendor Number	Date Ordered		Date Needed	Purchasing Agent	Terms
4001	8/15/01		9/1/01	J. Buell	2/10, n/30

Purchase Req. No.	Part No.	Quantity	Description	Unit Price	Extended Price
89631 89834 89851	86329 20671 45218		Engine Block Core Plug Brake Shoes Spring Compressors		

Prepared By :	BKG	Approved By :	RMS	Total Amount	

way. If receiving clerks are provided with quantity information, they may be tempted to accept deliveries on the basis of this information alone, rather than verify the quantity and condition of the goods being received. Also, price information shows the value of the inventory and encourages the theft of expensive items from the loading dock before they can be secured in the storeroom. Shipments that are short or contain damaged or incorrect items must be detected before the goods are accepted by the firm and placed into inventory. The blind copy is an important device in reducing this exposure.

Preparation of a Receiving Report. Upon completion of the physical count and inspection, the receiving clerk prepares a multipart **receiving report** stating the quantity and condition of the inventories. Figure 5–6 contains an example of a receiving report. One copy of the receiving report accompanies the physical inventories to either the raw materials storeroom or finished goods warehouse for safekeeping. Another copy goes to the purchasing department, where the purchasing clerk reconciles it with the open PO file. If the shipment is correct, the clerk closes the open PO file and files the purchase requisition, the PO, and the receiving report in the **closed purchase order file**.

A third copy of the receiving report goes to inventory control. Depending on the inventory valuation method in place, the inventory control procedures may vary somewhat among firms. Organizations that use a **standard cost system** carry their inventories at a predetermined standard value regardless of the price actually paid to the vendor. Figure 5–7 presents a copy of a standard cost inventory ledger.

FIGURE 5–6 Receiving Report

Hampshire Supply Co. Receiving Report			No. **62311**
Vendor *Jones and Harper Co.*		Shipped Via : *Vendor*	
Purchase Order No. *23591*		Date Received *9/1/01*	

Part No.	Quantity	Description	Condition
86329	*200*	*Engine Block Core Plug*	*Good*
20671	*100*	*Brake Shoes*	*Good*
45218	*10*	*Spring Compressors*	*Ear on one unit bent*

Received By: *RTS*	Inspected By: *LEW*	Delivered To: *DYT*

Posting to the standard cost ledger requires information only about the quantities received. Since the receiving report contains quantity information, it serves this purpose. Updating **actual cost inventory ledgers** requires additional financial information, such as a copy of the supplier's invoice when it arrives.

FIGURE 5–7 Inventory Subsidiary Ledger Using Standard Cost

HAMPSHIRE MACHINE CO.

Perpetual Inventory Record—Item #86329

Item Description	Units Received	Units Sold	Qnty On Hand	Reorder Point	Qnty On Order	EOC	Vendor Number	Standard Cost	Total Inven. Cost
Engine Block Core Plug	200		200	30	—	200	4001	1.10	220
		30	170						187
		20	150						165

Because the receiving report contains quantities only, it is insufficient as a source document for posting in this type of system. However, it does serve as a basis for recording the arrival of goods and their quantities. But the financial value of the inventory cannot be computed until the arrival of the invoice.

A fourth copy of the receiving report goes to the accounts payable department, where it is filed in the accounts payable pending file. The final copy of the receiving report is filed in the receiving department.

Accounts Payable Department

During the course of this transaction, the accounts payable department has received and temporarily filed copies of the purchase requisition, purchase order, and receiving report. The organization has received inventories from the vendor and has an obligation to pay for the goods.

However, at this point in the process, the firm may not have the financial information needed to record the transaction. The formal document for providing this information is the **supplier's invoice**.[2] If the firm has not yet received the invoice, it will defer recording the liability until the invoice arrives. This creates a slight lag (a few days) in the recording process, during which time the firm's liabilities are technically understated. As a practical matter, this misstatement is a problem only at period-end closing, when the firm prepares financial statements. To close the books, an estimate of the obligation's value is made until the invoice arrives. If the estimate is incorrect by a material amount, an adjusting entry must be made to correct the error. Since most AP procedures are triggered by the receipt of the invoice, accountants should be aware that unrecorded liabilities may exist at period-end closing.

When the invoice arrives, the accounts payable clerk reconciles the financial information with the documents in the pending file, records the transaction in the purchases journal, and posts it to the supplier's account in the accounts payable subsidiary ledger. Figure 5–8 shows the relationship between these accounting records.

Recall that the inventory valuation method will determine how inventory control will have recorded the receipt of inventories. If the firm is using the actual cost method, the accounts payable clerk sends a copy of the supplier's invoice to inventory control. If standard costs are used, this step is not necessary.

After recording the liability, the accounts payable clerk transfers all source documents (purchase requisition, purchase order, receiving report, and invoice) to the **open accounts payable file**. Typically, this file is organized by payment due date to ensure that debts are paid on the last possible date without missing due dates and losing discounts. We examine cash disbursements procedures later in this chapter. Finally, the accounts payable clerk summarizes the entries in the purchases journal for the period (or batch) and prepares a journal voucher for the general ledger department (see Figure 5–8). Assuming the organization uses the perpetual inventory method, the journal entry will be:

	DR	CR
Inventory—Control	6,800.00	
Accounts Payable—Control		6,800.00

---

2   Note that the supplier's invoice in the buyer's expenditure cycle is the sales invoice of the supplier's revenue cycle.

FIGURE 5-8

Relationship between Purchases Journal, Accounts Payable Subsidiary Ledger, and Journal Voucher

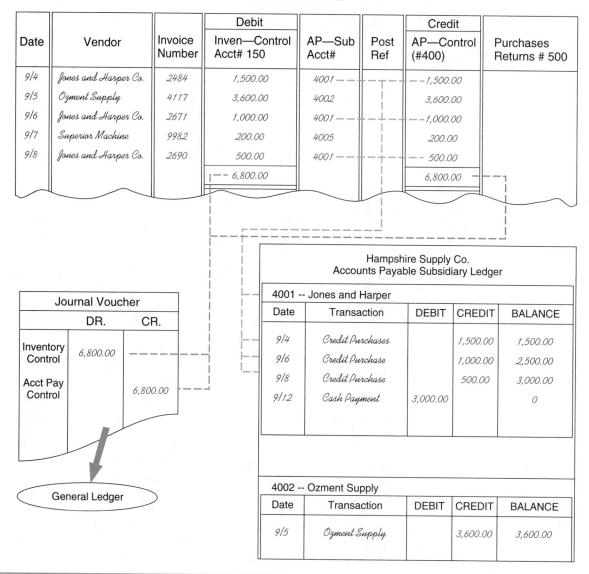

Hampshire Supply Co.
Purchases Journal

Date	Vendor	Invoice Number	Debit Inven—Control Acct# 150	AP—Sub Acct#	Post Ref	Credit AP—Control (#400)	Purchases Returns # 500
9/4	Jones and Harper Co.	2484	1,500.00	4001		1,500.00	
9/5	Ozment Supply	4117	3,600.00	4002		3,600.00	
9/6	Jones and Harper Co.	2671	1,000.00	4001		1,000.00	
9/7	Superior Machine	9982	200.00	4005		200.00	
9/8	Jones and Harper Co.	2690	500.00	4001		500.00	
			6,800.00			6,800.00	

Journal Voucher

	DR.	CR.
Inventory Control	6,800.00	
Acct Pay Control		6,800.00

General Ledger

Hampshire Supply Co.
Accounts Payable Subsidiary Ledger

4001 -- Jones and Harper

Date	Transaction	DEBIT	CREDIT	BALANCE
9/4	Credit Purchases		1,500.00	1,500.00
9/6	Credit Purchase		1,000.00	2,500.00
9/8	Credit Purchase		500.00	3,000.00
9/12	Cash Payment	3,000.00		0

4002 -- Ozment Supply

Date	Transaction	DEBIT	CREDIT	BALANCE
9/5	Ozment Supply		3,600.00	3,600.00

If the periodic inventory method is used, the entry will be:

	DR	CR
Purchases	6,800.00	
Accounts Payable—Control		6,800.00

Voucher Payable System

Many firms use a **voucher payable system** as an alternative to the accounts payable procedures described above. Under this system, the accounts payable department uses **cash disbursement vouchers** and maintains a voucher register. When the AP clerk reconciles the source documents as before, he or she then prepares a cash disbursement voucher. Figure 5–9 shows an example of a voucher.

Vouchers provide improved control over cash disbursements, and they allow firms to consolidate several payments to the same supplier on a single voucher, thus reducing the number of checks written.

The accounts payable clerk records the voucher in the **voucher register**, as illustrated in Figure 5–10. The voucher register reflects the accounts payable liability of the firm. The sum of the open (unpaid) vouchers in the register is also the firm's total accounts payable balance. For these reasons, many firms have replaced their accounts payable ledger with the voucher register. The flowchart in Figure 5–2 shows both methods in use.

The accounts payable clerk files the cash disbursement voucher, along with supporting source documents, in the **vouchers payable file**. This file is equivalent to the open accounts payable file discussed earlier and also is organized by due date.

General Ledger Department

The general ledger department receives a journal voucher from the accounts payable department and an account summary from inventory control. The general ledger clerk posts from the journal voucher to the inventory and accounts payable control accounts and reconciles the inventory control account and the inventory subsidiary summary. With this step, the purchases phase of the expenditure cycle is completed.

FIGURE 5–9

Cash
Disbursement
Voucher

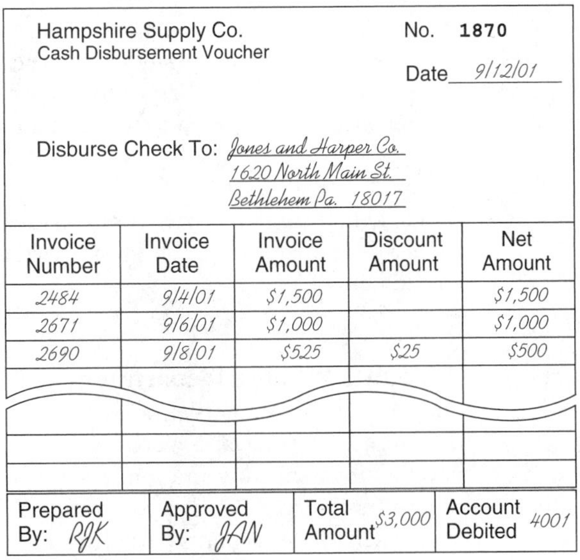

Hampshire Supply Co. Cash Disbursement Voucher			No. **1870**	
			Date _9/12/01_	
Disburse Check To: _Jones and Harper Co._ _1620 North Main St._ _Bethlehem Pa. 18017_				
Invoice Number	Invoice Date	Invoice Amount	Discount Amount	Net Amount
2484	9/4/01	$1,500		$1,500
2671	9/6/01	$1,000		$1,000
2690	9/8/01	$525	$25	$500
Prepared By: _RJK_	Approved By: _JAN_	Total Amount _$3,000_	Account Debited _4001_	

FIGURE 5–10   Voucher Register

		Paid								Misc. Debits	
Date	Voucher No.	Check No.	Date	Voucher Payable (credit)	Merchandise Debit	Supplies Debit	Selling Expense Debit	Administrative Expense Debit	Fixed Assets Debit	Acct. No.	Amount
9/12/01	1870	104	9/14	3,000	3,000						
9/13/01	1871			3,600		3,600					
9/14/01	1872	105	9/15	500			500				

Hampshire Supply Co. Voucher Register (table title)

THE CASH DISBURSEMENTS SYSTEMS

The cash disbursements system processes the payment of obligations created in the purchases system. The principal objective of this system is to ensure that valid creditors receive the correct amounts owed them when the obligation comes due. If the system makes payments early, the firm forgoes interest income it could have earned on the funds. However, if obligations are paid late, the firm will lose purchase discounts or may damage its credit standing.

Figure 5–11 presents a DFD depicting the basic information and resource flows of the cash disbursements system. The system comprises three processes:

1. The accounts payable process reviews the accounts payable file for items due and authorizes the cash disbursements process to make payment.
2. The cash disbursements process prepares and distributes the checks to the suppliers. Copies of the checks are returned to accounts payable as proof that the obligations were paid, and the accounts payable accounts are updated to remove the liabilities.
3. At the end of the period, both the cash disbursements and accounts payable processes send summary information to the general ledger. The information is reconciled and posted to the cash and accounts payable control accounts.

A MANUAL SYSTEM

A detailed document flowchart of a manual cash disbursements system is presented in Figure 5–12 (page 252). The tasks performed in each of the key processes are discussed below.

Accounts Payable Department

The cash disbursements process begins in the accounts payable department. Each day, the accounts payable clerk reviews the **open vouchers payable file** (or accounts payable) for items due and sends the vouchers and supporting documents (purchase requisition, purchase order, receiving report, and invoice) to the cash disbursements department. The accounts payable clerk debits the suppliers' accounts in the accounts payable subsidiary ledger and sends an account summary to the general ledger department.

FIGURE 5–11   DFD for Cash Disbursements System

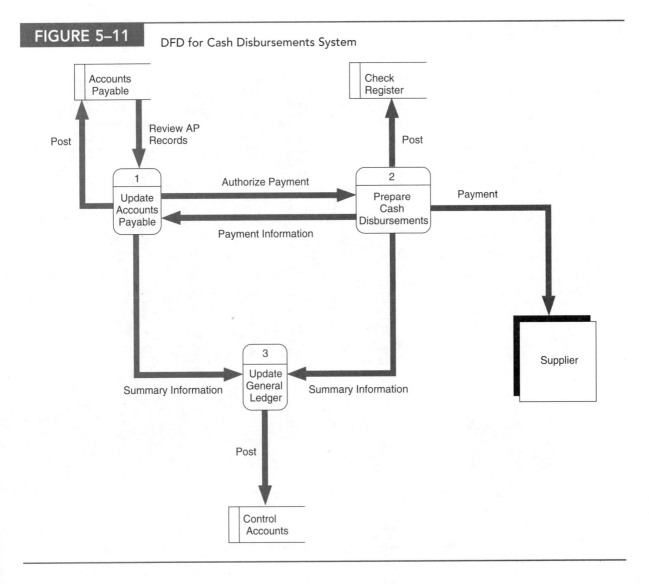

Cash Disbursements Department

The cash disbursements clerk receives the voucher packets and reviews the documents for completeness and clerical accuracy. For each disbursement, the clerk prepares a three-part check and records the check number, dollar amount, voucher number, and other pertinent data in the **check register**, also called the **cash disbursements journal**. Figure 5–13 (page 253) shows an example of a check register.

The check, along with the supporting documents, goes to the cash disbursements department manager, or treasurer, for his or her signature. The negotiable portion of the check is mailed to the supplier, and the clerk attaches a copy of the check to the voucher packet as proof of payment and files the third copy. The clerk marks the documents in the voucher packets as paid and returns them to the accounts payable department. Upon receipt of the voucher packet, the accounts payable clerk closes the open voucher by recording the check number in the voucher register and filing the voucher packet in the **closed voucher file**. Finally, the cash disbursements clerk

| FIGURE 5–12 | Cash Disbursements System |

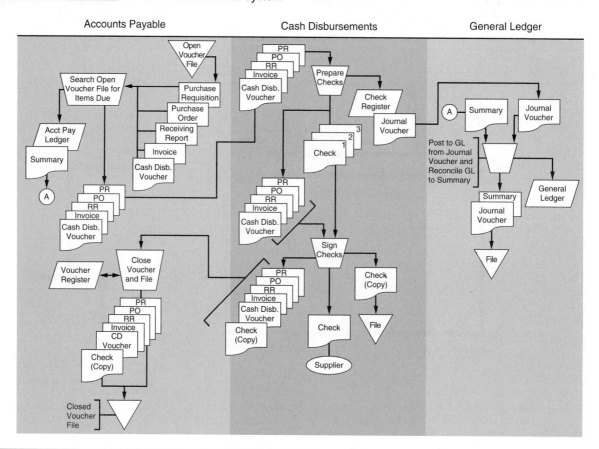

summarizes the entries made to the check register and sends a journal voucher with the following journal entry to the general ledger department:

	DR	CR
Accounts Payable	XXXX.XX	
Cash		XXXX.XX

General Ledger Department

The general ledger clerk receives the journal voucher from cash disbursements and the account summary from accounts payable. The voucher figures show the total reductions to the firm's obligations and cash account as a result of payments to suppliers. The general ledger clerk posts to the accounts payable control and cash accounts in the general ledger and reconciles the accounts payable control account with the accounts payable subsidiary summary. This concludes the cash disbursements procedures.

EXPENDITURE CYCLE CONTROLS

This section describes the primary internal controls in the expenditure cycle according to the control procedures specified in SAS 78. The main points are summarized in Table 5–1.

FIGURE 5–13   Cash Disbursements Journal (Check Register)

Cash Disbursements Journal

Date	Check No.	Voucher No.	Description	Credit Cash	Credit Purch. Disc.	GL / Subsidiary Account Debited	Posted	Vouch Pay 401	Freight-in 516	Op Expen 509	Other	Posted
9/4/01	101	1867	Martin Motors	500		Auto					500	✓
9/4/01	102	1868	Pen Power	100		Utility	✓			100		
9/12/01	103	1869	Acme Auto	500		Purchases					500	✓
9/14/01	104	1870	Jones and Harper	3,000				3,000				

TABLE 5–1

Summary of Expenditure Cycle Controls

CONTROL POINTS IN THE EXPENDITURE CYCLE

Control Activity	Purchases Processing System	Cash Disbursements System
Transactions authorization	Inventory control	Accounts payable authorizes payment.
Segregation of duties	Inventory control separate from purchasing and inventory custody. AP subsidiary ledger separate from the general ledger.	Separate AP subsidiary ledger, cash disbursements, and general ledger functions.
Supervision	Receiving department	
Accounting records	AP subsidiary ledger, general ledger, purchases requisition file, purchase order file, receiving report file.	Voucher payable file, AP subsidiary ledger, cash disbursements journal, general ledger cash accounts.
Access	Security of physical assets. Limit access to the accounting records above.	Proper security over cash. Limit access to the accounting records above.
Independent verification	Accounts payable reconciles source documents before liability is recorded. General ledger reconciles overall accuracy of process.	Final review by cash disbursements. Overall reconciliation by general ledger. Periodic bank reconciliation by controller.

Transaction Authorization

Purchases Subsystem. The inventory control department monitors inventory levels continually. As inventory levels drop to their predetermined reorder points, inventory control formally authorizes replenishment with a purchase requisition.

Formalizing the authorization process promotes efficient inventory management and ensures the legitimacy of purchases transactions. Without this step, purchasing agents could purchase inventories at their own discretion, being in a position both to authorize and to process the purchase transactions. Unauthorized purchasing can result in excessive inventory levels for some items, while others go out of stock. Either situation is potentially damaging to the firm. Excessive inventories tie up the organization's cash reserves, and "stockouts" cause lost sales and manufacturing delays.

Cash Disbursements Subsystem. The accounts payable department authorizes cash disbursements via the cash disbursement voucher. To provide effective control over the flow of cash from the firm, the cash disbursements clerk should not write checks without this explicit authorization. A cash disbursements journal (check register) containing the voucher number authorizing each check (see Figure 5–13) provides an audit trail for verifying the authenticity of every check written.

Segregation of Duties

Segregation of Inventory Control from the Warehouse. Within the purchases subsystem, the primary physical asset is inventory. Inventory control keeps the detailed records of the asset, while the warehouse has custody. At any point in time, an auditor should be able to reconcile inventory records to the physical inventory.

Segregation of the General Ledger and Accounts Payable from Cash Disbursements. The asset subject to exposure in the cash disbursements subsystem is cash. The records that control this asset are the accounts payable subsidiary ledger and the cash account in the general ledger. An individual with the combined responsibilities of writing checks, posting to the cash account, and maintaining accounts payable could perpetrate fraud against the firm. For instance, an individual with such access could withdraw cash and then adjust the cash account accordingly to hide the transaction. Also, he or she could establish fraudulent accounts payable (to an associate in a nonexistent vendor company) and then write checks to discharge the phony obligations. By segregating these functions (see Figures 5–2 and 5–12), we greatly reduce this type of exposure.

Supervision

The area that benefits most from supervision in the expenditure cycle is the receiving department. Large quantities of valuable assets flow through this area on their way to the warehouse. Close supervision here reduces the chances of two types of exposure: (1) failure to properly inspect the assets and (2) the theft of assets.

Inspection of Assets. When goods arrive from the supplier, receiving clerks must inspect items for proper quantities and condition (damage, spoilage, and so on). For this reason, the receiving clerk receives a blind copy of the original purchase order from purchasing. A blind purchase order has all the relevant information about the goods being received except for the quantities and prices. To obtain the information on quantities, which is needed for the receiving report, the receiving personnel are forced to physically count and inspect the goods. If receiving clerks were provided with quantity information through formal documentation (that is, the purchase order), they may be tempted to transfer this information to the receiving report without performing a physical count. Inspecting and counting the items received protects the firm from incomplete orders and damaged goods. Supervision is critical at this point to ensure that the clerks properly carry out these important duties. Incoming goods are accompanied by a packing slip containing quantity information that could be used to circumvent the inspection process. A supervisor should take custody of the packing slip while receiving clerks count and inspect the goods.

Theft of Assets. Receiving departments are sometimes hectic and cluttered during busy periods. In this environment, incoming inventories are exposed to theft until they are securely placed in the warehouse. Improper inspection procedures coupled with inadequate supervision can create a situation that is conducive to the theft of inventories in transit.

Accounting Records
The control objective of accounting records is to maintain an adequate audit trail for tracing a transaction from its source document to the financial statements. The expenditure cycle affects the following accounting records: accounts payable subsidiary ledger, voucher register, check register, and general ledger. The auditor's concern in the expenditure cycle is that obligations may be materially understated on financial statements due to unrecorded transactions. This is a normal occurrence at year-end closing simply because some supplier invoices do not arrive in time to record the liabilities. However, this could also happen as an attempt to intentionally misstate financial information. Hence, in addition to the routine accounting records, expenditure cycle systems must provide supporting information, such as the purchase requisition file, the purchase order file, and the **receiving report file**. By reviewing these peripheral files, auditors can obtain evidence of inventory purchases that have not been recorded as liabilities.

Access Controls
Direct Access. In the expenditure cycle, a firm must control access to physical assets such as cash and inventory. These control concerns are essentially the same as in the revenue cycle. Direct access controls include locks, alarms, and restricted access to areas that contain inventories and cash.

Indirect Access. A firm must limit access to documents that control its physical assets. For example, an individual with access to purchase requisitions, purchase orders, and receiving reports has the ingredients to construct a fraudulent purchase transaction. With the proper supporting documents, a fraudulent transaction can be made to look legitimate to the system and could be paid.

Independent Verification
Independent Verification by Accounts Payable. The accounts payable department plays a vital role in the verification of the work done by others in this system.

Copies of key source documents flow into this department for review and comparison. Each document contains unique facts about the purchase transaction, which the accounts payable clerk must reconcile before the firm recognizes an obligation. These include:

1. The purchase requisition, which shows that the firm needed the inventories and that the transaction was authorized.
2. The purchase order, which shows that the purchasing agent ordered only the needed inventories from a valid vendor.[3] This document should reconcile with the purchase requisition.
3. The receiving report, which is evidence of the physical receipt of the goods, their condition, and the quantities received. The reconciliation of this document with the previous two documents signifies that the organization has a legitimate obligation.
4. The supplier's invoice, which provides the financial information needed to record this obligation as an account payable. The accounts payable clerk verifies that the prices on the invoice are reasonable compared with the expected prices on the purchase order.

Independent Verification by the General Ledger Department. The general ledger department provides another independent verification in the system. This department receives journal vouchers from inventory control, accounts payable, and cash disbursements. From these summary figures, the general ledger clerk verifies that the total obligations recorded equal the total inventories received and that the total reductions in accounts payable equal the total disbursements of cash.

COMPUTER-BASED PURCHASES AND CASH DISBURSEMENTS APPLICATIONS

AUTOMATING PURCHASES PROCEDURES USING BATCH PROCESSING TECHNOLOGY

Many of the manual functions in the batch system presented in Figure 5–14 are the same as those in Figure 5–2. The principal difference is that the routine accounting tasks are automated. The following section describes the sequence of events as they occur in this system.

Data Processing Department: Step 1

The purchasing process begins in the data processing department, where the inventory control function is performed. The revenue cycle (in retailing firms) or the conversion cycle (in manufacturing firms) actually initiates this activity. When inventories are reduced by sales to customers or usage in production, the system determines if the affected items in the **inventory subsidiary file** have fallen to their re-

---

3   Firms often establish a list of valid vendors with whom they do regular business. Purchasing agents must acquire inventories only from valid vendors. This technique deters certain types of fraud such as an agent buying from suppliers with whom he or she has a relationship (a relative or friend) or buying at excessive prices from vendors in exchange for a kickback or bribe.

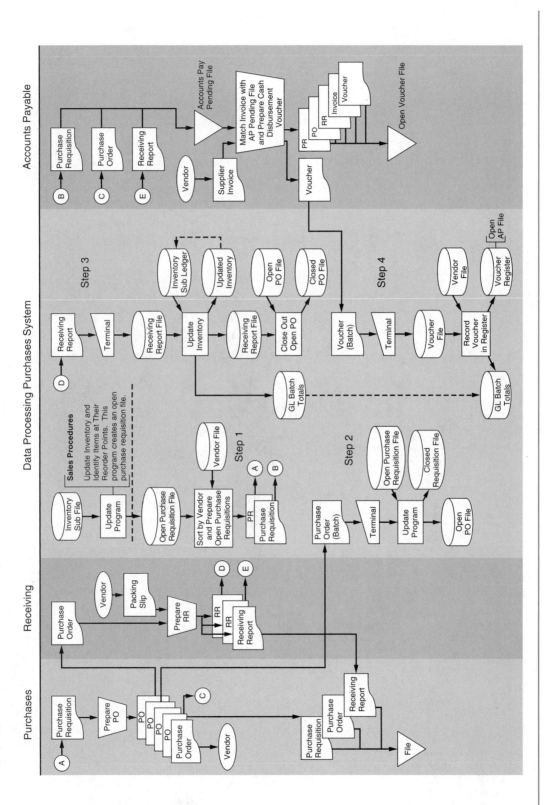

FIGURE 5-14

Batch Purchases System

FIGURE 5–14 *(continued)*

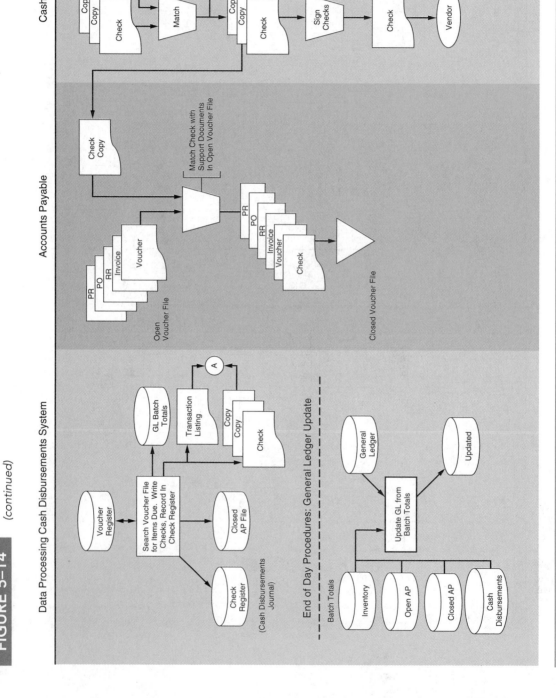

order points.[4] If so, a record is created in the open requisition file. Each record in the open requisition file defines a separate inventory item to be replenished. The record contains the inventory item number, a description of the item, the quantity to be ordered, the standard unit price, and the vendor number of the primary supplier. The information needed to create the requisition record is selected from the inventory subsidiary record. The inventory subsidiary record is then flagged "On Order" to prevent the item from being ordered again before it arrives. Figure 5–15 shows the record structures for the files used in this system.

FIGURE 5–15   Record Structures for Expenditure Cycle Files

| Inven Num | Description | Qnty on Hand | Reorder Point | Qnty On Order★ | EOQ | Vendor Number | Standard Cost | Total Inven. Cost | Inventory Master File |

| Pur Req Number | Inven Num | Qnty on Order | Vendor Number | Unit Standard Cost | Purchase Requisition File |

| Vendor Number | Address | Terms of Trade | Date of Last Order | Lead Time | Vendor File |

| PO Num | Pur Req Number | Inven Num | Qnty On Order | Vendor Number | Address | Standard Cost | Expected Invoice Amount | Rec Flag | Inven Flag | Open (and Closed) Purchase Order File |

| Voucher Number | Check Num | Invoice Num | Invoice Amount | Acct Cr | Acct DR | Vendor Number | Open Date | Due Date | Close Date |

Voucher Register (Open AP File)

★ A value in this field is a "flag" to the system not to order item a second time. When inventories are received, the flag is removed by changing this value to zero.

4   This may be batch or real time, depending on the revenue and conversion cycle systems that interface with the expenditure cycle. The raw materials and finished goods inventory files link these three transaction cycles together. The design of one system influences the others. For example, if sales processing (revenue cycle) reduces inventories in real time, the system will naturally identify inventory requirements in real time also. This is true even if the purchases system is batch-oriented.

At the end of the day, the system sorts the open requisition file by vendor number and consolidates multiple items from the same vendor onto a single requisition. Next, vendor mailing information is retrieved from the **valid vendor file** to produce purchase requisition documents. Copies of these documents go to manual procedures in the purchasing and accounts payable departments.

Purchasing Department

Upon receipt of the purchase requisition, the purchasing department prepares a five-part purchase order. Copies go to the vendor, accounts payable, receiving, data processing, and the purchasing department's own file.

The system in Figure 5–14 employs manual procedures to control the ordering process. A computer program identifies inventory requirements and prepares traditional purchase requisitions, thus allowing the purchasing agent to verify the purchase transaction before placing the order. Some firms use this technique to reduce the risk of placing unnecessary orders with vendors due to a computer error. However, such manual intervention creates delays in the ordering process. If sufficient computer controls are in place to prevent or detect purchasing errors, then more efficient ordering procedures can be implemented.

Before continuing with our example, we need to discuss alternative approaches for authorizing and ordering inventories. Figure 5–16 illustrates three different methods. In *alternative one*, the system advances the procedures shown in Figure 5–14 one step further. This system prepares the purchase order documents and sends them to the purchasing department for review and signing. The purchasing agent then mails the approved purchase orders to the vendors and distributes copies to other internal users.

The system shown in *alternative two* expedites the ordering process by distributing the purchase orders directly to the vendors and internal users, thus bypassing the purchasing department completely. This system produces a transaction list of items ordered for the purchasing agent's review.

Alternative three represents a reengineering technology called *electronic data interchange (EDI)*. The concept was introduced in Chapter 4 to illustrate its application to the revenue cycle. This method produces no physical documents (purchase orders or sales orders). Instead, the computer systems of both the buying and selling companies are connected via a special telecommunications link. The buyer and seller are parties in a trading partner arrangement in which the entire ordering process is automated and unimpeded by human intervention. EDI concepts and technologies are discussed in the Chapter 12.

In each of the three alternatives, the authorization and the ordering steps in the process are consolidated and performed by the computer system. Purchase requisition documents serve no purpose in such systems and are not produced. However, requisition records may still exist on magnetic disk or tape to provide an audit trail.

Data Processing Department: Step 2

Returning to Figure 5–14, the purchase order is used to create an open purchase order record and to transfer the corresponding record(s) in the open purchase requisition file to the closed purchase requisition file.

Receiving Department

When the goods arrive from vendors, the receiving clerk prepares a receiving report. Copies go to purchasing, accounts payable, and data processing.

FIGURE 5–16   Alternative Inventory Ordering Procedures

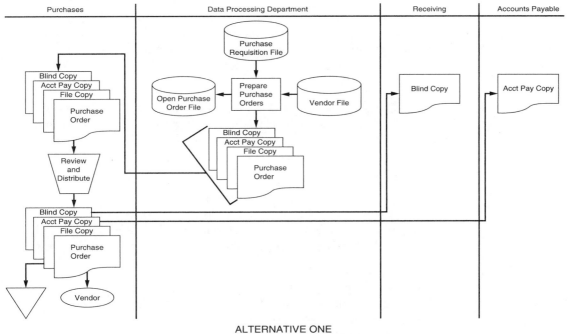

ALTERNATIVE ONE

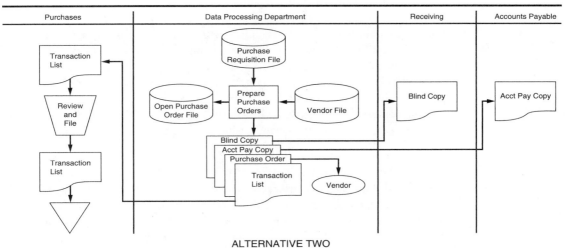

ALTERNATIVE TWO

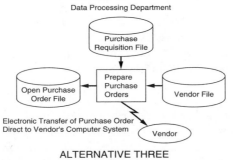

ALTERNATIVE THREE

Data Processing: Step 3

The data processing department runs a batch job (Step 3) that updates the inventory subsidiary file from the receiving reports and removes the "On Order" flag from the inventory records. The system calculates batch totals of inventory receipts for the general ledger update procedure and then closes the corresponding records in the open purchase order file to the closed purchase order file.

Accounts Payable

When the accounts payable clerk receives the supplier's invoice, he or she reconciles it with the supporting documents that were previously placed in the accounts payable pending file. The clerk then prepares a voucher, files it in the open voucher file, and sends a copy of the voucher to data processing.

Data Processing Department: Step 4

A batch program validates the voucher records against the valid vendor file, adds them to the voucher register (or open accounts payable subsidiary file), and prepares batch totals for posting to the accounts payable control account in the general ledger.

CASH DISBURSEMENTS PROCEDURES

Data Processing Department

Each day, the system scans the Due Date field of the voucher register (see Figure 5–15) for items due. Checks are printed for these items, and each check is recorded in the check register (cash disbursements journal). The check number is recorded in the voucher register to close the voucher and transfer the items to the **closed accounts payable file**. The checks, along with a transaction listing, are sent to the cash disbursements department. Finally, batch totals of closed accounts payable and cash disbursements are prepared for the general ledger update procedure.

At the end of the day, batch totals of open (unpaid) and closed (paid) accounts payable, inventory increases, and cash disbursements are posted to the accounts payable control, inventory control, and cash accounts in the general ledger. The totals of closed accounts payable and cash disbursements should balance.

Cash Disbursements Department

The cash disbursements clerk reconciles the checks with the transaction listing and submits the negotiable portion of the checks to management for signing. The checks are then mailed to the suppliers. One copy of each check goes to accounts payable, and the other copy is filed in cash disbursements along with the transaction listing.

Accounts Payable

Upon receipt of the check copies, the accounts payable clerk matches them with open vouchers and transfers these closed items to the closed voucher file. The expenditure cycle process concludes with this step.

REENGINEERING THE PURCHASES/CASH DISBURSEMENTS SYSTEM

The automated system described above simply replicates many of the procedures in a manual system. In particular, the accounts payable task of reconciling supporting documents with supplier invoices is labor intensive and costly. The following example shows how reengineering this process can produce considerable savings.

The Ford Motor Company employed over 500 clerks in its North American accounts payable department. Analysis of the function showed that a large part of the clerks' time was devoted to reconciling discrepancies between supplier invoices, receiving reports, and purchase orders. The first step in solving the problem was to change the business environment. Ford initiated trading partner agreements with suppliers in which they agreed in advance to terms of trade such as price, quantities to be shipped, discounts, and lead times. With these sources of discrepancy eliminated, Ford reengineered the work flow to take advantage of the new environment. The flowchart in Figure 5–17 depicts key features of a reengineered system.

Data Processing

The following tasks are performed automatically:

1. The inventory file is searched for items that have fallen to their reorder point.
2. A record is entered in the purchase requisition file for each item to be replenished.

| FIGURE 5–17 | Reengineered Purchases/Cash Disbursements System |

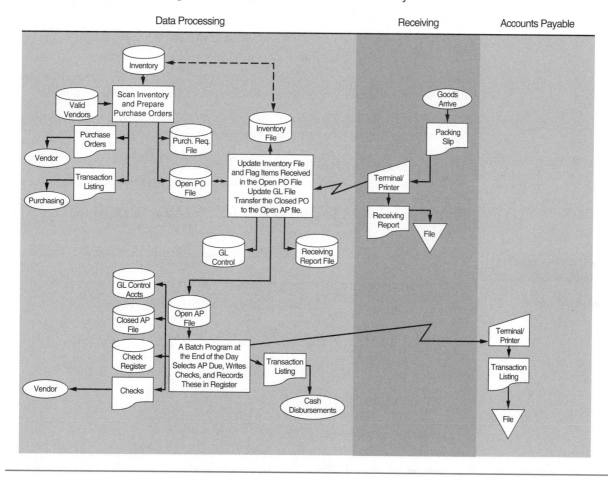

3. Requisitions are then consolidated according to vendor number.
4. Vendor mailing information is retrieved from the valid vendor file.
5. Purchase orders are prepared and added to the open purchase order file.
6. A transaction listing of purchase orders is sent to the purchasing department for review.

Receiving Department

When the goods arrive, the receiving clerk accesses the open purchase order file in real time by entering the purchase order number taken from the packing slip. The receiving screen, illustrated in Figure 5–18, then prompts the clerk to enter the quantities received for each item on the purchase order.

Data Processing

The following tasks are performed automatically by the system:

1. Quantities of items received are matched against the open purchase order record, and a "Y" value is placed in a logical field to indicate the receipt of inventories.
2. A record is added to the receiving report file.
3. The inventory subsidiary records are updated to reflect the receipt of the inventory items.
4. The general ledger inventory control account is updated.
5. The record is removed from the open purchase order file and added to the open accounts payable file, and a due date for payment is established.

Each day, the Due Date fields of the accounts payable records are checked for items due to be paid. The following procedures are performed for the selected items:

1. Checks are printed, signed, and distributed to the mail room for mailing to vendors. EDI vendors receive payment electronically. (This topic is discussed in Chapter 6.)
2. The payments are recorded in the check register file.
3. Items paid are transferred from the open accounts payable file to the closed accounts payable file.
4. The general ledger accounts payable and cash accounts are updated.

FIGURE 5–18

Receiving Screen

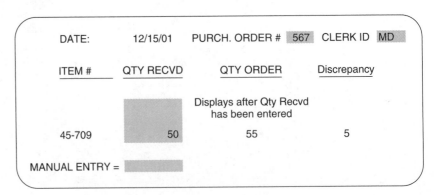

5. Reports detailing these transactions are transmitted via terminal to the accounts payable and cash disbursements departments for management review and filing.

Since the financial information about purchases is known in advance from the trading partner agreement, the **vendor's invoice** provides no critical information that cannot be derived from the receiving report. By eliminating this source of potential discrepancy, Ford was able to eliminate the task of reconciling vendor invoices with the supporting documents for the majority of purchase transactions. As a result of its reengineering effort, Ford was able to reduce its accounts payable staff from 500 to 125.

CONTROL
IMPLICATIONS

The technology control issues (i.e., those pertaining to the use of sequential files versus direct access files) are general in nature. The points made in the last chapter apply to the expenditure cycle also. Therefore, let's examine only the issues specific to this cycle by focusing on the differences between an automated versus a reengineered system.

The Automated System

Improved Inventory Control. The greatest advantage of the automated (batch) system over its manual counterpart is its improved ability to manage inventory needs. Inventory requirements are detected as they arise and are processed automatically. As a result, the risks of accumulating excessive inventory or of running out of stock are reduced. However, with this advantage comes a control concern. Authorization rules governing purchase transactions are consolidated within a computer program. Program errors or flawed inventory models can cause firms to be suddenly inundated with inventories or desperately short of stock. Therefore, it is extremely important to monitor automated decisions. A well-controlled system will provide management with adequate summary reports on inventory purchases, inventory turnover, spoilage, and slow-moving items.

Better Cash Management. This type of system promotes effective cash management by scanning the voucher file daily for items due, thus avoiding early payments and missed due dates. In addition, by writing checks automatically, the firm reduces labor cost, saves processing time, and promotes accuracy.

As a control against unauthorized payments, all entries in the voucher file are validated by comparing the vendor number on the voucher with a valid vendor file. If the vendor number is not on file, the record is presumed to be invalid and is diverted to an error file for management review.

In this system, a manager in the cash disbursements department physically signs the checks, thus providing control over the disbursement of cash. However, many computer systems automate check signing with special printing equipment, which is more efficient when check volume is high but relinquishes some control. To offset this exposure, firms often set a materiality threshold for check writing. Checks for amounts below the threshold are signed automatically, and those above the threshold are signed by an authorized manager or the treasurer.

Time Lag. A lag exists between the arrival of goods in the receiving department and recording inventory receipts in the inventory file. Depending on the type of sales order system in place, this lag may affect sales negatively. Because of this time lag, sales clerks will not know the current status of inventory, and sales may be lost.

Purchasing Bottleneck. In this hypothetical batch system, the purchasing department is directly involved with all purchase decisions. For many firms, this creates additional work that extends the time lag in the ordering process. A vast number of routine purchases could be automated. By freeing purchasing agents from routine work, such as preparing purchase orders and mailing them to the vendors, attention can be focused on problem orders (such as special items or those in short supply), and the purchasing staff can be reduced.

Excessive Paper Documents. The basic batch system is laden with paper documents. All operations departments create documents, which are sent to data processing and which data processing must then convert to magnetic media. A number of costs are associated with paper documents, since the paper must be purchased and the documents filed, stored, handled by internal mail carriers, and converted by data processing personnel. Organizations with high volumes of transactions benefit considerably from reducing or eliminating paper documents in their systems.

The Reengineered System

This system addresses many of the operational weaknesses found in the basic batch system. Specifically, the improvements in this system are that (1) it uses real-time procedures and direct access files to shorten the lag time in record keeping, (2) it eliminates routine manual procedures through automating, and (3) it achieves a significant reduction in paper documents by using electronic communications between departments and by storing records on direct access media. However, these operational improvements have the following control implications.

Segregation of Duties. This system removes the fundamental separation between authorization and transaction processing. Here, computer programs authorize and process purchase orders and authorize and issue checks to vendors. To compensate for this exposure, the system provides management with detailed transaction listings and summary reports. These documents describe the automated actions taken by the system and allow management to spot errors and any unusual events that warrant investigation.

Accounting Records and Access Controls. This system maintains accounting records exclusively on magnetic disks. To preserve the integrity of these records, the organization must implement controls that limit access to the disks. Unauthorized access to magnetic records carries the same consequences as access to source documents, journals, and ledgers in a manual environment. Organizations can employ a number of physical and software techniques to provide adequate access control. However, keep in mind that some techniques are costly, and management must justify these costs against their expected benefits.

Summary

The chapter examined procurement procedures involving the acquisition of raw materials and finished goods. Because most organizations conduct these activities on a credit basis, the information system needs to be designed to properly recognize and record obligations as they arise and to discharge them when they come due. Two expenditure cycle subsystems accomplish these tasks: the purchases system and the cash disbursements system. This chapter focused on the following areas:

1. The processes of each subsystem and the flow of information between them.
2. The documents, journals, and accounts needed to provide audit trails, maintain historical records, and support internal decision making and financial reporting.
3. The areas of exposure and the control techniques that reduce these risks.
4. The impact of technology on Items 1, 2, and 3 above.

From this perspective, we saw that basic batch systems manage inventory needs more efficiently than manual systems. In addition, batch systems promote effective cash management by identifying items due and by automatic check-writing. Real-time systems reduce the time lag between events and record keeping, eliminate paper in the system, and improve human productivity.

These improvements in efficiency carry control implications. Computers remove a fundamental separation of functions between authorizing and processing transactions. Also at risk is the integrity of accounting records. To control these risks, systems must be designed to provide users with documents and reports that permit independent verification and support audit trail needs.

Key Terms

accounts payable pending file   (241)
actual cost inventory ledgers   (246)
blind copy   (244)
cash disbursement vouchers   (249)
cash disbursements journal   (251)
check register   (251)
closed accounts payable file   (262)
closed purchase order file   (245)
closed voucher file   (251)
inventory subsidiary file   (256)
open accounts payable file   (247)
open purchase order file   (243)
open purchase requisition file   (241)

open vouchers payable file   (250)
purchase order   (243)
purchase requisition   (241)
receiving report   (245)
receiving report file   (255)
standard cost system   (245)
supplier's invoice   (247)
valid vendor file   (260)
vendor's invoice   (265)
voucher payable system   (249)
voucher register   (249)
vouchers payable file   (249)

Review Questions

1. Differentiate between a purchase requisition and a purchase order.
2. What purpose does a purchasing department serve?
3. Distinguish between an accounts payable file and a vouchers payable file.
4. What are the three logical steps of the cash disbursements system?
5. What general ledger journal entries are triggered by the purchases system? From which departments do these journal entries arise?
6. What two types of exposure can close supervision of the receiving department reduce?
7. How can a manual purchases cash disbursements system be reengineered to reduce discrepancies, be more accurate, and reduce processing costs?

8. What steps of independent verification does the general ledger department perform?
9. What is (are) the purpose(s) of maintaining a valid vendor file?

10. How do computerized purchasing systems help to reduce the risk of purchasing bottlenecks?

Discussion Questions

1. What three documents must accompany the payment of an invoice? Discuss where these three documents originate and the resulting control implications.
2. Are any time lags in recording economic events typically experienced in cash disbursements systems? If so, what are they? Discuss the accounting profession's view on this matter as it pertains to financial reporting.
3. Discuss the importance of supervision controls in the receiving department and the reasons behind blind fields on the receiving report, such as quantity and price.
4. Why do the inventory control and general ledger departments seem to "disappear" in computer-based purchasing systems (Figure 5–14)? Are these functions no longer important enough to have their own departments?

5. How does the procedure for determining inventory requirements differ between a basic batch processing system and batch processing with real-time data input of sales and receipts of inventory? What about for the procedures used by the receiving department?
6. What advantages are achieved in choosing
   a. a basic batch computer system over a manual system?
   b. a batch system with real-time data input over a basic batch system?
7. Discuss the major control implications of batch systems with real-time data input. What compensating procedures are available?
8. Discuss some specific examples in which information systems can reduce time lags and how the firm is positively affected by such time lags.

Multiple-Choice Questions

1. Which document helps to ensure that the receiving clerks actually count the number of goods received?
   a. packing list
   b. blind copy of purchase order
   c. shipping notice
   d. invoice
2. When the goods are received and the receiving report has been prepared, which ledger may be updated?
   a. standard cost inventory ledger
   b. inventory subsidiary ledger

   c. general ledger
   d. accounts payable subsidiary ledger
3. Which statement is NOT correct for an expenditure system with proper internal controls?
   a. Cash disbursements maintains the check register.
   b. Accounts payable maintains the accounts payable subsidiary ledger.
   c. Accounts payable is responsible for paying invoices.
   d. Accounts payable is responsible for authorizing invoices.

4. Which duties should be segregated?
   a. matching purchase requisitions, receiving reports, and invoices and authorizing payment
   b. authorizing payment and maintaining the check register
   c. writing checks and maintaining the check register
   d. authorizing payment and maintaining the accounts payable subsidiary ledger
5. Which documents would an auditor most likely choose to examine closely in order to ascertain that all expenditures incurred during the accounting period have been recorded as a liability?
   a. invoices
   b. purchase orders
   c. purchase requisitions
   d. receiving reports
6. Which task must still require human intervention in an automated purchases/cash disbursements system?

a. determination of inventory requirements
b. preparation of a purchase order
c. preparation of a receiving report
d. preparation of a check register

7. CMA 689 3-17
   Which of the following situations represents a strength in the internal control for purchasing and accounts payable?
   a. Prenumbered receiving reports are issued randomly.
   b. Invoices are approved for payment by the purchasing department.
   c. Unmatched receiving reports are reviewed on an annual basis.
   d. Vendors' invoices are matched against purchase orders and receiving reports before a liability is recorded.
   e. The purchasing department reconciles the accounts payable subsidiary vendor ledger with the general ledger control account.

Problems

1. Document Preparation
Create the appropriate documents (purchase requisition, purchase order, receiving report, inventory record, and disbursement voucher) and prepare any journal entries needed to process the following business events for Jethro's Boot & Western Wear Manufacturing Company (this is a manual system).
   a. On October 28, 20x4, the inventory subsidiary ledger for Item 2278, metal pins, indicates that the quantity on hand is 4,000 units (valued at $76), the reorder point is 4,750, and units are on order. The economic order quantity is 6,000 units. The supplier is Jed's Metal Supply Company (vendor number 83682). Our customer number is 584446. The current price per unit is $0.02. Inventory records are kept at cost. The goods should be delivered to Inventory Storage Room 2.
   b. On November 8, the goods were received (the scales indicated that 4,737 units were received).

   c. On November 12, an invoice (number 9886) was received for the above units, which included freight of $6. The terms were 1/10, net 30. Jethro's likes to keep funds available for use as long as possible without missing any discounts.

2. Flowchart Analysis
Examine the diagram on the following page and indicate any incorrect initiation and/or transfer of documentation. What problems could this cause?

3. Accounting Records and Files
Indicate which department—accounts payable, cash disbursements, data processing, purchasing, inventory, or receiving—has ownership over the following files and registers:
   a. open purchase order file
   b. purchase requisition file
   c. open purchase requisition file
   d. closed purchase requisition file
   e. inventory

Problem 2: Flowchart Analysis

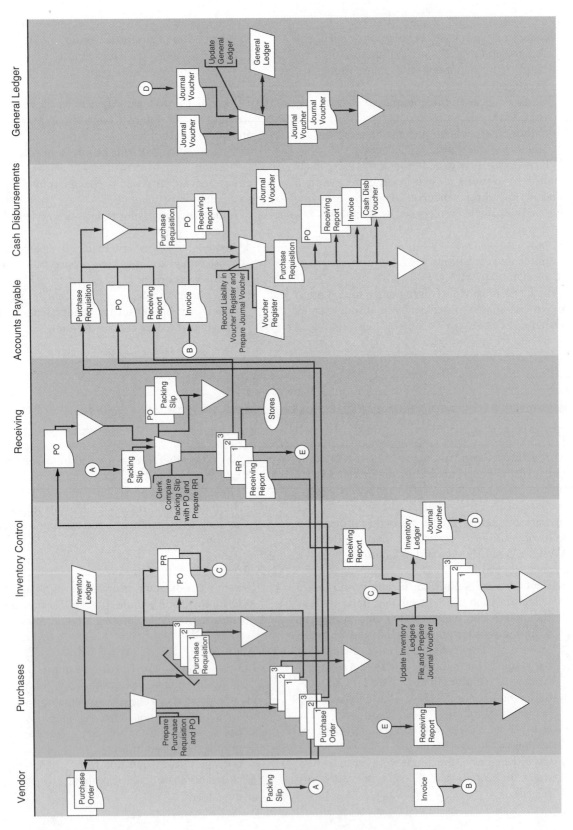

f. closed purchase order file
g. valid vendor file
h. voucher register
i. open vouchers payable file
j. receiving report file
k. closed voucher file
l. check register (cash disbursements journal)

4. Source Documents Identification
Explain, in detail, the process by which the information is obtained and the source of information for each of the fields in the expenditure cycle files. (See Figure 5–15 for a complete listing of files and fields.)

5. Data Processing
Explain how the processing procedures would differ, if at all, for the transactions listed in Problem 1 if a computer-based system with
a. a basic batch processing system were implemented.

b. a batch processing system with real-time data input were used.

6. Internal Control
Using the flowchart of a purchases system below, identify six major control weaknesses in the system. Discuss and classify each weakness in accordance with SAS 78.

7. Purchase Discounts Lost
Estimate the amount of money that could be saved by the accounts payable and cash disbursements departments if a basic batch processing system were implemented. Assume that the clerical workers cost the firm $12 per hour, that 13,000 vouchers are prepared, and that 5,000 checks are written per year. Assume that total cash disbursements to vendors amount to $5 million per year. Due to sloppy bookkeeping, the current system takes advantage of only about 25 percent of the discounts offered by vendors for

Problem 6: Internal Control

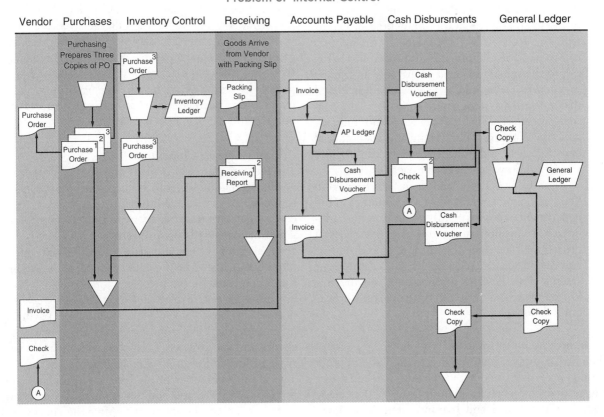

timely payments. The average discount is 2 percent if payment is made within ten days. Payments are currently made on the 15th day after the invoice is received. Make your own assumptions (and state them) regarding how long specific tasks will take. Also discuss any intangible benefits of the system. (Don't worry about excessive paper documentation costs.)

8. Data Processing Output

Using the information provided in Problem 7, discuss all transaction listings and summary reports that would be necessary for a batch system with real-time input of data.

9. CMA 1288 5-3
Internal Control

Lexsteel is a leading manufacturer of steel furniture. While the company has manufacturing plants and distribution facilities throughout the United States, the purchasing, accounting, and treasury functions are centralized at corporate headquarters.

While discussing the management letter with the external auditors, Ray Lansdown, controller of Lexsteel, became aware of potential problems with the accounts payable system. The auditors had to perform additional audit procedures to attest to the validity of accounts payable and cutoff procedures. The auditors have recommended that a detailed systems study be made of the current procedures. Such a study would not only assess the exposure of the company to potential embezzlement and fraud, but would also identify ways to improve management controls.

Landsdown has assigned the study task to Dolores Smith, a relatively new accountant in the department. Because Smith could not find adequate documentation of the accounts payable procedures, she interviewed those employees involved and constructed a flowchart of the current system. This flowchart is presented on the following page. A description of the current procedures follows.

Computer Resources Available

The host computer mainframe is located at corporate headquarters with interactive, remote job-entry terminals at each branch location. In general, data entry occurs at the source and is transmitted to an integrated database maintained on the host computer. Data transmission is made between the branch offices and the host computer over leased telephone lines. The software allows flexibility for managing user access and editing data input.

Procedures for Purchasing Raw Materials

Production orders and appropriate bills of materials are generated by the host computer at corporate headquarters. Based on these bills of materials, purchase orders for raw materials are generated by the centralized purchasing function and mailed directly to the vendors. Each purchase order instructs the vendor to ship the materials directly to the appropriate manufacturing plant. Assuming that the necessary purchase orders have been issued, the manufacturing plants proceed with the production orders received from corporate headquarters.

When goods are received, the manufacturing plant examines and verifies the count to the packing slip and transmits the receiving data to accounts payable at corporate headquarters. In the event that raw material deliveries fall behind production, each branch manager is given the authority to order materials and issue emergency purchase orders directly to the vendors. Data about the emergency orders and verification of materials receipt are transmitted via computer to accounts payable at corporate headquarters. Since the company employs a computerized perpetual inventory system, physical counts of raw materials are deemed not to be cost-effective and are not performed.

Accounts Payable Procedures

Vendor invoices are mailed directly to corporate headquarters and entered by accounts payable personnel when received; this often occurs before the receiving data are transmitted from the branch offices. The final day of the invoice term for payment is entered as the payment due date. This due date must often be calculated by the data entry person using information listed on the invoice.

Once a week, invoices due the following week are printed in chronological entry order on a payment listing, and the corresponding checks are drawn. The checks and the payment listing are sent to the treasurer's office for signing and mailing to the payee. The check number is printed by the computer and displayed on the check, and the payment listing is validated as the checks are signed. After the checks are

Problem 9: Internal Control

mailed, the payment listing is returned to accounts payable for filing. When there is insufficient cash to pay all the invoices, certain checks and the payment listing are retained by the treasurer until all checks can be paid. When the remaining checks are mailed, the listing is then returned to accounts payable. Often, weekly check mailings include a few checks from the previous week, but rarely are there more than two weekly listings involved.

When accounts payable receives the payment listing back from the treasurer's office, the expenses are distributed, coded, and posted to the appropriate plant or cost center accounts. Weekly summary performance reports are processed by accounts payable for each cost center and branch location reflecting all data entry to that point.

Required:

a. Identify and discuss three areas where Lexsteel Corporation may be exposed to fraud or embezzlement due to weaknesses in the procedures described, and recommend improvements to correct these weaknesses.

b. Describe three areas where management information could be distorted due to weaknesses in the procedures, and recommend improvements to correct these weaknesses.

c. Identify three strengths in the procedures described and explain why they are strengths.

Internal Control Cases

1. Teddy's Toys Wholesale Distributors
(Prepared by Jennifer Rush, Lehigh University)

Teddy's Toys is a medium-sized wholesale distributor of toys and games, located in Pennsylvania, that distributes throughout the northeastern portion of the United States. An English entrepreneur, Theodore E. Bear, established Teddy's in 1990. His previous experience as vice president of a major toy manufacturing company in England led Ted to take his talents overseas to try to create his own toy distribution center. Teddy's competition is limited to a few other small distributors, due to the limited region and the type of stores to which they sell. Teddy's size and cost base prevent competition between it and large manufacturers. Ted wanted to supply the smaller localized chains and single-standing retail stores around the region. His distribution center would handle the accounts of these smaller stores that larger distribution centers would not.

Ted was a risk-taker. He supplied the common, always popular lines of toys, but also held inventory of some select lines of toys that were relatively unknown. One toy in particular was one that held massive popularity in England due to its widely viewed children's television show. Ted brought a large supply with him to the United States in hopes that the popularity of the toy would make its way overseas. The TV show started to sweep the United States and toys from the show were in high demand. Since Teddy's was the only distribution center of its size to carry such a large stock of this particular toy, sales skyrocketed, causing the company to grow extremely rapidly.

The company currently employs 150 people full-time with many temporary workers hired for seasonal work. Sales are currently at $28 million and growing. The company does business with 10 large wholesale suppliers and various small suppliers. Teddy's has a very stock investment with ordering lead times of 2–3 days for shipment to their customers on in-stock items and 7–10 days lead time for out-of-stock items.

There are certain supplier problems that plague the company. Seasonal stockouts occur as well as excess inventories of products that don't sell. Because Ted is such a risk-taker by supplying different and unique items, there is an excess of inventory that raises carrying costs and takes up shelf space.

During the rapid expansion of the company, Ted concentrated more on developing a good reputation with a high level of customer satisfaction and creating a fun but stable work environment for his employees. Now that the company is firmly established and growing at a steady pace, Ted has the opportunity to take a step back and evaluate the system as a whole to identify current and potential problems that have surfaced throughout the daily operations.

One evening over dinner with his friend, Ernie N. Bertrand, who happens to be a consultant with a large accounting firm, Ted began discussing company problems. Always willing to help a friend, Ernie encouraged Ted to describe the company's expenditure cycle so he could determine where the bugs were.

"A typical day begins in the purchasing department. Brenda, my head purchasing agent, reviews the current inventory records to determine what items need to be reordered. We use a real-time computer system so our inventory records are always up to date, or so we think. We seem to have problems with the inventory records in particular in this system, which you will see as I continue. Once Brenda brings up the inventory requirements she prepares the purchase orders by computer and saves the form in the system, then creates hard copies. She uses one hard copy to send the purchase orders to our vendors via fax, then files it away, and the second copy goes to data processing for updating to the inventory and accounts payable records. However, at times she's found that after she has placed the orders, the inventory levels aren't exactly as she originally thought. They seem to change, either while she is placing the order or after, but we run into stock-outs and excess inventory problems because of these discrepancies."

Ernie thought about this a moment and asked," What type of computer system are you currently using?"

"We use a distributed data processing system connected through a local area network. We felt this type of system would satisfy our needs adequately, while keeping costs down. As you may know, a LAN system has a high degree of data currency, which is why I don't understand the inventory record inaccuracies.

"When the inventory comes in, Ken, in the receiving department, prepares a receiving report to verify the inventory received. He compares the inventory to the packing slip and the purchase orders placed by Brenda on the computer. He has access to a terminal that will pull up the particular purchase order's details when the PO number is entered. I feel Ken is always looking for a short

cut. Ken then sends copies of the receiving report to data processing for updating, and to accounts payable. He also files a copy of the report and the packing slip in his own files.

"When accounts payable receives the report, it is compared to the purchase order placed by Brenda on the computer and to the supplier invoice on file. The accounts payable clerk, Linda, then prepares a cash disbursement voucher, which is sent to data processing for entry. The copies of the receiving report and invoice are filed pending their need by the cash disbursements department. The cash disbursements clerk periodically checks this open voucher file for invoices coming due. The clerk prints a list of the invoices to be paid, which instructs the computer system to post to the check register and the accounts payable files.

"This is the department where it was recently discovered that two of my employees, Tom and the aforementioned Linda, had been stealing from me. The two are brother and sister, Tom being my former cash disbursements clerk. Linda is very knowledgeable about computer systems and teaches evening classes on programming at the local college. Apparently my systems designer had created a back door into the programming for his own use during the maintenance phase of our new system. He gave the managers in each department instructions on how to get into the system and to fix small problems that may occur when he was busy or not there to help. Linda used this weakness in the system to create a vendor, false purchase orders, and inventory receiving reports to keep the accounting records accurate. Tom wrote the appropriate checks as they came due and sent them to the vendors, keeping the fraudulent checks for himself. Copies of the legitimate checks written in cash disbursements were then sent to the accounts payable department for verification and filed. Linda then posted the payments to the accounts payable accounts. The two stole quite a bit of money form the company when a completely manual system was in place. The scam lasted another month under our new computer system before it was finally uncovered."

Ernie was aghast at the theft, "I never thought anyone would do such a thing to someone like you! You treat all your employees like family. How did Linda obtain the password to gain access to the created back door?"

"Apparently, the programmer used one easy password for everything he wanted to access. I guess it wasn't very hard for Linda to figure out. Now we have eliminated the back door and use a large number of difficult passwords. They are no longer easy to remember, so now the designer keeps a list posted in his office to keep track! Anyway, now everything seems to be running smoothly. Getting back to normal operations, at the end of the day, all of the accounts are updated in a batch to the control accounts in the general ledger.

"So that concludes our expenditure cycle. Do you see any problems?"

Required:

1. Create a data flow diagram of the current system.
2. Create a document flowchart of the existing system.
3. Analyze the internal control weaknesses in the system. Model your response according to the six categories of physical control activities specified in SAS 78.
4. Prepare a system flowchart of a redesigned computer-based system that resolves the control weaknesses that you identified.

2. Get Wet Pool Supply Company

(Prepared by Jana Clark and Amy Hamilton, Lehigh University)

Get Wet Company is currently one of the fastest-growing pool supply companies in the industry. The company is located in Florida, with company headquarters in Tampa and two branch stores in Miami and Panama City. Get Wet employs 50 people at the retail stores and about 100 employees at the headquarters. The retail store employees are hired to perform many of the mundane tasks involved with the business. These individuals are younger and less experienced and, as a result, Get Wet has a high employee turnover rate. Also, due to their rapid growth, the company is always looking to hire new employees.

Get Wet offers its customers a wide variety of products, including flotation devices (rafts and inner tubes), pool toys, pool chemicals, and basic pool-cleaning items. The supply company has a customer base that includes private pool owners and small municipal townships. Due to the wide array of products Get Wet offers its customers, the company relies on numerous vendors to fulfill its needs. These vendors include chemical suppliers, pool-cleaning item suppliers, and pool toy suppliers. Also, Get Wet relies on a general supplier, Speedy, for basic swimming and pool needs. The supplies are delivered to the company headquarters in Tampa and later distributed to the retail stores for storage in their stockrooms.

Get Wet's two branch stores have a history of seasonal sales because of the nature of the pool supply industry. Summer is by far the busiest season, due in part to tourism. In addition to these profits, Get Wet has recently landed a large account from Waterworld USA, one of Florida's largest water parks. Get Wet's president, John Poole, is delighted with the direction his company is headed, but he also feels the company may not be completely ready for this growth. It currently employs both low-level computer technology and manual procedures in its accounting system. John feels that the system needs to be revised in order to ensure that the company will be able to handle the new accounts now and in the future.

Purchases and Cash Disbursement Procedures

The process begins with Susie Swimmie, the warehouse clerk, reviewing the inventory subsidiary ledger. When she discovers that inventory has dropped below the predetermined reorder point, Susie prepares five copies of the purchase order. One copy of the purchase order is placed in the open purchase order file and another is sent to accounts payable. Two other copies are sent to the vendor. The remaining copy is sent to the receiving department where it is temporarily filed.

Upon receipt of the packing slip, Tommy Waters, the receiving clerk, pulls the purchase order from the temporary file and inspects the inventory. Tommy prepares four copies of the receiving report. Once this is done, he files the purchase order, the packing slip and a copy of the receiving report. One copy of the receiving report is sent with the merchandise to the warehouse department where Susie updates the inventory subsidiary ledger. Tommy sends the remaining copy to the accounts payable department.

The receipt of the purchase order, receiving report, and invoice by Phil Summers in the accounts payable department triggers the updating of both the accounts payable subsidiary ledger and the purchases journal. Phil then writes and signs the checks. A copy of the check, the purchase order, and the receiving report are filed in the accounts payable department. The original copy of the check is sent to the vendor in payment of the account. A daily summary of accounts payable and cash disbursed is sent to the general ledger department.

Mark Johnson uses the summary from the accounts payable department to post to the general ledger and reconcile the appropriate accounts involved. He then files the summary document in the general ledger department, completing the process.

Required:
1. Create a data flow diagram of the current system.
2. Create a document flowchart of the existing system.
3. Analyze the internal control weaknesses in the system. Model your response according to the six categories of physical control activities specified in SAS 78.
4. Prepare a system flowchart of a redesigned computer-based system that resolves the control weaknesses that you identified.

3. Trenton Net Company, Inc.
(Prepared by Sarah Swift and Jill Holloran, Lehigh University)

Trenton Net Company, Inc. was established in 1953 as a family-run manufacturer of nets, largely supplying the fishing industry. It has two manufacturing plants, one located in Trenton, New Jersey, and the other in Jonesport, Maine. As the fishing industry began to decline in Maine, Trenton Net expanded into different market segments to stay in business. As they diversified their products, the magnitude of their business expanded. Their products still include the original fishing nets but most of their sales now come from sport nets, amusement park nets, debris nets, material-handling nets, and various custom net orders.

In the Trenton plant, the company receives bulk nylon netting from their supplier, Johnson Netting Co., and manipulate the knotless netting

into products for their customers. In the Jonesport factory, the plant staff manufactures knotted netting from nylon rope that they manually tie together to create nets. The nylon rope is supplied by E.I. Dupont. Trenton Net has also started to carry other products besides nets since they have expanded their product line. To complement their nets they sell various hardware pieces that they purchase from various vendors. Trenton Net has also begun to sell accessories that complement their sport nets, such as baseball bats, baseballs, pitching machines, and other sports equipment which they buy from name-brand suppliers.

Trenton Net has incurred many problems in the past with regards to its inventory. A factory worker alerts the purchasing department when they are running low on netting material. At that point it may be too late and the job being manufactured will be delayed. If more orders come in for the same unavailable material these, too, will be delayed and sales may be lost. Trenton Net does not like to carry excess inventory of the sport accessories they offer because this area is still experimental and they are not sure if their customers will want to buy these products. Therefore, if an order is received for baseball bats, they may not be able to fill it on time because they will have to order it from their supplier.

The customers of Trenton Net Company vary greatly due to their large product base. Many universities and secondary schools buy items from Trenton Net for their sports complexes, such as baseball batting cages. Amusement parks use safety nets for their rides and construction workers rely on debris nets for on-site construction. Also, many companies that have warehouse facilities utilize netting in their daily operations and material storage.

As Trenton Net expanded into these new market segments, the CEO decided to gain exposure by advertising in the Thomas Register, an industrial trade advertising book. Trenton Net has also incurred significant advertising expense in trade show participation and various trade magazines. This investment has caused a dramatic increase in sales from $400,000 just five years ago, to just over $1,000,000 today. The physical size of Trenton Net has also expanded to just over 120 employees.

Description of Purchase Procedures

The purchases system begins when factory workers notice a need for more material and they alert a clerk in the purchases/accounts payable department of the inventory status. Once the clerk has been alerted he/she will prepare several purchase orders. One purchase order will be faxed to the supplier and then that PO and a duplicate will be mailed to the vendor. Another purchase order will go directly to the accounts payable pending file and a third will go to the open purchase order file. Finally, the last copy of the purchase order will be sent to the receiving department.

In the receiving department, when the goods arrive with a packing slip, a receiving clerk reconciles the goods with the PO and the packing slip. The goods are then marked with their contents and placed in the warehouse. The copy of the purchase order goes back to the purchases/accounts payable department and is used to close the open purchase order file. The packing slip is also sent to the purchases/accounts payable department to be filed in the accounts payable pending file.

When the invoice is received from the supplier in the purchases/accounts payable department, a clerk reconciles the invoice with the contents of the accounts payable pending file. Once all the information is checked for accuracy, the clerk will enter the information onto a microcomputer, which will update the purchases journal and the accounts payable subsidiary ledger. This event automatically triggers an update to the general ledger. The packing slip, vendor invoice, and purchase order are then filed in an open accounts payable file in this department.

Every day a clerk in the accounts payable/cash disbursements department reviews the open accounts payable file for bills that have come due. A clerk will send all the supporting documents from this file to a cash disbursements manager for review if a bill is noticed to be due. A manager then prepares the check on the microcomputer. Once he/she prepares the check, the accounting software program automatically updates the cash disbursements journal and the accounts payable subsidiary ledger. The general ledger is also automatically updated when changes are made to these accounting records. A manager then makes a photocopy of the check and stamps the real check with the president's signature. The stamped check is then mailed to the supplier. The supporting documents—the packing slip, invoice, purchase order, and check copy—are then used to close the open accounts payable file and are filed in the closed accounts payable file.

Required:

1. Create a data flow diagram of the current system.
2. Create a document flowchart of the existing system.
3. Analyze the internal control weaknesses in the system. Model your response according to the six categories of physical control activities specified in SAS 78.
4. Prepare a system flowchart of a redesigned computer-based system that resolves the control weaknesses that you identified.

4. Mom and Pop's Printing Press

(Prepared by Rick LaNeve and Hong Wai Ng, Lehigh University)

Mom and Pop's Printing Press is a former family-owned company that recently incorporated due to an increased need for capital. Mom and Pop's prints and distributes soft-cover books in bulk to a variety of customers, including schools, libraries, and general bookstores. The text materials are acquired on disk; Mom and Pop's then converts them to metal plates to be used in printing the finished books.

Mom and Pop's employs approximately 150 workers. The facility runs 24 hours a day, utilizing three shifts of workers, and caters to large clients. Mom and Pop's appears to be doing very well; just recently they won a major account from a rival printing press, forcing the rival out of business. Because of their incorporation, Mom and Pop's management decided to bring in an auditing team to review the system and look for potential problems.

Competition among Mom and Pop's suppliers is fierce. Management is concerned that the purchasing agent might be involved in a kickback fraud, since the cost of goods sold has risen disproportionately in recent months. Mom and Pop's keeps a very large inventory of paper and ink, since these are the two crucial components of production. If a stockout occurred, the receipt of a vital order would be six weeks late.

Purchases and Cash Disbursements Process

The purchasing agent reviews the inventory ledger and prepares a purchase order (5 copies) for the goods needed. One copy is sent to the vendor, one copy is sent to receiving, one copy is sent to accounting, one copy is sent to the warehouse, and the last copy is filed.

The packing slip from the incoming goods is reconciled against the purchase order. Once this reconciliation is done, the two are used to prepare a receiving report (4 copies) and are then filed. One receiving report is then sent to the warehouse, one to accounting, and two are placed in files.

The purchase order is used along with the receiving report to update the inventory records and post to the inventory ledgers. An inventory summary is also created at this step, and is sent to the accounting department.

The receiving report, purchase order, and invoice from the vendor are used to update the accounts payable ledger and the purchases journal. The receiving report, purchase order, invoice, and cash disbursement voucher created in the updating process are then filed. Another voucher is used along with the inventory summary created from the warehouse to post to the general ledger. The voucher and the inventory summary are then filed.

Cash Disbursements System

The receiving report, purchase order, invoice, and cash disbursement voucher are all in a file that is searched for items due. When an item is found to be due, the accounts payable ledger is updated, and the account summary is produced. The four documents are then used to prepare the checks. The checks are signed and sent to the supplier. The documents are then re-filed. A journal voucher is also prepared, which is reconciled with the account summary and used to update the general ledger. The account summary and the journal voucher are then filed.

Required:

1. Create a data flow diagram of the current system.
2. Create a document flowchart of the existing system.
3. Analyze the internal control weaknesses in the system. Model your response according to the six categories of physical control activities specified in SAS 78.
4. Prepare a system flowchart of a redesigned computer-based system that resolves the control weaknesses that you identified.

5. BSJ Limousine Service, Inc.

(Prepared by Sarah Blades, Lehigh University)

BSJ Limousine Service, Inc. is a luxury transportation service located in New York, New York. Founded in 1980, BSJ has been gaining market share steadily over the last decade. BSJ receives orders from customers to transport them to specified destinations. The company provides a top-quality service. The limousines are equipped with a full bar and a comfort leather interior.

The past two years have been extremely profitable for the relatively small company. With only 100 employees, BSJ has been experiencing control issues. Also, the manual transaction processing system, as well as the low-level computer technology the company uses, cannot support the volume of business. Out of the 100 employees, 60 are limousine drivers, 15 are administrative positions, 5 are executive positions, and 20 are maintenance positions. With the recent expansion, BSJ's employees are finding it difficult to carry on daily processes. Also, management is concerned about the possibility of fraudulent activity. For this reason, the company has hired Vinsinades, LLP to assess the organization's business processes.

On the expenditure cycle side, the main functions are the purchasing of and payment for the necessary inventory to maintain the fleet of limousines and stock the wet bar. There is a garage and a stockroom in which inventory is kept. Currently, there is no access control of the inventory. The limousine drivers restock the bar at there own discretion at the end of the day. The garage employees refuel and service the cars whenever needed. No records are kept of the used supplies. Once each week the garage manager takes a physical count of the supplies, updates the inventory ledger, and creates purchase requisitions for any necessary items.

The purchasing department clerk receives the purchase requisitions and creates purchase orders from them. When the goods are received in the garage, the garage manager and stockroom manager find their orders and verify that the orders match the sales invoice and a copy of the purchase order. Then a receiving report is created, filed, and forwarded to accounts payable where the purchase requisition, purchase order, and receiving report are filed awaiting the sales invoice. When the sales invoice arrives the liability is officially posted and the documents are ordered by due date in an open accounts payable file. The accounts payable subsidiary ledger is then sent to the general ledger department.

The accounts payable clerk checks the open accounts payable file to see if any bills are due. She creates and signs checks for the due accounts and makes copies of them. Then she puts copies in the files, closes the files, and updates the accounts payable file for the decrease in liability. The checks are summarized and the summary is sent to the general ledger department to be reconciled with the accounts payable journal voucher and then posted.

Required:
1. Create a data flow diagram of the current system.
2. Create a document flowchart of the existing system.
3. Analyze the internal control weaknesses in the system. Model your response according to the six categories of physical control activities specified in SAS 78.
4. Prepare a system flowchart of a redesigned computer-based system that resolves the control weaknesses that you identified.

6. PP&E Sports Emporium
(Prepared by Christina Eberhart, Lehigh University)
PP&E Sports Emporium is a large retailer of sporting goods equipment and apparel, similar to Sports Authority. However, PP&E is only a single store, not a chain. Some of its suppliers include Nike, Adidas, Reebok, Rawling, and Champion. PP&E attempts to target all age groups, from 5-year-olds playing little league baseball to 70-year-olds who are fishing and playing golf. The company's clientele also includes large sports teams from universities, high schools, and community sports programs. PP&E currently has about 100 employees between its sales staff and offices. The physical property includes the offices, sales floor, and warehouse.

Recently the company has been experiencing operational problems that suggest that the system may need improvement. Herman Hoffnagle, a consultant, has been asked to analyze the company's problems.

Purchases Procedures
Inventory levels are checked after sales are made. Periodically, the level of inventory is calculated by examining the most recent purchase orders and inventory records. The inventory control function is performed at the warehouse. Physical inventory is not counted frequently, usually only once every quarter. Once it is determined that more inventory must be ordered, Isabella, the inventory control clerk, prepares a purchase requisition to be sent to the purchasing department. One copy of the requisition is also filed in inventory control for future reference.

In the purchasing department, purchase requisitions are received by Pamela, the purchasing agent, and used to prepare a purchase order for each vendor. One copy of the purchase order is filed and copies of the purchase order are sent to the vendor, accounts payable department, and receiving department. As soon as a purchase order is received, accounts payable records a liability in the accounts payable subsidiary ledger.

Rafael, the receiving clerk, is entrusted to inspect and count the goods upon arrival to make sure they reconcile with the purchase order. Rafael both retrieves the inventory from the loading dock and secures it in the warehouse. A receiving report is then prepared stating the quantity and condition of the goods. Rafael files one copy of the receiving report, sends copies to accounts payable and inventory control, stores one copy with the inventory in the warehouse, and sends the fifth to purchasing. Once purchasing receives the receiving report, it is filed along with the purchase order in a closed purchase order file.

Lately, management has noticed complications involving the purchasing of inventory. When problems arose with reorder quantities, a physical inventory count was conducted and it was discovered that several thousand dollars worth of inventory was missing from the warehouse. Because goods are ordered based on quantities stated in the purchase order, and there were fewer goods actually in stock than had been purchased, not enough was being ordered and shortages were occurring frequently. Rafael is currently being investigated for the theft of this merchandise.

Accounts payable is one of the biggest departments at PP&E due to the large number of vendors with which the company does business. Amy and Alexander, the two accounts payable clerks, are cousins and owe thanks to their Uncle Bry for getting them jobs at PP&E. Accounts payable is done manually, with each clerk dedicated to different accounts. For example, Amy is responsible for payments to suppliers of baseball and lacrosse equipment and Alexander handles payments for tennis and golf equipment vendors. The bigger suppliers, such as Nike and Adidas, are divided between them. The reason for this division of accounts was to simplify each clerk's job, because the company had trouble in its early years keeping track of all their payments.

After the supplier's invoice is received by accounts payable, all source documents are transferred to an open accounts payable file, which is later used for cash disbursements. The liability was recorded when the purchase order was received to avoid a time lag, so the only step remaining is to send a journal voucher to the general ledger department. The general ledger clerk, Gary, then posts to the inventory and accounts payable control accounts and reconciles with the subsidiary accounts. At this point, the purchases processing phase is complete.

The next phase in the expenditure cycle, the cash disbursements system, handles the payment of those obligations that were created in the purchasing phase. Amy and Alexander review the open accounts payable file to find payments due to suppliers. When payments are due, invoices are sent to the cash disbursements department to be paid. The accounts payable clerks then debit the suppliers' accounts in the subsidiary ledger and send a summary to the general ledger.

Cash disbursements receives the invoices and writes a check to each vendor. Details regarding each check payment are recorded in a check register. The check is signed by the treasurer and mailed to the supplier, with one copy filed in the cash disbursements department. The general ledger department is then sent a voucher with an entry debiting accounts payable and crediting cash, and the voucher is reconciled with the accounts payable summary. This entry is then posted, the voucher and summary are filed, and the cash disbursements process is complete.

Another problem that has been spotted is that, on several occasions, invoices have been paid twice. For example, last month Carla, the cash disbursements clerk, noticed that she had written two checks for identical amounts to the same vendor within a two-day period. Suspecting that something was not right, Carla checked the vendor invoices and discovered that the vendor had indeed sent the same invoice twice, and PP&E had unknowingly paid the vendor twice. Knowing the magnitude of suppliers that PP&E does business with, Carla fears that this could have easily happened before and gone unnoticed.

Required:
1. Create a data flow diagram of the current system.
2. Create a document flowchart of the existing system.
3. Analyze the internal control weaknesses in the system. Model your response according to the six categories of physical control activities specified in SAS 78.
4. Prepare a system flowchart of a redesigned computer-based system that resolves the control weaknesses that you identified.

7. **Mitchell Law Firm**
(Prepared by Heather Dillon and Kellie Seaman, Lehigh University)
Annis Mitchell is a law firm operating from a main office in Tampa, Florida. The satellite offices for the firm are located in Ft. Myers, Naples, and Tallahassee, and there is also an associate office in Germany. The firm's clients include major national and local corporate businesses, as well as local individual clients. The firm employs 133 people: 65 lawyers, 42 secretaries, 10 in word processing, 4 in accounting, 8 in the mail room/records department, 2 in reception, and 2 in the administrator's office. The annual gross revenues are approximately $12 million, with all excess profits distributed to the shareholders (partners) of the firm.

General Information
The current accounting system is computerized, utilizing a batch approach, with some direct access capabilities. Time entry, receipts and disbursement entries, check processing, and various other functions are processed in batches. Functions such as correction of typographical errors in time entries and generation of bills is done on a direct access basis. The accounting department consists of Karen, Peggy, Heather,

and Frankie. Peggy and Heather are primarily responsible for billing and accounts receivable. Frankie enters cash disbursements into the system and processes the checks. Karen oversees all general ledger functions as well as receiving and verifying many of the firm's general bills, such as telephone and insurance. Heather and Karen both assist Frankie by entering disbursements and processing checks when needed.

Purchases System

There is no formal purchases system. The major purchases are simply for items such as office supplies. There is a stockroom, which is the charge of Susan, the facilities manager. Secretaries can order their own items, but for the most part Susan does the majority of the ordering, and she is responsible for major purchases such as furniture or other big equipment. The orders do not need to be approved, but the agreement of the administrator is usually a good thing to get if the payment is to be approved without problems. Which vendors are used is completely up to the discretion of the person ordering, with no formal vendor approval required. After the item is ordered, the person who did the ordering is the one who receives the item and the bill.

Cash Disbursements System

When a bill is received, or money is needed for some other reason, a three-part check request is filled out by the requester, usually the secretary. The request must be signed by an attorney, or by the secretary for the attorney, depending on their seniority in the firm. Many secretaries for the major partners or others that have been there for years are able to authorize routine check requests for such things as filing fees or other court costs. The check request is forwarded to the accounting department, along with any bills or other paperwork to support it. During the day, Heather, Frankie, or Karen posts the check requests to the system as a cash disbursement. The three-part checks are then printed, attached to the request, and taken to be signed. A senior partner or the administrator of the firm must sign checks for amounts over $50. Checks for amounts under $50 may be signed by a wider base of people, including some lower partners and two secretaries that have been with the firm for over ten years.

After the checks have been signed, Frankie, Heather, or Karen separate the copies. The original check and one copy of the request are forwarded to

the requester, who then forwards it to the payee. One copy of the check and another copy of the request are returned to the requester as well, who then puts it in the client or operating file as a record of the payment. The third copy of the check, the last copy of the request, and any supporting documentation is filed in the accounting department files, in order by check number.

General Ledger

All general ledger functions are performed automatically by the computerized accounting system. Karen is responsible for month-end reconciliation and review of the general ledger reports that are run with the monthly closing, in addition to determining which accounts to post a disbursement to.

Required:

1. Create a data flow diagram of the current system.
2. Create a document flowchart of the existing system.
3. Analyze the internal control weaknesses in the system. Model your response according to the six categories of physical control activities specified in SAS 78.
4. Make suggestions as to how these weaknesses can be resolved.

8. D & K Supplement Warehouse
(Prepared by, Kristin L. Ferris, Lehigh University)
D & K Supplement Warehouse (D&K) is a mail-order company specializing in vitamins, minerals, organic herbs, meal replacements, protein powders, and basic supplements. D&K sells these products mostly to body builders and various health-conscience people in the United States, but also has about a 15 percent customer base located internationally. The company, which is located in an industrial park in Bethlehem, Pennsylvania, has sales clerks taking phone orders 24 hours a day from customers who wish to purchase products from D&K's product lists and catalogs. Customers can find these product lists mainly in body builder and health magazines like *Flex* and *Prevention*, and in gyms and doctors' offices. D&K's catalog, containing their full list of products, is periodically mailed to current and potential customers, and also to anyone requesting it. Once an order is placed it takes five days for the order to reach the customer. D&K outsources their order deliveries to UPS.

D&K was started in 1990 to target those consumers who did not have time to stop at nutritional stores. It did not make a profit until 1993 because consumers had to become accustomed to the idea of ordering their nutritional products by phone. Once the concept caught on, D&K's profits soared. In 1994 and 1995, profits increased 30 percent each year. By 1996, the market became saturated and profits dropped 5 percent. The competition had also caught on to the concept. In 1997, profits were down 8 percent and from all reasonable indicators D&K should end 1998 with a 12 percent drop in profit. At this point in time, D&K's president knows they have a serious problem on their hands. The president found out that the competition is able to get their orders out to customers in two days, three days less than D&K. D&K just assumed their longer lead time was due to their highly manual system which they are planning to redesign in early 1999 with a highly computerized system. Despite the initial installation, purchase, and setup costs, the benefits of the redesigned system outweigh its costs and profits are to be generated within 1½ to 2 years. Also, D&K realized that their competitors were benefiting from D&K's initial market research and their organizational processes and strategies. Competitors were building off D&K's foundation, allowing them to have lower overhead costs and thus lower prices.

To get to the root of their problems, D&K has hired a local consulting firm to analyze their organization. The consultants are here today to begin reviewing D&K's operations.

Expenditure Cycle

Eric Jennings is the consultant assigned to the expenditure cycle. He would like to observe D&K's purchases and cash disbursements procedures by visiting all the departments involved in each cycle. Eric begins his review in the purchasing department where he speaks with Cindy, the purchasing agent. She explains that every Wednesday morning she sends some of the purchasing clerks into the warehouse to check the inventory bays for those items that need reordering. Each clerk jots down the relevant information needed to create a purchase order (PO) for each item being ordered. After a few hours the clerks return from the warehouse and begin to draw up the multipart POs. Once the clerks are done, Cindy is required to review and initial the POs. Cindy mentions that the POs

must be ready to go to the vendors by 1:00 to guarantee timely deliveries, so some weeks Cindy has her clerks initial some of the POs themselves. As soon as the POs are finished and sent to the vendors, Cindy takes one copy of each PO to the receiving department and files another copy in purchasing. Eric makes his notations and moves to the receiving area of the warehouse.

In receiving, Eric introduces himself to John, the receiving supervisor, and asks him about the receiving procedures. John begins by telling Eric that as long as Cindy has the POs ready by 1:00 on Wednesday the orders usually arrive by noon on Thursday. Eric then happens to notice that the plaque on John's door displays "Warehouse Manager" and questions John further about his responsibilities. John describes how he was put in charge of the entire warehouse. He not only oversees receiving, but packing and shipping as well. He also generates the various reports needed at the weekly meetings that he must attend. Eric steers him back to the issue of receiving to find out what happens when the truck arrives. John has Eric talk to Steve, a receiving clerk, who can give him more information since John is rarely around when the truck is unloaded. Steve tells Eric that he usually gets the packing slip from the driver and uses it to fill out the receiving report. Steve adds that he gives the receiving report to John, who uses it to update the inventory records. Then he takes a copy to purchasing for the file and finally files a copy in the receiving department. Eric thanks Steve for his time and makes his way to the accounts payable (AP) department. On the way, Eric runs into John again and decides to ask him a question or two about how he updates the inventory records. John explains that he uses the receiving report to update the inventory records on the computer terminal in his office, which is always locked. John further mentions that the software package he uses is just your average accounting software available at any supply store. Just then, John's name is announced over the intercom. He is needed on the phone, so Eric leaves John and goes to the AP department.

Sarah, the AP director, greets Eric and leads him into her office to talk. Sarah knows he wants to learn about D&K's AP procedures so she starts right in. She explains that upon receipt of a vendor's invoice, her clerks generate a cash disbursement voucher to authorize payment of the invoice. The voucher is prepared from the information on the invoice from the vendor. The AP clerks are supposed to open an unpaid vendor file, which includes the cash disbursement voucher and the invoice. Unpaid files are sent to the cash disbursements department as they come due. Once the voucher is created, the clerks are allowed to update the purchases journal and the AP ledger accounts on the computer terminal in the office, which automatically updates the corresponding general ledger accounts. The terminal sits on a desk in the middle of the department so that all clerks have access to the record keeping program, which is found only on that computer. The program is a basic accounting software package that was purchased at a local office supply store. Since all the AP clerks need to have access to the program to update the accounts they each are working with, the password is tacked on the wall next to the computer. This was the best solution the AP department came up with once everyone started to forget the password. Sarah also explained how not many other people stop by her department, so she figured this would not be a problem. Eric got enough information from Sarah and was ready to visit the cash disbursements department.

Sarah showed Eric to the cash disbursements (CD) department, where she introduced Eric to Aaron, the CD manager. Eric explains why he is there and asks Aaron to describe how D&K goes about paying their vendors. Aaron states that the CD clerks receive the CD vouchers from the AP department on a daily basis for those invoices that are due. The clerks review the voucher and the invoice for any corrections. If everything is correct, the clerks prepare a three-part check and record it in the check register. Aaron points out that he reviews the checks one last time before he signs them and sends them to the vendors. The copies of the checks are filed in both this department and the AP department. Eric remembers Sarah mentioning that when the copy of the check is sent to her department an AP clerk records the payment to the vendor in the computer. Eric writes down his final thoughts and says good-bye to Aaron. Now Eric has enough information about D&K's expenditure cycle and can analyze the internal control problems they have. Eric makes one last stop in the president's office to tell him he will be back next week to make his formal presentation to D&K's management.

Required:
1. Create a data flow diagram of the current system.
2. Create a document flowchart of the existing system.

3. Analyze the internal control weaknesses in the system. Model your response according to the six categories of physical control activities specified in SAS 78.
4. Prepare a system flowchart of a redesigned computer-based system that resolves the control weaknesses that you identified.

9. Kidswear Inc.

(Prepared by Nate Soron, Paul Troiano, and Alexis Yap, Lehigh University)

Kidswear, Inc. is a mail-order wholesaler of high-quality children's casual clothes. The company, which is located in Chicago, Illinois, carries a variety of manufacturer brands. Their warehouse and office are located on the same site. Kidswear employs 150 employees, mainly in their warehouse and sales order processing department. Gross sales for 1997 totaled ten million dollars.

Kidswear has long-standing relationships with fifteen major suppliers. All products are received FOB destination point to the warehouse. The company has agreements with all suppliers that standard ordering lead time is one week, however, recently Kidswear has been experiencing stockouts.

Kidswear customers are department stores and clothing stores. Orders are placed directly over the phone via the company's toll-free number. Currently Kidswear can process and ship via ground transportation in five days. Customers can expect to receive their orders in eight to ten business days. Customers pay on credit terms and are billed when their order is shipped. Kidswear is considering doing business over the Internet to increase their customer base.

This year Kidswear is expecting a decrease in sales revenue. A survey revealed that customers are unhappy with the back orders and long delivery lead time.

Expenditure Cycle

The purchasing function starts in the sales department when the sales records indicate that inventories have diminished to a certain level. The purchasing clerk notices this and prepares three copies of the purchase orders. One copy goes to the vendor, one goes to the warehouse, and one is filed in purchasing.

The warehouse files its copy of the purchase order until the goods arrive. Since Kidswear employs only one receiving clerk, when things get really busy the clerk has the carrier drop the goods off on the loading dock and signs for them immediately without inspection. Occasionally boxes accumulate and sit on the docks for hours as other employees work around them. When the receiving clerk checks the goods, he matches the packing slip against the purchase order and then prepares three receiving reports. One receiving report goes to purchasing, one is filed in the warehouse, and one goes to accounting along with the purchase order and the packing slip. The receiving clerk then updates the inventory subsidiary ledger and sends summary information to the accounting department to update the general ledger.

Accounting waits until it receives the invoice from the vendor and uses the invoice to update the purchasing journal and the accounts payable ledger. Using the purchasing journal and the summary report, accounting updates the general ledger. Then accounting sends the purchase order, the receiving report, and the invoice to the cash disbursements department.

The head of the cash disbursements department then prepares the checks, compares the appropriate records, and signs and mails the check to the vendor. The check register is then updated and a voucher is sent to accounting to update the general ledger. A copy of the check is filed along with the purchase order, the receiving report, and the invoice.

Required:
1. Create a data flow diagram of the current system.
2. Create a document flowchart of the existing system.
3. Analyze the internal control weaknesses in the system. Model your response according to the six categories of physical control activities specified in SAS 78.
4. Prepare a system flowchart of a redesigned computer-based system that resolves the control weaknesses that you identified.

10. D&F Music Club
(Prepared by Katie Daley and Gail Freeston, Lehigh University)
D&F is a distributor of CDs and cassettes that offers benefits such as discount prices and an introductory offer of 10 CDs or cassettes for a penny (not including the shipping and handling costs). Its primary target customers are college students;

its main marketing strategy is constant deals to club members. The company's main competitors in the industry are BMG and Columbia House, which both offer similar promotions. D&F started in 1993 with an office in Harrisburg, Pennsylvania, initially targeting college students in the surrounding area. They realized there was a high demand for discounted music merchandise and the convenience of delivery by mail within universities. After their second year, with a constant increase in customer orders, D&F relocated to Philadelphia because it was located near more colleges and universities. The move has had a positive effect on net profits and demand, supporting their decision to continue the growth of the company. D&F recently expanded their facility to be able to fulfill a higher demand for their services. Their customer base ranges from areas as close as Villanova University to as far as Boston College. As of 1998, there were 103 employees. Their prior year's gross sales were $125 million.

D&F's market share is on the rise, but is not yet comparable to the magnitude of BMG and Columbia House. However, the corporation's goals for the upcoming years include establishing itself as an industry player through increased customer satisfaction and loyalty. D&F is also considering the installation of a new information processing system. This system will reengineer their current business functions by reducing loopholes in their internal control problems.

D&F receives CDs and cassettes from various wholesale suppliers and music store chains, totaling 32 suppliers nationwide. The office has its own warehouse, stores its own merchandise, and is responsible for replenishing the inventory. D&F has had no substantial problems in the past with their suppliers. On the other hand, they have encountered problems with excess inventory, stockouts, and discrepancies with inventory records.

Expenditure Cycle
The purchasing of bulk orders of CDs and cassettes is the main function carried out within the expenditure cycle. The purchases system and the cash disbursements system comprise D&F Music Club's expenditure cycle. The three departments within the purchasing system are the warehouse, purchasing, and accounting.

The purchasing function begins in the warehouse, which stores the inventory of CDs and cassettes. Jim, the warehouse manager, compares inventory records with the various demand forecasts of each week, provided by the market research analyst teams, to determine the necessary orders to make. At the end of the week, Jim prepares the purchase requisition form for bulk orders to send to suppliers. Copies of the purchase requisition are then sent to the purchasing department.

Upon receipt of the purchase requisition, Sara, the supervisor in the purchasing department, determines the specific supplier for the bulk orders. Amanda, the purchasing clerk, is then given all the necessary information to prepare the purchase orders. (The company just recently hired Amanda after she lost her last job due to layoffs. Jim, the warehouse manager, was used as a principal reference, since he's been a friend of the family for years.) Copies of the purchase orders are sent to the supplier and accounting. A "blind copy" of the purchase order is also sent back to the warehouse to await the arrival of the goods.

When the warehouse receives the shipments, Dave, the warehouse clerk, is responsible for completing the blind copy of the purchase order, which involves counting the items and inspecting the goods for damage. Jim, the manager, is often too consumed in preparing the purchase requests to observe the receiving procedures of the warehouse. Dave has been a responsible and diligent employee for over three years; however, when he is in a rush, he has a tendency to copy the packing slip information directly onto the "blind copy" of the purchase order. The completed "blind copy" of the purchase order is then given to Michelle, another clerk within the warehouse who is responsible for preparing the receiving report and updating the inventory records. Copies of the receiving reports are filed within the warehouse and the purchasing department as well as sent to accounting for further processing.

Upon receipt of the invoice from the supplier, Diana, the clerk in accounting, compares this document to the respective purchase order and receiving report. If the invoice is accurate, Diana enters the information into the accounts payable ledger and updates the purchases journal. If there is an error in the invoice, Diana contacts the supplier directly regarding the discrepancy in the documents. The computer system automatically updates the general ledger with the input of information to the accounts payable ledger and the purchases journal.

After updating the respective journals and ledgers, Diana prepares a cash disbursement voucher to send to her supervisor. Evan, the head of the accounting department, receives the cash disbursement voucher from Diana and prepares the necessary checks for payment to the suppliers. The signed check is then sent to the supplier, with a copy of the check remaining in the files of the accounting department. Evan updates the check register and the general ledger is simultaneously updated.

Required:

1. Create a data flow diagram of the current system.
2. Create a document flowchart of the existing system.
3. Analyze the internal control weaknesses in the system. Model your response according to the six categories of physical control activities specified in SAS 78.

11. The Right Fit Company
(Prepared by Ryan Butler, Lehigh University)

The Right Fit Company consists of five stores in the Tri-State area that are in the sneaker retail business. The main store, located in Manhattan, is where the headquarters resides. The Right Fit Company is in business of selling high-quality sneakers at low prices. The vision statement for Right Fit is: The Right Fit Company's future depends upon the purchase of sneakers and related items at wholesale that will satisfy the customers in the Tri-State area.

The Right Fit Company buys directly from wholesalers and deals mainly with credit purchases. Right Fit's main customers consist of children and young adults, therefore, the sales are mostly cash sales (about 80 percent). Credit sales consist of sales made in which the local stores cannot meet the required inventory needed to complete the sale; most of the credit sales are made in bulk to local high school, college, and professional athletic teams. The sales to the athletic teams are mostly made in batches. The gross sales figures for previous years are as follows:

	Gross Sales
1993	$ 750,000
1994	875,000
1995	935,000
1996	1,100,000

The Right Fit Company has seen a 47 percent increase in gross profit since 1993. In 1996, credit sales amounted to $220,000. The credit sales mostly consist of sales made on The Right Fit credit card. As of December 31, 1996, Right Fit had a total of 120 employees: 80 salespeople, and 40 executives and their staff.

The Right Fit Company has had many problems with suppliers in the past. By being a small organization it is hard for Right Fit to purchase directly from Nike, Reebok, or any of the other large sneaker manufacturers. Right Fit deals mainly with five wholesalers in the Tri-State area. In the sneaker industry, one major problem that Right Fit must face is excess inventory. The Right Fit Company must find a way to limit inventory levels while maintaining customer satisfaction. The lead times from its current wholesalers is too great to keep up with sneaker technology. Sneaker Technology, as defined by Right Fit, is the changing styles of sneakers as new stars come upon the professional athlete horizon. It is almost impossible to carry every size of every shoe, so Right Fit must find a way to eliminate lead time, but lower inventory levels.

The president of the company, George Busch, focused the problem on the revenue and expenditure cycles. Right Fit has implemented low-level technology into its revenue cycle. Mr. Busch feels that it would benefit the company if they use computer technology only in the revenue cycle as a test run or evaluation period. Mr. Busch assigned his two closest friends, Dan Peacock and Cathy Powers, to review the cycles and eliminate the major problems. The major problems include lowering inventory levels while still satisfying the customer's demand, fulfilling sales orders with only one warehouse in Manhattan, keeping up with sneaker technology, and maintaining its status as the third-leading sneaker retailer in the Tri-State area behind Foot Locker and Kmart.

The Purchases Processing System
The existing system processes the expenditure cycle transactions as follows. The purchasing department has the sole responsibility of initiating the expenditure cycle. The purchasing department is responsible for determining when inventory levels have reached the re-order point. Once this has been determined, a purchase order is prepared. Once copy of the PO goes to accounts payable for filing in the AP pending file. The second copy of the PO goes to the vendor. A third and final copy is kept on file in the purchasing department.

The next event in the purchasing system is the receipt of inventory. Goods arrive from the vendor by truck at the receiving dock and the receiving clerk begins preparation of the receiving report. One copy of the receiving report accompanies the physical inventories to the warehouse for storage. Another copy goes to the purchasing department, where the purchasing clerk reconciles it with the open purchase order file. If the shipment is correct, the clerk closes the open purchase order file and files the PO and the receiving report in the closed purchase order file. A third and final copy is kept on file in the receiving department.

At this point in the process the accounts payable department has received and temporarily filed a copy of the PO. However, in order to record the transaction, a copy of the supplier's invoice must be received. When the invoice arrives, the accounts payable clerk reconciles the information with the PO in the pending file, records the transaction in the purchases journal, and posts it to the supplier's account in the accounts payable subsidiary ledger. After recording the liability, the accounts payable clerk transfers the PO and invoice to the open accounts payable file. The final step in the accounts payable department occurs when the clerk summarizes the entries in the purchases journal and prepares a journal voucher for the general ledger department. The purchasing process comes to a conclusion when the general ledger department receives a journal voucher from the accounts payable department.

The Cash Disbursements System
The cash disbursements process is initiated by the accounts payable department, which holds the invoice until the due date. The cash disbursements process formally begins when the due date occurs. On the due date, the accounts payable department prepares a cash disbursement voucher in the amount of the invoice. Next, three copies are made. The copies are forwarded to the cash disbursements department.

Next, the cash disbursements clerk receives the voucher and supporting documents for completeness and accuracy. For each disbursement, the clerk prepares a check and records the check number, dollar amount, and voucher number in the check register. The clerk then writes the check and signs it and the check is mailed to the supplier. The second copy of the check is sent to the accounts payable department and the third copy to a file in the cash disbursements department. The check register is now forwarded to the general ledger department.

The final stages of the cash disbursements process occur in the general ledger department. The general ledger department posts the amount paid the general ledger and files the copy. The accounts payable department then enters the check number in the voucher register and files the copy with the voucher.

Required:

1. Create a data flow diagram of the current system.
2. Create a document flowchart of the existing system.
3. Analyze the internal control weaknesses in the system. Model your response according to the six categories of physical control activities specified in SAS 78.
4. Prepare a system flowchart of a redesigned computer-based system that resolves the control weaknesses that you identified.

12. Grand Slam Company

(Prepared by Erin Kerler and Matt Ristau, Lehigh University)

Grand Slam Company is a top-of-the-line baseball equipment manufacturer that specializes in fielder's gloves but which also produces bats, balls, and other baseball accessories. The gloves made by Grand Slam are known in the industry to be one of the best gloves available on the market and are used by a large number of Major League Baseball players. Grand Slam is located in Dallas, Texas, and sells nationwide, concentrating heavily on the southern U.S. and California. It sells its product mainly to specialty sporting goods stores that focus on and are known for baseball equipment. Grand Slam has about 250 employees, with the majority in Dallas and the others located throughout the country on sales assignments.

Given the superior quality of the products manufactured by Grand Slam, the suppliers must provide them with the highest quality raw materials. Grand Slam has run into some problems finding a supplier that can provide them with the top-quality leather hides that it needs to make their gloves. They have tried various suppliers, and have had problems finding one that will send small shipments more frequently. The ones that can do this have problems with providing consistent quality.

Another factor that Grand Slam deals with is that the baseball equipment market is very much a seasonal market. This is a major reason for the concentration in the southern states—in this region baseball is played all year, as opposed to in the north where the weather doesn't allow for year-round baseball. However, the overall market still peaks around the first of March, and slowly declines throughout the rest of the year. Another market factor that Grand Slam recognizes is that baseball is becoming less popular with children. Basketball and soccer are gaining in popularity every year, and baseball is losing a large number of kids to these sports.

Grand Slam also has some internal problems that need to be addressed. The firm's revenue and expenditure cycles have various internal control weaknesses that should be looked into by the company's management. The company may be losing significant amounts of money through fraud or inefficiencies, and the company cannot afford to allow these potential problems to go unchecked.

Purchasing Procedures

The purchases and cash disbursements subsystems begin when raw materials inventory control reviews the levels of inventory and compares them to the materials needed. When necessary, a purchase requisition is sent to the purchasing department and the purchasing department prepares a three-part purchase order. One copy is sent to the supplier, one to raw materials inventory, and one is filed within the department.

Upon receival of the goods from the supplier, one worker in receiving counts the materials, prepares a three-part receiving report, and files one copy. One receiving report is sent to raw materials inventory control where the inventory records are updated, and the other receiving report is sent to the accounts payable department. Upon acquisition of the supplier's invoice, the accounts payable department reconciles the invoice with the receiving report and prepares a journal voucher to be sent to the general ledger department and a cash disbursement voucher that is filed in an open accounts payable file. Grand Slam's computer program searches this open file regularly for any payables that are due. These due records are pulled from the file and the cash disbursement voucher is sent to the cash disbursements department. A three-part check is written and signed. The original is sent in payment to the supplier while one copy is filed in the cash disbursements department and the other is sent with the cash disbursement voucher to the accounts payable department. The accounts payable department then closes that accounts payable record and sends a summary to the general ledger department where both the general ledger and accounts payable subsidiary ledger are updated.

Required:
1. Create a data flow diagram of the current system.
2. Create a document flowchart of the existing system.
3. Analyze the internal control weaknesses in the system. Model your response according to the six categories of physical control activities specified in SAS 78.
4. Prepare a system flowchart of a redesigned computer-based system that resolves the control weaknesses that you identified.

CHAPTER

6

The Expenditure Cycle Part II: Payroll Processing and Fixed Asset Procedures

As we saw in the last chapter, the objective of the expenditure cycle is to convert the organization's cash into the physical materials and the human resources that it needs to conduct business. In this chapter we examine expenditure cycle systems used to process labor and fixed asset transactions.

Again, we assume a credit-based environment in which resources are first acquired and then paid for at a later date. This chapter examines the principal features of two subsystems: payroll processing and fixed assets. The chapter is organized into two main sections. The first section provides an overview of the payroll process: the logical tasks, the key entities, the sources and uses of information, and the flow of key documents through an organization. We illustrate these features first with a manual system and then using computer-based approaches. The discussion of computer-based systems focuses on the operational and control implications of two alternative data processing methods. The second section repeats this general approach to explain the key elements of fixed asset systems.

LEARNING OBJECTIVES

After studying this chapter, you should:

- Recognize the fundamental tasks that constitute the payroll and fixed asset processes.
- Be able to identify the functional departments involved in payroll and fixed asset activities and trace the flow of these transactions through the organization.
- Be able to specify the documents, journals, and accounts that provide audit trails, promote the maintenance of historical records, and support internal decision making and financial reporting.
- Understand the exposures associated with payroll and fixed asset activities and recognize the controls that reduce these risks.
- Be aware of the operational features and the control implications of technology used in payroll and fixed asset systems.

OVERVIEW OF PAYROLL ACTIVITIES

Payroll processing is actually a special case purchases system. In theory, payroll checks could be processed through the regular accounts payable and cash disbursements system. However, as a practical matter, this approach would have a number of drawbacks, including:

1. A firm can design general expenditure procedures that apply to all vendors. However, payroll procedures differ greatly between classes of employees. For example, different procedures are used for hourly employees, salaried employees, piece workers, and commissioned employees. Also, payroll processing requires special accounting procedures for employee deductions and withholdings for taxes. Cash disbursements for trade accounts do not require special processing. Therefore, general expenditure systems are not designed to deal with these complications.

2. Writing checks to employees requires special controls. It is easier to conceal payroll fraud when payroll checks are combined with trade account checks.

3. General expenditure procedures are designed to accommodate a relatively smooth flow of transactions. Business enterprises are constantly purchasing inventories and disbursing funds to vendors. Naturally, they design systems to deal adequately with their normal level of transaction activity. Payroll activities are discrete rather than continuous. Disbursements to employees occur weekly, biweekly, or monthly. To periodically impose this processing burden on the general system would have an overwhelming peak-load effect.

Although specific payroll procedures vary among firms, Figure 6–1 presents a DFD depicting the general tasks of the payroll system in a manufacturing firm. The key points of the process are described below.

1. Payroll authorization and transaction details (hours worked) enter the payroll process from two different sources: personnel and production.

2. The payroll process reconciles this information, calculates the payroll, and distributes paychecks to the employees.

3. Cost accounting receives information regarding the time spent on each job from production. This is used for posting to the work-in-process (WIP) account.

4. Accounts payable receives payroll summary information from the payroll department and authorizes the cash disbursements department to deposit a single check, in the amount of the total payroll, in a special bank account on which the payroll is drawn.

5. The general ledger process reconciles summary information from cost accounting, accounts payable, and cash disbursements. Control accounts are updated to reflect these transactions.

MANUAL PAYROLL SYSTEM

Figure 6–2 (pages 294–295) presents a flowchart detailing the above procedures in the context of a manual system. The key tasks are discussed below.

Personnel

The personnel department prepares and submits to the payroll department various **personnel action forms**. These documents identify employees authorized to receive

FIGURE 6-1   DFD of Payroll Procedures

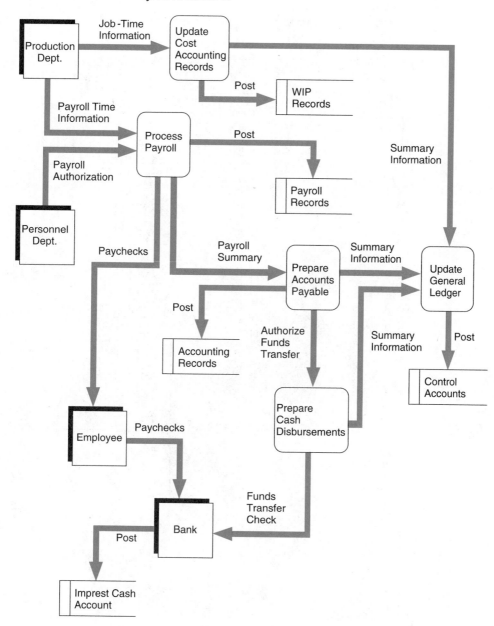

a paycheck and are used to reflect changes in hourly pay rates, payroll deductions, and job classification. Figure 6–3 (page 296) shows a personnel action form used to advise payroll of an increase in an employee's salary.

Production

Production employees prepare two types of time records: job tickets and time cards. **Job tickets** capture the total amount of time that individual workers spend on each

FIGURE 6–2

Manual Payroll System

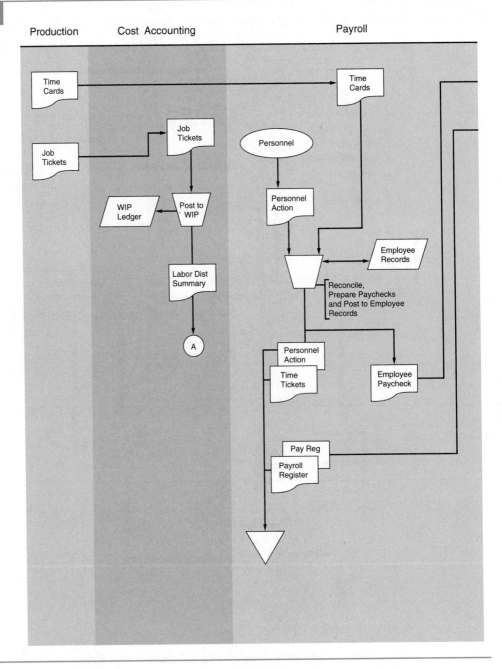

production job. These documents go to cost accounting (conversion cycle), where they are used to allocate direct labor charges to WIP accounts. **Time cards** capture the total time the employee is at work. These go to payroll for calculating the amount of the employee's paycheck. Figure 6–4 (page 297) illustrates a job ticket, and Figure 6–5 (page 298) illustrates a time card.

Each day at the beginning of the shift, employees place their time cards in a special clock that records arrivals and departures. They "clock out" for their lunch period and at the end of the shift. This time card is the formal record of daily atten-

FIGURE 6-2

(continued)

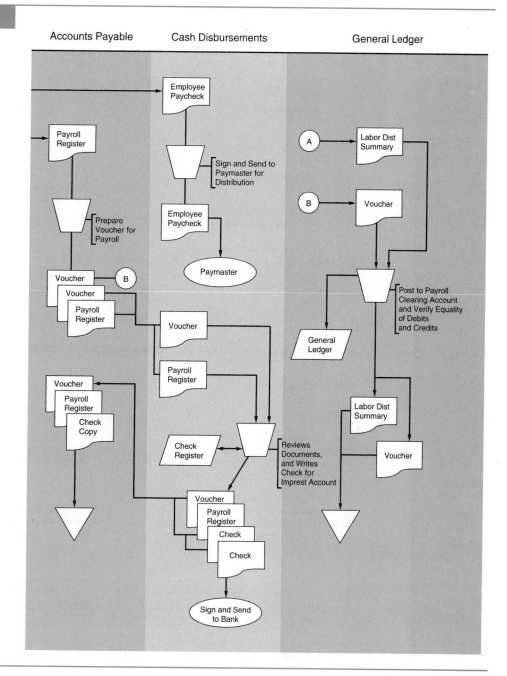

dance. At the end of the week, the supervisor reviews the time cards, signs them, and sends them to the payroll department.

Cost Accounting

Cost accounting uses the job tickets to allocate labor costs to work-in-process accounts as direct labor or overhead. These charges are summarized in a **labor distribution summary** and forwarded to the general ledger department.

FIGURE 6–3

Personnel Action Form

Salary Increase Recommendation

Based on the attached appraisal form, the following recommendation is made for:

Name: Jane Doe
Position: Accounting Clerk
Social Security Number: 111 – 22 – 3333

Current Salary: 23,520.00
Current Bonus Level: 00%
Last Increase Date: 08/22/00
Next Increase Date: 08/22/01

Current Performance Rating:
(from attached appraisal)   good

Salary Increase Guidelines:
Outstanding: 6–9%   9–12 months
Superior: 4–6%   12 months
Good: 3–4%   12–15 months
Provisional: 0%   Review again in 90 days.

In view of the Current Performance and the Salary Increase Guidelines, I recommend the following salary treatment:

Percentage Increase: 4   %
New Salary: $ 24,460
Effective Date: 8 / 22 / 01

Promotions:
In the case of a promotion, a standard 5% increase for the promotion and a pro-rated merit increase (based on time since last merit increase) are appropriate. The next increase will be considered from the date of promotion.

Other Considerations:
In some situations, it is possible to advance a salary beyond the above guidelines as an exception, with the President's approval. Some typical situations are, but are not limited to, equity adjustment and job reevaluation. If such is the case here, please provide justification below:

Approvals: J. R. Johnson   Supervisor
                    H. M. Mills   Director of Personnel

Exception approval if needed: N/A   President

Payroll

The payroll department receives pay rate and withholding data from the personnel department and hours-worked data from the production department. A clerk in payroll then performs the following tasks:

FIGURE 6–4   Job Ticket

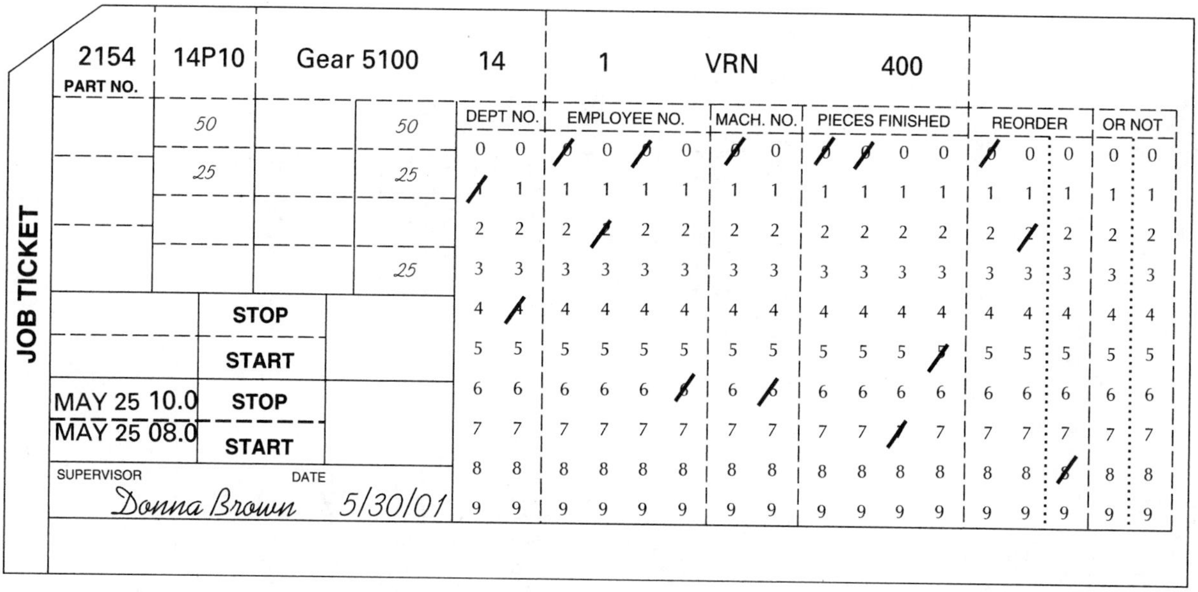

1. Prepares the **payroll register** (Figure 6–6, page 299) showing gross pay, deductions, overtime pay, and net pay.
2. Enters the above information into the **employee payroll records** (Figure 6–7, page 300).
3. Prepares **paychecks** (Figure 6–8, page 301) for employees.
4. Sends the paychecks to cash disbursements and a copy of the payroll register to accounts payable.
5. Files the time cards, personnel action form, and copy of the payroll register.

Accounts Payable Department

The accounts payable clerk reviews the payroll register for correctness and prepares two copies of a cash disbursement voucher for the amount of the payroll. One copy, along with the payroll register, goes to cash disbursements. The other copy goes to the general ledger department.

Cash Disbursements

A manager in cash disbursements receives the payroll checks and then reviews, signs, and sends them to the paymaster for distribution to the employees.

A clerk receives the cash disbursement voucher and payroll register. A single check for the entire amount of the payroll is written and deposited in the **payroll imprest account**. The employee paychecks are drawn on this account, which is used only for payroll. Funds must be transferred from the general cash account to this imprest account before the paychecks can be cashed. Finally, the clerk sends a copy of the check with the disbursement voucher and the payroll register to the accounts payable department, where they are filed.

FIGURE 6–5

Time Card

No.	_447–32–4773_		Pay End	_June 15, 2001_				
Name	_Joe Smith_		Signature	_JAM_				

			Out	In		M	8:02
			In	Out		M	12:70
		SUNDAY	Out	In	MONDAY	M	13:34
			In	Out		M	17:05
			Out	In		TU	8:00
			In	Out		TU	11:06
		SATURDAY	Out	In	TUESDAY		
			In	Out			
			Out	In		W	8:15
			In	Out		W	12:35
		FRIDAY	Out	In	WEDNESDAY	W	13:04
			In	Out		W	17:06
			Out	In		TH	12:02
			In	Out		TH	16:02
		THURSDAY	Out	In	THURSDAY	TH	16:98
			In	Out		TH	21:08
			Out	In		FR	8:14
			In	Out		FR	11:75
		WEDNESDAY	Out	In	FRIDAY	FR	12:42
			In	Out		FR	17:32
			Out	In		SA	9:08
			In	Out		SA	12:00
		TUESDAY	Out	In	SATURDAY		
			In	Out			
			Out	In			
			In	Out			
		MONDAY	Out	In	SUNDAY		
			In	Out			
	SECOND WEEK				FIRST WEEK		

K14-32

FIGURE 6–6

Payroll Register

HC HAMPSHIRE SUPPLY COMPANY

Payroll register for period ending   10/31/01
Checks: All
Employee(s): All

Check# 5000   Paid to Emp# CAS : CASEY, SUE

PAY	Hours	Rate	Gross	DEDUCTIONS	
Regular	173.33		1,000.00	SD SDI	9.00
Overtime			0.00	HL INSUR	100.00
Sick			0.00	SV SAVINGS	100.00
Holiday			0.00		0.00
Vacation			0.00	Fed. withholding	16.25
			0.00	Addl. fed. withholding	0.00
				State withholding	21.77
Totals	173.33		1,000.00	Social Security	62.00
				Medicare	14.50
Days worked	21			NET PAY	676.48

Check# 5001   Paid to Emp# JON : JONES, JESSICA

PAY	Hours	Rate	Gross	DEDUCTIONS	
Regular	173.33	15.00	2,599.95	SD SDI	23.40
Overtime		30.00	0.00	HL INSUR	100.00
Sick		15.00	0.00	SV SAVINGS	260.00
Holiday		45.00	0.00		0.00
Vacation		15.00	0.00	Fed. withholding	256.24
			0.00	Addl. fed. withholding	0.00
				State withholding	116.98
Totals	173.33		2,599.95	Social Security	161.20
				Medicare	37.70
Days worked	21			NET PAY	1,644.43

Check# 5002   Paid to Emp # ROB : ROBERTS, WILLIAM

PAY	Hours	Rate	Gross	DEDUCTIONS	
Regular	173.33	15.00	2,599.95	SD SDI	23.40
Overtime		30.00	0.00	HL INSUR	100.00
Sick		15.00	0.00	SV SAVINGS	260.00
Holiday		45.00	0.00		0.00
Vacation		15.00	0.00	Fed. withholding	396.07
			0.00	Addl. fed. withholding	0.00
				State withholding	208.04
Totals	173.33		2,599.95	Social Security	161.20
				Medicare	37.70
Days worked	21			NET PAY	1,413.54

FIGURE 6–7

Employee
Payroll Record

H₂C HAMPSHIRE SUPPLY COMPANY

Employee pay and earnings information

Period Ending   10/31/01

Emp# : JON   SS# :   682–63–0897   JESSICA JONES

Rate: 15.00/ hour

Addl   FITW/ check: 0.00

Normal deduction(s)			Amount
Ded 1 SD	%	0.9000	0.00
Ded 2 HL	%	0.0000	100.00
Ded 3 SV	%	10.0000	0.00
Ded 4	%	0.0000	0.00

Earnings:

	– Quarter to date –		— Year to date —	
	Hours	Amount	Hours	Amount
Regular	173.3	2,599.95	173.3	2,599.95
Overtime	0.0	0.00	0.0	0.00
Sick	0.0	0.00	0.0	0.00
Vacation	0.0	0.00	0.0	0.00
Holiday	0.0	0.00	0.0	0.00
	0.0	0.00	0.0	0.00

Withholding:		
FIT	256.24	256.24
SIT	116.98	116.98
Social Security	161.20	161.20
Medicare	37.70	37.70
Deductions:		
SDI	23.40	23.40
HEALTH INSUR	100.00	100.00
SAVINGS	260.00	260.00
	0.00	0.00

FIGURE 6–8 Employee Paycheck

HAMPSHIRE SUPPLY COMPANY

5001

HOURS		RATE	REGULAR EARNINGS	OVERTIME EARNINGS	OTHER PAY			GROSS	PERIOD ENDING
REGULAR	OVERTIME				UNITS	RATE	AMOUNT		
173.33	00.00	R 15/Hr OT 30/Hr	$2,599.95	$00.00	Holiday Sick Vacat.	45.00 15.00 15.00	00.00 00.00 00.00	2,599.95	10/31/01
									TOTAL GROSS
									2,599.95

DEDUCTIONS

F.I.C.A.	FED. W/H	STATE W/H	YEAR TO DATE F.I.C.A.	YEAR TO DATE FED. W/H	YEAR TO DATE STATE W/H	OTHER		CONTROL NUMBER
161.20 37.70	256.24	116.98 37.70	161.20	256.24	116.98	SDI HI SAV	23.40 100.00 260.00	682-63-0897
								TOTAL DEDUCTIONS
								955.52

EMPLOYEE'S NAME AND SOC. SEC. NO.		NET PAY
JONES, JESSICA 682-63-0897	**HAMPSHIRE SUPPLY COMPANY** 406 LAKE AVE. PH. 323-555-7448 SEATTLE, CA 92801	1,644.43

No. 5001

HAMPSHIRE SUPPLY COMPANY
406 LAKE AVE. PH. 323-555-7448
SEATTLE, CA 92801

STATE BANK
4000 PENNSYLVANIA AVE.
UMA CA 98210

PAY: One Thousand Six Hundred Forty-Four and 43/100 dollars

AMOUNT $*******1,644.43

TO THE ORDER OF

JESSICA JONES
72 N. LOTUS AVE #1
SAN GABRIEL CA 91775-8321

DATE
October 31, 2001

00000 0 00000 00 0

General Ledger

The general ledger department receives the labor distribution summary from cost accounting and the disbursement voucher from accounts payable. The disbursement voucher shows the total amount of wages payable and its breakdown into cash, taxes payable, and other deductions. With this information, the general ledger clerk makes the following accounting entries:

FROM THE LABOR DISTRIBUTION SUMMARY

	DR	CR
Work-in-Process (Direct labor)	XXX.XX	
Factory Overhead (Indirect labor)	XXX.XX	
Wages Payable		XXX.XX

FROM DISBURSEMENT VOUCHER

	DR	CR
Wages Payable	XXX.XX	
Cash		XXX.XX
Fed. Income Tax Withholdings Payable		XXX.XX
State Income Tax Withholdings Payable		XXX.XX
FICA Income Tax Withholdings Payable		XXX.XX
Group Insurance Premiums Payable		XXX.XX
Pension Fund Withholdings Payable		XXX.XX
Union Dues Payable		XXX.XX

The debits and credits from these entries must equal. If they do not, there is an error in the calculation of either labor distribution charges or payroll. When the equality has been verified, the clerk files the voucher and labor distribution summary.

PAYROLL CONTROLS

Transaction Authorization

The personnel action form provides an important authorization control in a payroll system. This document is essential for preventing payroll fraud by identifying authorized employees. A common form of fraud is to submit time cards to payroll on behalf of employees who are no longer with the firm. The personnel action form permits the payroll department to maintain a current list of employees, which is compared to the time cards.

Segregation of Duties

The timekeeping function should be separated from the personnel function. The personnel department provides payroll with pay-rate information for authorized hourly employees. There may be a range of pay rates based on experience, job classification, seniority, and merit. If this information was provided directly by the production department, an employee might change the information and perpetrate a fraud. To control against this, pay-rate information should come from an independent source—the personnel department.

Supervision

Another area at risk is timekeeping. Sometimes employees will "clock in" for another worker who is late or absent. Supervisors should observe the clocking process and reconcile the time cards with actual attendance.

Accounting Records

The audit trail for payroll includes the following documents:

1. Time cards, job tickets, and disbursement vouchers.
2. Journal information, which comes from the labor distribution summary and the payroll register.
3. Subsidiary ledger accounts, which contain the employee records and various expense accounts.
4. The general ledger accounts: payroll control, cash, and payroll clearing (an imprest account).

Access Controls

The assets associated with the payroll system are labor and cash. Both can be misappropriated through improper access to accounting records. A dishonest individual can misrepresent on the time cards the amount of labor rendered and thus embezzle cash. The control over access to source documents and records in a payroll system is important, as it is in all expenditure cycle systems.

Independent Verification

The following are examples of independent verification controls in the payroll system:

1. *Verification of time.* Before sending time cards to payroll, the supervisor must verify their accuracy and sign them.
2. *Paymaster.* The use of an independent paymaster to distribute checks (rather than the normal supervisor) helps verify the existence of the employees. The supervisor may be party to a payroll fraud by pretending to distribute paychecks to nonexistent employees.
3. *Accounts payable.* The accounts payable clerk verifies the accuracy of the payroll register before creating a disbursement voucher that transfers funds to the imprest account.[1]
4. *General ledger.* The general ledger department provides verification of the overall process by reconciling the labor distribution summary and the payroll disbursement voucher.

COMPUTER-BASED PAYROLL SYSTEMS

AUTOMATING THE PAYROLL SYSTEM WITH BATCH PROCESSING

Because payroll systems run infrequently (weekly or monthly), they are often well suited to batch processing and sequential files. Figure 6–9 shows a flowchart for such a system. The manual functions in this automated system are essentially the same as in the previous system. The data processing department receives the personnel action forms, job tickets, and time cards, which it converts to sequential files. Batch computer programs perform the detailed record keeping, check-writing, and general ledger functions.

---

1   This can also be classified as an authorization control. Accounts payable actually authorizes the funding for the payroll with a disbursement voucher.

FIGURE 6–9   Batch Payroll System with Sequential Files

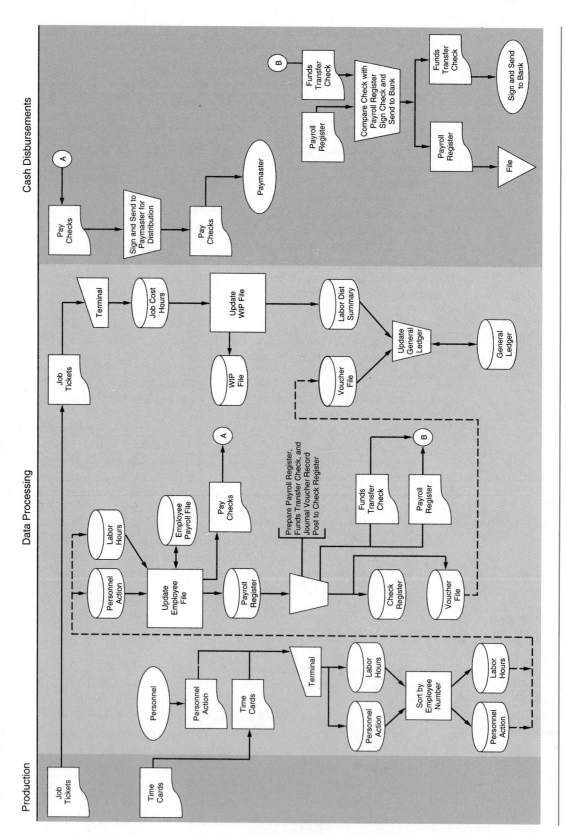

Control Implications

The strengths and weaknesses of this system are similar to those in the batch system for general expenditures discussed earlier. This system promotes accounting accuracy and reduces check-writing errors. Beyond this, it does not significantly enhance operational efficiency; however, for many types of organizations, this level of technology is adequate.

REENGINEERING THE PAYROLL SYSTEM

For moderate-sized and large organizations, payroll processing is often integrated within the **human resource management (HRM) system**. The HRM system captures and processes a wide range of personnel-related data, including employee benefits, labor resource planning, employee relations, employee skills, personnel actions (pay rates, deductions, and so on), as well as payroll. HRM systems must support real-time access to personnel files for purposes of direct inquires and recording changes in employee status as they occur. Figure 6–10 illustrates a payroll system as part of an HRM system.

This system differs from the simple automated system in the following ways: (1) operations departments transmit transactions to data processing via terminals, (2) direct access files are used for data storage, and (3) many processes are now performed in real time. We discuss the key operating features of this system below.

Personnel

The personnel department makes changes to the employee file in real time via terminals. These changes include additions of new employees, deletions of terminated employees, changes in dependents, changes in withholding, and changes in job status (pay rate).

Cost Accounting

The cost accounting department enters job cost data (real time or daily) to create the **labor usage file**.

Timekeeping

Upon receipt of the approved time cards from the supervisor at the end of the week, the timekeeping department creates the current **attendance file**.

Data Processing

At the end of the work period, the following tasks are performed in a batch process:

1. Labor costs are distributed to various work-in-process, overhead, and expense accounts.
2. An on-line labor distribution summary file is created. Copies of the file go to the cost accounting and general ledger departments.
3. An on-line payroll register is created from the attendance file and the **employee file**. Copies of the files go to the accounts payable and cash disbursements departments.
4. The employee records file is updated.

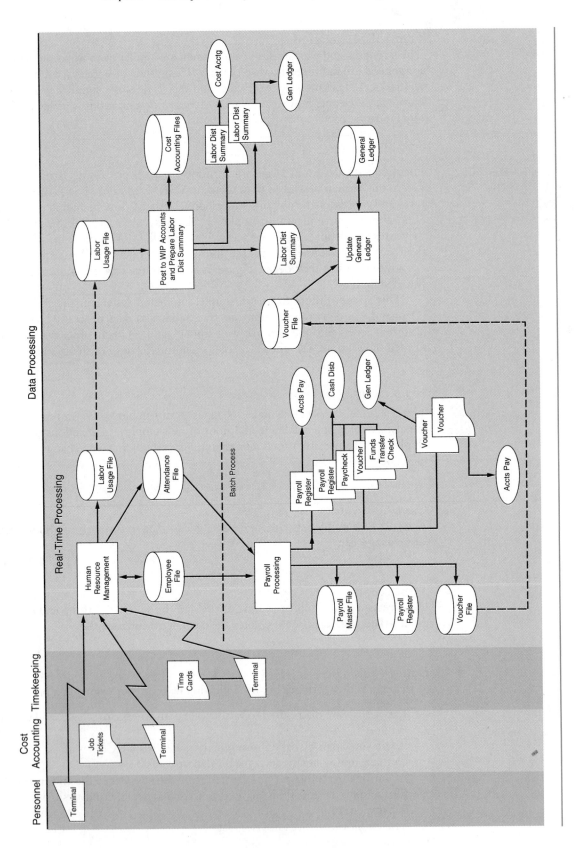

FIGURE 6–10   Payroll System with Real-Time Elements

5. Payroll checks are prepared and signed. They are sent to the treasurer for review and reconciliation with the payroll register. The paychecks are then distributed to the employees.[2]
6. The disbursement voucher file is updated and a check is prepared for the funds transfer to the imprest payroll account. The check and a hard copy of the disbursement voucher go to cash disbursements. One copy of the voucher goes to the general ledger department, and the final copy goes to accounts payable.
7. At the end of processing, the system retrieves the labor distribution summary file and the disbursements voucher file and updates the general ledger file.

Control Implications

The features of the payroll system with real-time elements provide many of the operational benefits discussed earlier, including reductions in the lag time between events and recording, paper, and clerical labor. These features also carry control implications. Many tasks once performed by humans are now performed by computers. Computer-based systems must produce adequate records for independent verification and audit purposes. Finally, controls must be designed to protect against unauthorized access to data files and computer programs.

THE FIXED ASSET SYSTEM

Fixed assets are the property, plant, and equipment used in the operation of a business. These are relatively permanent items that often collectively represent the largest financial investment by the organization. Examples of fixed assets include land, buildings, furniture, machinery, and motor vehicles. A firm's fixed asset system processes transactions pertaining to the acquisition, maintenance, and disposal of its fixed assets. An effective system will support management decisions, financial reporting, and reporting to regulatory agencies, and it will possess adequate internal controls. The specific objectives of the fixed asset system are to:

1. Process the acquisition of fixed assets as needed and in accordance with formal management approval and procedures.
2. Maintain adequate accounting records of asset acquisition, cost, description, and physical location in the organization.
3. Maintain accurate depreciation records for depreciable assets in accordance with acceptable methods.
4. Provide management with information to help it plan future fixed asset investments.
5. Properly record the retirement and disposal of fixed assets.

The fixed asset system shares some characteristics with the expenditure cycle presented in Chapter 5, but two important differences distinguish these systems. First, the expenditure cycle processes routine acquisitions of raw material inventories for the production function and finished goods inventories for the sales function. The

---

2   For added internal control, many companies encourage their employees to have their checks directly deposited in their bank accounts.

fixed asset system processes nonroutine transactions for a wider group of users in the organization. Managers in virtually all functional areas of the organization make capital investments in fixed assets, but these transactions occur with less regularity than inventory acquisitions. Because fixed asset transactions are unique, they require specific management approval and explicit authorization procedures. In contrast, organizations often automate the authorization procedures for expenditure cycle transactions to deal effectively with the large volume of routine acquisitions.

The second difference between these systems is that organizations usually treat inventory acquisitions as an expense of the current period, while they capitalize fixed assets that yield benefits for multiple periods. Since the productive life of a fixed asset extends beyond one year, its acquisition cost is apportioned over its lifetime and depreciated in accordance with accounting conventions and statutory requirements. Therefore, fixed asset accounting systems include cost allocation and matching procedures that are not part of routine expenditure systems. Because of these distinguishing characteristics, we have separated the discussion of fixed asset procedures from the expenditure cycle.

THE LOGIC OF A FIXED ASSET SYSTEM

Figure 6–11 presents the general logic of the fixed asset system. The process involves three tasks: asset acquisition, asset maintenance, and asset disposal.

Asset Acquisition

Asset acquisition usually begins with the departmental manager (user) recognizing the need to obtain a new or replace an existing fixed asset. Authorization and approval procedures involved in the transaction will depend on the asset's cost. In these decisions, department managers often possess the general authority to approve the purchase of less expensive fixed assets. However, for capital expenditures above a specified materiality threshold, the manager must seek explicit approval. Typically, this involves a formal capital investment analysis to evaluate the costs and benefits of the request. As part of this analysis, management will often solicit bids from several suppliers.

Once the request is approved and a supplier is selected, the fixed asset acquisition task is similar to the expenditure cycle process described in Chapter 5. There are two noteworthy differences. First, the receiving department delivers the asset into the custody of the user/manager rather than a central store or warehouse. Second, the fixed asset department, not inventory control, performs the record keeping function.

Asset Maintenance

Asset maintenance involves adjusting the fixed asset subsidiary account balances as the assets (excluding land) depreciate over time or with usage. Some common depreciation methods in use are straight-line, sum-of-the-years'-digits, double-declining balance, and units of production. The method of depreciation and the period used should reflect, as closely as possible, the asset's actual decline in utility to the firm. Accounting conventions and IRS rules sometimes specify the depreciation parameters to be used. For example, businesses must depreciate new office buildings using the straight-line method and use a period of at least 40 years. The depreciation of fixed assets used to manufacture products is charged to manufacturing overhead and then

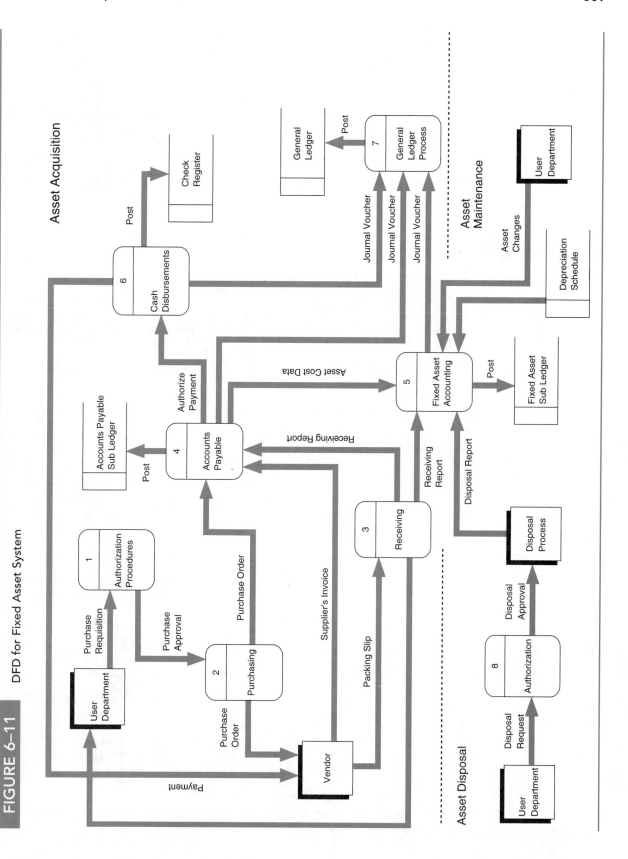

FIGURE 6-11   DFD for Fixed Asset System

allocated to work-in-process in the conversion cycle. Depreciation charges of assets not used in manufacturing are treated as expenses in the current period.

Depreciation calculations are internal transactions that the fixed asset system must process without the benefit of an explicit economic event or source document to trigger the action. An important record used to initiate this task is the **depreciation schedule**. A separate depreciation schedule, such as the one illustrated in Figure 6–12, will be prepared by the system for each fixed asset recorded in the fixed asset subsidiary ledger.

A depreciation schedule shows when and how much depreciation to record. It also shows when to stop taking depreciation on fully depreciated assets. This infor-

FIGURE 6–12

Depreciation Schedule

OZMENT'S INDUSTRIAL SUPPLY
ASSET LISTING WITH DEPRECIATION SCHEDULES
FROM 200 THROUGH 200

Code	Type	Description	Month#	Depn. exp.	Acc. depn.	Book value
200	OFF&F					
	OFFICE FURNITURE					
	Depn. method: SYD					
	Life in years: 5					
	Date acquired 2/01/01					
	Date retired					
	Cost	5,500.99				
	Residual	500.00				
	Acc. Depn.	2,222.23				
			1	138.89	138.89	5,361.11
			2	138.89	277.78	5,222.22
			3	138.89	416.67	5,083.33
			4	138.89	555.56	4,944.44
			5	138.89	694.45	4,805.55
			6	138.89	833.34	4,666.66
			7	138.89	972.23	4,527.77
			8	138.89	1,111.12	5,388.88
			9	138.89	1,250.01	4,249.99
			10	138.89	1,388.90	4,111.10
			•	•	•	•
			•	•	•	•
			•	•	•	•
			52	27.78	4,777.80	722.20
			53	27.78	4,805.58	694.42
			54	27.78	4,833.36	666.64
			55	27.78	4,861.14	638.86
			56	27.78	4,888.92	611.08
			57	27.78	4,916.70	583.30
			58	27.78	4,944.48	555.52
			59	27.78	4,672.26	527.74
			60	27.78	5,000.04	499.96

Assets listed: 1

mation in a management report is also useful for planning asset retirement and replacement.

Asset maintenance also involves adjusting asset accounts to reflect the cost of physical improvements that increase the asset's value or extend its useful life. Such enhancements, which are themselves capital investments, are processed the same as new asset acquisitions.

Finally, the fixed asset system must promote accountability by keeping track of the physical location of each asset. Unlike inventories that are usually consolidated in secure areas, fixed assets are distributed throughout the organization and are subject to increased risk from theft and misappropriation. When one department transfers custody of an asset to another department, information about the transfer should be recorded in the fixed asset subsidiary ledger. Each subsidiary record should indicate the current location of the asset. The ability to locate and verify the physical existence of fixed assets is an important component of the audit trail.

Asset Disposal

When an asset has reached the end of its useful life or when management decides to dispose of it, the asset must be removed from the fixed asset subsidiary ledger. The bottom left portion of Figure 6–11 illustrates the **asset disposal** process. It begins when the responsible manager issues a request to dispose of the asset. Like any other transaction, the disposal of an asset requires proper approval. The disposal options open to the firm are to sell, scrap, donate, or retire the asset in place. A disposal report describing the final disposition of the asset goes to the fixed asset accounting department to authorize its removal from the ledger.

COMPUTER-BASED FIXED ASSET SYSTEM

Figure 6–13 illustrates a computer-based fixed asset system. For our discussion, we are demonstrating a real-time system. However, organizations that process large numbers of fixed asset transactions may employ batch processing instead. To simplify the flowchart and to focus on the key features of the system, we have omitted the processing steps for accounts payable and cash disbursements. The top portion of the flowchart presents the fixed asset acquisition procedures, the center portion presents fixed asset maintenance procedures, and the bottom portion presents the asset disposal procedures.

Acquisition Procedures

The process begins when the fixed asset accounting clerk receives a receiving report and a cash disbursement voucher. These documents provide evidence that the firm has physically received the asset and show its cost. The clerk uses a computer terminal to create a record of the asset in the fixed asset subsidiary ledger. Figure 6–14 presents a possible record structure for this file.

Notice that in addition to the historic cost information, the clerk enters data specifying the asset's useful life, its salvage (residual) value, the depreciation method to be used, and the asset's location in the organization.

The fixed asset system automatically updates the fixed asset control account in the general ledger and prepares journal vouchers for the general ledger department as evidence of the entry. The system also produces reports for accounting

FIGURE 6–13   **Computer-Based Fixed Asset System**

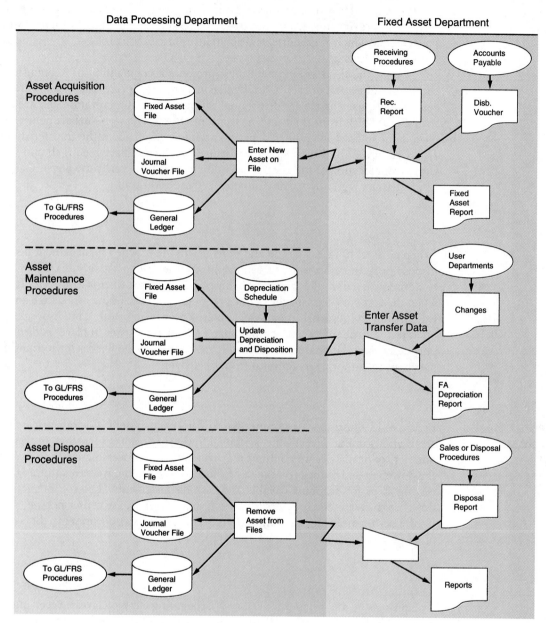

Based on the depreciation parameters contained in the fixed asset records, the system prepares a depreciation schedule for each asset when its acquisition is originally recorded. The schedule is stored on computer disk to facilitate future depreciation calculations.

management. Figure 6–15 illustrates the fixed asset status report showing the cost, the accumulated depreciation (if any), and residual value for each of the firm's fixed assets.

FIGURE 6–14

Fixed Asset Record Structure

ITEM NUMBER	LOCATION	DESCRIP.	ASSET TYPE	ASSET LIFE/ MONTHS	COST	RESIDUAL VALUE	DEPR. METHOD	PERIOD/ MONTH	RETIRE DATE	ACCUM. DEPN.	BOOK VALUE
200	Rm. 182	Photocopier	Off&F	60	5,500.00	500.00	SYD	5	N/A	694.45	4,805.55

FIGURE 6–15

Asset Status Report

**OZMENT'S INDUSTRIAL SUPPLY
ASSET LISTING**

Code	Type	Description
100	OFF&F	
	COMPUTER SYSTEM	
	Depn. method: SL	
	Life in years: 5	
	Date acquired 1/01/01	
	Date retired	
	Cost	40,000.00
	Residual	4,000.00
	Acc. Depn.	10,800.00
200	OFF&F	
	OFFICE FURNITURE	
	Depn. method: SL	
	Life in years: 5	
	Date acquired 2/01/01	
	Date retired	
	Cost	5,500.00
	Residual	500.00
	Acc. Depn.	2,222.23
300	MACH	
	SNOWBLOWER	
	Depn. method: DDB	
	Life in years: 5	
	Date acquired 2/01/01	
	Date retired	
	Cost	1,000.00
	Residual	0.00
	Acc. Depn.	499.96
400	MACH	
	TRUCK	
	Depn. method: SL	
	Life in years: 3	
	Date acquired 12/01/01	
	Date retired	
	Cost	2,000.00
	Residual	0.00
	Acc. Depn.	2,333.31

Asset Maintenance

The fixed asset system uses the depreciation schedules to record end-of-period depreciation transactions automatically. The specific tasks include (1) calculating the current period's depreciation, (2) updating the accumulated depreciation and book value fields in the subsidiary records, (3) posting the total amount of depreciation to the affected general ledger accounts (depreciation expense and accumulated depreciation), and (4) recording the depreciation transaction by adding a record to the journal voucher file. Finally, a fixed asset depreciation report, shown in Figure 6–16, is sent to the fixed asset department for review.

Department managers must report any changes in the custody or status of assets to the fixed asset department. A clerk using a computer terminal records such changes in the fixed asset subsidiary ledger.

Disposal Procedures

The disposal report formally authorizes the fixed asset department to remove from the ledger an asset disposed of by the user department. When the clerk deletes the record from the fixed asset subsidiary ledger, the system automatically (1) posts an adjusting entry to the fixed asset control account in the general ledger, (2) records any loss or gain associated with the disposal transaction, and (3) prepares a journal voucher record. A fixed asset status report containing details of the deletion is sent to the fixed asset department for review.

FIGURE 6–16

Fixed Asset
Depreciation
Report

OZMENT'S INDUSTRIAL SUPPLY
DEPRECIATION CALCULATIONS LISTING THROUGH
6/30/02 POSTED AS BATCH #1327

Code	Method		Description	Depn. Expense
100	SL	5 yr	COMPUTER SYSTEM	3,600.00
200	SYD	5 yr	OFFICE FURNITURE	694.44
300	DDB	5 yr	SNOWBLOWER	133.33
400	SL	3 yr	DELIVERY TRUCK	0.00
500	SL	3 yr	DELIVERY TRUCK	0.00
600	SL	3 yr	TRUCK	2,333.31

Assets listed: 6		Total	6,761.08

GL summary:

615	DEPRECIATION EXPENSE	6,761.08	
151	ACCUM DEPN. EQUIPMENT		6,761.08

CONTROLLING
THE FIXED
ASSET SYSTEM

Because of the similarities between the fixed asset system and the expenditure cycle, many of the controls are the same and have already been discussed. Our discussion of fixed asset controls will thus focus on three areas of principal difference between these systems: authorization, supervision, and independent verification.

Authorization Controls

Fixed asset acquisitions should be formal and explicitly authorized. Each transaction should be initiated by a written request from the user or department. In the case of high-value items, there should be an independent approval process that evaluates the merits of the request on a cost-benefit basis.

Supervision Controls

Because capital assets are widely distributed throughout the organization, they are more susceptible to theft and misappropriation than inventories that are secured in a warehouse. Therefore, management supervision is an important element in the physical security of fixed assets. Supervisors must ensure that fixed assets are being used in accordance with the organization's policies and business practices. For example, microcomputers purchased for individual employees should be secured in their proper location and should not be removed from the premises without explicit approval. Company vehicles should be secured in the organization's motor pool at the end of the shift and should not be taken home for personal use unless authorized by the appropriate supervisor.

Independent Verification Controls

Periodically, the internal auditor should review the asset acquisition and approval procedures to determine the reasonableness of factors used in the analysis. These include the useful life of the asset, the original financial cost, the proposed cost savings as a result of acquiring the asset, the discount rate used, and the capital budgeting method used in the analysis.

The internal auditor should verify the location, condition, and fair value of the organization's fixed assets against the fixed asset records in the subsidiary ledger. In addition, the automatic depreciation charges calculated by the fixed asset system should be reviewed and verified for accuracy and completeness. System errors that miscalculate depreciation can result in the material misstatement of operating expenses, reported earnings, and asset values.

Summary

The chapter began with an examination of payroll procedures. The discussion focussed on fundamental tasks; the functional departments; and the documents, journals, and accounts that constitute the payroll system. Common exposures and controls that reduce risks inherent in payroll activities were explained. In addition, the operational features and the control implications of technology used in payroll systems were reviewed.

The second section of the chapter presented the typical features of the fixed asset system. Fixed asset accounting involves three classes of procedures: asset acquisition, asset maintenance, and asset disposal. We examined the files, procedures, and reports that constitute the fixed asset system. We concluded our discussion by reviewing the principal risks and controls in the system.

Key Terms

asset acquisition (308)
asset disposal (311)
asset maintenance (308)
attendance file (305)
depreciation schedule (310)
employee file (305)
employee payroll records (297)
fixed assets (307)
human resource management (HRM) system (305)

job tickets (293)
labor distribution summary (295)
labor usage file (305)
paychecks (297)
payroll imprest account (297)
payroll register (297)
personnel action form (292)
time cards (294)

Review Questions

1. Which document is used by cost accounting to allocate direct labor charges to work-in-process?
2. Which department authorizes changes in employee pay rates?
3. Why should the employee's supervisor not distribute paychecks?
4. Why should employee paychecks be drawn against a special checking account?
5. Why should employees clocking on and off the job be supervised?
6. What is a personnel action form?
7. What tasks does a payroll clerk perform upon receipt of hours-worked data from the production department?
8. What documents are included in the audit trail for payroll?
9. What are the strengths and weaknesses of a batch process with sequential files?
10. What are the strengths and weaknesses of a batch system with direct access files?

11. What are the objectives of a fixed asset system?
12. How do fixed asset systems differ from purchases systems?
13. What are three tasks of the fixed asset system?
14. What information is found on the depreciation schedule? How can this information be verified?
15. Why is it crucial to the integrity of the financial statements that the fixed asset department be informed of asset improvements and disposals?
16. What is the auditor's role with respect to the fixed asset system?
17. Which department performs the formal record keeping function for fixed assets?
18. What document shows when fixed assets are fully depreciated?
19. Who should authorize disposal of fixed assets?
20. Assets used for production are secured in a warehouse. Who has custody of fixed assets?

Discussion Questions

1. What is the importance of the job ticket? Illustrate the flow of this document and its information from inception to impact on the financial statements.

2. Are any time lags in recording economic events typically experienced in payroll systems? If so, what are they? Discuss the accounting profession's view on this matter as it pertains to financial reporting.

3. What advantages are achieved in choosing
   a. a basic batch computer system over a manual system?
   b. a batch system with real-time data input over a basic batch system?

4. Discuss the major control implications of batch systems with real-time data input. What compensating procedures are available?

5. Discuss some specific examples in which information systems can reduce time lags and how the firm is positively affected by such time lags.

6. Discuss some service industries that may require their workers to use job tickets.

7. Payroll is often used as a good example of when batch processing using magnetic tapes is considered appropriate. Why is payroll typically considered a good application for this type of storage device?

8. If an asset that is not fully depreciated is sold or disposed, but the fixed asset records are not adjusted, what effect will this have on the financial statements?

9. Discuss the fundamental risk and control issues associated with fixed assets that are different from raw materials and finished goods.

10. Describe an internal control that would prevent an employee from removing a computer and then reporting it as scrapped.

11. Describe an internal control that would prevent the payment of insurance premiums on an automobile that is no longer owned by the company.

12. Describe an internal control that would prevent the charging of depreciation expense to the maintenance department for a sweeper that is now located in and used by the engineering department.

13. Describe an internal control that would prevent the acquisition of office equipment that is not needed by the firm.

14. What negative consequences result when fixed asset records include assets that are no longer owned by the firm?

Multiple-Choice Questions

1. The document that captures the total amount of time that individual workers spend on each production job is called a
   a. time card.
   b. job ticket.
   c. personnel action form.
   d. labor distribution form.

2. An important reconciliation in the payroll system is
   a. the general ledger department compares the labor distribution summary from cost accounting to the disbursement voucher from accounts payable.
   b. the personnel department compares the number of employees authorized to receive a paycheck to the number of paychecks prepared.
   c. the production department compares the number of hours reported on job tickets to the number of hours reported on time cards.
   d. the payroll department compares the labor distribution summary to the hours reported on time cards.

3. Which internal control is not an important part of the payroll system?
   a. supervisors verify the accuracy of employee time cards
   b. paychecks are distributed by an independent paymaster
   c. the accounts payable department verifies the accuracy of the payroll register before transferring payroll funds to the general checking account
   d. the general ledger department reconciles the labor distribution summary and the payroll disbursement voucher

4. Which duties should be segregated?
   a. matching purchase requisitions, receiving reports, and invoices and authorizing payment
   b. authorizing payment and maintaining the check register
   c. writing checks and maintaining the check register
   d. authorizing payment and maintaining the accounts payable subsidiary ledger

5. CMA 686 3-12

   In a well-designed internal control structure, two tasks that should be performed by different persons are
   a. preparation of purchase orders and authorization of monthly payroll.
   b. preparation of bank reconciliations and recording of cash disbursements.
   c. distribution of payroll checks and approval of credit sales.
   d. posting of amounts from both the cash receipts journal and cash disbursements journal to the general ledger.
   e. posting of amounts from the cash receipts journal to the general ledger and distribution of payroll checks.

6. Which transaction is not processed in the fixed asset system?
   a. purchase of building
   b. repair of equipment
   c. purchase of raw materials
   d. sale of company van

7. Depreciation
   a. is calculated by the department that uses the fixed asset.
   b. allocates the cost of the asset over its useful life.
   c. is recorded weekly.
   d. results in book value approximating fair market value.

8. Depreciation records include all of the following information about fixed assets except

   a. the economic benefit of purchasing the asset.
   b. the cost of the asset.
   c. the depreciation method being used.
   d. the location of the asset.

9. Which control is not a part of the fixed asset system?
   a. formal analysis of the purchase request
   b. review of the assumptions used in the capital budgeting model
   c. development of an economic order quantity model
   d. estimates of anticipated cost savings

10. Objectives of the fixed asset system do not include
    a. authorizing the acquisition of fixed assets.
    b. recording depreciation expense.
    c. computing gain and/or loss on the disposal of fixed assets.
    d. maintaining a record of the fair market value of all fixed assets.

11. Which of the following is not a characteristic of the fixed asset system?
    a. acquisitions are routine transactions requiring general authorization
    b. retirements are reported on an authorized disposal report form
    c. acquisition cost is allocated over the expected life of the asset
    d. transfer of fixed assets among departments is recorded in the fixed asset subsidiary ledger

Problems

1. **Payroll Fraud**

   A common form of payroll fraud is payments to nonexistent employees or employees that were previously terminated but who still receive paychecks.

   Required:
   Explain how this type of fraud is committed and describe the control techniques that can reduce the risk.

2. **Payroll Fraud**

   A common form of payroll fraud is paying employees for time that they did not actually work,

   such as fraudulent overtime charges or claiming payment for days that they did not attend work.

   Required:
   Explain how this fraud is committed and describe the controls that can reduce the risk.

3. **Payroll Controls**

   Sherman Company employs 400 production, maintenance, and janitorial workers in eight separate departments. In addition to supervising operations, the supervisors of the departments are responsible for recruiting, hiring, and firing workers within their areas of responsibility. The organization attracts casual labor and experiences a 20 to 30 percent turnover rate in employees per year. A portion of Sherman Company's payroll procedures are as follows:

Employees clock on and off the job each day to record their attendance on time cards. Each department has it own clock machine that is located in an unattended room away from the main production area. Each week, the supervisors gather the time cards, review them for accuracy, and sign and submit them to the payroll department for processing. In addition, the supervisors submit personnel action forms to reflect newly hired and terminated employees. From these documents, the payroll clerk prepares payroll checks and updates the employee records. The supervisor of the payroll department signs the paychecks and sends them to the department supervisors for distribution to the employees. A payroll register is sent to accounts payable for approval. Based on this approval, the cash disbursements clerk transfers funds into a payroll clearing account.

Required:
Discuss the risks for payroll fraud in the Sherman Company payroll system. What controls would you implement to reduce the risks? Use the SAS 78 framework of control activities to organize your response.

4. **Internal Control**
   Discuss any control weaknesses found in the flowchart in the next column. Recommend any necessary changes.

5. **Human Resource Data Management**
   In a payroll system with real-time processing of human resource management data, control issues become very important. List some items in this system that could be very sensitive or controversial. Also describe what types of data must be carefully guarded to ensure that they are not altered. Discuss some control procedures that might be put into place to guard against unwanted changes to employees' records.

6. **Payroll Flowchart Analysis**
   Discuss the risks depicted by the payroll system flowchart on the next page. Describe the internal

Problem 4: Internal Control

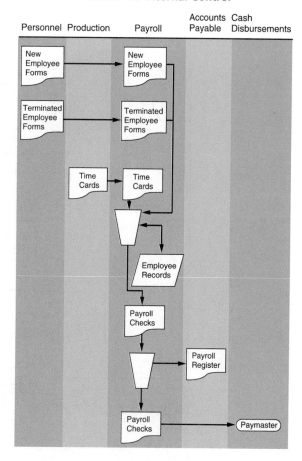

control improvements to the system that are needed to reduce these risks.

7. **Comprehensive Flowchart Analysis**
   Discuss the internal control weaknesses in the expenditure cycle flowchart on page 321. Structure your answer in terms of the SAS 78 control activities covered in Chapters 5 and 6.

8. **Fixed Asset System**
   The fixed asset acquisition procedures for Turner Brothers, Inc. are as follows:

   Supervisors in the user departments determine their fixed asset needs and submit bids or orders directly to contractors, vendors, or suppliers. In the case of competitive bidding, the user makes the final selection of the vendor and negotiates the prices paid. The assets are delivered directly to the user areas. The users inspect and

Problem 6: Payroll Flowchart Analysis

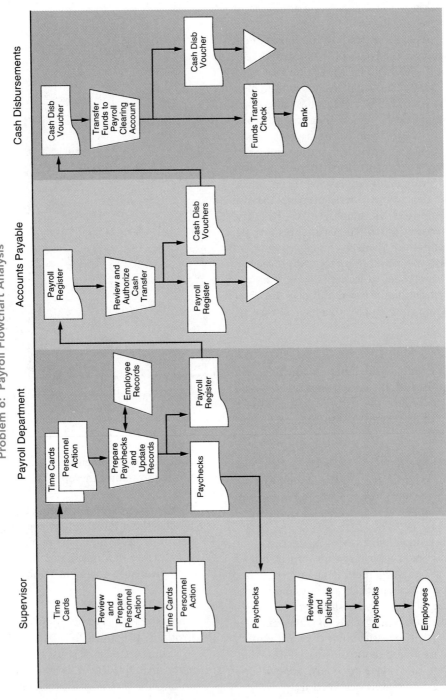

Problem 7: Comprehensive Flowchart Analysis

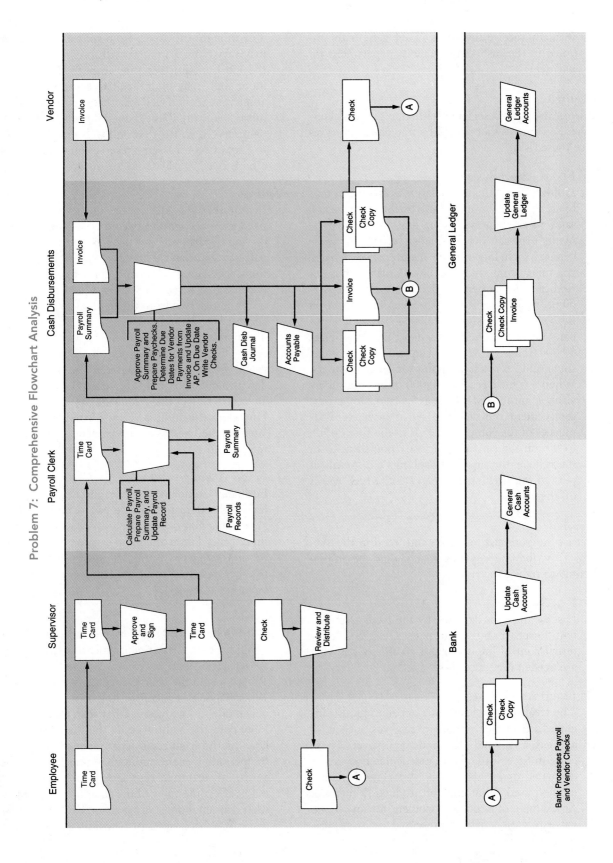

formally receive the assets. They submit the invoice to the cash disbursements department for payment.

Required:

Discuss the risks associated with this process. Describe the controls that should be implemented to reduce these risks.

9. Fixed Asset System

Holder Co. maintains a large fleet of automobiles, trucks, and vans for use by their service and sales force. Supervisors in the various departments maintain the fixed asset records for these vehicles including routine maintenance, repairs, and mileage information. This information is periodically submitted to the fixed asset department, which uses it to calculate depreciation on the vehicle. To assure a reliable fleet, the company disposes of vehicles when they accumulate 80,000 miles of service. Depending on usage, some vehicles reach this point sooner than others. When a vehicle reaches 80,000 miles, the supervisor is authorized to use it in trade for a new replacement vehicle or to sell it privately. Employees of the company are given the first option to bid on the retired vehicles. Upon disposal of the vehicle, the supervisor submits a disposal report to the fixed asset department, which writes off the asset.

Required:

Discuss the potential for abuse and fraud in this system. Describe the controls that should be implemented to reduce the risks.

10. Fixed Asset Flowchart Analysis

Discuss the risks depicted by the fixed asset system flowchart on the next page. Describe the internal control improvements to the system that are needed to reduce these risks.

11. Fixed Asset System

The treatment of fixed asset accounting also includes accounting for mineral reserves, such as oil and gas, coal, gold, diamonds, and silver. These costs must be capitalized and depleted over the estimated useful life of the asset. The depletion method used is the units of production method. An example of a source document for an oil and gas exploration firm is presented on page 324.

The time to drill a well from start to completion may vary from 3 to 18 months, depending upon the location. Further, the costs to drill two or more wells may be difficult to separate. For example, the second well may be easier to drill since more is known about the conditions of the field or reservoir, and the second well may be drilled to help extract the same reserves more quickly or efficiently.

Required:

a. In Figure 6–11, the source documents for the fixed asset accounting system come from the receiving department and the accounts payable department. For an oil and gas firm, where do you think the source documents come from?

b. Assume that a second well is drilled to help extract the reserves from the field. How would you allocate the drilling costs?

c. The number of reserves to be extracted is an estimate. These estimates are constantly being revised. How does this affect the fixed asset department's job? Does Figure 6–13 need to be altered to reflect these adjustments?

d. How does the auditor verify the numbers calculated by the fixed asset department at the end of the period?

12. Fixed Asset System

Fittipaldi Company recently purchased a patent for a radar detection device for $8 million. This radar detection device has been proven to detect three times better than any existing radar detector on the market. Fittipaldi expects four years to pass before any competitor can devise a technology to beat its device.

Required:

a. Why does the $8 million represent an asset? Should the fixed asset department be responsible for its accounting?

b. Where would the source documents come from?

c. What happens if a competitor comes out with a new model in two years rather than four?

d. How does the auditor verify the numbers calculated by the fixed asset department at the end of the period? Is it the auditor's responsibility to be aware of external regulatory conditions that might affect the value of the patent? For example, what if seven more states prohibit the use of radar detectors? (Two states now prohibit their use.)

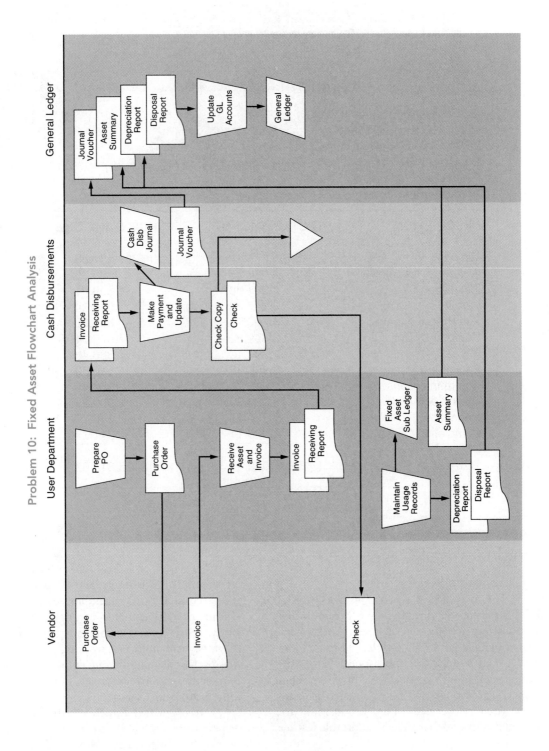

Problem 10: Fixed Asset Flowchart Analysis

Problem 11: Fixed Asset System

WILDCAT EXPLORATION COMPANY
P.O. Box 5478
Baton Rouge, Louisiana 56758

JOINT INTEREST BILLING

INVOICE DATE: August 23, 2001
INVOICE NO.: DNS3948
TERM: net 20 days from receipt
BILLING PERIOD: September 19—August 19, 2000
Property: Dutch North Sea–K/11
Percentage Interest: .1875

DESCRIPTION	TOTAL AMOUNT	PERCENTAGE DUE
Tubing	$291,876.69	$ 37,851.88
Wellhead Assembly	976.25	183.05
Installation Cost	6,981.38	1,309.01
Permits	3,297.28	618.24
Site Prep & Cleanup	4,298.78	806.02
Contract Drilling	415,345.82	77,877.34
Bits	7,394.12	1,386.40
Equipment Rental	8,109.33	1,520.50
Communications	812.77	152.49
Testing and Drafting	15,980.23	2,996.29
Inspection	3,980.13	746.27
Completion Costs	1,980.11	371.27
TOTAL	$671,032.89	$125,818.67

Internal Control Cases

1. BSJ Limousine Service, Inc.
(Prepared by Brianne Vincent, Lehigh University)

BSJ Limousine Service, Inc. is a luxury transportation service located in New York, New York. Founded in 1980, BSJ has been gaining market share steadily over the last decade. BSJ receives orders from customers to transport them to specified destinations. The company provides a top quality service. The limousines are equipped with a full bar and a comfortable leather interior.

BSJ Limousine Service, Inc. has 100 employees, consisting of 5 executives, 15 administrators, 20 maintenance workers, and 60 drivers. Each of these classifications of employees can be found within the departments through out the company. BSJ is a flexible company and does its best to satisfy its employees' working preferences. BSJ has part-time and full-time employees. They also pay some employees on an hourly basis while others are paid a salary.

Payroll in BSJ Limousine, Inc. is a separate expenditure system. The cycle used by payroll is weekly and begins each Monday. Every Monday the department supervisors send payroll a department employee pay report, which is a list of the employees in their department and their pay rate or salary. Along with this list are the time cards used by the employees paid on a time-worked basis and a list of any employees who missed days of work the previous week.

The payroll department uses this information for several tasks. First, they compare the employee lists given to them by the supervisors and the employees on the personnel action form they receive from the personnel department every month. If an employee is not on the personnel action form the department makes a note to verify that this employee is added to the personnel action form they receive the following month. The data is then used by payroll to calculate the employee's pay for the week and is also entered into each employee payroll record.

After all employee pay has been calculated the payroll register is made and a check is written and signed by the payroll department. A copy of the check, the personnel action form, time cards and the department employee pay form are filed in the payroll department. The checks and employee department pay form are returned to each supervisor on Friday to be distributed to the employees.

A copy of the payroll register is sent to the cash disbursements department so they can update the related cash accounts and know how much cash the general account will decrease by that week. Cash disbursements also creates a cash disbursement voucher that they send to the bank to authorize the paychecks to be cashed. A copy of the payroll register and cash disbursement voucher are filed in the cash disbursements department and another copy of these documents are sent to the general ledger department so that the proper accounting entries can be made. The general ledger department also receives a copy of the department employee pay form and reconciles this summary of labor with the payroll register form and cash disbursement voucher. The forms are then filed in the department.

Required:

1. Create a data flow diagram of the current system.
2. Create a document flowchart of the existing system.
3. Analyze the internal control weaknesses in the system. Model your response according to the six

categories of physical control activities specified in SAS 78.
4. Prepare a system flowchart of a redesigned computer-based system that resolves the control weaknesses that you identified.

2. Get Wet Pool Supply Company
(Prepared by Jana Clark and Amy Hamilton, Lehigh University)

Get Wet Company is currently one of the fastest-growing pool supply companies in the industry. The company is located in Florida, with company headquarters in Tampa and two branch stores in Miami and Panama City. Get Wet employs 50 people at the retail stores and about 100 employees at the headquarters. The retail store employees are hired to perform many of the mundane tasks involved with the business. These individuals are younger and less experienced and, as a result, Get Wet has a high employee turnover rate. Also, due to its rapid growth, the company is always looking to hire new employees.

Get Wet offers its customers a wide variety of products, including flotation devices (rafts and inner tubes), pool toys, pool chemicals, and basic pool-cleaning items. The supply company has a customer base that includes private pool owners and small municipal townships. Due to the wide array of products Get Wet offers its customers, the company relies on numerous vendors to fulfill its needs. These vendors include chemical suppliers, pool-cleaning item suppliers, and pool toy suppliers. Also, Get Wet relies on a general supplier, Speedy, for basic swimming and pool needs. The supplies are delivered to the company headquarters in Tampa and later distributed to the retail stores for storage in their stockrooms.

Get Wet's two branch stores have a history of seasonal sales because of the nature of the pool supply industry. Summer is by far the busiest season, due in part to tourism. In addition to these profits, Get Wet has recently landed a large account from Waterworld USA, one of Florida's largest water parks. Get Wet's president, John Poole, is delighted with the direction his company is headed, but he also feels the company may not be completely ready for this growth. It currently employs both low-level computer technology and manual procedures in its accounting system. John feels that the system needs to be revised in order to ensure that the company will be able to handle the new accounts now and in the future. Below is a description of Get Wet's payroll procedures.

Payroll Procedures

Not much has changed since the early days of the company. It is a simple system and John always thought it worked quite well and met Get Wet's needs. Each employee has a time card and all hours are kept on it. Get Wet's payroll is calculated by the accounts payable department. Recently, this department has been feeling the effects of Get Wet's growth, and John has been getting complaints that it is becoming more difficult for them to handle all the work that have to do.

Fannie Flipper in the accounts payable department receives the personnel action forms from the personnel department and the time cards from production. These two documents are then reconciled, but there has been some concern about how accurate the personnel action forms are due to a high employee turnover rate. Once reconciled, Fannie prepares the paychecks based on information from employee records, posts to the appropriate accounts, and prepares the payroll register. She then develops the cash disbursement voucher.

The paychecks prepared by Fannie in accounts payable are sent to the cash disbursements department where the paychecks are sent to the appropriate supervisor for distribution to the employees. Also sent to the cash disbursements department from accounts payable are the cash disbursement voucher and payroll register. Genie Diver, the manager in cash disbursements, writes a payroll check and deposits it in Get Wet's payroll clearing account. She then sends the voucher, payroll register, and copy of the check back to accounts payable, where they are filed.

Mark Splash in the general ledger department receives the voucher and posts to the general ledger and files the voucher. This signals the completion of Get Wet's payroll procedures.

Required:

1. Create a data flow diagram of the current system.
2. Create a document flowchart of the existing system.
3. Analyze the internal control weaknesses in the system. Model your response according to the six

categories of physical control activities specified in SAS 78.
4. Prepare a system flowchart of a redesigned computer-based system that resolves the control weaknesses that you identified.

3. PP&E Sports Emporium

(Prepared by Bryan Perler, Lehigh University)

PP&E Sports Emporium is a large retailer of sporting goods equipment and apparel, similar to Sports Authority. However, PP&E is only a single store, not a chain. Some of its suppliers include Nike, Adidas, Reebok, Rawling, and Champion. PP&E attempts to target all age groups, from 5-year-olds playing little league baseball to 70-year-olds who are fishing and playing golf. The company's clientele also includes large sports teams from universities, high schools, and community sports programs. PP&E currently has about 100 employees between its sales staff and offices. The physical property includes the offices, sales floor, and warehouse.

Recently the company has been experiencing operational problems that suggest that the system may need improvement. Herman Hoffnagle, a consultant, has been asked to analyze the company's problems. The following describes Herman's review of the payroll procedures

Payroll Procedures

When employees show up for work each day, they are required to punch their time cards. The clock machine is in an unsupervised area. Tammy, the timekeeping clerk, tries to keep track of the employees, but is often distracted by many other things. Every Friday, Tammy submits the time cards to Pamela, the payroll clerk.

Pamela copies all time cards and files the copies in the employees' folders. She uses employee wage records and tax tables to calculate the net pay for each employee. She sends a copy of the payroll register to the accounts payable department, and files a copy in the payroll department. She updates the employee records with the earnings, and prepares the payroll summary and sends it to the cash disbursements department along with the paychecks. Unbeknownst to her, however, some supervisors have been submitting time cards for employees that no longer work for the company.

After receiving the payroll summary, Alex, an accounts payable clerk, authorizes the cash disbursements department to proceed with posting the earnings and paychecks to the check register. Alex then updates the cash disbursements journal. The treasurer signs all the paychecks and gives the paychecks to the supervisors for distribution. The supervisors distribute the checks to the employees and keep the falsified ones. Finally, both the accounts payable and cash disbursements departments send a summary of transactions to the general ledger department.

Gary, the general ledger clerk, is having a difficult time reconciling the summaries that he has received. As a result, one of the most important verification and reconciliation steps in the cycle is not being effectively completed. After meticulously analyzing the payroll cycle, Herman reassures PP&E's management that he has a solution to their problems.

Required:
1. Create a data flow diagram of the current system.
2. Create a document flowchart of the existing system.
3. Analyze the internal control weaknesses in the system. Model your response according to the six categories of physical control activities specified in SAS 78.
4. Prepare a system flowchart of a redesigned computer-based system that resolves the control weaknesses that you identified.

4.   FALS Beverage Payroll System
(Prepared by Michael Mendelson, Lehigh University)
After six years of operation, FALS Beverage Company has reached the level of $50 million in revenue. It currently supplies 500 customers with various beverages ranging from iced tea to beer. Most of its customers are large restaurants, bars, and smaller beverage distributors. FALS's competition consists of three other beverage distributors that share the same geographic territory. Competition is fierce among the four beverage distributors and each is currently trying to diversify as much as possible.

Of the 120 people employed by FALS, approximately 60 of them are truck drivers. The rest are management, staff, and warehouse workers. One supervisor, Ryan Nash, controls the

warehouse. His duties include keeping track of inventory, placing new orders, and supervising the packers that work in the warehouse. The following describes the payroll procedures for FALS truck drivers and warehouse personnel.

Truck drivers and warehouse packers manually clock in and out each day. Every two weeks, Nash takes the time cards to the payroll clerk, John Schmelzer. Schmelzer takes the time cards and prepares the paychecks. Once prepared, he records them in the payroll register. After the paychecks are recorded, they are sent to the cash disbursements clerk, Sandra Buell. Buell matches the time cards with each employee, checks the amount, then signs the paychecks. After receiving her signature, the paychecks are sent to Nash to be distributed to the employees. Buell then sends the payroll register to the accounting department where the general ledger is updated.

Required:
1. Create a data flow diagram of the current system.
2. Create a document flowchart of the existing system.
3. Analyze the internal control weaknesses in the system. Model your response according to the six categories of physical control activities specified in SAS 78.

5.   The Right Fit Company
(Prepared by Jonathan Wowak, Lehigh University)
The Right Fit Company consists of five stores in the Tri-State area that are in the sneaker retail business. The main store, located in Manhattan, is where the headquarters resides. The Right Fit Company is in business of selling high-quality sneakers at low prices. As of December 31, 2001, Right Fit had a total of 120 employees consisting of sales staff, administrative staff, and management.

Payroll System
Every two weeks employees enter data from their time card into a terminal located in each of the stores. After the data is entered, the computer runs a check on the employee through an employee history file. Upon verification, a personnel action form is created, and the data is transmitted to Eji Paige in the payroll department.

Eji remains at his terminal every other Friday because he has payroll data coming in from all of the stores. Eji then prepares the paychecks from the time cards and the personnel action forms, and sends them to Jon Venezia in the cash disbursements department. Eji also prepares three copies of the payroll registers, one of which is filed, one is sent to the cash disbursements department, and the other is sent to Sharon Trusa in the accounts payable department. The time cards and the personnel action forms are filed.

Jon Venezia in cash disbursements signs and sends the checks to the employees directly. Jon takes the payroll register and writes and signs a payroll clearing check that will be sent to the bank to cover the employee paychecks. Sharon Trusa, in accounts payable, verifies and copies the payroll register. One copy of the payroll register is filed and the other is sent to Michelle Remorenko in the general ledger department. Michelle uses the payroll register from the accounts payable department and posts to the control accounts. The payroll register is then filed.

Required:
1. Create a data flow diagram of the current system.
2. Create a document flowchart of the existing system.
3. Analyze the internal control weaknesses in the system. Model your response according to the six categories of physical control activities specified in SAS 78.
4. Prepare a system flowchart of a redesigned computer-based system that resolves the control weaknesses that you identified.

6. Santa's Attic—Purchases and Payroll Procedures
(Prepared by Elizabeth Caufield and Michelle Asadourian, Lehigh University)

Purchases System
Santa's Attic purchases raw materials for production, such as plastics, wood, metal, and certain fabric. Judy, the inventory clerk in the warehouse department, is responsible for all purchasing activity. Within the warehouse department, Judy reviews the inventory records and decides when certain materials need to be repurchased. She then prepares a single purchase requisition and five copies of the purchase order form. Judy includes all of the necessary information on all copies of the form, including the material to be purchased, the price of the good, the quantity needed, and the requested delivery date. Once completed, two copies of the PO form are sent to the vendor along with the order. One is placed in the open purchase order file in the warehouse, and one is used to update the inventory control records that are kept in the warehouse department. The final copy of the PO is forwarded to the receiving department.

The materials are received by Harry, the receiving clerk, who creates four copies of a receiving report based on the packing slip and purchase order information. Two of the receiving reports are forwarded to the warehouse, where one is used to update inventory records and the other is filed. One copy of the receiving report is also maintained within the receiving department and is filed along with the packing slip and the purchase order. The third copy is sent to the accounts payable department, where it is filed in a pending file until the vendor's invoice arrives. The two documents are then reconciled. Once the receiving report and the vendor invoice are reconciled, Joanna, the accounts payable clerk, records the liability to the purchases journal and posts the total amount due to the general ledger.

Payroll System
Santa's Attic production workers each have time cards that they punch at a time clock in the morning when they arrive. They clock out in the evening when they leave. The time clock is located in an unattended room at the entrance to the plant. At the end of the week, their supervisor approves the time cards by reviewing and signing them. He then sends the time cards to the cash disbursements department. Supervisors do not keep their own attendance records. Rose, in cash disbursements, receives the time cards and reconciles them with personnel records stored on a PC database. Access to the database is very restricted. Personnel can only update the records once a year. Rose's database view displays employee demographic information but does not display salary information. Rose prepares the paychecks and signs them. She then prepares the payroll register using information from the time cards. John in accounts payable, receives the payroll register and updates the general ledger. Rose hands the prepared paychecks to the supervisors of each department for distribution to the workers. The paychecks are written from the general cash account.

Required:

1. Create a data flow diagram of the purchases and payroll systems.
2. Create a document flowchart of the purchases and payroll systems.
3. Analyze the internal control weaknesses in both systems. Model your response according to the six categories of physical control activities specified in SAS 78.

7. XMK International—Fixed Asset System
(Prepare by Badaoui Boulos, Lehigh University)

XMK International is a Philadelphia-based manufacturer of television components. A large component of the company's fixed assets is comprised of office equipment, personal computers, and specialized testing and manufacturing equipment. The supervisor of a user department in need of a new fixed asset selects the item and prepares a three-part purchase order. One copy of the PO is sent to the supplier. The supervisor sends a second copy to accounts payable, where it placed in the open fixed asset purchase file. The third copy is filed in the user department. The asset, along with a packing slip, arrives at the user department. Upon receiving an invoice from the supplier, accounts payable records the liability, which is paid on the due date. The AP clerk prepares a journal voucher and sends it to the general ledger department.

User departments are responsible for the custody, security, maintenance, and ultimate disposal of the asset. Each user department maintains a fixed asset subsidiary ledger of the items acquired and maintained by it. Changes in asset status (depreciation, repairs, and disposal) are reported to the general ledger in the form of journal vouchers from the user departments.

Required:

1. Create a data flow diagram of the fixed asset system.
2. Create a document flowchart of the fixed asset system.
3. Analyze the internal control weaknesses of the system. Model your response according to the six categories of physical control activities specified in SAS 78.

4. Prepare a system flowchart of a redesigned computer-based system that resolves the control weaknesses that you identified.

8. Williams Beverages—Fixed Asset and Payroll Systems
(Prepared by Shen Lu and Jason Stokes, Lehigh University)

Williams Beverages is a supplier of malt beverage products to the Lehigh Valley and surrounding areas. Dick Williams, a native of Bethlehem, Pennsylvania, founded the company in 1955. Currently the firm employs 175 people. They have 60 truck drivers that deliver the beverages to customers, 40 warehouse workers, and the remainder are employed in administrative and support positions. Currently Williams runs two shifts in the warehouse, and one shift for the support function.

The Pennsylvania Liqueur Control Board (PLCB) has many regulations on how a supplier may conduct business. The main provisions that Williams must follow are:

1. No credit sales for the transfer of alcoholic beverages, all sales must be cash or cash equivalent.
2. All business must be performed between Monday and Saturday.
3. All employees must have reached their eighteenth birthday.

Williams Beverages receives its inventory from many domestic suppliers, all of which have long-term exclusive contracts with Williams. Williams also is a major supplier of imported beers from all over the globe. The company supplies the malt products it receives to retail beer distributors throughout Lehigh Valley. The distributors either call or fax orders to Williams. Williams owns its own fleet of delivery trucks. The company offers quantity discounts for large orders. Lead times for delivering to customers range from one day to two weeks.

The Fixed Asset System

Daniel Jefferson has been the fixed asset manager for sixteen years. He is a trusted employee of the company, and has been given greater responsibility in recent years. Daniel is in charge of the acquisition, maintenance, and time logging of the fixed assets that Williams Beverages owns. In his tenure, he has implemented a program to buy all delivery trucks rather than lease them. The added equity that owning provides over leasing has allowed Williams to employ leverage into acquiring new assets. Recently, however, management has become concerned about the rise in maintenance costs. The average maintenance bill has increased by 15 percent over the last two years. Management is considering leasing once again, and selling the trucks that they now own. Before taking any major steps, they have decided to investigate the fixed asset department.

Daniel Jefferson is responsible for selecting repair companies and negotiating maintenance and repair terms with them. Daniel selected Fix 'Em All Repairs for all the needed work. Jessica Jefferson, his wife, is the office manger of the repair shop. Daniel fills out the work-orders as maintenance comes due and repairs are needed. Fix 'Em All Repairs bills Williams Beverages at the end of the month for services rendered. Upon receipt of the bill, the accounts payable department processes the payment, which takes five business days. Daniel makes the necessary entries to the general ledger.

Payroll System

Management at Williams trusts the employees to be accurate in this task. Jim Richmond is the treasurer at Williams Beverages. He has been working in the accounting department since the early 1960s. Because of his extended service, he has been entrusted with many responsibilities. One of his responsibilities is to maintain the personnel files. He supplies this information for payroll processing purposes.

The employees prepare their time sheets when they arrive, and note when they leave. At the end of the work week, each department sends the employee time sheets to Jim for approval. After he approves all the time sheets, he then sends them and the personnel action form to the payroll office to be processed. The paychecks are drawn on the company's general cash account. After preparing the payroll register, the payroll department sends the paychecks and the payroll register to the accounts payable department for review. Accounts payable then sends a journal voucher to the general ledger department, files the payroll register, and sends the paychecks to Jim for signing and distribution to the employees.

Required:

1. Create a data flow diagram for the fixed asset and payroll systems.
2. Create a document flowchart for the fixed asset and payroll systems.
3. Analyze the internal control weaknesses in each of the two systems. Model your response according to the six categories of physical control activities specified in SAS 78.
4. Prepare a system flowchart for each of the two redesigned computer-based systems that resolves the control weaknesses that you identified.

9. Philly Designer Phones—Comprehensive Case

(Prepared by Bonny Bustin, Melissa Clymer, and Andrea Vardaro, Lehigh University)

Philly Designer Phones, Inc. (PDP) is a manufacturer of stylish portable and cellular telephones. Founded in 1994, PDP is the successful producer in this industry. With a base of 112 employees, the company has one main location in Philadelphia, Pennsylvania.

Customers

Philly Designer Phones, Inc. mainly distributes their products to electronic store chains in the northeast region of the United States, however, they have received some orders from the West Coast. The company's terms of trade include net 30 to 45 day limits, if the 5 percent discount is not recognized in the specified three-day time period. The company intends to launch a new marketing campaign that will focus on increasing sales throughout the United States. If this proves successful, the company is prepared to expand its operations to other locations throughout the country.

The company also sells its product through "high-tech" catalogues, even though its largest source of income is from the store orders. In 2000, gross sales increased to $25 million, as compared to $10 million in 1999. A further increase in sales is expected with the release of the 2001 financial statements.

Suppliers

PDP deals with numerous suppliers. It has no trading partner arrangements, and selects suppliers based on the best price on the specific part being purchased. A consequence of this is that the company has had problems with raw material and component quality, as well as delivery problems. The terms of payment differ for each supplier, and frequently payments are late, resulting in lost discounts. In addition, PDP experiences stockouts and occasionally overstocks items.

Purchases System

The purchases cycle begins in the inventory department. Every Friday, John, a clerk in the inventory department, reviews his records to determine the amount of supplies to be ordered for the following week. John prepares three copies of a purchase requisition and sends one to the purchasing department, one to the accounting department, and uses the third to update the inventory records in the inventory department. With this information he then updates his records, posts to the inventory ledger, and produces a summary of the activity of the inventory department.

After receiving a purchase requisition, Pat in the purchases department must choose an appropriate supplier from the supplier table. Because the supplier table has so many vendors, Pat has a difficult time choosing what company to order from. PDP often gets stuck with faulty merchandise from nonreputable vendors. Pat uses the purchase requisition to prepare a purchase order noting the quantity needed, expected unit prices, and the terms and conditions of the purchase. She sends a copy to the accounting department, the receiving department, and the inventory department; two copies to the vendor; and files the last copy in the open purchase order file.

Ryan in the receiving department receives a copy of the purchase order with all the information regarding the purchase, which he files away until the goods are received. A packing slip is included with each order of merchandise. Because PDP orders small parts in bulk quantity, the receiving department does not have time to inspect or count the merchandise. Upon receipt of the inventory, an employee in the receiving department will compare the vendor's packing slip with the purchase order. If the numbers correctly match, the parts are dumped into different bins and the purchase order and packing slip are filed away.

After the goods are received, the invoice is sent to Mary in the accounting department. The invoice is matched against the purchase requisition and the purchase order. All outstanding balances are paid upon receipt of the invoice. Mary updates accounts payable, posts to the accounts payable subsidiary ledger and the purchases journal, and then creates a cash disbursement voucher. Kevin reviews the accounts payable subsidiary ledger for items which are due and then prepares and signs the checks for the suppliers. The original check is sent to the supplier, while a copy is filed in the accounting department. An employee in the accounting department uses the other copy to update the accounting records.

Fixed Asset System

Users of the equipment in each department decide when new equipment needs to be ordered. Each user sends a purchase requisition to the purchases department. Three copies of the purchase order are prepared. One copy goes to the vendor, one goes to Mary in the accounts payable department, and one is filed in the purchases department. When the new equipment arrives, Ryan in the receiving department inspects it and sends a receiving report to accounts payable. Mary in accounts payable authorizes payment upon receipt of the supplier's invoice and sends a cash disbursement voucher to Kevin, the cash disbursements clerk. He sends a check to the vendor and updates the general ledger control accounts.

Payroll System

In the production departments, each employee completes a job ticket and time card for the workweek. At the end of every week, the production department supervisors send the job tickets to the cost accounting department, where they are posted to the work-in-process account, and a completed labor distribution summary is sent to the general ledger department. The supervisor sends the time cards to the payroll department. They are reconciled and posted to the individual employee records, and the employee paychecks are prepared. The paychecks are then sent to the cash disbursements department.

Kevin, the cash disbursement clerk, reconciles and signs the paychecks, and places the amounts in the payroll summary, which he sends to the general ledger department. Once signed, the paychecks are given to the department supervisors for distribution to the employees. Finally, the general ledger clerk, Angela, reconciles the labor distribution summary with the payroll summary and updates the general ledger.

Required:

1. Create a data flow diagram for each of the three systems just described.
2. Create a document flowchart for each system.
3. Analyze the internal control weaknesses of each system. Model your response according to the six categories of physical control activities specified in SAS 78.

10. Jumes Grocery—Comprehensive Case

(Prepared by Cheryl Hoops, Gregory McDonald, and Mike Rosen, Lehigh University)

Jumes Grocery is a chain of grocery stores that sell a variety of goods from quality deli meats and fresh fruit, supplied by local farmers, to routine grocery items, supplied by nationally known suppliers. Dick Jumes, an 18-year-old immigrant to Great Neck, New York, founded the first market in 1975. Since 1975, Jumes Grocery has grown to include 13 locations and 251 employees across Long Island, spanning Nassau and Suffolk Counties.

For 1998, Jumes Grocery as a whole experienced roughly $19.5 million in gross sales. A major contributor was the Oyster Bay branch, which alone brought $2.5 million to the company. Compared to its competitors, Jumes Grocery performed rather well. Consumers prefer its family-owned business atmosphere compared to the commercial grocery stores.

A head manager represents every local branch of Jumes Grocery. For the most part, the head manager is responsible for all functional processes within the store. Head manager responsibilities include managing supplier relationships, human resources, and accounting transactions, and maintaining the store itself. Under the head manager are supervisors who are allocated leadership positions in different departments and who oversee part-time employees, who keep the appearance of the stores satisfactory by stocking the shelves and displays throughout the stores. To perform operations, Jumes Grocery currently uses an unsophisticated system that employs low-level technology and manual procedures. Each location uses standalone microcomputers to perform certain accounting functions, but for the most part the company relies on the efficiency of its managers.

Although Jumes Grocery is performing well against its competitors, the owners are concerned that if they do not implement changes as well as an upgrade in computer technology they will no longer continue to supply Long Island with the freshest groceries. As a result, they hired the CMG consulting group to examine the current weaknesses in operations and to make suggestions for changes in the future. The following documents are the results for the purchases, cash disbursements, payroll, and fixed assets systems.

Purchases System

The logical activities that constitute the purchases subsystem are consistent for all locations of Jumes Grocery. Although the activities are consistent, there are some differences that create a complicated system for the company as a whole. For example, the purchases manager at each location is responsible for his or her own suppliers. If the manager needs a product he or she chooses a supplier using his or her own discretion. There is no formal approval from the central office for suppliers. Once a supplier is chosen, each store follows the steps described below.

1. The purchasing function begins with sales representatives from suppliers periodically observing the shelves and displays at each individual location and recognizing the need to restock inventory. Inventory declines by direct sales to the customers or by spoilage of perishable goods. In addition, sales representatives may observe that certain products are unsaleable at a particular location, at which point the goods are returned to the supplier and replaced with more successful products. The sales representatives create a purchase requisition and meet with the purchases managers of the individual store locations. Together the sales rep and the purchases manager prepare a purchase order, deciding on the quantity and delivery time. The supplier subsequently submits a bill.

2. At the intended delivery date, Jumes Grocery stores receive the goods from the suppliers. Goods received are unloaded from the delivery trucks and stocked in the shelves and displays by part-time employees.

3. The unloading personnel send the information about the deliveries to the purchases managers. The purchases managers reconcile the receiving

information against the purchase orders and record an obligation of payment for some future date, depending on the terms with the supplier.

4. After compiling all the necessary information, the purchases managers send summaries of the inventory and obligation information by FedEx to the CFO, Colleen O'Herlihy, at the central office. There the general ledger records the information from all the store locations collectively and posts to the accounts payable and inventory control accounts.

A Detailed Look
Rockville Centre's Purchases Subsystem

Nabisco Incorporated is one of the many suppliers for the Rockville Centre (RVC) branch of Jumes Grocery. Once a week Tom Hamm, a sales representative from Nabisco's Westbury sales office, inspects the shelves and displays in the RVC store and prepares the appropriate purchase requisition for the cookies and crackers needed. Tom then meets with Jeff Hoops, RVC's purchases manager, and they collectively prepare a purchase order. Tom takes a copy of the PO back to Nabisco, another copy is sent to Sharon Hoops, who is in charge of the receiving department, and Jeff files the last copy along with the purchase requisition in the Nabisco file. Nabisco later sends Jeff a sales invoice, which is filed as well.

There is a short time lag between Tom Hamm's visit to the store and the delivery of the Nabisco products. When the delivery trucks arrive, Sharon Hoops accepts the delivery after comparing the purchase order and the packing slip. The employees then proceed to unload and stock the cookies and crackers in the store. If damaged goods are detected they are stored in the back of the grocery until the next delivery, when they are sent back to Nabisco.

After delivery, Sharon prepares a receiving report and sends it to Jeff Hoops. Jeff reconciles the report against the PO and the sales invoice on file, then updates the actual cost inventory ledgers as well as accounts payable. Finally, Jeff summarizes all the purchasing information and prepares a journal voucher to be delivered by FedEx to Colleen O'Herlihy at the central office. When Colleen receives this information she updates the inventory and accounts payable control accounts in the general ledger. It is important to note that the summary information from all the branches is collaborated in the same accounts at the

central office. In other words, there is one single accounts payable control account embodying all locations. The purchases phase is now complete.

Cash Disbursements Subsystem

The cash disbursements process, like the purchases process, is identical for every branch of Jumes Grocery. Continuing from the purchases subsystem, the general cash disbursements steps are listed below.

1. The purchases manager is responsible for establishing an obligation for payment. When the obligations are near due, he/she sends summary information to the central office in order to trigger the wiring of funds.

2. Colleen O'Herlihy reviews the summary information from the individual locations and, based on the totals, wires the correct amount of funds to the individual branch accounts from the main Jumes Grocery account.

3. The cash disbursements process then prepares and distributes checks to the suppliers. Copies of the checks are kept on file in the individual stores as proof of payment, and the appropriate liabilities are removed.

4. At the end of the process, the purchases manager sends summary information and a copy of the checks by FedEx to the central office where the general ledger posts to the cash and accounts payable control accounts.

A Detailed Look
Rockville Centre's Cash Disbursements Subsystem

RVC's cash disbursements process begins with Jeff Hoops. Periodically, Jeff reviews the accounts payable records for payments due and sends the total amount of payments to Colleen O'Herlihy in Great Neck. Colleen reviews the summary information and wires the necessary funds from the main bank account to Rockville Centre's individual bank account.

Once Jeff receives notice that the funds have been wired, he proceeds to have an employee prepare the checks and record the data in the cash disbursements journal. The employee then submits the checks to Jeff for his signature. The formal checks are delivered to the appropriate suppliers and two copies are filed.

Finally, Jeff summarizes the entries made to the check register and sends a journal voucher as well as one copy of the checks to Colleen O'Herlihy. Colleen reviews the information, then posts to the cash and accounts payable control accounts in the general ledger. This concludes the cash disbursements procedures.

The Payroll System
A General Look

All of the payroll activities are focused around the main store located in Great Neck, New York. The remaining twelve stores follow the procedures set forth by the main store since that is where Colleen O'Herlihy is situated. All employees are paid on a biweekly basis and are paid directly by the employer, Jumes Grocery. Located at the Great Neck office, the payroll department consists of three people. Colleen O'Herlihy is one of the three people on this team. Currently, every two weeks the department follows the steps described below.

1. The pay period ends on every other Thursday. On this day, the time card totals are calculated by each employee and are either faxed or hand delivered (if on-site) to the Great Neck location.

2. The payroll department receives the time card totals. Employee records are referenced as to tax and deduction information. New employees are added to the records after their first pay period. Therefore, for the first pay period human resources supplies payroll with the information they need to process the paycheck.

3. Paychecks are distributed to the employees of the Great Neck location by one of the payroll staff, usually Colleen O'Herlihy.

4. For the other employees, the paychecks are sent to their managers. Therefore, each location receives a package of paychecks every two weeks. Since they use a carrier that allows anyone to sign for the package, the paychecks may or may not be distributed by the manager.

5. Employees do not have to sign for the paychecks when they receive them.

A Detailed Look
Atlantic Beach's Payroll Subsystem

The Atlantic Beach location receives its paychecks by carrier every other Thursday. It becomes a mystery of who has the checks since the carrier does not look for anyone in particular and lets anyone sign for them. Kenny Abile is usually the employee who happens to sign for the paycheck package most of the time. He then distributes the paychecks to the location's employees. Upon giving the paycheck to an employee, the employee is not required or asked to sign for the

acceptance of the paycheck. For the employees that are not present to receive the checks, Kenny keeps the check at his desk until the employee's return. Once all the checks are distributed, the package envelope is discarded and the payroll system has ended.

Fixed Asset System

The fixed asset subsystem for Jumes Grocery is comprised of two basic functions. Both the asset acquisition function and the maintenance/disposal function are the responsibility of the store manager. The process of acquiring fixed assets is consistent throughout the chain of stores, yet each store has the autonomy to choose a supplier. Freezers, refrigerators, delivery vans, and store shelving are the most common fixed asset purchases. Land and any building purchases are only to be conducted by Dick Jumes and are dealt with on a case-by-case basis. The manager handbook reads, "Managers may purchase fixed assets at their discretion to ensure unruffled continuation of operations." There is no formal capital investment analysis done by headquarters. Once a manager decides a purchase is necessary, the store follows the steps described below.

1. The manager chooses a supplier and then negotiates terms of the contract/purchase order, which may include trade-ins, delivery date, applicable financing, warranties, and service.

2. Once a contract is agreed upon, the manager sends the contract/purchase order to the supplier. The supplier processes the purchase order and the manager makes an arrangement to pick up the asset or the supplier delivers it. The manager receives a copy of the purchase order and invoice from the supplier.

3. The supplier mails an additional copy of the purchase order and invoice to the manager, who files it in the store's fixed asset records.

4. The manager then sends a form with details of the transaction, along with copies of the purchase order, invoice, and capital needs, to the accounts payable department at headquarters in Great Neck.

5. Headquarters then transfers the capital needs to the store's account through the cash disbursements process.

6. Payments to suppliers are made through the cash disbursements process.

Guidelines are listed in the handbook to give managers an idea of the useful life of typical fixed assets, but these are not viewed as regulations. There are no formal authorizations to purchase or dispose of assets. When a manager decides an asset needs to be disposed of, general company policy is to trade the asset in for value when acquiring replacement, transfer it to another store, or scrap it. The manager has the ultimate decision on the disposal of fixed assets. Delivery drivers submit daily mileage in a travel log to managers. Assistant managers are responsible for ensuring vehicles pass state inspections and routine maintenance is performed.

A Detailed Look
Oyster Bay's Fixed Asset Subsystem
Oyster Bay (OB) is Jumes Grocery's third largest and second oldest store. In 1998, OB increased sales from the previous year 140 percent to $2.3 million, mostly attributed to an aggressive and innovative grocery delivery campaign where customers receive brochures with weekly specials. Customers can then phone in complete grocery orders that Jumes guarantees to deliver within two hours. Due to the increased demand for delivery, the OB branch expanded its fleet of delivery vans from four to seven. On January 7, Tim McDonald, manager of the Oyster Bay store, felt one of the existing vans, a 1992 Dodge Caravan, had too many miles on it and had outlived its usefulness. He contacted his college roommate, DJ Fox at Fox

Chevrolet in Little Neck, to purchase four Chevy Blazers. McDonald contracted Fox Chevrolet to purchase two new Blazers for $26,500 each, and two used Blazers: a 1997 for $19,800 and a 1999 for $22,300. All vehicles were delivered on February 1. The old Caravan was traded in for $4,000 credit towards the new vehicles. McDonald sent a purchase order for the vehicles to Fox on January 9. Fox then mailed copies of the invoice back to McDonald, who filed them. The vehicles were delivered on the agreed-upon date with a copy of the invoice. McDonald updated accounts payable and then compiled a transaction summary report that was sent to the cash disbursements system.

Required:
1. Create a data flow diagram for each of the three systems described above.
2. Create a document flowchart for each system.
3. Analyze the internal control weaknesses of each system. Model your response according to the six categories of physical control activities specified within SAS 78.
4. Describe the revisions that could be made to the three systems that resolve the control weaknesses that you identified.

CHAPTER

7

The Conversion Cycle

A company's conversion cycle transforms (converts) input resources, such as raw materials, labor, and overhead, into finished products or services for sale. The conversion cycle is most formal and apparent in manufacturing firms. However, this cycle exists, conceptually, in certain service industries, such as health care, consulting, and public accounting. In this discussion of the conversion cycle, we shall assume a manufacturing environment.

U.S. manufacturers are in a period of dynamic transformation. Rapid swings in consumer demands, shorter product life cycles, and foreign competition have radically changed the rules of the marketplace. In attempting to cope with these changes, manufacturers are beginning to conduct business in a dramatically new way. The term *world-class* defines this new era of business. Figure 7–1 presents the manufacturing environment as a continuum, with traditional firms at one end and world-class firms at the other. At points along this line are firms in various stages of transformation as they move toward world-class status.

Relatively few firms have achieved world-class status. Many are moving in that direction; many more remain traditional. To deal with the diversity of practices, this chapter has been divided into four major sections. The first outlines the defining characteristics of a world-class organization. The second section describes the traditional manufacturing environment. It examines the batch production process and the traditional accounting information system within this setting. The third section deals with the world-class manufacturing environment. Here, we become acquainted with the significant assumptions, philosophies, objectives, and technologies associated with world-class firms. The fourth section addresses the implications for accounting and AIS. Here, we will see how world-class competition is influencing changes in accounting techniques, information reporting, and information systems. The chapter concludes by presenting the key features of a world-class information system.

LEARNING OBJECTIVES

After studying this chapter, you should:

- Understand the basic elements and procedures encompassing a traditional production process.
- Understand the data flows and procedures in a traditional cost accounting system.
- Be familiar with the accounting controls found in a traditional environment.
- Understand the operating features, philosophies, and technologies that characterize a world-class company.
- Understand the objectives of just-in-time systems and recognize the implications of maintaining excessive inventories in the world-class environment.
- Recognize the importance of quality in the world-class environment.
- Understand the shortcomings of traditional accounting methods in the world-class environment.
- Be familiar with the characteristics of a world-class information system.

FIGURE 7–1

Continuum of
Manufacturing
Practices

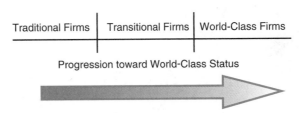

The Manufacturing Environment

| Traditional Firms | Transitional Firms | World-Class Firms |

Progression toward World-Class Status

WORLD-CLASS COMPANIES

The **world-class company** is a company that has achieved high standards and has undergone fundamental changes from traditional forms of organization and management. This type of company continuously pursues improvement in all aspects of its operations, including its manufacturing procedures. Let's examine some of the characteristics that distinguish world-class manufacturers from traditional firms.

A world-class company profitably meets the needs of its customers. Its goal is not simply to satisfy customers but to positively delight them. This is not something that can be done once and then forgotten. With competitors aggressively seeking new ways to increase market share, a world-class firm must continue to delight its customers.

The philosophy of customer satisfaction permeates the world-class firm. All of its activities, from the acquisition of raw materials to selling the finished product, form a "chain of customers." Each activity is dedicated to serving its customer, that is, the next activity in the process. The final paying customer is the last in the chain.

Products in a world-class company are produced in teams comprising members from all functional areas within the firm—engineering and production to marketing and procurement. To activate the talents of everyone on the team, decisions in this setting are pushed to the lowest level in the organization. The result is a flat organizational structure requiring high-quality, cross-functional information.

Achieving world-class status carries significant implications for accounting and accounting information systems. Traditional information produced under conventional accounting techniques does not adequately support the needs of the world-class firm. These companies need new accounting methods and new information systems that:

1. Show what matters to its customers (such as quality and service).
2. Identify profitable products.
3. Identify profitable customers.
4. Identify opportunities for improvement in operations and products.
5. Encourage the adoption of value-added activities and processes within the organization and identify those that do not add value.
6. Efficiently support multiple users with both financial and nonfinancial information.

The role played by accounting information is a critical determinant in a firm's success as a world-class competitor and will be a major focus of this chapter.

THE TRADITIONAL MANUFACTURING ENVIRONMENT

The traditional conversion cycle consists of two subsystems: the production system and the cost accounting system. The **production system** involves the planning, scheduling, and control of the physical product through the manufacturing process. This includes determining raw materials requirements, authorizing the release of raw materials into production and the work to be performed, and directing the movement of work in process through the various stages of manufacturing. The **cost accounting system** monitors the flow of cost information related to production. Information produced by this system is used for inventory valuation, budgeting, cost control, performance reporting, and such management decisions as "make-or-buy" decisions.

In the traditional **manufacturing environment**, these subsystems tend to be separate rather than integrated. Therefore, we will examine them separately.

THE PRODUCTION SYSTEM

Depending on the product being manufactured, a company will employ one of the following production methods:

Continuous processing creates a homogeneous product through a continuous series of standard procedures. Cement and petrochemicals are produced by this manufacturing method. Typically, under this approach firms attempt to maintain finished goods inventory at levels needed to meet expected sales demand. The sales forecast in conjunction with information on current inventory levels triggers this process.

Batch processing produces discrete groups (batches) of product. Each item in the batch is similar, requiring the same raw materials and operations. To justify the cost of setting up and retooling for each batch run, the number of items in the batch is usually large. This is the most common method of production. It is used to manufacture such products as automobiles, household appliances, and computers. The triggering mechanism for this process is the need to maintain finished goods inventory levels in accordance with projected sales requirements.

Make-to-order processing involves the fabrication of discrete products in accordance with customer specifications. This process is initiated by sales orders rather than depleted inventory levels.

The actual procedures that make up the production system will vary with the manufacturing method in use. The following discussion will focus on the batch processing system. This system determines in advance the exact quantity and type of input materials, as well as the physical operations required to produce each batch.

Documents in the Batch Processing System

Let's begin our study of the batch processing system with an examination of the documents that trigger and support batch activities. The most common of these are briefly described below.

1. The **sales forecast** shows the expected demand for the firm's finished goods for a given period. The marketing function usually produces a forecast of annual demand by product. For firms with seasonal swings in sales, this is broken down

into shorter periods (quarterly or monthly) that can be revised in accordance with prevailing economic conditions. In many industries, the sales forecast is an essential production planning document.

2. The **production schedule** is the formal plan and authorization to begin production. This document describes the specific products to be made, the quantities to be produced in each batch, and the manufacturing timetable for starting and completing production. Figure 7–2 contains an example of a production schedule.

3. The **bill of materials** (BOM), an example of which is illustrated in Figure 7–3, specifies the types and quantities of the raw materials and subassemblies

FIGURE 7–2

Production Schedule

Batch Num	Qnty Units	OPER #1 Start	Complete	OPER #2 Start	Complete	OPER #3 Start	Complete
1237	800	1/2/01	1/5/01			1/8/01	1/23/01
1567	560	1/3/01	1/8/01	1/9/01	1/15/01	1/16/01	1/18/01
1679	450			1/2/01	1/5/01	1/8/01	1/10/01
4567	650	1/5/01	1/10/01	1/11/01	1/15/01	1/16/01	1/23/01
5673	1000	•	•	•	•	•	•
•	•	•	•	•	•	•	•
•	•	•	•	•	•	•	•

ABC COMPANY   PRODUCTION SCHEDULE   JAN 2001

FIGURE 7–3

Bill of Materials

BILL OF MATERIALS

PRODUCT ENGINE TR6 2500 CC — NORMAL BATCH QNTY 100

Material Item Num	Description	Quantity Reg/Unit Product
28746	Crank shaft	1
387564	Main bearing set	4
735402	Piston	6
663554	Connecting rods	6
8847665	Rod bearing set	6
663345	Core plug 2"	6
663546	Core plug 1 1/2"	4

used in producing a single unit of finished product. The raw materials requirements for an entire batch are determined by multiplying the BOM times the number of items in the batch.

4. A **route sheet**, illustrated in Figure 7–4, shows the production path a particular batch of product follows during manufacturing. It is similar conceptually to a BOM. Whereas the BOM specifies material requirements, the route sheet specifies the sequence of operations (machining or assembly) and the standard time allocated to each task.

5. The **work order** (or production order) draws from BOMs and route sheets to specify the materials and production (machining, assembly, and so on) for each batch. These, together with move tickets (described next), initiate the manufacturing process in the production departments. Figure 7–5 presents a work order.

6. A **move ticket**, shown in Figure 7–6, records work done in each work center and authorizes the movement of the job or batch from one work center to the next.

7. A **materials requisition** authorizes the storekeeper to release materials (and subassemblies) to individuals or work centers in the production process. This document usually specifies only standard quantities. Materials needed in excess of standard amounts require separate requisitions that may be identified explicitly as excess materials requisitions. This allows for closer control over the production process by highlighting excess material usage. In some cases, less than the standard amount of material is used in production. When this happens, the work centers return the unused materials to the storeroom accompanied by a materials return ticket. Figure 7–7 presents a format that could serve all three purposes.

The Batch Production Process

The flowchart in Figure 7–8 (pages 344–345) illustrates the flow of information through a typical batch production system. The functions and interrelationships of each phase in the production system are briefly described. Let's first look at the production planning and control phase of the system. This phase involves two main

---

FIGURE 7–4

Route Sheet

ROUTE SHEET

PRODUCT
ENGINE TR6
2500 CC

Work Center	Operation	Description	Standard Time/Unit	
			Set Up	Process
101	1a	Mill block and fit studs	.6	1.6
153	4a	Clean block and fit crank	.3	1.5
154	1	Fit pistons and bearings	.1	.7
340	2	Fit water pump, fuel pump, oil pump, and cylinder head	.1	1.4

FIGURE 7–5   Work Order

WORK ORDER #5681

| PART NAME: | Drawing # |
| ENGINE CRANK SHAFT | CS-87622 |

MATERIAL:
CRANK CASTING

Work Center	Operation	Description	Standard Hrs		Actual Proc	Unit Compltd	Units Scrap	Insp #
			Set Up	Proc				
184	21	Draw castings from stores	—	2.2	2.5	100	0	
186	23	Turn journals and main bearings per specs	2.3	14.9	16.00	99	1	
156	01	Balance crank	4.0	21.5	32.00	99	0	
•	•	•	•	•	•	•	•	•
•	•	•	•	•	•	•	•	•

FIGURE 7–6

Move Ticket

MOVE TICKET

| Batch Num: | 1292 |
| Units: | 100 |

Move to:	Work Center 153
Operation:	4a
Start Date:	1/8/01
Finish Date:	1/10/01
Qnty Received:	100
Received By:_____	

procedures: the specification of **materials and operations requirements** and production scheduling.

Establishing the raw material requirements for a batch of any given product entails analyzing what is needed versus what is available in the raw materials inventory. Operations requirements are determined by examining the machining and other manufacturing tasks needed to produce a unit of finished product. Primary determinants for both materials and operations requirements are the sales forecast, the inventory status report, and engineering specifications for the finished product.

When producing nonstandard batches or custom products, the specification of materials and operations requirements can become quite involved due to the detailed analysis necessary to prepare the BOMs and route sheets. For standard products,

FIGURE 7–7

Materials Requisition,
Excess Materials
Requisition, and
Materials Return
Ticket

MATERIALS REQUISITION/RETURNS

Issued To: _____   **Work Order Number**_____
  Date: _____

Material Item #	Description	Quantity Issued	Unit Cost	Extended Cost

Authorized By: _____
Received By: _____
Cost Accounting: _____

however, the BOMs and route sheets can be prepared in advance and filed. Clerks can simply retrieve these as needed from the BOM and route sheet files, thus reducing the complexity of this phase in the production process.

Also produced in the planning and control step are the purchase requisitions (if needed) for additional raw materials. Procedures for preparing purchase orders and acquiring inventories are the same as those described in Chapter 5.

The second procedure carried out under planning and control is production scheduling. The schedule for a production run is prepared by the production scheduling clerk and is based on the information provided in BOMs and route sheets. The scheduling clerk also prepares work orders, move tickets, and materials requisitions for each batch in the production run. Before releasing these documents to the various work centers, the clerk creates an open work order file and sends a copy of the work order to cost accounting.

The work orders, move tickets, and materials requisitions prepared by the scheduling clerk flow through the various work centers in accordance with the route sheet. To provide a simplified illustration of the manufacturing phase of the production system, Figure 7–8 shows only one work center.

The manufacturing phase begins when workers obtain raw materials from storekeeping in exchange for materials requisitions. These materials, as well as the machining and the labor required to manufacture the product, are applied in compliance with the work order. When the task is complete, the supervisor or other authorized person fills out and signs the move ticket for that work center. The completed move ticket authorizes the batch to proceed to the next work center. As evidence that this stage of production has been completed, a copy of the move ticket is sent back to production planning and control to update the open work order file. Upon receipt of the last move ticket, the open work order file is closed. The finished product along with a copy of the work order goes to the finished goods warehouse. A copy of the work order also goes to inventory control to update the finished goods inventory records.

As one might expect, work centers also fulfill an important role in recording labor time costs. This task is handled by work center supervisors, who, at the end of each

FIGURE 7–8   Batch Production Process

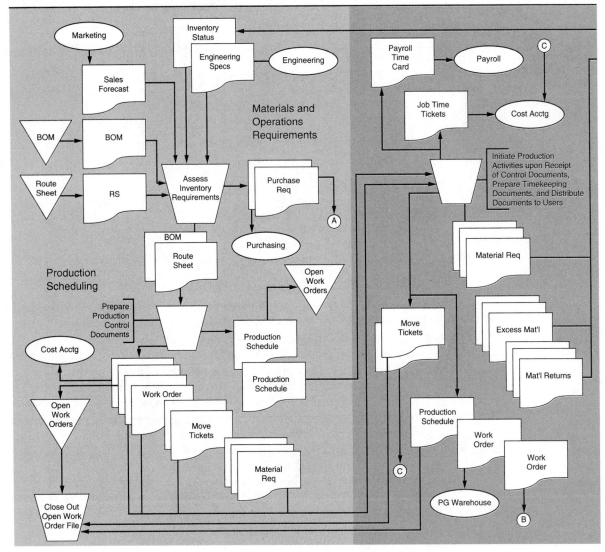

work week, send employee time cards and job tickets to the payroll and cost accounting departments, respectively.

The remaining phase of the production system is inventory control, which has three main functions in the production process. First, it triggers the entire process by providing production planning and control with an inventory status report of raw materials and finished goods. Second, inventory control personnel are continually involved in updating the raw materials inventory records from materials requisitions, excess materials requisitions, and materials return tickets. Finally, upon receipt of the work order from the last work center, inventory control records the completed production in the finished goods inventory records.

FIGURE 7–8 (continued)

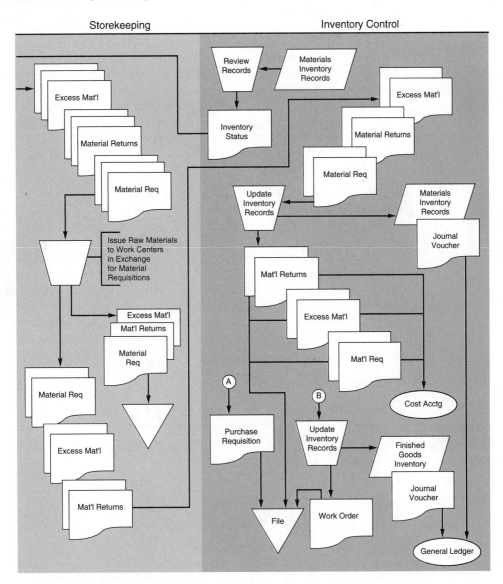

THE ECONOMIC ORDER QUANTITY MODEL

The objective of inventory control is to minimize total inventory cost while ensuring that adequate inventories exist to meet current demand. Inventory models used for achieving this objective help answer two fundamental questions:

1. When should inventory be purchased?
2. How much inventory should be purchased?

The simplest and most commonly used inventory model is the **economic order quantity (EOQ) model**. However, the EOQ model is based on assumptions that may not always reflect the economic reality. These assumptions are:

1. Demand for the product is constant and known with certainty.
2. The lead time—the time between placing an order for inventory and its arrival—is known and constant.
3. All inventories in the order arrive at the same time.
4. The total cost per year of placing orders is a variable that decreases as the quantities ordered increase. Ordering costs include the cost of preparing documentation, contacting vendors, processing inventory receipts, maintaining vendor accounts, and writing checks.
5. The total cost per year of holding inventories (carrying costs) is a variable that increases as the quantities ordered increase. These costs include the opportunity cost of invested funds, storage costs, property taxes, and insurance.
6. There are no quantity discounts. Therefore, the total purchase price of inventory for the year is constant.

The objective of the EOQ model is to reduce total inventory costs. The significant parameters in this model are the carrying costs and the ordering costs. Figure 7–9 illustrates the relationship between these costs and order quantity. As the quantity ordered increases, the number of ordering events decreases, causing the total annual cost of ordering to decrease. However, as the quantity ordered increases, average inventory on hand increases, causing the total annual inventory carrying cost to increase. Because the total purchase price of inventory is constant (Assumption 6), we minimize total inventory costs by minimizing the total carrying cost and total ordering costs. The point at which the combined total cost curve is minimized is the intersection of the ordering cost curve and the carrying cost curve. This is the economic order quantity.

FIGURE 7–9

The Relationship of Total Inventory Cost and Order Quantity

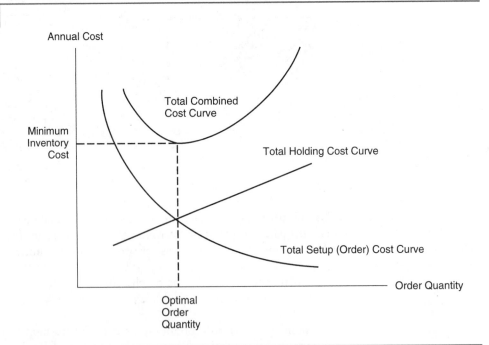

The following equation is used to determine the EOQ:

$$Q = \sqrt{\frac{2DS}{H}}$$

where: Q = economic order quantity
D = annual demand in units
S = the fixed cost of placing each order
H = the holding or carrying cost per unit per year

To illustrate the use of this model, consider the following example:

A company has an annual demand of 2,000 units, a per-unit order cost of $12, and a carrying cost per unit of $0.40. Using these values, we calculate the EOQ as follows:

$$Q = \sqrt{\frac{2DS}{H}}$$

$$Q = \sqrt{\frac{2(2,000)(12)}{0.40}}$$

$$Q = \sqrt{120,000}$$

$$Q = 346$$

Now that we know how much to purchase, let's consider the second question: When do we purchase?

The **reorder point** (ROP) is usually expressed as follows:

$$ROP = I \times d$$

where: I = lead time
d = daily demand (total demand/number of working days)

In simple models, both I and d are assumed to be known with certainty and are constant. For example, if:

d = 5 units, and
I = 8 days, then
ROP = 40 units.

The assumptions of the EOQ model produce the saw-toothed inventory usage pattern illustrated in Figure 7–10. Values for Q and ROP are calculated separately for each type of inventory item. Each time inventory is reduced by sales or used in production, its new quantity on hand (QOH) is compared to its ROP. When QOH = ROP, an order is placed for the amount of Q. In our example, when inventory drops to 40 units, the firm orders 346 units.

If the parameters d and I are stable, the firm should receive the ordered inventories just as the quantity on hand reaches zero. However, if either or both parameters are subject to variation, then additional inventories called **safety stock** must be added to the reorder point to avoid unanticipated stockout conditions. Figure 7–11 shows an additional 10 units of safety stock to carry the firm through a lead time that could vary from eight to ten days. The new reorder point is 50 units. Stockouts result in either lost sales or back-orders. A back-order is a customer order that cannot be filled

FIGURE 7–10

Inventory Usage

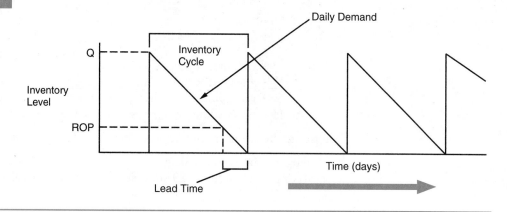

because of a stockout and will remain unfilled until the supplier receives replenishment stock.

When an organization's inventory usage and delivery patterns depart significantly from the assumptions of the EOQ model, more sophisticated models such as the *back-order quantity model* and the *production order quantity model* may be used. However, a discussion of these models is beyond the scope of this text.

FIGURE 7–11

The Use of Safety Stock to Prevent Stockouts

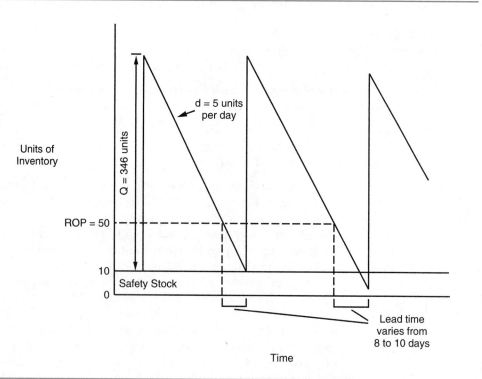

THE COST ACCOUNTING SYSTEM

The cost accounting subsystem of the conversion cycle records the financial effects of the events occurring in the production process. Figure 7–12 represents typical information flows and tasks in the cost accounting system. The cost accounting process for a given production run begins when the production planning and control department sends a copy of the original work order to the cost accounting department. The clerk creates a new cost record for the batch that is beginning production and files this in the work-in-process (WIP) file. This file acts as the subsidiary ledger for the WIP control account in the general ledger.

As materials and labor are added throughout the production process, documents reflecting these events flow into cost accounting. Inventory control sends copies of materials requisitions, excess materials requisitions, and materials returns. The various work centers send job tickets and completed move tickets. These documents, along with standards provided by the standard cost file, enable cost accounting clerks to update the affected WIP accounts with the standard charges for direct labor, material, and manufacturing overhead (MOH). Deviations from standard usage are recorded in variance accounts. Common calculated variances include material usage, direct labor, and MOH.

FIGURE 7–12   Cost Accounting Procedures

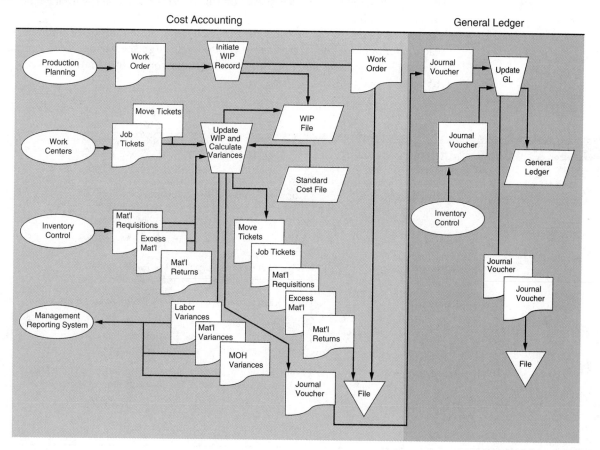

The receipt of the last move ticket for a batch signals the completion of the production process. At this point, the clerk removes the cost sheet from the WIP file. This represents a transfer of product from WIP to the finished goods (FG) inventory. Periodically, summary information regarding charges (debits) to WIP, reductions (credits) to WIP, and variances are recorded on a journal voucher and sent to the general ledger department for posting to the control accounts.

CONTROLS IN THE TRADITIONAL ENVIRONMENT

Recall from previous chapters the six general classes of internal control activities: transaction authorization, segregation of duties, supervision, access control, accounting records, and independent verification. Specific controls as they apply to the conversion cycle are summarized in Table 7–1 and further explained below.

Transaction Authorization

The following describes the transaction authorization procedure in the conversion cycle.

1. In the traditional manufacturing environment, the production activity is authorized by production planning and control via a formal work order. This document reflects production requirements, which is the difference between the expected demand for products (based on the sales forecast) and the finished goods inventory on hand.
2. Move tickets signed by the supervisor in each work center authorize activities for each batch and for the movement of products through the various work centers.
3. Materials requisitions and excess materials requisitions authorize the storekeeper to release materials to the work centers.

TABLE 7–1	Summary of Conversion Cycle Controls

Control Class	Control Points in the System
Transaction authorization	Work orders, move tickets, and materials requisitions.
Segregation of duties	1. Inventory control separate from RM and FG inventory custody. 2. Cost accounting separate from work centers. 3. GL separate from other accounting functions.
Supervision	Supervisors oversee usage of raw materials and timekeeping.
Access	Limit physical access to finished goods, raw materials stocks, and production processes. Use formal procedures and documents to release materials into production.
Accounting records	Work orders, cost sheets, move tickets, job tickets, materials requisitions, WIP records, FG inventory file.
Independent verification	Cost accounting function reconciles all cost of production. General ledger reconciles overall system.

Segregation of Duties

One objective of this control procedure is to separate the tasks of transaction authorization and transaction processing. As a result, the production planning and control department is organizationally segregated from the work centers.

Another control objective is to segregate record keeping from asset custody. The following separations apply:

1. Inventory control maintains accounting records for raw materials (RM) and (FG) inventories. This activity is kept separate from the materials storeroom and from the FG warehouse functions, which have custody of these assets.
2. Similarly, the cost accounting function accounts for work in process and should be separate from the work centers in the production process.

Finally, to maintain the independence of the general ledger function as a verification step, the general ledger (GL) department must be separate from departments keeping subsidiary accounts. Therefore, the GL department is organizationally segregated from inventory control and cost accounting.

Supervision

The following supervision procedures apply to the conversion cycle:

1. The supervisors in the work centers oversee the usage of raw materials in the production process. This helps to ensure that all materials released from stores are used in production and that waste is minimized. Employee time cards and job tickets must also be checked for accuracy.
2. Supervisors also observe and review timekeeping activities. This promotes accurate employee time cards and job tickets.

Access Control

The conversion cycle allows both direct and indirect access to assets.

Direct Access to Assets. The nature of the physical product and the production process influences the type of access controls needed.

1. Firms often limit access to sensitive areas, such as storerooms, production work centers, and finished goods warehouses. Control methods used include identification badges, security guards, observation devices, and various electronic sensors and alarms.
2. The use of standard costs provides a type of access control. By specifying the quantities of material and labor authorized for each product, the firm limits unauthorized access to those resources. To obtain excess quantities requires special authorization and formal documentation.

Indirect Access to Assets. Assets, such as cash and inventories, can be manipulated through access to the source documents that control them. In the conversion cycle, critical documents include materials requisitions, excess materials requisitions, and employee time cards. A method of control that also supports an audit trail is the use of prenumbered documents.

Accounting Records

As we have seen in preceding chapters, the objective of this control technique is to establish an audit trail for each transaction. In the conversion cycle, this is accomplished through the use of work orders, cost sheets, move tickets, job tickets, materials requisitions, the WIP file, and the FG inventory file. By prenumbering source documents and referencing these in the WIP records, a company can trace every item of FG inventory back through the production process to its source. This is essential in detecting errors in production and record keeping, locating batches "lost" in production, and performing periodic audits.

Independent Verification

Verification steps in the conversion cycle are performed as follows:

1. Cost accounting reconciles the materials and labor usage taken from materials requisitions and job tickets with the prescribed standards. Cost accounting personnel may then identify departures from prescribed standards, which are formally reported as variances. In the traditional manufacturing environment, calculated variances are an important source of data for the management reporting system.
2. The general ledger department also fulfills an important verification function by checking the total movement of products from work in process to finished goods. This is done by reconciling journal vouchers from cost accounting and summaries of the inventory subsidiary ledger from inventory control.
3. Finally, internal and external auditors periodically verify the raw materials and finished goods inventories on hand through a physical count. They compare actual quantities against the inventory records and make adjustments to the records when necessary.

THE WORLD-CLASS ENVIRONMENT

The traditional conversion cycle just described still represents procedures in many manufacturing firms in the United States. In the past two decades, however, manufacturing has seen radical changes as firms seek world-class status. In this section, we explore the nature of these changes. We begin with a brief account of factors influencing the world-class environment.

In the mid-1950s, the United States was the undisputed leader in manufacturing among industrialized nations. Mass-production processes, perfected early in the century, provided economies of scale that gave American industry a distinct competitive advantage. Firms achieved low unit costs by producing a narrow range of products in large lot sizes. Demand for these products was stable over time, yielding an extended period for cost recovery. In many respects, this was a seller's market. A line attributed to Henry Ford characterizes the mass-production philosophy: "Americans can have any color Model T they want, as long as it's black."

Today, the dominance of foreign goods in American stores reflects a world very different from 20 or 30 years ago. U.S. industries have seen an erosion of their market shares and a blunting of their competitive edge. The automobile and electronics industries are clear examples of this phenomenon. One argument for the change in status quo asserts that significantly lower labor costs have given foreign firms a competitive advantage. While perhaps true at the beginning of the decline, wage competition now explains only a small portion of the total picture. A better explanation is found in the market factors that have redefined competitive advantage, factors that American industry failed to recognize immediately.

Since the mid-1970s, the factors that govern competitive advantage have shifted away from an emphasis on costs alone to an emphasis on customer satisfaction, product diversity, and the ability to respond rapidly to changing consumer demand. Figure 7–13 portrays the trends in competitive advantage factors over time.

For many years U.S. manufacturers ignored these trends and continued with "business as usual" while foreign competitors seized the leadership role. Through innovations in business philosophy, production processes, and technology, along with a relentless pursuit of customer satisfaction, they emerged as serious contenders in an arena once dominated by the United States. Today, U.S. manufacturers are responding to the changes that they can no longer ignore by achieving manufacturing flexibility.

MANUFACTURING FLEXIBILITY

Modern consumers want quality products, they want them quickly, and they want variety of choice. This demand profile imposes a fundamental conflict on traditional manufacturers, whose structured and inflexible orientation renders them ineffective in this environment.

In contrast, world-class competitors meet the challenges of modern consumerism through flexible manufacturing systems. Consider the following examples of flexibility among world-class automobile manufacturers. One firm has the flexibility to completely retool for a change from one model to another in 2.5 minutes. One

---

FIGURE 7–13   Trends in Competitive Advantage

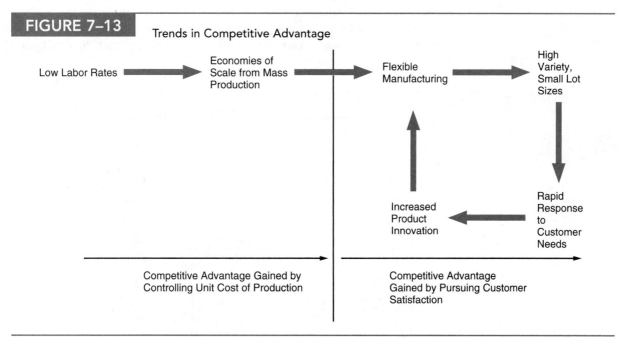

SOURCE: Adaped from J.D. Blackburn, "Trends in Manufacturing," *Cost Accounting, Robotics, and the New Manufacturing Environment* (Sarasota, Fla.: American Accounting Association, 1987).

manufacturer can produce 600 different end items on a single production line. Another firm can switch paint colors on its production line in a few seconds. This allows customized painting to customer orders without having to run a whole batch of vehicles through at one color.

Achieving **manufacturing flexibility** incorporates four operational characteristics: (1) physical reorganization of the production facilities, (2) automation of the manufacturing process, (3) reduction of inventories, and (4) high product quality. Let's consider each of these characteristics and look at some emerging trends.

PHYSICAL REORGANIZATION OF THE PRODUCTION FACILITIES

Traditional manufacturing processes tend to evolve in piecemeal fashion over years into snake-like sequences of activities. Products move back and forth across shop floors, and upstairs and downstairs through different activities. Figure 7–14 shows a traditional factory layout. The inefficiencies inherent in the layout of traditional plants add handling costs, conversion time, and even inventories to the manufacturing process. Furthermore, because production activities are usually organized along functional lines, there is a tendency for parochialism among employees. This "us versus them" mentality is contrary to the team attitude and creates bottlenecks in the process.

A flexible manufacturing system is a much-simplified process. Figure 7–15 illustrates this idea. The flexible production system is organized into flows. Computer-controlled machines, robots, and manual tasks that constitute the flow activities are grouped together physically into factory units called *cells*. This arrangement shortens the physical distances between the activities, thus reducing setup and processing time, handling costs, and inventories in the flow.

AUTOMATION OF THE MANUFACTURING PROCESS

Automation is at the heart of a well-functioning manufacturing environment. By replacing labor with automation, a firm can be more efficient and therefore more competitive. Automation also contributes directly to the other operating characteristics of inventory reduction and increased quality. However, the deployment of automation

---

FIGURE 7–14

The Traditional Factory Layout

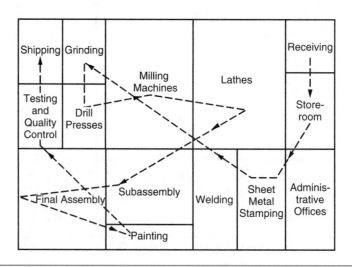

FIGURE 7–15

Flexible
Production
System

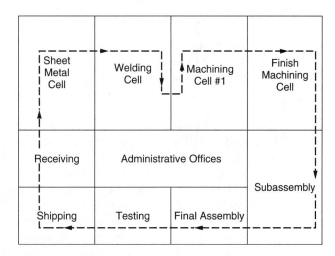

among U.S. manufacturers varies considerably. Figure 7–16 presents automation as a continuum with the traditional manufacturing model at one end and the fully computer-integrated manufacturing model at the other.

Traditional Manufacturing

The traditional manufacturing environment consists of a range of different types of machines, each controlled by a single operator. Since these machines require a great deal of setup time, the cost of set up must be absorbed by large production runs. The machines and their operators are organized into functional departments, such as milling, grinding, and welding. The work in process follows a circuitous route through the different operations across the factory floor.

Islands of Technology

Islands of technology describes an environment where modern automation exists in the form of islands that stand alone within the traditional setting. The islands employ

FIGURE 7–16

The Automation
Continuum

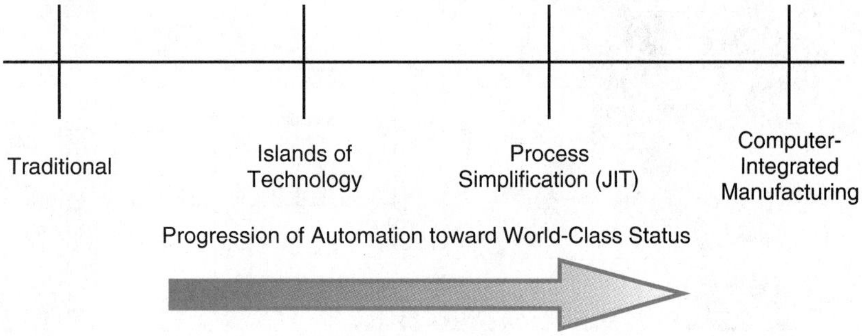

Traditional   Islands of   Process   Computer-
                  Technology   Simplification (JIT)   Integrated
                                                         Manufacturing

Progression of Automation toward World-Class Status

computer numerical controlled (CNC) machines that can perform multiple operations with less human involvement. CNC machines contain computer programs for all the parts that are manufactured by the machine. Under a CNC configuration, humans still load, set up, and unload the machines. However, a particularly important benefit of CNC technology is that little setup time (and cost) is needed to change from one operation to another.

Process Simplification

Process simplification focuses on reducing the complexity of the physical manufacturing layout of the shop floor. Various types of CNC machines are arranged in **cells** to produce an entire part from start to finish in one location. Unlike standard CNC machines, there is no human involvement in a cell. For example, Nissan employs a multi-operation cell in the manufacture of heavy-duty truck axles. The machine takes an 800-pound axle and performs over 40 operations (turning, grinding, drilling, and so on) without any form of human involvement. The less complex physical layout of a cell reduces the distance a part must travel in manufacturing. This in turn saves on production time and significantly reduces inventories in-transit.

Computer-Integrated Manufacturing

Computer-integrated manufacturing (CIM) is a completely automated environment. A CIM facility is organized into group technology cells using no human labor in the manufacturing process. In addition to CNC machines, the process employs automated storage and retrieval systems and robotics. Figure 7–17 shows the physical relationship between these technologies.

FIGURE 7–17   Computer-Integrated Manufacturing System

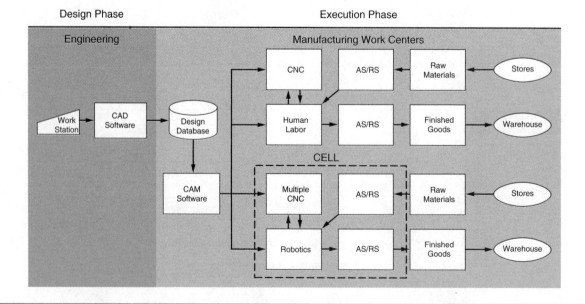

Automated Storage and Retrieval Systems (AS/RS). Many firms have increased productivity and profitability by replacing traditional forklifts and their human operators with **automated storage and retrieval systems (AS/RS)**. Harley-Davidson went from 60 forklift operators down to five. AS/RS are computer-controlled conveyor systems that carry raw materials from stores to the shop floor and finished products to the warehouse. The operational advantages of AS/RS technology over manual systems include reduced errors, improved inventory control, and lower storage costs.

Robotics. **Robotics** involves the use of robots, special CNC machines that are useful in hazardous environments or for performing dangerous and monotonous tasks that are prone to causing accidents.

The remainder of the section outlines a number of information technologies used to plan and control the production process. These are computer-aided design (CAD), computer-aided manufacturing (CAM), manufacturing resources planning (MRP II), enterprise resources planning (ERP), and electronic data interchange (EDI). Manufacturing and nonmanufacturing firms employ ERP and EDI technologies. Hence, they will be examined within a broader context later, in separate chapters.

Computer-Aided Design

Engineers use **computer-aided design (CAD)** to design better products faster. CAD systems increase engineers' productivity, improve accuracy by automating repetitive design tasks, allow firms to be more responsive to market demands, and interface with the CAM and MRP II systems, as well as the external environment. The relation between these systems is shown in Figure 7–18.

Product design has been revolutionized through CAD technology. The technology was first applied to the aerospace industry in the early 1960s but has since been adopted by every industry. CAD technology has been extended to the design and evaluation of the manufacturing *process* for new products. This results in the specification of detailed steps and procedures (routing information) for the work center personnel. Advanced CAD systems can design both product and process simultaneously. Thus, aided by CAD, management can evaluate the technical feasibility of the product and determine its "manufacturability."

CAD technology greatly shortens the time frame between initial and final design. This allows firms to adjust their production quickly to changes in market demand. It also allows them to respond to customer requests for unique products. The CAD system's interface to the external communication network (EDI) is required so that the world-class manufacturer can share its product design specifications with its vendors and customers. This communications link also allows the world-class manufacturer to receive product design specifications electronically from its customers and suppliers for its review.

Computer-Aided Manufacturing

Computer-aided manufacturing (CAM) focuses on the shop floor and the use of computers to control the physical manufacturing process. At one time, the most common type of machines in manufacturing were general-purpose machines, such as drill presses, lathes, and milling machines. The objective of early automation was to

FIGURE 7–18

Relationship between
CAD and CAM
Technology

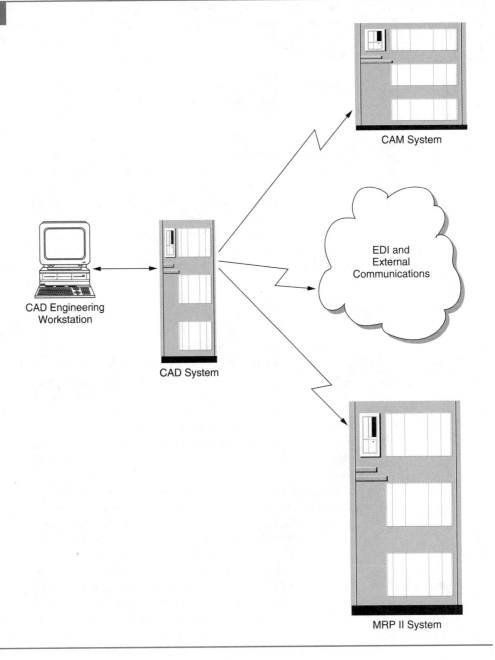

increase the productivity of labor. Today, CAM provides greater precision, speed, and control than human production processes. The objective behind CAM is to *replace* labor through automation. As shown in Figure 7–19, CAM systems monitor and control the production process and routing through the use of process control, numerical control, and robotics equipment. A world-class manufacturer will derive several benefits from deploying a CAM system: improved process productivity, improved cost and time estimates, improved process monitoring, improved process quality, decreased setup times, and reduced labor costs.

FIGURE 7–19

Computer-Aided
Manufacturing System

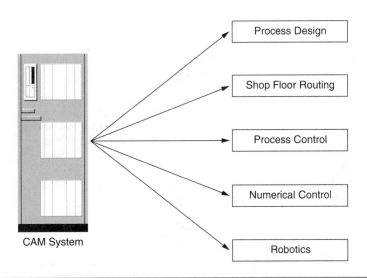

CAM System

Process Design

Shop Floor Routing

Process Control

Numerical Control

Robotics

MRP II, EDI, and ERP

Manufacturing resources planning II (MRP II) is an extension of a simpler concept still in use called **materials requirements planning (MRP)**. Figure 7–20 illustrates an MRP system, which "explodes" individual work orders to create a BOM and determine inventory requirements in advance of production. This approach was designed to minimize inventory-carrying costs in mass-production industries. MRP is simply an automated version of a traditional production planning and control process. On the other hand, MRP II is a reengineering technique that integrates several business processes.

MRP II is not confined to the management of inventory. It is both a system and a philosophy for coordinating the activities of the entire firm. As such, MRP II systems incorporate techniques to execute the production plan, provide feedback, and control the process. Figure 7–21 shows the integration of systems under an MRP II environment.

The MRP II system will produce a bill of materials for the product, fit the production of the product into the master production schedule, produce a rough-cut capacity plan based on machine and labor availability, produce a materials requirements plan that will schedule the delivery of the raw materials on a just-in-time basis, design a final capacity plan for the factory, and manage the raw materials and finished goods inventories. Figure 7–22 (page 362) shows in detail the highly integrated nature of the MRP II concept. MRP II integrates product design and the factory production process with the order entry, accounting information, and activity-based costing systems, which will allow the world-class manufacturer to establish, communicate, and execute production schedules while controlling costs and maintaining the lowest level of inventory possible. The world-class manufacturer can realize a considerable number of significant benefits from a highly integrated MRP II system, including the following:

- Improved customer service.
- Reduced inventory investment.
- Increased productivity.

FIGURE 7–20

Overview of
MRP System

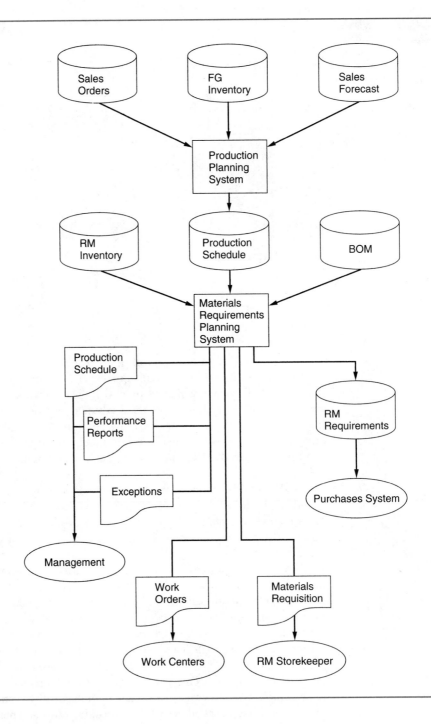

- Improved cash flow.
- Assistance in achieving long-term strategic goals.
- Help in managing change (that is, new product development or specialized product development for customers or by vendors).
- Flexibility in the production process.

FIGURE 7–21   The Integration of Manufacturing and Financial Systems within the MRP II Environment

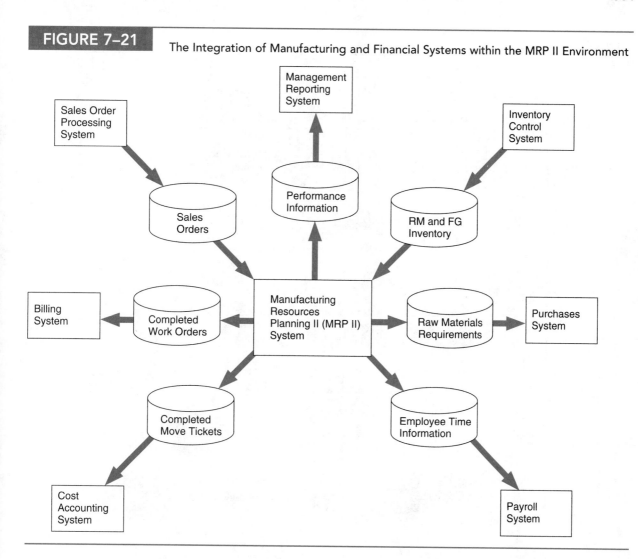

MRP II has evolved into the large suites of software called **enterprise resource planning (ERP)** systems. These huge commercial packages support the information needs of the entire organization, not just the manufacturing functions. An ERP can calculate resource requirements, schedule production, manage changes to product configurations, allow for future planned changes in products, and monitor shop floor production. In addition, the ERP provides order entry, cash receipts, procurement, and cash disbursement functions along with full financial and managerial reporting capability.

A world-class organization will have an ERP system that is capable of external communications with its customers and suppliers through **electronic data interchange (EDI)**. The EDI communications link (either via Internet or direct connection) will allow the firm to electronically receive sales orders and cash receipts from customers, send invoices to customers, send purchase orders to vendors, receive invoices from vendors and pay them, as well as send and receive shipping documents. EDI is a central element of many electronic commerce systems. We will revisit this important topic in Chapter 12.

FIGURE 7–22   MRP II System: Production Capability Planning Modules

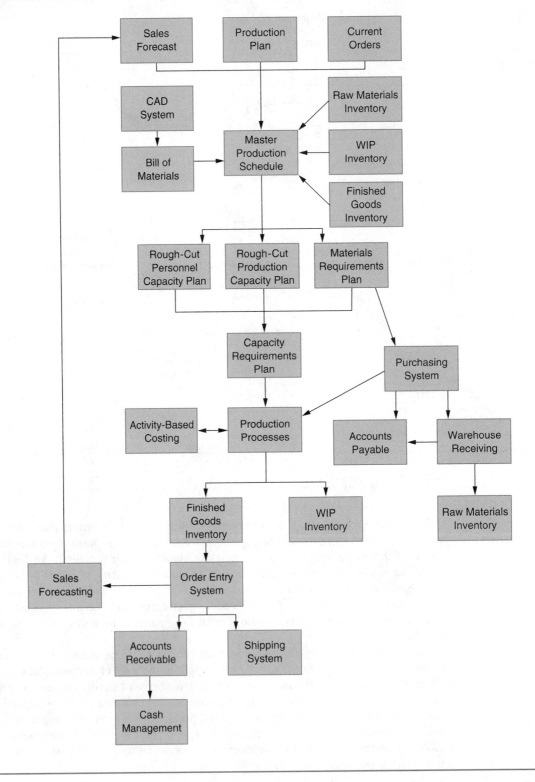

<table>
</table>

REDUCTION OF INVENTORIES

The hallmark of world-class manufacturing firms is their success in inventory reduction. Such firms often experience annual inventory turnovers of 100 times per year. While other firms carry weeks and even months of inventories, world-class firms have only a few days or sometimes even a few hours of inventory. Why is this important? What is wrong with maintaining inventories?

The Evils of Inventories

There are three main reasons it is advantageous for a company to reduce its inventories.

1. Inventories cost money. Inventories represent an investment in materials, labor, and overhead that cannot be realized until they are sold. Also, there are other costs associated with inventory that are often hidden. Inventories must be transported throughout the factory. They must be handled, stored, and counted. In addition, inventories lose their value through obsolescence.
2. Inventories camouflage production problems. If machine capacity imbalances in the manufacturing process are causing bottlenecks, work-in-process inventory builds up at the bottlenecks. If customer orders and production are out of sync, inventories build up.
3. Willingness to maintain inventories can precipitate overproduction. Because of setup cost constraints, firms tend to overproduce inventories in large batches to absorb the allocated costs and create the image of improved efficiency. The true cost of this dysfunctional activity is hidden in excess inventories.

These inventory-driven problems promote inefficiency, reduce profitability, and erode a firm's competitiveness. Many manufacturing problems can be solved by reducing inventories.

How Can Firms Reduce Their Inventories?

Firms have successfully reduced their inventories by adopting the **just-in-time (JIT)** manufacturing model. However, JIT is more than an inventory reduction technique. JIT is a philosophy that attacks the manufacturing problems described above through process simplification as well as inventory reduction.

Under the JIT approach, inventories arrive in small quantities from vendors several times per day "just in time" to go into production. JIT supports a pull manufacturing process. As production capacity upstream becomes available, the manufacturing process pulls small batches (or a single item) of product into the next work center. Rather than periodically taking in large batches, JIT promotes a continuous flow of production through the process pulled along by idle capacity. Unlike the traditional push process, JIT does not create batches of semi-finished inventories at bottlenecks. In fact, under this philosophy, the firm eliminates bottlenecks and reduces the distances between cells and work centers. Hence, fewer inventories are in transit at any point in time. The JIT concept rests heavily on the following assumptions:[1]

---

1   R. D'Amore, "Just in Time Systems," in *Cost Accounting, Robotics, and the New Manufacturing Environment* (Sarasota, Fla.: American Accounting Association, 1987).

Zero Defects. Continuous processing requires raw materials, work in process, and finished goods with zero defects. Some world-class manufacturing firms define this as fewer than 200 defects per million parts produced.

Zero Setup Time. Long machine setup procedures add cost and delays to the process. Firms should strive to reduce setup time to less than five minutes.

Small Lot Sizes. To achieve a machine utilization of about 95 percent and a continuous flow of product through the process, lot sizes must be small. Some should be no more than one day's worth of inventory in the production cycle.

Zero Inventories. To reiterate a subtle but important point made earlier, JIT is not simply an inventory reduction technique. Rather, JIT depends upon inventory reduction. A successful JIT firm may achieve inventory turnover of 100 times a year.

Zero Lead Times and Reliable Vendors. A JIT firm must have established and cooperative relationships with vendors. Late deliveries, defective raw materials, or incorrect orders will shut down production immediately. There are no inventory reserves to draw on in a JIT system.

Team Attitude. JIT relies heavily on the team attitude of all employees involved in the process. This includes those in purchasing, receiving, manufacturing, shipping—everyone. Each employee must be vigilant of problems that threaten the continuous flow operation of the production line. JIT requires a constant state of quality control along with the authority to take immediate action.

When Toyota first introduced JIT, its production employees had the authority to shut down the line when defects were discovered. In the early days, the line was often shut down to bring attention to a problem. Whether a defective part from a vendor or a faulty machine in a cell, the problem was properly addressed so that it did not recur. After an adjustment period, the process stabilized.

PRODUCT QUALITY

There are two basic reasons why quality is important to a world-class manufacturer. First, poor quality is very expensive to the firm. Consider the cost of scrap, reworking, scheduling delays, extra inventories to compensate for defective parts, warranty claims, and field service. These costs can represent between 25 to 35 percent of total product cost.

Second, quality is a basis on which world-class manufacturers compete. Quality has ceased to be a trade-off against price. Consumers demand quality and seek the lowest-priced quality product.

How Can Firms Improve Quality?

One way firms can improve quality is to place control points throughout the manufacturing process to identify "out of control" operations as they happen. Through early detection of problems, firms can better manage the situation. The alternative is the traditional end-of-process quality control procedure. Under this approach, products are examined upon their completion. The manufacturer may discover, too late, that an entire batch of product is scrap.

Statistical process control is a method for controlling automated production systems. A single manufacturing process may employ hundreds of control points that are monitored for out-of-control conditions. Many firms have used this method with great success.

IMPLICATIONS FOR ACCOUNTING AND AIS

The new manufacturing environment carries profound implications for accounting and AIS. In this section, we examine the nature of the changes underway and on the horizon. This discussion addresses two areas of reformation: (1) changes in accounting techniques and (2) changes in information reporting.

CHANGES IN ACCOUNTING TECHNIQUES

What's Wrong with Traditional Accounting Information?
Traditional cost accounting information emphasizes financial performance rather than manufacturing performance. The techniques and conventions used for so many years do not support the new objectives of world-class manufacturing firms. The following are the most commonly cited deficiencies of traditional accounting systems.

Inaccurate Cost Allocations. Traditional accounting systems do not accurately trace costs to products and processes. One consequence of new technologies is a restructuring of manufacturing cost patterns. Figure 7–23 shows the changing relationship between direct labor, direct materials, and overhead cost in different manufacturing environments. In the traditional manufacturing environment, direct labor is a much larger component of total manufacturing costs than in the CIM environment. Overhead, on the other hand, is a far more significant element of cost in advanced technology manufacturing. In this setting, traditional cost accounting procedures are grossly inadequate. To understand the problem, let's consider how overhead charges are traditionally applied to products. All components of overhead, such as indirect labor, depreciation of machinery, utilities, and insurance, are pooled. This cost pool is then allocated to production on the basis of direct labor hours. The following characteristics of the CIM environment show us why the traditional allocation of overhead is inadequate.

1. In traditional manufacturing, the overhead cost component is relatively small—about 10 to 40 percent of total manufacturing cost. However, overhead is the largest component in CIM.
2. Direct labor charges in CIM are substantially smaller—between 1 to 10 percent of total cost—than they are in traditional manufacturing.
3. Direct labor charges are not easily traced to products in the CIM environment. An advantage of CIM is flexible batch sizes. It is not necessary to produce lots of predetermined amounts. Products can even be manufactured in single-item lots. In addition, operators may be assigned to more than one machine at a time. It becomes very difficult to assign labor time accurately to individual products being produced simultaneously in variable quantities.

For traditional allocations to be correct, there must be a direct relationship between labor and technology. In CIM, this relationship is diametric rather than complementary. When the cost pool is large and the allocation method ambiguous, any

FIGURE 7–23   Changes in Cost Structure between Different Manufacturing Environments

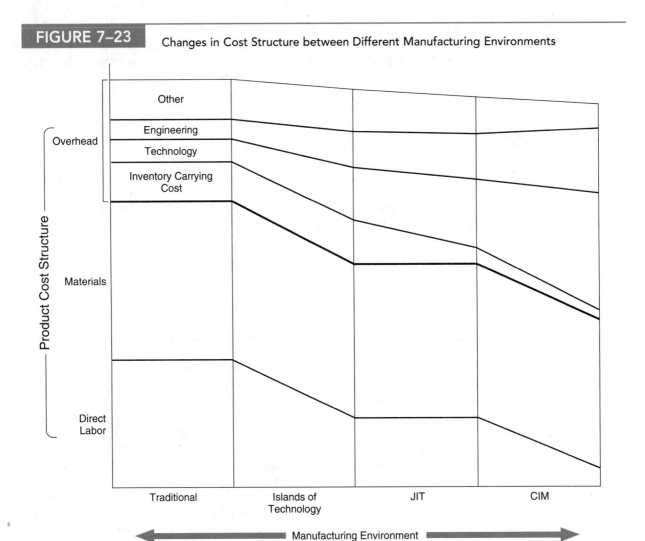

SOURCE: Adapted from J. A. Brimson, "Bringing Cost Management up to Date," *Manufacturing Engineering* (June 1988): 49.

miscalculation in assigning labor is magnified many times in the calculation of overhead. Figure 7–24 illustrates the significance of this problem. The figure shows the product cost profile common to many companies. The curved line represents the products' true cost, as calculated under the activity-based costing method (ABC)[2]; the straight line represents the allocated cost using conventional accounting. For low-volume, high-variety products, the true cost is as much as 600 percent of the allocated cost. Errors of this magnitude can devastate a company's ability to make crucial decisions. Without accurate cost information, firms cannot:

1. Focus on profitable markets.
2. Service profitable customers.

---

2   We discuss ABC later in the chapter.

| FIGURE 7–24 | A Profile of Costing Differences between ABC and Traditional Methods |

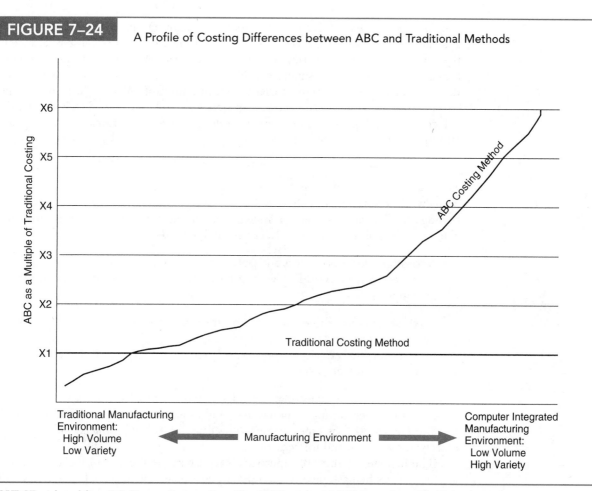

SOURCE: Adapted from P. B. Turney, *Common Cents: The ABC Breakthrough* (Hillsboro, Ore.: Cost Technology, 1991): 5.

3. Accurately measure the cost of product designs.
4. Accurately measure the cost of process designs.

Time Lag. Traditional accounting data for management reporting is essentially historic. Data thus lag behind the actual manufacturing activities on the assumption that control can be applied after the fact to correct errors. But shop floor managers in a JIT setting need immediate information about abnormal deviations. They must know in real time about a machine breakdown or a robot out of control. After-the-fact information is too late to be useful.

Financial Orientation. The orientation of traditional accounting information does not adequately identify defective products or processes. Accounting data use dollars as a standard unit of measure for comparability between items being evaluated. Decisions linking functional areas and different management levels in the firm demand information that has no common basis. These include the functionality of a product or process, improving product quality, and shortening delivery time. Attempts to force these data into a common financial measure may distort the problem and promote bad decisions.

Emphasis on Standard Costs. Conventional accounting emphasizes standard costs and variance analysis. The objectives underlying these conventions lose relevance in the new manufacturing environment. As we have seen, modern production methods are capital-intensive and assume zero defects in both materials and processes. Under these circumstances, traditional variances are insignificant. When defects, deviations, or out-of-control activities do occur, managers need to know immediately. Under the JIT concept, such problems need attention long before a traditional accounting system can generate a variance report.

How Can We Solve These Problems?

Many world-class companies have found solutions to these problems in activity-based costing. ABC is an information system that provides managers with information about activities and cost objects. Let's first define these terms:

> **Activities** describe the work performed in a firm. Preparing a purchase order, readying a product for shipping, or operating a lathe are examples of activities.

> **Cost objects** are the reasons for performing activities. These include products, services, vendors, and customers. For example, the task of preparing a sales order (the activity) is performed because a customer (the cost object) wishes to place an order.

The underlying assumptions of **activity-based costing (ABC)** contrast sharply with traditional cost accounting assumptions. Traditional accounting assumes that products cause costs. ABC assumes that activities cause costs and products (and other cost objects) create a demand for activities.

The first step in the ABC approach is to determine the cost of the activity. The activity cost is then assigned to the relevant cost object by means of an **activity driver**. This factor measures the activity consumption by the cost object. For example, if drilling holes in a steel plate is the activity, the number of holes is the activity driver.

Traditional accounting systems often use only one activity driver. For instance, overhead costs, collected into a single cost pool, are allocated to products on the basis of direct labor hours. A world-class company using ABC may have dozens of activity cost pools, each with a unique activity driver. Figure 7–25 illustrates the allocation of overhead costs to products under ABC. ABC allocates costs to products more accurately than traditional methods. To emphasize the magnitude of the difference possible between these methods, review Figure 7–25. With improved cost information, firms are better able to analyze such critical decisions as pricing, product mix, product design, and process design.

CHANGES IN INFORMATION REPORTING

We are on the threshold of significant change in the role of management accounting information. Historically, the management accounting function was limited to reporting financially oriented information relating to operations. Today, serving the needs of a world-class management team means breaking out of these narrow confines. Management accountants must now provide new information on the state of business activities that is very different from that traditionally produced.

FIGURE 7–25   Allocation of Manufacturing Costs under ABC

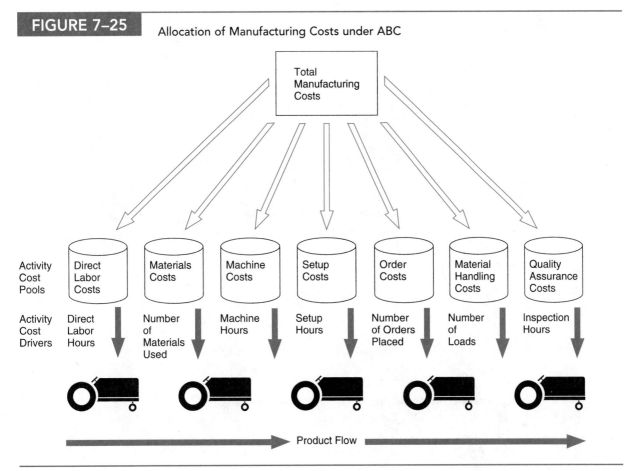

SOURCE: Adapted from P. B. Turney, *Common Cents: The ABC Breakthrough* (Hillsboro, Ore.: Cost Technology, 1991): 96.

Activity Management

In some organizations, managing business activities is merely a custodial task. This can never be the case in a world-class company. Activity management must be a relentless and continuous quest for improvement. Managers must thus understand which activities should be performed and how best to perform them. Two underlying objectives guide managers in this challenge:

1. Managers should deploy resources to activities that yield maximum benefit.
2. Managers should seek to improve those factors most important to their customers.

The following discussion provides examples of activity management tasks that require support from a new class of accounting information.

Evaluating Manufacturing Activities. The need for information about operations has led to the development of a second generation of ABC. Figure 7–26 illustrates the new ABC model, which has two dimensions. The vertical dimension is the cost assignment model that we examined in Figure 7–25. It shows the allocation of costs to

| FIGURE 7–26 | Two-Dimensional ABC Model |

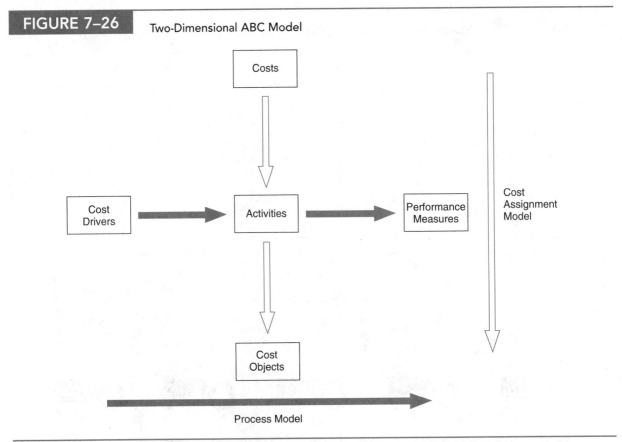

SOURCE: Adapted from P. B. Turney, *Common Cents: The ABC Breaktbrough* (Hillsboro, Ore.: Cost Technology, 1991): 98.

activities first and then to cost objects. The horizontal dimension is the process model. It reflects the organization's need for a new category of information about the cause of activities and performance measures for those activities. The ABC process model can provide critical information about cost drivers and performance measures to help managers answer such questions as:

1. Which activities require the most resources?
2. What types of resources are required?
3. Where can costs be reduced?

The information produced by the process model is primarily nonfinancial and falls well outside the domain of traditional accounting information.

Identifying Nonessential Activities. Activities are either essential or they are not. Essential activities add value in one of two ways. First, the activity has value to the customer. For example, balancing the wheels of each car off the production line is essential because the customer demands a car that rides smoothly. Second, the activity adds value to the organization. For example, the activity of preparing financial statements has no immediate value for the customer. However, because of the firm's legal obligation to do so, this activity has value to the firm and is essential. Nonessential activities add no value and should be eliminated. For example, in a zero defects manufacturing environment, traditional quality control activities at the end of the process become nonessential. Likewise, in this setting, the traditional accounting activities of calculating material usage variances and accounting for scrap are of no value to the organization.

Identifying Cost Drivers. The reduction of unnecessary activities rests on the proper identification of cost drivers. The **cost driver** is the cause of the cost. Managers cannot manage unnecessary activities unless they understand their driving forces. For instance, if the movement of work in process from one operation to another adds no value, it should be eliminated. How do we do this? We must first identify the cost driver for this activity. In this case, it is the physical distance between operations. By reorganizing the need to place these activities in physical sequence, the firm removes the cost driver (distance) and the nonessential activity (moving the product).

Comparing Activities to Benchmarks. In assessing the value added by activities, managers often compare key activities with similar activities elsewhere in the firm or in other firms. This is called **benchmarking**. For example, the firm may rate its key activities on such factors as quality, lead times, flexibility, cost, and customer satisfaction and compare these against the best practices of an industry leader.

Establishing Links between Key Activities. In the previous section, we discussed the importance of team effort in managing a world-class company. From the shop floor to the CEO, each manager (armed with the appropriate information) must act quickly and decisively within his or her sphere of activity. It becomes essential that members of the team, at all levels, understand their performance measures, can spot a problem as it emerges, and recognize their roles in its resolution.

Effective coordination requires information that links decision making and performance measures to the firm's **critical success factors** (CSFs). CSFs are items of such importance that failure to meet any one of them would cause the firm to fail. Although specific CSFs vary among firms, the following general categories apply to most manufacturing companies:[3]

- *Product quality*. The firm's product must meet or exceed the customer's expectations.
- *Process quality*. The firm must minimize the amount of process variation that results in scrap or reworking the product.
- *Customer service*. The firm must adequately meet the customer's demand for finished products. The customer may be either the end consumer or an internal customer, such as the next department in the manufacturing process.
- *Resource management*. The firm must optimize the use of raw materials, labor, and fixed assets in the manufacture of its products.
- *Flexibility*. The firm must be responsive and adaptable to changes in its environment. This includes changes in the product market, in suppliers, and in the legal environment.

No single individual can influence a CSF. Improving a CSF comes from coordinated action at each decision point. Figure 7–27 shows an example of how this can be

---

3   M. E. Beischel and R. K. Smith, "Linking the Shop Floor to the Top Floor," *Management Accounting* (October 1991): 25, 26.

FIGURE 7-27   Linking Performance Measure at Levels Throughout the Organization

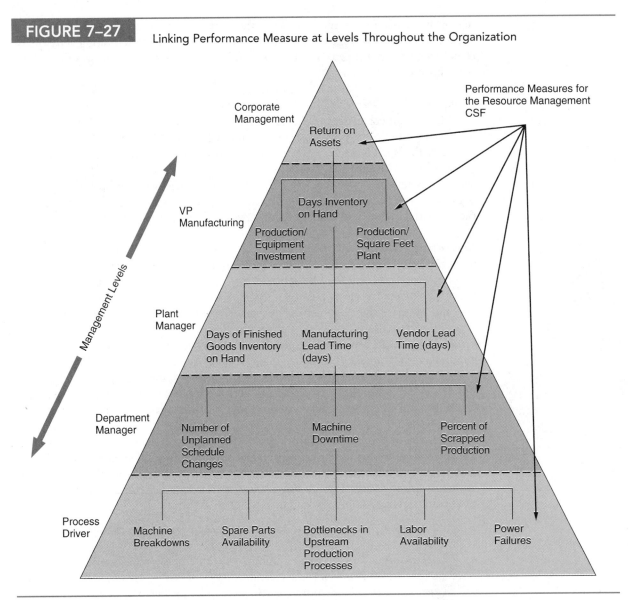

SOURCE: Adapted from M. E. Beischel and R. K. Smith, "Linking the Shop Floor to the Top Floor," *Management Accounting* (October 1991): 26.

accomplished for the resource management CSF. The diagram shows some of the performance measures that influence the *resource management* CSF at each management level. To improve this CSF, each manager must control his or her performance measures and recognize the influence they have on the next level in the organization. For example, when the department manager properly manages specific items, such as machine downtime, percent of scrapped production, and the number of unplanned schedule changes, the manager knows he or she is contributing to the overall resource management goal of the firm.

Note two additional points to be made from Figure 7–27. First, at higher management levels, performance measures are broader and more aggregated, while at lower levels they are more detailed and specific. Second, this approach integrates financial and nonfinancial information within a common reporting structure, thus extending the role of accounting beyond its traditional boundary. Accommodating the broader spectrum of management needs with both financial and nonfinancial information has been the topic of much interest. However, doing so requires a new accounting model that can support multiple user views. Such a model is REA (resources, events, and agents), which is examined at length in Chapter 10.

THE WORLD-CLASS INFORMATION SYSTEM

The key to a world-class information system (WCIS) is the integration of all the system's functional and technological components. Integration is the glue that binds the system together and includes basic accounting applications, activity-based costing, materials requirements planning, capacity planning, inventory control, bill of materials, the master production schedule, forecasting, order entry, computer-aided design, computer-aided manufacturing, and EDI communications links.

In this section we introduce the concept of a WCIS. It begins with a review of the traditional information system to illustrate the sharp contrast to a world-class system. As an example of a WCIS, we overview the general features of a system called *SAP*. SAP is the market leader among a class of information systems known as *enterprise resource planning* (ERP) systems. In recent years, SAP has secured a prominent position and is regarded by many as the standard by which other ERPs are judged. Because of the importance of ERP to accounting information systems, we continue the treatment of this material in Chapter 11. This section concludes with a review of control issues related to WCIS.

CHARACTERISTICS OF THE TRADITIONAL INFORMATION SYSTEM

In the traditional manufacturing environment, technology is generally employed in a haphazard fashion and without a plan. The objective is often to solve a specific, recurring problem for a specific department without regard to integrating the technology into the whole process. The result is isolated islands of technology that are not integrated and often can be integrated only at considerable expense. This is true not only of shop floor automation technology but also of information systems and business applications.

Information technology employed by a traditional manufacturer will likely consist of a mainframe to handle the primary accounting functions, such as the sales order processing, purchases processing, and payroll. These basic accounting applications may or may not be integrated. The mainframe applications will be primarily batch-oriented, and only a few real-time systems will exist.

The mainframe will probably have some type of job costing and inventory control systems for finished goods and raw materials. However, in many traditional manufacturing environments, the cost accounting system is kept on a separate personal computer (PC), which requires a considerable amount of manual data entry to keep it up to date. In fact, the cost accounting system may be nothing more than a spreadsheet.

Generally, PCs are used by traditional manufacturers to solve stand-alone business problems, and connectivity to the mainframe through networking is an afterthought and cumbersome. Many of the PCs were purchased by the various functional departments to solve their own business problems and are deployed haphazardly. Unlike the mainframe applications, which generate authorization documents and reports in support of the organization's internal control system, PC-based systems have little or no internal controls placed on them. Therefore, the potential for errors and irregularities (fraud) is significant.

The traditional manufacturer's information system depends heavily on paper-based transactions, which must be entered and reentered as the paper moves from one department or work center to the next. The duplication of effort is substantial in this environment, which increases the chance of data entry errors and promotes a rather poor level of data integrity.

Finally, the traditional manufacturer's telecommunications network is usually confined to the firm's internal environment. Normally, there is no external communications capability, or even desire to possess the capability, unless the firm is forced to implement EDI by a customer or a supplier. Not only is the traditional manufacturer's implementation of technology a series of isolated islands, the traditional manufacturer itself is an isolated island in relation to the global business community.

SAP: An Example of a World-Class Information System

SAP AG is a German company that was founded in 1972 in Waldorf, Germany, by a couple of IBM employees. Opening their operation, the goal was to create an integrated business package to serve large organizations in the manufacturing industry. The software, also named SAP, supports key business processes related to sales, marketing, manufacturing, and human resources. In English, the term *SAP* stands for *Systems, Applications, and Products in Data Processing*.

SAP Products
SAP has two primary products—R/2 and R/3. R/2 is SAP's original system. It is mainframe-based, batch-oriented, highly structured, and less flexible than the newer R/3 system. SAP R/3 is a distributed system that runs under a number of operating systems and network configurations. Most of SAP's new business is in R/3 implementation. To date, more than 20,000 companies have installed R/3 systems. R/2 is still a pervasive system that SAP AG has promised to maintain and improve through the year 2004. The discussion that follows, however, relates to the R/3 system.

R/3 Overview
The R/3 system supports hundreds of business processes and handles multiple languages and international currencies to support the global expansion of the user organization. It can be customized to interact with EDI and other systems written in standard languages such as C, C++, COBOL, and SQL. Currently R3 supports limited commerce on the World Wide Web. SAP is expected to extend this capability to automatically process sales and order supplies when inventory is low. Theoretically, this could be done with little or no user intervention.

The R/3 architecture is a hierarchical structure. The underlying basis is the first layer in the foundation on which the R/3 system is built. This includes the application modules, the network architecture, and the hardware platform. The database, which may be distributed among multiple computers, is the lowest layer in the system. The database tables contain the transaction details needed to support multiple user needs. The data dictionary describes the *views* of the multiple users of the system. This layer provides the mapping of data relationships between the business entities.

SAP R/3 was developed as a client/server architecture (the specifics of this type of network architecture are discussed in Chapter 12). The system works on multiple hardware platforms including Windows NT PCs, UNIX Systems (multiuser workstations), and the IBM AS 400 (minicomputers). R/3 also supports multiple databases including Informix, Oracle, DB2, ADABAS D, MS SQL, and DB2/4000.

R/3 provides predefined business modules that support over 1,000 business processes organized in the following four general categories: financial, logistics, human resources, and business process support. A few years ago, organizations would have had to design and program custom applications in-house to support these functions. R/3 users can mix and match pre-fabricated software components to assemble an ERP application that meets their business requirements. One of the driving forces behind the ERP revolution is that system maintenance will be cheaper (over the long term) than maintaining many separate in-house developed applications. A more important motive, however, is the desire by many organizations to move closer to world-class status through business processes reengineering. An integrated R/3 system can improve customer service, reduce production time of products, increase productivity, and improve decision making. The operational features of R/3 and several other world-class ERP systems are presented in Chapter 11.

CONTROL ISSUES IN THE WCIS

The high degree of automation associated with a WCIS creates a number of unique control issues of concern to accountants. Our objective at this point is to draw attention to the potential risks that must be addressed by management and accountants. Since the solutions to these problems involve an understanding of technologies that we have not yet studied, our discussion of control techniques must be deferred to Chapters 15 and 16, where these issues and their solutions will be revisited.

The Paperless Environment

A WCIS can virtually eliminate the traditional paper flow in the order-delivery-invoice-payment cycle because the system enables transactions to be initiated, recorded, approved, and executed electronically. Paper documents are extremely expensive in terms of handling costs and data entry errors. Therefore, paper documents are printed, handled, and filed only when absolutely necessary. A portion of the paper reduction comes from the extensive use of source data automation, particularly bar coding. Where feasible, all raw materials and finished goods inventory items should be bar-coded. The ideal situation is to have the raw materials bar-coded by the supplier. To track and monitor labor charges as well as authorizations and security considerations, employees use either bar-coded or magnetic strip-encoded identification cards. In fact, all resources (materials, portable equipment, and employees) that move around the factory floor should be bar-coded for tracking and monitoring purposes.

The paperless environment has a significant impact on a firm's internal control system. It results in control evidence being found in machine-readable formats that may be at locations that transcend traditional organizational boundaries. There may be no traditional documents for the internal or external auditors to examine.

Automatic Transactions

The extensive use of EDI for processing transactions eliminates traditional source documents bearing signatures and evidencing authorization of transactions. Based on the occurrence of an event such as the receipt of a sales order or inventories falling to their reorder point, transactions are automatically initiated by the MRP system and transmitted by EDI. Given the lack of human involvement in the transaction processing system, the control concerns focus on the validity, completeness, and accuracy of automatically generated transactions. The only paper document may be the original contract between the trading parties. Management and accountants seek the following assurances regarding the system's performance:

- The system places orders only when inventory is needed.
- Inventory orders are placed only with approved vendors.
- The quantity of items ordered is correct for the needs of the organization.
- Programmed procedures correctly match electronic control documents (i.e., the purchase order, receiving report, and invoice) before initiating the payment function.

Networking Considerations

A WCIS will be designed around a series of local area networks, minicomputers, and/or mainframes, depending on the needs of the manufacturer. The network architecture may involve the distribution of databases and/or transaction processing responsibility among various users at multiple locations. Distributed technology has implications for the accuracy and consistency of accounting records. For example, auditors are concerned that the general ledger accounts accurately reflect the sum total of transactions processed at multiple distributed locations. We examine distributed databases in Chapter 9 and network architectures in Chapter 12.

Summary

This chapter has examined the conversion cycle, whereby a company transforms input resources (materials, labor, and capital) into marketable products and services. The principal aim has been to highlight the changing manufacturing environment of the contemporary business world and to show how it calls for a shift away from traditional forms of business organization and activities toward a "world-class" way of doing business. We have seen how companies that are attempting to achieve world-class status must pursue manufacturing flexibility through increased automation, inventory reduction, and improved product quality.

We have also seen that achieving world-class status requires significant departures from traditional accounting techniques. In response to deficiencies in traditional accounting methods, world-class companies have adopted activity-based costing, which provides a more precise and accurate allocation of costs to products. New techniques in activity management complement ABC and enable managers to better understand the nature of activities and cost drivers. New accounting models are needed that allow organizations to combine both financial and nonfinancial data in an integrated database that will support the needs of multiple users. Finally, we examined the key features of a world-class information system and briefly addressed potential control issues.

Key Terms

activities   (368)

activity-based costing (ABC)   (368)

activity driver   (368)

automated storage and retrieval systems (AS/RS)   (357)

benchmarking   (371)

bill of materials   (340)

cells   (356)

computer-aided design (CAD)   (357)

computer-aided manufacturing (CAM)   (357)

computer-integrated manufacturing (CIM)   (356)

computer numerical control (CNC)   (356)

cost accounting system   (339)

cost driver   (371)

cost objects   (368)

critical success factors   (371)

economic order quantity (EOQ) model   (345)

electronic data interchange (EDI)   (361)

enterprise resource planning (ERP)   (361)

islands of technology   (355)

just-in-time (JIT)   (363)

manufacturing environment   (339)

manufacturing flexibility   (354)

manufacturing resources planning II (MRP II)   (359)

materials and operations requirements   (342)

materials requirements planning (MRP)   (359)

materials requisition   (341)

move ticket   (341)

process simplification   (356)

production schedule   (340)

production system   (339)

reorder point   (347)

robotics   (357)

route sheet   (341)

safety stock   (347)

sales forecast   (339)

statistical process control   (365)

work order   (341)

world-class company   (338)

Review Questions

1. What is a world-class firm? What characteristics do world-class information systems need to have to provide sufficient information to world-class firms?

2. What activities are involved in the production system? The cost accounting system?

3. Distinguish between continuous, batch, and made-to-order processing.

4. What documents trigger and support batch processing systems?

5. What are the primary determinants for both materials and operations requirements?

6. What three main functions does inventory control serve in the production process?

7. What document triggers the beginning of the cost accounting process for a given production run?

8. What documents are necessary in order for cost accounting clerks to update the WIP accounts with standard charges?

9. What types of management reports are prepared by the cost accounting system?

10. What document signals the completion of the production process?

11. What functions should be separated in order to segregate record keeping from asset custody?

12. What are the four operating characteristics U.S. manufacturing firms need to incorporate to regain their competitive advantage?

13. Distinguish between computer-aided design and computer-aided manufacturing.

14. What is meant by the statement that inventories camouflage production problems and can cause overproduction? What is wrong with overproduction if you already own the raw materials?

15. Upon what assumptions does the JIT method heavily depend?

16. Distinguish between activities and cost objects in activity-based costing.

17. Differentiate between essential and nonessential activities.
18. What are some critical success factors common to most manufacturing firms?
19. What are the inputs and outputs of an MRP system?

Discussion Questions

1. Discuss the importance to the cost accounting department of the move ticket and some of the job duties that the work center supervisor performs.
2. How realistic are the assumptions of the EOQ model? Discuss each assumption individually.
3. Explain why the economic order quantity is the intersection of the ordering cost curve and the carrying cost curve.
4. Since the supervisors in the work centers oversee the usage of raw materials in production, explain why the work centers do not keep the records of the work in process.
5. Explain how prenumbered documents help to provide indirect access control over assets.
6. What role does the general ledger department play in the conversion cycle?
7. How have U.S. manufacturers adjusted their emphasis in response to competitive factors since the mid-1970s?

8. What is meant by manufacturing flexibility and how do firms achieve it?
9. Identify three areas where computer-aided design software applications are being used directly by the consumer to aid in designing the product.
10. How can poor quality be expensive to the firm, especially if low-cost raw materials are used to reduce cost of goods sold and hence raise net income?
11. Discuss how an emphasis on financial performance of cost centers as measured by traditional cost accounting information may lead to inefficient and ineffective production output.
12. How can ABC be used to switch the management of business activities from a custodial task to a continuous improvement activity?

Multiple-Choice Questions

1. CMA 1283 5-24
   Which of the following items is irrelevant for a company that is attempting to minimize the cost of a stockout?
   a. cost of placing an order
   b. contribution margin on lost sales
   c. storage cost of inventory
   d. size of the safety stock
   e. probability of being out of stock
2. CMA 1288 5-28
   The fundamental economic order quantity model
   a. provides for fluctuating lead times during reorder cycles.
   b. is relatively insensitive to errors in demand, procurement costs, and carrying costs.
   c. focuses on the trade-off between production costs and carrying costs.

   d. is stochastic in nature.
   e. is best used in conjunction with a periodic inventory system.
3. CMA 1289 5-19
   The formula to determine the economic order quantity is
   EOQ = 2AD/K
   A = the annual unit demand
   D = the cost per order
   K = the cost of carrying one unit per year
   Solden Corporation has annual sales of 10,000 units per year at a unit cost of $5. Storage and other costs are 10 percent of the unit cost, and the incremental order cost is $16. The economic order quantity for Solden Corporation is
   a. 1,789 units.
   b. 800 units.

c. 25 units.
d. 56 units.
e. 400 units.

Questions 4 though 6 are based on the diagram below, which represents the economic order quantity model.

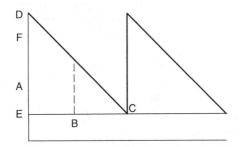

4. CMA 1289 5-16
   Which line segment represents the reorder lead time?
   a. AB
   b. AE
   c. AF
   d. BC
   e. AC

5. CMA 1289 5-17
   Which line segment identifies the quantity of safety stock maintained?
   a. AB
   b. AE
   c. AC
   d. BC
   e. EF

6. CMA 1289 5-18
   Which line segment represents the length of time to consume the total quantity of materials ordered?
   a. DE
   b. BC
   c. AC

d. AE
e. AD

7. CMA 690 5-30
   Many manufacturing and retail organizations are giving increased attention to potential gains to be derived from just-in-time purchasing. Which of the following is not a perceived benefit of JIT purchasing?
   a. increased cash discounts on purchases
   b. a reduction in the number of suppliers
   c. a reduction in purchasing paperwork through the use of longer-term contracts with suppliers
   d. less checking on quality and quantity of goods received from suppliers
   e. a reduction in the total value of inventories on hand

8. CMA 691 4-4
   A decrease in inventory order costs will
   a. decrease the economic order quantity.
   b. increase the reorder point.
   c. have no effect on the economic order quantity.
   d. increase the economic order quantity.
   e. decrease the holding cost percentage.

9. CMA 691 4-5
   An increase in inventory holding costs will
   a. decrease the economic order quantity.
   b. increase the safety stock required.
   c. have no effect on the economic order quantity.
   d. increase the economic order quantity.
   e. decrease the number of orders issued per year.

10. Which of the following is NOT an operational characteristic incorporated into manufacturing flexibility?
    a. reduction of inventories
    b. high product quality
    c. reduction of accounts receivables
    d. automation of the manufacturing process

Problems

1. **Document Flowchart**
   Diagram the sequence in which the following source documents are prepared.
   a. bill of materials
   b. work order

   c. sales forecast
   d. materials requisition
   e. move ticket
   f. production schedule
   g. route sheet

2. Economic Order Quantity

A bicycle manufacturer projects that it will produce 10,000 bicycles this year. For each bicycle, it orders two bicycle wheels from one of its suppliers. The firm has 200 bicycle wheels in beginning inventory and would like to have only 100 bicycle wheels in ending inventory at the end of this year. It estimates that this year's cost per order will be 10 percent less than last year's cost per order due to a new transaction processing system. Last year's cost per order is estimated to be $14 per unit. Last year's carrying cost was $2.25 per unit per year. This year, the carrying cost per unit is expected to rise 15 percent due to an increase in insurance rates.

a. Compute the EOQ amount.

b. What is the reorder point if the lead time to order is five days?

3. Economic Order Quantity

A manufacturing firm has determined that the EOQ amount is 275 units, the daily demand is 40 units, and the lead time to reorder is usually four days but can be as long as six days. Compute the reorder point and the required safety stock amount.

4. Internal Control

Examine the flowchart below and determine any control threats. Discuss specifically the control problems, the possible dangers, and any corrective procedures you would recommend.

5. Manufacturing Processes

Consider a pizzeria that sells pizza, pasta, lasagna, meatball sandwiches, and sodas. Discuss the methods in which the products would be manufactured under

a. the traditional manufacturing environment.

b. computer-integrated manufacturing.

6. Zero Defects Process

Playthings, a toy manufacturer specializing in toys for toddlers, is considering switching to a just-in-time manufacturing process. The CEO has been talking with the production consultants,

Problem 4: Internal Control

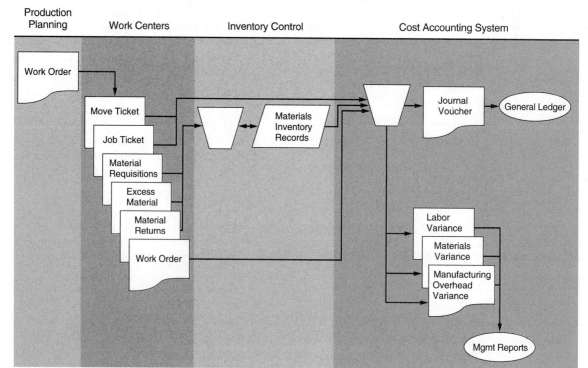

who tell her that a new philosophy must be embraced; if a defective part of an out-of-control process is detected, no more units should be made until the process is corrected. The consultants estimate that the production process may occasionally be shut down anywhere from 30 minutes to 7 hours. Discuss the advantages and disadvantages of such a system.

7. **Activity Drivers**
   Scholz Publishing Company is in the process of switching to an activity-based costing system. In the past, it has allocated overhead based upon the number of machine hours used for a job. The following processes are included in the production process once the document has been proofed.
   a. printing of pages in the book
   b. printing of color pictures

c. collating the text with pictures
d. cutting the paper to the appropriate size
e. printing the covers
f. cutting the covers to the appropriate size
g. binding the pages into the book
h. printing book jackets, if a book jacket is required
i. cutting the book jackets, if required
j. placing the book jackets on the book, if required
k. packing the books into boxes for shipment

Determine the most logical activity driver for each process. Discuss the advantages of using the activity driver you choose over machine hours for allocating overhead.

Internal Control Cases

1. **Blades R Us—Comprehensive Case**
   (Prepared by Edward P. Kiernan and Abigail Olken, Lehigh University)
   Blades R Us is a growing manufacturing firm that produces high-pressure turbine blades. They supply these to airline companies as replacement parts for use in large commercial jet engines. The high-pressure turbine is the segment of the engine that undergoes the most stress and heat. This requires that these parts be replaced frequently, so Blades R Us operates a relatively large firm with constant demand for their products. They operate out of Philadelphia, Pennsylvania, with a workforce of approximately one thousand employees. Their annual output is based on demand, yet at full capacity they have the ability to produce 100,000 blades a year. The company's largest suppliers are casting houses, which take a rough shape of the final product to very demanding specifications given by Blades. Blades R Us then does the final detail work to bring it to FAA regulations.

   The general business environment of Blades R Us is one in which they see expansion in their future. This is because of the recent boom in the commercial airline industry. In addition, with the recent attention to airline safety and the discov-

ery of bogus parts used in engines, the airlines will be doing better checks and needing to replace parts more frequently to insure safety.

Blades R Us has been around for some time, and therefore has no computer-operated accounting systems. Some of the problems the company faces include (a) lack of inventory control; (b) keeping track of items in production or production that was completed in one day; (c) a need for trends and tracking of largest customers so that future demand might be more accurate; (d) supervisory issues dealing with theft of parts, near substandard parts, and hiding of scrap; and (e) large inventories on hand of both finished goods and raw materials.

Procurement Procedures
The company reviewed the records associated with the raw materials inventory files. Mr. Sampson, the inventory manager, was in charge of this procedure. Once he finished his manual review of the inventory he issued two purchase requisitions. He kept one of the purchase requisitions in the inventory department, filing it in a cabinet. He sent the second purchase requisition to the purchasing department.

Ms. Connolly in the purchasing department would take the requisition and complete a purchase order in triplicate. One copy was sent to the supplier, the second was filed in the purchases department filing cabinet, and the third was sent back to Mr. Sampson in the inventory department. Mr. Sampson would use this PO to update his inventory records so he knew exactly how much inventory was on hand at all times. Once the inventory was updated, the PO was put into the filing cabinet in the inventory department with the original purchase requisition.

The supplier would receive the purchase order and send the requested blades, including a packing slip with the shipment. At the same time shipment was made the supplier would also send an invoice to the accounts payable department.

In receiving, Mr. Hiro simply used the packing slip that was included with the goods to make three copies of the receiving report. The first copy was sent to the purchasing department where it was filed. The second copy was sent to accounts payable, and the third copy was filed by Mr. Hiro in the filing cabinet.

The accounts payable department would file the receiving report received by Mr. Hiro until the invoice from the supplier arrived. Then, Mr. Maldonado would check both the receiving report and invoice to make sure everything that was sent was actually received. Mr. Maldonado would then hand off the documents to Mr. Bailey so that he could do the appropriate posting and filing of the checked documents. Mr. Bailey would post the changes to the voucher register and purchases journal, sending a journal voucher to the general ledger department after the purchases journal was updated. Mr. Bailey would then put the receiving report and invoice in the appropriate file. Also in accounts payable, Mr. Dresden would be scanning the records to see when it was time to write checks to the different vendors. Whenever a due date arrived, Mr. Dresden would write a check in two copies. The first copy would be filed in the cabinet and the other would be sent to the appropriate vendor. Then Mr. Dresden would update the accounts payable subsidiary ledger, sending an account summary to the general ledger department.

The general ledger was a tight ship. Mr. Callahan would receive the account summary and journal voucher and then post the necessary changes to the general ledger. After posting the documents were filed in the general ledger department.

Conversion Cycle Procedures

The conversion cycle at Blades R Us begins with the production planning and control department receiving the inventory levels from the finished goods warehouse. If the number of a given part in the finished goods warehouse is below the set minimum then production for the part is to be run. The production planning and control department gathers the bill of materials and the route sheet for that part and makes up the production schedule and work orders. A copy of the work order, route sheet, bill of materials, and production schedule is filed at the production planning and control department. A copy of the production schedule, work order, and bill of materials is sent to the work centers.

Once the work centers receive the paperwork from the production planning and control department production is initiated. The work order is sent to the finished goods warehouse, and the production schedule and route sheet are filed. Time cards are filled out and given to the payroll department. Materials requisition forms are filled out in order to attain the necessary materials; one is filed and the other is sent to the inventory control department.

When inventory control receives the materials requisition they send the desired material to the work center, update the inventory records, and then file the material requisition. The inventory control department makes the decision to buy raw materials based on a predetermined minimum of parts in inventory and a set order number. The inventory records are periodically reviewed, and when the number of a part in inventory falls below the set minimum a purchase requisition is completed. One copy is sent to the purchasing department and the other is filed. The purchasing department sends inventory control a purchase order which it then uses to update its inventory records. The purchase order is then filed.

Blades R Us has made the decision to try and become a world-class company. They realize that they will have to make many fundamental changes in order to achieve this goal. One of the first steps that they have decided to take is to implement an MRP system. They feel this will help them to keep better track of their inventories, work in process, and customer demands and trends. They also realize that there are many weaknesses in the other pieces of their conversion cycles and they would like to take steps in improving those as well.

Required:
1. Create a data flow diagram of the current system.
2. Create a document flowchart of the existing system.

3. Analyze the internal control weaknesses in the system. Model your response according to the six categories of physical control activities specified in SAS 78.
4. Prepare a system flowchart of a redesigned computer-based system that resolves the control weaknesses that you identified.

2. Jack Inc.
(Prepared by Scot Pasquale and Kyle Smith, Lehigh University)
Jack Inc. has been a manufacturer of automotive jacks since 1970. Originally, Jack had only one customer—the General Motors plant in Detroit, Michigan. Eventually business expanded into Canada, and Jack began producing for GM's assembly plant in Oshawa, Ontario. By 1985, the company began supplying the rest of the Big Three (The Ford Motor Company and Chrysler) North American auto manufacturers and by 1990, Jack had gained a piece of the Japanese market. Jack supplies Toyota, Nissan, and Honda with automotive jacks for their assembly operations in North America and in Japan.

Conversion Cycle
At the start of the year each automobile manufacturer provides Jack's with an order that is based on budgeted sales predictions. However, this order is guaranteed for only the first month; after that each automobile manufacturer can update their orders on a monthly basis. Jack's current system requires orders for raw materials to be placed with suppliers on a quarterly basis. While the order provides a general idea of what is to be expected, orders from the automobile manufacturers can increase or decrease dramatically after the initial month.

Under the current batch production process in the conversion cycle, the blanket order is sent directly to the production, planning, and control phase. In this phase, the material and operation requirements are determined. It is here that the necessary production documents (bills of materials, route sheets) are created and combined with inventory status reports from inventory control and the required engineering specifications from the engineering department in order to create a purchase requisition. Currently the production scheduling phase falls under the responsibility of the work center. At the work center, the supervisor in charge prepares work orders, move tickets,

and materials requisitions. These documents are sent to the cost accounting department and are also used to create an open work order file. The work center also retains copies of these documents so they can be used to initiate production activities. Under the current system, once production is initiated, any excess material is immediately scrapped. The work center also prepares the necessary timekeeping documents (payroll time card and job tickets) and sends this information to the cost accounting department as well. Upon completion of the production cycle, the production schedule and move tickets are used to close the open work order file, while one copy of the work order is sent to the finished goods warehouse and another is sent to inventory control.

At the start of the production phase, a copy of the materials requisition is sent to storekeeping so that the necessary raw materials can be issued to the work center. A copy of the materials requisition is kept on file in storekeeping.

Inventory control is involved in the batch production process throughout the entire operation. It releases the inventory status document to production, planning, and control so that materials and operations requirements can be determined. A copy of the materials requisition document is received from storekeeping so that inventory files can be updated. Once files are updated the materials requisition is sent to cost accounting, while the updated files are also used to prepare a journal voucher that is sent to the general ledger department. A copy of the materials requisition, purchase requisition, and work order documents are kept on file in inventory control.

Once the cost accounting department has received all the necessary information from the other departments, the work-in-process file is updated. All work center documents (move tickets, job tickets, materials requisitions, excess materials, and materials returns), along with a copy of the work order, are filed in the cost accounting department. At the end of the phase the cost accounting department prepares a journal voucher and sends it to the general ledger department. This journal voucher along with the one sent by inventory control are used to update the general ledger. Both journal vouchers are kept on file in the general ledger department.

Required:
1. Create a data flow diagram of the current system.
2. Create a document flowchart of the existing system.

3. Analyze the internal control weaknesses in the system. Model your response according to the six categories of physical control activities specified in SAS 78.

4. Prepare a system flowchart of a redesigned computer-based system that resolves the control weaknesses that you identified.

3. Automotive Component Corporation—Activity-Based Costing Case

(Prepared by Trey Johnston, Lehigh University)

Automotive Component Corporation (ACC) began in 1955 as a small machine shop supplying the Big Three automakers. The business is now a $2 billion component manufacturing firm. During the three decades from 1955 to 1985, ACC expanded from a common machine shop to a modern manufacturing operation with CNC machines, automatic guided vehicles (AGVs), and a world-class quality program. Consequently, ACC's direct labor cost component has decreased significantly since 1955 from 46 percent to 11 percent. ACC's current cost structure is as follows:

Manufacturing overhead	43.6%
Materials	27.1%
Selling and administrative expenses	17.8%
Labor	11.5%

Despite efforts to expand, revenues leveled off and margins declined in the late 1980s and early 1990s. ACC began to question its investment in the latest flexible equipment and even considered scrapping some. Bill Brown, ACC's controller, explains.

> At ACC, we have made a concerted effort to keep up with current technology. We invested in CNC machines to reduce setup time and setup labor and to improve quality. Although we accomplished these objectives, they did not translate to our bottom line. Another investment we made was in AGVs. Our opinion at the time was that the reduction in labor and increased accuracy of the AGVs combined with the CNC machines would allow us to be competitive on the increasing number of small-volume orders. We have achieved success in this area, but once again, we have not been able to show a financial benefit from these programs.

> Recently, there has been talk of scrapping the newer equipment and returning to our manufacturing practices of the early eighties. I just don't believe this could be the right answer but, as our margins continue to dwindle, it becomes harder and harder to defend my position.

With these sentiments in mind, Bill decided to study the current costing system at ACC in detail. He had attended a seminar recently that discussed some of the problems that arise in traditional cost accounting systems. Bill felt that some of the issues discussed in the meeting directly applied to ACC's situation.

The speaker mentioned that activity-based costing was a tool corporations could use to better identify their true product costs. He also mentioned that better strategic decisions could be made based on the information provided from the activity-based reports. Bill decided to form an ABC team to look at the prospect of implementing ABC at ACC. The team consisted of two other members: Sally Summers, a product engineer with a finance background, and Jim Schmidt, an industrial engineer with an MBA.

Sally had some feelings about the current state of ACC:

> ACC is a very customer-focused company. When the automakers demanded small-volume orders, we did what we could to change our manufacturing processes. The problem is that no one realized that it takes just as long for the engineering department to design a ten-component part and process for a small-volume order as it does for a ten-component large-volume order. Our engineering departments cannot handle this kind of workload much longer. On top of this, we hear rumors about layoffs in the not-too-distant future.

Jim felt similarly:

> Sally is correct. As an industrial engineer, I get involved in certain aspects of production that are simply not volume dependent. For example, I oversee first-run inspections. We run a predetermined number of parts before each full run to ensure the process is under control. Most of the in-

spections we perform on the automobile components are looking for burrs, which can severely affect fit or function downstream in our assembly process. Many times, we can inspect sample part runs right on the line. The real consumption of resources comes from running a sample batch, not only inspecting each part.

To begin its study, the team obtained a cost report from the plant cost accountant. A summary of the product costs are as follows:

Product Costs

	Product		
	101	102	103
Material	$ 5.46	$ 4.37	$ 3.09
Direct labor	1.43	1.55	1.80
Overhead (labor- hour basis)	5.44	5.89	6.85
Total	$12.33	$11.81	$11.74

ACC has been determining product costs basically the same way as it did in 1955. Raw material cost is determined by multiplying the number of components by the standard raw material price. Direct labor cost is determined by multiplying the standard labor hours per unit by the standard labor rate per hour. Manufacturing overhead is allocated to product based on direct labor content.

The team then applied the traditional 20 percent markup to the three products. This represents the target price that ACC tries to achieve on its products. They then compared the target price to the market price. ACC was achieving its 20 percent target gross margin on Product 101, but not on Products 102 or 103, as illustrated below.

Product Price

	Product		
	101	102	103
Traditional cost	$12.33	$11.81	$11.74
Target selling price	14.79	14.17	14.08
Target gross margin	20%	20%	20%
Market price	14.79	14.05	13.61
Actual gross margin	20%	19%	16%

Bill was concerned; he remembered the conference he had attended. The speaker had mentioned examples of firms headed in a downward

spiral because of a faulty cost system. Bill asked the team, "Is ACC beginning to show signs of a faulty cost system?"

Next, the team looked at the manufacturing overhead breakdown (Figure 1, on the following page). The current cost accounting system allocated 100 percent of this overhead to product based on labor dollars. The team felt ACC could do a better job of tracing costs to products based on transaction volume. Jim explains:

> The manufacturing overhead really consists of the six cost pools shown in Figure 1. Each of these activity cost pools should be traced individually to products based on the proportion of transactions they consume, not the amount of direct labor they consume.

The team conducted the following interviews to determine the specific transactions ACC should use to trace costs from activities to products.

John "Bull" Adams, the supervisor in charge of material movement, provided the floor layout shown in Figure 2 on the following page and commented on his department's workload:

> Since ACC began accepting small-volume orders, we have had our hands full. Each time we design a new part, a new program must be written. Additionally, it seems the new small-volume parts we are producing are much more complex than the large-volume parts we produced just a few years ago. This translates into more moves per run. Consequently, we wind up performing AGV maintenance much more frequently. Sometimes I wish we would get rid of those AGVs; our old system of forklifts and operators was much less resistant to change.

Sara Nightingale, the most experienced jobsetter at ACC, spoke about the current status of setups:

> The changeover crew has changed drastically recently. Our team has shifted from mostly mechanically skilled maintenance people to a team of highly trained programmers and mechanically skilled people. This shift has greatly reduced our head count. Yet, the majority of our work is still spent on setup labor time.

Case 3: Figure 1

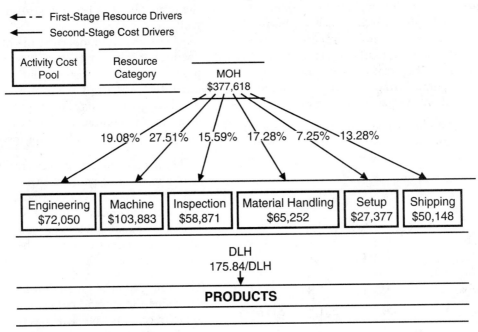

Case 3: Figure 2

Phil Johnson, the shipping supervisor, told the team what he felt drove the activity of the shipping department:

The volume of work we have at the shipping department is completely dependent on the number of trucks we load. Recently, we have been filling more trucks per day with less volume. Our workload has increased, not decreased. We still have to deal with all of the paperwork and administrative hassles for each shipment. Also, the smaller trucks they use these days are side-loaders, and our loading docks are not set up to handle these trucks. Therefore, it takes us a while to coordinate our docks.

Once the interviews were complete, the team went to the systems department to request basic product information on the three products ACC manufactured. The information is shown in Figure 3.

Required:
The team has conducted all of the required interviews and collected all of the necessary information in order to proceed with its ABC pilot study.
1. The first three steps in an activity-based cost implementation is to define the resource categories, activity centers, and first-stage resource drivers. These steps have already been completed at ACC, and the results are displayed in Figure 1. Using the information from the case, perform the next step for the implementation team and determine the second-stage cost drivers ACC should use in its ABC system. Support your choices with discussion.
2. Using the second-stage cost drivers identified in part (1), compute the new product costs for Products 101, 102, and 103.
3. Modify Figure 2 and include the cost drivers identified in part (1).
4. Compare the product costs computed under the current cost accounting system to the product costs computed under the activity-based system. Explain the differences in product cost.
5. Given the new information provided by the ABC system, recommend a strategy ACC should pursue to regain its margins and comment on specific improvements that would reduce ACC's overhead burden in the long run.

4. Horox, Inc.—Internal Controls Assessment
(Prepared by Chris Horrocks, Lehigh University)
Horox, Inc. is a manufacturer of portable compact disc (CD) players located outside of Philadelphia, Pennsylvania. It employs 1,500

Case 3: Figure 3

Basic Product Information

	101	102	103	Total
Production				
Quantity	10,000 units	20,000 units	30,000 units	60,000 units
Runs	10 runs	4 runs	3 runs	17 runs
Shipments				
Quantity	10,000 units	20,000 units	30,000 units	60,000 units
Shipments	20 shipments	4 shipments	3 shipments	27 shipments
Manufacturing cost				
Raw material				
Components	16 components	9 components	6 components	
Cost per component	$0.34 per component	$0.49 per component	$0.52 per component	
Labor usage*				
Setup labor	15.93 hours per run	63.68 hours per run	90.15 hours per run	684 hours
Run labor	0.05 hours per part	0.04 hours per part	0.03 hours per part	2,148 hours
Machine usage**	0.03 hours per part	0.02 hours per part	0.02 hours per part	1,297 hours
Other overhead				
Engineering				$72,050
Inspection				58,871
Material handling				65,252
Material moves	500 feet per run	350 feet per run	250 feet per run	
Shipping				$50,148

*Labor = $40 per hour; including fringe benefits
**Machine cost = $80 per hour

workers at a centrally located, 15-acre production facility. Horox distributes its products worldwide through three nearby distribution centers. Sales are currently $20 million per year and growing. Horox was formed ten years ago; the company's management was relatively inexperienced and lacking in technical knowledge. Since 1987, Horox has been expanding into new research areas; in the past three years, the company has reported enormous profits in its financial statements.

Horox, Inc. currently uses very little computer technology in its conversion cycle except on the shop floor, where up-to-date machinery is in place. The process begins in the storekeeping department.

In the storekeeping department, Mr. Wall controls the inventory and keeps the inventory records. He checks daily on the inventory control files to assess the amount of goods in various inventories. He then sends an inventory status report to production planning and control.

The production planning and control department is led by Mr. Goody. Once the inventory status report is received, as well as the sales forecasts from marketing, Mr. Goody takes a copy of the bill of materials and route sheet and assesses the inventory requirements. If the inventory amounts are adequate, Mr. Goody then prepares a production schedule, work order, move tickets, and materials requisitions, which he then sends to the work centers. Mr. Goody then sends a purchase requisition to the purchasing and storekeeping departments.

Mr. Goody also heads the various work centers, and the supervisors of the different work centers report to him. These supervisors, upon receipt of the above documents, send the materials requisitions to the storekeeping department. In the storekeeping department, Mr. Wall then sends back to the work center the necessary materials. He then files a copy of the materials requisition and updates the raw materials inventory ledger. At the end of each day, he sends a copy of the materials requisitions to the cost accounting department. He also sends a journal voucher for the use of materials and a journal voucher for finished goods to the general ledger department.

In the work centers, the managers of each center collect the employees' time cards and send them to cost accounting, along with a copy to payroll. They also send the job and move tickets, which outline the various costs that have been incurred, to cost accounting.

Ms. Tower, who heads the cost accounting department, collects all of the data, determines the overall cost, compares it to the standard costs, and determines the variances. Only the total variances are compared; the information is then used to evaluate managers and supervisors of the various departments. Ms. Tower then updates the work-in-process files and finished goods inventory files. She then creates a journal voucher and sends it to the general ledger department.

In the general ledger department, the information from the journal vouchers is entered into the general ledger computer program, where the files are updated. The journal vouchers are filed.

Required:
1. Create a data flow diagram of the current system.
2. Create a document flowchart of the existing system.
3. Analyze the internal control weaknesses in the system. Model your response according to the six categories of physical control activities specified in SAS 78.
4. Prepare a system flowchart of a redesigned computer-based system that resolves the control weaknesses that you identified.

5. **Atlantis Scuba Gear—Internal Controls Assessment**
(Prepared by Anne Toolan, Lehigh University)
The production process at Atlantis involves the planning, scheduling, and controlling of the physical product through the manufacturing process. Atlantis's manufacturing process begins in the production planning and control department where Mary determines the materials and operations requirements and combines information from various departments to assess inventory requirements needed to produce a product. Marketing provides the sales forecast, engineering provides the engineering specifications, and inventory provides the inventory status. When this information is combined with the bill of materials and route sheet, Mary is able to prepare a purchase requisition document. The purchase

requisition is then sent to purchasing and inventory control.

Hope is also part of the production planning and control department. Her job is to prepare production and control documents by comparing the bill of materials and route sheets. The documents produced are the move ticket, work order, and materials requisitions. A copy of the work order, move ticket, and materials requisitions documents are sent to cost accounting. The other two copies are sent to Ken, the manager in the work center.

Once Ken receives the production control documents, he initiates production. Unfortunately for Atlantis, Ken is not a good supervisor. One of Ken's duties is to review the job tickets, which are sent to cost accounting, and the employee time cards, which are sent to payroll. Ken doesn't pay attention to the amount of time his employees spend working, so they can easily enter any time onto their time cards. Ken also doesn't pay close attention to the production process and the use of raw materials. Ken sends the materials requisitions to the inventory department, but never sends back any excess material or returns. Materials are left in the work center department and are used in the future if they run out of material.

Steve in the inventory department takes the materials requisitions from the work center and releases the raw materials to the work centers. Steve then files a copy of the materials requisitions and updates the inventory records with the other two copies. He then updates the materials inventory records and creates a journal voucher that is sent to the accounting department. The finished goods inventory is updated and a journal voucher is created and sent to the accounting department. A copy of the materials requisitions is filed and the other copy is sent to accounting.

The cost accounting department at Atlantis monitors the flow of cost information related to production. Information flows from the production planning, work centers, and inventory departments. The production department sends a work order to Sherry in cost accounting, which is used to initiate work-in-process recording, and then the work order is filed. The work center sends a job ticket and the production planning and control department sends a materials requisi-

tion. Sherry then updates the work in process and calculates the variances. Sherry creates a journal voucher and then updates the general ledger after she compares it with the journal voucher from inventory. Finally, Sherry files both journal vouchers.

Required:

1. Create a data flow diagram of the current system.
2. Create a document flowchart of the existing system.
3. Analyze the internal control weaknesses in the system. Model your response according to the six categories of physical control activities specified in SAS 78.
4. Prepare a system flowchart of a redesigned computer-based system that resolves the control weaknesses that you identified.

6. **Bumper Cars, Ltd.—Inventory Management and Control**
   (Prepared by Julie Fisch and Melinda Bowman, Lehigh University)

In 1983, Mr. Amusement created Bumper Cars, Ltd., a company whose main concern was the manufacture and repair of the exterior shells of bumper cars used in amusement parks. Although the company functioned on a small scale for a few years, it has recently expanded to some new areas, including larger-scale amusement parks such as Coney Island. Despite the recent increase in business, Bumper Cars still operates as a small company with limited technology invested in computer systems. Many departments run totally manual systems. Due to the expansion, however, Mr. Amusement has taken a serious look at the setup of his company and determined that some problems exist. The most pressing problem is in the area of inventory management and control.

Inventory Control Department

At Bumper Cars, raw materials are stored in a warehouse until they are transferred to the production department for manufacturing. The inventory control department, which consists of three workers employed under the inventory manager, Ms. Coaster, work with the inventory at the raw materials stage. Each worker's responsibilities involve periodic inventory counts, along with the day-to-day jobs of storing and transferring inventory. Each day, when the workers transfer the inventory to work in process, they also attempt to keep track of the levels of inventory to inform the purchasing department to reorder if the stock of materials becomes too low. However, in their attempt to achieve efficient and speedy transfers of raw materials to manufacturing, the workers find it very difficult and inconvenient to constantly check for low levels of inventory. As a result, the inventory frequently runs out before the workers reorder, thus causing a gap in raw materials needed for production.

Production Department

The production department receives the goods from inventory control, then puts them into production. Recently, however, Mr. Ferris, the production manager, complained to the president about the inconvenience caused by the lack of raw materials at crucial periods of production. As he stated at an important managerial meeting:

> Each week, we have a certain number of orders that must be filled, along with an indeterminable and changing number of repair requests. When we receive these orders, we immediately start work in order to fill our quotas on time. Lately, however, my workers have been handicapped by the fact that the raw materials are not available to put into production at the times we need them. During these lags, production stops, workers become idle, and back-orders pile up. Although we inform the inventory control and purchases departments of the problem right away, it still takes time for them to order and get the inventory to the warehouse. Then, it takes even more time for them to get the inventory to us in production. As a result, when we finally receive the necessary materials, my workers are forced to work overtime and at an unreasonable rate to meet demand. This up-and-down method of working is bad for general morale in my department. My workers tend to become lazy, expecting a lag to occur. Also, requests for repairs become nearly impossible to fulfill, because we never know if the materials needed to fix the problem will be available. Usually, we fall so far behind on regular production during these lags that we must concentrate all our efforts just to meet daily demand. As a

result, our repair business has dropped steadily over the past year. I feel that these production lags are extremely detrimental to our expanding business and we should immediately work on finding a solution.

Possible Solutions

As a result of Mr. Ferris's complaints, Bumper Cars realized that some changes must be made. Basically, the company determined that both the inventory control and production departments needed reorganization at a reasonable cost. Another managerial meeting of all the department heads took place specifically to discuss this problem. Each manager came to the meeting with his or her own ideas for a possible solution. Mr. Flume, the controller, aggressively suggested that a new companywide computer system be installed. This system would solve the inventory control problems by keeping up-to-date records of the inventory available at any given time. At the same time, the system could be set up to reduce paperwork in the accounting and finance departments. In addition, this computer could link all the departments, thus alleviating communication breakdowns. Finally, the computer could be linked to the company from which Bumper Cars ordered its inventory, so that as soon as materials became low, it could immediately reorder before a problem developed.

At this point in the meeting, the president, Mr. Amusement, jumped up and exclaimed:

> Wait a minute! This system would solve our problems, but as you all know, we are not a large company. The cost of implementing a companywide computer system would be excessive. We would have to consider research, installation, maintenance, and repair costs involved in developing a complex system such as this one. When you take everything into consideration, I'm not sure if the costs would greatly exceed the benefits. Let's search for some other less costly, but still efficient, solutions.

Mr. Ferris, the production manager, then offered a second possible solution. After agreeing that a computer system might be too expensive, he went on to suggest:

> Since my main problem is meeting demand after a backlog has occurred, a possible solu-

tion might be to hire temporary workers to help alleviate the overload problem. These workers would not cost too much because they would not receive benefits, but they would help solve the immediate problem. They would then be trained for production, so if people leave the production department, it would be easy to find replacements. As a result, production could continue with a minimum of problems and lags.

The managers discussed Mr. Ferris's suggestion for a few minutes. Then, Ms. Coaster, the inventory control manager, stood up and offered a third solution for the inventory problems. She explained:

Although Mr. Ferris's plan might work, I feel that the real root of the problem lies in my department rather than in the area of production. It seems that the problem is that my employees have too many tasks to perform all at once. Therefore, what we really need are more employees in the inventory control department to continually check and recheck inventory levels. Then my other employees could concentrate solely on the transfer of raw materials to production. By this separation of tasks, I feel we could efficiently solve our inventory problems. Also, the cost of hiring a few more people would not be excessive.

By the end of the meeting, management still had not made a decision. They had identified the need to reorganize, but they could not decide which approach would be the best for the company.

Required:
Using the information about Bumper Cars, Ltd., along with your own knowledge, either agree or disagree with the various solutions suggested by the company's employees, then discuss what you feel is the best solution for the company's inventory problem.

CHAPTER

8

General Ledger, Financial Reporting, and Management Reporting Systems

This chapter examines the objectives, operational features, and control issues of three related systems: the general ledger system (GLS), the financial reporting system (FRS), and the management reporting system (MRS). Because of the operational interdependency of the GLS and FRS, it is generally convenient to view them as a single, integrated system (GL/FRS). In this chapter, however, we consider the GLS and FRS first as separate systems and then as an integrated system.

The MRS provides management with information needed for planning and controlling business activities. The MRS is distinguishable from the FRS in two key respects. First, the general ledger is the primary data source for the FRS. The MRS, on the other hand, draws upon financial and nonfinancial data from operations as well as traditional general ledger data. Hence, MRS applications may be either stand-alone systems or they may be integrated into other AIS applications such as the order entry system or the procurement system.

The second distinction is that the financial reporting performed by the FRS is mandatory, while MRS applications are *discretionary*. Neither the applications themselves nor the content, timing, or format of the information they produce are mandated by authoritative bodies such as the IRS, SEC, or AICPA. Organization management implements MRS applications at its discretion based on its need for information.

Before examining the features and functions of the GLS, FRS, and MRS applications, the chapter opens with a review of data coding schemes, which are essential to their effective operation.

LEARNING OBJECTIVES

After studying this chapter, you should:

- Understand the purpose of data coding and be able to identify the respective features, advantages, and disadvantages of the various numeric and alphabetic coding schemes.
- Understand the operational features of the GLS, FRS, and MRS.
- Be able to identify the principle operational controls governing the GLS, FRS, and MRS.
- Understand the management decision-making process.
- Recognize the role of management principles in information systems design.
- Understand the effect of decision type and management level on information needs.
- Know the difference between structured and unstructured decisions.
- Know the different report types and the attributes common to all reports.
- Understand the elements of a responsibility accounting system.
- Be aware of behavioral issues in management reporting.

DATA CODING SCHEMES

The subject of data coding is not unique to the systems covered in this chapter. All AIS applications (including those discussed in previous chapters) use codes to represent various aspects of economic activity. But coding is especially important for the GLS portion of the GL/FRS, which is the point where all the subsystems of the AIS come together. We might say that all subsystems are connected via flows of information to the GLS, as the spokes of a wheel are attached to the hub. Figure 8–1 presents this relationship.

To do business, an organization must effectively coordinate these flows. Without some method of identifying and channeling transaction and account information, vital communications between AIS subsystems would be chaotic and unmanageable. Data coding provides just such a method, and the GLS is the logical place to introduce coding and to specify its applicability for the entire AIS. We can begin to appreciate the importance of coding by briefly examining a system that does not use codes.

A SYSTEM WITHOUT CODES

Firms process large volumes of transactions and accounts that have attributes similar to others within the same class. These common attributes are, in fact, the basis for

FIGURE 8–1

Relationship of GLS to Other Information Subsystems

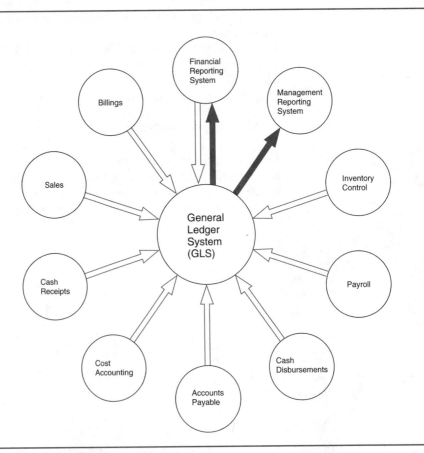

classifying such accounts and transactions. For instance, a firm's accounts receivable file may contain accounts for several different customers with the same name and similar addresses. To process transactions accurately against the correct accounts, the firm must be able to distinguish one from another. This task becomes particularly difficult as the number of similar attributes and items in the class increase.

To illustrate, consider the most elemental item a machine shop wholesaler firm might carry in its inventory—a machine nut. Assume that the total inventory of nuts has only three distinguishing attributes: size, material, and thread. As a result, this entire class of inventory can be distinguished solely on the basis of these three features. Let's assume the following:

1. The size attribute ranges from / inch to 1 fl inches in diameter in increments of $1/64$ of an inch, giving 96 sizes of nuts.
2. For each size subclass, four materials are available: brass, copper, mild steel, and case-hardened steel.
3. Each of these size and material subclasses come in three different threads: fine, standard, and coarse.

By these assumptions, this class of inventory could contain 1,152 separate items (96 ˇ 4 ˇ 3). The identification of a single nut in this class requires a description in terms of these distinguishing attributes. To illustrate, consider the following journal entry to record the receipt of $1,000 worth of half-inch, case-hardened steel nuts with standard threads supplied by Industrial Parts Manufacturer of Cleveland, Ohio.

	DR	CR
Inventory-nut, fi inch, case-hardened steel, standard thread	1,000	
A/P—Industrial Parts Manufacturer, Cleveland, Ohio		1,000

This uncoded approach takes a great deal of recording space, is time consuming to record, and is obviously prone to many types of errors. The negative effects of this approach may be seen in many parts of the organization:

1. *Sales staff.* To properly identify the items sold requires the transcription of large amounts of details onto source documents. Apart from the time and effort involved, this tends to encourage clerical errors and incorrect shipments.
2. *Warehouse personnel.* Locating and picking goods for shipment are impeded, and shipping errors will likely result.
3. *Accounting personnel.* Postings to ledger accounts will require searching through the subsidiary files using lengthy descriptions as the key. This will be painfully slow, and postings to the wrong accounts will be common.

A SYSTEM WITH CODES

These problems are solved, or at least greatly reduced, by using codes to represent each item in the inventory and supplier accounts. Let's assume the inventory item in our previous example had been assigned the numeric code 896, and the supplier in the AP account is given the code number 321. The coded version of the previous journal entry can now be greatly simplified:

ACCOUNT	DR	CR
896	1,000	
321		1,000

This is not to suggest that detailed information about the inventory and the supplier is of no interest to the organization. Obviously it is! These facts will be kept in reference files and used for such purposes as the preparation of parts lists, catalogs, bills of material, and mailing information. The inclusion of such details, however, would clutter the task of transaction processing and could prove dysfunctional.

With just this simple example, we begin to see the importance of data coding. Some of the common uses of codes in AIS are to:

1. Concisely represent large amounts of complex information that would otherwise be unmanageable.
2. Provide a means of accountability over the completeness of the transactions processed.
3. Identify unique transactions and accounts within a file.
4. Support the audit function by providing an effective audit trail.

The following discussion examines some of the more commonly used coding techniques and explores their respective advantages and disadvantages.

NUMERIC AND ALPHABETIC CODING SCHEMES

Sequential Codes

As the name implies, **sequential codes** represent items in some sequential order (ascending or descending). A common application of numeric sequential codes is the prenumbering of source documents. At printing, each document is given a unique sequential code number. This becomes the transaction number that allows the system to track each transaction processed and to identify any lost or out-of-sequence documents.

Advantages. Sequential coding supports the reconciliation of a batch of transactions, such as sales orders, at the end of processing. If the transaction processing system detects any gaps in the sequence of transaction numbers, it alerts management to the possibility of a missing or misplaced transaction. By tracing the transaction number back through the stages in the process, management can eventually determine the cause and effect of the error. Without sequentially numbered documents, problems of this sort are difficult to detect and resolve.

Disadvantages. Sequential codes carry no information content beyond their order in the sequence. For instance, a sequential code assigned to a raw material inventory item tells us nothing about the attributes of the item (type, size, material, warehouse location, and so on). Also, sequential coding schemes are difficult to change. Inserting a new item at some midpoint requires renumbering the subsequent items in the class accordingly. In applications where record types must be grouped together logically and where additions and deletions occur regularly, this coding scheme is inappropriate.

Block Codes

A numeric **block code** is a variation on sequential coding that remedies in part the disadvantages just described. This approach can represent whole classes of items by restricting each class to a specific range within the coding scheme. A common application of block coding is the construction of a **chart of accounts**.

A well-designed and comprehensive chart of accounts is the basis for the general ledger and, thus, is critical to a firm's financial and management reporting systems.

The more extensive the chart of accounts, the more precisely a firm can classify its transactions and the greater the range of information it can provide both internal and external users. Figure 8–2 presents an example of a chart of accounts that uses block codes.

Notice that each account type is represented by a unique range of codes or blocks. Thus, balance sheet and income statement account classifications and subclassifications can be depicted. In this example, each of the accounts consists of a three-digit code. The first digit is the "blocking" digit and represents the account classification, for example, current asset, liability, or expense. The other digits in the code are sequentially assigned.

Advantages. Block coding allows for the insertion of new codes within a block without having to reorganize the entire coding structure. For example, if advertising expense is account number 626, the first digit indicates that this account is an operating expense. As new types of expense items are incurred and have to be specifically accounted for, they may be added sequentially within the 600 account classification. This three-digit code accommodates 100 individual items (X00 through X99) within each block. Obviously, the more digits in the code range, the more items per block there can be.

Disadvantages. As with the sequential codes, the information content of the block code is not readily apparent. For instance, account number 626 means nothing until matched against the chart of accounts, which identifies it as advertising expense.

Group Codes

Numeric **group codes** are used to represent complex items or events involving two or more pieces of related data. The code consists of zones or fields that possess

---

FIGURE 8–2

Chart of Accounts

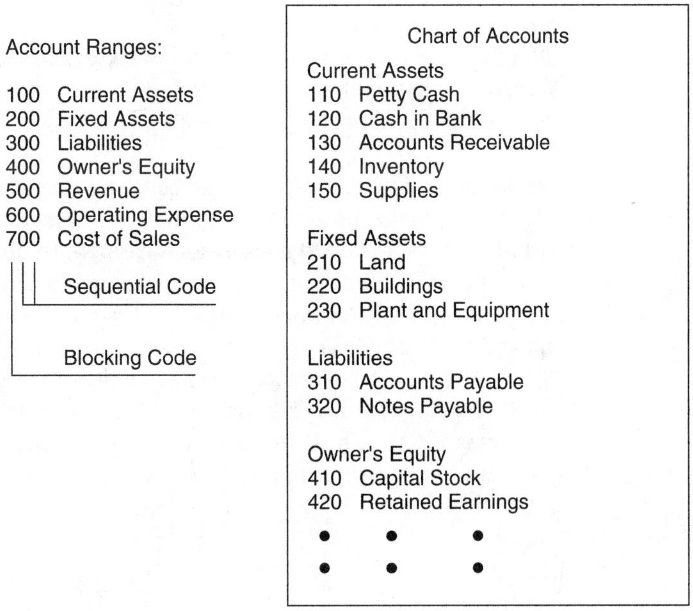

Account Ranges:

100	Current Assets
200	Fixed Assets
300	Liabilities
400	Owner's Equity
500	Revenue
600	Operating Expense
700	Cost of Sales

Sequential Code

Blocking Code

Chart of Accounts

Current Assets
110 Petty Cash
120 Cash in Bank
130 Accounts Receivable
140 Inventory
150 Supplies

Fixed Assets
210 Land
220 Buildings
230 Plant and Equipment

Liabilities
310 Accounts Payable
320 Notes Payable

Owner's Equity
410 Capital Stock
420 Retained Earnings

specific meaning. For example, a department store chain might code sales order transactions from its branch stores as follows:

Store Number	Dept. Number	Item Number	Salesperson
04	09	476214	99

Advantages. Group codes have a number of advantages over sequential and block codes, including:

1. They facilitate the representation of large amounts of diverse data.
2. They allow complex data structures to be represented in a hierarchical form that is logical and more easily remembered by humans.
3. They permit detailed analysis and reporting both within an item class and across different classes of items.

Using the example above to illustrate, Store Number 04 could represent the Hamilton Mall store in Allentown; Dept. Number 09 represents the sporting goods department; Item Number 476214 is a hockey stick; and Salesperson 99 is Jon Innes. With this level of information, a corporate manager could measure profitability by store, compare the performance of similar departments across all stores, track the movement of specific inventory items, and evaluate sales performance by employees within and between stores.

Disadvantages. Ironically, the primary disadvantage of group coding results from its success as a classification tool. Because group codes can effectively present diverse information, they tend to be overused. There is the possibility that unrelated data will be linked simply because it can be done. Overuse can also lead to unnecessarily complex group codes that cannot be easily interpreted. Finally, overuse can increase storage costs, promote clerical errors, and increase processing time and effort.

Alphabetic Codes

Alphabetic codes may be used for many of the same purposes as numeric codes. Alphabetic characters may be assigned sequentially (in alphabetical order) or may be used in block and group coding techniques.

Advantages. The capacity to represent large numbers of items is increased dramatically through the use of pure alphabetic codes or alphabetic characters imbedded within numeric codes (**alphanumeric codes**). In our earlier example of a chart of accounts using a three-digit code with a single blocking digit, the coding scheme is limited to representing only ten blocks of accounts—0 through 9. However, when an alphabetic character is used for blocking, the number of possible blocks is increased to 26—A through Z. Furthermore, while the two-digit sequential portion of that code has the capacity of only 100 items (10^2), a two-position alphabetic code can represent 676 items (26^2). Thus, by using alphabetic codes in the same three-digit storage space, we see a geometric increase in the potential code range from

$$(10 \text{ blocks} \times 100 \text{ items each}) = 1,000 \text{ items}$$

to

$$(26 \text{ blocks} \times 676 \text{ items each}) = 17,576 \text{ items}$$

Disadvantages. The primary drawbacks with alphabetic coding are (1) as with numeric codes, there is difficulty rationalizing the meaning of codes that have been sequentially assigned; and (2) sorting records that are coded alphabetically tend to be more difficult for users.

Mnemonic Codes

Mnemonic codes are alphabetic characters in the form of acronyms and other combinations that convey meaning. For example, a student enrolling in college courses may enter the following course codes on the registration form:

Course Type	Course Number
Acctg	101
Psyc	110
Mgt	270
Mktg	300

This combination of mnemonic and numeric codes conveys a good deal of information about these courses; with a little analysis, we can deduce that "Acctg" is accounting, "Psyc" is psychology, "Mgt" is management, and "Mktg" is marketing. The sequential number portion of the code indicates the level of each course. Another example of the use of mnemonic codes is assigning state codes in mailing addresses:

Code	Meaning
NY	New York
CA	California
OK	Oklahoma

Advantages. The mnemonic coding scheme does not require the user to memorize meaning; the code itself conveys a high degree of information about the item that is being represented.

Disadvantages. Although mnemonic codes are useful for representing classes of items, they are limited in their ability to represent items within a class. For example, the entire class of accounts receivable could be represented by the mnemonic code AR, but we would quickly exhaust meaningful combinations of alphabetic characters if we attempted to represent the individual accounts that make up this class. These accounts would be represented better by sequential, block, or group coding techniques.

THE GENERAL LEDGER SYSTEM

Figure 8–1 characterizes the GLS as a hub connected to the other systems of the firm through spokes of information flows. Take a moment to review this figure. Transaction cycles process individual events that are recorded in special journals and subsidiary accounts. Summaries of these transactions flow into the GLS and become sources of input for the management reporting system (MRS) and FRS.

The bulk of the flows into the GLS come from the transaction cycle subsystems. However, note that information also flows from the FRS as feedback into the GLS. We shall explore this point more thoroughly later. Other, less frequent events, such as stock transactions, mergers, and lawsuit settlements, for which there may be no formal processing cycle in place, are entered into the GLS directly.

THE JOURNAL VOUCHER

A document called the *journal voucher*, shown in Figure 8–3, is the input source to the general ledger. A journal voucher, which can be used to represent summaries of similar transactions or a single unique transaction, identifies the financial amounts and general ledger accounts that are affected. Routine transactions, adjusting entries, and closing entries are all entered into the general ledger from journal vouchers. Since journal vouchers must be approved by a responsible manager, they provide effective controls against unauthorized general ledger entries. The traditional general journal is not used in systems that use journal vouchers. Most organizations have replaced the general journal with a journal voucher file.

THE GLS DATABASE

The GLS database includes a variety of transaction files, master files, reference files, and archive files. While these will vary from firm to firm, the following examples are fairly representative.

The **general ledger master file** is the principle file in the GLS database. The basis of this file is the firm's coded chart of accounts. Each record in the general ledger master is either a separate GL account (for example, sales) or the control account (such as AR—control) for a corresponding subsidiary file in the transaction processing system (TPS). The FRS draws upon the GL master to produce the firm's financial statements. The MRS also uses this file to support internal information needs. Figure 8–4 illustrates the structure of a typical GL master file.

The **general ledger history file** has the same format as the GL master. The primary purpose of this file is to present comparative financial reports on a historic basis.

The *journal voucher file* (discussed in Chapter 4) is the total of the journal vouchers processed in the current period. By providing a record of all general ledger transactions, this file serves the same purpose as the traditional general journal.

FIGURE 8–3

Journal Voucher

Journal Voucher		Number: JV6 - 03 Date: 6/26/01	
Acct Num	Account Name	Amount DR.	CR.
130	Accts Rec.	$5,500	
502	Sales		$5,500

Explanation: To Record Total Credit Sales for 6/26/01.

Approved By: J. R. Martin   Posted By: S.D. Smith

FIGURE 8–4

Record Layout for
a General Ledger
Master File

Account Number	Account Description	Acct Class A = Asset L = Liab R = Rev E = Expense OE = Equity	Normal Balance D = Debit C = Credit	Beginning Balance	Total Debits This Period	Total Credits This Period	Current Balance

The **journal voucher history file** contains journal vouchers for past periods. This historic information supports management's stewardship responsibility to account for resource utilization. Both the current and historic journal voucher files are important links in the firm's audit trail.

The **responsibility center file** contains the revenues, expenditures, and other resource utilization data for each responsibility center in the organization. The MRS draws upon these data for input in the preparation of responsibility reports for management.

Finally, the **budget master file** contains budgeted amounts for revenues, expenditures, and other resources for responsibility centers. These data, in conjunction with the responsibility center file, are the basis for responsibility accounting, which is discussed later in the chapter.

GLS PROCEDURES

The GLS update process is conceptually simple, as represented by the manual system in Figure 8–5. Journal vouchers flow from transaction processing systems and other sources into the general ledger department. Routinely, these are summary transactions from subsidiary accounts and special journals located in the transaction cycles. As we shall see, less frequent transactions from the fixed asset system, along with adjusting and reversing entries from the financial reporting system, also enter the GLS in this way. Let's now turn our attention to the financial reporting system portion of the GL/FRS.

THE FINANCIAL REPORTING SYSTEM

The responsibility for providing stewardship information to external parties is, to a great extent, prescribed by law and professional standards. Much of this information is in the form of traditional financial statements, tax returns, and documents required by regulatory agencies. This reporting obligation is met via the FRS component of the GL/FRS.

The primary recipients of financial statement information are external users, such as stockholders, creditors, and government agencies. Generally speaking, outside users of information are interested in the performance of the organization as a

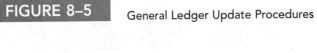

FIGURE 8–5   General Ledger Update Procedures

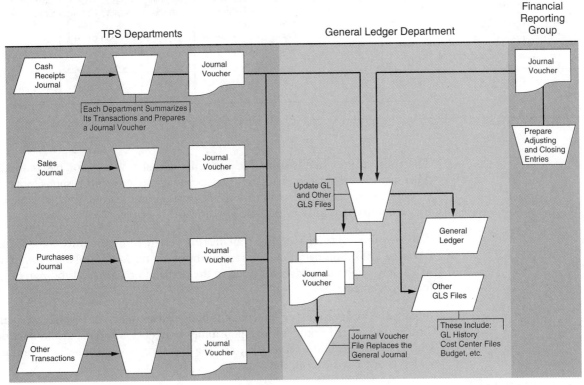

whole. Therefore, they require information that allows them to observe trends in performance over time and to make comparisons between different organizations. Given the nature of these needs, financial reporting information must be prepared and presented by all organizations in a manner that is generally accepted and understood by external users.

SOPHISTICATED USERS WITH HOMOGENEOUS INFORMATION NEEDS

Because the community of external users is vast and their individual information needs may vary, financial statements are aimed at a general audience. They are prepared on the proposition that the audience comprises **sophisticated users** with relatively homogeneous information needs. In other words, it is assumed that users of financial reports understand the conventions and accounting principles that are applied and that the statements have information content that is useful. As we shall see in Chapter 16, no such simplifying assumptions are made for the internal (management) user. Managers tend to require very specialized information.

FRS ACTIVITIES

Sources of input to the FRS include the current general ledger master file, the general ledger history file, and direct input (adjusting and closing entries) from the financial reporting group. The most common output of the FRS are financial statements, including the balance sheet, income statement, and statement of cash flows. These reports, based on the general ledger master file, are sent stockholders, creditors, and other interested outsiders. The FRS may also produce financial analysis reports, comparative financial statements, tax returns, and special reports for regulatory bodies, such as the Securities and Exchange Commission.

THE FINANCIAL ACCOUNTING PROCESS

The FRS is actually the final step in the entire **financial accounting process** that begins in the transaction cycles. To place this in proper perspective, we must consider this process in relation to the other information subsystems. Figure 8–6 presents this intersystem view.

The financial accounting process begins with a clean slate at the start of a new fiscal year. Only the balance sheet (permanent) accounts are carried forward from the previous year. From this point, the process proceeds with the following steps:

1. *Capture the transaction.* Within each transaction cycle, transactions are recorded on the appropriate source documents.
2. *Record in special journal.* Each transaction is entered into the journal—the book of original entry. Recall that frequently occurring classes of transactions, such as sales, are captured in special journals. Those that occur infrequently are recorded in the general journal or directly on a journal voucher.
3. *Post to subsidiary ledger.* The details of each transaction are posted to the affected subsidiary accounts.
4. *Post to general ledger.* Periodically, journal vouchers, summarizing the entries made to the special journals and subsidiary ledgers, are prepared and posted to the general ledger accounts.
5. *Prepare the unadjusted trial balance.* At the end of the accounting period, the ending balance of each account in the general ledger is placed on a worksheet next to its account caption. They are evaluated in total for debit-credit equality.
6. *Make adjusting entries.* Adjusting entries are made to the worksheet to correct errors and to reflect unrecorded transactions during the period, such as depreciation.
7. *Journalize and post adjusting entries.* Journal vouchers for the adjusting entries are prepared and posted to the appropriate accounts in the general ledger.
8. *Prepare the adjusted trial balance.* From the adjusted balances, a trial balance is prepared that contains all the entries that should be reflected in the financial statements.
9. *Prepare the financial statements.* The balance sheet, income statement, and statement of cash flows are prepared using the adjusted trial balance.
10. *Journalize and post the closing entries.* Journal vouchers are prepared for entries that close out the income statement (temporary or nominal) accounts and transfer the income or loss to retained earnings. Finally, these entries are posted to the general ledger.
11. *Prepare the post-closing trial balance.* A trial balance worksheet containing only the balance sheet accounts may now be prepared to indicate the balances being carried forward to the next accounting period.

The financial accounting process described above has three distinct phases (refer to Figure 8–6), each of which involves elements of one or more information subsystem:

Phase 1—**Daily procedures**. The TPS subsystems capture daily transactions on source documents, record these in special journals, post the individual transactions to subsidiary ledgers, and prepare journal vouchers.

FIGURE 8–6   Intersystem View of Financial Accounting Process

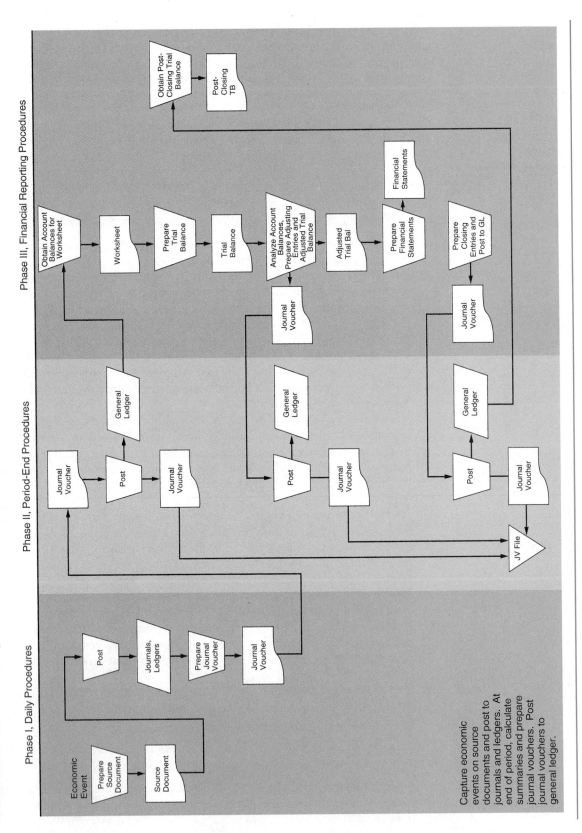

Phase II—**Period-end procedures**. Journal vouchers are entered into the general ledger periodically. This involves both the TPS and GLS. The frequency of updates to the general ledger determines the degree of integration of these systems. In highly integrated systems, general ledger updates are part of daily procedures.

Phase III—**Financial reporting procedures**. The analysis of general ledger accounts and the steps leading to the production of financial statements (the preparation of trial balances, adjusting entries, closing entries, and so on) involve both the FRS and GLS. Note how the GLS and FRS both send and receive data in an iterative exchange. This relationship illustrates why these systems are often viewed as a single system—the GL/FRS.

Now that we have analyzed these systems individually, we shall treat them as a single, integrated system for the remainder of this chapter.

CONTROLLING THE GL/FRS

The activities of the GL/FRS are exclusively accounting tasks. Unlike transaction processing, which also involves flows of physical resources, control concerns in the GL/FRS pertain only to the accuracy and reliability of accounting information. The potential exposures in this system consist of:

1. A defective audit trail.
2. Unauthorized access to the general ledger.
3. General ledger accounts that are out of balance with subsidiary accounts.
4. General ledger account balances that are wrong because of unauthorized or incorrect journal vouchers.

If not controlled, these exposures may cause financial statements and other reports to be misstated and, thus, misleading to their users. The potential consequences are litigation, significant financial loss for the firm, and regulatory agency sanctions.

GL/FRS CONTROL ISSUES

Our study of GL/FRS controls shall follow the framework prescribed by SAS 78, which by now is familiar to you.

Transaction Authorization
Entries into the general ledger are summaries of transactions and are subject to the same controls. The journal voucher is the document that authorizes an entry to the general ledger. Journal vouchers have numerous sources such as the cash receipts processing, sales order processing, and the financial reporting group. It is vital to the integrity of the accounting records that the journal vouchers be properly authorized by a responsible manager at the source department.

Segregation of Duties
In previous chapters, we have seen how the general ledger provides verification control for the accounting process. To do so, the task of updating the general ledger must

be separate from all accounting and asset custody responsibility within the organization. Therefore, general ledger clerks should not:

1. Have record keeping responsibility for special journals or subsidiary ledgers.
2. Prepare journal vouchers.
3. Have custody of physical assets.

Access Controls

Unauthorized access to the general ledger accounts can result in errors, fraud, and misrepresentations in financial statements. Recall that access control has two elements: direct access and indirect access. Concerns over direct access are reduced by ensuring that journal vouchers are posted only by authorized individuals.

Exposure to indirect access stems from poor control over journal vouchers in the source departments. Lost or stolen journal vouchers can be used to make unauthorized entries to the general ledger. Prenumbering and logging these documents at their source provides a means of accountability. Through subsequent review and reconciliation of the log, missing vouchers are identified by gaps in the number sequence and draw attention to the potential exposure.

Accounting Records

The general ledger database is an important component of the system of accounting records a firm must maintain. When properly based on an adequate chart of accounts, these records fully describe the economic activities of the firm. An important aspect of this recording function is maintenance of the audit trail.

As discussed in Chapter 2, the audit trail is a record of the path that a transaction follows through the input, processing, and output phases of a transaction processing system. Documentation is necessary so that an interested party can determine the propriety of transactions. The audit trail is thus a network of documents, journals, and ledgers designed to ensure that a transaction can be accurately traced through the system from initiation to final disposition. An individual should be able to follow the flow of a transaction (with the aid of a document flowchart) from its initiation and capture onto a source document, to the recording of the transaction in a special journal and subsidiary ledger, to the posting to the general ledger, and finally to the financial statements. Conversely, one should be able to start with the summarized financial statements and locate the individual transactions constituting it.

An audit trail is necessary for several reasons: (1) to provide the ability to answer inquiries, for example, from customers or vendors; (2) to be able to reconstruct files if they are completely or partially destroyed; (3) to provide historical data required by auditors; (4) to fulfill government regulations; and (5) to provide a means for preventing, detecting, and correcting errors. An audit trail makes the prevention of errors easier because the details are conveniently organized in logical files, facilitating the processing of those files. Moreover, an audit trail helps to detect errors because the details that make up a total balance (such as accounts payable) can be tallied periodically and compared to the control account. The audit trail also facilitates the correction of errors because the details are readily available for making the necessary changes.

Independent Verification

Throughout this chapter and in previous chapters dealing with transaction cycles, we have portrayed the general ledger function as an independent verification step within the AIS. Journal vouchers, summarizing transaction activity, flow from various operating departments into the GL/FRS, where they are independently reconciled and posted to the general ledger accounts. The GL/FRS produces two operational reports that provide proof of the accuracy of this process. These reports are the journal voucher listing and the general ledger change report. The **journal voucher listing** provides relevant details about each journal voucher the GL/FRS receives as input. This report balances the debits and credits of the transactions and, for purposes of analysis, classifies them by batch, date, and transaction type (for example, credit sales).

The **general ledger change report** presents the effects of journal voucher transactions on the general ledger accounts. Figure 8–7 and Figure 8–8, respectively, provide examples of these two reports. The use of computer technology greatly enhances the preparation of these essential control reports and of other complex reports, such as financial statements, budgets, and tax returns. In the next section, we examine the effects of technology on the design, the operation, and the control of the GL/FRS.

COMPUTER-BASED GL/FRS

Organizations that use the general ledger solely for financial reporting may find that a batch system, which uses sequential files, meets their needs and provides a high degree of security. Such a system is simple to operate, and controlling access to the general ledger is easy to achieve. When the general ledger is used to support a wider

FIGURE 8–7

Journal Voucher Listing

Date	JV Num	Description	Account Number	Debit	Credit
6/26/01	JV6 - 01	Cash receipts	10100	109,000	
			20100		50,000
			10600		44,000
			10900		15,000
6/26/01	JV6 - 02	Credit sales	20100	505,000	
			50200		505,000
6/26/01	JV6 - 03	Inventory usage	30300	410,000	
			17100		410,000
•	•	•	•	•	•
•	•	•	•	•	•
•	•	•	•	•	•
6/26/01	JV - 12	Cash disbursements	90310	102,100	
			10100		102,100
				6,230,000	6,230,000

FIGURE 8–8	General Ledger Change Report

General Ledger Change Report

Date	Acct	Description	JV Ref	Balance	Debits	Credits	Net Change	New Balance
6/26/01	10100	Cash receipts	JV6 - 01 JV6 - 12	1,902,300	109,000	102,100	6,900	10,909,200
6/26/01	20100	Cash receipts Credit sales	JV6 - 01 JV6 - 02	2,505,600	505,000	50,000	455,000	2,960,600
•	•	•	•	•	•	•	•	•
•	•	•	•	•	•	•	•	•
•	•	•	•	•	•	•	•	•
6/26/01	90310	Cash disburs.	JV6 - 12	703,500	102,100		102,100	811,600
6/26/01	17100	Inven. usage	JV6 - 03	1,600,500		410,000	410,000	2,010,500

Control Totals:

	Debits	Credits
Previous Balance	23,789,300	23,789,300
Total Net Change	6,230,000	6,230,000
Current Balance	30,019,300	30,019,300

range of tasks within the organization, however, a system that uses real-time processing and direct access files may be necessary. In this section we examine a traditional automated GL/FRS and a reengineered approach using a **computer-based GL/FRS**.

AUTOMATED GL/FRS USING BATCH PROCESSING AND SEQUENTIAL FILES

Figure 8–9 shows a batch GL/FRS using sequential files for the GL database. This automated system reflects fairly faithfully the manual procedures depicted in Figure 8–6. The strengths and weaknesses of the system are outlined below.

Strengths

Control. The greatest advantage of this system is control. Journal vouchers from the operating departments can be approved, validated, and balanced prior to entering them into the general ledger. Since the GL update is an end-of-day batch process, the entire GL is reproduced each day. In the event of a processing error that materially effects the general ledger, the previous day's balances are available as backup. While this may seem like an archaic method of maintaining the general ledger, some large organizations that use sophisticated real-time transaction processing systems opt for a batch GL/FRS with sequential files because of the backup control that it provides.

Reporting. This system can support management with limited summary feedback reports on transaction activity.

FIGURE 8–9   GL/FRS Using Sequential Files

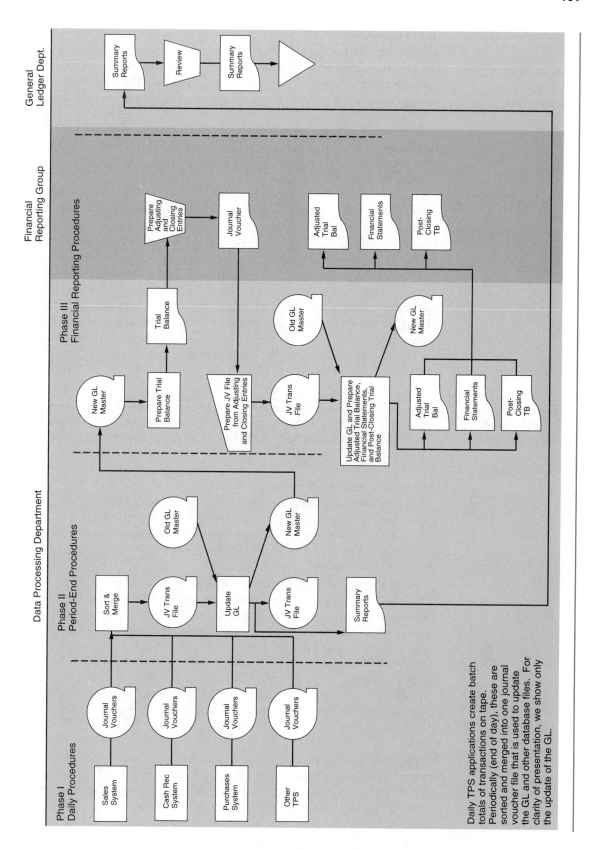

Weaknesses

Inefficiency. The sequential file approach is a conservative use of technology that employs the computer primarily as an accounting tool. This system does not appreciably improve efficiency in operations or facilitate a reduction in labor. For instance, the journal vouchers from the financial reporting group are manually prepared on paper documents. This adds to the operating costs of the system. Journal vouchers must be purchased, prepared, filed, handled by internal mail carriers, and converted to tape or disk by data processing personnel. When transaction volumes are high, these costs can be excessive. Using technology to remove paper from a system will improve **internal efficiency**.

Infrequent Reconciliation. In our discussion of transaction cycles in Chapters 4 through 7, we saw that the frequency of updates to the general ledger has control implications. Infrequent (daily or weekly) updates restrict management to an end-of-period review of overall operations. The technology employed in the GL/FRS influences the general ledger update frequency. The sequential file technique in Figure 8–9 forces the recreation of the entire general ledger master with each update. As an operational matter, therefore, an end-of-day update approach is the most feasible. When the general ledger is updated frequently (after each batch), however, it allows management to monitor the overall process and evaluate whether internal controls are functioning as intended. We examine such a system next.

REENGINEERED
GL/FRS USING
DIRECT ACCESS
FILES

Figure 8–10 shows a reengineered GL/FRS that enables end users to update the general ledger after each batch of transactions is processed. The new system also integrates the GL/FRS with MRS, which is discussed in the next chapter.

Strengths and Weaknesses

The reengineered system overcomes the weaknesses of the traditional system outlined above. Since it does not recreate the entire general ledger each time it is updated, the GL update and reconciliation can now occur as a step within the transaction cycle. The approach greatly facilitates the timely identification of errors when transaction batches are out of balance.

The use of direct access files has additional benefits for management reporting. The organization's MRS provides internal users with financial and nonfinancial information. Internal managers require more frequent and timely information than external users of traditional financial statements. Since some of this information comes from general ledger database files, the use of the direct access approach facilitates management's access to these important data. A traditional GL/FRS that employs batch processing, sequential files, and infrequent updates does not adequately serve the needs of management. Making the general ledger database available to numerous internal users, however, also creates control problems that must be addressed. These include the following.

Segregation of Duties. The system in Figure 8–10 removes the fundamental separation between transaction authorization and processing. Here, end-user systems authorize and process entries directly to the general ledger. To compensate for this potential exposure, the system should provide the end user and general ledger departments with detailed listings of journal voucher and account activity reports.

FIGURE 8–10   GL/FRS Using Direct Access Files

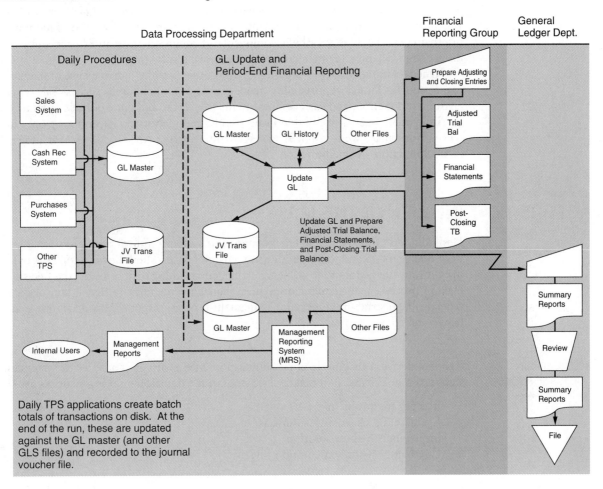

These documents advise users of the automated actions taken by the system so that errors and unusual events, which warrant investigation, can be identified.

Accounting Records and Access Controls.   General ledger records are stored on magnetic disks that can be readily accessed by end-user systems. To preserve the integrity of these records, the organization must implement controls that limit access to them. A number of control techniques are available that will restrict access to authorized users and ensure that authorized users do not exceed their access privileges. Such techniques, however, must be consciously implemented and conscientiously maintained. We shall study these controls in Chapter 15.

THE MANAGEMENT REPORTING SYSTEM

Although discretionary in nature, the MRS has long been informally regarded as an important element in the internal control system of the organization. A reporting system that directs management's attention to problems on a timely basis also promotes effective management and thus supports the organization's business objectives. The control implications of the MRS have now been recognized officially in SAS 78, which requires management to provide formal means for *monitoring* the function of internal controls. This may be accomplished through separate audit procedures (as discussed in Chapter 17) or by ongoing monitoring activities.

One technique for achieving ongoing monitoring is the judicious use of management reports. Timely reports allow managers in functional areas such as sales, purchasing, production, and cash disbursements to oversee and control their operations. By summarizing activities, highlighting trends, and identifying exceptions from normal performance, well-designed management reports provide evidence of internal control function—or malfunction.

FACTORS THAT INFLUENCE THE MRS

Designing an effective management reporting system requires an understanding of what managers do and the types of problems they face. The following topics provide insight into the factors that influence management information needs: the decision-making process; management principles; management function, level, and decision type; problem structure; types of management reports; responsibility accounting; and behavioral considerations.

THE DECISION-MAKING PROCESS

Rational decision making is not a single spontaneous act. It is a series of systematic steps taken by the decision maker. The steps in the **decision-making process** are to:

1. Identify the problem.
2. Evaluate the alternative solutions.
3. Implement the best solution.
4. Conduct post-implementation review.

Identify the Problem
A decision maker usually cannot solve a problem until he or she properly identifies it. Therefore, this first step in the process is critical. Problems themselves are often not observable. Instead, we observe the symptoms of problems. We must recognize this distinction, because treating a symptom as a problem can lead to faulty decisions. For example, a doctor observes that a patient has a temperature of 104 degrees, but this is not a problem. It is a symptom. The root cause (the problem) of the high temperature may be one of any number of viruses, infections, or diseases. To determine the specific problem may require additional tests and a great deal of data. If the doctor forgoes further testing and simply administers aspirin to the patient, the temperature may indeed return to normal, but its cause will go unidentified and untreated. In other words, the doctor has treated the symptom, not the problem. The aspirin (the solution) may make the patient appear well when, in fact, he or she is getting sicker.

We can apply this analogy to a business situation. Consider the division manager who observes a declining trend in the organization's profit margin. Like the patient's temperature, the reduced profit is a symptom, not the problem. The root cause may be ineffective marketing, poor quality control in the production process, a backlog in sales order processing, or a combination of problems. The manager must identify the underlying cause through further analysis before he or she can prescribe a treatment. A hasty fix can simply mask these symptoms and have disastrous consequences for the long-term health of the organization.

Evaluating Alternative Solutions

Having identified the problem, the decision maker faces alternative courses of action. At the very least, he or she faces the option of taking action or not taking action. If there are no alternatives open, then there is no decision to make.

In making a decision, the manager must identify and consider all feasible options. The domain of options identified at this point sets the constraints on the quality of the final decision. It is usually better to disprove the virtue of an option than simply assume it has none, only to discover later that an opportunity was lost.

To illustrate this step, consider the decision-making process of a production manager who must renovate an aging production line. Let us assume that the manager has the following three options:

1. Increase the labor force and keep the existing production line equipment.
2. Reduce significantly (or eliminate) the labor force and automate the production line with a new but unproven technology.
3. Retain the labor force and upgrade the equipment with a proven technology.

Decision Criteria. Several critical factors or **decision criteria** form the basis for making a decision. These criteria may be either tangible or intangible. Tangible decision criteria are those that we can quantify, such as cost information, increased productive capacity in units, and speed of operation. Intangible decision criteria cannot normally be quantified. These are qualitative issues and include such things as behavioral implications, political consequences, and changes in quality of life.

In evaluating alternative solutions, the decision maker must identify all relevant decision criteria. However, because tangible criteria are much easier to deal with than intangibles, there is a tendency to ignore the latter. This is a potential pitfall in decision making, because intangibles can be the most important factors in a decision. Ignoring any important factors (tangible or intangible) will result in a suboptimal decision.

One way of dealing with intangibles is to attempt to quantify them. Table 8–1 demonstrates a quantification process that uses the weighted score table technique. Let's look at the use of this technique.

Identifying Decision Criteria and Assigning Weights. To simplify our production line example, assume that only the five decision criteria listed in the first column are relevant to the decision. The first one, improvement in efficiency, is a tangible factor. We can measure efficiency by comparing units of production to units of input resources. And we can estimate and express in financial terms the fourth factor, potential cost savings. The other decision criteria are intangibles that have no quantifiable units of measure.

We assign each of these five factors a numeric value as a weight (shown in the second column). This weight represents the relative (subjective) importance of each factor to the decision. The value of the weight reflects the decision maker's judgment of the relative importance of each factor to the decision. The five factors total 100 percent because these alone are relevant to the decision. Notice that 60 percent of this decision is influenced by intangible factors.

| TABLE 8–1 | **Weighted Score Table** |

| | | ALTERNATIVES | | | | | | |
| DECISION CRITERIA | WEIGHT | A | | B | | C | |
		RS	WS	RS	WS	RS	WS
Improvement in efficiency	30	1	30	5	150	4	120
Flexibility of operations	20	4	80	2	40	5	100
Impact on employee relations	20	2	40	(4)	(80)	2	40
Potential cost savings	10	(2)	(20)	5	50	1	10
Likelihood of success	20	3	60	1	20	4	80
TOTAL	100%		190		180		350

Rating Each Alternative. The next step in the decision-making process is to evaluate the relative impact of each alternative on the decision criteria. Here, we assign a raw score (RS) to each using a scale of minus (5) to 5. For example, Alternative A is given an RS of 1 for the first decision criterion. On the other hand, Alternative B is given a score of 5 for the same factor. This means that the decision maker rates Alternative B superior to Alternative A on its ability to improve the efficiency of operations. If this were the only relevant factor in the decision, then Alternative B would be the rational choice. However, there are four other factors that the decision maker must consider in the same way.

Calculating Weighted Scores. The next step is to calculate the weighted score (WS) of each decision factor and each alternative by multiplying the weight by the RS value. Thus, an RS of 5 for Alternative B and a weight of 30 yields a WS of 150. By summing the column of weighted scores for each alternative, we derive the alternative's total weighted score. The table shows that Alternative C, with a total WS of 350, is the best choice.

The weighted score approach provides structure to the decision process by focusing only on the decision criteria that are common to all the alternatives. Without a structured approach, the volume of facts generated by competing proposals can overwhelm the decision maker and distract attention from the key issues.

Implementing the Best Solution

The **implementation** stage of the decision-making process involves a good deal of detailed planning. This is also the most protracted and time-consuming portion of the decision-making process. The decision maker must consider all resources necessary to implement the decision. This may require developing a detailed implementation plan with deadlines and checkpoints to ensure that all phases of the implementation proceed on schedule. These phases include:

- Arranging for the financing of the project.
- Negotiating contracts with vendors and contractors.
- Obtaining licenses, building permits, and zoning authorizations.
- Organizing retraining programs for employees who are faced with new practices, procedures, and equipment.
- Planning the changeover from the old system to the new one.[1]

Once the manager develops the plan, implementation can begin in earnest. Large and complex projects frequently encounter delays and cost overruns, but similar problems can plague smaller projects as well. A single subcontractor who fails to perform according to the plan may cause a ripple effect that delays the completion of the entire project. For example, in the construction of a building, if the plumber falls behind the work schedule, the plasterers cannot install the drywall. This delays the painting, which delays the carpeting, which delays finishing work, and so forth.

Some problems, such as delays due to unseasonable weather or sudden union disputes at the vendor company, are beyond the manager's control. However, signals precede many problems. A well-informed manager will have the information to recognize potential problems and will develop a contingency or backup plan to be implemented when problems are imminent. The success of the project may depend on the effectiveness of the manager's contingency planning.

The management reporting system plays a vital role in this phase of the decision-making process. The MRS can help the manager gather, analyze, and assemble pieces of information to identify potential problem areas. It can also alert the manager to checkpoints and critical deadlines.

Conducting a Post-Implementation Review

The final step in the decision-making process is to conduct a **post-implementation review** of the newly implemented project. This is best done after a reasonable settling-in period has passed. The objectives of the review are to determine if both the decision and the decision-making process were sound. An independent group, such as the internal audit department, evaluates the project using the standards of performance that were anticipated during the planning phases. Post-implementation reviews provide valuable insight into the thoroughness of problem identification, the adequacy and completeness of decision criteria, the weighting scheme used, the appropriateness of the scoring process, and the effectiveness of the implementation plan. Obviously, the review process does little to benefit the project under scrutiny. The real benefit from this step is the improvement of future decisions.

The MRS plays a role in the post-implementation review stage by capturing performance data, performing analysis, and reporting on the project's success. In addition, the review process provides insight into the MRS. A flawed decision-making process may be due to deficiencies in the quality, quantity, or nature of information

---

1   This last item may be either a "phased approach," which occurs gradually and is generally less traumatic to the organization, or the "cold turkey" approach, which occurs abruptly. For most organizations, a phased approach is most likely to succeed.

the system provides. This is an opportunity for systems designers to fine-tune the information system.

Management principles provide insight into management information needs. The principles that most directly influence the MRS are formalization of tasks, responsibility, authority, span of control, and management by exception.

Formalization of Tasks

The **formalization of tasks** principle suggests that management should structure the firm around the tasks it performs rather than around individuals with unique skills. Under this principle, organizational areas are subdivided into tasks that represent full-time job positions. Each position must have clearly defined limits of responsibility.

The purpose of formalization of tasks is to avoid an organizational structure in which the organization's performance, stability, and continued existence depend on specific individuals. The **organizational chart** in Figure 8–11 shows some typical job positions in a manufacturing firm. Notice how this is similar to the decomposition of a firm into its functional areas (Chapter 1). However, an organizational chart shows the management titles of each position and the name of the manager who fills that position.

Although a firm's most valuable resource is its employees, it does not own the resource. Sooner or later, key individuals leave and take their skills with them. By formalizing tasks, the firm can more easily recruit individuals to fill standard positions left open by those who leave. In addition, the formalization of tasks promotes internal control. With employee responsibilities formalized and clearly specified, management can construct an organization that avoids assigning incompatible tasks to an individual.

Implications for the MRS. Formalizing the tasks of the firm allows specification of the information needed to support the tasks. Thus, when a personnel change occurs, the information needed by the new employee will be essentially the same as for his or her predecessor. The information system must focus on the task, not the individual performing the task. Otherwise, information requirements would need to be reassessed with the appointment of each new individual to the position. Also, internal control is strengthened by restricting information based on need, as defined by the task, rather than the whim or desire of the user.

Responsibility and Authority

The principle of **responsibility** refers to an individual's obligation to achieve desired results. Responsibility is closely related to the principle of **authority**. If a manager delegates responsibility to a subordinate, he or she must also grant the subordinate the authority to make decisions within the limits of that responsibility. In a business organization, managers delegate responsibility and authority downward through the organizational hierarchy from superior to subordinates.

Implications for the MRS. The principles of responsibility and authority define the vertical reporting channels of the firm through which information flows. The manager's location in the reporting channel influences the scope and detail of the infor-

FIGURE 8–11   Organizational Chart for a Manufacturing Firm

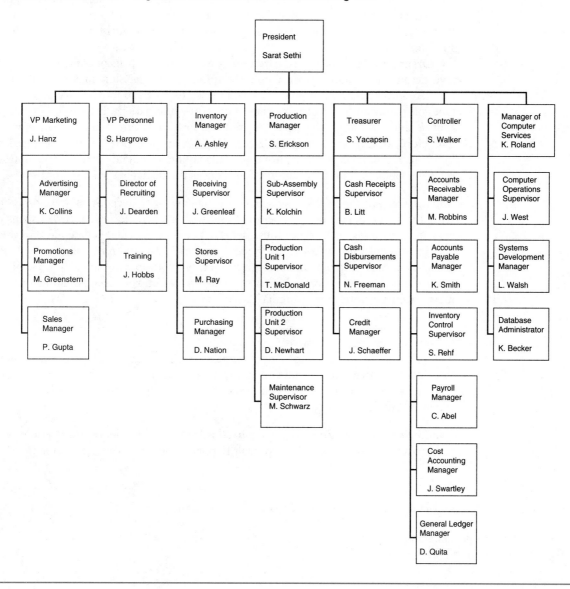

mation reported. Managers at higher levels usually require more highly summarized information. Managers at lower levels receive information that is more narrow and detailed. In designing a reporting structure, the analyst must consider the manager's position in the reporting channel.

Span of Control

A manager's **span of control** refers to the number of subordinates directly under his or her control. The size of the span has an impact on the organization's physical structure. A firm with a narrow span of control has fewer subordinates reporting directly to managers. These firms tend to have tall, narrow structures with several layers of management. Firms with broad spans of control (more subordinates reporting to each manager) tend to have wide structures, with fewer levels of management. Figure 8–12 illustrates the relationship between span of control and organizational structure.

Organizational behavior research suggests that wider spans of control are preferable because they allow more employee autonomy in decision making. This may translate into better employee morale and increased motivation. However, an important consideration in setting the span of control is the nature of the task. The more routine and structured the task, the more subordinates one manager can control. Therefore, routine tasks tend to have a broad span of control. Less structured or highly technical tasks often require a good deal of management participation on task-related problems. This close interaction reduces the manager's span of control.

Implications for the MRS. Managers with narrow spans of control are closely involved with the details of the operation and with specific decisions. Broad spans of control remove managers from these details. These managers delegate more of their decision-making authority to their subordinates. The different management approaches require different information. Managers with narrow spans of control require more detailed reports. Managers with broad control responsibilities operate most effectively with more summarized information.

Management by Exception

The principle of **management by exception** suggests that managers should limit their attention to potential problem areas (i.e., exceptions) rather than being involved with every activity or decision. Thus, managers maintain control without being overwhelmed by details.

Implications for the MRS. Managers need information that identifies operations or resources at risk of going out of control. Reports should support management by ex-

FIGURE 8–12   Impact of Span of Control on Organizational Structure

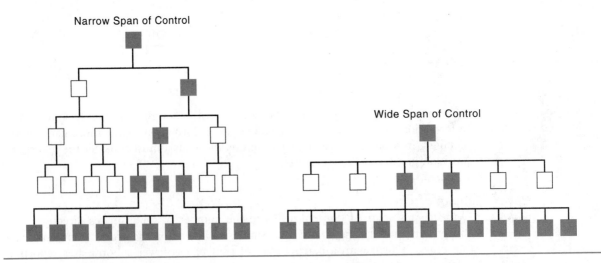

ception by focusing on changes in key factors that are symptomatic of potential problems. Unnecessary details that may draw attention away from important facts should not be in the reports. For example, an inventory exception report may be used to identify items of inventory that turn over more slowly or go out of stock more frequently than normal. Management attention must be focused on these exceptions. The majority of inventory items that fluctuate within normal levels should not be included in the report.

MANAGEMENT FUNCTION, LEVEL, AND DECISION TYPE

The management functions of planning and control have a profound effect on the management reporting system. The planning function is concerned with making decisions about the future activities of the organization. Planning can be long-range or short-range. Long-range planning usually encompasses a period of between 1 and 5 years, but this varies among industries. For example, a public utility may plan 15 years ahead in the construction of a new power plant, while a computer manufacturer deals in a time frame of only 1 or 2 years in the planning of its new products. Long-range planning involves a variety of tasks, including setting the goals and objectives of the firm, planning the growth and optimum size of the firm, and deciding on the degree of diversification among the firm's products.

Short-term planning involves the implementation of specific plans that are needed to achieve the objectives of the long-range plan. Examples include planning the marketing and promotion for a new product, preparing a production schedule for the month, and providing department heads with budgetary goals for the next three months.

The control function ensures that the activities of the firm conform to the plan. This entails evaluating the operational process (or individual) against a predetermined standard and, when necessary, taking corrective action. Effective control takes place in the present time frame and is triggered by feedback information that advises the manager about the status of the operation being controlled.

Planning and control decisions are frequently classified into four categories: strategic planning, tactical planning, managerial control, and operational control. Figure 8–13 relates these decisions to managerial levels.

Strategic Planning Decisions

Figure 8–13 shows that top-level managers make **strategic planning decisions**, including:

- Setting the goals and objectives of the firm.
- Determining the scope of business activities, such as desired market share, markets the firm wishes to enter or abandon, the addition of new product lines and the termination of old ones, and merger and acquisition decisions.
- Determining or modifying the organization's structure.
- Setting the management philosophy.

Strategic planning decisions have the following characteristics:

- They have long-term time frames. Because they deal with the future, managers making strategic decisions require information that supports forecasting.
- They require highly summarized information. Strategic decisions focus on general trends rather than detail-specific activities.

FIGURE 8–13

Management Level
and Decision Type

- They tend to be nonrecurring. Strategic decisions are usually one-time events. As a result, there is little historic information available to support the specific decision.
- Strategic decisions are associated with a high degree of uncertainty. The decision maker must rely on insight and intuition. Judgment is often central to the success of the decision.
- They are broad in scope and have a profound impact on the firm. Once made, strategic decisions permanently affect the organization at all levels.
- Strategic decisions require external as well as internal sources of information.

Tactical Planning Decisions

Tactical planning decisions are subordinate to strategic decisions and are made by middle management (see Figure 8–13). These decisions are shorter term, more specific, recurring, have more certain outcomes, and have a lesser impact on the firm than strategic decisions. For example, assume that the president of a manufacturing firm makes the strategic decision to increase sales and production by 100,000 units over the prior year's level. One tactical decision that must result from this is setting the monthly production schedule to accomplish the strategic goal.

Management Control Decisions

Management control involves motivating managers in all functional areas to use resources, including materials, personnel, and financial assets, as productively as possible. The supervising manager compares the performance of his or her subordinate manager to preestablished standards. If the subordinate does not meet the standard, the supervisor must take corrective action. When the subordinate meets or exceeds expectations, he or she may be rewarded.

Uncertainty surrounds **management control decisions** because it is difficult to separate the manager's performance from that of his or her operational unit. We often lack both the criteria for specifying management control standards and the objective techniques for measuring performance. For example, assume that a firm's top management places its most effective and competent middle manager in charge of a business segment that is performing poorly. The manager's task is to revitalize the operations of the unit, and doing so requires a massive infusion of resources. The segment will operate in the red for some time until it establishes a foothold in the market. Measuring the performance of this manager in the short term may be difficult. Traditional measures of profit, such as return on investment (which measures the performance of the operational unit itself), would not really measure the manager's performance. We shall examine this topic in more depth later in the chapter.

Operational Control Decisions

Operational control ensures that the firm operates in accordance with preestablished criteria. Figure 8–13 shows that operations managers exercise operational control. **Operational control decisions** are narrower and more focused than strategic and tactical decisions because they are concerned with the routine tasks of operations. Operational control decisions are more structured than management control decisions, more dependent on details than planning decisions, and have a shorter time frame than tactical or strategic decisions. These decisions are associated with a fairly high degree of certainty. In other words, the identified symptoms are good indicators of the root problem, and corrective actions tend to be obvious. This degree of certainty makes it easier to establish meaningful criteria for measuring performance. Operational control decisions have three basic elements: setting standards, evaluating performance, and taking corrective action.

Standards. Standards are preestablished levels of performance that managers believe are attainable. Standards apply to all aspects of operations, including sales volume, quality control over production, costs for inventory items, material usage in the production of products, and labor costs in production. Once established, these standards become the basis for evaluating performance.

Performance Evaluation. The decision maker compares the performance of the operation in question against the standard. The difference between the two is the **variance**. For example, a price variance for an item of inventory is the difference between the expected price—the standard—and the price actually paid. If the actual price is greater than the standard, the variance is said to be unfavorable. If the actual price is less than the standard, the variance is favorable.

Taking Corrective Action. After comparing the performance to the standard, the manager takes action to remedy any out-of-control condition. However, recall from Chapter 3 that we must apply extreme caution when taking corrective action. An inappropriate response to performance measures may have undesirable results. For example, to achieve a favorable price variance, the purchasing agent may pursue the low-price vendors of raw materials and sacrifice quality. If the lower quality raw materials result in excessive quantities going into production, the firm will experience an unfavorable material usage variance. The unfavorable usage variance may completely offset the favorable price variance and produce an unfavorable total variance.

Table 8–2 classifies strategic planning, tactical planning, management control, and operational control decisions in terms of time frame, scope, level of details, recurrence, and certainty.

| TABLE 8–2 | Classification of Decision Types by Decision Characteristics |

DECISION CHARACTERISTIC	DECISION TYPE			
	Strategic Planning	Tactical Planning	Management Control	Operational Control
Time frame	Long term	Medium	Medium	Short
Scope	High impact	Medium impact	Lower impact	Lowest impact
Level details	Highly summarized	Detailed	Moderately summarized	Highly detailed
Recurrence	Nonrecurring	Periodic recurring	Periodic recurring	Frequent recurring
Certainty	Uncertain	Highly certain	Uncertain	Highly certain

PROBLEM STRUCTURE

The structure of a problem reflects how well the decision maker understands the problem. Structure has three elements.[2]

1. Data—the values used to represent factors that are relevant to the problem.
2. Procedures—the sequence of steps or decision rules used in solving the problem.
3. Objectives—the results the decision maker desires to attain by solving the problem.

When all three elements are known with certainty, the problem is structured. Payroll calculation is an example of a **structured problem**:

1. We can identify the data for this calculation with certainty (hours worked, hourly rate, withholdings, tax rate, and so on).
2. Payroll procedures are known with certainty:

$$\text{Gross pay} = \text{Hours worked} \times \text{Pay rate}$$
$$\text{Net pay} = \text{Gross pay} - \text{Taxes} - \text{Withholdings}$$

3. The objective of payroll is to discharge the firm's financial obligation to its employees.

Structured problems do not present unique situations to the decision maker and, because their information requirements can be anticipated, they are well suited to traditional data processing techniques. In effect, the analyst who designs the procedures and programs for the system solves the problem.

---

2 Adapted from F. L. Luconi, T. W. Malone, and M. S. Scott Morton, "Expert Systems: The Next Challenge for Managers," *Sloan Management Review* (Summer 1986). Reprinted in P. Gray, W. R. King, E. R. McLean, and H. J. Watson, *MOIS: Management of Information Systems* (Chicago: Dryden Press, 1989): 69–84.

Unstructured Problems

Problems are unstructured when any of the three characteristics identified previously are not known with certainty. In other words, an **unstructured problem** is one for which we have no precise solution techniques. Either the data requirements are uncertain, the procedures are not specified, or the solution objectives have not been fully developed. Such a problem is normally complex and engages the decision maker in a unique situation. In these situations, the systems analyst cannot fully anticipate user information needs, rendering traditional data processing techniques ineffective.

Figure 8–14 illustrates the relationship between problem structure and organizational level. We see from the figure that lower levels of management deal more with fully structured problems, while upper management deals with unstructured problems. Middle-level managers tend to work with partially structured problems. Keep in mind that these structural classifications are generalizations. Top managers also deal with some highly structured problems, and lower-level managers sometimes face problems that lack structure.

Figure 8–14 also shows the use of information systems by different levels of management. The traditional information system deals most effectively with fully structured problems. Therefore, operations management and tactical management receive the greatest benefit from these systems. Because management control and strategic planning decisions lack structure, the managers who make these decisions do not receive adequate support from traditional systems alone.

TYPES OF MANAGEMENT REPORTS

Reports are the formal vehicles for conveying information to managers. The term *report* tends to imply a written message presented on sheets of paper. In fact, a **management report** may take any physical form the user desires or needs. It could be a paper document or an electronic image displayed on a computer terminal. The report may express information in verbal, numeric, or graphic form, or any combination of these.

FIGURE 8–14

Problem Structure Management Level and Information System Usage

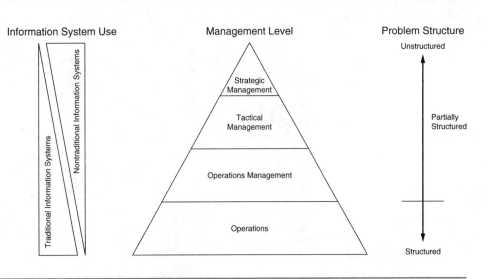

Report Objectives

Chapter 1 made the distinction between information and data. Recall that information leads the user to an action. Therefore, to be useful, reports must have **information content**. Their value is the effect they have on users. This is expressed in two general reporting objectives: (1) to reduce the level of uncertainty associated with a problem facing the decision maker and (2) to influence the behavior of the decision maker in a positive way. Reports that fail to accomplish these objectives lack information content and have no value. In fact, reliance on such reports may lead to dysfunctional behavior. Later in the chapter, we examine causes of dysfunctional behavior. Management reports fall into two broad classes: programmed reports and ad hoc reports.

Programmed Reporting

Programmed reports provide information to solve problems that users have anticipated. There are two subclasses of programmed reports: scheduled reports and on-demand reports. The management reporting system produces **scheduled reports** according to an established time frame. This could be daily, weekly, quarterly, and so on. Examples of such reports are a daily listing of sales, a weekly payroll action report, and annual financial statements. **On-demand reports** are triggered by events, not by the passage of time. For example, when inventories fall to their preestablished reorder points, the system sends an inventory reorder report to the purchasing agent. Another example is an accounts receivable manager responding to a customer problem over the telephone. The manager can, on demand (at the push of a computer key), display the customer's account history on the computer screen. Note that this query capability is the product of an anticipated need. This is quite different from the ad hoc reports that we discuss next. Table 8–3 lists examples of typical programmed reports and identifies them as scheduled or on-demand.

TABLE 8–3	Examples of Programmed Reports	
Type of Report	**Scheduled**	**On-Demand**
Planning Reports:		
Financial budgets	X	
Materials requirements reports		X
Sales forecast reports	X	
Production schedules		X
Projected cash flows reports	X	
Control Reports:		
Cost center reports	X	
Profit center reports	X	
Profitability by line of product	X	
Quality control reports		X
Labor distribution reports	X	
Inventory exception reports		X
Equipment utilization reports	X	

Report Attributes

To be effective, a report must possess the following attributes: relevance, summarization, exception orientation, accuracy, completeness, timeliness, and conciseness. Each of these **report attributes** is discussed below.

Relevance. Each element of information in a report must support the manager's decision. Irrelevancies waste resources and may even be dysfunctional by distracting a manager's attention from the information content of the report.

Summarization. Reports should be summarized according to the level of the manager within the organizational hierarchy. In general, the degree of summarization becomes greater as information flows from lower management upward to top management.

Exception Orientation. Control reports should identify activities that are at risk of going out of control and should ignore activities that are under control. For example, consider a purchasing agent with ordering responsibility for an inventory of 10,000 different items. If the agent received a daily report containing the actual balances of every item, he or she would search through 10,000 items to identify a few that need reordering. This would be a time-consuming and error-prone task. An exception-oriented report would identify only those inventory items that have fallen to their reorder levels. From this report, the agent could easily prepare purchase orders.

Accuracy. Information in reports must be free of material errors. A material error will cause the user to make the wrong decision (or fail to make a required decision). We often sacrifice accuracy for timely information. In situations that require very quick responses, the manager must factor this trade-off into the decision-making process.

Completeness. Information must be as complete as possible. Ideally, no piece of information that is essential to the decision should be missing from the report. Like the attribute of accuracy, we sometimes must sacrifice completeness in favor of timely information.

Timeliness. If managers always had time on their side, they may never make bad decisions. However, managers cannot always wait until they have all the facts before they act. Timely information that is sufficiently complete and accurate is more valuable than perfect information that comes too late to use. Therefore, the MRS must provide managers with timely information. Usually, information can be no older than the period to which it pertains. For example, if each week a manager decides on inventory acquisitions based on a weekly inventory status report, the information in the report should be no more than a week old.

Conciseness. Information in the report should be presented as concisely as possible. Reports should use coding schemes to represent complex data classifications and provide all the necessary calculations (such as extensions and variances) for the user. In addition, information should be clearly presented with titles for all values.

Ad Hoc Reporting

Managers cannot always anticipate their information needs. This is particularly true for top and middle management. In the dynamic business world, problems arise that require new information on short notice and there may be insufficient time to write traditional computer programs to produce the required information. In the past, these needs often went unsatisfied. However, advances in database technology have made direct inquiry and report generation capabilities widely available to users. Managers with limited computer background can quickly produce **ad hoc reports** from a terminal or microcomputer, without the assistance of data processing professionals.

Increases in computing power, point-of-transaction scanners, and continuous reductions in data storage costs over the past two decades have enabled organizations to accumulate massive quantities of raw data. Management recognizes that information is at the heart of business operations and that they can make use of stored data to gain valuable insight into their business. This data resource is now being tapped to support ad hoc reporting needs through a concept known as *data mining*.

Data mining is the process of selecting, exploring, and modeling large amounts of data to uncover relationships and global patterns that exist in large databases but are "hidden" among the vast amount of facts. This involves sophisticated techniques such as *database queries* and *artificial intelligence* that model real-world phenomena from data collected from a variety of sources, including transaction processing systems, customer history databases, and demographics data from external sources such as credit bureaus. Managers employ two general approaches to data mining: *verification* and *discovery*.

The **verification model** uses a drill-down technique to either verify or reject a user's hypothesis. For example, assume a marketing manager needs to identify the best target market, as a subset of the organization's entire customer base, for an ad campaign for a new product. The data mining software will examine historical data about the firm's customer purchase and demographic information to reveal comparable purchases and the demographic characteristics shared by those purchasers. This subset of the customer base can then be used to focus the promotion campaign.

The **discovery model** uses data mining to discover previously unknown but important information that is hidden within the data. This model employs inductive learning to infer information from detailed data by searching for recurring patterns, trends, and generalizations. This approach is fundamentally different from the verification model in that the data are searched with no specific hypothesis driving the process. For example, a company may apply discovery techniques to identify customer-buying patterns and gain a better understanding of customer motivations and behavior.

A central feature of a successful data mining initiative is a **data warehouse** of archived operational data. A data warehouse is a relational database management system that has been designed specifically to meet the needs of data mining. The warehouse is a central location that contains operational data about current events (within the past 24 hours) as well as events that have transpired over many years. Data are coded and stored in the warehouse in detail and at various degrees of aggregation to facilitate identification of recurring patterns and trends.

Management decision making can be greatly enhanced through data mining, but only if the appropriate data have been identified, collected, and stored in the data warehouse. Since many of the important issues related to data mining and warehousing require an understanding of relational database technology, these topics are examined further in the next chapter.

RESPONSIBILITY
ACCOUNTING

A large part of management reporting involves **responsibility accounting**. This concept implies that every economic event that affects the organization is the responsibility of and can be traced to an individual manager. The responsibility accounting system personalizes performance by saying to the manager, "This is your original budget and this is how your performance for the period compares to your budget." Most organizations structure their responsibility reporting system around areas of responsibility in the firm. A fundamental principle of this concept is that responsibility-area managers are accountable only for items (costs, revenues, and investments) that they control.

The flow of information in responsibility systems is both downward and upward through the information channels. Figure 8–15 illustrates this pattern. These top-down and bottom-up information flows represent the two phases of responsibility accounting: (1) creating a set of financial performance goals (budgets) pertinent to the manager's responsibilities and (2) reporting and measuring actual performance as compared to these goals.

Setting Financial Goals: The Budget Process

The **budget** process helps management achieve its financial objectives by establishing measurable goals for each organizational segment. This mechanism conveys to the segment managers the standards that senior managers will use for measuring their performance. Budget information flows downward and becomes increasingly detailed as it moves to lower levels of management. Figure 8–16 shows the distribution of budget information through three levels of management.

Measuring and Reporting Performance

Performance measurement and reporting take place at each operational segment in the firm. This information flows upward as **responsibility reports** to senior levels of management. Figure 8–17 shows the relationship between levels of responsibility

FIGURE 8–15

Upward and
Downward Flow
of Information

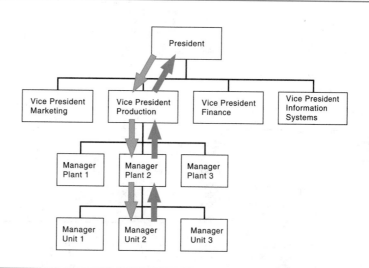

FIGURE 8–16

Top-Down Flow of
Budget Information

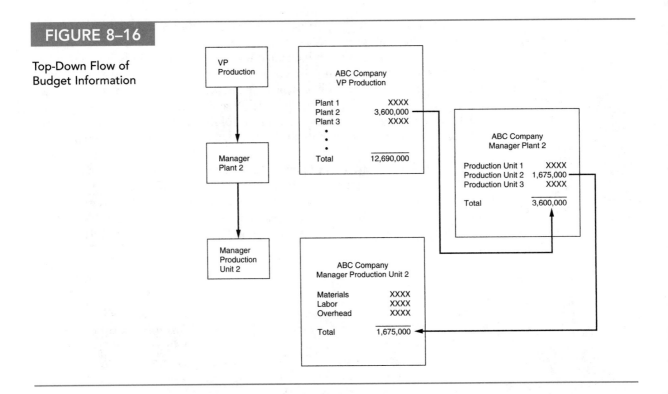

FIGURE 8–17

The Bottom-Up Flow of Performance Information

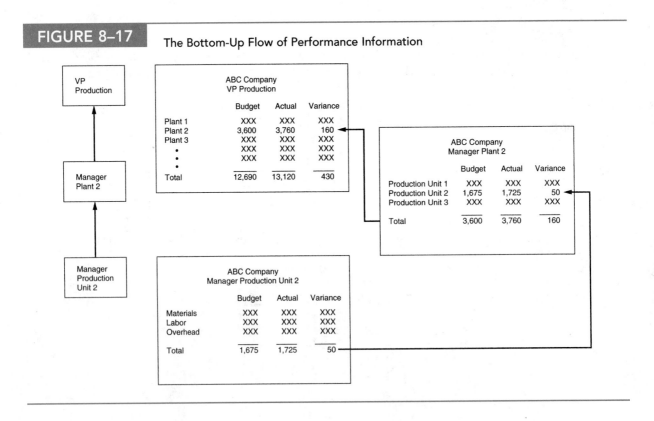

reports. Notice how the information in the reports becomes increasingly summarized at each higher level of management.

Responsibility Centers

To achieve accountability, business entities frequently organize their operations into units called **responsibility centers**. The most common forms of responsibility centers are cost centers, profit centers, and investment centers.

Cost Centers. A **cost center** is an organizational unit with responsibility for cost management within budgetary limits. For example, a production department may be responsible for meeting its production obligation while keeping production costs (labor, materials, and overhead) within the budgeted amount. The performance report for the cost center manager reflects its controllable cost behavior by focusing on budgeted costs, actual costs, and variances from budget. Figure 8–18 gives an example of a cost center performance report. Performance measurements should not consider costs that are outside of the manager's control, such as investments in plant equipment or depreciation on the building.

Profit Centers. A **profit center** manager has responsibility for both cost control and revenue generation. For example, the local manager of a national department store chain may be responsible for decisions about:

- Which items of merchandise to stock in the store.
- What prices to charge.
- The kind of promotional activities for products.

FIGURE 8–18

Cost Center
Performance
Report

	PLANT UNIT 2 CONTROLLABLE COST REPORT		
PLANTWIDE CONTROLLABLE COSTS			
	Budget	Actual	Variance
Materials			
Drilling Dept.	XXX	XXX	XX
Milling Dept.	XXX	XXX	XX
Assembly Ship	XXX	XXX	XX
Direct Labor			
Drilling Dept.	XXX	XXX	XX
Milling Dept.	XXX	XXX	XX
Assembly Ship	XXX	XXX	XX
Controllable Overhead			
Drilling Dept.	XXX	XXX	XX
Milling Dept.	XXX	XXX	XX
Assembly Ship	XXX	XXX	XX
Total Controllable Costs	XXXXX	XXXXX	XXX

- The level of advertising.
- The size of the staff and the hiring of employees.
- Building maintenance and limited capital improvements.

The performance report for the profit center manager is different from that of the cost center. However, the reporting emphasis for both should be on controllable items. Figure 8–19 is an example of a profit center report. While only controllable items are used to assess the manager's performance, the profit center itself is assessed by its contribution after noncontrollable costs.

Investment Centers.   The manager of an **investment center** has the general authority to make decisions that profoundly affect the organization. Assume that a division of a corporation is an investment center with the objective of maximizing the return on its investment assets. The division manager's range of responsibilities include cost management, product development, marketing, distribution, and capital disposition through investments of funds in projects and ventures that earn a desired rate of return. Figure 8–20 illustrates the performance report for an investment center.

BEHAVIORAL
CONSIDERATIONS

Goal Congruence

Earlier in this chapter, we touched on the management principles of authority, responsibility, and the formalization of tasks. When properly applied within an organization, these principles promote **goal congruence**. Lower-level managers pursuing their own objectives contribute in a positive way to the objectives of their superiors. For example, by controlling costs, a production supervisor contributes to the division

---

FIGURE 8–19

Profit Center
Performance
Report

XYZ COMPANY PROFIT STATEMENT			
Sales		XXX	
Less:			
Cost of goods sold	XXX		
Gross profit		XXX	
Less controllable costs:		XXX	
Controllable overhead	XXX		
Controllable operating expenses	XXX		
Controllable operating profit		XXX	(Measure of management performance)
Depreciation on noncontrollable fixed assets	XXX		
Contribution after noncontrollable costs		XXX	(Measure of profit center performance)

FIGURE 8–20

Investment Center
Performance
Report

XYZ COMPANY DIVISION INCOME STATEMENT			
Sales		XXX	
Less:			
Cost of goods sold	XXX		
Gross profit		XXX	
Less controllable costs:		XXX	
Controllable overhead	XXX		
Depreciation on noncontrollable			
fixed assets	XXX		
Controllable operating profit		XXX	(Measure of management performance)
Less noncontrollable costs:			
Divisional overhead	XXX		
Allocated centralized charges	XXX		
Net income before taxes		XXX	(Measure of investment center performance)

manager's goal of profitability. Thus, as individual managers serve their best interests, they also serve the best interests of the organization.

A carefully structured management reporting system plays an important role in promoting and preserving goal congruence. On the other hand, a badly designed MRS can cause dysfunctional actions that are in opposition to the organization's objectives. Two pitfalls that cause managers to act dysfunctionally are information overload and inappropriate performance measures.

Information Overload

Information overload occurs when a manager receives more information than he or she can assimilate. This happens when designers of the reporting system do not properly consider the manager's organizational level and span of control. For example, consider the information volume that would flow to the president if the reports were not properly summarized (refer to Figure 8–15). The details required by lower-level managers would quickly overload the president's decision-making process. Although the report may have many of the information attributes discussed earlier (complete, accurate, timely, and concise), it is useless if not properly summarized.

Information overload causes managers to disregard their formal information and rely on informal cues to help them make decisions. Thus, the formal information system is replaced by heuristics (rules of thumb), tips, hunches, and guesses. The resulting decisions run a high risk of being suboptimal and dysfunctional.

Inappropriate Performance Measures

Recall that one purpose of a report is to stimulate behavior consistent with the objectives of the firm. When **inappropriate performance measures** are used, however, the report can have the opposite effect. Let's see how this can happen using a common performance measure—return on investment (ROI).

Assume that the corporate management of an organization evaluates division management performance solely on the basis of ROI. Each manager's objective is to maximize ROI. Naturally, the organization wants this to happen through prudent cost management and increased profit margins. However, when ROI is used as the single criterion for measuring performance, the criterion itself becomes the focus of attention and object of manipulation. We illustrate this point with the multiperiod investment center report in Figure 8–21. Notice how ROI went up in the second and third years. On the surface, this looks like favorable performance. However, a closer analysis of the cost and revenue figures gives a different picture. Actual sales were below budgeted sales for 2001, but the shortfall in revenue was offset by reductions in discretionary operating expenditures (employee training and plant maintenance). The ROI figure is further improved by reducing investments in inventory and plant equipment to lower the asset base.

The manager took actions that increased ROI but were dysfunctional to the organization. Usually, such tactics can succeed in the short run only. As the plant equipment starts to wear out, customer dissatisfaction increases (because of stockouts) and employee dissent becomes epidemic. The ROI figure will then begin to reflect the economic reality. However, by that time the manager may have been promoted based on the perception of good performance, and the successor will inherit the problems left behind.

FIGURE 8–21

Multiperiod
Investment
Center Report

YEAR	ACTUAL			BUDGET
	1999	2000	2001	2001
Sales	1,780.0	2,670.0	3,204.0	3,560.0
Less segment variable costs:				
Materials	445.0	667.5	801.0	890.0
Labor	89.0	133.5	89.0	178.0
Supplies	35.6	53.4	64.1	71.2
Less discretionary costs				
employee training	53.4	62.3	44.5	71.2
Maintenance	89.0	97.9	71.2	106.8
Less segment committed costs:				
Depreciation	213.6	284.8	284.8	356.0
Rent	142.4	178.0	195.8	249.2
Total cost	1,068.0	1,477.4	1,550.4	1,922.4
Contribution	712.0	1,192.6	1,653.6	1,637.6
Investment in assets				
Accounts receivable	178.0	267.0	320.4	356.0
Inventory	356.0	534.0	480.6	712.0
Fixed assets	2,830.2	4,565.7	4,984.0	6,016.4
Less accounts payable	(267.0)	(400.5)	(623.0)	(534.0)
Net investment	3,097.2	4,966.2	5,162.0	6,550.4
Return on investment	23%	24%	32%	25%

The use of any single criterion as a performance measure can lead to dysfunctional behavior. Consider the following examples:

1. The use of price variance to evaluate a purchasing agent can affect the quality of the items purchased.
2. The use of quotas (such as units produced) to evaluate a supervisor can affect quality control, material usage efficiency, labor relations, and plant maintenance.
3. The use of profit measures such as ROI, net income, and contribution margin can affect plant investment, employee training, inventory reserve levels, customer satisfaction, and labor relations.

Effective performance measures consider all relevant aspects of a manager's responsibility. In addition to measures of general performance (such as ROI), management should measure trends in key variables such as sales, cost of goods sold, operating expenses, and asset levels. There are also nonfinancial measures that serve as indicators of management performance, including product leadership, personnel development, employee attitudes, and public responsibility. The use of a single criterion can impose personal goals on managers that conflict with organizational goals and result in dysfunctional behavior.

Summary

This chapter began by examining the general ledger system and the financial reporting system, two operationally interdependent systems that are vital to the economic activities of the organization. We first learned the importance of data coding schemes and their role in the GLS and TPS as a means of coordinating and managing a firm's transactions. In examining the major types of numeric and alphabetic coding schemes, we saw how each has certain advantages and disadvantages. We then turned to a more direct examination of the GLS, focusing on the files that typically make up a GLS database and on standard GLS procedures. Turning to the FRS, we then examined how financial information is provided to both external and internal users. A step-by-step outline of the financial reporting process was presented.

Next, the GLS and the FRS were examined as a single, integrated physical system (GL/FRS). Our principle focus here was on the standard operational controls that govern this system and on the use of computer technology for improved efficiency in reporting and record keeping.

This chapter then examined discretionary information systems. Discretionary systems are not subject to the professional guidelines and legal statutes that govern the design, operation, and control of nondiscretionary systems. Specifically, the chapter examined discretionary systems that constitute the management reporting system. The information needs of managers are influenced by several factors, including the decision-making process, management principles, management level and decision type, problem structure, types of management reports, responsibility accounting, and behavioral considerations. The chapter investigated the impact of each factor on the design of the MRS. A large part of the management reporting system is based on the idea of responsibility accounting. Under this concept, information flows in two directions. Budget information flows downward to responsibility centers, and performance information flows up from these centers to senior levels of management.

The chapter concluded with a discussion of the causes of dysfunctional behavior. The purpose of a reporting system is to influence behavior. However, a poorly designed system can have a negative or dysfunctional influence on the user. Designers of MRSs must recognize the potential consequences of information overload and the use of inappropriate performance measures.

Key Terms

ad hoc reports   (426)
alphabetic codes   (398)
alphanumeric codes   (398)
authority   (416)
block code   (396)
budget   (427)
budget master file   (401)
chart of accounts   (396)
computer-based GL/FRS   (408)
cost center   (429)
daily procedures   (403)
data mining   (426)
data warehouse   (426)
decision criteria   (413)
decision-making process   (412)
discovery model   (426)
financial accounting process   (403)
financial reporting procedures   (405)
general ledger change report   (407)
general ledger history file   (400)
general ledger master file   (400)
goal congruence   (430)
group codes   (397)
implementation   (414)
inappropriate performance measures   (431)
information content   (424)
information overload   (431)
internal efficiency   (410)
investment center   (430)

journal voucher history file   (401)
journal voucher listing   (407)
management by exception   (418)
management control decisions   (420)
management report   (423)
mnemonic codes   (399)
on-demand reports   (424)
operational control decisions   (421)
organizational chart   (416)
period-end procedures   (405)
post-implementation review   (415)
profit center   (429)
programmed reports   (424)
report attributes   (425)
responsibility   (416)
responsibility accounting   (427)
responsibility center file   (401)
responsibility centers   (429)
responsibility reports   (427)
scheduled reports   (424)
sequential codes   (396)
sophisticated users   (402)
span of control   (417)
strategic planning decisions   (419)
structured problem   (422)
tactical planning decisions   (420)
unstructured problem   (423)
variance   (421)
verification model   (426)

Review Questions

1. What are some of the more common uses of data codes in AIS?
2. Compare and contrast the relative advantages and disadvantages of sequential, block, group, alphabetic, and mnemonic codes.
3. What information is contained in a journal voucher?
4. How are journal vouchers used as a control mechanism?

5. What information is contained in the general ledger master file?
6. What is the purpose of the general ledger history file?
7. What is the purpose of a responsibility center file?
8. List the primary users of the FRS and discuss their information needs.
9. What are the eleven steps, in order, of the financial accounting process?

10. What assumption is made regarding the external users of financial statements?
11. When are adjusting entries made to the worksheet and what is their purpose? When are the corresponding voucher entries made?
12. What are the three distinct phases of the financial accounting process? How often are each of these performed?
13. What are the purposes of an audit trail? What is meant by a defective audit trail? How can a defective audit trail be prevented?
14. What tasks should the general ledger clerk not be allowed to do?
15. What are two operational reports produced by the GL/FRS that provide proof to the accuracy of the process?
16. Explain which of the four potential exposures in the GLS may be controlled better by a close examination of the journal voucher listing.
17. What are the steps involved in a rational decision-making process?
18. Distinguish between a symptom and a problem. How would you categorize a decline in the market price of an organization's publicly traded stock?
19. Distinguish between tangible and intangible decision criteria. Discuss their relative importance and the techniques used to measure them.
20. List some of the tasks involved in the implementation phase of the decision-making process.
21. What is the purpose of a post-implementation review?
22. Explain how the formalization of tasks promotes internal control.
23. Explain why it is important that both responsibility and authority are appropriately assigned to employees.
24. Distinguish between narrow and wide span of control. Give an example of tasks appropriate to each type.
25. How does management by exception help to alleviate information overload by a manager?

26. Identify instances for which feedback becomes useless in helping to control activities.
27. Contrast the four decision types—strategic planning, tactical planning, management control, and operational control—by the five decision characteristics—time frame, scope, level of details, recurrence, and certainty.
28. What are the three elements that distinguish structured and unstructured problems? Give an example of each type of problem. Which type of problem is more suitable to a transaction processing system?
29. What management levels are more likely to deal with unstructured problems? With structured problems? Why?
30. What are two objectives that enable reports to be considered useful?
31. List and define the seven report attributes.
32. What is responsibility accounting?
33. What are the two phases of responsibility accounting?
34. What are the three most common forms of responsibility centers?
35. What is goal congruence?
36. What is data mining?
37. What is a data warehouse?
38. What is information overload?
39. Explain some characteristics of reports that may cause dysfunctional behavior by a manager.
40. Explain how ad hoc reports have allowed managers to make more timely and better-quality decisions. Give an example.
41. Explain how exception reporting would be invaluable to the manager of a credit department.
42. What types of variances are found on cost center reports? Explain what each variance is measuring and why this information is important.
43. Distinguish between a profit center and an investment center. Draw a diagram illustrating the relationship between cost, profit, and investment centers.

Discussion Questions

1. Discuss some of the problems associated with general ledger systems that do not have data coding schemes.
2. For each of the following items, indicate whether a sequential, block, group, alphabetic, or mnemonic code would be most appropriate (you may

list multiple methods; give an example and explain why each method is appropriate):
   a. state codes
   b. check number
   c. chart of accounts
   d. inventory item number
   e. bin number (inventory warehouse location)
   f. sales order number
   g. vendor code
   h. invoice number
   i. customer number
3. Discuss any separation of duties necessary to control against unauthorized entries to the general ledger. What other control procedures regarding the general ledger should be employed?
4. Discuss the various sources of data for the FRS output and how this data is processed into information (output) for the different external users.
5. Explain how erroneous journal vouchers may lead to litigation and significant financial losses for a firm.
6. Is the potential for the general ledger accounts being out of balance with subsidiary accounts increased or decreased as a result of converting from a manual general ledger system to a computerized general ledger system? Why?
7. Ultimately, is the purpose of an audit trail to follow a transaction from its input through its processing and finally to the financial statements or vice-versa? Explain your answer.
8. When converting from a manual-based GLS to a computer-based batch processing system, do labor requirements increase or decrease? Explain your answer by discussing specific tasks.
9. Discuss the benefits that may be realized in switching from a computerized batch processing system to a direct access storage system. Also, discuss any additional control implications.
10. In Figure 8–10, what files would probably be included in the category of "other files"?
11. Discuss the following statement made by a manager's boss during the implementation phase of a project: "These cost overruns and inadequacies in the new system you developed are a result of rushing to implement a solution. Not enough time was spent identifying the problem or generating and evaluating alternatives!"
12. Why should post-implementation reviews NOT be conducted immediately following implementation?

13. Controls are only as good as the predetermined standard on which they are based. Discuss the preceding comment and give an example.
14. If management control and strategic planning decisions do not receive a high level of support from traditional information systems, then where does the support come from?
15. In terms of decision-making capabilities, which type of report do you think is generally more important—scheduled reports or on-demand reports? Explain your answer and give an example of each type of report.
16. Scheduled reports may contain some information that is relevant to some decisions and irrelevant to other decisions. Why are some scheduled reports designed this way, rather than multiple reports being generated for various decision-making purposes?
17. Sometimes a trade-off must be made between information accuracy and timeliness. Give an example where it is imperative to make an estimate now, rather than wait a couple of weeks for an exact number.
18. Figure 8–15 illustrates both upward and downward flows of information. What are the downward flows and their purpose? What about the upward flows? Are the downward and upward flows related?
19. Distinguish between the verification model and the discovery model approaches to data mining.
20. Explain how a data warehouse database is fundamentally different from a transaction processing database.
21. Why are cost centers considered to be more appropriate than profit centers for production departments?
22. Explain how a production quota used to evaluate a supervisor can adversely affect quality control, material usage efficiency, and labor relations.
23. Explain and give an example as to how a manager can manipulate the return on investment figure in the short run. Why are these manipulations bad for the company in the long run? Suggest some alternative performance evaluation and compensation schemes.
24. Comment on the following statement: "More information is always preferred to less; you can never have too much information."

Multiple-Choice Questions

1. CIA 586 III-39
   Sequential access means that
   a. data are stored on magnetic tape.
   b. the address of the location of data is found through the use of either an algorithm or an index.
   c. each record can be accessed in the same amount of time.
   d. to read record 500, records 1 through 499 must be read first.

2. A chart of accounts would best be coded using a(n) _____ coding scheme.
   a. alphabetic
   b. mnemonic
   c. block
   d. sequential

3. Which of the following statements is NOT true?
   a. Sorting records that are coded alphabetically tends to be more difficult for users than sorting numeric sequences.
   b. Mnemonic coding requires the user to memorize codes.
   c. Sequential codes carry no information content beyond their order in the sequence.
   d. Mnemonic codes are limited in their ability to represent items within a class.

4. Which file has as its primary purpose to present comparative financial reports on a historic basis?
   a. journal voucher history file
   b. budget master file
   c. responsibility file
   d. general ledger history file

5. Which of the following statements is true?
   a. Journal vouchers, detailing transaction activity, flow from various operational departments into the GLS, where they are independently reconciled and posted to the journal voucher history file.
   b. Journal vouchers, summarizing transaction activity, flow from the accounting department into the GLS, where they are independently reconciled and posted to the general ledger accounts.
   c. Journal vouchers, summarizing transaction activity, flow from various operational departments into the GLS, where they are independently reconciled and posted to the general ledger accounts.

   d. Journal vouchers, summarizing transaction activity, flow from various operational departments into the GLS, where they are independently reconciled and posted to the journal voucher history file.

6. Which of the following statements best describes a computer-based GL/FRS?
   a. Most firms derive little additional benefit from a real-time FRS.
   b. Batch processing is typically not appropriate for transaction processing of GLS.
   c. The sequential file approach is an inefficient use of technology.
   d. A batch system with direct access files recreates the entire database each time the file is updated.

7. A coding scheme in the form of acronyms and other combinations that convey meaning is a(n)
   a. sequential code.
   b. block code.
   c. alphabetic code.
   d. mnemonic code.

8. Which of the following is NOT a potential exposure of the GL/FRS?
   a. a defective audit trail
   b. general ledger accounts that are out of balance with subsidiary accounts
   c. unauthorized access to the check register
   d. unauthorized access to the general ledger

9. Which task should the general ledger perform?
   a. update the general ledger
   b. prepare journal vouchers
   c. have custody of physical assets
   d. have record keeping responsibility for special journals of subledgers

10. CMA 689 4-25
    Hersh Company uses a performance reporting system that reflects the company's decentralization of decision making. The departmental performance report shows one line of data for each subordinate who reports to the group vice president. The data presented show the actual costs incurred during the period, the budgeted costs, and all variances from budget for that subordinate's department. Hersh Company is using a type of system called
    a. contribution accounting.
    b. cost-benefit accounting.

    c. flexible budgeting.

    d. program budgeting.

    e. responsibility accounting.

11. CMA 1290 3-16

    All of the following are characteristics of the strategic planning process except the

    a. emphasis on both the short and long run.

    b. analysis and review of departmental process.

    c. review of the attributes and behavior of the organization's competition.

    d. analysis of external economic factors.

    e. analysis of consumer demand.

12. CMA 691 3-5

    Kallert Manufacturing uses budgets only as a planning tool. Management has decided that it would be beneficial to also use budgets for control purposes. To implement this change, the management accountant must

    a. appoint a budget director.

    b. organize a budget committee.

    c. develop forecasting procedures.

    d. report daily to operating management any deviations from plan.

    e. synchronize the budgeting and accounting system with the organizational structure.

13. CMA 691 3-6

    The budgeting process should be one that motivates managers and employees to work toward organizational goals. Which of the following is least likely to motivate managers?

    a. setting budget targets at attainable levels

    b. participation by subordinates in the budgetary process

    c. use of management by exception

    d. holding subordinates accountable for the items they control

    e. having top management set budget levels

14. CMA 691 3-10

    Wong Company uses both strategic planning and operational budgeting. Which of the following items would normally be considered in a strategic plan?

    a. setting a target of 12 percent return on sales

    b. maintaining the image of the company as the industry leader

    c. setting a market price per share of stock outstanding

    d. distributing monthly reports for departmental variance analysis

    e. tightening credit terms for customers to 2/10, n/30

15. CMA 691 3-13

    Long-range planning as a management function is more important

    a. at top management levels.

    b. at middle management levels.

    c. at lower management levels.

    d. for staff functions than line functions.

    e. for line functions than staff functions.

16. CMA 691 3-28

    The basic purpose of a responsibility accounting system is

    a. budgeting.

    b. motivation.

    c. authority.

    d. variance analysis.

    e. pricing.

17. CMA 1291 3-8

    A segment of an organization is referred to as a profit center if it has

    a. authority to make decisions affecting the major determinants of profit, including the power to choose its markets and sources of supply.

    b. authority to make decisions affecting the major determinants of profit, including the power to choose its markets and sources of supply, and significant control over the amount of invested capital.

    c. authority to make decisions over the most significant costs of operations, including the power to choose the sources of supply.

    d. authority to provide specialized support to other units within the organization.

    e. responsibility for combining the raw materials, direct labor, and other factors of production into a final product.

18. CMA 1291 3-9

    A segment of an organization is referred to as an investment center if it has

    a. authority to make decisions affecting the major determinants of profit, including the power to choose its markets and sources of supply.

    b. authority to make decisions affecting the major determinants of profit, including the power to choose its markets and sources of supply, and significant control over the amount of invested capital.

    c. authority to make decisions over the most significant costs of operations, including the power to choose the sources of supply.

d. authority to provide specialized support to other units within the organization.

e. responsibility for developing markets for and selling of the output of the organization.

Problems

1. General Ledger System Overview

Draw a diagram depicting the relationship between the general ledger master file, control accounts, subsidiary files, and financial statements.

2. Financial Accounting Process

The following contains the various steps of the financial accounting process. Place these steps in the proper order and indicate whether each step is a function of the TPS, GLS, or FRS.

*   Record transaction in special journal
*   Make adjusting entries
*   Capture the transaction
*   Prepare the post-closing trial balance
*   Prepare the adjusted trial balance
*   Prepare the financial statements
*   Journalize and post the adjusting entries
*   Post to the subsidiary ledger
*   Post to the general ledger
*   Journalize and post the closing entries
*   Prepare the unadjusted trial balance

3. Coding Scheme

Devise a coding scheme using block and sequential codes for the following chart of accounts for Jensen Camera Distributors.

Cash
Accounts receivable
Office supplies inventory
Prepaid insurance
Inventory
Investments in marketable securities
Delivery truck
Accumulated depreciation—delivery truck
Equipment
Accumulated depreciation—equipment
Furniture and fixtures
Accumulated depreciation—furniture and fixtures
Building
Accumulated depreciation—building
Land
Accounts payable
Wages payable
Taxes payable
Notes payable
Bonds payable
Common stock
Paid-in capital in excess of par
Treasury stock
Retained earnings
Sales
Sales returns and allowances
Dividend income
Cost of goods sold
Wages expense
Utility expense
Office supplies expense
Insurance expense
Depreciation expense
Advertising expense
Fuel expense
Interest expense

4. Coding Scheme

Devise a coding scheme for the warehouse layout on the following page. Be sure to use an appropriate coding scheme that allows the inventory to be located efficiently from the picking list.

5. Internal Control

Leslie Epstein, an employee of Bormack Manufacturing Company, prepares journal vouchers for general ledger entries. Due to the large number of voided journal vouchers caused by errors, the journal vouchers are not prenumbered by the printer; rather, Leslie numbers them as she prepares each journal voucher. She does, however, keep a log of all journal vouchers written so that she does not assign the same number to two journal vouchers. Biweekly, Leslie posts the journal vouchers to the general ledger and any necessary subsidiary accounts. Bimonthly, she reconciles the subsidiary accounts to their control accounts in the general ledger and makes sure the general ledger accounts balance.

Required:

Discuss any potential control weaknesses and problems in this scenario.

Problem 4: Coding Scheme

WAREHOUSE LAYOUT

Three warehouse locations—Warehouses 1, 2, and 3
Each warehouse is organized by aisles.

Aisle A

Aisle B

Aisle C

Aisle D

Aisle E

WAREHOUSE LAYOUT—(CONT.)

Each aisle is separated into a right and left side, with 7 shelves of goods and 17 partitions, with each storage area called a "bin."

6. Direct Access System

Crystal Corporation processes its journal vouchers using sequential files similar to the process outlined in Figure 8–9. To improve customer satisfaction, the sales system is going to be converted to a direct access filing system. Redraw Figure 8–9 to reflect this change in the GL/FRS.

7. Direct Access System

The top management team at Olympia, Inc. wishes to have on-line access to the major items in the general ledger. The general ledger is processed using a sequential file processing system, which is updated nightly. Adjust Figure 8–9 to accommodate this request by top management, assuming that the nightly updates to the general ledger are sufficient.

8. Internal Control

Expand Figures 8–9 and 8–10 to incorporate the journal voucher listing and general ledger change report as control mechanisms. Also discuss the specific controls they impose on the system.

9. Rankings of Alternatives

Assume that you have just evaluated the data presented on the following page in the weighted score table. The results indicate that Alternative B has the highest score. As the decision maker, you are extremely uncomfortable with Alternative B. You feel comfortable with the rankings of 1 to 5, with 5 being the best score, for each of the criteria rankings. You realize, however, that the weight for each criterion is subjective. How can you alter the weights so that the

Problem 9: Rankings of Alternatives

WEIGHTED SCORE TABLE
ALTERNATIVES

DECISION CRITERIA	WEIGHT	A RS	A WS	B RS	B WS	C RS	C WS
Increased efficiency	20	2	40	5	100	6	60
Impact on employee relations	20	3	60	2	40	3	60
Impact on customer relations	20	5	100	3	60	3	60
Potential cost savings	25	3	75	5	125	4	100
Likelihood of success	15	5	75	3	45	4	60
TOTAL	100%		350		370		340

outcome favors Alternative A (your personal favorite)? What does this process tell you about the relative importance of each of the decision criteria?

10. Organizational Chart
Prepare an organizational chart for your university. (Your campus phone directory catalogue may be helpful.)

11. Decision Level
Classify the following decisions as being characteristic of strategic planning, tactical planning, managerial control, or operational control.
- Determining the mix of products to manufacture this year
- Examining whether the number of defective goods manufactured is within a certain range
- Expanding a product line overseas
- Determining the best distribution route
- Examining whether the cost of raw materials is within a certain range
- Examining whether personnel development cost is rising
- Employing more automated manufacturing this year
- Examining whether the amount of scrap material is acceptable
- Building a new plant facility
- Examining whether employees' attitudes are improving

- Examining whether production levels are within a predicted range
- Making purchasing arrangements with a new supplier
- Increasing production capabilities this year by purchasing a more efficient piece of machinery
- Closing down a plant

12. Report Categorization
Classify the following reports as being either scheduled or on-demand reports.
- Cash disbursements listing
- Overtime report
- Customer account history
- Inventory stockout report
- Accounts receivable aging list
- Duplicate paycheck report
- Cash receipts listing
- Machine maintenance report
- Vendor delivery record report
- Journal voucher listing
- Investment center report
- Maintenance cost overrun report

13. CMA Adapted 1288 2-4 Organizational Structure and Span of Control
Relco Industries recently purchased Arbeck, Inc., a manufacturer of electrical components used by the construction industry. Roland Ford has been ap-

pointed as chief financial officer of Arbeck and has been asked by Martha Sanderson, president of Relco, to prepare an organizational chart for his department at Arbeck. The chart that Ford has prepared is shown below.

Ford believes that the treasurer's department should include the following employees: assistant treasurer, manager of accounts receivable and 4 subordinates, manager of investments and 3 subordinates, and manager of stockholder relations and 2 subordinates, for a total of 13 employees besides the treasurer. The controller's department should consist of an assistant controller, a manager of general accounting and 4 subordinates, a manager of fixed asset control and 3 subordinates, and a manager of cost accounting with 4 subordinates, for a total of 15 employees besides the controller.

When Ford presented his plans (Chart A) to Sanderson, she told him that she believed the organi-

zational structure was too tall and showed him, by drawing Chart B, how she had envisioned his department at Arbeck. There would be a reduction in personnel, and 10 employees would report directly to the treasurer, while 13 employees would report directly to the controller.

Ford replied that he believed the span of control was too broad for both the treasurer and the controller and would create problems. Sanderson said that she preferred a flat organizational structure as she believed that its benefits outweighed the problems that could arise from too great a span of control.

Required:

a. For the organizational structure proposed by Ford, chief financial officer, describe the
   1. advantages and disadvantages of that structure.
   2. impact of the resulting span of control.
   3. effect on employee behavior.
b. For the flat organizational structure proposed by Sanderson, president, describe the
   1. advantages and disadvantages of that structure.
   2. impact of the resulting span of control.
   3. effect on employee behavior.
c. When determining the appropriate span of control for Arbeck, Inc., discuss the factors that Ford and Sanderson should consider.

14. CMA Adapted 691 T-1 Organizational Structure and Span of Control

Barnes Corporation recently purchased Parker Machine Company, a manufacturer of sophisticated parts for the aircraft industry. Donald Jenkins has been appointed vice president of production of Parker and has been asked by Beverly Kiner, president of Barnes, to prepare an organizational chart for his department at Parker. The chart that Jenkins prepared is presented in Chart A on the next page.

When Jenkins presented his chart to Kiner, she told him that she preferred a flat organizational structure and showed him how she envisioned his department at Parker by drawing the chart presented in Chart B. Kiner's chart reduced a layer of management personnel and increased the number of people reporting directly to the manager of planning and control and the manager of manufacturing.

Jenkins expressed concern about the broad span of control depicted in Kiner's chart, as he believed this might cause problems for the two managers. Kiner said that she believed that the benefits of a flat orga-

Problem 13: Organizational Structure and Span of Control

Chart A

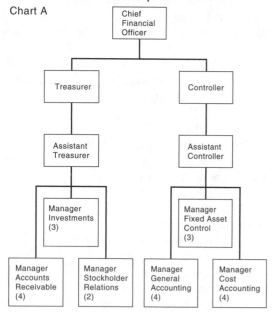

Chart B

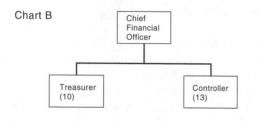

Problem 14: Organizational Structure and Span of Control

Chart A

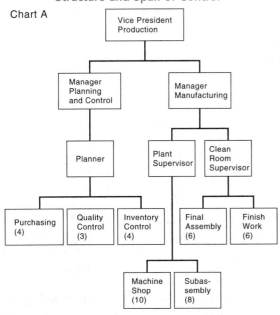

Chart B

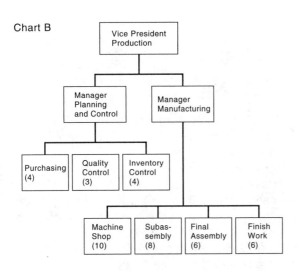

nizational structure outweighed the problems that could arise from too great a span of control.

Required:

a. For the organizational structure proposed by Jenkins, describe
   1. the advantages and disadvantages of that structure.
   2. the impact of the resulting span of control.
   3. the effect of the organizational structure on employee behavior.

b. For the flat organizational structure proposed by Kiner, describe
   1. the advantages and disadvantages of that organizational structure.
   2. the impact of the resulting span of control.
   3. the effect of the organizational structure on employee behavior.

c. When determining the appropriate span of control for Parker Machine Company, discuss the factors that Jenkins and Kiner should consider.

15. CMA Adapted 1287 2-Y8 Organizational Structure

While attending night school to earn a degree in computer engineering, Stan Wilson had worked for Morlot Container Company (MCC) as an assembly line supervisor. MCC was located near Wilson's hometown and had been a prominent employer in the area for many years. MCC's main product was milk cartons that were distributed throughout the midwest for use by milk processing plants. The technology at MCC was stable, and the assembly lines were monitored very closely. MCC employed a standard cost system because cost control was considered important. The employees who manned the assembly lines were generally unskilled workers who had been with the company for many years; the majority of these workers belonged to the local union.

Wilson was glad he was nearly done with school because he found the work at MCC to be repetitive and boring, even as a supervisor. The supervisors were monitored almost as closely as the line workers, and standard policies and procedures existed that applied to most situations. Most of MCC's management had been with the company for several years and believed in clear lines of authority and well-defined responsibilities. While he knew he had performed well against the company's standards, Wilson also knew that there probably would be little opportunity for advancement or significant compensation increases.

After receiving his degree, Wilson went to work in the research and development department of Alden Computers, a five-year-old company specializing in educational computer systems for elementary schools. The company was customer-oriented and willing to tailor its computer systems to the needs of the end users. The customization of its systems, combined with continual changes in technology, resulted in a job-shop orientation in the company's production facility. The employees who assembled Alden's systems were skilled technicians who worked closely with the engineering staff.

Wilson was gratified by the respect and authority his newly acquired knowledge and skills afforded him at Alden. If changes were required in his area of expertise, Wilson often made recommendations about how the work should proceed and was involved in decisions on new product development. The company's management team frequently "rolled up its sleeves" and worked alongside the technicians when production problems arose; the lines of authority were sometimes difficult to distinguish, and decisions were often made by the expert on the spot. Wilson believed that his skills were appreciated at Alden, and he would be fairly compensated for his professional expertise.

Required:

a. Morlot Container Company and Alden Computers represent two different types of organizational structures. In terms of each of the following points, explain how MCC differs from Alden Computers.
   1. General organizational structure and climate
   2. Bases of authority
   3. Evaluation criteria
   4. Bases of compensation
b. Both structures have potential benefits or can create problems. Discuss the features of the
   1. structure used by Alden Computers that might benefit MCC.
   2. structure used by Alden that might create problems for Alden.
   3. structure used by MCC that might benefit Alden Computers.

16. CMA Adapted 691 T-Y9
Performance Measures

The Star Paper Division of Royal Industries is located near Los Angeles. A major expansion of the division's only plant was completed in April 2001. The expansion consisted of an addition to the existing building, additions to the production-line machinery, and the replacement of obsolete and fully depreciated equipment that was no longer efficient or cost-effective.

On May 1, 2001, George Harris became manager of Star. Harris had a meeting with Marie Fortner, vice president of operations for Royal, who explained to Harris that the company measured the performance of divisions and division managers on the basis of return on gross assets (ROA). When Harris asked if other measures were used in conjunction with ROA, Fortner replied, "Royal's top management prefers to use a single performance measure. Star should do well this year now that it has expanded and replaced all of that old equipment. You should have no problem exceeding the division's historical rate. I'll check with you at the end of each quarter to see how you are doing."

Fortner called Harris after the first quarter results were completed because Star's ROA was considerably below the historical rate for the division. Harris told Fortner that he did not believe that ROA was a valid performance measure for Star. Fortner indicated that she would discuss this with others at headquarters and get back to Harris. However, there was no further discussion of the use of ROA, only reports on divisional performance at the end of the second and third quarters. Now that the fiscal year has ended, Harris has received the memorandum shown below.

Harris is looking forward to meeting with Fortner as he plans to pursue the discussion about the

Problem 16: Performance Measures

TO: George Harris, Star Paper Division
FROM: Marie Fortner, Royal Industries
SUBJECT: Divisional Performance

The operating results for the fourth quarter and for our fiscal year ended on April 30 are now complete. Your fourth quarter return on gross assets was only 9 percent, resulting in a return for the year of slightly under 11 percent. I recall discussing your low return after the first quarter and reminding you after the second and third quarters that this level of return is not considered adequate for the Star Paper Division.

The return on gross assets at Star has ranged from 15 to 18 percent for the past five years. An 11 percent return may be acceptable at some of Royal's other divisions, but not at a proven winner like Star, especially in light of your recently improved facility. Please arrange to meet with me in the near future to discuss ways to restore Star's return on gross assets to its former level.

appropriateness of ROA as a performance measure for Star. While the ROA for Star is below historical levels, the division's profits for the year are higher than at any previous time. Harris is going to recommend that ROA be replaced with multiple criteria for evaluating performance—namely, dollar profit, receivable turnover, and inventory turnover.

Required:

a. Identify general criteria that should be used in selecting performance measures to evaluate operating managers.

b. Describe the probable cause of the decline in the Star Paper Division's return on gross assets during the fiscal year ended April 30, 2001.

c. On the basis of the relationship between Fortner and Harris, as well as the memorandum from Fortner, discuss apparent weaknesses in the performance evaluation process at Royal Industries.

d. Discuss whether the multiple performance evaluation criteria suggested by Harris would be appropriate for the evaluation of the Star Paper Division.

17. CMA Adapted 1286 2-5
Responsibility Accounting

Family Resorts, Inc. is a holding company for several vacation hotels in the northeastern and mid-Atlantic states. The firm originally purchased several old inns, restored the buildings, and upgraded the recreational

facilities. The inns have been well received by vacationing families, because many services are provided that accommodate children and afford parents time for themselves. Since the completion of the restoration ten years ago, the company has been profitable.

Family Resorts has just concluded its annual meeting of regional and district managers. This meeting is held each November to review the results of the previous season and to help the managers prepare for the upcoming year. Before the meeting, the managers submitted proposed budgets for their districts or regions as appropriate. These budgets have been reviewed and consolidated into an annual operating budget for the entire company. The 2001 budget has been presented at the meeting and was accepted by the managers.

To evaluate the performance of its managers, Family Resorts uses responsibility accounting. Therefore, the preparation of the budget is given close attention at headquarters. If major changes need to be made to the budgets submitted by the managers, all affected parties are consulted before the changes are incorporated. Below and on the following page are two pages from the budget booklet that all managers received at the meeting.

Required:

a. Responsibility accounting has been used effectively by many companies, both large and small.

Problem 17: Responsibility Accounting

FAMILY RESORTS, INC.
RESPONSIBILITY SUMMARY
($000 omitted)

Reporting Unit: Family Resorts		Reporting Unit: Maine District	
Responsible Person: President		Responsible Person: District Manager	
Mid-Atlantic Region	$ 605	Harbor Inn	$ 80
New England Region	365	Camden Country Inn	60
Unallocated costs	(160)	Unallocated costs	(35)
Income before taxes	$ 810	Total contribution	$ 105
Reporting Unit: New England Region		Reporting Unit: Harbor Inn	
Responsible Person: Regional Manager		Responsible Person: Innkeeper	
Vermont	$ 200	Revenue	$ 600
New Hampshire	140	Controllable costs	(455)
Maine	105	Allocated costs	(65)
Unallocated costs	(80)		
		Total contribution	$ 80
Total contribution	$ 365		

Problem 17: Responsibility Accounting

FAMILY RESORTS, INC.
CONDENSED OPERATING BUDGET—MAINE DISTRICT
FOR THE YEAR ENDING DECEMBER 31, 2000
($000 OMITTED)

	Family Resorts	Region		New England District				Maine District Inns		
		Mid-Atlantic	New England	Not Allocated[1]	Vermont	New Hampshire	Maine	Not Allocated[2]	Harbor	Camden Country
Net sales	$7,900	$4,200	$3,700		$1,400	$1,200	$1,100		$600	$500
Cost of sales	4,530	2,310	2,220		840	720	660		360	300
Gross margin	$3,370	$1,890	$1,480		$ 560	$ 480	$ 440		$240	$200
Controllable expenses										
Supervisory	$ 240	$ 130	$ 110		$ 35	$ 30	$ 45	$ 10	$ 20	$ 15
Training	160	80	80		30	25	25		15	10
Advertising	500	280	220	$ 50	55	60	55	15	20	20
Repairs and maintenance	480	225	255	—	90	85	80	—	40	40
Total controllable expenses	$1,380	$ 715	$ 665	$ 50	$ 210	$ 200	$ 205	$ 25	$ 95	$ 85
Controllable contribution	$1,990	$1,175	$ 815	$(50)	$ 350	$ 280	$ 235	$(25)	$145	$115
Expenses controlled by others										
Depreciation	$ 520	$ 300	$ 220	$ 30	$ 70	$ 60	$ 60	$ 10	$ 30	$ 20
Property taxes	200	120	80		30	30	20		10	10
Insurance	300	150	150	—	50	50	50	—	25	25
Total expenses controlled by others	$1,020	$ 570	$ 450	$ 30	$ 150	$ 140	$ 130	$ 10	$ 65	$ 55
Total contribution	$ 970	$ 605	$ 365	$(80)	$ 200	$ 140	$ 105	$(35)	$ 80	$ 60
Unallocated costs[3]	160									
Income before taxes	$ 810									

[1]Unallocated expenses include a regional advertising campaign and equipment used by the regional manager.
[2]Unallocated expenses include a portion of the district manager's salary, district promotion costs, and a district manager's car.
[3]Unallocated costs include taxes on undeveloped real estate, headquarters' expense, legal fees, and audit fees.

1. Define responsibility accounting.
2. Discuss the benefits that accrue to a company using responsibility accounting.
3. Describe the advantages of responsibility accounting for the managers of a firm.

b. Family Resorts, Inc.'s budget was accepted by the regional and district managers. Based on the facts presented, evaluate the budget process employed by Family Resorts by addressing the following:
   1. What features of the budget presentation shown on the previous page are likely to make the budget attractive to managers?
   2. What recommendations, if any, could be made to the budget preparers to improve the budget process? Explain your answer.

18. CMA Adapted 688 2-2
Management by Exception

Some executives believe that it is extremely important to manage "by numbers." This form of management requires that all employees with departmental or divisional responsibilities spend time understanding the company's operations and how they are reflected by the company's financial reports. Because of the managers' increased comprehension of the financial reports and the activities that they represent, their subordinates will become more attuned to the meaning of financial reports and the important signposts that can be detected in these reports. Companies use a variety of numerical measurement systems, including standard costs, financial ratios, human resource forecasts, and operating budgets.

Required:
a. Discuss the following aspects of a standard cost system:
   1. Discuss the characteristics that should be present to encourage positive employee motivation.
   2. Discuss how the system should be implemented to positively motivate employees.
b. The use of variance analysis often results in management by exception.
   1. Explain the meaning of "management by exception."
   2. Discuss the behavioral implications of management by exception.
c. Explain how employee behavior could be adversely affected when actual-to-budget comparisons are used as the basis for performance evaluation.

19. CMA Adapted 1287 2-Y6
Variance Analysis

Engineers Education Association (EEA) is a volunteer membership organization providing educational and professional services to its members. The professional staff is organized into four divisions with a total of 14 operating departments.

EEA adopted an annual budget program many years ago as a means for planning and controlling activities. Each department of EEA prepares an annual budget in consultation with its respective volunteer committee(s). After a series of reviews by both the professional staff and the volunteer structure, the budget is adopted. The professional staff is expected to comply with the budget in conducting its activities and operations.

The EEA's accounting department generates monthly income statements that present actual performance as compared to budget for each department of EEA. The November 2001 statement for the publications department is reproduced on the following page. Accompanying the report this month was a memorandum from EEA's president, Daniel Riley, which is also presented in the next column.

Marie Paige, publications manager, was having lunch with Jon Franklin, continuing education manager, when the following conversation about Riley's memorandum took place.

Paige: The volunteers must be giving Riley some static—the memo doesn't sound like him.

Franklin: I think you're right. One of EEA's problems is that membership is down.

Paige: I heard that both growth and retention are bad. This is confirmed by my results. A set percentage of the membership dues of each member is assigned to us each month for the magazine subscription. This amount is down 12 percent. I have no control over this number because only members get the magazine.

Franklin: I wonder if the results are really as bad as they look. For instance, accounting has divided all of the annual budget figures by 12 to derive the monthly figures. This is okay for some things but not for most. What about you?

Paige: I agree. I don't know why they do that when we spend so much time up front developing the annual budget. I know what Riley is attempting, but I don't think he is going to get the results he wants. I know

Problem 19: Variance Analysis

EEA—PUBLICATIONS DEPARTMENT
INCOME STATEMENT
FOR THE MONTH ENDED NOVEMBER 30, 2001
($000 OMITTED)

			Variance	
	Budget	Actual	Dollar	Percent
Revenues				
Subscriptions	$ 9.5	$ 8.4	$ (1.1)	(11.6)
Library subscriptions	3.4	3.3	(.1)	(2.9)
Research publications	13.6	15.2	1.6	11.8
Advertising	64.0	50.1	(13.9)	(21.7)
List rentals	15.2	13.9	(1.3)	(8.6)
Total revenue	$105.7	$90.9	$(14.8)	(14.0)
Operating expenses				
Salaries and wages	$ 24.0	$22.0	$ 2.0	8.3
Employee benefits	4.8	4.4	.4	8.3
Temporary help	0.0	1.5	(1.5)	(ERR)
Outside services	1.0	2.5	(1.5)	(150.0)
Education and training	0.5	0.0	.5	100.0
Promotion and advertising	7.5	4.0	3.5	46.6
Typesetting	8.0	12.0	(4.0)	(50.0)
Production printing	46.0	40.4	5.6	12.2
Postage, freight, and handling	12.0	11.0	1.0	8.3
Supplies	1.0	.8	.2	20.0
Total expenses	$104.8	$98.6	$ 6.2	5.9
Contribution	$ .9	$ (7.7)	$ (8.6)	(955.6)

Problem 19: Variance Analysis

December 12, 2001

TO: Department Managers
FROM: Daniel Riley, President
SUBJECT: Performance Analysis

The November 2001 operating results for your department are attached. The results for the entire organization and most departments are unfavorable as compared to budget. In fact, our results for the first three months of this fiscal year are substantially below budget.

I want to determine our problems as quickly as possible. Prepare an explanation of all unfavorable (negative) variances by line item that exceed budget by 5 percent or more, and present a plan to eliminate such variances in the future. Remember that you played a key role in the development of the budget and you have a responsibility to achieve the budget figures. These negative variances must be eliminated if we are to get back on steam.

Please submit your analysis to your divisional director and accounting by noon, Monday, December 17. Divisional directors will meet at 10 A.M. on Tuesday, December 18, to review these analyses.

he wants to eliminate the negative variances, but some positive variances are really not favorable! We should be analyzing all significant variances—positive and negative.

Franklin: What are you going to do—analyze just the negatives? Should we do anything before we prepare our reports?

Required:

a. The monthly income statements prepared by EEA's accounting department for each department of EEA are a form of communication.

  1. Explain why the departmental income statements are considered a form of communication.

  2. In terms of the format of the income statement presented for the publications department, evaluate EEA's departmental income statement as a communication device.

b. Paige stated that all significant variances should be analyzed because some positive variances are not favorable. Discuss why EEA's departments should be analyzing all significant variances, both positive (favorable) and negative (unfavorable). As support for your answer, identify a positive variance from the publications department's income statement that may not be favorable to EEA's operations and explain why.

c. Recommend a course of action that Paige or Franklin could take to encourage Riley to have all significant variances reviewed.

ADVANCED TECHNOLOGIES IN ACCOUNTING INFORMATION SYSTEMS

9

Database Management Systems

This chapter deals with the database approach to managing an organization's data resources. The database model is a particular philosophy whose objectives are supported by specific strategies, techniques, hardware, and software that are very different from those associated with flat file environments.

Chapter 1 drew a distinction between two general data-management approaches: the flat file model and the database model. Since the best way to present the virtues of the database model is by contrast with the flat file model, the first section of this chapter examines how traditional flat file problems are resolved under the database approach. Important features of modern relational databases are covered later in the chapter. The second section describes in detail the functions and relationship between four primary elements of the database environment: the users, the database management system (DBMS), the database administrator (DBA), and the physical database. The third section is devoted to an in-depth explanation of the characteristics of the relational model. A number of database design topics are covered including data modeling, deriving relational tables from ER diagrams, the creation of user views, and data normalization techniques. The fourth section concludes the chapter with a discussion of distributed databases issues. It examines three possible database configurations in a distributed environment: centralized, partitioned, and replicated databases.

LEARNING OBJECTIVES

After studying this chapter, you should:

- Understand the operational problems inherent in the flat file approach to data management that gave rise to the database concept.
- Understand the relationships among the defining elements of the database environment.
- Be familiar with the operational characteristics of the relational database model.
- Be familiar with the operational stages in database design including conceptual design, logical design, and physical design.
- Understand the anomalies caused by unnormalized databases and the need for data normalization.
- Be familiar with the operational features of distributed databases and recognize the issues that need to be considered in deciding on a particular database configuration.

OVERVIEW OF THE FLAT FILE VS. DATABASE APPROACH

Figure 9–1 illustrates the **flat file** approach to data management. In this environment, users *own* their data files. Exclusive ownership of data is a natural consequence of two problems associated with the legacy-system era. The first is a business culture that erects barriers between organizational units that inhibits entity-wide integration of data. The second problem stems from limitations in flat file management technology that requires data files to be structured to the unique needs of the primary user. Thus the same data, used in slightly different ways by different users, may need to be restructured and reproduced in physically different files. To illustrate, the contents of the files in the figure are represented conceptually with letters. Each letter could signify a single **data attribute** (field), a record, or an entire file. Note also that data element B is present in all user files. This is called **data redundancy**, which is the cause of significant data management problems in three areas: **data storage**, **data updating**, and **currency of information**. Each of these, and a fourth problem, **task-data dependency**, which is not directly related to data redundancy, is examined below.

DATA STORAGE

Chapter 1 showed that an efficient information system captures and stores data only once and makes this single source available to all users who need it. In the flat file environment, this is not possible. To meet the private data needs of users, organizations

---

FIGURE 9–1   Flat File Data Management

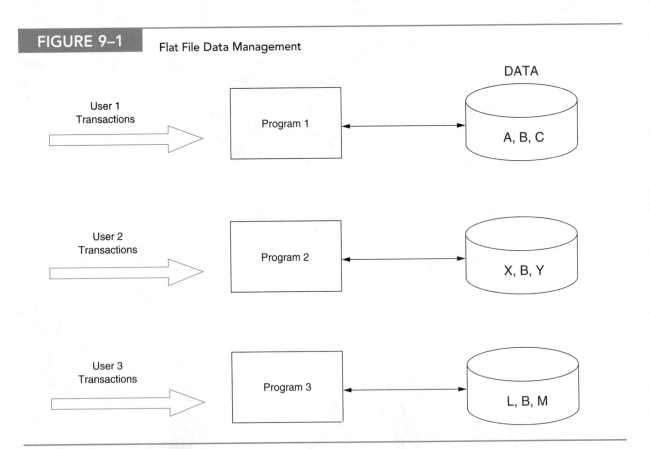

must incur the costs of both multiple collection and multiple storage procedures. Some commonly used data may be duplicated dozens, hundreds, or even thousands of times, creating excessive storage costs.

DATA UPDATING

Organizations have a great deal of data stored on master files and reference files that require periodic updating to reflect operational and economic changes. For example, a change in a customer's name or address must be reflected in the appropriate master files. This piece of information may be important to several user departments in the organization, such as sales, billing, credit, customer services, sales promotion, and catalog sales. When users keep separate files, any such change must be made separately for each user. This adds significantly to the cost of data management.

CURRENCY OF INFORMATION

In contrast to the problem of performing multiple updates is the problem of failing to update the files of all users affected by a change. If update messages are not properly disseminated, then some users may not record the change, but will perform their duties and make decisions based on outdated data.

TASK-DATA DEPENDENCY

Another problem with the flat file approach is the user's inability to obtain additional information as his or her needs change. This problem is called *task-data dependency*. The user's information set is constrained by the data that he or she possesses and controls. For example, in Figure 9–1, if the information needs of User 1 change to include Data L, User 1's program would not have access to these data. Although Data L exists in the files of another user, keep in mind the culture of this environment. Users do not interact as members of a user community. They act independently. As such, User 1 may be unaware of the presence of Data L elsewhere in the organization. In this environment, it is very difficult to establish a mechanism for the formal sharing of data. Therefore, Data L would need to be created from scratch. This will take time, inhibit User 1's performance, add to data redundancy, and drive data management costs even higher.

THE DATABASE APPROACH

Figure 9–2(a) presents a simple overview of the database approach with the same users and data requirements as in Figure 9–1. The most obvious change from the flat file model is the pooling of data into a common database that is shared by all the users.

TRADITIONAL PROBLEMS SOLVED

Data sharing (the absence of ownership) is the central concept of the database approach. Let's see how this resolves the problems identified.

- *No data redundancy*. Each data element is stored only once, thereby eliminating data redundancy and reducing storage costs.
- *Single update*. Because each data element exists in only one place, it requires only a single update procedure. This reduces the time and cost of keeping the database current.
- *Current values*. A change to the database made by any user yields current data values for all other users. For example, if User 1 records a customer address change, User 3 has immediate access to this current information.

FIGURE 9–2(a)

The Database
Concept

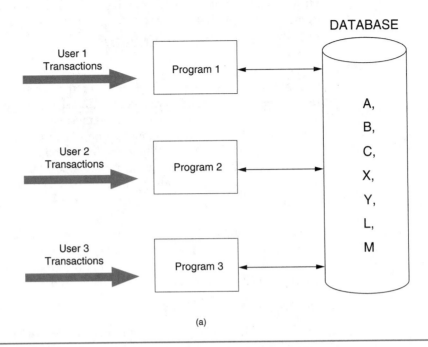

(a)

- *Task-data independence.* Users have access to the full domain of data available to the firm. As users' information needs expand beyond their immediate domain, the new needs can be more easily satisfied than under the flat file approach. Users are constrained only by the limitations of the data available to the firm (the entire database) and the legitimacy of their need to access it.

CONTROLLING ACCESS TO THE DATABASE

The database approach places all the firm's information eggs in one basket. It becomes critical, therefore, to take very good care of the basket. The example in Figure 9–2(a) has no provision for controlling access to the database. Assume Data X is sensitive, confidential, or secret information that only User 3 is authorized to access. How can the organization prevent others from gaining unauthorized access to it?

THE DATABASE MANAGEMENT SYSTEM

Figure 9–2(b) adds a new element to Figure 9–2(a). Standing between the users' programs and the physical database is the **database management system (DBMS)**. The purpose of the DBMS is to provide controlled access to the database. The DBMS is a special software system that is programmed to know which data elements each user is authorized to access. The user's program sends requests for data to the DBMS, which validates and authorizes access to the database in accordance with the user's level of authority. If the user requests data that he or she is not authorized to access, the request is denied. As you might imagine, the organization's procedures for assigning user authority are important control issues for accountants to consider.

THREE CONCEPTUAL MODELS

The database approach is not represented by a single architecture. Early database models are as different from modern database models as they were from traditional

FIGURE 9–2(b)

The Database
Concept

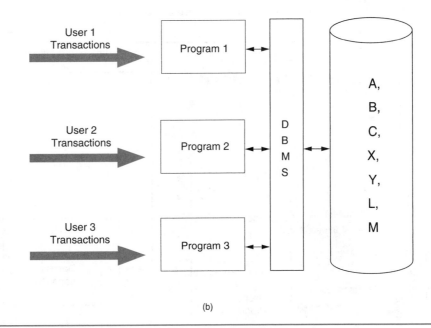

(b)

flat files. The most common database approaches used for business information systems are the **hierarchical**, the **network**, and the **relational models**. Because of certain conceptual similarities, the hierarchical and network databases are termed **navigational** or **structured models**. The way that data are organized in these early database systems forces users to *navigate* between data elements using predefined *structured* paths. The relational model is far more flexible by allowing users to create new and unique paths through the database to solve a wider range of business problems.

Although their limitations are severe and their demise is inevitable, hierarchical and network models still exist as legacy systems that support mission-critical functions in some companies. Most modern systems, however, employ relational databases. The main text of the chapter focuses on the relational model. The key features of structured database models are outlined in the appendix to this chapter.

ELEMENTS OF THE DATABASE ENVIRONMENT

Figure 9–3 presents a breakdown of the database environment into four primary elements: *users*, the *DBMS*, the *database administrator*, and the *physical database*. In this section we examine each of these elements.

USERS

Figure 9–3 shows how **users** access the database in two ways. First, access can be achieved via user programs prepared by systems professionals. User programs send data access requests (calls) to the DBMS, which validates the requests and retrieves the data for processing. Under this mode of access, the presence of the DBMS is transparent to the users. Data processing procedures (both batch and real-time) for

FIGURE 9–3   Elements of the Database Concept

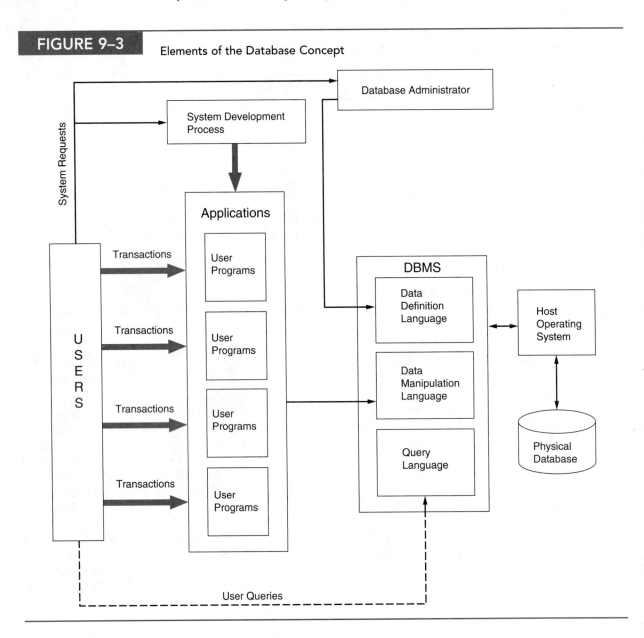

transactions such as sales, cash receipts, and purchases are essentially the same as they would be in the flat file environment.

The second method of database access is via direct query, which requires no formal user programs. The DBMS has a built-in query facility that allows authorized users to process data independent of professional programmers. The query facility provides a "friendly" environment for integrating and retrieving data to produce ad hoc management reports. This feature is an attractive incentive for users to adopt the database approach.

DATABASE MANAGEMENT SYSTEM

The second element of the database approach depicted in Figure 9–3 is the database management system. The DBMS provides a controlled environment to assist (or prevent) user access to the database and to efficiently manage the data resource. Each

DBMS model accomplishes these objectives differently, but some typical features include:

1. *Program development.* The DBMS contains **application development software**. Both programmers and end users may employ this feature to create applications to access the database.
2. *Backup and recovery.* During processing, the DBMS periodically makes backup copies of the physical database. In the event of a disaster (disk failure, program error, or malicious act) that renders the database unusable, the DBMS can recover to an earlier version that is known to be correct. Although some data loss may occur, without the backup and recovery feature the database would be vulnerable to total destruction.
3. *Database usage reporting.* This feature captures statistics on what data are being used, when they are used, and who uses them. The database administrator (DBA) uses this information to help in assigning user authorization and in maintaining the database. We discuss the role of the DBA later in this section.
4. *Database access.* The most important feature of a DBMS is to permit authorized user access to the database. Figure 9–3 shows the three software modules that facilitate this task. These are the data definition language, data manipulation language, and the query language.

Data Definition Language

Data definition language (DDL) is a programming language used to define the physical database to the DBMS. The definition includes the names and the relationship of all data elements, records, and files that constitute the database. There are three levels, called *views*, in this definition: the internal view, the conceptual view (schema), and the user view (subschema). Figure 9–4 shows the relationship between these views.

Internal View. The **internal view** presents the physical arrangement of records in the database. This is the lowest level of representation, which is one step removed from the physical database. The internal view describes the structure of records, the linkages between them, and the physical arrangement and sequence of records in a file. There is only one internal view of the database.

Conceptual View (Schema). The conceptual view or **schema** represents the database logically and abstractly, rather than the way it is physically stored. This view allows users' programs to call for data without knowing or needing to specify how the data are arranged or where they reside in the physical database. There is only one conceptual view for a database.

User View (Subschema). The **user view** defines how a particular user sees the database. This is the portion of the database that an individual user is authorized to access. To the user, the user view *is* the database. Unlike the internal and conceptual views, there are many distinct user views. For example, a user in the personnel department may view the database as a collection of employee records and is unaware of the supplier and inventory records seen by the users in the inventory control department.

DBMS Operation. To illustrate the roles of these views, let's look at the typical sequence of events that occurs in accessing data through a DBMS. The following description is hypothetical, and certain technical details are omitted.

FIGURE 9-4   Overview of DBMS Operation

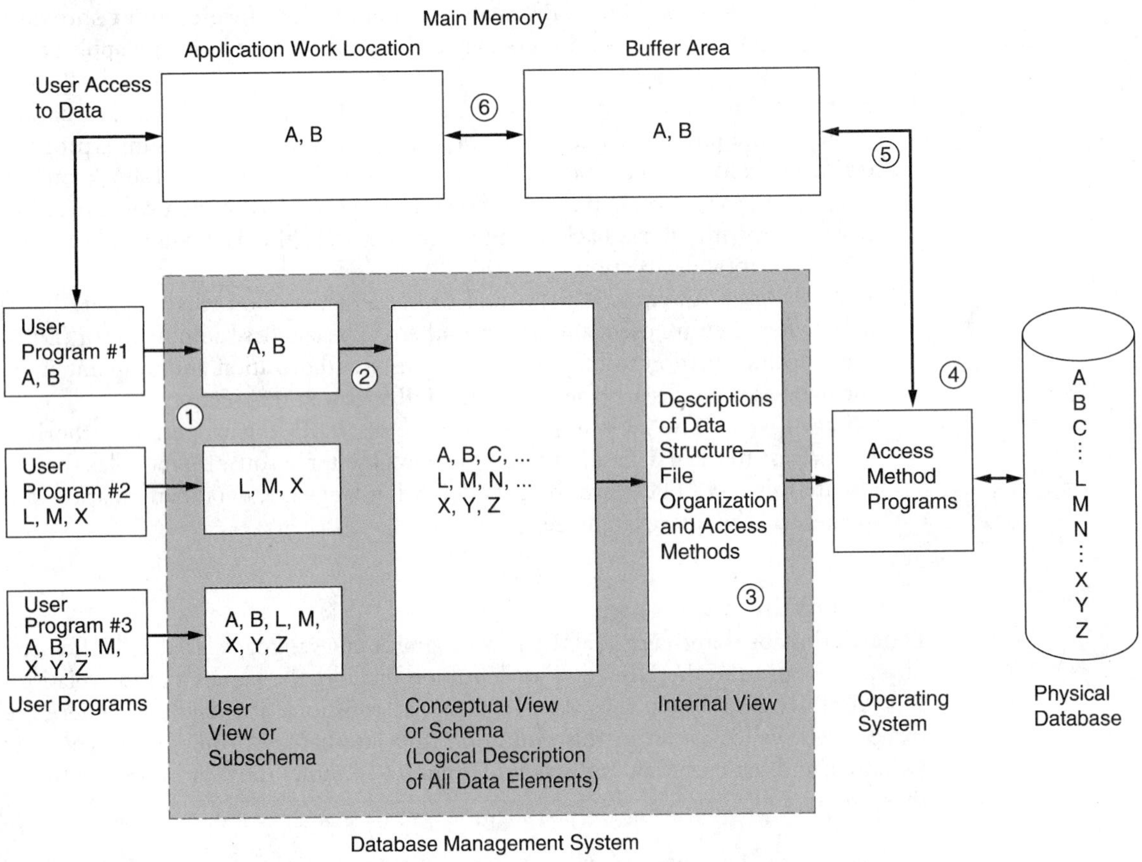

1. A user program sends a request (call) for data to the DBMS. The call is written in a special data manipulation language (discussed later) that is embedded in the user program.
2. The DBMS analyzes the request by matching the called data elements against the user view and the conceptual view. If the data request matches, it is authorized, and processing proceeds to Step 3. If it does not match the views, access is denied.
3. The DBMS determines the data structure parameters from the internal view and passes them to the operating system, which performs the actual data retrieval. Data structure parameters describe the organization and **access method** (an operating system utility program), for retrieving the requested data.
4. Using the appropriate access method, the operating system interacts with the disk storage device to retrieve the data from the physical database.
5. The operating system then stores the data in a main memory buffer area managed by the DBMS.
6. The DBMS transfers the data to the user's work location in main memory. At this point, the user's program is free to access and manipulate the data.
7. When processing is complete, Steps 4, 5, and 6 are reversed to restore the processed data to the database.

Data Manipulation Language

Data manipulation language (DML) is the proprietary programming language that a particular DBMS uses to retrieve, process, and store data. Entire user programs may be written in the DML or, alternatively, selected DML commands can be inserted into programs that are written in universal languages, such as PL/1, COBOL, and FORTRAN. Inserting DML commands enables standard programs, which were originally written for the flat file environment, to be easily converted to work in a database environment. The use of standard language programs also provides the organization with a degree of independence from the DBMS vendor. If the organization decides to switch its vendors to one that uses a different DML, it will not be necessary to rewrite all the user programs. By replacing the old DML commands with the new commands, user programs can be modified to function in the new environment.

Query Language

The query capability of the DBMS permits end users and professional programmers to access data in the database directly without the need for conventional programs. IBM's **structured query language (SQL,** pronounced *sequel*) has emerged as the standard query language for both mainframe and microcomputer DBMSs. SQL is a fourth-generation, nonprocedural language with many commands that allow users to input, retrieve, and modify data easily. The SELECT command is a powerful tool for retrieving data. The example in Figure 9–5 illustrates the use of the SELECT command to produce a user report from a database called Inventory.

SQL is an efficient data processing tool. Although not a natural English language, SQL requires far less training in computer concepts and fewer programming skills than many languages. In fact, many database query systems require no SQL knowledge at all. Users select data visually by "pointing and clicking" at the desired attributes. The visual user interface then generates the necessary SQL commands automatically. This feature places ad hoc reporting and data processing capability in the hands of the user/manager. By reducing reliance on professional programmers, managers are better able to deal with problems that "pop up."

THE DATABASE ADMINISTRATOR

Refer to Figure 9–3 and note the administrative position of **database administrator (DBA).** This position does not exist in the flat file environment. The DBA is responsible for managing the database resource. The sharing of a common database by multiple users requires organization, coordination, rules, and guidelines to protect the integrity of the database.

In large organizations, the DBA function may consist of an entire department of technical personnel under the database administrator. In smaller organizations, DBA responsibility may be assumed by someone within the computer services group. The duties of the DBA fall into the following areas:[1] database planning; database design; database implementation; database operation and maintenance; and database change and growth. Table 9–1 presents a breakdown of specific tasks within these broad areas.

Organizational Interactions of the DBA

Figure 9–6 shows some of the organizational interfaces of the DBA. Of particular importance is the relationship among the DBA, the end users, and the systems

---

1   Adapted from F. R. McFadden and J. A. Hoffer, *Database Management*, 3rd ed. (Redwood City, CA: Benjamin/Cummings Publishing, 1991): 343.

FIGURE 9–5   Example of SELECT Command Used to Query an Inventory Database

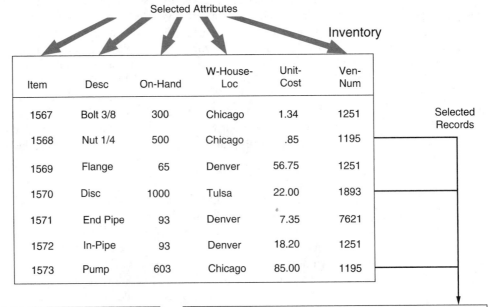

SQL Command

SELECT   Item, Desc, On-Hand,
             W-House-Loc, Ven-Num

FROM   Inventory

WHERE   On-Hand > 300

Report Produced

TABLE 9–1   **Functions of the Database Administrator**

Database Planning:	**Implementation:**
Develop organization's database strategy	Determine access policy
Define database environment	Implement security controls
Define data requirements	Specify test procedures
Develop data dictionary	Establish programming standards
Design:	**Operation and Maintenance:**
Logical database (schema)	Evaluate database performance
External users' views (subschemas)	Reorganize database as user needs demand
Internal view of database	Review standards and procedures
Database controls	
	Change and Growth:
	Plan for change and growth
	Evaluate new technology

FIGURE 9–6

Organizational
Interactions of
the Database
Administrator

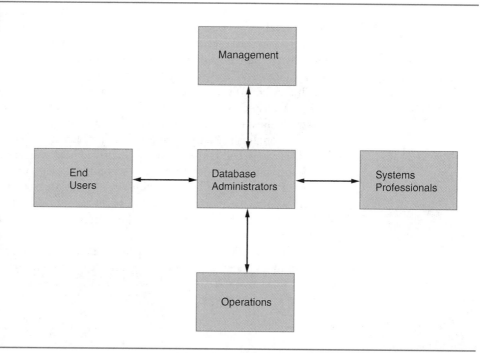

professionals of the organization. Refer again to Figure 9–3 during the examination of this relationship.

As information needs arise, users send formal requests for computer applications to the systems professionals (programmers) of the organization. The requests are handled through formal systems development procedures, which produce the programmed applications. Figure 9–3 shows this relationship as the line from the users block to the systems development process block. The user requests also go to the DBA, who evaluates these to determine the user's database needs. Once this is established, the DBA grants the user access authority by programming the user's view (subschema). This relationship is shown as the lines between the user and the DBA and between the DBA and DDL module in the DBMS. By keeping access authority separate from systems development (application programming), the organization is better able to control and protect the database. Intentional and unintentional attempts at unauthorized access are more likely to be discovered when these two groups work independently. The rationale for this separation of duties is developed in Chapter 15.

The Data Dictionary

Another important function of the DBA is the creation and maintenance of the **data dictionary**. The data dictionary describes every data element in the database. This enables all users (and programmers) to share a common view of the data resource, thus greatly facilitating the analysis of user needs.

THE PHYSICAL DATABASE

The fourth major element of the database approach as presented in Figure 9–3 is the **physical database**. This is the lowest level of the database. The physical database consists of magnetic spots on magnetic disks. The other levels of the database (the user view, conceptual view, and internal view) are abstract representations of the physical level.

At the physical level, the database is a collection of records and files. Relational databases are based on the **indexed sequential file** structure. This structure, illustrated in Figure 9–7, uses an index in conjunction with a sequential file organization. It facilitates both direct access to individual records and batch processing of the entire file. Multiple indexes can be used to create a cross-reference, called an **inverted list**, which allows even more flexible access to data. Two indexes are shown in Figure 9–7. One contains the employee number (primary key) for uniquely locating records in the file. The second index contains record addresses arranged by year-to-date earnings. Using this non-unique field as a secondary key permits all employee records to be viewed in ascending or descending order according to earnings. Alternatively, individual records with selected earnings balances can be displayed. Indexes may be created for each attribute in the file, allowing data to be viewed from a multitude of perspectives.

The next section examines the principles that underlay the relational model and the techniques, rules, and procedures for creating relational tables from indexed sequential files. You will also see how tables are linked to other tables to permit complex data representations.

THE RELATIONAL DATABASE MODEL

E. F. Codd originally proposed the principles of the relational model in the late 1960s.[2] The formal model has its foundations in relational algebra and set theory, which provide the theoretical basis for most of the data manipulation operations used. The relational model represents data in the form of two-dimensional tables. Figure 9–8 presents an example of a database table called Customer.

FIGURE 9–7   Indexed Sequential File

Emp Num Index

Key Value	Record Address
101	1
102	2
103	3
104	4
105	5

Employee Table

Emp Num	Name	Address	Skill Code	YTD Earnings
101	L. Smith	15 Main St.	891	15000
102	S. Buell	107 Hill Top	379	10000
103	T. Hill	40 Barclay St.	891	20000
104	M. Green	251 Ule St.	209	19000
105	H. Litt	423 Rauch Ave.	772	18000

YTD Earnings Index

Key Value	Address
20000	3
19000	4
18000	5
15000	1
10000	2

---

2   C. J. Date, *An Introduction to Database Systems*, vol. 1, 4th ed. (Reading, MS: Addison-Wesley, 1986): 99.

FIGURE 9–8

A Relational Table
Called Customer

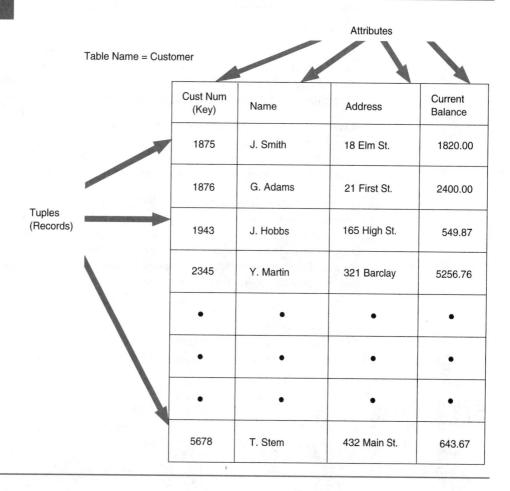

Table Name = Customer

Attributes

Tuples
(Records)

Cust Num (Key)	Name	Address	Current Balance
1875	J. Smith	18 Elm St.	1820.00
1876	G. Adams	21 First St.	2400.00
1943	J. Hobbs	165 High St.	549.87
2345	Y. Martin	321 Barclay	5256.76
•	•	•	•
•	•	•	•
•	•	•	•
5678	T. Stem	432 Main St.	643.67

DATABASE TERMINOLOGY

The relational model has its own terminology. The database table is called a *relation*. Across the top of the relation are **attributes** (data elements) forming columns. Intersecting the columns and forming rows in the relation are *tuples*. A tuple, which was given a precise definition by Codd when he first introduced it, corresponds approximately to a record. From here on, the terms *record* and *table* will be used in place of *tuple* and *relation*, respectively.

Properly designed tables possess the following four characteristics:

1. All occurrences at the intersection of a row and a column are a single value. No multiple values (repeating groups) are allowed.
2. The attribute values in any column must all be of the same class.
3. Each column in a given table must be uniquely named. However, different tables may contain columns with the same name.
4. Each row in the table must be unique in at least one attribute. This attribute is the primary key.

Table Associations

Database tables exist in relation to other tables. This is called an **association**. There are three fundamental table associations: one-to-one, one-to-many, and many-to-many. These associations are represented by the data structure diagrams shown in Figure 9–9.

One-to-One Association. Figure 9–9(a) shows the one-to-one (1:1) association. This means that for every record occurrence in Table X, there is zero or one occurrence in Table Y. In business terms, for every employee record in the employee file, there is a single (or zero for new employees) record in the year-to-date earnings file.

One-to-Many Association. Figure 9–9(b) shows the one-to-many (1:M) association. For every record occurrence in Table X, there is zero, one, or many occurrences in Table Y. To illustrate, for every customer record in the customer table, there is zero, one, or many sales order records in the Sales Order table.

Many-to-Many Association. Figure 9–9(c) illustrates a many-to-many (M:M) association, which is a two-way relationship. For each record occurrence in Tables X and Y, there is zero, one, or many records in Tables Y and X, respectively. An M:M association often exists between a firm's inventory records and its vendor records. A particular inventory item may be supplied by one or more vendors. At the same time, a single vendor supplies one or more items of inventory.

Linkages between Relational Tables

The linkages between relational tables needed to achieve the associations described above are formed using embedded keys, as illustrated in Figure 9–10. Associations are

---

FIGURE 9–9   Record Associations

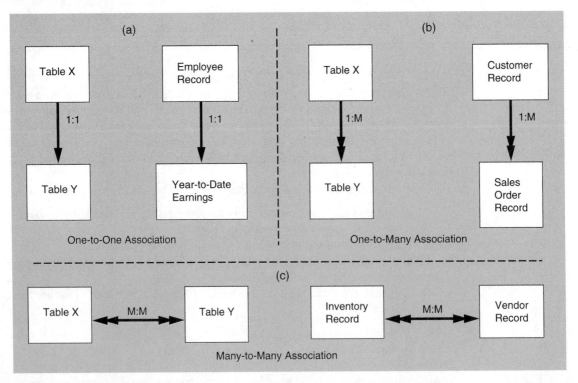

FIGURE 9–10   Linkages between Relational Tables

formed by an attribute that is common to both tables. For example, the primary key of the Customer table (Cust Num) is embedded as a foreign key in both the Sales Invoice and Cash Receipts tables. Similarly, the primary key in the Sales Invoice table (Invoice Num) is a foreign key in the Line Item table. Note that the Line Item table uses a composite primary key comprising two fields—Invoice Num and Item Num. Both fields are needed to identify each record in the table uniquely, but only the invoice number portion of the key provides the logical link to the Sales Invoice table.

The DBMS makes the physical connection between records in the related tables by searching the specified tables for records with a known key value. For example, if a user wants all the invoices for Customer 1875, the systems will search the Sales Invoice table for records with a foreign key value of 1875. We see from Figure 9–10 that there is only one occurrence—invoice number 1921. To obtain the line item details for this invoice, a search is made of the Line Item table for records with a foreign key value of 1921. Two records are retrieved.

The nature of the association between two tables determines the method used for assigning foreign keys. These methods will be examined later in the section that deals with designing a relational database.

The Defining Rules for Relational Database Systems

From a purist's point of view, a fully relational system is one that conforms to 12 stringent rules outlined by Codd.[3] As a practical matter, however, not all of Codd's rules are equally important. Some are critical but some are not. Therefore, other theorists have proposed less rigid requirements for assessing the relational standing of a system.[4] Accordingly, a system is relational if it:

> Supports the relational algebra functions of *restrict, project,* and *join* without requiring any definitions of access paths (links) to support these operations.

These requirements are examined below:

Restrict: Extracts specified rows from a specified table. This operation, illustrated in Figure 9–11(a), creates a virtual table (one that does not physically exist) that is a subset of the original table.

Project: Extracts specified attributes (columns) from a table to create a virtual table. This is presented in Figure 9–11(b).

Join: Builds a new physical table from two tables consisting of all concatenated pairs of rows, from each table. See Figure 9–11(c).

Although restrict, project, and join is not the complete set of relational algebra functions, it is a useful subset. Most business information needs are satisfied with these operations alone. The next section demonstrates the use of SQL to perform these functions.

DESIGNING RELATIONAL DATABASES

This section examines the steps involved in creating a relational database. Keep in mind that this process is a subset of a much larger systems development process that involves extensive analysis of user needs, which are not covered at this time. That body of material is the subject of Chapters 13 and 14. Thus, the starting point is actually the result of a considerable amount of preliminary work that has identified, in great detail, the key elements of the system that is under development. With this backdrop, the focus will be on the three primary phases of database design: **conceptual database design**, **logical database design**, and **physical database design**.

CONCEPTUAL DATABASE DESIGN

Conceptual database design involves discovering and analyzing the organization's data needs. Through discussions with users and analysis of business rules, the database designer identifies the key entities in the system and the data pertaining to them that are important and which need to be captured and maintained. These findings are formally represented by a data model. The primary tool used in data modeling is the

---

3   For a complete discussion of these rules see McFadden and Hoffer, *Database Management*: 698–703.
4   Date, *An Introduction to Database Systems*: 320–26.

| FIGURE 9–11 | The Relational Algebra Function—Restrict, Project, and Join |

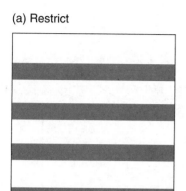

(a) Restrict

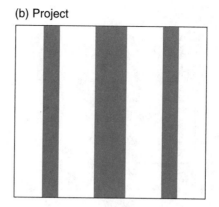

(b) Project

(c) Join

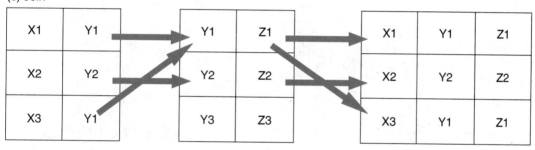

entity relationship (ER) diagram. The ER diagram employs three basic symbols to depict the entities or data objects in the system:

1. *Entities* are nouns that are depicted by rectangles on an ER diagram. An entity is a resource, an event, or an individual involved in the business process.
2. *Attributes* are data that describe the characteristics or properties of entities. These are represented by labeled circles attached to entities.
3. *Relationships* among entities are depicted by diamond symbols. They are expressed in verb form such as selects, updates, prepares, or examines.

The ER diagram of a proposed new purchases system is represented by Figure 9–12. Only a few entity attributes are illustrated in the example to keep the diagram simple. To avoid cluttering an ER diagram, many data modeling tools do not use the attribute symbol. Instead, the user can access an attribute list for each entity simply by selecting the object with the mouse pointer.

The degree of association between two entities is represented by *cardinality*—the number of records in one file that are linked to a single record in another file. Cardinality reflects 1:1, 1:M, and M:M associations. The cardinality of a particular relationship depends on the organization's **business rules**. The following describes the business rules implicit in Figure 9–12:

FIGURE 9–12 ER Diagram for Purchases System

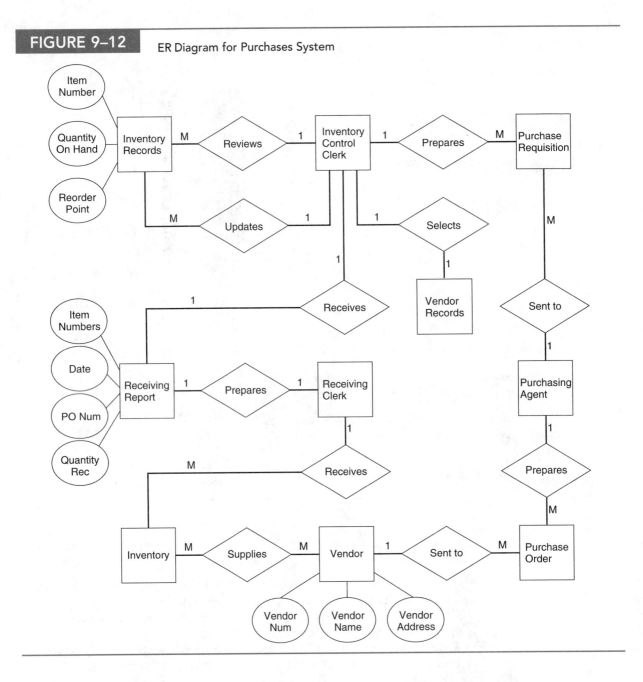

1. The inventory control clerk reviews the inventory records for items that are below their reorder point and prepares one purchase requisition for each inventory item to be reordered. The clerk selects one vendor from the vendor records.
2. The purchase requisitions are sent to the purchasing agent, who combines many of them (by vendor) onto a single purchase order.
3. The agent sends the purchase order to the vendor.
4. The vendor sends inventory items to the receiving clerk, who prepares a receiving report. (Many vendors may supply the same items.)
5. The inventory control clerk updates the inventory records after receiving the receiving report.

A user view is the set of data a user needs to take an action or make a decision. Each entity in Figure 9–12 (inventory, inventory records, inventory control clerk, purchase requisition, purchasing agent, purchase order, vendor, vendor records, receiving clerk, and receiving report) is a candidate for a user view that will need to be supported by one or more database tables. Some entities, such as the purchase requisition and the purchase order, may be adequately represented by a single view. The inventory entity, on the other hand, may need more than one view. For example, one view may be an inventory listing that shows each item on hand, its warehouse location, its average cost, and certain supplier information. An inventory status report that shows only items that need to be reordered could constitute a second view. A third view of the inventory entity could be a report of selected inventory items with long turnover periods. This may be used by management and auditors to identify slow moving or obsolete inventory that needs to be written down or written off.

Some of the entities portrayed in Figure 9–12 can be disqualified as candidates for a user view because they are redundant or pertain to other business processes. For example, the inventory clerk, purchasing agent, and receiving clerk are entities in both the purchases process and in the personnel system (not shown). Assuming that personnel data about these entities would be captured by the personnel system, they will be eliminated as candidates for user views in *this* system. Similarly, the entities of inventory and vendor are redundant with the entities of inventory records and vendor records, respectively. Eliminating the redundant entities leaves us with the five viable entities shown Figure 9–13.

The relevant data attributes associated with these entities should be determined by careful analysis of user needs and may include both financial and nonfinancial data. A possible list of data attributes is provided in Figure 9–14. At this point we are ready to proceed to the next stage in the design process.

LOGICAL DATABASE DESIGN

This section examines the process of converting conceptual user views into the underlying base tables of the database. These tables will ultimately be used to produce the physical views that the end user will use for decision making.

FIGURE 9–13

Five Database
Tables of the
Purchases System

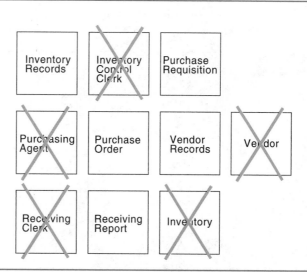

FIGURE 9–14

Partial List of
Attributes

INVENTORY
  Part number
  Description
  Quantity on hand
  Reorder point
  Unit price
  Order quantity
  Purchase requisition number

PURCHASE ORDER
  Purchase order number
  Inventory part number(s)
  Description
  Order quantity
  Unit price
  Vendor (number)
  Expected delivery date
  Order date
  Total cost of purchase
  Vendor name
  Vendor address
  Vendor telephone number

PURCHASE REQUISITION
  Purchase requisition number
  Inventory part number
  Description
  Order quantity

  Expected purchase price
  Vendor (number)
  Expected delivery date
  Order date
  Purchase order number

RECEIVING REPORT
  Receiving report number
  Purchase order number
  Inventory part number(s) received
  Condition code
  Quantity received
  Date received
  Carrier code
  Bill of lading number
  Prepaid
  Collect
  Vendor name
  Vendor address

VENDOR
  Vendor number
  Vendor name
  Vendor address
  Vendor telephone number
  Terms of trade
  Lead time

The first step in this process is to create an unnormalized table for each of the five candidate views in Figure 9–13 and assign each table a primary key. Although several base tables may be required to support a single view, for the moment each candidate view will be represented as a single unnormalized table. Any additional tables that are needed will be produced later. Figure 9–15 shows the five unnormalized tables with their primary keys.

FIGURE 9–15

Tables and
Primary Keys

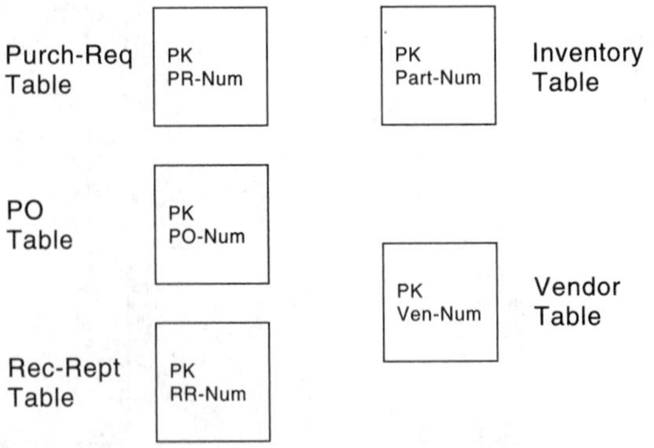

Purch-Req Table — PK PR-Num

PK Part-Num — Inventory Table

PO Table — PK PO-Num

PK Ven-Num — Vendor Table

Rec-Rept Table — PK RR-Num

Determine Relationships among the Tables

Next we need to specify the associations between the tables. Recall that three types of data associations may exist: one-to-one (1:1), one-to-many (1:M), and many-to-many (M:M). Associations represent business rules. Sometimes the rules are obvious and are the same for all organizations. For example, the normal association between a Customer table and an Invoice table is 1:M. This signifies that one customer may have many invoices (sales events). Most organizations would not restrict their customers to a single sale. If they were to do so, however, this rule will be represented as a 1:1 association between the tables.

Sometimes the association between entities is not apparent because different rules may apply in different organizations. For example, the association between the Inventory table and the Supplier table may be 1:M or M:M. A 1:M association reflects the policy of always buying a particular inventory item from the same vendor. The vendor, however, may supply multiple items. Such a policy could reflect an exclusive trading partner relationship between the organization and its vendors. Alternatively, an organization may choose to buy the same products from multiple vendors to avoid excessive reliance on a single vendor. Each vendor also supplies many different items of inventory. The business rule in this case is represented by an M:M association between the tables. The important point to be made here is that the organization's business rules will impact the structure of the database tables. If the database is to function properly, its designers need to understand the business rules of the organization as well as the specific needs of the individual user. Figure 9–16 illustrates the entity associations in this example. The underlying business rules are explained below.

1. There is a 1:1 association between the Inventory and Purchase Requisition tables. Each inventory item that falls below its reorder point is represented by a single corresponding record in the Purchase Requisition table. Similarly, each record in the Purchase Requisition table is associated with only one inventory item. A further assumption here is that the Purchase Requisition table contains only *open* items. Once the item is received from the supplier the requisition record is closed, removed from the table, and copied to a closed Invoice table. This archive table is not shown in our example.

FIGURE 9–16

Relations
between
Tables

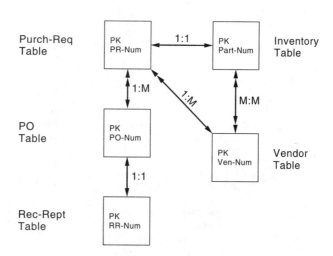

2. There is an M:M association between the Inventory and Vendor tables. This means that inventory items may be supplied by one or more vendors, and each vendor may supply one or more items of inventory.

3. There is a 1:M association between the Vendor and Purchase Requisition tables. Although many vendors supply the same items, a single vendor is selected for each purchase event (requisition). However, each vendor may be associated with many purchase requisitions.

4. There is a 1:M association between the Purchase Order and Purchase Requisition tables. Each purchase order record may be associated with multiple requisitions to the same vendor, but each requisition is associated with only one purchase order record.

5. There is a 1:1 association between the Purchase Order and Receiving Report tables. A single receiving report record reflects the receipt of goods that are specified on a single purchase order record. Multiple purchase orders are not combined on a single receiving report.

Place Foreign Keys in Tables

Now that logical associations between the tables have been established, links must be created between them. Tables in relational database systems are linked via embedded foreign keys. Figure 9–17 shows the embedded keys for all the tables in the example. The key-assignment rules for linking tables are discussed below.

Keys in 1:1 Associations. Where there is a 1:1 association between tables, it does not matter which primary key is used as the foreign key in the related table. For example, Part-Num (primary key of Inventory table) could serve as the foreign key in the Purchase Requisition table. Alternatively, PR-Num (primary key of the Purchase Requisition table) could be the foreign key in the Inventory table. In this instance, there is an advantage to using the latter option. The presence of a key value in the PR-Num (FK) field in the inventory record indicates that the item is "on order." This

---

FIGURE 9–17

Embedded Keys
within Tables

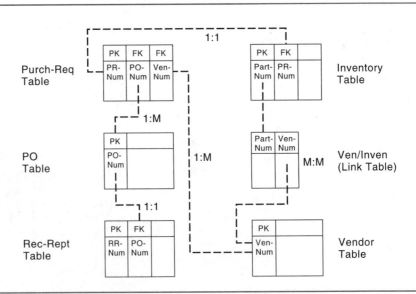

field is assigned a value when a purchase requisition record is created, which occurs only when quantity-on-hand (QOH) falls below the reorder point. If the system detects that QOH is below the reorder point, and there is no value in the PR-Num field, then and only then should a purchase requisition record be created. This prevents the same items from being ordered multiple times. When the inventory is received and posted to the Inventory table, the value in the PR-Num field will be returned to its normal (zero) state.

Keys in 1:M Associations. Where there is a 1:M association, the primary key of the 1 side is embedded in the table of the M side. Therefore, in forming the link between the Purchase Order and Purchase Requisition tables, PO-Num will be the foreign key in the Purchase Requisition table. Similarly, the primary key Ven-Num (Vendor table) is embedded in the Purchase Requisition table.

Keys in M:M Associations. To represent the M:M association between the Inventory and Vendor databases, a link table called Ven/Inven is created. The link table has a combined key consisting of Part-Num and Ven-Num. This table could be used to contain data that are unique to a specific item and a specific vendor, such as price or special terms. In the example, the link table contains only keys for linkage purposes.

Add Database Attributes and Normalize the Tables

Now the attributes listed in Figure 9–14 can be added to the table structures. To avoid serious anomalies associated with unnormalized data, normalization procedures need to be performed. A detailed explanation of the normalization process and associated anomalies is provided at the end of this section. Additional explanation in is the appendix to the chapter.

Simply stated, normalization involves dividing an unnormalized database into smaller tables until all attributes in the resulting tables are uniquely and wholly dependent on (explained by) the primary key. When this is achieved, the tables are in **third normal form (3NF)**. Currently, not all the tables in Figure 9–18 are in 3NF. Briefly, the normalization problems to be resolved are:

1. The attributes Part-Num, Description, Order-Quantity, and Unit Price in the Purchase Order table constitute **repeating group** data. This means that when a particular purchase order contains more than one item, then multiple values will exist for *part number*, *description*, *quantity ordered*, and *price* in the purchase order record. Multiple values for attributes cannot be stored efficiently within a single record. These repeating group data need to be removed from the Purchase Order table, placed is a separate table, and assigned a new key.
2. The attributes Part-Num, Quantity Received, and Condition Code are repeating groups in the Receiving Report table, and also need to be removed to another table.
3. The Purchase Requisition, Purchase Order, and Receiving Report tables contain data that are not dependent on their primary keys. These data have **transitive dependencies** on another attribute within their respective tables. Normally, transitive dependencies need to be removed from their existing tables and placed in a new table. In our example, however, these data are also redundant with data that currently exist in other tables, making it unnecessary to create any additional tables for this purpose.

Figure 9–19 illustrates the structures of 3NF base tables that solve these problems. The primary and foreign keys linking the tables are represented by dotted lines. The

FIGURE 9–18   Unnormalized Tables for Purchases System

Inventory Table

PK						FK
Part-Num	Desc.	QOH	Reorder-Point	Order-Qnty	Unit Price	PR-Num

Purch-Req Table

PK								FK
PR-Num	Part-Num	Desc.	Order-Qnty	Unit Price	Ven-Num	Expected Del Date	Order Date	PO-Num

PO Table

PK	Repeating Group										
PO-Num	Part-Num	Desc.	Order-Qnty	Unit Price	Ven-Num	Expected Del Date	Order Date	Total Cost	Vendor Name	Vendor Address	Tel-Num

Rec-Rept Table

PK	FK	Repeating Group									
RR-Num	PO-Num	Part-Num	Qnty Received	Condition Code	Carrier Code	Date Received	Vendor Name	Vendor Address	Freight Bill Num	Pre-Paid	Collect

Vendor Table

PK					
Ven-Num	Vendor Name	Vendor Address	Tel-Num	Terms	Lead Time

Ven/Inven Table

PK	PK
Ven-Num	Part-Num

normalization process resulted in the creation of two new base tables called RR Line Item and PO Line Item. Each record in the RR Line Item table represents an individual item on the receiving report. The table has a combined key comprising RR-Num and Part-Num. Both keys are needed to uniquely identify each line item record. The RR-Num portion of the key provides the link to the Receiving Report table that contains general data about the receipt. The Part-Num portion of the key is used to access the Inventory table to update the QOH field from the Qnty Received field of the Line Item record.

The PO Line Item table contains only the PO-Num and the Part-Num. This combined key uniquely defines each item on the purchase order. The PO-Num component of the composite key provides a link to the Purchase Order table. The Part-Num element of the key is a link to the Inventory table where Description, Order Quantity, and Unit Price data reside.

The normalized base tables should be rich enough to support the views of all system users. For example, the purchase order in Figure 9–19, which could be the data entry screen for a purchasing clerk, has been constructed from the attributes of several base tables. To illustrate the relationship, the fields in the view are cross-referenced via circled numbers to the attributes in the supporting base tables. Keep in mind that these base tables would also provide data for many other views not shown here, including receiving reports, purchase requisition listing, inventory status report, vendor purchases activity report, and more.

The purchase order in Figure 9–19 is an example of a **physical user view**, which would be created through the query feature of the database management system. The

FIGURE 9–19

Normalized Tables

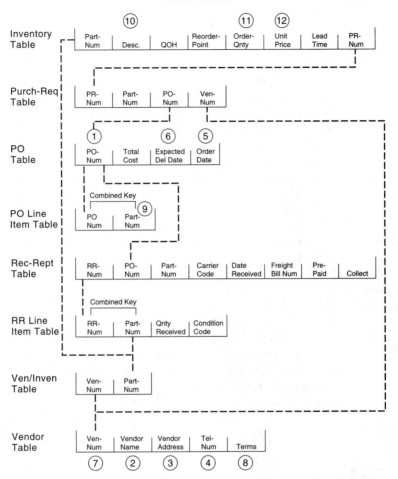

Base Tables

User's View—Purchase Order

technical task of producing physical views varies among DBMS products. A generic explanation of this process is discussed later in the section that deals with the physical design of the database.

The Data Normalization Process

In this section, the **data normalization** process is explored, which requires an in-depth understanding of the user's information needs and the organization's business rules. The process begins by designing the views (output reports, documents, and input screens) needed by the user. These views may be created on a word processor, a graphics program, or simply with paper and pencil. At this point the view is simply a graphical representation of the physical view the user will eventually have when the project is completed.

As a matter of efficiency, many views of many users may be considered together. This is particularly so when the views are based on the same set of base tables. For illustration purposes, however, the normalization process will be based on the inventory status report illustrated in Figure 9–20. This view provides the purchasing agent with information about inventory items to be ordered and the suppliers (vendors) of the inventory.

The Importance of Data Normalization

Correctly designed database tables are critical to the operational success of the DBMS. Poorly designed tables can cause processing problems that restrict, or even deny, users access to the information they need.

Data normalization is a process that promotes effective database design by grouping data attributes into tables that comply to specific conditions. There are several possible levels of normalization. Usually, designers of business databases normalize tables to the 3NF level.

FIGURE 9–20   Inventory Status Report

Ajax Manufacturing Co.
Inventory Status Report

Part Number	Description	Quantity On Hand	Reorder Point	Order Quantity	Supplier Number	Name	Address	Telephone
1	Bracket	100	150	500	22 24 27	Ozment Sup Buell Co. B&R Sup	123 Main St. 2 Broadhead Westgate Mall	555-7895 555-3436 555-7845
2	Gasket	440	450	1000	22 24 28	Ozment Sup Buell Co. Harris Manuf	123 Main St. 2 Broadhead 24 Linden St.	555-7895 555-3436 555-3316
3	Brace	10	10	50	22 24 28	Ozment Sup Buell Co. Harris Manuf	123 Main St. 2 Broadhead 24 Linden St.	555-7895 555-3436 555-3316
• • •	• • •	• • •	• • •	• • •	• • •	• • •	• • •	• • •

Tables that have not been normalized are associated with three types of problems called **anomalies**: the *update anomaly*, the *insertion anomaly*, and the *deletion anomaly*. One or more of these anomalies will exist in tables that are normalized at lower levels such as **first normal form (1NF)** and **second normal form (2NF)**, but tables in 3NF are free of anomalies.

To demonstrate the three anomalies, the user view in Figure 9–20 is represented as a single unnormalized table called Inventory in Figure 9–21. While it is possible to represent simple user views with a single 3NF table, complex views usually require more than one table. The user view in Figure 9–20, for example, cannot be represented by the single table depicted in Figure 9–21 without incurring the anomalies described below.

Update Anomaly.   The **update anomaly** results from data redundancy in an unnormalized table. To illustrate, notice that Supplier Number 22 provides each of the three inventory items (Part Num 1, 2, 3) shown in Figure 9–21. The data attributes pertaining to Supplier Number 22 (Name, Address, and Tele Num) are thus repeated in every record of every inventory item that Supplier Number 22 provides. Any change in the supplier's name, address, or telephone number must be made to each of these records in the table. In the example, this means three different updates. To better appreciate the implications of the update anomaly, consider a more realistic situation where the vendor supplies 10,000 different items of inventory. Any update to an attribute must then be made 10,000 times.

Insertion Anomaly.   To demonstrate the effects of the **insertion anomaly**, assume that a new vendor has entered the marketplace. The organization does not yet purchase from the vendor, but may wish to do so in the future. In the meantime, the organization wants to add the vendor to the database. This is not possible because the primary key for the Inventory table is Part Num. Since the vendor does not supply the organization with any inventory items, the supplier data cannot be added to the table.

Deletion Anomaly.   The **deletion anomaly** involves the unintentional deletion of data from a table. To illustrate, assume that Supplier Number 27 provides the

FIGURE 9–21   Unnormalized Database Table

Inventory Table

Part Num	Description	Quantity On Hand	Reorder Point	EOQ	Supplier Number	Name	Address	Tele Num
1	Bracket	100	150	500	22	Ozment Sup	123 Main St.	555-7895
1	Bracket	100	150	500	24	Buell Co.	2 Broadhead	555-3436
1	Bracket	100	150	500	27	B&R Sup	Westgate Mall	555-7845
2	Gasket	440	450	1000	22	Ozment Sup	123 Main St.	555-7895
2	Gasket	440	450	1000	24	Buell Co.	2 Broadhead	555-3436
2	Gasket	440	450	1000	28	Harris Manuf	24 Linden St.	555-3316
3	Brace	10	10	50	22	Ozment Sup	123 Main St.	555-7895
3	Brace	10	10	50	24	Buell Co.	2 Broadhead	555-3436
3	Brace	10	10	50	28	Harris Manuf	24 Linden St.	555-3316

Primary Key / Nonkey Attributes

company with only one item: Part Number 1. If the organization discontinues this item of inventory and deletes it from the table, the data pertaining to Supplier Number 27 will also be deleted. Although the company may wish to retain the supplier's information for future use, the current table design prevents it from doing so.

The presence of the deletion anomaly is less conspicuous, but potentially more serious than the update and insertion anomalies. A flawed database design that prevents the insertion of records or requires the user to perform excessive updates attracts attention quickly. However, the deletion anomaly may go undetected, and the user may be unaware of the loss of important data until it is too late. A poorly structured database can result in the unintentional loss of critical accounting records and the destruction of the audit trail. Hence, the design of database tables carries internal control significance that accountants need to recognize.

Data Normalization Rules

A normalization process that formally examines anomaly-causing dependencies known as *repeating groups*, **partial dependencies**, and *transitive dependencies* is presented in the appendix to this chapter. Here, an intuitive approach is followed to normalizing data. Simply stated, eliminating the three anomalies involves a process of systematically splitting unnormalized complex tables into smaller tables that meet two conditions:

1. All nonkey attributes in the table are dependent on the primary key.
2. All nonkey attributes are independent of the other nonkey attributes.

In other words, a normalized table is one in which the primary key of a table wholly and uniquely defines each attribute in the table. Furthermore, none of the table attributes are defined by another attribute other than the primary key. When these conditions are met, the table is in 3NF. If, however, one or more attributes violates these conditions, they need to be removed and placed in a separate table and assigned an appropriate key.

Splitting Unnormalized Tables

Not all the data attributes in Figure 9–21 are defined by the primary key Part Num. In fact, two distinct sets of data reside in this table as it currently stands: data about inventory and data about suppliers. The nonkey attributes of Name, Address, and Tele Num are not dependent on (defined by) Part Num. Rather, these attributes are dependent on the nonkey attribute Supplier Number. The solution is to remove the supplier data from the Inventory table and place them in a separate table, which we will call Supplier. Figure 9–22 shows the two 3NF base tables, Inventory and Supplier, along with a third table called Part/Supplier, which links the two. This linking technique will be explained later.

Normalizing the tables has eliminated the three anomalies. First, the update anomaly is resolved because data about each supplier exist in only one location—the Supplier table. Any change in the data about an individual vendor is made only once, regardless of how many items it supplies. Second, the insert anomaly is solved, because new vendors can be added to the supplier table even if they are not currently supplying the organization with inventory. For example, Supplier Number 30 in the table does not supply any inventory items. Finally, the deletion anomaly is eliminated. The decision to delete an inventory item from the database will not result in the unintentional deletion of the supplier data as well, since these data reside independently in different tables.

FIGURE 9–22   Normalized Database Tables

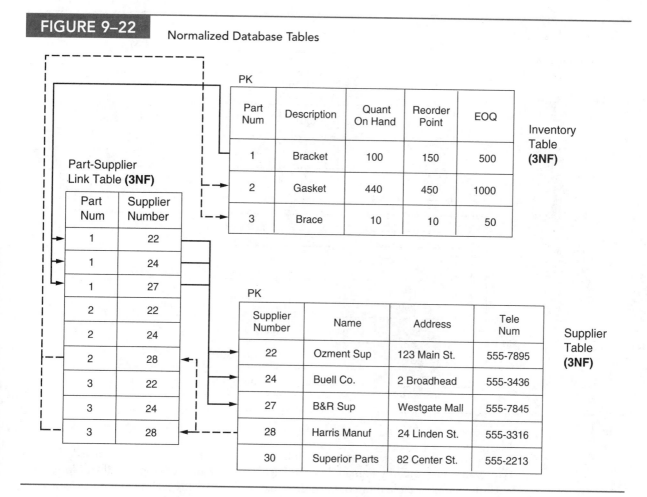

Linking Normalized Tables

When unnormalized tables are split into multiple 3NF tables, they need to be linked together so that the data in them can be related and made accessible to users. The degree of association between the resulting tables (i.e., 1:1, 1:M, or M:M) determines how the linking occurs. Three key-assignment rules were introduced earlier in this section. While the 1:1 association involves a simplistic solution, the 1:M and M:M associations require further explanation. To demonstrate the logic behind the 1:M key-assignment rule, consider two alternative business rules for purchasing inventory from suppliers.

> Business Rule 1. Each vendor supplies the firm with three (or less) different items of inventory but each item is supplied by only one vendor.

This somewhat unrealistic, but logically possible, business rule describes a limited 1:M association between the Inventory and Supplier tables.

Recall that in a 1:M association, the primary key on the "1" side is embedded as a foreign key on the "many" side. Following this rule the designer would modify the inventory table structure to include the Supplier Number as illustrated in Figure 9–23. Under this approach, each record in the Inventory table will now contain the value of the key field of the vendor that supplies that item. By contrast, Figure 9–24

FIGURE 9–23

Applying the 1:M
Key-Assignment Rule

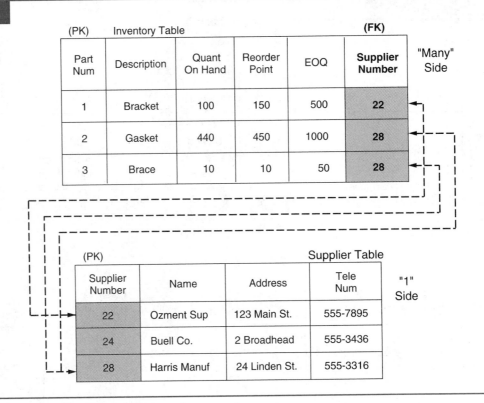

shows what the table structure might look like if the designer reversed the key-assignment rule by embedding the Part Num key in the Supplier table. Notice that the Supplier table now contains three part number fields each linking to an associated record in the Inventory table. Only the links to part numbers 1, 2, and 3 are shown. Although this technique violates the key-assignment rule, these table structures would work. They work, however, only because the upper limit of the "many" side of the association is known and is very small (limited to three). How would this table structure look if we assume a more realistic business rule like the one below?

> Business Rule 2. Each vendor supplies the firm with any number of inventory items but each item is supplied by only one vendor.

This is a true 1:M association where the upper limit of the "many" side of the association is unbounded. In other words the vendor may supply one item of inventory or ten thousand. How many fields must we add to the Supplier table structure to accommodate all possible links to the Inventory table? Here we can see the logic behind the 1:M key-assignment rule. The structure in Figure 9–23 still works under this business rule, whereas the technique illustrated in Figure 9–24 does not.

Now re-examine the association in Figure 9–22. These tables illustrate a M:M association described by the following business rule:

> M:M Business Rule. Each vendor supplies the firm with any number of inventory items but each item may be supplied by any number of vendors.

This business rule is evident by examining the contents of the Inventory Status Report (the user view) in Figure 9–20. Each part number shown has multiple suppli-

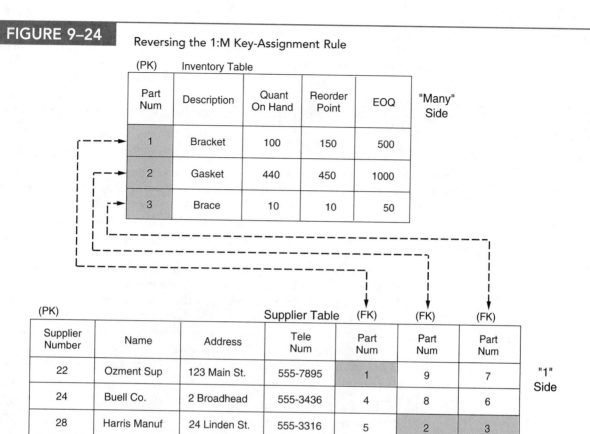

FIGURE 9–24   Reversing the 1:M Key-Assignment Rule

ers and each supplier may supply multiple items. For example, Ozment Supply provides items 1, 2, and 3.

Recall that an M:M association between base tables requires the creation of a separate link table rather than using embedded foreign keys as links. The logic that prevented us (in the previous example) from embedding the primary key from the "many" side table of an unbounded 1:M association into the table of the "one" side applies here. Neither table can donate an embedded key to the other because both are on the "many" side. The only solution, therefore, is to create a new link table containing the key fields of the other two tables.

The link table (Part/Supplier) in Figure 9–22 contains the primary keys for the records in the Inventory table (Part Num) and the related Supplier table (Supplier Number). Via the link table, every inventory record can be linked to each supplier of the item, and every supplier can be linked to the inventory items that it supplies. For example, by searching the Inventory table for Part Num 1, we see that suppliers 22, 24, and 27 supply this item. Searching in the opposite direction, supplier 28 provides part numbers 2 and 3. A separate record in the link table represents each unique occurrence of a supplier/inventory association. For example, if supplier 24 provides 500 different items, 500 link records are needed to depict these associations.

Accountants and Data Normalization

Database normalization is a technical matter that is usually the responsibility of systems professionals. However, the subject has implications for internal control that make it the concern of accountants, also. For example, the update anomaly can generate conflicting and obsolete database values; the insertion anomaly can result in unrecorded transactions and incomplete audit trails; and the deletion anomaly can cause the loss of accounting records and the destruction of audit trails. Although most accountants will not be responsible for normalizing an organization's databases, they should have an understanding of the process and be able to determine whether a table is properly normalized.

PHYSICAL DATABASE DESIGN

The Inventory, Supplier, and Part-Supplier tables created thus far are theoretical (on paper), not physical. The next step is to create the physical tables and populate them with data. This is an involved step that must be carefully planned and executed, and may take many months in a large installation. Once this is done, the physical user views can be produced.

The query function of a relational DBMS allows the system designer to easily create user views from base tables. The designer simply tells the DBMS which tables to use, their primary and foreign keys, and the attributes to select from each table. Older DBMSs require the designer to specify these parameters in SQL or another query language. Newer systems allow this to be done visually. The designer simply points and clicks at the tables and the attributes. From this visual representation, the DBMS generates the SQL commands for the query to produce the view.

The SQL commands to produce the actual inventory status report (the physical view) illustrated in Figure 9–20 are given below.

SELECT inventory.part-num, description, quant-on-hand, reorder-point, EOQ, part-supplier.part-num, part-supplier.supplier-number, supplier.supplier-number, name, address, tele-num,

FROM inventory, part-supplier, supplier

WHERE inventory.part-num=part-supplier.part-num AND part-supplier. supplier-number=supplier.supplier-number AND quant-on-hand≤reorder-point

- The SELECT command identifies all the attributes to be contained in the view. When the same attribute appears in more than one table (e.g., part-num) the source table name must also be specified.
- The FROM command identifies the tables used in creating the view.
- The WHERE command specifies how rows in the Inventory, Part-Supplier and Supplier tables are to be matched to create the view. In this case, the three tables are algebraically joined on the primary keys Part-Num and Supplier-Number.
- Multiple expressions may be linked with the AND, OR, and NOT operators. In this example, the last expression uses AND to restrict the records to be selected with the logical expression *quant-on-hand≤reorder-point*. Only records whose quantities on hand have fallen to or below their reorder points will be selected for the view. The user will not see the many thousands of other inventory items that have adequate quantities available.

To view data, the user executes the query program. Each time this is done, the query builds a new view with current data. The resulting view is based on a **virtual table** derived from the underlying base tables. A virtual table does not physically exist as a set of rows and columns. Rather, it is a partial representation (subrows and subcolumns) of the actual physical base tables. However, the user perceives the view as his or her personal database. By restricting the user's access to the view, rather than permitting access to the underlying base tables, the user is limited to authorized data only.

A report program is used to make the view visually attractive and easy to use. Column headings can be added, fields summed, and averages calculated to produce a hard-copy or computer screen report that resembles the original user report in Figure 9–20. The report program can suppress unnecessary data from the view such as duplicated fields and the key values in the Part-Supplier link table. These keys are necessary to build the view but are not needed in the actual report.

DATABASES IN A DISTRIBUTED ENVIRONMENT

Chapter 1 introduced the concept of **distributed data processing (DDP)** as an alternative to the centralized approach. Most modern organizations use some form of distributed processing and networking to process their transactions. Some companies process all of their transactions in this way. An important consideration in planning a distributed system is the location of the organization's database. In addressing this issue, the planner has two basic options: databases can be *centralized* or they can be distributed. Distributed databases fall into two categories: *partitioned* and *replicated* databases. This section examines issues, features, and trade-offs that should be carefully evaluated in deciding how databases should be distributed.

CENTRALIZED DATABASES

Under the **centralized database** approach, remote users send requests via terminals for data to the central site, which processes the requests and transmits the data back to the user. The central site performs the functions of a file manager that services the data needs of the remote users. The centralized database approach is illustrated in Figure 9–25.

Earlier in the chapter, three primary advantages of the database approach were presented: the reduction of data storage costs, the elimination of multiple update procedures, and the establishment of **data currency** (the firm's data files reflect accurately the effects of its transactions). Achieving data currency is critical to database integrity and reliability. However, in the DDP environment, this can be a challenging task.

Data Currency in a DDP Environment

During data processing, account balances pass through a state of **temporary inconsistency** where their values are incorrectly stated. This occurs during the execution of any accounting transaction. To illustrate, consider the computer logic for recording the credit sale of $2,000 to customer Jones.

	INSTRUCTION	DATABASE VALUES AR-Jones	AR-Control
	START		
1	Read AR-Sub account (Jones)	1500	
2	Read AR-Control account		10000
3	Write AR-Sub account (Jones) + $2000	3500	
4	Write AR-Control account + $2000		12000
	END		

Immediately after the execution of Instruction Number 3, and before the execution of Instruction Number 4, the AR-Control account value is temporarily inconsistent by the sum of $2,000. Only after the completion of the entire transaction is this inconsistency resolved. In a DDP environment, such temporary inconsistencies can

FIGURE 9–25

Centralized Database

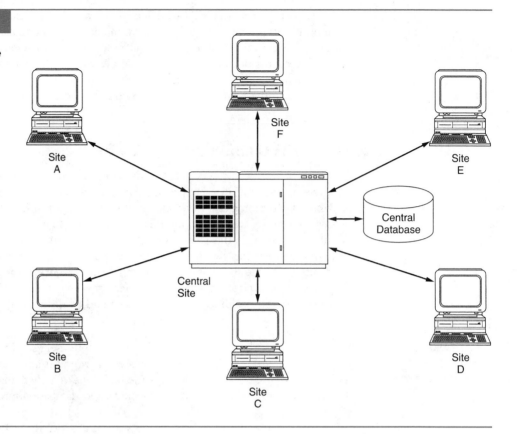

result in the permanent corruption of the database. To illustrate the potential for damage, look at a slightly more complicated example. Using the same computer logic as before, consider the processing of two separate transactions from two remote sites: Transaction 1 (T1) is the sale of $2,000 on account to customer Jones from Site A; Transaction 2 (T2) is the sale of $1,000 on account to customer Smith from Site B. The following logic shows the possible interweaving of the two processing tasks and the effect on data currency.

		INSTRUCTION	DATABASE VALUES Central Site		
SITE A	SITE B		AR-Jones	AR-Smith	AR-Control
T1	T2	START			
1		Read AR-Sub account (Jones)	1500		
	1	Read AR-Sub account (Smith)		3000	
2		Read AR-Control account			10000
3		Write AR-Sub account (Jones) + $2000	3500		
	2	**Read AR-Control account**			10000
4		Write AR-Control account + $2000			12000
	3	Write AR-Sub account (Smith) + $1000		4000	
	4	Write AR-Control account + $1000 END			11000

Notice that Site B seized the AR-Control data value of $10,000 when it was in an inconsistent state. By using this value to process its transaction, Site B effectively destroyed the record of Transaction T1 that had been processed by Site A. Therefore, instead of $13,000, the new AR-Control balance is misstated at $11,000.

Database Lockout

To achieve data currency, simultaneous access to individual data elements by multiple sites needs to be prevented. The solution to this problem is to use a **database lockout,** which is a software control (usually a function of the DBMS) that prevents multiple simultaneous accesses to data. The previous example can be used to illustrate this technique: immediately upon receiving the access request from Site A for AR-Control (T1, Instruction Number 2), the central site DBMS places a lock on AR-Control to prevent access from other sites until Transaction T1 is complete. Thus, when Site B requests AR-Control (T2, Instruction Number 2), it is placed on "wait" status until the lock is removed. Only then can Site B access AR-Control and complete Transaction T2.

DISTRIBUTED DATABASES

Distributed databases can be distributed using either the partitioned or replicated technique.

Partitioned Databases

The **partitioned database** approach splits the central database into segments or partitions that are distributed to their primary users. The advantages of this approach are:

- Users' control is increased by having data stored at local sites.
- Transaction processing response time is improved by permitting local access to data and reducing the volume of data that must be transmitted between sites.
- Partitioned databases can reduce the potential for disaster. By having data located at several sites, the loss of a single site cannot terminate all data processing by the organization.

The partitioned approach, which is illustrated in Figure 9–26, works best for organizations that require minimal data sharing among users at remote sites. To the extent that remote users share common data, the problems associated with the centralized approach still apply. Requests for data from other sites must now be managed by the primary user. Selecting the optimum host location for the partitions will minimize data access problems. This requires an in-depth analysis of end-user data needs.

The Deadlock Phenomenon. In a distributed environment, it is possible that multiple sites will lock out each other, thus preventing each from processing its transactions. For example, Figure 9–27 illustrates three sites and their mutual data needs. Notice that Site 1 has requested (and locked) Data A and is waiting for the removal of the lock on Data C to complete its transaction. Site 2 has a lock on C and is waiting for E. Finally, Site 3 has a lock on E and is waiting for A. A **deadlock** occurs here because there is mutual exclusion to data, and the transactions are in a "wait" state until the locks are removed. This can result in transactions being incompletely processed and corruption of the database. A deadlock is a permanent condition that must be resolved by special software that analyzes each deadlock condition to determine the best solution. Because of the implications for transaction processing, accountants should be aware of the issues pertaining to deadlock resolutions.

FIGURE 9-26

The Partitioned
Database Approach

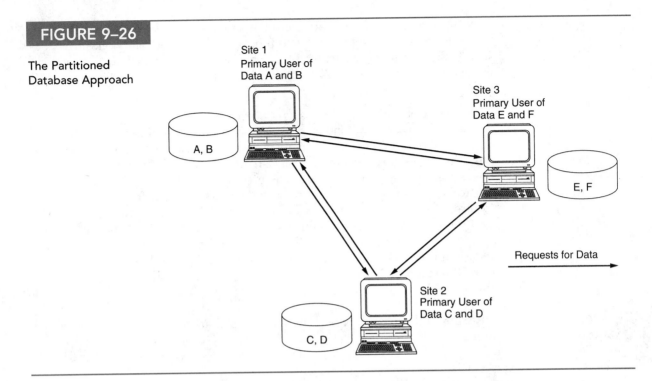

Deadlock Resolution. Resolving a deadlock usually involves sacrificing one or more transactions. These must be terminated to complete the processing of the other transactions in the deadlock. The preempted transactions must then be reinitiated. In

FIGURE 9-27

The Deadlock
Condition

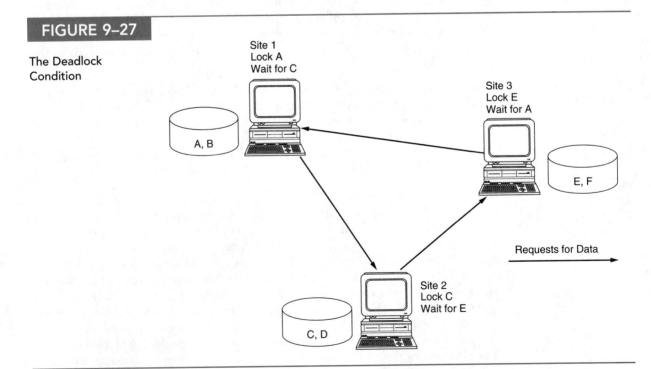

preempting transactions, the deadlock resolution software attempts to minimize the total cost of breaking the deadlock. Although not an easy task to automate, some of the factors that influence this decision are:

1. The resources currently invested in the transaction. This may be measured by the number of updates that the transaction has already performed and that must be repeated if the transaction is terminated.
2. The transaction's stage of completion. In general, deadlock resolution software will avoid terminating transactions that are close to completion.
3. The number of deadlocks associated with the transaction. Because terminating the transaction breaks all deadlock involvement, the software should attempt to terminate transactions that are part of more than one deadlock.

Replicated Databases

In some organizations, the entire database is replicated at each site. **Replicated databases** are effective in companies where there exists a high degree of data sharing but no primary user. Since common data are replicated at each site, the data traffic between sites is reduced considerably. Figure 9–28 illustrates the replicated database model.

The primary justification for a replicated database is to support read-only queries. With data replicated at every site, data access for query purposes is ensured, and lockouts and delays due to network traffic are minimized. However, a problem arises when replicated databases need to be updated by transactions and current copies of the database must be maintained at all sites.

Since each site processes only its local transactions, the common data attributes that are replicated at each site will be updated by different transactions and thus, at any point in time, will possess uniquely different values. Using the data from the earlier example, Figure 9–29 illustrates the effect of processing credit sales for Jones at Site A and Smith at Site B. After the transactions are processed, the value shown for the common AR-Control account is inconsistent ($12,000 at Site A and $11,000 at Site B) and incorrect at both sites.

FIGURE 9–28

Replicated Database
Approach

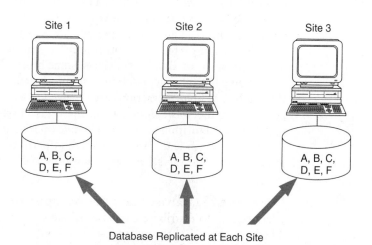

Database Replicated at Each Site

FIGURE 9–29   Replicated Databases Updated Independently

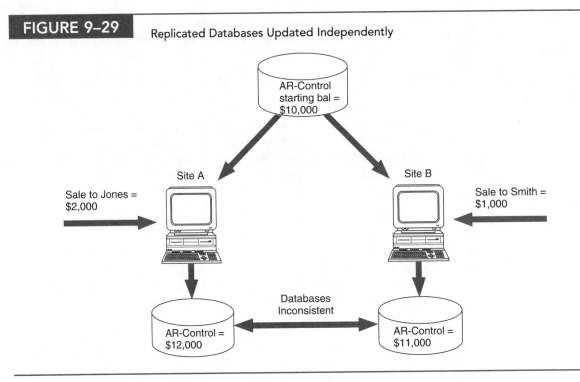

Concurrency Control

Database concurrency is the presence of complete and accurate data at all remote sites. System designers need to employ methods to ensure that transactions processed at each site are accurately reflected in the databases at all other sites. This task, while problematic, has implications for accounting records and is a matter of concern for accountants.

A commonly used method for **concurrency control** is to serialize transactions by time-stamping. This involves labeling each transaction by two criteria. First, special software groups transactions into classes to identify potential conflicts. For example, read-only (query) transactions do not conflict with other classes of transactions. Similarly, accounts payable and accounts receivable transactions are not likely to use the same data and do not conflict. However, multiple sales order transactions involving both read and write operations will potentially conflict.

The second part of the control process is to time-stamp each transaction. A systemwide clock is used to keep all sites, some of which may be in different time zones, on the same logical time. Each time stamp is made unique by incorporating the site's ID number. When transactions are received at each site, they are examined first for potential conflicts. If conflicts exist, the transactions are entered into a serialization schedule. An algorithm is used to schedule updates to the database based on the transaction time stamp and class. This method permits multiple interleaved transactions to be processed at each site as if they were serial events.

Distributed Databases and the Accountant

The decision to distribute databases is one that should be entered into thoughtfully. There are many issues and trade-offs to consider. Some of the most basic questions to be addressed are:

- Should the organization's data be centralized or distributed?
- If data distribution is desirable, should the databases be replicated or partitioned?
- If replicated, should the databases be totally replicated or partially replicated?
- If the database is to be partitioned, how should the data segments be allocated among the sites?

The choices involved in each of these questions impact the organization's ability to maintain database integrity. The preservation of audit trails and the accuracy of accounting records are key concerns. Clearly, these are decisions that the modern accountant should understand and influence intelligently.

Summary

This chapter examined the database approach to data management and showed how this approach enables business organizations to overcome data redundancy and the associated problems that plague the flat file approach to data management. It showed that the database concept comprises four dynamically interrelated components: users, the database management system, the database administrator, and the physical database. The DBMS stands between the physical database and the user community. Its principal function is to provide a controlled and secure environment for the database. This is achieved through software modules, such as a query language, a data definition language, and a data manipulation language. The DBMS also provides security against human error and natural disaster through various backup and recovery modules.

Three common database models were examined—the hierarchical, network, and relational models. Database models are abstract representations of data about entities, events, and activities, and their relationships within an organization. The purpose of these models is to represent such attributes in a way that is understandable to users. The focus of attention was on the relational model. A number of database design topics were covered, including data modeling, the creation of user views from ER diagrams, and data normalization techniques. Finally, the chapter presented a number of issues associated with distributed databases. It examined three possible database configurations in a distributed environment: centralized, partitioned, and the replicated databases.

Appendix

THE HIERARCHICAL DATABASE MODEL

The earliest database management systems were based on the *hierarchical* data model. This was a popular approach to data representation because it reflected, more or less faithfully, many aspects of an organization that are hierarchical in relationship. Also, it was an efficient data processing tool for highly structured problems. Figure 9–30 presents a data structure diagram showing a portion of a hierarchical database.

The hierarchical model is constructed of sets of files. Each set contains a *parent* and a *child*. Notice that File B, at the second level, is both the child in one set and the parent in another set. Files at the same level with the same parent are called *siblings*. This structure is also called a *tree structure*. The file at the most aggregated level in the tree is the *root* segment, and the file at the most detailed level in a particular branch is called a *leaf*.

FIGURE 9–30   Hierarchical Data Model

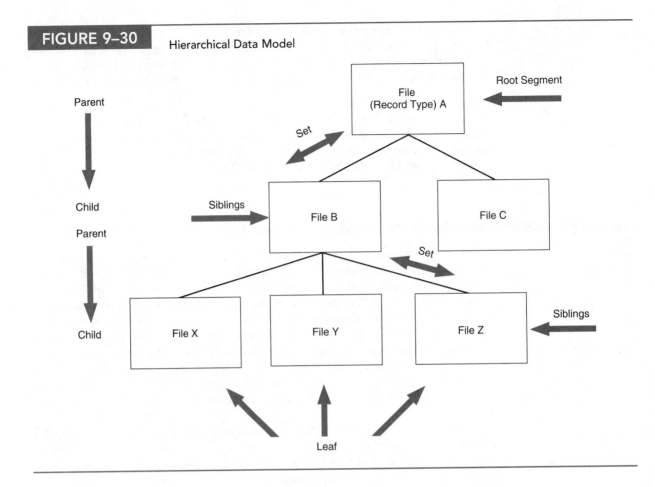

A Navigational Database

The hierarchical data model is called a *navigational database* because traversing it requires following a predefined path. This is established through pointers (discussed in Chapter 2) that create explicit linkages between related records. The only way to access data at lower levels in the tree is from the root and via the pointers down the navigational path to the desired records. For example, consider the partial database in Figure 9–31. To retrieve an invoice line item record, the DBMS must first access the customer record (the root). That record contains a pointer to the sales invoice record, which points to the invoice line item record.

Limitations of the Hierarchical Model

The hierarchical model presents a limited view of data relationships. Based on the proposition that all business relationships are hierarchical (or can be represented as such), this model does not always reflect reality. The following rules, which govern the hierarchical model, reveal its operating constraints:

1. A parent record may have one or more child records. For example, in Figure 9–31, customer is the parent of both sales invoice and cash receipts.
2. No child record can have more than one parent.

The second rule is often restrictive and limits the usefulness of the hierarchical model. Many firms need a view of data associations that permit multiple parents, such

FIGURE 9–31

Portion of a
Hierarchical
Database

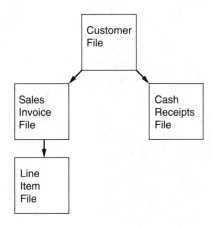

as that represented by Figure 9–32(a). In this example, the sales invoice file has two natural parents: the customer file and the salesperson file. A specific sales order is the product of both the customer's purchase activity and a salesperson's selling efforts. Management, wishing to keep track of sales orders by customer and by salesperson, will want to view sales order records as the logical child of both parents. This relationship, although logical, violates the single parent rule of the hierarchical model. Figure 9–32(b) shows the most common way of resolving this problem. By duplicating the sales invoice file, two separate hierarchical representations are created. Unfortunately, this improved functionality is achieved at a cost—increased data redundancy. The network model, examined next, deals with this problem more efficiently.

THE NETWORK DATABASE MODEL

The *network* model is a variation of the hierarchical model. The principal distinguishing feature between the two is that the network model allows a child record to have multiple parents. The multiple ownership rule is flexible in allowing complex

FIGURE 9–32

Multiple Parent
Association

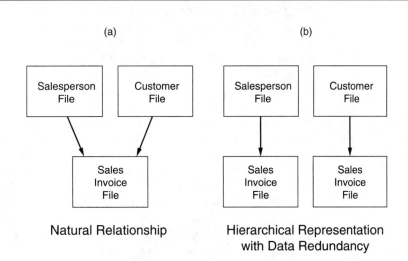

(a)   (b)

Natural Relationship   Hierarchical Representation
                                                      with Data Redundancy

relationships to be represented. Figure 9–32(a) illustrates a simple network model in which the sales invoice file has two parent files—Customer and Salesperson.

The navigational DBMS dominated the data processing industry for many years, although the current trend is overwhelmingly toward the relational model. Many hierarchical and network systems still exist and continue to be maintained and upgraded by their manufacturers.

DATA STRUCTURES

Data structures are the bricks and mortar of the database. The data structure allows records to be located, stored, and retrieved, and enables movement from one record to another. Chapter 2 examined data structures commonly used by flat file systems. These include *sequential*, *indexed*, *hashing*, and *pointer* structures. These basic structures form the foundation for the more complex *hierarchical* and *network* database structures discussed below.

HIERARCHICAL MODEL DATA STRUCTURE

Figure 9–33 shows the data structures and linkages between files for the partial database in Figure 9–31. Since the purpose is to illustrate the navigational nature of the data structure, the content of the records has been simplified.

Assume that a user of this system is using a query program to retrieve all the data pertinent to a particular sales invoice (Invoice Number 1921) for a customer John Smith (Account Number 1875). The access method used for this situation is the **hierarchical indexed direct access method (HIDAM)**. Under this method, the root segment (customer file) of the database is organized as an indexed file. Lower-level records (sales invoice, invoice line item, and cash receipts records) use pointers in a linked-list arrangement. This allows both efficient processing of the root records, for tasks such as updating accounts receivable and billing customers, and direct access of detail records for inquiries.

The access method retrieves the primary key—Cust Num 1875—entered by the user via the query program and compares this against the index for the root segment. Upon matching the key with the index, it directly accesses John Smith's customer record. Notice the customer record contains only summary information. The current balance figure represents the total dollar amount owed ($1,820) by John Smith. This is the difference between the sum of all sales to this customer minus all cash received in payment on the account. The supporting details about these transactions are contained in the lower-level sales invoice and cash receipts records. In response to the user's inquiry for data pertaining to Invoice Number 1921, the access method follows the invoice record pointer to the sales invoice file.

The sales invoice file is a randomly organized file of invoices for all customers arranged in a series of linked lists. The records in each linked list have a common property—they all relate to a specific customer. The first record in the list—the head record—has a pointer to the next in the list (if one exists), which points to the next, and so on. The pointer in the customer record (the level above) directs the access method to the head record in the appropriate linked list. The access method then compares the key value sought (Invoice Number 1921) against each record in the list until it finds a match. The records in the sales invoice file contain only summary information about sales transactions. Pointers in these records identify the supporting detail records (the specific items sold) in the invoice line item file. The structure of the line item file is also a linked-list arrangement. Starting with the head record, the access method retrieves the entire list of line items for Invoice Number 1921. In this list there are two records. The sales invoice and line item records are returned to the user's application for processing.

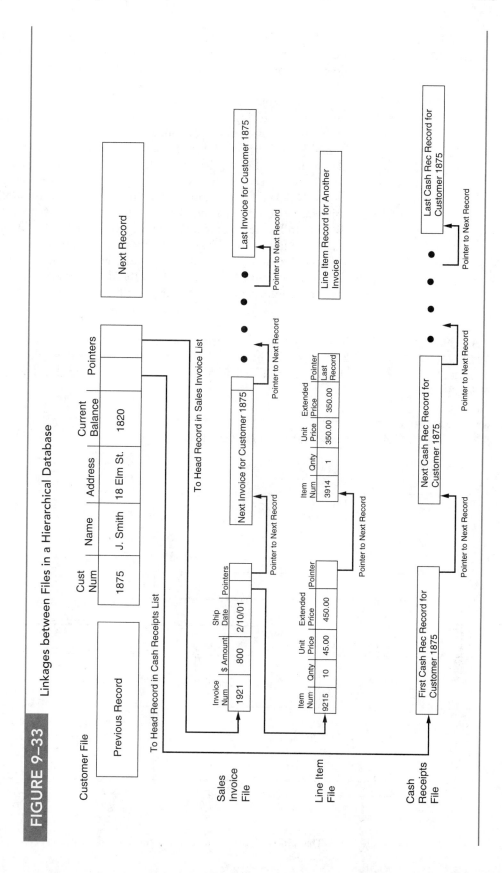

FIGURE 9-33   Linkages between Files in a Hierarchical Database

NETWORK MODEL DATA STRUCTURE

As with the hierarchical model, the network model is a navigational database with pointers creating explicit linkages between records. Whereas the hierarchical model allows only one path, the network model supports multiple paths to a particular record. Figure 9–34 shows the linkages for the data structure in Figure 9–32(a).

The structure can be accessed at either of the root level records (salesperson or customer) by hashing their respective primary keys (SP Num or Cust Num) or by reading their addresses from an index. A pointer field in the parent record explicitly defines the path to the child record, as discussed earlier. Notice the structure of the sales invoice file. In this example, each child now has two parents and contains explicit links to other records that form linked lists related to each parent. For example, Invoice Number 1 is the child of Salesperson Number 1 and Customer Number 5. This record structure has two links to related records. One of these is a salesperson (SP) link to Invoice Number 2. This represents a sale by Salesperson Number 1 to Customer Number 6. The second pointer is the customer (C) link to Invoice Number 3. This represents the second sale to Customer Number 5, which was processed this time by Salesperson Number 2. Under this data structure, management can track and report sales information pertaining to both customers and sales staff.

THE DATA NORMALIZATION PROCESS

In this appendix, the normalization process is applied to the unnormalized table in Figure 9–35.[5] The table represents a view of student enrollment data for the registrar of a university. The data, as presented in the unnormalized table, satisfy the registrar's

---

FIGURE 9–34   Linkages in a Network Database

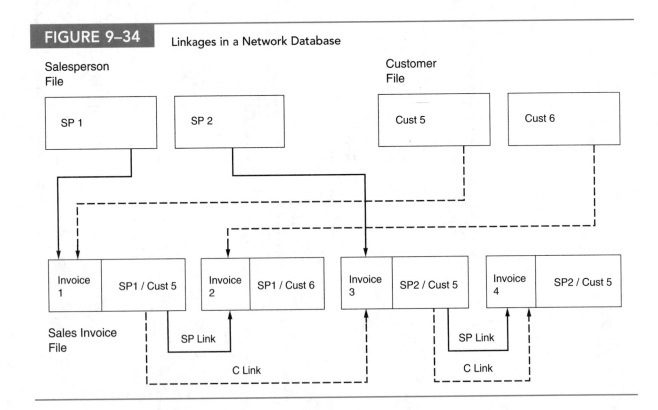

---

5   This section is based on an excellent example by McFadden and Hoffer, *Database Management*: 223–30.

FIGURE 9–35   Unnormalized Database of Student Enrollments

Stdnt Num	Stdnt	Major	Course	Crse Desc	Instr	Off Hrs	Loc	Tel Num	Grade
86432	Sethi	Acctg	Acc 315	Fin Acct	Ray	9–11	442	8-4545	A
			Acc 324	Mgt Acc	Smith	8–10	448	8-8945	A
			Math 21	Calc	Jones	1–3	323	8-2345	B
86789	Archer	Mgt	Mgt 1	Intro Mgt	Buell	4–5	463	8-3436	C
			Hist 1	U.S. Hist	Patch	9–11	342	8-2378	B
98653	Mills	Acctg	Acc 371	Ind Stdy	Ray	9–11	442	8-4545	B
			Math 21	Calc	Jones	1–3	323	8-2345	B
			Mgt 1	Intro Mgt	Buell	4–5	463	8-3436	C

information needs. The current structure of the table, however, does not comply with the requirements of a relational database management system and will not function properly. The table must be normalized to accommodate the needs of both the DBMS and the registrar. Data normalization is the process of systematically reducing a complex table to a set of simple efficient tables that meet two conditions:

1. All nonkey attributes in the table are dependent on (defined by) the primary key.
2. All nonkey attributes are independent of the other nonkey attributes.

When these conditions are met, the table in question is in third normal form (3NF). Although tables can be further normalized to fourth and fifth normal form, these levels of precision are beyond most business needs. Achieving the state of 3NF involves the systematic process presented in Figure 9–36.

Beginning with an unnormalized table, the first step in the process is to identify and remove any repeating groups. Repeating groups are multiple data values at the intersection of rows and columns. When this is done, the table is in first normal form (1NF). The next step is to identify and remove any partial dependencies. These are nonkey attributes that are dependent on (defined by) only part of the primary key. This condition exists only when the primary key is a composite key. At this point, the table is in second normal form (2NF). The last step, which places the table in 3NF, is to remove any transitive dependencies. These are nonkey attributes dependent on another nonkey attribute in the table. With these basic goals in mind, let's now apply the normalization process to the Student Enrollment table.

Remove Repeating Groups

This example contains repeating groups of data. Because a student may take more than one course, the data unique to each additional course constitutes a repeating group. There is no single primary key that defines the repeating group data in an unnormalized table. We can see this clearly in Figure 9–37 by looking at the relationship between Stdnt Num (the candidate primary key) and the other attributes.

There is a 1:1 association between Stdnt Num and the Stdnt and Major attributes.[6] In other words, the two nonkey attributes (Stdnt and Major) are uniquely

---

6   This assumes that the student is allowed to have only one major at a time.

FIGURE 9–36

Steps in the
Normalization
Process

Normalization of Data

This is a series of steps that achieve the following two objectives:
1. All nonkey attributes are dependent upon the primary key,
2. All nonkey attributes are independent of the other nonkey
   attributes.
When these objectives are met, the data file is in the third normal
form (3NF).

The normalization process involves systematically splitting the data
file until the above objectives are met. The following describes the
steps in the process:

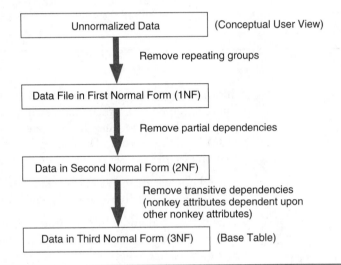

defined by the primary key (Stdnt Num). There is a 1:M association, however, between Stdnt Num and the other attributes. These repeating group attributes are not uniquely defined by Stdnt Num. The lack of dependency between Stdnt Num and the repeating group attributes prevents it from being the primary key for the table as

FIGURE 9–37

Relationship between
Candidate Key and
Other Attributes

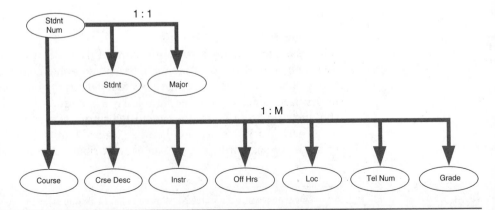

it currently exists because the first normalization condition stated has not been met. Note that no other attribute in the table qualifies as the primary key either.

Figure 9–38 shows that the repeating groups problem is solved by dividing the unnormalized table into two new tables: Student and Course-Grade. The Student table now meets the normalization conditions. The attributes Stdnt and Major are both defined by the primary key Stdnt Num and are independent of each other. This table is in 3NF.

The Course-Grade table is in 1NF. The primary key for this table is a composite key: Stdnt Num and Course. This is the only key that uniquely identifies the attribute Grade. While this table no longer contains repeating groups, a good deal of data redundancy exists. The attributes Instr, Loc, and Off Hrs are repeated for every student in every course the instructor teaches. Data redundancy and the partial relationships in the table (which will be explained shortly) lead to anomalies that negatively affect the performance of the database in three areas: updating records, inserting records, and deleting records. Before moving to the next step in the normalization process, let's briefly examine each of these anomalies.

Update Anomaly. Assume that Mgt 1, Introduction to Management, is an introductory course with 600 students registered. Assume the decision has been made to change the name of the course to Principles of Management. The current course title appears in each student record registered for this course. The user will need to search the entire Course-Grade table for each student enrolled in Mgt 1 and modify the course name 600 times. This is a consequence of data redundancy.

FIGURE 9–38   Removing Repeating Groups from Unnormalized Data

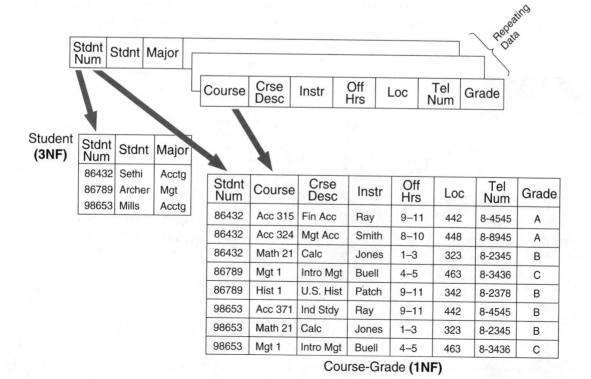

Course-Grade (1NF)

Insertion Anomaly. Suppose the registrar wants to add a new course—Acc 398, Advanced Managerial Topics—to the Course-Grade table. Currently, no students are enrolled in the course. Because Stdnt Num is part of the primary key, the registrar is unable to record this course until at least one student registers.

Deletion Anomaly. Suppose only one student is registered for the course Acc 371, Independent Study. Assume the student permanently leaves the university and is deleted from the Course-Grade table. The data about the course and the instructor will be lost because it cannot exist in the table without the primary key. This is undesirable, because the course and the instructor still exist, and the registrar wants and needs to retain these data. This problem occurs because the Stdnt Num is part of a composite primary key and the course and instructor data are not defined by this portion of the key. In other words, these data are only *partially* dependent on the primary key.

Remove Partial Dependencies

The next step in the normalization process is to remove all partial dependencies. Partial dependencies occur only in tables with a composite primary key. Figure 9–39 shows the relationship between the primary key and the nonkey attributes.

Notice that course and instructor data are dependent only on the Course portion of the composite key. The Grade attribute, however, is dependent on the entire key. For each student in each course, there is a single grade. By removing the partially dependent attributes, we create the two new tables: Stdnt-Grade and Course-Instr, shown in Figure 9–40.

The Stdnt-Grade table meets the conditions for 3NF. The Course-Instr table is in 2NF since it is free of repeating groups and partial dependencies. The three anomalies discussed above are reduced significantly by this new table. Because of the reduced data redundancy in the table, the most apparent improvement pertains to the update anomaly. Now each course is listed only once, rather than once for every stu-

FIGURE 9–39   Attributes Partially Dependent on Primary Key

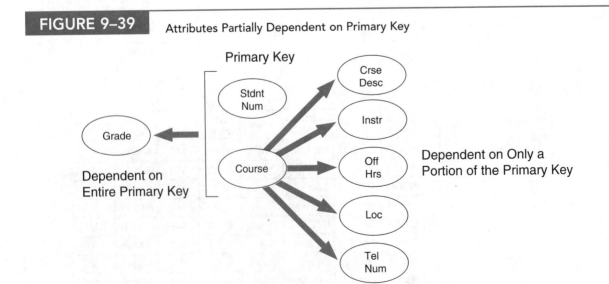

FIGURE 9–40

Removing Partial
Dependencies from
Data Table

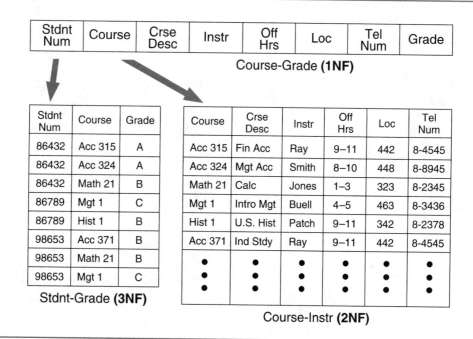

Course-Grade (**1NF**)

Stdnt Num	Course	Crse Desc	Instr	Off Hrs	Loc	Tel Num	Grade

Stdnt Num	Course	Grade
86432	Acc 315	A
86432	Acc 324	A
86432	Math 21	B
86789	Mgt 1	C
86789	Hist 1	B
98653	Acc 371	B
98653	Math 21	B
98653	Mgt 1	C

Stdnt-Grade (**3NF**)

Course	Crse Desc	Instr	Off Hrs	Loc	Tel Num
Acc 315	Fin Acc	Ray	9–11	442	8-4545
Acc 324	Mgt Acc	Smith	8–10	448	8-8945
Math 21	Calc	Jones	1–3	323	8-2345
Mgt 1	Intro Mgt	Buell	4–5	463	8-3436
Hist 1	U.S. Hist	Patch	9–11	342	8-2378
Acc 371	Ind Stdy	Ray	9–11	442	8-4545
•	•	•	•	•	•
•	•	•	•	•	•
•	•	•	•	•	•

Course-Instr (**2NF**)

dent. Although diminished in the 2NF table, the insertion and deletion anomalies still exist because of transitive dependencies. They are resolved in the next step.

Remove Transitive Dependencies
The instructor attributes (Off Hrs, Loc, Tel Num) are defined not by the course that the instructor teaches, but by the instructor, as illustrated in Figure 9–41. This is a transitive dependency that causes update, insertion, and deletion anomalies similar to those discussed earlier.

Update Anomaly. Under the current table structure, the instructor data must be repeated for every occurrence of a course taught. For example, Ray teaches Acc 315 and Acc 371. In each of these records, Loc, Off Hrs, and Tel Num are listed. Any change in these instructor attributes must be changed for each occurrence.

Insertion Anomaly. The insertion anomaly prevents the registrar from adding data about an instructor unless he or she is currently teaching a course. Therefore, the registrar cannot maintain information about new faculty, who are not yet teaching, nor existing faculty, who are on sabbatical leave.

Deletion Anomaly. The deletion anomaly causes the unintentional destruction of data. Assume that an instructor is teaching only one course that for some reason is canceled. By deleting the course from the table, the instructor data is also destroyed.
     The transitive dependency is resolved by creating two new tables—Course and Instructor, as illustrated in Figure 9–42. Both of these tables are in 3NF. The anomalies associated with the original Course-Instr table no longer exist. Instructor data now reside independently from course data in separate tables that facilitate efficient updates, insertions, and deletions.

FIGURE 9–41

Transitive Relationship between the Nonkey Attribute Instructor and Other Instructor Attributes

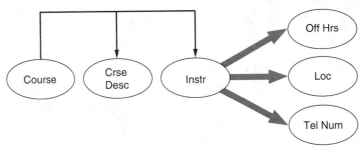

Transitive Dependency on the Attribute Instr

Embedded Keys

At this point, we have systematically reduced the unnormalized Stdnt-Grade table to four normalized base tables: Student, Stdnt-Grade, Course, and Instructor. Figure 9–43 shows how the four base tables are linked together by common attributes. The primary key of one table is an embedded key in the related table. Specifically, Stdnt Num is the common attribute between the Student and Stdnt-Grade tables; Course is common to both the Stdnt-Grade and the Course tables,[7] and Instr is the attribute common to both the Course and Instructor tables. From these four normalized ta-

FIGURE 9–42

Remove Transitive Dependencies from Database

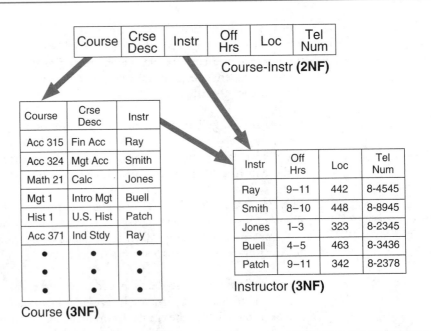

Course-Instr (2NF)

Course	Crse Desc	Instr
Acc 315	Fin Acc	Ray
Acc 324	Mgt Acc	Smith
Math 21	Calc	Jones
Mgt 1	Intro Mgt	Buell
Hist 1	U.S. Hist	Patch
Acc 371	Ind Stdy	Ray
•	•	•
•	•	•
•	•	•

Course (3NF)

Instr	Off Hrs	Loc	Tel Num
Ray	9–11	442	8-4545
Smith	8–10	448	8-8945
Jones	1–3	323	8-2345
Buell	4–5	463	8-3436
Patch	9–11	342	8-2378

Instructor (3NF)

---

7   Remember, Stdnt-Grade has a composite key (Stdnt Num and Course). Thus, we can access this table by using the entire key or either component.

FIGURE 9–43

Four Tables Linked by
Common Attributes

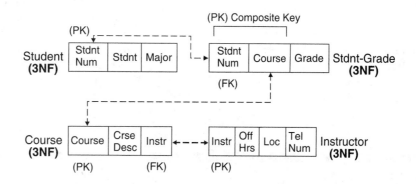

bles, the student enrollment information needed by the registrar can be derived. The physical user view that presents this information can take the form of a computer screen or a hard-copy report. The underlying base tables will be transparent to the user.

Key Terms

Review Questions

1. Give five general duties of the database administrator.
2. What are the four primary elements of the database environment?
3. How are the network and hierarchical models different?
4. What flat file data management problems are solved as a result of using the database concept?
5. What are four ways in which database management systems provide a controlled environment to manage user access and the data resources?
6. Explain the relationship between the three levels of the data definition language. As a user, which level would you be most interested in?
7. What is the internal view of a database?
8. What is SQL?
9. What is a data dictionary and what purpose does it serve?
10. Give an application for a partitioned database.
11. What are the criteria that influence the selection of the data structure?
12. Give an application for a replicated database.
13. Discuss and give an example of one-to-one, one-to-many, and many-to-many record associations.
14. Why is a hierarchical database model considered to be a navigational database? What are some limitations of the hierarchical database model?
15. Explain how a separate linking file works in a many-to-many association.
16. What are the four characteristics of properly designed relational database tables?
17. What do the relational features restrict, project, and join mean?
18. What is data normalization?
19. Explain how the SELECT and WHERE commands help a user to view the necessary data from multiple database files (tables).
20. What is a virtual table?
21. How can a poorly designed database result in unintentional loss of critical records?

Discussion Questions

1. In the flat file data management environment, users are said to own their data files. What is meant by the "ownership" concept?
2. Discuss the potential aggravations you might face as a student as a result of your university using a flat file data management environment, that is, different files for the registrar, library, parking, and so on.
3. Discuss why control procedures over access to the data resource become more crucial under the database approach than in the flat file environment. What role does the DBMS play in helping to control the database environment?
4. What is the relationship between a database and a user view?
5. Discuss the two ways in which users can access the database in a database environment.
6. Explain how data linkages in the navigational and relational models are fundamentally different.
7. Explain the purpose of an ER diagram during the conceptual design of the database.

8. SQL has been said to place power in the hands of the user. What does this statement mean?
9. Discuss the importance of the role of the database administrator. Why wasn't such a role necessary in the flat file environment? What are the tasks performed by the DBA?
10. As users determine new computer application needs, requests must be sent to both the system programmers and the DBA. Why is it important that these two groups perform separate functions, and what are these functions?
11. Why is a separate link table required when a M:M association exits between related tables?
12. As an accountant, why would you need to be familiar with data normalization techniques?
13. How does a database lockout contribute to financial data integrity?
14. How does concurrency control contribute to financial data integrity?
15. In a relational database environment, certain accounting records (journals, subsidiary ledgers, and event general ledger accounts) may not exist. How is this possible?

Multiple-Choice Questions

1. The mechanism for identifying the data attributes that a particular user has permission to access is found in the
   a. operating system view.
   b. systems design view.
   c. database schema.
   d. user view.
   e. application program.
2. The database approach has several unique characteristics not found in traditional (flat file) systems. Which of the following statements does not apply to the database model?
   a. Database systems have data independence; that is, the data and the programs are maintained separately except during processing.
   b. Database systems contain a data definition language that helps describe each schema and subschema.
   c. The database administrator is the part of the software package that instructs the operating aspects of the program when data are retrieved.
   d. A primary goal of database systems is to minimize data redundancy.
   e. Database systems provide increased accessibility to data and flexibility in its usage.
3. One of the first steps in the creation of a relational database is to
   a. integrate accounting and nonfinancial data.
   b. plan for increased secondary storage capacity.
   c. order data mining software that will facilitate data retrieval.
   d. create a data model of the key entities in the system.
   e. study the need for a larger central processing unit.

4. Database currency is achieved by
   a. implementing partitioned databases at remote sites.
   b. employing data cleansing techniques.
   c. ensuring that the database is secure from accidental entry.
   d. an external auditor's reconciliation of reports from multiple sites.
   e. a database lockout that prevents multiple simultaneous access.
5. The installation of a database management system is likely to have the least impact on
   a. data redundancy.
   b. entity-wide sharing of common data.
   c. exclusive ownership of data.
   d. the logic needed to solve a problem in an application program.
   e. the internal controls over data access.
6. The functions of a database administrator are
   a. database planning, data input preparation, and database design.
   b. data input preparation, database design, and database operation.
   c. database design, database operation, and equipment operations.
   d. database design, database implementation, and database planning.
   e. database operations, database maintenance, and data input preparation.
7. A relational database system contains the following inventory data: part number, description, quantity-on-hand, and reorder point. These individual items are called
   a. attributes.
   b. relations.

c. associations.

d. occurrences.

8. Which of the following is a characteristic of a relational database system?

   a. All data within the system are shared by all users to facilitate integration.

   b. Database processing follows explicit links that are contained within the records.

   c. User views limit access to the database.

d. Transaction processing and data warehousing systems share a common database.

9. Partitioned databases are most effective when

   a. users in the system need to share common data.

   b. primary users of the data are clearly identifiable.

   c. read-only access is needed at each site.

   d. all of the above.

Problems

1. **DBMS Versus Flat File Processing**

   Werner Manufacturing Corporation has a flat file processing system. The information processing facility is very large. Different applications, such as order processing, production planning, inventory management, accounting systems, payroll, and marketing systems, use separate tape and disk files. The corporation has recently hired a consulting firm to investigate the possibility of switching to a database management system. Prepare a memo to the top management team at Werner explaining the advantages of a DBMS. Also, discuss the necessity of a database administrator and the job functions this person would perform.

2. **Access Methods**

   For each of the following file processing operations, indicate whether a sequential file, indexed random file, indexed sequential access method (ISAM), hashing, or pointer structure works the best. You may choose as many as you wish for each step. Also indicate which would perform the least optimally.

   a. Retrieve a record from the file based upon its primary key value.

   b. Update a record in the file.

   c. Read a complete file of records.

   d. Find the next record in a file.

   e. Insert a record into a file.

   f. Delete a record from a file.

   g. Scan a file for records with secondary keys.

3. **Database Design**

   Design a relational database system for a large costume rental store. The store has approxi-

mately 3,200 customers each year. It is stocked with over 500 costumes in various sizes. The rental costumes and other items that may be purchased by the customer (e.g., makeup and teeth) are purchased from approximately 35 different suppliers. Design the necessary database files. Make sure they are in third normal form, and indicate the necessary linkages.

4. **Database Design**

   Sears Roebuck, the most well-known and oldest mail-order retailer in the country, discontinued its mail-order operations a few years ago. Other mail-order marketers are using information systems to trim printing and postage costs of their catalogs. They also want to more effectively target their customers. Explain how an appropriately designed coding system for inventory items (see Chapter 8) incorporated in a relational database system with SQL capabilities could allow more cost-efficient and effective mail-order operations. Sketch the necessary database table structure.

5. **Database Deadlock**

   How is a lockout different from a deadlock? Give an accounting example to illustrate why a database lockout is necessary and how a deadlock can occur. Use actual table names in your example.

6. **Structured Query Language**

   The vice president of finance has noticed in the aging of the accounts receivable that the amount of overdue accounts is substantially higher than anticipated. He wants to investigate this problem. To do so, he requires a report of overdue accounts containing the attributes shown in the top half of the table below. The bottom half of the table contains the data fields and relevant files in the relational database system. Further, he wants to alert the salespeople of any customers not paying their bills on time. Using the SQL commands given in this chapter, write the code necessary to generate a report of overdue accounts that are greater than $5,000 and over 30 days due. Each customer has an assigned salesperson.

7. Distributed Databases

The XYZ company is a geographically distributed organization with several sites around the country. Users at these sites need rapid access to common data for read-only purposes. Which distributed database method is best under these circumstances? Explain your reasoning.

8. Distributed Databases

The ABC Company is a geographically distributed organization with several sites around the country. Users at these sites need rapid access to data for transaction processing purposes. The sites are autonomous; they do not share the same customers, products, or suppliers. Which distributed database method is best under these circumstances? Explain your reasoning.

9. Normalization of Data

On the next page is a table of data for a library. Normalize this data into the third normal form, preparing it for use in a relational database environment. The library's computer is programmed to compute the due date to be 14 days after the check-out date. Document the steps necessary to normalize the data similar to the procedures found in the chapter. Index any fields necessary and show how the databases are related.

10. Normalization of Data

On the next page is a table of data for a veterinarian practice. Normalize this data into the third normal form, preparing it for use in a relational database environment. Document the steps necessary to normalize the data similar to the procedures found in the chapter. Index any fields necessary and show how the databases are related.

Problem 6: Structured Query Language

REPORT ATTRIBUTES

Salesperson Name, Salesperson Branch Office, Customer Number, Customer Name, Amount Overdue, Last Purchase Date, Goods Delivered?, Amount of Last Sales Order, Amount of Last Payment, Date of Last Payment

FILES AVAILABLE:

Salesperson Table	Customer Table	Sales Order Table
Salesperson Name	Customer Number	Sales Order Number
Salesperson Number	Customer Name	Customer Number
Commission Rate	Customer Address1	Order Date
Rank	Customer Address2	Amount
Branch	Salesperson Number	Delivery Date
Date of Hire	Last Sales Order Number	
	Year-to-Date Purchases	
	Account Balance	
	Overdue Balance	
	Amount of Last Payment	
	Date of Last Payment	

Problem 9: Normalization of Data

Student ID Number	Student First Name	Student Last Name	Number of Books Out	Book Call No	Book Title	Date Out	Due Date
678-98-4567	Amy	Baker	4	hf351.j6	Avalanches	09-02-01	09-16-01
678-98-4567	Amy	Baker	4	hf878.k3	Tornadoes	09-02-01	09-16-01
244-23-2348	Ramesh	Sunder	1	i835.123	Politics	09-02-01	09-16-01
398-34-8793	James	Talley	3	k987.d98	Sports	09-02-01	09-16-01
398-34-8793	James	Talley	3	d879.39	Legal Rights	09-02-01	09-16-01
678-98-4567	Amy	Baker	4	p987.t87	Earthquakes	09-03-01	09-17-01
244-23-2348	Ramesh	Sunder	1	q875.i76	Past Heroes	09-03-01	09-17-01

Problem 10: Normalization of Data

Patient ID Number	Patient Name	Owner ID Number	Owner Last Name	Owner First Name	Address1	Address2	Date	Animal Code	Animal Description	Service Code	Service Description	Service Charge
417	Beau	Magel	Magee	Elaine	23 Elm St	Houston, TX	01/10/00	GR	Golden Retriever	238	Rabies Shot	15.00
417	Beau	Magel	Magee	Elaine	23 Elm St	Houston, TX	01/12/00	GR	Golden Retriever	148	Flea Dip	25.00
417	Beau	Magel	Magee	Elaine	23 Elm St	Houston, TX	01/15/00	GR	Golden Retriever	337	Bloodwork II	20.00
632	Luigi	Cacil	Caciolo	Tony	8 Oak St	Houston, TX	01/27/00	DN	Dalmation	238	Rabies Shot	15.00
632	Luigi	Cacil	Caciolo	Tony	8 Oak St	Houston, TX	02/16/00	DN	Dalmation	500	Kennel-medium	9.00
632	Luigi	Cacil	Caciolo	Tony	8 Oak St	Houston, TX	02/18/00	DN	Dalmation	500	Kennel-medium	9.00
632	Luigi	Cacil	Caciolo	Tony	8 Oak St	Houston, TX	03/01/00	DN	Dalmation	148	Flea Dip	25.00
168	Astro	Jetsl	Jetson	George	3 Air Rd	Sprockley, TX	03/14/00	MX	Canine-mixed	368	Ear Cleaning	17.00

11. Normalization of Data

Prepare the base tables, in third normal form, needed to produce the user view below.

12. Normalization of Data

Prepare the base tables, in third normal form, needed to produce the user view below.

13. Normalization of Data

Prepare the 3NF base tables needed to produce the sales report view on the following page.

14. Normalization of Data

Prepare the 3NF base tables needed to produce the sales invoice view on the page 509.

15. Table Linking

Refer to text in Problem 15 on page 510.

16. ER Diagram

Using the ER diagram of a payroll system given on page 511, apply the following database design procedures:

a. Determine the candidate views and create a table for each. Assign a name and primary key to each table.

b. Show the association (cardinality) between the related tables and assign embedded keys.

c. Create a reasonable set of data attributes for each table.

d. Normalize all tables.

17. Prepare ER Diagram for Purchases Procedures

The business rules that constitute the purchases system for the Safe Buy Grocery Stores chain are similar at all the store locations. The purchase manager at each location is responsible for selecting his or her local suppliers. If the manager needs a product he or she chooses a supplier using his or her own discretion. Once a supplier is chosen, each store follows the steps described below.

1. The purchasing function begins with sales representatives from suppliers periodically observing the shelves and displays at each

Problem 11: Normalization of Data

USER VIEW									
Part Num	**Description**	**QOH**	**Reorder Point**	**EOQ**	**Unit Cost**	**Ven Num**	**Ven Name**	**Ven Address**	**Tel**
132	Bolt	100	50	1000	1.50	987	ABC Co.	654 Elm St	555 5498
143	Screw	59	10	100	1.75	987	ABC Co.	654 Elm St	555 5498
760	Nut	80	20	500	2.00	742	XYZ Co.	510 Smit	555 8921
982	Nail	100	50	800	1.00	987	ABC Co.	654 Elm St	555 5498

Problem 12: Normalization of Data

USER VIEW									
Part Num	**Description**	**QOH**	**Reorder Point**	**EOQ**	**Unit Cost**	**Ven Num**	**Ven Name**	**Ven Address**	**Tel**
132	Bolt	100	50	1000	1.50	987	ABC Co.	654 Elm St	555 5498
					1.55	750	RST Co.	3415 8th St	555 3421
					1.45	742	XYZ Co.	510 Smit	555 8921
982	Nail	100	50	800	1.00	987	ABC Co.	654 Elm St	555 5498
					1.10	742	XYZ Co.	510 Smit	555 8921
					1.00	549	LMN Co.	18 Oak St	555 9987

Sales Report

Customer Number: 19321
Customer Name   : Jon Smith
Address   : 520 Main St.,City

Invoice Num	Date	Invoice Total	Part Num	Quantity	Unit Price	Ext'd Price
12390	11/11/01	$850	2	5	$20	$100
			1	10	50	500
			3	25	10	250
12912	11/21/01	$300	4	10	$30	$300

Customer Total: $1,150

* * *   * * * *   * * * *   * * * *   * * * *   * * * *   * * *

Customer Number: 19322
Customer Name   : Mary Smith
Address   : 2289 Elm St., City

Invoice Num	Date	Invoice Total	Part Num	Quantity	Unit Price	Ext'd Price
12421	11/13/01	$1,000	6	10	$20	$200
			1	2	50	100
			5	7	100	700
12901	11/20/01	$500	4	10	$30	$300
			2	10	20	200

Customer Total: $1,500

* * *   * * * *   * * * *   * * * *   * * * *   * * * *   * * *

Next Customer
   •
   •
   •
Next Customer

individual location and recognizing the need to restock inventory. Inventory declines by direct sales to the customers or by spoilage of perishable goods. In addition, the supplier's sales representatives may observe certain products are unsalable at a particular location, at which point the goods are returned to the supplier and replaced with more successful products. The sales representatives create a purchase requisition and meet with the purchase manager of the individual store locations. Together the sales representative and the purchase manager prepare a purchase order

deciding the quantity and delivery time phase. The supplier subsequently submits a bill.

2. At the intended delivery date, Safe Buy Grocery Stores receive the goods from the suppliers. Goods received are unloaded from the delivery trucks and stocked in the shelves and displays around the store by part-time employees.

3. The unloading personnel send the information about the deliveries to the purchase managers. The purchase managers reconcile the receiving information against the purchase orders and record an obligation of payment for

Problem 14: Normalization of Data

SOLD TO:	S & J SUPPLY CO 598 RIDGE LANE CINCINNATI, OHIO 45240					**INVOICE**

SHIP TO:	S & J SUPPLY CO 598 RIDGE LANE CINCINNATI, OHIO 45240					

TERMS	CUSTOMER PURCHASE ORDER NO.	CUSTOMER NO.	SOLD BY	SHIP VIA	DATE	INVOICE NO.
2–10 NET 30	P87654	102.912	7	OUR TRUCK	NOV. 15, 01	12347

CODE	QUANTITY	DESCRIPTION	PRICE	UNIT	GROSS	DISCOUNT	NET
12314522	10	CUTTING TIP TT–3	2.80	EA	28.00	00	28.00
12415710	10	SCREWDRIVER 6"	1.90	EA	19.00	38	18.62
15611410	5	WELDING GLOVE–10	1.50	PR	7.50	15	7.35
12488806	10	OSK	1.00	EA	10.00	00	10.00
							63.97
				TAX		5.0%	3.20
				HANDLING			75.00
							92.17

YOU MAY DEDUCT 1% IF THIS INVOICE IS PAID BY DEC. 30, 01

some future date, depending on the terms with the supplier.

Required:
Prepare an ER diagram that reflects the business rules and procedures outlined above.

18. Prepare ER Diagram for Fixed Asset Procedures

The business rules that constitute the fixed asset procedures for the Safe Buy Grocery Stores chain are similar at all the store locations. The store manager at each location is responsible for identifying the need to acquire assets and for selecting the vendor. Freezers, refrigerators, delivery vans, and store shelving are examples of fixed asset purchases. Once the need has been identified, each store follows the procedure described next.

The manager sends the purchase order to the supplier. The supplier delivers the asset to the receiving clerk, who prepares a receiving report and sends it to the fixed asset department. The fixed asset clerk maintains the inventory records and depreciation schedules. The vendor mails the invoice to the manager who reviews it and forwards the invoice to the cash disbursement clerk. The clerk prepares a check and sends it to the vendor.

Required:
Prepare an ER diagram that reflects the business rules and procedures outlined above.

Problem 15: Table Linking

Several related tables with their primary keys (PK) are shown below. Place the foreign key(s) in the tables to link them according to the associations shown (e.g., 1:M and M:M). Create any new table(s) that may be needed.

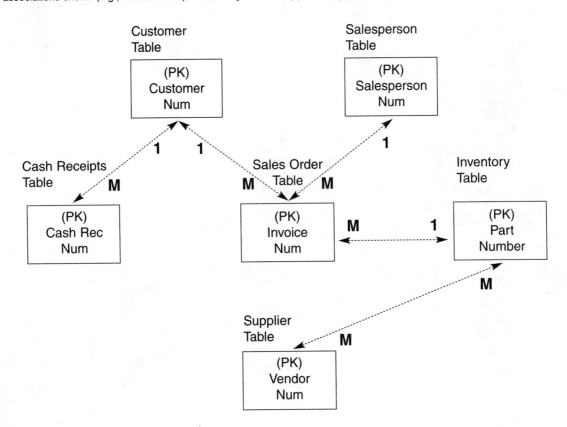

Problem 16: ER Diagram

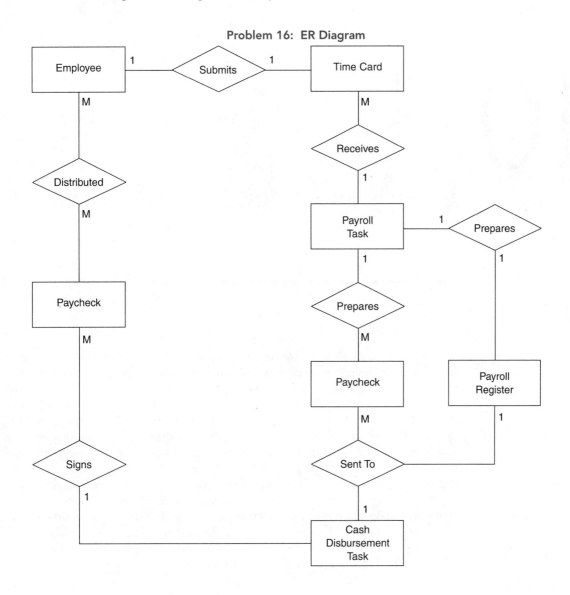

CHAPTER

10

The REA Approach to Business Process Modeling*

This chapter examines the resources, events, and agents (REA) model as a means of specifying and designing accounting information systems that serve the needs of all the users within an organization. The chapter is comprised of three major sections. The first introduces the REA approach and identifies a number of problems associated with traditional accounting practice that can be resolved through an REA approach. The second section examines traditional database applications and their limitations. While superior to flat file systems, traditional database systems suffer from serious problems that limit their usefulness. An important limitation is their almost exclusive support of financial information users and their inadequacy at meeting the growing need for nonfinancial information. A second limitation is their inability to respond to noneconomic events that may be of extreme importance to an organization. The third section provides a detailed examination of the REA model. The steps involved in developing an REA model are presented and compared to the traditional ER approach to modeling business processes.

---

*   This chapter was co-authored by Alan Sangster, Open University Business School, Milton Keynes, United Kingdom.

LEARNING OBJECTIVES

After studying this chapter, you should:

- Recognize the limitations of the traditional database system.
- Be aware of the benefits of adopting an REA approach to information systems compared to a traditional approach.
- Be aware of the implications of REA for the accounting profession.
- Be aware of the steps involved in preparing an REA model of a business process.
- Appreciate the importance of identifying the attributes of entity relations in relational database design.
- Appreciate the difference between an REA model representation of a business process and an ER diagram representation.

THE REA APPROACH

Central to the REA philosophy is the recognition that information systems should support the information needs of all users of information in the organization. This section addresses the changing information needs of modern management, the limitations of traditional accounting in meeting those needs, and the role of REA as a potential solution.

USER VIEWS

You will recall from Chapter 9 that a **user view** is the set of data that a particular user needs to achieve his or her assigned tasks. For example, a general ledger clerk's user view will include the organization's chart of accounts, but not detailed transaction data. A sales manager's view may include detailed customer sales data organized by product, region, and salesperson. A production manager's view may include finished goods inventory on hand, available manufacturing capacity, and vendor lead times.

A problem arises in meeting these diverse needs when the collection, summarization, storage, and reporting of transaction and resource data are dominated by a single view that is inappropriate for entity-wide purposes. The accounting profession has been criticized in recent years for focusing too narrowly on the role of accounting information. Many believe that the profession should shift its emphasis away from debits, credits, double-entry accounting, and GAAP towards providing useful information for decision making and helping organizations identify and control business risk. As the primary providers of information, however, accountants have dictated the set of data used by organizations.

Modern managers need both financial and nonfinancial information in formats and at levels of aggregation that the traditional GAAP-based accounting systems are generally incapable of providing. The response within organizations to the single view of accounting information has been to create separate information systems to support each user's view. This has resulted in organizations with multiple information systems that are frequently unconnected electronically. Virtually all data entered into one system needs to be re-entered into the others. With such widespread duplication of data, accuracy and currency are serious problems. Often, these information systems provide different answers to the same requests for information, which leads to confusion, poor decision making, and inappropriate actions.

Future accountants will increasingly face enterprise-wide information systems that are designed to overcome the information shortcomings outlined above. These systems will be based on the relational database model and will be event-oriented rather that account-oriented. Such a system is REA. The modern accountant needs to be responsive, proactive, and equipped with an understanding of the REA approach, its power, and its flexibility.

THE REA MODEL

The **REA model** is an alternative accounting framework for modeling an organization's critical resources, events, and agents (REA) and the relationships between them. Once adopted, both accounting and nonaccounting data about these phenomena can be identified, captured, and stored in a centralized database. From this repository, user views can be constructed that meet the needs of all users in the organization. The availability of multiple views allows flexible use of transaction data and enables the development of accounting information systems that are free of the weaknesses identified earlier.

REA was proposed in 1982 as a theoretical model for accounting.[1] At that time, technology was not sufficiently powerful to translate the theory of REA into practice. Advances in database technology have now focused renewed attention on REA as a practical alternative to the traditional accounting framework.

The REA model requires that phenomena be characterized in a manner consistent with the development of multiple user views. Business data must not be pre-formatted or artificially constrained and must reflect all relevant aspects of the underlying economic events. As such, REA **data modeling** does not include traditional accounting elements such as journals, ledgers, charts of accounts, and double entry (debits and credits) accounting. (Though it can be used to create any or all of them if required.)

Organizations that use REA produce financial statements and reports directly from the event-driven detailed data, rather than from traditional ledgers and journals. The key elements of the REA model are discussed below.

Resources

Economic **resources** are the assets of the organization. They are defined as objects that are both scarce and under the control of the enterprise. This definition departs from the traditional model since it does not include anything that can be derived from other data, such as accounts receivable, which is an artifact record used simply to store and transmit data. (Accounts receivable is derived as the difference between sales to customers and the cash received in payment of sales.)

It should be noted that when relevant to the planning, evaluation, and control of events, the resources within an REA model include the locations where significant events occur, such as cash tills, inventory records, and inquiry desks.

Events

Economic **events** are phenomena that affect changes in resources. They can result from activities such as production, exchange, consumption, and distribution. Economic events are the critical information elements of the accounting system and should be captured in a highly detailed form to provide a rich database. Under the REA modeling approach, events are divided into three classes, *operating events* (what happens), *information events* (what is recorded), and *decision/management events* (what is done as a result). Only operating events, however, are included in the REA model.

Agents

Economic **agents** are individuals and departments that participate in an economic event. They are parties both inside and outside the organization with discretionary power to use or dispose of economic resources. Examples of agents include sales clerks, production workers, shipping clerks, customers, and vendors.

ADVANTAGES OF THE REA MODEL

Organizations that use the REA approach can derive the following advantages.

More Efficient Operations

Firms using the REA approach may experience improved operational efficiency in three ways:

---

1   W. E. McCarthy, "The REA Accounting Model: A Generalized Framework for Accounting Systems in a Shared Data Environment," *The Accounting Review* (July 1982): 554–577.

1. The REA approach to modeling business processes will help managers identify nonvalue-added activities that can be eliminated from operations.
2. The storage of both financial and nonfinancial data in the same central database reduces the need for multiple data collection, storage, and maintenance procedures.
3. Storing financial and nonfinancial data about business events in detailed form permits the support of a wider range of management decisions.

Increased Productivity

Improving the operational efficiency of individual departments by eliminating nonvalue-added activities will generate excess capacity. This additional capacity can be redirected to increase the overall productivity of the firm.

Competitive Advantage

By supporting multiple user views, the REA model provides managers with more relevant, timely, and accurate information. This will translate into better customer service, higher quality products, and flexible production processes.

VALUE CHAIN ANALYSIS

The competitive advantage benefits of adopting the REA approach are most clearly seen from the perspective of the **value chain**. These are the activities that add value or usefulness to an organization's products and services. To remain competitive, most organizations must differentiate between their various business activities, prioritizing them on the basis of their value in achieving organizational objectives. Organizations need to be increasingly adaptable and responsive to changes in the environment in which they operate. This includes their industry, suppliers, customers, and other external influences that impact upon performance. Furthermore, organization management needs to continuously review and improve the effective and efficient utilization of resources to maximize the attainment of their organization's objectives.

Decision makers need to look beyond the internal operations and functions of their organizations. One approach adopted for this purpose is known as **value chain analysis**. This analysis distinguishes between primary activities—those that create value—and support activities—those that assist in the achievement of the primary activities. Through applying this analysis, an organization is able to look beyond itself and maximize its ability to create value by, for example, incorporating the needs of its customers in its products, or the flexibility of its suppliers in scheduling its production.

Traditional information systems are not well suited to supporting many value chain activities. Organizations that have applied value chain analysis have generally done so outside the traditional accounting information system by providing such information separately to the decision makers. Frequently, this involved the creation of separate information systems with all the resulting problems outlined above. It is fairly obvious that the adoption of a single information system framework that supplies all the needed information is preferable.

DATABASE APPLICATIONS

Before considering REA modeling further, we need to first look at traditional database applications. Specifically, the operational characteristics of revenue and expenditure cycle applications that use relational databases and how they differ from equivalent flat file systems will be examined. We shall then be better prepared to look further at REA modeling and understand how an REA model may be used for developing relational databases that support business processes.

ORDER ENTRY AND CASH RECEIPTS SYSTEM

A quick review of the order entry system flowchart in Figure 10–1 shows that the business processes in this database application are not fundamentally different from its flat file counterpart that was studied in Chapter 4. Orders are received, credit is checked, goods are shipped, and customers are billed just as before.

The most significant difference between the two approaches is the method of storing data. Relational tables have replaced the flat files that emulate classical accounting records including journals, subsidiary ledgers, and the general ledger. The transaction data captured by flat file systems are artificially structured to meet the needs of financial reporting. These systems are account-based in their orientation. This orientation often results in the loss of rich details that are needed by other users. In a relational database environment it is possible to focus on economic transactions rather than the accounting *artifacts* that merely capture the financial effects of these events. If the transaction is captured in sufficient detail, the financial values needed for financial reporting can be calculated from the transaction database. However, this rich database can also support the needs of other users.

Many organizations adopt a compromise position and maintain both a traditional general ledger for financial reporting and a transaction database for operations support. Figure 10–2 illustrates the structures of the database tables represented in Figure 10–1. An explanation of their usage is given below.

Customer Table

The **Customer table** contains address and credit information about customers. The Credit Limit value is used to validate sales transactions. If the sum of the customer's outstanding account balance and the amount of current sales transaction exceeds the pre-established credit limit, then the transaction is rejected.

Sales Invoice Table

The **Sales Invoice table**, along with the Line Item table (discussed next), captures sales transactions for the period. A sales invoice record is created when credit approval is granted. When the order is shipped to the customer, the date is placed in the Shipped Date field to signify the event and to flag the record "open." When cash receipts are received, they are matched to the open invoice record, which is then closed by placing the current date in the Closed Date field. Also, the Remittance Number, which is the primary key of the of the Remittance table, is added to the invoice record as a cross-reference.

The Sales Invoice table may be used to replace some traditional accounting records. First, since it contains the total amount due for each invoice, summing the Invoice Amount field for all records in the table yields total sales (equivalent to the Sales Journal) for the period. The accounts receivable balance (AR Subsidiary Ledger) for a particular customer is calculated by summing the Invoice Amount fields for all of the customer's open invoices. Total accounts receivable (General Ledger, AR—Control) is the sum of all the open invoice records in the entire table.

Line Item Table

The **Line Item table** contains a record of every item sold to the organization's customers. Since a single transaction can involve one or more products, each record in the Sales Invoice table is associated with (linked to) one or more records in this table.

FIGURE 10-1 Database Sales Order Entry and Cash Receipts System

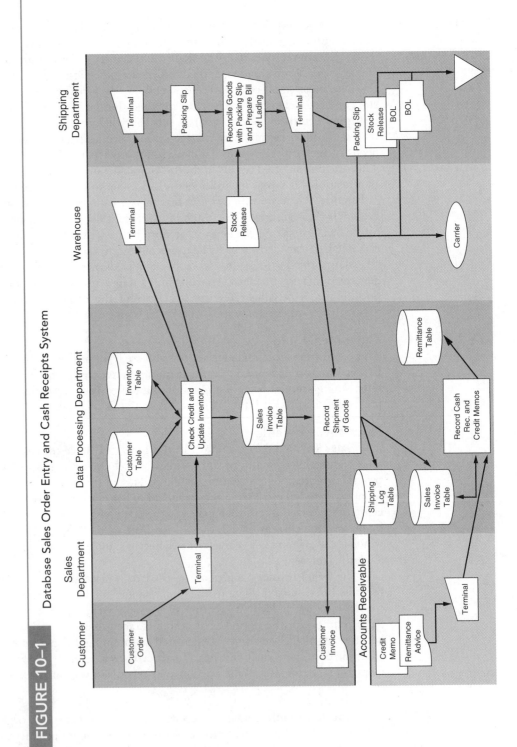

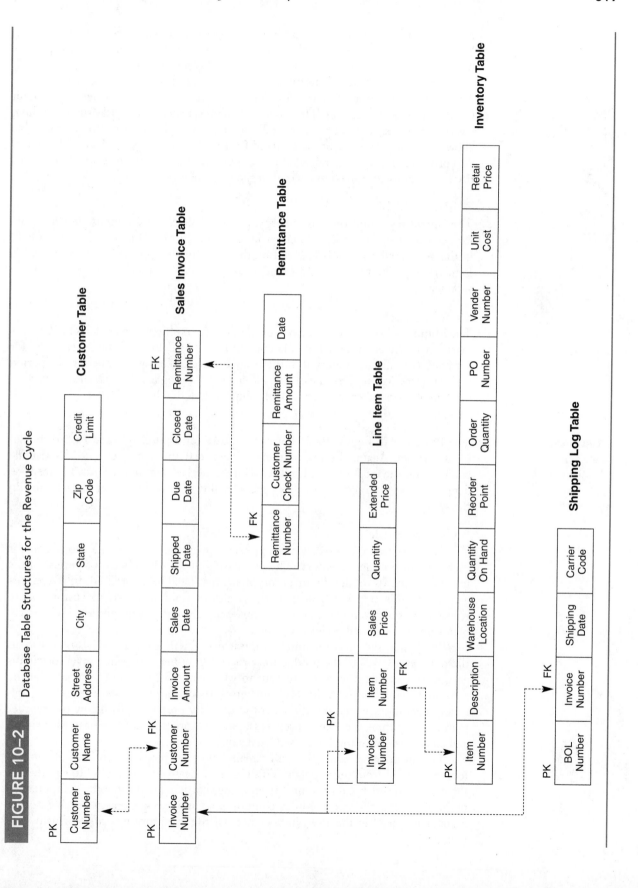

FIGURE 10–2   Database Table Structures for the Revenue Cycle

Notice that the table contains two primary keys—Invoice Number and Item Number. Both keys are needed to uniquely define each record in the table. They also provide links to related records in the Sales Invoice and Inventory tables.

Cost of goods sold is determined by linking each Line Item table record to the Inventory table and multiplying the Quantity field value in the former by the Unit Cost field value in the latter. This table also supports operational tasks such as billing, customer service, marketing, and auditing. For example, sales details in the table allow marketing to evaluate the demand for the organization's products. These data also provide audit evidence needed to corroborate the accuracy of price times quantity calculations that are summarized in the sales invoices.

Inventory Table

The **Inventory table** contains quantity, price, supplier, and warehouse location data for each item of inventory. When products are sold, the Quantity On Hand field in the associated records is reduced by the value of the Quantity field in the Line Item record. The Quantity On Hand field is increased by inventory receipts from suppliers.

Shipping Log Table

The **Shipping Log table** is a record of all sales orders shipped to customers. The primary key of the table is the bill of lading number. The data in this table are useful for verifying that all sales reflected in the Sales Invoice table were shipped in the period under review. As a tool for measuring efficiency, shipping log data can also be used to determine if customer orders are being shipped in a timely manner.

PURCHASES AND CASH DISBURSEMENTS SYSTEM

The flowchart in Figure 10–3 shows a database for a purchases and cash disbursements system. Again, the main difference between this approach and the flat file equivalent is the focus on events rather than classical accounting records. Figure 10–4 depicts the table structures for this system. Following is a discussion of each table in the system.

Inventory Table

The *Inventory table* contains quantity, price, supplier, and warehouse location data for each item of product inventory. The purchasing process begins with a review of the inventory records to identify inventory items that need to be ordered. In a retail organization, this step is performed when sales of finished goods to customers are recorded in the inventory records. In this case, the purchasing process involves replenishing the finished goods inventory.

Purchasing systems of manufacturing firms replenish raw materials inventory as these items are used in the production process. In either case, when inventory items are sold or used in production, the Quantity On Hand field is reduced accordingly by a computer application. With each inventory reduction, the system tests for a "reorder" condition, which occurs when the quantity on hand falls below the reorder point. At that time, the system prepares a purchase order, which is sent to the vendor, and adds a record to the Purchase Order table.

The quantity on hand value will remain below the reorder point until the inventory is received from the supplier. This may take days or even weeks. To signify that the item is on order and prevent it from being reordered each time the computer application detects the same reorder condition, a computer-generated purchase order number is placed in the PO Number field of the inventory record. Normally, this field is blank.

FIGURE 10–3   Database Purchases/Cash Disbursements System

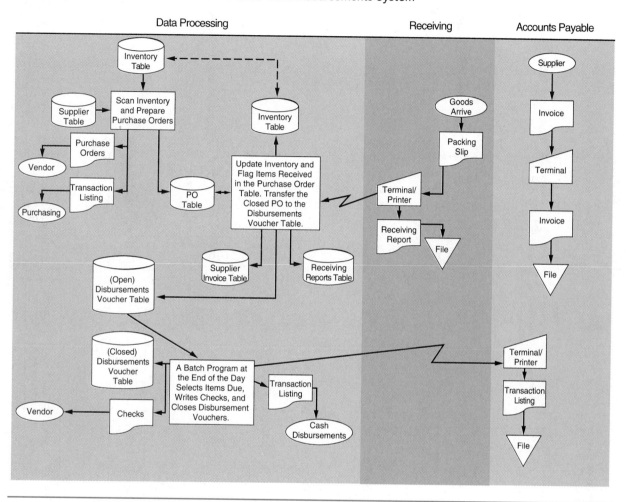

Purchase Order Table

The **Purchase Order table** contains records of purchases placed with suppliers. The record remains open until the inventory arrives. Placing the receiving report number in the designated field closes the record.

Purchase Order Line Item Table

The **PO Line Item table** contains a record of every item ordered. Since a single transaction can involve one or more products, each record in the Purchase Order table is associated with (linked to) one or more records in this table. Notice that the table contains two primary keys—Purchase Order Number and Item Number. Both keys are needed to uniquely define each record in the table. They also provide links to related records in the Purchase Order and Inventory tables.

Receiving Report Table

When the ordered items arrive from the supplier, they are counted and inspected and receiving documents are prepared. Via a terminal, the receiving clerk enters

FIGURE 10–4 File Structures for the Expenditure Cycle

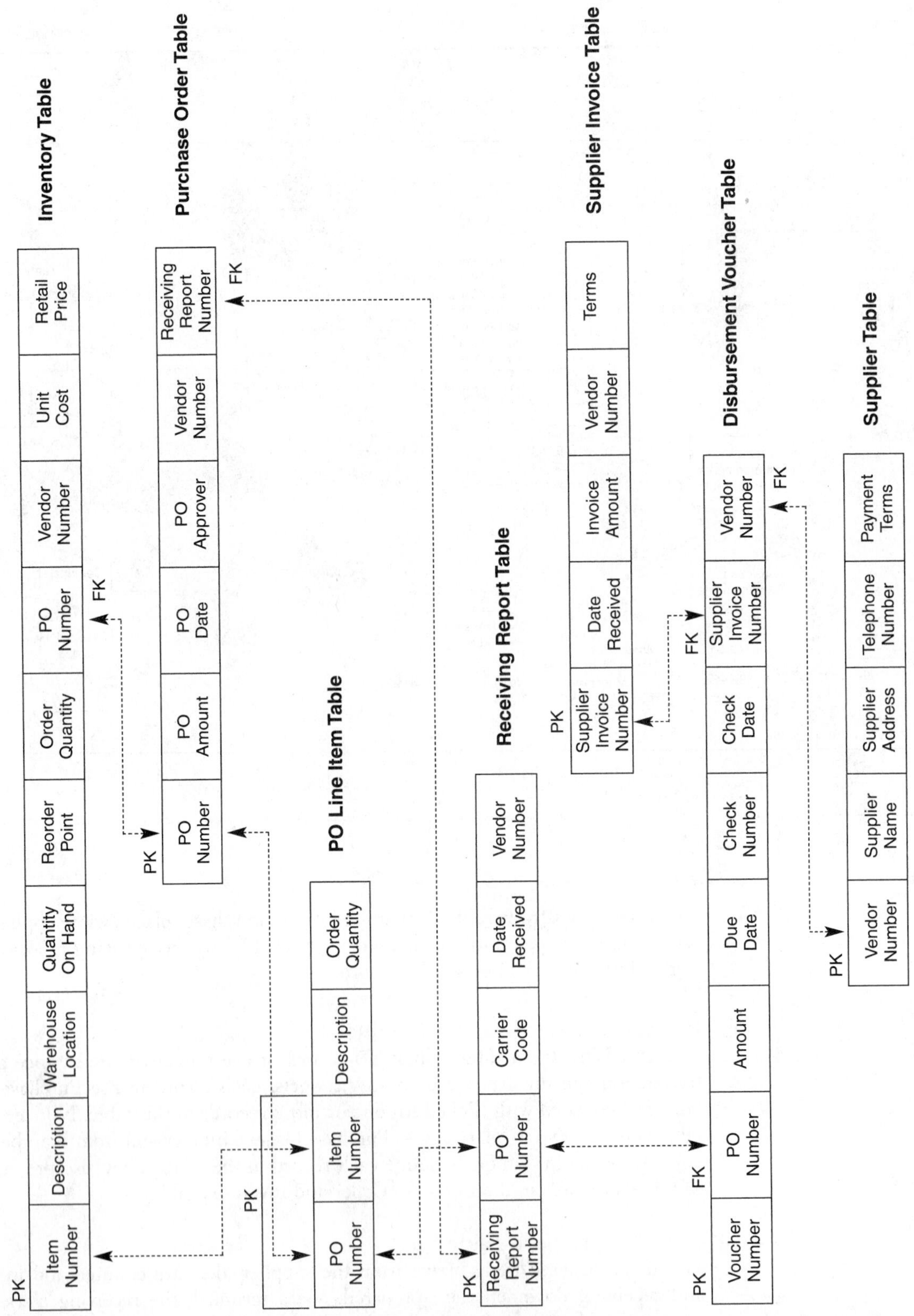
Inventory Table
PK
Item Number
Description
Warehouse Location
Quantity On Hand
Reorder Point
Order Quantity
PO Number
FK
Vendor Number
Unit Cost
Retail Price
Purchase Order Table
PK
PO Number
PO Amount
PO Date
PO Approver
Vendor Number
Receiving Report Number
FK
PO Line Item Table
PK
PO Number
Item Number
Description
Order Quantity
Receiving Report Table
PK
Receiving Report Number
PO Number
Carrier Code
Date Received
Vendor Number
Supplier Invoice Table
PK
Supplier Invoice Number
Date Received
Invoice Amount
Vendor Number
Terms
Disbursement Voucher Table
PK
Voucher Number
FK
PO Number
Amount
Due Date
Check Number
Check Date
FK
Supplier Invoice Number
Vendor Number
FK
Supplier Table
PK
Vendor Number
Supplier Name
Supplier Address
Telephone Number
Payment Terms

information about the items received in the **Receiving Report table**. The system automatically performs the following tasks: (1) increases the Quantity On Hand field in the inventory record(s); (2) removes the reorder condition by resetting the PO Number field to its normal blank state; (3) creates a record in the Receiving Report table; and (4) closes the purchase order record by placing the receiving report number in the designated field.

Disbursement Voucher Table

For most companies, discrepancies between amounts ordered, received, and billed are legitimate concerns that must be resolved before payment to the vendor is approved. Because of its complexity, this reconciliation is often a manual process that is triggered by receipt of the supplier's invoice. The accounts payable clerk reviews the supporting records in the Purchase Order and Receiving Report tables and compares them to the invoice. If the items, quantities, and prices match, then a cash disbursement voucher is created and a record is added to the Supplier Invoice table. Based on the supplier's terms of trade and the company's payment policy, the payment due date is determined and placed in the disbursement voucher record.

Each payment day, the cash disbursements application automatically selects the items due, flags them "paid" by entering the current date in the Check Date field, and cuts the check, which is then mailed to the supplier.

The **Disbursement Voucher table** provides three important pieces of information that are traditionally contained in formal accounting records. First, it is a record of checks written in payment of trade accounts for the period and thus replaces the traditional Cash Disbursements Journal. Second, the sum of the open items (unpaid vouchers) for a particular vendor is equivalent to the Accounts Payable Subsidiary Ledger for the vendor. Finally, the total of all unpaid vouchers in the table constitutes the company's accounts payable (General Ledger) balance.

LIMITATIONS OF TRANSACTION-BASED SYSTEMS

While the system just described represents a marked improvement over the traditional flat file approach, it has serious shortcomings. This system is **transaction-based**, which allows the user to capture in great detail information related to *economic events* such as sales to customers and purchases from suppliers. A look at the database tables, however, shows that they are designed to capture only financial transaction data. Nonfinancial data are not captured. Furthermore, *noneconomic* events are ignored by this system. An example of a noneconomic event is a customer who enters a place of business, browses, inquires about products, but does not buy. Information about such customer behavior may be very important to an organization. This type of event would, however, not be captured by a transaction-based system such as the one above. As we will see, REA is an **event-based** (or sometimes called a **pattern-based**) system. The distinction is more than semantic. An REA system is responsive to both economic and noneconomic phenomena, permitting the creation of much richer databases that can support the information needs of all users within the organization.

TRADITIONAL APPROACH TO MODELING BUSINESS PROCESSES

Under the traditional approach to relational database design, an entity relationship (ER) diagram is used to model the relationships between an organization's critical resources, events, and agents. The principle elements of an ER diagram were discussed in Chapter 2. Figure 10–5 shows how this technique can be used to depict a simplified model of a manufacturing firm.

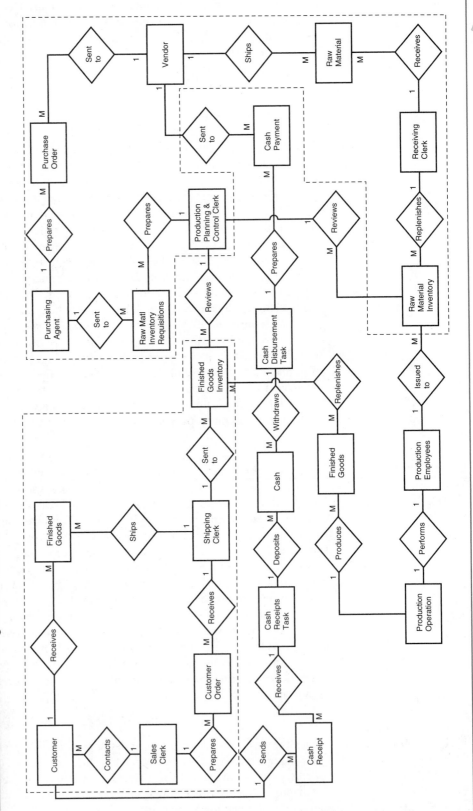

FIGURE 10–5   ER Diagram of a Manufacturing Firm

The **sales business process** is shown in the upper left of the figure surrounded by a dashed border, and the procurement business process is shown in the top and bottom right surrounded by a dashed border.

This ER representation is suitable if a traditional approach to database design is being followed. A different form of model is developed, however, under the REA approach. As illustrated in the next section, REA modeling is more detailed and necessitates an additional consolidating step involving relation cardinalities prior to designing the information system's base tables. Thereafter, the relational database design follows a process similar to that outlined in Chapter 9.

DEVELOPING AN REA MODEL

Having introduced the basic concepts of the REA model and its potential advantages over the traditional approach, let's now look at how REA models are developed. Central to this approach is the concept of an event. One business process may consist of several events. Before developing an REA model, events must be classified as either:

- **Operating events**, which are activities that produce goods and services.
- **Information events**, which are activities associated with recording, maintaining, and reporting information.
- **Decision/management events**, which are activities that lead to decisions being made and implemented.

These classes of events are all linked in a circular fashion: Decision/management events trigger operating events. Operating events trigger information events. Information events trigger decision/management events, and so on. In a manual information system, it is fairly easy to distinguish between these three classes of events. Unfortunately, the greater complexity of computerized information systems makes it much less clear where one class ends and another begins. Nevertheless, from the perspective of control and relevance to the item of interest, it is important that they are separately identified when an REA model is being developed.

Starting with the most straightforward, it is generally not difficult to identify which are decision/management events. These involve decisions relating to planning, evaluation, and control. For example, to purchase or not to purchase, to sell or not to sell, to hire or not to hire, to request a report, to request information, and to implement a new control measure are all decision/management events.

Information events produce the information that enables decisions to be made. These include the acts of recording, amending, updating, or maintaining. The following are examples of information events:

- recording new customer data,
- updating inventory records following a sale,
- amending the details of a customer who has changed address,
- preparing cost estimates for new products,
- preparing credit rating reports on potential customers,
- preparing an analysis of applicant data for a position in the organization,
- preparing sales invoices,
- preparing purchase orders,
- preparing divisional performance reports.

Operating events are the physical activities associated with business processes. Because of accounting students' information orientation, they sometimes have difficulty separating operating events from information events. For example, taking a customer's order, shipping the product to the customer, receiving raw materials from the supplier, and paying for inventories received are operating events. Preparing the sales invoice, recording shipments in the shipping log, recording inventory receipts in the ledger, and preparing a cash disbursement voucher for payment to the supplier are the related, but different, information events.

To identify operating events within a business process we can employ an approach used by many disciplines when trying to discover what has occurred. Operating events are revealed through the answers to a series of questioning verbs: Who did it? What happened? When did it happen? Where did it happen? What was involved? How did it happen?

To illustrate the process of developing an REA model, the following case is used.

Horizon Books

Horizon Books is a bookstore in downtown Philadelphia. It carries an inventory of approximately 5,000 books. Customers come in and browse the shelves, select their books, and take them to one of three cashiers, positioned in different parts of the store. One of the cashiers is situated at an information desk where customers can discover whether a particular book is in stock, place orders for books not currently available in the bookstore, and collect and pay for books previously ordered. The cashier at the information desk has a book database that is consulted for every query. There are no credit sales. All customers pay for their purchases at the time of purchase.

STEP 1

As a first step, the operating events that are to be included in the model are identified. These are the events that support the strategic objectives of the organization and about which information is needed. At its simplest, the model could have only one event, the sale. But that would mean gathering no data about the time a customer spent browsing before purchase. It would also mean gathering no data about customers who inquired but left without purchasing. To capture these data an *arrival* event, a *departure* event, and an *inquiry* event need to be included in the model. For the sake of simplicity, assume that Horizon Books does not require information about customer arrivals and departures at this time. Information is needed, however, for a customer payment event and a customer inquiry event.

STEP 2

The operating events identified now need to be organized in sequence of occurrence. While many sales will occur without an inquiry preceding them, whenever an inquiry takes place, it will precede any subsequent sale arising from it. Hence, the sequence of events in the model is inquiry, sale, and payment. This is shown as in Figure 10–6. Notice how each event is shown as verb-object. Note also that the verb is represented from the perspective of the organization, not the customer.

STEP 3

Next the resources and agents involved in each operating event must be identified. This is most easily done by answering *who, what,* and *where* questions about each event. For example, the following questions may be asked. Who was involved? What was involved? Where did it take place?

FIGURE 10–6

Horizon Books REA
Sales Model Events
of Interest

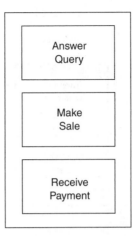

In the case of the Answer Query event, the customer and a cashier were involved, the inventory database was involved, and it occurred at the information desk. The Make Sale event involved the customer, a cashier and the book sold. The event took place at a cash register. The Receive Payment event involved the customer, a cashier, cash, and took place at a cash register.

This model is presented in Figure 10–7. Notice that resources are illustrated on the left, events in the middle, and agents on the right of the figure. An REA model is typically drawn without the column headings and dividers. They are shown in Figure 10–7 to illustrate the correct placement of the objects. Headings and dividers are not shown in subsequent diagrams.

STEP 4

The next step is to identify the links between the resources, events, and agents. Start from each event and connect it to the resources and agents that are involved in the event. Next draw a line connecting events that are logically related. This graphical representation is shown in Figure 10–8.

You learned how to construct relational tables in Chapter 9. Since REA models are used to build relational databases, an REA-based information system exhibits all the features of a relational database. Look at the relational table called Customer in Figure 10–9 (page 530), which has been reproduced from Chapter 9.

In an REA accounting system, where there is a mixture of cash and credit sales, cash customers can all be assigned the same identifier within the Customer table. In terms of Figure 10–9, this could be represented in the line:

Cust Num	Name	Address	Current Balance
0	Cash	0	0

However, Horizon Books operates a cash-sales-only policy. In a traditional accounting system where all sales are for cash, no data would be maintained for a customer and there would be no customer data table. When the form of settlement is cash, it can be argued that from a purely financial point of view we need not to know who paid the cash. We only need to know that cash has been received. If each cash sale is identified uniquely to separate the transactions then there is no need for a Customer table.

FIGURE 10–7

Horizon Books
Resources, Events,
and Agents Labeled to
Show Their Positions

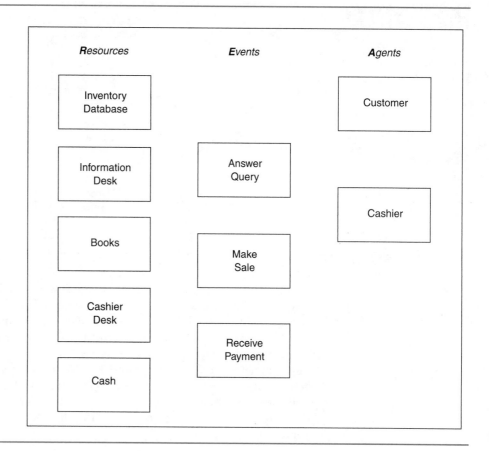

On the other hand, an advantage of REA is to capture a far wider range of data about events. These would include the age and gender of the customer, the type of books that the customer likes to read, and the customer's name and address. With this information the bookshop can send the customer details of new books and special events. Thus, even where all sales are for cash, under an REA-based information system the Customer table will not only exist but will likely have many more attributes than would typically appear in a traditional information system.

STEP 5

The next step is to assign the **cardinalities** of all the entity relationships. Recall from Chapter 9 that three fundamental record associations (cardinalities) were defined and used when constructing an ER diagram, one-to-one (1:1), one-to-many (1:M), and many-to-many (M:M). An entity in a relation with cardinality of *one* could have zero or one instance in that relation. An entity in a relation with a cardinality of *many* could have zero, one, or many instances in that relation.

Consider the relationship between an entity called *customer* and another called *inventory* in an antique store. Assume *inventory* is comprised of unique items of antique furniture. The cardinality would be defined as one-to-many (1:M). You could have zero or one *customers* who buy each item of *inventory* (antique furniture) and zero, one, or many items of *inventory* may be bought by each *customer*. The cardinality rules defined in Chapter 9 and applied in the description of the ER diagrams in that chap-

FIGURE 10–8

Horizon Books REA
Sales Process
Relationships

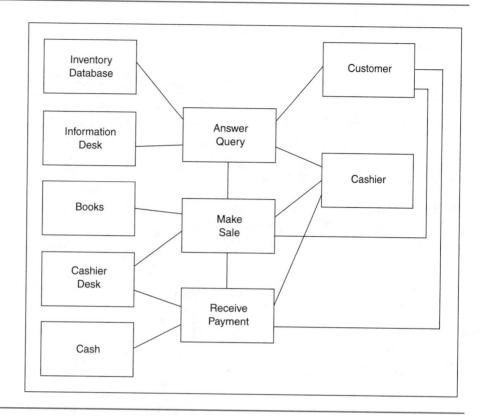

ter resulted in cardinalities that gave the maximum instances of each entity in the relation, one-to-many (1:M).

Under the REA approach, five forms of associations are used when constructing the REA model. These are zero-to-one (0,1), zero-to-many (0,M), one-to-one (1,1), one-to-many (1,M), and many-to-many (M,M). The difference between the Chapter 9 definition and the REA definition is that the REA model requires that both the minimum and maximum instances for each entity in a relation be defined.

Thus, the cardinality of the *customer* entity in the *inventory:customer* relation is defined as (0,1) and the *inventory* entity's cardinality is defined as (0,M). The cardinality of the relation would be one-to-many (1:M) as in Chapter 9, but the REA model would show both minimum and maximum instances for each entity, not just the maximum instances as in the case of the ER diagram.

Note that the actual design of the relational base tables follows the same process whether they are derived from a traditional ER or an REA model. Only the maximum cardinalities are used to define the links between the tables. By documenting the REA model in this way, however, more information is available than is found in traditional ER diagrams of the same business process. The increased level of detail in the REA model makes it far easier to identify what occurs during the process being modeled. This added information adds to the richness of the database and also improves planning, evaluation, and control of the business processes. Let's now see how this works in practice by further developing the REA model for Horizon Books.

In the case of Horizon Books' *customer:make sale* entity relationship, the existence of one *customer* may result in zero, one, or many *make sales* occurring. This is

FIGURE 10–9

A Relational Table
Called Customer

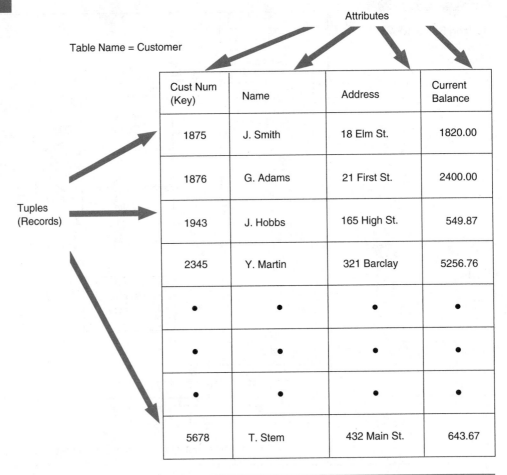

FIGURE 10–10

Horizon Books
Customer:Make Sale
Cardinalities

represented in the REA model of the process using the notation (0,M) to represent the minimum and maximum cardinality. Similarly, the existence of one *make sale* arises from the existence of one and only one *customer* entity, represented as (1,1) in the REA model. This is shown in Figure 10–10.

Sometimes, when defining the cardinalities of an entity relation, it helps to imagine that you are standing on top of one of the entity boxes and looking at the other. Imagine what you see. If you are on top of the customer entity box what minimum and maximum sales can you see? You can see as few as zero (the customer may wish to buy nothing) or a maximum greater than one (if the customer decides to buy more

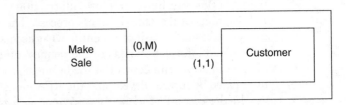

than one item). Thus the *make sale* entity in this relation is zero-to-many (0,M). Now, stand on the other entity box. How many *customers* do you see buying a specific item? The minimum is one. For the *make sale* entity to exist there must be a *customer*. Furthermore, since only one customer can buy a specific item, the maximum cardinality is also one. The cardinalities of the *customer* entity in this relation is, therefore, one-to-one (1,1).

Using these principles, cardinalities are assigned to the relations in the REA model for the sales process of Horizon Books. These cardinalities are illustrated in Figure 10–11.

REA MODELS VERSUS ER DIAGRAMS

To illustrate the differences between the REA and ER modeling refer to Figure 10–12. Although not obvious at first glance, this is an REA model of the same process described by the traditional ER diagram in Figure 10–5. The areas modeled in Figure 10–12 correspond to the sales and procurement processes outlined with the dashed borders in Figure 10–5.

The **entities** in both REA- models and ER diagrams are represented by rectangles, and lines connect them. The lines connecting the ER diagram entities are intersected by diamond relationship symbols containing verbs, which indicate what

---

FIGURE 10–11

The REA Model for
the Sales Process of
Horizon Books

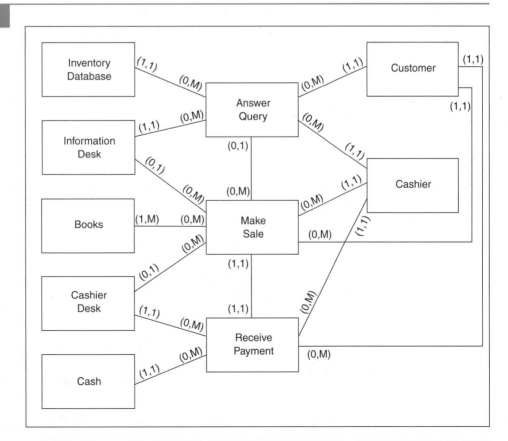

FIGURE 10–12

REA Model of a
Manufacturing Firm

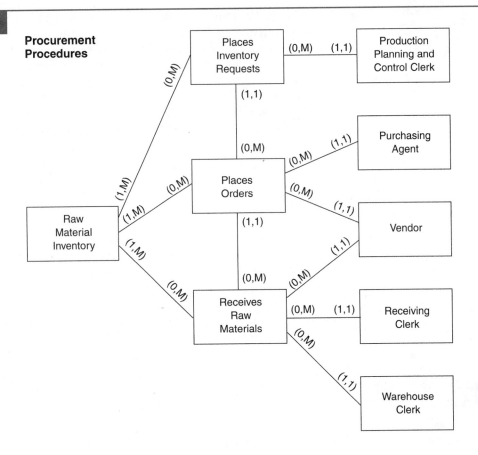

**Procurement
Procedures**

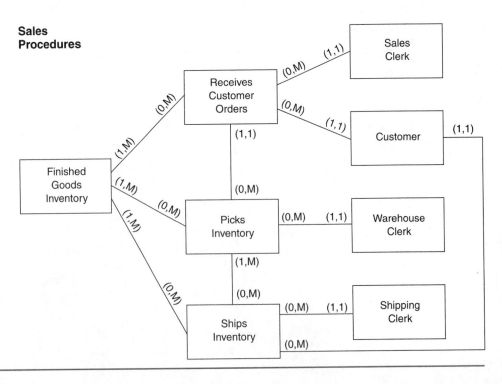

**Sales
Procedures**

occurs in the relationship. In effect, each diamond symbol represents an event. ER diagrams, however, represent a much broader set of events than do REA models. These include operating events (receives), information events (prepares, or updates), and decision events (reviews). In contrast, only operating events are included in an REA model, and only those of strategic importance.

While in some respects the REA model is simpler than the corresponding ER diagram, it provides more relevant information. The REA approach allows the systems designer to focus on key events that facilitate the design and placement of controls. Because information and decision-making events are isolated from the primary operating events, the differing controls required over these classes of events can be more easily identified and inserted into the business process.

It is in these crucial differences that the benefits of preparing an REA model become apparent. The ER diagram is a data modeling tool that enables organizations to view each business process in detail and to ensure alignment between the processes and the relational database in which data relating to them are stored. Its primary purpose is to identify the data attributes that represent the conceptual user views that must be supported by the base tables. In other words, the ER model is view-oriented.

The REA model pinpoints where the organization can plan, evaluate, and control significant operating events within the business process. In addition to being a systems analyst's tool, it is a management tool. REA focuses upon business activities within business processes. It is event-based.

DEFINING THE ENTITY ATTRIBUTES

The REA model can be used to define entity **attributes**. Consider the procurement procedures presented in Figure 10–12. The following describes the accounting phenomena associated with this process.

- The operating *events* in the process are placing inventory requests, placing the order, and receiving the inventory. The data elements describing these events should be specified in sufficient detail to support all user needs. To illustrate, the financial and nonfinancial data for the Places Orders event include:

  Financial
  Vendor name
  Vendor address
  Inventory item number
  Quantity to be ordered
  Unit cost
  Purchase order number
  Order date

  Nonfinancial
  Vendor lead time
  Carrier used
  On-time delivery record
  Incomplete shipments record
  Damaged shipments record
  Price disputes record

- Raw materials inventory is the economic *resource* affected by the event. The data attributes needed to specify this resource and the changes that are made to it would include:

  Financial
  Inventory item number
  Description
  Quantity on hand
  Reorder point
  Economic order quantity
  Supplier

  Nonfinancial
  Turnover rate
  Lead time
  Usage rate
  Warehouse location
  Stockout history
  Scrap history
  Delayed arrival history

- The primary *agents* are production planning and control clerks, the purchasing agent, the vendor, the receiving clerks, and the warehouse clerks. All of the relevant attributes describing these agents would be specified and modeled into the database. Using the vendor as an example, these data include:

Financial	*Nonfinancial*
Vendor name	On-time delivery record
Vendor address	Damaged goods record
Vendor telephone number	Average lead time
Amount owed to vendor	Help line support
Value of total purchases to date	EDI access
Terms of trade offered	Internet access

Consider now the sales procedures in Figure 10–12. The following describes the accounting phenomena associated with this process.

- The *events* in the process are receiving the customer order, picking the finished goods inventory, and shipping the inventory. The data elements describing these events should be specified in sufficient detail to support all user needs. To illustrate, the financial and nonfinancial data for the Receives Customer Order event include:

Financial	*Nonfinancial*
Customer name	Customer credit rating
Customer address	Carrier used
Inventory item number	On-time delivery record
Quantity ordered	Incomplete shipments record
Unit price	Damaged shipments record
Sales order number	Complaints record
Order date	

- Finished goods inventory is the economic *resource* affected by the event. The data attributes needed to specify this resource and the changes that are made to it include:

Financial	*Nonfinancial*
Inventory item number	Turnover rate
Description	Lead time
Quantity on hand	Usage rate
Production reorder point	Warehouse location
Economic order quantity	Stockout history
	Scrap history
	Delayed production history

- The primary *agents* are the sales clerks, the customer, the warehouse clerks, and the shipping clerks. All of the relevant attributes describing these agents would be specified and modeled into the database. Using the customer as an example, these data include:

Financial	*Nonfinancial*
Customer name	Customer credit rating
Customer address	Damaged goods record
Customer telephone number	On-time payment record
Amount owed by customer	Customer volume record
Value of total sales to date	EDI access
Terms of trade offered	Internet access

Data requirements of other business processes such as production, cash receipts, etc., would be obtained in this fashion and combined to produce an overall schema of data requirements. Both accounting and nonaccounting requirements would contribute to the overall database. In the process of combining data requirements, it is important to recognize and eliminate any redundancies from the model. For example, the raw materials inventory resource is also an element of the production process. Similarly, the vendor is also an agent in the cash disbursement process.

The data requirements for resources, events, and agents associated with multiple business processes must be integrated, not modeled separately. Hence, while each business process is modeled separately, the same underlying database tables are used across all the models. The same Customer table will be used in the sales model and in the cash collection model; and the same Vendor table will be used in the purchase model as in the cash disbursement model, etc.

Once the attributes have been defined, the database tables can be designed. The process of assigning primary and foreign keys and table normalization to support user views is no different from that described in Chapter 9, and is not repeated here.

CREATING USER VIEWS

The REA approach can generate an information system capable of supporting multiple views. As a result, the various possible views must be accounted for at an early stage in model development. This is achieved through defining a range of data attributes that cover the desired range of views.

This usually involves an extensive analysis of user information needs. Once the analysis is complete, the designer can derive the set of data attributes (the conceptual user view) necessary to produce these inputs and outputs. As the physical representation of the conceptual user view, the reports, documents, and computer screens, are called **physical views**. They help the designer understand key relationships among the data.

Once the attributes have been identified, the forms and procedures to collect event, resources, and agent data can be designed and the base tables can be populated. Once this is done, a query interface can be created to produce views and reports.

The query interface must encompass all conceivable views and the format for the reports resulting from each query needs to be determined. The following three figures present examples of the physical views of three users. The first view is for a purchasing agent who needs information about inventory items to be ordered and the suppliers of the inventory. Figure 10–13 depicts the inventory status report that conveys this information. The second user view is for a sales manager who needs a breakdown of daily sales activity organized by customer and product. Figure 10–14 shows the sales report containing this information. Finally, the third view, for the general ledger department, presents a listing of journal vouchers summarizing the day's business activity. The journal voucher report is portrayed in Figure 10–15. These views were all obtained from the same database. They each satisfy the information needs of a user and they show the data at the required level of details.

Flexibility in user view design is one of REA's strengths. User views should be capable of being amended in any way that the individual user wishes. To illustrate, let's return to the Horizon Books example. If the sales manager of the company wants to know whether each sale resulted from an initial customer inquiry, that information could be easily provided in a report. Similarly, as shown in Figure 10–16 (page 538), a report could be produced for the Horizon Books purchasing manager showing the time spent on each customer inquiry, the nature of the inquiry, whether the inquiry resulted in a sale, and the demographic details of the customer who made the inquiry. This could then be used to identify potential new topics or authors Horizon Books should carry.

FIGURE 10–13
Inventory Status Report

Ajax Manufacturing Co.
Inventory Status Report

Part Number	Description	Quantity On Hand	Reorder Point	Order Quantity	Supplier Number	Name	Address	Telephone
1	Bracket	100	150	500	22 24 27	Ozment Sup Buell Co. B&R Sup	123 Main St. 2 Broadhead Westgate Mall	555-7895 555-3436 555-7845
2	Gasket	440	450	1000	22 24 28	Ozment Sup Buell Co. Harris Manuf	123 Main St. 2 Broadhead 24 Linden St.	555-7895 555-3436 555-3316
3	Brace	10	10	50	22 24 28	Ozment Sup Buell Co. Harris Manuf	123 Main St. 2 Broadhead 24 Linden St.	555-7895 555-3436 555-3316
⋮	⋮	⋮	⋮	⋮	⋮	⋮	⋮	⋮

Summary

This chapter examined the REA model as a means of specifying and designing accounting information systems that serve the needs of all users in an entity. It began by defining the key elements of REA and outlining its advantages, such as efficient operations, increased productivity, and competitive advantage. The competitive advantage benefits of REA are most clearly seen from the perspective of the value chain. Before delving into REA, the chapter examined the advantages and disadvantages of traditional database design. While superior to flat file systems, traditional database systems have serious limitations. Foremost among these is that they support primarily the needs of financial information users. Also, they are economic event-driven and unresponsive to noneconomic events that may be of extreme importance to an organization. Next, the chapter examined the steps involved in developing an REA model of a business process. These include the following:

1. Identify the operating events that are to be included in the model. These are the operating events of interest, about which we wish to gather information. Typically, these are the events of strategic significance to the organization.
2. Organize the operating events into their sequence of occurrence.
3. Identify the resources and agents involved in each operating event.
4. Identify the links between these resources, events, and agents.
5. Define the entity relations by assigning cardinalities to them.

Using a manufacturing firm as an example, the REA and ER models of sales and procurement processes were compared. The similarities and differences between the two approaches were highlighted. Based on the REA model of these business processes, a set of financial and nonfinancial data that would meet the need of multiple users was derived. The chapter concluded with a discussion of REA's flexibility in producing and amending user views.

FIGURE 10–14	Sales Report

Customer Number: 19321
Customer Name : Jon Smith
Address   : 520 Main St.,City

Invoice #	Date	Invoice Total	Part Num	Quantity	Unit Price	Ext'd Price
12390	11/11/01	$850	2	5	$20	$100
			1	10	50	500
			3	25	10	250
12912	11/21/01	$300	4	10	$30	$300

Customer Total: $1,150

* * *   * * * *   * * * *   * * * *   * * * *   * * * *   * * *

Customer Number: 19322
Customer Name : Mary Smith
Address   : 2289 Elm St., City

Invoice #	Date	Invoice Total	Part Num	Quantity	Unit Price	Ext'd Price
12421	11/13/01	$1,000	6	10	$20	$200
			1	2	50	100
			5	7	100	700
12901						
	11/20/01	$500	4	10	$30	$300
			2	10	20	200

Customer Total: $1,500

* * *   * * * *   * * * *   * * * *   * * * *   * * * *   * * *

Next Customer

-
-
-

Next Customer

FIGURE 10–15	

Journal Voucher
Report

Journal Voucher Report

JV Num	Date	Title	Acct Num	Debit	Credit
1	9/20/01	Cash	101	1000	
		Acct Rec	103	2000	
		Sales	401		3000
2	9/20/01	Cost of Goods Sold	501	2500	
		Inventory	108		2500
•	•	•	•	•	•
•	•	•	•	•	•
•	•	•	•	•	•

FIGURE 10–16   Customer Inquiry Report

Customer Inquiry Report 2/14/01 – 7/14/01										
Inq Num	Date	Cust Num	m/f	Age	Topic	Author	In Store	Sale	Time Spent	Comments
483	2/14	217	m	26	collecting	—	yes	yes	5	—
484	2/14	142	f	19	—	Wood, F	no	no	7	—
485	2/14	723	f	54	aerobics	Banks, J	yes	no	3	too expensive
.	.	.	.	.	.	.	.	.	.	.
.	.	.	.	.	.	.	.	.	.	.

Key Terms

agents (515)
attributes (533)
cardinalities (528)
Customer table (517)
data modeling (515)
decision/management events (525)
Disbursement Voucher table (523)
entities (531)
events (515)
event-based (523)
information events (525)
Inventory table (520)
Line Item table (517)
operating events (525)

pattern-based (523)
physical views (535)
PO Line Item table (521)
Purchase Order table (521)
REA model (514)
Receiving Report table (523)
resources (515)
sales business process (525)
Sales Invoice table (517)
Shipping Log table (520)
transaction-based (523)
user view (514)
value chain (516)
value chain analysis (516)

Review Questions

1. What is a user view?
2. What other type of information do modern managers need apart from financial information?
3. In the term *REA model*, what does the "R" stand for?
4. In the term *REA model*, what does the "E" stand for?
5. In the term *REA model*, what does the "A" stand for?
6. What form of view is provided by an REA-based information system?
7. Define "economic resources."
8. Define "economic events."
9. Define "economic agents."
10. What is represented in the diamond boxes within an ER diagram?
11. Value chain analysis distinguishes between which two primary activities?
12. Define "operating event."
13. Define "information event."
14. Define "decision/management event."
15. What criteria do you apply when deciding which operating events are to be included in an REA model?

16. What form of questions do you use in order to identify the resources and agents involved in each event?
17. List the steps involved in preparing an REA model of a business process.
18. What do you need to do in order to prepare an REA model for use in the development of a relational database?

Discussion Questions

1. Discuss the primary differences between flat file and traditional database systems.
2. Explain how a Sales Invoice table can be used to replace traditional accounting records.
3. Explain how a Disbursement Voucher table can be used to replace traditional accounting records.
4. Discuss the limitations of transaction-based systems.
5. Discuss why adherence by accountants to a single, GAAP-based view is inappropriate.
6. What do you think the implications of accountants' adherence to a single, GAAP-based view are for the accounting profession?
7. Discuss why the REA approach empowers accountants to meet the needs of modern managers.
8. Distinguish between resources, events, and agents.
9. Compare and contrast the appearance and content of an ER diagram with that of an REA model.
10. Discuss the advantages of adopting an REA modeling approach over a traditional approach to information system development.
11. Discuss how adopting a value chain perspective reveals advantages of the REA approach to information system development.
12. Discuss the relationship between operating events, information events, and decision/management events.
13. Discuss the differences between the cardinalities defined in an ER diagram and those defined in an REA model, and their usefulness in the development of relational databases.

Multiple-Choice Questions

1. Which of the following is included in an REA model?
   a. operating events
   b. information events
   c. decision events
   d. management events
2. The "R" in REA stands for
   a. ratios.
   b. relationships.
   c. reserves.
   d. resources.
3. Which of the following is not an example of the cardinalities included in an REA model?
   a. one-to-one
   b. many-to-one
   c. many-to-many
   d. none, they all are
4. Which of the following statements is correct?
   a. The REA model requires that phenomena be characterized in a manner consistent with the development of a single user view.
   b. The REA model requires that phenomena be characterized in a manner consistent with the development of selected user views.
   c. The REA model requires that phenomena be characterized in a manner consistent with the development of unique user views.
   d. The REA model requires that phenomena be characterized in a manner consistent with the development of multiple user views.
5. Which of the following is not an advantage of the REA model?
   a. increased productivity
   b. greater efficiency
   c. less complex database development
   d. more relevant and timely information

6. Which of the following is incorrect?
   a. Operating events trigger information events.
   b. Decision/management events trigger operating events.
   c. Information events trigger operating events.
   d. Information events trigger decision/management events.
7. When designing an REA model, events need to be organized in sequence of
   a. completion.
   b. length.
   c. ease of analysis.
   d. occurrence.
8. In an REA model, each event is described from the perspective of the
   a. user.
   b. organization.
   c. designer.
   d. customer.
9. Which of the following is not an example of a physical view?
   a. reports
   b. documents
   c. electronic images
   d. data tables

Problems

1. REA Model Extract
Prepare an REA model depicting the issuance of raw materials into the manufacturing process.
a. List the specific data elements that would be necessary to describe the issuance of raw materials into the manufacturing process.
b. Identify the
   1. economic resources affected.
   2. underlying economic event.
   3. primary agents involved.

2. REA Model Extract
Prepare an REA model depicting the shipping of finished goods to a customer.
a. List the specific data elements that would be necessary to describe the shipping of finished goods to the customer.
b. Identify the
   1. economic resources affected.
   2. underlying economic event.
   3. primary agents involved.

3. REA model
Prepare an REA model for the sales business process from the following amended version of the Horizon Books case.

Horizon Books
Horizon Books is a bookstore in downtown Philadelphia. It carries an inventory of approximately 5,000 books. Customers come in and browse the shelves, select their books, and take them to the cashier. In addition to the cashier's desk, there is also an information desk where customers can discover whether a particular book is in stock, place orders for books not currently available in the bookstore, and collect books previously ordered. The employee at the information desk has a book database that is consulted for every query. There are no credit sales. All customers pay for their purchases at the time of purchase.

4. REA model
Prepare an REA model for the sales business process from the following amended version of the Horizon Books case.

Horizon Books
Horizon Books is a bookstore in downtown Philadelphia. It carries an inventory of approximately 5,000 books. Customers come in and browse the shelves, select their books, and take them to the cashier. At the cashier's desk they can also discover whether a particular book is in stock, place orders for books not currently available in the bookstore, and collect and pay for books previously ordered. The cashier has a book database that is consulted for every query. There are no credit sales. All customers pay for their purchases at the time of purchase.

5. Cardinalities

Redraw Figure 10–11 showing the collapsed cardinalities between the entities required for the design of a relational database for Horizon Books.

6. REA Model

(Prepared by Todd Feinman, Coopers & Lybrand LLP)

F&Y is in the industry of selling computers. Its main competition is other major mail-order computer companies. Its market share is small compared to the industry leaders, but it hopes to increase its share by becoming more responsive to its customers' orders through reengineering its sales order processing system. F&Y has 147 employees, and the main office is located in St. Paul, Minnesota.

F&Y sells desktop computer systems that it primarily manufactures itself, with a few parts purchased from third-party companies. It offers many different packages to accommodate its end-user customers, about 15 different bundles in all. Customers pay on credit terms and receive a satisfaction guarantee for 30 days after receipt of their computers. F&Y's suppliers include a few different microcomputer chip and software manufacturers whose products F&Y packages with its computers. F&Y's warehouse is located at the main office in St. Paul.

Last year, F&Y's market share dropped in comparison to its competition. A survey revealed that one reason was because customers were not getting their computers on time. The lead times were too long and were always a day or two late. Customer orders need to be sent out the day they are received, and inventory records need to be updated as orders are placed to be able to accurately tell customers how long a lead time is or whether a back-order is necessary. The board of directors also suspects that internal control weaknesses exist that might lead to internal fraud.

When customers need to order new computers for their homes or offices, they call F&Y to place an order. All sales are made via an order document. F&Y gives these to its usual customers to complete; it may be mailed or faxed to the company, or a telephone order may be placed. In this case, sales representatives transcribe the order to a formal sales order document. Existing customers pay via credit, usually through existing accounts, while new customers must have a new account established. A customer's account record includes his or her name, address, phone number, background history with the company, and F&Y's formally assigned unique customer number. Usually Sam, from the sales department, will create the formal sales order and send it to Chris in the credit department.

Chris's job is to check the customer's credit and make sure he or she has the funds available to pay for the order. If this is so, the customer receives a credit approval, and Chris creates a stock release so that the order can continue to be processed. Credit that is not approved gets filed, and Chris calls the customer to notify him or her that the order has been canceled. For approved credit, Chris staples the approved sales order to the stock release and sends it to the warehouse (shipping) department.

Willie, a warehouse employee, receives the stock release, picks the goods, and calls either Federal Express, UPS, or a service requested by the customer. Willie then proceeds to update the inventory subsidiary ledger to account for the computers he is going to load on the trucks. When Willie is too busy to ship the computers, he can ask another employee to do it because once inside the warehouse, any employee can transport any item out of the warehouse onto a delivery truck. Due to this easy transportation of goods, F&Y wants to ensure that it is not easy for unauthorized people to get into the warehouse. F&Y implemented codes rather than keys, to open the warehouse doors since keys can be stolen or lost. Willie now prepares the bills of lading and shipping notices. The shipping companies arrive every day at 4:30 P.M., and Willie gives them the bill of lading, shipping notice, and computers to be shipped. After he knows the goods are on their way to the customer, the stock release, copy of shipping notice, and sales order are stapled together and sent to Barb, in the billing department.

Barb receives and files the stock release, prepares the invoice, makes a copy of it, and mails it to the customer. Every Friday afternoon, Barb updates the sales journal and then sends the original invoice, sales order, stock release, and shipping notice to the accounts receivable department.

Adam, in the accounting (accounts receivable) department, files the documents that Barb sent him and updates the accounts receivable and general ledger for the customer's account. The accounts receivable is sorted according to customer number for Adam's ease, since each customer number is unique. Every week he goes through the accounts and calls customers who are overdue on the payments. If a customer defaults on payment, Adam reclassifies the account as "doubtful."

When a customer receives his or her goods and invoice, the company is usually mailed a check for payment. Mickey, in the mail room, receives the checks and sends them to cash receipts. Mickey's boss, Muhammad, also works in the mail room, but is too busy with administrative work in his office behind closed doors to supervise the opening of the mail. This structure allows mail room clerks like Mickey to listen to music while they work and not disturb Muhammad. Mickey also happens to be Adam's (accounts receivable) son. Adam thought it would be wise to get his son's foot in the company's door by getting him a low-level job in the mail room.

Carol, the cash receipts clerk, receives the checks and stores them in her top drawer until the end of the week, at which point she prepares a deposit slip and deposits the checks at the Bank of New York. Carol returns from the bank with a bank receipt, files it, and updates the cash receipts journal.

At the end of each month, Adam makes sure all transactions are reconciled in the general ledger. If they are not, he asks the corresponding department to verify the books and report back to him. Usually the department in question can identify and correct the problem and tell Adam what adjusting entries to make.

Upon receipt of the goods, the customer sends F&Y the payment check as described above.

a. Prepare the REA model of the sales/collection business process of F&Y Computer Sales.
b. List the information events in the process and classify each of them as either recording, reporting, or maintaining events.
c. List the decision/management events in the process.

7.   REA Model

(Prepared by Megan Gillette, Lehigh University)

Horox, Inc. is a manufacturer of portable compact disc (CD) players. It is located outside of Philadelphia, Pennsylvania, and employs 1,500 workers at a centrally located, 15-acre production facility. It distributes its products worldwide through three nearby distribution centers. Sales are currently $20 million per year and growing. Horox was formed ten years ago; its management was relatively inexperienced and its technical knowledge was lacking. Since 1997, Horox has been expanding into new research areas and in the past three years has reported enormous profits in its financial statements.

Its major competitors for the small market share it has are electronic giants. Horox has managed to edge its way into retail chains and privately owned stores through the aggressiveness and wit of its sales staff. Horox supplies the major electronic chains and department stores, requiring payment for all orders within 30 days of the order or upon receipt.

The salespersons work partly on salary and partly on commissions. Since the salespersons are traveling to retailers most of the time, the purchase orders come in throughout the day over the fax machine or by telephone to Eddie in the sales department. Eddie has been with the company for a long time; he knows the sales process well and performs credit checks simultaneously with sales order processing. Once Eddie prepares copies of the sales order, he sends a copy to billing and two copies to the inventory warehouse. He files one copy.

Once the sales orders reach Rosemary in the inventory warehouse, she prepares the packing slip and collects the CD players from inventory. Rosemary then updates the inventory records and sends the merchandise, a copy of the sales order, and the packing slip to Kelly in the shipping department. She files one copy of the sales order. Once received by the shipping department, Kelly prepares two shipping notices and bills of lading.

Once the order is ready to be distributed to the customer, it is sent out with the bills of lading, shipping notice, and packing slip. Kelly files one copy of the sales order and shipping notice.

In the billing department, the sales order is processed into an invoice with prices. The remittance advice is also created. Both are sent out to the customer as a bill. The sales journal is updated by Tim, the billing clerk. The sales department reconciles with the billing department periodically.

Once the customer receives the bill requesting payment, he or she sends a check along with the remittance advice back to the company. Here the mail room sorts the checks by company and gives the checks and remittance advices accompanying the checks to Katie, the billing department secretary. Katie updates the cash receipts journal and credits the customer's account. Katie deposits the checks in the company account at the bank. She then files the remittance advice in a file for two months, and afterwards she discards them.

a. Prepare the REA model of the sales/collection business process of Horox Inc.
b. List the information events in the process and classify each of them as either recording, reporting, or maintaining events.
c. List the decision/management events in the process.

8. REA Model

(Prepared by Michael Steinberg, Reich & Co.)

Dicky's Dental Supply (DDS) is a dental supply distributor located in Haverstraw, New York. It was founded in 1985 and has grown rapidly since then. Though the company has expanded, the founder, owner, and president Rebecca "Dicky" Howe still makes all executive decisions. DDS purchases dental supplies from manufacturers and sells them to all dentists located within an 80-mile radius of the company. Through a high volume of bulk sales and a low labor cost, DDS has developed into quite a profitable enterprise.

The revenue cycle begins in the sales department, where an operator takes telephone orders from area dentists and prepares four copies of a sales order. The operator files one copy in the sales file, sends two copies to the billing department, and sends the last one to the warehouse.

The warehouse manager checks the sales order against the current inventory records and notes on the sales order any part of the order that cannot be filled. She then instructs the stockperson which goods to prepare for shipment and prepares two copies of a shipping notice. The sales order becomes the packing slip and is attached to the shipment, which is sent out at the end of the day via Unified Parcel Service. The warehouse manager adjusts the inventory account, and one copy of the shipping notice is filed. The other copy is delivered to billing.

The billing clerk compares the shipping notice with the two sales orders he received from

the sales department. He adjusts the sales orders, if necessary, and one becomes the invoice and remittance advice, which is sent to the customer. The billing clerk uses the other updated sales order to adjust the sales journal and file the sales order. At the end of the day, journal vouchers from billing and the warehouse are sent to the accounting office, where the senior accountant updates the general ledger.

The cash receipts function begins when the mail room receives a check, along with an attached remittance advice, that identifies the customer and account number. The mail room separates the checks and remittance advices, delivering the checks to the cash receipts clerk and the remittance advices to the accounts receivable clerk. The cash receipts clerk endorses the checks, updates the cash receipts journal, and prepares a journal voucher of cash receipts. At the end of the day, she deposits the checks in the company's checking account and sends the journal voucher to the general ledger. The accounts receivable clerk updates the accounts receivable subsidiary ledger and files the remittance advice. The senior accountant gathers all batch totals and updates the general ledger accounts from the journal voucher.

a. Prepare the REA model of the sales/collection business process of Dicky's Dental Supply.
b. List the information events in the process and classify each of them as either recording, reporting, or maintaining events.
c. List the decision/management events in the process.

9. REA Model

(Prepared by Heather Racki, Bob's Stores)

The Heatheria Company was founded five years ago by Elizabeth Robinson. It is a retailing company that buys dresses at wholesale and distributes them to upscale stores. The Heatheria expenditure cycle is based on four basic goals: to order goods as needed, to make sure they are received in good condition, to store the goods without loss, and to record transactions properly and accurately.

A purchase is the first procedure in the expenditure cycle. Every Friday, Susan, a clerk in the inventory control department, checks her accounts to determine the amount to be ordered for the following week. To confirm whether her records are accurate, Susan compares her accounts to John's in receiving. After adjusting her records, Susan prepares a purchase requisition, noting the quantities to be reordered and the requested delivery date. The quantities are determined by the economic order quantity. Susan then sends copies to Heather in purchasing and David in accounts payable and files a copy for herself.

After receiving a purchase requisition, Heather must choose an appropriate supplier and prepare a purchase order. Using the supplier file, Heather is able to select the supplier that best fits her needs. She then gives Beth, a purchasing clerk, all of the information concerning the sale. At the end of the day, Beth prepares a purchase order containing the quantities needed, the expected unit prices, and the terms and conditions negotiated. Copies of the purchase order are sent to the supplier, inventory control, receiving, and accounts payable. Beth files a copy for her department.

As the dresses arrive, John counts them and examines each one for defects. Any goods that are unacceptable are sent back to the supplier. John informs Chuck of the number of dresses that are accepted. Chuck prepares a receiving report and sends copies to accounts payable, purchasing, and inventory control. One copy is kept and filed with the packing slip. Chuck enters the quantity of dresses received into the inventory accounts.

Shortly after the goods are received, an invoice is sent to accounts payable. David compares the purchase order, receiving report, and invoice. If the invoice prices and quantities match those of the purchase order and all the goods have been received, David approves the invoice. If not, David writes the errors onto an error report. The error report is then sent to Jennifer, who settles all discrepancies with the supplier.

Once the invoice is approved, David enters the transactions into the accounts payable ledger and purchases journal. Next, he sends the invoice to Maria, head of the accounts payable department. Upon receiving the invoice, Maria prepares a prenumbered cash disbursements voucher and signs it. She records all vouchers in the vouchers register and posts them to the general ledger. George in the general accounting department is sent the vouchers for approval. After authorizing them, George places the vouchers in a bin.

Each Friday, Maria collects the unpaid vouchers from George's bin and then prepares prenumbered checks. Upon completing the checks, Maria enters each one into the check register and posts everything to the general ledger. She then sends the checks to George, who signs and mails them.

a. Prepare the REA model of the acquisition/payment business process of The Heatheria Company.

b. List the information events in the process and classify each of them as either recording, reporting, or maintaining events.

c. List the decision/management events in the process.

10. REA Model

(Prepared by Kate Cannon, Lehigh University)

Horox, Inc. is a manufacturer of portable compact disc (CD) players. It is located outside of Philadelphia, Pennsylvania, and employs 1,500 workers at a centrally located, 15-acre production facility. It distributes its products worldwide through three nearby distribution centers. Sales are currently $20 million per year and growing. Horox was formed ten years ago; its management was relatively inexperienced and its technical knowledge was lacking. Since 1997, Horox has been expanding into new research areas and in the past three years has reported enormous profits in its financial statements.

Its major competitors for the small market share it has are electronic giants. Horox has managed to edge its way into retail chains and privately owned stores through the aggressiveness and wit of its sales staff. Horox supplies the major electronic chains and department stores, requiring payment for all orders within 30 days of the order or upon receipt.

Within the expenditure cycle, the company needs to purchase raw materials such as plastics and special computer chips and send these materials to the conversion cycle. The expenditure cycle also maintains the payroll department. John, a purchasing department clerk, monitors the inventory levels and determines whether purchases are necessary. He then prepares a purchase requisition. If purchases are needed, he prepares six purchase order forms. Two purchase orders are sent directly to the vendor. One is placed in an open purchase order file in the purchasing department, and the other is used to update the records of the purchasing department. Accounts payable and the receiving department also are sent a purchase order. Upon receiving the goods with a packing slip, the receiving department creates five receiving reports. A receiving report is sent to the stores and the accounts payable department. Two receiving reports are sent to the purchasing department, where one is filed and one is used to update records. The final report is filed in the receiving department with the purchase order and packing slip. Vendors send the accounts payable department invoices, which are updated to the accounts payable subsidiary ledger and the purchases journal and filed. A voucher is created from the purchases journal, and it is sent to the general ledger.

In the cash disbursements department, Larry prepares and signs the checks for the suppliers. He receives the information from the accounts payable department such as the purchase requisition, purchase order, receiving report, invoice, and the cash disbursement voucher. After preparation of the checks, these documents are sent back to the accounts payable department, and a journal voucher is sent to general ledger. A copy of the check is filed after the original is sent to the supplier. Within the general ledger, the journal voucher is reconciled with the summary sent by the accounts payable department. After reconciliation, the voucher and the summary are filed.

a. Prepare the REA model of the acquisition/ payment business process of Horox, Inc.
b. List the information events in the process and classify each of them as either recording, reporting, or maintaining events.
c. List the decision/management events in the process.

11. REA Model
(Prepared by Patrick Gilbride, Fleet Bank)
Lava Typewriter Manufacturing (LTM) is a regional producer of business machines. LTM employs 120 production and office workers. The general accounting record keeping of LTM

is predominantly manual. "One Write" style records are maintained for accounts payable, purchases, payroll, cash disbursements, and the general journal. Selected information from the general journal and other journals is manually input to a series of Lotus worksheets to produce trial balances and other reports.

Every two weeks, the payroll supervisor initiates the payroll cycles. She calculates each employee's gross pay, overtime pay, taxes, and so forth. These calculations are entered into the payroll register and sent to the accounts payable clerk who checks the calculations and notifies the payroll supervisor of any errors. Errors are corrected immediately in the payroll register. The accounts payable clerk posts the obligations to the payroll subsidiary ledger. The totals from this ledger are sent to the general ledger clerk and entered into the computer. Meanwhile, the payroll supervisor calls Automatic Data Processing (ADP), a service bureau, and faxes it all of the information necessary for the checks. ADP cuts the checks and sends them to the payroll supervisor, along with two copies of a list of payment details for each employee.

The payroll supervisor sends the accounts payable clerk one of the copies of the payment details list and files the other. The accounts payable clerk posts the payments to the payroll subsidiary ledger. The payroll supervisor sends the checks to the payroll clerk who places them in individual envelopes and then mails them to the employees.

At the end of the day on which the checks were mailed, the payroll supervisor sends batch totals of the payments to the general ledger clerk, who posts them to the computer.

a. Prepare the REA model of the payroll business process of Lava Typewriter Manufacturing (LTM).
b. List the information events in the process and classify each of them as either recording, reporting, or maintaining events.
c. List the decision/management events in the process.

11

Enterprise Resource Planning Systems

Until recent years most large and mid-sized organizations designed and programmed custom information systems in-house. This resulted in an array of stand-alone systems that were designed to the unique needs of specific users. While these systems dealt with their designated tasks efficiently, they did not provide strategic decision support at the enterprise level because they lacked the integration needed for information transfer across organization boundaries. Today the trend in information systems is toward implementing highly integrated enterprise-oriented systems. These are not custom packages designed for a specific organization. Instead, they are generalized systems that incorporate the best business practices in use. Organizations mix and match these prefabricated software components to assemble an **enterprise resource planning (ERP)** system that best meets their business requirements. This means that an organization may need to change the way that it conducts business to take full advantage of the ERP.

This chapter is comprised of five major sections and an appendix. The first outlines the key features of a generic ERP system by comparing the function and data storage techniques of a traditional flat file or database system to that of an ERP. The second section describes various ERP configurations related to servers, databases and bolt-on software. Data warehousing is the topic of the third section. A data warehouse is a relational or multidimensional database that supports on-line analytical processing (OLAP). The fourth section examines risks associated with ERP implementation. The fifth section reviews the internal control and auditing issues related to ERPs. The discussion follows the SAS 78 framework. The chapter appendix reviews the leading ERP software products. Some of the functionality and distinguishing features of these systems are highlighted.

LEARNING OBJECTIVES

After studying this chapter, you should:

- Understand the general functionality and key elements of ERP systems.
- Understand the various aspect of ERP configuration including servers, databases, and the use of bolt-on software.
- Understand the purpose of data warehousing as a strategic tool and recognize the issues related to the design, maintenance, and operation of a data warehouse.
- Recognize the risks associated with ERP implementation.
- Be aware of the key considerations related to ERP implementation.
- Understand the internal control and auditing implications associated with ERPs.
- Be able to identify the leading ERP products and be familiar with their distinguishing features.

WHAT IS AN ERP?

ERP systems are multiple module software packages that evolved primarily from traditional manufacturing resource planning (MRP II) systems. The term ERP was coined by the Gartner Group and has become widely used in recent years. The objective of ERP is to integrate key processes of the organization such as order entry, manufacturing, procurement and accounts payable, payroll, and human resources. By so doing a single computer system can serve the unique needs of each functional area. Designing one system that serves everyone is an undertaking of massive proportions. Under the traditional model each functional area or department has its own computer system optimized to the way that it does its daily business. ERP combines all of these into a single, integrated system that accesses a single database to facilitate the sharing of information and to improve communications across the organization.

To illustrate, consider the traditional model for a manufacturing firm illustrated in Figure 11–1. This company employs a **closed database architecture**, which is similar in concept to the basic flat file model. Under this approach a database management system is used to provide minimal technological advantage over flat file systems. The DBMS is little more than a private but powerful file system. As with the flat file approach, the data remains the property of the application. Thus distinct, separate, and independent databases exist. As is true with the flat file architecture, there is a high degree of data redundancy in a closed database environment.

When a customer places an order, it begins a paper-based journey around the company where it is keyed and rekeyed into the systems of several different departments. These redundant tasks cause delays, lost orders, and promote data entry errors. During transit through the various systems, the status of the order may be unknown at any point in time. For example, responding to a customer query, the marketing department may be unable to look into the production database to determine

---

FIGURE 11–1   Traditional Information System

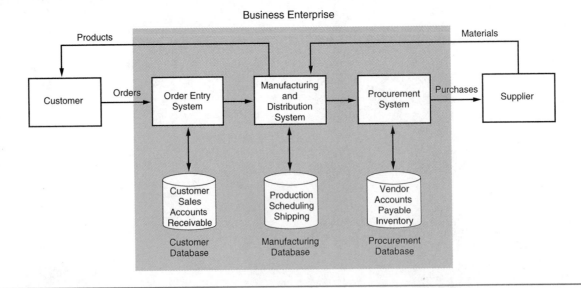

whether an order has been manufactured and shipped. Instead, the frustrated customer is told "You will need to call manufacturing." Similarly, the procurement of raw materials from suppliers is not linked to customer orders until they reach the manufacturing stage. This results in delays, as manufacturing awaits the arrival of needed materials, or in excessive investment in inventories to avoid stockouts.

The lack of effective communication between systems in the traditional model is often the consequence of a fragmented systems design process. Each system tends to be designed as a solution to a specific operational problem rather than as part of an overall strategy. Furthermore, since systems designed in-house emerge independently and over time, they are often constructed on different and incompatible technology platforms. Thus special procedures and programs need to be created so that older mainframe systems using flat files can communicate with newer distributed systems that use relational databases. Special software "patches" are also needed to enable commercial systems from different vendors to communicate with each other as well as with custom systems that were developed in-house. While communications between such a hodgepodge of systems is possible, it is highly fragmented and not conducive to efficient operations.

ERP systems support a smooth and seamless flow of information across the organization by providing a standardized environment for a firm's business processes and a common operational database that supports communications. An overview of ERP is presented in Figure 11–2. Data in the operational database are modeled,

---

FIGURE 11–2   ERP System

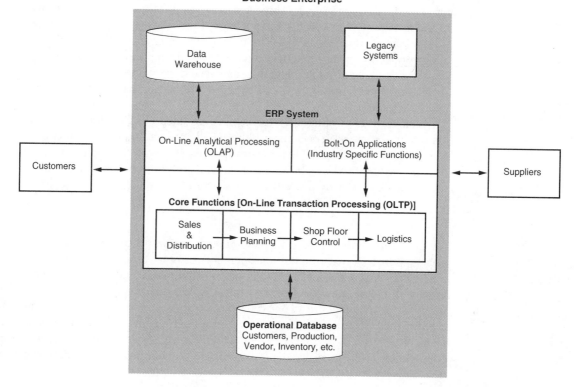

structured, and stored in accordance with the internal attributes of the data. They remain independent of any specific application. Extensive data sharing among users occurs through application-sensitive views that present the data in a way that meets all user needs.

ERP CORE APPLICATIONS

ERP functionality falls into two general groups of applications: *core applications* and *business analysis applications*. **Core applications** are those applications that operationally support the day-to-day activities of the business. If these applications fail so does the business. Typical core applications would include but are not limited to sales and distribution, business planning, production planning, shop floor control, and logistics. Core applications are also called *on-line transaction processing (OLTP)* applications. Figure 11–2 illustrates these functions applied to a manufacturing firm.

Sales and distribution functions handle order entry and delivery scheduling. This includes checking on product availability to ensure timely delivery and verifying customer credit limits. Unlike the previous example, customer orders are entered into the ERP only once. Since all users access a common database, the status of an order can be determined at any point. In fact, the customer may be able to dial in over the Internet and check the status of the order directly. Such integration reduces manual activities, saves time, and decreases human error.

Business planning consists of forecasting demand, planning product production, and the detailed routing information that describes the sequence and the stages of the actual production process. Capacity planning and production planning can be very complex; therefore, some ERPs provide simulation tools to help managers decide how to avoid shortages in materials, labor, or plant facilities. Once the master production schedule is complete, the data enter the MRP (materials requirements planning) module, which provides three key pieces of information: an exception report, a materials requirements listing, and inventory requisitions. The exception report identifies potential situations such as late delivery of materials that will result in rescheduling production. The materials requirements listing shows the details of vendor shipments and expected receipts of products and components needed for the order. Inventory requisitions are used to trigger material purchase orders to vendors for items not in stock.

Shop floor control involves the detailed production scheduling, dispatching, and job costing activities associated with the actual production process. Finally, the logistics application is responsible for assuring timely delivery to the customer. This consists of inventory and warehouse management, and shipping. Most ERPs also include their procurement activities within the logistics function.

ON-LINE ANALYTICAL PROCESSING

An ERP is more than simply an elaborate transaction processing system. It is a decision support tool that supplies management with real-time information and permits timely decisions that are needed to improve performance and achieve competitive advantage. **On-line analytical processing (OLAP)** includes decision support, modeling, information retrieval, ad hoc reporting/analysis, and what-if analysis. Some ERPs support these functions with their own industry-specific modules that can be added to the core system. Other ERP vendors have designed their systems to accept and communicate with specialized *bolt-on* packages that are produced by third-party vendors. Sometimes the user organization's decision support requirements are so unique that they need to integrate in-house legacy systems into the ERP.

However business analysis applications are obtained or derived, central to their successful function is a data warehouse. A **data warehouse** is a database constructed for quick searching, retrieval, ad hoc queries, and ease of use. The data is normally extracted periodically from an operational database or from a public information service. An ERP system could exist without having a data warehouse; similarly, organizations that have not implemented an ERP may deploy data warehouses. The trend, however, is that organizations that are serious about competitive advantage deploy both. The recommended data architecture for an ERP implementation includes separate operational and data warehouse databases. Issues related to the creation and operation of a data warehouse will be examined later in the chapter.

ERP SYSTEM CONFIGURATIONS

SERVER CONFIGURATIONS

Most ERP systems are based on the **client-server model**, which is discussed in detail in the next chapter. Briefly, the client-server model is a form of network topology in which a user's computer or terminal (the client) accesses the ERP programs and data via a host computer called the server. While the servers may be centralized, the clients are usually located at multiple locations throughout the enterprise. Two basic architectures are the *two-tier model* and the *three-tier model* described below.

Two-Tier Model

In a typical **two-tier model**, the server handles both application and database duties. Client computers are responsible for presenting data to the user and passing user input back to the server. Some ERP vendors use this approach for local area network (LAN) applications where the demand on the server is restricted to a relatively small population of users. This configuration is illustrated in Figure 11–3.

Three-Tier Model

The database and application functions are separated in the **three-tier model**. This architecture is typical of large ERP systems that use wide area networks (WANs) for connectivity among the users. Satisfying client requests requires two or more network connections. Initially, the client establishes communications with the application server. The application server then initiates a second connection to the database server. Figure 11–4 presents the three-tier model.

OLTP VERSUS OLAP SERVERS

When implementing an ERP system that will include a data warehouse, a clear distinction needs to be made between the competing types of data processing: *on-line transaction processing* and *on-line analytical processing*. **On-line transaction processing (OLTP)** events consist of large numbers of relatively simple transactions such as updating accounting records that are stored in several related tables. For example, an order entry system retrieves all of the data relating to a specific customer to process a sales transaction. Relevant data are selected from the Customer table, Invoice table, and detail Line Item table. Each table contains an embedded key (i.e., customer number), which is used to relate rows between different tables. The transaction processing activity involves updating the customer's current balance and inserting new records into the Invoice and Line Item tables. The relationships between records in such OLTP transactions are generally simple and only a few records are actually retrieved or updated in a single transaction.

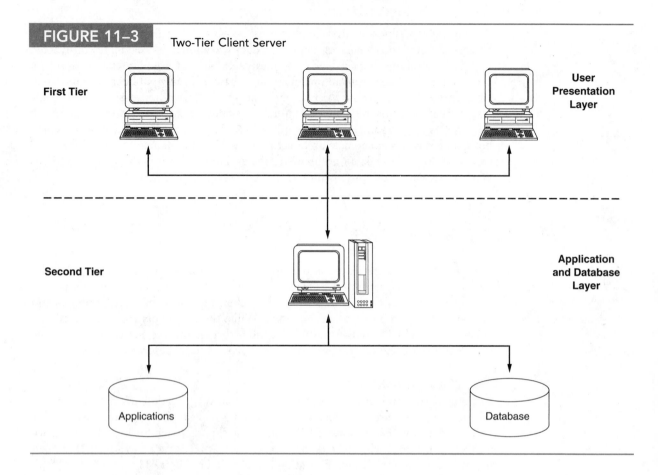

FIGURE 11–3   Two-Tier Client Server

First Tier

User Presentation Layer

Second Tier

Application and Database Layer

Applications

Database

On-line analytical processing (OLAP) can be characterized as on-line transactions that:[1]

- Access very large amounts of data (e.g. several years of sales data).
- Analyze the relationships between many types of business elements such as sales, products, geographic regions, and marketing channels.
- Involve aggregated data such as sales volumes, budgeted dollars, and dollars spent.
- Compare aggregated data over hierarchical time periods (e.g. monthly, quarterly, yearly).
- Present data in different perspectives such as sales by region, sales by distribution channel, or sales by product.
- Involve complex calculations between data elements such as expected profit as a function of sales revenue for each type of sales channel in a particular region.
- Respond quickly to user requests so that they can pursue an analytical thought process without being stymied by system delays.

An example of an OLAP transaction is the aggregation of sales data by region, product type, and sales channel. The OLAP query may need to access vast amounts of sales data over a multiyear period to find sales for each product type within each

---

1   "Data Mining Techniques," The Queen's University of Belfast,
http://www.pcc.qub.ac.uk/tec/courses/datamining/stu_notes/dm_book_4.html.

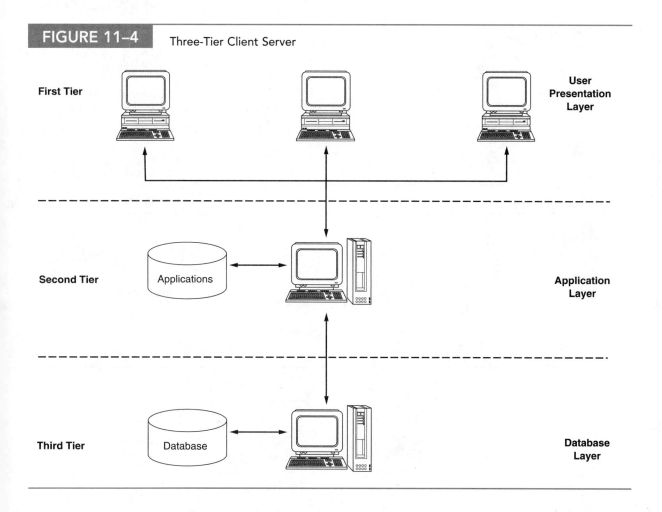

FIGURE 11–4   Three-Tier Client Server

region. The user can further refine the query to identify sales volume by product for each sales channel within a given region. Finally, the user may decide to perform year-to-year or quarter-to-quarter comparisons for each sales channel. An OLAP application must be able to support this analysis on-line with rapid response.

The difference between OLAP and OLTP can be summarized as follows. OLTP applications support mission-critical tasks through simple queries of operational databases. OLAP applications support management-critical tasks through analytical investigation of complex data associations that are captured in data warehouses. OLAP and OLTP have specialized requirements that are in direct conflict. Figure 11–5 shows how the client-server architecture enables organizations to deploy separate and specialized application and database servers to resolve these conflicting data management needs. OLAP servers support common analytical operations including *consolidation*, *drill-down*, and *slicing and dicing*.

Consolidation is the aggregation or roll-up of data. For example, sales offices data can be rolled up to districts and districts rolled up to regions.

Drill-down permits the disaggregation of data to reveal the underlying details that explain certain phenomena. For example, the user can drill down from total Sales Returns for a period to identify the actual products returned and the reasons for their return.

FIGURE 11–5	OLTP and OLAP Client Server

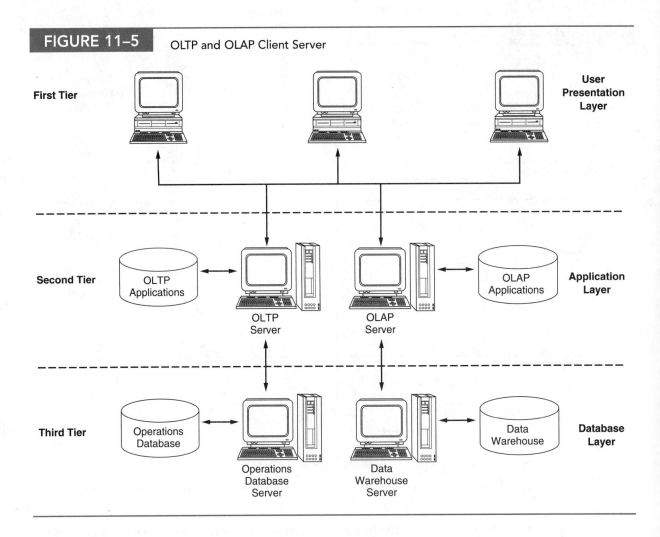

Slicing and dicing enables the user to examine data from different viewpoints. One slice of data might show sales within each region. Another slice presents sales by product across regions. Slicing and dicing is often performed along a time axis to depict trends and patterns.

OLAP servers allow users to analyze complex data relationships. The physical database itself is organized in such a way that related data may be rapidly retrieved across multiple dimensions. OLAP database servers thus need to be efficient when storing and processing multidimensional data. Later in the chapter data modeling and storage techniques that improve data warehouse efficiency will be examined. In contrast, relational databases for operations are modeled and optimized to handle OLTP applications. They concentrate on reliability and transaction processing speed, instead of decision support need.

DATABASE CONFIGURATION

ERP systems are comprised of thousands of database tables. Each table is associated with business processes that are coded into the ERP. The ERP implementation team, which includes key users and IT professionals, selects specific database tables and processes by setting switches in the system. Determining how all the switches need to be set for a given configuration requires a deep understanding of the existing processes used in operating the business. Often, however, choosing table settings involves decisions to reengineer the company's processes so that they comply with the best business practices in use. In other words, the company typically changes its processes to accommodate the ERP rather than modifying the ERP to accommodate the company.

BOLT-ON SOFTWARE

Many organizations have found that ERP software alone cannot drive all the processes of the company. These firms use a variety of **bolt-on software** provided by third-party vendors. The decision to use bolt-on software requires careful consideration. Most of the leading ERP vendors have entered into partnership arrangements with third-party vendors that provide specialized functionality. The least risky approach is to choose the bolt-on that is endorsed by the ERP vendor. Some organizations, however, take a more independent approach. Domino's Pizza is a case in point.

Domino's Pizza

Domino's U.S. distribution delivered 338 million pizzas in 1998.[2] The company manufactures an average of 4.2 million pounds of dough per week in its 18 U.S. distribution centers. A fleet of 160 trucks carries the dough along with other food and paper products to the 4,500 U.S. Domino's franchises. Domino's has no cutoff time for ordering supplies. Therefore, a franchise can call and adjust its order even after the truck has rolled away from the distribution center. To help anticipate demand Domino's uses forecasting software from Prescient Systems Inc., which bolts on to their PeopleSoft ERP system. In addition, they use a system from Manugistics Inc. to schedule and route the delivery trucks. Each truck has an on-board computer system that feeds data into a time-and-attendance system from Kronos Inc., which connects to the PeopleSoft human resources module. Domino's also has an extensive data warehouse. To anticipate its market, Domino's performs data mining with software from Cognos Inc. and Hyperion Solutions Corp.

Domino's had been using these and other applications before it implemented an ERP. The company did not want to retire its existing applications, but discovered that the legacy system required data fields that the ERP did not provide. For instance, the routing system tells the truck drivers which stores to visit and in what order. The ERP system did not have a data field for specifying the delivery stop sequence. This information, however, was needed by the warehousing system to tell loaders what to put in the trucks and in what order. Having confidence in its in-house IT staff, Domino's management decided to take the relatively drastic step of modifying the ERP software to include these fields.

Supply Chain Management

Another development regarding the bolt-on software issue is the rapid convergence between ERP and bolt-on software functionality. **Supply chain management (SCM)** software is a case in point. The supply chain is the set of activities associated with moving goods from the raw materials stage through to the consumer. This includes procurement, production scheduling, order processing, inventory management, transportation, warehousing, customer service, and forecasting the demand for

---

2   Slater, D. "'The Ties That Bolt,' Enterprise Resource Planning," *CIO Magazine* (April 15, 1999): 4–9.

goods. SCM systems are a class of application software that supports this task. Successful supply chain management coordinates and integrates these activities into a seamless process. In addition to the key functional areas within the organization, SCM links all of the partners in the chain, including vendors, carriers, third-party logistics companies, and information systems providers. Organizations can achieve competitive advantage by linking the activities in its supply chain more efficiently and effectively than its competitors.

Recognizing this need, ERP vendors have moved decisively to add SCM functionality to their ERP products. ERP systems and SCM systems are now on converging paths. SAP and Oracle have recently added an SCM module, while Baan and PeopleSoft both have acquired smaller SCM vendors to integrate their SCM software into future releases. On the other hand, SCM software vendors are also expanding their functionality to appear more like ERP systems. As larger ERP vendors move into the mid-size company market the smaller SCM and ERP vendors will likely be pushed out of business.

DATA WAREHOUSING

Data warehousing is one of the fastest growing IT issues before businesses today. Not surprisingly, data warehousing functionality is being incorporated into all leading ERP systems. A *data warehouse* is a *relational* or *multidimensional* database that may consume hundreds of gigabytes or even terabytes of disk storage. When the data warehouse is organized for single department or function, it is often called a **data mart**. Rather than containing hundreds of gigabytes of data for the entire enterprise, a data mart may have only tens of gigabytes of data. Other than size, we make no distinction between a data mart and a data warehouse. The issues discussed in this section apply to both.

The process of data warehousing involves extracting, converting, and standardizing an organization's operational data from ERP and legacy systems and loading it into a central archive—the data warehouse. Once loaded into the warehouse, data are accessible via various query and analysis tools that are used for *data mining*. Data mining, which was introduced in Chapter 8, is the process of selecting, exploring, and modeling large amounts of data to uncover relationships and global patterns that exist in large databases but are "hidden" among the vast amount of facts. This involves sophisticated techniques that use *database queries* and *artificial intelligence* to model real-world phenomena from data collected from the warehouse.

Most organizations implement a data warehouse as part of a strategic IT initiative that involves an ERP system. Implementing a successful data warehouse involves installing a process for gathering data on an ongoing basis, organizing it into meaningful information, and delivering it for evaluation. The data warehousing process has the following essential stages:[3]

- Modeling data for the data warehouse.
- Extracting data from operational databases.
- Cleansing extracted data.

---

3   Fiore, P. "Everyone is Talking About Data Warehousing," *Evolving Enterprise*, Vol. 1, Number 1 (Spring 1998): 2.

- Transforming data into the warehouse model.
- Loading the data into the data warehouse database.

MODELING DATA FOR THE DATA WAREHOUSE

Chapters 9 and 10 stressed the importance of data normalization to eliminate three serious anomalies: the *update anomaly*, the *insertion anomaly*, and the *deletion anomaly*. Normalizing data in an operational database is necessary to accurately reflect the dynamic interactions among entities. Data attributes are constantly updated, new attributes are added, and obsolete attributes are deleted on a regular basis. While a fully normalized database will yield the flexible model needed for supporting multiple users in this dynamic operational environment, it also adds to complexity that translates into performance inefficiency.

The Warehouse Consists of De-Normalized Data

Because of the vast size of a data warehouse, such inefficiency can be devastating. A three-way join between tables in a large data warehouse may take an unacceptably long time to complete and may be unnecessary. In the data warehouse data model, the relationship among attributes does not change. Since historical data are static in nature, nothing is gained by constructing normalized tables with dynamic links.

For example, in an operational database system, Product X may be an element of work-in-process in Department A this month and part of Department B's work-in-process next month. In a properly normalized data model, it would be incorrect to include Department A's work-in-process data as part of a Sales Order table that records an order for Product X. Only the product item number would be included in the Sales Order table as a foreign key linking it to the Product table. Relational theory would call for a join (link) between the Sales Order table and Product table to determine the production status (which department the product is in, currently) and other attributes of the product. From an operational perspective, complying with relational theory is important because the relation changes as the product moves through different departments over time. Relational theory does not apply to a data warehousing system because the Sales Order /Product relation is stable.

Wherever possible, therefore, normalized tables pertaining to selected events may be consolidated into de-normalized tables. Figure 11–6 illustrates how sales order data is reduced to a single de-normalized Sales Order table for storage in a data warehouse system.

EXTRACTING DATA FROM OPERATIONAL DATABASES

Data extraction is the process of collecting data from operational databases, flat files, archives, and external data sources. Operational databases typically need to be out of service when data extraction occurs to avoid data inconstancies. Because of their large size and the need for a speedy transfer to minimize the downtime, little or no conversion of data occurs at this point. A technique called **changed data capture** can dramatically reduce the extraction time by capturing only newly modified data. The extraction software compares the current operational database with an image of the data taken at the last transfer of data to the warehouse. Only the data that have changed in the interim are captured.

Extracting Snapshots Versus Stabilized Data

Transaction data stored in the operational database go through several stages as economic events unfold. For example, a sales transaction first undergoes credit approval, then the product is shipped, then billing occurs, and finally payment is received. Each

FIGURE 11-6   De-Normalized Data

A Normalized Representation for an Operational Database System

Customer Table

Customer Number	Name	Street	City	State
34675	John Smith	10 Elm	Bath	PA

Invoice Table

Invoice Number	Invoice Date	Shipped Date	Invoice Amount	Customer Number
8866376	06/12/00	06/23/00	600	34675

Line Item Table

Invoice Number	Item Number	Quantity	Price	Extended Price
8866376	j683	2	200	400
8866376	r223	5	40	200

B De-Normalized Representation for Data Warehouse System

Sales Order Table

Customer Number	Name	Street	City	State	Invoice Number	Invoice Date	Shipped Date	Invoice Amount	Item Number	Quantity	Price	Extended Price
34675	John Smith	10 Elm	Bath	PA	8866376	06/12/00	06/23/00	600	j683	2	200	400
34675	John Smith	10 Elm	Bath	PA	8866376	06/12/00	06/23/00	600	r223	5	40	200

of these events changes the state of the transaction and associated accounts such as inventory, accounts receivable, and cash.

A key feature of a data warehouse is that the data contained in it are in a nonvolatile (stable) state. Typically, transaction data are loaded into the warehouse only when the activity on them has been completed. Potentially important relationships between entities may, however, be absent from data that are captured in this stable state. For example, information about cancelled sales orders will probably not be reflected among the sales orders that have been shipped and paid for before they are placed in the warehouse. One way to reflect these dynamics is to extract the operations data in "slices of time." These slices provide snapshots of business activity. For example, decision makers may want to observe sales transactions approved, shipped, billed, and paid at various points in time along with snapshots of inventory levels at each state. Such data may be useful in depicting trends in the average time taken to approve credit or ship goods that might help explain lost sales.

CLEANSING EXTRACTED DATA

Data cleansing involves filtering out or repairing invalid data prior to being stored in the warehouse. Operational data are "dirty" for many reasons. Clerical, data entry, and computer program errors can create illogical data such as negative inventory quantities, misspelled names, and blank fields. Data cleansing also involves transforming data into standard business terms with standard data values. Data are often combined from multiple systems that use slightly different spellings to represent common terms, such as "cust," "cust_id," or "cust_no." Some operational systems may use entirely different terms to refer to the same entity. For example, a bank customer with a certificate of deposit and an outstanding loan may be called a *Lender* by one system and a *Borrower* by another. The source application may use cryptic or difficult-to-understand terms for a number of reasons. For example, some older legacy systems were designed at a time when programming rules placed severe restrictions on naming and formatting data attributes. Also, a commercial application may assign attribute names that are too generic for the needs of the data warehouse user. Businesses that purchase commercial data, such as competitive performance information or market surveys, need to extract data from whatever format the external source provides and reorganize them according to the conventions used in the data warehouse. During the cleansing process, therefore, the attributes taken from multiple systems need to be transformed into uniform standard business terms. This tends to be an expensive and labor-intensive activity, but one that is critical in establishing data integrity in the warehouse. Figure 11–7 illustrates the role of data cleansing in building and maintaining a data warehouse.

TRANSFORMING DATA INTO THE WAREHOUSE MODEL

A data warehouse is comprised of both detail and summary data. To improve efficiency, data can be transformed into summary views before they are loaded into the warehouse. For example, many decision makers may need to see product sales figures summarized for a week, a month, a quarter, or annually. It may not be practical to summarize information from detail data every time the user needs it. A data warehouse that contains the most frequently requested summary views of data can reduce the amount of processing time during analysis. Referring again to Figure 11–7 we see the creation of summary views over time. These are typically created around business entities such as customers, products, and suppliers. Unlike operational views, which are virtual in nature with underlying base tables, data warehouse views are physical tables. Most OLAP software will, however, permit the user to construct virtual views from detail data when one does not already exist.

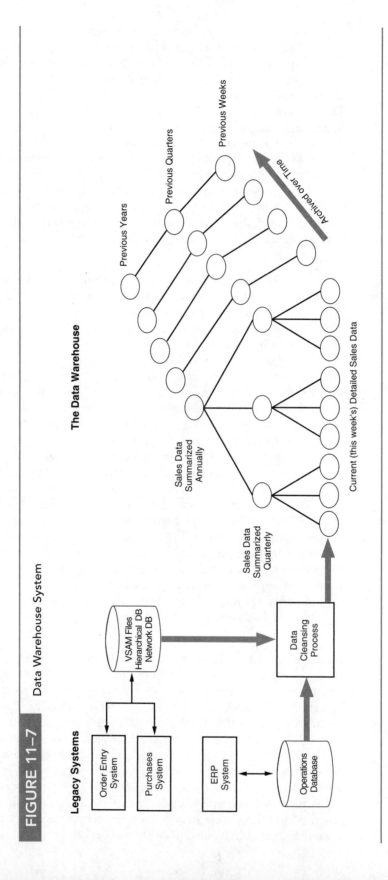

FIGURE 11-7 Data Warehouse System

A data warehouse will often provide multiple summary views based on the same detailed data such as customers or products. For example, several different summary views may be generated from sales order detail data. These may include summaries by product, by customer, and by region. From such views an analyst can drill down into the underlying detail data. Many business problems require a review of detail data to fully evaluate a trend, pattern, or anomaly exhibited in the summarized reports. Also, a single anomaly in detail data may manifest itself differently in different summary views.

LOADING THE DATA INTO THE DATA WAREHOUSE DATABASE

Most organizations have found that data warehousing success requires that the data warehouse be created and maintained separately from the operational (transaction processing) databases. This point is developed further below.

Internal Efficiency

One reason for a separate data warehouse is that the structural and operational requirements of transaction processing and data mining systems are fundamentally different, making it impractical to keep both operational (current) and archive data in the same database. Transaction processing systems need a data structure that supports performance, whereas data mining systems need data organized in a manner that permits broad examination and the detection of underlying trends.

Integration of Legacy Systems

The continued influence of legacy systems is another reason that the data warehouse needs to be independent of operations. A remarkably large number of business applications continue to run in the mainframe environment of the 1970s. By some estimates, more than 70 percent of business data for large corporations still resides in the mainframe environment. The data structures employed by these systems are often incompatible with the architectures of modern data mining tools. Hence, transaction data that are stored in navigational databases and VSAM systems often end up in large tape libraries that are isolated from the decision process. A separate data warehouse provides a venue for integrating the data from legacy and contemporary systems into a common structure that supports entity-wide analysis.

Consolidation of Global Data

Finally, the emergence of the global economy has brought about fundamental changes in business organizational structure and has profoundly changed the information requirements of business entities. Decision makers in the global corporation are challenged by unique business complexities. For example, they need to assess the profitability of products built and sold in multiple countries with volatile currencies. Such challenges add complexity to data mining. A separate centralized data warehouse is an effective means of collecting, standardizing, and assimilating data from diverse sources.

In conclusion, the creation of a data warehouse separate from operational systems is a fundamental data warehousing concept. Many organizations now consider data warehouse systems to be key components of their IS strategy. As such, they allocate considerable resources to build data warehouses concurrently with the operational systems being implemented.

DECISIONS SUPPORTED BY THE DATA WAREHOUSE

By making the data warehouse as flexible and friendly as possible, it becomes accessible by many end users. Some decisions supported by a data warehouse are not fundamentally different from those that are supported by traditional databases. Other information uses such as multidimensional analysis and information visualization are not possible with traditional systems. Some users of the data warehouse need routine reports based on traditional queries. When standard reports can be anticipated in advance, they can be provided automatically as a periodic product. Automatic generation of standard information reduces access activity against the data warehouse and will improve its efficiency in dealing with more esoteric needs.

Drill-down capability is a useful data analysis technique associated with data mining. Drill-down analysis begins with the summary views of data described above. When anomalies or interesting trends are observed, the user "drills down" to lower-level views and ultimately into the underlying detail data. Obviously, such analysis cannot be anticipated like a standard report. Drill-down capability is an OLAP feature of data mining tools available to the user. Tools for data mining are evolving rapidly to satisfy the decision maker's need to understand the business unit's behavior in relation to key entities including customers, suppliers, employees, and products. Standard reports and queries produced from summary views can answer many "what" questions, but drill-down capability answers the "why" and "how" questions. Table 11–1 summarizes some of the applications of data mining in decision support.

SUPPORTING SUPPLY CHAIN DECISIONS FROM THE DATA WAREHOUSE

The primary reason for data warehousing is to optimize business performance. Many organizations feel that more strategic benefit can be gained by sharing data externally. By providing customers and suppliers with the information they need when they need it, the company can improve its relationships and provide better service. The potential gain to the giving organization is seen in a more responsive and efficient supply chain. Using Internet technologies and OLAP applications an organization can share its data warehouse with its trading partners and, in effect, treat them like divisions of the firm. A few examples of this approach are outlined below.[4]

> Western Digital Corporation, a leading manufacturer of hard drives, plans to grant certain suppliers access to its data warehouse so they can view performance data on their parts. Because Western Digital maintains a limited engineering staff, the company relies on its suppliers to act as strategic partners in product development. Providing suppliers with performance data allows them to make improvements and participate in the engineering process. The suppliers improve their parts, which in turn improves Western Digital's products.

The company's data warehouse holds more than 600 gigabytes of raw data collected from more than 100,000 drives that it manufactures each day. Approximately 800 attributes are collected on each drive, all of which can be analyzed using OLAP software. The systems feeding the warehouse include ERP applications, data from trouble-call centers, data from failure-analysis systems, and field test data from customer sites and service centers. The company routinely searches the data warehouse for failure information on every drive that it manufactures. All failures and their causes can be linked back to the supplier.

GM's supply chain data warehouse will be available via the Web to more than 5,000 suppliers worldwide. The suppliers can log on to a secure Web site and query information on the quantities of supplies shipped, delivery times, and prices. This in-

---

4   Davis, B., "Data Warehouses Open Up," *Information Week On Line News in Review*, (June 28, 1999).

TABLE 11–1	**Applications of Data Mining**

Business Field	Application
Banking/Investments	Detect patterns of fraudulent credit card use
	Identify "loyal" customers and predict those likely to change their credit card affiliation
	Examine historical market data to determine investors' stock trading rules
	Predict credit card spending of key customer groups
	Identify correlations between different financial indicators
Health Care and Medical Insurance	Predict office visits from historical analysis of historical patient behavior
	Identify successful and economical medical therapies for different illnesses
	Identify which medical procedures tend to be claimed together
	Predict which customers will buy new policies
	Identify behavior patterns associated with high-risk customers
	Identify indicators of fraudulent behavior
Marketing	Identify buying patterns based on historical customer data
	Identify relationships among customer demographic data
	Predict response to various forms of marketing and promotion campaigns

formation will help GM suppliers optimize their product planning, their ability to source materials, and their shipping-fulfillment processes.

MIM Health Plans Inc., an independent pharmacy benefits–management company, lets its customers view warehouse data to promote better buying decisions. For instance, benefits managers can view reports and drill down into the warehouse to see claims costs, overall costs, the number of prescriptions ordered in a given time period, the number of brand versus generic drugs, and other decision metrics.

RISKS ASSOCIATED WITH ERP IMPLEMENTATION

The benefits from ERP can be significant, but they do not come without some risk to the organization. An ERP system is not a silver bullet that will, by its mere existence, solve an organization's problems. If that were the case, there would never be ERP failures, but there have been many. This section examines some of the risk issues that need to be considered.

BIG BANG VERSUS
PHASED-IN
IMPLEMENTATION

Implementing an ERP system has more to do with changing the way an organization does business than it does with technology. As a result, most ERP implementation failures are due to cultural problems within the firm that stand in opposition to the objective of process reengineering. Strategies for implementing ERP systems to achieve this objective follow two general approaches: the *big bang* and the *phased-in* approach.

The **big bang** method is the more ambitious and risky of the two. Organizations taking this approach attempt to switch operations from their old legacy systems to the new system in a single event that implements the ERP across the entire company. While this method has certain advantages, it has been associated with numerous system failures. Since the new ERP system means new ways of conducting business, getting the entire organization on board and in sync can be a daunting task. On day one of the implementation no one within the organization will have had any experience with the new system. In a sense, everyone in the company is a trainee learning a new job. The new ERP will initially meet with opposition because using it involves compromise. The legacy systems with which everyone in the organization was familiar had been honed over the years to meet exact needs. In most cases, ERP systems have neither the range of functionality nor the familiarity of the legacy systems that they replace. Also, because a single system is now serving the entire organization, individuals at data input points often find themselves entering considerably more data than they did previously with the more narrowly focused legacy system. As a result, the speed of the new system often suffers, causing disruptions to daily operations. These problems are typically experienced whenever any new system is implemented. The magnitude of the problem is the issue under the big bang approach where everyone in the company is affected. Once the initial adjustment period has passed and the new culture emerges, however, the ERP becomes an effective operational and strategic tool that provides competitive advantage to the firm.

Because of the disruptions associated with the big bang, the **phased-in** approach has emerged as a popular alternative. It is particularly suited to diversified organizations whose units do not share common processes and data. In these types of companies, independent ERP systems can be installed in each business unit over time to accommodate the adjustment periods needed for assimilation. Common processes and data (such as the general ledger function) can be integrated across the organization without disrupting operations throughout the firm.

Organizations that are not diversified can also employ the phased-in approach. The implementation usually begins with one or more key processes, such as order entry. The goal is to get ERP up and running concurrently with legacy systems. As more of the organization's functions are converted to ERP, legacy systems are systematically retired. In the interim the ERP is interfaced to legacy systems. During this period, the objectives of *system integration* and *process reengineering*, which are fundamental to the ERP model, are not achievable. To take full advantage of the ERP, process reengineering will still need to occur. Otherwise, the organization will have simply replaced its old legacy system with a very expensive new one.

OPPOSITION TO
CHANGES TO THE
BUSINESSES
CULTURE

To be successful, all functional areas of the organization need be involved in determining the culture of the firm and in defining the new system's requirements. The firm's willingness and ability to undertake a change of the magnitude of an ERP implementation is an important consideration. If the corporate culture is such that change is not tolerated or desired, then an ERP implementation will not be successful.

The technological culture must also be assessed. Organizations that lack technical support staff for the new system or have a user base that is unfamiliar with computer technology face a steeper learning curve and a potentially greater barrier to acceptance of the system by its employees.

CHOOSING THE WRONG ERP

Since ERP systems are prefabricated systems, users need to determine whether a particular ERP fits their organization's culture and its business processes. A common reason for system failure is when the ERP does not support one or more important business processes. In one example, a textile manufacturer in India implemented an ERP only to discover afterwards that it did not accommodate a basic need. The textile company had a policy of maintaining two prices for each item of inventory that it sold. One price was used for the domestic market and a second price, which was four times higher, was for export sales. The ERP that the user implemented was not designed to allow two different prices for the same inventory item. The changes needed to make the ERP work were both extensive and expensive. Serious system disruptions resulted from this oversight. Furthermore, modifying an ERP program and database can introduce potential processing errors and can make updating the system to later versions difficult.

Goodness of Fit

Management needs to make sure that the ERP they choose is right for their company. No single ERP system is capable of solving all the problems of all organizations. For example, SAP's R/3 was designed primarily for manufacturing firms with highly predictable processes that are relatively similar to those of other manufacturers. It may not be the best solution for a service-oriented organization that has a great need for customer-related activities conducted over the Internet.

Finding a good functionality fit requires a software selection process that resembles a funnel, which starts broad and systematically becomes more focused. It begins with a large number of software vendors that are potential candidates. Evaluation questions are asked of vendors in iterative rounds. Starting with a large population of vendors and a small number of high-level qualifier questions the number of vendors is reduced to a manageable few. With proper questioning, more than half the vendors are removed from contention with as few as 10 to 20 questions. In each succeeding round, the questions asked become more detailed and the population of vendors decreases.

When a business's processes are truly unique, the ERP system must be modified to accommodate industry-specific (bolt-on) software or to work with custom-built legacy systems. Some organizations, such as telecommunications service providers, have unique billing operations that cannot be satisfied by off-the-shelf ERP systems. Before embarking on the ERP journey, the organization's management needs to assess whether they can and should reengineer their business practices around a standardized model.

System Scalability Issues

If an organization's management expects business volumes to increase substantially during the life of the ERP system, then they have a scalability issue that needs to be addressed. **Scalability** is the system's ability to grow smoothly and economically as user requirements increase. The term *system* in this context refers to the technology platform, application software, network configuration, or database. *Smooth and economical growth* is the ability to increase system capacity at an acceptable incremental cost per unit of capacity without encountering limits that would demand a system upgrade or replacement. *User requirements* pertain to volume-related activities such as transaction processing volume, data entry volume, data output volume, data storage volume, or increases in the user population.

To illustrate scalability, four dimensions of scalability are important: size, speed, workload, and transaction cost. In assessing scalability needs for an organization, each of these dimensions in terms of the ideal of linear scaling must be considered.[5]

Size. With no other changes to the system, if database size increases by a factor of x, then query response time will increase by no more than a factor of x in a scalable system. For example, if business growth causes the database to increase from 100GB to 500GB, then transactions and queries that previously took one second will now take no more than five seconds.

Speed. An increase in hardware capacity by a factor of x will decrease query response time by no less than a factor of x in a scalable system. For example, increasing the number of input terminals (nodes) from one to twenty will increase transaction processing time proportionately. Transactions that previously took twenty seconds will now take no more than one second in a system with linear scaling.

Workload. If workload in a scalable system is increased by a factor of x, then response time or throughput can be maintained by increasing hardware capacity by a factor of no more than x. For example, if transaction volume increased from 400 per hour to 4,000 per hour, the previous response time can be achieved by increasing the number of processors by a factor of ten in a system that is linearly scalable.

Transaction cost. In a scalable system, increases in workload do not increase transaction cost. Therefore, an organization should not need to increase system capacity faster than demand. For example, if the cost of processing a transaction in a system with one processor is ten cents, then it should still cost no more than ten cents when the number of processors is increased to handle larger volumes of transactions.

Vendors of ERP systems sometimes advertise scalability as if it were a single dimension factor. In fact, it is a multifaceted issue. Some systems accommodate growth in user populations better than others. Some systems can be scaled to provide more efficient access to large databases when business growth demands it. All systems, however, have their scaling limits. Since infinite scalability is impossible, prospective users need to assess their needs and determine how much scalability they want to purchase up front and what form it should take. The key is to anticipate specific scalability issues before making an ERP investment and before the issues become reality.

CHOOSING THE WRONG CONSULTANT

Implementing an ERP system is an event that most organizations will undergo only once. Success of the projects rests on skills and experience that typically do not exist in-house. Because of this, virtually all ERP implementations involve an outside consulting firm, which coordinates the project, helps the organization to identify its

---

5   Winter, R., "Scalable Systems: Lexicology of Scale," *Intelligent Enterprise Magazine* (March 2000): 68–74.

needs, develops a requirements specification for the ERP, selects the ERP package, and manages the cutover. ERP consulting has grown into a $20 billion per year market. The fee for a typical implementation is normally between three and five times the cost of the ERP software license.

Consulting firms with large ERP practices have at times been desperately short of human resources. This was especially true in the mid- to late 1990s when thousands of clients were rushing to implement ERP systems before the new millennium and thus avoid Y2K problems. As demand for ERP implementations grew beyond the supply of qualified consultants, more and more stories of botched projects materialized.

A frequent complaint is that consulting firms promise experienced professionals but deliver incompetent trainees. They have been accused of employing a bait-and-switch maneuver to get contracts. At the initial engagement interview the consulting firm introduces their top consultants who are sophisticated, talented, and persuasive. The client agrees to the deal, incorrectly assuming that these individuals, or others with similar qualifications, will actually implement the system. The following three lawsuits that have been filed against the consultants of failed ERP projects give some sense of the potential problem.

> In 1999, W.L. Gore & Associates, makers of GoreTex, filed a $3.5 million lawsuit against Deloitte & Touche (D&T) Consulting whom they had hired to implement an ERP system. Gore charged D&T with breach of contract, fraud, and negligence related to the project. In addition, they named PeopleSoft (the designer of the ERP system) in the lawsuit for certifying D&T.

> Another lawsuit against D&T was filed by SunLite Casual Furniture. They charged the consulting firm with "maliciously indoctrinating in SunLite a total dependency on D&T that D&T hoped would result in lucrative fees for years to come."

> The trustees for the bankrupt FoxMeyer's drugs filed a lawsuit against Andersen Consulting and SAP for a failed implementation of an R/3 system. They are claiming $500 million in damages on the grounds that the system failure pushed the firm into bankruptcy in 1996.

The jury is literally still out on these cases. The problem has been equated to the airline industry's common practice of overbooking flights. Some suggest that consulting firms, not wanting to turn away business, are guilty of overbooking their consulting staff. The consequences, however, are far graver than the inconvenience of missing a flight, and a free hotel room and a meal cannot compensate for the damages done. Therefore, before engaging an outside consultant, management should:

- Interview the staff proposed for the project and draft a detailed contract specifying which members of the consulting team will be assigned to which tasks.
- Establish in writing how staff changes will be handled.
- Conduct reference checks of the proposed staff members.
- Align the consultants' interests with those of the organization by negotiating a pay-for-performance scheme based on achieving certain milestones in the project. For example, the actual amount paid to the consultant may be between 85 to 115 percent of the contracted fee, based on whether a successful project implementation comes in under or over schedule.
- Set a firm termination date for the consultant to avoid consulting arrangements becoming interminable, resulting in dependency and an endless stream of fees.

Total cost of ownership (TCO) for ERP systems varies greatly from company to company. For medium- to large-sized implementations costs range from hundreds of thousands to hundreds of millions of dollars. TCO includes hardware, software, consulting services, internal personnel costs, installation, and upgrades and maintenance to the system for the first two years after implementation. The risk comes in the form of underestimated and unanticipated costs. Some of the more commonly experienced problems occur in the following areas.

Training. Training costs are invariably higher than estimated because management focuses primarily on the cost of teaching employees the new software. This is only part of the needed training. Employees also need to learn new procedures, which is often overlooked during the budgeting process.

System Testing and Integration. ERP is a holistic model in which one system drives the entire organization, in theory. The reality, however, is that many organizations use their ERP as a backbone system that is attached to legacy systems and other bolt-on systems, which support unique needs of the firm. Integrating these disparate systems with the ERP may involve writing special conversion programs or even modifying the internal code of the ERP. Integration and testing are done on a case-by-case basis, thus the cost is extremely difficult to estimate in advance.

Database Conversion. A new ERP system usually means a new database. Data conversion is the process of transferring data from the legacy system's flat files to the ERP's relational database. When the legacy system's data are reliable, the conversion process may be accomplished through automated procedures. Even under ideal circumstances, a high degree of testing and manual reconciliation is necessary to ensure that the transfer was complete and accurate. More often, the data in the legacy system are not reliable (sometimes called dirty). Empty fields and corrupted data values cause conversion problems that demand human intervention and data rekeying. Also, and more importantly, the structure of the legacy data is likely to be incompatible with the reengineered processes of the new system. Depending on the extent of the process reengineering involved, the entire database may need to be converted through manual data entry procedures.

Develop Performance Measures

Since ERPs are extremely expensive to implement, many managers are often dismayed at the apparent lack of cost savings that they achieve in the short term. In fact, a great deal of criticism about the relative success of ERPs relates to whether they provide benefits that outweigh their cost. To assess benefits, management first needs to know what they want and need from the ERP. They should then establish key performance measures such as reductions in inventory levels, inventory turnover, stockouts, and average order fulfillment time that reflect their expectations. To monitor performance in such key areas, some organizations establish an independent *value assessment group* that reports to top management. Although financial break-even on an ERP will take years, by developing focused and measurable performance indicators, an operational perspective on its success can be developed.

ERP systems can wreak havoc in the companies that install them. In a Deloitte Consulting survey of 64 Fortune 500 companies, 25 percent of the firms surveyed admitted that they experienced a drop in performance in the period immediately following implementation. The reengineering of business processes that often accompanies ERP implementation is the most commonly attributed cause of performance problems. Operationally speaking, when business begins under the ERP system everything looks and works differently from the way it did with the legacy system. An adjustment period is needed for everyone to reach a comfortable point on the learning curve. Depending on the culture of the organization and attitudes toward change within the firm, adjustment may take longer in some firms than in others. The list of major organizations that have experienced serious disruptions includes Dow Chemical, Boeing, Dell Computer, Apple Computer, Whirlpool Corporation, and Waste Management. The most notorious case in the press was Hershey Foods Corporation, which had trouble processing orders through its new ERP system and was unable to ship products.

As a result of these disruptions, Hershey's 1999 third-quarter sales dropped by 12.4 percent compared to the previous year's sales, and earnings were down by 18.6 percent. Hershey's problem has been attributed to two strategic errors related to system implementation. First, because of schedule overruns, they decided to cutover to the new system during their busy season. The inevitable snags that arise from implementations of complex systems like SAP's R/3 are easier to deal with during slack business periods. Secondly, many experts feel that Hershey attempted to do too much in a single implementation. In addition to the R/3 system, they implemented a customer relations management system and logistics software from two different vendors, which had to interface with R/3. The ERP and these bolt-on components were all implemented using the big bang approach.

IMPLICATIONS FOR INTERNAL CONTROL AND AUDITING

As with any system, the internal control and audit of ERP systems are issues. Key concerns are examined below within the framework of SAS 78.

TRANSACTION AUTHORIZATION

A key benefit of an ERP system is its tightly integrated architecture of modules. This structure, however, also poses potential problems for transaction authorization. For example, the bill of materials drives many manufacturing systems. If the procedures over the creation of the bill of materials are not configured correctly, every component that uses the bill of materials could be affected. Controls need to be built in to the system to validate transactions before they are accepted and acted upon by other modules. Because of their real-time orientation, ERPs are more dependent on programmed controls than on human intervention, as was the case with legacy systems. The challenge for auditors in verifying transaction authorization is to gain a detailed knowledge of the ERP system configuration as well as a thorough understanding of the business processes and the flow of information between system components.

SEGREGATION OF DUTIES

Operational decisions in ERP-based organizations are pushed down to a point as close as possible to the source of the event. Manual processes that normally require segregation of duties are thus often eliminated in an ERP environment. For example, shop supervisors may order inventories from suppliers and receiving dock personnel may post inventory receipts to the inventory records in real time. Furthermore, ERP forces together many different business functions such as order entry, billing, and accounts payable under a single integrated system. Organizations using ERP systems must establish new security, audit, and control tools to ensure duties are properly segregated.

To help resolve the segregation of duties problem, SAP, the leading ERP system, employs a configuration technique called *user role*. Each role is associated with a specific set of activities that are assigned to an authorized user of the ERP system. SAP currently provides over 150 predefined user roles, which limit a user's access to only certain functions and associated data. The system administrator assigns roles to users of the system when it is configured. These can be customized as needed. When the user logs onto the system, a role-based menu appears, which limits the user to the specified tasks. Auditors should ensure that roles are assigned in accordance with job responsibilities on a "need-to-know" basis.

SUPERVISION

An often-cited pitfall of an ERP implementation is that management does not fully understand is impact on business. Too often, after the ERP is up and running, only the implementation team understands how it works. Because their traditional roles will be changed, supervisors need to acquire an extensive technical and operational understanding of the new system. Typically, when an organization implements an ERP many decision-making responsibilities are pushed down to the shop floor level. The employee-empowered philosophy of ERP should not eliminate supervision as an internal control. Instead, it should provide substantial efficiency benefits. Supervisors should have more time to manage the shop floor and, through improved monitoring capability, increase their span of control.

ACCOUNTING RECORDS

ERP systems have the ability to streamline the entire financial reporting process. In fact, many organizations can and do close their books daily. OLTP data can be manipulated quickly to produce ledger entries, accounts receivable and payable summaries, and financial consolidation for both internal and external users. Traditional batch controls and audit trails are no longer needed in many cases. This risk is mitigated by improved data entry accuracy through the use of default values, cross-checking, and specified user views of data.

In spite of ERP technology, some risk to accounting record accuracy may still exist. Because of the close interfaces with customers and suppliers, some organizations run the risk that corrupted or inaccurate data may be passed from these external sources and corrupt the accounting database. Additionally, many organizations need to import data from legacy systems into their ERP systems. These data may be laden with problems such as duplicate records, inaccurate values, or incomplete fields. Consequently, strict data cleansing is an important control. Special *scrubber* programs are used as interfaces between the ERP and the exporting systems to reduce these risks and ensure that the most accurate and current data is being received.

ACCESS CONTROLS

Security is perhaps one of the most critical control issues in an ERP implementation. The goal of security in these systems is to provide confidentiality, integrity, and availability of necessary information. Security weaknesses can result in the revealing of trade secrets to competitors and other unauthorized access. Some security professionals argue that computer systems should be restricted to user-specific tasks. Others argue that everyone should have access to all company information. The most sensible resolution to these opposing views is to impose security limitations to data based on a risk assessment. Security administrators should tightly control the more sensitive and risky data within the organization.

Access to the Data Warehouse

Access control is a vital feature of a data warehouse that is shared with customers and suppliers. The organization should establish procedures to oversee the authorization of individuals at customer and supplier sites that will be granted access to their data warehouses. Access privileges should be specified for each outside user and controlled by passwords. User views need to be created to limit outsider access to only approved data. Internet sessions should be managed through a firewall and use encryption and digital signatures to maintain confidentiality.[6] Firewalls, which are a combination of hardware and software that protect the resources of a private network, help to secure data from unauthorized internal and external users. Auditing tools for intrusion detection are available to assist in mitigating security risks. Periodic audits should include a risk assessment and review of access levels granted to both internal and external users based on their job descriptions.

Contingency Planning

In addition to access security, detailed contingency plans must be developed for computer and business operations that can be invoked instantly in the event of a disaster. These plans need to be developed prior to the cutover to a new ERP system. Related to this is the need for backup procedures in the event of a server failure. Two general approaches are outline briefly below, but a more extensive discussion is presented in Chapters 15 and 16.

Centralized organizations with highly integrated business units may need a single global ERP system that is accessed via the Internet or private lines from around the world to consolidate data from subsidiary systems. A server failure under this model could leave the entire organization unable to process transactions. To control against this, two linked servers can be connected in redundant backup mode. All production processing is done on one server. If it fails, processing is automatically transferred to the other. Organizations that want more security and resilience may arrange servers in a cluster of three or more that dynamically share the workload. Processing can be redistributed if one or more of the servers in the cluster fails.

Companies whose organizational units are autonomous and do not share common customers, suppliers, or product lines often choose to install regional servers. This approach permits independent processing and spreads the risk associated with server failure. For example, BP Amoco implemented SAP's R/3 into 17 separate business groups.

Independent Verification

Since ERP systems employ OLTP, traditional independent verification controls such as reconciling batch control numbers are meaningless. Similarly, process reengineering to improve efficiency also changes the nature of independent verification. For example, the traditional three-way match of the purchase order, receiving report, and invoice serves no purpose in an EDI environment in which the vendor's check is cut when the order is placed. The focus of independent verification needs to be redirected from the transaction level to one that views overall performance. ERP systems come with canned controls and can be configured to produce performance reports that should be used as assessment tools. Internal auditors also play an important role in this new environment and need to acquire a thorough technical background and

---

6   Firewalls, encryption, and digital signatures are discussed in Chapters 12 and 16.

comprehensive understanding of the ERP system. Ongoing independent verification efforts can be conducted only by a team well-versed in ERP technology.

AUDITING THE DATA WAREHOUSE

As part of an information system audit the auditor designs a procedure to gather evidence relating to various management assertions pertaining to the firm's financial statements. As part of this procedure the auditor often performs an **analytical review** of account balances to identify relationships between accounts and risks that are not otherwise apparent. Analytical procedures may indicate trends, even in adequately controlled organizations, that lead the auditor to extend the number and nature of substantive tests that he or she subsequently performs.[7] On the other hand, such evidence can provide assurance that transactions and accounts are reasonably stated and complete and may thus permit the auditor to reduce substantive testing (this material is discussed at length in Chapter 17).

The vast amount of data contained in the data warehouse is an excellent resource for performing time-series and ratio analysis. In the case of the revenue cycle, an analytical review will provide the auditor with an overall perspective for trends in sales, cash receipts, sales returns, and accounts receivable. For example, the auditor may compare reported sales for the quarter with those for the same period in previous years. Ratio analysis may be used to compare total sales to cost of goods sold, sales to accounts receivable, and allowance for doubtful accounts to accounts receivable. Significant variations in account balances over time, or unusual ratios, may signify financial statement misrepresentations. Accounts receivable may be examined in time slices for changes in balances relative to sales. This can indicate whether the organization's credit policy is being properly and consistently applied. Another useful audit procedure for identifying potential audit risks involves scanning thousands or even millions of records for unusual transactions and abnormal account balances.

In the case of the expenditure cycle, an analytical review can provide the auditor with an overall perspective for trends in accounts payable and related expenses. Current expenses may be compared to historical expenses and management budgets. For example, the auditor may compare current payroll expenses for the quarter with those for the same period in previous years. Unusual trends or variances should be examined for cause.

The auditor may use drill-down techniques to identify unusually high levels of business activity with a particular supplier. Excessive purchases from a single supplier could represent an abnormal business dependency that may prove harmful to the firm if the supplier raises prices or cannot deliver on schedule. It may also signify a fraudulent relationship involving kickbacks to purchasing agents or other management. On the other hand, a large number of vendors with small balances may be evidence of a highly inefficient purchasing process. In such cases management may need to consolidate business activity. Various corporate surveys have estimated the cost of processing a purchase order at between $50 and $125. Restricting the number of vendors with whom the organization does business can reduce this expense.

---

7   Substantive tests are tests of details as opposed to tests of controls. For example, an auditor may examine the details of invoices to verify that their amounts were properly calculated and recorded in the accounts. Substantive testing can be time consuming. Extensive substantive tests will add cost and delays to the audit. The amount of substantive testing performed is influenced in part by the quality of internal controls in place. Based on evidence provided by testing internal controls and analytical reviews the auditor may decide to reduce or expand the amount of substantive testing to be performed.

While an organization's data warehouse is an excellent resource for per analytical reviews, the auditor needs to understand the procedures used to p the warehouse. As illustrated, data cleansing is an important phase in the maintenance of a warehouse. To be useful as an OLAP tool the data warehouse needs to be free of contamination. Erroneous data (such as negative inventory values, missing fields, and other clerical errors) that are a natural part of operational databases are identified and repaired (or rejected) in the cleansing process prior to their entering the data warehouse. The auditor must, therefore, be careful of the reliance placed on this resource. Since the data warehouse exists in an artificially pristine state, it may not be a suitable substitute for the operational database when assessing tests of process controls and performing substantive tests.[8]

Summary

This chapter opened by comparing the function and data storage techniques of a traditional flat file or database system to that of an ERP. An important distinction was drawn between OLTP and OLAP applications. Similarly, the differences between the ERP's operational database and the data warehouse was discussed. Next, ERP configurations were examined related to servers, databases, and bolt-on software. Supply chain management (SCM) as an area of contention was discussed. ERP vendors are moving quickly to provide SCM functionality. Simultaneously, SCM vendors are encroaching on traditional ERP territory. Data warehousing was the topic of the third section. A data warehouse is a relational or multidimensional database that supports on-line analytical processing (OLAP). A number of data warehouse issues were discussed, including data modeling, data extraction from operational databases, data cleansing, data transformation, and loading data into the warehouse. The fourth section examined common risks associated with ERP implementation. Among these are the risks associated with the big bang approach, internal opposition to changing the way a company does its business, choosing the wrong ERP model, choosing the wrong consultant, cost overrun issues, and disruptions to operations. Also presented were a number of issues to consider when implementing an ERP. These include selecting a system that is a good fit for the organization, understanding that the term "scalability" can mean different things to different people, potential problems associated with customizing the software, the need for assigning performance measures, and the need to control outside consultants. The chapter concluded with a review of the internal control and auditing issues related to ERPs.

Appendix

LEADING ERP PRODUCTS

The ERP market constitutes products from dozens of vendors of all sizes. This appendix reviews the key features and distinguishing characteristics of the industry leaders including SAP, J.D.Edwards, Oracle, PeopleSoft, and Baan. The purpose is to provide overview and insight into the underlying philosophies of these vendors. Specific system characteristics and functionality, however, undergo changes on a regular basis. To obtain current and detailed information on these products the reader should visit the vendors' Web pages.

---

8   For a more complete discussion of this material see Hall, J. A., *Information Systems Auditing and Assurance*, (South-Western College Publishing, 2000).

SAP is the largest of the ERP vendors. At the time of this writing it has an estimated 10 million licensed users worldwide with over 20,000 installations using its R/3 base product. The customer list consists of firms of all sizes in 19 different industries including aerospace, automobile, banking, chemicals, consumer goods, higher education, and utilities. Currently SAP is expanding its traditional ERP solution to an Internet and e-business approach. Traditionally SAP has targeted larger organization clients but, as is the case for all ERP vendors, they are now focusing on medium-sized and smaller customers.

R/3 employs a three-tier client server architecture. One tier is used for presentation of end-user data. This includes an *Internet enabling layer* that creates an open system providing integration with many different operating systems through Internet data transfer protocols. These Internet standards are explained in Chapter 12. The second tier is used to host the application and perform data processing. The third tier provides access to the database.

SAP's Key Features and Functions

SAP R/3 is comprised of multiple modules that are fully integrated or can be taken and used individually. The basic functions are organized according to the following four categories of applications: financial, logistics, human resources, and business process. Each of these is outlined below.

Financial

Financial Accounting. The financial accounting module collects and manages all the financial data for external and internal reporting. This is the backbone system that connects and integrates other SAP business modules. The financial accounting module includes the following general accounting activities: general ledger, accounts payable, accounts receivable, treasury (cash management), foreign exchange, and activity-based cost accounting.

Controlling. This module is a management tool for reporting and controlling costs in support of the following business activities: cost center accounting, job order accounting, project accounting, and profitability analysis.

Fixed Asset Management. This module supports the management of corporate assets including fixed, leased, and real estate. For example, a major purchase could either be assigned as an asset for depreciation, assigned to a project, or declared an expense. The fixed asset module supports the following tasks: asset acquisition, repair, sale of an asset, retirement, and depreciation.

Interactive Requests. The user can display and maintain current customer data on the Internet. Through this module, customers can be given access to interest rates being charged, account balances, and billing status. Current sales and services-rendered information can be provided. For example, a utility company can show the current level of electricity, water, or gas usage by the customer.

Logistics

The logistics modules support all phases of manufacturing from quoting a job to delivery of the product. Each of the main modules is discussed below.

Available-to-Promise. The available-to-promise (ATP) module allows a customer to obtain information about the manufacturer's production and schedule in real time.

The customer connects to SAP via the Internet and enters the product, quantity, and planned delivery date. The ATP system responds with a quote and a promised delivery date for the product.

Sales and Distribution. This application module supports all the typical tasks associated with the sales and distribution of products to customers including order processing, delivery processing, and billing. In addition, the order entry module allows customers to access the seller's home page over the Internet and access an electronic catalog of products. Product descriptions employ multimedia technology including photographs, audio, and graphics. The system allows the customer to browse, reserve inventory, request production of subassemblies, and enter orders that are built to order. The order status module allows the customer to check the status of the order over the Internet. The system optimizes all the tasks and activities in sales, delivery, and billing, including the following tasks.

Product Planning. The product planning module supports a number of manufacturing scenarios including forecasting based on user demand, internal consumption, or sales history. This system connects to MRP II and EDI via the materials management module.

Materials Management. The materials management module tells the user what is in stock and defines the procurement and vendor evaluation process. Specific processes supported by this module are material procurement, inventory management, reorder point processing, vendor invoice verification, material valuation, and vendor evaluation.

Service Calls. Customers can place product service requests via the Internet into the company's service log by selecting from a list of predefined potential problems. SAP's service module assigns the problem a service number and advises the customer when the problem will be addressed under the terms of the customer's service contract.

Preventive Maintenance. The world-class manufacturer cannot afford to have its production equipment fail unexpectedly. The decision to remove plant and equipment from service to perform preventive maintenance (PM), therefore, becomes a critical strategic decision. SAP's PM module permits the collection of equipment usage readings that are used for scheduling PM. Information relating to wear, consumption, or units produced can be automatically collected via counters located at strategic points in the production process. For example, an electricity meter connected to an electrically powered production unit can serve as a usage counter. Personnel at remote sites can enter usage information into the system via the Internet.

Human Resources

The human resources module helps the organization manage its employee resources including hiring, work scheduling, and payroll processing. Management can obtain current information on overtime worked, labor time and costs charged to individual jobs, and travel expenses. The following routine business tasks are supported: payroll, time management, travel expense accounting, employee benefits, recruitment, and workforce planning.

In addition to the above, SAP's Who Is Who application improves communication among employees by providing personal information on the Intranet (the Internet used for internal communication). The module maintains current Internet addresses, telephone numbers, fax numbers, and employee photographs, which can be accessed from the Internet using various search criteria.

Business Process Support

Business process support comprises two classes of modules: the workflow management and the industry solution modules. These modules provide a framework for controlling all the application modules discussed previously. Using a centralized data repository, the process support modules permit a smooth flow of information between sales, manufacturing, finance, purchasing, etc. The workflow management module automates the business process according to specified business procedures and rules. It notifies users of activities that have been successfully completed and of open items that need attention. The industry solution module is a set of SAP processes that have been customized to a specific industry. Customized procedures have been developed for the following industries: consumer packaged goods, utilities and telecommunications, health care, process industries (chemical and pharmaceutical), oil and gas, high technology and electronics, and automotive.

Supply Chain Management

The inclusion of SCM functionality is a recent focus for ERP vendors. The objective is to provide a total-solution system for their clients. SCM components are not included in all ERP systems, but along with improved Internet connectivity (discussed next), SCM issues are at the forefront of ERP development. SAP supports supply chain management with its *advanced planner and optimizer* system. This module helps improve demand forecasting and production efficiencies for the firm. Another module called the *logistics execution system* aids in efficient flow of inventory items along the supply chain and allows integration with outside systems.

Electronic Commerce Support

More and more companies are using electronic commerce to support business-to-business and business-to-consumer processes such as procurement, customer service, and sales order processing. Providing clients with an ERP system that can interact directly with systems used by their customers and suppliers is a primary objective. Many ERP vendors are going the way of Internet order fulfillment to satisfy this requirement. This approach is a departure from the traditional EDI systems in which partnering with another firm was essential for the systems to interact.

R/3 can link to the Internet to execute electronic commerce transactions. For example, a warehouse supervisor can use R/3 to create a requisition for an item of material directly from the shop floor. The system will automatically access the Internet in real time, scan the list of authorized suppliers, select a supplier based on relevant criteria (such as price, quantity needed, terms of trade, and lead time), and then place the order over the Internet.

SAP uses industry standard interfaces such as XML (Extensible Markup Language) to better support integration to outside systems. This helps facilitate the exchange of information with customers and vendors along the supply chain that utilize different ERP systems.

J.D. EDWARDS

J.D. Edwards' ERP philosophy is in sharp contrast to SAP's. Rather than creating a highly structured and tightly integrated system, they employ a *configurable network computing* approach, which provides a flexible system that is open enough to accept the best-practices modules of other vendors. In other words, if the client wants to use the SCM system of another vendor, the J.D. Edwards (JDE) system should accommodate it. Their architecture allows highly configurable, distributed applications to run on a variety of platforms without users or analysts knowing which platforms or which databases are involved in any given tasks. JDE's client base is drawn from the following industries: automotive, energy/chemical, government/education/utilities, pharmaceuticals, consumer package goods, industrial fabrication and assembly, architecture/engineering/construction, mining, real estate, and electronics.

JDE is built on a distributed object network-centric architecture with both client server and browser access to enterprise applications. Internet media objects, data marts, and data mining can be incorporated into this environment. Most ERPs offer configurability at the point of system implementation but if the business environment changes in the future, highly structured ERPs may be too rigid accommodate them easily. JDE users can reconfigure after the design phase to adjust for changes in organizational structure, technology, etc. JDE's architecture is written at a high level of abstraction that sorts out platform differences and thus allows the business solution to run in almost any configuration on any platform. This allows simplified configurability and upgrades. Their platform independent solutions include AS/400 (DB2), RS/6000 (DB2 or Oracle), HP 9000 (DB2 or Oracle), Windows NT servers (SQL Server, DB2, or Oracle), and Internet.

JDE Distinguishing Features

Flexibility. JDE's software flexibility allows business managers to have direct access to configure and change certain system functions. The advantages are that users take immediate ownership of the system and IT professionals do not make business decisions that they are not qualified to make. For example, the business staff has the ability to make changes to user views and output reports without relying on the IT staff to make the changes for them. Business staff can also change the look of input screens through a visually-oriented point and click environment. This functionality is based on a separation of *business activators* and *technology activators* that allow the professionals in each area to control their area of expertise.

An example of a **business activator** is the *grid options activator*, which allows business users to control the display and data entry screens. The business user can change color, size, and style of the font to their preference. Other business activators JDE provides include charting, navigation, printer/e-mail, security, language, currency, and 19 others. An example of a **technology activator** is the *just-in-time installation* activator that allows a technology professional to distribute user configurations and changes such as a sales order input screen to the users throughout the organization via the network. JDE provides a number of other technology activators including version control, object configuration manager, EDI, and open data access.

JDE's flexibility differentiates them from their competition by giving business managers the ability to control the business decisions without involving IT unnecessarily. The power of decision making is thus placed into the most qualified hands. Users think of the ERP as their system rather than one that was thrust upon them by others. This sense of ownership is necessary for acceptance of the significant changes that accompany all ERP implementations.

Modularity. Another distinguishing feature of the JDE system software is modularity. Client organizations have the option of implementing one piece of the ERP system or the entire enterprise package. The core function modules include Manufacturing & Distribution Suites, Financial Foundation Suite, and Payroll & Human Resource Suite. JDE has also developed industry-specific applications such as Energy & Chemical Suite, Services Suite, and Public Services Solutions for Government,

Education, Utilities, and Not-for-Profits. In addition to these suites, JDE has developed a supply chain management solution called SCOREx. During implementation JDE provides preconfigured Industry Practice Models to allow the client to start with industry standard practices, which they can later modify if necessary.

ORACLE

Oracle was founded in 1977 by Larry Ellison. The Oracle database was the first DBMS to incorporate the SQL language. Now Oracle offers a variety of application development tools and is a major promoter of the network computer. Currently Oracle is the world's leading supplier of software for information management, and the world's second largest independent software company. With annual revenues of about $10 billion, the company offers its database, development tools, and ERP application products, along with related consulting, education, and support services, in more than 145 countries around the world.

Oracle's client list includes many large and mid-sized companies from the following industries: education, telecommunications, chemical/pharmaceutical, high technology, media/Internet, government, energy, financial services, health care, manufacturing, consumer sector, retail, transportation, utilities, aerospace/defense, automotive, and metals. Organizations that employ a competitor's ERP will most likely implement it over an Oracle database. Their core system is organized into modules for manufacturing, supply chain management, financials, projects, human resources, and front office.

Oracle's Distinguishing Features
Oracle is tailored to an e-business focus. With Oracle's Internet-based applications versus the standard client-server-based applications, their technology easily supports e-business. Internet applications centralize their ERP system into a few professionally managed servers. This technology also consolidates data into a few global databases and distributes information via a global network. The old client-server applications that all of Oracle's competitors are still using (some are developing and starting to use Internet capabilities at this time) distribute complexity onto every user's desktop PC and fragment information into many little database servers spread out in many locations

Internet-Based Software
Oracle's ERP is an Internet-based system rather than a traditional client-server approach. Oracle users access the ERP applications via an Intranet[9] server using a standard Internet browser. Oracle is the first ERP software company to develop and deploy 100 percent Internet-enabled enterprise software across its entire product line. This approach promotes lower cost of operations, supports thousands of users, and provides a better return on investment because of the rapid implementation and longer software life. Oracle software runs on PCs, workstations, minicomputers, mainframes, and massive parallel computers.

Customizable
During implementation Oracle applications can be customized to the client's needs by setting various switches that enable or disable functions and database tables. When

---

9   Intranets are standard Internet connections that are used for communications within an organization. This topic is discussed in the next chapter.

upgrades are necessary, the custom parts of the applications are upgraded along with the basic software. Therefore, clients do not need to start from scratch with each new release.

PEOPLESOFT

When PeopleSoft was founded in 1987, its products supported primarily the human resource management and finance functions. Today, PeopleSoft has expanded into an enterprise-wide system. PeopleSoft's core application suite focuses on the functions that are fundamental to most organizations—managing materials, people, finances, and projects. Its product portfolio includes applications that support a wide range of businesses including manufacturing, education, financial services, public sector, retail, U.S. government, service industries, communications, utilities, and transportation.

PeopleSoft is built on the concept of open architecture, which allows organizations to configure the application to integrate with existing internal systems. Products are supported through three-tier configurations for wide area networks (WANs) and two-tier configurations for local area networks (LANs). Additionally, PeopleSoft gives its customers a choice of leading platforms and is flexible enough to migrate from one to another if necessary. The preferred platforms include DEC Open VMS, IBM DB2, Novell Netware, Informix, OS/400, MS SQL Server, Unix, Oracle, Windows 95/98/NT, Sybase, and IBM S390.

PeopleSoft's Distinguishing Features

Rapid Implementation. The PeopleSoft suite of products was developed on a common platform and employs a modular approach, which allows organizations to implement additional applications rapidly.

Advanced Planning and Scheduling. PeopleSoft was the first ERP vendor to incorporate advanced planning and scheduling directly into its ERP system. This gave the company a competitive advantage in the manufacturing sector by providing an interface for handling multiple constraints in production planning simultaneously.

BAAN

Baan is a software company that specializes in enterprise-wide applications. Founded in the Netherlands in 1978 by Jan and Paul Baan, it has become a major ERP vendor operating in more than 80 countries. Baan includes modules for manufacturing, finance, project estimating, and management and distribution. These integrate with other Baan modules including supply chain management. Baan products appear in the following industries: aerospace and defense, automotive, consumer packaged goods, electronics, engineering and construction, forest products, industrial equipment, primary metals, semiconductor, specialty chemicals, and wholesale. Baan's ERP system supports multiple languages, tax structures, and currencies including the Euro. It is built on the concept of open architecture that allows customers to configure applications to work with their existing internal systems. The preferred platforms are UNIX, NT, and AS/400.

Baan's Distinguishing Features

Best-of-Class Applications. The Baan ERP Suite assembles best-of-class components and keeps them current through subsequent releases. This enables enterprises to update their information infrastructure in manageable incremental initiatives. Baan clients are able to choose state-of-the-art software solutions from Baan and hundreds of its technology partner companies. The client organization can effectively configure its ERP's functionality from many different vendors to suit each business need across the company's value chain.

Evergreen Delivery. Baan's partnering arrangements with technology firms provides an ongoing stream of new component applications. Baan customers can implement an "assemble to order" system that grows with business needs. This can prove to be less costly and less risky than the big bang model.

Workflow Modeling and Maintenance Modules. Baan has two unique industry leading modules—Baan DEMse and Baan Maintenance—that allow it to service unique needs. The Maintenance module is very useful for industries like aviation, while DEMse provides graphic business control models that are the best in the industry.

Key Terms

analytical review   (572)
big bang   (564)
bolt-on software   (555)
business activator   (577)
changed data capture   (557)
client-server model   (551)
closed database architecture   (548)
consolidation   (553)
core applications   (550)
data mart   (556)
data warehouse   (551)

drill-down   (553)
enterprise resource planning (ERP)   (546)
on-line analytical processing (OLAP)   (550)
on-line transaction processing (OLTP)   (551)
phased-in   (564)
scalability   (565)
slicing and dicing   (554)
supply chain management (SCM)   (555)
technology activator   (577)
three-tier model   (551)
two-tier model   (551)

Review Questions

1. Define ERP.
2. What is the closed database architecture?
3. Define core applications and give some examples.
4. Define OLAP and give some examples.
5. What is the client-server model?
6. Describe the two-tier client-server model.
7. Describe the three-tier client-server model.
8. What is bolt-on software?
9. What is SCM software?
10. What is changed data capture?
11. What is a data warehouse?
12. What is data mining?
13. What does data cleansing mean?
14. Why are de-normalized tables used in data warehouses?
15. What is the drill-down approach?
16. What is the big bang approach?
17. What is scalability?
18. What is a business activator?
19. What is a technology activator?
20. What is Baan's Evergreen Delivery?
21. How is the Oracle database different from relational databases?
22. What is the OLAP operation called consolidation?
23. What is the OLAP operation of drill-down?
24. What is meant by the term "slicing and dicing"?

Discussion Questions

1. How are OLTP and OLAP different? Explain, giving some examples.
2. Distinguish between the two-tier and three-tier client-server models. Describe when each would be used.
3. Why do ERP systems need bolt-on software? Give an example of bolt-on software.
4. Your organization is considering acquiring bolt-on software for your ERP system. What approaches are open to you?
5. Explain why the data warehouse needs to be separate from the operational database.
6. Data in a data warehouse are in a stable state. Explain how this can hamper data mining analysis. What can an organization do to alleviate this problem?
7. This chapter stressed the importance of data normalization when constructing a relational database. Why then is it important to de-normalize data in a data warehouse?
8. What problems does the data cleansing step attempt to resolve?
9. How are the summary views in a data warehouse different from views in an operational database?
10. Would drill-down be an effective audit tool for identifying an unusual business relationship between a purchasing agent and suppliers in a large

organization with several hundred suppliers? Explain.
11. Disruptions to operations are a common side effect of implementing an ERP. Explain the primary reason for this.
12. ERP systems use the best practices approach in designing their applications. Yet goodness of fit is considered to be an important issue when selecting an ERP. Shouldn't the client just be able to use whatever applications the ERP system provides?
13. Explain the issues of size, speed, workload, and transaction as they relate to scalability.
14. Explain how SAP uses roles as a way to improve internal control.
15. How would you deal with the problem of file server backup in a highly centralized organization?
16. How would you deal with the problem of file server backup in a decentralized organization with autonomous divisions that do not share common operational data?
17. Distinguish between the OLAP operations of consolidation and drill-down.
18. When would slicing and dicing be an appropriate OLAP tool? Give an example.

Multiple-Choice Questions

1. Closed database architecture is
   a. a control technique intended to prevent unauthorized access from trading partners.
   b. a limitation inherent in traditional information systems that prevents data sharing.
   c. a data warehouse control that prevents unclean data from entering the warehouse.
   d. a technique used to restrict access to data marts.
   e. a database structure used by many of the leading ERPs to support OLTP applications.
2. Which of the following is typically not part of an ERP's core applications?
   a. OLTP applications
   b. sales and distribution applications
   c. business planning applications
   d. OLAP applications
   e. shop floor control applications

3. Which of the following is typically not part of an ERP's OLAP applications?
   a. decision support systems
   b. information retrieval
   c. ad hoc reporting/analysis
   d. logistics
   e. what-if analysis
4. Which of the following comments describes a data warehouse least well?
   a. is constructed for quick searching and ad hoc queries
   b. contains data that are normally extracted periodically from operational database
   c. contains data from a public information service
   d. is an integral part of all ERP systems
   e. may be deployed by organizations that have not implemented an ERP

582 Chapter 11 Enterprise Resource Planning Systems

5. Which statement is not true?
   a. In a typical two-tier client-server architecture, the server handles both application and database duties.
   b. Client computers are responsible for presenting data to the user and passing user input back to the server.
   c. Two-tier architecture is for local area network (LAN) applications where the demand on the server is restricted to a relatively small population of users.
   d. The database and application functions are separated in the three-tier model.
   e. In three-tier client-server architectures, one tier is for user presentation, one is for database and applications access, and the third is for Internet access.

6. Which statement is not true?
   a. Drill-down capability is an OLAP feature of data mining tools available to the user.
   b. The data warehouse should be separate from operational systems.
   c. De-normalization of data involves dividing the data into very small tables that support detailed analysis.
   d. Some decisions supported by a data warehouse are not fundamentally different from those that are supported by traditional databases.
   e. Data cleansing involves transforming data into standard business terms with standard data values.

7. Which statement is least accurate?
   a. Implementing an ERP system has more to do with changing the way an organization does business than it does with technology.
   b. The phased-in approach to ERP implementation is particularly suited to diversified organizations whose units do not share common processes and data.
   c. Since the primary reason for implementing an ERP is to standardize and integrate operations, diversified organizations whose units do not share common processes and data do not benefit and tend not to implement ERPs.
   d. To take full advantage of the ERP, process reengineering will need to occur.

e. A common reason for ERP failure is that the ERP does not support one or more important business processes of the organization.

8. Which statement is least true?
   a. A defining feature of ERPs is that they are infinitely scaleable.
   b. The reengineering of business processes that often accompanies ERP implementation is the most commonly attributed cause of performance problems.
   c. No single ERP system is capable of solving all the problems of all organizations.
   d. When a business's processes are truly unique, the ERP system must be modified to accommodate industry-specific (bolt-on) software or to work with custom-built legacy systems.
   e. Scalability is the system's ability to grow smoothly and economically as user requirements increase.

9. Auditors of ERP systems
   a. need not be concerned about segregation of duties because these systems possess strong computer controls.
   b. focus on output controls such as independent verification to reconcile batch totals.
   c. may be concerned that the data in the data warehouse is too clean and free from errors.
   d. do not see the data warehouse as an audit or control issue at all because financial records are not stored there.
   e. need not review access levels granted to users since these are determined when the system is configured and never change.

10. Which statement is most correct?
   a. SAP is more suited to service industries than manufacturing clients.
   b. J.D. Edwards' ERP is designed to accept the best practices modules of other vendors.
   c. Oracle evolved from a human resources system.
   d. PeopleSoft is the world's leading supplier of software for information management.
   e. Baan's Evergreen Delivery policy ensures free upgrades of bolt-on software.

Problems

1. Data Warehouse Access Control

You are the CEO of a large organization that implemented a data warehouse for internal analysis of corporate data. The operations manager has written you a memo advocating opening the data warehouse to your suppliers and customers. Explain any merit to this proposal. What are the control issues, if any?

2. Project Implementation

Your organization is planning to implement an ERP system. Some managers in the organization favor the big bang approach. Others are advocating a phased-in approach. The CEO has asked you, as project leader, to write a memo summarizing the advantages and disadvantages of each approach and to make a recommendation. This is a traditional organization with a strong internal hierarchy. The company was acquired in a merger two years ago and the ERP project is an effort on the part of the parent company to standardize business processes and reporting across the organization. Prior to this the organization had been using a general ledger package that it acquired in 1979. Most of the transaction processing is a combination of manual and batch processing. Most employees think that the legacy system works well. At this point the implementation project is behind schedule.

3. Data Warehousing

EuroTunnel is a company that transports thousands of vehicles and passengers through the Channel Tunnel between Britain and France each day. Initially, the company employed a single Travellog booking system for both its ticketing and marketing operations. As tunnel usage grew, the ticketing sales staff were soon processing more than 5,000 transactions daily. At the same time, EuroTunnel's marketing department was accessing the Travellog system to generate analysis reports and forecast sales. The conflicting demand for marketing analysis data and on-line ticket sales transactions caused an information gridlock. As large marketing inquiries were running, ticket sales and other on-line transactions were delayed and the company began to experience an information crisis. EuroTunnel's IS department had to come up with a solution quickly.

Required:
Outline the key elements and operational features of a data warehouse solution that resolves EuroTunnel's conflicting needs for information.

4. Selecting a Consultant

You are the chief information officer for a moderate-sized organization that has decided to implement an ERP system. The CEO has met with a consulting ERP firm based on a recommendation from a personal friend at his club. At the interview the president of the consulting firm introduced the chief consultant who was charming, personable, and seemed very knowledgeable. The CEO's first instinct was to sign a contract with the consultant, but he decided to hold off until he had gotten your input.

Required:
Write a memo to the CEO presenting the issues and the risks associated with consultants. Also outline a set of procedures that could be used as a guide in selecting a consultant.

5. Auditing ERP Databases

You are an independent auditor attending an engagement interview with the client. The client organization has recently implemented a data warehouse. Management is concerned that the audit tests that you perform will disrupt operations. They suggest that instead of running tests against the live operational database, you draw the data for your analytical reviews and substantive tests of details from the data warehouse. They point out that operational data is copied weekly into the warehouse and everything you need will be contained there. This will enable you to perform your tests without disrupting routine operations. You agree to give this some thought and get back with the client with your answer.

Required:
Draft a memo to the client outlining your response to their proposal. Mention any concerns that you might have.

SAP R/3 Exercises

The exercises in this section pertain to SAP's R/3 system, which is made available through the Internet Development and Educational System (IDES) Web site. The instruction booklet that comes with this text provides access to the site (see the booklet instructions for detailed access procedures).

The exercises below fall into three categories: Selling Services, Procurement, and Business to Business (B2B) Procurement. The first assignment in each category is accompanied by detailed walkthrough instructions and screen images that are contained in the SAP instruction booklet. The screen images illustrate what the user should see at each step of the process. The instructions and screen images may be also viewed on-line at http://hall.swcollege.com. The other exercises in each category follow the same general procedures but use different transaction data.

SAP Exercise 1
Access the IDES site and perform the *Selling Services* procedures described in the SAP instruction booklet.

Required:
To demonstrate successful completion of the operations, print the pages identified in the instructions and submit them to your instructor.

SAP Exercise 2
Using the same procedure as described by SAP 1, apply the following changes using the Roles tab in place of the Processes tab.

During this business process you:

1. Create a sales order for the service requested by your customer.

    Roles → Order Processing Clerk → Order Processing → Create Order

2. Confirm the time you have worked for the customer on this service order.

    Roles → Consultant → Confirm Working Hours

3. Bill the services provided.

    Roles → Order Processing → Order Processing → Bill Order

4. Determine the costs, revenues, and revenue in excess of billings (REB) at period end for this service order. These values represent the operating result for the order.

    Roles → Management Accountant → Settle Sales Document → Execute Result Analysis

5. Settle the costs and revenues of the service order to Profitability Analysis and settle the REB to Financial Accounting.

    Roles → Management Accountant → Settle Sales Document → Execute Settlement

6. Enter the incoming payment in accounts receivable accounting.

    Roles → Financial Accountant → Customers → Enter Incoming Payment

Mamane will be implementing an IT system and has approached your company for consulting services. Mamane requires the services of Mr. Michael Curtis (Employee ID 10005) over a four-day period beginning on Friday and ending on Monday. Mr. Curtis worked 5 hours on Saturday, and 8 hours for each of the remaining days. Print a copy of the screen at the end of each phase outlined in Exercise 1. Do not perform the Analyze Contribution Margin segment.

Required:
To demonstrate successful completion of the operations, print the pages identified in the instructions and submit them to your instructor.

SAP Exercise 3
Using the same procedure as SAP 2, apply the following changes. Foxbox Corporation has approached your company for consulting services. You will need to create only one service order. Upon further investigation, you have determined that it requires the services of two consultants. You will assign Ms. Caren Johnson-Hudson (Employee ID 10004) and Mr. Matthew Carter (Employee ID 10009) to this service order. Upon completion, both employees must confirm their working hours. Ms. Johnson-Hudson worked 8 hours the first two days and 6 the final day. Mr. Carter worked 8 hours the first day, 6 hours the second, and was not required for the third. Print a copy of the screen at the end of each phase outlined in Exercise 1. Do not perform the Analyze Contribution Margin segment.

Required:
To demonstrate successful completion of the operations, print the pages identified in the instructions and submit them to your instructor.

SAP Exercise 4
Access the IDES site and perform the *Procuring Consumable Materials Selling Services* procedures described in the SAP instruction booklet.

Required:
To demonstrate successful completion of the operations, print the pages identified in the instructions and submit them to your instructor.

SAP Exercise 5

Use the following procedure to purchase consumable material.

During this business process you:

1. Create a purchase order for the office supplies.

    Roles → Buyer → Purchase Order → Create Purchase Order

2. Enter the goods receipt when the materials are delivered.

    Roles → Buyer → Goods Receipt → Enter Goods Receipt

3. Enter the incoming invoice sent to you by the vendor.

    Roles → Buyer → Invoice Receipt → Enter Incoming Invoice

4. Enter the outgoing payment to pay the vendor.

    Roles → Financial Accountant → Vendors → Enter Outgoing Payment

You will purchase 20 Network Cards from IBM Online at a cost of $199 each. You will need to follow the procedure listed above, using the Roles tab instead of the Processes tab.

Required:

To demonstrate successful completion of the operations, print the pages identified in the instructions and submit them to your instructor.

SAP Exercise 6

Using the same procedures as SAP 5 above:

Purchase several items from Aspect Online. These include 13 GB Hard Drive (Qty 200, $150 ea.), 40 GB Hard Drive 7200 rpm (Qty 150, $300 ea.), and 48 bit Photo Scanner (Qty 100, $600 ea.). You will need to follow the procedure listed above, using the Roles tab instead of the Processes tab.

Required:

To demonstrate successful completion of the operations, print the pages identified in the instructions and submit them to your instructor.

SAP Exercise 7

Access the IDES site and perform the *Procuring Consumable Materials via B2B* procedures described in the SAP instruction booklet.

Required:

To demonstrate successful completion of the operations, print the pages identified in the instructions and submit them to your instructor.

SAP Exercise 8

Follow the same procedure as SAP 7 to purchase 200 "Round World" Design Keyboards from the eStationary catalog. Use "Keyboard" for the name of the shopping basket.

Required:

To demonstrate successful completion of the operations, print the pages identified in the instructions and submit them to your instructor.

SAP Exercise 9

Use the same procedures as SAP7. In this exercise, purchase the following items from the Requisite Technology Catalog: Panasonic PANS70 monitor (20 units), Panasonic PANE110 monitor (10 units), and the Verbatim S600C Personal Scanner (10 units). Use "Video" for the name of the shopping basket.

Required:

To demonstrate successful completion of the operations, print the pages identified in the instructions and submit them to your instructor.

CHAPTER

12

Electronic Commerce Systems

Upon hearing the term "electronic commerce" many people think of browsing an electronic catalogue on the Web or going Internet shopping at a virtual mall. While this aspect of electronic commerce is rapidly growing and potentially the most important, it is not the entire story. Simply stated, electronic commerce (EC) involves the electronic processing and transmission of data. This is a broad definition that encompasses many diverse activities, including the electronic buying and selling of goods and services, on-line delivery of digital products, electronic funds transfer (EFT), electronic trading of stocks, and direct consumer marketing. Electronic commerce is not an entirely new phenomenon. Many companies have engaged in electronic data interchange (EDI) over private networks for decades. Driven by the Internet revolution, however, electronic commerce is dramatically expanding and undergoing radical changes. This fast-moving environment has engendered an array of innovative markets and trading communities. While electronic commerce promises enormous opportunities for consumers and businesses, its effective implementation and control are urgent challenges facing organization management and accountants.

To properly evaluate the potential exposures and risks in this environment, the modern accountant must be familiar with the technologies and techniques that underlie electronic commerce. Hardware failures, software errors, and unauthorized access from remote locations can expose the organization's accounting system to unique threats. For example, transactions can be lost in transit and never processed, electronically altered or rearranged to change their financial effect, corrupted by transient signals on transmission lines, and diverted to or initiated by the perpetrator of a fraud.

This chapter deals with three aspects of electronic commerce: (1) the intra-organizational usage of networks to support distributed data processing; (2) traditional business-to-business transactions conducted via EDI systems; and (3) Internet-based commerce including business-to-consumer and business-to-business relationships. The chapter examines the technologies, topologies, and applications of EC in these three areas. It presents the risks associated with electronic commerce, reviews security and assurance techniques used to reduce risk and promote trust, and concludes with a discussion of electronic commerce's implications for the accounting profession.

LEARNING OBJECTIVES

After studying this chapter, you should:

- Be acquainted with the basic network topologies that are employed to achieve connectivity within an Intranet.
- Understand the function of network software and know how it is employed to manage communications sessions and avoid data collision.
- Understand the operational characteristics of EDI technology and its application in coordinating the sales and procurement activities of organizations in a trading partner relationship.
- Be familiar with the basic technologies and layered approach to protocols used in Internet communications.
- Be familiar with the business opportunities and risks associated with electronic commerce.
- Understand the key security and assurance issues pertaining to electronic commerce.

INTRA-ORGANIZATIONAL ELECTRONIC COMMERCE

Distributed data processing was introduced in Chapter 1 as an alternative to the centralized model. Most modern organizations use some form of distributed processing to process their transactions; some companies process all of their transactions in this way. Networks owned or leased by organizations for internal business use are called Intranets. The section examines several Intranet topologies and techniques for network control.

NETWORK TOPOLOGIES

A **network topology** is the physical arrangement of the components (nodes, servers, communications links, and so on) of the network. In this section, we examine the features of five basic network topologies: star, hierarchical, ring, bus, and client-server. Most networks are a variation on, or combination of, these basic models. However, before proceeding, a working definition for some of the terms that will be used in the following sections are presented.

Local Area Networks and Wide Area Networks

One way of distinguishing between networks is the geographic area covered by their distributed sites. Networks are usually classified as either *local area networks* (LANs) or *wide area networks* (WANs). **Local area networks** are often confined to a single room in a building, or they may link several buildings within a close geographic area. However, a LAN can cover distances of several miles and connect hundreds of users. The computers connected to a LAN are called nodes.

When networks exceed the geographic limitations of the LAN, they are called **wide area networks**. Because of the distances involved and the high cost of telecommunication infrastructure (telephone lines and microwave channels), WANs are often commercial networks (at least in part) that are leased by the organization. The nodes of a WAN may include microcomputer workstations, minicomputers, mainframes, and LANs. The WAN may be used to link geographically dispersed segments of a single organization or to connect multiple organizations in a trading partner arrangement.

Network Interface Cards

The physical connection of workstations to the LAN is achieved through a **network interface card (NIC)**, which fits into one of the expansion slots in the microcomputer. This device provides the electronic circuitry needed for inter-node communications. The NIC works with the network control program to send and receive messages, programs, and files across the network.

Servers

LAN nodes often share common resources such as programs, data, and printers, which are managed through special-purpose computers called **servers**, as depicted in Figure 12–1. When the server receives requests for resources, the requests are placed in a queue and are processed in sequence.

In a distributed environment, there is often a need to link networks together. For example, users of one LAN may share data with users on a different LAN. Networks are linked via combinations of hardware and software devices called *bridges* and *gate-*

FIGURE 12–1

LAN with File and
Print Servers

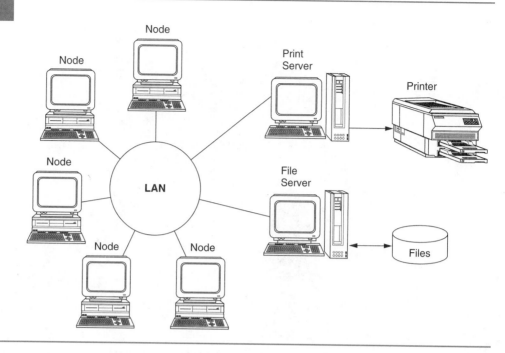

ways. Figure 12–2 illustrates this technique. **Bridges** provide a means for linking LANs of the same type, such as an IBM token ring to another IBM token ring. **Gateways** connect LANs of different types and are also used to link LANs to WANs. With these definitions in mind, we now turn our attention to the five basic network topologies.

Star Topology
The **star topology** shown in Figure 12–3 describes a network of computers with a large central computer (the host) at the hub that has direct connections to a

FIGURE 12–2

Bridges and Gateways
Linking LANs and
WANs

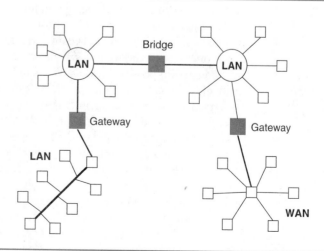

FIGURE 12–3

Star Network

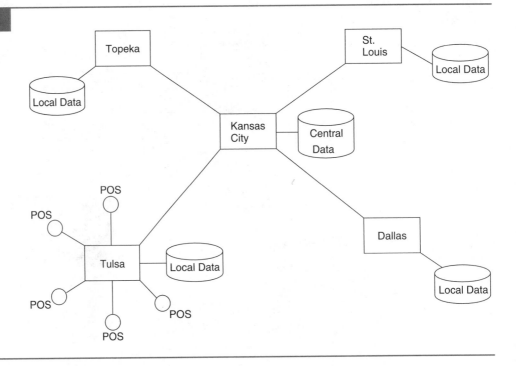

periphery of smaller computers. Communications between the nodes in the star are managed and controlled from the host site.

The star topology is often used for a WAN, in which the central computer is a mainframe. The nodes of the star may be microcomputer workstations, minicomputers, mainframes, or a combination. Databases under this approach may be distributed or centralized. A common model is to partition local data to the nodes and centralize the common data. For example, consider a department store chain that issues its own credit cards. Each node represents a store in a different metropolitan area. In Figure 12–3, these are Dallas, St. Louis, Topeka, and Tulsa. The nodes maintain local databases such as records for customers holding credit cards issued in their areas and records of local inventory levels. The central site—Kansas City—maintains data common to the entire regional area, including data for customer billing, accounts receivable maintenance, and overall inventory control. Each local node is itself a LAN, with point-of-sales (POS) terminals connected to a minicomputer at the store.

If one or more nodes in a star network fail, communication between the remaining nodes is still possible through the central site. However, if the central site fails, individual nodes can function locally but cannot communicate with the other nodes.

Transaction processing in this type of configuration could proceed as follows. Sales are processed in real time at the POS terminals. Local processing includes obtaining credit approval, updating the customer's available credit, updating the inventory records, and recording the transaction in the transaction file (journal). At the end of the business day, the nodes transmit sales and inventory information to the central site in batches. The central site updates the control accounts, prepares customer bills, and determines inventory replenishment for the entire region.

The assumption underlying the star topology is that primary communication will be between the central site and the nodes. However, limited communication between the nodes is possible. For example, assume a customer from Dallas was in Tulsa and made a purchase from the Tulsa store on credit. The Tulsa database would not contain the customer's record, so Tulsa would send the transaction for credit approval to Dallas via Kansas City. The approved transaction would then be returned by Dallas to Tulsa via Kansas City. Inventory and sales journal updates would be performed at Tulsa.

The transaction processing procedure above would differ somewhat depending on the database configuration. For example, if local databases are partial replicas of the central database, credit queries could be made directly from Kansas City. However, this would require keeping the central database current with all the nodes.

Hierarchical Topology

A **hierarchical topology** is one where a host computer is connected to several levels of subordinate smaller computers in a master-slave relationship. This structure is applicable to firms with many organizational levels that must be controlled from a central location. For example, consider a manufacturing firm with remote plants, warehouses, and sales offices, such as the one illustrated in Figure 12–4. Sales orders from the local sales departments are transmitted to the regional level, where they are summarized and uploaded to the corporate level. Sales data, combined with inventory and plant capacity data from manufacturing, are used to compute production requirements for the period, which are downloaded to the regional production scheduling system. At this level, production schedules are prepared and distributed to the local production departments. Information about completed production is uploaded from the production departments to the regional level, where production summaries are prepared and transmitted to the corporate level.

Ring Topology

The **ring topology** illustrated in Figure 12–5 eliminates the central site. All nodes in this configuration are of equal status; thus, responsibility for managing

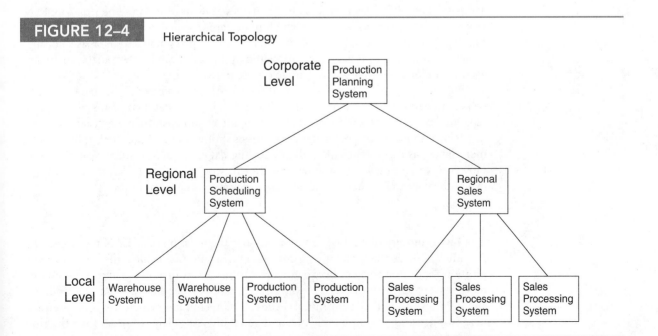

FIGURE 12–4   Hierarchical Topology

FIGURE 12–5

Ring Topology

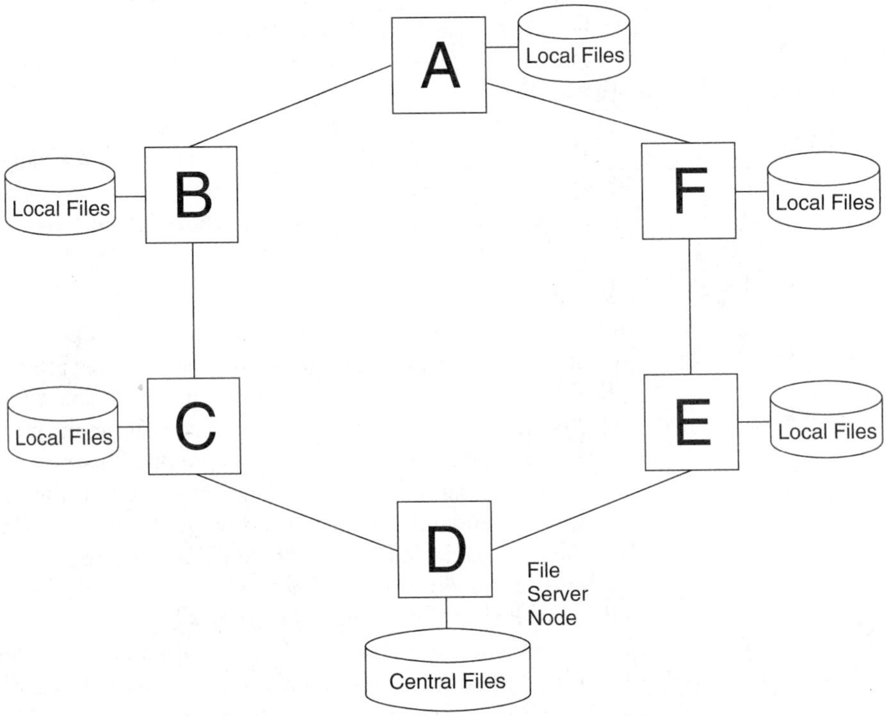

communications is distributed among the nodes. Every node on the ring has a unique electronic address, which is attached to messages such as an address on an envelope. If Node A wishes to send a message to Node D, the message is received, regenerated, and passed on by Nodes B and C until it arrives at its destination. The ring topology is a *peer-to-peer arrangement* in which all nodes are of equal status. This is a popular topology for LANs. The peer nodes manage private programs and databases locally. However, common resources that are shared by all nodes can be centralized and managed by a file server that is also a node on the network ring.

The ring topology may also be used for a WAN, in which case the databases may be partitioned rather than centralized. For example, consider a company with widely separated warehouses, each with different suppliers and customers and each processing its own shipping and receiving transactions. In this case, where there is little common data, it is more efficient to distribute the database than to manage it centrally. However, when one warehouse has insufficient stock to fill an order, it can communicate through the network to locate the items at another warehouse.

Bus Topology

The **bus topology** illustrated in Figure 12–6 is the most popular LAN topology. It is so named because the nodes are all connected to a common cable—the bus. Communications and file transfers between workstations are controlled centrally by one or more servers. As with the ring topology, each node on the bus has a unique address, and only one node may transmit at a time. The technique, which has been used for over two decades, is simple, reliable, and generally less costly to install than the ring topology.

FIGURE 12–6

Bus Topology

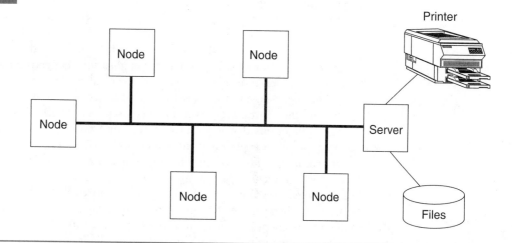

Client-Server Topology

The term *client-server* is often misused to describe any type of network arrangement. In fact, the **client-server topology** has specific characteristics that distinguish it from the other topologies. Figure 12–7 illustrates the approach.

To explain the client-server difference, let's review the features of a traditional distributed system. DDP can result in considerable data "traffic jams." Users

FIGURE 12–7

Client-Server Topology

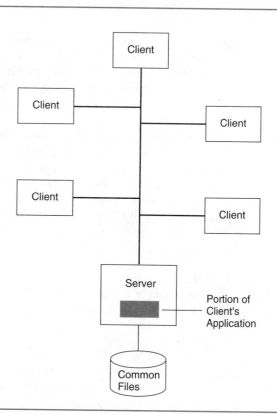

competing for access to shared data files experience queues, delays, and lockouts. A factor influencing the severity of this problem is the structure of the database in use. For example, assume that User A requests a single record from a database table located at a central site. To meet this request, the file server at the central site must lock and transmit the entire table to User A. The search for the specific record is performed at the remote site by the user's application. When the record is updated, the entire file is then transmitted back to the central site.

The client-server model distributes the processing between User A's (client) computer and the central file server. Both computers are part of the network, but each is assigned functions that it performs best. For example, the record-searching portion of an application is placed at the server, and the data manipulation portion is on the client computer. Thus, only a single record, rather than the entire file, must be locked and sent to the client for processing. After processing, the record is returned to the server, which restores it to the table and removes the lock. This approach reduces traffic and allows more efficient use of shared data. Distributing the record-searching logic of the client's application to the server permits other clients to access different records in the same file simultaneously. The client-server approach can be applied to any topology (i.e., ring, star, or bus). Figure 12–7 illustrates the client-server model applied to a bus topology.

NETWORK CONTROL

In this section, we examine methods for controlling communications between the physical devices connected to the network. **Network control** exists at several points in the network architecture. The majority of network control resides with software in the host computer, but control also resides in servers and terminals at the nodes and in switches located throughout the network. The purpose of network control is to perform the following tasks:

1. Establish a communications session between the sender and the receiver.
2. Manage the flow of data across the network.
3. Detect and resolve data collisions between competing nodes.
4. Detect errors in data caused by line failure or signal degeneration.

DATA COLLISION

To achieve effective network control, there must be an exclusive link or session established between a transmitting and a receiving node. Only one node at a time can transmit a message on a single line. Two or more signals transmitted simultaneously will result in a **data collision**, which destroys both (all) messages. When this happens, the messages must be retransmitted. There are several techniques for managing sessions and controlling data collisions, but most of them are variants of three basic methods: polling, token passing, and carrier sensing.

Polling
Polling is the most popular technique for establishing a communication session in WANs. One site, designated the "master," polls the other "slave" sites to determine if they have data to transmit. If a slave responds in the affirmative, the master site locks the network while the data are transmitted. The remaining sites must wait until they are polled before they can transmit. The polling technique illustrated in Figure 12–8 is well suited to both the star and the hierarchical topologies. There are two primary advantages to polling. First, polling is *noncontentious*. Because nodes can send data only when requested by the master node, two nodes can never access the net-

FIGURE 12–8

Polling Method of
Controlling Data
Collisions

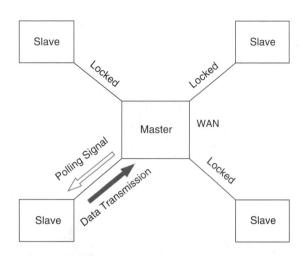

work at the same time. Data collisions are, therefore, prevented. Second, an organization can set *priorities* for data communications across the network. Important nodes can be polled more often than less important nodes.

Token Passing

Token passing involves transmitting a special signal—the token—around the network from node to node in a specific sequence. Each node on the network receives the token, regenerates it, and passes it to the next node. Only the node in possession of the token is allowed to transmit data.

Token passing can be used with either ring or bus topologies. On a ring topology, the token passing sequence is determined by the order in which the nodes are physically connected. With a bus, the sequence is logical, not physical. The token is passed from node to node in a predetermined order to form a logical ring. Token bus and token ring configurations are illustrated in Figure 12–9. Since nodes are permitted to transmit only when they possess the token, the node wishing to send data across the network seizes the token upon receiving it. Holding the token blocks other nodes from transmitting and ensures that no data collisions will occur. After the transmitting node sends its message and receives an acknowledgment signal from the receiving node, it releases the token. The next node in sequence then has the option of either seizing the token and transmitting data or passing the token on to the next node in the circuit.

A major advantage of token passing is its *deterministic* access method, which avoids data collisions. This is in contrast to the *random* access approach of carrier sensing (discussed below). IBM's version of token ring is emerging as an industry standard.

Carrier Sensing

Carrier sensing is a random access technique that detects collisions when they occur. This technique, which is formally labeled *carrier sensed multiple access with collision detection (CSMA/CD)*, is used with the bus topology. The node wishing to transmit

FIGURE 12–9

Token Passing
Approach to
Controlling Data
Collision

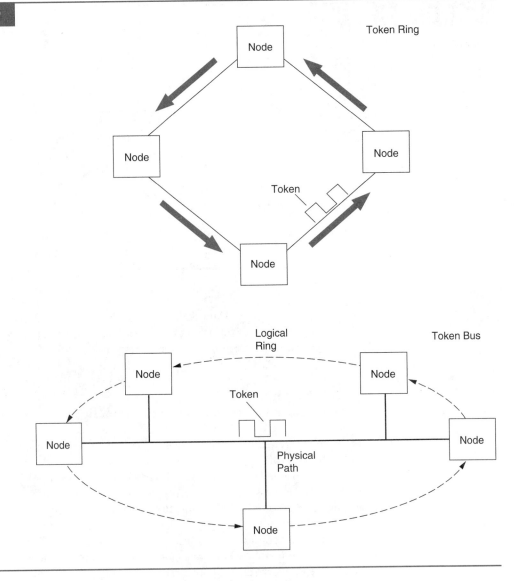

"listens" to the bus to determine if it is in use. If it senses no transmission in progress (no carrier), the node transmits its message to the receiving node. This approach is not as fail-safe as token passing. Collisions can occur when two or more nodes, unaware of each other's intent to transmit, do so simultaneously when they independently perceive the line to be clear. When this happens, the network server directs each node to wait a unique and random period of time and then retransmit the message. In a busy network, data collisions are more likely to occur, thus resulting in delays while the nodes retransmit their messages. Proponents of the token passing approach point to its collision-avoidance characteristic as a major advantage over the CSMA/CD model.

Ethernet is the best-known LAN software that uses the CSMA/CD standard. The Ethernet model was developed by Xerox Corporation in the 1970s. In 1980, Digital Equipment Corporation, in a joint venture with Intel Corporation, published the specifications for a LAN based on the Ethernet model.[1] The greatest advantage of Ethernet is that it is established, reliable, and well understood by network specialists. Ethernet also has a number of economic advantages over token ring: (1) the technology, being relatively simple, is well suited to the less costly twisted-pair cabling, whereas token ring works best with more expensive coaxial cable; (2) the network interface cards used by Ethernet are much less expensive than those used in the token ring topology; and (3) Ethernet uses a bus topology, which is easier to expand.

ELECTRONIC DATA INTERCHANGE (EDI)

To coordinate sales and production operations and to maintain an uninterrupted flow of raw materials, many organizations enter into a trading partner agreement with their suppliers and customers. This agreement is the foundation for a fully automated business process called **electronic data interchange (EDI)**. A general definition of EDI is:

> The intercompany exchange of computer-processable business information in standard format.

The definition reveals several important features of EDI. First, EDI is an interorganization endeavor. A firm does not engage in EDI on its own. Second, the transaction is processed automatically by the information systems of the trading partners. In a pure EDI environment, there are no human intermediaries to approve or authorize transactions. Authorizations, mutual obligations, and business practices that apply to transactions are all specified in advance under the trading partner agreement. Third, transaction information is transmitted in a standardized format. Therefore, firms with different internal systems can exchange information and do business. Figure 12–10 shows an overview of an EDI connection between two companies. Assume that the transaction in Figure 12–10 is the purchase of inventory by the customer (Company A) from the supplier (Company B). Company A's purchases system automatically creates an electronic purchase order (PO), which it sends to its translation software. Here, the PO is converted to a standard format electronic message ready for transmission. The message is transmitted to Company B's translation software, where it is converted to the supplier's internal format. Company B's sales order processing system receives the customer order, which it processes automatically.

Figure 12–10 shows a direct communications link between companies. But many companies choose to use a third-party **value-added network (VAN)** to connect to their trading partners. Figure 12–11 illustrates this arrangement. The originating company transmits its EDI messages to the network rather than directly to the trading partner's computer. The network directs each EDI transmission to its destination and deposits the message in the appropriate electronic mailbox. The messages stay in the mailboxes until the receiving companies' systems retrieve them. The network is called a *value-added network* because it provides service by managing the distribution of the messages between trading partners. VANs can also provide an important degree of control over EDI transactions. EDI control issues are examined in Chapter 16.

---

[1]   The Ethernet, a Local Area Network Version 1.0. Digital Equipment Corporation, Maynard, Mass.; Intel Corporation, Santa Clara, Calif.; and Xerox Corporation, Stanford, Conn.

FIGURE 12-10

Overview of EDI

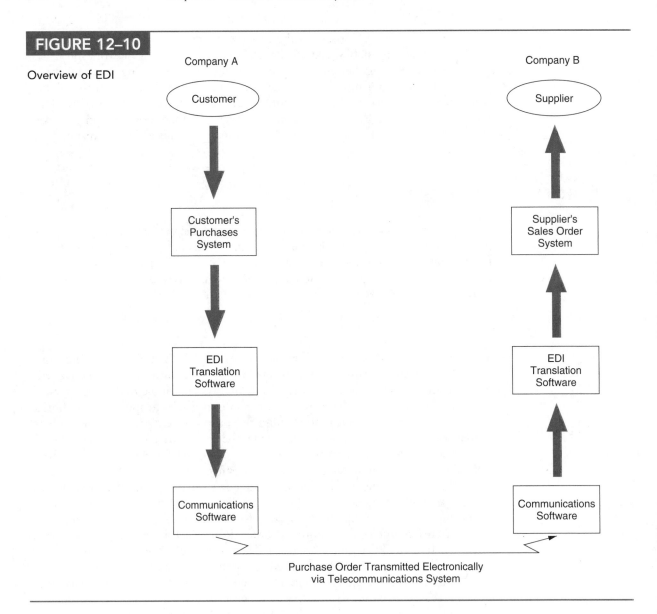

Purchase Order Transmitted Electronically
via Telecommunications System

EDI STANDARDS

Key to EDI success is the use of a standard format for messaging between dissimilar systems. Over the years, both in the United States and internationally, a number of formats have been proposed. The standard in the United States is the **American National Standards Institute (ANSI)** X.12 format. The standard used internationally is the **EDI For Administration, Commerce, and Transport (EDIFACT)** format. Figure 12–12 illustrates the X.12 format.

The electronic envelope contains the electronic address of the receiver, communications protocols, and control information. This is the electronic equivalent of a traditional paper envelope. A functional group is a collection of transaction sets (electronic documents) for a particular business application, such as a group of sales invoices or purchase orders. The transaction set is the electronic document and

FIGURE 12–11

Value-Added
Network and EDI

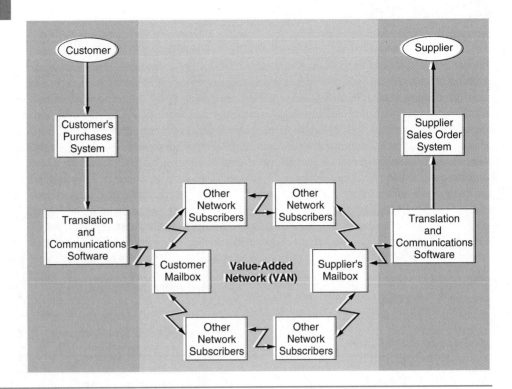

comprises data segments and data elements. Figure 12–13 relates these terms to a conventional document.[2]

Each data segment is an information category on the document, such as part number, unit price, or vendor name. The data elements are specific items of data related to a segment. In the example in Figure 12–13, these include such items as REX-446, $127.86, and Ozment Supply.

BENEFITS OF EDI

EDI has made considerable inroads in a number of industries, including automotive, groceries, retail, health care, and electronics. Following are some common EDI cost savings that justify the approach.

Data keying. EDI reduces or even eliminates the need for data entry.

Error reduction. Firms using EDI see reductions in data keying errors, human interpretation and classification errors, and filing (lost document) errors.

Reduction of paper. The use of electronic envelopes and documents reduces drastically the paper forms in the system.

Postage. Mailed documents are replaced with much cheaper data transmissions.

---

2   J. M. Cathey, "Electronic Data Interchange: What the Controller Should Know," *Management Accounting* (November 1991): 48.

FIGURE 12–12

The X.12 Format

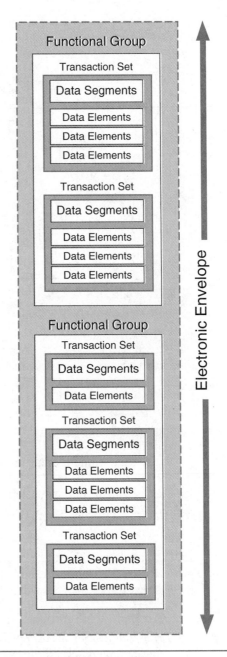

SOURCE: B. K. Stone, *One to Get Ready:*
How to Prepare Your Company for EDI
(CoreStates, 1988): 12.

Automated procedures. EDI automates manual activities associated with purchasing, sales order processing, cash disbursements, and cash receipts.

Inventory reduction. By ordering directly as needed from vendors, EDI reduces the lag time that promotes inventory accumulation.

FIGURE 12–13   Relationship between X.12 Format and a Conventional Source Document

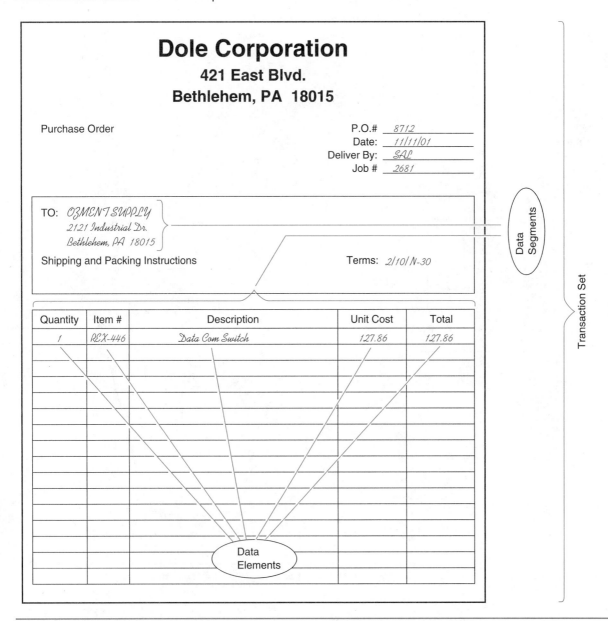

SOURCE: J. M. Cathey, "Electronic Data Interchange: What the Controller Should Know," *Management Accounting* (November 1991): 4.

FINANCIAL EDI

Using EDI for cash disbursement and cash receipts processing is more complicated than using EDI for purchasing and selling activities. **Electronic funds transfer (EFT)** requires intermediary banks between trading partners. This arrangement is shown in Figure 12–14. Purchase invoices are received and automatically approved for payment by the buyer's EDI system. On the payment date, the buyer's system automatically makes an EFT to its originating bank (OBK). The OBK removes funds from the buyer's account and transmits them electronically to the automatic clearing

FIGURE 12–14   EFT Transactions between Trading Partners

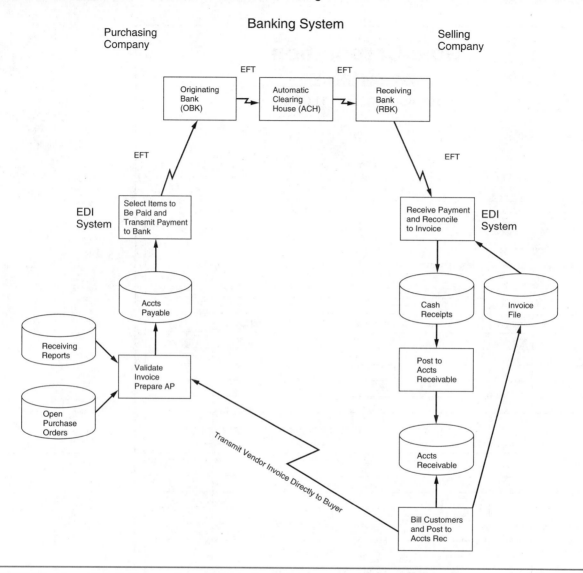

SOURCE: Adapted from B. K. Stone, *One to Get Ready: How to Prepare Your Company for EDI* (CoreStates, 1988): 62.

house (ACH) bank. The ACH is a central bank that carries accounts for its member banks. The ACH transfers the funds from the OBK to the receiving bank (RBK), which in turn applies the funds to the seller's account.

Transferring funds by EFT poses no special problem. A check can easily be represented within the X.12 format. The problem arises with the remittance advice information that accompanies the check. Remittance advice information is often quite extensive because of complexities in the transaction. The check may be in payment of multiple invoices or only a partial invoice. There may be disputed amounts because of price disagreements, damaged goods, or incomplete deliveries. In traditional systems, these disputes are resolved by modifying the remittance advice and/or attaching a letter explaining the payment.

Converting remittance information to electronic form can result in very large records. Members of the ACH system are required to accept and process only EFT formats limited to 94 characters of data—a record size sufficient for only very basic messages. Not all banks in the ACH system support the ANSI standard format for remittances, ANSI 820. In such cases, remittance information must be sent to the seller by separate EDI transmission or conventional mail. The seller must then implement separate procedures to match bank and customer EDI transmissions in applying payments to customer accounts.

Recognizing the void between services demanded and those supplied by the ACH system, many banks have established themselves as **value-added banks (VAB)** to compete for this market. A VAB can accept electronic disbursements and remittance advices from its clients in any format. It converts EDI transactions to the ANSI X.12 and 820 formats for electronic processing. In the case of non-EDI transactions, the VAB writes traditional checks to the creditor. The services offered by VABs allow their clients to employ a single cash disbursement system that can accommodate both EDI and non-EDI customers.

INTERNET COMMERCE

Internet commerce has been the source of more intense interest and excitement than any other computer-related or communications topic. It has enabled thousands of business enterprises of all sizes and millions of consumers to congregate and interact in a worldwide virtual shopping mall. Along with enormous opportunities, however, the electronic marketplace has engendered unique risks and problems that need to be resolved if this is to become the business model for the 21st century. This section examines the technologies, benefits, risks, and security techniques associated with Internet commerce.

INTERNET TECHNOLOGIES

The Internet is a large network comprised of over 100,000 interconnected smaller networks located around the world. The Internet was originally developed for the U.S. military, and later became widely used for academic and government research. In recent years the Internet has rapidly evolved into a worldwide information highway. This growth is attributed to three factors. First, in 1995, national commercial telecom companies such as MCI, Sprint, and UUNET took control of the backbone elements of the Internet and have continued to enhance their infrastructures. Regional Internet service providers (ISPs) can link into these backbones to connect their subscribers, and smaller ISPs can either connect directly to the national backbones or into the regional ISPs. Second, on-line services such as CompuServe and AOL connect to the Internet for e-mail, thus enabling users of different services to communicate with each other. Third, the development of graphics-based Web browsers such as Netscape Navigator and Microsoft's Internet Explorer made accessing the Internet a simple task. The Internet thus became the domain of ordinary people with PCs rather than scientists and computer hackers. As a result, the Web has grown exponentially and continues to grow daily. Its greatest potential as a conduit for worldwide commercial activity is now about to be realized.

Packet Switching
The Internet employs communications technologies based on **packet switching**. Figure 12–15 illustrates this technique, whereby messages are divided into small

FIGURE 12–15

Message Packet
Switching

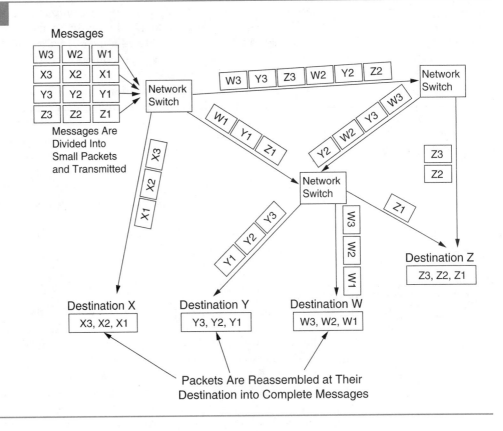

Messages

Messages Are
Divided Into
Small Packets
and Transmitted

Packets Are Reassembled at Their
Destination into Complete Messages

packets for transmission. Individual packets of the same message may take different routes to their destination. Each packet contains address and sequencing codes so they can be reassembled into the original complete message at the receiving end. The choice of transmission path is determined according to criteria that achieve optimum utilization of the long-distance lines, including the degree of traffic congestion on the line, the shortest path between the end points, and the line status of the path (that is, working, failed, or experiencing errors). Network switches provide a physical connection for the addressed packets only for the duration of the message; the line then becomes available to other users. The first international standard for wide area packet switching networks was X.25, which was defined when all circuits were analog and very susceptible to noise. Subsequent packet technologies, such as frame relay and SMDS (Switched Multimegabit Data Service) were designed for today's almost-error-free digital lines.

Virtual Private Networks

In the last section we examined the use of private networks for EDI. In reality many of these are **virtual private networks** (VPN). A VPN is a private network within a public network. For years, common carriers have built VPNs that from the client's perspective are private but which physically share backbone trunks with other users. VPNs have been built on X.25 and frame relay technologies. Today, Internet-based VPNs are of great interest. To maintain security and privacy in this setting, however, requires encryption and authentication controls discussed later in the chapter.

Extranets

Another variant on Internet technology is the **extranet**. This is a password-controlled network for private users rather than the general public. Extranets are used to provide access between trading partner internal databases. Any Internet-based site containing information intended for private consumption may use an extranet configuration.

World Wide Web

The World Wide Web (Web) is an Internet facility that links user sites locally and around the world. In 1989, Tim Berners-Lee of the European Center for Nuclear Research (CERN) in Geneva developed the Web as a means of sharing nuclear research information over the Internet. The fundamental format for the Web is a text document called a **Web page** that has embedded HTML (Hypertext Markup Language) codes that provide the formatting for the page as well as hypertext links to other pages. The linked pages may be stored on the same server or on a server anywhere in the world. HTML codes are simple alphanumeric characters that can be typed with a text editor or word processor. Most word processors now support Web publishing features that allow text documents to be converted to HTML format. This feature allows users without programming knowledge to produce Web pages and present information about themselves or their companies.

Web pages are maintained at **Web sites**, which are computer servers that support HTTP (Hypertext Transfer Protocol). The pages are accessed and read via a Web browser such as Netscape Navigator or Internet Explorer. Accessing a Web site requires entering the URL (Uniform Resource Locator) address of the site in the Web browser. When an Internet user visits a Web site, his or her point of entry is typically the site's **home page**. This HTML document serves as a directory to the site's contents and other pages. Through browsers, the Web provides point-and-click access to the largest collection of on-line information in the world. The Web has also become a multimedia delivery system that supports audio, video, videoconferencing, and 3-D animation. The ease of Web page creation and navigation via browsers has driven the unprecedented growth of the Web. In 1994, there were approximately 500 Web sites in the world; today there are millions.

Internet Addresses

The Internet uses three types of addresses for communications: (1) e-mail address; (2) Web site (URL) address; and (3) the addresses of individual computers attached to a network (IP address). Each of these is discussed below.

E-Mail Address. The format for an e-mail address is USER NAME @ DOMAIN NAME. For example, the address of the author of this textbook is jah0@lehigh.edu. There are no spaces between any of the words. The user name (or in this case user ID) is jah0. A domain name is an organization's unique name combined with a top-level domain (TLD) name. In the example above, the unique name is "Lehigh" and TLD is "edu." Following are the top-level domain names:

.com   commercial
.net   network provider
.org   nonprofit organization
.edu   education and research
.gov   government

.mil   military agency
.int   international intergovernmental

Outside of the U.S., the top-level domain names consist of the country code such as .uk for United Kingdom and .es for Spain. The Internet Ad Hoc Committee (IAHC) has introduced a category called a generic top-level domain (gTLD), which includes the following:

.firm   a business
.store   goods for sale
.web   WWW activities
.arts   culture/entertainment
.rec   recreation/entertainment
.info   information service
.nom   individual/personal

The Internet e-mail addressing system allows the user to send e-mail directly to the mailboxes of users of all major on-line services such as America Online and Compu-Serve.

URL Address. The **URL (Uniform Resource Locator)** is the address that defines the path to a facility or file on the Web. URLs are typed into the browser to access Web site home pages and individual Web pages, and can be embedded in Web pages, to provide hypertext links to other pages. The general format for a URL is: **protocol prefix**, **domain name**, **subdirectory name**, and **document name**. The entire URL is not always needed. For example, to access the South-Western College Publishing company's home page, only the following *protocol* and *domain name* are required:

http://www.swcollege.com

The protocol prefix is "http://" and the domain name "www.swcollege.com." From this home page the user can activate hyperlinks to other pages as desired. The user can go directly to a linked page by providing the complete address and separating the address components with slashes. For example,

http://www.swcollege.com/hall.html

Subdirectories can be several levels deep. To reference them each must be separated with a slash. For example, the elements of the following URL for a hypothetical sporting goods company are described below.

http://www.flyfish.com/equipment/rods/brand_name.html
http://   protocol prefix (most browsers default to HTTP if a
                     prefix is not typed)
www.flyfish.com/   domain name
equipment/   subdirectory name
rods/   subdirectory name
brand_name.html   document name (Web page)

IP Address. Every computer node and host attached to the Internet must have a unique IP (Internet protocol) address. For a message to be sent, the IP addresses of both the sending and the recipient nodes must be provided. Currently, IP addresses are represented by a 32-bit data packet. The general format is four sets of numbers separated by periods. The decomposition of the code into its component parts varies depending upon the class to which it is assigned. Class A, class B, and class C coding schemes are used for large, medium, and small networks, respectively. To illustrate the coding technique, the IP address 128.180.94.109 translates into:

128.180	Lehigh University
94	Business Department Faculty Server
109	A faculty member's office computer (node)

PROTOCOLS

The term **protocol** has been used several times in this section. Let's now take a closer look at the meaning of this term. An important element of network control is achieved through protocols. They are the rules and standards governing the design of hardware and software that permit users of networks that have been manufactured by different vendors to communicate and share data. The general acceptance of protocols within the network community provides both standards and economic incentives for the manufacturers of hardware and software. Products that do not comply with prevailing protocols will have little utility to prospective customers.

The data communications industry borrowed the term *protocol* from the diplomatic community. Diplomatic protocols define the rules by which the representatives of nations communicate and collaborate during social and official functions. These formal rules of conduct are intended to avoid international problems that could arise through the misinterpretation of ambiguous signals passed between diplomatic counterparts. The greatest potential for error naturally exists between nations with vastly dissimilar cultures and conventions for behavior. Establishing a standard of conduct through protocols that all members of the diplomatic community understand and practice minimizes the risk of miscommunications between nations of different cultures.

An analogy may be drawn to data communications. A communications network is a community of computer users who also must establish and maintain unambiguous lines of communication. If network members all had homogeneous needs and operated identical systems, this would not be much of a problem; however, networks are characterized by heterogeneous systems components. Typically, network users employ hardware devices (PCs, printers, monitors, data storage devices, modems, and so on) and software (user applications, network control programs, and operating systems) that are produced by a variety of vendors. Passing messages effectively from device to device in such a multivendor environment requires ground rules or protocols.

What Functions Do Protocols Perform?

Protocols serve network functions in several ways.[3] First, they facilitate the physical connection between the network devices. Through protocols, devices are able to identify themselves to other devices as legitimate network entities and thus initiate (or terminate) a communications session.

Second, protocols synchronize the transfer of data between physical devices. This involves defining the rules for initiating a message, determining the data transfer rate between devices, and acknowledging message receipt.

Third, protocols provide a basis for error checking and measuring network performance. This is done by comparing measured results against expectations. For example, performance measures pertaining to storage device access times, data

---

3   H. M. Kibirige, *Local Area Networks in Information Management* (Greenwood Press, 1989).

transmission rates, and modulation frequencies are critical to controlling the network's function. The identification and correction of errors thus depends on protocol standards that define acceptable performance.

Fourth, protocols promote compatibility among network devices. To successfully transmit and receive data, the various devices involved in a particular session must conform to a mutually acceptable mode of operation, such as synchronous or asynchronous and duplex or half-duplex. Without protocols to provide such conformity, messages sent between devices will be distorted and garbled.

Finally, protocols promote network designs that are flexible, expandable, and cost-effective. Users are free to change and enhance their systems by selecting from the best offerings of a variety of vendors. Manufacturers must, of course, construct these products in accordance with established protocols.

The Layered Approach to Network Protocol

The first networks used several different protocols that emerged in a rather haphazard manner. These protocols often provided poor interfaces between devices and sometimes resulted in irreconcilable incompatibilities. Also, early protocols were structured and inflexible, thus limiting network growth by making system changes difficult. A change in the architecture at a node on the network could have an unpredictable effect on an unrelated device at another node. Technical problems such as these can translate into unrecorded transactions, destroyed audit trails, and corrupted databases. Out of this situation emerged the contemporary model of layered protocols. The purpose of a layered protocol model is to create a modular environment that reduces complexity and permits changes to one layer without adversely affecting another.

The data communication community, through the **International Standards Organization**,[4] has developed a layered set of protocols called the **Open System Interface (OSI)**. The OSI model provides standards by which the products of different manufacturers can interface with one another in a seamless interconnection at the user level. Figure 12–16 shows the seven-layer OSI model. The OSI standard has the following general features. First, each layer in the model is independent, allowing the development of separate protocols specifically for each layer. Second, the layers at each node communicate logically with their counterpart layers across nodes. The physical flow of data and parameters passes between layers. Each layer performs specific subtasks that support the layer above it and are in turn supported by the layer below it. Third, the model distinguishes between the tasks of data communications and data manipulation. The first four layers are dedicated to data communications tasks, which are a function of hardware devices and special software. The last three layers support data manipulation, which is a function of user applications and operating systems. The specific function of each layer is described below.

Layer Functions

Physical Layer. The **physical layer**, the first and lowest level in the protocol, defines standards for the physical interconnection of devices to the electronic circuit. This

---

4   The International Standards Organization is a voluntary group comprising representatives from the national standards organizations of its member countries. The ISO works toward the establishment of international standards for data encryption, data communications, and protocols.

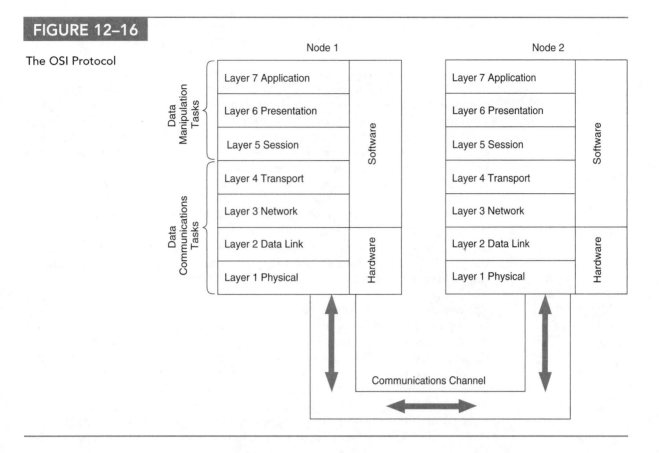

FIGURE 12–16

The OSI Protocol

level is concerned with pin connections to devices, the wiring of workstations, and cabling standards. An example of a standard at this layer is the RS-232 connector cable that is used by virtually all microcomputer manufacturers.

Data Link Layer. **Data link layer** protocols are concerned with the transmission of packets of data from node to node based on the workstation address. This includes message origination, acknowledgment of message receipt, and error detection and retransmission.

Network Layer. **Network layer** protocols deal with the routing and relaying of data to different LANs and WANs based on the network address. They specify how to identify nodes on a network and regulate the sequencing of messages to the nodes. In addition, this third layer describes how packet data are transferred between networks with different architectures, thus permitting the synchronization of data.

Transport Layer. The purpose of the **transport layer** is to ensure delivery of the entire file or message across individual networks and multiple networks, regardless of the number and type of dissimilar devices involved. If a transmission error is detected, this layer defines the retransmission methods to ensure the complete and accurate delivery of the message.

In addition, the transport layer seeks the connection between users that best meets the users' needs for message packeting and multiplexing messages. These protocols provide the logic for segmenting long messages into smaller units and, at the receiving end, reassembling the packets into the original message.

Session Layer. A **session layer** is a specific connection between two users or entities on the network. The purpose of this layer is to guarantee a correct and synchronized connection. At this level, the protocols for starting a session may require a user password to establish the legitimacy of the connection. Protocols may also determine priorities of sessions and rules for interrupting and reestablishing the session. For example, the transmission of a large document may be interrupted by a transmission of higher priority. Session protocols define the rules for such interrupts and the procedures for resuming the original transmission.

Presentation Layer. In the **presentation layer**, data in transit are often in a format that is very different from that required by the user's application. During transmission, data may be compressed to increase transfer speeds, blocked for efficiency, and encrypted for security. Presentation protocols provide the rules for editing, formatting, converting, and displaying data to the user's system.

Application Layer. The **application layer** provides the overall environment for the user or the user's application to access the network. This layer provides what are called "common application services." These services—common to all communicating applications—include protocols for network management, file transfer, and e-mail. The uniqueness of user applications makes this layer the least amenable to general standards. By their very nature, protocols at this level impinge upon application structure and function. Consequently, these are the least rigorously defined rules. Most of the protocols here tend to be vendor defined. For example, an individual vendor's DBMS may provide the application layer protocols for managing file transfers.

INTERNET PROTOCOLS

TCP/IP (Transfer Control Protocol/Internet Protocol) is the basic protocol that permits communication between Internet sites. It was invented by Vinton Cerf and Bob Kah under contract from the U.S. Department of Defense to network dissimilar systems. This protocol controls how individual packets of data are formatted, transmitted, and received. This is known as a reliable protocol because delivery of all the packets to the designation are guaranteed. If delivery is interrupted by hardware or software failure the packets are automatically retransmitted.

The TCP portion of the protocol supports the transport function of the OSI model. This ensures that the total number of data bytes transmitted were received. The IP component provides the routing mechanism. Every server and computer in a TCP/IP network requires an IP address, which is either permanently assigned or dynamically assigned at startup. The IP part of the TCP/IP protocol supports the network layer of the OSI model. It contains a network address and is used to route messages to different networks. IP receives message packets from the transport protocol and delivers them to the data link layer.

While TCP/IP is the fundamental communications protocol for the Internet, the following are some of the more common protocols that are used for specific tasks.

HTTP and HTTP-NG

HTTP (Hypertext Transfer Protocol) controls Web browsers that access the Web. When the user clicks on a link to a Web page, a connection is established and the

Web page is displayed, then the connection is broken. **HTTP-NG (HyperText Transport Protocol-Next Generation)** is an enhanced version of the HTTP protocol that will enable it to meet the increasing performance requirements anticipated for the 21st century.

Document Format and Access Protocols

HTML (Hyper Text Markup Language) is the document format used to produce Web pages. HTML defines the page layout, fonts, and graphic elements as well as hypertext links to other documents on the Web. HTML is derived from **SGML (Standard Generalized Markup Language)**, which was designed for document sharing and is an international standard. **XML (EXtensible Markup Language)** is a document format that is more flexible than HTML and allows customizable tags (format codes). Commercial XML (cXML) was introduced in 1999 to define the characteristic of business transactions. It is expected to become a common standard for electronic commerce transactions that use XML. **DHTML (Dynamic HTML)** is a combination of HTML enhancements that allows animation, interaction, and dynamic updating of Web pages. For example, DHTML Web pages can return values from a search in contrast with a static HTML pages that cannot change. **DOM (Document Object Model)** is a programming interface for accessing HTML and XML documents from a Web browser. It specifies the representation of objects in a Web page. DHTML uses DOM to access and dynamically update the contents of a Web page and to make changes as desired.

File Transfer Protocols

FTP (File Transfer Protocol) is used to transfer text files, programs, spreadsheets, and databases across the Internet. **TELNET** is a terminal emulation protocol used on TCP/IP-based networks. It allows users to run programs and review data from a remote terminal or computer. TELNET is an inherent part of the TCP/IP communications protocol. While both protocols deal with data transfer, FTP is useful for downloading entire files from the Internet; TELNET is useful for perusing a file of data as if the user were actually at the remote site.

Mail Protocols

SNMP (Simple Network Mail Protocol) is the most popular protocol for transmitting e-mail messages. Other e-mail protocols are **POP (Post Office Protocol)** and **IMAP (Internet Message Access Protocol)**.

Security Protocols

SSL (Secure Sockets Layer) is a low-level encryption scheme used to secure transmissions in higher-level (HTTP) format. **PCT (Private Communications Technology)** is a security protocol that provides secure transactions over the Web. PCT encrypts and decrypts a message for transmission. Most Web browsers and servers support PCT and other popular security protocols such as SSL. **SET (Secure Electronic Transmission)** is an encryption scheme developed by a consortium of technology firms and banks (Netscape, Microsoft, IBM, Visa, Mastercard, etc.) to secure credit card transactions. Customers making credit card purchases over the Internet transmit their encrypted credit card number to the merchant, who then transmits the number to the bank. The bank returns an encrypted acknowledgment to the merchant. The customer need not worry about an unscrupulous merchant decrypting the customer's credit card number and misusing the information. **PEM (Privacy Enhanced Mail)** is a standard for secure e-mail on the Internet. It supports encryption, digital signatures, and digital certificates as well as both private and public key methods (discussed later).

Network News Transfer Protocol
NNTP (Network News Transfer Protocol) is used to connect to Usenet groups on the Internet. Usenet newsreader software supports the NNTP protocol.

BENEFITS FROM INTERNET COMMERCE

It is almost impossible to find an industry that is not affected by the Internet. Business-to-business e-commence in 1998 was $43 billion. This is expected to reach $1.3 trillion by the year 2003. Over the same time frame business-to-consumer e-commerce will grow from $8 billion to $108 billion.[5] These projections reflect the potential significant benefits attainable through e-commerce, some of which include:

- Access to a worldwide customer and/or supplier base
- Reductions in inventory investment and carrying costs
- The rapid creation of business partnerships to fill market niches as they emerge
- Reductions in retail prices through lower marketing costs
- Reductions in procurement costs
- Better customer service

Internet Business Models
Not all organizations will enjoy all the benefits listed above. The degree of benefits attained from e-commerce depends on the level of the organization's commitment to it as a business strategy. This can occur on three levels as discussed below.

Information Level. At the **information level** of activity an organization uses the Internet to display information about the company, its products, services, and business policies. This level involves little more than creating a Web site. This is the first step taken by most firms as they enter the virtual marketplace. When customers access the Web site, they generally first visit the home Web page. This is an index to the site's contents through other Web pages. Large organizations often create and manage their Web sites internally. Smaller companies have their sites hosted on servers that are maintained by an ISP. To be successful at this level the organization must ensure that:

- Information displayed on the Web site is current, complete, and accurate;
- Customers can find the site and successfully navigate through it;
- An adequate hardware and software infrastructure exists to facilitate quick access during high usage periods; and
- Information stored on the site is accessed only by authorized users.

Transaction Level. Organizations involved at the **transaction level** use the Internet to accept orders from customers and/or to place them with their suppliers. This in-

---

5   Forrester Research, Cambridge, Massachusetts, www.forrester.com, 1999.

volves engaging in business activities with total strangers from remote parts of the world. These may be customers, suppliers, or potential trading partners. Many of the risks that are discussed later in the chapter relate to this (and to the next) level of e-commerce. Success in this domain involves creating an environment of trust by resolving some key concerns. These include:

- Ensuring that data used in the transaction are protected from misuse.
- Verifying the accuracy and integrity of business processes used by the potential customer, partner, or supplier.
- Verifying the identity and physical existence of the potential customer, partner, or supplier.
- Establishing the reputation of the potential customer, partner, or supplier.

Distribution Level. Organizations operating on the **distribution level** are using the Internet to sell and deliver digital products to customers. These include subscriptions to on-line news services, software products and upgrades, and music and video products. In addition to all the concerns identified at the transaction level, firms involved in this aspect of e-commerce are concerned that products are delivered successfully and only to legitimate customers.

Dynamic Virtual Organizations

Perhaps the greatest potential benefit to be derived from e-commerce is the firm's ability to forge dynamic business alliances with other organizations to fill unique market niches as the opportunities arise. These may be long-lasting partnerships or one-time ventures. Electronic partnering of business enterprises forms a **dynamic virtual organization** that benefits all parties involved. For example, consider a company that markets millions of different products including books, music, software, and toys over the Internet. If this were a traditional organization created to serve walk-in customers, it would need a massive warehouse to store the extensive physical inventories of the products that it sells. It would also need to make significant investments in inventory and personnel to maintain stocks, fill customer orders, and control the environment. A virtual organization does not need this physical infrastructure. Figure 12–17 illustrates the partnering relationship that is possible in a virtual organization.

The selling organization maintains a Web site for advertising product offerings. The products themselves are not physically in the custody of the seller, but are stored at the trading partner organization's (manufacturers, publishers, and distributors) facilities. The seller provides customers with product descriptions, consumer reports, prices, availability, and expected delivery times. This information comes from trading partners through an Internet connection. The seller validates customer orders placed through the Web site and automatically dispatches these to the trading partner firm, which actually ships the product. Low-cost EDI Web browser translation systems are available that translate data entered from Web forms into the X.12 format for EDI processing.

The virtual organization can expand, contract, or shift its product line and services by simply adding or eliminating trading partners. To fully exploit this flexibility, organizations often forge relationships with perfect strangers. Managers in both firms need to make rapid determinations as to the competence, compatibility, and capacity of potential partners to discharge their responsibilities. These and other security-related risks are potential impediments to e-commerce that will be examined later.

FIGURE 12–17

Dynamic Virtual
Organization

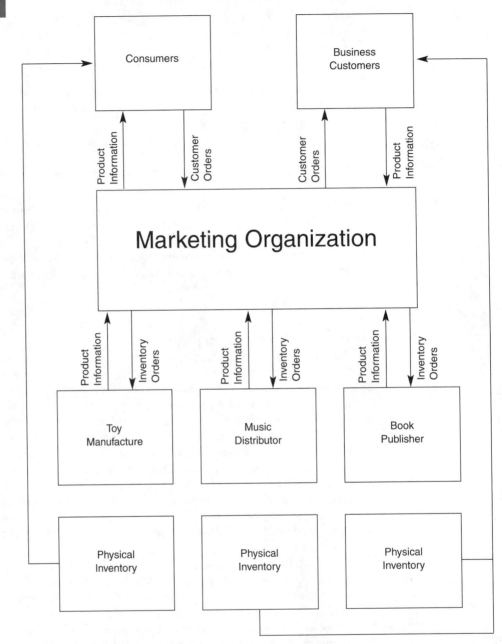

RISKS ASSOCIATED WITH ELECTRONIC COMMERCE

As a vehicle for processing business transactions, the potential for electronic commerce is almost unlimited. Reliance on electronic commerce, however, opens new areas for concern about unauthorized access to confidential information. As LANs become the platform for mission-critical applications and data, proprietary information, customer data, and financial records are at risk. Organizations connected to their customers and business partners via the Internet are particularly exposed. Without adequate protection, firms open their doors to computer hackers, vandals, thieves, and industrial spies both internally and from around the world.

The paradox of networking is that networks exist to provide user access to shared resources, yet the most important objective of any network is to control access. Hence, for every productivity argument in favor of remote access, there is a security argument against it. Organization management must seek a balance between improved performance and the associated risks.

This section opens with a definition of electronic commerce risk. We then examine the internal risks posed by Intranets and dishonest employees with the technical knowledge and position to perpetrate frauds and malicious acts. Finally, we turn our attention to the Internet and the risks faced by both consumers and business entities in this relatively new business frontier.

WHAT IS RISK?

Business **risk** is the possibility of loss or injury that can reduce or eliminate an organization's ability to achieve its objectives. In terms of electronic commerce, risk relates to the loss, theft, or destruction of data or the use or generation of data or computer programs that financially or physically harms an organization.

INTRANET RISKS

Intranets consist of small LANs and large WANs that may contain thousands of individual nodes. Intranets are used to connect employees within a single building, between buildings on the same physical campus, and between geographically dispersed locations. Typical Intranet activities include e-mail routing, transaction processing between business units, and linking to the outside Internet.

Intranet threats are spawned internally by unauthorized and illegal employee activities. Their motives for doing harm may be vengeance against the company, the challenge of breaking into unauthorized files, or to profit from selling trade secrets or embezzling assets. The threat from employees (both current and former) is significant because of their intimate knowledge of system controls and the lack of controls. Trade secrets, operations data, accounting data, and confidential information to which the employee has access are at the greatest risk. Discharged employees, or those that leave under contentious circumstance, are particularly troubling.

Intercepting Network Messages

The individual nodes on most Intranets are connected to a shared channel across which travel user IDs, passwords, confidential e-mails, and financial data files. The unauthorized interception of this information by a node on the network is called sniffing. The exposure is even greater when the Intranet is connected to the Internet. Commercially available sniffer software is routinely used by network administrators to analyze network traffic and to detect bottlenecks. Sniffer software, however, can also be downloaded from the Internet. In the hands of the computer criminal, sniffer software can be used to intercept and view data sent across a shared Intranet channel. The potential situation raises serious concerns for auditors in financial institutions and the human resources departments of most large corporations.[6]

---

6   Patrick Dryden, News—*Computerworld Online* (January 12, 1998).

Accessing Corporate Databases

Intranets connected to central corporate databases increase the risk that data will be viewed, corrupted, changed, or copied by an employee. Social security numbers, customer listings, credit card information, recipes, formulas, and design specifications may be downloaded and sold. Employees with access privileges to financial accounts have been bribed by outsiders to electronically write off an account receivable or erase an outstanding tax bill. A 1998 Computer Security Institute (CSI) study reported that financial fraud losses of this sort averaged $387,000. The study found that the average loss from corporate espionage was over $1 million. Total losses from insider trade secret theft have been estimated to exceed $24 billion per year.

Who Are the Greatest Threats?

We know from earlier chapters that an organization's internal controls are typically aimed at lower-level employees. According to one study, however, middle managers are most often prosecuted for insider crimes.[7] Middle managers often possess access privileges that allow them to override controls. Information systems employees within the organization are another group empowered with override privileges that may permit access to mission-critical data. A 1997 study revealed that 19 of the 104 firms surveyed were the victims of fraudulent acts committed by the organization's IS employees.

What Can Be Done?

A factor that contributes to computer crime is the reluctance by many organizations to prosecute the criminals. The CSI study revealed that only 17 percent of the firms that experienced an illegal intrusion reported it to a law enforcement agency. Eighty five percent of the firms that did not report the intrusions cited fear of negative publicity as the justification for their silence.

Many computer criminals are repeat offenders. An organization can significantly reduce its hiring risk and avoid criminal acts by performing background checks on prospective employees. In the past employee backgrounding was difficult to achieve because former employers, fearing legal action, were reluctant to disclose negative information to prospective employers. A "no comment" policy prevailed. The relatively new legal doctrine of *negligent hiring liability* is changing this. This doctrine effectively requires employers to check into an employee's background. Increasingly, courts are holding employers responsible for criminal acts perpetrated by employees both on and off the job that a background check could have prevented. Many states have passed laws that protect a former employer from legal action when providing work-related performance information about a former employee when (1) the inquiry comes from a prospective employer, (2) the information is based on credible facts, and (3) the information is given without malice.[8]

Uncontrolled Expansion of Intranets

Not all risks to the organization are the result of criminal activity. Well intended but ill-conceived network decisions also create a serious threat. Low cost and relative ease

7   Financial Executives Institute, Safety Nets: Secrets of Effective Information Technology Controls, An Executive Report (June 1997).
8   M. Greenstein, and T. Fineman, *Electronic Commerce: Security, Risk Management and Control* (Irwin McGraw-Hill, 2000): 146.

of implementation have fuelled the uncontrolled growth of Intranets in many organizations. In a discovery search of Intranet sites, Boeing Co. identified over one million Web pages hosted on 2,300 Web sites.[9] Management is concerned that additional, yet undiscovered, sites still exist. The unsanctioned proliferation of Intranet sites contributes to risk. Such sites represent private group decisions that are unsupported and unprotected by the organization's information technology department. They are a blind spot in the organization's perimeter defenses that exposes it to additional outside threats from the Internet.

INTERNET RISKS

This section looks at some of the more significant risks associated with Internet commerce. First the risks related to consumer privacy and transaction security are examined. The risk to business entities from fraud, malicious acts, and network failures are then reviewed.

Risks to Consumers

As more and more people connect, Internet fraud is on the rise. The National Consumer League reported that Internet fraud rose by 600 percent between 1997 and 1998.[10] According to the U.S. Securities and Exchange Commission, the number of e-mail complaints alleging fraud has risen from approximately 12 per day in 1997 to between 200 and 300 per day in 1999.[11] In a recent experiment to detect and remedy Internet security weaknesses, researchers working for the National Research Institute for Mathematics and Computer Science in Amsterdam cracked the international security code used to protect credit card numbers, stock transactions, and other secure information transmitted over the Internet. A team of professionals from around the world, including employees of Microsoft and Sun Microsystems, participated in this project. While the technology needed to replicate the experiment is expensive and difficult to obtain, should it fall into the hands of computer criminals and hackers, the loss of confidence in electronic commerce would be incalculable.[12]

It is not surprising that many consumers view the Internet as an unsafe place to do business. In particular, they worry about the security of credit card information left on Web sites and the confidentiality of their transactions. This section examines some of the more common threats to consumers from cyber criminals. The next section will look at some the risks business entities face when doing business on the Web.

Theft of Credit Card Numbers. The perception that the Internet is not secure for credit card purchases is considered to be the biggest barrier to e-commerce. Are Internet companies negligent or even fraudulent in the way they collect, use, and store credit card information? One hacker successfully stole 100,000 credit card numbers with a combined credit limit of $1 billion from an Internet service provider's customer files. He was arrested when he tried to sell the information to an undercover FBI agent.

---

9   Carol Sliwa, "Maverick Intranets a Challenge for IT," *Computerworld Online* (March 15, 1999).
10   "Internet Fraud Watch," The National Consumer League (Washington, D.C.).
11   "Securities Fraud: The Internet Poses Challenges to Regulators and Investors," United States General Accounting Office (Washington, D.C., March 22, 1999).
12   National Research Institute for Mathematics and Computer Science (Amsterdam, Netherlands, September 1999).

Another fraud scheme is to establish a fraudulent business operation that captures credit card information. For example, the company may take orders to deliver flowers on Mother's Day. When the day arrives, the company goes out of business and disappears from the Web. Of course, the flowers are never delivered and the credit card information collected is either sold or used by the perpetrator.

Theft of Passwords. One form of Internet fraud involves establishing a Web site for the purpose of stealing a visitor's password. To access the Web page, the visitor is asked to register and provide an e-mail address and password. Many people use the same password for different applications such as ATM services, e-mail, and employer-network access. In the hopes that the Web site visitor falls into this pattern of behavior, the cyber criminal uses the captured password to break into the victim's accounts.

Consumer Privacy. Concerns about the lack of privacy are discouraging consumers from engaging in Internet commerce. One poll revealed that:[13]

- Almost two-thirds of non-Internet users would start using the Internet if they could be assured that their personal information was protected; and
- Privacy is the number one reason that individuals are avoiding Internet commerce.

Many coalitions have been formed to lobby for stronger privacy measures. The Center for Democracy and Technology (CDT), Electronic Frontier Foundation (EFF), and Electronic Privacy Information Center (EPIF) are three prominent groups. One aspect of privacy involves the way in which Web sites capture and use "cookies."

Cookies are files containing user information that are created by the Web server of the site being visited and are then stored on the visitor's own computer hard drive. Cookies contain the URLs of sites visited by the user. When the site is revisited the user's browser sends the specific cookies to the Web server. The original intent behind the cookie was to improve efficiency in processing return visits to sites where users are required to register for services. For example, on the user's first visit to a particular Web site, the URL and User ID may be stored as a cookie. On subsequent visits, the Web site retrieves the User ID, thus saving the visitor from rekeying the information.

Cookies allow Web sites to off-load the storage of routine information about vast numbers of visitors. It is far more efficient for a Web server to retrieve this information from a cookie file stored on the user's computer than to search through millions of such records stored at the Web site. Most browsers have preference options to disable cookies or to warn the user before accepting one.

The privacy controversy over cookies relates to what is captured in a cookie and how the information is used. For example, the cookie may be used to create a profile of user preferences for marketing purposes. The profile could be based on the pages accessed or the options selected during the site visit, the time of day or night of the visit, and the length of time spent at the site. The profile could also include the user's e-mail address, zip code, home phone number, and any other information the user is willing to provide to the Web site.

---

13   "Privacy . . . A Weak Link in the Cyber-Chain," PricewaterhouseCoopers E-Business Leaders Series, www.pcwglobal.com, 1999.

This type of information is useful to on-line marketing firms that sell advertising for thousands of Internet customers hawking their products. The user profile enables the marketing firm to customize ads and to target them to electronic consumers. To illustrate, lets assume a user visiting an on-line bookstore browses sports car and automobile racing listings. This information is stored in a cookie and transmitted to the on-line marketing firm, which then sends JavaScript ads for general automotive products to the bookstore's Web page to entice the visitor to click on the ads. Each time the consumer visits the site, the contents of the cookie will be used to trigger the appropriate ads. User profile information can also be compiled into a mailing list, which is sold and used in the traditional way for solicitation.

Cookies and Consumer Security. Another concern over the use of cookies relates to security. Cookies are text (.txt) files that can be read with any text editor. Some Web sites store user passwords in cookies. If the passwords are not encrypted (discussed later) before being stored, then anyone with access to the computer can retrieve the cookies and the passwords. Thus, when a computer in the workplace is shared by multiple employees, the cookies file, which is stored in a common directory, may be reviewed by all users of the computer.

A related form of risk comes from criminal or malicious Web sites. As the user browses the site, a JavaScript program such as the "Frieburg Bug" is uploaded to the user's computer. The program secretly scans the hard drive for the cookies file and copies it to the Web site where it is reviewed for passwords.

Risks to Businesses

There is a tendency to think that the risks associated with Internet commerce fall entirely onto the consumer's shoulders. Business entities are also at risk from fraud and system failures. IP spoofing and denial of service attacks are two significant fraud issues that are examined below. The section concludes with a brief discussion of the threat from technology failure.

IP Spoofing. **IP spoofing** is a form of masquerading to gain unauthorized access to a Web server and/or to perpetrate an unlawful act without revealing one's identity. To accomplish this the perpetrator disguises his or her identity by replacing the IP address of the originating server with that of another server. A criminal may use IP spoofing to make a message appear to be coming from a trusted or authorized source and thus slip through controls systems designed to accept transmissions from certain (trusted) host computers and block out others. This technique could be used to crack into corporate networks to perpetrate frauds, conduct acts of espionage, or destroy data. For example, a hacker may "spoof" a manufacturing firm with a false sales order that appears to come from a legitimate customer. If the spoof goes undetected the manufacturer will incur the costs of producing and delivering a product that was never ordered.

Denial of Service Attacks. A **denial of service attack** is an assault on a Web server to prevent it from servicing users. While such attacks can be aimed at any type of Web site, they are particularly devastating to business entities that cannot receive and process business transactions from their customers.

When a user establishes a connection on the Internet through TCP/IP, a three-way handshake takes place. The connecting server sends an initiation code called a *SYN (SYNchronize) packet* to the receiving server. The receiving server then acknowledges the request by returning a **SYN-ACK (SYNchronize-ACKnowledge)** packet. Finally the initiating host machine responds with an *ACK packet code*. The attack is accomplished by not sending the final acknowledgment to the server's SYN-ACK response, which causes the server to keep signaling for acknowledgement until the server times out.

The individual or organizations perpetrating the denial of service attack transmits hundreds of SYN packets to the targeted receiver but never responds with an ACK to complete the connection. As a result, the ports of the receiver's server are clogged with incomplete communication requests that prevent legitimate transactions from being received and processed. Organizations under attack have been prevented from receiving Internet messages for days at a time.

If the target organization could identify the server that is launching the attack, the firewall (discussed later) could be programmed to ignore all communication from that site. Such attacks, however, are difficult to prevent because IP spoofing is used to disguise the source of the messages. IP spoofing programs that randomize the source address of the attacker have been written and publicly distributed over the Internet. Therefore, to the receiving site it appears that the transmissions are coming from all over the Internet.

Technology Failures. Web service disruption caused by hardware failure can cause an e-business organization to lose both customers' credibility and sales revenues. Organizations are also at risk if their network connections become degraded by unforeseen demand that overloads their systems. Such failures cause lost revenues in the short run, but in the long run both current and potential customers may move forever to more reliable suppliers. On August 6, 1999, 3,000 ISPs, banks, and corporations (among them the Chicago Board of Trade) started to lose their Internet connections when MCI's network began to fail for the first of 10 frustrating days. The problem was eventually solved and MCI offered customers two days of service for every one they missed. Industry analysts, however, compared MCI's technical handling of the problem unfavorably to their competitor AT&T, which solved a similar problem in only two days. Many also criticize MCI's tight-lipped handling of the situation. Lack of open and timely communication about the crisis damaged their credibility. Customers wanting to know when they could reconnect were especially enraged. Such breakdowns are likely to occur in the future, but the lesson to be learned is clear. Whether a business uses a large ISP such as MCI or a small one, they should ensure that the ISP has a backup link to the Internet.[14]

Malicious Programs. Viruses and other forms of malicious programs such as worms, logic bombs, and Trojan horses pose a threat to both Internet and Intranet users. Malicious programs are, however, not exclusively an electronic commerce issue; database management, operating systems security, and application integrity are also threatened. Because of the broad-based implications of the risk it is examined at length in Chapter 15.

Areas of General Concern

The specific consumer and business risks addressed above can be summarized in the four areas of general concern that are discussed as follows.[15]

---

14   Brad Stone, "MCI: Meltdown and Misconnection," *Newsweek* (August 30, 1999).
15   M. Greenstein, and T. Fineman, *Electronic Commerce: Security, Risk Management and Control* (Irwin McGraw-Hill, 2000): 42.

Data Security.   The term **data security** pertains to the level of protection over stored and transmitted data. Before consumers and trading partners do electronic business with a Web-based company, they need to know about the quality of security measures that are in place to protect their transmitted data. They are concerned about the security of internal databases containing business and personal information. They need assurance that these data will be protected from unauthorized access and unintentional harm from both outsiders and those within the organization.

Business Policies.   E-commerce consumers and trading partners are concerned about **business policies** of the firm with whom they do business. They need to know if the organization's policies are publicly stated and consistently followed. Some of the more common concerns relate to the company's policies regarding billing and payment, merchandise returns, shipping products, and tax collection on sales.

Privacy.   **Privacy** pertains to the level of confidentiality employed by an organization in managing customer and trading partner data. Privacy applies also to data collected by Web sites from visitors who are not actual customers. Specific concerns include:

- Does the organization have a stated privacy policy?
- What information on customers, trading partners, and visitors does the company capture?
- Does the organization share or sell its customer, trading partner, or visitor information?
- Can individuals and business entities verify and update the information captured about them?
- What mechanisms are in place to assure the consistent application of stated privacy policies?

Business Process Integrity.   **Business process integrity** pertains to the accuracy, completeness, and consistency with which an organization processes its business transactions. In traditional EDI environments, assurance about these issues is provided through a trading partner agreement that is negotiated in advance of trading relations. In the *dynamic virtual organization* environment, potential trading partners need this information quickly since there may not be time to negotiate a formal trading partner agreement. Business process concerns relate primarily to internal control adequacy. Specific questions that need to be answered include:

- Does the company have adequate controls to ensure that it does not lose sales orders?
- How does the company process bills and account information?
- Are controls in place to ensure that payments are posted accurately and in a timely manner?
- What controls ensure that customer orders are shipped on time and are correct?

The following section examines security and assurance techniques that can help resolve these concerns and establish a basis of trust that is essential to the future of electronic commerce.

SECURITY, ASSURANCE, AND TRUST

Trust is the catalyst for increasing e-commerce. Both consumers and businesses are drawn to organizations that are perceived to have integrity. Organizations must convey a sense that they are competent and conduct business fairly with their customers, trading partners, and employees. This is a two-pronged problem. First, the company must implement the technology infrastructure and controls needed to provide for adequate security. Second, the company must assure potential customers and trading partners that adequate safeguards are in place and working. According to Forrester Research, organizations are expected to spend the bulk of their security budgets in three key areas: *data encryption, digital authentication*, and *firewalls*.[16] These security techniques are outlined below, but are presented in more detail in Chapter 16. This chapter concludes with a review of assurance initiatives underway to promote trust in e-commerce.

ENCRYPTION

Encryption is the conversion of data into a secret code for storage in databases and transmission over networks. The sender uses an encryption algorithm to convert the original message (called cleartext) into a coded equivalent (called ciphertext). At the receiving end the ciphertext is decoded (decrypted) back into cleartext. The encryption algorithm uses a **key**, which is a binary number that is typically from 40 to 128 bits in length. The more bits in the key the stronger the encryption method. Today, nothing less than 128-bit algorithms are considered truly secure. Two commonly used methods of encryption are data encryption standard (DES) and public key encryption.

The **data encryption standard (DES)** approach uses a single key known to both the sender and the receiver of the message. To encode a message, the sender provides the encryption algorithm with the key, which produces the ciphertext message. This is transmitted to the receiver's location, where it is decoded using the same key to produce a cleartext message. Since the same key is used for coding and decoding, control over the key becomes an important security issue. The more individuals that need to exchange encrypted data, the greater the chance that the key will become known to an unauthorized intruder who could intercept a message and read it, change it, delay it, or destroy it.

Public Key Encryption

To overcome the above problem, the **public key encryption** technique was devised. This approach uses two different keys: one for encoding messages and the other for decoding them. The recipient has a private key used for decoding that is kept secret. The encoding key is public and published for everyone to use. This approach is illustrated in Figure 12–18.

Receivers never need to share private keys with senders, thus reducing the likelihood that they fall into the hands of an intruder. The most trusted public key encryption method is **RSA (Rivest-Shamir-Adleman)**. This method is, however, computationally intensive and much slower than DES encryption. Sometimes, both DES and RSA are used together in what is called a **digital envelope**.

DIGITAL AUTHENTICATION

Not all security concerns are resolved by encryption alone. For example, how does the supplier (receiver) know for sure that a purchase order (message) for 1,000 units of product sent by a customer (sender) was not intercepted by a hacker during

---

16   Forrester Research, Cambridge, Massachusetts, www.forrester.com, 1998.

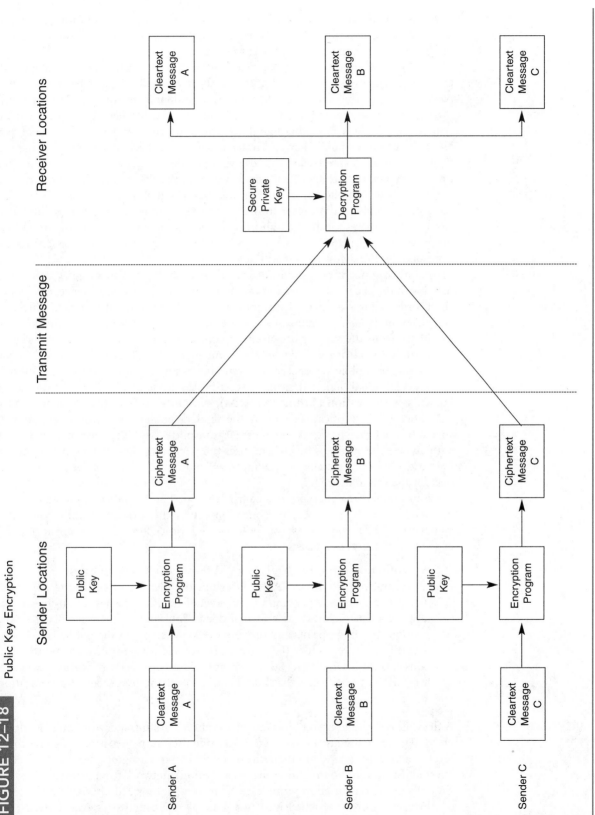

FIGURE 12–18   Public Key Encryption

transmission and altered to read 100,000? If such an alteration went undetected, the supplier would incur the labor, material, manufacturing, and distribution costs for the order. Litigation between the innocent parties may ensue.

A **digital signature** is an electronic authentication technique that ensures the transmitted message originated with the authorized sender and that it was not tampered with after the signature was applied. The digital signature is derived from a mathematically computed digest of the document that has been encrypted with the sender's private key. Both the digital signature and the text message are encrypted using the receiver's public key and transmitted to the receiver. At the receiving end, the message is decrypted using the receiver's private key to produce the digital signature (encrypted digest) and the cleartext version of the message. Finally the receiver uses the sender's public key to decrypt the digital signal to produce the digest. The receiver recalculates the digest from the cleartext using the original hashing algorithm and compares this to the transmitted digest. If the message is authentic, the two digest values will match. If even a single character of the message was changed in transmission, the digest figures will not be equal.

Another concern facing the receiver is determining if a message actually originated with the expected sender. For example, suppose that the supplier receives a purchase order addressed from Customer A for 100,000 units of product, which was actually sent from an unknown computer criminal. Once again, significant costs would accrue to the suppler organization upon action on this fraudulent message.

A **digital certificate** is like an electronic identification card that is used in conjunction with a public key encryption system to verify the authenticity of the message sender. Also called digital IDs, digital certificates are issued by trusted third parties known as **certification authorities (CAs)**, such as Veri-Sign, Inc., Mountain View, CA. The digital certificate is actually the sender's public key that has been digitally signed by the CA. The digital certificate is transmitted with the encrypted message to authenticate the sender. The receiver uses the CA's public key to decrypt the sender's public key (which is attached to the message) and then uses the sender's public key to decrypt the actual message.

Since public key encryption is central to digital authentication, public key management becomes an important control point in this process. **Public key infrastructure (PKI)** constitutes the policies and procedures for administering this activity. A PKI system consists of:

1. A certification authority that issues and revokes digital certificates.
2. A registration authority (RA) that verifies the identity of certificate applicants. The process varies depending on the level of certification desired. It involves establishing one's identity with formal documents such as a driver's license, notarization, and fingerprints and proving one's ownership of the public key.
3. A certification repository (CR), which is a publicly accessible database that contains current information about current certificates and a certification revocation list (CRL) of certificates that have been revoked and the reasons for revocation.

FIREWALLS

A **firewall** is a system used to insulate an organization's Intranet from outside intruders. They can be used to authenticate an outside user of the network, verify his or her level of access authority, and then direct the user to the program, data, or service requested. In addition to insulating the organization's network from external networks, firewalls can also be used to protect LANs from unauthorized internal access.

Firewalls can be grouped into two general types: network-level firewalls, and application-level firewalls. **Network-level firewalls** provide low cost and low security access control. They route messages to their destinations based on the source and destination addresses attached to incoming message packets. **Application-level firewalls** provide a high level of customizable network security, but can be extremely expensive. These systems are configured to run security applications called *proxies* that permit routine services such as e-mail to pass through the firewall, but can perform sophisticated functions such as verifying user authentication.

ASSURANCE

In response to consumer demand for evidence that a Web-based business is trustworthy, a number of "trusted" third-party organizations are offering seals of *assurance* that businesses can display on their Web site home pages. To legitimately bear the seal, the company must show that it complies with certain business practices, capabilities, and controls. This section reviews six seal-granting organizations: *Better Business Bureau (BBB), TRUSTe, Veri-Sign, Inc., International Computer Security Association (ICSA), AICPA/CICA WebTrust*, and *AICPA/CICA SysTrust*.

Better Business Bureau

The Better Business Bureau (BBB) is a nonprofit organization that has been promoting ethical business practices through self-regulation since 1912. The BBB has extended its mission to the Internet through a wholly owned subsidiary called BBBOnline, Inc. To qualify for the BBBOnline seal an organization must:

- Become a member of the BBB.
- Provide information about the company's ownership, management, address, and phone number. This is verified by a physical visit to the company's premises.
- Be in business for at least one year.
- Promptly respond to customer complaints.
- Agree to binding arbitration for unresolved disputes with customers.

The assurance provided by BBBOnline relates primarily to concern about business policies, ethical advertising, and consumer privacy. BBBOnline does not verify controls over transaction processing integrity and data security issues.

TRUSTe

Founded in 1996, TRUSTe is a nonprofit organization dedicated to improving consumer privacy practices among Internet businesses and Web sites. To qualify to display the TRUSTe seal the organization must:

- Agree to follow TRUSTe privacy policies and disclosure standards.
- Post a privacy statement on the Web site disclosing the type of information being collected, the purpose for collecting information, and with whom it is shared.
- Promptly respond to customer complaints.
- Agree to site compliance reviews by TRUSTe or an independent third party.

TRUSTe addresses consumer privacy concerns exclusively and provides a mechanism for posting consumer complaints against it members. If a member organization is found to be out of compliance with TRUSTe standards, its right to display the trust seal may be revoked.

Veri-Sign, Inc.

Veri-Sign, Inc. was established as a for-profit organization in 1995. Veri-Sign, Inc. provides assurance regarding the security of transmitted data. The organization does not verify security of stored data or address concerns related to business policies, business processes, or privacy. Their mission is to "provide digital certificate solutions that enable trusted commerce and communications." Their products allow customers to transmit encrypted data and verify the source and destination of transmissions. Veri-Sign, Inc. issues three classes of certificates to individuals, businesses, and organizations. To qualify for class three certification the individual, business, or organization must provide a third-party confirmation of name, address, telephone number, and Web site domain name.

ICSA

The International Computer Security Association (ICSA) established its Web Certification Program in 1996. ICSA certification addresses data security and privacy concerns. It does not deal with concerns about business policy and business processes. Organizations that qualify to display the ICSA seal have undergone an extensive review of firewall security from outside hackers. Organizations must be recertified on an annual basis and undergo at least two surprise checks each year.

AICPA/CICA WebTrust

The AICPA and CICA established the WebTrust program in 1997. To display the AICPA/CICA WebTrust seal the organization undergoes an examination according to the AICPA's Standards for Attestation Engagements, No. 1, by a specially Web-certified CPA or CA. The examination focuses on the areas of business practices (policies), transaction integrity (business process), and information protection (data security). The seal must be renewed every 90 days.

AICPA/CICA SysTrust

In July 1999, the AICPA/CICA introduced an exposure draft describing a new assurance service called SysTrust. It is designed to increase management, customer, and trading partner confidence in systems that support entire businesses or specific processes. The assurance service involves the public accountant evaluating the system's reliability against four essential criteria: availability, security, integrity, and maintainability.

The potential users of SysTrust are trading partners, creditors, shareholders, and others who rely on the integrity and capability of the system. For example, Virtual Company is considering outsourcing some of its vital functions to third-party organizations. Virtual needs assurance that the third parties' systems are reliable and adequate to provide the contracted services. As part of the outsourcing contract, Virtual requires the servicing organizations to produce a clean SysTrust report every three months.

In theory, the SysTrust service will enable organizations to differentiate themselves from their competitors. Those organizations that undergo a SysTrust engagement will be perceived as competent service providers and trustworthy. They will be more attuned to the risks in their environment and equipped with the necessary controls to deal with the risks.[17]

---

17   AICPA/CICA SysTrust Principle and Criteria for Systems Reliability, American Institute of Certified Public Accountants, Inc. and Canadian Institute of Chartered Accountants (1999): 3.

IMPLICATIONS FOR THE ACCOUNTING PROFESSION

The issues discussed in this chapter carry many implications for auditors and the public accounting profession. This section concludes the chapter with a discussion of new directions for auditing techniques, auditor education, and future business opportunities and services that arise from electronic commerce.

A NEW AUDIT PARADIGM

As key functions such as inventory procurement, sales processing, shipping notification, and cash disbursements are performed automatically, digitally, and in real-time, auditors are faced with the challenge of developing new methods of monitoring and verifying economic events. The traditional after-the-fact audit approach adds little value in the fast-changing virtual world of electronic commerce.

Continuous Auditing

Continuous process auditing techniques need to be developed that will enable the auditor to review transactions at frequent intervals or as they occur. To be effective such an approach will need to employ **intelligent control agents** (computer programs) that embody auditor-defined heuristics that search electronic transactions for anomalies. Upon finding unusual events, the control agent will first search for similar events to identify a pattern.[18] If the anomaly cannot be explained, the agent alerts the auditor with an alarm or exception report.

Real-time continuous auditing is becoming increasingly important because of the rising need to produce accurate and reliable financial information on short notice. For example, organizations may need to provide prospective trading partners and other stakeholders with financial status information before entering into a business transaction.

Electronic Audit Trails

Transactions processed by traditional systems are triggered by source documents that leave a paper audit trail, which can be reviewed using traditional audit techniques. In an EDI environment, electronic transactions are generated automatically by a trading partner's computer, relayed by the VAN, and processed by the client's computer without human intervention. Since there is no paper audit trail, the auditor must employ nontraditional techniques. Validating such transactions may involve the client, its trading partners, and the value-added networks (VANs) that connect them. In this setting audits may be extended to the critical systems of the parties involved in the transactions. This could take the form of direct review of these systems or a collaboration between the auditors of the trading partners and VANs.

New Skills Needed by Auditors of Smaller Clients

In the past, the challenge of auditing EDI and other forms of electronic transactions was limited to larger firms with larger clients. Access to the Internet has allowed

---

18   Kogan, A., F. Sudit, and M. Vasarhelyi, "Some Auditing Implications of Internet Technology." http://rutgers.edu/Accounting/raw/miklos/tcon3.htm.

much smaller organizations to engage in EDI with trading partners and Web-based commerce with consumers. The generally smaller accounting firms that serve these organizations will now need to audit paperless transactions. Their success will in part depend on their ability to attract a new breed of accounting graduates that will possess strong technical skills.

The skills needed to perform in this new environment will include knowledge of operating systems, computer programming, network technology, and security techniques such as firewalls and authentication techniques. These skills are also essential to providing WebTrust and SysTrust assurance services. The new breed of accountant is more akin to a computer scientist than a bookkeeper.

REDEFINITION OF TRADITIONAL AUDITING CONCERNS

Traditional audit concerns pertaining to the confidentiality of client data, authentication of transactions, nonrepudiation of transactions, data integrity, and access controls take on new meaning in the electronic commerce environment.

Confidentiality of Data

As system designs become increasingly open to accommodate trading partner transactions, mission-critical information is at the risk of being exposed to intruders both from inside and outside the organization. Accountants need to understand the cryptographic techniques used to protect the confidentiality of stored and transmitted data. They need to assess the quality of encryption tools used and the effectiveness of key management procedures used by certification authorities. Furthermore, the term *mission-critical* defines a set of information that extends beyond the traditional financial concerns of accountants. This broader set demands a more holistic approach to assessing internal controls that ensure the confidentiality of data.

Authentication

In traditional systems, the authenticity of a sales order from a trading partner or customer was determined by the business paper on which it was written. In electronic commerce systems, determining the identity of the customer is not as simple a task. With no physical forms to review and approve, authentication is accomplished through digital signatures and digital certificates. Accountants must develop and understand these technologies and their application to perform their assurance function.

Nonrepudiation

Accountants are responsible for assessing the accuracy, completeness, and validity of transactions that constitute client sales, accounts receivable, purchases, and liabilities. Transactions that can be unilaterally repudiated by a trading partner can lead to uncollected revenues or legal action. In traditional systems, signed invoices, sales agreements, and other physical documents provide proof that a transaction occurred. As with the problem of authentication, electronic commerce systems can also use digital signatures and digital certificates to promote nonrepudiation. This technology has specific implication for the accounting profession. Because public accounting firms enjoy a high degree of public confidence, they are natural candidates for certification authorities.

Data Integrity

A nonrepudiated transaction from an authentic trading partner may still be intercepted and rendered inaccurate in a material way. In a paper-based environment, such alterations are easy to detect. Digital transmissions, however, pose much more of a problem. To assess data integrity, accountants must become familiar with the concept of computing a digest of a document and the role of digital signatures in data transmissions.

Access Controls

Controls need to be in place that prevent or detect unauthorized access to an organization's information system. Organizations whose systems are connected to the Internet are at greatest risk from outside intruders. Accounting firms need to be expert in assessing their clients' access controls. Many firms are now performing penetration tests, designed to assess the adequacy of their clients' access control by imitating known techniques used by hackers and crackers.

DEVELOPMENT OF NEW BUSINESS LINES AND SERVICES

Electronic commerce creates a number of new business problems that the public accounting profession is well positioned to exploit. Some of these involve expanding the assurance services already being provided including assessing systems reliability (*SysTrust*) for nonattest purposes, and Web site risk analysis and assurance (*WebTrust*). Other opportunities that take the profession into new areas include:[19]

- Providing electronic transaction processing services for organizations that need to outsource this function.
- Developing, authenticating, and storing digital signatures used in electronic transactions.
- Providing certificate authority services.

A CHANGING LEGAL ENVIRONMENT

Accountants have traditionally served their clients by assessing risk (both business and legal) and devising techniques to mitigate and control risk. This risk assessment role is greatly expanded by Internet commerce, whose legal framework is still evolving in a business environment fraught with new and unforeseen risks. To estimate its client's exposure to legal liability in this setting, the public account must understand the potential legal implications (both domestic and international) of actions taken by the client's electronic commerce system. The act of creating a Web page from which customers may order goods opens the organization to the national and international business communities and also exposes it to multiple and possibly conflicting legal statutes. Legal issues relating to taxes, privacy, security, intellectual property rights, and libel are of particular concern. For example, if a company has its corporate headquarters and inventory warehouse in one country and its Internet transaction processing systems in another, where did the sale originate for tax purposes?

The legal issues associated with electronic commerce have and will continue to create new opportunities for the profession. Accounting firms will need to provide their clients with rapid and accurate advice on a wide range of legal questions. In response to demand for such services, large firms such as PricewaterhouseCoopers are expanding their pool of international legal talent.

---

19   Greenstein and Feinman: 57.

Summary

This chapter focused on three aspects of electronic commerce: (1) the intra-organizational usage of networks to support distributed data processing; (2) traditional business-to-business transactions conducted via EDI; and (3) Internet commerce, including business-to-consumer and business-to-business relationships.

Intranet architectures and the respective features of the star, hierarchical, ring, bus, and client-server topologies were examined. Network control techniques are employed to manage communication sessions and to deal with the threat of data collisions. EDI systems are used to conduct business-to-business electronic commerce. Key in its success is the use of a standard format for communicating between dissimilar systems. The United States uses the American National Standards Institute (ANSI) X.12 format. The standard used internationally is the EDIFACT (EDI For Administration, Commerce, and Transport) format.

Internet commerce has been the source of intense interest since it enables thousands of business enterprises of all sizes and millions of consumers to congregate and participate in worldwide commerce. The chapter examined Internet technologies, including packet switching, the World Wide Web, Internet addressing, and protocols. The discussion of protocols focused on the layered approach exemplified in the Open System Interface model. The OSI model embeds protocols in seven separate layers and thus provides for effective communications between users who employ a variety of different hardware and software devices. Several advantages of Internet commerce were reviewed, including access to worldwide markets, reductions in inventory, creation of business partnerships, reductions in prices, and better customer service.

Electronic commerce is associated with unique risks. The primary concerns posed by Intranets come from employees. Internet risks were characterized as a number of specific fraud schemes that threaten consumer privacy and the security of transmitted and stored data. Several measures were examined that can reduce risks and promote an environment of security and trust. These include data encryption, digital certificates, firewalls, and third-party trust seals for Web sites.

The chapter concluded with a review of implications for accountants and the profession. The issues covered included continuous process auditing, electronic audit trails, changing skill sets of auditors, redefinition of traditional auditing concerns, new business opportunities for accountants, and the changing legal environment.

Key Terms

American National Standards Institute (ANSI) (598)
application layer (610)
application-level firewalls (625)
bridges (589)
bus topology (592)
business policies (621)
business process integrity (621)
carrier sensing (595)
certification authorities (CAs) (624)
client-server topology (593)
continuous process auditing (627)
cookies (618)
data collision (594)
data encryption standard (DES) (622)
data link layer (609)
data security (621)
denial of service attack (619)
DHTML (Dynamic HTML) (611)
digital certificate (624)
digital envelope (622)
digital signature (624)
distribution level (613)
document name (606)
DOM (Document Object Model) (611)
domain name (606)

Review Questions

1. What is a network topology?
2. What is a WAN?
3. Distinguish between network bridges and gateways.
4. Define EDI.
5. What is a VAN?
6. What is the X.12 standard?
7. Distinguish between the terms *network*, *network architecture*, and *network topologies*.
8. List five basic network topologies.
9. What purpose does a network interface card serve?
10. Does the star topology foster centralized or distributed data processing? Explain your answer.
11. How do the bus and ring topologies differ?
12. In the client-server mode, which end does the searching of the file, which end does the processing, and what part of the database needs to be locked?
13. What services are provided by a VAB?
14. What is the World Wide Web?
15. Name the three types of addresses used on the Internet.
16. Describe the elements of an e-mail address.

17. List the primary top-level domain names used in the United States.
18. What are the roles of VABs and VANs in EDI?
19. What is message packet switching?
20. What are some of the ways in which EDI can generate cost savings for a firm?
21. Explain data collision and discuss three basic methods of avoiding collisions. What are their relative merits?

22. Networks would be inoperable without protocols. Explain the importance of protocols and what functions they perform.
23. Describe Open System Interface (OSI).
24. Define the Internet.
25. What is the Internet's basic protocol?
26. Discuss the elements of the URL address.
27. What does the HTTP protocol do?

Discussion Questions

1. Explain the purpose of the two elements of the TCP/IP protocol.
2. Explain the purpose of each of the layers in the OSI protocol model.
3. Distinguish between the FTP and TELNET protocols.
4. Discuss the three levels of Internet business models.
5. What is a dynamic virtual organization?
6. Define risk in an electronic commerce setting.
7. What important factor has contributed to computer crime and what can be done?
8. How can Intranet expansion increase risk to an organization?
9. Differentiate between a LAN and a WAN. Do you have either or both at your university or college?
10. What purpose is served by protocols?
11. What is the paradox of networking?
12. As the information superhighway progresses and electronic data interchange increases in popularity, interfaces between organizational computers are becoming a necessity. Discuss what steps are being taken to foster these types of interfaces.
13. Electronic funds transfers are widely used by payroll departments and individuals to pay their personal bills, so why are they so infrequently used by businesses for cash disbursements?

14. EDI systems tied into inventory control models in conjunction with just-in-time inventory systems have been said to be beneficial in many ways; however, a mistake made by one firm in over-ordering can mushroom into overproduction for many firms. Explain how this can happen.
15. What are cookies and why are they used?
16. What privacy concerns pertain to cookies?
17. What security concerns pertain to cookies?
18. Discuss IP spoofing.
19. Explain a denial of service attack.
20. Discuss the four areas of general concern—data security, business policy, privacy, and business process integrity—as they relate to e-commerce.
21. Distinguish between DES and public key encryption.
22. What is a digital envelope?
23. What is a digital signature?
24. What is a digital certificate? How is it different from a digital signature?
25. Distinguish between a network-level firewall and an application-level firewall.
26. Discuss the key aspects of the following five seal-granting organizations: Better Business Bureau (BBB), TRUSTe, Veri-Sign, Inc., International Computer Security Association (ICSA), and AICPA/CICA WebTrust.

Multiple-Choice Questions

1. Which of the following statements is correct?
   a. TCP/IP is the basic protocol that permits communication between Internet sites.
   b. TCP/IP controls Web browsers that access the Web.
   c. TCP/IP is the document format used to produce Web pages.

d. TCP/IP is used to transfer text files, programs, spreadsheets, and databases across the Internet.

e. TCP/IP is a low-level encryption scheme used to secure transmissions in higher-level (HTTP) format.

2. Which of the following best describes a system of computers that connects the internal users of an organization that is distributed over a wide geographic area?

a. LAN

b. Internet

c. decentralized network

d. multidrop network

e. Intranet

3. Sniffer software is

a. used by malicious Web sites to sniff data from cookies stored on the user's hard drive.

b. used by network administrators to analyze network traffic.

c. used by bus topology Intranets to sniff for carriers before transmitting a message to avoid data collisions.

d. an illegal program downloaded from the Web to sniff passwords from the encrypted data of Internet customers.

e. illegal software for decoding encrypted messages transmitted over a shared Intranet channel.

4. Which of the following statements is true?

a. Cookies were originally intended to facilitate advertising on the Web.

b. Cookies always contain encrypted data.

c. Cookies are text files and never contain encrypted data.

d. Cookies contain the URLs of sites visited by the user.

e. Web browsers cannot function without cookies.

5. A message that is contrived to appear to be coming from a trusted or authorized source is called

a. a denial of service attack.

b. digital signature forging.

c. Internet Protocol spoofing.

d. URL masquerading.

e. a SYN-ACK packet.

6. A digital signature

a. is the encrypted mathematical value of the message sender's name.

b. is derived from the digest of a document that has been encrypted with the sender's private key.

c. is derived from the digest of a document that has been encrypted with the sender's public key.

d. is the computed digest of the sender's digital certificate.

e. allows digital messages to be sent over an analog telephone line.

7. Which of the following statements about the client-server model is correct?

a. It is best suited to the token-ring topology because the random-access method used by this topology detects data collisions.

b. It distributes both data and processing tasks to the server node. The client-server model can use the bus or ring topology.

c. It is most effective when used as a bus topology because its deterministic access method avoids collisions and prevents data loss during transmissions.

d. It is more efficient than the bus or ring topologies because it transmits an entire file of records to the requesting node rather than only a single record.

e. It is not used in conjunction with either the bus or ring topologies.

8. Which of the following statements is correct?

a. A bridge is used to connect a LAN and a WAN.

b. Packet switching combines the messages of multiple users into a "packet" for transmission. At the receiving end, the packet is disassembled into individual messages and distributed to the user.

c. The decision to partition a database assumes that no identifiable primary user exists in the organization.

d. Message switching is used to establish temporary connections between network devices for the duration of a communications session.

e. A deadlock is a temporary phenomenon that disrupts transaction processing. It will resolve itself when the primary computer completes processing its transaction and releases the data needed by the other nodes.

Problems

1. System Configuration

A local newspaper in Austin, Texas, receives its stories from two main sources—its own reporters and the wire services. Each of the reporters has a microcomputer on his or her desk. The writer types the story and carries the story on diskette to the editor's desk. The editor makes cuts and sends the story back to the writer for revision. The diskette is then sent to the editor for final approval. After final approval, the story is sent to the printer for typesetting. Stories that come in over the wire are first marked up by a reporter and then typed. From there, they follow much the same process as internally generated stories. When two reporters are collaborating on a story, they must pass the diskette back and forth between themselves. Writers reporting from the field must come back to the office to prepare the stories for editorial review. In rare instances, they may dictate a very important story over the phone.

Discuss the weaknesses in this system. What type of communication system would you suggest for this newspaper?

2. Data Communications Configuration

The big accounting firms prepare their working papers using electronic spreadsheets. They also use electronic mail capabilities that allow them to transmit these spreadsheets over telecommunication lines. Considering that the staff accountants who prepare the working papers are usually at the client's office and the manager in charge of the job may be at another site or at the accounting firm's main office, what type of data communication configuration is being employed? What are any potential advantages and disadvantages of this method?

3. CMA Adapted 1286 5-2
Distributed Data Processing

Vincent Maloy, director of special projects and analysis for Milok Company, is responsible for preparing corporate financial analyses and monthly projections, and for reviewing and presenting to upper management the financial impacts of proposed strategies. Data for these financial analyses and projections are obtained from reports developed by Milok's systems department and generated from its mainframe computer. Additional data are obtained through terminals via a data inquiry system. Reports and charts for presentations are then prepared by hand and typed. Maloy has tried to have final presentations generated by the computer but has not always been successful.

The systems department has developed a package using a terminal emulator to link a microcomputer to the mainframe computer. This allows the microcomputer to become part of the current data inquiry system and enables data to be downloaded to the microcomputer's disk. The data are in a format that allows printing or further manipulation and analyses using commercial software packages, such as spreadsheet analysis. The special projects and analysis department has been chosen to be the first users of this new computer terminal system.

Maloy questioned whether the new system could do more for his department than implementing the program modification requests that he has submitted to the systems department. He also believes that his people would have to become programmers.

Lisa Brandt, a supervisor in Maloy's department, has decided to prepare a briefing for Maloy on the benefits of integrating microcomputers with the mainframe computer. She has used the terminal inquiry system extensively and has learned to use spreadsheet software to prepare special analyses, sometimes with multiple alternatives. She also tried the new package while it was being tested.

Required:

a. Identify five enhancements to current information and reporting that Milok Company should be able to realize by integrating microcomputers with its mainframe computer.

b. Explain how the utilization of computer resources would be altered as a result of integrating microcomputers with the company's mainframe computer.

c. Discuss what security of the data is gained or lost by integrating microcomputers with the company's mainframe computer.

4. **CMA Adapted 1288-5Y6**
   Distributed Data Processing
   In the last two decades, there has been a transition from a centralized mainframe computer environment to a distributed network where an organization has the ability to share computer processing. One of the fastest-growing segments of the computer industry is the local area network, which is said to be the wave of the future. LANs permit the transfer of information between microcomputers, word processors, data storage devices, printers, and voice and telecommunication devices. Current opinion holds that the flow of organizational communications has been enhanced by the transition from the optimization of computers experienced in the traditional distributed network to the optimization of human resources in the LAN environment.

   Required:
   a. Describe the reasons why an organization would choose a distributed network over the traditional centralized computer environment.
   b. Compare and contrast the characteristics of a traditional distributed computer network with those of a local area network as they are related to the
       1. utilization of computer hardware.
       2. user interaction and the sharing of electronic information.
   c. Identify and explain three problems that can result from the use of local area networks.

5. **Electronic Data Interchange**
   The purchase order for one firm is the source document for the sales order of another firm. Consider the following purchase order and sales order data elements stored for two firms. Discuss any differences that may be problematic in transferring information between the two firms.

   Purchasing Firm:
   GH BETTIS
   A Division of Galveston-Houston Corp.
   1200 Post Oak Blvd.
   P.O. Box 4768
   Houston, TX 77637-9877

   Data Elements
   Vendor Number
   Vendor Name
   Vendor Address
   Vendor City
   Vendor State
   Vendor Country
   Vendor Zip Code
   Purchase Order No.
   Date
   Shipment Destination Code
   Vendor Part No.
   Item Description
   Quantity Ordered
   Unit Price
   Total

   Selling Firm:
   Oakland Steel Company
   469 Lakeland Blvd.
   Chicago, IL 60613-8888

   Data Elements
   Customer Number
   Customer Name
   Customer Address
   Customer City
   Customer State
   Customer Country
   Customer Zip Code
   Purchase Order No.
   Sales Order No.
   Date
   Shipping Company
   Vendor Part No.
   Item Description
   Quantity Ordered
   Unit Price
   Total
   Discount Offered
   Tax
   Freight Charges

6. **Internal Controls Assessment and**
   Electronic Data Interchange
   Gresko Toys Factory
   (Prepared by Robertos Karahannas,
   Lehigh University)
   Gresko Toys was started in the early 1960s by Mr. and Mrs. Gresko. Initially, the company was small and few toys were produced. The talent and skills of Mr. Gresko were by far the major assets of the company. Toys then were mainly made of wood and had few or no electronic parts; they were mainly manually operated and included toy cars,

several kinds of dolls, and toy guns. Gresko toys became part of the Pennsylvania tradition. Kids loved them and parents had no choice but to buy them.

Gresko toys quickly expanded, and by 1969 it reported a sales volume of $400,000, $50,000 of which was profit. Such profits caught the attention of other businesspeople, who began entering the market. The innovative spirit of some competitors through the introduction of fancy, battery-operated toys stole some of Gresko's market share. As the competition became more intense, the Greskos saw their market share declining even further. Children liked battery-operated toys.

Mr. Gresko saw this as both a threat and a challenge. He would not give up, however. He knew that he needed better machinery to make competitive toys. With a loan from the local bank and his savings, he sought and bought what he needed. After a period of training and test marketing, Gresko toys were again in the market, boosting sales. The company was generating orders that the factory could not handle. The workforce rose from a low of 50 to a high of 350. Most of the workforce was on the factory floor. More equipment was purchased, and the company has been expanding since then.

Today, the company sells $20 million worth of toys per year. The president of the company is Mrs. Gresko. Mr. Gresko felt that he should be on the factory floor managing production. Under him are the purchasing agent supervising a buyer, the warehouse manager managing two inventory clerks, a chief engineer, and a supervisor who is in charge of the factory workers. The controller of the company is Randi, the Greskos' elder daughter. An accounting clerk, a cashier, and a personnel manager work for her. Finally, Bob, the Greskos' only son, is the sales manager. A credit manager and two salespeople work for him.

Company Information

At present, the company's profit margin is 9 percent, only 2 percent below the industry average. According to Mr. Gresko, $850,000 in sales was lost last year due to insufficient inventory of parts. Due to the seasonal nature of the market and the short popularity span of most toys, Gresko customers require fast delivery of the ordered toys; if the parts are not available, it takes at least two weeks to get the paperwork ready, order the parts, and have them delivered by the suppliers.

Some customers cannot wait that long; others order the toys and subsequently cancel the order if it takes too long to complete. Often orders are accepted on the assumption that the parts are readily available in the warehouse; when they are not, orders are delayed for weeks. A missing part not only delays an order but also the whole assembly line.

To alleviate the problem, many parts are rushed in, thus raising tremendously the cost of the toys. The fine quality of the products allows for slight price increases to make up for part of the extra cost, but customers have already complained about such price fluctuations.

The Greskos are on good terms with their suppliers. After all, the market is so competitive that a reliable supplier is crucial to a firm's survival. Most of their major suppliers are located in Pennsylvania, where the Greskos have about 35 percent of the market share. However, those suppliers deal with the Greskos' competitors as well. There are about a dozen suppliers with whom the Greskos deal; eight of them supply about 95 percent of all inventory parts.

Even though good supplier relations are crucial to Gresko Toys, suppliers have often complained about Gresko's promptness in paying. The Greskos demand on-time delivery; the payment of the supplier invoice, however, is usually not timely. Mr. Gresko said that he does not have the time to run from the factory to the accounting department to make sure payments are on time. Late payments, however, also mean a loss of the 2 percent discount offered by the suppliers for early payment.

Besides resulting in lost sales, insufficient inventory of parts also delays the whole assembly line. Workers spend much time switching jobs. A just-in-time inventory system would, according to Mr. Gresko, be more appropriate for the factory. If the parts were available in the warehouse, the machines could be set up on an assembly-line fashion and operated on scheduled runs. But the fact that the necessary parts are frequently missing, forcing production to switch to another job, is a major obstacle to a just-in-time inventory system.

The Purchasing Cycle

Gresko Toys is very involved in purchasing the parts used in the production of toys. The company uses a periodic inventory system. When sales orders are received, Bob Gresko sends a copy to the production floor. This copy is used to trigger production as well as to indicate the potential need of parts not available in inventory. The inventory clerks search for parts;

when parts are out of stock, the inventory clerks issue two copies of a purchase requisition. This requisition is approved by Mr. Gresko before a purchase order is issued. One copy is sent to the purchasing manager and the other to the accounting department.

The buyer checks the suppliers' prices for the needed parts. Based on cost as well as past experience with a particular supplier, two suppliers are recommended. The purchasing manager subsequently decides on the supplier, and a purchase order is issued. Four copies of the purchase order are issued. The first copy is sent to the supplier, the second is filed by the purchasing manager, the third is sent to the warehouse, and the fourth is sent to the accounting department. All purchase order copies are filed by supplier number.

Approximately a week after the initiation of the purchase, the parts are received. The warehouse manager along with the inventory clerks inspect and count the received parts. The purchase order copy previously received by the purchasing manager is used as the basis of comparison. A receiving report in three parts is prepared. If prices and quantities received agree with those ordered and with the information on the packing slip received by the carrier, the parts are accepted. If any differences exist, Mr. Gresko is called in to decide whether to accept or reject the parts. On many occasions, acceptance of parts will be delayed for days until the suppliers are informed and an agreement is reached.

One copy of the receiving report is sent to the purchasing manager and another to the accounting department. The original copy is kept at the warehouse. The accounting clerk files the receiving report along with the purchase requisition and the purchase order by supplier number. The clerk also prepares the necessary journal entry and credits the related supplier in the subsidiary ledger. When the supplier sends the invoice, the accounting clerk matches the information to the purchase requisition, purchase order, and receiving report and prepares a disbursement voucher. This voucher is used for two purposes. It initiates the journal entry for the disbursement of cash, and it is used by the cashier to issue a check. Randi Gresko, as well as Mrs. Gresko, must sign the checks before they are sent to the suppliers.

Electronic Data Interchange

In search of anything that could improve the present system at the Gresko Toys factory, Mr. Gresko came across the electronic data interchange (EDI) system. One of his suppliers had attended a conference on EDI and had supplied Mr. Gresko with the conference material. Looking at the present system, Mr. Gresko tried to find EDI applications that would benefit the company's operations and at the same time improve its financial position.

For EDI to be implemented, certain databases will need to be established. An inventory master file with all relevant information is the key to the system. Predetermined order quantities and minimum inventory levels will need to be set for each item based on forecasts. At the warehouse, the inventory clerks will be constantly updating this database. When inventory levels drop below acceptable levels, an EDI purchase requisition will be issued to the purchasing department.

A supplier master file with related information on supplier performance will be accessed to identify potential suppliers. Depending on how advanced the system is, the computer or the purchasing manager will choose the proper supplier and issue an EDI order. This means that the factory's suppliers will also need to be using EDI.

Various ways of developing EDI links with suppliers are available. In the Gresko case, developing an independent system seems more appropriate; it is cheaper and perhaps easier to convince suppliers to join in. Software is readily available in the market and is easy to set up. Someone, however, should help set up the EDI links with the suppliers.

Once an EDI order is issued, the supplier will receive the message instantaneously. The open purchase order will be kept in a database until the receipt of the parts. Any changes to the order can be made by accessing the particular transmitted order and making the change. Suppliers can send the parts as well as their invoices more quickly. An EDI invoice can be sent to the Gresko factory upon shipment.

On arrival of the parts, the receiving clerk will prepare a receiving report and file it in a receiving database file. This report will be used to verify prices by accessing the purchase order. Credit terms, volume discounts, trade allowances, and other adjustments to quoted prices can be settled through EDI transmitted messages. If adjustments due to disagreements occur, the transaction is entered into the adjusted database file. The inventory master file is also updated, and the open purchase order is closed. In addition, the supplier history file and the accounts payable file are updated, and an evaluated receipts settlement (ERS) is established.

An ERS is a database containing records to be used for the payment of suppliers. The EDI order is matched against the receiving and adjusted database files. Such a comparison creates a payment input file that indicates the scheduled payment date within which any discount can be obtained, the latest possible payment date, and the remittance record for such payments.

At the beginning of every day, the treasurer (who presently does not exist) should receive a listing of the payment input file; this listing will indicate what has to be paid and when. The treasurer will initiate an EDI payment pending the approval of Mrs. Gresko. Upon approval and the transmission of the payment, the supplier records as well as the accounts payable records will be automatically updated. For an electronic funds transfer to occur, the banks that serve Gresko and its suppliers will also need to be using EDI. If such intermediary banks are not using EDI, Gresko and its suppliers will need to rely on a manual system of cash disbursement to settle their transactions.

Conclusion

Mr. Gresko has hired you to look at the present accounting system and his suggested EDI implementation plan. He wants you to identify the problem areas and look into the feasibility of setting up EDI links with the company's suppliers.

Required:

a. Draw a document flowchart of the present accounting system at Gresko.
b. What control problems, if any, exist in the accounting system?
c. Draw a document flowchart of the accounting system of the Gresko Toys factory using EDI as suggested by Mr. Gresko.
d. Do some research on your own. What EDI options, other than the one suggested by Mr. Gresko, are available to the Gresko Toys factory?
e. Discuss the possible implementation of an EDI system at the Gresko Toys factory. What areas should Mr. Gresko concentrate on, and what are the related issues associated with implementing EDI at the factory?

7. Electronic Fraud

In a recent financial fraud case, city employees in Brooklyn, New York, accessed electronic databases to defraud the city of $20 million. Several employees in collusion with the former deputy tax collector completely erased or reduced $13 million in property taxes and $7 million in accrued interest owed by taxpayers. In exchange for this service, the taxpayers paid the employees involved bribes of 10 to 30 percent of their bills.

Required.

Discuss the control techniques that could prevent or detect this fraud.

8. Santa'sAttic.com

Santa'sAttic.com is an on-line retailer/manufacturer of children's toys. Its main competitors are larger e-commerce toy companies including Amazon.com; Yahoo Shopping, which includes ToysRUs.com and KBKids.com; and all of the other retail stores with on-line shopping. It has a low market share compared to the industry leaders, and is possibly a victim of Internet fraud. The CEO of Santa'sAttic.com has noticed that the level of accounts receivable has been quite high in comparison to prior years. He is wondering if this is a sign of weak internal controls. He has also heard through the grapevine that some of his customers were noticing unauthorized charges on their credit cards, and is wondering if there may be on-line security issues to deal with as well. For this reason, you have been contacted to help Santa'sAttic.com restructure its company to prevent possible company failure.

Santa'sAttic.com employs 100 individuals, 75 of which work directly on the manufacturing line and 25 of which hold administrative positions. Its customer base consists mainly of individuals, but also smaller toy stores, day care centers, and schools. Santa'sAttic. com works on a cash basis with its customers and accepts all major credit cards. It has running credit balances with all of its suppliers. Its credit terms are 2/10 n30. Santa'sAttic.com currently has only one warehouse, which is located in Cooperstown, New York. Being the technical genius that he is, the vice president of marketing took it upon himself to design the company Web site. The Web site has pages where customers can view all of the products and prices. There is a virtual shopping cart available for each customer once he/she has set up a demographical information account. If the customer chooses to make a purchase, he/she simply clicks on the direct link to the shopping cart from the product that he/she wishes to purchase and proceeds to the checkout. Here the customer is prompted to choose a payment method and enter the shipping address. Once this information has been entered, the customer chooses a shipping method. All shipping is done through U.S. Mail, UPS, Federal Express, Airborne Express, or Certified Mail. The customer is then informed of the total price and the date to expect shipment.

Within the purchasing system, Santa'sAttic.com purchases raw materials for production, such as plastics, wood, metal, and certain fabrics. There is no formal purchasing department at Santa'sAttic.com. Judy, the inventory clerk in the warehouse department, is responsible for all purchasing activity. Within the warehouse department, Judy has access to the inventory records and knows when certain materials have to be repurchased. If materials are needed, she prepares a single purchase requisition and also five copies of the purchase order form. Judy includes all of the necessary information on all copies of the form, including the material to be purchased, the price of the material, the quantity needed, and the requested delivery date. Once completed, two copies of the form are sent to the vendor along with the order. One is placed in the open purchase order file in the warehouse, and one is used to update the inventory records that are also kept within the warehouse department. The final copy is forwarded to the receiving department.

The materials are received by Harry, the receiving clerk, who creates four copies of a receiving report based on the packing slip and purchase order information. Two of these receiving reports are forwarded to the warehouse, where one is used to update inventory records and the other is filed. One copy of the receiving report is also maintained within the receiving department and is filed along with the packing slip and the purchase order. The final copy is sent to the accounts payable department, where it is reconciled with the vendor invoice.

Once the receiving report and the vendor invoice are reconciled in the accounts payable department, the liability is posted to the purchases journal and the total amount due is paid to the vendor. Finally, both the receiving report and the invoice are filed within the accounts payable de-

partment and the liability is posted to the general ledger by Joanna, the accounts payable clerk.

Santa'sAttic.com's production workers each have timecards that they punch at a punch-in station in the morning when they arrive, and again in the evening when they leave. The punch-in station is located at the entrance to the plant and is not monitored. At the end of the week, the supervisor authorizes the timecards by reviewing them and signing them, and then sends the timecards to cash disbursements. Supervisors do not keep their own attendance records. Rose, in cash disbursements, receives the timecards and reconciles them with personnel records on the company database to verify the timecards for accuracy. All personnel records are maintained in a database. Access to the database is very restricted. Personnel can update the records only once a year. Rose's only view displays employee demographic information and does not allow access to salary information. Rose prepares the paychecks and signs them. She then prepares the payroll register using only information gained from the timecards. Sally in accounts payable receives a copy of the payroll register and uses it to update the general ledger. Accounts payable receives no information besides the payroll register. Rose, in cash disbursements, hands the prepared paychecks to the supervisors of each department for distribution. All checks are written directly from the company's only cash account. Supervisors distribute the checks directly to the employees and themselves.

Engaging in electronic commerce has exposed Santa'sAttic.com to a whole new nature of risks within its real-time revenue cycle. A customer has the option of paying for the product by credit card or personal check. Upon entering the credit card information, it becomes attached to the customer's e-mail file. This information includes the type of card, the customer's name as it appears on the card, the credit card number, and the expiration date. Once an order is placed, an employee reviews the order in question, verifies credit, and enters the transaction into Santa'sAttic.com's main database.

The main problem with this system is that orders have been placed with the company where the customer in question honestly denies ever submitting orders. It turns out that many of these orders have been placed by their children, without the customer's knowledge. The children were able to gain access to their parent's account after the system recognized cookies in the hard drive. When the children went to the Web site, the page recognized them as the users of the account and gave them authorized access to make purchases.

Another problem with the information in the revenue cycle has been that hackers have been able to enter the database and obtain information concerning customers. This unauthorized access has sent top management in a frenzy knowing that their customer information is insecure.

Required:

a. Discuss the control and security weaknesses in this system.

b. Make specific recommendations for improving controls.

4

SYSTEMS DEVELOPMENT ACTIVITIES

13

The Systems Development Process, Part I: Introduction to the Systems Development Life Cycle

One of the most valuable assets of the modern business organization is a responsive, user-oriented information system. A well-designed system can increase productivity, reduce inventories, eliminate nonvalue-added activities, improve customer service and management decisions, and coordinate activities throughout the organization.

This chapter examines several related topics. The first section in the chapter introduces the systems development life cycle (SDLC). This multistage procedure is used to guide the development of information systems in many organizations. The second section examines two automated techniques that improve the systems development process. These are prototyping and computer-aided software engineering. The third section reviews the objectives and activities associated with the first two stages in the SDLC process—systems planning and systems analysis. The third stage in the SDLC process—Conceptual systems design—is covered in the final section of the chapter.

LEARNING OBJECTIVES

After studying this chapter, you should:

- Be able to identify the seven stages in the SDLC.
- Be familiar with common problems that can lead to failure in the systems development process.
- Understand how prototyping and computer-aided software engineering can be employed in the systems development process.
- Understand the importance of strategic planning for systems.
- Understand what transpires during systems analysis.
- Understand the basic features of both the structured and object-oriented approaches to systems design.
- Have a general understanding of how accountants participate in the SDLC activities covered in the chapter.

IN-HOUSE SYSTEMS DEVELOPMENT

Organizations usually acquire information systems in two ways: (1) they develop customized systems in-house through formal systems development activities and (2) they purchase commercial systems from software vendors. Numerous commercial vendors offer high-quality, general-purpose information systems. These vendors primarily serve organizations with generic information needs. Typically, their client firms have business practices so standardized that they can purchase predesigned information systems and employ them with little or no modifications. However, many organizations require systems that are highly tuned to their unique operations. These firms design their own information systems through in-house systems development activities.

Each approach has its advantages and disadvantages, but they are not mutually exclusive options. A firm may satisfy some of its information systems needs by purchasing commercial software and develop other systems in-house. This chapter is concerned primarily with in-house systems development. The issues pertaining to the purchase of commercial software are discussed in the next chapter.

THE SYSTEMS DEVELOPMENT LIFE CYCLE

Many moderate- and large-sized firms maintain an internal computer services group that designs customized computer systems to meet the organization's unique information requirements. These systems are developed through a formal process called the **systems development life cycle (SDLC)**, which is depicted in Figure 13–1.

The objectives and sequence of SDLC activities are logical and generally accepted by experts in the systems community. However, the number and the names of specific stages within this process are matters of some disagreement. Different authorities have proposed SDLC models with as few as 4 and as many as 14 specific activities. From an accounting point of view, the number of actual stages is of no

---

FIGURE 13–1   Systems Development Life Cycle

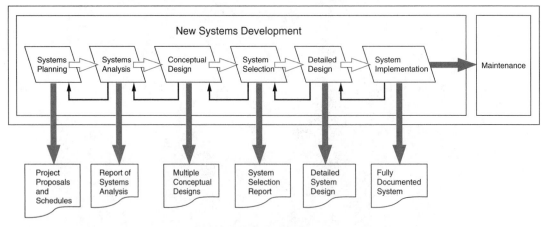

Required Documentation

particular importance. We are concerned about the substance and the consistent application of this process, however it is defined. The SDLC in Figure 13–1 is a seven-stage process consisting of two major phases: new systems development and maintenance.

New Systems Development

The first six stages of the SDLC describe the activities that all new systems should undergo. **New systems development** involves five steps: identify the problem, understand what is to be done, consider alternative solutions, select the best solution, and, finally, implement the solution. Notice that each stage of the SDLC produces a set of documentation that marks the completion of the stage.

Two chapters are devoted to this body of material. In this chapter, we look at systems planning, systems analysis, and conceptual design. The next chapter covers system selection, detailed design, and system implementation.

Maintenance

Once a system is implemented, it enters the second phase in its life cycle—maintenance. **Maintenance** involves changing systems to accommodate changes in user needs. This may be relatively trivial, such as modifying the system to produce a new report or changing the length of a data field. Maintenance may also be more extensive, such as making major changes to an application's logic and user interface. For some organizations, the systems maintenance period of the SDLC may last from five to ten years. However, businesses that must respond to frequent changes in technology or business processes may see shorter system life spans. When it is no longer feasible for the organization to maintain and continue with its current system, the system is scrapped, and a new systems development life cycle begins.

Maintenance represents a significant resource outlay compared to initial development costs. Over a system's life span, as much as 80 to 90 percent of its total cost may be incurred in the maintenance phase. We shall investigate the accounting implications of maintenance in Chapters 15 and 17 as part of our treatment of computer controls and auditing.

Front End and Back End

The first four stages in the SDLC are often called *front end activities*. These are concerned with what the system should do. The last three stages are the *back end activities*. These stages deal with the technical issues of how the physical system will accomplish its objectives.

Participants in Systems Development

The participants in systems development can be classified into three broad groups: systems professionals, end users, and stakeholders.

Systems professionals are systems analysts, systems designers, and programmers. These individuals actually build the system. They gather facts about problems with the current system, analyze these facts, and formulate a solution to solve the problems. The product of their efforts is a new system.

End users are those for whom the system is built. There are many users at all levels in an organization. These include managers, operations personnel, accountants, and internal auditors. In some organizations, it is difficult to find someone who is not a user. During systems development, systems professionals work with the primary users to obtain an understanding of the users' problems and a clear statement of their needs.

As defined in Chapter 1, **stakeholders** are individuals either within or outside the organization who have an interest in the system but are not end users. These include accountants, internal auditors, external auditors, and the internal steering committee that oversees systems development.[1] We shall discuss the steering committee later in this chapter. For the moment, let's examine the role of accountants in systems development.

Why Are Accountants Involved with SDLC?

The SDLC process is of interest to accountants for two reasons. First, the creation of an information system represents a significant financial transaction that consumes both financial and human resources. Systems development is like any manufacturing process that produces a complex product through a series of stages. Such transactions must be planned, authorized, scheduled, accounted for, and controlled. Accountants are as concerned with the integrity of this process as they are with any manufacturing process that has financial resource implications.

The second and more pressing concern for accountants is with the products that emerge from the SDLC. The quality of accounting information systems rests directly on the SDLC activities that produce them. These systems are used to deliver accounting information to internal and external users. The accountant's responsibility is to ensure that the systems apply proper accounting conventions and rules, and possess adequate controls. Therefore, accountants are concerned with the quality of the process that produces accounting information systems. For example, a sales order system produced by a defective SDLC may suffer from serious control weaknesses that introduce errors into the financial accounting records.

How Are Accountants Involved with SDLC?

Accountants are involved in systems development in three ways. First, accountants are users. All systems that process financial transactions impact the accounting function in some way. Like all users, accountants must provide a clear picture of their problems and needs to the systems professional. For example, accountants must specify accounting techniques to be used, internal control requirements (such as audit trails), and special algorithms (such as depreciation models).

Second, accountants participate in systems development as members of the development team. Their involvement often extends beyond the development of strictly AIS applications. Systems that do not process financial transactions may still draw on accounting data. The accountant may be consulted to provide advice or to determine if the proposed system constitutes an internal control risk.

Third, accountants are involved in systems development as auditors. Accounting information systems must be auditable. Some computer audit techniques require special features that must be designed into the system. The auditor/accountant has a stake in such systems and must be involved early in their design.

---

1   Accountants and auditors are end users of some systems but are stakeholders in all accounting information systems.

IMPROVING SYSTEMS DEVELOPMENT THROUGH AUTOMATION

Systems development projects are not always success stories. In fact, by the time they are implemented, some systems are obsolete or defective and must be replaced. Estimates hold that up to 25 percent of all systems projects fail. That is, they are terminated prematurely and never implemented, or they must be redesigned within six months of implementation. Historically, the SDLC has been plagued by three problems that account for most systems failures. These problems are discussed below.

1. *Poorly specified systems requirements.* Systems development is not a precise science. The process involves human communications and the sharing of ideas between users and systems professionals. This information exchange is often imperfect. Mistakes are made in identifying problems and needs, new ideas emerge as the true nature of the problem unfolds, and people simply change their minds about what they really want and need from the system.

    Because of this uncertainty, the SDLC tends not to be a smooth, linear process, where one stage is completed before the next one begins. In reality, the process is iterative or cyclical. Notice the two arrows between each block in Figure 13–1 and how they point in opposite directions. For example, it is not uncommon for a systems designer to return to the analysis stage from the conceptual design stage to gather additional information as his or her perception of the problem changes.

    The cyclical nature of this process results in time-consuming false starts, much repeated work, and pressure from all fronts to get the job done. Too often, the result is a system that is poorly designed, over budget, and behind schedule.

2. *Ineffective development techniques.* The problems cited above are amplified by ineffective techniques for presenting, documenting, and modifying systems specifications. In the worst-case scenario, systems development tools are simply paper, pencils, rulers, templates, and erasers. The situation is improved considerably by the use of PC-based graphics software that permits original designs and changes to be made electronically. Nevertheless, days or even weeks of work may need to be redone because of a change in a system's specifications.

3. *Lack of user involvement in systems development.* The major cause of systems failure is the lack of end user involvement during critical development stages. At one time, computer systems development was thought to be the exclusive domain of the systems professionals. During this period, users (including accountants) abdicated their traditional responsibility for systems design. Too often, this led to business problems because systems designs reflected the analyst's perception of information needs rather than the perception of accountants and other users. Systems often lacked adequate controls and audit trails.

Today, we recognize that user involvement in a system's development is the key to its ultimate success. However, achieving competent user involvement is still difficult to accomplish. There are two reasons for this: (1) users tend to become discouraged when they discover the amount of time they must actually invest and (2) communication between end users and systems professionals is generally not fluent. It is often said that these groups speak different languages. Each tends to resort to its own jargon when communicating with the other. Therefore, much time is spent identifying user problems and needs and formulating acceptable solutions. Miscommunications between users and systems professionals lead to mistakes that, sometimes, are discovered too late.

These problems have led researchers to seek ways to improve the development process. The focus of this effort has been on techniques to reduce development time, facilitate better information transfer, encourage user involvement, and improve overall systems quality. In the following sections, we consider two widely used techniques: prototyping and computer-aided software engineering (CASE).

PROTOTYPING

Prototyping is a technique for providing users a preliminary working version of the system. The prototype is built quickly and inexpensively with the intention that it will be modified. The objective of this technique is for the prototype to represent "an unambiguous functional specification, serve as a vehicle for organizing and learning, and evolve ultimately into a fully implemented" system.[2] As the users work with the prototype and make suggestions for changes, both they and the systems professional develop a better understanding of the true requirements of the system.

The costs of a prototype model are kept low by reducing its features to the essential elements. For example, the prototype system will not contain the complex code necessary to perform transaction validation, exception-handling capabilities, and internal controls. Typically, prototypes are limited to user input screens, output reports, and some principle functions.

When incorporated in the front end stages of the SDLC, prototyping is an effective tool for establishing user requirements. Once these are obtained, the prototype is discarded. This throwaway prototyping is used for developing structured applications, such as accounting systems.[3] An alternative technique continues the prototyping process until the system is completed. This approach is used for developing decision support systems and expert systems. Figure 13–2 illustrates the prototyping model.

FIGURE 13–2   Prototyping Techniques

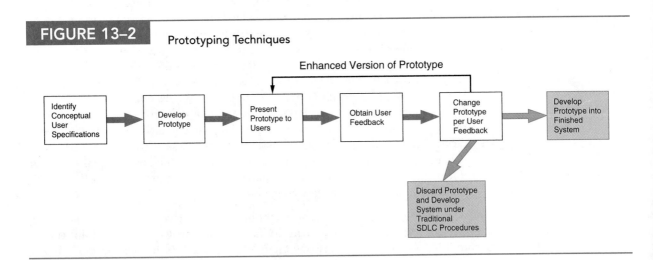

---

2   J. C. Emery, *Management Information Systems: The Critical Strategic Resource* (New York: Oxford University Press, 1987): 325.

3   V. Zwass, *Management Information Systems* (Dubuque, Iowa: Wm. C. Brown, 1992): 740.

THE CASE
APPROACH

Computer-aided software engineering (CASE) technology involves the use of computer systems to build computer systems. CASE tools are commercial software products consisting of highly integrated applications that support a wide range of SDLC activities. This methodology was developed to increase the productivity of systems professionals, improve systems design quality, and expedite the SDLC.

Most CASE products comprise both upper and lower tools or applications. Upper CASE tools support the conceptual activities of analysis and design. Lower CASE tools support the physical activities associated with system implementation and program maintenance. Figure 13–3 presents the CASE spectrum of support in relation to the relevant stages of the SDLC. CASE tools are used to define user requirements, create physical databases from conceptual user views, produce systems design specifications, automatically generate computer program code, and facilitate the maintenance of programs created by both CASE and non-CASE techniques. Figure 13–4 presents an overview diagram of a comprehensive CASE system. The sections below follow the main points of this diagram.

Central Repository

The heart of the CASE system is the **central repository**. Essentially, this is a database of attributes, relations, and elements that describe all the applications created under the CASE system. These items include:

1. Definitions of all databases.
2. Systems documentation, such as context diagrams, data flow diagrams, and structure charts.
3. The program code.
4. Reusable program modules.
5. User prototype screens.

The central repository system helps to integrate the activities of systems designers working on the same project or on separate but related projects. For example, if the

---

FIGURE 13–3   CASE Spectrum of Support Tools for the SDLC

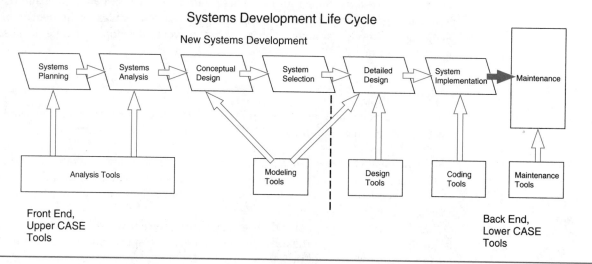

FIGURE 13–4   Overview of CASE System

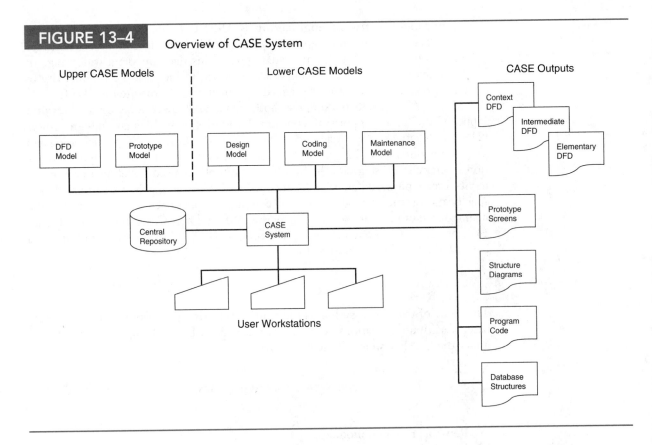

size or the name of a data attribute must be changed, then all the applications that use that attribute must also be changed. In a moderate-sized firm, this could involve hundreds of programs. Normally, this would require many days of manual searching to identify the affected programs. However, the central repository system can quickly identify and list the applications that use the attribute being changed. Another example of the integration of activities is the ability to reuse program code. Different applications may use the same routines. These routines can be created, tested, and then used many times. The central repository stores reusable modules for immediate implementation in other systems. This reduces the overall development time of subsequent applications.

CASE Models

CASE products employ several functional models that can be used to support activities in different phases of the SDLC. The following models are representative.

The Data Flow Diagram Model. We introduced the data flow diagram in Chapter 2. This section presents a more extensive use of this documentation technique. The DFD uses a set of symbols to represent the processes, data sources, data flows, and process sequences of a current or proposed system.

As a systems design tool, DFDs are used to represent multiple levels of detail. From the most general to the most detailed, these are, respectively, the context level, the intermediate level, and the elementary level.

The Context Level DFD. The analyst can use the context level DFD to present an overview model of the business activities and the primary transactions processed by the system. Figure 13–5 presents an example of a context diagram of the revenue cycle for a company. The context diagram is a very high-level representation of the system. It does not include a detailed definition of data files and specific procedures. The focus is on the overall relationship between the entities (data, sources of data, and processes) in the system. This relationship is represented by symbols, lines, and arrows that show the direction of the data flows.

The Intermediate Level DFD. The next step is to explode the context level DFD into one or more intermediate level DFDs, as illustrated in Figure 13–6. Notice how Process 1.0 in Figure 13–5 is decomposed into the following subprocesses.

    1.1 Sales Approval
    1.2 Ship Goods
    1.3 Bill Customer
    1.4 Update Accounts Receivable

Several levels of intermediate DFDs may be needed to present enough detail for the systems professional and user to fully understand the system. In this example, we show only one intermediate level.

The Elementary Level DFD. Figure 13–7 presents the elementary level DFD for Process 1.3 in Figure 13–6. An elementary level DFD provides a clear and precise definition of all elements of a portion of the system. In this example, Process 1.3 (bill customer) is explained in detail. Other elementary level DFDs will be required for Processes 1.1, 1.2, and 1.4.

The preparation of DFDs in a non-CASE environment can be time-consuming for the analyst. Because of inevitable changes in specifications during the system's development, the analyst may produce many versions of the DFD documents before arriving at the final product. The graphics capability of CASE tools greatly expedites this task by providing functions for labeling, modifying, and rearranging the DFD. However, the CASE DFD is more than simply a graphic representation of the

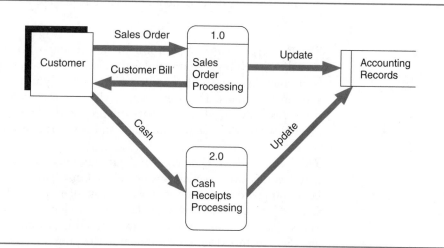

FIGURE 13–5

Context Level Data
Flow Diagram for the
Revenue Cycle

FIGURE 13–6   Intermediate Level Data Flow Diagram for Sales Order Processing System

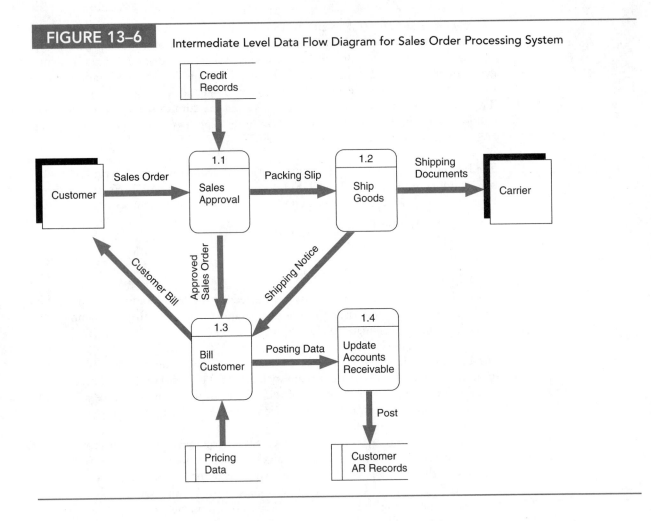

system. The elementary level DFD is the physical input to lower CASE models that automatically produce program code and database tables. Any and all changes to the system during its development and maintenance are thus made directly through the DFD.

The Prototype Model. The prototype model supports the prototyping concept presented earlier. This is a powerful feature that helps ensure that user requirements are being met. Systems professionals can immediately provide users with input screens and report formats. The user can thus visualize certain features of the system before it is actually designed and evaluate the proposed system. Any changes can be implemented before the system is designed and at virtually no cost to the project schedule.

The Design Model. The logic of the design model is based upon the concept of system decomposition, which was introduced in Chapter 1. Recall that any system can be decomposed from the top down into smaller and smaller subsystems, each with a specific function. The design model takes the elementary level DFD as input and produces from this a structure diagram. The DFD is a model of the conceptual system, and the structure diagram is a model of the program code that constitutes the physi-

FIGURE 13–7   Elementary Level Data Flow Diagram for the Billing Process

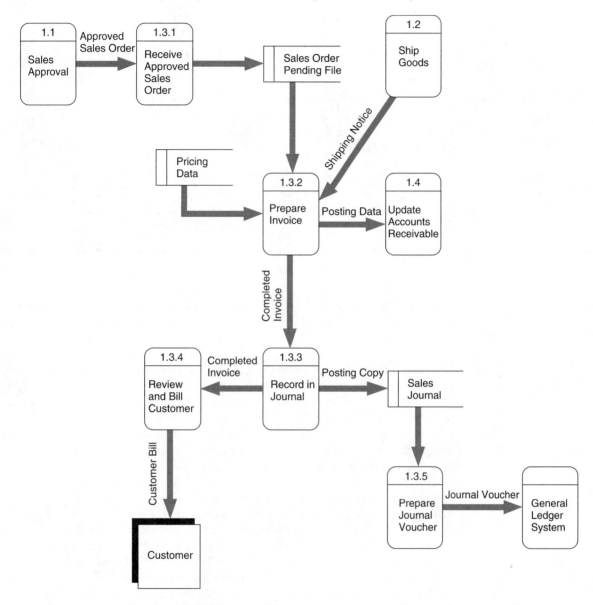

cal system. Figure 13–8 shows a structure diagram for the elementary level DFD in Figure 13–7. The structure diagram shows the overall relationship between the modules that constitute the system. Each of these modules represents a separate program that must be coded, unless it already exists as a reusable program module. We examine the issue of reusable modules later in the chapter.

Many CASE tools document the details of each module in the form of pseudocode or structured English. Pseudocode tells the reviewers (analyst, auditor, or programmer) of the structure diagram exactly what the module is supposed to do,

FIGURE 13-8   Structure Diagram for Elementary Level DFD of the Billing Process in Figure 13-7

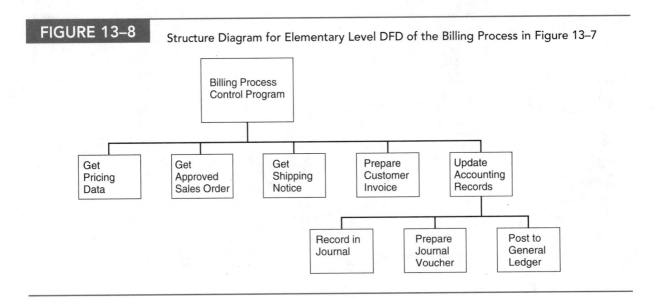

regardless of the programming language used. We examine more closely the relationship between DFDs and structure diagrams, and the use of pseudocode, in Chapter 14.

The Coding Model. One of the great labor-saving advantages of CASE is its facility for transforming the structure diagram into computer modules. Many top-end CASE tools produce program source code, such as COBOL, C, and C++. These source programs must then be compiled (translated) into executable machine code modules.

Some CASE tools convert the structure diagrams directly to machine code and eliminate the source-code stage. The reason for this is to preserve the integrity between the conceptual system model (the DFD) and the physical system (the program). Sometimes during maintenance or original development, systems specialists are tempted to make design changes directly to the source code. If these changes are not also made to the DFDs and structure diagrams that specify the system, there will be a discrepancy between what the documentation that describes what the program does and the actual program. By eliminating the source code, the systems professional is forced to make all systems changes via the DFDs. The CASE tool will then modify the structure diagrams and rewrite the computer (machine level) code automatically. This ensures that the system's description is always consistent with the program code.

The nonsource code approach has two implications for accountants, auditors, and management. The first is a potential control issue. The program source code is part of the system documentation. To properly design their test procedures, auditors sometimes need to review the source code. If it is not available, this may hamper testing and force the auditor to employ alternative, less efficient, and more costly procedures. Second, the nonsource code approach can have the effect of committing the firm to a particular CASE tool and vendor. By creating source code as a by-product of the development process, the application remains independent of the CASE system. Should the firm's management decide to switch to another vendor, current applications can still be maintained. Most CASE tools will accept source programs written in standard source code.

The Maintenance Model. Eighty to 90 percent of the total cost of a system is expended during the maintenance phase of the SDLC. This is often referred to as the "iceberg effect." Figure 13–9 illustrates this phenomenon. All systems must be maintained throughout their lives, and some iceberg effect is inevitable. However, poorly designed systems can significantly contribute to the problem. To make a change to a computer program in a non-CASE environment, the maintenance programmer must first thoroughly review the program code in an attempt to understand the original programmer's logic. This review often requires a great deal of time and is protracted by awkward, inefficient, and redundant program logic. Even companies that use CASE tools will have some badly designed systems. Often these systems are old and precede CASE usage.

The CASE maintenance model facilitates program maintenance and greatly reduces the iceberg effect. Applications originally developed under CASE are relatively easy to maintain. The maintenance programmer reviews the documentation for the application and makes the required changes, at the conceptual level, to the DFDs. The CASE system then makes the changes to the structure diagrams and program code automatically. Finally, the programmer thoroughly tests and installs the modified application.

CASE tools can also be used to maintain applications that were not originally developed under the CASE system. The CASE maintenance model provides two such tools for this purpose: reverse engineering and reengineering. Reverse engineering extracts from the source code meaningful design specifications that the maintenance programmer can use to understand the application logic. Reengineering restructures and documents the old source code logic to conform to CASE standards. This in-

FIGURE 13–9

The Iceberg Effect

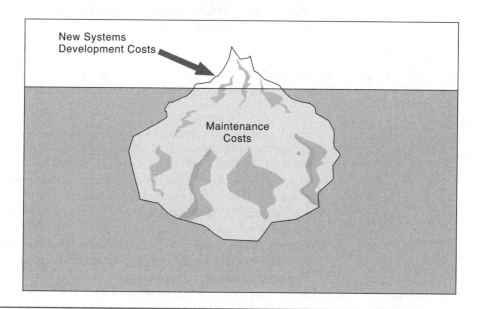

New Systems Development Costs

Maintenance Costs

cludes preparing DFDs and structure diagrams. Thus, future maintenance of the system can proceed as if the application were originally created under CASE.

Advantages of CASE

The following is a list of the commonly cited advantages of the CASE approach.

1. *Reduced system complexity.* CASE systems are more easily comprehended than traditional methods and support structured logic concepts.
2. *Increased flexibility.* The systems development process does not usually proceed in a purely linear fashion in which each stage is totally complete before the next one begins. Rather, it tends to be a cyclical process. It will be necessary to return to a previous stage if proceeding to the next stage will result in a flawed design or an improper implementation. As the details of the problem unfold in the downstream stages, it may be necessary to reconsider and revise upstream models. Compared to manual techniques, CASE provides a great deal of flexibility to the analyst in making such revisions.
3. *Capacity to review alternative designs.* Because CASE systems can be rapidly produced and changed, users and systems specialists can review prototypes of many alternative designs before committing to a particular system.
4. *Quicker development process.* The development process under CASE is three to six times faster than traditional methods, depending on the complexity of the system and the degree of CASE expertise within the firm.
5. *Promotion of user involvement.* Through its prototyping features, CASE has great potential for improving user involvement in the development process. We discuss this point in more detail in the next section.
6. *Reusable program code and documentation.* The central repository feature allows CASE systems to share common program modules and documentation.
7. *Reduced maintenance cost.* By maintaining the system at the conceptual level, maintenance time and programming errors are reduced. This translates into a more efficient process that responds more quickly to user needs. The iceberg effect is reduced by as much as 50 percent.

Disadvantages of CASE

In spite of these many virtues, CASE is not without its disadvantages, including:

1. *Product cost.* The cost of a CASE system is proportional to its features and sophistication. Microcomputer CASE tools with limited features may be obtained for hundreds of dollars. Fully equipped CASE tools for a mainframe environment can cost hundreds of thousands of dollars.
2. *Start-up time and cost.* Developing a pool of CASE expertise within the organization takes time. Systems professionals must be trained, and the learning curve for sophisticated CASE systems is steep.
3. *Incompatible CASE tools.* The hundreds of CASE products on the market are often incompatible with one another. This limits a firm's choices when selecting CASE tools and tends to tie the firm to a single product and vendor.
4. *Program inefficiency.* The source code produced by CASE tools is not as efficient as code written by a skilled programmer. To improve program efficiency, programmers often modify the CASE-generated modules. This practice can produce discrepancies between the DFD system logic and the program logic.

SYSTEMS PLANNING AND SYSTEMS ANALYSIS

We are now ready to begin our examination of the SDLC. All the stages in the SDLC are enhanced to some degree by the techniques discussed in the previous section. In practice, some are affected more than others, but none of them depends solely on these techniques. Therefore, we shall treat the SDLC subject matter conceptually. That is, the focus will be on *what* is done rather than *how* it is done. The remainder of this chapter is devoted to the first three stages of the SDLC (see Figure 13–10). In this section, we examine stages one and two—systems planning and systems analysis. We study stage three of the DSLC—conceptual systems design—in the last section.

SYSTEMS PLANNING

The objective of **systems planning** is to link individual system projects or applications to the strategic objectives of the firm. In fact, the basis for the systems plan is the organization's business plan, which specifies where the firm plans to go and how it will get there. Figure 13–11 presents the relationship between these plans and the strategic objectives of the firm. There must be congruence between the individual projects and the business plan, or the firm may fail to meet its objectives. Effective systems planning provides this goal congruence.

Who Should Do Systems Planning?

Most firms that take systems planning seriously establish a systems steering committee to provide guidance and review the status of system projects. The composition of the **steering committee** may include the chief executive officer, the chief financial officer, the chief information officer, senior management from user areas, the

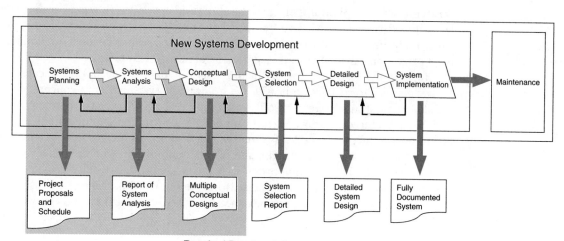

FIGURE 13–10   Systems Development Life Cycle

Required Documentation

FIGURE 13–11   Relationship between Systems Plans and Organizational Objectives

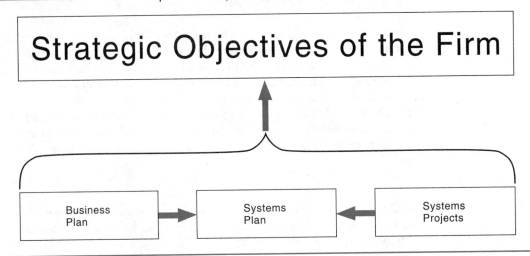

internal auditor, and senior management from computer services. The committee may also be supplemented by external parties, such as management consultants and the firm's external auditors. Typical responsibilities for a steering committee include:

1. Resolving conflicts that arise from new systems.
2. Reviewing projects and assigning priorities.
3. Budgeting funds for systems development.
4. Reviewing the status of individual projects under development.
5. Determining at various checkpoints throughout the SDLC whether to continue with the project or terminate it.

Systems planning occurs at two levels: strategic systems planning and project planning.

STRATEGIC SYSTEMS PLANNING

Strategic systems planning involves the allocation of systems resources at the macro level. It usually deals with a time frame of three to five years. This process is very similar to budgeting resources for other strategic activities, such as product development, plant expansions, market research, and manufacturing technology.

Technically, strategic systems planning is not part of the SDLC because the SDLC pertains to specific applications. The strategic systems plan is concerned with the allocation of such systems resources as employees (the number of systems professionals to be hired), hardware (the number of workstations, minicomputers, and mainframes to be purchased), software (the funds to be allocated to new systems projects and for systems maintenance), and telecommunications (the funds allocated to networking and EDI). It is important that the strategic plan avoid excessive detail. The plan must allow systems specialists to make informed decisions by considering such relevant factors as price, performance measures, size, security, and control.

Why Perform Strategic Systems Planning?
Perhaps no aspect of a firm's business activities is as volatile and unpredictable as information systems planning. Who can look five years into the future and accurately

predict the state of systems technology? Because of this volatility, any long-term plans a firm makes are likely to change. How, therefore, can a firm do strategic systems planning? Why should it do it?

There are three justifications for strategic systems planning:

1.   A plan that changes constantly is better than no plan at all. Strategic planning charts the path the firm will follow to reach its information systems goal. Even if it means making many midcourse adjustments, planning is superior to simply wandering in the wilderness.
2.   Strategic planning reduces the crisis component in systems development. A formal plan is a model for identifying and prioritizing user needs. It allows management to consider future needs, recognize problems in their early stages, and even anticipate needs before the symptoms of underlying problems emerge. In the absence of a plan, the trigger that stimulates systems development is the recognition of a problem. Often problems reach a crisis level before they receive attention, which adversely affects the quality of the solution.
3.   Strategic systems planning provides authorization control for the SDLC. The SDLC is similar to the fixed asset system described in Chapter 6. In this case, the fixed asset is the new system, and the acquisition process is the SDLC. Systems planning is the authorization step for this transaction. The strategic systems plan lays out authorization rules to ensure that decisions to develop specific systems are congruent with the objectives of the firm. Investing in the wrong systems can be just as damaging to a firm as investing in the wrong plant and equipment.

PROJECT PLANNING

The purpose of **project planning** is to allocate resources to individual applications within the framework of the strategic plan. This involves identifying areas of user needs, preparing proposals, evaluating each proposal's feasibility and contribution to the business plan, prioritizing individual projects, and scheduling the work to be done. The product of this phase consists of two formal documents: the project proposal and the project schedule.

The remainder of this section deals with project planning, which includes the following steps:

1.   Recognizing the problem.
2.   Defining the problem.
3.   Specifying system objectives.
4.   Determining project feasibility.
5.   Preparing a formal project proposal.
6.   Evaluating and prioritizing competing proposals.
7.   Producing a project schedule.
8.   Announcing the new system project.

We conclude the section by examining the accountant's role in systems planning.

RECOGNIZING THE PROBLEM

The need for a new, improved information system may be manifested in various symptoms. In the early stages of a problem, these symptoms may seem vague and innocuous or may go unrecognized. However, as the underlying source of the problem grows in severity, so do its symptoms, until they are alarmingly apparent. At this point, operations may have reached a state of crisis. The point at which the problem is recognized is therefore important. This is often a function of the philosophy of a firm's management. The reactive management philosophy characterizes an extreme position; in contrast to this is the philosophy of proactive management.

Reactive management responds to problems only when they reach a crisis state and can no longer be ignored. This approach creates a great deal of pressure to quickly solve the problem once it has been recognized. Too often, this results in hurried analysis, incomplete problem identification, shortcuts in design, poor user participation, and the final product of a generally suboptimal solution.

Proactive management stays alert to subtle signs of problems and aggressively looks for ways to improve the organization's systems. This management style is more likely to recognize symptoms early and, therefore, implement better solutions. Early problem detection avoids the crisis stage and provides the time necessary for a complete and thorough study.

Who Reports Problem Symptoms?

Typically, symptoms are first reported by lower-level managers and operations personnel. Being in continuous contact with their systems, these individuals are quick to notice operational difficulties with customers, suppliers, and the financial community. As a result, most systems requests originate with lower-level management.

Occasionally, top management initiates systems requests. This usually occurs when the firm is seeking competitive advantage rather than merely improved operational performance from the system. Systems initiated at this level tend to have a profound impact on the organization and its activities.

On rare occasions, computer specialists will identify problem symptoms and will initiate a systems solution. However, computer specialists are seldom involved with the daily operations of systems and are not likely to be aware of problems until contacted by users.

DEFINING THE PROBLEM

It is tempting to take a leap in logic from symptom recognition to problem definition. The manager (user) must avoid this. It is important to keep an open mind and avoid drawing conclusions about the nature of the problem that may direct attention and resources in the wrong direction. For example, increased product returns, excessive delays in product shipments to customers, excessive overtime for operations personnel, and slow inventory turnover rates are all problem symptoms. These are evidence of underlying problems, but do not, in themselves, define the problems. The manager must learn enough about the problem to intelligently pursue a solution. However, the manager cannot collect all the information needed to accurately define the problem and specify a solution. This would require a detailed system evaluation. The manager must specify the nature of the problem as he or she sees it based on the nature of the difficulties identified.

The manager reports this problem definition to the computer systems professionals within the firm. This begins an interactive process between the systems professionals and the user, which results in a formal project proposal that will go before the steering committee for approval. The following three stages in the planning phase—specifying system objectives, determining project feasibility, and preparing a formal project proposal—represent the cooperative efforts of the manager and the systems professional.

SPECIFYING SYSTEM OBJECTIVES

There must be harmony between the strategic objectives of the firm and the operational objectives of the information system. Broad strategic objectives shape the narrower functional objectives at the tactical and operations levels. These functional objectives lead to the identification of information needs and serve to set out the operational objectives for the information system.

For example, a firm might have the strategic objective of maintaining a 15 percent market share. To achieve this objective, let's assume the production function must produce 500,000 units of product within certain budgetary constraints. The production managers charged with this responsibility must, therefore, receive information pertaining to such critical factors as production levels, production costs, available plant capacity, and workforce capacity and requirements.

The operational objectives of the information system are to satisfy these identified information needs. At this point in the SDLC, we need only define the objectives in general terms. Later in the process, we will translate these into precise system requirements.

DETERMINING PROJECT FEASIBILITY

A preliminary **project feasibility** study is conducted at this early stage to determine how best to proceed with the project. By assessing the major constraints on the proposed system, management can evaluate the project's feasibility, or likelihood for success, before committing large amounts of financial and human resources. Some important feasibility issues are discussed below.

Technical feasibility is concerned with whether the system can be developed under existing technology or if new technology is needed. As a general proposition, the technology in the marketplace is far ahead of most firms' ability to apply it. Therefore, from an availability viewpoint, technical feasibility is not usually an issue. For most firms, the real issue is their desire and ability to apply available technology. Given that technology is the physical basis for most of the system's design features, this aspect bears heavily on the overall feasibility of the proposed system.

Economic feasibility pertains to the availability of funds to complete the project. In Chapter 14, as part of system justification and selection, we shall perform a cost-benefit analysis to identify the best system design for the cost. At this point, we are concerned with management's financial commitment to this project in view of other competing capital projects under consideration. The level of available economic support directly impacts the operational nature and scope of the proposed system.

Legal feasibility identifies any conflicts between the proposed system and the company's ability to discharge its legal responsibilities. In previous chapters, we have studied the need to comply with the control requirement laid down in the Foreign Corrupt Practices Act of 1977 and SAS 78. In addition, many regulations and statutes deal with invasion of privacy and the confidentiality of stored information. We must be certain the proposed system falls inside all legal boundaries.

Operational feasibility shows the degree of compatibility between the firm's existing procedures and personnel skills and the operational requirements of the new system. Implementing the new system may require adopting new procedures and retraining operations personnel. The question that must be answered is, can enough procedural changes be made, personnel retrained, and new skills obtained to make the system operationally feasible?

Schedule feasibility relates to the firm's ability to implement the project within an acceptable time. This feasibility factor impacts both the scope of the project and whether it will be developed in-house or purchased from a software vendor. If the project, as originally envisioned, cannot be produced internally by the target date, then its design, its acquisition method, or the target date must be changed.

PREPARING A FORMAL PROJECT PROPOSAL

The **systems project proposal** provides management with a basis for deciding whether or not to proceed with the project. The formal proposal serves two purposes. First, it summarizes the findings of the study conducted to this point into a general recommendation for a new or modified system. This enables management to evaluate the perceived problem along with the proposed system as a feasible solution. Second, the proposal outlines the linkage between the objectives of the proposed system and the business objectives of the firm. It shows that the proposed new system complements the strategic direction of the firm. Figure 13–12 shows an example of a project proposal.

EVALUATING AND PRIORITIZING COMPETING PROPOSALS

After a manageable number of system proposals have been received, members of the steering committee and systems professionals evaluate the pros and cons of each proposal. This is the first major decision point in a project's life cycle. If the committee approves a proposal, the project will undergo further detailed study and development. If a proposal is rejected, it will not be considered further within the current budgeting period. The proposals that remain under consideration are then evaluated on their relative merits, and a priority level is assigned to each. This process is outlined below.

FIGURE 13–12

System Project Proposal

```
                              Project Proposal
  Requested by: ____J.J. Johnson_____   Date: __11/13/01__

  Nature of System Requested: _Inventory Control System_____
  _____

  Reason for New System: __Better manage inventory, reduce obsolescence,
   increase turnover, and reduce inventory carrying costs_____
  _____

  Resource Requirements of New System:
              High      Moderate    Low
  Personnel    ☐          ☐         ☑
  Hardware     ☐          ☑         ☐
  Software     ☐          ☑         ☐

  Rate project's feasibility factors on a scale of 1 to 10 where 10 is most feasible:

  Technical Feasibility      _9_
  Economic Feasibility       _8_
  Legal Feasibility          _10_
  Operational Feasibility    _10_
  Schedule Feasibility       _8_

  Project Priority:  High _✓_   Moderate ____   Low ____
```

Assessing the Strategic Contribution of the System

An important step in the evaluation process is to identify those proposals that promise the greatest potential in supporting the business objectives of the firm. Two important strategic objectives are improved operational productivity and improved decision making.

Improved Operational Productivity. The proposed system should improve operational performance by eliminating nonessential activities and their associated costs. For example, a new EDI system may contribute to the firm's productivity by automating purchase processing activities. This may permit the firm to decrease costs by eliminating or reducing such tasks as carrying excess inventory, analyzing inventory requirements, preparing purchase requisitions and orders, and mailing purchase orders to vendors.

Improved Decision Making. We saw in Chapter 1 that a fundamental objective of an information system is to support management decisions. By providing quality information, an information system reduces uncertainty and improves management decisions. Furthermore, systems can relieve the burden on managers by automating highly structured decision making, thus freeing the managers to focus their attention on more complicated and unstructured problems.

Prioritizing Competing Proposals

Once each proposal has been evaluated in terms of its strategic contribution, the entire set of competing proposals can be prioritized. One method is to assign scores (say, from 1 to 10) to each proposal's five feasibility factors and strategic factors. These individual scores are converted to a composite score using a priority table. Figure 13–13 shows this process as applied to six competing proposals. The table gives management a comparative view of each project's feasibility and strategic potential. In this example, Projects X, L, and Z all have high priority scores and are candidates for development in the current fiscal year. Projects Y and Q are of moderate priority. They

FIGURE 13–13

Project Priority Table

Priority Factors	Project Proposals					
	L	M	Q	X	Y	Z
Strategic Factors						
Operational Productivity	8	3	5	9	8	8
Improved Decisions	9	2	4	9	9	8
Feasibility Factors						
Technical	8	1	7	8	5	7
Economic	9	2	6	8	4	9
Legal	8	3	7	9	6	8
Operational	9	2	8	9	5	8
Schedule	9	2	7	8	5	8
Composite Score	60	15	44	60	42	56

are worthy of further development but not within the current budget period. These projects will be reconsidered by the steering committee at a later date, along with any new proposals. Project M has low priority and is not a candidate for development.

PRODUCING A PROJECT SCHEDULE

The next step in the planning phase is to produce a **project schedule**. This document formally presents management's commitment to the project. Figure 13–14 illustrates a project schedule. The project schedule is a budget of the time and costs for all the phases of the SDLC. These phases will be completed by a project team selected from systems professionals, end users, and other specialists such as accountants and internal auditors. The composition of the team and the competence and dedication of its members are critical to the success of the new system.

ANNOUNCING THE NEW SYSTEM PROJECT

The last step of the planning process—management's formal announcement of the new system to the rest of the organization—is the most delicate aspect of the SDLC. This is an exceedingly important communiqué that, if successful, will pave the way for the new system and help ensure its acceptance among the user community.

A new system can sometimes generate considerable political backlash that may threaten its success. For example, not all users may understand the objectives of the

FIGURE 13–14   System Project Schedule

Project Schedule

Project Name _____   Date _____

Budget of Resources

Hardware Costs	XXXXX
Site Preparation	XXXX
Personnel Training	XXXX
Software Development	XXXXX
Total Resource Commitment	XXXXXX

Time Schedule of SDLC Phases

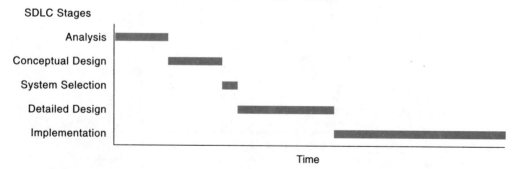

new system. In fact, some users may feel threatened by the uncertainty surrounding the system. As we have seen, new systems must improve the productivity and efficiency of operations. These objectives sometimes translate into organizational restructuring that erodes the personal power base of some users. Because of operational changes, some employees may be displaced or may be required to undergo retraining to function in the new workplace.

The fears that take root and grow in this environment of uncertainty are often revealed in acts of opposition, both overt and covert, to the new system. To minimize opposition, top management must quell unnecessary fears and fully explain the business rationale for the system before any formal development begins. If lower management and operating staff are assured that the new system will be beneficial, the project's chances for success are vastly improved.

We see the benefits of this top-down communication in the composition of the system project teams. End-user managers who view the new system as a potential benefit to their jobs, rather than a threat to their personal well being, are more likely to comply and cooperate with the project team's objectives. Managers are often called on to provide representatives to the project teams who must contribute information vital to the analysis and design of the system. The choice of representatives can shape the very nature of the system and determine its success or failure. When a manager supports the project, he or she will naturally assign the best and most experienced employees to the team. By so doing, business problems will be more clearly identified, operational constraints more accurately specified, and the resulting solutions more completely formulated.

THE ACCOUNTANT'S ROLE IN SYSTEMS PLANNING

During the planning process, accountants are often called on to provide expertise in evaluating the feasibility of projects. Their skills are particularly needed in specifying aspects of economic and legal feasibility. Also, in their role as auditor, accountants must routinely examine the systems planning phase of the SDLC. History has shown that careful systems planning is a cost-effective control technique in the systems development process. Planning greatly reduces the risk of producing unneeded, unwanted, inefficient, and ineffective systems. Both internal and external accountants are interested in ensuring that adequate systems planning takes place.

SYSTEMS ANALYSIS

We now move on to the second phase in the SDLC—systems analysis. **Systems analysis** is actually a two-step process involving first a survey of the current system and then an analysis of the user's needs. A business problem must be fully understood by the systems analyst before he or she can formulate a solution. An incomplete or defective analysis will lead to an incomplete or defective solution. Therefore, systems analysis is the foundation for the rest of the SDLC.

The deliverable product of this phase is a formal systems analysis report, which presents the findings of the analysis and recommendations for the new system.

THE SURVEY STEP

Most systems are not developed from scratch. Usually, some form of information system and related procedures are currently in place. The analyst often begins the analysis by determining what elements, if any, of the current system should be preserved as part of the new system. This involves a rather detailed **system survey**. Facts pertaining to preliminary questions about the system are gathered and analyzed. As the analyst obtains a greater depth of understanding of the problem, he or she develops more specific questions for which more facts must be gathered. This process may go on through several iterations. When all the relevant facts have been gathered and analyzed, the analyst arrives at an assessment of the current system. Surveying the current system has both disadvantages and advantages.

Disadvantages of Surveying the Current System

Perhaps the most compelling argument against a current system survey centers on a phenomenon known as the *current physical tar pit*.[4] This is the tendency on the part of the analyst to be "sucked in" and then "bogged down" by the task of surveying the current dinosaur system.

Some argue that current system surveys stifle new ideas. By studying and modeling the old system, the analyst may develop a constrained notion about how the new system should function. The result is an improved old system rather than a radically new approach. An example is the implementation of an ERP system. The task of reviewing current organizational procedures may serve no purpose since the successful implementation of an ERP depends on reengineering these processes to employ the best business practices of the industry.

Advantages of Surveying the Current System

There are three advantages to studying the current system. First, it is a way to identify what aspects of the old system should be kept. Some elements of the system may be functionally sound and can provide the foundation for the new system. By fully understanding the current system, the analyst can identify those aspects worth preserving or modifying for use in the new system.

Second, when the new system is implemented, the users must go through a conversion process whereby they formally break away from the old system and move to the new one. The analyst must determine what tasks, procedures, and data will be phased out with the old system and which will continue. To specify these conversion procedures, the analyst must know not only what is to be done by the new system but also what was done by the old one. This requires a thorough understanding of the current system.

Finally, by surveying the current system, the analyst may determine conclusively the cause of the reported problem symptoms. Perhaps the root problem is not the information system at all; it may be a management or employee problem that can be resolved without redesigning the information system. We may not be able to identify the root cause of the problem if we discard the existing system without any investigation into the symptoms.

Gathering Facts

The survey of the current system is essentially a fact-gathering activity. The facts gathered by the analyst are pieces of data that describe key features, situations, and relationships of the system. System facts fall into the following broad classes:

---

4   W. Keuffel, "House of Structure," *Unix Review* 9 (February 1991): 36.

Data Sources. These include external entities, such as customers or vendors, as well as internal sources from other departments.

Users. These include both managers and operations users.

Data Stores. Data stores are the files, databases, accounts, and source documents used in the system.

Processes. Processing tasks are manual or computer operations that represent a decision or an action triggered by information.

Data Flows. Data flows are represented by the movement of documents and reports between data sources, data stores, processing tasks, and users.

Controls. These include both accounting and operational controls and may be manual procedures or computer controls.

Transaction Volumes. The analyst must obtain a measure of the transaction volumes for a specified period of time. Many systems are replaced because they have reached their capacity. Understanding the characteristics of a system's transaction volume and its rate of growth are important elements in assessing capacity requirements for the new system.

Error Rates. Transaction errors are closely related to transaction volume. As a system reaches capacity, error rates increase to an intolerable level. Although no system is perfect, the analyst must determine the acceptable error tolerances for the new system.

Resource Costs. The resources used by the current system include the costs of labor, computer time, materials (such as invoices), and direct overhead. Any resource costs that disappear when the current system is eliminated are called *escapable costs*. Later, when we perform a cost-benefit analysis, escapable costs will be treated as benefits of the new system.

Bottlenecks and Redundant Operations. The analyst should note points where data flows come together to form a bottleneck. At peak-load periods, these can result in delays and promote processing errors. Likewise, delays may be caused by redundant operations, such as unnecessary approvals or sign-offs. By identifying these problem areas during the survey phase, the analyst can avoid making the same mistakes in the design of the new system.

Fact-Gathering Techniques

Systems analysts use several techniques to gather the above-cited facts. These include *observation*, *task participation*, *personal interviews*, and *reviewing key documents*.

Observation. Observation involves passively watching the physical procedures of the system. This allows the analyst to determine what gets done, who performs the task, when they do it, how they do it, why they do it, and how long it takes.

Task Participation. Participation is an extension of observation, whereby the analyst takes an active role in performing the user's work. This allows the analyst to experience first-hand the problems involved in the operation of the current system. For example, the analyst may work on the sales desk taking orders from customers and preparing sales orders. The analyst can determine that documents are improperly designed, that insufficient time exists to perform the required procedures, or that peak-load problems cause bottlenecks and processing errors. With hands-on experience, the analyst can often envision better ways to perform the task.

Personal Interviews. Interviewing is a method of extracting facts about the current system and user perceptions about the requirements for the new system. The instruments used to gather these facts may be open-ended questions or formal questionnaires.

Open-ended questions allow users to elaborate on the problem as they see it and offer suggestions and recommendations. Answers to these questions tend to be difficult to analyze, but they give the analyst a feel for the scope of the problem. The analyst in this type of interview must be a good listener and able to focus on the important facts. Examples of open-ended questions are: "What do you think is the main problem with our sales order system?" and "How could the system be improved?"

Questionnaires are used to ask more specific, detailed questions and to restrict the user's responses. This is a good technique for gathering objective facts about the nature of specific procedures, volumes of transactions processed, sources of data, users of reports, and control issues.

Reviewing Key Documents. The organization's documents are another source of facts about the system being surveyed. Examples of these include the following:

- Organizational charts
- Job descriptions
- Accounting records
- Charts of accounts
- Policy statements
- Descriptions of procedures
- Financial statements
- Performance reports
- System flowcharts
- Source documents
- Transaction listings
- Budgets
- Forecasts
- Mission statements

Following the fact-gathering phase, the analyst formally documents his or her impressions and understanding about the system. This will take the form of notes, system flowcharts, and various levels of DFDs.

THE ANALYSIS STEP

Systems analysis is an intellectual process that is commingled with fact gathering. The analyst is simultaneously analyzing as he or she gathers facts. The mere recognition of a problem presumes some understanding of the norm or desired state. It is therefore difficult to identify where the survey ends and the analysis begins.

System Analysis Report

The event that marks the conclusion of the systems analysis phase is the preparation of a formal **systems analysis report**. This report presents to management or the steering committee the survey findings, the problems identified with the current system, the user's needs, and the requirements of the new system. Figure 13–15 contains a possible format for this report. The primary purpose for conducting systems analysis is to identify user needs and specify requirements for the new system. The report should set out in detail what the system must do rather than how to do it. The requirements statement within the report establishes an understanding between systems professionals, management, users, and other stakeholders. This document constitutes a formal contract that specifies the objectives and goals of the system. The systems analysis report should establish in clear terms the data sources, users, data files, general processes, data flows, controls, and transaction volume capacity.

The systems analysis report does not specify the detailed design of the proposed system. For example, it does not specify processing methods, storage media, record structures, and other details needed to design the physical system. Rather, the report

---

FIGURE 13–15

Outline of Main Topics in a Systems Analysis Report

Systems Analysis Report

I. Reasons for System Analysis
   A. Reasons specified in the system project proposal
   B. Changes in reasons since analysis began
   C. Additional reasons

II. Scope of Study
   A. Scope as specified by the project proposal
   B. Changes in scope

III. Problems Identified with Current System
   A. Techniques used for gathering facts
   B. Problems encountered in the fact-gathering process
   C. Analysis of facts

IV. Statement of User Requirements
   A. Specific user needs in key areas, such as:
      1. Output requirements
      2. Transaction volumes
      3. Response time
   B. Nontechnical terms for a broad-based audience, including:
      1. End users
      2. User management
      3. Systems management
      4. Steering committee

V. Resource Implications
   A. Preliminary assessment of economic effect
   B. Is economic feasibility as stated in proposal reasonable?

VI. Recommendations
   A. Should the project continue?
   B. Has analysis changed feasibility, strategic impact, or priority of the project?

remains at the objectives level to avoid placing artificial constraints on the conceptual design phase. Several possible designs may serve the user's needs, and the development process must be free to explore all of these.

<table>
<tr><td>

THE ACCOUNTANT'S ROLE IN SYSTEMS ANALYSIS

</td><td>

Accountants have the background and training to contribute significantly to the systems analysis process. As a preliminary step to every financial audit, accountants conduct a systems survey to understand the essential elements of the current system. The accountant's experience and knowledge in this area can be a valuable resource to the systems analyst. Similarly, the accountant's understanding of end-user information needs, internal control standards, audit trail requirements, and mandated procedures is of obvious importance to the task of specifying new system requirements.

</td></tr>
</table>

The firm's auditors (both external and internal) are stakeholders in the proposed system. In Chapter 17, we will see how certain audit techniques (such as the embedded audit module and the integrated test facility) must be designed into the system during the SDLC. Often, advanced audit features cannot be easily added to existing systems. Therefore, the accountant/auditor should be involved in the needs analysis of the proposed system to determine if it is a good candidate for advanced audit features and, if so, which features are best suited for the system.

CONCEPTUAL SYSTEMS DESIGN

The purpose of the conceptual design phase is to produce several alternative conceptual systems that satisfy the system requirements identified during systems analysis. By presenting users with a number of plausible alternatives, the systems professional avoids imposing preconceived constraints on the new system. The user will evaluate these conceptual models and settle on the alternatives that appear most plausible. These alternative designs then go to the systems selection phase of SDLC (which will be discussed in Chapter 14), where their respective costs and benefits are compared and a single optimum design is chosen.

This section describes two approaches to **conceptual systems design**: the structured design approach and the object-oriented design approach. The structured approach develops each new system from scratch from the top down. Object-oriented design builds systems from the bottom up through the assembly of reusable modules rather than creating each system from scratch. This has been a particularly successful approach for developing commercial software such as large ERP systems. Users select the functionality they need from an inventory standard objects to produce a customized system. We first examine the structured design approach and then the object-oriented design approach.

<table>
<tr><td>

THE STRUCTURED DESIGN APPROACH

</td><td>

The **structured design** approach is a disciplined way of designing systems from the top down. It consists of starting with the "big picture" of the proposed system that is gradually decomposed into more and more detail until it is fully understood. Under this approach the business process under design is usually documented by data flow and structure diagrams (discussed earlier in this chapter). Figure 13–16 shows the use of these techniques to depict the top-down decomposition of a hypothetical business process.

</td></tr>
</table>

We can see from these diagrams how the systems designer follows a top-down approach. The designer starts with an abstract description of the system and, through

FIGURE 13–16 Top-Down Decomposition of the Structured Design Approach

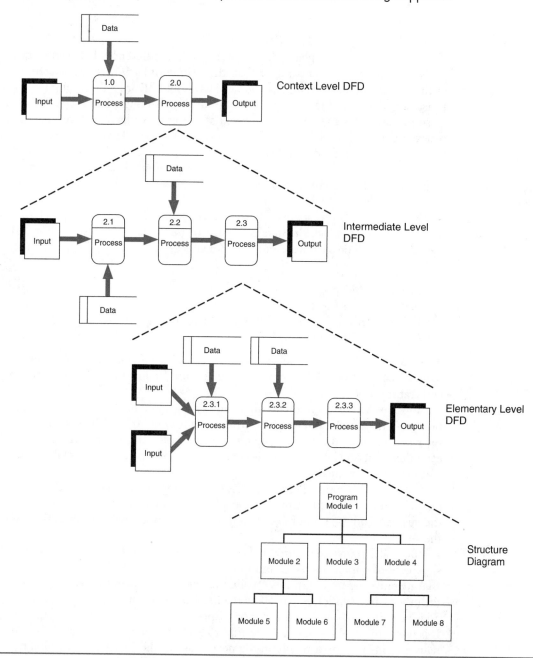

successive steps, redefines this view to produce a more detailed description. In our example, Process 2.0 in the context diagram is decomposed into an intermediate level DFD. Process 2.3 in the intermediate DFD is further decomposed into an elementary DFD. This decomposition could involve several levels to obtain sufficient details. Let's assume that three levels are sufficient in this case. The final step transforms

Process 2.3.3 into a structure diagram that defines the program modules that will constitute the process.

How Much Design Detail Is Needed?

The conceptual design phase should highlight the differences between critical features of competing systems rather than their similarities. Therefore, system designs at this point should be general. The designs should identify all the inputs, outputs, processes, and special features necessary to distinguish one alternative from another. In some cases, this may be accomplished at the context diagram level. In situations where the important distinctions between systems are subtle, designs may need to be represented by lower-level DFDs and even with structure diagrams. However, detailed DFDs and structure diagrams are more commonly used at the detailed design phase of the SDLC. We shall discuss the transition from detailed DFD to structure diagram in Chapter 14.

Figure 13–17 presents two alternative conceptual designs for a purchasing system. These designs lack the details needed to implement the system. For instance, they do not include such necessary components as:

- Database record structures.
- Processing details.
- Specific control techniques.
- Formats for input screens and source documents.
- Output report formats.

The designs do, however, possess sufficient detail to demonstrate how the two systems are conceptually different in their functions. To illustrate, let's examine the general features of each system.

Option A is a traditional batch purchasing system. The initial input for the process is the purchase requisition from inventory control. When inventories reach their predetermined reorder points, new inventories are ordered according to their economic order quantity. Transmittal of purchase orders to suppliers takes place once a day via the U.S. mail.

In contrast, Option B employs EDI technology. The trigger to this system is a purchase requisition from production planning. The purchases system determines the quantity and the vendor and then transmits the order on-line via EDI software to the vendor.

Both alternatives have pros and cons. A benefit of Option A is its simplicity of design, ease of implementation, and lower demand for systems resources than Option B. A negative aspect of Option A is that it requires the firm to carry inventories. On the other hand, Option B may allow the firm to reduce or even eliminate inventories. This benefit comes at the cost of more expensive and sophisticated system resources. It is premature, at this point, to attempt to evaluate the relative merits of these alternatives. This is done formally in the next phase in the SDLC. At this point, system designers are concerned only with identifying plausible system designs.

THE OBJECT-ORIENTED DESIGN APPROACH

The **object-oriented design** approach is to build information systems from reusable standard components or objects. This approach may be equated to the process of building an automobile. Car manufacturers do not create each new model from scratch. New models are actually built from standard components that also go into

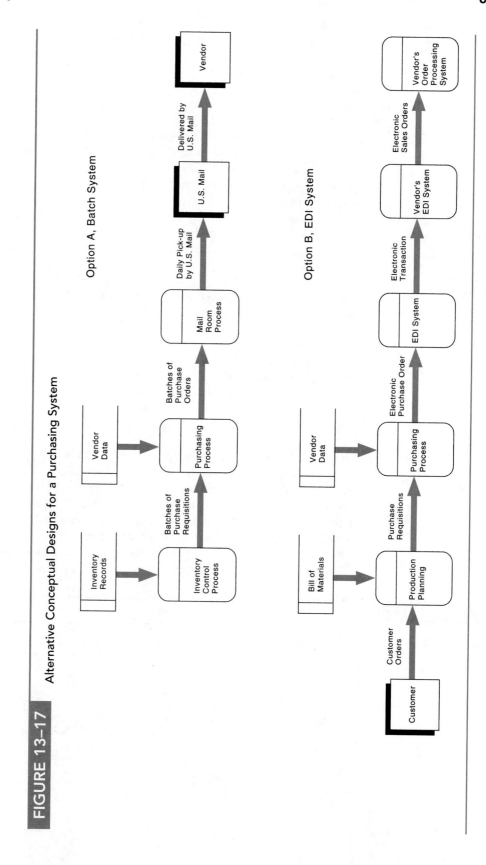

FIGURE 13–17   Alternative Conceptual Designs for a Purchasing System

Option A, Batch System

Option B, EDI System

other models. For example, each model of car produced by a particular manufacturer may use the same type of engine, gearbox, alternator, rear axle, radio, and so on. Some of the car's components will be industry-standard products that are used by other manufacturers. Such things as wheels, tires, spark plugs, and headlights fall into this category. In fact, it may be that the only component actually created from scratch for a new car model is the body.

The automobile industry operates in this fashion to stay competitive. By using standard components, car manufacturers minimize production and maintenance costs. At the same time, they can remain responsive to consumer demands for new products and preserve manufacturing flexibility by mixing and matching components according to the customer's specification.

The concept of reusability is central to the object-oriented design approach to systems design. Once created, standard modules can be used in other systems with similar needs. Ideally, the systems professionals of the organization will create a library (inventory) of modules that can be used by other systems designers within the firm. The benefits of this approach are similar to those stated for the automobile example. They include reduced time and cost for development, maintenance, and testing and improved user support and flexibility in the development process.

Elements of the Object-Oriented Design Approach

A distinctive characteristic of the object-oriented design approach is that both data and programming logic, such as integrity tests, accounting rules, and updating procedures, are encapsulated in modules to represent objects. The following discussion deals with the principle elements of this approach.

Objects. **Objects** are equivalent to nouns in the English language. For example, vendors, customers, inventory, and accounts are all objects. These objects possess two characteristics: attributes and operations. Attributes are equivalent to adjectives in the English language and serve to describe the objects. **Operations** are equivalent to verbs and show actions that are performed on objects and that may change their attributes. Figure 13–18 illustrates these characteristics with a nonfinancial example. The object in this example is an automobile whose attributes are make, model, year,

---

FIGURE 13–18

Characteristics
of Objects

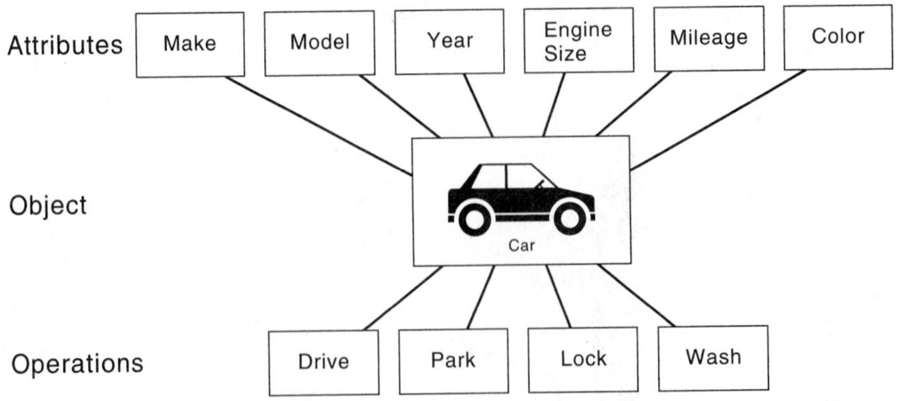

engine size, mileage, and color. Operations (also called *methods*) that may be performed on this object include drive, park, lock, and wash. Note that if we perform a drive operation on the object, the mileage attribute will be changed.

Figure 13–19 illustrates these points with an inventory accounting example. In this example, the object is inventory and its attributes are part number, description, quantity on hand, reorder point, order quantity, and supplier number. The operations that may be performed on inventory are reduce inventory (from product sales), review available quantity on hand, reorder inventory (when quantity on hand is less than the reorder point), and replace inventory (from inventory receipts). Again, note that performing any of the operations will change the attribute quantity on hand.

Classes and Instances. An **object class** is a logical grouping of individual objects that share the same attributes and operations. An **instance** is a single occurrence of an object within a class. For example, Figure 13–20 shows the inventory class consisting of several instances or specific inventory types.

Inheritance. **Inheritance** means that each object instance inherits the attributes and operations of the class to which it belongs. For example, all instances within the inventory class hierarchy share the attributes of part number, description, and quantity on hand. These attributes would be defined once and only once for the inventory

FIGURE 13–19

Characteristics of an
Inventory Object

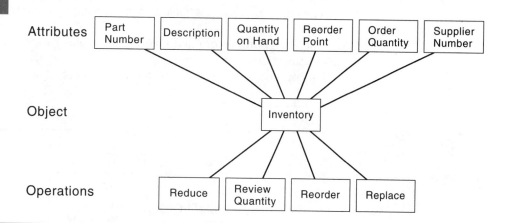

FIGURE 13–20

Relationship between
Object Class and
Instance

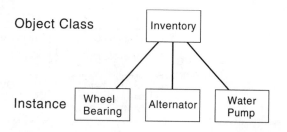

object. Thus, the object instances of wheel bearing, water pump, and alternator will inherit these attributes. Likewise, these instances will inherit the operations (reduce, review, reorder, and replace) defined for the class.

Object classes can also inherit from other object classes. For example, Figure 13–21 shows an object hierarchy made up of an object class called control and three subclasses called accounts payable, accounts receivable, and inventory.

All three object subclasses have certain control operations in common. For example, no account should be updated without first verifying the primary key (that is, Ven-Num, Cust-Num, or Part-Num) of the record being updated. This operation (and others) may be specified for the control object (once and only once) and then inherited by all the subclass objects to which this method applies.

Entity Relationship Diagram

The entity relationship (ER) diagram introduced in Chapter 2 as a documentation technique for database designs is used also to represent object-oriented systems. Figure 13–22 illustrates the use of an ER diagram to depict an object-oriented design for a sales order system.

The following steps describe the process:

1. Each customer places one or more customer orders.
2. Many orders (in batches) initiate the transaction process.
3. One or more inventory items are picked from inventory and sent to each customer.
4. The transaction process updates many accounting records and prepares many invoices.
5. The accounting record and invoice objects inherit many control attributes and operations from the control object.
6. One or more invoices are sent to each customer.

FIGURE 13–21

Inheritance between Classes

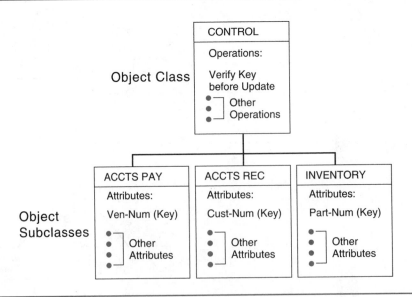

FIGURE 13–22

Object-Oriented
Design of Sales Order
System

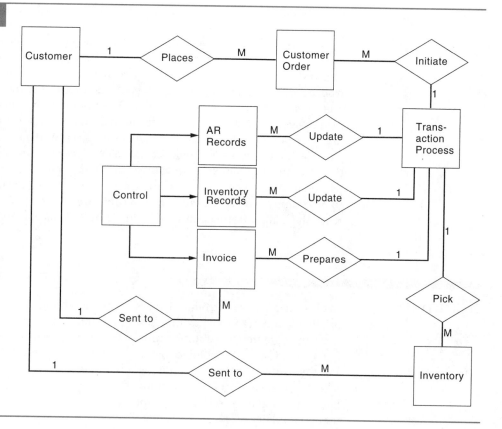

At the implementation phase of the SDLC, programmers using **object-oriented programming (OOP)** will program the attributes and operations that constitute the object modules represented in the ER diagram. The resulting modules will encapsulate the attributes and operations unique to the object and will inherit other attributes and operations common to the object class. For example, referring to Figure 13–22 and Step 5, the control operations needed by the objects that update the accounts receivable and inventory records and prepare the invoices are inherited from the control object module.

Because object-oriented designs support the objective of reusability, portions of systems, or entire systems, can be created from modules that already exist. For example, any future system that requires the control attributes and operations specified by the existing control module (for example, verify primary key before updating record) can inherit these operations. The object-oriented design approach also promotes ease of maintenance. A single change to an attribute or operation in one object class is automatically changed for all the object instances and subclasses that inherit the attribute.

THE ROLE OF ACCOUNTANTS IN CONCEPTUAL SYSTEMS DESIGN

The accountant plays an important role in the conceptual design of the system. We established in Chapter 1 that designing an AIS was a joint effort between the accounting function of the organization and systems professionals. Accountants are responsible for the conceptual system (the logical information flows), and systems professionals are responsible for the physical system (the technical task of building the system). If important accounting considerations are not conceptualized at this point, they may be overlooked completely, thus exposing the organization to financial loss and potential litigation. While participating in the conceptual design process, the accountant must be aware that each alternative system must be adequately controlled, that audit trails must be preserved, and that accounting conventions and legal requirements must be understood. This does not mean that these issues must be specified in detail at this point. It does mean that they should be recognized as items that must be addressed during the detailed design phase of the system.

The auditor is a stakeholder in all financial systems and, thus, has an interest in the conceptual design stage of the system. The auditability of a system depends in part on its design characteristics. Some computer auditing techniques require systems to be designed with special audit features that are integral to the system. For such systems, these audit features must be included in the conceptual design.

Summary

In this chapter, we introduced the systems development life cycle (SDLC). After briefly identifying problems that have traditionally thwarted the successful development of computer-based information systems, we proceeded to examine how prototyping and CASE technologies have been used to improve the development process. We then turned to a detailed discussion of the steps involved in systems planning. The importance of strategic planning was emphasized throughout, as was the importance of taking into consideration the diverse needs and concerns of the prospective user community.

Next we discussed systems analysis. This process begins with an intensive survey of an organization's existing information system and culminates in the preparation of a systems analysis report.

The chapter concluded with a review of the conceptual design of the system. The structured approach was shown to employ a top-down method, wherein design begins with an abstract and general picture of a proposed system and proceeds to provide a more detailed description of the system's features. With an eye toward evaluation, it was emphasized that detailed descriptions of competing systems should highlight differences between their crucial features. We then examined the object-oriented approach, which employs a bottom-up methodology in which systems are constructed from reusable standard components or modules. Its emphasis on reusability allows significant reductions in development and maintenance costs.

Key Terms

central repository   (649)
computer-aided software engineering (CASE)
    (649)
conceptual systems design   (670)
economic feasibility   (661)
end users   (645)

inheritance   (675)
instance   (675)
maintenance   (645)
new systems development   (645)
object class   (675)
object-oriented design   (672)

Review Questions

1. What are the seven stages, in order, of the systems development life cycle? Which stages are considered front end and which are considered back end?
2. Distinguish between systems professionals, end users, and stakeholders.
3. What is the role of the accountant in the SDLC? Why might accountants be called on for input into the development of a nonaccounting information system?
4. What are the three problems that account for most system failures?
5. Why is it often difficult to obtain competent and meaningful user involvement in the SDLC?
6. Is the SDLC a step-by-step procedure that must be followed precisely, or is it more interactive and recursive? Explain your answer.
7. How does a prototype differ from the final product? Why discard the prototype? What role does the end user play in prototyping?
8. What functions do CASE tools serve?
9. Distinguish between upper and lower CASE tools.
10. What is a central repository in a CASE system?
11. How can program code be reused?
12. What is a data flow diagram? What are the different levels from most general to most detailed? Draw the common symbols used.
13. What is the relationship between an elementary level DFD and a structure diagram? Which must be prepared first?
14. Is pseudocode programming language specific? How about the coding model?
15. What is the difference between source code and machine code? Why is it preferable to have the CASE tools convert the structure diagrams into machine code rather than source code?
16. What is the iceberg effect? How can CASE tools help to minimize this phenomenon?
17. Distinguish between reverse engineering and reengineering.
18. Contrast the advantages and disadvantages of CASE tools. What should determine whether CASE is used?
19. Explain why a survey of the current system may serve no purpose when an organization is planning to implement an ERP.
20. Why is it crucial that the strategic objectives of the firm be considered when conducting the systems planning phase?
21. Who should sit on the systems steering committee? What are their typical responsibilities?
22. Why is strategic systems planning not technically considered to be part of the SDLC?
23. What is strategic systems planning, and why should it be done?
24. What is the purpose of project planning, and what are the various steps?
25. Contrast proactive and reactive management styles. Which style would you prefer for your organization? Why?
26. What purposes do system objectives serve? Should they be broadly or narrowly defined? Why?
27. What is the purpose of a project schedule?
28. Why can the formal announcement of a new system technique be crucial?
29. Discuss the various feasibility measures that should be considered. Give an example of each.
30. What are the broad classes of facts that need to be gathered in the system survey?

31. What are the primary fact-gathering techniques?
32. What are the relative merits and disadvantages of a current system survey?
33. What is the primary objective of the conceptual systems design phase?
34. What are two approaches to conceptual systems design?
35. How much design detail is needed in the conceptual design phase?

36. What is an object, and what are its characteristics in the object-oriented approach? Give two examples.
37. Distinguish between object classes and instances.
38. What is meant by inheritance? Give an example.
39. Why is the object-oriented approach particularly suited to ERP system design?
40. What is the accountant's primary role in the conceptual design of the system?

Discussion Questions

1. Accounting educators are discussing ways to incorporate communication skills, both oral and written, into accounting information systems courses. Why do you think these skills are deemed crucial for proper execution of the SDLC?

2. Comment on the following statement: "The maintenance stage of the SDLC involves making trivial changes to accommodate changes in user needs."

3. Discuss how rushing the system's requirements stage may delay or even result in the failure of a systems development process. Conversely, discuss how spending too long in this stage may result in "analysis paralysis."

4. Discuss the independence issue when audit firms also provide consulting input into the development and selection of new systems.

5. Should the systems development tasks be performed by users of the system or by systems professionals who are trained specifically in systems development techniques? Why?

6. Data flow diagrams are often described as exploding from one level to the next. What is meant by "exploding"? Also, data flow diagrams must reconcile from the general level to the next level of detail. What is meant by "reconcile"? How do you think CASE tools help in this procedure?

7. What issues are accountants concerned with when determining their preference for CASE tools that convert structure diagrams into machine code or source code? What are the costs associated with each?

8. Is a good strategic plan detail-oriented?

9. Distinguish between a problem and a symptom. Give an example. Are these usually noticed by upper-, middle-, or lower-level managers?

10. What purposes does the systems project proposal serve? How are these evaluated and prioritized? Is the prioritizing process objective or subjective?

11. Most firms underestimate the cost and time requirements of the SDLC by as much as 50 percent. Why do you think this occurs? In what stages do you think the underestimates are most dramatic?

12. A lack of support by top management has led to the downfall of many new systems projects during the implementation phase. Why is this support so important?

13. Many new systems projects grossly underestimate transaction volumes simply because they do not take into account how the new, improved system can actually increase demand. Explain how this can happen and give an example.

14. What documentation techniques are used in the structured design approach to conceptual design? What is the purpose of each of these documentation techniques, and how do they vary from each other? How much detail is provided?

15. Compare and contrast the structured design approach and the object-oriented design approach. Which do you feel is most beneficial? Why?

16. Do you think legal feasibility is an issue for a system that incorporates the use of machines to sell lottery tickets?

Multiple-Choice Questions

1. CMA 1282 5-9

   The role of an information system steering committee should be to

   a. initiate all computer applications, set computer applications priorities, control access to the computer room, and keep the computer file library.

   b. prepare control totals, maintain systems documentation, and perform follow-up on errors.

   c. assign duties to systems personnel, prepare and monitor systems implementation plans, and prepare flowcharts of systems applications.

   d. review systems project proposals, long-range systems plans, and the performance of the systems department and approve major acquisitions in consideration of overall plans.

   e. decide on specific information needs, prepare detailed plans for systems evaluations, set priorities for writing programs, and decide which equipment will be purchased.

2. CIA 582 IV-8

   Many people believe that a data processing department should have a long-range plan. Which of the following is NOT likely to appear in a long-range plan?

   a. organizational goals and objectives

   b. detailed flowcharts for each computer program that will be developed

   c. schedule of the development of each project

   d. identification of the hardware, personnel, and financial resources that will be required

   e. forecast of future hardware developments

3. CIA 584 II-36

   In reviewing a feasibility study for a new computer system, the auditor should ascertain that the study

   a. considered costs, savings, controls, profit improvement, and other benefits analyzed by application area.

   b. provided the preliminary plan for converting existing manual systems and clerical operations.

   c. provided management with assurance from qualified, independent consultants that the use of a computer system appeared justified.

   d. included a report by the internal audit department that evaluated internal control features for each planned application.

4. CMA 686 5-2

   The most important factor in planning for a system change is

   a. having an auditor as a member of the design team.

   b. using state-of-the-art techniques.

   c. concentrating on software rather than hardware.

   d. involving top management and people who use the system.

   e. selecting a user to lead the design team.

5. CMA 678 5-5

   In the context of a feasibility study, technical feasibility refers to whether

   a. a proposed system is attainable, given the existing technology.

   b. the systems manager can coordinate and control the activities of the systems department.

   c. an adequate computer site exists for the proposed system.

   d. the proposed system will produce economic benefits exceeding its costs.

   e. the system will be used effectively within the operating environment of an organization.

6. CIA Adapted 581 I-24

   For an automated system to provide for continuity and effective control over the proposed data processing activities, the systems development process should be performed in a certain order. Which of the following sequences lists the computer systems development phases in the order in which they should be performed?

   a. implementation planning, development of user specifications, systems planning, and programming

   b. development of user specifications, development of technical specifications, implementation planning, and programming

   c. training of user department personnel, implementation planning, and system testing

   d. implementation planning, programming, conversion, and system testing

   e. systems planning, development of conceptual specifications, development of detailed specifications, and programming

7. CMA 1281 5-13

   The stage of a systems study that would include up-to-date organizational charts; description of

the present system; complete flowcharts for the present system; forms and layouts of all input and output documents (along with samples) used in the present system; and summaries of interviews, review sessions, and personal observations regarding the present system is
a. problem definition.
b. problem analysis.
c. systems design.
d. program analysis.
e. documentation and maintenance.

8. CMA 678 5-4
A systems survey is being conducted to obtain an accurate perspective on the existing system and to identify weaknesses that can be corrected by the new system. Which of the following steps is NOT considered part of this systems survey?
a. Interviews are conducted with operating people and managers.
b. The complete documentation of the system is obtained and reviewed.

c. Measures of processing volume are obtained for each operation.
d. Equipment sold by various computer manufacturers is reviewed in terms of capability, cost, and availability.
e. Work measurement studies are conducted to determine the time required to complete various tasks or jobs.

9. CMA 1281 5-12
Kesta Company is doing a systems development study. The study started with broad organizational goals and the types of decisions made by organizational executives. This study supports a model of information flow and, ultimately, design requirements. This approach to systems development is called
a. bottom-up.
b. network.
c. top-down.
d. strategic.
e. sequential.

Problems

1. **Systems Planning**

A new systems development project is being planned for Reindeer Christmas Supplies Company. The invoicing, cash receipts, and accounts payable modules are all going to be updated. The controller, Kris K. Ringle, is a little anxious about this project. The last systems development project that affected his department was not very successful, and the employees in the accounting department did not accept the new system very well at first. He feels that the systems personnel did not interact sufficiently with the users of the systems in the accounting department. Prepare a memo from Ringle to the head of the information systems department, Sandy Klaus. In this memo, provide some suggestions for including the accounting personnel in the systems development project. Give persuasive arguments as to why prototyping would be helpful to the workers in the accounting department.

2. **CASE Tools**

Reeve Lumber Company has a small information systems department consisting of five people. A backlog of approximately 15 months exists for re-

quests for new systems applications to even be considered. Both information users and systems personnel are unhappy with this state of affairs. The users feel that the systems department is not responsive enough to their needs, while the systems personnel feel overworked, frustrated, and unappreciated. Janet Hubert, the manager of the systems department, has decided that she needs to take a proactive measure. She is requesting the funds to purchase a CASE system for approximately $75,000 that takes about two months to install and train workers on how to use it. The president of the company, Mike Cassidy, initially responded by questioning the wisdom of taking the systems personnel away from their duties when they are backlogged so they can learn a system. Prepare a memo from Hubert to Cassidy. In the memo, outline the expected benefits of purchasing and using a CASE system and address Cassidy's concern regarding the two-month training and implementation period.

3. **Data Flow Diagrams**

Sawicki Music Supply is a mail-order business that accepts merchandise orders by telephone and mail. All payments must be prepaid with a major credit card. Once an order is received, the item is either found in inventory and shipped immediately, the item is not found in inventory and is ordered from the manufacturer, or a notice is sent to the customer indicating the item is no longer stocked.

Prepare a context, intermediate, and elementary level data flow diagram for Sawicki Music Supply. For the elementary level diagram, explode the inventory function.

4. Data Flow Diagrams

Examine the following context and intermediate (Level 1) data flow diagrams and indicate what is incorrect about them.

5. CASE Tools

Atlantis Corporation, a manufacturer of recreational boating, has an accounting information

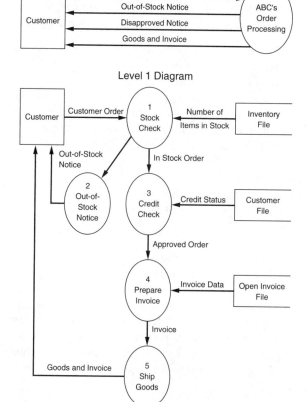

Problem 4: Data Flow Diagrams

Context Level Diagram

Level 1 Diagram

system that is 17 years old. The maintenance programmers have been patching and updating the old program code for over a decade now. The auditors (both internal and external) are becoming anxious about the state of the programs since it is becoming almost impossible to follow their logic sequences and algorithms. Recently, the information systems (IS) department acquired some CASE modules for developing new systems. The manager of the IS department has suggested that Atlantis purchase a reverse engineering module to help the situation. The internal auditors think it would be helpful to purchase and employ a reengineering module instead. Prepare a document that explains each type of module and its relative merits. Recommend which module you believe is more appropriate.

6. Problem Identification

Classify each of the following as a problem or a symptom. If it is a symptom, give two examples of a possible underlying problem. If it is a problem, give two examples of a possible symptom that may be detected.

a. declining profits
b. defective production process
c. low-quality raw materials
d. shortfall in cash balance
e. declining market share
f. shortage of employees in the accounts payable department
g. shortage of raw material due to a drought in the Midwest
h. inadequately trained workers
i. decreasing customer satisfaction

7. Systems Development and Implementation

Kruger Designs hired a consulting firm three months ago to redesign the information system used by the architects. The architects will be able to use state-of-the-art CAD programs to help in designing the products. Further, they will be able to store these designs on a network server where they and other architects may be able to call them back up for future designs with similar components. The consulting firm has been instructed to develop the system without disrupting the architects. In fact, top management believes that the best route is to develop the system and then to "introduce" it to the architects during a training session. Management does not want the architects to spend precious billable hours guessing about the new system or putting work off until the new system is working. Thus, the consultants are operating in a backroom under a shroud of secrecy.

a. Do you think that management is taking the best course of action for the announcement of the new system? Why?

b. Do you approve of the development process? Why?

8. **Systems Analysis**

Consider the following dialogue between a systems professional, Joe Pugh, and a manager of a department targeted for a new information system, Lars Meyer:

Pugh: The way to go about the analysis is to first examine the old system, such as reviewing key documents and observing the workers perform their tasks. Then we can determine which aspects are working well and which should be preserved.

Meyer: We have been through these types of projects before and what always ends up happening is that we do not get the new system we are promised; we get a modified version of the old system.

Pugh: Well, I can assure you that will not happen this time. We just want a thorough understanding of what is working well and what is not.

Meyer: I would feel much more comfortable if we first started with a list of our requirements. We should spend some time up-front determining exactly what we want the system to do for my department. Then you systems people can come in and determine what portions to salvage if you wish. Just don't constrain us to the old system!

a. Obviously these two workers have different views on how the systems analysis phase should be conducted. Comment on whose position you sympathize with the most.

b. What method would you propose they take? Why?

9. **Systems Design**

Vince Malloy and Katy Smith, both systems personnel at Shamrock Steelworks, are designing a new expenditure cycle system. Vince has worked for Shamrock for twelve years and has been involved in many systems development projects. Katy recently began working for Shamrock. She has four years experience in systems development with another comparably sized organization. Yesterday, Vince and Katy met to determine their plan for approaching the conceptual system design. Below is an excerpt of some dialogue that occurred in that meeting.

Katy: I really think that the new system can be designed more efficiently if we use an object-oriented design approach. Further, future enhancements and maintenance will be easier if we use an object approach.

Vince: The method you are suggesting is a creation of modules. I do not have a problem with that concept in general. I just prefer using a top-down approach to design the system. We have been using that system for the past twelve years, and it has worked out OK.

Katy: Sure, your systems have worked for you, but perhaps they can be developed more efficiently, not to mention maintaining them. Further, we have approximately a two-year backlog of projects. Changing to a more efficient design system may help us to reduce that wait.

Vince: We may not end up with the system we want if we do not consider the "big picture." I am afraid if we get too tied to using existing modules for future projects, that we may design suboptimal systems that will require more maintenance and have shorter lives in the long run. What good will the more "efficient" system do us then?

Required:
Prepare a response by Katy, and develop a strategy for systems design that will address both of their concerns.

10. **Conceptual Design**

Prepare two alternative conceptual designs for both an accounts payable system and an accounts receivable system. Discuss the differences in concept between the different designs. From a cost perspective, which is more economical? From a benefits perspective, which is more desirable? Which design would you prefer and why?

Systems Development Cases

Several systems development cases that draw upon the material in this and the next chapter are available online at http://hall.swcollege.com.

The Systems Development Process, Part II: System Selection, Detailed Design, and System Implementation

We saw in the last chapter that the purpose of the conceptual design phase of the SDLC is to produce several alternative proposals that satisfy the system requirements that were identified during systems analysis. By presenting users with a number of plausible alternatives, systems professionals avoid imposing preconceived constraints on the new system.

This chapter covers the system selection, detailed design, and system implementation phases of the SDLC. It describes the procedures by which decision makers evaluate competing conceptual systems to settle on the one that appears most plausible from an operational and cost-beneficial perspective. The selected system then proceeds to the final phases of the SDLC, where it is designed in detail and implemented. In the detailed design phase system components including user views, database tables, business processes, and controls are meticulously specified. These components are presented formally in a detailed design report, which constitutes a set of "blueprints" for creating input screen formats, output report layouts, database structures, and application process logic. Finally, these completed plans are used in the implementation phase to physically construct the system.

LEARNING OBJECTIVES

After studying this chapter, you should:

- Be able to identify the range of factors that should be considered in a detailed feasibility study.
- Be able to identify and discuss the three major steps involved in a cost-benefit analysis of proposed information systems.
- Understand the advantages and disadvantages of the commercial software option, and be able to discuss the decision-making process used to select commercial software.
- Be able to identify the sequence of events that constitute the detailed design phase of the SDLC.
- Understand the design procedure for both hard-copy and electronic input and output media.
- Understand how the process component of a system is designed.
- Understand the principle features of a system implementation, including the use of PERT and Gantt charts to create an implementation schedule.
- Be familiar with the different types of system documentation and the purposes they serve.
- Understand the procedures employed in database and system conversion.

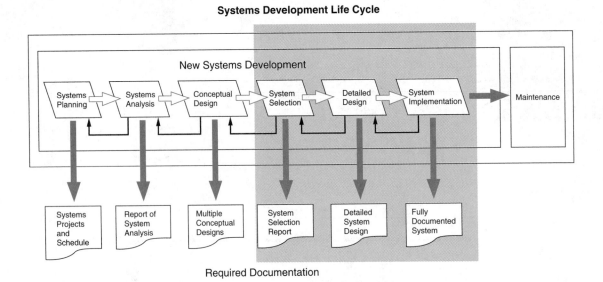

The following text appears within the figure:

Systems Development Life Cycle

New Systems Development

Systems Planning → Systems Analysis → Conceptual Design → System Selection → Detailed Design → System Implementation → Maintenance

| Systems Projects and Schedule | Report of System Analysis | Multiple Conceptual Designs | System Selection Report | Detailed System Design | Fully Documented System |

Required Documentation

SYSTEMS EVALUATION AND SELECTION

The next phase in the SDLC is the procedure for selecting the one system from the set of alternative conceptual designs that will go to the detailed design phase. The **systems evaluation and selection** phase is an optimization process that seeks to identify the best system. This decision represents a critical juncture in the SDLC. At this point there is a great deal of uncertainty about the system, and a poor decision can be disastrous. The purpose of a formal evaluation and selection procedure is to structure this decision-making process and thereby reduce both uncertainty and the risk of making a poor decision.

There is no magic formula to ensure a good decision. Ultimately, the decision comes down to management judgment. The objective is to provide a means by which management can make an informed judgment. This selection process involves two steps:

1. Perform a detailed feasibility study.
2. Perform a cost-benefit analysis.

The results of these evaluations are then reported formally to the steering committee for final system selection.

PERFORM A DETAILED FEASIBILITY STUDY

We begin the system selection process by reexamining the feasibility factors that were evaluated on a preliminary basis as part of the systems proposal. Originally, the scores assigned to these factors were based largely on the judgment and intuition of the systems professional. Now that specific system features have been conceptualized, the designer has a clearer picture of these factors. Also, at the proposal stage, these factors were evaluated for the entire project. Now they are evaluated for each alternative conceptual design.

Independent Evaluation

The task of performing a **detailed feasibility study** should be performed by informed but independent evaluators. Objectivity is essential to a fair assessment of each design. This group should consist of the project manager, a user representative, and systems professionals who are not part of the project but have expertise in the specific areas covered by the feasibility study. Also, for operational audit reasons, the group should contain a member of the internal audit staff. The feasibility factors that were introduced in the last chapter provide a framework for identifying the key issues that evaluators should consider.

Technical Feasibility. In evaluating technical feasibility, a well-established and understood technology represents less risk than an unfamiliar one. If the systems design calls for established technology, the feasibility score will be high, say 9 or 10. The use of technology that is new (first release) and unfamiliar to systems professionals who must install and maintain it, or is a hybrid of several vendors' products, is a more risky option. Depending on the number and combination of risk factors, the feasibility score for such technology will be lower.

Legal Feasibility. In financial transaction processing systems, the legality of the system is always an issue. However, legality is also an issue for nonfinancial systems that process sensitive data, such as hospital patient records or personal credit ratings. Different systems designs may represent different levels of risk when dealing with such data. The evaluator should be concerned that the conceptual design recognizes critical control, security, and audit trail issues and that the system does not violate laws pertaining to rights of privacy and/or the use and distribution of information.

Operational Feasibility. The availability of well-trained, motivated, and experienced users is the key issue in evaluating the operational feasibility of a design. If users lack these attributes, the move to a highly technical environment may be risky and will require extensive retraining. This may also affect the economic feasibility of the system. On the other hand, a user community that is comfortable with technology is more likely to make a smooth transition to an advanced technology system. The operational feasibility score of each alternative design should reflect the expected ease of this transition.

Schedule Feasibility. At this point in the design, the system evaluator is in a better position to assess the likelihood that the system will be completed on schedule. The technology platform, the systems design, and the need for user training may influence the original schedule. The systems development technology being used is another influence. The use of CASE, JAD, and prototyping can significantly reduce the development time of any systems design option.

Economic Feasibility. The preliminary economic feasibility study was confined to assessing management's financial commitment to the overall project. This is still a relevant issue. If the economic climate has changed since the preliminary study or if one or more of the competing designs does not have management's support, this should now be determined.

The original feasibility study could specify the project's costs only in general terms. Now that each competing design has been conceptualized and expressed in terms of its unique features and processes, designers can be more precise in their estimates of the costs of each alternative. The economic feasibility study can now be taken a step further by performing a cost-benefit analysis.

PERFORM A COST-BENEFIT ANALYSIS

Cost-benefit analysis helps management determine whether (and by how much) the benefits received from a proposed system will outweigh its costs. This technique is frequently used for estimating the expected financial value of business investments. However, in this case, the investment is an information system, and the costs and benefits are more difficult to identify and quantify than those of traditional capital projects. Although imperfect for this setting, cost-benefit analysis is employed because of its simplicity and the absence of a clearly better alternative. In spite of its limitations, cost-benefit analysis, combined with feasibility factors, is a useful tool for comparing competing systems designs.

There are three steps in the application of cost-benefit analysis: identify costs, identify benefits, and compare costs and benefits. We discuss each of these steps below.

Identify Costs

One method of identifying costs is to divide them into two categories: one-time costs and recurring costs. *One-time costs* include the initial investment to develop and implement the system. *Recurring costs* include operating and maintenance costs that recur over the life of the system. Table 14–1 shows a breakdown of typical one-time and recurring costs.

One-Time Costs

Hardware Acquisition. This includes the cost of mainframe, minicomputers, microcomputers, and peripheral equipment, such as tape drives and disk packs. The cost figures for items can be obtained from the vendor.

TABLE 14–1   **One-Time and Recurring Costs**

ONE-TIME AND RECURRING COSTS

One-Time Costs
- Hardware acquisition
- Site preparation
- Software acquisition
- Systems design
- Programming and testing
- Data conversion from old system to new system
- Training personnel

Recurring costs
- Hardware maintenance
- Software maintenance contracts
- Insurance
- Supplies
- Personnel

Site Preparation. This involves such frequently overlooked costs as building modifications (for example, adding air conditioning or making structural changes), equipment installation (which may include the use of heavy equipment), and freight charges. Estimates of these costs can be obtained from the vendor and the subcontractors who do the installation.

Software Acquisition. These costs apply to all software purchased for the proposed system, including operating system software (if not bundled with the hardware), network control software, and commercial applications (such as accounting packages). Estimates of these costs can be obtained from vendors.

Systems Design. These are the costs incurred by systems professionals performing the planning, analysis, and design functions. Technically, such costs incurred up to this point are "sunk" and irrelevant to the decision. The analyst should estimate only the costs needed to complete the detailed design.

Programming and Testing. Programming costs are based on estimates of the personnel-hours required to write new programs and modify existing programs for the proposed system. System testing costs involve bringing together all the individual program modules for testing as an entire system. This must be a rigorous exercise if it is to be meaningful. The planning, testing, and analysis of the results may demand many days of involvement from systems professionals, users, and other stakeholders of the system. The experience of the firm in the past is the best basis for estimating these costs.

Data Conversion. These costs arise in the transfer of data from one storage medium to another. For example, the accounting records of a manual system must be converted to magnetic form when the system becomes computer-based. This can represent a significant task. The basis for estimating conversion costs is the number and size of the files to be converted.

Training. These costs involve educating users to operate the new system. This could be done in an extensive training program provided by an outside organization at a remote site or through on-the-job training by in-house personnel. The cost of formal training can be easily obtained. The cost of an in-house training program includes instruction time, classroom facilities, and lost productivity.

Recurring Costs
Hardware Maintenance. This involves the cost of upgrading the computer (increasing the memory), as well as preventive maintenance and repairs to the computer and peripheral equipment. The organization may enter into a maintenance contract with the vendor to minimize and budget these costs. Estimates for these costs can be obtained from vendors and existing contracts.

Software Maintenance. These costs include upgrading and debugging operating systems, purchased applications, and in-house developed applications. Maintenance contracts with software vendors can be used to specify these costs fairly accurately. Estimates of in-house maintenance can be derived from historical data.

Insurance. This covers such hazards and disasters as fire, hardware failure, vandalism, and destruction by disgruntled employees.

Supplies. These costs are incurred through routine consumption of such items as printer ribbons and paper, magnetic disks, magnetic tapes, and general office supplies.

Personnel. These are the salaries of individuals who are part of the information system. Some employee costs are direct and easily identifiable, such as the salaries of operations personnel exclusively employed as part of the system under analysis. Some personnel involvement (such as the database administrator and computer room personnel) is common to many systems. Such personnel costs must be allocated on the basis of expected incremental involvement with the system.

Identify Benefits

The next step in the cost-benefit analysis is to identify the benefits of the system. These may be both tangible and intangible.

Tangible Benefits. *Tangible benefits* are benefits that can be measured and expressed in financial terms. Table 14–2 lists several types of tangible benefits.

Tangible benefits fall into two categories: those that increase revenue and those that reduce costs. For example, assume a proposed EDI system will allow the organization to reduce inventories and at the same time improve customer service by reducing stockouts. The reduction of inventories is a cost-reducing benefit. The proposed system will use fewer resources (inventories) than the current system. The value of this benefit is the dollar amount of the carrying costs saved by the annual reduction in inventory. The estimated increase in sales due to better customer service is a revenue-increasing benefit.

When measuring cost savings, it is important to include only escapable costs in the analysis. Escapable costs are directly related to the system, and they cease to exist when the system ceases to exist. Some costs that appear to be escapable to the user are not truly escapable and, if included, can lead to a flawed analysis. For example, data processing centers often "charge back" their operating costs to their user constituency through cost allocations. The charge-back rate they use for this includes both fixed costs (allocated to users) and direct costs created by the activities of individual users. Figure 14–1 illustrates this technique.

TABLE 14–2	**Tangible Benefits**

TANGIBLE BENEFITS
Increased Revenues
Increased sales within existing markets
Expansion into other markets
Cost Reduction
Labor reduction
Operating cost reduction (such as supplies and overhead)
Reduced inventories
Less expensive equipment
Reduced equipment maintenance

FIGURE 14-1

DP Center Cost
Charge-Back to
User Areas

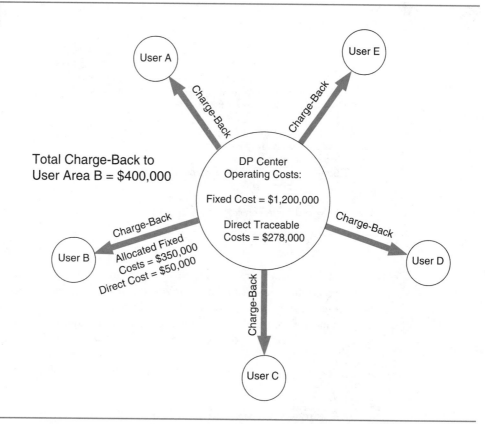

User A

User E

Total Charge-Back to
User Area B = $400,000

DP Center
Operating Costs:

Fixed Cost = $1,200,000

Direct Traceable
Costs = $278,000

Charge-Back

Charge-Back

Charge-Back

Charge-Back

Charge-Back

User B

Allocated Fixed
Costs = $350,000
Direct Cost = $50,000

User D

User C

Assume the management in User Area B proposes to acquire a computer system and perform its own data processing locally. One benefit of the proposal is the cost savings derived by escaping the charge-back from the current data processing center. Although the user may see this as a $400,000 annual charge, only the direct cost portion ($50,000) is escapable by the organization as a whole. Should the proposal be approved, the remaining $350,000 of the charge-back does not go away. This cost must now be absorbed by the remaining users of the current system.

Intangible Benefits. Table 14–3 lists some common categories of *intangible benefits*. Although intangible benefits are often of overriding importance in information system decisions, they cannot be easily measured and quantified. For example, assume that a proposed point-of-sale system for a department store will reduce the average time to process a customer sales transaction from eleven minutes to three minutes. The time saved can be quantified and produces a tangible benefit in the form of an operating cost saving. An intangible benefit is improved customer satisfaction; no one likes to stand in long lines to pay for purchases. But what is the true value of this intangible benefit to the organization? Increased customer satisfaction may translate into increased sales. More customers will buy at the store—and may be willing to pay slightly more to avoid long checkout lines. But how do we quantify this translation? Assigning a value is often highly subjective.

Systems professionals draw upon many sources in attempting to quantify intangible benefits and manipulate them into financial terms. Some common techniques

TABLE 14–3	**Intangible Benefits**

INTANGIBLE BENEFITS

Increased customer satisfaction
Improved employee satisfaction
More current information
Improved decision making
Faster response to competitor actions
More efficient operations
Better internal and external communications
Improved planning
Operational flexibility
Improved control environment

include customer (and employee) opinion surveys, statistical analysis, expected value techniques, and simulation models. Though systems professionals may succeed in quantifying some of these intangible benefits, more often they must be content to simply state the benefits as precisely as good judgment permits.

Because they defy precise measurement, intangible benefits are sometimes exploited for political reasons. By overstating or understating these benefits, a system may be pushed forward by its proponents or killed by its opponents.

Compare Costs and Benefits

The last step in the cost-benefit analysis is to compare the costs and benefits identified in the first two steps. The two most common methods used for evaluating information systems are net present value and payback.

The Net Present Value Method. Under the **net present value method**, the present value of the costs is deducted from the present value of the benefits over the life of the system. Projects with a positive net present value are economically feasible. When comparing competing projects, the optimal choice is the project with the greatest net present value. Figure 14–2 illustrates the net present value method by comparing two competing designs.

The example is based on the following data:

	Design A	Design B
Project completion time	1 year	1 year
Expected useful life of system	5 years	5 years
One-time costs (thousands)	$300	$140
Recurring costs (thousands)		
incurred in beginning of Years 1 through 5	$45	$55
Annual tangible benefits (thousands)		
incurred in end of Years 1 through 5	$170	$135

If costs and tangible benefits alone were being considered, then Design A would be selected over Design B. However, the value of intangible benefits, along with the design feasibility scores, must also be factored into the final analysis.

FIGURE 14–2

Net Present Value
Method of Cost-
Benefit Analysis

Year Time	Beginning End Year Outflows	Inflows	Year Time	Beginning End Year Outflows	Inflows
0	$(300,000)		0	$(140,000)	
1	(45,000)	170,000	1	(55,000)	135,000
2	(45,000)	170,000	2	(55,000)	135,000
3	(45,000)	170,000	3	(55,000)	135,000
4	(45,000)	170,000	4	(55,000)	135,000
5	(45,000)	170,000	5	(55,000)	135,000
PV Out	$(479,672)		PV Out	$(359,599)	
PV In	$628,428		PV In	$499,089	
NPV	$148,810		NPV	$139,490	
Interest Rate	8.00%				

The Payback Method. The **payback method** is a variation of break-even analysis. The break-even point is reached when total costs equal total benefits. Figure 14–3(a) and (b) on pages 696 and 697 illustrates this approach using the data from the previous example.

The total-cost curve consists of the one-time costs plus the present value of the recurring costs over the life of the project. The total benefits curve is the present value of the tangible benefits. The intersection of these lines represents the number of years into the future when the project breaks even, or pays for itself. The shaded area between the benefit curve and the total-cost curve represents the present value of future profits earned by the system.

In choosing an information system, payback speed is often a decisive factor. With brief product life cycles and rapid advances in technology, the effective lives of information systems tend to be short. Using this criterion, Design B, with a payback period of four years, would be selected over Design A, whose payback will take four and one-half years. The length of the payback period often takes precedence over other considerations represented by intangible benefits.

PREPARE SYSTEMS SELECTION REPORT

The deliverable product of the systems selection process is the **systems selection report**. This formal document consists of a revised feasibility study, a cost-benefit analysis, and a list and explanation of intangible benefits for each alternative design. On the basis of this report, the steering committee will select a single system that will go forward to the next phase of the SDLC—detailed design.

COMMERCIAL SYSTEMS PACKAGES

This chapter has reviewed the conceptual design and selection procedures for systems being developed in-house. However, not all systems are acquired in this fashion. A growing number of systems are purchased from software vendors. Faced with many

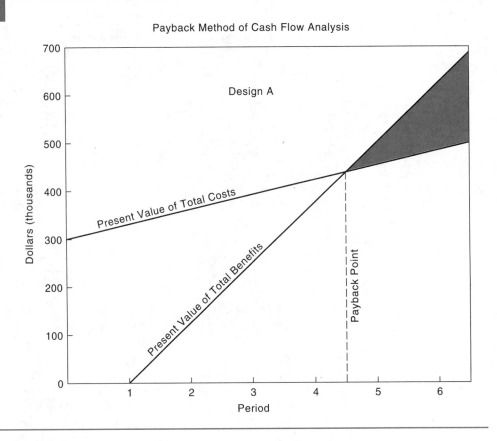

FIGURE 14–3(a)

Discounted Payback
Method of Cost-
Benefit Analysis

competing packages, each with unique features and attributes, management must choose the system and the vendor that best serves the needs of the organization. Making the optimal choice requires that this be an informed decision.

Before moving on to the next phase of the SDLC, we will examine the issues surrounding the purchase of commercial software. Our discussion will focus primarily on a technique that can help structure and evaluate the many intangible factors that complicate the process of selecting commercial software.

TRENDS IN COMMERCIAL SOFTWARE

Four factors have stimulated the growth of the commercial software market: (1) the relatively low cost of general commercial software as compared to customized software; (2) the emergence of industry-specific vendors who target their software to the needs of particular types of businesses; (3) a growing demand from businesses that are too small to afford an in-house systems development staff; and (4) the trend toward downsizing of organizational units and the resulting move toward the distributed data processing environment, which has made the commercial software option more appealing to larger organizations. Indeed, organizations that maintain their own in-house systems development staff will purchase commercial software when the nature of their need permits. Commercial software can be divided into a number of general groups, which are now discussed.

FIGURE 14–3(b)

(continued)

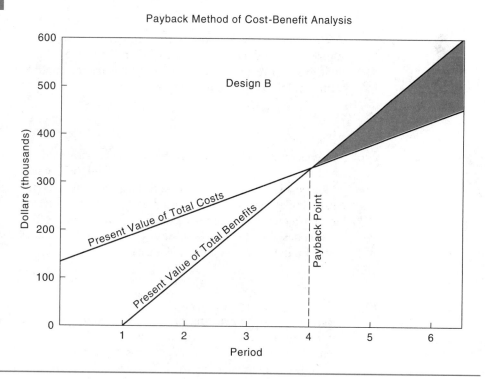

Payback Method of Cost-Benefit Analysis

Turnkey Systems

Turnkey systems are completely finished and tested systems that are ready for implementation. Often these are general-purpose systems or systems customized to a specific industry. Turnkey systems are usually sold only as compiled program modules, and users have limited ability to customize such systems to their specific needs. Some turnkey systems have software options that allow the user to customize input, output, and some processing through menu choices. Other turnkey system vendors will sell their customers the source code if program changes are desired. For a fee, the user or the vendor can then customize the system by reprogramming the original source code. Some examples of turnkey systems are described below.

General Accounting Systems. General accounting systems are designed to serve a wide variety of user needs. By mass producing a standard system, the vendor is able to reduce the unit cost of these systems to a fraction of in-house development costs. Powerful systems of this sort can be obtained for under $2,000.

To provide as much flexibility as possible, general accounting systems are designed in modules. This allows users to purchase the modules that meet their specific needs. Typical modules include accounts payable, accounts receivable, payroll processing, inventory control, general ledger, financial reporting, and fixed asset.

Special-Purpose Systems. Some software vendors have targeted their systems to selected segments of the economy. For example, the medical field, the banking industry, and government agencies have unique accounting procedures, rules, and conventions that general-purpose accounting systems do not always accommodate.

Software vendors have thus developed standardized systems to deal with industry-specific procedures.

Office Automation Systems. Office automation is the use of computer systems to improve the productivity of office workers. Examples of office automation systems include word processing packages, database management systems, spreadsheet programs, and desktop publishing systems.

Backbone Systems

As we learned in Chapter 1, **backbone systems** provide a basic system structure on which to build. Backbone systems come with all the primary processing modules programmed. The vendor designs and programs the user interface to suit the client's needs. This approach can produce highly customized systems. But customizing a system is expensive and time-consuming. Many vendors thus employ object-oriented systems design, which takes advantage of reusable modules and thereby reduces the costs of tailoring the system to the user.

Vendor-Supported Systems

Vendor-supported systems are hybrids of custom systems and commercial software. Under this approach, the vendor develops (and maintains) custom systems for its clients. The systems themselves are custom products, but the systems development service is commercially provided. This option is popular in the health care and legal services industries. Since the vendor serves as the organization's in-house systems development staff, the client organization must rely on the vendor to provide custom programming and on-site maintenance of systems. Much of each client's system may be developed from scratch, but by using an object-oriented approach, vendors can produce common modules that can be reused in other client systems. This approach helps to reduce development costs charged to the client firms.

ERP Systems

ERP systems are difficult to classify into a single category since they have characteristics of all of the above. They are prewritten systems, which in some cases are implemented as turnkey applications. On the other hand, they can be modified to meet user needs. An ERP may be installed as a backbone system that interfaces with other legacy systems or it may constitute an entirely new system. Because of their complexity, ERP systems are most often vendor-supported packages that are installed by an outside service provider.

ADVANTAGES OF COMMERCIAL SOFTWARE

Implementation Time

Custom systems often take a long time to develop. Months or even years may pass before a custom system can be developed through in-house procedures. Unless the organization successfully anticipates future information needs and schedules application development accordingly, it may experience long periods of unsatisfied need. However, commercial software can be implemented almost immediately upon recognizing a need. The user does not have to wait.

Cost

In-house development costs must be wholly absorbed by a single user. However, since the cost of commercial software is spread across many users, the unit cost is reduced to a fraction of the cost of a system developed in-house.

Reliability

Most reputable commercial software packages are thoroughly tested before their release to the consumer market. Any system errors not discovered during testing are likely to be uncovered by user organizations shortly after release and corrected. Although no system is certified as being free from errors, commercial software is less likely to have errors than an equivalent in-house system.

DISADVANTAGES OF COMMERCIAL SOFTWARE

Independence

Purchasing a vendor-supported system makes the firm dependent on the vendor for maintenance. The user runs the risk that the vendor will cease to support the system or even go out of business. This is perhaps the greatest disadvantage of vendor-supported systems.

The Need for Customized Systems

The prime advantage of in-house development is the ability to produce applications to exact specifications. This advantage also describes a disadvantage of commercial software. Sometimes, the user's needs are unique and complex, and commercially available software is either too general or too inflexible.

Maintenance

Business information systems undergo frequent changes. Remember the iceberg effect of systems maintenance discussed in the last chapter. If the user's needs change, it may be difficult or even impossible to modify commercial software. On the other hand, in-house development provides users with proprietary applications that can be economically maintained.

BYPASSING THE SDLC

Whenever an application is general enough to be satisfied by commercial software, this option should be seriously considered. There are several points within the SDLC at which the system designer can decide to pursue this option. It may be clear at the conceptual design phase (or before) that an application is a candidate for this approach. If so, nothing may be gained by continuing with the remainder of SDLC activities and investing the resources to design the system in detail. In other cases, management may decide to pursue a detailed design to ensure that all user requirements are completely specified prior to choosing a commercial package.

CHOOSING A PACKAGE

Having made the decision to purchase commercial software, the systems development team is now faced with the task of choosing the package that best satisfies the organization's needs. On the surface, there may appear to be no clear-cut best choice from the many options available. The following four-step procedure can help structure this decision-making process by establishing decision criteria and identifying key differences between options.

Step 1: Needs Analysis

As with in-house development, the commercial option begins with an analysis of user needs. These are formally presented in a statement of systems requirements that provides a basis for choosing between competing alternatives. For example, the stated requirement of the new system may be to:

1. Support the accounting and reporting requirements of federal, state, and local agencies.
2. Provide access to information in a timely and efficient manner.
3. Simultaneously support both accrual accounting and fund accounting systems.
4. Increase transaction processing capacity.
5. Reduce the cost of current operations.
6. Improve user productivity.
7. Reduce processing errors.
8. Support batch and real-time processing.
9. Provide automatic general ledger reconciliations.
10. Be expandable and flexible to accommodate growth and changes in future needs.

The systems requirements should be as detailed as the user's technical background permits. Detailed specifications enable users to narrow the search to only those packages most likely to satisfy their needs. Although computer literacy is a distinct advantage in this step, the technically inexperienced user can still compile a meaningful list of desirable features that the system should possess. For example, the user should address such items of importance as compliance with accounting conventions, special control and transaction volume requirements, and so on.

Step 2: Send Out the Request for Proposals

Systems requirements are summarized in a document called a **request for proposal (RFP)** that is sent to each prospective vendor. A letter of transmittal accompanies the RFP to explain to the vendor the nature of the problem, the objectives of the system, and the deadline for proposal submission.

The RFP provides a format for vendor responses and thus a comparative basis for initial screening. Some vendors will choose not to respond to the RFP, while others will propose packages that clearly do not meet the stated requirements. The reviewer should attempt to select from these responses those proposals that are feasible alternatives.

Step 3: Gather Facts

In this next step in the selection process, the objective is to identify and capture relevant facts about each vendor's system. The following describes techniques for fact gathering.

Vendor Presentations. At some point during the review, vendors should be invited to make formal presentations of their systems at the user's premises. This provides the principle decision makers and users an opportunity to observe the product firsthand.

Technical demonstrations are usually given at these presentations using modified versions of the packages that run on microcomputers. This provides an opportunity to obtain answers to detailed questions. Sufficient time should therefore be allotted for an in-depth demonstration followed by a question-and-answer period. If vendor representatives are unable or unwilling to demonstrate the full range of system capabilities or to deal with specific questions from the audience, this may indicate a functional deficiency of the system.

Failure to gain satisfactory responses from vendor representatives may also be a sign of their technical incompetence. The representatives either do not understand the user's problem or their own system and how it relates to the user's situation. In either case, the user has cause to question the vendor's ability to deliver a quality product and to provide adequate support.

Benchmark Problems. One often-used technique for measuring the relative performance of competing systems is to establish a benchmark problem for them to solve. The benchmark problem could consist of important transactions or tasks performed by key components of the system. In the benchmark example illustrated in Figure 14–4, both systems are given the same data and processing task. The results of processing are compared on criteria such as speed, accuracy, and efficiency in performing the task.

Vendor Support. For some organizations, vendor support is an important criterion in systems selection. The desired level of support should be carefully considered. Organizations with competent in-house systems professionals may need less vendor support than firms without such internal resources. Support can vary greatly from vendor to vendor. Some vendors provide full-service support, including:

- Client training.
- User and technical documentation.
- Warranties.

FIGURE 14–4

Benchmark Approach to Testing Competing Software

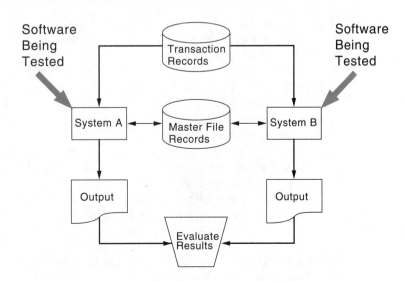

- Maintenance programs to implement system enhancements.
- Toll-free help numbers.
- Annual seminars to obtain input from users and apprise them of the latest developments.

At the other extreme, some vendors provide virtually no support. The buyer should be wary of a promise of support that seems too good to be true, because it probably is. The level of support the vendor provides can account for a large portion of its product's price. To avoid "dump and run" vendors, the buyer must be prepared to pay for support.

Contact User Groups. A vendor's current user list is an important source of information. The prospective user, not the vendor, should select a representative sample of users with the latest version of the package and with similar computer configurations. A standard set of questions directed to these users will provide information for comparing packages. The following list is an example of the type of questions to ask:

- When did you purchase the package?
- Which other vendors did you review?
- Why did you select this package?
- Are you satisfied with the package?
- Are you satisfied with the vendor support?
- Does the system perform as advertised?
- Were modifications required?
- What type of training did the vendor provide?
- What is the quality of the documentation?
- Have any major problems been encountered?
- Do you subscribe to the vendor's maintenance program?
- If so, do you receive enhancements?

To reiterate an important point, the prospective user, not the vendor, should select the user references. This provides for a more objective appraisal and reduces the possibility of receiving biased information from "showcase" installations.

Step 4: Analyze the Findings and Make a Final Selection

The final step in the selection process is to analyze the facts and choose the best package. The principle problem is dealing with the many qualitative aspects of this decision. A popular technique for structuring and analyzing qualitative variables is the "weighted factor matrix." The technique requires constructing a table similar to the one illustrated in Table 14–4. This table shows a comparison between only two proposals, those of Vendor A and Vendor B. In practice, the approach can be applied to all the vendors under consideration.

The table presents the relevant decision criteria under the heading "Factor." Each decision factor is assigned a weight that implies its relative importance to the user. Two steps are critical to this analysis technique: (1) identify all relevant decision factors and (2) assign realistic weights to each factor. As these factors represent all of the relevant decision criteria, their weights should total 100 percent. These weights will likely vary among decision makers. One reviewer may consider vendor support an important factor and thus assign a high numeric value to its weight. Another decision maker may give this a low weight because support is not important in his or her firm, relative to other factors.

TABLE 14–4	**Weighted Factor Matrix**					
			PROPOSAL A		PROPOSAL B	
Factor	Weight	Raw Score	Weighted Score	Raw Score	Weighted Score
Response time	10	5	50	4	40
Compatibility	9	3	27	5	45
Reputation and experience	5	3	15	5	25
Ability to deliver on schedule	7	4	28	5	35
Range of capabilities	15	4	60	4	60
Modularity	12	4	48	3	36
User friendliness	15	4	60	3	45
Supports database	9	2	18	5	45
Supports networking	3	2	6	5	15
Vendor support	15	4	60	3	45
Total	100		372		391

After assigning weights, each vendor package is evaluated according to its performance in each factor category. Based upon the facts gathered in the previous steps, each individual factor is scored on a scale of 1 to 5, where 1 is poor performance and 5 is excellent. The weighted scores are computed by multiplying the raw score by the weight for each factor. Using the previous example, a weight of 15 for vendor support is multiplied by a score of 4 for Vendor A and 3 for Vendor B, yielding the weighted scores of 60 and 45, respectively.

The weighted scores are then totaled, and each vendor is assigned a composite score. This is the vendor's overall performance index. Table 14–4 shows a score for Vendor B of 391 and 372 for Vendor A. This composite score suggests that Vendor B's product is rated slightly higher than Vendor A's.

This analysis must be taken a step further to include financial considerations. For example, assume Proposal A costs $150,000 and Proposal B costs $190,000. An overall performance/cost index is computed as follows.

$$\text{PROPOSAL A: } \frac{372}{\$150,000} = 2.48 \text{ per } \$1,000$$

$$\text{PROPOSAL B: } \frac{391}{\$190,000} = 2.06 \text{ per } \$1,000$$

This means that Proposal A provides 2.48 units of performance per $1,000 versus only 2.06 units per $1,000 from Proposal B. Therefore, Proposal A provides the greater value for the cost.

The option with the highest performance/cost ratio is the more economically feasible choice. Of course, this analysis rests on the user's ability to identify all relevant decision factors and assign to them weights that reflect their relative importance to the decision. If any relevant factors are omitted or if their weights are misstated, the results of the analysis will be misleading.

THE ROLE OF ACCOUNTANTS IN SYSTEMS EVALUATION AND SELECTION

The primary concern for accountants is that the economic feasibility of the proposed system is measured as accurately as possible. Specifically, the accountant should ensure that:

1. Only escapable costs are used in calculations of cost savings benefits.
2. Reasonable interest rates are used in measuring present values of cash flows.
3. One-time and recurring costs are completely and accurately reported.
4. Realistic useful lives are used in comparing competing projects.
5. Intangible benefits are assigned reasonable financial values.

Errors, omissions, and misrepresentations in the accounting for such items can distort the analysis and result in a suboptimal decision.

Accountants should likewise be involved in the selection of commercial software. All systems that process financial transactions are of concern to accountants, because the integrity of accounting information rests directly upon the quality of these systems. Systems that process transactions incorrectly, fail to comply with accounting standards, or fail to produce an audit trail may expose the organization to financial loss. To minimize such problems, the procedures by which commercial software is acquired come under close scrutiny by accountants.

DETAILED SYSTEMS DESIGN

The purpose of the **detailed design phase** is to produce a detailed description of the proposed system that both satisfies the system requirements identified during systems analysis and is in accordance with the conceptual design. In this phase, all system components—user views, database tables, processes, and controls—are meticulously specified. At the end of this phase, these components are presented formally in a detailed design report. This report constitutes a set of "blueprints" that specify input screen formats, output report layouts, database structures, and process logic. These completed plans then proceed to the final phase in the SDLC—system implementation—where the system is physically constructed.

THE DESIGN SEQUENCE

The **detailed systems design** phase of the SDLC follows a logical sequence of events: create a data model of the business process, define conceptual user views, design the normalized database tables, design the physical user views (output and input views), develop the process modules, specify the system controls, and perform a system walkthrough. In this section, each of the design steps is examined in detail.

An Iterative Approach

Typically, the design sequence listed above is not a purely linear process. Inevitably, system requirements change during the detailed design phase, causing the designer to revisit previous steps. For example, a last-minute change in the process design may influence data collection requirements that, in turn, changes the user view and requires alterations to the database tables.

To deal with this material as concisely and clearly as possible, the detailed design phase is presented here as a neat linear process. However, the reader should recognize its circular nature. This characteristic has control implications for both accountants and management. For example, a control issue that was previously resolved may need to be revisited as a result of modifications to the design.

DATA MODELING, CONCEPTUAL VIEWS, AND NORMALIZED TABLES

Data modeling is the task of formalizing the data requirements of the business process as a conceptual model. The primary documentation instrument used for data modeling is the entity relationship (ER) diagram. This technique is used to depict the entities or data objects in the system. Once the entities have been represented in the data model, the data attributes that define each entity can then be described. They should be determined by careful analysis of user needs and may include both financial and nonfinancial data. These attributes represent the **conceptual user views** that must be supported by *normalized database tables*. To the extent that the data requirements of all users have been properly specified in the data model, the resulting databases will support multiple user views. Data modeling, defining user views, and designing normalized base tables were described in Chapter 9 and its appendix. In the interest of space, these procedures are not reexamined here.

DESIGN PHYSICAL USER VIEWS

The physical views are the media for conveying and presenting data. These include output reports, documents, and input screens. The remainder of this section deals with a number of issues related to the design of physical user views. The discussion examines output and input views separately.

Design Output Views

Output is the information produced by the system to support user tasks and decisions. Table 14–5 presents examples of output produced by several AIS subsystems. At the transaction processing level, output tends to be extremely detailed. Revenue and expenditure cycle systems produce control reports for lower-level management and operational documents to support daily activities. Conversion cycle systems produce reports for scheduling production, managing inventory, and cost management. These systems also produce documents for controlling the manufacturing process.

The general ledger/financial reporting system (GL/FRS) and the management reporting system (MRS) produce output that is more summarized. The intended users of these systems are management, stockholders, and other interested parties outside the firm. The GL/FRS is a nondiscretionary reporting system that produces formal reports required by law. These include financial statements, tax returns, and other reports demanded by regulatory agencies. The output requirements of the GL/FRS tend to be predictable and stable over time and between organizations.

The management reporting system serves the needs of internal management users. MRS applications may be stand-alone systems or they may be integrated in the revenue, conversion, and expenditure cycles to produce output that contains both financial and nonfinancial information. The MRS produces problem-specific reports that vary considerably between business entities.

Output Attributes. Regardless of their physical form, whether operational documents, financial statements, or discretionary reports, output views should possess the

TABLE 14–5	**Examples of System Outputs**

System	Output
Expenditure cycle	Purchase orders Cash disbursement voucher Payment check Purchases summary report Cash disbursements summary
Revenue cycle	Sales invoice Remittance advice Bill of lading Packing slip Customer statements Deposit slips Cash receipts prelist Sales summary Cash receipts summary
Conversion cycle	Purchase requisitions Work orders Move tickets Materials requisitions Production schedules Job tickets Employee time cards Work-in-process status reports Summary of changes to finish goods
General ledger and financial reporting system	Financial statements Comparative financial statements Tax returns Reports to regulatory agencies

Management Reporting System	Various status and analysis reports such as:
	    Inventory turnover reports
	    Inventory status reports
	    Vendor analysis reports
	    Budget and performance reports

following attributes: relevance, summarization, exceptions orientation, timeliness, accuracy, completeness, and conciseness.

Relevance. Each element of information output must support the user's decision or task. Irrelevant facts waste resources and detract attention from the information content of the output. Output documents that contain unnecessary facts tend to be cluttered, take time to process, cause bottlenecks, and promote errors.

Summarization. Reports should be summarized according to the level of the user in the organization. The degree of summarization increases as information flows upward from lower-level managers to top management. We see this characteristic clearly in the responsibility reports represented in Figure 14–5.

FIGURE 14–5

Responsibility Reports Showing Consolidation of Information

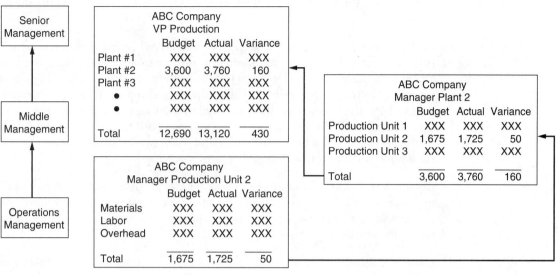

Exception Orientation. **Operations control reports** should identify activities that are about to go out of control and ignore those that are functioning within normal limits. This allows managers to focus their attention on areas of greatest need. An example of this is illustrated with the inventory reorder report presented in Figure 14–6. Only the items that need to be ordered are listed on the report.

FIGURE 14–6

Inventory Reorder Report

Sports Car Factory
Inventory Reorder Report

12975

Date: 11/22/01

The following inventory items have fallen below normal levels:

Part	Description	Primary Vendor	Order Quantity	Quantity On Hand	Average Daily Usage
47782	Exhaust Header	2378	10	2	1
6671	Wheel Bearing	2378	500	25	20
9981	Ball Joint	2401	200	10	20

Timeliness. Timely information that is reasonably accurate and complete is more valuable than perfect information that comes too late to be useful. Therefore, the system must provide the user with information that is timely enough to support the desired action.

Accuracy. Information output must be free of material errors. A material error is one that causes the user to take an incorrect action or to fail to take the correct action. Operational documents and low-level control reports usually require a high degree of accuracy. However, for certain planning reports and reports that support rapid decision making, the system designer may need to sacrifice accuracy to produce information that is timely. Managers cannot always wait until they have all the facts before they must act. The designer must seek a balance between the competing needs for accuracy and timeliness when designing output reports.

Completeness. Information must be as complete as possible. Ideally, no piece of information essential to the task or decision should be missing from the output. As with the accuracy attribute, the designer must sometimes sacrifice completeness in favor of timely information.

Conciseness. Information output should be presented as concisely as possible within the report or document. Output should use coding schemes to represent complex data classifications. Also, information should be clearly presented with titles for all values. Reports should be visually pleasing and logically organized.

Output Reporting Techniques. While recognizing that differences in cognitive styles exist among managers, systems designers must determine the output type and format most useful to the user. Some managers prefer output that presents information in tables and matrices. Others prefer information that is visually oriented in the form of graphs and charts. The issue of whether the output should be hard copy (paper) or electronic must also be addressed.

Despite predictions for two decades or more, we have not yet achieved a paperless society. On the contrary, trees continue to be harvested and paper mills continue to be productive. In some firms, top management receives hundreds of pages of paper output each day. Paper documents also continue to flow at lower organizational levels.

On the other hand, many firms are moving to paperless audit trails and support daily tasks with electronic documents. Insurance companies, law firms, and mortgage companies make extensive use of electronic documents. The problems associated with paper documents (purchasing, handling, storage, and disposal) are greatly reduced or eliminated by the use of electronic output. However, the use of electronic output has obvious implications for accounting and auditing.

The query and report-generating features of modern database management systems permit the manager to quickly create standard and customized output reports. Custom reports can present information in different formats, including text, matrices, tables, and graphs. Section 1 in the chapter appendix examines these formats and provides some examples.

Design Input Views

Data input views are used to capture the relevant facts about the resources, events, and agents involved in business process transactions. In this section, we divide input into two classes: hard-copy input and electronic input.

Design Hard-Copy Input. Businesses today still make extensive use of paper input documents. In designing **hard copy** documents, the system designer must keep in mind several aspects of the physical business process. Several of these are discussed below.

Handling. How will the document be handled? Will it be on the shop floor around grease and oil? How many hands must it go through? Is it likely to get folded, creased, or torn? Input forms are part of the audit trail and must be preserved in legible form. If they are to be subjected to physical abuse, they must be made of high-quality paper.

Storage. How long will the form be stored? What is the storage environment? Length of storage time and environmental conditions will influence the appearance of the form. Data entered onto poor-quality paper may fade under extreme conditions. Again, this may have audit trail implications. A related consideration is the need to protect the form against erasures.

Numbers of Copies. Source documents are often created in multiple copies to trigger multiple activities simultaneously and provide a basis for reconciliation. For example, the system may require that individual copies of sales orders go to the warehouse, the shipping department, billing, and accounts receivable. Manifold forms are often used in such cases. A manifold form produces several carbon copies from a single writing. The copies are normally color-coded to facilitate distribution to the correct users.

Form Size. The average number of facts captured for each transaction affects the size of the form. For example, if the average number of items received from the supplier for each purchase is 20, the receiving report should be long enough to record them all. Otherwise, additional copies will be needed, which will add to the clerical work, clog the system, and promote processing errors.

Standard forms sizes are full-size, 8fi by 11 inches; and half size, 8fi by 5fi inches. Card form standards are 8 by 10 inches and 8 by 5 inches. The use of nonstandard forms can cause handling and storage problems and should be avoided.

Form Design. Clerical errors and omissions can cause serious processing problems. Input forms must be designed to be easy to use and collect the data as efficiently and effectively as possible. This requires that forms be logically organized and visually comfortable to the user. Two techniques used in well-designed forms are zones and embedded instructions.

Zones. **Zones** are areas on the form that contain related data. Figure 14–7 provides an example of a form divided into zones. Each zone should be constructed of lines, captions, or boxes that guide the user's eye to avoid errors and omissions.

Embedded Instructions. **Embedded instructions** are contained within the body of the form itself rather than on a separate sheet. It is important to place instructions directly in the zone to which they pertain. If an instruction pertains to the entire form, it should be placed at the top of the form. Instructions should be brief and unambiguous. As an instructive technique, active voice is stronger, more efficient (needing fewer words), and less ambiguous than passive voice. For example, the first instruction below is written in passive voice. The second is in active voice.

1. This form should be completed in ink.
2. Complete this form in ink.

FIGURE 14–7

Zones of a Form

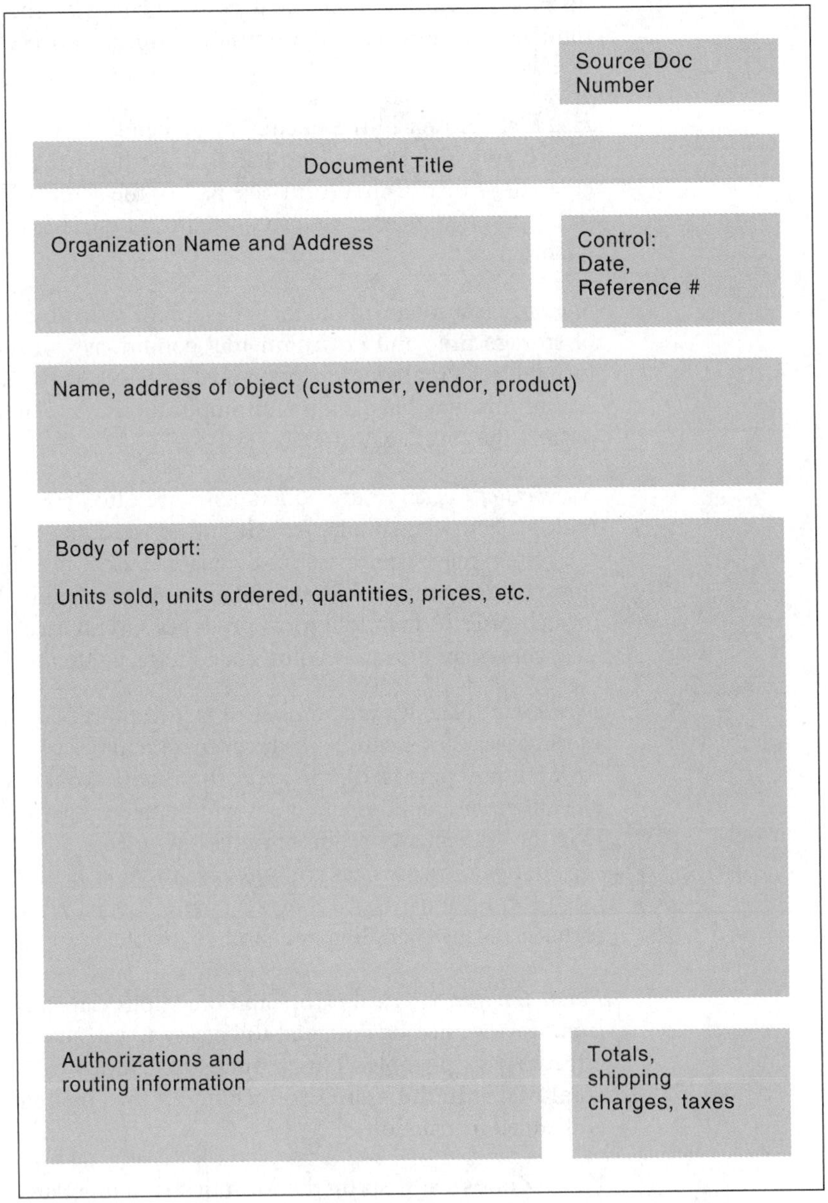

Notice the difference: the second sentence is stronger, shorter, and clearer than the first; it is an instruction rather than a suggestion.

Design Electronic Input. **Electronic input techniques** fall into two basic types: input from source documents and direct input. Figure 14–8 illustrates the difference in these techniques. Input from source documents involves the collection of data on paper forms that are then transcribed to electronic forms in a separate operation. Direct input procedures capture data directly in electronic form, via terminals at the source of the transaction.

FIGURE 14–8

Input from Source
Document and
Direct Input

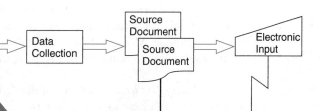

Input from Source Documents

Input from Source Documents. Firms use paper source documents for a number of reasons. Some firms prefer to maintain a paper audit trail that goes back to the source of an economic event. Some companies capture data onto paper documents because direct input procedures may be inconvenient or impossible. Other firms achieve economies of scale by centralizing electronic data collection from paper documents.

An important aspect of this approach is to design input screens that visually reflect the source document. The captions and data fields should be arranged on the electronic form exactly as they are on the source document. This minimizes eye movement between the source and the screen and maximizes throughput of work.

Direct Input. Direct data input requires that data collection technology be distributed to the source of the transaction. A very common example of this is the point-of-sale terminal in a department store.

An advantage of direct input is the reduction of input errors that plague downstream processing. By collecting data once, at the source, clerical errors are reduced since the subsequent transcription step associated with paper documents is eliminated. The more times a transaction is manually transcribed, the greater the potential for error.

Direct data collection uses **intelligent forms** for on-line editing that help the user complete the form and make calculations automatically. The input screen is attached to a computer that performs logical checks on the data being entered. This reduces input errors and improves the efficiency of the data collection procedures. During data entry, the intelligent form will detect transcription errors, such as illegal characters in a field, incorrect amounts, and invalid item numbers. A beep can be used to draw attention to an error, an illegal action, or a screen message. Thus, corrections to input can be made on the spot.

Given minimal input, an intelligent form can complete the input process automatically. For example, a sales clerk need enter into the terminal only the item numbers and quantities of products sold. The system will automatically provide the descriptions, prices, price extensions, taxes, and freight charges and calculate the grand total. Many time-consuming and error-prone activities are eliminated through this technique. Modern relational database packages have a *screen painting* feature that allows the user to quickly and easily create intelligent input forms.

Data Entry Devices. A number of data entry devices are used to support direct electronic input. These include point-of-sale terminals, magnetic ink character recognition devices, optical character recognition devices, automatic teller machines, and voice recognition devices.

DESIGN THE SYSTEM PROCESS

Now that the database tables and user views for the system have been designed, we are ready to design the process component. This starts with the DFDs that were produced in the general design phase. Depending on the extent of the activities performed in the general design phase, the system may be specified at the context level or may be refined in lower-level DFDs. The first task is to decompose the existing DFDs to a degree of detail that will serve as the basis for creating structure diagrams. The structure diagrams will provide the blueprints for writing the actual program modules.

Decompose High-Level DFDs

To demonstrate the decomposition process, we will use the intermediate DFD of the purchases and cash disbursements system illustrated in Figure 14–9. This DFD was decomposed from the context-level DFD (Figure 13–17, Option A) originally prepared in the conceptual design phase. We will concentrate on the accounts payable process numbered 1.4 in the diagram. This process is not yet sufficiently detailed to produce program modules.

Figure 14–10 shows Process 1.4 decomposed into the next level of detail. Each of the resulting subprocesses is numbered with a third-level designator, such as 1.4.1, 1.4.2, 1.4.3, and so on. We will assume that this level of DFD provides sufficient detail to prepare a structure diagram of program modules. Many CASE tools will automatically convert DFDs to structure diagrams. However, to illustrate the concept, we will go through the process manually.

Design Structure Diagrams

The creation of the **structure diagram** requires analysis of the DFD to divide its processes into input, process, and output functions. Figure 14–11 on page 715 presents a structure diagram showing the program modules based on the DFD in Figure 14–10.

The Modular Approach

The modular approach presented in Figure 14–11 involves arranging the system in a hierarchy of small discrete modules, each of which performs a single task. Correctly designed modules possess two attributes: they are loosely coupled, and they have strong cohesion. **Coupling** measures the degree of interaction between modules.

FIGURE 14–9 DFD for Purchases and Cash Disbursements System

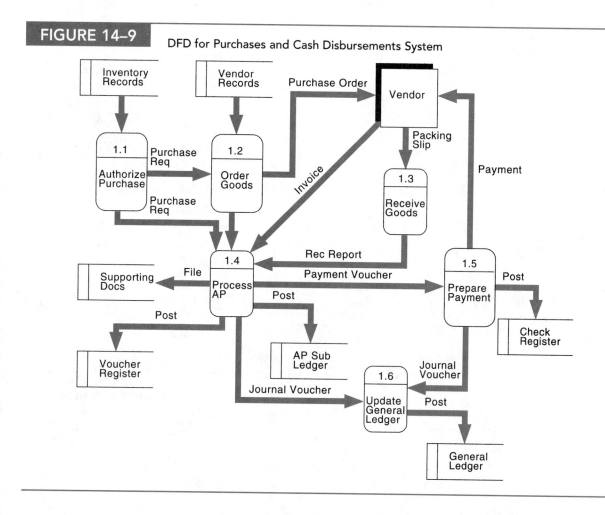

Interaction is the exchange of data between modules. A loosely coupled module is independent of the others. Modules with a great deal of interaction are tightly coupled. Figure 14–12 shows the relationship between modules in loosely coupled and tightly coupled designs.

In the loosely coupled system, the process starts with Module A. This module controls all the data flowing through the system. The other modules interact only with this module to send and receive data. Module A then redirects the data to other modules.

Cohesion refers to the number of tasks a module performs. Strong cohesion means that each module performs a single, well-defined task. Returning to Figure 14–11, Module D gets receiving reports and only that. It does not compare reports to open purchase orders, nor does it update accounts payable. These tasks are performed by separate modules.

Modules that are loosely coupled and strongly cohesive are much easier to understand and easier to maintain. Maintenance is an error-prone process, and it is not uncommon for errors to be accidentally inserted into a module during maintenance. Thus, changing a single module within a tightly coupled structure can have an impact on the other modules with which it interacts. Look again at the tightly coupled structure in Figure 14–12. These interactions complicate maintenance by extending the

FIGURE 14–10

Lower-Level DFD for
AP Process 1.4

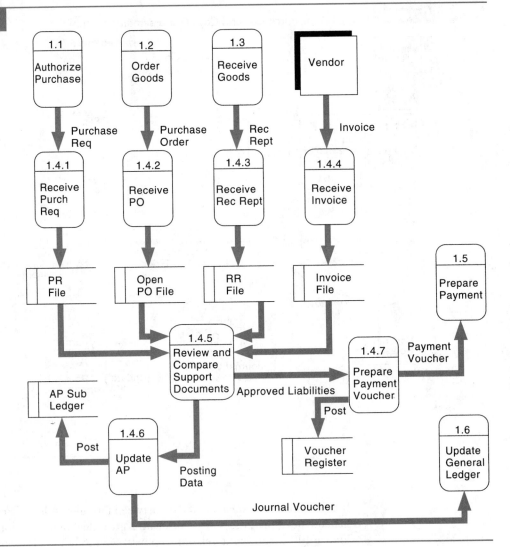

process to the other modules. Similarly, modules with weak cohesion—those that perform several tasks—are more complex and difficult to maintain.

Pseudocode the System Modules

Each module in Figure 14–11 represents a separate computer program. The higher-level programs will communicate with lower-level programs through "call" commands. System modules are coded in the implementation phase. When we get to that phase, we will examine programming language options. At this point, the designer must specify the functional characteristics of the modules through other techniques.

Next, we illustrate how **pseudocode** may be used to describe the function of Module F in Figure 14–11. This module authorizes payment of accounts payable by validating the supporting documents.

FIGURE 14-11   Structure Diagram for AP Process

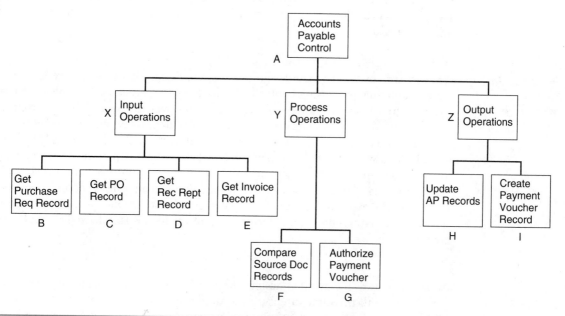

COMPARE-DOCS (Module F)
    READ PR-RECORD FROM PR-FILE
    READ PO-RECORD FROM PO-FILE
    READ RR-RECORD FROM RR-FILE
    READ INVOICE-RECORD FROM INVOICE-FILE
    IF ITEM-NUM, QUANTITY-RECEIVED, TOTAL-AMOUNT
        IS EQUAL FOR ALL RECORDS
            THEN PLACE "Y" IN AUTHORIZED FIELD OF PO-RECORD
    ELSE READ ANOTHER RECORD

The use of pseudocode for specifying module functions has two advantages. First, the designer can express the detailed logic of the module, regardless of the programming

FIGURE 14-12

Weakly and Tightly Coupled Modules

Loosely Coupled Modules

Tightly Coupled Modules

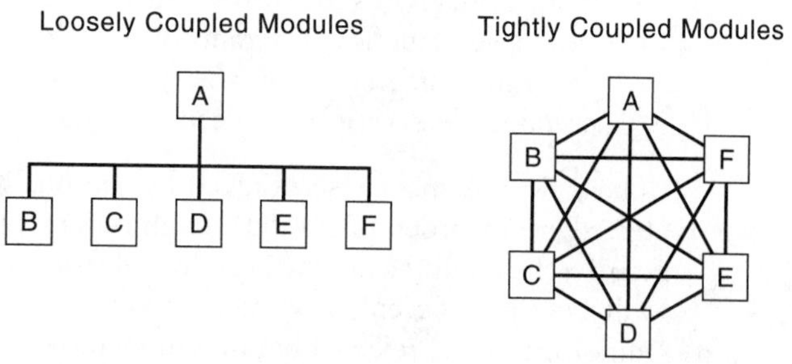

language to be used. Second, although the end user may lack programming skills, he or she can be actively involved in this technical but crucial step. Section 2 of the chapter appendix provides a complete example of pseudocoding based on the structure diagram in Figure 14–11.

DESIGN SYSTEM CONTROLS

The last step in the detailed design phase is the design of system controls. This includes computer processing controls, database controls, manual controls over input to and output from the system, as well as controls over the operational environment (for example, distributed data processing controls). In practice, many controls that are specific to a type of technology or technique will, at this point, have already been designed, along with the modules to which they relate. This step in the design phase allows the design team to review, modify, and evaluate controls with a systemwide perspective that did not exist when each module was being designed independently. Because of the extensive nature of computer-based system controls, treatment of this aspect of the systems design is deferred to Chapters 15 and 16, where they can be covered in depth.

PERFORM A SYSTEM DESIGN WALKTHROUGH

After completing the detailed design, the development team usually performs a system design **walkthrough** to ensure the design is free from conceptual errors that could become programmed into the final system. Many firms have formal, structured walkthroughs conducted by a **quality assurance group**. This is an independent group of programmers, analysts, users, and internal auditors. The job of this group is to simulate the operation of the system to uncover errors, omissions, and ambiguities in the design. Most system errors emanate from poor designs rather than programming mistakes. Detecting and correcting errors in the design thus reduces costly reprogramming later.

Review System Documentation

The **detailed design report** documents and describes the system to this point. This report includes:

- Designs of all screen outputs, reports, and operational documents.
- Entity relationship (ER) diagrams describing the data relations in the system.
- Third normal form designs for database tables specifying all data elements.
- An updated **data dictionary** describing each data element in the database.
- Designs for all screen inputs and source documents for the system.
- Context diagrams for the overall system.
- Low-level data flow diagrams of specific system processes.
- Structure diagrams for the program modules in the system, including a pseudocode description of each module.

These documents are scrutinized by the quality control group, and any errors detected are recorded in a walkthrough report. Depending on the extent of the system errors, the quality assurance group will make a recommendation. The system design will be either accepted without modification, accepted subject to modification of minor errors, or rejected because of material errors.

At this point, a decision is made either to return the system for additional design or to proceed to the next phase—systems implementation. Assuming the design goes forward, the documents just mentioned constitute the "blueprints" that guide programmers and system designers in constructing the physical system.

SYSTEM IMPLEMENTATION

The system is now ready to be implemented. In this final phase of the SDLC, database structures are created and populated with data, applications are coded and tested, equipment is purchased and installed, employees are trained, and the system is documented. This phase concludes with the conversion to the new system and termination of the old system.

The implementation process engages the efforts of designers, programmers, database administrators, users, and accountants. The activities in this phase entail extensive costs and will often consume more personnel hours than all other phases of the SDLC combined. All the steps in this stage warrant careful management. Nevertheless, not all steps are part of every systems implementation and not all are of direct concern to accountants. For example, the implementation activities of ordering equipment from vendors, preparing the site, installing equipment, and training employees are not performed with each new system. Moreover, these are technical tasks that do not usually involve the accounting function.

This section focuses on those activities that have the greatest direct implications for accountants and auditors. These include managing the systems implementation, developing system software, documenting the system, converting the databases, converting to the new system, and conducting the post-implementation review.

MANAGING THE SYSTEM IMPLEMENTATION

The first step in the implementation phase is to create an implementation schedule. Two popular techniques for this purpose are the PERT chart and the Gantt chart. We will briefly discuss how a project may be managed using these methods.

PERT Charts

The project evaluation and review technique (PERT) reflects the relationship among the many activities that constitute the implementation process. Figure 14–13 presents a **PERT chart** for a hypothetical project. The principal features of this diagram are:

1. *Activities*—the tasks to be completed in the project. These are labeled (and lettered A through H) on the lines, along with the time estimate for their completion. For example, the programming activity (C) is estimated to take nine weeks.
2. *Events* that mark the completion of one activity and the beginning of the next. The events in this diagram are numbered 1 through 7.
3. *Paths*—routes through the diagram that connect the events from the first to the last.
4. *Critical path*—the path with the greatest overall time. The critical path in this project is C-F-G-H, with a total time of 18 (9 + 3 + 2 + 4) weeks. Any time delays in the activities along this path will extend the overall project time, which is why this path is critical.

Gantt Charts

The **Gantt chart** is a horizontal bar chart that presents time on a horizontal plane and activities on a vertical plane. Figure 14–14 illustrates a Gantt chart for a project

FIGURE 14–13   PERT Chart for System Project

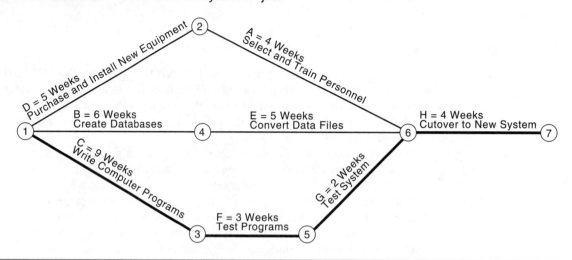

FIGURE 14–14   Gantt Chart

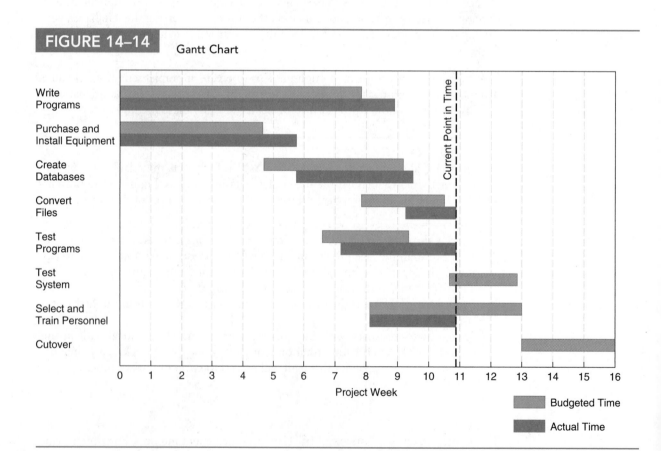

including several typical implementation activities. The time associated with each activity is represented by a bar marking its starting and ending dates. The Gantt chart is popular because it can show the current status of the project at a glance. By comparing projected time and work completed to date, we can see which projects are on, ahead of, or behind schedule.

DEVELOPING
APPLICATION
SOFTWARE

The objective of **software development** is to produce high-quality applications from the detailed design specifications. This may be accomplished in-house or through the purchase of commercial software. The decision to use vendor-supplied software may occur at any of several places within the SDLC. We discussed the commercial software option earlier in the chapter.

Assuming the in-house development option is chosen the next decision is to select a programming language from among the various languages that are available and suitable to the application. These include *procedural languages* like COBOL, *event-driven languages* like Visual Basic, or *object-oriented programming (OOP) languages* like Java or C++. This section presents a brief overview of various programming approaches. Systems professionals will make their decision based on the nature of the application and the needs of the user.

Procedural Languages

A **procedural language** requires the programmer to specify the precise order in which the program logic is executed. Procedural languages are often called **third-generation languages** (3GLs). Examples of 3GLs include COBOL, FORTRAN, C, and PL1. In business (particularly in accounting) applications, COBOL was the dominant language for years. COBOL has great capability for performing highly detailed operations on individual data records and handles large files very efficiently. On the other hand, it is an extremely "wordy" language that makes programming a time-consuming task. COBOL has survived as a viable language because many of the "legacy systems" written in the 1970s and 1980s, which were coded in COBOL, are still in operation today. Major retrofits and routine maintenance to these systems need to be coded in COBOL. Upward of 12 billion lines of COBOL code are executed daily in the United States.

Event-Driven Languages

Event-driven languages are no longer procedural. Under this model, the program's code is not executed in a predefined sequence. Instead, external actions or "events" that are initiated by the user dictate the control flow of the program. For example, when the user presses a key, or "clicks" on an icon on the computer screen, the program automatically executes code associated with that event. This is a fundamental shift from the 3GL era. Now, instead of designing applications that execute sequentially from top to bottom in accordance with the way the programmer *thinks* they should function, the user is in control.

Microsoft's Visual Basic is the most popular example of an event-driven language. The syntax of the language is simple yet powerful. Visual Basic is used to create real-time and batch applications that can manipulate flat files or relational databases. It has a screen-painting feature that greatly facilitates the creation of sophisticated *graphical user interfaces (GUI)*.

Object-Oriented Languages

We discussed the object-oriented approach in Chapter 13. Central to achieving the benefits of this approach is developing software in an **object-oriented programming (OOP) language**. The most popular true OOP languages are Java and Smalltalk. However, the learning curve of OOP languages is steep. The time and cost of retooling for OOP is the greatest impediment to the transition process. Most firms are not prepared to discard millions of lines of traditional COBOL code and retrain their programming staffs to implement object-oriented systems. Therefore, a compromise, intended to ease this transition, has been the development of hybrid languages, such as Object COBOL, Object Pascal, and C++.

Programming the System

Regardless of the programming language used, modern programs should follow a *modular approach*. This technique produces small programs that perform narrowly defined tasks. The following three benefits are associated with modular programming.

Programming Efficiency. Modules can be coded and tested independently, which vastly reduces programming time. A firm can assign several programmers to a single system. Working in parallel, the programmers each design a few modules. These are then assembled into the completed system.

Maintenance Efficiency. Small modules are easier to analyze and change, which reduces the start-up time during program maintenance. Extensive changes can be parceled out to several programmers simultaneously to shorten maintenance time.

Control. By keeping modules small, they are less likely to contain material errors of fraudulent logic. Since each module is independent of the others, errors are contained within the module.

Software Testing

Programs must be thoroughly tested before they are implemented. Program testing issues of direct concern to accountants are discussed in this section.

Testing Individual Modules. Completed modules should be tested independently by programmers before being implemented. This usually involves the creation of test data. Depending on the nature of the application, this could include test transaction files, test master files, on both. Figure 14–15 illustrates the test data approach. This and several other testing techniques are examined in detail in Chapter 17.

Assume the module under test is the Update AP Records program (Module H) represented in Figure 14–11. The approach taken is to test the application thoroughly within its range of functions. To do this, the programmer must create some test accounts payable master file records and test transactions. The transactions should contain a range of data values adequate to test the logic of the application, including both "good" and "bad" data. For example, the programmer may create a transaction with an incorrect account number to see how the application handles such errors. The programmer will then compare the amounts posted to accounts payable records to see if they tally with precalculated results. Tests of all aspects of the logic will be performed in this way, and the test results will be used to identify and correct errors in the logic of the module.

FIGURE 14–15

The Test Data
Technique

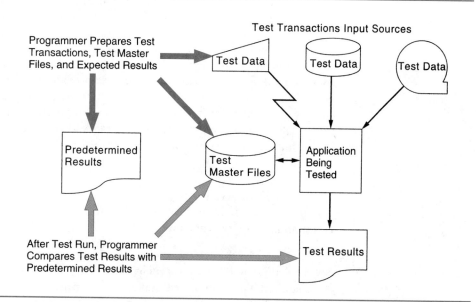

Testing the Entire System. When all modules have been coded and tested, they must
be brought together and tested as a whole. Systemwide testing should be directed by
user personnel as a prelude to the formal system cutover. The procedure involves
using the system to process hypothetical data. The outputs of the system are then reconciled with predetermined results, and the test is documented to provide evidence
of the system's performance. Finally, when those conducting the tests are satisfied
with the results, a formal acceptance document should be completed. This is an explicit acknowledgment by the user that the system in question meets stated requirements. The user acceptance document becomes important in reconciling differences
and assigning responsibility during the post-implementation review of the system.

Saving Test Data. The preparation of test data is a tedious, time-consuming activity.
These data should be saved for future use by the auditor during system reviews. By
preserving the test data, we create what is called a *base case*, which documents how the
system performed at a point in time. At any future point, the base case data should
generate the same results. The only differences between base case results and current
test results will be explained by system changes (maintenance) that have occurred
since system implementation. Hence, the base case provides a reference point for analyzing the effects of system changes and eases the burden of creating test data.

DOCUMENTING THE SYSTEM

The system's **documentation** describes how the system works. In this section, we
consider the documentation requirements of four groups: systems designers and programmers, computer operators, end users, and accountants.

Designer and Programmer Documentation
Systems designers and programmers need documentation to debug errors and perform maintenance on the system. This group is involved with the system on a highly

technical level, which requires both general and detailed information. Some of this is provided through DFDs, ER diagrams, and structure diagrams. In addition, system flowcharts, program flowcharts, and listings of program code are important forms of documentation. The *system flowchart* shows the relationship of input files, programs, and output files. However, it does not reveal the logic of individual programs that constitute the system. The *program flowchart* provides a detailed description of the sequential and logical operation of the program. Each program in the system's flowchart is represented by a separate program flowchart. From these, the programmer can visually review and evaluate the program's logic. The program code should itself be documented with comments that describe each major program segment.

Operator Documentation

Computer operators use documentation describing how to run the system called a **run manual**. The typical contents of a run manual include:

- The name of the system, such as Purchases System.
- The run schedule (daily, weekly, time of day, and so on).
- Required hardware devices (tapes, disks, printers, or special hardware).
- File requirements specifying all the transaction (input) files, master files, and output files used in the system.
- Run time instructions describing the error messages that may appear, actions to be taken, and the name and telephone number of the programmer on call, should the system fail.
- A list of users who receive the output from the run.

For security and control reasons, system flowcharts, logic flowcharts, and program code listings are not part of the operator documentation. Operators should not have access to the details of a system's internal logic. We will discuss this point more fully in Chapter 15.

User Documentation

Users need documentation describing how to use the system. User tasks include such things as entering input for transactions, making inquiries of account balances, updating accounts, and generating output reports. The nature of user documentation will depend upon the user's degree of sophistication with computers and technology. Thus, before designing user documentation, the systems professional must assess and classify the user's skill level. The following is one classification scheme:

- Novices
- Occasional users
- Frequent light users
- Frequent power users

Novices have little or no experience with computers and may be embarrassed to ask questions. Novices also know little about their assigned tasks. User training and documentation for novices must be extensive and detailed.

Occasional users once understood the system but have forgotten some essential commands and procedures. They require less training and documentation than novices.

Frequent light users are familiar with limited aspects of the system. Although functional, they tend not to explore beneath the surface and lack depth of knowledge. This group knows only what it needs to know and requires training and documentation for unfamiliar areas.

Frequent power users understand the existing system and will readily adapt to new systems. They are intolerant of detailed instructions that waste their time. They like to find shortcuts and use macro commands to improve performance. This group requires only abbreviated documentation.

With these classes in mind, user documentation often takes the form of a user handbook, as well as on-line documentation. The typical **user handbook** will contain the following items:

- An overview of the system and its major functions
- Instructions for getting started
- Descriptions of procedures with step-by-step visual references
- Examples of input screens and instructions for entering data
- A complete list of error message codes and descriptions
- A reference manual of commands to run the system
- A glossary of key terms
- Service and support information

On-line documentation will guide the user interactively in the use of the system. Some commonly found on-line features include tutorials and help features.

Tutorials. On-line tutorials can be used to train the novice or the occasional user. The success of this technique is based on the tutorial's degree of realism. Tutorials should not restrict the user from access to legitimate functions.

Help Features. On-line help features range from simple to sophisticated. A simple help feature may be nothing more than an error message displayed on the screen. The user must "walk through" the screens in search of the solution to the problem. More sophisticated help is context-related. When the user makes an error, the system will send the message, "Do you need help?" The help feature analyzes the context of what the user is doing at the time of the error and provides help with that specific function (or command).

Account (Auditor) Documentation

With responsibility for the design of certain security procedures, accounting controls, and audit trails, accountants are stakeholders in all AIS applications. For these tasks, accountants may draw upon all of the documentation described before. As internal and external auditors, accountants also require document flowcharts of manual procedures. We have encountered numerous examples of document flowcharts in the chapters dealing with the revenue, expenditure, and conversion cycles. Document flowcharts differ from DFDs in an important way. DFDs describe the overall logic of the system. Document flowcharts show explicitly the flow of information between departments, the departments in which tasks are actually performed, and the specific types and number of documents that carry information. A physical view such as this is needed to understand the segregation of duties, the adequacy of source documents, and the location of files that support the audit trail. Document flowcharts are not always included as part of the system's documentation. When not provided, auditors must create their own during the audit process.

<table>
<tr><td>

CONVERTING THE DATABASES

</td><td>

Database conversion is a critical step in the implementation phase. This is the transfer of data from its current form to the format or medium required by the new system. The degree of conversion depends on the technology leap from the old system to the new one. Some conversion activities are very labor-intensive, requiring data to be entered into new databases manually. For example, the move from a manual system to a computer system will require converting files from paper to magnetic disk or tape. In other situations, data transfer may be accomplished by writing special conversion programs. A case in point is changing the file structure of the databases from sequential direct access files. In any case, data conversion is risky and must be carefully controlled. The following precautions should be taken:

1. *Validation.* The old database must be validated before conversion. This requires analyzing each class of data to determine whether it should be reproduced in the new database.
2. *Reconciliation.* After the conversion action, the new database must be reconciled against the original. Sometimes this must be done manually, record by record and field by field. In many instances, this process can be automated by writing a program that will compare the two sets of data.
3. *Backup.* Copies of the original files must be kept as backup against discrepancies in the converted data. If the current files are already in magnetic form, they can be conveniently backed up and stored. However, paper documents can create storage problems. When the user feels confident about the accuracy and completeness of the new databases, the paper documents may be destroyed.

</td></tr>
</table>

<table>
<tr><td>

CONVERTING TO THE NEW SYSTEM

</td><td>

The process of converting from the old system to the new one is called the **cutover**. A system cutover will usually follow one of three approaches: cold turkey, phased, or parallel operation.

Cold Turkey Cutover

Under the **cold turkey cutover** approach (also called the "Big Bang" approach), the firm switches to the new system and simultaneously terminates the old system. When implementing simple systems, this is often the easiest and least costly approach. With more complex systems, it is the riskiest. Cold turkey cutover is akin to skydiving without a reserve parachute. As long as the main parachute functions properly, there is no problem. But things don't always work the way they are supposed to. System errors that were not detected during the walkthrough and testing steps may materialize unexpectedly. Without a backup system, an organization can find itself in serious trouble.

Phased Cutover

Sometimes an entire system cannot, or need not, be cutover at once. The **phased cutover** begins operating the new system in modules. For example, Figure 14–16 shows how we might implement a system, starting with the sales subsystem, followed by the inventory control subsystem, and finally the purchases subsystem.

</td></tr>
</table>

FIGURE 14–16

Phased Cutover

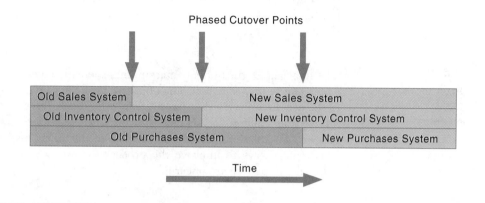

By phasing in the new system in modules, we reduce the risk of a devastating system failure. However, the phased approach can create incompatibilities between new subsystems and yet-to-be-replaced old subsystems. This problem may be alleviated by implementing special conversion systems that provide temporary interfaces during the cutover period.

Parallel Operation Cutover

Parallel operation cutover involves running the old system and the new system simultaneously for a period of time. Figure 14–17 illustrates this approach, which is the most time-consuming and costly of the three. Running two systems in parallel essentially doubles resource consumption. During the cutover period, the two systems require twice the source documents, twice the processing time, twice the databases, and twice the output production.

The advantage of parallel cutover is the reduction in risk. By running two systems, the user can reconcile outputs to identify errors and debug errors before

FIGURE 14–17

Parallel Operation
Cutover

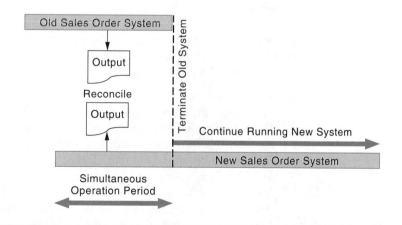

running the new system solo. Parallel operation should usually extend for one business cycle, such as one month. This allows the user to reconcile the two outputs at the end of the cycle as a final test of the system's functionality.

POST-IMPLEMENTATION REVIEW

The final step in the implementation phase actually takes place some months later in a *post-implementation review*. The objective is to measure the success of the system and of the process after the dust has settled. Although systems professionals strive to produce systems that are on budget, on time, and meet user needs, this does not always happen. The post-implementation review of the newly installed system can provide insight into ways to improve the process for future systems. The areas discussed below are of particular concern.

System Design Adequacy

The physical features of the system should be reviewed to see if they meet user needs. The reviewer should seek answers to the following types of questions:

1. Does the output from the system possess such characteristics of information as relevance, timeliness, completeness, accuracy, and so on?
2. Is the output in the format most useful and desired by the user (such as tables, graphs, electronic, hard copy, and so on)?
3. Are the databases accurate, complete, and accessible?
4. Were data lost, corrupted, or duplicated by the conversion process?
5. Are input forms and screens properly designed and meeting user needs?
6. Are the users using the system properly?
7. Does the processing appear to be correct?
8. Can all program modules be accessed and executed properly, or does the user ever get stuck in a loop?
9. Is user documentation accurate, complete, and easy to follow?
10. Does the system provide the user adequate help and tutorials?

Accuracy of Time, Cost, and Benefit Estimates

The task of estimating time, costs, and benefits for a proposed system is complicated by uncertainty. This is particularly true for large projects involving many activities and long time frames. The more variables in the process, the greater the likelihood for material error in the estimates. History is often the best teacher for decisions of this sort. Therefore, a review of actual performance compared to budgeted amounts provides critical input for future budgeting decisions. From such information, we can learn where mistakes were made and how to avoid them the next time. The following questions provide some insight:

1. Were PERT and Gantt chart estimates accurate to within 10 percent?
2. What were the areas of significant departures from budget?
3. Were departures from the budget controllable (internal) in the short run or noncontrollable (for example, supplier problems)?
4. Were estimates of the number of lines of program code accurate?
5. Was the degree of rework due to design and coding errors acceptable?
6. Were actual costs in line with budgeted costs?
7. Are users receiving the expected benefits from the system?
8. Do the benefits seem to have been fairly valued?

THE ROLE OF ACCOUNTANTS

As the preceding discussion has already suggested, the role of accountants in the detailed design and implementation phases should be significant. Most system failures are due to poor designs and improper implementation. Being a major stakeholder in all financial systems, accountants must apply their expertise in this process to guide and shape the finished system. Specifically, accountants should get involved in the following ways.

Provide Technical Expertise

The detailed design phase involves precise specifications of procedures, rules, and conventions to be used in the system. In the case of an AIS, these specifications must comply with GAAP, GAAS, SEC regulations, and IRS codes. Failure to so comply can lead to legal exposure for the firm. For example, choosing the correct depreciation method or asset valuation technique requires a technical background not necessarily possessed by systems professionals. The accountant must provide this expertise to the systems design process.

Specify Documentation Standards

In the implementation phase, the accountant plays a role in specifying system documentation. Since financial systems must periodically be audited, they must be adequately documented. The accountant must actively encourage adherence to effective documentation standards.

Verify Control Adequacy

The applications that emerge from the SDLC must possess controls that are in accordance with the provisions of SAS 78. This requires the accountant's involvement at both the detailed design and implementation phases. Controls may be programmed or manual procedures. Some controls are part of the daily operation of the system, while others are special actions that precede, follow, or oversee routine processing. The extent of control techniques makes it impossible to treat them within this chapter. Instead, we have devoted the next two chapters to the study of control concepts and design.

Summary

This chapter has examined systems evaluation and selection, detailed design, and system implementation phases of the SDLC. Systems evaluation and selection is an important step in which an organization attempts to assess the respective merits of proposed systems. To ensure a correct decision at this crucial stage, management must gather and weigh relevant information regarding the various systems under consideration. This is done through a detailed feasibility study and a careful cost-benefit analysis. Since success at this stage depends, in large part, on an accurate identification of prospective costs and benefits, we devoted special attention to the principle one-time and recurring costs that systems generate and to the various tangible and intangible benefits they can be expected to yield.

We examined the issue of commercial software, an option that businesses are increasingly using. After briefly identifying the pros and cons of commercial software, we examined a four-step procedure that can be employed in the selection of commercial software packages.

In examining the detailed design phase, we initially saw how the design of system components requires adherence to a logical sequence. The first step in the sequence is to model the data requirements of the system and develop conceptual user views. The second step is to design the normalized database tables. This step in the detailed design includes creating database tables, determining table relationships, embedding foreign keys, specifying table attributes, normalizing the tables, and updating the data dictionary.

We then proceeded to the third step of the design sequence—designing the physical user views. Our discussion here focused on the design of hard-copy and electronic output and input media. The next step of the design sequence was process design, which begins by decomposing existing DFDs and then constructs structure diagrams that provide the basis for process modules. At this stage of system design, we saw how pseudocoding can be used to describe the various functions of system modules. Next we introduced the issue of system controls. Detailed treatment of this extensive and important body of material will take place in Chapters 15 and 16. The final step in the detailed design phase is to perform a system walkthrough. The purpose of the walkthrough is to identify system errors prior to implementation and thereby avoid costly reprogramming after the system is up and running.

Once a walkthrough has been performed, system implementation begins with the development of an implementation schedule. Our discussion of system implementation focused on the in-house development and testing of software and the process of documenting the system, which is especially important for accountants. We concluded by examining database conversion, the cutover to the new system, and the post-implementation review, which constitute the final steps in the system implementation phase.

Appendix

**SECTION 1:
OUTPUT
REPORTING
ALTERNATIVES**

This section presents various output design alternatives, along with a number of example output reports.

Tables and Matrices

Tables and matrices can be used to summarize large amounts of information. A *table* is a report arranged in columns and rows, such as the supplier analysis report in Figure 14–18. This table shows columns of evaluation data for suppliers with whom the firm does business. This is an effective means for comparing and contrasting relevant facts.

A *matrix* is a rectangular arrangement of data into rows and columns. Each element (the intersection of a row and a column) is a data value. This form of report is particularly useful for presenting binary state relations—the presence or absence of a state—among elements. Figure 14–19 is a matrix report showing which vendors supply which major inventory items.

Graphs and Charts

Graphs and *charts* present numeric data as geometric shapes. This visual approach to reporting presumes that a picture is worth a thousand words. Certainly this is true

FIGURE 14–18

Supplier Analysis
Report

Attribute	VENDOR			
	Acme Motors	Morgan Supply	Norton Co.	The Roadster Factory
Yrs in Business	1fi	4	9	3
Terms of Trade	2/10, n/30 offers quantity discounts	40% off retail, no quantity discounts	2/10, n/30, offers quantity discounts	Wholesale price list, no quantity discounts
Price Structure	Competitive	Lowest-priced supplier	Competitive	
Lead Time	5–7 days	7–10 days	7–10 days for most Items	3 days guaranteed
Rush Service	1 day delivery at 3% charge	None	None	Overnight—2% charge
Delivery Reliability	Good	Good	Poor	Good

FIGURE 14–19

Matrix Report
Showing Vendors
(columns) and
Inventory (rows)
Provided

Inventory Item Supplied	Vendor			
	Acme Motors	Morgan Supply	Norton Co.	The Roadster Factory
109873 k	X	X	X	X
109873 q	X		X	X
1098745		X		X
1098746	X		X	
•		X		
•				X
•	X		X	
•		X		
•		X		
•	X	X		
•		X		
•			X	
•	X			X
•			X	X
7893279				X
8237419	X			X
9495581	X	X	X	
				X

when conveying such summarized messages as "the big picture" and trends over time, and comparing the performance of multiple products. For these purposes, visual reports are far more effective than numeric reports alone. In this section, we examine five visual reporting techniques: line graph, scatter graph, bar graph, pie chart, and layer chart.

Line Graph. The simple line graph is used to show the fluctuations in an item of interest over time. Figure 14–20 illustrates this approach. We can use different colors and different shaped lines to track multiple items. In Figure 14–20, the solid line is projected sales and the dashed line is actual sales. The increments of the scale (sales dollars) should be small enough to detect material fluctuations. However, in using line graphs, we must guard against using a scale that is too small, because it might portray an exaggerated picture to the user.

Scatter Graph. The purpose of a scatter graph is to reveal relationships among underlying data. To illustrate, Figure 14–21 superimposes a line graph and scatter graph. The line graph shows only the movement from Point A to Point B in the form of a trend line that takes the average path through the data. In some instances, this could result in the loss of important information to the user. The points in the scatter graph show the degree of dispersion associated with the underlying activity.

Bar Graph. The purpose of a bar graph is to show the relationship of total quantities or proportions. Figure 14–22 uses a vertical bar graph to show the relationship over time between actual computer usage for a firm and budgeted usage.

The height of the bars represents the total amount of computer usage. If we were to plot the top points of each bar, we could construct a line graph showing the trend in usage and the relationship between actual and budgeted usage. However, the emphasis of a bar graph is on total amounts at specific points rather than on trends.

The horizontal bar graph is used to compare multiple items in the same time frame. For example, Figure 14–23 compares output from four production plants for the month of January.

FIGURE 14–20

Line Graph Showing
Fluctuations in Sales
Over Time—One-
Month Intervals

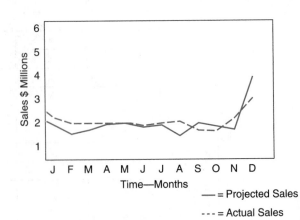

FIGURE 14–21

Scatter Graph
Superimposed
on Line Graph

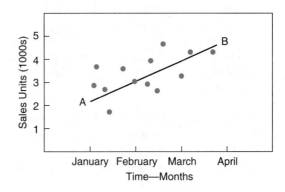

FIGURE 14–22

Bar Graph Showing
Actual Computer
Usage to Budgeted
Usage—Shows CPU
Hours per Month

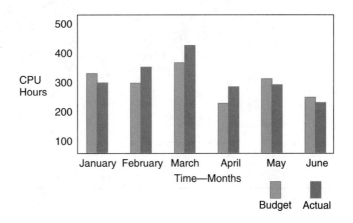

FIGURE 14–23

Horizontal Bar Graph
Comparing Production
of Multiple Plants

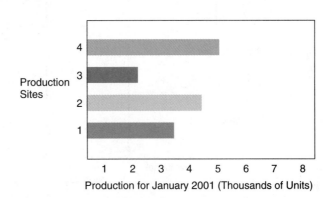

Pie Chart. A pie chart presents the proportional relationship of different items to the whole. For example, Figure 14–24 shows the proportions of several items that together constitute total manufacturing cost. We can differentiate the segments by using color or by exploding them slightly from the rest of the pie. To maintain the visual power of the message, however, the designer should attempt to restrict the number of segments. Too many pie wedges make differentiation difficult and complicate the chart.

Layer Chart. A layer chart also shows proportional relationships but allows the addition of another dimension, such as time or condition. Figure 14–25 illustrates this by showing the change in the proportion of individual item costs to total manufacturing cost under different technology bases.

FIGURE 14–24

Pie Chart for
Manufacturing Costs

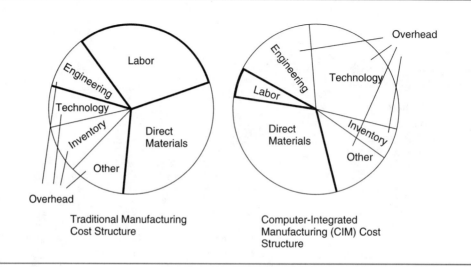

Traditional Manufacturing
Cost Structure

Computer-Integrated
Manufacturing (CIM) Cost
Structure

FIGURE 14–25

Layer Chart of Cost
Proportion Changes
Under Different
Technology Bases

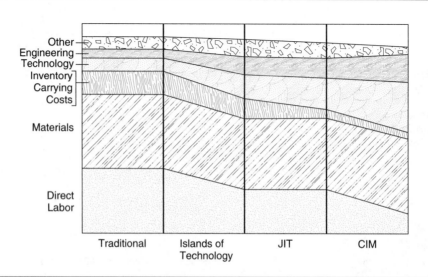

Colors

Colors can greatly enhance the usefulness of a report. Choosing colors that are widely spaced on the color spectrum—such as red, green, and blue—provides for the greatest visual discrimination. This approach can be used to present data that are being compared or contrasted within a report. The level of color intensity can be used to emphasize material items or to deemphasize normal (or less important) data. For example, the variance report in Figure 14–26 shows budgeted amounts, actual amounts, and the variance from budget for each line item.

High-intensity color is used here to draw attention to line items with a material variance (for example, a variance greater than 10 percent). Line items whose variance is under this materiality threshold are deemed under control and are deemphasized by the use of low-intensity color.

SECTION 2: PSEUDOCODING THE SYSTEM MODULES

This section provides an example of the pseudocoding technique. This method is used to represent the functional characteristics of program modules before they are actually programmed. The pseudocode for the structure diagram in Figure 14–11 is presented below.

```
CONTROL PROGRAM (Module A)
    PERFORM INPUT-OPERATION
    PERFORM PROCESS-OPERATION UNTIL END OF FILE
    PERFORM OUTPUT-OPERATION
    END

INPUT-OPERATION (Module X)
    IF PURCHASE REQUISITION PERFORM GET-PR
    IF PURCHASE ORDER PERFORM GET-PO
    IF RECEIVING REPORT PERFORM GET-RR
    IF INVOICE PERFORM GET-INVOICE

GET-PR (Module B)
    READ PR-RECORD AND STORE IN PR-FILE
```

FIGURE 14-26

Variance Report Using Intensity to Highlight Material Variances

Sports Car Factory
Cost Variance Report for Production Dept. 6

Date 11/20/01

CVAR 1

Item	Budget	Actual	(Over) Under Budget
Direct labor	36,000	36,800	< 800 >
Direct materials	122,000	141,600	< 19,600 >
Job setup	4,000	3,600	400
Supplies	2,200	2,330	<130>
Scheduled maintenance	1,200	1,200	0

GET-PO (Module C)
  READ PO-RECORD AND STORE IN PO-FILE

GET-RR (Module D)
  READ RR-RECORD AND STORE IN RR-FILE

GET-INVOICE (Module E)
  READ INVOICE-RECORD AND STORE IN INVOICE-FILE

PROCESS-OPERATION (Module Y)
  PERFORM COMPARE-DOCS
  PERFORM AUTHORIZE-PAYMENT

COMPARE-DOCS (Module F)
  READ PR-RECORD FROM PR-FILE
  READ PO-RECORD FROM PO-FILE
  READ RR-RECORD FROM RR-FILE
  READ INVOICE-RECORD FROM INVOICE-FILE
  IF ITEM-NUM, QUANTITY-RECEIVED, TOTAL-AMOUNT
    EQUAL FOR ALL RECORDS
    THEN PLACE "Y" IN AUTHORIZED FIELD OF PO-RECORD
  ELSE READ ANOTHER RECORD

AUTHORIZE-PAYMENT (Module G)
  READ PO-RECORD FROM PO-FILE
  IF AUTHORIZED EQUALS "Y"
    THEN ADD VOUCHER-REC TO VOUCH-JOURNAL FILE
    MOVE PO-NUM, TOTAL-AMOUNT, DUE-DATE, VENDOR-NUM
    TO VOUCHER-REC IN VOUCH-JOURNAL FILE
  ELSE READ ANOTHER RECORD

OUTPUT-OPERATION (Module Z)
  PERFORM UPDATE-AP
  PERFORM PREPARE-VOUCHER

UPDATE-AP (Module H)
  READ PO-RECORD FROM PO-FILE
  IF AUTHORIZED EQUALS "Y"
    THEN ADD AP-RECORD TO AP-FILE
    MOVE TOTAL-AMOUNT, DUE-DATE, VENDOR-NUM
    TO AP-RECORD IN VOUCH-JOURNAL FILE
  ELSE READ ANOTHER RECORD

PREPARE-VOUCHER (Module I)
  READ VOUCHER-RECORD FROM VOUCH-JOURNAL FILE
  IF DUE-DATE EQUALS TODAYS DATE
    THEN WRITE CD-VOUCHER
  ELSE READ ANOTHER RECORD

Key Terms

cost-benefit analysis   (690)
coupling   (712)
cutover   (724)
data dictionary   (716)
data modeling   (705)
database conversion   (724)
detailed design phase   (704)
detailed design report   (716)
detailed feasibility study   (689)
detailed systems design   (704)
documentation   (721)
electronic input techniques   (710)
embedded instructions   (709)
event-driven languages   (719)
Gantt chart   (717)
hard copy   (709)
intelligent forms   (711)
net present value method   (694)
object-oriented programming (OOP) language
   (720)

on-line documentation   (723)
operations control reports   (707)
parallel operation cutover   (725)
payback method   (695)
PERT chart   (717)
phased cutover   (724)
procedural language   (719)
pseudocode   (714)
quality assurance group   (716)
request for proposal (RFP)   (700)
run manual   (722)
software development   (719)
structure diagram   (712)
systems evaluation and selection   (688)
systems selection report   (695)
third-generation languages   (719)
turnkey systems   (697)
user handbook   (723)
walkthrough   (716)
zones   (709)

Review Questions

1. Who should be included in the group of independent evaluators performing the detailed feasibility study?
2. What makes the cost-benefit analysis more difficult for information systems than most other investments an organization may make?
3. Classify each of the following as either one-time or recurring costs:
   a. training personnel
   b. initial programming and testing
   c. systems design
   d. hardware costs
   e. software maintenance costs
   f. site preparation
   g. rent for facilities
   h. data conversion from old system to new system
   i. insurance costs
   j. installation of original equipment
   k. hardware upgrades
4. Distinguish between escapable and inescapable costs. Give an example of each.
5. Distinguish between tangible and intangible benefits.
6. What is a systems selection report?

7. What are the four factors that have stimulated the growth of commercial software?
8. Explain the net present value and the payback methods. Which method do you prefer? Why?
9. Distinguish between turnkey and backbone systems. Which is more flexible?
10. What are the four steps involved in choosing a package?
11. What is an RFP?
12. What is the role of the accountant in evaluation and selection?
13. Discuss the relative merits of in-house programs versus commercially developed software.
14. List, in sequential order, the system components that are designed in the detailed design phase.
15. What is data modeling? What is its primary tool?
16. What are the three basic symbols in an ER diagram?
17. Distinguish between primary and foreign keys.
18. What is a data dictionary?
19. What document is used to determine which tables of data are necessary?
20. Once the conceptual links between tables have been determined, how are the physical links incorporated?

21. What attributes should output views possess?
22. Why is the quality of the paper a major consideration in the design of a hard-copy input?
23. What are the two classes of design input views?
24. What are zones?
25. In what form should embedded instructions be written—active or passive voice? Why?
26. What are the relative merits of input from source documents and direct input?
27. What is pseudocode? Are end users or systems designers involved in this process?
28. What are the controls designated in the systems controls stage?
29. Typically, which is more difficult to detect and more costly to fix—a design flaw in the processes or a programming error?
30. Who is included in the quality assurance group? What are their tasks? What documents do they need to perform their tasks?
31. Which activities during the systems implementation phase have the greatest implications for accountants and auditors?
32. Which chart, a PERT or a Gantt, shows the project status at a glance for a given point in time? Which method illustrates the critical path at a glance?
33. Discuss the relative merits and drawbacks to 3GL. How might changing technology affect some of these issues in the future?
34. What is a hybrid language?
35. What are the advantages to the modular programming approach?
36. Why should test data be saved after it has been used?
37. Explain the importance of documentation by the systems programmers.
38. What documents not typically needed by other stakeholders do accountants and auditors need for the new system?
39. What very important precautions must be taken during the data conversion procedures?

Discussion Questions

1. Critical thinking can be defined as suspending judgment until all the issues have been considered. Why do you think critical thinking skills are important during the systems evaluation and selection phase?
2. How does the detailed feasibility study differ from the feasibility study conducted during the systems proposal stage? Is the work redundant?
3. How are the various feasibility factors scored? Is this an objective or subjective procedure? Are all factors equally weighted?
4. Intangible benefits are usually extremely difficult to quantify accurately. Some designers argue that if you understate them, then conservative estimates are produced. Any excess benefits will be greatly welcomed but not required for the new system to be a success. What are the dangers of this viewpoint?
5. If a firm decides early on to go with a special-purpose system, such as SAP, based upon the recommendations of the external audit firm, should the SDLC be bypassed?
6. Explain how benchmarking works. Should this be conducted on the vendor's computer or the customer's computer? What about technical presentations by the vendor? Why?
7. Discuss how important the weights are that are assigned to factors in the final selection process. What method might you suggest be used to investigate the appropriateness of the weights?
8. Who should select the contact user group—the vendor or the prospective user? Why?
9. What processes should be used to develop useful and meaningful output? Who should be involved in the development process?
10. Are input requirements or output requirements examined to determine the attributes of tables? Should all of these attributes physically be in the data file? Why or why not?
11. Are direct input systems (i.e., point-of-sale using bar codes) error free? Why or why not?
12. Why is it necessary to decompose the DFD to a level of high detail before preparing the structure diagram? How do you know when to stop this process?
13. A good structure diagram should be loosely coupled yet strongly cohesive. How can you achieve both characteristics simultaneously? What impli-

cations do these characteristics have on error-prone problems during maintenance?

14. Why bother with pseudocode? Why not spend the time developing actual source code?

15. During a test data procedure, why should the developers bother testing "bad" data?

16. During implementation, if the system is behind schedule and if each program module is tested and no problems are found, is it necessary to test all modules in conjunction with one another? Why or why not?

17. Run manuals for computer operators are similar in theory to the checklists that airplane pilots use for takeoffs and landings. Explain why these are important.

18. How might the decision to use CASE tools affect the choice of a programming language?

19. What are the three implementation (cutover) methods? Which appears to be the most costly up front? Which could very likely end up being the most costly in the long run?

20. Who conducts the post-implementation review? When should it be conducted? If an outside consulting firm were hired to design and implement the new system, or a canned software package were purchased, would a post-implementation review still be useful?

21. Discuss the importance of involving accountants in the detailed design and implementation phases. What tasks should they perform?

Multiple-Choice Questions

1. Which of the following is NOT a one-time cost?
   a. site preparation
   b. insurance
   c. software acquisition
   d. data conversion

2. Which of the following is NOT an advantage of commercial software?
   a. independence
   b. cost
   c. reliability
   d. implementation time

3. CMA 1287 5-6
   The process of developing specifications for hardware, software, personnel hours, data resources, and information products required to develop a system is referred to as
   a. systems analysis.
   b. systems feasibility study.
   c. systems maintenance.
   d. systems implementation.
   e. systems design.

4. CMA 689 5-4
   The analysis tool for the systems analyst and steering committee to use in selecting the best systems option is
   a. cost-benefit analysis.
   b. systems design.
   c. decision tree analysis.
   d. user selection.
   e. pilot testing.

5. CMA 1289 5-8
   In determining the need for system changes, several types of feasibility studies can be made. The most commonly recognized feasibility studies are
   a. legal, environmental, and economic.
   b. environmental, operational, and economic.
   c. technical, economic, legal, and practical.
   d. practical, technical, and operational.
   e. technical, operational, and economic.

6. CMA 1290 4-13
   The technique that recognizes the time value of money by discounting the after-tax cash flows for a project over its life to time period zero using the company's minimum desired rate of return is called the
   a. net present value method.
   b. capital rationing method.
   c. payback method.
   d. average rate of return method.
   e. accounting rate of return method.

7. Johnson Company is planning to acquire a $250,000 computer that will provide increased efficiencies, thereby reducing annual operating costs by $80,000. The computer will be depreciated by the straight-line method over a 5-year life with no salvage value at the end of 5 years. Assuming a 40 percent income tax rate, the machine's payback period is
   a. 3.13 years.
   b. 3.21 years.

c. 3.68 years.
d. 4.81 years.
e. 5.21 years.

Questions 8 and 9 are based on the following information and deal with a critique of the cost-benefit analysis portion of the feasibility study.

When management decides to implement a management information system in a segment of the company, the decision is often based upon a feasibility study conducted by the systems department. Listed below are terms and examples of them used in the section of the study dealing with the cost-benefit analysis.

Terms	*Examples*
Tangible cost	Development cost
Intangible cost	Imputed interest
Tangible benefits	Cost displacement
Intangible benefits	Improved decisions

The feasibility study identifies the major benefits of the new management information system. Many of the benefits are intangible, such as improved decision-making capability and effectiveness, better customer relations, and improved employee morale.

8. CMA Adapted 679 5-9
   The estimated category that ordinarily would have the greatest uncertainty as to its precise value is
   a. the tangible costs.
   b. the intangible costs.
   c. the tangible benefits.
   d. the intangible benefits.
   e. none of the above because they are equally precise.

9. CMA Adapted 679 5-10
   Which of the following statements best describes what is usually true regarding the estimates included in feasibility studies?
   a. Development time and cost are usually less than estimated; benefits are stated accurately.
   b. Development time and cost are usually less than estimated; benefits are usually greater than estimated.
   c. Development cost and benefits are usually greater than estimated; development time is usually less than estimated.
   d. Development time and cost are usually greater than estimated; benefits are usually less than estimated.

e. Development time, cost, and benefits are usually greater than estimated.

10. Which of the following is NOT an output attribute?
    a. relevance
    b. exception orientation
    c. zones
    d. accuracy

11. Which of the following is NOT a principle feature of a PERT chart?
    a. starting and ending dates
    b. events
    c. paths
    d. activities

12. CMA 1289 5-3
    Coding in data processing assigns a unique identification number or key to each data record. Which of the following statements about coding is incorrect?
    a. A primary key is the main code used to store and locate records within a file.
    b. Records can be sorted, and temporary files created, using codes other than their primary keys.
    c. Secondary keys are used when the primary keys cannot be found.
    d. A given data record may have more than one secondary key.

13. CMA 691 4-30
    The least risky strategy for converting from a manual to a computerized accounts receivable system would be a
    a. direct conversion.
    b. parallel conversion.
    c. pilot conversion.
    d. database conversion.
    e. file conversion.

14. CMA 691 4-29
    Errors are most costly to correct during
    a. programming.
    b. conceptual design.
    c. analysis.
    d. detailed design.
    e. implementation.

15. CMA 685 5-22
    A useful tool for formatting computer input and file records is a
    a. document flowchart.
    b. printer layout chart.
    c. record layout sheet.

d. work distribution analysis.

e. decision table.

16. CMA 1287 5-6

The process of developing specifications for hardware, software, personnel hours, data resources, and information products required to develop a system is referred to as

a. systems analysis.

b. systems feasibility study.

c. systems maintenance.

d. systems implementation.

e. systems design.

17. CMA 678 5-2

When designing a computer-based information system, the initial step in the systems design process is to determine

a. the required output.

b. the source documents that serve as the basis for input.

c. the processing required.

d. the decisions for which data will be required.

e. the file information required during processing.

18. CMA 1282 5-12

Characteristics of an accounting application that might influence the selection of data entry devices and media for a computerized accounting system are

a. timing of feedback needs relative to input, need for documentation of an activity, and the necessity for reliability and accuracy.

b. cost considerations, volume of input, complexity of activity, and liquidity of assets involved.

c. need for documentation, necessity for accuracy and reliability, volume of output, and cost considerations.

d. relevancy of data, volume of input, cost considerations, volume of output, and timing of feedback needs relative to input.

e. type of file used, reliability of manufacturer's service, volume of output, and cost considerations.

19. CIA 1187 III-32

User acceptance is part of which phase of the system development life cycle?

a. implementation

b. general systems design

c. program specification and implementation planning

d. detailed systems design

20. CMA 1287 5-26

The program evaluation and review technique (PERT) is widely used to plan and measure progress toward scheduled events. PERT is combined with cost data to produce a PERT-cost analysis to

a. calculate the total project cost inclusive of the additional slack time.

b. evaluate and optimize trade-offs between time of an event's completion and its cost to complete.

c. implement computer-integrated manufacturing concepts.

d. avoid the problem of time variance analysis.

e. calculate expected activity times.

21. CMA 689 5-25

A Gantt chart

a. shows the critical path for a project.

b. is used for determining an optimal product mix.

c. shows only the activities along the critical path of a network.

d. does not necessarily show the critical path through a network.

e. is used in queuing analysis.

22. CMA 684 5-21

When using the PERT method for network analysis, the critical path through the network is the

a. shortest path through the network.

b. longest path through the network.

c. path with the most slack.

d. path with the most variability in estimated times.

e. least-cost path.

Problems

1. **Systems Design and Selection**

The Denver International Airport was plagued with problems prior to and immediately after its opening. After reading the following article, discuss where you think problems went wrong in either the conceptual design and/or the system selection stages.

Copyright 1996 Information Access Company, a
Thomson Corporation Company
ASAP
Copyright 1996 Reed Publishing USA
Modern Materials Handling
April 15, 1996

HEADLINE: Reengineering for the 21st century; contains related articles about the Denver Airport and the Gulf War; the 1990s 50th Anniversary Issue

SECTION: Vol. 51; No. 5; Pg. 90; ISSN: 0026-8038

A major materials handling story of the 1990s was the 16-month delay in the opening of the new Denver International Airport due to problems with the high-tech baggage handling system. Considered to be an enormous technological leap even by today's high-tech standards, the system design called for a series of complicated and highly variable routings of individually-powered baggage carriers.

Designers, however, grossly underestimated the difficulties of dealing with the high level of complexity in the system design. Unrealistic schedules, software problems, and the lack of a backup system all contributed to a string of delays. Not until a $50 million backup system based on conventional conveyor technology was built and the initial scope of the automated system greatly scaled back was the airport able to open on February 28, 1995.

Although disastrous from a public relations perspective, the experience at Denver will prove invaluable in terms of the lessons learned about developing large-scale, technologically-advanced systems. Gaining a better understanding of the kinds of extraordinary challenges that are routinely encountered in dealing with complex systems should help today's designers ask more of the right questions up-front instead of after the fact.

2. **Systems Design**

Robin Alper, a manager of the credit collections department for ACME Building Supplies, is extremely unhappy with a new system that was installed three months ago. Her complaint is that the data flows from the billing and accounts receivable departments are not occurring in the manner originally requested. Further, the updates to the database files are not occurring as frequently as she had envisioned. Thus, the hope that the new system would provide more current

and timely information has not materialized. She claims that the systems analysts spent three days interviewing her and other workers. During that time, she and the other workers thought they had clearly conveyed their needs. She feels as if their needs were ignored and their time was wasted.

What went wrong during the systems design process? What suggestions would you make for future projects?

3. **Attributes and Operations**

Prepare a list of attributes and operations for the following items:
a. general ledger
b. accounts payable ledger
c. accounts receivable ledger

4. **Systems Design**

Robert Hamilton was hired six months ago as the controller of a small oil and gas exploration and development company, Gusher, Inc., headquartered in Beaumont, Texas. Before working at Gusher, Hamilton was the controller of a larger petroleum company, Eureka Oil Company, based in Dallas. The joint interest billing and fixed asset accounting systems of Gusher are outdated, and frequent processing problems and errors have been occurring. Hamilton immediately recognized these problems and informed the president, Mr. Barton, that it was crucial to install a new system. Barton concurred and met with Hamilton and Sally Jeffries, the information systems senior manager. Barton instructed Jeffries to make the new system a top priority. Basically, he told Jeffries to deliver the system to meet Hamilton's needs as soon as possible.

Jeffries left the meeting feeling overwhelmed since the IS department is currently working on two other very big projects, one for the production department and the other for the geological department. The next day, Hamilton sent a memo to Jeffries indicating the name of a system he had 100 percent confidence in—Amarillo Software—and he also indicated that he would very much like this system to be purchased as soon as possible. He stated that the system had been used with much success during the past four years in his previous job.

When commercial software is purchased, Jeffries typically sends out requests for proposals to at least six different vendors after conducting a careful analysis of the needed requirements. However, due to the air of urgency demonstrated in the meeting with the president and the over-worked systems staff, she decided to go along with Hamilton's wishes and sent only one RFP, which went to Amarillo Software. Amarillo promptly returned the completed questionnaire. The purchase price ($75,000) was within the bud-geted amount. Jeffries contacted the four refer-ences provided and was satisfied with their comments. Further, she felt comfortable since the system was for Hamilton, and he had used the system for four years.

The plan was to install the system during the month of July and try it for the August transac-tion cycle. Problems were encountered, however, during the installation phase. The system processed extremely slowly on the hardware plat-form owned by Gusher. When Jeffries asked Hamilton how the problem had been dealt with at Eureka, he replied that he did not remember having such a problem. He called the systems manager from Eureka and discovered that Eureka has a much more powerful mainframe than Gusher. Further investigation revealed that Gusher has more applications running on its mainframe than Eureka does, since Eureka uses a two-mainframe distributed processing platform.

Further, the data transfer did not go smoothly. A few data elements being stored in the system were not available as an option in the Amarillo system. Jeffries found that the staff at Amarillo was very friendly when she called, but they could not always identify the problem over the phone. They needed to come out to the site and investigate. Hamilton was surprised at the delays between requesting an Amarillo consultant to come out and the time in which he or she ac-tually arrived. Amarillo explained that it had to fly a staff member from Dallas to Beaumont for each trip. The system finally began to work somewhat smoothly in January, after a grueling fiscal year-end close in October. Hamilton's staff view the project as an unnecessary inconvenience. At one point, two staff accountants threatened to quit. The extra consulting fees amounted to $35,000. Further, the systems department at Gusher spent 500 more hours during the implementation process than it had expected. These additional hours caused other projects to fall behind schedule.

Required:
Discuss what could have been done differently during the design phase. Why were most of the problems en-countered? How might a detailed feasibility study have helped?

5. **Cost-Benefit Analysis**
   Listed on the following page are some probabil-ity estimates of the costs and benefits associated with two competing projects.
   a. Compute the net present value of each alter-native. Round the cost projections to the near-est month. Determine what happens to the answer if the probabilities of the recurring costs are incorrect and a more accurate esti-mate is as follows:

	A		B
.10	$ 75,000	.4	$ 85,000
.55	95,000	.4	100,000
.35	105,000	.2	110,000

   b. Repeat Step (a) for the payback method.
   c. Which method do you feel provides the best source of information? Why?

6. **Data Flow Diagram**
   The detailed data flow diagram in Figure 14–10 decomposes the DFD for the expenditure cycle in Figure 14–9. Further decompose the process numbered 1.4.4, Receive Invoice, into more de-tail.

7. **PERT Chart**
   The Peabody Coal Corporation recently com-pleted the final feasibility report for a new gen-eral ledger accounting system. It has hired a consulting firm to program and install the new system. The consulting firm is charging $350,000 for the remaining tasks to be performed. These tasks are to be performed over the next ten months as detailed in the Gantt chart on the next page. The consulting firm is extremely concerned with the project staying on schedule since it is re-ceiving a flat fee. The release of the final payment is contingent upon the system performing as stated in the contract and upon Peabody receiv-ing appropriate documentation of the system.

Problem 5: Cost-Benefit Analysis

COST OF CAPITAL = .14

	A Probability	Amount	B Probability	Amount
Project completion time	0.5	12 months	0.6	12 months
	0.3	18 months	0.2	18 months
	0.2	24 months	0.1	24 months
Expected useful life	0.6	4 years	0.5	4 years
	0.25	5 years	0.3	5 years
	0.15	6 years	0.2	6 years
One-time costs	0.35	$ 200,000	0.2	$210,000
	0.4	250,000	0.55	250,000
	0.25	300,000	0.25	260,000
Recurring costs	0.1	$ 75,000	0.4	$ 85,000
	0.55	95,000	0.4	100,000
	0.35	105,000	0.2	110,000
Annual tangible benefits starting with weighted average completion date	0.3	$ 220,000	0.25	$215,000
	0.5	233,000	0.5	225,000
	0.2	240,000	0.25	235,000

Problem 7: Gantt Chart

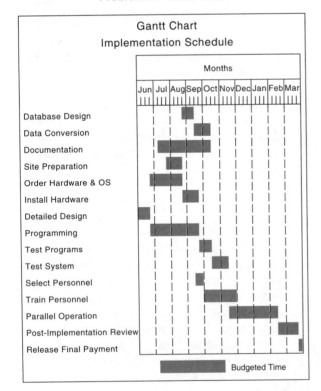

Gantt Chart
Implementation Schedule

Required:

a. Prepare a PERT diagram and indicate the critical path.

b. What happens to the time frame of the implementation of the project if the manufacturer is four weeks late shipping the hardware?

c. What happens if the data conversion does not go smoothly and takes an additional three weeks?

d. Who should conduct the post-implementation review? What activities should be conducted during this review? Do you think enough time has been allotted for this activity?

8. PERT and Gantt Charts

The lottery commission of a state with about $500 million a year in revenue has looked to modern technology for increasing lottery sales. The strategy is to place self-service sales machines around the state. Customers simply fill out the bubbles on the form and insert the form into the computer. If they wish, they may enter their numbers directly into the computer and skip the form altogether. The machine accepts cash and automatic teller machine cards. The lottery commission is very excited about this project because it thinks it could boost lottery ticket sales by as much as 30 percent.

The systems department has finished the final feasibility report and has determined the following estimates for implementing the system. It plans on purchasing a larger, more powerful mainframe computer to handle the processing of the transactions. The manufacturer has promised a delivery date of three months from the time the order is placed. The lottery sales machines must be special ordered and require a lead time of five months. The plan is to initially order 15 machines and test them for 12 weeks. If all goes well, the lottery commission will order a total of 500 machines, with 20 delivered and installed each month. This order will not be placed until the results of the pilot test have been analyzed.

The writing of the programs is expected to take six weeks. The testing of the programs on the mainframe is expected to take four weeks, with an additional three weeks once the sales machines have been received. Another two weeks of testing by the state gaming commission is expected. The design of the databases is expected to take only two weeks. Not much data transfer is expected to be necessary, so only three weeks is budgeted for this task.

An estimated 20 employees need to be hired and trained to install and maintain these machines around the state. The hiring process is expected to take six weeks, and the training should take an additional six weeks. The documentation should be completed before the training of the new employees. The documentation should take about three months. As soon as the gaming commission signs off on the programs, the 15 machines are to be installed at test sites around the state. Four weeks are allotted for this installation procedure. A one-week testing period is planned, with commission employees going to the sites and using the machines. An additional week is planned to review the results of these tests. The

pilot test then begins and runs for eight weeks. The data will be analyzed for four weeks after the pilot test. The final order for the additional machines will be placed after the data analysis is conducted and the demand for the number of machines is more accurately determined.

Required:
a. Prepare a PERT chart for the above process. Identify the critical path.
b. Prepare a Gantt chart for the above process.

9. **CMA Adapted 688 5-10**
   PERT Chart
   Consider the estimated times and costs associated with a particular project shown below.

Required:
a. Determine the critical path.
b. Determine the total expected cost of the project.
c. Determine the incremental cost of completing the project in 12 weeks.

10. **CMA 786 5-Y6**
    PERT Chart
    Silver Aviation assembles small aircraft for commercial use. The majority of Silver's business is with small freight airlines serving areas where the airport does not accommodate larger planes. The remainder of Silver's customers are commuter airlines and individuals who use planes in their businesses. Silver recently expanded into Central and South America and expects to double its sales over the next three years.

Problem 9: PERT Chart

ACTIVITY	NORMAL ACTIVITY TIME	NORMAL ACTIVITY COST	CRASH TIME	CRASH ACTIVITY COST
A–B	2 weeks	$1,000	2 weeks	$ 1,000
A–C	1	800	1	800
B–D	2	1,500	2	1,500
B–E	5	5,100	3	10,200
C–D	4	2,500	3	3,500
D–E	1	600	1	600
E–F	4	1,700	4	1,700
E–G	3	1,200	2	2,600
F–H	3	1,400	2	2,100
G–H	3	1,300	3	1,300

To schedule work and keep track of all projects, Silver uses the program evaluation and review technique (PERT). The PERT diagram for the construction of a single cargo plane is shown below. The PERT diagram shows that there are four alternative paths, with the critical path being ABGEFJK.

Bob Peterson, president of Coastal Airlines, has recently placed an order with Silver Aviation for five cargo planes. At the time of contract negotiations, Peterson agreed to a delivery time of 13 weeks (five working days per week) for the first plane, with the balance of the planes being delivered at the rate of one every four weeks. Because of problems with some of the aircraft Coastal is using, Peterson has contacted Grace Vander, sales manager for Silver Aviation, to ask about improving the delivery date of the first cargo plane. Vander replied that she believed the schedule could be shortened by as much as ten working days, or two weeks, but the cost of construction would increase as a result. Peterson said he would be willing to consider the increased costs, and they agreed to meet the following day to review a revised schedule that Vander would prepare.

Because Silver Aviation has assembled aircraft on an accelerated basis before, the company has compiled a list of crash costs for this purpose. Vander used the data shown in the Crash Cost Listing table to develop a plan to cut ten working days from the schedule at a minimum increase in cost to Coastal Airlines.

Upon completing her plan, Vander was pleased that she could report to Peterson that Silver would be able to cut ten working days from the schedule. The associated increase in cost would be $6,600. Presented on the following page is Vander's plan for the accelerated delivery of the cargo plane starting from the regularly scheduled days and costs.

Required:

a. PERT is a form of network analysis.
  1. Explain how the expected regular times for each activity are derived in using PERT.
  2. Define the term *critical path* and explain why path ABGEFJK is the critical path in this situation.
b. Evaluate the accelerated delivery schedule prepared by Grace Vander.

1. Explain why Vander's plan as presented is unsatisfactory.
2. Revise the accelerated delivery schedule so that Coastal Airlines will take delivery of the first plane two weeks (ten working days) ahead of schedule at the least incremental cost to Coastal.
3. Calculate the incremental costs Bob Peterson will have to pay for this revised accelerated delivery.

11. Detailed Systems Design
Below is an ER diagram for the expenditure cycle.

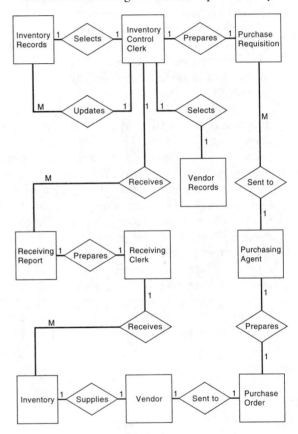

Required:

a. List the entity database tables and describe which entities need representing from an AIS perspective.
b. For each item identified as relevant to AIS, prepare a list of database tables along with primary and embedded foreign keys.
c. Prepare database tables showing attributes in normalized form.

Problem 10: PERT Chart

PERT diagram

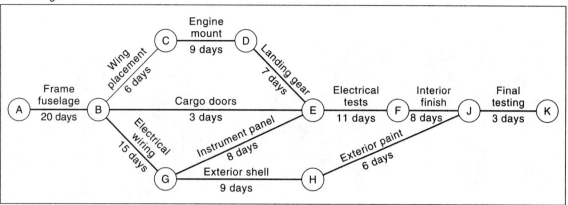

Crash Cost Listing

	Activity	Expected Activity Times		Direct Cost		Added Crash Cost per Reduced Day
		Regular	Crash	Regular	Crash	
AB	Frame fuselage	20 days	16 days	$12,000	$16,800	$1,200
BC	Wing placement	6	5	3,600	5,000	1,400
CD	Engine mount	9	7	6,600	8,000	700
DE	Landing gear	7	5	5,100	6,700	800
BE	Cargo doors	3	3	1,400	1,400	—
BG	Electrical wiring	15	13	9,000	11,000	1,000
GE	Instrument panel	8	6	5,700	8,300	1,300
EF	Electrical tests	11	10	6,800	7,600	800
GH	Exterior shell	9	7	4,200	5,200	500
FJ	Interior finish	8	7	3,600	4,000	400
HJ	Exterior paint	6	5	3,600	4,000	400
JK	Final testing	3	2	3,500	4,400	900
				$65,100	$82,400	

Vander's plan for accelerated delivery

Completion Time	Activity Crashed	Additional Cost per Day	Total Direct Cost
65 days			$65,100
64	HJ by 1 day	$ 400	65,500
63	FJ by 1 day	400	65,900
61	GH by 2 days	500	66,900
59	CD by 2 days	700	68,300
58	EF by 1 day	800	69,100
56	DE by 2 days	800	70,700
55	BG by 1 day	1,000	71,700

Systems Development Cases

Several systems development cases that draw upon the material in this and the next chapter are available on-line at http://hall.swcollege.com.

PART 5

COMPUTER CONTROLS AND AUDITING

CHAPTER

15

Controlling Computer-Based Information Systems, Part I

This chapter begins an examination of internal control issues related to the computer-based information system (CBIS) environment. Because of the extensive nature of the topic, and its importance to accountants, two chapters are devoted to this body of material. Our study of internal control has thus far been confined to manual systems. The introduction of computer technology, however, dramatically transforms the environment to create an entirely new set of problems that need to be controlled. This chapter and the next examine the unique nature of CBIS exposures and the techniques for managing these risks.

This chapter begins with a review of the fundamental control concerns underlying SAS 78 and provides an overview of how they translate to the CBIS environment. Following this overview is a framework for control that identifies ten areas of risk unique to a CBIS environment. The remainder of the chapter explores the first six of these areas and prescribes specific techniques to reduce the risks. The remaining four areas of risk will be examined in Chapter 16.

LEARNING OBJECTIVES

After studying this chapter, you should:

- Understand how the unique features of a CBIS environment must be taken into account to achieve the control objectives specified in SAS 78.
- Be able to identify the principal threats to the operating system and the control techniques used to minimize the possibility of actual exposures.
- Be familiar with the various techniques used to control access to the database.
- Understand the nature of incompatible functions in a CBIS environment.
- Be familiar with the controls necessary to regulate systems development and maintenance activities.
- Be familiar with the controls and precautions required to ensure the security of an organization's computer facilities and the recovery options available in the event of a disaster.

EFFECTS OF CBIS ON TRADITIONAL CONTROL ACTIVITIES

To this point, the text has presented internal control activities from the perspective of manual systems only. Our study has focused on the SAS 78 control activities of transaction authorization, segregation of duties, supervision, access control, adequate accounting records, and independent verification. These control activities have emerged in response to fundamental risks, which, under different technological scenarios, change in their nature but do not go away. The purpose of this section is to reconcile traditional control concerns with the CBIS environment.

TRANSACTION AUTHORIZATION

Authorization procedures are controls that ensure that an organization's employees process only valid transactions within the scope of their prescribed authority. For example, in a manual purchasing system, the purchase of inventories from a designated vendor when inventory levels fall to their reorder points requires an authorization. In this environment, management and auditors can verify compliance with established authorization rules by observing the employees involved and reviewing their work.

In a CBIS environment, transactions are often authorized by rules embedded within computer programs. For example, a program in a purchasing system will determine when, how much, and from which vendor inventories are ordered. Such transactions may be initiated automatically, with no human involvement. In this setting, however, it may be difficult to assess whether these transactions comply with management's wishes. Is the firm buying inventory only when it is needed? Is it buying correct quantities? Is it buying from approved vendors? Because automated authorization procedures are unobserved by management, control failure may go unnoticed until the firm experiences some adverse symptoms. In the case of purchase authorizations, symptoms of a problem may take the form of inventory stockouts or an excessive buildup of inventory. Unfortunately, by the time the problem is recognized, the firm may have incurred substantial financial losses.

In a CBIS environment, the responsibility for achieving appropriate transaction authorization rests directly on the accuracy and the integrity of the computer programs that perform these tasks. Control techniques that promote program accuracy and integrity will be explored later in the chapter.

SEGREGATION OF DUTIES

In a manual system, an important control activity is the separation of incompatible duties during transaction processing. Individuals are given responsibility for performing only limited aspects of the transaction to achieve the three control objectives originally illustrated in Figure 3-8 and reproduced in Figure 15–1.

Objective 1. Transaction authorization is separate from transaction processing. For example, in a purchases system, the inventory control function authorizes a purchase that is acted upon by purchasing agents and others. In a sales order processing system, the credit department authorizes the sales department to process a sales order.

Objective 2. Asset custody is separate from record keeping responsibilities. For example, the cash receipts department handles cash, while the accounts receivable and general ledger departments record these transactions. Likewise, physical inventories are secured in warehouses and storerooms, while their records are maintained separately by the inventory control group.

FIGURE 15–1

Segregation of Duties

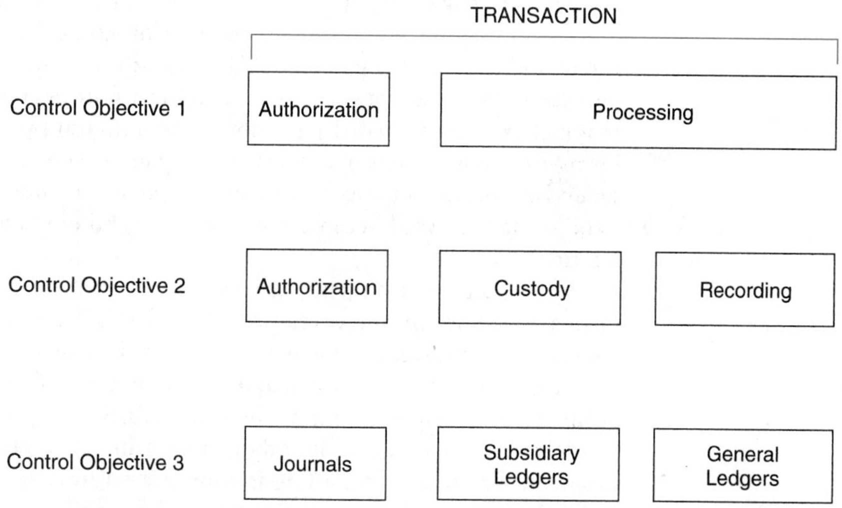

Objective 3. The organization should be structured so that a successful fraud requires collusion between two or more individuals with incompatible responsibilities. For example, no individual should have sufficient access to accounting records to perpetrate a fraud. Hence, journals, subsidiary ledgers, and the general ledger are maintained separately. For most people, the thought of approaching another employee with the proposal to collude in a fraud presents an insurmountable psychological barrier. The fear of rejection and subsequent disciplinary action discourages solicitations of this sort. However, when employees with incompatible responsibilities work together daily in close quarters, the resulting familiarity will tend to erode this barrier. For this reason, the segregation of incompatible tasks should be physical as well as organizational. Indeed, concern about personal familiarity on the job is the justification for establishing rules prohibiting nepotism.

In a CBIS environment, separation of duties is not identical to that in a manual system. For example, a computer program may authorize a purchase, process the purchase order, and record the account payable. When the supplier's invoice arrives, a program will reconcile it to the purchase order, determine the amount to be paid, and print a check in payment of the liability. Thus, in the CBIS environment, a computer program may perform many tasks that are deemed incompatible in the manual environment.

This is not to say that separation of duties plays no role in the CBIS environment. Instead, the control emphasis shifts to activities that can threaten application integrity. For example, once the proper functioning of a program is established at system implementation, it must be preserved throughout the application's life cycle. The activities of *program development*, *program operations*, and *program maintenance* are the primary CBIS functions that must be adequately separated.

SUPERVISION

Supervision is often used as a compensating control in situations where an adequate separation of duties is not possible for economic or practical reasons. Adequate supervision is especially important in small organizations or in small functional units of larger firms where individual employees must perform incompatible tasks.

An underlying assumption of supervision control is that the firm employs competent and trustworthy personnel. Obviously, no company could function for long on the alternative assumption that its employees are incompetent and dishonest. The "competent and trustworthy employee" assumption promotes supervisory efficiency. Firms can thus establish a managerial span of control whereby a single manager supervises several employees. In manual systems, maintaining a span of control tends to be straightforward because both manager and employees are at the same physical location.

In a CBIS environment, supervisory control must be more elaborate than in manual systems for three reasons. The first relates to the problem of attracting competent employees. The technology of data processing creates an exceedingly complex environment that demands a unique class of employees. Those who design, program, maintain, and operate the firm's CBIS must possess highly specialized skills. These individuals operate in a dynamic setting characterized by a high rate of staff turnover. The task of restaffing is complicated further by rapid changes in technology, which tend to frustrate management's ability to assess the competence of prospective employees.

The second reason reflects management's concern over the trustworthiness of data processing personnel in high-risk areas. Some systems professionals serve in positions of authority that permit direct and unrestricted access to the organization's programs and data. The combination of technical skill and opportunity, in the hands of an individual who is mischievous or corrupt, represents a significant exposure to the organization.

The third reason is management's inability to adequately observe employees in a CBIS environment. The activities of employees engaged in data processing are frequently hidden from management's direct observation. For example, data processing personnel may be distributed in the user areas and perform their functions remotely and electronically; thus, supervisory controls must be designed into the CBIS to compensate for the lack of direct supervision.

ACCOUNTING RECORDS

In a manual system, organizations must keep accounting records in the form of source documents, journals, and ledgers. These records provide an audit trail of essential information for tracing transactions from their initiation to their final disposition. Organizations maintain this information to conduct their day-to-day operations, prepare financial statements, and support periodic audits. Thus, adequate accounting records become a critical element of internal control that the firm's management and accountants are obliged to maintain and their auditors obliged to review.

In a CBIS environment, documents and audit trails may assume very different and unfamiliar forms. In some types of CBIS, no physical source documents exist. Source documents and ledger accounts are kept magnetically on various mass storage devices. Journals, in the traditional sense, do not exist in this environment. Instead, journal entries, or their equivalent transaction records, are often fragmented and stored in normalized database files. The audit trails between these various magnetic records may take the form of pointers, hashing techniques, indexes, or embedded keys. To meet their respective responsibilities, the firm's management, accountants, and auditors must understand the operational principles of the data management systems in use.

ACCESS CONTROL

Access to the firm's assets should be limited only to authorized personnel. Uncontrolled access exposes assets to misappropriation, illegal use, theft, and destruction. Assets are at risk to both direct and indirect access. Controls over direct access include physical security devices, such as locks, safes, fences, restricted areas, and various alarm systems. Indirect access is accomplished by accessing accounting records that control the physical assets' distribution or ownership. For example, an individual with access to all the relevant accounting records can destroy the audit trail that describes a particular sales transaction. Thus, by removing the records of the transaction, including the account receivable balance, the sale may never be billed and the firm will never receive payment for the items sold. In a manual system, indirect access control is accomplished by controlling the use of documents and records and by segregating the duties of those who must access and process these records.

In a CBIS environment, accounting records tend to be concentrated within the data processing center on mass storage devices. Data consolidation exposes the organization to two threats: (1) computer fraud and (2) losses from disasters.

Fraud. An individual with the proper skills and unrestricted access to accounting records is in a prime position to perpetrate and conceal a fraud. Because all the necessary records are in one location, the perpetrator does not have to gain access to several different places and is thus more likely to achieve his or her objective without detection.

Disasters. Natural disasters such as fires, earthquakes, or floods, or even less sensational events such as vandalism or hardware failures, can destroy (or corrupt) the organization's data, including its accounting records. If the firm is unable to recover essential records, it may not be able to continue in business.

Another access control problem unique to the CBIS environment is controlling access to computer programs. During the development phase, computer applications undergo a great deal of scrutiny and testing to expose logic errors. However, errors and fraud exposures are more likely to occur in the maintenance phase. During this period, an application may be modified many times and is subjected to two forms of exposure. First, during authorized program maintenance, unintentional errors are sometimes programmed into applications along with the intended changes. Second, illegal access to applications can be used to make fraudulent program changes.

Access control in a CBIS environment covers many levels of exposure. Controls that address these exposures include techniques designed to limit personnel access authority, restrict access to computer programs, provide physical security for the data processing center, ensure adequate backup for data files, and provide disaster recovery capability. Some access controls are technological procedures and devices, while others are physical barriers implemented through the organizational segregation of duties. But underlying all access control techniques is the fundamental principle of "need to know." Individuals should be granted access to data, programs, and restricted areas only when a need in connection with their assigned tasks has been demonstrated. This principle should never be violated.

INDEPENDENT VERIFICATION

Verification procedures are independent checks of the accounting system to identify errors and misrepresentations. Verification differs from supervision because it takes place after the fact, by an individual who is not directly involved with the transaction or task being verified. Supervision takes place while the activity is being performed, by a supervisor with direct responsibility for the transaction or task. Through independent verification procedures, management can assess (1) the performance of individuals, (2) the integrity of the transaction processing system, and (3) the correctness of data contained in accounting records. Examples of independent verifications include:

- The reconciliation of batch totals at periodic points during transaction processing.
- The comparison of physical assets with accounting records.
- The reconciliation of subsidiary accounts with control accounts.
- Reviews by management of reports that summarize business activity.
- Periodic audits by independent external and internal auditors.

Independent verifications are needed in the manual environment because employees sometimes make mistakes or forget to perform necessary tasks. In a computer environment, many of these tasks are performed by computer programs. Being precise machines, computers will always do what their programs specify. If these programs are accurate and complete, there is no reason to perform an independent check on their functioning as an ongoing operational procedure. Once again, our concern rests with application integrity. In the CBIS environment, accountants and auditors perform their independent verification function by evaluating controls over systems development and maintenance activities and occasionally by reviewing the internal logic of programs. This is called *EDP auditing*. Commonly used EDP auditing techniques will be examined in Chapter 17.

GENERAL CONTROL FRAMEWORK FOR CBIS EXPOSURES

This section introduces a framework for viewing CBIS exposures, which is presented in Figure 15–2. The areas of greatest potential risk are indicated by the circled numbers, which correspond to the following ten control topics.

1. Operating system controls
2. Data management controls
3. Organizational structure controls
4. Systems development controls
5. Systems maintenance controls
6. Computer center security and controls
7. Internet and Intranet controls
8. Electronic data interchange controls
9. Personal computer controls
10. Application controls

CBIS internal controls are divided into the two broad categories of *general controls* and *application controls*.[1] General controls apply to a wide range of exposures that systematically threaten the integrity of all applications processed within the CBIS environment. General controls are topics 1 through 9. Application controls (topic 10) are narrowly focused on exposures associated with specific systems, such as payroll, accounts receivable, and so on. The remainder of this chapter is devoted to examining control topics 1 through 6. Topics 7 through 10 are covered in Chapter 16. The order

---

1   The Committee of Sponsoring Organizations of the Treadway Commission, (New York, 1991): 115.

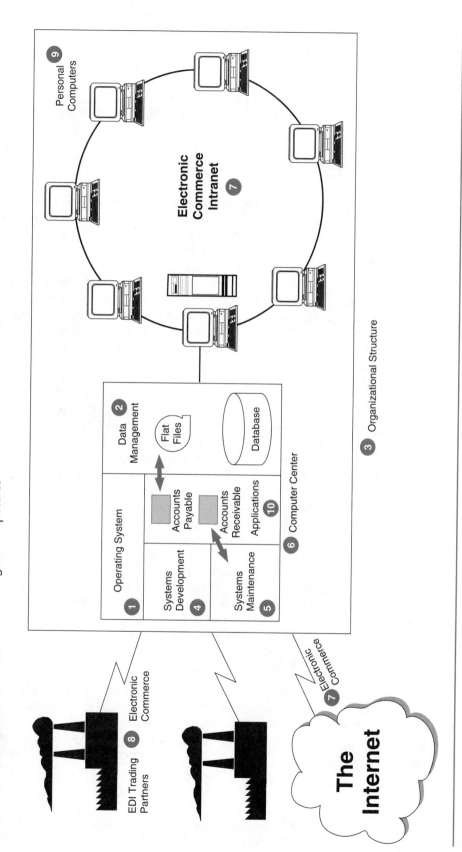

FIGURE 15-2   Framework for Viewing CBIS Exposures

in which these topics are covered represents an attempt to deal with this material efficiently and logically; it should not be taken to imply the relative importance of these topics.

The primary areas of risk, the nature of the exposures, and the control techniques used to reduce the exposures are summarized in Table 15–1. The remainder of the chapter presents a detailed explanation of these issues.

OPERATING SYSTEM CONTROLS

The **operating system** is the computer's control program. It allows users and their applications to share and access common computer resources, such as processors, main memory, databases, and printers. The modern accountant needs to recognize the operating system's role in the overall control picture to properly assess the risks that threaten the accounting system.

If operating system integrity is compromised, controls within individual accounting applications may also be circumvented or neutralized. Because the operating system is common to all users, the larger the computer facility, the greater the scale of potential damage. Thus, with more and more computer resources being shared by an ever-expanding user community, operating system security becomes an important control issue.

The operating system performs three main tasks. First, it translates high-level languages, such as COBOL, FORTRAN, BASIC, and SQL, into the machine-level language that the computer can execute. The language translator modules of the operating system are called **compilers** and **interpreters**. The control implications of language translators are examined later in the chapter.

Second, the operating system allocates computer resources to users, workgroups, and applications. This includes assigning memory work space (partitions) to applications and authorizing access to terminals, telecommunications links, databases, and printers.

Third, the operating system manages the tasks of job scheduling and multiprogramming. At any point in time, numerous user applications (jobs) are seeking access to the computer resources under the control of the operating system. Jobs are submitted to the system in three ways: (1) directly by the system operator, (2) from various batch-job queues, and (3) through telecommunications links from remote workstations. To achieve efficient and effective use of finite computer resources, the operating system must schedule job processing according to established priorities and balance the use of resources among the competing applications.

To perform these tasks consistently and reliably, the operating system must achieve five fundamental control objectives.[2]

1. The operating system must protect itself from users. User applications must not be able to gain control of, or damage in any way, the operating system, thus causing it to cease running or destroy data.

2. The operating system must protect users from each other. One user must not be able to access, destroy, or corrupt the data or programs of another user.

---

2   F. M. Stepczyk, "Requirements for Secure Operating Systems," *Data Security and Data Processing*, Vol. 5; Study Results: TRW Systems, Inc. (New York: IBM Corporation, 1974): 25–73.

TABLE 15–1	Summary of CBIS Exposures and Controls

Area of Risk	Nature of Exposure	Control Techniques
1. Operating System	Accidental and intentional threat, including attempts to access data illegally, violate user privacy, or perform malicious acts.	Access privilege control, password control, virus control, audit trail control, and fault tolerance control
2. Data Management	Inadequate backup of data and unauthorized access to data by authorized and unauthorized personnel.	BACKUP CONTROL: Grandparent-parent-child backup procedures, direct access file backup, and database backup and recovery procedures. ACCESS CONTROLS: Subschemas, passwords, authorization rules, user-defined procedures, encryption, biometric devices, and inference controls.
3. Organizational Structure	Programmers and operators who perform incompatible functions may perpetrate program fraud. Documentation standards may be inadequate to support audit tasks. Data files in tape libraries are subject to loss, destruction, and illegal access.	The functions of programming, computer operations, tape librarian, and database administrator should be organizationally segregated.
4. Systems Development	The development of unauthorized projects resulting in the misapplication of financial resources. Projects are improperly prioritized, resulting in inefficient allocation of resources. Newly implemented systems contain material errors, fraud, or fail to meet user needs. Poor-quality systems documentation impedes audit and maintenance activities.	Systems authorizations, user specification activities, technical design activities, internal audit participation, program testing, and user test and acceptance procedures.
5. Systems Maintenance	Unauthorized changes can result in program errors, fraud, incorrect information presented in financial statements and to users, systems failures, and severe disruptions to operations.	Program maintenance authorizations, user involvement, technical specifications, program testing, documentation, and source program library software control.
6. Computer Center	Loss and theft of physical equipment and system disruption caused by software failure, hardware failure, power outages, and physical disasters.	Physical construction, location, limited access to computer facilities, air conditioning, backup power supply, and disaster recovery planning.

3. The operating system must protect users from themselves. A user's application may consist of several modules stored in separate memory locations, each with its own data. One module must not be allowed to destroy or corrupt another module.

4. The operating system must be protected from itself. The operating system is also made up of individual modules. No module should be allowed to destroy or corrupt another module.

5. The operating system must be protected from its environment. In the event of a power failure or other disaster, the operating system should be able to achieve a controlled termination of activities from which it can later recover.

OPERATING SYSTEM SECURITY

Operating system security involves policy, procedures, and controls that determine who can access the operating system, which resources (files, programs, printers) they can access, and what actions they can take. The following security components are found in secure operating systems: *log-on procedure, access token, access control list,* and *discretionary access control.*

Log-On Procedure

A formal **log-on procedure** is the operating system's first line of defense against unauthorized access. When the user initiates the process, he or she is presented with a dialog box requesting the user's ID and password. The system compares the ID and password to a database of valid users. If the system finds a match, then the log-on attempt is authenticated. If, however, the password or ID is entered incorrectly, the log-on attempt fails and a message is returned to the user. The message should not reveal whether the password or the ID caused the failure. The system should allow the user to reenter the log-on information. After a specified number of attempts (usually no more than five), the system should lock out the user from the system.

Access Token

If the log-on attempt is successful, the operating system creates an **access token** that contains key information about the user, including user ID, password, user group, and privileges granted to the user. The information in the access token is used to approve all actions attempted by the user during the session.

Access Control List

Access to system resources such as directories, files, programs, and printers are controlled by an **access control list** assigned to each resource. These lists contain information that defines the access privileges for all valid users of the resource. When a user attempts to access a resource, the system compares his or her ID and privileges contained in the access token with those contained in the access control list. If there is a match, the user is granted access.

Discretionary Access Control

The central system administrator usually determines who is granted access to specific resources and maintains the access control list. In distributed systems, however, resources may be controlled (owned) by end users. Resource owners in this setting may be granted **discretionary access control**, which allows them to grant access privileges to other users. For example, the controller, who is the owner of the general ledger, grants read-only privileges to a manager in the budgeting department. The accounts payable manager, however, is granted both read and write permission to the ledger. Any attempt by the budgeting manager to add, delete, or change the general ledger will be denied. The use of discretionary access control needs to be closely supervised to prevent security breaches due to its liberal use.

THREATS TO OPERATING SYSTEM INTEGRITY

Operating system control objectives are sometimes not achieved because of flaws in the operating system that are exploited either accidentally or intentionally. Accidental threats include hardware failures that cause the operating system to crash. Operating system failures are also caused by errors in user application programs that the operating system cannot interpret. Accidental system failures may cause whole segments of memory to be "dumped" to disks and printers, resulting in the unintentional disclosure of confidential information.

Intentional threats to the operating system are most commonly attempts to illegally access data or violate user privacy for financial gain. However, a growing form of threat is from destructive programs from which there is no apparent gain. These exposures come from three sources:

1. Privileged personnel who abuse their authority. Systems administrators and systems programmers require unlimited access to the operating system to perform maintenance and to recover from system failures. Such individuals may use this authority to access users' programs and data files.
2. Individuals, both internal and external to the organization, who browse the operating system to identify and exploit security flaws.
3. An individual who intentionally (or accidentally) inserts a computer virus or other form of destructive program into the operating system.

OPERATING SYSTEM CONTROL TECHNIQUES

This section of the text describes a variety of control techniques for preserving operating system integrity.

Controlling Access Privileges

User access privileges are assigned to individuals and to entire workgroups authorized to use the system. Privileges determine which directories, files, applications, and other resources an individual or group may access. They also determine the types of actions that can be taken. Recall that the system administrator or the owner of the resource may assign privileges. Management should be concerned that individuals are not granted privileges that are incompatible with their assigned duties. Consider, for example, a cash receipts clerk who is granted the right to access and make changes to the accounts receivable file.

Overall system security is influenced by the way access privileges are assigned. Privileges should, therefore, be carefully administered and closely monitored for compliance with organizational policy and principles of internal control.

Password Control

A **password** is a secret code entered by the user to gain access to systems, applications, data files, or a network server. If the user cannot provide the correct password, the operating system should deny access. Although passwords can provide a degree of security, when imposed on nonsecurity-minded users, password procedures can result in end-user behavior that actually circumvents security. The most common forms of contra-security behavior include:

- Forgetting passwords and being locked out of the system.
- Failing to change passwords on a frequent basis.

- The post-it syndrome, whereby passwords are written down and displayed for others to see.
- Simplistic passwords that are easily anticipated by a computer criminal.

Reusable Passwords. The most common method of password control is the **reusable password**. The user defines the password to the system once and then reuses it to gain future access. Most operating systems set only basic standards for password acceptability. The quality of the security provided by a reusable password depends on the quality of the password itself. If the password pertains to something personal about the user, such as a child's name, pet's name, birth date, or hair color, it can be deduced by a computer criminal. Even if the password is derived from nonpersonal data, such as a string of keystrokes (such as A-S-D-F) or the same letter used multiple times, the computer criminal can use a frequency table to run through the most common passwords very quickly. Reusable passwords that contain random letters and digits are more difficult to crack, but are also more difficult for the user to remember.

To improve access control, management should discourage the use of "weak" passwords. Inexpensive software is available that automatically scans password files and notifies the security administrator when weak passwords are detected, thus assuring that only "smart" passwords are used on the system. An alternative to the standard reusable password is the *one-time* password.

One-Time Passwords. The **one-time password** was designed to overcome the problems just discussed. Under this approach, the user's password changes continuously. To access the operating system, the user must provide both a secret reusable personal identification number (PIN) and the current one-time-only password for that point in time. The problem, of course, is how to advise the valid user of the current password.

One technology employs a credit card–sized device (smart card) that contains a microprocessor programmed with an algorithm that generates, and electronically displays, a new and unique password every 60 seconds. The card works in conjunction with special authentication software located on a mainframe host or network server computer. Each user's card is synchronized to the authentication software, so that at any point in time both the smart card and the network software are generating the same password for the same user.

To access the network, the user enters the PIN followed by the current password displayed on the card. The password can be used one time only. If, for example, a computer hacker intercepts the password and PIN during transmission and attempts to use them within the one-minute time frame, access will be denied. Also, if the smart card should fall into the hands of a computer criminal, access cannot be achieved without the PIN.

Another one-time password technique uses a *challenge/response* approach to achieve the same end. When the user attempts to log on, the network authentication software issues a six-character code (the challenge) that can be either scanned optically by the card or entered into the card via its built-in keypad. The card's internal algorithm then generates a one-time password (the response) that is entered by the user through the keyboard of the remote terminal. If the firewall recognizes the current password, access is permitted.

Controlling Against Viruses and Other Destructive Programs

Destructive programs such as viruses are responsible for millions of dollars of corporate losses annually. The losses are measured in terms of data corruption and destruction, degraded computer performance, hardware destruction, violations of privacy, and the personnel time devoted to repairing the damage. The discussion that follows outlines some of the more common types of destructive programs.

Virus. A **virus** is a program (usually destructive) that attaches itself to a legitimate program to penetrate the operating system. The virus destroys application programs, data files, and operating systems in a number of ways. One common technique is for the virus to simply replicate itself over and over within the main memory, thus destroying whatever data or programs are resident. One of the most insidious aspects of a virus is its ability to spread throughout the system and to other systems before perpetrating its destructive acts. Typically, a virus will have a built-in counter that will inhibit its destructive role until the virus has copied itself a specified number of times to other programs and systems. The virus thus grows geometrically, which makes tracing its origin extremely difficult.

Microcomputers are a major source of virus penetration. When connected in a network or a mainframe, an infected microcomputer can upload the virus to the host computer. Once in the host, the virus can spread throughout the operating system and to other users.

Due to the heavy dependency on connectivity, the proliferation of microcomputers, and the need for extensive application programming, it may be impossible to eliminate the threat of viruses from the modern business environment. Sometimes, viruses are created internally by disgruntled employees in positions of power; other times, they are created outside the organization and are brought inside by unsuspecting users with legitimate access privileges to the system. Understanding how viruses work and how they are passed between systems is critical to their effective control.

Virus programs usually attach themselves to the following types of files:

1. An .EXE or .COM program file
2. An .OVL (overlay) program file
3. The boot sector of a disk
4. A device driver program

When a virus-infected program is executed, the virus searches the system for uninfected programs and copies itself into these programs. The virus may thus spread to the applications of other users or to the operating system itself.

Personal computers are the most common source of virus infestation. Their proliferation in business and society, combined with their relatively unsophisticated operating systems, has created a fertile environment in which viruses can grow and spread. A major contributing factor to the spread of viruses is the sharing of programs among users. The downloading of public-domain programs from network bulletin boards and the exchange of illegal "bootleg" software are the primary methods of virus transfer. Because of the lack of control features in microcomputer operating systems, microcomputers connected to mainframes pose a serious threat to the mainframe environment as well. For example, an application programmer may develop and test programs on a microcomputer and then upload the finished system to the mainframe. If a virus is in the microcomputer on which the program is developed, it can spread to the mainframe via the new application. When this program is executed, the virus can then spread to other applications on the mainframe.

Worm. The term **worm** is used interchangeably with virus. A worm is a software program that "burrows" into the computer's memory and replicates itself into areas of idle memory. The worm systematically occupies idle memory until the memory is exhausted and the system fails. Worms differ from viruses in that the replicated worm modules remain in contact with the original worm that controls their growth. The replicated virus modules, on the other hand, grow independently of the initial virus.

Logic Bomb. A **logic bomb** is a destructive program, such as a virus, that is triggered by some predetermined event. Quite often a date (such as Friday the 13th, April Fool's Day, or a birthday) will be the logic bomb's trigger. The famous Michelangelo virus (triggered by his birth date) is an example of a logic bomb. Logic bombs have also been triggered by events of less public prominence, such as the dismissal of an employee. For example, during the customary two-week severance period, a terminated programmer may embed a logic bomb in the system that will activate six months after his or her departure from the firm.

Back Door. A **back door** (also called a *trap door*) is a software program that allows unauthorized access to a system without going through the normal (front door) log-on procedure. Programmers who want to provide themselves with unrestricted access to the programs that they are developing for users may create a log-on procedure that will accept both the user's private password and their own secret password, thus creating a back door to the system. The purpose of the back door may be to provide easy access to perform program maintenance, or it may be to perpetrate a fraud or insert a virus into the system.

Trojan Horse. A **Trojan horse** is a program whose purpose is to capture IDs and passwords from unsuspecting users. The program is designed to mimic the normal log-on procedures of the operating system. When the user enters his or her ID and password, the Trojan horse stores a copy of them in a secret file. At some later date, the author of the Trojan horse uses these IDs and passwords to access the system and masquerade as an authorized user.

Threats from destructive programs can be substantially reduced through a combination of technology controls and administrative procedures. The following examples are relevant to most operating systems.

- Purchase software only from reputable vendors and accept only those products that are in their original, factory-sealed packages.
- Issue an entity-wide policy pertaining to the use of unauthorized software or illegal (bootleg) copies of copyrighted software.
- Examine all upgrades to vendor software for viruses before they are implemented.
- Inspect all public-domain software for virus infection before using.
- Establish entity-wide procedures for making changes to production programs.
- Establish an educational program to raise user awareness regarding threats from viruses and malicious programs.
- Install all new applications on a stand-alone computer and thoroughly test them with antiviral software prior to implementing them on the mainframe or LAN server.
- Routinely make backup copies of key files stored on mainframes, servers, and workstations.
- Wherever possible, limit users to read and execute rights only. This allows users to extract data and run authorized applications, but denies them the ability to write directly to mainframe and server directories.
- Require protocols that explicitly invoke the operating system's log-on procedures in order to bypass Trojan horses. A typical scenario is one in which a user sits

down to a terminal that is already displaying the log-on screen and proceeds to enter his or her ID and password. This, however, may be a Trojan horse rather than the legitimate procedure. Some operating systems allow the user to directly invoke the operating system log-on procedure by entering a key sequence such as CTRL + ALT + DEL. The user then knows that the log-on procedure on the screen is legitimate.

- Use antiviral software (also called *vaccines*) to examine application and operating system programs for the presence of a virus and remove it from the affected program. Antiviral programs are used to safeguard mainframes, network servers, and personal computers. Most antiviral programs run in the background on the host computer and automatically test all files that are uploaded to the host. However, the software works only on known viruses. If a virus has been modified slightly (mutated), there is no guarantee that the vaccine will work. It is therefore important to maintain the current version of the vaccine.

Controlling Audit Trails

Audit trails are logs that can be designed to record activity at the system, application, and user level. When properly implemented, audit trails provide an important detective control to help accomplish security policy objectives. Many operating systems allow management to select the level of auditing to be provided by the system. This determines which events will be recorded in the log. An effective audit policy will capture all significant events without cluttering the log with trivial activity. Each organization needs to decide where the threshold between information and irrelevant facts lies. Audit trails typically consist of two types of audit logs: (1) detailed logs of individual keystrokes and (2) event-oriented logs.

Keystroke Monitoring. **Keystroke monitoring** involves recording both the user's keystrokes and the system's responses. This form of log may be used after the fact to reconstruct the details of an event or as a real-time control to monitor or prevent unauthorized intrusion. Keystroke monitoring is the computer equivalent of a telephone wiretap. Some situations may justify this level of surveillance. In some circumstances, however, keystroke monitoring may be regarded as a violation of privacy. Before implementing this type of control, management and auditors should consider the possible legal, ethical, and behavioral implications.

Event Monitoring. **Event monitoring** summarizes key activities related to users, applications, and system resources. Event logs typically record the IDs of all users accessing the system; the time and duration of a user's session; programs that were executed during a session; and the files, databases, printers, and other resources accessed.

Audit Trail Objectives

Audit trails can be used to support security objectives in three ways: (1) detecting unauthorized access to the system, (2) facilitating the reconstruction of events, and (3) promoting personal accountability.

Detecting Unauthorized Access. Detecting unauthorized access can occur in real time or after the fact. The primary objective of real-time detection is to protect the system from outsiders who are attempting to breach system controls. A real-time audit trail can also be used to report on changes in system performance that may indicate infestation by a virus or worm. Depending upon how much activity is being logged and reviewed, real-time detection can impose a significant overhead on the operating system, which can degrade operational performance. After-the-fact detection logs can be stored electronically and reviewed periodically or as needed. When properly designed, they can be used to determine if unauthorized access was accomplished, or attempted and failed.

Reconstructing Events. Audit analysis can be used to reconstruct the steps that led to events such as system failures, security violations by individuals, or application processing errors. Knowledge of the conditions that existed at the time of a system failure can be used to assign responsibility and to avoid similar situations in the future. Audit trail analysis also plays an important role in accounting control. For example, by maintaining a record of all changes to account balances, the audit trail can be used to reconstruct accounting data files that were corrupted by a system failure.

Personal Accountability. Audit trails can be used to monitor user activity at the lowest level of detail. This capability is a preventive control that can be used to influence behavior. Individuals are less likely to violate an organization's security policy if they know that their actions are recorded in an audit log.

An audit log can also serve as a detective control to assign personal accountability for actions taken. Serious errors and the abuse of authority are of particular concern. It may be easier to prevent unauthorized intruders from accessing a system than to ensure that authorized users act only in accordance with their assigned authority. For example, an accounts receivable clerk is authorized to access customer records. The audit log may disclose that the clerk has been printing an inordinate number of records, which could indicate that the clerk is selling customer information.

Implementing an Audit Trail

The information contained in audit logs is useful to accountants in measuring the potential damage and financial loss associated with application errors, abuse of authority, or unauthorized access by outside intruders. Logs also provide valuable evidence for assessing both the adequacy of controls in place and the need for additional controls. Audit logs, however, can generate data in overwhelming detail. Important information can easily get lost among the superfluous details of daily operation. Thus, poorly designed logs can actually be dysfunctional. Protecting exposures with the potential for material financial loss should drive management's decision as to which users, applications, or operations to monitor, and how much detail to log. As with all controls, the benefits of audit logs must be balanced against the costs of implementating them.

Fault Tolerance Controls

Fault tolerance is the ability of the system to continue operation when part of the system fails due to hardware failure, application program error, or operator error. Various levels of fault tolerance can be achieved by implementing redundant system components. These include:

> **Redundant arrays of inexpensive disks (RAID).** There are several types of RAID configurations. Essentially, each method involves the use of parallel disks that contain redundant elements of data and applications. If one disk fails, the lost data are automatically reconstructed from the redundant components stored on the other disks.

> **Uninterruptible power supplies.** In the event of a power supply failure, short-term backup power is provided to allow the system to shut down in a controlled

manner. This will prevent data loss and corruption that would otherwise result from an uncontrolled system crash.

Multiprocessing. The simultaneous use of two or more processors improves throughput under normal operation. During a processor failure, the redundant processors balance the workload and provide complete backup.

Implementing fault tolerance control ensures that there is no single point of potential system failure. Total failure can occur only in the event of the failure of multiple components.

DATA MANAGEMENT CONTROLS

Controls over data management fall into two general categories: access controls and backup controls. **Access controls** are designed to prevent unauthorized individuals from viewing, retrieving, corrupting, or destroying the entity's data. **Backup controls** ensure that in the event of data loss due to unauthorized access, equipment failure, or physical disaster the organization can recover its files and databases.

ACCESS CONTROLS

Users of flat file systems maintain exclusive ownership of their data. In spite of the data integration problems associated with this model, it creates an environment in which unauthorized access to data can be effectively controlled. When not in use by the owner, a flat file is closed to other users and may be taken off-line and physically secured in the data library. In contrast, the need to integrate and share data in the database environment means that databases must remain on-line and open to all potential users.

In the shared database environment, access control risks include corruption, theft, misuse, and destruction of data. These threats originate from both unauthorized intruders and authorized users who exceed their access privileges. Several database control features are reviewed below.

User Views

The **user view** or subschema is a subset of the total database that defines the user's data domain and provides access to the database. Figure 15–3(a) illustrates the role of the user view. In a centralized database environment, the database administrator (DBA) has primary responsibility for user view design but works closely with users and systems designers in this task. Access privileges to the database, as defined in their views, should be commensurate with the users' legitimate needs.

Although user views can restrict user access to a limited set of data, they do not define task privileges such as read, delete, or write. Often, several users may share a single user view but have different authority levels. For example, users Smith, Jones, and Adams in Figure 15–3(a) all may have access to the same set of data: account number, customer name, account balance, and credit limit. Let's assume that all have read-authority, but only Jones has authority to modify and delete the data. Effective access control requires additional security measures, discussed next.

Database Authorization Table

The **database authorization table** contains rules that limit the actions a user can take. This technique is similar to the access control list used in the operating system. Each user is granted certain privileges that are coded in the authority table, which is

FIGURE 15–3(a)

Subschema Restricting
Access to Database

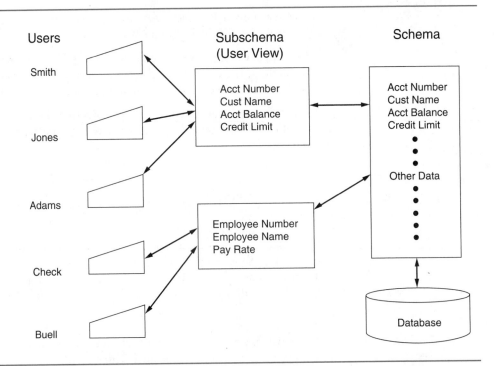

used to verify the user's action requests. For example, Figure 15–3(a) shows that Jones, Smith, and Adams have access to the same data attributes via a common user view, but the authorization table in Figure 15–3(b) shows that only Jones has the authority to modify and delete the data. Each row in the authority table indicates the level of action (read, insert, modify, or delete) that individuals can take based on their entering the correct password.

User-Defined Procedures

A **user-defined procedure** allows the user to create a personal security program or routine to provide more positive user identification than a single password can. For example, in addition to a password, the security procedure asks a series of personal

FIGURE 15–3(b)

Database
Authorization
Table

Dept	Accounts Rec			Billings	
User	Jones	Smith	Adams	Check	Buell
Password	Bugs	Dog	Katie	Lucky	Star
Authority:					
Read	Y	Y	Y	Y	Y
Insert	Y	N	Y	Y	N
Modify	Y	N	N	Y	N
Delete	Y	N	N	N	N

questions (such as the user's mother's maiden name), which only the legitimate user is likely to know.

Data Encryption

Many database systems use encryption procedures to protect highly sensitive data, such as product formulas, personnel pay rates, password files, and certain financial data. **Data encryption** uses an algorithm to scramble selected data, thus making it unreadable to an intruder "browsing" the database. In addition to protecting stored data, encryption is used for protecting data that are transmitted across networks. Various encryption techniques are discussed in Chapter 16.

Biometric Devices

The ultimate in user authentication procedures is the use of **biometric devices**, which measure various personal characteristics, such as fingerprints, voice prints, retina prints, or signature characteristics. These user characteristics are digitized and stored permanently in a database security file or on an identification card that the user carries. When an individual attempts to access the database, a special scanning device captures his or her biometric characteristics, which it compares with the profile data stored internally or on the ID card. If the data do not match, access is denied. Biometric technology is currently being used to secure ATM cards and credit cards.

Inference Controls

One advantage of the database query capability is that it provides users with summary and statistical data for decision making. For example, managers might ask the following questions:

- What is the total value for inventory items with monthly turnover less than three?
- What is the average charge to patients with hospital stays greater than eight days?
- What is the total cost of Class II payroll for department XYZ?

Answers to these types of questions are needed routinely for resource management, facility planning, and operations control decisions. Legitimate queries sometimes involve access to confidential data. Thus, individual users may be granted summary and statistical query access to confidential data to which they normally are denied direct access.

To preserve the confidentiality and integrity of the database, **inference controls** should be in place to prevent users from inferring, through query features, specific data values that they otherwise are unauthorized to access. Inference controls attempt to prevent three types of compromises to the database.[3]

1. *Positive compromise*—the user determines the specific value of a data item.
2. *Negative compromise*—the user determines that a data item does not have a specific value.
3. *Approximate compromise*—the user is unable to determine the exact value of an item but is able to estimate it with sufficient accuracy to violate the confidentiality of the data.

The payroll database table presented in Figure 15–4 will be used to illustrate how inference techniques are used to compromise a database. The salary field in the table is

---

3   R. Weber, *EDP Auditing Conceptual Foundations and Practice*, 2d ed. (New York: McGraw-Hill, 1988): 564.

FIGURE 15–4

Payroll Database
Containing
Confidential
Data

Payroll Database

Empl Num	Name	Job Title	Salary	Sex	Other Data	
5439	Jim Jones	Consultant	50,000	Male	●	●
9887	Sam Smith	Lawyer	60,000	Male	●	●
8765	Mary Swindle	Lawyer	65,000	Female	●	●
4462	Bob Haub	Manager	60,000	Male	●	●
7742	Joan Hess	Consultant	50,000	Female	●	●
5532	Ben Huber	Lawyer	62,000	Male	●	●
8332	John Enis	Lawyer	63,000	Male	●	●
9662	Jim Hobbs	Consultant	70,000	Male	●	●
3391	Joe Riley	Manager	75,000	Male	●	●

the confidential data being sought. Assuming that no inference controls are in place, a user wanting to determine the salary of Mary Swindle, a staff lawyer, could make the following queries:

Q. How many lawyers are female?
A. One.
Q. What is the average salary of all who are female and lawyers?
A. $65,000.

Since she is the only female lawyer, Mary Swindle's salary is explicitly provided by the query system through this statistical feature. This sort of compromise may be prevented by implementing the following inference control rule that places restrictions on the size of the query set to which the system will respond:

The system will not respond to queries where fewer than two records satisfy the query.

However, a determined and creative user may easily circumvent this control with the following queries:

Q. What is the total salary for the payroll database?
A. $555,000.

Q. What is the total salary for all not lawyers and not female?
A. $490,000.

Swindle's salary can be calculated in this example by subtracting $490,000 from $555,000. Preventing this compromise requires further restrictions on the query set size. This may be accomplished with the following additional inference control rule:

> The system will not respond to queries where greater than $(n - 2)$ records satisfy the query (where n is the number of records in the database).

Under this rule, neither query would have been satisfied.

BACKUP CONTROLS

Data can be corrupted and destroyed by malicious acts from external hackers, disgruntled employees, disk failure, program errors, fires, floods, and earthquakes. To recover from such disasters, organizations must implement policies, procedures, and techniques that systematically and routinely provide backup copies of critical files.

Backup Controls in the Flat File Environment

The backup technique employed will depend on the media and the file structure. Sequential files (both tape and disk) use a backup technique called grandparent-parent-child (GPC). This backup technique is an integral part of the master file update process. Direct access files, on the other hand, need a separate backup procedure. Both methods are outlined below.

GPC Backup Technique. Figure 15–5 illustrates the **grandparent-parent-child (GPC)** backup technique that is used in sequential file batch systems. The backup procedure begins when the current master file (the parent) is processed against the transaction file to produce a new updated master file (the child). With the next batch of transactions, the child becomes the current master file (the parent), and the original parent becomes the backup (grandparent) file. The new master file that emerges from the update process is the child. This procedure is continued with each new batch of transactions, creating generations of backup files. When the desired number of backup copies is reached, the oldest backup file is erased (scratched). If the current master file is destroyed or corrupted, processing the most current backup file against the corresponding transaction file can reproduce it.

The systems designer determines the number of backup master files needed for each application. Two factors influence this decision: (1) the financial significance of the system and (2) the degree of file activity. For example, a master file that is updated several times a day may require 30 or 40 generations of backup, while a file that is updated only once each month may need only four or five backup versions. This decision is important, because certain types of system failures can result in the destruction of large numbers of backup versions within the same family of files.

The author was witness to one system failure that destroyed, through accidental erasure, over 150 master files in only a few hours. The destruction began by erasing the most current master file (parent) in each application being processed. Then, one by one, the older generations were systematically scratched. Some systems lost as many as 20 backup copies. In fact, the accounts payable system had only one backup version left when the error was finally detected and stopped. Reconstruction of files after such a disaster requires locating the most current remaining backup version and methodically reprocessing the batches of past transactions until the current version of the master file is reproduced. This will also recreate all the intermediate generations of the master file. When using the GPC approach for financial systems, management

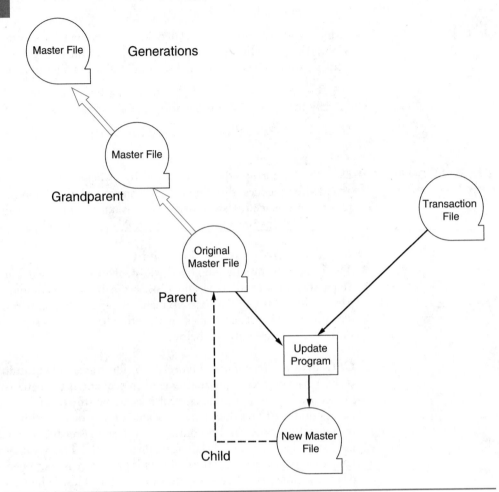

FIGURE 15–5

Grandparent-Parent-Child Approach

and auditors should be involved in determining the needed number of backup files. Insufficient backup can result in the total destruction of accounting records. Most operating systems permit the creation of up to 256 generations for each application.

Direct Access File Backup. Data values in direct access files are changed in place through a process called *destructive replacement*. Therefore, once a data value is changed, the original value is destroyed, leaving only one version (the current version) of the file. To provide backup, direct access files must be copied before being updated. Figure 15–6 illustrates this process.

The timing of the **direct access backup** procedures will depend upon the processing method being used. Backup of files in batch systems is usually scheduled prior to the update process. Real-time systems pose a more difficult problem. Since transactions are being processed continuously, the backup procedure takes place at specified intervals throughout the day (for example, every 15 minutes).

If the current version of the master file is destroyed through a disk failure or corrupted by a program error, it can be reconstructed with a special recovery program from the most current backup file. In the case of real-time systems, transactions

FIGURE 15–6

Backup of Direct
Access Files

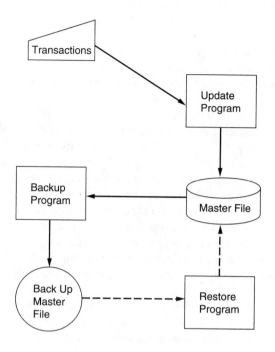

Real-Time Processing System

Real-time systems use timed backup. Transactions processed between backup runs will have
to be reprocessed after restoration of the master file.

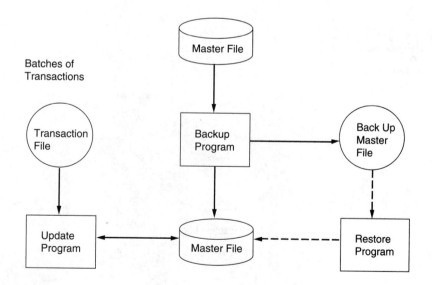

Batch Processing System

In a batch processing system using direct access files, the master file is backed up before
the update run.

processed since the last backup and prior to the failure will be lost and will need to be reprocessed to restore the master file to current status.

Off-Site Storage. As an added safeguard, backup files created under both the GPC and direct access approaches should be stored off-site in a secure location. **Off-site storage** is discussed further in the section dealing with disaster recovery planning.

Backup Controls in the Database Environment

Since data sharing is a fundamental objective of the database approach, this environment is particularly vulnerable to damage from individual users. One unauthorized procedure, one malicious act, or one program error can deprive an entire user community of its information resource. Also, because of data centralization, even minor disasters such as a disk failure can affect many or all users. When such events occur, the organization needs to reconstruct the database to pre-failure status. This can be done only if the database was properly backed up in the first place. Most mainframe DBMSs have a backup and recovery system similar to the one illustrated in Figure 15–7. This system provides four backup and recovery features: database backup, a transaction log, checkpoints, and a recovery module. Each of these is described below.

Backup. The backup feature makes a periodic backup of the entire database. This is an automatic procedure that should be performed at least once a day. The backup copy should then be stored in a secure remote area.

Transaction Log (Journal). The **transaction log** feature provides an audit trail of all processed transactions. It lists transactions in a transaction log file and records the resulting changes to the database in a separate database change log.

FIGURE 15–7

Database Backup and Recovery

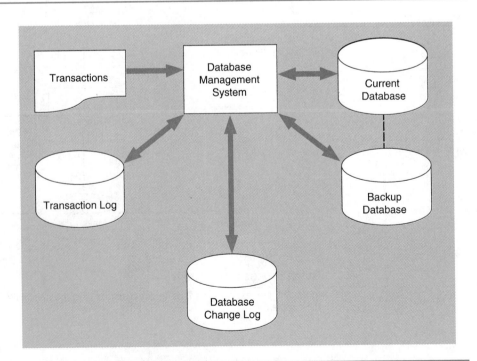

Checkpoint Feature.   The **checkpoint** facility suspends all data processing while the system reconciles the transaction log and the database change log against the database. At this point, the system is in a "quiet state." Checkpoints occur automatically several times an hour. If a failure occurs, it is usually possible to restart the processing from the last checkpoint. Thus, only a few minutes of transaction processing must be repeated.

Recovery Module.   The **recovery module** uses the logs and backup files to restart the system after a failure.

ORGANIZATIONAL STRUCTURE CONTROLS

Previous chapters have addressed the importance of segregating incompatible duties in manual systems. In a manual environment, operational tasks must be separated to:

1. Segregate the task of transaction authorization from transaction processing.
2. Segregate record keeping from asset custody.
3. Divide transaction processing tasks among individuals so that the perpetration of a fraud will require collusion between two or more individuals.

The tendency in a CBIS environment is to consolidate activities. A single application may authorize, process, and record all aspects of a transaction. Thus, the focus of segregation control shifts from the operational level (transaction processing tasks now performed by computer programs) to higher-level organizational relationships within the computer services function. The interrelationships among systems development, systems maintenance, database administration, and computer operations activities are of particular concern.

The following section examines organizational control issues within the context of two general models—the centralized model and the distributed model. In Chapter 1, you studied the operational characteristics and principal features of these models. While these are often presented as extreme alternative structures, in reality, many firms possess elements of both models.

SEGREGATION OF DUTIES WITHIN THE CENTRALIZED FIRM

Figure 15–8 contains an organizational chart of a centralized computer services function. A similar organizational chart was presented in Chapter 1 to provide the basis for discussing computer services tasks. It is reexamined here to study the control objectives behind separating these tasks. If the positions represented in this chart are unfamiliar, you should review the relevant sections in Chapter 1 at this time.

Separating Systems Development from Computer Operations

The segregation of systems development (both new systems development and maintenance) and operations activities is of the greatest importance. The relationship between these groups should be extremely formal, and their responsibilities should not be commingled. Systems development and maintenance professionals should create (and maintain) systems for users. Operations staff should run these systems and have no involvement in their design. Consolidating these functions invites fraud. With detailed knowledge of the application's logic and control parameters and access to computer functions, an individual could make unauthorized changes to the application during its execution. Such changes may be temporary ("on the fly") and will disappear without a trace when the application terminates.

FIGURE 15–8   Organizational Chart of a Centralized Computer Services Function

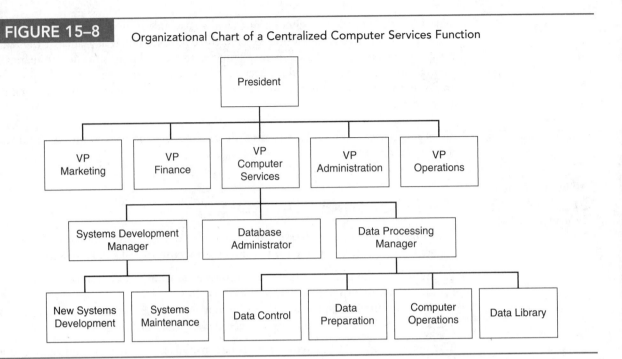

Separating the Database Administrator from Other Functions

Another important organizational control is the segregation of the database administrator function from other computer services functions. The DBA function is responsible for a number of critical tasks pertaining to database security, including creating the database schema, creating user subschemas (views), assigning access authority to users, monitoring database usage, and planning for future expansion. Delegating these responsibilities to others who perform incompatible tasks threatens database integrity. Figure 15–8 shows how the DBA function is organizationally independent. However, special note should be taken of the separation of the DBA from systems development.

Separating the DBA from Systems Development. Programmers produce applications that access, update, and retrieve information from the database. This chapter and Chapter 9 illustrate how database access control is achieved through the creation of a subschema or user view, which is a DBA responsibility. Giving responsibility for subschema definition to programmers effectively destroys access control and can neutralize the DBMS's ability to detect unauthorized access attempts.

Separating New Systems Development from Maintenance

Some companies organize their systems development function into two groups: systems analysis and programming. This organizational alternative is presented in Figure 15–9.

The systems analysis group works with the user to produce a detailed design of the new system. The programming group codes the programs according to these design specifications. Under this approach, the programmer who codes the original programs also maintains the system during the maintenance phase of the SDLC. Although a popular arrangement, this approach promotes two types of control problems: inadequate documentation and fraud.

FIGURE 15–9

Alternative
Organization
of Systems
Development

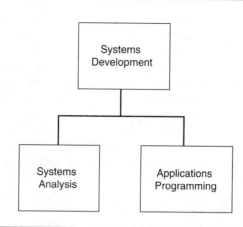

Inadequate Documentation. Poor-quality systems documentation is a chronic problem for many firms. This is particularly true in companies that do not use CASE tools with automatic documentation features. There are at least two explanations for this phenomenon. First, documenting a system is not as interesting as designing, testing, and implementing it. Systems professionals much prefer to move on to an exciting new project rather than document one that is completed. Pressure from users demanding new systems makes the decision to move on to something else even easier.

The second reason for poor documentation is job security. When a system is poorly documented, it is difficult to interpret, test, and debug. Therefore, the programmer who understands the system (the one who coded it) is in a position of power and becomes relatively indispensable. However, when the programmer leaves the firm, the system must be maintained by a new programmer unfamiliar with it. The new programmer may have to study the detailed code of the application to glean an understanding of its logic. Depending upon the complexity of the system, the transition period can be long and costly.

Program Fraud. When the original programmer of a system also has maintenance responsibility, the potential for fraud is increased. Program fraud involves making unauthorized changes to program modules for the purpose of committing an illegal act. The original programmer may successfully conceal the fraudulent code among the thousands of lines of legitimate code and the hundreds of modules that constitute a system. However, for the fraud to work successfully, the programmer must have continued and unrestricted access to these programs. To control the situation, the programmer must protect the fraudulent code from accidental detection by another programmer (during maintenance) or by the auditor. Therefore, being vested with sole responsibility for maintenance is an important element in the duplicitous programmer's scheme. Through this maintenance authority, the programmer may freely access the system, disabling fraudulent a code during audits and then restoring the code when the coast is clear. Frauds of this sort may go on for years without detection.

An Alternative Structure for Systems Development

Figure 15–8 presents a superior organizational structure in which the systems development function is separated into two different groups: new systems development and systems maintenance. The new systems development group is responsible for designing, programming, and implementing new systems projects. Upon successful implementation, responsibility for the system's ongoing maintenance falls to the systems maintenance group. This restructuring has implications that directly address the two control problems described previously.

First, documentation standards are improved because the maintenance group requires documentation to perform its maintenance duties. Without complete and adequate documentation, the formal transfer of system responsibility from new systems development to systems maintenance simply cannot occur.

Second, denying the original programmer future access to the program deters program fraud. That the fraudulent code, once concealed within the system, is out of the programmer's control and may later be discovered increases the risk associated with program fraud. The success of this control depends on the existence of other controls that limit, prevent, and detect unauthorized access to programs (such as source program library controls). Organizational separations alone cannot prevent such unauthorized access. However, they are critical to creating the environment in which unauthorized access can be prevented.

Separating the Data Library from Operations

The data library is usually a room adjacent to the computer center that provides safe storage for the off-line data files, such as magnetic tapes and removable disk packs. Access to the library should be controlled by a data librarian who is responsible for the receipt, storage, retrieval, and custody of data files. The librarian must keep a detailed log of each file, including file name, serial number, contents, creation date, and retention dates. The librarian issues scratch tapes (when their expiration dates are exceeded) to computer operators in accordance with system requests. When the program run is complete, the operator returns the file(s) to the librarian for storage.

The separation of the librarian from operations is important for the physical security of off-line data files. However, for many organizations, the volume of tape file usage is insufficient to justify a full-time librarian. The trend in recent years toward real-time and direct access batch systems has reduced the need for sequential tape storage. Thus, firms with modest tape usage—which still may represent several hundred tape volumes—often assign librarian functions to selected operators who perform these tasks on an ad hoc basis in addition to their usual operator functions.

It is essential that operators who are assigned library tasks understand the control importance of this apparently mundane responsibility. Management should maintain strict control over who performs library functions to ensure that these responsibilities are not assumed by other operators during busy periods. This apparently innocuous transgression creates an environment of shared responsibility that inevitably deteriorates into one of no responsibility. In such an environment, data security suffers. The potential exposure can be illustrated through the following three scenarios.

1. Computer centers become very busy at times. Rushed operators, hurrying to start the next job, may forget to return to the library the tapes used by the program that has just completed processing. Lacking a librarian with the formal responsibility to account for the disposition of all tapes files, these tapes may remain in a corner of the computer room for days, exposed to physical damage, loss, theft, or corruption.

2. Inexperienced individuals filling in as librarian during busy periods may return a tape to the wrong storage location in the library. When needed again, the librarian may not be able to find the tape. This is analogous to placing an important

book in a randomly selected shelf space in a library. How does one go about relocating it?

3. The librarian is directly responsible for implementing the firm's scratch tape policy. The librarian issues expired tapes to operators as scratch tapes (to be written over) for another program. Inexperienced librarians have been known to issue current tapes, thinking they were scratch tapes. In one such incident, over 100 tape master files were destroyed.

THE DISTRIBUTED MODEL

Chapter 1 examined the impact on organizational structure of moving to a distributed data processing model in which computer services are controlled by end-user departments. The effect of this is to consolidate some computer functions that are traditionally separated and to distribute some activities that are consolidated under the centralized model. In spite of the many advantages provided by DDP, the approach carries control implications that accountants should recognize. These are discussed below.

Incompatibility

Distributing responsibility for the purchases of software and hardware can result in uncoordinated and poorly conceived decisions. Organizational users, working independently, may select different and incompatible operating systems, technology platforms, spreadsheets, word processing, and database packages. System incompatibilities can greatly impair intraorganization communications.

Redundancy

Autonomous systems development activities throughout the firm can result in each one essentially reinventing the wheel. Programs created by one user that could be used with little or no change by others will be redesigned from scratch rather than shared. Likewise, data common to many users may be reproduced, resulting in a high level of data redundancy.

Consolidating Incompatible Activities

The distribution of computer services functions to user areas can result in the creation of many very small units. Achieving an adequate segregation of duties may not be possible. In small businesses one person maybe responsible for program development, program maintenance, and computer operations.

Acquiring Qualified Professionals

End users are often unqualified to evaluate the technical credentials and relevant experience of prospective computer services employees. Also, because the organizational unit into which these candidates are entering is small, opportunities for personal growth, continuing education, and promotion are limited. For these reasons, computer services units under the distributed model have difficulty attracting highly qualified personnel.

Lack of Standards

For the above reasons, standards for systems development, documentation, and evaluating performance tend to be unevenly applied or nonexistent in the DDP environment.

CREATING A
CORPORATE
COMPUTER
SERVICES
FUNCTION

The completely centralized and the distributed models represent extreme positions on a continuum of structural alternatives. The needs of most firms fall somewhere between these end points. For these firms, the control problems associated with DDP can, to some extent, be overcome by implementing a **corporate computer services function**. Figure 15–10 illustrates this organizational approach.

The corporate computer services function is greatly reduced in size and status from that of the centralized model shown in Figure 15–8. In some firms, this corporate group provides systems development and database management for systems that serve the entire organization rather than an individual user. This group also provides technical advice and expertise to distributed computer service functions, as represented by the dotted lines in Figure 15–10. Some of the services that it provides are described below.

Central Testing of Commercial Software and Hardware

The corporate computer services group is better able to evaluate the merits of competing vendor software and hardware. Systems features, controls, and compatibility with industry and organizational standards can be evaluated most efficiently by a cen-

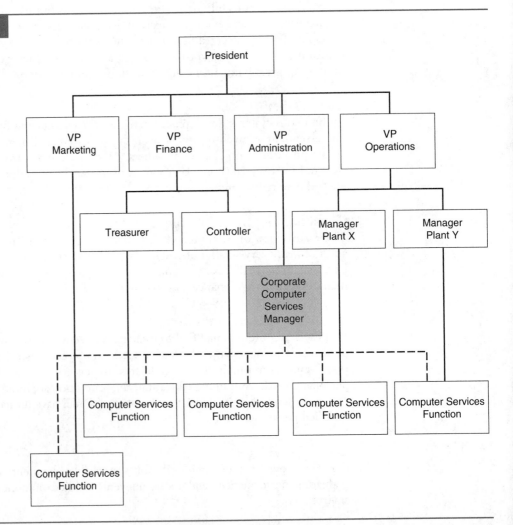

FIGURE 15–10

Distributed
Organization with
Corporate Computer
Services Function

tral, technically astute group such as this. Test results can then be distributed to user areas as standards for guiding acquisition decisions.

User Services

A valuable feature of the corporate group is its user services function. This activity provides technical help to users during the installation of new software and in troubleshooting hardware and software problems. The creation of an electronic bulletin board for users is an excellent way to distribute information about common problems and allows the sharing of user-developed programs with others within the organization. The user services staff in many organizations teaches technical courses for end users and their computer services staff; this raises the level of user awareness and promotes the continued education of technical personnel.

Standard-Setting Body

The relatively poor control environment imposed by the DDP model can be improved by establishing some central guidance. The corporate group can contribute to this goal by establishing and distributing to user areas appropriate standards for systems development, programming, and documentation.

Personnel Review

The corporate group is probably better equipped than users to evaluate the technical credentials of prospective systems professionals. Although the systems professional will actually be part of the user group, the involvement of the corporate group in employment decisions can render a valuable service to the organization.

SYSTEMS DEVELOPMENT CONTROLS

Chapters 13 and 14 presented the systems development life cycle (SDLC) as a seven-phase process by which organizations satisfy their formal information needs. A point made during the introduction of that material was that no significance should be attached to the number of phases that constitute the SDLC, which may vary from firm to firm. The focus of the accountant in reviewing the adequacy of the SDLC should be on the control objectives of these activities. This section and the next examine eight controllable activities that distinguish an effective SDLC.

CONTROLLING NEW SYSTEMS DEVELOPMENT ACTIVITIES

The six activities discussed below deal with the authorization, development, and implementation of the original system.

Systems Authorization Activities

All systems must be properly authorized to ensure their economic justification and feasibility. As with any transaction, systems authorizations should be formal. Typically, this requires that each new system request be submitted in written form by users to systems professionals who have both the expertise and authority to evaluate and approve (or reject) the request.

User Specification Activities

Users must be actively involved in the systems development process. User involvement should not be stifled by the prospect of a high degree of technical complexity in the system. Regardless of the technology involved, the user can create a detailed written description of the logical needs that must be satisfied by the system. The creation of a user specification document often involves the joint efforts of the user and systems professionals. However, it is most important that this document remain a statement of user needs. It should describe the user's view of the problem, not that of the systems professionals.

Technical Design Activities

The technical design activities in the SDLC translate the user specifications into a set of detailed technical specifications of a system that meets the user's needs. The scope of these activities includes systems analysis, general systems design, feasibility analysis, and detailed systems design. The adequacy of these activities is measured by the quality of the documentation that emerges from each phase. Documentation is both a control and evidence of control and is critical to the system's long-term success. Specific documentation requirements were discussed in Chapter 14.

Internal Audit Participation

The internal auditor plays an important role in the control of systems development activities, particularly in organizations whose users lack technical expertise. The internal auditor can serve as a liaison between users and the systems professionals to ensure an effective transfer of knowledge. An internal audit group, astute in computer technology and with a solid grasp of the business problems of users, is thus invaluable to the organization during all phases of the SDLC. The auditor should become involved at the inception of the SDLC process to make conceptual suggestions regarding system requirements and controls. Auditor involvement should continue throughout all phases of the development process and into the maintenance phase.

Program Testing

All program modules must be thoroughly tested before they are implemented. Figure 15–11 shows a program testing procedure involving the creation of hypothetical master files and transactions files that are processed by the modules being tested. The results of the tests are then compared against predetermined results to identify programming and logic errors. For example, in testing the logic of the accounts receivable update module illustrated in Figure 15–11, the programmer might create an accounts receivable master file record for John Smith with a current balance of $1,000 and a sales order transaction record for $100. Before performing the update test, the programmer concludes that a new balance of $1,100 should be created. To verify the module's internal logic, the programmer compares the actual results obtained from the run with the predetermined results. This is a very simple example of a program test. Actual testing would be extensive and involve many transactions that test all aspects of the module's logic.

   Program testing is time-consuming, the principal task being the creation of meaningful test data. However, this is not a one-time activity. As we shall see in Chapter 17, some aspects of information systems auditing involve program testing that continues throughout the application's operational life. To facilitate the efficient implementation of audit objectives, test data prepared during the implementation phase must be preserved for future use. This will give the auditor a frame of reference for designing and evaluating future audit tests. For example, if a program has undergone no maintenance changes since its implementation, the test results from the audit should be identical to the original test results. Having a basis for comparison, the auditor can thus quickly verify the integrity of the program code. On the other hand, if changes have occurred, the original test data can provide evidence regarding these changes. The auditor can thus focus attention upon those areas.

FIGURE 15–11

Program Testing
Procedures

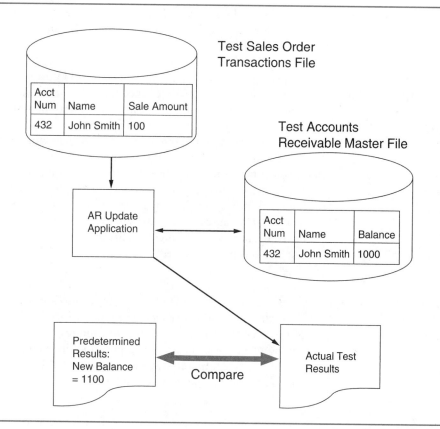

Test Sales Order
Transactions File

Acct Num	Name	Sale Amount
432	John Smith	100

Test Accounts
Receivable Master File

Acct Num	Name	Balance
432	John Smith	1000

AR Update
Application

Predetermined
Results:
New Balance
= 1100

Compare

Actual Test
Results

User Test and Acceptance Procedures

Just before implementation, the individual modules of the system must be tested as a unified whole. A test team comprising user personnel, systems professionals, and internal audit personnel subjects the system to rigorous testing. Once the test team is satisfied that the system meets its stated requirements, the system is formally accepted by the user department(s).

The formal test and acceptance of the system are considered by many to be the most important control over the SDLC. It is imperative that user acceptance be documented. Before implementation, this is the last point at which the user can determine the system's adequacy and acceptability. Although discovering a major flaw at this juncture is costly, discovering the flaw during production operations can be devastating.

SYSTEMS MAINTENANCE CONTROLS

The last two controllable activities pertain to systems maintenance. On implementation, the system enters the maintenance phase of the SDLC. This is the longest period in the SDLC, often spanning several years. It is important to recognize that systems do not remain static throughout this period. Rather, they undergo substantive changes that constitute, in dollars, an amount many times their original implementation cost. To illustrate the magnitude of resources devoted during this period, maintenance was characterized in Chapter 13 as that portion of an iceberg below the water line. The nature and extent of systems maintenance activities create great potential for exposure, which requires explicit control procedures.

MAINTENANCE AUTHORIZATION, TESTING, AND DOCUMENTATION

Little purpose is served by imposing control in the systems development process, only to abandon it in the maintenance phase. Post-implementation access to systems via maintenance activities increases the possibility of systems corruption. Logic may be corrupted either by the accidental introduction of errors or intentional acts to defraud. To minimize the potential exposure, all maintenance actions should require, as a minimum, four controls: formal authorizations, technical specifications, testing, and documentation updates. In other words, maintenance activities should be given essentially the same treatment as new development. The extent of the change and its potential impact on the system should govern the degree of control applied. When maintenance causes extensive changes to program logic, additional controls should be invoked, such as involvement by the internal auditor and the implementation of user test and acceptance procedures.

SOURCE PROGRAM LIBRARY CONTROLS

Even with the above maintenance procedures in place, application integrity can be jeopardized by individuals gaining unauthorized access to programs. The remainder of this section deals with control techniques and procedures for preventing and detecting unauthorized access to application programs.

In larger computer systems, application program modules are stored in source code form on magnetic disks called the *source program library (SPL)*. Figure 15–12

FIGURE 15–12   Uncontrolled Access to the Source Program Library

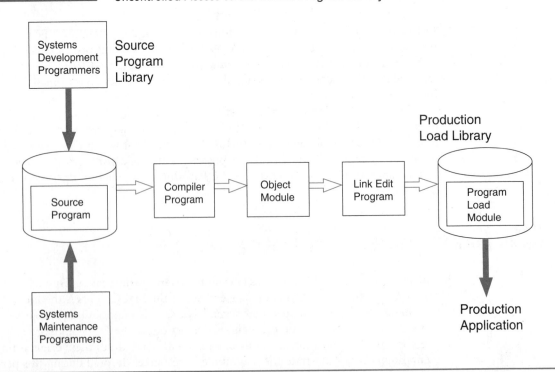

illustrates the relationship between the SPL and other key components of the operating environment. This material presumes an understanding of the program compilation process. If you are uncertain about the meaning of the terms *source program*, *compiler*, and *load module*, review the section on language translators on the book's Web page located at http://hall.swcollege.com.

For a program to be executed as a production application, it must first be compiled and linked into a load module that the computer can process. As a practical matter, programs in their compiled form are considered to be secure and free from the threat of unauthorized modification. Program changes (both authorized maintenance and unauthorized changes) are accomplished by first making changes to the source code on the SPL and then recompiling and linking the program to create a new load module that incorporates the changed code. Therefore, the SPL is a sensitive area that, to preserve application integrity, must be properly controlled.

THE WORST CASE SITUATION: NO CONTROLS

Figure 15–12 shows the SPL without controls. This arrangement has the potential to create two serious forms of exposure:

1. Access to programs is completely unrestricted. Programmers and others can access any programs stored in the library, and there is no provision for detecting an unauthorized intrusion.
2. Because of these control weaknesses, programs are subject to unauthorized changes. Hence, there is no basis for relying on the effectiveness of other controls (maintenance authorization, program testing, and documentation). In other words, with no provision for detecting unauthorized access to the SPL, the program's integrity cannot be verified.

Control is in conflict with operational flexibility and efficiency. For these reasons, controlling the SPL is sometimes opposed by systems professionals who must work daily within this environment. To achieve a mutually acceptable control-flexibility trade-off between the needs of systems professionals and accountants, both must understand the exposures that are created when control features are not employed or are routinely circumvented. In spite of the exposure described above, the no-controls approach is often the choice (perhaps inadvertently) that management makes.

A CONTROLLED SPL ENVIRONMENT

To control the SPL, protective features and procedures must be explicitly addressed, and this requires the implementation of an *SPL management system (SPLMS)*. Figure 15–13 illustrates the use of this technique.

The black box surrounding the SPL signifies the SPLMS. This software is used to control four routine but critical functions: (1) storing programs on the SPL, (2) retrieving programs for maintenance purposes, (3) deleting obsolete programs from the library, and (4) documenting program changes to provide an audit trail of the changes.

You may have recognized the similarities between the SPL management system and a database management system. This is a valid analogy, the difference being that SPL software manages program files and DBMSs manage data files. SPLMSs may be supplied by the computer manufacturer as part of the operating system or may be purchased through software vendors. Some organizations, to provide special control features, develop their own SPL software.

The mere presence of an SPLMS does not guarantee program integrity. Again, we can draw an analogy with the DBMS. To achieve data integrity, the DBMS must

FIGURE 15–13   Source Program Library under the Control of SPL Management Software

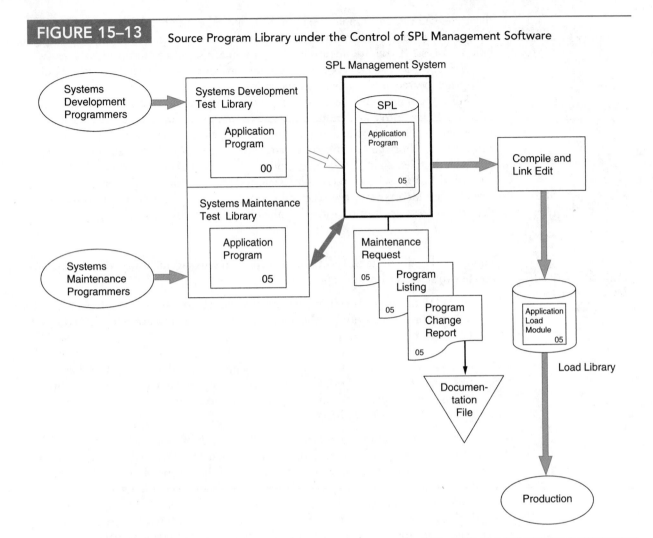

be properly used; control does not come automatically—it must be planned. Likewise, an SPL requires specific planning and control techniques to ensure program integrity. The control techniques discussed below address only the most vulnerable areas and should be considered minimum SPL controls.

Password Control
One form of access control over the SPL is provided by assigning passwords. This is similar to password controls used in a DBMS to protect data files. Every financially significant program stored in the SPL can be assigned a separate password. As previously discussed, passwords have drawbacks. When more than one person is authorized to access a program, preserving the secrecy of a shared password is a problem. As more authorized personnel have a need to know the password, the potential for losing control of the password increases. Since responsibility for the secrecy of a shared password lies with the group rather than with an individual, personal accountability is reduced, and individuals within the group may take less care in protecting the password.

Separation of Test Libraries

Figure 15–13 illustrates an improvement on the shared password approach through the creation of separate password-controlled libraries (or directories) for each programmer. Under this concept, a strict separation is maintained between the production programs that are subject to maintenance in the SPL and those being developed. Production programs are copied into the programmer's library for maintenance and testing purposes only. Direct access to the production SPL is limited to a specific librarian group that must approve all requests to modify, delete, and copy programs. Passwords for production programs can be changed regularly and disclosed only on a need-to-know basis.

A relatively cost-free enhancement to this control feature is the implementation of program naming conventions. The name assigned a program clearly distinguishes it as being either a test or a production program. When a program is copied from the production SPL to the programmer's library, it is given a temporary "test" name. When the program is returned to the SPL, it is renamed with its original production name. This technique greatly reduces the risk of accidentally running an untested version of a program in place of the production program.

Audit Trail and Management Reports

An important feature of SPL management software is the creation of reports that enhance management control and the audit function. The most useful of these are program modification reports, which describe in detail all program changes (additions and deletions) to each module. These reports should be part of the documentation file of each application to form an audit trail of program changes over the life of the application. During an audit, these reports can be reconciled against program maintenance requests to verify that only those changes requested were actually implemented. For example, if a programmer attempted to use a legitimate maintenance action as an opportunity to commit program fraud, the unauthorized code changes would be presented in the program modification report. These reports can be produced as hard copy and on disk and can be governed by password control, thus limiting access to management and auditors only.

Program Version Numbers

The SPLMS assigns a version number automatically to each program stored on the SPL. When programs are first placed in the libraries (at implementation), they are assigned a version number of zero. With each modification to the program, the version number is increased by one. For instance, after five authorized maintenance changes, the production program will be Version 05, as illustrated in Figure 15–3. This feature, when combined with audit trail reports, provides evidence for identifying unauthorized changes to program modules. An unauthorized change is signaled by a version number on the production load module that cannot be reconciled to the number of authorized changes. For example, if ten changes were authorized but the production program is Version 12, then one of two possibilities explains this discrepancy: (1) authorized changes occurred that are unsupported by documentation or (2) unauthorized changes were made to the program that increased the version numbers. We shall discuss the use of this feature as an audit tool in Chapter 17.

Controlling Access to Maintenance Commands

Powerful maintenance commands are available for most library systems that can be used to alter or eliminate program passwords, alter the program version (modification) number, and temporarily modify a program without generating a record of the modification.

There are a number of legitimate technical reasons why systems designers must sometimes use these commands. However, if not controlled, maintenance commands open the possibility of unrecorded, and perhaps unauthorized, program modifications. Hence, access to the maintenance commands themselves should be password controlled, and the authority to use them should be controlled by management or the security group.

COMPUTER CENTER SECURITY AND CONTROLS

Fires, floods, wind, sabotage, earthquakes, or even power outages can deprive an organization of its data processing facilities and bring to a halt those functions that are performed or aided by the computer. Although the likelihood of such a disastrous event is remote, the consequences to the organization could be serious. If a disaster occurs the organization not only loses its investment in data processing facilities, but more importantly, it also loses its ability to do business.

The objective of this section is to present computer center controls that help create a secure environment. We will begin with a look at controls designed to prevent and detect threats to the computer center. However, no matter how much is invested in control, some disasters simply cannot be anticipated and prevented. What does a company do to prepare itself for such an event? How will it recover? These questions are at the heart of the organization's disaster recovery plan. The second half of this section deals with issues pertaining to the development of a disaster recovery plan.

COMPUTER CENTER CONTROLS

Accountants routinely examine the physical environment of the computer center as part of their annual audit. Exposures in these areas have a great potential impact on information, accounting records, transaction processing, and the effectiveness of other, more conventional, internal controls. The following are some of the control features that contribute directly to the security of the computer center environment.

Physical Location

The physical location of the computer center affects the risk of disaster directly. To the extent possible, the computer center should be away from human-made and natural hazards, such as processing plants, gas and water mains, airports, high-crime areas, flood plains, and geological faults.

Construction

Ideally, a computer center should be located in a single-story building of solid construction with controlled access (discussed below). Utility (power and telephone) and communications lines should be underground. The building windows should not open. An air filtration system should be in place that is capable of excluding pollens, dust, and dust mites.

Access

Access to the computer center should be limited to the operators and other employees who work there. Programmers and analysts who need access to correct program errors should be required to sign in and out. The computer center should maintain accurate records of all such events to verify access control. The main entrance to the computer center should be through a single door, though fire exits with alarms are necessary. To achieve a higher level of security, access should be monitored by closed-circuit cameras and video recording systems.

Air Conditioning

Computers function best in an air-conditioned environment. For mainframe computers, providing adequate air conditioning is often a requirement of the vendor's warranty. Computers operate best in a temperature range of 70 to 75 degrees Fahrenheit and a relative humidity of 50 percent. Logic errors can occur in computer hardware when temperatures depart significantly from this optimal range. Also, the risk of circuit damage from static electricity is increased when humidity drops. High humidity, on the other hand, can cause molds to grow and paper products (such as source documents) to swell and jam equipment.

Fire Suppression

The most common threat to a firm's computer equipment is from fire. Half of the companies that suffer fires go out of business because of the loss of critical records, such as accounts receivable. The implementation of an effective fire suppression system requires consultation with specialists. Some of the major features of such a system are listed below.

1. Automatic and manual alarms should be placed in strategic locations around the installation. These alarms should be connected to permanently staffed fire-fighting stations.
2. There must be an automatic fire extinguishing system that dispenses the appropriate type of suppressant (carbon dioxide or halon) for the location. For example, spraying water and certain chemicals on a computer can do as much damage as the fire.
3. There should be manual fire extinguishers placed at strategic locations.
4. The building should be of sound construction to withstand water damage caused by fire suppression equipment.
5. Fire exits should be clearly marked and illuminated during a fire.

Power Supply

Commercially provided electrical power presents several problems that can disrupt the computer center operations, including total power failures, brownouts, power fluctuations, and frequency variations. The equipment used to control these problems includes voltage regulators, surge protectors, generators, and batteries. The extent and configuration of control equipment needed will depend on the firm's ability to withstand such disruptions and the power company's record for providing reliable service. This can be an expensive control decision and requires extensive analysis and the advice of experts.

DISASTER RECOVERY PLANNING

Some disasters cannot be prevented or evaded. Recent events include Hurricane Andrew in Florida, widespread flooding in the Midwest, earthquakes in California, and the bombing of the World Trade Center. The survival of a firm affected by such a disaster depends on how it reacts. With careful contingency planning, the full impact of a disaster can be absorbed and the organization can still recover.

A **disaster recovery plan (DRP)** is a comprehensive statement of all actions to be taken before, during, and after a disaster, along with documented, tested procedures that will ensure the continuity of operations. Although the details of each plan are unique to the needs of the organization, all workable plans possess common features. The remainder of this section is devoted to a discussion of these essential features: providing second-site backup, identifying critical applications, performing backup and off-site storage procedures, creating a disaster recovery team, and testing the DRP.

Providing Second-Site Backup

A necessary ingredient in a DRP is that it provides for duplicate data processing facilities following a disaster. Among the options available are mutual aid pact, empty shell, recovery operations center, and internally provided backup.

Mutual Aid Pact. A **mutual aid pact** is an agreement between two or more organizations (with compatible computer facilities) to aid each other with their data processing needs in the event of a disaster. In such an event, the "host" company must disrupt its processing schedule to process the critical applications of the disaster-stricken company. In effect, the host company itself must go into an emergency operation mode (and cut back on the processing of its lower-priority applications) to accommodate the sudden increase in demand for its EDP resources.

Reciprocal agreements of this sort are a popular option. This is partly because they are relatively cost-free (as long as no disaster occurs) and provide some degree of psychological comfort. In fact, plans of this sort tend to work better in theory than in practice. To rely on such an arrangement for substantive relief during a disaster requires a level of faith and untested trust that is uncharacteristic of sophisticated management and its auditors.

The Empty Shell. An option that is growing in popularity is the **empty shell** or "cold site" plan. This arrangement usually involves two or more user organizations that buy or lease a building and remodel it into a computer site, but without the computer and peripheral equipment. For example, shells are normally equipped with raised floors and air conditioning. In the event of a disaster, the shell is available and ready to receive whatever hardware the temporary user requires to run its essential data processing systems.

Although an improvement over mutual aid pacts, the shell approach has two major problems. First, recovery depends on the timely availability of the necessary computer hardware to restore the data processing function. Management must obtain assurances from hardware vendors that filling the organization's needs will be given priority in the event of a disaster. An unanticipated hardware supply problem at this critical juncture could be a fatal blow.

The second problem with this approach is the potential for competition among users for the shell resources. For example, a widespread natural disaster, such as a flood or earthquake, may destroy the data processing capabilities of several shell members located in the same geographic area. Those affected by the disaster would be faced with a second major problem: how to allocate the limited facilities of the shell among them. The situation is analogous to a sinking ship that has an inadequate number of lifeboats. What equitable criteria should be used for assigning lifeboat seats?

The period of confusion following a disaster is not an ideal time to negotiate such property rights. Therefore, before entering into an arrangement to share the cost of shell facilities, management, accountants, and auditors should consider the potential problems of overcrowding and geographic clustering of members. Quotas—limiting the number of members by size of firm and geographic location—should provide effective control.

The Recovery Operations Center. A variation on the empty shell approach is the completely equipped **recovery operations center (ROC)** or "hot site." Because of the heavy investment involved, ROCs are typically shared among many companies. These firms either buy shares in or become subscribers to the ROC, paying a monthly fee for rights to its use.

ROCs may be tailor-equipped to serve the needs of their members, or they may be designed to accommodate a wide range of computer systems. The advantage of the ROC option over the empty shell is a vastly reduced initial recovery period, since the facilities are ready for use. In the event of a major disruption, a subscriber can occupy the premises and, within a few hours, resume processing critical applications. Accountants and managers should recognize, however, that the problems of over-crowding and geographic clustering of subscribers also apply to ROCs.

Internally Provided Backup. Larger organizations with multiple data processing centers may prefer the self-reliance provided by creating internal excess capacity. This permits firms to develop standardized hardware and software configurations, which ensure functional compatibility among their data processing centers and minimize cutover problems in the event of a disaster.

Identifying Critical Applications

Another essential element of a DRP is to identify the critical applications and data files of the firm. Recovery efforts must concentrate on restoring those applications that are critical to the short-run survival of the organization. Obviously, over the long term, all applications must be restored to pre-disaster business activity levels. However, the DRP should not attempt to restore the organization's data processing facility to 100 percent capacity. Rather, the plan should focus on short-run survival. In any disaster scenario, it is the firm's short-run survivability that is at risk.

For most organizations, short-term survival requires the restoration of those functions that generate cash flows sufficient to satisfy short-term obligations. For example, assume that the following items affect the cash flow position of a particular firm:

- Customer sales and service
- Fulfillment of legal obligations
- Accounts receivable maintenance and collection
- Production and distribution decisions
- Purchasing functions
- Communications between branches or agencies
- Public relations

The computer applications that support these items directly are critical. Hence, these applications should be so identified and prioritized in the restoration plan.

Application priorities may change over time, and these decisions must be re-assessed regularly. Systems are constantly revised and expanded to reflect changes in user requirements. Similarly, the DRP must be updated to reflect new developments and identify critical applications. Up-to-date priorities are important, because they affect other aspects of the strategic plan. For example, changes in application priorities may cause changes in the nature and extent of second-site backup requirements and specific backup procedures.

The task of identifying critical items and prioritizing applications requires the active participation of user departments, accountants, and auditors. Too often, this task is incorrectly viewed as a technical "computer" issue and delegated to systems professionals. Although the technical assistance of a systems professional will be required, this is a business decision and should be made by those best equipped to understand the problem.

Performing Backup and Off-Site Storage Procedures

All data files, application documentation, and supplies needed to perform critical functions should be specified in the DRP. Backup and storage procedures to safeguard these critical resources should be routinely performed by data processing personnel.

Backup Data Files. Databases should be copied daily to tape or disks and secured off-site. In the event of a disruption, reconstruction of the database is achieved by updating the most current backup version with subsequent transaction data. Likewise, master files and transaction files should be protected. Techniques for data backup were discussed earlier.

Backup Documentation. The system documentation for critical applications should be backed up and stored off-site in much the same manner as data files. The large volumes of material involved and constant application revisions complicate the task. The process can be made more efficient through the use of CASE documentation tools.

Backup Supplies and Source Documents. The firm should provide backup inventories of supplies and source documents used in the critical applications. Examples of critical supplies are check stocks, invoices, purchase orders, and any other special-purpose forms that cannot be obtained immediately. The DRP should specify the types and quantities needed of these special items. Because they are such an integral part of the daily operations, these items are often overlooked by disaster contingency planners. At this point, it is worth noting that a copy of the current DRP document should also be stored off-site at a secure location.

Creating a Disaster Recovery Team

Recovering from a disaster depends on timely corrective action. Failure to perform essential tasks (such as obtaining backup files for critical applications) prolongs the recovery period and diminishes the prospects for a successful recovery. To avoid serious omissions or duplication of effort during implementation of the contingency plan, task responsibility must be clearly defined and communicated to the personnel involved.

Figure 15–14 presents an organizational chart depicting the composition of a disaster recovery team. The team members should be experts in their areas and have assigned tasks. Following a disaster, team members will delegate subtasks to their subordinates. It should be noted that traditional control concerns do not apply in this setting. The environment created by the disaster may make it necessary to violate control techniques, such as segregation of duties, access controls, and supervision.

Testing the DRP

The most neglected aspect of contingency planning is testing the plans. Nevertheless, DRP tests are important and should be performed periodically. Tests provide measures of the preparedness of personnel and identify omissions or bottlenecks in the plan.

A test is most useful when the simulation of a disruption is a surprise. When the mock disaster is announced, the status of all processing affected by it should be

FIGURE 15–14

Disaster
Recovery
Team

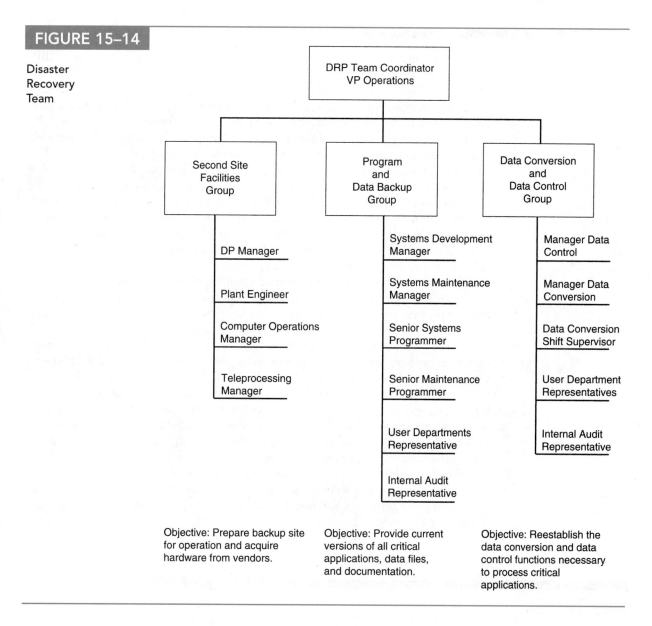

Objective: Prepare backup site for operation and acquire hardware from vendors.

Objective: Provide current versions of all critical applications, data files, and documentation.

Objective: Reestablish the data conversion and data control functions necessary to process critical applications.

documented. This provides a benchmark for subsequent performance assessments. The plan should be carried through as far as is economically feasible. Ideally, this will include the use of backup facilities and supplies.

The progress of the plan should be noted at key points throughout the test period. At the conclusion of the test, the results can be analyzed and a DRP performance report prepared. The degree of performance achieved provides input for decisions to modify the DRP or schedule additional tests. The organization's management should seek measures of performance in each of the following areas: (1) the effectiveness of DRP team personnel and their knowledge levels, (2) the degree of conversion success (that is, the number of lost records), (3) an estimate of financial loss due to lost records or facilities, and (4) the effectiveness of program, data, and documentation backup and recovery procedures.

Summary

This chapter examined some of the internal control issues that arise within a CBIS environment. Initially, it discussed how the unique features of a CBIS environment affect control activities outlined in SAS 78. It then focused on several major areas of the CBIS environment that are susceptible to exposure threats and examined a variety of control techniques that are used to deal with these threats.

First, the chapter examined threats to the security and integrity of the operating system and the data resource. The principal threats to these vital areas of the CBIS are (1) unauthorized access for financial gain or other illicit purposes, (2) intentional or unintentional insertion of viruses into the operating system, and (3) loss of data due to system malfunctions. Although exposures to viruses can never be fully eliminated, this threat can be significantly reduced through user education, antivirus software, and sound procedures in acquiring software. Unauthorized access to data can be effectively controlled through the use of techniques such as subschemas, authorization rules, user-defined procedures, and data encryption. Backup and recovery techniques can be used to safeguard the data resource against system malfunctions.

Next, the chapter examined exposures that arise in connection with organizational structure, systems development, and systems maintenance. In these general areas, exposures are controlled through a variety of access control techniques and, even more important, through the segregation of incompatible duties. Minimizing exposures requires the formation of a program library, which is separate from operations and subject to careful operational and access control.

Finally, the chapter examined threats to the security of the actual computer center, which come primarily in the form of environmental hazards and disasters. To ensure the physical security of its computer equipment, a firm must first choose a location that is not susceptible to human-made or natural hazards. The building that houses the computer equipment must be soundly and strategically constructed and equipped with systems that regulate air filtration, temperature, and humidity. An adequate fire suppression system is also required, since fire is the most common threat to the computer center. In addition to these preemptive measures, a firm must have a disaster recovery plan in place.

Key Terms

access control list   (758)

access controls   (765)

access token   (758)

audit trails   (763)

back door   (762)

backup controls   (765)

biometric devices   (767)

checkpoint   (773)

compilers   (756)

corporate computer services function   (778)

data encryption   (767)

database authorization table   (765)

direct access backup   (770)

disaster recovery plan (DRP)   (787)

discretionary access control   (758)

empty shell   (788)

event monitoring   (763)

fault tolerance   (764)

grandparent-parent-child (GPC)   (769)

inference controls   (767)

interpreters   (756)

keystroke monitoring   (763)

logic bomb   (762)

log-on procedure   (758)

multiprocessing   (765)

mutual aid pact   (788)

off-site storage   (772)

one-time password   (760)

operating system   (756)
operating system security   (758)
password   (759)
recovery module   (773)
recovery operations center (ROC)   (789)
redundant arrays of inexpensive disks (RAID)   (764)
reusable password   (760)

transaction log   (772)
Trojan horse   (762)
uninterruptible power supplies   (764)
user view   (765)
user-defined procedure   (766)
virus   (761)
worm   (761)

Review Questions

1. How do automated authorization procedures differ from manual authorization procedures?
2. Explain why certain duties that are deemed incompatible in a manual system may be combined in a CBIS environment. Give an example.
3. What are the three primary CBIS functions that must be separated?
4. Explain how the audit trail differs between a manual system and a CBIS.
5. What exposures do data consolidation in a CBIS environment pose?
6. Give examples of independent verifications.
7. Differentiate between general and application controls. Give two examples of each.
8. What are the five control objectives of an operating system?
9. What are the three main tasks performed by the operating system?
10. What is the purpose of an access control list?
11. What are the four techniques that a virus could use to infect a system?
12. What is an access token?
13. Explain discretionary access control.
14. What is event monitoring?
15. What is keystroke monitoring?
16. What is fault tolerance?
17. What are redundant arrays of inexpensive disks (RAID)?
18. What is a vaccine and what are its limitations?
19. Explain the grandparent-parent-child backup technique. Is it used for sequential files or direct access techniques? Why? How many generations can be backed up?
20. Distinguish between data access and access privileges. Give an example by designing and explaining a database authorization table.
21. What are inference controls? Why are they needed?
22. What are the four basic backup and recovery features necessary in a DBMS? Briefly explain each.
23. What are the primary reasons for separating operational tasks?
24. What problems may occur as a result of combining applications programming and maintenance tasks in one position?
25. What is the role of a data librarian? Why is this role so important?
26. Why is poor-quality systems documentation a prevalent problem?
27. Why is it important to separate the data library from operations?
28. What is the role of a corporate computer services department? How does this differ from other configurations?
29. What are the five control implications of distributed data processing?
30. List the six systems development controls discussed in the chapter. List the two systems maintenance controls.
31. Explain how program testing is conducted and the importance of test data.
32. List the control features that directly contribute to the security of the computer center environment.

Discussion Questions

1. The personnel in the CBIS area are responsible for producing and maintaining the controls in the systems. How is the supervision of these personnel different from the supervision of staff employees working in a manual system environment?

2. How can human behavior be considered one of the biggest potential threats to operating system integrity?

3. A bank in California has 13 branches spread throughout northern California, each with its own minicomputer where its data are stored. Another bank has 10 branches spread throughout California, with the data being stored on a mainframe in San Francisco. Which system do you think is more vulnerable to unauthorized access? Excessive losses from disaster?

4. Why would a systems programmer create a back door if he or she has access to the program in his or her day-to-day tasks?

5. Discuss the issues that need to be considered before implementing keystroke monitoring.

6. Explain how an access token and an access control list are used to approve or deny access.

7. Explain how a Trojan horse may be used to penetrate a system.

8. Discuss six ways that threats from destructive programs can be substantially reduced through a combination of technology controls and administrative procedures.

9. Explain the three ways that audit trails can be used to support security objectives.

10. Explain how poorly designed audit trail logs can actually be dysfunctional.

11. Many authorities believe that 90 percent of all computer fraud acts are not prosecuted by the employer. What do you think accounts for this lack of prosecution? Discuss the importance of the establishment of a formal policy for taking disciplinary (or legal) action against security violations.

12. Why is it dangerous to allow programmers to create user subschemas and assign access authority to users? What unethical technique do programmers sometimes use when they are not allowed to assign access authority to users?

13. Is access control of greater concern in the flat file or database file environment?

14. How can passwords actually circumvent security? What actions can be taken to minimize this?

15. Explain how the one-time password approach works.

16. End-user computing has become extremely popular in distributed data processing organizations. The end users like it because they feel they can more readily design and implement their own applications. Does this type of environment always foster more efficient development of applications? Explain your answer.

17. Discuss how a controlled SPL environment can help to deter unauthorized changes to programs. Can the use of maintenance commands mitigate these controls?

18. Compare and contrast the following disaster recovery options: mutual aid pact, empty shell, recovery operations center, and internally provided backup. Rank them from most risky to least risky, as well as from most costly to least costly.

19. Who should determine and prioritize the critical applications? How is this done? How frequently is it done?

Multiple-Choice Questions

1. A user's application may consist of several modules stored in separate memory locations, each with its own data. One module must not be allowed to destroy or corrupt another module. This is an objective of
   a. operating system controls.
   b. data resource controls.
   c. computer center and security controls.
   d. application controls.

2. A program that attaches to another legitimate program but does not replicate itself is called a
   a. virus.
   b. worm.
   c. Trojan horse.
   d. logic bomb.

3. For those instances where individual users may be granted summary and statistical query access to confidential data to which they normally are denied access, which type of control is MOST suitable?
   a. user-defined procedures
   b. data encryption
   c. inference controls
   d. biometric devices

4. Which of the following is NOT a control implication of distributed data processing?

a. redundancy
b. user satisfaction
c. incompatibility
d. lack of standards

5. Which of the following disaster recovery techniques may be least optimal in the case of a widespread natural disaster?
   a. empty shell
   b. mutual aid pact
   c. internally provided backup
   d. they are all equally beneficial

6. Which of the following is NOT a potential threat to computer hardware and peripherals?
   a. low humidity
   b. high humidity
   c. carbon dioxide fire extinguishers
   d. water sprinkler fire extinguishers

7. CMA 685 5-24
   Computer accounting control procedures are referred to as general or application controls. The primary objective of application controls in a computer environment is to
   a. ensure that the computer system operates efficiently.
   b. maintain the accuracy of the inputs, files, and outputs for specific applications.
   c. ensure the separation of incompatible functions in the data processing departments.
   d. provide controls over the electronic functioning of the hardware.

e. plan for the protection of the facilities and backup for the systems.

8. CMA 685 5-31
   The identification of users who have permission to access data elements in a database is found in the
   a. operating system.
   b. systems manual.
   c. database schema.
   d. database file definition.
   e. application programs.

9. CMA 686 5-4
   An integrated group of programs that supervises and supports the operations of a computer system as it executes users' application programs is called a(n)
   a. operating system.
   b. database management system.
   c. utility program.
   d. language processor.
   e. object program.

10. CMA 687 5-6
    A checkpoint or restart procedure is primarily designed to recover from
    a. programming errors.
    b. data input errors.
    c. the failure to have all input data ready on time.
    d. computer operator errors.
    e. hardware failures.

Problems

1. Internal Control

In reviewing the processes procedures and internal controls of one of your audit clients, Steeplechase Enterprises, you notice the following practices in place. Steeplechase has recently installed a new EDP system that affects the accounts receivable, billing, and shipping records. A specifically identified computer operator has been permanently assigned to each of the functions of accounts receivable, billing, and shipping. Each of these computer operators is assigned the responsibility of running the program for transaction processing, making program changes, and reconciling the computer log. In order to prevent any one operator from having exclusive access to the tapes and documentation, these three computer operators randomly rotate the custody and control tasks every two weeks over the magnetic tapes and the system documentation. Access controls to the computer room consist of magnetic cards and a digital code for each operator. Access to the computer room is not allowed to either the systems analyst or the computer operations supervisor.

The documentation for the EDP system consists of the following: record layouts, program listings, logs, and error listings.

Once goods are shipped from one of Steeplechase's three warehouses, warehouse personnel forward shipping notices to the accounting department. The billing clerk receives the shipping notice and accounts for the manual sequence of the shipping notices. Any missing notices are investigated. The billing clerk also manually enters the price of the item, prepares daily totals (supported by adding machine tapes) of the units shipped and the amount of sales. The shipping notices and adding machine tapes are sent to the computer department for data entry.

The computer output generated consists of a two-copy invoice and remittance advice and a daily sales register. The invoices and remittance advice are forwarded to the billing clerk, who mails one copy of the invoice and remittance advice to the customer and files the other copy in an open invoice file, which serves as an accounts receivable document. The daily sales register contains the total of units shipped and sales amounts. The computer operator compares the computer-generated totals to the adding machine tapes.

Required:
Identify the control weaknesses present and make a specific recommendation for correcting each of the control weaknesses.

2. Internal Control

Gustave, CPA, during its preliminary review of the financial statements of Comet, Inc., found a lack of proper segregation of duties between the programming and operating functions. Comet owns its own computing facilities. Gustave, CPA, diligently intensified the internal control study and assessment tasks relating to the computer facilities. Gustave concluded in its final report that sufficient compensating general controls provided reasonable assurance that the internal control objectives were being met.

Required:
What compensating controls are most likely in place?

3. CMA Adapted 1289 3-4
Internal Control

Oakdale, Inc. is a subsidiary of Solomon Publishing and specializes in the publication and distribution of reference books. Oakdale's sales for the past year exceeded $18 million, and the company employed an average of 65 employees. Solomon periodically sends a member of its internal audit department to audit the operations of each of its subsidiaries. Katherine Ford, Oakdale's treasurer, is currently working with Ralph Johnson of Solomon's internal audit staff. Johnson has just completed a review of Oakdale's investment cycle and prepared the following report.

General
Throughout the year, Oakdale has made both short-term and long-term investments in securities; all securities are registered in the company's name. According to Oakdale's bylaws, long-term investment activity must be approved by its board of directors, while short-term investment activity may be approved by either the president or the treasurer.

Transactions
Oakdale has a computer link with its broker; thus, all buy and sale orders are transmitted electronically. Only individuals with authorized passwords may initiate certain types of transactions. All purchases and sales of short-term securities in the year were made by the treasurer. In addition, two purchases and one sale of long-term securities were executed by the treasurer. The long-term security purchases were approved by the board. The president, having on-line authorization access to all transactions, was able to approve a sale of a long-term security. The president is given access to authorize all transactions engaged in by the firm. Because the treasurer is listed with the broker as the company's contact, all revenue from these investments is received by this individual, who then forwards the checks to accounting for processing.

Documentation
Purchase and sales authorizations, along with brokers' advices, are maintained in an electronic file with authorized access by the treasurer. Brokers' advices are received verbally on the phone, and this advice is noted on a broker advice form. This form is filed by the treasurer. The certificates for all long-term investments are kept in a safe deposit box at the local bank; only the president of Oakdale has access to this box. An inventory of this box was made, and all certificates were accounted for. Certificates for short-term investments are kept in a locked metal box in the accounting office. Other documents, such as long-term contracts and legal agreements, are also kept in this box. There are three keys to the box held by the president, treasurer, and the accounting manager. The accounting manager's key is available to all accounting personnel, should they require documents kept in this box. Certificates of investments may take

up to four weeks to receive after the purchase of the investment. An electronic inventory list is kept perpetually. The data is keyed in by accounting personnel who receive a buy/sale transaction sheet from the treasurer. The president, treasurer, and accounting manager all have passwords to access and update this inventory list. The accounting manager's password is known by two of the accounting supervisors in case the inventory list needs to be updated when the accounting manager is not available. Documentation for two of the current short-term investments could not be located in this box; the accounting manager explained that some of the investments are for such short periods of time that formal documentation is not always provided by the broker.

Accounting Records

Deposits of checks for interest and dividends earned on investments are recorded by the accounting department, but these checks could not be traced to the cash receipts journal maintained by the individual who normally opens, stamps, and logs incoming checks. These amounts are journalized monthly to an account for investment revenue. Electronic payments for investment purchases are authorized by the treasurer. If the amount is in excess of $15,000, an authorization code given by the treasurer or president is necessary.

Each month, the accounting manager and the treasurer prepare the journal entries required to adjust the short-term investment account. There was insufficient backup documentation attached to the journal entries reviewed to trace all transactions; however, the balance in the account at the end of last month closely approximates the amount shown on the statement received from the broker. The amount in the long-term investment account is correct, and the transactions can be clearly traced through the documentation attached to the journal entries. No attempts are made to adjust either account to the lower of aggregate cost or market.

Required:

To achieve Solomon Publishing's objective of sound internal control, the company believes the following four controls are basic for an effective system of accounting control.

- Authorization of transactions
- Complete and accurate record keeping
- Physical control
- Internal verification

a. Describe the purpose of each of the four controls listed above.

b. Identify an area in Oakdale's investment procedures that violates each of the four controls listed above.

c. For each of the violations identified, describe how Oakdale can correct it.

4. **CMA 1290 4-2**
    Internal Control
    Arlington Industries manufactures and sells component engine parts for large industrial equipment. The company employs over 1,000 workers for three shifts, and most employees work overtime when necessary. Arlington has had major growth in its production and has purchased a mainframe computer to handle order processing, inventory management, production planning, distribution operations, and accounting applications. Michael Cromley, president of Arlington, suspects that there may be internal control weaknesses due to the quick implementation of the computer system. Cromley recently hired Kathleen Luddy as the internal control accountant.

    Cromley asked Luddy to review the payroll processing system first. Luddy has reviewed the payroll process, interviewed the individuals involved, and compiled the flowchart shown on the following page. The following additional information concerns payroll processing:

    - The personnel department determines the wage rate of all employees at Arlington. Personnel starts the process by sending an authorization form for adding an employee to the payroll to the payroll coordinator, Marjorie Adams. After Adams inputs this information into the system, the computer automatically determines the overtime and shift differential rates for the individual, updating the payroll master files.
    - Arlington uses an external service to provide monthly payroll tax updates. The company receives a magnetic tape every month that the data processing department installs to update the payroll master file for tax calculations.
    - Employees at Arlington use a time clock to record the hours worked. Every Monday morning, Adams collects the previous week's time cards and begins the computerized processing of payroll information to produce

Problem 4: Internal Control

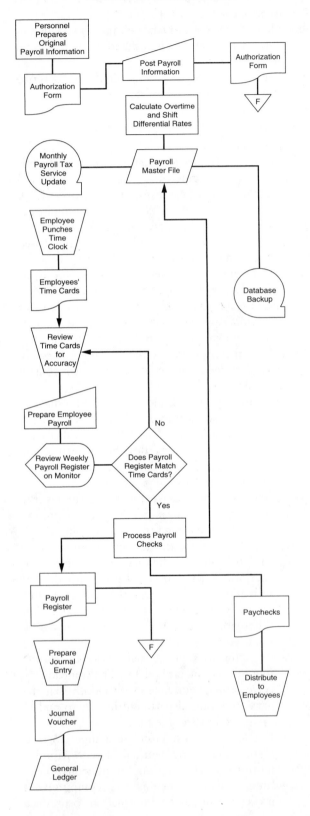

paychecks the following Friday. Adams reviews the time cards to ensure that the hours worked are correctly totaled; the system will determine whether overtime has been worked or a shift differential is required.

- All other processes displayed on the flowchart are performed by Adams. The system automatically assigns a sequential number to each payroll check produced. The checks are stored in a box next to the computer printer to provide immediate access. After the checks are printed, Adams uses an automatic check-signing machine to sign the checks with an authorized signature plate that Adams keeps locked in a safe.

- After the check processing is completed, Adams distributes the checks to the employees, leaving the checks for the second- and third-shift employees with the appropriate shift supervisor. Adams then notifies the data processing department that she is finished with her weekly processing, and data processing makes a backup of the payroll master file to magnetic tape for storage on the tape shelves in the computer room.

Required:

By referring to the information above and the flowchart, identify and describe:

a. Five different areas in Arlington's payroll processing system where the system controls are inadequate.

b. Two different areas in Arlington's payroll processing system where the system controls are satisfactory.

5. **Operating System Exposures and Controls**

Listed below are five scenarios. For each scenario, discuss the potential consequences and give a prevention technique.

a. The systems operator opened a bag of burned microwave popcorn directly under a smoke detector in the computing room where two mainframes, three high-speed printers, and approximately 40 tapes are housed. The extremely sensitive smoke detector triggered the sprinkler system. Three minutes passed before the sprinklers could be turned off.

b. A system programmer intentionally placed an error into a program that causes the operating system to fail and dump certain confidential information to disks and printers.

c. Jane, a secretary, was laid off. Her employer gave her three weeks notice. After two weeks, Jane realized that finding another job was going to be very tough, and she became bitter. Her son told her about a virus that had infected the computers at school. He had a disk infected with the virus. Jane took the disk to work and copied the disk onto the network server, which is connected to the company's mainframe. One month later, the company realized that some data and application programs had been destroyed.

d. Robert discovered a new sensitivity analysis public-domain program on the Internet. He downloaded the software to his microcomputer at home, then took the application to work and placed it onto his networked personal computer. The program had a virus on it that eventually spread to the company's mainframe.

e. Murray, a trusted employee and a systems engineer, had access to both the computer access control list and user passwords. He was recently hired away by the firm's competitor for twice his old salary. After leaving, Murray continued to browse through his old employer's data, such as price lists, customer lists, bids on jobs, and so on. He passed this information on to his new employer.

6. **CMA 689 5-Y5**
Disaster Recovery Plans
The headquarters of Gleicken Corporation, a private company with $3.5 million in annual sales, is located in California. Gleicken provides for its 150 clients an on-line legal software service that includes data storage and administrative activities for law offices. The company has grown rapidly since its inception three years ago, and its data processing department has expanded to accommodate this growth. Because Gleicken's president and sales personnel spend a great deal of time out of the office soliciting new clients, the planning of the EDP facilities has been left to the data processing professionals.

Gleicken recently moved its headquarters into a remodeled warehouse on the outskirts of the city. While remodeling the warehouse, the architects retained much of the original structure, including the wooden-shingled exterior and exposed wooden beams throughout the interior. The minicomputer distributive processing hardware is situated in a large open area with high ceilings and skylights. The openness makes the data processing area accessible to the rest of the staff and encourages a team approach to problem solving. Before occupying the new facility, city inspectors declared the building safe; that is, it had adequate fire extinguishers, sufficient exits, and so on.

In an effort to provide further protection for its large database of client information, Gleicken instituted a tape backup procedure that automatically backs up the database every Sunday evening, avoiding interruption in the daily operations and procedures. All tapes are then labeled and carefully stored on shelves reserved for this purpose in the data processing department. The departmental operator's manual has instructions on how to use these tapes to restore the database, should the need arise. A list of home phone numbers of the individuals in the data processing department is available in case of an emergency. Gleicken has recently increased its liability insurance for data loss from $50,000 to $100,000.

This past Saturday, the Gleicken headquarters building was completely ruined by fire, and the company must now inform its clients that all of their information has been destroyed.

Required:

a. Describe the computer security weaknesses present at Gleicken Corporation that made it possible for a disastrous data loss to occur.

b. List the components that should have been included in the disaster recovery plan at Gleicken Corporation to ensure computer recovery within 72 hours.

c. What factors, other than those included in the plan itself, should a company consider when formulating a disaster recovery plan?

7. **Database Authorization Table**
The following information is stored in two relational database files:

Employee Master File
Social Security number
Name
Address
Date hired

Hourly wage rate
Marital status
Number of exemptions

Weekly Payroll
Social Security number
Hours worked
Deductions
Bonuses

Required:
a. Bogey works in personnel and Bacall works in payroll. Prepare a database authorization table that you feel is appropriate for Bogey and Bacall for these two files.
b. Discuss any potential exposure if the right prevention devices are not in place or if Bogey and Bacall collude.

8. Separation of Duties

Transferring people from job to job within the organization is the philosophy at Arcadia Plastics. Management feels that job rotation deters employees from feeling that they are stagnating in their jobs and promotes a better understanding of the company. The computer services personnel typically work for six months as a data librarian, one year as a systems developer, six months as a database administrator, and one year in systems maintenance. At that point, they are assigned to a "permanent" position.

Required:
Discuss the importance of separation of duties within the information systems department. How can Arcadia Plastics have both job rotation and well-separated duties?

9. CMA 1287 5-3
End-User Computing

The internal audit department of Hastone Manufacturing Company recently concluded a routine examination of the company's computer facilities. The auditor's report identified as a weakness the fact that there had been no coordination by the data processing services department in the purchase of microcomputer systems for the individual departments of Hastone. Among the 12 microcomputers in the organization, there are three different hardware manufacturers. In addition, there are four to five different software vendors for spreadsheets, word processing, and database applications, along with some networking applications for clusters of microcomputers.

Microcomputers were acquired in the operating departments to allow employees in each department to conduct special analyses. Many of the departments also wanted the capability to download data from the mainframe. Therefore, each operating department had requested guidance and assistance from the data processing services department. Data processing, however, responded that it was understaffed and must devote full effort to its main priority, the mainframe computer system.

In response to the internal audit report, the director of data processing services, Stan Marten, issued the following memorandum.

TO: All Employees
FROM: Stan Marten, Director
REFERENCE: Microcomputer Standardization

Policies must be instituted immediately to standardize the acquisition of microcomputers and applications software. The first step is to specify the spreadsheet software that should be used by all personnel. From now on, everyone will use Micromate. All microcomputer hardware should be MS-DOS compatible. During the next month, we will also select the standard software for word processing and database applications. You will use only the user packages that are prescribed by the data processing services department. In the future, any new purchases of microcomputers, hardware, or software must be approved by the director of data processing services.

Several managers of other operating departments have complained about Marten's memorandum. Apparently, before issuing this memorandum, Marten had not consulted with any of the microcomputer users regarding their current and future software needs.

Required:
a. When acquiring microcomputers for various departments in an organization, describe the factors related to:
  1. Computer hardware that needs to be considered during the initial design and set-up phase of the microcomputer environment.
  2. Operating procedures and system controls that need to be considered.

b.   Discuss the benefits of having standardized hardware and software for microcomputers in an organization.

c.   Discuss the concerns that the memorandum is likely to create for the microcomputer users at Hastone Manufacturing.

10. **CMA Adapted 688 5-Y6**
    End-User Computing
    List the problems inherent in the use, by others, of spreadsheet models developed by users who are not trained in the procedural controls of system design and development.

16

Controlling Computer-Based Information Systems, Part II

This chapter continues the treatment of CBIS controls begun in Chapter 15. Figure 16–1 reproduces the CBIS exposure framework presented in the previous chapter. Chapter 15 examined the exposures and control techniques for the items numbered 1 through 6 on the diagram. This chapter examines items 7 through 10, which include Internet and Intranet risks, electronic data interchange, personal computers, and computer applications. Table 16–1 provides an overview of the nature of the risks and the control techniques used in the general control areas 7 through 9. Recall that general controls deal with systemic exposures that affect the CBIS environment. The chapter also examines application control techniques that relate to item 10 in Figure 16–1.

LEARNING OBJECTIVES

After studying this chapter, you should:

- Be familiar with the principal risks associated with electronic commerce conducted over Intranets and the Internet and to understand the control techniques used to reduce these risks.
- Recognize the unique exposures that arise in connection with electronic data interchange (EDI) and understand how these exposures can be reduced.
- Be aware of the exposures which threaten firms that rely on personal computers for their information needs and understand the controls that are necessary to reduce risks in this environment.
- Be able to explain the principal input, processing, and output controls that are used to ensure the integrity of computer applications.

FIGURE 16–1   Framework for Viewing CBIS Exposures

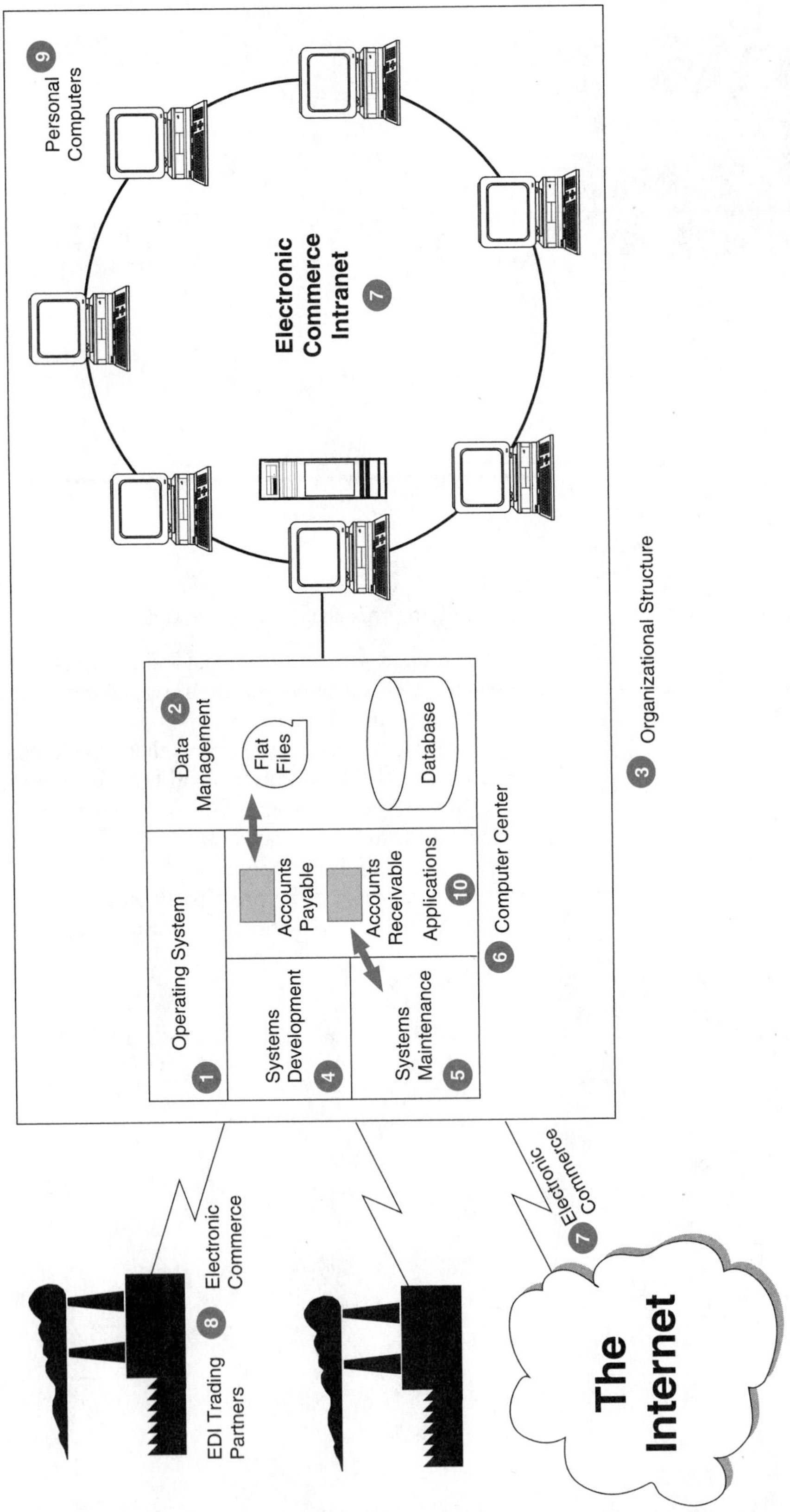

TABLE 16–1	**Summary of CBIS Exposures and Controls**	
Area of Risk	**Nature of Exposure**	**Control Techniques**
7. Internet and Intranet	Loss, destruction, and corruption of data from equipment failure and subversive activities from inside the organization and via the Internet.	CONTROLLING EQUIPMENT FAILURE: Parity checks, echo checks, and backup. CONTROLLING SUBVERSIVE THREATS: Access controls, message encryption, digital signatures, digital certificates and firewalls. MESSAGE CONTROL: Sequence numbering, authentication codes, transaction log, request-response polling.
8. Electronic Data Interchange	Processing of unauthorized, invalid, and illegal transactions. Illegal access by trading partners to databases. Absence of source documents disrupts the traditional audit trail, which inhibits the auditor's ability to verify the completeness and accuracy of transactions.	Authorization and validation controls, access controls, and audit trail controls implemented at various points within the trading partners' systems and at the VAN.
9. Personal Computers	Financial loss from program errors and fraud because of inadequate segregation of functions. Destruction and corruption of data due to uncontrolled access to files and hardware failures. Inadequate data backup and recovery features.	Organization controls, access controls, backup controls, systems selection and acquisition controls, disk locks, encryption, multilevel password.

INTERNET AND INTRANET CONTROLS

Chapter 12 examined the operational characteristics of several network topologies used in Internet and Intranet communications. Network topologies consist of various configurations of (1) communications lines (twisted pair wires, coaxial cable, microwaves, and fiber optics), (2) hardware components (modems, multiplexers, servers, and front-end processors), and (3) software (protocols and network control systems). The technology of network communications exposes an organization's computer systems to two general categories of risk:

1. *Risks from subversive threats.* These include, but are not limited to, a computer criminal intercepting a message transmitted between the sender and the receiver, a computer hacker gaining unauthorized access to the organization's network, and a denial of service attack from a remote location of the Internet.

2. *Risks from equipment failure.* For example, transmissions between senders and receivers can be disrupted, destroyed, or corrupted by equipment failures in the communications system. Equipment failure can also result in the loss of databases and programs stored on the network server.

Firewalls

Organizations connected to the Internet or other public networks often implement an electronic "firewall" to insulate their Intranet from outside intruders. A **firewall** is a system that enforces access control between two networks. To accomplish this:

- All traffic between the outside network and the organization's Intranet must pass through the firewall.
- Only authorized traffic between the organization and the outside, as specified by formal security policy, is allowed to pass through the firewall.
- The firewall must be immune to penetration from both outside and inside the organization.

Firewalls can be used to authenticate an outside user of the network, verify his or her level of access authority, and then direct the user to the program, data, or service requested. In addition to insulating the organization's network from external networks, firewalls can also be used to insulate portions of the organization's Intranet from internal access. For example, a LAN controlling access to financial data can be insulated from other internal LANs. There are a number of firewall products on the market. Some of these provide a high level of security while others are less effective. While the technology is constantly evolving, firewalls can be grouped into two general types: network-level firewalls, and application-level firewalls.

Network-level firewalls provide low cost and low security access control. This type of firewall consists of a **screening router** that examines the source and destination addresses that are attached to incoming message packets. The firewall accepts or denies access requests based on filtering rules that have been programmed into it. Similar to an intelligent PBX, the firewall directs incoming calls to the correct internal receiving node. Network-level firewalls are insecure because they are designed to facilitate the free flow of information rather than restrict it. This method does not explicitly authenticate outside users. Using IP spoofing, hackers can disguise their message packets to look as if they came from an authorized user and thus gain access to the host's network.

Application-level firewalls provide a high level of customizable network security, but can be extremely expensive. These systems are configured to run security applications called *proxies* that permit routine services such as e-mail to pass through the firewall, but can perform sophisticated functions such as logging or user authentication for specific tasks. Application-level firewalls also provide comprehensive transmission logging and auditing tools for reporting unauthorized activity. If an outside user attempts to connect to an unauthorized service or file, the network administrator or security group can be notified immediately.

The highest level of firewall security is provided by a *dual-homed* system. This approach, illustrated in Figure 16–2, has two firewall interfaces. One screens incoming requests from the Internet, the other provides access to the organization's Intranet. Direct communication to the Internet is disabled and the two networks are fully isolated. All access is performed by proxy applications that impose separate log-on procedures.

Choosing the right firewall involves a trade-off between convenience and security. Ultimately, organization management, in collaboration with accountants and

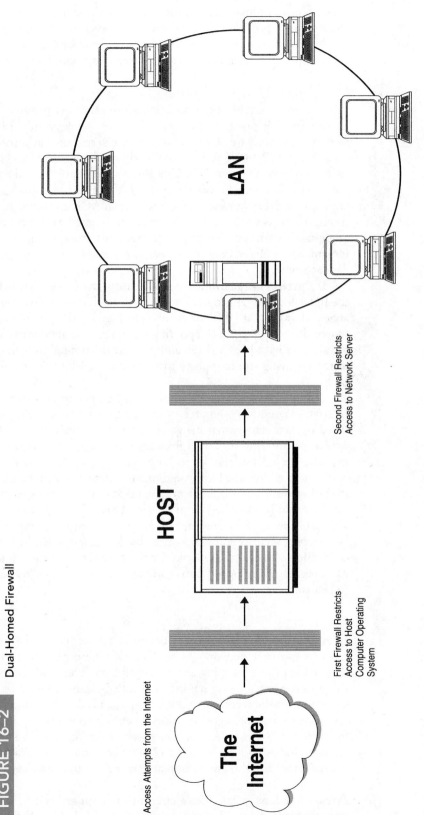

FIGURE 16–2 Dual-Homed Firewall

network professionals, must come to grips with what constitutes acceptable risk. The more security provided by the firewall, however, the less convenient it is for authorized users to pass through it. An excessive level of control could, therefore, negatively impact the organization's ability to conduct commerce on the Internet.

Controlling Denial of Service Attacks

When a user establishes a connection on the Internet through TCP/IP, a three-way handshake takes place. The connecting server sends an initiation code called a *SYN packet* to the receiving server. The receiving server then acknowledges the request by returning a *SYN/ACK packet*. Finally, the initiating host machine responds with an *ACK packet code*. Computer hackers and crackers have devised a malicious act called a *denial of service attack*, in which the attacker transmits hundreds of SYN packets to the targeted receiver but never responds with an ACK to complete the connection. As a result, the ports of the receiver's server are clogged with incomplete communication requests that prevent legitimate transactions from being received and processed. Organizations under attack have been prevented from receiving Internet messages for days at a time.

If the target organization could identify the server that is launching the attack, the firewall could be programmed to ignore all communication from that site. Such attacks, however, are difficult to prevent because IP spoofing is used to disguise the source of the messages. IP spoofing programs that randomize the source address of the attacker have been written and publicly distributed over the Internet. Therefore, to the receiving site it appears that the transmissions are coming from all over the Internet.

Denial of service attacks can severely hamper an organization's ability to use the Internet to conduct commerce. Although this activity cannot currently be prevented, there are two actions that management and accountants can take to limit the exposure. First, Internet sites with firewalls must engage in a policy of social responsibility. The firewalls at the source sites can be programmed to block messages with noninternal addresses. This would prevent attackers from hiding their locations from the targeted site and would assure the organization's management that no undetected attacks could be launched from its site. This strategy will not, however, prevent attacks from areas of the Internet that do screen outgoing transmissions.

Second, security software is available for the targeted sites that scan for half-open connections. The software looks for SYN packets that have not been followed by an ACK packet. The clogged ports can then be restored to allow legitimate connections to be made

Encryption

Encryption is the conversion of data into a secret code for storage in databases and transmission over networks. The discussion here pertains to transmitted data, but these basic principles apply also to stored data. The sender uses an encryption algorithm to convert the original message called cleartext into a coded equivalent called ciphertext. At the receiving end the ciphertext is decoded (decrypted) back into cleartext. The encryption algorithm uses a **key**, which is a binary number that is typically from 56 to 128 bits in length. The more bits in the key the stronger the encryption method. Today, nothing less than 128 bit algorithms are considered truly secure. Two general approaches to encryption are *private key* and *public key* encryption.

Private Key Encryption. **Data encryption standard (DES)** is a private-key encryption technique designed in the early 1970s by IBM. The DES algorithm uses a single key known to both the sender and the receiver of the message. To encode a message, the sender provides the encryption algorithm with the key, which is used to produce a ciphertext message. The message enters the communication channel and is transmitted to the receiver's location, where it is stored. The receiver decodes the message with a decryption program that uses the same key employed by the sender. Figure 16–3 illustrates this technique.

The primary problem with the DES approach is that a perpetrator may discover the key and intercept and decipher the message. The more individuals who need to know the key, the greater the probability of it falling into the wrong hands.

Triple-DES encryption is an enhancement to standard DES that provides considerably more security. Two forms of triple-DES encryption are EEE3 and EDE3. **EEE3** uses three different keys to encrypt the message three times. **EDE3** uses one key to encrypt the message. A second key is used to decode it. The resulting message is garbled because the key used for decoding is different from the one that encrypted it. Finally, a third key is used to encrypt the garbled message. The use of multiple keys greatly reduces the chances of breaking the cipher. Triple-DES encryption is thought to be very secure and is used by major banks to transmit transactions. Unfortunately, it is also very slow. The EEE3 and EDE3 techniques are illustrated in Figure 16–4.

All private-key techniques suffer from the same problem. They are effective only when used within small exclusive groups. If the keys become known to outsiders, messages can be intercepted, interpreted, and altered. Encrypting data transmitted between large numbers of relative strangers (such as transactions between Internet businesses and customers) needs another approach. The solution to this problem is public key encryption.

FIGURE 16–3

The Data Encryption
Standard Technique

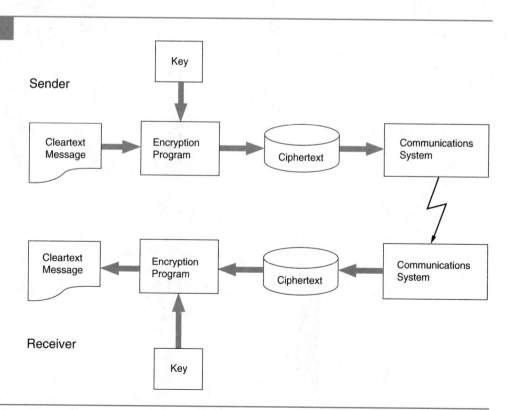

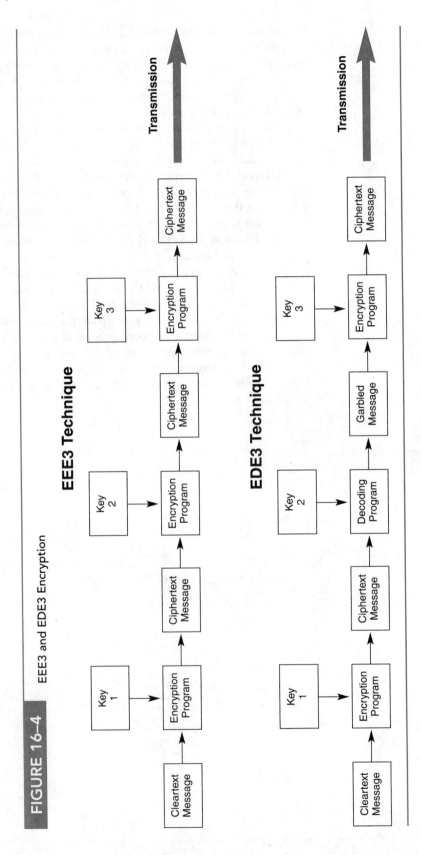

FIGURE 16–4   EEE3 and EDE3 Encryption

Public Key Encryption. The **public key encryption** technique uses two different keys: one for encoding messages and the other for decoding them. Each recipient has a private key that is kept secret and a public key that is published. The sender of a message uses the receiver's public key to encrypt the message. The receiver then uses his or her private key to decrypt the message. Users never need to share their private keys to decrypt messages, thus reducing the likelihood that they fall into the hands of a criminal.

RSA (Rivest-Shamir-Adleman) is a highly secure public key cryptography method. This method is, however, computationally intensive and much slower than standard DES encryption. Sometimes, both DES and RSA are used together in what is called a **digital envelope**. The actual message is encrypted using DES to provide the fastest decoding. The DES private key needed to decrypt the message is encrypted using RSA and transmitted along with the message. The receiver first decodes the DES key, which is then used to decode the message.

Digital Signatures

A **digital signature** is electronic authentication that cannot be forged. It ensures that the message or document transmitted originated with the authorized sender and that it was not tampered with after the signature was applied. The digital signature is derived from the computed digest of the document that has been encrypted with the sender's private key. Figure 16–5 illustrates this process. The sender uses a one-way hashing algorithm to calculate a **digest** of the text message. The digest is a mathematical value calculated from the text content of the message. The digest is then encrypted using the sender's private key to produce the digital signature. Next, the digital signature and the text message are encrypted using the receiver's public key and transmitted to the receiver. At the receiving end, the message is decrypted using the receiver's private key to produce the digital signature (encrypted digest) and the cleartext version of the message. The receiver then uses the sender's public key to decrypt the digital signal to produce the digest. Finally, the receiver recalculates the digest from the cleartext using the original hashing algorithm and compares this to the decoded digest. If the message is authentic, the two digest values will match. If even a single character of the message was changed in transmission, the digest figures will not be equal.

Digital Certificate

The above process proves that the message received was indeed sent by the sender and was not tampered with during transmission. However, it does not prove that the sender is who he or she claims to be. The sender could be an impersonator. To verify the sender's identity requires a **digital certificate**, which is issued by a trusted third party called a **certification authority** (CA). A digital certificate is used in conjunction with a public key encryption system to authenticate the sender of a message. The process for certification varies depending on the level of certification desired. It involves establishing one's identity with formal documents such as a driver's license, notarization, and fingerprints and proving one's ownership of the public key. After verifying the owner's identity the CA creates the certification, which is the owner's public key, and other data that has been digitally signed by the CA.

The digital certificate is transmitted with the encrypted message to authenticate the sender. The receiver uses the public key of the CA, which is widely publicized, to decrypt the sender's public key attached to the message. The sender's public key is then used to decrypt the message.

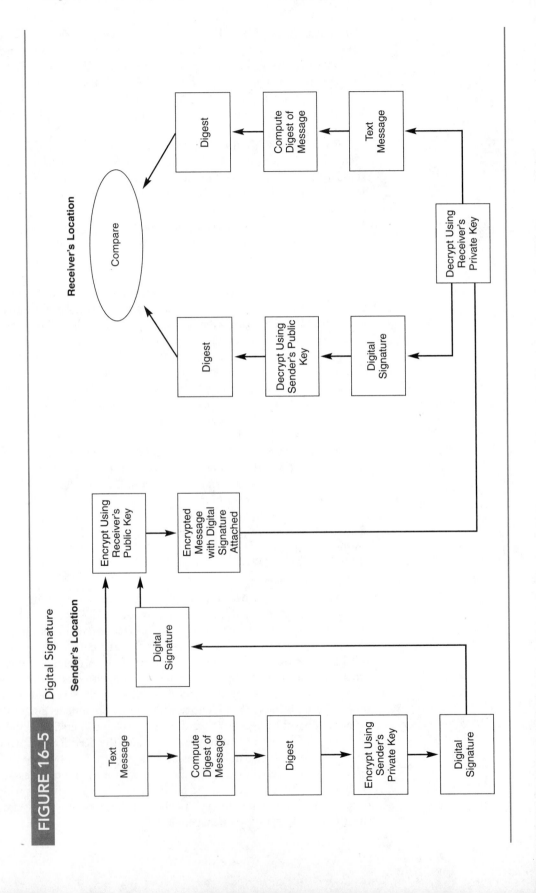

FIGURE 16–5   Digital Signature

Message Sequence Numbering

An intruder in the communications channel may attempt to delete a message from a stream of messages, change the order of messages received, or duplicate a message. Through **message sequence numbering**, a sequence number is inserted in each message, and any such attempt will become apparent at the receiving end.

Message Transaction Log

An intruder may successfully penetrate the system by trying different password and user ID combinations. Therefore, all incoming and outgoing messages, as well as attempted (failed) access, should be recorded in a **message transaction log**. The log should record the user ID, the time of the access, and the terminal location or telephone number from which the access originated.

Request-Response Technique

An intruder may attempt to prevent or delay the receipt of a message from the sender. When senders and receivers are not in constant contact, the receiver may not know that the communications channel has been interrupted and that messages have been diverted. With the **request-response technique**, a control message from the sender and a response from the receiver are sent at periodic, synchronized intervals. The timing of the messages should follow a random pattern that will be difficult for the intruder to determine and circumvent.

Call-Back Devices

As we have seen, networks can be equipped with security features such as passwords, authentication devices, and encryption. The common weakness to all of these technologies is that they impose the security measure *after* the criminal has connected to the LAN server. Many feel that the key to network security is to keep the intruder off the LAN to begin with.

A **call-back device** requires the dial-in user to enter a password and be identified. The system then breaks the connection to perform user authentication. If the caller is authorized, the call-back device dials the caller's number to establish a new connection. This limits access from only authorized terminals or telephone numbers and prevents an intruder masquerading as a legitimate user.

CONTROLLING RISKS FROM EQUIPMENT FAILURE

Previous sections examined controls for reducing the likelihood and effects of component failure. These include hardware acquisition procedures, virus control procedures, the physical security of the data center, and adequate backup procedures. This section will examine additional controls that apply more specifically to data communications components.

Line Errors

The most common problem in data communications is data loss due to **line error**. The bit structure of the message can be corrupted through noise on the communications lines. *Noise* is random signals that can interfere with the message signal when they reach a certain level. These random signals may be caused by electric motors, atmospheric conditions, faulty wiring, defective components in equipment, or noise spilling over from an adjacent communications channel. If not detected, bit structure changes to transmitted data can be catastrophic to the firm. For example, in the case of a database update program, the presence of line errors can result in incorrect transaction values being posted to the accounts. The following two techniques are commonly used to detect and correct such data errors before they are processed.

Echo Check. The **echo check** involves the receiver of the message returning the message to the sender. The sender compares the returned message with a stored copy of the original. If there is a discrepancy between the returned message and the original, suggesting a transmission error, the message is retransmitted. This technique reduces, by one half, throughput over communications channels. Throughput can be increased by using full-duplex channels, which allow both parties to transmit and receive simultaneously.

Parity Check. The **parity check** incorporates an extra bit (the parity bit) into the structure of a bit string when it is created or transmitted. Parity can be both vertical and horizontal (longitudinal). Figure 16–6 illustrates both types of parity. Vertical parity adds the parity bit to each character in the message when the characters are originally coded and stored in magnetic form. For example, the number of 1 bits in the bit structure of each character is counted. If the number is even (say there are four 1 bits in a given eight-bit character) the system assigns the parity bit a value of one. If the number of 1 bits is odd, a 0 parity bit is added to the bit structure.

The concern is that during transmission, a 1 bit will be converted to a 0 bit or vice versa, thus destroying the bit structure integrity of the character. In other words, the original character is incorrectly presented as a different yet valid character. An error of this sort, if it goes undetected, could have a devastating effect on financial numbers. But this error can be detected at the receiving end by a parity check. The 1 bits are again counted by the system and should always equal an odd number. If a 1 bit is added to or removed from the bit structure during transmission, the number of 1 bits for the character will be even, which would signal that an error has occurred.

The problem with using vertical parity alone is the possibility of an error that changes two bits in the structure simultaneously, thus retaining the parity of the character. In fact, some estimates indicate a 40 to 50 percent chance that line noise will corrupt more than one bit within a character. This potential is greatly reduced by

FIGURE 16–6

Vertical and Horizontal Parity Using Odd Parity

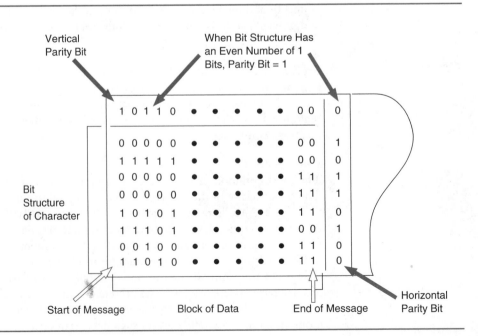

using horizontal parity in conjunction with vertical parity. Referring to Figure 16–6, notice the parity bit following each block of characters. The combination of vertical and horizontal parity provides a higher degree of protection from line errors.

Backup Control for Networks

Data backup in networks is accomplished in several different ways depending on the network's complexity. In small networks, a single workstation may be assigned the backup and restore functions for the other nodes. As networks grow to include more nodes and increased data sharing, backup is usually assigned at the network server level. Enterprise-level networks can be very large and include multiple servers. These network environments are likely to control mission-critical data, and a server failure could mark disaster for the organization. Because of the large number of users, enterprise-level networks undergo continuous change to accommodate shifts in user needs. In such a dynamic setting, organization management must be able to centrally monitor and control backup procedures.

Restricting access to backup files in enterprise-level networks is a control issue requiring specific attention. The organization's mission-critical backup data are exposed to the same access threats as its production data. Many backup products provide access control features such as encryption and password management similar to those discussed earlier in this section. At the very least, user management should ensure that the backup management package under consideration is compatible with the network's existing access control features.

Finally, backup redundancy is advisable in enterprise-level networks. Some top-end products permit dynamic allocation of backup devices and automatic notification of backup status. If an assigned backup device fails, the data are automatically routed to a working device. The backup management system immediately notifies the network administrator of the failure via e-mail or pager.

ELECTRONIC DATA INTERCHANGE CONTROLS

Previous chapters illustrated how EDI substantially changes the way companies do business. This environment creates unique control issues that accountants must recognize. Before examining these issues, let's first review the EDI concept. Figure 16–7 illustrates the data flow through the basic elements of an EDI system that links two trading partners—the customer (Company A) and the vendor (Company B). When Company A wishes to place an order with Company B, Company A's purchases system automatically creates and sends an electronic purchase order to its EDI translation software. The translation software converts the purchase order from Company A's internal format to a standard format, such as ANSI X.12. Next, the communications software adds the protocols to the message to prepare it for transmission over the communication channel. The transmission may be either a direct connection between the trading partners or an indirect connection through a value-added network (VAN). At Company B, the process is reversed, yielding a sales order in Company B's internal format, which is processed automatically by its sales order system.

The absence of human intervention in this process presents a unique twist to traditional control problems, including ensuring that transactions are authorized and valid, preventing unauthorized access to data files, and maintaining an audit trail of transactions. Techniques for dealing with these issues are following.

FIGURE 16–7

EDI System

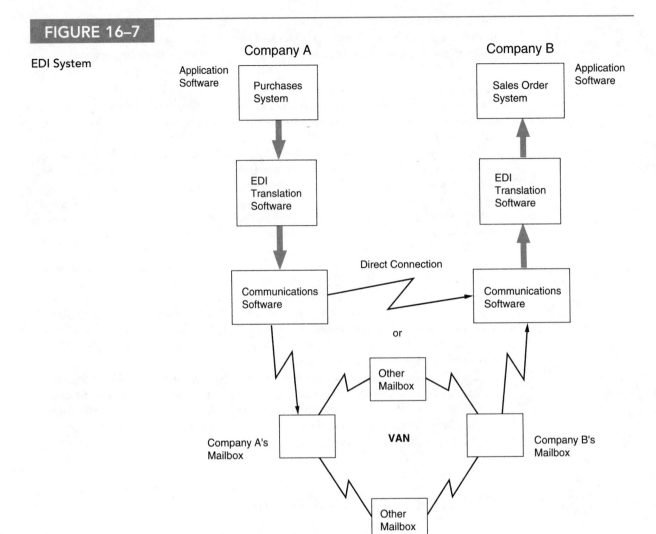

**TRANSACTION
AUTHORIZATION
AND VALIDATION**

Both the customer and the supplier must establish that the transaction being processed is to (or from) a valid trading partner and is authorized. This can be accomplished at three points in the process.

1. Some VANs have the capability of validating passwords and user ID codes for the vendor by matching these against a valid customer file. Any unauthorized trading partner transactions are rejected by the VAN before they reach the vendor's system.
2. Before being converted, the translation software can validate the trading partner's ID and password against a validation file in the firm's database.
3. Before processing, the trading partner's application software can validate the transaction by referencing the valid customer and vendor files.

ACCESS CONTROL

The degree of access control in the system will be determined by the trading agreement between the trading partners. For EDI to function smoothly, the trading partners must allow a degree of access to private data files that would be forbidden in a traditional environment. For example, before placing an order, the customer's system may need to access the vendor's inventory files to determine if inventories are available. Also, to avoid the vendor having to prepare an invoice and the customer having to match it against a purchase order, the partners may agree that the prices on the purchase order will be binding on both parties. In such a scenario, the customer must periodically access the vendor's price list file to keep pricing information current. Alternatively, the vendor may need access to the customer's price list to update prices.

To guard against unauthorized access, each company must establish valid vendor and customer files. Inquiries against databases can thus be validated, and unauthorized attempts at access can be rejected. User authority tables can also be established, which specify the degree of access a trading partner is allowed. For example, the partner may be authorized to read inventory or pricing data but not change any values. Again, some VANs can screen and reject unauthorized access attempts by trading partners.

EDI AUDIT TRAIL

The absence of source documents in EDI transactions disrupts the traditional audit trail and restricts the ability of accountants to verify the validity, completeness, timing, and accuracy of transactions. One technique for restoring the audit trail is to maintain a control log, which records the transaction's flow through each phase of the EDI system. Figure 16–8 illustrates how this approach may be employed.

As the transaction is received at each stage in the process, an entry is made into the log. In the customer's system, the transaction log can be reconciled to ensure that all transactions initiated by the purchases system were correctly translated and communicated. Likewise, in the vendor's system, the control log will establish that all messages received by the communications software were correctly translated and processed by the sales order system.

PERSONAL COMPUTER CONTROLS

The PC environment possesses significant features that characterize and distinguish it from the mainframe and client-server environments. The most important of these features are listed below. In general, PC systems:

- Are relatively simple to operate and program and do not require extensive professional training to use.
- Frequently are controlled and operated by the end users rather than by systems administrators.
- Usually employ interactive data processing rather than batch processing.
- Typically run commercial software applications designed to minimize effort. Usually, data are entered by end users and may be uploaded to a mainframe or network server for further processing.
- Often are used to access data on mainframe and client-server systems that are downloaded for local processing.
- Allow users to develop their own software (such as spreadsheets and databases).

PC OPERATING SYSTEMS

The operating system is booted and resides in the computer's primary memory as long as it is turned on. The operating system has several functions. It controls the CPU, accesses RAM, executes programs, receives input from the keyboard or other

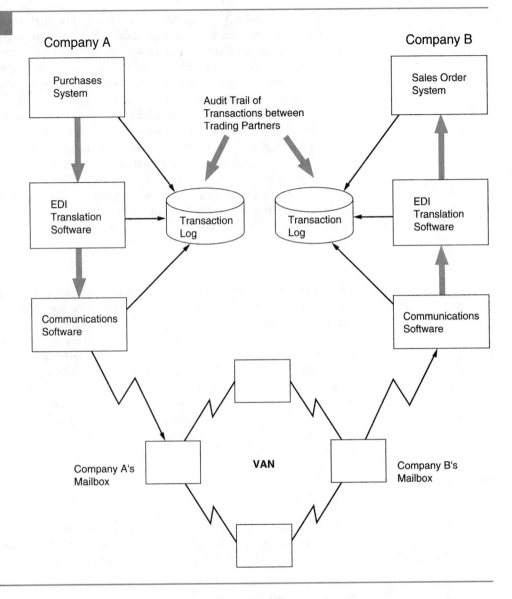

FIGURE 16–8

EDI System Using
Transaction Control
Log for Audit Trail

input device, retrieves and saves data to and from secondary storage devices, displays data on the monitor, controls the printer, and performs other functions that control the hardware system.

The operating system contains two types of instructions. *System-resident commands* are active in primary memory at all times to coordinate input/output requests and execute programs. *Disk-resident commands* reside on a secondary storage device until a request is made to execute these special-purpose utility programs.

At one time, the most popular operating system for the IBM-compatible computer was *DOS (Disk Operating System)*. Microsoft Corporation sells this product under the name MS-DOS (Microsoft Disk Operating System) and licenses another version, called PC-DOS, to IBM for use in its personal computers. An enormous number of microcomputers ran versions of DOS; as a result, there is an abundance of application software for DOS computers.

DOS was written for the microcomputer technology of the early 1980s. Even though there have been numerous improvements to the software since its introduction, limitations still exist. For example, application programs running on DOS computers have direct access to only 640,000 bytes of primary memory.

Newer operating systems, such as Microsoft Windows 98, have broken the 640,000-byte barrier, providing direct access to millions of bytes of memory. These operating systems take advantage of today's more powerful microprocessor chips, such as the Intel Pentium, which address more memory and run faster than the older microprocessors. Some operating systems employ *multitasking*, which allows more than one task to be executed at a time in a single-user computer. Operating systems that address more memory can run several tasks simultaneously.

The computer's operating system defines the family of software that the computer can use. *Application software* is written for a particular operating system. For example, the user of an IBM-compatible microcomputer running the Windows 3.1 operating system must select programs from the available software written for that operating system. The user of an IBM-compatible microcomputer with a different operating system, such as Windows 98 or NT, can select from a much broader set of software.

In both mainframe and microcomputer environments, the computer's operating system is an important element of the internal control structure. Mainframes, being multiuser systems, are designed to maintain a separation between end users and permit only authorized users to access data and programs. Unauthorized attempts to access data or programs can be thwarted by the security system. In contrast, PCs provide only minimal security over data files and programs. This control weakness is inherent in the philosophy behind the design of PC operating systems. Intended primarily as single-user systems, they are designed to make computer use easy and to facilitate access, not restrict it. This philosophy, while necessary to promote end-user computing, is sometimes at odds with internal control objectives. The data stored on microcomputers that are shared by multiple users are exposed to unauthorized access, manipulation, and destruction. Once a computer criminal gains access to the user's microcomputer, there may be little or nothing in the way of control to prevent him or her from stealing or manipulating the data stored on the internal hard drive.

The advanced technology and power of modern PC systems stand in sharp contrast to the relatively unsophisticated operational environment in which they exist. Controlling this environment rests heavily on physical controls. Some of the more significant risks and possible control techniques are outlined on the following pages.

WEAK ACCESS CONTROL

Security software that provides log-on procedures is available for PCs. Most of these programs, however, become active *only* when the computer is booted from the hard drive. A computer criminal attempting to circumvent the log-on procedure may do so by forcing the computer to boot from the A: drive, whereby an uncontrolled operating system can be loaded into the computer's memory. Having bypassed the computer's stored operating system and security package, the criminal has unrestricted access to data and programs on the hard disk.

Disk locks are devices that prevent unauthorized individuals from accessing the floppy disk drive of a computer. One form of disk lock is a memory-resident program that prevents the computer from being booted from the A: drive. The lock will also prevent the A: drive from being used to run programs, upload data and programs to the hard disk, or download from the hard disk. This form of disk lock is password-controlled so it can be disabled as needed by an authorized user.

Certain risks are associated with the use of disk locks. In the event of a hard disk failure that prevents the computer from being booted from the hard disk, users can usually boot the computer from the A: drive and recover the system, or at least retrieve vital data. However, with a memory-resident disk lock in place, the user may be denied access to the A: drive. Being unable to boot from either drive permanently prevents access to data and programs. An alternative solution is to use a physical disk lock rather than the memory-resident type. This device fits into the A: drive like a floppy disk to prevent its use and is secured with a physical lock and key.

<table>
<tr><td>

INADEQUATE SEGREGATION OF DUTIES

</td><td>

In PC environments, particularly those of small companies, an employee may have access to multiple applications that process incompatible transactions. For example, a single individual may be responsible for entering all transaction data, including sales orders, cash receipts, invoices, and disbursements. Typically, the general ledger and subsidiary accounts are updated automatically from these input sources. This degree of authority is similar, in a manual system, to assigning accounts receivable, accounts payable, cash receipts, cash disbursement, and general ledger responsibility to the same person. The exposure is compounded when the operator is also responsible for the development (programming) of the applications that he or she runs. In small-company operations, there may be little that can be done to eliminate these inherent conflicts of duties. However, multilevel password control can reduce the risks.

</td></tr>
</table>

Multilevel Password Control

Multilevel password control is used to restrict employees who are sharing the same computers to specific directories, programs, and data files. This technique uses stored authorization tables to further limit an individual's access to read-only, data input, data modification, and data deletion capability. While not a substitute for traditional control techniques such as employee supervision and management reports that detail all transactions and their effects on account balances, multilevel password control can greatly enhance the small organization's control environment.

<table>
<tr><td>

INADEQUATE BACKUP PROCEDURES

</td><td>

To preserve the integrity of mission-critical data and programs, organizations need formal backup procedures. Adequate backup of critical files is actually more difficult to achieve in simple environments than it is in sophisticated ones. In mainframe and network environments, backup is controlled automatically by the operating system, using specialized software and hardware. The responsibility of providing backup in the PC environment falls to the user. Often, because of lack of computer experience and training, users fail to appreciate the importance of backup procedures until it is too late.

</td></tr>
</table>

Computer failure, usually disk failure, is the primary cause of significant data loss in the PC environment. If the hard drive of the microcomputer fails, it may be impossible to recover the data stored on the disk. Formal procedures for making backup copies of critical data (and program) files can reduce this threat considerably. There are a number of options available for dealing with this problem.

Floppy Disk Backup

Files can be backed up to floppy disks at routine periods during processing and stored away from the computer. In the event of a microcomputer failure, the data file can be reconstructed from the backup disks. This requires a conscious effort on the part of the user. Failure to back up data even one time can result in its loss.

Dual Internal Hard Drives

Microcomputers can be configured with two physical internal hard disks. One disk can be used to store production data while the other stores the backup files. A batch program, run prior to or immediately after each data processing session, can copy the data file to the backup disk. Thus, backup is almost transparent to the user and involves a minimum of effort. This is a useful technique for the backup of large files that cannot be stored effectively on floppy disks. If one of the internal hard drives fails, the data files can be retrieved from the remaining hard drive.

External Hard Drives

A popular backup option is the external hard drive with removable disk cartridge, which can store more than a gigabyte of data per cartridge. When a cartridge is filled, the user can remove it and insert a new one. Removable drives offer the advantages of unlimited storage capacity, portability, and physical security. This technology does not materially degrade computer performance since the disk access speed for external hard drives compares favorably with internal hard drives.

External hard drives can be used as an effective and simple backup technique. Dual external drives can be used to store both production and backup files. By using two separate drives, backup can be performed automatically before, during, or after the data processing session. Hence, the user does not need to physically switch cartridges and consciously perform the backup procedures, and the chance for human error is reduced. Also, with both versions of the data file residing on external drives, access control is improved. Both the backup and the original can be removed and stored in separate locations away from the microcomputer.

Tape Backup Devices

The most common type of archive device for PCs is magnetic tape. These may be internal or external devices and provide efficient and inexpensive backup. In normal backup mode, a single tape can store about 1.6 gigabytes of data. In compressed mode, a tape can store up to 3.2 gigabytes.

INADEQUATE SYSTEMS DEVELOPMENT AND MAINTENANCE PROCEDURES

Chapter 15 examined the control issues surrounding the development and maintenance of computer applications. The microcomputer environment lacks both the operating system features and the segregation of duties necessary to provide the necessary control. Management must thus compensate for these inherent exposures with other, more conventional control techniques. The following examples help reduce the risk.

Use Commercial Software

To the extent possible, users should acquire commercial software from reputable vendors for their PC accounting applications. Many of the hundreds of packages on the market are general-purpose accounting systems. Others are special-purpose systems designed to meet the unique needs of specific industries. Commercial software purchased from a reputable vendor will normally be thoroughly tested and is highly reliable.

Software Selection Procedures

Even small firms should employ formal software selection procedures that include the following steps:

- Conduct a formal analysis of the problem and user needs.
- Solicit bids from several vendors.
- Evaluate the competing products in terms of their ability to meet the identified needs. (At this point, it is often wise to seek the help of a professional consultant.)
- Contact current users of prospective commercial packages to get their opinions about the product.
- Make a selection. (The firm should keep in mind the degree of support it will need and should be sure that the vendor is willing and able to provide that support.)

APPLICATION CONTROLS

Application controls deal with exposures within specific applications, such as payroll, purchases, and cash disbursements systems. Application controls, which may be manual actions or procedures programmed into an application, fall into three broad categories: input controls, processing controls, and output controls.

INPUT CONTROLS

The data collection component of the information system is responsible for bringing data into the system for processing. Input controls at this stage attempt to ensure that these transactions are valid, accurate, and complete. Data input procedures can be either source document-triggered (batch) or direct input (real-time).

Direct input can employ real-time editing techniques to identify and correct errors immediately and thus significantly reduce the number of errors that enter the system. On the other hand, source document input requires more human involvement and is more prone to clerical errors than direct input procedures. Some types of errors entered on the source documents cannot be detected and corrected during the data input stage. Dealing with these may require retracing the transaction to its source (such as contacting the customer) to correct the mistake.

Classes of Input Control

For presentation convenience and to provide structure to this discussion, input controls are divided into the following broad classes:

- Source document controls
- Data coding controls
- Batch controls
- Validation controls
- Input error correction
- Generalized data input systems

These control classes are not mutually exclusive divisions. Some control techniques could fit logically into more than one class.

Source Document Controls

In systems that use physical source documents to initiate transactions, careful control must be exercised over these instruments. Source document fraud can be used to remove assets from the organization. For example, an individual with access to purchase orders and receiving reports could fabricate a purchase transaction to a nonexistent supplier. If these documents were entered into the data processing stream, along with a fabricated vendor's invoice, the system could process these documents as if a legitimate transaction had taken place. In the absence of other compensating controls to detect this type of fraud, the system would create an account payable and subsequently write a check in payment.

To control against this type of exposure, the organization must implement control procedures over source documents to account for each document, as described below.

Use Prenumbered Source Documents. Source documents should come prenumbered from the printer with a unique sequential number on each document. Source document numbers permit accurate accounting of document usage and provide an audit trail for tracing transactions through accounting records. We discuss this further in the next section.

Use Source Documents in Sequence. Source documents should be distributed to the users and used in sequence. This requires that adequate physical security be maintained over the source document inventory at the user site. When not in use, documents should be locked away. At all times, access to source documents should be limited to authorized persons.

Periodically Audit Source Documents. Missing source documents should be identified by reconciling document sequence numbers. Periodically, the auditor should compare the numbers of documents used to date with those remaining in inventory plus those voided due to errors. Documents not accounted for should be reported to management.

Data Coding Controls
Coding controls are checks on the integrity of data codes used in processing. A customer's account number, an inventory item number, and a chart of accounts number are all examples of data codes. Three types of errors can corrupt a data code and cause processing errors: transcription, single transposition, and multiple transposition.

Transcription errors fall into three classes:

1. Addition errors occur when an extra digit or character is added to the code. For example, inventory item number 83276 is recorded as 832766.
2. Truncation errors occur when a digit or character is removed from the end of a code. In this type of error, the inventory item above would be recorded as 8327.
3. Substitution errors are the replacement of one digit in a code with another. For example, code number 83276 is recorded as 83266.

There are two types of **transposition errors**. *Single transposition errors* occur when two adjacent digits are reversed. For instance, 83276 is recorded as 38276. *Multiple transposition errors* occur when nonadjacent digits are transposed. For example, 83276 is recorded as 87236.

Any of these errors can cause serious problems in data processing if they go undetected. For example, a sales order for customer 732519 that is transposed into 735219 will be posted to the wrong customer's account. A similar error in an inventory item code on a purchase order could result in ordering unneeded inventory and failing to order inventory that is needed. These simple errors can severely disrupt operations.

Check Digits. One method for detecting data coding errors is a check digit. A **check digit** is a control digit (or digits) added to the code when it is originally assigned that allows the integrity of the code to be established during subsequent processing. The check digit can be located anywhere in the code, as a prefix, a suffix, or embedded someplace in the middle. The simplest form of check digit is to sum the digits in the code and use this sum as the check digit. For example, for the customer account code 5372 the calculated check digit would be:

$$5 + 3 + 7 + 2 = 17$$

By dropping the tens column, the check digit 7 is added to the original code to produce the new code 53727. The entire string of digits (including the check digit) becomes the customer account number. During data entry, the system can recalculate the check digit to ensure that the code is correct. This technique will detect only transcription errors. For example, if a substitution error occurred and the above code were entered as 52727, the calculated check digit would be 6 (5 + 2 + 7 + 2 = 16 = 6), and the error would be detected. However, this technique would fail to identify transposition errors. For example, transposing the first two digits yields the code 35727, which still sums to 17 and produces the check digit 7. This error would go undetected.

There are many check digit techniques for dealing with transposition errors. A popular method is modulus 11. Using the code 5372, the steps in this technique are outlined below:

1. *Assign weights.* Each digit in the code is multiplied by a different weight. In this case, the weights used are 5, 4, 3, and 2, shown as follows:

Digit		Weight	
5	x	5 =	25
3	x	4 =	12
7	x	3 =	21
2	x	2 =	4

2. *Sum the products.* (25 + 12 + 21 + 4 = 62).
3. *Divide by the modulus.* We are using modulus 11 in this case, giving: 62/11 = 5 with remainder of 7.
4. *Subtract the remainder from the modulus to obtain the check digit.* (11 − 7 = 4 [check digit]).
5. *Add the check digit to the original code to yield the new code:* 53724.

Using this technique to recalculate the check digit during processing, a transposition error in the code will produce a check digit other than 4. For example, if the code above was incorrectly entered as 35724, the recalculated check digit would be 6.

When Should Check Digits Be Used? The use of check digits introduces storage and processing inefficiencies and therefore should be restricted to essential data, such as primary and secondary key fields. All check digit techniques require one or more additional spaces in the field to accommodate the check digit. In the case of modulus 11, if step 3 above produces a remainder of 1, the check digit of 10 will require two additional character spaces. If field length is a limitation, one way of handling this problem is to disallow codes that generate the check digit 10. This would restrict the range of available codes by about 9 percent.

Batch Controls

Batch controls are an effective method of managing high volumes of transaction data through a system. The objective of batch control is to reconcile output produced by the system with the input originally entered into the system. This provides assurance that:

- All records in the batch are processed.
- No records are processed more than once.
- An audit trail of transactions is created from input through processing to the output stage of the system.

Batch control is not exclusively an input control technique. Controlling the batch continues through all phases of the system. The topic is addressed here because batch control is initiated at the input stage.

Achieving batch control objectives requires grouping similar types of input transactions (such as sales orders) together in batches and then controlling the batches throughout data processing. Two documents are used to accomplish this task: a batch transmittal sheet and a batch control log. Figure 16–9 shows an example of a batch transmittal sheet. The batch transmittal sheet captures relevant information about the batch, such as:

1. A unique batch number.
2. A batch date.
3. A transaction code (indicating the type of transactions, such as a sales order or cash receipt).
4. The number of records in the batch (record count).
5. The total dollar value of a financial field (batch control total).
6. The total of a unique nonfinancial field (hash total).

FIGURE 16–9

Batch Transmittal Sheet

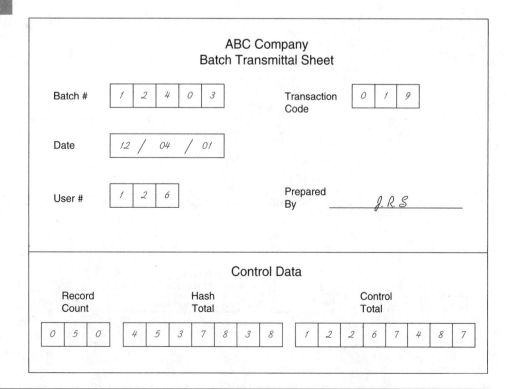

Usually, the batch transmittal sheet is prepared by the user department and is submitted to data control along with the batch of source documents. Sometimes the data control clerk, acting as a liaison between the users and the data processing department, prepares the transmittal sheet. Figure 16–10 illustrates the batch control process.

The data control clerk receives transactions from users assembled in batches of 40 to 50 records. The clerk assigns each batch a unique number, date-stamps the documents, and calculates (or recalculates) the batch control numbers, such as the total dollar amount of the batch and a hash total (discussed later). The clerk enters the batch control information in the batch control log and submits the batch of documents, along with the transmittal sheet, to the data entry department. Figure 16–11 shows a sample batch control log.

The data entry group codes and enters the transmittal sheet data onto the transaction file, along with the batch of transaction records. The transmittal data may be added as an additional record in the file or placed in the file's internal trailer label. (Internal labels are discussed later in this section.) The transmittal sheet becomes the batch control record and is used to assess the integrity of the batch during processing. For example, the data entry procedure will recalculate the batch control totals to make sure the batch is in balance. The transmittal record shows a batch of 50 sales order records with a total dollar value of $122,674.87 and a hash total of 4537838. At various points throughout and at the end of processing, these amounts are recalcu-

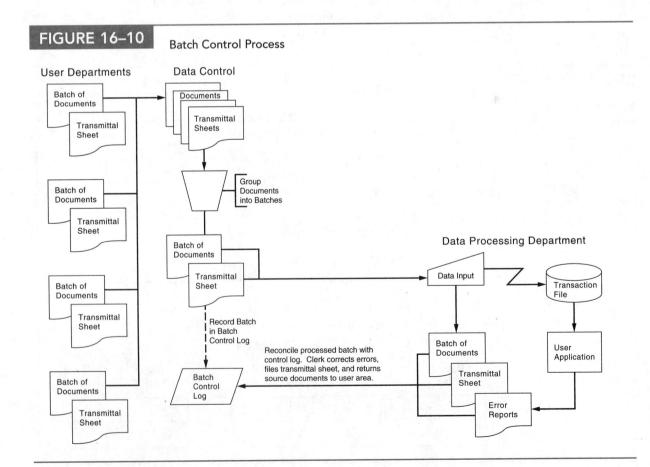

FIGURE 16–10   Batch Control Process

FIGURE 16–11

Batch Control Log

Batch #	Date	Time	Rec By	Control Total	Hash Total	Record Count	Submitted Date	Time	Returned Date	Time	Error Code	Reconciled By
End User							Data Processing					
12 403	12/4/01	9:05	B.R.	1,22,674.87	4537838	50	12/4/01	9:55	12/4/01	11:05	0	PMR

lated and compared to the batch control record. If the procedure recalculates the same amounts, the batch is in balance.

After processing, the output results are sent to the data control clerk for reconciliation and distribution to the user. The clerk updates the batch control log to record that the processing of the batch was completed successfully.

Hash Totals. The term **hash total**, which was used in the preceding discussion, refers to a simple control technique that uses nonfinancial data to keep track of the records in a batch. Any key field, such as a customer's account number, a purchase order number, or an inventory item number, may be used to calculate a hash total. In the example below, the sales order number (SO#) field for an entire batch of sales order records is summed to produce a hash total.

```
        SO#
       14327
       67345
       19983
         •
         •
         •
         •
       88943
       96543
      4537838   (hash total)
```

Let's see how this seemingly meaningless number can be of use. Assume that after this batch of records leaves data control, but prior to data input, someone replaced one of the sales orders in the batch with a fictitious record of the same dollar amount. How would the batch control procedures detect this irregularity? Both the record count and the dollar amount control totals would be unaffected by this act. However, unless the perpetrator obtained a source document with exactly the same sales order number (which would be impossible, since they should come uniquely prenumbered from the printer), the hash total calculated by the batch control procedures would not balance. Thus, the irregularity would be detected.

Validation Controls

Input **validation controls** are intended to detect errors in transaction data before the data are processed. Validation procedures are most effective when they are performed as close to the source of the transaction as possible. However, depending on the type of CBIS in use, input validation may occur at various points in the system. For example, some validation procedures require making references against the current master file. CBISs using real-time processing or batch processing with direct access master files can validate data at the input stage. Figure 16–12 illustrates these techniques.

If the CBIS uses batch processing with sequential files, the transaction records being validated must first be sorted in the same order as the master file. Validating at the data input stage in this case may require considerable additional processing. Therefore, as a practical matter, some validation procedures are performed by each processing module prior to updating the master file record. This approach is shown in Figure 16–13.

The problem with this technique is that a transaction may be partially processed before data errors are detected. Dealing with a partially complete transaction will require special error-handling procedures. Error-handling controls will be discussed later in this section.

There are three levels of input validation controls:

1. Field interrogation
2. Record interrogation
3. File interrogation

Field Interrogation. **Field interrogation** involves programmed procedures that examine the characteristics of the data in the field. The following are some common types of field interrogation.

FIGURE 16–12

Validation during Data Input

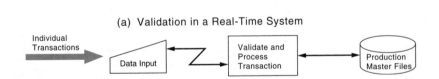

(a) Validation in a Real-Time System

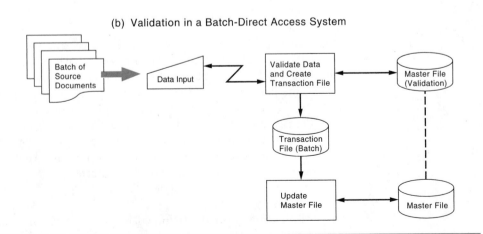

(b) Validation in a Batch-Direct Access System

FIGURE 16–13

Validation in Batch
Sequential File System

Note: For simplifica-
tion, the necessary
re-sorting of the
transaction file
between update
processes is not
shown.

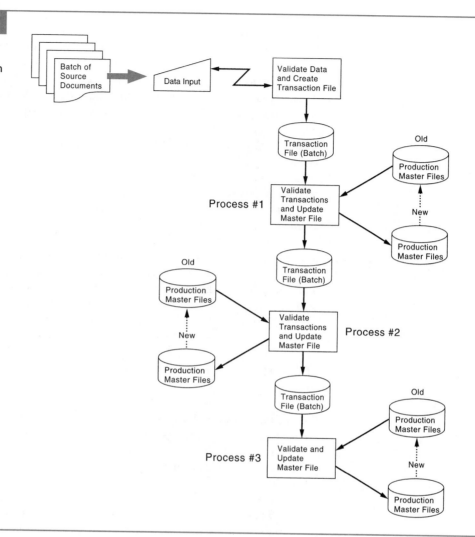

Missing data checks are used to examine the contents of a field for the presence of blank spaces. Some programming languages are restrictive as to the justification (right or left) of data within the field. If data are not properly justified or if a character is missing (has been replaced with a blank), the value in the field will be improperly processed. In some cases, the presence of blanks in a numeric data field may cause a system failure. When the validation program detects a blank where it expects to see a data value, this will be interpreted as an error.

Numeric-alphabetic data checks determine whether the correct form of data is in a field. For example, a customer's account balance should not contain alphabetic data. As with blanks, alphabetic data in a numeric field may cause serious processing errors.

Zero-value checks are used to verify that certain fields are filled with zeros. Some program languages require that fields used in mathematical operations are initiated with zeros prior to processing. This control may trigger an automatic corrective control to replace the contents of the field with zero if it detects a nonzero value.

Limit checks determine if the value in the field exceeds an authorized limit. For example, assume the firm's policy is that no employee works more than 44 hours per week. The payroll system validation program can interrogate the hours-worked field in the weekly payroll records for values greater than 44.

Range checks assign upper and lower limits to acceptable data values. For example, if the range of pay rates for hourly employees in a firm is between 8 and 20 dollars, all payroll records can be checked to see that this range is not exceeded. The purpose of this control is to detect keystroke errors that shift the decimal point one or more places. It would not detect an error where a correct pay rate of, say, 9 dollars is incorrectly entered as 15 dollars.

Validity checks compare actual values in a field against known acceptable values. This control is used to verify such things as transaction codes, state abbreviations, or employee job skill codes. If the value in the field does not match one of the acceptable values, the record is determined to be in error.

This is a frequently used control in cash disbursement systems. One form of cash disbursement fraud involves manipulating the system into making a fraudulent payment to a nonexistent vendor. To prevent this, the firm may establish a list of valid vendors with whom it does business exclusively. Thus, before payment of any trade obligation, the vendor number on the cash disbursement voucher is matched against the valid vendor list by the validation program. If the code does not match, payment is denied, and the transaction is reviewed by management.

Check digit controls identify keystroke errors in key fields by testing the internal validity of the code. This control technique was discussed earlier in the section.

Record Interrogation. **Record interrogation** procedures validate the entire record by examining the interrelationship of its field values. Some typical tests are discussed below.

Reasonableness checks determine if a value in one field, which has already passed a limit check and a range check, is reasonable when considered along with other data fields in the record. For example, an employee's pay rate of 18 dollars per hour falls within an acceptable range. However, this rate is excessive when compared to the employee's job skill code of 693; employees in this skill class never earn more than 12 dollars per hour.

Sign checks are tests to see if the sign of a field is correct for the type of record being processed. For example, in a sales order processing system, the dollar amount field must be positive for sales orders but negative for sales returns transactions. This control can determine the correctness of the sign by comparing it with the transaction code field.

Sequence checks are used to determine if a record is out of order. In batch systems that use sequential master files, the transaction files being processed must be sorted in the same order as the primary keys of the corresponding master file. This requirement is critical to the processing logic of the update program. Hence, before each transaction record is processed, its sequence is verified relative to the previous record processed.

File Interrogation. The purpose of **file interrogation** is to ensure that the correct file is being processed by the system. These controls are particularly important for master files, which contain permanent records of the firm and which, if destroyed or corrupted, are difficult to replace.

Internal label checks verify that the file processed is the one the program is actually calling for. Files stored on magnetic tape are usually kept off-line in a tape library. These files have an external label that identifies them (by name and serial number) to the tape librarian and operator. External labeling is typically a manual procedure and, like any manual task, prone to errors. The wrong external label may be mistakenly affixed to a file when it is created. Thus, when the file is called for again, the wrong file will be retrieved and placed on the tape drive for processing. Depending on how the file is being used, this may result in its destruction or corruption. To prevent this, the operating system creates an internal header label that is placed at the beginning of the file. An example of a header label is shown in Figure 16–14.

To ensure that the correct file is about to be processed, the system matches the file name and serial number in the header label with the program's file requirements. If the wrong file has been loaded, the system will send the operator a message and suspend processing. It is worth noting that while label checking is generally a standard feature, it is an option that can be overridden by programmers and operators.

Version checks are used to verify that the version of the file being processed is correct. In a grandparent-parent-child (GPC) approach, many versions of master files and transactions may exist. The version check compares the version number of the files being processed with the program's requirements.

An *expiration date check* prevents a file from being deleted before it expires. In a GPC system, for example, once an adequate number of backup files is created, the oldest backup file is scratched (erased from the disk or tape) to provide space for new files. Figure 16–15 illustrates this procedure.

FIGURE 16–14

Header Label on
Magnetic Tape

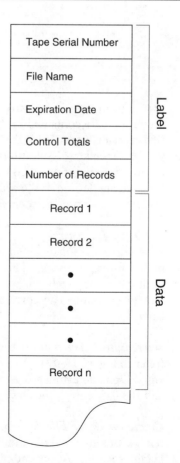

FIGURE 16–15

FIGURE 16–15   Scratch Tape Approach Using Retention Date

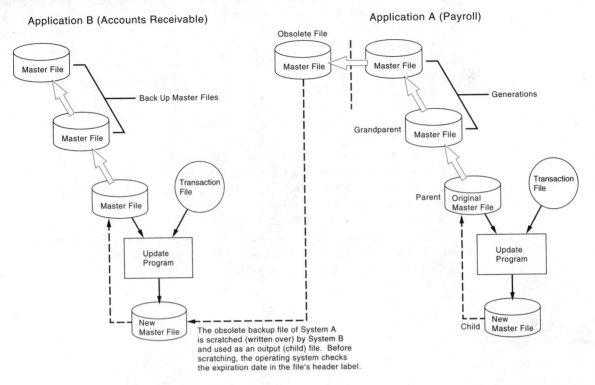

To protect against destroying an active file by mistake, the system first checks the expiration date contained in the header label (see Figure 16–14). If the retention period has not yet expired, the system will generate an error message and abort the scratch procedure. Expiration date control is an optional measure. The length of the retention period is specified by the programmer and based on the number of backup files that are desired. If the programmer chooses not to specify an expiration date, the control against such accidental deletion is eliminated.

Input Error Correction

When errors are detected in a batch, they must be corrected and the records resubmitted for reprocessing. This must be a controlled process to ensure that errors are dealt with completely and correctly. There are three common error-handling techniques: (1) immediate correction, (2) create an error file, and (3) reject the entire batch.

Immediate Correction. If the system is using the direct data validation approach (refer to Figure 16–12), error detection and correction can also take place during data entry. Upon detecting a keystroke error or an illogical relationship, the system should halt the data entry procedure until the user corrects the error.

Create an Error File. When delayed validation is being used, such as in batch systems with sequential files, individual errors should be flagged to prevent them from being processed. At the end of the validation procedure, the records flagged as errors are removed from the batch and placed in a temporary error holding file until the errors can be investigated.

Some errors can be detected during data input procedures. However, as was mentioned earlier, some validation tests are performed by the update module. Thus, error records may be placed on the error file at several different points in the process, as illustrated by Figure 16–16. At each validation point, the system automatically adjusts the batch control totals to reflect the removal of the error records from the batch. In a separate procedure, an authorized user representative will later make corrections to the error records and resubmit them as a separate batch for reprocessing.

Errors detected during processing require careful handling. These records may already be partially processed. Therefore, simply resubmitting the corrected records to the system via the data input stage may result in processing portions of these transactions twice. There are two methods for dealing with this complexity. The first is to reverse the effects of the partially processed transactions and resubmit the corrected records to the data input stage. The second method is to reinsert corrected records to the processing stage in which the error was detected. In either case, batch control procedures (preparing batch control records and logging the batches) apply to the resubmitted data, just as they do for normal batch processing.

Reject the Batch. Some forms of errors are associated with the entire batch and are not clearly attributable to individual records. An example of this type of error is an

FIGURE 16–16

Use of Error File in Batch Sequential File System with Multiple Resubmission Points

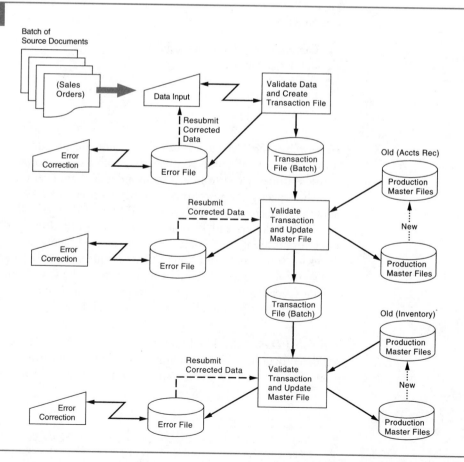

imbalance in a batch control total. Assume that the transmittal sheet for a batch of sales orders shows a total sales value of $122,674.87, but the data input procedure calculated a sales total of only $121,454.32. What has caused this? Is the problem a missing or changed record? Or was the batch control total incorrectly calculated by the data control clerk? The most effective solution in this case is to cease processing and return the entire batch to data control to evaluate, correct, and resubmit.

Batch errors are one reason for keeping the size of the batch to a manageable number. Too few records in a batch make batch processing inefficient. Too many records make error detection difficult, create greater business disruption when a batch is rejected, and increase the possibility of mistakes when calculating batch control totals.

Generalized Data Input Systems

To achieve a high degree of control and standardization over input validation procedures, some organizations employ a **generalized data input system (GDIS)**. This technique includes centralized procedures to manage the data input for all the organization's transaction processing systems. The GDIS approach has three advantages. First, it improves control by having one common system perform all data validation. Second, GDIS ensures that each AIS application applies a consistent standard for data validation. Third, GDIS improves systems development efficiency. Given the high degree of commonalty in input validation requirements for AIS applications, a GDIS eliminates the need to recreate redundant routines for each new application. Figure 16–17 shows the primary features of this technique. A GDIS has five major components:[1]

1. Generalized validation module
2. Validated data file
3. Error file
4. Error reports
5. Transaction log

Generalized Validation Module. The generalized validation module (GVM) performs standard validation routines that are common to many different applications. These routines are customized to an individual application's needs through parameters that specify the program's specific requirements. For example, the GVM may apply a range check to the HOURLY RATE field of payroll records. The limits of the range are 6 dollars and 15 dollars. The range test is the generalized procedure; the dollar limits are the parameters that customize this procedure. The validation procedures for some applications may be so unique as to defy a general solution. To meet the goals of the generalized data input system, the GVM must be flexible enough to permit special user-defined procedures for unique applications. These procedures are stored, along with generalized procedures, and invoked by the GVM as needed.

Validated Data File. The input data that are validated by the GVM are stored on a validated data file. This is a temporary holding file through which validated transactions flow to their respective applications. The file is analogous to a tank of water

1   Ron Weber, *EDP Auditing Conceptual Foundations and Practice*, 2d ed. (New York: McGraw-Hill, 1988): 424–27.

FIGURE 16–17

Generalized Data
Input System

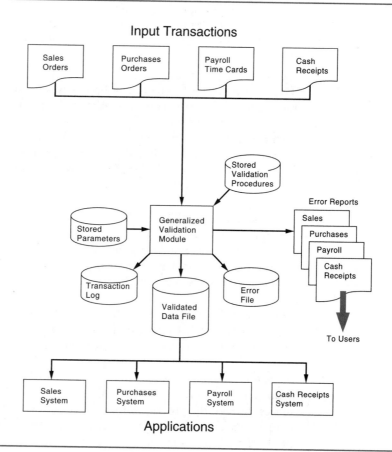

whose level is constantly changing, as it is filled from the top by the GVM and emptied from the bottom by applications.

Error File.   The error file in the GDIS plays the same role as a traditional error file. Error records detected during validation are stored in the file, corrected, and then resubmitted to the GVM.

Error Reports.   Standardized error reports are distributed to users to facilitate error correction. For example, if the HOURLY RATE field in a payroll record fails a range check, the error report will display an error message stating the problem. The report will also present the contents of the failed record, along with the acceptable range limits taken from the parameters.

Transaction Log.   The transaction log is a permanent record of all validated transactions. From an accounting records point of view, the transaction log is equivalent to the journal and is an important element in the audit trail. However, only successful transactions (those that will be completely processed) should be entered in the journal. If a transaction is to undergo additional validation testing during the processing phase (which could result in its rejection), it should be entered in the transaction log only after it is completely validated. This issue is discussed further in the next section under "Audit Trail Controls."

PROCESSING CONTROLS

After passing through the data input stage, transactions enter the processing stage of the system. Processing controls are divided into three categories: run-to-run controls, operator intervention controls, and audit trail controls.

Run-to-Run Controls

The preparation of batch control figures was previously discussed as an element of input control. **Run-to-run controls** use batch figures to monitor the batch as it moves from one programmed procedure (run) to another. These controls ensure that each run in the system processes the batch correctly and completely. Batch control figures may be contained in either a separate control record created at the data input stage or an internal label. Specific uses of run-to-run control figures are described below.

Recalculate Control Totals. After each major operation in the process and after each run, dollar amount fields, hash totals, and record counts are accumulated and compared to the corresponding values stored in the control record. If a record in the batch is lost, goes unprocessed, or is processed more than once, this will be revealed by the discrepancies between these figures.

Transaction Codes. The transaction code of each record in the batch is compared to the transaction code contained in the control record. This ensures that only the correct type of transaction is being processed.

Sequence Checks. In systems that use sequential master files, the order of the transaction records in the batch is critical to correct and complete processing. As the batch moves through the process, it must be re-sorted in the order of the master file used in each run. The sequence check control compares the sequence of each record in the batch with the previous record to ensure that proper sorting took place.

Figure 16–18 illustrates the use of run-to-run controls in a revenue cycle system. This application comprises four runs: (1) data input, (2) accounts receivable update, (3) inventory update, and (4) output. At the end of the accounts receivable run, batch control figures are recalculated and reconciled with the control totals passed from the data input run. These figures are then passed to the inventory update run, where they are again recalculated, reconciled, and passed to the output run. Errors detected in each run are flagged and placed in an error file. The run-to-run (batch) control figures are then adjusted to reflect the deletion of these records.

Operator Intervention Controls

Systems sometimes require operator intervention to initiate certain actions, such as entering control totals for a batch of records, providing parameter values for logical operations, and activating a program from a different point when reentering semi-processed error records. Operator intervention increases the potential for human error. Systems that limit operator intervention through **operators intervention controls** are thus less prone to processing errors. Although it may be impossible to eliminate operator involvement completely, parameter values and program start points should, to the extent possible, be derived logically or provided to the system through look-up tables.

Audit Trail Controls

The preservation of an audit trail is an important objective of process control. In an accounting system, every transaction must be traceable through each stage of

FIGURE 16–18

Run-to-Run Controls

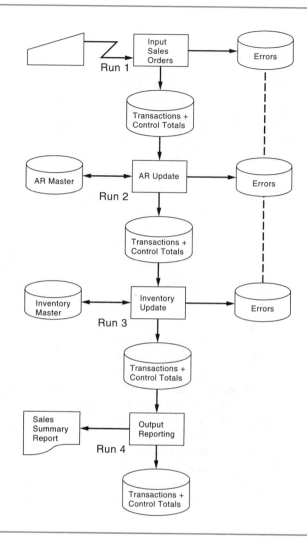

processing from its economic source to its presentation in financial statements. In a CBIS environment, the audit trail can become fragmented and difficult to follow. It thus becomes critical that each major operation applied to a transaction be thoroughly documented. The following are examples of techniques used to preserve audit trails in a CBIS.

Transaction Logs. Every transaction successfully processed by the system should be recorded on a transaction log, which serves as a journal. Figure 16–19 shows this arrangement.

There are two reasons for creating a transaction log. First, the transaction log is a permanent record of transactions. The validated transaction file produced at the data input phase is usually a temporary file. Once processed, the records on this file are erased (scratched) to make room for the next batch of transactions. Second, not all of the records in the validated transaction file may be successfully processed. Some of these records may fail tests in the subsequent processing stages. A transaction log should contain only successful transactions—those that have changed account

FIGURE 16–19   Transaction Log to Preserve the Audit Trail

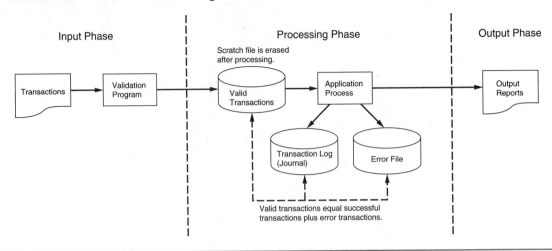

balances. Unsuccessful transactions should be placed in an error file. The transaction log and error files combined should account for all the transactions in the batch. The validated transaction file may then be scratched with no loss of data.

Transaction Listings. The system should produce a (hard-copy) transaction listing of all successful transactions. These listings should go to the appropriate users to facilitate reconciliation with input.

Log of Automatic Transactions. Some transactions are triggered internally by the system. An example of this is when inventory drops below a preset reorder point, and the system automatically processes a purchase order. To maintain an audit trail of these activities, all internally generated transactions must be placed in a transaction log.

Listing of Automatic Transactions. To maintain control over automatic transactions processed by the system, the responsible end user should receive a detailed listing of all internally generated transactions.

Unique Transaction Identifiers. Each transaction processed by the system must be uniquely identified with a transaction number. This is the only practical means of tracing a particular transaction through a database of thousands or even millions of records. In systems that use physical source documents, the unique number printed on the document can be transcribed during data input and used for this purpose. In real-time systems, which do not use source documents, each transaction should be assigned a unique number by the system.

Error Listing. A listing of all error records should go to the appropriate user to support error correction and resubmission.

OUTPUT CONTROLS   Output controls ensure that system output is not lost, misdirected, or corrupted and that privacy is not violated. Exposures of this sort can cause serious disruptions to operations and may result in financial losses to a firm. For example, if the checks produced by a firm's cash disbursements system are lost, misdirected, or destroyed, trade accounts and other bills may go unpaid. This could damage the firm's credit rating and result in lost discounts, interest, or penalty charges. If the privacy of certain types of output is violated, a firm could have its business objectives compromised, or it could even become legally exposed. Examples of privacy exposures include the disclosure of trade secrets, patents pending, marketing research results, and patient medical records.

The choice of controls employed to protect system output is influenced by the type of processing method in use. Generally, batch systems are more susceptible to exposure and require a greater degree of control than real-time systems. This section examines output exposures and controls for both methods.

Controlling Batch Systems Output

Batch systems usually produce output in the form of hard copy, which typically requires the involvement of intermediaries in its production and distribution. Figure 16–20 shows the stages in the output process and serves as the basis for the rest of this section.

The output is removed from the printer by the computer operator, separated into sheets and separated from other reports, reviewed for correctness by the data control clerk, and then sent through interoffice mail to the end user. Each stage in this

---

FIGURE 16–20

Stages in the
Output Process

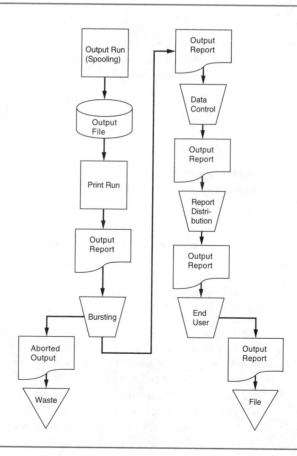

process is a point of potential exposure where the output could be reviewed, stolen, copied, or misdirected. An additional exposure exists when processing or printing goes wrong and produces output that is unacceptable to the end user. These corrupted or partially damaged reports are often discarded in waste cans. Computer criminals have successfully used such waste to achieve their illicit objectives.

Techniques for controlling each phase in the output process are examined below. Keep in mind that not all of these techniques will necessarily apply to every item of output produced by the system. As always, controls are employed on a cost-benefit basis that is determined by the sensitivity of the data in the reports.

Output Spooling. In large-scale data processing operations, output devices such as line printers can become backlogged with many programs simultaneously demanding these limited resources. This can cause a bottleneck, which adversely affects the throughput of the system. Applications waiting to print output occupy computer memory and block other applications from entering the processing stream. To ease this burden, applications are often designed to direct their output to a magnetic disk file rather than to the printer directly. This is called **spooling**. Later, when printer resources become available, the output files are printed.

The creation of an output file as an intermediate step in the printing process presents an added exposure. A computer criminal may use this opportunity to perform any of the following unauthorized acts:

1. Access the output file and change critical data values (such as dollar amounts on checks). The printer program will then print the corrupted output as if it was produced by the output run. Using this technique, a criminal may effectively circumvent the processing controls designed into the application.
2. Access the file and change the number of copies of output to be printed. The extra copies may then be removed without notice during the printing stage.
3. Make a copy of the output file to produce illegal output reports.
4. Destroy the output file before output printing takes place.

The auditor should be aware of these potential exposures and ensure that proper access and backup procedures are in place to protect output files. The nature and extent of file access and backup controls were discussed in Chapter 15.

Print Programs. When the printer becomes available, the print run program produces hard-copy output from the output file. Print programs are often complex systems that require operator intervention. Four common types of operator actions are:

1. Pausing the print program to load the correct type of output documents (check stocks, invoices, or other special forms).
2. Entering parameters needed by the print run, such as the number of copies to be printed.
3. Restarting the print run at a prescribed checkpoint after a printer malfunction.
4. Removing printed output from the printer for review and distribution.

Print program controls are designed to deal with two types of exposures presented by this environment: (1) the production of unauthorized copies of output and (2) employee browsing of sensitive data. Some print programs allow the operator to specify more copies of output than the output file calls for, which allows for the possibility of producing unauthorized copies of output. One way to control this is to employ output document controls similar to the source document controls discussed earlier. This is feasible when dealing with prenumbered invoices for billing customers or prenumbered check stock. At the end of the run, the number of copies specified by the output file can be reconciled with the actual number of output documents used. In cases where output documents are not prenumbered, supervision may be the most effective control technique. A security officer can be present during the printing of sensitive output.

To prevent operators from viewing sensitive output, special multipart paper can be used, with the top copy colored black to prevent the print from being read. This type of product, which is illustrated in Figure 16–21, is often used for payroll check printing. The receiver of the check separates the top copy from the body of the check, which contains readable details. An alternative privacy control is to direct the output to a special remote printer that can be closely supervised.

Bursting. When output reports are removed from the printer, they go to the bursting stage to have their pages separated and collated. The concern here is that the bursting clerk may make an unauthorized copy of the report, remove a page from the report, or read sensitive information. The primary control against these exposures is supervision. For very sensitive reports, bursting may be performed by the end user.

Waste. Computer output waste represents a potential exposure. It is important to properly dispose of aborted reports and the carbon copies from multipart paper removed during bursting. Computer criminals have been known to sift through trash cans searching for carelessly discarded output that is presumed by others to be of no value. From such trash, computer criminals may obtain a key piece of information about the firm's market research, the credit ratings of its customers, or even trade secrets that they can sell to a competitor. Computer waste is also a source of technical data, such as passwords and authority tables, which a perpetrator may use to access the firm's data files. Sensitive computer output can easily be destroyed by passing it through a paper shredder.

Data Control. In some organizations, the data control group is responsible for verifying the accuracy of computer output before it is distributed to the user. Normally, the data control clerk will review the batch control figures for balance; examine the report body for garbled, illegible, and missing data; and record the receipt of the report in the data control batch control log. For reports containing highly sensitive data, the end user may perform these tasks. In this case, the report will bypass the data control group and go directly to the user.

Report Distribution. The primary risks associated with report distribution include reports being lost, stolen, or misdirected in transit to the user. A number of control measures can minimize these exposures. For example, when reports are generated, the name and address of the user should be printed on the report. For multicopy reports, an address file of authorized users should be consulted to identify each recipient of the report. Maintaining adequate access control over this file becomes highly important. If an unauthorized individual was able to add his or her name to the authorized user list, he or she would receive a copy of the report.

For highly sensitive reports, the following distribution techniques can be used:

1. The reports may be placed in a secure mailbox to which only the user has the key.
2. The user may be required to appear in person at the distribution center and sign for the report.
3. The report may be delivered to the user by a security officer or special courier.

End-User Controls. Once in the hands of the user, output reports should be reexamined for any errors that may have evaded the data control clerk's review. Users are in

FIGURE 16–21   Multipart Check Stock

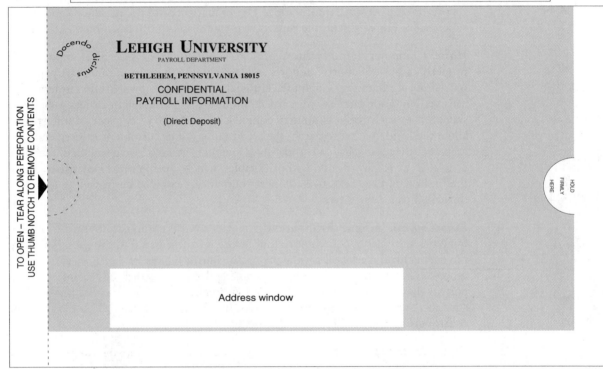

a far better position to identify subtle errors in reports that are not disclosed by an imbalance in control totals. Errors detected by the user should be reported to the appropriate computer services management. Such errors may be symptoms of an improper systems design, incorrect procedures, errors inserted by accident during systems maintenance, or unauthorized access to data files or programs.

Once a report has served its purpose, it should be stored in a secure location until its retention period has expired. Factors influencing the length of time a hard-copy report is retained include:

1. Statutory requirements specified by government agencies, such as the IRS.
2. The number of copies of the report in existence. When there are multiple copies, certain of these may be marked for permanent retention, while the remainder can be destroyed after use.
3. The existence of magnetic or optical images of reports that can act as permanent backup.

When the retention date has passed, reports should be destroyed in a manner consistent with the sensitivity of their contents. Highly sensitive reports should be shredded.

Controlling Real-Time Systems Output

Real-time systems direct their output to the user's computer screen, terminal, or printer. This method of distribution eliminates the various intermediaries in the journey from the computer center to the user and thus reduces many of the exposures discussed above. The primary output threat to real-time output is the interception, disruption, destruction, or corruption of the output message as it passes along the communications link. This threat comes from two types of exposures: (1) exposures from equipment failure and (2) exposures from subversive acts, whereby a computer criminal intercepts the output message transmitted between the sender and the receiver. Techniques for controlling communications exposures were discussed previously in this chapter.

Summary

This chapter concluded the discussion of the CBIS control issues that began in Chapter 15. First, it examined the three remaining general control areas—communications, electronic data interchange, and microcomputers. In each of these areas, control measures are required to minimize exposures that have systemwide ramifications. The chapter discussion then turned to the topic of application controls, which deals with exposures that threaten the integrity of specific computer applications, such as payroll, purchases, and cash disbursement systems.

In examining data communications and networking, it was found that communication links are susceptible to exposures from both criminal subversion and equipment failure. Subversive threats to a communications system can be minimized through a variety of access control measures including firewalls, data encryption, and call-back devices. Equipment failure in this area comes principally in the form of line errors, which are caused by noise in communications lines and can be effectively reduced through echo checks and parity checks. Equipment failure can also result in the loss of stored data. Therefore, adequate backup procedures are critical in a network environment.

The discussion then turned to EDI, where firms are faced with a variety of exposures that arise in connection with an environment void of human intermediaries to authorize or review transactions. Controls in an EDI environment are achieved primarily through programmed procedures to authorize transactions, limit access to data files, and ensure that transactions processed by the system are valid.

The topic of microcomputers was discussed next. The microcomputer environment is characterized by inadequate segregation of duties, ease of access to data resources, and uncontrolled systems development and maintenance procedures, all of which constitute substantial exposures to an organization. These exposures can be minimized through access controls, backup procedures, and sound policies governing computer software purchases.

Finally, the chapter turned to the issue of application controls, which fall into three broad categories: input controls, processing controls, and output controls. Input controls, which govern the gathering and insertion of data into the system, attempt to ensure that all data transactions are valid, accurate, and complete. Processing controls attempt to preserve the integrity of individual records and batches of records within the system and ensure that an adequate audit trail is preserved. The goal of output controls is to ensure that information produced by the system is not lost, misdirected, or subject to privacy violations.

Key Terms

application-level firewalls   (806)
batch controls   (824)
call-back device   (813)
certification authority   (811)
check digit   (823)
data encryption standard (DES)   (808)
digest   (811)
digital certificate   (811)
digital envelope   (811)
digital signature   (811)
disk locks   (819)
echo check   (814)
EDE3   (809)
EEE3   (809)
encryption   (808)
field interrogation   (828)
file interrogation   (830)
firewall   (806)
generalized data input system (GDIS)   (834)
hash total   (827)

key   (808)
line error   (813)
message sequence numbering   (813)
message transaction log   (813)
multilevel password control   (820)
network-level firewalls   (806)
operators intervention controls   (836)
parity check   (814)
public key encryption   (811)
record interrogation   (830)
request-response technique   (813)
RSA (Rivest-Shamir-Adleman)   (811)
run-to-run controls   (836)
screening router   (806)
spooling   (840)
transcription errors   (823)
transposition errors   (823)
triple-DES encryption   (809)
validation controls   (827)

Review Questions

1. What are the risks from subversive threats?
2. What are the risks from equipment failure?
3. What is a firewall?
4. Distinguish between network-level and application-level firewalls.

5. What are the most common forms of contra-security behavior?
6. What is a three-way handshake?
7. What are denial of service attacks? Can they be thwarted?

8. How does public key encryption work?
9. What is a digital envelope?
10. What is a digital signature?
11. Categorize each of the following as either an equipment failure control or an unauthorized access control.
    a. Message authentication
    b. Parity check
    c. Call-back device
    d. Echo check
    e. Line error
    f. Data encryption
    g. Request-response technique
12. Will a vertical parity check always catch a data transmission error? Why or why not?
13. At what three points in an electronic data interchange transaction and validation process can authorization and validation be accomplished?
14. What is the purpose of a valid vendor file?
15. What techniques are available in the microcomputer environment to reduce access exposure?
16. What is a mitigating control to inadequate segregation of duties in microcomputer environments?
17. What advantage do dual external hard drives offer over dual internal hard drives?
18. What are the broad classes of input controls?
19. Explain the importance of source documents and associated control techniques.
20. Give one example of an error that is detected by a check digit control.
21. What are the primary objectives of a batch control?
22. Classify each of the following as either a field, record, or file interrogation.
    a. Limit check
    b. Validity check
    c. Version check
    d. Missing data check
    e. Sign check
    f. Expiration date check
    g. Numeric-alphabetic data check
    h. Sequence check
    i. Zero-value check
    j. Header label check
    k. Range check
    l. Reasonableness check
23. Compare the three common error-handling techniques discussed in the text.
24. What are the five major components of a GDIS?
25. What are the three categories of processing controls?
26. If all of the inputs have been validated before processing, then what purpose do run-to-run controls serve?
27. What is the objective of a transaction log?
28. How can spooling present an added exposure?

Discussion Questions

1. Discuss some of the risks from subversive threats and how they can be controlled.
2. Discuss the risks from equipment failure and how they can be controlled.
3. Does every organization that has a LAN need a firewall?
4. What is a denial of service attack?
5. Why might an individual launch a denial of service attack on a company's Internet connection?
6. Discuss the various ways in which data encryption may be used. Which way provides the most control?
7. What is RSA encryption?
8. Explain the triple-DES encryption techniques know as EEE3 and EDE3.
9. Distinguish between a digital signature and a digital certificate.
10. Describe a digest within the context of a digital signature.
11. What is a digital envelope?
12. Describe multilevel password control.
13. Why is inadequate segregation of duties a problem in the personal computer environment?
14. Why is the request-response technique important? Discuss the reasons an intruder may wish to prevent or delay the receipt of a message.
15. Is backup redundancy inefficient?
16. Discuss how the widespread use of laptop and notebook computers is making data encryption standards more easily penetrable.
17. Discuss the unique control problems created by EDI.
18. "In an EDI system, only the customer needs to verify that the order being placed is from a valid supplier and not vice versa." Do you agree with this statement? Why or why not?
19. Discuss how EDI creates an environment in which sensitive information, such as inventory

amounts and price data, is no longer private. What potential dangers exist if the proper controls are not in place? Give an example.

20. President Clinton wanted to require manufacturers of data encryption software to give the CIA and FBI their decryption algorithms. Do you agree with this type of policy? What are the issues?

21. Give an example of a field that may be used in various processes in the revenue cycle. Explain how a generalized validation module can help to reduce system development time and maintenance time.

22. What types of output would be considered extremely sensitive in a university setting? Give three examples and explain why the information would be considered sensitive. Discuss who should and should not have access to each type of information.

23. Discuss how the printer controls presented in this chapter may break down in personal computing LAN environments where a laser printer is shared.

24. Why is the use of prenumbered source documents important in systems that use paper data input forms?

25. What are the three classes of transcription errors?

26. What is the purpose of a check digit?

27. Does a hash total need to be based on a financial data field? Explain.

28. Discuss the three common methods of handling errors in transaction files.

29. Why is computer waste disposal a potential internal control issue?

Multiple-Choice Questions

1. Hackers can disguise their message packets to look as if they came from an authorized user and gain access to the host's network using a technique called
   a. spoofing.
   b. spooling.
   c. dual-homed.
   d. screening.

2. Transmitting numerous SYN packets to a targeted receiver, but not responding to an ACK, is
   a. a DES message.
   b. the request-response technique.
   c. a denial of service attack.
   d. a call-back device.

3. CMA 685 5-28
   Routines that use the computer to check the validity and accuracy of transaction data during input are called
   a. operating systems.
   b. edit programs.
   c. compiler programs.
   d. integrated test facilities.
   e. compatibility tests.

4. CMA 686 5-10
   An edit of individual transactions in a direct access file processing system usually
   a. takes place in a separate computer run.
   b. takes place in an on-line mode as transactions are entered.
   c. takes place during a backup procedure.
   d. is not performed due to time constraints.
   e. is not necessary.

5. CMA Adapted 686 5-13
   An example of an input control is
   a. making sure that output is distributed to the proper people.
   b. monitoring the work of programmers.
   c. collecting accurate statistics of historical transactions while gathering data.
   d. recalculating an amount to ensure its accuracy.
   e. having another person review the design of a business form.

6. A control designed to validate a transaction at the point of data entry is
   a. recalculation of a batch total.
   b. a record count.
   c. a check digit.
   d. checkpoints.
   e. recalculation of hash total.

7. CMA 687 5-8
   In a manual system, records of current activity are posted from a journal to a ledger. In a computer system, current records from a(n)
   a. table file are updated to a transaction file.

b. index file are updated to a master file.
c. transaction file are updated to a master file.
d. master file are updated to a year-to-date file.
e. current balance file are updated to an index file.

8. CMA 1287 5-1
The primary functions of a computerized information system include
a. input, processing, and output.
b. input, processing, output, and storage.
c. input, processing, output, and control.
d. input, processing, output, storage, and control.
e. collecting, sorting, summarizing, and reporting.

9. CMA 1287 5-16
An employee in the receiving department keyed in a shipment from a remote terminal and inadvertently omitted the purchase order number. The best systems control to detect this error would be a
a. batch total.
b. completeness test.
c. sequence check.
d. reasonableness test.
e. compatibility test.

10. CMA 1287 5-15
In an automated payroll processing environment, a department manager substituted the time card for a terminated employee with a time card for a fictitious employee. The fictitious employee had the same pay rate and hours worked as the terminated employee. The best control technique to detect this action using employee identification numbers would be a
a. batch total.
b. record count.
c. hash total.
d. subsequent check.
e. financial total.

11. CMA 1287 5-17
The reporting of accounting information plays a central role in the regulation of business operations. The importance of sound internal control practices is underscored by the Foreign Corrupt Practices Act of 1977, which requires publicly owned U.S. corporations to maintain systems of internal control that meet certain minimum standards. Preventive controls are an integral part of virtually all accounting processing systems, and much of the information generated by the accounting system is used for preventive control purposes. Which of the following is not an essential element of a sound preventive control system?
a. separation of responsibilities for the recording, custodial, and authorization functions
b. sound personnel practices
c. documentation of policies and procedures
d. implementation of state-of-the-art software and hardware
e. physical protection of assets

Problems

1. **Access Control**
Design a well-controlled system in terms of access controls for a major insurance company that equips each salesperson (life, property, and investments) with a laptop. Each salesperson must transmit sales data daily to corporate headquarters. Further, the salespeople use their laptops to connect to the company's e-mail system.

2. **Input Validation**
Identify the types of input validation techniques for the following inputs to the payroll system. Explain the controls provided by each of these techniques.
a. Operator access number to payroll file

b. Add new employee
c. Employee name
d. Employee number
e. Social Security number
f. Rate per hour or salary
g. Marital status
h. Number of dependents
i. Cost center
j. Regular hours worked
k. Overtime hours worked
l. Total employees this payroll period

3. **Internal Control and Fraud**
Charles Hart, an accounts payable clerk, is an hourly employee. He never works a minute past

5 P.M. unless the overtime has been approved. Charles has recently found himself faced with some severe financial difficulties. He has been accessing the system from his home during the evening and setting up an embezzlement scheme. As his boss, what control technique(s) discussed in this chapter could you use to help detect this type of fraud?

4. Internal Control and Fraud

Stephanie Baskill, an unemployed accounting clerk, lives one block from Cleaver Manufacturing Company. While walking her dog last year, she noticed some material resource planning manuals in the dumpsters. Curious, she took the manuals home with her. She found that the documentation in the manual was dated two months ago, so she thought that the information must be fairly current. Over the next month, Stephanie continued to collect all types of manuals from the dumpster during her dog-walking excursions. Cleaver Manufacturing Company was apparently updating all of its documentation manuals and placing them on-line. Eventually, Stephanie found manuals about critical inventory reorder formulas, the billing system, the sales order system, the payables system, and the operating system. Stephanie went to the local library and read as much as she could about this particular operating system.

To gain access to the organization, she took a low profile position as a cleaning woman. By snooping through offices and guessing at passwords, watching people who were working late type in their passwords, and ultimately printing out lists of user IDs and passwords using a Trojan horse virus, Stephanie was able to obtain all the necessary passwords she needed to set herself up as a supplier, customer, systems operator, and systems librarian. Further, as a cleaning woman, she had access to all areas in the building.

As a customer, she was able to order enough goods so that the inventory procurement system would automatically trigger a need for a purchase of raw materials. Then, as a supplier, Stephanie would stand ready to deliver the goods at the specified price. She then covered her tracks by adjusting the transaction logs once the bills were paid. Stephanie was able to embezzle, on average, $125,000 a month. About 16 months after she

began working at Cleaver, the controller saw her arrive at a very expensive French restaurant one evening, driving a Jaguar. He told the internal auditors to keep a close watch on her, and they were able to catch her in the act.

Required:
a. What weaknesses in the organization's control structure must have existed to permit this type of embezzlement?
b. What specific control techniques and procedures could have helped prevent or detect this fraud?

5. CMA 690 5-1
Internal Control and Fraud

It is estimated that several hundred million dollars are lost annually through computer crime. The first conviction of a computer hacker under the Computer Fraud and Abuse Act of 1986 occurred in 1988. There have been other cases of computer break-ins reported in the news, as well as stories of viruses spreading throughout vital networks. While these cases made the headlines, most experts maintain that the number of computer crimes publicly revealed represents only the tip of the iceberg. Companies have been victims of crimes but have not acknowledged them to avoid adverse publicity and not advertise their vulnerability.

Although the threat to security is seen as external, through outside penetration, the more dangerous threats are of internal origin. Management must recognize these problems and commit to the development and enforcement of security programs to deal with the many types of fraud that computer systems are susceptible to on a daily basis. The primary types of computer systems fraud include (1) input manipulation, (2) program alteration, (3) file alteration, (4) data theft, (5) sabotage, and (6) theft of computer time.

Required:
For the six types of fraud identified above, explain how each is committed. Also, identify a different method of protection against each type of fraud and describe how it operates. The same protection method should not be used for more than one type of fraud; that is, six different methods must be identified and described. Use the following format.

Type of Fraud	Explanation	Description of Protection Methods
a.		
b.		
c.		
d.		
e.		
f.		

6. CMA 1290 4-3
Internal Control and End-User Computing

The National Commercial Bank has 15 branches and maintains a mainframe computer system at its corporate headquarters. National has recently undergone an examination by the state banking examiners, and the examiners have some concerns about National's computer operations.

During the last few years, each branch has purchased a number of microcomputers to communicate with the mainframe in the emulation mode. Emulation occurs when a microcomputer attaches to a mainframe computer and, with the use of the appropriate software, can act as if it is one of the mainframe terminals. The branch also uses these microcomputers to download information from the mainframe and, in the local mode, manipulate customer data to make banking decisions at the branch level. Each microcomputer is initially supplied with a word processing application package to formulate correspondence to the customers, a spreadsheet package to perform credit and financial loan analyses beyond the basic credit analysis package on the mainframe, and a database management package to formulate customer market and sensitivity information. National's centralized data processing department is responsible only for mainframe operations; microcomputer security is the responsibility of each branch.

Because the bank examiners believe National is at risk, they have advised the bank to review the recommendations suggested in a letter issued by banking regulatory agencies in 1988. This letter emphasizes the risks associated with end-user operations and encourages banking management to establish sound control policies. More specifically, microcomputer end-user operations have outpaced the implementation of adequate controls and have taken processing control out of the centralized environment, introducing vulnerability in new areas of the bank.

The letter also emphasizes that the responsibility for corporate policies identifying management control practices for all areas of information processing activities resides with the board of directors. The existence, adequacy, and compliance with these policies and practices will be part of the regular banking examiners' review. The three required control groups for adequate information system security as they relate to National are (1) processing controls, (2) physical and environmental controls, and (3) spreadsheet program development controls.

Required:

For each of the three control groups listed:
a. Identify three types of controls for microcomputer end-user operations where National Commercial Bank might be at risk, and
b. Recommend a specific control procedure that National should implement for each type of control you identified. Use the following format for your answer.

Control Types	Recommended Procedures

7. CMA 691 4-2
Processing Controls
Internal Control

Unless adequate controls are implemented, the rapid advance of computer technology can reduce a firm's ability to detect errors and fraud. Therefore, one of the critical responsibilities of the management team in firms where computers are used is the security and control of information service activities.

During the design state of a system, information system controls are planned to ensure the reliability of data. A well-designed system can prevent both intentional and unintentional alteration or destruction of data. These data controls can be classified as (1) input controls, (2) processing controls, (3) output controls, and (4) storage controls.

Required:

For each of the four data control categories listed, provide two specific controls and explain how each control contributes to ensuring the reliability of data. Use the following format for your answer.

Control Category	Specific Controls	Contribution to Data Reliability

8. Input Controls and Data Processing

You have been hired by a catalog company to computerize its sales order entry forms. Approximately 60 percent of all orders are received over the telephone, with the remainder either mailed or faxed in. The company wants the phone orders to be input as they are received. The mail and fax orders can be batched together in groups of 50 and submitted for keypunching as they become ready. The following information is collected for each order:

- Customer number (if customer does not have one, one needs to be assigned)
- Customer name
- Address
- Payment method (credit card or money order)
- Credit card number and expiration date (if necessary)
- Items ordered and quantity
- Unit price

Required:

Determine control techniques to make sure that all orders are entered accurately into the system. Also, discuss any differences in control measures between the batch and the real-time processing.

9. CMA 686 5-2
Input Controls and Telecommunications

Intex Corporation is a multinational company with approximately 100 subsidiaries and divisions, referred to as reporting units. Each reporting unit operates autonomously and maintains its own accounting information system. Each month, the reporting units prepare the basic financial statements and other key financial data on prescribed forms. These statements and related data are either mailed or telexed to corporate headquarters in New York City for entry into the corporate database. Top and middle management at corporate headquarters use the database to plan and direct corporate operations and objectives.

Under the current system, the statements and data are to be received at corporate headquarters by the twelfth working day following the end of the month. The reports are logged, batched, and taken to the data processing department for coding and entry into the database. Approximately 15 percent of the reporting units are delinquent in submitting their data, and three to four days are required to receive all of the data. After the data are loaded into the system, data verification programs are run to check footings, cross-statement consistency, and dollar range limits. Any errors in the data are traced and corrected, and reporting units are notified of all errors by form letters.

Intex Corporation has decided to upgrade its computer communications network. The new system would allow a more timely receipt of data at corporate headquarters and would provide numerous benefits to each of the reporting units.

The systems department at corporate headquarters is responsible for the overall design and implementation of the new system. It will use current computer communications technology by installing smart computer terminals at all reporting units. These terminals will provide two-way computer communications and serve as microcomputers that can use spreadsheet and other applications software. As part of the initial use of the system, the data collection for the corporate database would be performed through these terminals.

The financial statements and other financial data currently mailed or telexed would be entered by terminals. The required forms would initially be transmitted (downloaded) from the headquarters computer to the terminals of each reporting unit and stored permanently on disk. Data would be entered on the forms appearing on the reporting unit's terminal and stored under a separate file for transmission after the data are checked.

The data edit program would also be downloaded to the reporting units so the data could be verified at the unit location. All corrections would be made before transmitting the data to headquarters. The data would be stored on disk in proper format to maintain a unit file. Data would either be transmitted to corporate headquarters immediately or retrieved by the computer at corporate headquarters as needed. Therefore, data arriving at corporate headquarters would be free from errors and ready to be used in reports.

Charles Edwards, Intex's controller, is very pleased with the prospects of the new system. He believes that the data will be received from the reporting units two to three days faster and that data accuracy will be much improved. However, Edwards is concerned about data security and integrity during the transmission of data between the reporting units and corporate headquarters. He has scheduled a meeting with key personnel from the systems department to discuss these concerns.

Required:
Intex could experience data security and integrity problems when transmitting data between the reporting units and corporate headquarters.
a. Identify and explain the data security and integrity problems that could occur.
b. For each problem identified, identify and explain a control procedure that could be employed to minimize or eliminate the problem. Use the following format to present your answer.

Problem Identification and Explanation	Control Procedure and Explanation

10. Preventive Controls

Listed below are five scenarios. For each scenario, discuss the possible damages that can occur. Suggest a preventive control.
a. An intruder taps into a telecommunications device and retrieves the identifying codes and personal identification numbers for ATM cardholders. (The user subsequently codes this information onto a magnetic coding device and places this strip on a piece of cardboard.)

b. Due to occasional noise on a transmission line, electronic messages received are extremely garbled.
c. Due to occasional noise on a transmission line, data being transferred is lost or garbled.
d. Important strategic messages are being temporarily delayed by an intruder over the telecommunications lines.
e. Electronic messages are being altered by an intruder before being received by the user.

11. Internal Control and End-User Computing

Until a year ago, Dagwood Printing Company had always operated in a centralized computer environment. Now, 75 percent of the office employees have a PC. Users have been able to choose their own software packages, and no documentation of end-user-developed applications has been required. Next month, each PC will be linked into a LAN and to the company's mainframe.

Required:
a. Outline a plan of action for Dagwood Printing Company to ensure that the proper controls over hardware, software, data, people, procedures, and documentation are in place.
b. Discuss any exposures the company may face if the above plan is not implemented.

CHAPTER

17

Information Systems Auditing and Assurance

Recent developments in information technology (IT) have had a tremendous impact on the field of auditing. In this text we have seen how IT has inspired the reengineering of traditional business processes to promote more efficient operations and to improve communications within the entity and between the entity and its customers and suppliers. These advances, however, have introduced new risks that require unique internal controls. They have engendered the need for new techniques for evaluating controls and for assuring the security and accuracy of corporate data and the information systems that produce it.

This chapter presents an overview of computer auditing. It begins with a discussion of alternative audit approaches and presents the general structure of an audit. It then reviews audit objectives and procedures used to test controls related to the general areas of risk that were discussed in Chapters 15 and 16. Finally, it examines audit objectives and methods used to perform tests of controls and substantive tests related to specific applications.

LEARNING OBJECTIVES

After studying this chapter, you should:

- Understand the general purpose of an audit and have a firm grasp of the basic conceptual elements of the audit process.
- Know the difference between internal and external auditing and be able to explain the relationship between these two types of auditing.
- Understand how auditing objectives and tests of control are determined by the control structure of the firm that is being audited.
- Be familiar with the audit objective and tests of control for each of the nine general control areas.
- Understand the auditing techniques that are used to verify the effective functioning of application controls.
- Understand the auditing techniques used to perform substantive tests in a CBIS environment.

ATTEST SERVICES VERSUS ASSURANCE SERVICES

An important starting point for this body of material is to draw a distinction between the auditor's traditional attestation function and the emerging field of assurance services. The attest service is defined as:

> an engagement in which a practitioner is engaged to issue, or does issue, a written communication that expresses a conclusion about the reliability of a written assertion that is the responsibility of another party. (SSAE No. 1, AT Section 100.01)

The following requirements apply to attestation services:

- Attestation services require written assertions and a practitioner's written report.
- Attestation services require the formal establishment of measurement criteria or their description in the presentation.
- The levels of service in attestation engagements are limited to examination, review, and application of agreed-upon procedures.

Assurance services constitute a broader concept that encompasses, but is not limited to, attestation. The relationship between these services is illustrated in Figure 17–1.

Assurance services are professional services that are designed to improve the quality of information, both financial and nonfinancial, used by decision makers. The domain of assurance services is intentionally unbounded so that it does not inhibit the growth of future services that are currently unforeseen. For example, assurance services may be contracted to provide information about the quality or marketability of a product. Alternatively, a client may need information about the efficiency of a production process or the effectiveness of its network security system. Assurance services are intended to help people make better decisions by improving information. This information may come as a by-product of the attest function, or it may ensue from an independently motivated review.

The evolution of the accounting profession is expected to follow the assurance services model. All of the Big Five professional services firms have now renamed their traditional audit functions "Assurance Services." The organizational unit responsible

---

FIGURE 17–1

Relationship between Assurance Services and Attest Services

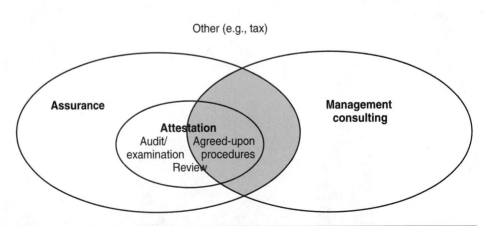

SOURCE: Based on the AICPA *Special Committee Report on Assurance Services.*

for conducting IT audits is named either *IT Risk Management*, *Information Systems Risk Management*, or *Operational Systems Risk Management (OSRM)* and typically is a division of assurance services.

The material outlined in this chapter relates to tasks normally conducted by OSRM professionals while performing an IT audit. In the pages that follow we examine what constitutes an audit, who performs audits, and how audits are structured. Keep in mind, however, that in many cases the purpose of the audit task, rather than the task itself, defines the service being rendered. Therefore, the issues and procedures described in this text apply to the broader context of assurance services, which include, but are not limited to, attest services. They also relate directly to the internal audit function.

What Is a Financial Audit?

A financial audit is an independent attestation performed by an expert—the auditor—who expresses an opinion regarding the presentation of financial statements. The auditor's role is similar in concept to a judge who collects and evaluates evidence and renders an opinion. A key concept in this process is *independence*. The judge must remain independent in his or her deliberations. The judge cannot be an advocate of either party in the trial, but must apply the law impartially based on the evidence presented. Likewise, the independent auditor collects and evaluates evidence and renders an opinion based on the evidence. Throughout the audit process, the auditor must maintain his or her independence from the client organization. Public confidence in the reliability of the company's internally produced financial statements rests directly on the statements being evaluated by an independent expert auditor.

The public expression of the auditor's opinion is the culmination of a systematic audit process that involves three conceptual phases: (1) familiarization with the organization's business, (2) evaluating and testing internal controls, and (3) assessing the reliability of financial data. The specific elements of the audit process are examined later in this section.

Auditing Standards

The product of the attestation function is a formal written report that expresses an opinion about the reliability of the assertions contained in the financial statements. The auditor's report expresses an opinion as to whether the financial statements are in conformity with *generally accepted accounting principles*. External users of financial statements are presumed to rely on the auditor's opinion about the reliability of financial statements in making decisions. To do so, users must be able to place their trust in the auditor's competence, professionalism, integrity, and independence. Auditors are guided in their professional responsibility by the ten *generally accepted auditing standards (GAAS)* presented in Table 17–1.

Auditing standards are divided into three classes: general qualification standards, field work standards, and reporting standards. GAAS establishes a framework for prescribing auditor performance, but it is not sufficiently detailed to provide meaningful guidance in specific circumstances. To provide specific guidance, the American Institute of Certified Public Accountants (AICPA) issues *Statements on Auditing Standards (SASs)* as authoritative interpretations of GAAS. SASs are often referred to as *auditing standards*, or *GAAS*, although they are not the ten generally accepted auditing standards.

Statements on Auditing Standards

The first SAS (SAS 1) was issued by the AICPA in 1972. Since then, many SASs have been issued to provide auditors with guidance on a spectrum of topics, including

TABLE 17–1	**Generally Accepted Auditing Standards**

General Standards	Standards of Field Work	Reporting Standards
1. The auditor must have adequate technical training and proficiency.	1. Audit work must be adequately planned.	1. The auditor must state in the report whether financial statements were prepared in accordance with generally accepted accounting principles.
2. The auditor must have independence of mental attitude.	2. The auditor must gain a sufficient understanding of the internal control structure.	2. The report must identify those circumstances in which generally accepted accounting principles were not applied.
3. The auditor must exercise due professional care in the performance of the audit and the preparation of the report.	3. The auditor must obtain sufficient, competent evidence.	3. The report must identify any items that do not have adequate informative disclosures.
		4. The report shall contain an expression of the auditor's opinion on the financial statements as a whole.

methods of investigating new clients, procedures for collecting information from attorneys regarding contingent liability claims against clients, and techniques for obtaining background information on the client's industry.

Statements on auditing standards are regarded as authoritative pronouncements because every member of the profession must follow their recommendations or be able to show why an SAS does not apply in a given situation. The burden of justifying departures from SAS falls upon the individual auditor.

EXTERNAL AUDITING VERSUS INTERNAL AUDITING

External auditing is often called **independent auditing** because it is done by certified public accountants who are independent of the organization being audited. External auditors represent the interests of third-party stakeholders in the organization, such as stockholders, creditors, and government agencies. Because the focus of the external audit is on the financial statements, this type of audit is called a *financial audit*.

The Institute of Internal Auditors defines **internal auditing** as an independent appraisal function established within an organization to examine and evaluate its activities as a service to the organization.[1] Internal auditors perform a wide range of activities on behalf of the organization, including conducting financial audits, examining an operation's compliance with organizational policies, reviewing the organization's compliance with legal obligations, evaluating operational efficiency, detecting and pursuing fraud within the firm, and conducting IT audits.

The characteristic that conceptually distinguishes internal auditors from external auditors is their respective constituencies: external auditors represent outsiders, and

---

1   Institute of Internal Auditors, Standards of Professional Practice of Internal Auditing (Orlando, Fla.: Institute of Internal Auditors, 1978).

internal auditors represent the interests of the organization. Nevertheless, in this capacity, internal auditors often cooperate with and assist external auditors in performing financial audits. This is done to achieve audit efficiency and reduce audit fees. For example, a team of internal auditors can perform tests of computer controls under the supervision of a single external auditor.

The independence and competence of the internal audit staff determine the extent to which external auditors may cooperate with and rely on work performed by internal auditors. Some internal audit departments report directly to the controller. Under this arrangement, the internal auditor's independence is compromised, and the external auditor is prohibited by professional standards from relying on evidence provided by the internal auditors. In contrast, external auditors can rely in part on evidence gathered by internal audit departments that are organizationally independent and that report to the board of directors' audit committee. A truly independent internal audit staff adds value to the audit process. Internal auditors can gather audit evidence throughout a fiscal period; external auditors can then use this evidence at year end to conduct more efficient, less disruptive, and less costly audits of the organization's financial statements.

WHAT IS AN INFORMATION TECHNOLOGY (IT) AUDIT?

An IT audit focuses on the computer-based aspects of an organization's information system. This includes assessing the proper implementation, operation, and control of computer resources. Since most modern information systems employ information technology, the IT audit is typically a significant component of all external (financial) and internal audits.

The Elements of Auditing

To this point, we have painted a broad picture of auditing. Let's now fill in some details. The following definition of auditing is applicable to external auditing, internal auditing, and IT auditing:

> Auditing is a systematic process of objectively obtaining and evaluating evidence regarding assertions about economic actions and events to ascertain the degree of correspondence between those assertions and established criteria and communicating the results to interested users.[2]

This seemingly obtuse definition contains several important points that are examined below.

A Systematic Process. Conducting an audit is a systematic and logical process that applies to all forms of information systems. While important in all audit settings, a systematic approach is particularly important in the IT environment. The lack of physical procedures that can be visually verified and evaluated injects a high degree of complexity into the IT audit. Therefore, a logical framework for conducting an audit in the IT environment is critical to help the auditor identify important processes and data files.

Management Assertions and Audit Objectives. The organization's financial statements reflect a set of **management assertions** about the financial health of the

---

2   AAA Committee on Basic Auditing Concepts, "A Statement of Basic Auditing Concepts," *Accounting Review,* supplement to vol. 47, 1972.

entity. The task of the auditor is to determine whether the financial statements are fairly presented. To accomplish this, the auditor establishes **audit objectives**, designs procedures, and gathers evidence that corroborate or refute management's assertions. These assertions fall into five general categories:

- The **existence or occurrence** assertion affirms that all assets and equities contained in the balance sheet exist and that all transactions in the income statement actually occurred.
- The **completeness** assertion declares that no material assets, equities, or transactions have been omitted from the financial statements.
- The **rights and obligations** assertion maintains that assets appearing on the balance sheet are owned by the entity and that the liabilities reported are obligations.
- The **valuation or allocation** assertion states that assets and equities are valued in accordance with generally accepted accounting principles and that allocated amounts such as depreciation expense are calculated on a systematic and rational basis.
- The **presentation and disclosure** assertion alleges that financial statement items are correctly classified (e.g., long-term liabilities will not mature within one year) and that footnote disclosures are adequate to avoid misleading the users of financial statements.

Generally, auditors develop their audit objectives and design **audit procedures** based on the preceding assertions. The example in Table 17–2 outlines these procedures.

Audit objectives may be classified into two general categories. Those in Table 17–2 relate to transactions and account balances that directly impact financial reporting. The second category pertains to the information system itself. This includes the audit objectives for assessing controls over manual operations and computer technologies used in transaction processing. Both categories of audit objectives and the associated audit procedures are discussed later in the chapter.

Obtaining Evidence. Auditors seek evidential matter that corroborates management assertions. In the IT environment, this involves gathering evidence relating to the reliability of computer controls as well as the contents of databases that have been processed by computer programs. Evidence is collected by performing tests of controls, which establish whether internal controls are functioning properly, and substantive tests, which determine whether accounting databases fairly reflect the organization's transactions and account balances.

Ascertaining the Degree of Correspondence with Established Criteria. The auditor must determine whether weaknesses in internal controls and misstatements found in transactions and account balances are material. In all audit environments, assessing *materiality* is an auditor judgment. In an IT environment, however, this decision is complicated further by technology and a sophisticated internal control structure.

Communicating Results. Auditors must communicate the results of their tests to interested users. Independent auditors render a report to the audit committee of the board of directors or stockholders of a company. The audit report contains, among other things, an **audit opinion**. This opinion is distributed along with the financial report to interested parties both internal and external to the organization. IT auditors often communicate their findings to internal and external auditors, who can then integrate these findings with the non-IT aspects of the audit.

TABLE 17–2	**Audit Objectives and Audit Procedures Based on Management Assertions**	

Management Assertion	Audit Objective	Audit Procedure
Existence or Occurrence	Inventories listed on the balance sheet exist.	Observe the counting of physical inventory.
Completeness	Accounts payable include all obligations to vendors for the period.	Compare receiving reports, supplier invoices, purchase orders, and journal entries for the period and the beginning of the next period.
Rights and Obligations	Plant and equipment listed in the balance sheet are owned by the entity.	Review purchase agreements, insurance policies, and related documents.
Valuation or Allocation	Accounts receivable are stated at net realizable value.	Review entity's aging of accounts and evaluate the adequacy of the allowance for uncorrectable accounts.
Presentation and Disclosure	Contingencies not reported in financial accounts are properly disclosed in footnotes.	Obtain information from entity lawyers about the status of litigation and estimates of potential loss.

THE STRUCTURE OF AN IT AUDIT

The IT audit is generally divided into three phases: audit planning, tests of controls, and substantive testing. Figure 17–2 illustrates the steps involved in these phases.

Audit Planning

The first step in the IT audit is **audit planning**. Before the auditor can determine the nature and extent of the tests to perform, he or she must gain a thorough understanding of the client's business. A major part of this phase of the audit is the analysis of audit risk (discussed later). The objective of the auditor is to obtain sufficient information about the firm to plan the other phases of the audit. The risk analysis incorporates an overview of the organization's internal controls. During the review of controls, the auditor attempts to understand the organization's policies, practices, and structure. In this phase of the audit, the auditor also identifies the financially significant applications and attempts to understand the controls over the primary transactions that are processed by these applications.

The techniques for gathering evidence at this phase include questionnaires, interviewing management, reviewing systems documentation, and observing activities. During this process, the IT auditor must identify the principal exposures and the controls that attempt to reduce these exposures. Having done so, the auditor proceeds to the next phase, where he or she tests the controls for compliance with preestablished standards.

Tests of Controls

The objective of the **tests of controls** phase is to determine whether adequate internal controls are in place and functioning properly. To accomplish this, the auditor

FIGURE 17–2

FIGURE 17–2

Phases of an IT Audit

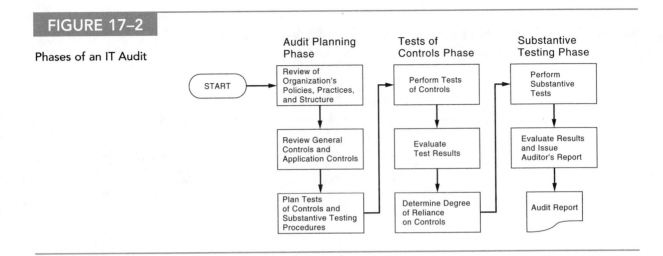

performs various tests of controls. The evidence-gathering techniques used in this phase may include both manual techniques and specialized computer audit techniques. Several such methods are examined later in this text.

At the conclusion of the tests of controls phase, the auditor must assess the quality of the internal controls. The degree of reliance the auditor can ascribe to internal controls affects the nature and extent of substantive testing. The relationship between tests of controls and substantive tests is discussed later.

Substantive Testing

The third phase of the audit process focuses on financial data. This involves a detailed investigation of specific account balances and transactions through what are called **substantive tests**. For example, a customer confirmation is a substantive test sometimes used to verify account balances. The auditor selects a sample of accounts receivable balances and traces these back to their source—the customers—to determine if the amount stated is in fact owed by a bona fide customer. By so doing, the auditor can verify the accuracy of each account in the sample. Based on such sample findings, the auditor is able to draw conclusions about the fair value of the entire accounts receivable asset.

Some substantive tests are physical, labor-intensive activities such as counting cash, counting inventories in the warehouse, and verifying the existence of stock certificates in a safe. In an IT environment, the information needed to perform substantive tests (such as account balances and names and addresses of individual customers) is contained in data files that often must be extracted using computer-assisted audit tools and techniques (CAATTs) software. The role of CAATTs in performing traditional substantive tests is examined later in the chapter.

ASSESSING AUDIT RISK AND DESIGNING TESTS OF CONTROLS

Audit risk is the probability that the auditor will render an unqualified (clean) opinion on financial statements that are, in fact, materially misstated. Material misstatements may be caused by errors or irregularities or both. Errors are unintentional mistakes. Irregularities are intentional misrepresentations to perpetrate a fraud or to mislead the users of financial statements. The auditor's objective is to minimize audit risk by performing tests of controls and substantive tests.

AUDIT RISK COMPONENTS

The three components of audit risk are inherent risk, control risk, and detection risk.

Inherent Risk

Inherent risk is associated with the unique characteristics of the business or industry of the client.[3] Firms in declining industries have greater inherent risk than firms in stable or thriving industries. Auditors cannot reduce the level of inherent risk. Even in a system protected by excellent controls, financial data and, consequently, financial statements can be materially misstated.

To illustrate inherent risk, assume that the audit client's financial statements show an accounts receivable balance of $10 million. Unknown to the auditor and the client, several customers with accounts receivable totalling $2 million are about to go out of business. These accounts, which are a material component of the total accounts receivable balance of $10 million, are not likely to be collected. To represent these accounts as an asset in the financial statements would be a material misstatement of the firm's economic position.

Control Risk

Control risk is the likelihood that the control structure is flawed because controls are either absent or inadequate to prevent or detect errors in the accounts.[4] To illustrate control risk, consider the following partial customer sales record, which is processed by the sales order system.

Quantity	Unit Price	Total
10 Units	$20	$2,000

Assuming the Quantity and Unit Price fields in the record are correctly presented, then the extended amount (Total) value of $2,000 is in error. An AIS with adequate controls should prevent or detect such an error. If, however, controls are lacking and the value of Total in each record is not validated before processing, then the risk of undetected errors entering the data files increases.

Auditors reduce the level of control risk by performing tests of internal controls. In the preceding example, the auditor could create test transactions, including some with incorrect Total values, which are processed by the application in a test run. The results of the test will indicate that price extension errors are not detected and are being incorrectly posted to the accounts receivable file.

Detection Risk

Detection risk is the risk that auditors are willing to take that errors not detected or prevented by the control structure will also not be detected by the auditor.[5] Auditors set an acceptable level of detection risk (planned detection risk) that influences the level of substantive tests that they perform. For example, more substantive testing would be required when the planned detection risk is 1 percent than when it is 5 percent.

---

3   Auditing Standards Board, AICPA Professional Standards (New York: AICPA), 1994 AU Section 312.20.
4   *Ibid.*
5   *Ibid.*

Tests of controls and substantive tests are auditing techniques used for reducing total audit risk. The relationship between tests of controls and substantive tests varies according to the auditor's risk assessment of the organization. The stronger the internal control structure, the lower the control risk and the less substantive testing the auditor must do. This is because the likelihood of errors in the accounting records is reduced. In other words, when controls are strong, the auditor may limit substantive testing. However, the weaker the internal control structure, the greater the control risk and the more substantive testing the auditor must perform to reduce total audit risk. Evidence of weak controls forces the auditor to extend substantive testing to search for misstatements in financial data caused by control errors as well as business problems inherent to the organization.

Because substantive tests are labor-intensive and time-consuming, they are expensive. Increased substantive testing translates into longer and more disruptive audits and higher audit costs. Thus, management's best interests are served by having a strong internal control structure.

TESTS OF GENERAL CONTROLS

This section examines auditing procedures used for verifying the adequacy of general controls. Our primary purposes are to understand (1) the auditing objectives in each general control area and (2) the nature of the tests that auditors perform to achieve these objectives. The discussion is organized around the following auditing areas:

1. Operating system controls
2. Data management controls
3. Organizational structure controls
4. Systems development controls
5. Systems maintenance controls
6. Computer center security and controls
7. Internet and Intranet controls
8. Electronic data interchange controls
9. Personal computer controls

These auditing areas should look familiar because they correspond to the general control areas discussed in Chapters 15 and 16. The auditing of application controls is a distinct issue and will be treated separately in the next section.

The introductory discussion of basic auditing concepts has indicated that the auditing objective for any given firm will be determined by that firm's control structure. That is to say, one aim of the auditing process is to ascertain whether a firm's **control objectives** are being achieved; toward this end, tests of controls are performed to determine whether specific control techniques are in place and properly functioning. Given this essential relationship between the auditing process and the firm's internal control structure, the ensuing discussion of EDP auditing will presuppose familiarity with the control issues covered in Chapters 15 and 16. Key points from this body of material are summarized in Table 17–3. If you are unclear about any of these exposures and controls, you should go back to these earlier chapters and review the material.

Before determining the kinds of evidence to be gathered in the review of internal controls, the auditor needs to identify the appropriate audit objectives. Audit objectives follow from two kinds of knowledge acquired in the risk analysis phase of the audit:

TABLE 17–3	**Summary of CBIS Exposures and Controls**		
	Area of Risk	**Nature of Exposure**	**Control Techniques**
	1. Operating System	Accidental and intentional threat, including attempts to access data illegally, violate user privacy, or perform malicious acts.	Access privilege control, password control, virus control, audit trail control, and fault tolerance control
	2. Data Management	Inadequate backup of data and unauthorized access to data by authorized and unauthorized personnel.	BACKUP CONTROL: Grandparent-parent-child backup procedures, direct access file backup, and database backup and recovery procedures. ACCESS CONTROLS: Subschemas, passwords, authorization rules, user-defined procedures, encryption, biometric devices, and inference controls.
	3. Organizational Structure	Programmers and operators who perform incompatible functions may perpetrate program fraud. Documentation standards may be inadequate to support audit tasks. Data files in tape libraries are subject to loss, destruction, and illegal access.	The functions of programming, computer operations, tape librarian, and database administrator should be organizationally segregated.
	4. Systems Development	The development of unauthorized projects resulting in the misapplication of financial resources. Projects are improperly prioritized, resulting in inefficient allocation of resources. Newly implemented systems contain material errors, fraud, or fail to meet user needs. Poor-quality systems documentation impedes audit and maintenance activities.	Systems authorizations, user specification activities, technical design activities, internal audit participation, program testing, and user test and acceptance procedures.
	5. Systems Maintenance	Unauthorized changes can result in program errors, fraud, incorrect information presented in financial statements and to users, systems failures, and severe disruptions to operations.	Program maintenance authorizations, user involvement, technical specifications, program testing, documentation, and source program library software control.
	6. Computer Center	Loss and theft of physical equipment and system disruption caused by software failure, hardware failure, power outrages, and physical disasters.	Physical construction, location, limited access to computer facilities, air conditioning, backup power supply, and disaster recovery planning.

(continued)

TABLE 17–3   *(continued)*

Area of Risk	Nature of Exposure	Control Techniques
7. Internet and Intranet	Loss, destruction, and corruption of data from equipment failure and subversive activities from inside the organization and via the Internet.	CONTROLLING EQUIPMENT FAILURE: Parity checks, echo checks, and backup. CONTROLLING SUBVERSIVE THREATS: Access controls, message encryption, digital signatures, digital certificates and firewalls. MESSAGE CONTROL: Sequence numbering, authentication codes, transaction log, request-response polling.
8. Electronic Data Interchange	Processing of unauthorized, invalid, and illegal transactions. Illegal access by trading partners to databases. Absence of source documents disrupts the traditional audit trail, which inhibits the auditor's ability to verify the completeness and accuracy of transactions.	Authorization and validation controls, access controls, and audit trail controls implemented at various points within the trading partners' systems and at the VAN.
9. Personal Computers	Financial loss from program errors and fraud because of inadequate segregation of functions. Destruction and corruption of data due to uncontrolled access to files and hardware failures. Inadequate data backup and recovery features.	Organization controls, access controls, backup controls, systems selection and acquisition controls, disk locks, encryption, multilevel password.

1. An understanding of exposures that threaten the organization's activities.
2. An understanding of the existing internal control structure.[6]

A complete treatment of this topic is beyond the scope of this chapter. For purposes of conceptual clarity, however, it will be useful to keep in mind the general relationship between risks, controls, audit objectives, and audit procedures. This relationship is illustrated below, using the data management category from Table 17–3 as an example.

- *Risk:* The intentional destruction, corruption, or theft of data by an unauthorized user or by an authorized user who has exceeded his or her access privileges.

6   L. F. Konrath, *Auditing Concepts and Applications: A Risk Analysis Approach* (St. Paul: West Publishing, 1993): 107.

- *Control:* Access privileges to the database are controlled by an authority table.
- *Audit objective:* To verify that users are allowed to access only the data that they need to perform their authorized tasks.
- *Audit procedure:* Choose a sample of users and verify that their access privileges as stated in the authorization table are consistent with their organizational functions.

A many-to-many relationship exists between risks and controls. A single risk may require many controls, and a single control technique may reduce many forms of risk. The risks and control techniques relating to the nine categories of general controls were examined at length in Chapters 15 and 16. Corresponding audit objectives and audit procedures are addressed in the next section. If you are uncertain about the nature of the risks and control techniques related to any of the audit areas, please review the appropriate sections in Chapters 15 and 16.

TESTING OPERATING SYSTEM CONTROLS

We learned in Chapter 15 that the **operating system** is the computer's control program. It allows users and their applications to share and access common computer resources, such as processors, main memory, databases, and printers. If operating system integrity is compromised, controls within individual accounting applications may also be circumvented or neutralized. Because the operating system is common to all users, the larger the computer facility, the greater the scale of potential damage. The following areas of operating system control are examined in this section: *access privileges, password policy, virus control, audit trail control,* and *fault tolerance.*

Audit Objectives Relating to Access Privileges
The objective of the auditor is to verify that access privileges are granted in a manner that is consistent with the need to separate incompatible functions and is in accordance with organizational policy.

Audit Procedures Relating to Access Privileges
- Review the organization's policies for separating incompatible functions and ensure that they promote reasonable security.
- Review the privileges of a selection of user groups and individuals to determine if their access rights are appropriate for their job descriptions and positions. The auditor should verify that individuals are granted access to data and programs based on their need to know.
- Review personnel records to determine whether privileged employees undergo an adequately intensive security clearance check in compliance with company policy.
- Review employee records to determine whether users have formally acknowledged their responsibility to maintain the confidentiality of company data.
- Review the users' permitted log-on times. Permission should be commensurate with the tasks being performed.

Audit Objectives Relating to Passwords
The auditor's objective here is to ensure that the organization has an adequate and effective password policy for controlling access to the operating system.

Audit Procedures Relating to Passwords
- Verify that all users are required to have passwords.
- Verify that new users are instructed in the use of passwords and the importance of password control.

- Determine that procedures are in place to identify weak passwords. This may involve the use of software for scanning password files on a regular basis.
- Assess the adequacy of password standards such as length and expiration interval.
- Review the account lockout policy and procedures. Most operating systems allow the system administrator to define the action to be taken after a certain number of failed log-on attempts. The auditor should determine how many failed log-on attempts are allowed before the account is locked. The duration of the lockout also needs to be determined. This could range from a few minutes to a permanent lockout that requires formal reactivation of the account.

Audit Objective Relating to Viruses and Other Destructive Programs

The key to computer virus control is prevention through strict adherence to organizational policies and procedures that guard against virus infection. The auditor's objective is to verify that effective management policies and procedures are in place to prevent the introduction and spread of destructive programs, including viruses, worms, back doors, logic bombs, and Trojan horses.

Audit Procedures Relating to Viruses and Other Destructive Programs

- Through interviews, determine that operations personnel have been educated about computer viruses and are aware of the risky computing practices that can introduce and spread viruses and other malicious programs.
- Review operations procedures to determine if floppy disks are routinely used to transfer data between workgroups.
- Verify that system administrators routinely scan workstations and file servers for viruses.
- Verify that new software is tested on stand-alone workstations prior to being implemented on the host or network server.
- Verify that the current version of antiviral software is installed on the server and that upgrades are regularly downloaded to workstations.

Audit Objectives Relating to Automated Audit Trails

Audit trails are logs that can be designed to record activity at the system, application, and user level. When properly implemented, they can support security objectives in three ways: (1) detecting unauthorized access to the system, (2) facilitating the reconstruction of events, and (3) promoting personal accountability.

The auditor's objective is to ensure that the auditing of users and events is adequate for preventing and detecting abuses, reconstructing key events that preceded systems failures, and planning resource allocation.

Audit Procedures Relating to Automated Audit Trails

Most operating systems provide some form of audit manager function to specify the events that are to be audited. The auditor should verify that the event audit trail has been activated according to organizational policy.

- Many operating systems provide an audit log viewer that allows the auditor to scan the log for unusual activity. These can be reviewed on screen or by archiving the file for subsequent review. The auditor can use general-purpose data extraction tools for accessing archived log files to search for defined conditions such as:
  - Unauthorized or terminated user
  - Periods of inactivity

- Activity by user, workgroup, or department
- Log-on and log-off times
- Failed log-on attempts
- Access to specific files or applications
- The organization's security group has the responsibility to monitor and report on security violations. The auditor should select a sample of security violation cases and evaluate their disposition to assess the effectiveness of the security group.

Audit Objectives Relating to Fault Tolerance

Fault tolerance is the ability of the system to continue operation when part of the system fails due to hardware failure, application program error, or operator error. Various levels of fault tolerance can be achieved by implementing redundant system components. The auditor's objective is to ensure that the organization is employing an appropriate level of fault tolerance.

Audit Procedures Relating to Fault Tolerance

- Most systems that employ redundant arrays of inexpensive disks (RAID) provide a graphical mapping of their redundant disk storage. From this mapping, the auditor should determine if the level of RAID in place is adequate for the organization, given the level of business risk associated with disk failure.
- If the organization is not employing RAID, the potential for a single point of system failure exists. The auditor should review with the system administrator alternative procedures for recovering from a disk failure.
- Determine that copies of boot disks have been made for each server on the network in the event of a boot sector failure. Since boot disks can be used to bypass the normal boot process, they should be secured and access to them restricted to the system administrator.

TESTING DATA MANAGEMENT CONTROLS

The auditor's responsibility for reviewing data management controls includes controls in both the flat file and database environment. These environments differ in their data management techniques and controls. In the flat file environment, users own their data exclusively and do not share this resource with other users. In the database environment, data sharing is the fundamental objective. Each of these approaches has unique exposures and requires specific control techniques. Figure 17–3 illustrates backup techniques commonly found in both approaches.

Diagram A shows the grandparent-parent-child (GPC) technique for sequential files, Diagram B illustrates backup where direct access files are used, and Diagram C shows database backup and recovery procedures. The ensuing discussion covers control objectives and tests of controls relevant to both the flat file and database environments.

Audit Objectives Relating to Data Management

The auditor's objective is to verify that controls over data management are sufficient to preserve the integrity and physical security of the database. This general objective translates into three specific objectives around which the auditor can design procedures. These are (1) that backup of data files is adequate to facilitate the recovery of lost, destroyed, or corrupted data; (2) that individuals who are authorized to use the database are limited to accessing only the data needed to perform their duties; and (3) that individuals who are unauthorized are denied access to the database.

FIGURE 17–3	Data Resource Backup Techniques

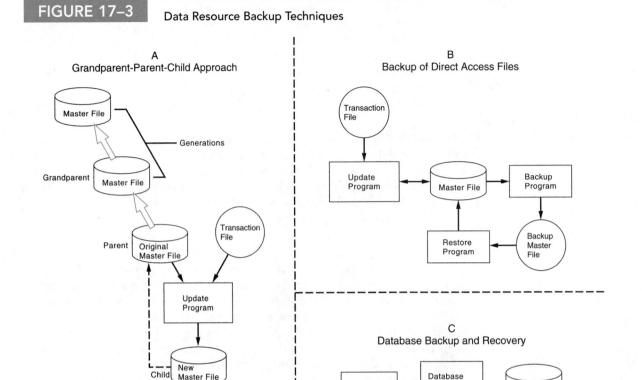

Audit Procedures for Testing Backup Controls

Sequential File (GPC) Backup. The auditor should select a sample of systems and determine from the system documentation that the number of GPC backup files specified for each system is adequate. Systematic errors and disasters may destroy several backup versions of a particular data file. If an insufficient number of backup files exists, recovery may be impossible.

Direct Access File Backup. The auditor should select a sample of applications and identify the direct access files being updated in each system. From system documentation and through observation, the auditor can verify that each of these is copied to tape or disk before being updated.

Database Backup. Backup in a database environment should be a routine activity. The auditor should verify that such automatic backup procedures are in place and functioning. Production databases should be copied at regular intervals (perhaps several times an hour) for recovery purposes in the event of a systems failure. The auditor should establish that the frequency of such backup procedures is adequate for the needs of the organization, and copies of the database are stored off-site for further security.

Audit Procedures for Testing Access Controls

Responsibility for Authority Tables and Subschemas. The auditor should verify that database administration (DBA) personnel retain exclusive responsibility for creating authority tables and designing user subschemas. Evidence of compliance can come from three sources: (1) by reviewing company policy and job descriptions, which specify these technical responsibilities; (2) by examining programmer authority tables for access privileges to data definition language (DDL) commands; and (3) through personal interviews with programmers and DBA personnel.

Appropriate Access Authority. The auditor can select a sample of users and verify that their access privileges stored in the authority table are consistent with their organizational functions.

Biometric Controls. The auditor should evaluate the costs and benefits of biometric controls. Generally, these would be most appropriate where highly sensitive data are accessed by a very limited number of users.

Inference Controls. The auditor should verify that database query controls exist to prevent unauthorized access via inference. The auditor can test controls by simulating access by a sample of users and attempting to retrieve unauthorized data via inference queries.

Encryption Controls. The auditor should verify that sensitive data, such as passwords, are properly encrypted. This can be done by printing the file contents to hard copy.

TESTING ORGANIZATIONAL STRUCTURE CONTROLS

The organization of the information technology (IT) function has implications for the nature of internal controls, which, in turn, has implications for the audit. Even the most sophisticated control techniques can be circumvented if inadequate segregation of duties exist. Chapter 15 examined the nature of the underlying exposures along with the segregation controls that reduce the risk of these exposures.

Audit Objectives Relating to Organizational Structure

The auditor's objective is to verify that individuals in incompatible areas are segregated in accordance with the level of potential risk and in a manner that promotes a working environment. This is an environment in which formal, rather than casual, relationships exist between incompatible tasks.

Audit Procedures Relating to Organizational Structure

The following tests of controls would enable the auditor to achieve the control objectives.

- Obtain and review the corporate policy on computer security. Verify that the security policy is communicated to responsible employees and supervisors.
- Review relevant documentation, including the current organizational chart, mission statement, and job descriptions for key functions, to determine if individuals or groups are performing incompatible functions.
- Review systems documentation and maintenance records for a sample of applications. Verify that maintenance programmers assigned to specific projects are not also the original design programmers.
- Through observation, determine that the segregation policy is being followed in practice. Review operations room access logs to determine whether programmers enter the facility for reasons other than system failures.

- Review user rights and privileges to verify that programmers have access privileges consistent with their job descriptions.

**TESTING SYSTEMS
DEVELOPMENT
CONTROLS**

Chapters 13 and 14 presented the systems development life cycle (SDLC) as a multiphase process by which organizations produce information systems. While the number of phases that constitute the SDLC will vary from firm to firm, the auditor is concerned that an organization's stated SDLC procedures are properly applied to all applications. Failure to comply with formal procedures and controls can result in a number of serious exposures to the firm.

Audit Objectives Relating to Systems Development

The auditor's objectives are to ensure that (1) SDLC activities are applied consistently and in accordance with management's policies to all systems development projects; (2) the system as originally implemented was free from material errors and fraud; (3) the system was judged to be necessary and justified at various checkpoints throughout the SDLC; and (4) system documentation is sufficiently accurate and complete to facilitate audit and maintenance activities.

Tests of Systems Development Controls

The following are tests of systems development controls.

Ongoing Involvement of Internal Audit Staff. Firms with independent internal audit staffs may conduct tests of SDLC controls on an ongoing basis. This audit activity may, in fact, be built into the SDLC at various checkpoints. By having internal audit representatives on project teams, each project can be reviewed for compliance with management's policies through all phases of the SDLC. Errors and irregularities may thus be detected early and corrected.

Review SDLC Documentation. The auditor should select a sample of completed projects (completed in both the current period and previous periods) and review the documentation for evidence of compliance with SDLC policies. Specific points for review should include determining that:

- User and computer services management properly authorized the project.
- A preliminary feasibility study showed that the project had merit.
- A detailed analysis of user needs was conducted that resulted in alternative general designs.
- A cost-benefit analysis was conducted using reasonably accurate figures.
- The project's documentation shows that the detailed design was an appropriate and accurate solution to the user's problem.
- Test results show that the system was thoroughly tested at both the individual module and the total system level before implementation. (To confirm these test results, the auditor may decide to retest selected elements of the application.)
- There is a checklist of specific problems detected during the conversion period, along with evidence that they were corrected in the maintenance phase.
- Systems documentation complies with organizational requirements and standards.

**TESTING SYSTEMS
MAINTENANCE
CONTROLS**

If an application has undergone maintenance (and even if it has not), its integrity may have been compromised since implementation. The auditor's investigation must, therefore, extend into the maintenance phase to determine that application integrity still exists.

In Chapter 15, we saw how uncontrolled program changes can increase a firm's exposure to financial loss from programming errors. Some programming errors are subtle, resulting in the creation and distribution of incorrect information that goes undetected by the user. Other forms of errors are more apparent and result in system failures that can disrupt data processing and even bring operations to a halt. In addition to these exposures, program fraud more easily takes root in an environment of poorly controlled maintenance and can go undetected for years.

Audit Objectives Relating to Systems Maintenance

The auditor's objectives are to detect unauthorized program maintenance (which may have resulted in significant processing errors or fraud) and to determine that (1) maintenance procedures protect applications from unauthorized changes, (2) applications are free from material errors, and (3) program libraries are protected from unauthorized access.

Each of these objectives will be examined in turn, focusing on the tests of controls that are necessary to achieve the objective. The discussion will assume that the organization employs source program library (SPL) software to control program maintenance. It should be noted that without SPL software, it can be difficult to achieve these audit objectives. The procedures described below are illustrated in Figure 17–4.

Audit Procedures for Identifying Unauthorized Program Changes

To establish that program changes were authorized, the auditor should examine the audit trail of program changes for a sample of applications that have undergone

---

FIGURE 17–4   Auditing SPL Software System

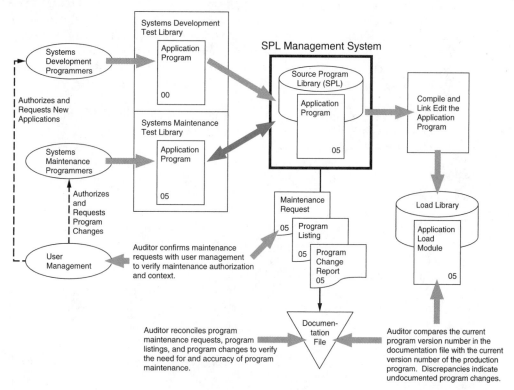

maintenance. The auditor can confirm that authorization procedures were followed by performing the following tests of controls.

Reconcile Program Version Numbers. The permanent file of the application should contain program change authorization documents that correspond to the current version number of the production application. In other words, if the production application is in its tenth version, there should be ten program change authorizations in the permanent file as supporting documentation.[7] Any discrepancies between version numbers and supporting documents may indicate that unauthorized changes were made.

Confirm Maintenance Authorization. The program maintenance authorization should indicate the nature of the change requested and the date of the change. It should also be signed and approved by the appropriate management from both computer services and the user departments. The auditor should confirm the facts contained in the maintenance authorization and verify the authorizing signatures with the managers involved.

Audit Procedures for Identifying Application Errors

The auditor can determine that programs are free from material errors by performing three types of tests of controls: reconcile the source code, review the test results, and retest the program.

Reconcile the Source Code. Each application's permanent file should contain the current program listing and listings of all changes made to the application. These documents describe in detail the application's maintenance history. In addition, the nature of the program change should be clearly stated on the program change authorization document. The auditor should select a sample of applications and reconcile each program change with the appropriate authorization documents. The modular approach to systems design (creating applications that comprise many small discrete program modules) greatly facilitates this testing technique. The reduced complexity of these modules enhances the auditor's ability to identify irregularities that indicate errors, omissions, and potentially fraudulent programming codes.

Review Test Results. Every program change should be thoroughly tested before being implemented. Program test procedures should be properly documented by test objectives, test data, and processing results, which support the programmer's decision to implement the change. The auditor should review this record for each significant program change to establish that testing was sufficiently rigorous to identify any errors.

Retest the Program. The auditor can retest the application to confirm its integrity. We examine several techniques for application testing later in this chapter.

Audit Procedures for Testing Access to Libraries

The existence of a secure program library is central to preventing errors and program fraud. One method is to assign library access rights exclusively to individuals who act

---

7   In most systems, a program in its original (unmodified) state has a version number of 00. Thus, ten changes will give a version number of 10.

as librarians. Their function is to retrieve applications from the program libraries for maintenance and to restore the modified programs to the library. In this arrangement, programmers perform program maintenance and testing in their own "private" libraries but do not have direct access to the program library.

The auditor should establish that the program library and private libraries are protected from unauthorized access by performing the following tests of controls.

Review Programmer Authority Tables. The auditor can select a sample of programmers and review their access authority. The programmer's authority table will specify the libraries a programmer may access. These authorizations should be matched against the programmer's maintenance authority to ensure that no irregularities exist.

Test Authority Table. The auditor should simulate the programmer's access privileges and then violate the authorization rules by attempting to access unauthorized libraries. Any such attempts should be denied by the operating system.

TESTING COMPUTER CENTER SECURITY

Auditors routinely examine the physical environment of the computer center as part of their audit. As seen in Chapter 15, risks from fire, floods, civil disorder, and sabotage pose a potentially serious threat to information, accounting records, transaction processing capability, and even the firm's survival.

Audit Objectives Relating to Computer Center Security

The auditor's objective is to evaluate the controls governing computer center security. Specifically, the auditor must verify that (1) physical security controls are adequate to reasonably protect the organization from physical exposures; (2) insurance coverage on equipment is adequate to compensate the organization for the destruction of, or damage to, its computer center; (3) operator documentation is adequate to deal with routine operations as well as system failures; and (4) the organization's disaster recovery plan is adequate and feasible.

Audit Procedures for Assessing Physical Security Controls

The following are tests of physical security controls.

Tests of Physical Construction. The auditor should determine that the computer center is solidly built of fireproof material. There should be adequate drainage under the raised floor to allow water to flow away in the event of water damage from a fire in an upper floor or from some other source. In addition, the auditor should evaluate the physical location of the computer center. The facility should be located in an area that minimizes its exposure from fire, civil unrest, and other hazards.

Tests of the Fire Detection System. The auditor should establish that fire detection and suppression equipment, both manual and automatic, are in place and are tested regularly. The fire detection system should detect smoke, heat, and combustible fumes. The adequacy of these devices can be determined by reviewing official fire marshal records of tests that are stored at the computer center.

Tests of Access Control. The auditor must establish that routine access to the computer center is restricted to authorized employees. Details about visitor access (by programmers and others), such as arrival and departure times, purpose, and frequency of access, can be obtained by reviewing the access log. To establish the veracity of this document, the auditor may covertly observe the process by which access is permitted.

Tests of the Backup Power Supply. The computer center should perform periodic tests of the backup power supply to ensure that it has sufficient capacity to run the computer and air conditioning. These are extremely important tests, and their results should be formally recorded. As a firm's computer function develops, its backup power needs are likely to grow proportionally. Indeed, without such tests, an organization may be unaware that it has outgrown its backup capacity until it is too late.

Audit Procedures for Verifying Insurance Coverage

The auditor should annually review the organization's insurance coverage on its computer hardware, software, and physical facility. The auditor must verify that all new acquisitions are listed on the policy and that obsolete equipment and software have been deleted. The insurance policy should reflect management's needs in terms of extent of coverage and cost. For example, the firm may wish to be partially self-insured and require minimum coverage. On the other hand, the firm may seek complete replacement-cost coverage.

Audit Procedures for Verifying Adequacy of Operator Documentation

Computer operators use documentation called a *run manual* to run certain aspects of the system. In particular, large batch systems often require special attention from operators. During the course of the day, computer operators may execute dozens of computer programs that each process multiple files and produce multiple reports. To achieve effective data processing operations, the run manual must be sufficiently detailed to guide operators in their tasks. The auditor should review the run manual for completeness and accuracy. The typical contents of a run manual include:

- The name of the system, such as "Purchases System."
- The run schedule (daily, weekly, time of day).
- Required hardware devices (tapes, disks, printers, or special hardware).
- File requirements specifying all the transaction (input) files, master files, and output files used in the system.
- Run-time instructions describing the error messages that may appear, actions to be taken, and the name and telephone number of the programmer on call, should the system fail.
- A list of users who receive the output from the run.

The auditor should also verify that other systems documentation, such as systems flowcharts, logic flowcharts, and program code listings, are not part of the operation documentation. Operators should not have access to the operational details of a system's internal logic.

Audit Procedures for Assessing the Disaster Recovery Plan

The auditor should verify that the management disaster recovery plan (DRP) is realistic for dealing with a catastrophe that could deprive the organization of its computer resource. The following tests focus on the areas of greatest concern.

Second-Site Backup. The auditor should evaluate the adequacy of the backup site arrangement. System incompatibility and human nature can both greatly reduce the effectiveness of the mutual aid pact. Auditors should be skeptical of such arrangements for two reasons. First, the sophistication of the computer system can make it difficult to find a potential partner with an identical or even a compatible configuration. Second, most firms do not have the necessary excess capacity to support a disaster-stricken partner while also processing their own work. When it comes to the "crunch," the management of the firm untouched by disaster may have little appetite for the sacrifices that must be made to honor the agreement.

More viable but expensive alternatives to the mutual aid pact are the empty shell and the recovery operation center. These, too, must be examined carefully. The auditor should be concerned about the number of members in these arrangements and their geographic dispersion. A widespread disaster may create a demand that cannot be satisfied by the backup facility.

Critical Application List. The auditor should review the list of critical applications to ensure that it is complete. Missing applications can result in failure to recover. However, the same is true for restoring unnecessary applications. To include applications on the critical list that are not needed to achieve short-term survival can misdirect resources and distract attention from the primary objective during the recovery period.

Backup Critical Applications. The auditor should verify that copies of critical programs are stored off-site. In the event of a disaster or system failure, the production applications can then be reconstructed from the backup versions.

Backup Critical Data Files The auditor should verify that critical data files are backed up in accordance with the DRP. Data backup procedures were discussed in the examination of data resource controls.

Backup Supplies, Source Documents, and Documentation. The system documentation, supplies, and source documents needed to restore and run critical applications should be backed up and stored off-site. The auditor should verify that the types and quantities of items specified in the DRP exist in a secure location. Examples of critical supplies are check stock, invoices, purchase orders, and any other special-purpose forms that cannot be obtained immediately.

The Disaster Recovery Team. The DRP should clearly list the names, addresses, and emergency telephone numbers of the disaster recovery team members. The auditor should verify that members of the team are current employees and are aware of their assigned responsibilities. On one occasion, while reviewing a firm's DRP, the author discovered that a team leader listed in the plan had been deceased for nine months.

TESTING INTERNET AND INTRANET CONTROLS

Chapter 12 showed that Internet and Intranet communications are susceptible to a variety of threats from equipment failure and subversive acts. Auditors are concerned about the adequacy of the communications controls that prevent loss, destruction, corruption, or illegal interception of transmitted signals. Recall that important control techniques used to reduce these risks include various line control devices, message logs, firewalls, encryption techniques, and network backup procedures.

Audit Objectives Relating to Internet and Intranet Controls

The auditor's objective is to verify the security and integrity of the electronic commerce transactions by determining that controls (1) can detect and correct message loss due to equipment failure, (2) can prevent and detect illegal access both internally and from the Internet, (3) will render useless any data that are successfully captured by a perpetrator, and (4) are sufficient to preserve the integrity and physical security of data connected to the network.

Tests of Data Communications Controls

To achieve these control objectives, the auditor can perform the following tests of controls:

1. Select a sample of messages from the transaction log and examine them for garbled contents caused by line noise. The auditor should verify that all corrupted messages were successfully retransmitted.
2. Review the message transaction logs to verify that all messages were received in their proper sequence.
3. Test the operation of the call-back feature by placing an unauthorized call from outside the installation.
4. Review security procedures governing the administration of data encryption keys.
5. Verify the encryption process by transmitting a test message and examining the contents at various points along the channel between the sending and receiving locations.
6. Review the adequacy of the firewall in achieving the proper balance between control and convenience based on the organization's business objectives and potential risks. Criteria for assessing the firewall effectiveness include:
    - *Flexibility.* The firewall should be flexible enough to accommodate new services as the security needs of the organization change.
    - *Proxy services.* Adequate proxy applications should be in place to provide explicit user authentication to sensitive services, applications, and data.
    - *Filtering.* Strong filtering techniques should be designed to deny all services that are not explicitly permitted. In other words, the firewall should specify only those services the user is permitted to access, rather than specifying the services that are denied.
    - *Segregation of systems.* Systems that do not require public access should be segregated from the Internet.
    - *Audit tools.* The firewall should provide a thorough set of audit and logging tools that identify and record suspicious activity.
    - *Probe for weaknesses.* To validate security, the auditor (or a professional security analyst) should periodically probe the firewall for weaknesses just as a computer Internet hacker would do. A number of software products are currently available for identifying security weaknesses.[8]
7. Review password control procedures to ensure that passwords are changed regularly and that weak passwords are identified and disallowed. Reviewing a sample of user passwords taken from the password file can do this. The auditor should also verify that the password file is encrypted and that the encryption key is properly secured.
8. Audit procedures for verifying adequate backup include:
    - The auditor should verify that backup is performed routinely and frequently to facilitate the recovery of lost, destroyed, or corrupted data.
    - Network databases should be copied at regular intervals (perhaps several times an hour). A balance must be sought between the inconvenience of frequent backup activities and the business disruption caused by excessive reprocessing that is needed to restore the database after a failure.

[8] Examples include Security Administrator Tool for Analyzing Networks (SATAN), Internet Security Scanner (ISS), Gabriel, and Courtney.

- The auditor should verify that automatic backup procedures are in place and functioning, and that copies of files and databases are stored off-site for further security.

TESTING ELECTRONIC DATA INTERCHANGE CONTROLS

Electronic data interchange is the intercompany exchange of computer-processible business information in standard format. EDI transactions are conducted automatically by the trading partners' respective information systems. In a pure EDI environment, no human intermediaries approve or authorize transactions. The absence of human intervention creates unique audit risks.

Audit Objectives Relating to EDI

The auditor's objectives are to determine that (1) all EDI transactions are authorized, validated, and in compliance with the trading partner agreement; (2) no unauthorized organizations gain access to database records; (3) authorized trading partners have access only to approved data; and (4) adequate controls are in place to ensure a complete audit trail of all EDI transactions.

Audit Procedures Relating to EDI

To achieve these control objectives, the auditor may perform the following tests of controls.

Tests of Authorization and Validation Controls. The auditor should establish that trading partner identification codes are verified before transactions are processed. To accomplish this, the auditor should (1) review agreements with the VAN facility to validate transactions and ensure that information regarding valid trading partners is complete and correct and (2) examine the organization's valid trading partner file for accuracy and completeness.

Tests of Access Controls. Security over the valid trading partner file and databases is central to the EDI control framework. The auditor can verify control adequacy in the following ways:

1. The auditor should determine that access to the valid vendor or customer file is limited to authorized employees only. The auditor should verify that access to this file is controlled by password and authority tables and that the data are encrypted.
2. The degree of access a trading partner should have to the firm's database records (such as inventory levels and price lists) will be determined by the trading agreement. The auditor should reconcile the terms of the trading agreement against the trading partner's access privileges stated in the database authority table.
3. The auditor should simulate access by a sample of trading partners and attempt to violate access privileges.

Tests of Audit Trail Controls. The auditor should verify that the EDI system produces a transaction log that tracks transactions through all stages of processing. By selecting a sample of transactions and tracing these through the process, the auditor can verify that key data values were recorded correctly at each point.

TESTING PERSONAL COMPUTER CONTROLS

The advanced technology and power of modern personal computer systems stand in sharp contrast to the relatively unsophisticated operational environment in which they exist. The exposures associated with PC systems were presented in Chapter 16.

Controlling this environment rests heavily on physical security rather than the software techniques used to control the more sophisticated mainframe and client-server environments. The audit objectives and procedures described below address four areas of primary concern: unauthorized access, segregation of functions, backup control, and systems development and maintenance.

Audit Objectives Relating to Access

The objective of the auditor is to verify that controls are in place to protect data, programs, and computers from unauthorized access, manipulation, destruction, and theft.

Audit Procedures Relating to Access

The auditor should verify that PCs and their files are physically controlled. Desktop computers should be anchored to reduce the opportunity to remove them. On computers containing mission-critical data, locks should be in place to disable input from the keyboard and the A: drive.

Audit Objectives Relating to Segregation of Duties

The auditor's objective is to verify that adequate supervision and operating procedures exist to compensate for lack of segregation between the duties of users, programmers, and operators.

Audit Procedures Relating to Segregation of Duties

- The auditor should verify from organizational charts, job descriptions, and observation that the programmers of applications performing financially significant functions do not also operate those systems. In smaller organizational units where functional segregation is impractical, the auditor should verify that there is adequate supervision over these tasks.
- The auditor should confirm that reports of processed transactions, listings of updated accounts, and control totals are prepared, distributed, and reconciled by appropriate management at regular and timely intervals.
- Where appropriate, the auditor should determine that multilevel password control is used to limit access to data and applications.

Audit Objectives Relating to Backup

The auditor's objective is to verify that backup procedures are in place to prevent data and program loss due to hardware failures.

Audit Procedures Relating to Backup

- If removable hard drives are used, the auditor should verify that the drives are removed and stored in a secure location when not in use.
- By selecting a sample of backup files, the auditor can verify that backup procedures are being followed. By comparing data values and dates on the backup disks to production files, the auditor can assess the frequency and adequacy of backup procedures.
- The auditor should verify that the application source code is physically secured (such as in a locked safe) and that only the compiled version is stored on the microcomputer.

Audit Objectives Relating to Systems Development and Maintenance

The auditor's objective is to verify that systems selection and acquisition procedures produce applications that are high quality, free from errors and viruses, and protected from unauthorized changes.

Audit Procedures Relating to Systems Development and Maintenance

Review Systems Selection and Acquisition Controls. The auditor should verify that commercial software packages employed on microcomputers were purchased from reputable vendors. The auditor should review the selection and acquisition procedures to ensure that user needs were fully considered and that the purchased software satisfies those needs.

Review Virus Control Techniques. Strict adherence to organizational policies and procedures that guard against virus infection is critical to effective virus control. The auditor should verify that such policies and procedures exist and that they are being followed. But policy alone will not deter a resolute perpetrator. The organization must therefore resort to additional technical controls in the form of antivirus software.

The auditor can obtain corroborating evidence of virus control adequacy by performing the following tests:

1. The auditor should verify that the organization follows a policy of purchasing software from reputable vendors only.
2. The auditor should review the organization's policy for using antiviral software. This policy may include the following points:
   - Antiviral software should be installed on all microcomputers and invoked as part of the startup procedure when the computers are turned on. This will ensure that all key sectors of the hard disk are examined before any data are transferred through the network.
   - All upgrades to vendor software should be checked for viruses before they are implemented.
   - All public-domain software should be examined for virus infection before it is used.
   - Current versions of antiviral software should be available to all users.
3. The auditor should verify that only authorized software is loaded on personal computers.

TESTING COMPUTER APPLICATION CONTROLS

This section and the next examine several popular techniques for auditing computer applications. These techniques fall into two classes: (1) techniques for testing application controls and (2) techniques for examining transaction details and account balances—*substantive testing*.

Earlier in the chapter we introduced the concept of audit objectives for transactions and account balances that are derived from management assertions about financial statement presentation. These assertions are *existence or occurrence, completeness, accuracy, rights and obligations, valuation or allocation* and *presentation and disclosure*. Depending upon the type of account being considered, a particular management assertion has different implications for the audit objective that needs to be developed. Once developed, achieving the audit objectives requires designing audit procedures to gather evidence that either corroborates or refutes the underlying management assertions. Generally, this involves a combination of tests of controls and substantive tests of details.

The development of audit objectives relating to transactions and account balances is beyond the scope of this chapter. Only techniques that show *how* auditors gather evidence are examined. The more conceptual question of *why* is not covered.

Techniques used for testing computer program controls provide information about the accuracy and completeness of an application's processes. These tests follow two general approaches: (1) the black box (around the computer) approach and (2) the white box (through the computer) approach. Substantive testing techniques provide the auditor with evidence about the details underlying a transaction or account balance. These techniques involve extracting data from files and databases.

The remainder of this section deals with tests of program controls. First, the black box approach is examined. Then, several white box testing techniques are reviewed. Substantive testing is the subject of the final section in this chapter.

BLACK BOX APPROACH

Auditors performing black box testing do not rely on a detailed knowledge of the application's internal logic. Instead, they seek to understand the functional characteristics of the application by analyzing flowcharts and interviewing knowledgeable personnel in the client's organization. With an understanding of what the application is supposed to do, the auditor tests the application by reconciling production input transactions processed by the application with output results. The output results are analyzed to verify the application's compliance with its functional requirements. Figure 17–5 illustrates the black box approach.

The advantage of the black box approach is that the application need not be removed from service and tested directly. This approach is feasible for testing applications that are relatively simple. However, complex applications—those that receive input from many sources, perform a variety of operations, or produce multiple outputs—require a more focused testing approach to provide the auditor with evidence of application integrity.

WHITE BOX APPROACH

The white box approach relies on an in-depth understanding of the internal logic of the application being tested. The white box approach includes several techniques for testing application logic directly. These techniques use small numbers of specially created test transactions to verify specific aspects of an application's logic and controls. In this way, auditors are able to conduct precise tests, with known variables, and

FIGURE 17–5

Auditing around the Computer—The "Black Box" Approach

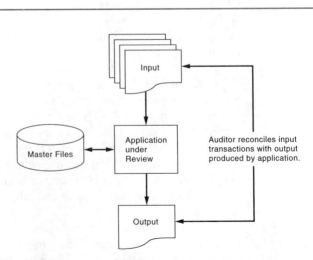

obtain results that they can compare against objectively calculated results. The most common types of tests of controls include the following:[9]

1. **Authenticity tests**, which verify that an individual, a programmed procedure, or a message (such as an EDI transmission) attempting to access a system is authentic. Authenticity controls include user IDs, passwords, valid vendor codes, and authority tables.

2. **Accuracy tests**, which ensure that the system processes only data values that conform to specified tolerances. Examples include range tests, field tests, and limit tests.

3. **Completeness tests**, which identify missing data within a single record and entire records missing from a batch. The types of tests performed are field tests, record sequence tests, hash totals, and control totals.

4. **Redundancy tests**, which determine that an application processes each record only once. Redundancy controls include the reconciliation of batch totals, record counts, hash totals, and financial control totals.

5. **Access tests**, which ensure that the application prevents authorized users from unauthorized access to data. Access controls include passwords, authority tables, user-defined procedures, data encryption, and inference controls.

6. **Audit trail tests**, which ensure that the application creates an adequate audit trail. This includes evidence that the application records all transactions in a transaction log, posts data values to the appropriate accounts, produces complete transaction listings, and generates error files and reports for all exceptions.

7. **Rounding error tests**, which verify the correctness of rounding procedures. Rounding errors occur in accounting information when the level of precision used in the calculation is greater than that used in the reporting. For example, interest calculations on bank account balances may have a precision of five decimal places, whereas only two decimal places are needed to report balances. If the remaining three decimal places are simply dropped, the total interest calculated for the total number of accounts may not equal the sum of the individual calculations.

Figure 17–6 shows the logic for handling the rounding error problem. This technique uses an accumulator to keep track of the rounding differences between calculated and reported balances. Note how the sign and the absolute value of the amount in the accumulator determines how the customer account is affected by rounding. To illustrate, the rounding logic is applied to three hypothetical bank balances. (See the table on page 883.) The interest calculations are based on an interest rate of 5.25 percent.

Failure to properly account for the rounding difference above can result in an imbalance between the total (control) figure and the sum of the detail figures for each account. Poor accounting for rounding differences can also present an opportunity for fraud.

Rounding programs are particularly susceptible to so-called salami frauds. **Salami fraud** tends to affect a large number of victims, but the harm to each is immaterial. This type of fraud takes its name from the analogy of slicing a large salami (the fraud objective) into many thin pieces. Each victim assumes one of these small pieces and is unaware of being defrauded. For example, a programmer, or someone with access to the rounding program above, can perpetrate a salami fraud by

---

9   R. Weber, *EDP Auditing Conceptual Foundations and Practice*, 2d ed. (New York: McGraw-Hill, 1988): 38.

FIGURE 17–6

Rounding Error
Algorithm

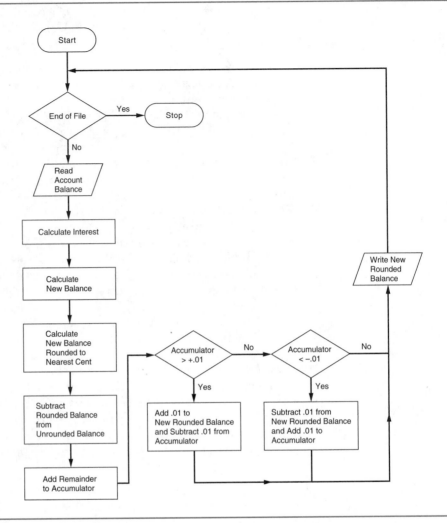

SOURCE: Adapted from R. Weber, *EDP Auditing Conceptual Foundations and Practice*, 2d ed. (New York: McGraw-Hill, 1988): 493.

modifying the rounding logic as follows: at the point in the process where the algorithm should increase the customer's account (that is, the accumulator value is > +.01), the program instead adds one cent to another account—the perpetrator's account. Although the absolute amount of each fraud transaction is small, given the thousands of accounts processed, the total amount of the fraud can become significant over time.

Most large public accounting firms have developed special audit software that can detect excessive file activity. In the case of the salami fraud, there would be thousands of entries into the computer criminal's personal account that may be detected by the audit software. A clever programmer may disguise this activity by funneling these entries through several intermediate accounts, which are then posted to a smaller number of intermediate accounts and finally to the programmer's personal account. By using many levels of accounts in this way, the activity to any single account is reduced and may go undetected by the audit software. There will be a trail, but it can be complicated. The auditor can also use audit software to detect the existence of unauthorized (dummy) files that contain the intermediate accounts used in such a fraud.

Record 1

Beginning accumulator balance	.00861
Beginning account balance	2,741.78
Calculated interest	143.94345
New account balance	2,885.72345
Rounded account balance	2,885.72
Adjusted accumulator balance	.01206 (.00345 + .00861)
Ending account balance	**2,885.73 (round up 1 cent)**
Ending accumulator balance	.00206 (.01206 − .01)

Record 2

Beginning accumulator balance	.00206
Beginning account balance	1,893.44
Calculated interest	99.4056
New account balance	1,992.8456
Rounded account balance	1,992.85
Adjusted accumulator balance	−.00646 (.00206 − .0044)
Ending account balance	**1,992,85 (no change)**
Ending accumulator balance	−.00646

Record 3

Beginning accumulator balance	−.00646
Beginning account balance	7,423.34
Calculated interest	389.72535
New account balance	7,813.06535
Rounded account balance	7,813.07
Adjusted accumulator balance	−.01111 (.00646 − .00465)
Ending account balance	**7,813.06 (round down 1 cent)**
Ending accumulator balance	.00111

WHITE BOX TESTING TECHNIQUES

To illustrate how application controls are tested, this section describes five **computer-assisted audit tools and techniques (CAATTs)** approaches: the test data method, base case system evaluation, tracing, integrated test facility, and parallel simulation.

Test Data Method

The **test data method** is used to establish application integrity by processing specially prepared sets of input data through production applications that are under review. The results of each test are compared to predetermined expectations to obtain an objective evaluation of application logic and control effectiveness. The test data technique is illustrated in Figure 17–7. To perform the test data technique, a copy of the current version of the application must be obtained by the auditor. In addition, test transaction files and test master files must be created. As illustrated in the figure, test transactions may enter the system from magnetic tape, disk, or via an input terminal. Results from the test run will be in the form of routine output reports, transaction listings, and error reports. In addition, the auditor must review the updated master files to determine that account balances have been correctly updated. The test results are then compared with the auditor's expected results to determine if the application is functioning properly. This comparison may be performed manually or through special computer software.

FIGURE 17–7

The Test Data
Technique

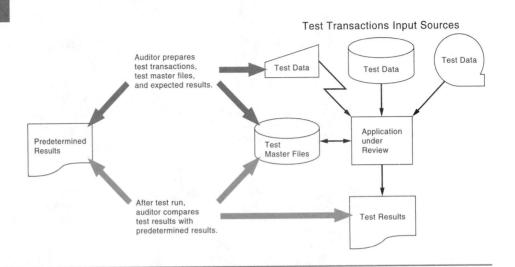

Figure 17–8 lists selected fields for hypothetical transactions and accounts receivable records prepared by the auditor to test a sales order processing application. The figure also shows an error report of rejected transactions and a listing of the updated accounts receivable master file. Any deviations between the actual results obtained and those expected by the auditor may indicate a logic or control problem.

Creating Test Data. When creating test data, it is important that auditors prepare a complete set of both valid and invalid transactions. If test data are incomplete, auditors might fail to examine critical branches of application logic and error checking routines. Test transactions should test every possible input error, logical process, and irregularity.

Gaining knowledge of the application's internal logic sufficient to create meaningful test data frequently requires a large investment of time. However, the efficiency of this task can be improved through careful planning during systems development. The test data used to test program modules during the implementation phase of the SDLC should be saved for future use by the auditor. If the application has undergone no maintenance since its initial implementation, current audit test results should equal the test results obtained at implementation. However, if the application has been modified, the auditor can create additional test data that focus on the areas of the program changes.

Base Case System Evaluation

There are several variants of the test data technique. When the set of test data in use is comprehensive, the technique is called the **base case system evaluation (BCSE)**. BCSE tests are conducted with a set of test transactions containing all possible transaction types. These are processed through repeated iterations during systems development testing until consistent and valid results are obtained. These results are the base case. When subsequent changes to the application occur during maintenance, their effects are evaluated by comparing current results with base case results.

Tracing

Another type of the test data technique called **tracing** performs an electronic walk-through of the application's internal logic. The tracing procedure involves three steps:

FIGURE 17–8   Example of Test Data and Test Results

Test Transaction File

REC NUM	CUST NUM	CUSTOMER NAME	PART NUM	DESCRIPTION	QNTY	UNIT PRICE	TOTAL PRICE
1	231893	Smith, Joe	AX-612	Water Pump	1	20.00	20.00
2	231893	Azar, Atul	J-912	Gear	3	15.00	45.00
3	245851	Jones, Mary	123-LM	Hose	20	20.00	400.00
4	256519	Lang, Tony	Y-771	Spacer	5	2.00	10.00
5	259552	Tuner, Agnes	U-734	Bushing	5	25.00	120.00
6	175995	Hanz, James	EA-74	Seal	1	3.00	3.00
7	267991	Swindle, Joe	EN-12	Rebuilt Engine	1	1,220.00	1,220.00

Original Test AR Master File

CUST NUM	CUSTOMER NAME	CUSTOMER ADDRESS	CREDIT LIMIT	CURRENT BALANCE
231893	Smith, Joe	1520 S. Maple, City	1,000.00	400.00
256519	Lang, Tony	18 Etwine St., City	5,000.00	850.00
267991	Swindle, Joe	1 Shady Side, City	3,000.00	2,900.00

Updated Test AR Master File

CUST NUM	CUSTOMER NAME	CUSTOMER ADDRESS	CREDIT LIMIT	CURRENT BALANCE
231893	Smith, Joe	1520 S. Maple, City	1,000.00	420.00
256519	Lang, Tony	18 Etwine St., City	5,000.00	860.00
267991	Swindle, Joe	1 Shady Side, City	3,000.00	2,900.00

Error Report

REC NUM	CUST NUM	CUSTOMER NAME	PART NUM	DESCRIPTION	QNTY	UNIT PRICE	TOTAL PRICE	EXPLANATION OF ERROR
2	231893	Azar, Atul (X)	J-912	Gear	3	15.00	45.00	CUSTOMER NAME does not correspond to CUST # 231893
3	245851 (X)	Jones, Mary	123-LM	Hose	20	20.00	400.00	Check digit error in CUST # field
5	259552	Tuner, Agnes	U-734	Bushing	5	25.00	120.00 (X)	Price extension error
6	175995 (X)	Hanz, James	EA-74	Seal	1	3.00	3.00	Record out of sequence
7	267991	Swindle, Joe	EN-12	Rebuilt Engine	1	1,220.00 (X)	1,220.00 (X)	Credit limit error

1. The application under review must undergo a special compilation to activate the trace option.
2. Specific transactions or types of transactions are created as test data.
3. The test data transactions are traced through all processing stages of the program, and a listing is produced of all programmed instructions that were executed during the test.

Implementing tracing requires a detailed understanding of the application's internal logic. Figure 17–9 illustrates the tracing process using a portion of the logic for a

FIGURE 17–9

Tracing

Payroll Transaction File

Time Card #	Employee Number	Name	Year	Pay Period	Reg Hrs	OT Hrs
8945	33456	Jones, J.J.	2001	14	40.0	3.0

Payroll Master File

Employee Number	Hourly Rate	YTD Earnings	Dependents	YTD Withhold	YTD FICA
33276	15	12,050	3	3,200	873.62
33456	15	13,100	2	3,600	949.75

Computer Program Logic

```
0001   Read Record from Transaction File
0010   Read Record from Master File
0020   If Employee Number (T) = Employee Number (M)
0030       Wage = (Reg Hrs + [OT Hrs x 1.5] ) x Hourly Rate
0040       Add Wage to YTD Earnings
0050       Go to 0001
0060   Else Go to 0010
```

Trace Listing
0001, 0010, 0020, 0060, 0010, 0020, 0030, 0040, 0050

payroll application. The example shows records from two payroll files—a transaction record showing hours worked and two records from a master file showing pay rates. The trace listing at the bottom of Figure 17–9 identifies the program statements that were executed and the order of execution. Analysis of trace options indicates that Commands 0001 through 0020 were executed. At that point, the application transferred to Command 0060. This occurred because the employee number (the key) of the transaction record did not match the key of the first record in the master file. Then Commands 0010 through 0050 were executed.

Advantages of Test Data Techniques

There are three primary advantages of test data techniques. First, they employ through-the-computer testing, thus providing the auditor with explicit evidence concerning application functions. Second, if properly planned, test data runs can be employed with only minimal disruption to the organization's operations. Third, they require only minimal computer expertise on the part of auditors.

Disadvantages of Test Data Techniques

The primary disadvantage of test data techniques is that auditors must rely on computer services personnel to obtain a copy of the application for test purposes. This entails a risk that computer services may intentionally or accidentally provide the auditor with the wrong version of the application and may reduce the reliability of the audit evidence. In general, audit evidence collected by independent means is more reliable than evidence supplied by the client.

A second disadvantage of these techniques is that they provide a static picture of application integrity at a single point in time. They do not provide a convenient means of gathering evidence about ongoing application functionality. There is no evidence that the application being tested today is functioning as it did during the year under test.

A third disadvantage of test data techniques is their relatively high cost of implementation, which results in audit inefficiency. The auditor may devote considerable time to understanding program logic and creating test data. The following section shows how automating testing techniques can resolve these problems.

THE INTEGRATED TEST FACILITY

The **integrated test facility (ITF)** approach is an automated technique that enables the auditor to test an application's logic and controls during its normal operation. The ITF is one or more audit modules designed into the application during the systems development process. In addition, ITF databases contain "dummy" or test master file records integrated with legitimate records. Some firms create a dummy company to which test transactions are posted. During normal operations, test transactions are merged into the input stream of regular (production) transactions and are processed against the files of the dummy company. Figure 17–10 illustrates the ITF concept.

ITF audit modules are designed to discriminate between ITF transactions and routine production data. This may be accomplished in a number of ways. One of the simplest and most commonly used is to assign a unique range of key values exclusively to ITF transactions. For example, in a sales order processing system, account numbers between 2000 and 2100 can be reserved for ITF transactions and will not be assigned to actual customer accounts. By segregating ITF transactions from legitimate transactions in this way, routine reports produced by the application are not corrupted by ITF test data. Test results are produced separately on storage media or hard-copy output and distributed directly to the auditor. Just as with the test data techniques, the auditor analyzes ITF results against expected results.

FIGURE 17–10

The ITF Technique

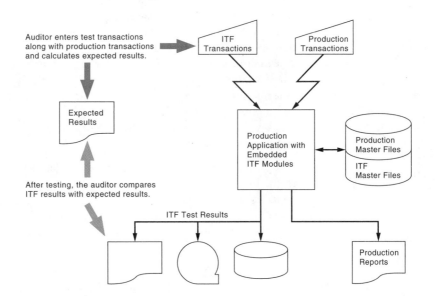

Advantages of ITF

The ITF technique has two advantages over test data techniques. First, ITF supports ongoing monitoring of controls as required by SAS 78. Second, applications with ITF can be economically tested without disrupting the user's operations and without the intervention of computer services personnel. Thus, ITF improves the efficiency of the audit and increases the reliability of the audit evidence gathered.

Disadvantages of ITF

The primary disadvantage of ITF is the potential for corrupting the data files of the organization with test data. Steps must be taken to ensure that ITF test transactions do not materially affect financial statements by being improperly aggregated with legitimate transactions. This problem is remedied in two ways: (1) adjusting entries may be processed to remove the effects of ITF from general ledger account balances or (2) data files can be scanned by special software that remove the ITF transactions.

PARALLEL SIMULATION

Parallel simulation requires the auditor to write a program that simulates key features or processes of the application under review. The simulated application is then used to reprocess transactions that were previously processed by the production application. This technique is illustrated in Figure 17–11. The results obtained from the simulation are reconciled with the results of the original production run to establish a basis for making inferences about the quality of application processes and controls.

Creating a Simulation Program

A simulation program can be written in any programming language. However, because of the one-time nature of this task, it is a candidate for fourth-generation language generators. Most public accounting firms provide a simulation feature in their generalized audit software (GAS).[10] The steps involved in performing parallel simulation testing are outlined below.

1. The auditor must first gain a thorough understanding of the application under review. Complete and current documentation of the application is required to construct an accurate simulation.
2. The auditor must then identify those processes and controls in the application that are critical to the audit. These are the processes to be simulated.
3. The auditor creates the simulation using a fourth-generation language or generalized audit software.
4. The auditor runs the simulation program using selected production transactions and master files to produce a set of results.
5. Finally, the auditor evaluates and reconciles the test results with the production results produced in a previous run.

Simulation programs are usually less complex than the production applications they represent. Because simulations contain only the application processes, calculations, and controls relevant to specific audit objectives, the auditor must carefully evaluate differences between test results and production results. Differences in output results occur for two reasons: (1) the inherent crudeness of the simulation program and

---

10   Although generalized audit software (GAS) can be used for testing internal controls, it is primarily a substantive testing technique. For this reason, this technology is discussed in the section that deals with substantive testing.

FIGURE 17–11

Parallel Simulation
Technique

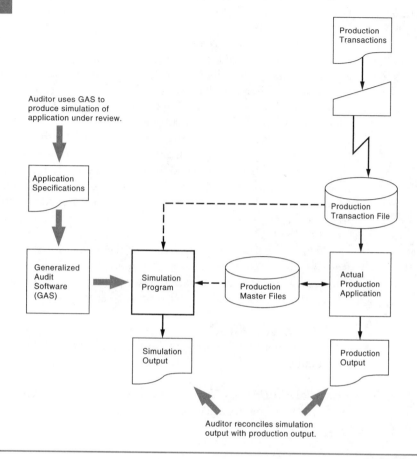

Auditor reconciles simulation
output with production output.

(2) real deficiencies in the application's processes or controls, which are made apparent by the simulation program.

SUBSTANTIVE TESTING TECHNIQUES

Most audit testing occurs in the substantive testing phase of the audit. These procedures are called *substantive tests* because they are used to substantiate dollar amounts in account balances. Substantive tests include but are not limited to the following:

1. Determining the correct value of inventory.
2. Determining the accuracy of prepayments and accruals.
3. Confirming accounts receivable with customers.
4. Searching for unrecorded liabilities.

Most of the records needed to perform these tests are stored in magnetic files and databases. Before substantive tests can be performed, these data must first be extracted from their host media and presented to the auditor in usable form. The two CAATTs examined in this section assist the auditor in selecting, accessing, and organizing data used for performing substantive tests.

THE EMBEDDED
AUDIT MODULE

Embedded audit module (EAM) techniques use one or more specially programmed modules embedded in a host application to select and record predetermined types of transactions for subsequent analysis. This approach is illustrated in Figure 17–12.

As the selected transaction is being processed by the host application, a copy of the transaction is stored in an audit file for subsequent review. The EAM approach allows material transactions to be captured throughout the audit period. Captured transactions are made available to the auditor at period end or at any time during the period, thus significantly reducing the amount of work the auditor must do to identify significant transactions for substantive testing.

To begin data capturing, the auditor specifies to the EAM the parameters and materiality threshold of the transactions set to be captured. For example, assume that the auditor establishes a $50,000 materiality threshold for transactions processed by a sales order processing system. Transactions equal to or greater than $50,000 will be copied to the audit file. From this set of transactions, the auditor will select a subset to be used for substantive tests. Transactions that fall below this threshold will be ignored by the EAM.

While primarily a substantive testing technique, EAMs may also be used to monitor controls on an ongoing basis as required by SAS 78. For example, transactions selected by the EAM can be reviewed for proper authorization, completeness and accuracy of processing, and correct posting to accounts.

Disadvantages of EAMs

The EAM approach has two significant disadvantages. The first pertains to operational efficiency and the second is concerned with EAM integrity.

Operational Efficiency. From the user's point of view, EAMs decrease operational performance. The presence of an audit module within the host application may cre-

---

FIGURE 17–12

Embedded Audit
Module Technique

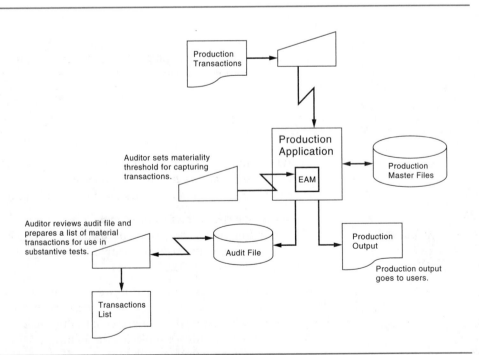

ate significant overhead, especially when the amount of testing is extensive. One approach for relieving this burden from the system is to design modules that may be "turned on and off" by the auditor. Doing so will, of course, reduce the effectiveness of the EAM as an ongoing audit tool.

Verifying EAM Integrity. The EAM approach may not be a viable audit technique in environments with a high level of program maintenance. When host applications are undergoing frequent changes, the EAMs embedded within the hosts will also require frequent modifications. The integrity concerns raised earlier regarding application maintenance apply equally to EAMs. The integrity of EAM directly affects the quality of the audit process. Auditors must therefore evaluate the EAM integrity. This would be accomplished in the same way as testing the host application controls.

GENERALIZED AUDIT SOFTWARE

Generalized audit software (GAS) is the most widely used CAATT for IS auditing. GAS allows auditors to access electronically coded data files and perform various operations on their contents. Many public accounting firms have developed versions of GAS, but these have very similar features. The following audit tasks can be performed using GAS:

1. Footing and balancing entire files or selected data items.
2. Selecting and reporting detailed data contained on files.
3. Selecting stratified statistical samples from data files.
4. Formatting results of tests into reports.
5. Printing confirmations in either standardized or special wording.
6. Screening data and selectively including or excluding items.
7. Comparing two files and identifying any differences.
8. Recalculating data fields.

The widespread popularity of GAS is due to four factors: (1) GAS languages are easy to use and require little EDP background on the part of the auditor, (2) GAS may be used on any type of computer because it is hardware independent, (3) auditors can perform their tests on data independent of a computer service professional, and (4) GAS can be used to audit the data files of many different applications (in contrast with EAMs, which are application specific).

Using GAS to Access Simple Structures
Gaining access to flat file structures is a simple process, as illustrated in Figure 17–13. In this example, an inventory file is read directly by the GAS, which extracts key information needed for the audit, including the quantity on hand, the dollar value, and the warehouse location of each inventory item. The auditor's task is to verify the existence and value of the inventory by performing a physical count of a representative sample of the inventory on hand. Thus, on the basis of a materiality threshold provided by the auditor, the GAS selects the sample records and prepares a report with the key information.

Using GAS to Access Complex Structures
Gaining access to complex structures, such as those maintained by database management systems, poses more of a problem for the auditor. Not all GAS products on the market may be capable of accessing every type of file structure. Most DBMSs, however, have utility features that will reformat complex structures into flat files. Rather than accessing the complex structure directly, an intermediate flat file is produced, which the GAS accesses. Figure 17–14 shows this technique.

FIGURE 17–13

Using GAS to Access
Simple File Structure

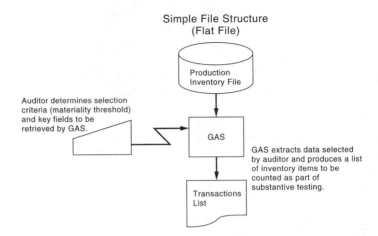

Simple File Structure
(Flat File)

Production
Inventory File

Auditor determines selection
criteria (materiality threshold)
and key fields to be
retrieved by GAS.

GAS

GAS extracts data selected
by auditor and produces a list
of inventory items to be
counted as part of
substantive testing.

Transactions
List

FIGURE 17–14

Using GAS to Access
Complex File
Structures

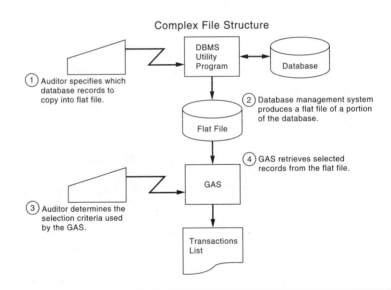

Complex File Structure

① Auditor specifies which
database records to
copy into flat file.

DBMS
Utility
Program

Database

② Database management system
produces a flat file of a portion
of the database.

Flat File

④ GAS retrieves selected
records from the flat file.

GAS

③ Auditor determines the
selection criteria used
by the GAS.

Transactions
List

To illustrate the file flattening process, consider the complex database structure presented in Figure 17–15. The database structure uses pointers to integrate three related files—Customer, Sales Invoice, and Line Item—in a hierarchical arrangement. It would be difficult if not impossible to extract audit evidence from a structure of this complexity using GAS. A simpler flat file version of this structure is illustrated in Figure 17–16 (on page 894). The single flat file presents the three record types as a sequential structure that can be easily accessed by GAS.

Audit Issue Pertaining to the Creation of Flat Files

The auditor must sometimes rely on computer services personnel to produce a flat file from the database. There is a risk that database integrity will be compromised by

FIGURE 17–15   Complex Database Structure

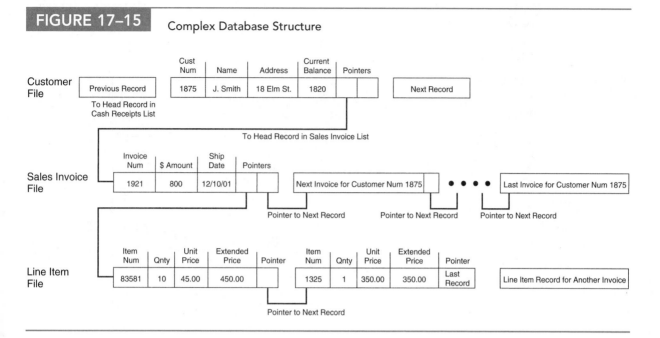

the procedure used to create the flat file. For example, if the auditor is confirming accounts receivable, certain fraudulent accounts in the original database may be intentionally omitted from the flat file that is produced. The sample of confirmations drawn from the flat file may therefore be unreliable. Auditors skilled in a DBMS query language, such as SQL, can avoid this problem by extracting data directly from the database.

Summary

This chapter examined the primary features of information systems auditing. The general purpose of a financial audit is to assess the fair presentation of financial statements. IS auditing plays an important role in the financial audit by verifying the reliability of the control structures for organizations that employ computer-based information systems. Although the specific procedures of an IS audit will vary according to differences in control structures, an IS audit will follow a three-phased process comprising risk analysis, tests of controls, and substantive testing. Much of this chapter focused on tests of controls for the nine general control areas and application controls. In examining each of the general control areas, auditors employ a variety of tests of controls designed to verify the adequacy of a firm's access controls and the soundness of its policies governing the physical security of the computer system. To verify the integrity of application controls, auditors can use several CAATTs, including the test data method, the integrated test facility, and parallel simulation.

This chapter concluded with an examination of substantive testing techniques. Substantive tests are designed to provide evidence about the underlying details of financial transactions and statement balances. As part of an IS audit, substantive testing involves locating, retrieving, and evaluating accounting data that are stored in databases and flat files. Two popular CAATTs for this purpose are the embedded audit module and generalized audit software.

FIGURE 17–16

Flat Version of a
Complex File
Structure

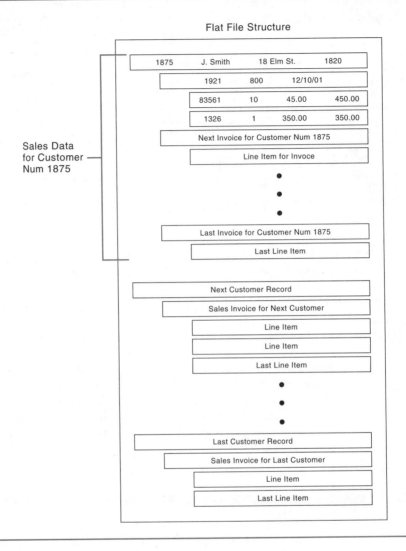

Flat File Structure

Sales Data
for Customer
Num 1875

| 1875 | J. Smith | 18 Elm St. | 1820 |

| 1921 | 800 | 12/10/01 |

| 83561 | 10 | 45.00 | 450.00 |

| 1326 | 1 | 350.00 | 350.00 |

Next Invoice for Customer Num 1875

Line Item for Invoce

•
•
•

Last Invoice for Customer Num 1875

Last Line Item

Next Customer Record

Sales Invoice for Next Customer

Line Item

Line Item

Last Line Item

•
•
•

Last Customer Record

Sales Invoice for Last Customer

Line Item

Last Line Item

Key Terms

access tests   (881)
accuracy tests   (881)
assurance services   (854)
audit objectives   (858)
audit opinion   (858)
audit planning   (859)
audit procedures   (858)
audit risk   (860)
audit trail tests   (881)
authenticity tests   (881)
base case system evaluation (BCSE)   (884)
completeness   (858)

completeness tests   (881)
computer-assisted audit tools and techniques
    (CAATTs)   (883)
control objectives   (862)
control risk   (861)
detection risk   (861)
embedded audit module (EAM)   (890)
external auditing   (856)
existence or occurrence   (858)
generalized audit software (GAS)   (891)
independent auditing   (856)
inherent risk   (861)

integrated test facility (ITF)   (887)
internal auditing   (856)
management assertions   (857)
operating system   (865)
parallel simulation   (888)
presentation and disclosure   (858)
redundancy tests   (881)
rights and obligations   (858)

rounding error tests   (881)
salami fraud   (881)
substantive tests   (860)
test data method   (883)
tests of controls   (859)
tracing   (884)
valuation or allocation   (858)

Review Questions

1. What is the purpose of an audit?
2. Discuss the concept of independence within the context of an audit.
3. What is the meaning of the term *attest services*?
4. What are assurance services?
5. What are the conceptual phases of an audit? How do they differ between general auditing and IT auditing?
6. Distinguish between internal and external auditors.
7. What are the four primary elements described in the definition of auditing?
8. Explain the concept of materiality.
9. What tasks do auditors perform during audit planning, and what techniques are used?
10. Distinguish between tests of controls and substantive testing.
11. What is audit risk?
12. Distinguish between errors and irregularities. Which do you think concern auditors the most?
13. Distinguish between inherent risk and control risk. How do internal controls affect inherent risk and control risk, if at all? What is the role of detection risk?
14. What is the relationship between tests of controls and substantive tests?
15. What are the primary general audit objectives?
16. What are three tests of controls that may be implemented to obtain corroborating evidence regarding virus control?
17. What are the specific objectives of auditors in auditing data management?
18. Define the term CAATT.
19. What is the purpose of an access control list?
20. What types of documents would an auditor review in testing organizational structure controls? Why is it also important to observe actual behavior?
21. What tests may be conducted for identifying unauthorized program changes?
22. What tests may be conducted for identifying application errors?
23. What are some tests of physical security controls?
24. What are some tests of data communications controls?
25. What are the auditor's primary concerns in an audit of EDI objectives? What tests are conducted?
26. What is meant by auditing around the computer versus auditing through the computer? Why is this so important?
27. What are some white box tests?
28. What is an embedded audit module?
29. Explain what GAS is and why it is so popular with larger public accounting firms. Discuss the independence issue related to GAS.

Discussion Questions

1. Discuss the differences between the attest function and assurance services.
2. Explain the audit objectives of existence or occurrence, completeness, rights and obligations, valuation or allocation, and presentation and disclosure.
3. An organization's internal audit department is usually considered to be an effective control

mechanism for evaluating the organization's internal control structure. Birch Company's internal auditing function reports directly to the controller. Comment on the effectiveness of this organizational structure.

4. Why would a systems programmer create a back door if he or she has access to the program in his or her day-to-day tasks?

5. Discuss why any distinction between IS auditing and financial auditing is not meaningful.

6. A CPA firm has many clients. For some of its clients, it relies very heavily on the work of the internal auditors; for others it does not. The amount of reliance affects the fees charged. How can the CPA firm justify the apparent inconsistency of fees charged in a competitive marketplace?

7. Accounting firms are very concerned that their employees have excellent communication skills, both oral and written. Explain why this is important by giving examples of where these skills would be necessary in each of the three phases of an audit.

8. Discuss how the process of obtaining evidence in a CBIS is inherently different than in a manual system.

9. Some internal controls can be tested objectively. Discuss some internal controls that you think are relatively more subjective to assess in terms of adequacy than others.

10. Give a specific example, other than the one in the chapter, to illustrate the relationship between exposure, control, audit objective, and tests of control.

11. The systems development life cycle is a methodology. Why are auditors responsible for evaluating the controls in this process?

12. What factors do you think might cause an auditing team to spend more time than average on tests to identify application errors? For unauthorized program changes?

13. Discuss the subjective nature of auditing computer center security.

14. A recent wave of thefts has occurred of notebook computers containing sensitive data. Thieves dressed as pizza delivery persons or parcel couriers steal these computers. What recommendation can an audit team make to protect this data?

15. Explain how an embedded audit module works and why auditors may choose not to use it.

16. Compare and contrast the following techniques based on costs and benefits:
    • test data method
    • base case system evaluation
    • tracing
    • integrated test facility
    • parallel simulation

Multiple-Choice Questions

1. Which of the following is NOT a task performed in the audit planning phase?
   a. reviewing an organization's policies and practices
   b. determining the degree of reliance on controls
   c. reviewing general controls
   d. planning substantive testing procedures

2. Which of the following risks is least controllable by the auditor?
   a. inherent risk
   b. control risk
   c. detection risk
   d. all are equally controllable

3. Reviewing database authority tables is a(n)
   a. access control.
   b. organizational structure control.
   c. data resource control.
   d. operating resource control.

4. Which of the following is NOT a test for identifying application errors?
   a. reconciling the source code
   b. reviewing test results
   c. retesting the program
   d. testing the authority table

5. Which of the following is NOT a data communications control objective?
   a. maintaining the critical application list
   b. correcting message loss due to equipment failure
   c. preventing illegal access
   d. rendering useless any data that are successfully captured by a perpetrator

6. Which of the following is NOT a common type of white box test of controls?
   a. completeness tests
   b. redundancy tests

c. inference tests

d. authenticity tests

7. An electronic walkthrough of the application's internal logic is called

   a. a salami logic test.

   b. an integrated test.

   c. tracing.

   d. a logic bomb test.

8. CIA 581 1-27

   Which of the following would strengthen organizational control over large-scale electronic data processing activities?

   a. requiring the user departments to specify the minimum standards of control that are necessary to handle transactions and to process data

   b. requiring that requests for data processing services be submitted directly to the console operator of the EDP department

   c. having the librarian report to the supervisor of computer operations rather than to the manager of computer operations

   d. assigning limited responsibility to the user departments for identifying minimum standards of control over handling transactions

   e. none of the above

9. CIA 586 I-13

   An internal auditor noted the following points when conducting a preliminary survey in connection with the audit of an EDP department. Which of the following would be considered a safeguard in the control system on which the auditor might rely?

   a. Programmers and computer operators correct daily processing problems as they arise.

   b. The control group works with user organizations to correct rejected input.

   c. New systems are documented as soon as possible after they begin processing live data.

   d. The average tenure of employees working in the EDP department is ten months.

Problems

1. Audit Plan

Rainbow Paint Company, a medium-sized manufacturing firm, has no internal auditing department. It recently hired a new accounting firm to perform the external audit.

Required:

Outline an audit plan to examine operating system control, program maintenance controls, and organizational system controls. Include in your plan the audit objectives, exposures, necessary controls, and test of controls. Also, be sure to include any documentation the auditors should request.

2. Audit Plan

The auditors for Golden Gate Company have a gut feeling that liabilities may be unrecorded. Their initial suspicions stem from a radical decline in accrued liabilities from last year. Golden Gate's records are all computerized.

Required:

Devise a plan to search through the data files to perform the substantive test of searching for unrecorded liabilities.

3. Exposure Identification and Plan of Action

Two years ago an external auditing firm supervised the programming of embedded audit modules for Previts Office Equipment Company. During the audit process this year, the external auditors requested that a transaction log of all transactions be copied to the audit file. The external auditors noticed large gaps in dates and times for transactions being copied to the audit file. When they inquired about this, they were informed that increased processing of transactions had been burdening the mainframe system and that operators frequently had to turn off the EAM to allow the processing of important transactions in a timely fashion. In addition, much maintenance had been performed during the past year on the application programs.

Required:

Outline any potential exposures and determine the courses of action the external auditors should use to proceed.

4. **Exposure Identification and Plan of Action**

The internal auditors of Brown Electrical Company report to the controller. Due to changes made in the past year to several of the transaction processing programs, the internal auditors created a new test data set. The external auditors requested that the old data set also be run. The internal auditors embarrassingly explained that they overwrote the original test data set.

Required:

Outline any potential exposures and determine the courses of action the external auditor should take.

5. **Exposure Identification and Plan of Action**

As the manager of the external audit team, you realize that the embedded audit module only writes "material" invoices to the audit file for the accounts receivable confirmation process. You are immediately concerned that the accounts receiv-

able account may be substantially overstated this year and for the prior years in which this EAM was used.

Required:

Explain why you are concerned since all "material" invoices are candidates for confirmation by the customer. Outline a plan for determining if the accounts receivable are overstated.

6. **Audit Objectives and Procedures**

As an auditor, discuss any concerns that you would have, and any actions that you would take, in the following situation:

You are conducting substantive tests on the accounts receivable file to verify its accuracy. The file is large, and you decide to test only a sample of the records. Because of the complexity of the database structure you cannot access the database directly. The client's systems programmer uses a utility program to write a query that produces a flat file, which he provides you for testing purposes.

Internal Control Cases

1. **CMA 1290 4-Y7**
   Generalized Audit Software

The internal audit department of Sachem Manufacturing Company is considering buying computer software that will aid in the auditing process. Sachem's financial and manufacturing control systems are completely automated on a large mainframe computer. Melinda Robinson, the director of internal audit, believes that Sachem should acquire computer audit software to assist in the financial and procedure audits that her department conducts. The types of software packages that Robinson is considering are described below.

- A generalized audit software package that assists in basic audit work, such as the retrieval of live data from large computer files. The department would review this information using conventional audit investigation techniques. More specifically, the department could perform criteria selection, sampling, basic computations for quantitative analysis, record

handling, graphical analysis, and the printing of output (confirmations).
- An integrated test facility package that uses, monitors, and controls dummy test data through existing programs and checks the existence and adequacy of program data entry controls and processing controls.
- A control flowcharting package that provides a graphical presentation of the data flow of information through a system, pinpointing control strengths and weaknesses.
- A program (parallel) simulation and modeling package that uses actual data to conduct the same systemized process by using a different computer-logic program developed by the auditor. The package can also be used to seek answers to difficult audit problems (involving many comparisons and computations) within statistically acceptable confidence limits.

Required:

a. Without regard to any specific computer audit software, explain to the internal auditor the general advantages of using computer audit software to assist with audits.

b. Describe the audit purpose facilitated and the procedural steps to be followed by the internal auditor to use a(n)

1. generalized audit software package.
2. integrated test facility package.
3. control flowcharting package.
4. program (parallel) simulation and modeling package.

2. CMA 6898 3-3
Audit Committee Software

Micro Dynamics, a developer of database software packages, is a publicly held company whose stock is traded over the counter. The company recently received an enforcement release proceeding through an SEC administrative law judge that cited the company for inadequate internal controls. In response, Micro Dynamics has agreed to establish an internal audit function and strengthen its audit committee.

A manager of the internal audit department has been hired as a result of the SEC enforcement action to establish an internal audit function. In addition, the composition of the audit committee has been changed to include all outside directors. Micro Dynamics has held its initial planning meeting to discuss the roles of the various participants in the internal control and financial reporting process. Participants at the meeting included the company president, the chief financial officer, a member of the audit committee, a partner from Micro Dynamics' external audit firm, and the newly appointed manager of the internal audit department. Comments by the various meeting participants are presented below.

President: "We want to ensure that Micro Dynamics complies with the SEC's enforcement release and that we don't find ourselves in this position again. The internal audit department should help to strengthen our internal control system by correcting the problems. I would like your thoughts on the proper reporting relationship for the manager of the internal audit department."

CFO: "I think the manager of the internal audit department should report to me since much of the department's work is related to financial issues. The audit committee should have oversight responsibilities."

Audit committee member: "I believe we should think through our roles more carefully. The Treadway Commission has recommended that the audit committee play a more important role in the financial reporting process; the duties of today's audit committee have expanded beyond mere rubber-stamp approval. We need to have greater assurance that controls are in place and being followed."

External audit firm partner: "We need a close working relationship among all of our roles. The internal audit department can play a significant role in monitoring the control systems on a continuing basis and should have strong ties to your external audit firm."

Internal audit department manager: "The internal audit department should be more involved in operational auditing, but it also should play a significant monitoring role in the financial reporting area."

Required:

a. Describe the role of each of the following in the establishment, maintenance, and evaluation of Micro Dynamics' system of internal control.

1. Management
2. Audit committee
3. External auditor
4. Internal audit department

b. Describe the responsibilities that Micro Dynamics' audit committee has in the financial reporting process.

3. CMA 1290 4-Y8
Role of Internal Auditor

Leigh Industries has an internal audit department consisting of a director and four staff auditors. The director of internal audit, Diane Bauer, reports to the corporate controller, who receives copies of all internal audit reports. In addition, copies of all internal audit reports are sent to the audit committee of the board of directors and the individual responsible for the area of activity being audited.

In the past, the company's external auditors have relied on the work of the internal audit department to a substantial degree. However, in recent months, Bauer has become concerned that the objectivity of the internal audit function is being affected by the nonaudit work being performed by the department. This possible loss of objectivity could result in more extensive testing and analysis by the external auditors. The percentage of nonaudit work performed by the internal auditors has steadily increased to about 25 percent of the total hours worked. A sample of five recent nonaudit activities is presented below.

- One of the internal auditors assisted in the preparation of policy statements on internal control. These statements included such things as policies regarding sensitive payments and the safeguarding of assets.
- Reconciling the bank statements of the corporation each month is a regular assignment of one of the internal auditors. The corporate controller believes this strengthens the internal control function because the internal auditor is not involved in either the receipt or the disbursement of cash.
- The internal auditors are asked to review the annual budget each year for relevance and reasonableness before the budget is approved. At the end of each month, the corporate controller's staff analyzes the variances from budget and prepares explanations of these variances. These variances and explanations are then reviewed by the internal audit staff.
- One of the internal auditors has been involved in the design, installation, and initial operation of a new computerized inventory system. The auditor was primarily concerned with the design and implementation of internal accounting controls and conducted the evaluation of these controls during the test runs.
- The internal auditors are sometimes asked to make the accounting entries for complex transactions as the employees in the accounting department are not adequately trained to handle such transactions. The corporate controller believes this gives an added measure of assurance to the accurate recording of these transactions.

Required:

a. Define objectivity as it relates to the internal audit function.
b. For each of the five nonaudit activities presented, explain whether the objectivity of Leigh Industries' Internal Audit Department has been materially impaired. Consider each situation independently.

c. The director of internal audit reports directly to the corporate controller.
   1. Does this reporting relationship affect the objectivity of the internal audit department? Explain your answer.
   2. Would your evaluation of the five situations in question (b) change if the director of internal audit reported to the audit committee of the board of directors? Explain your answer.

4. **CMA 1287 3-Y6**
Role of Internal Auditors
The impact of employee and management fraud is staggering in terms of dollar costs and effects on the victims. Presented below are three independent cases of employee wrongdoing.

- A retail store that was part of a national chain experienced an abnormal inventory shrinkage in its audiovisual department. The internal auditors, noting this shrinkage, included an in-depth evaluation of the department in the scope of their audit of the store. During their review, the auditors were "tipped" by an employee that a particular customer bought a large number of small electronic components and that the customer always went to a certain cashier's checkout line. The auditors' work revealed that the cashier and the customer had colluded to steal a number of electronic components. The cashier did not record the sale of several items the customer took from the store.
- Internal auditors discovered a payroll fraud in a large hospital when they conducted a surprise review of the distribution of paychecks. The supervisors of each department distributed paychecks to employees and were supposed to return unclaimed checks to the payroll department. When the auditors took control of, and followed up on, an unclaimed paycheck for an employee in the food service department, they discovered that the employee had quit four months before. The employee and the supervisor had an argument, and the employee had simply left and never returned. The supervisor had continued to turn in a time card for the employee and, when the paychecks came from distribution, had taken the unclaimed checks and cashed them.
- While performing an audit of cash disbursements in a manufacturing firm, internal audi-

tors discovered a fraud perpetrated by an accounts payable clerk. The clerk had made copies of supporting documents and used the copies to support duplicate payments to a vendor of materials used in the manufacturing process. The clerk, who had opened a bank account in a name similar to that of the vendor, took the duplicate checks and deposited them in the bank account.

Required:
a. Explain the internal auditor's general role in detecting errors and irregularities.
b. Discuss the steps that an internal auditor should take when fraud is suspected.
c. For each of the three situations presented, describe the recommendations that the internal auditors should make to prevent similar problems in the future.

5. CMA 686 3-Y6
Audit of Systems Planning
AndreCo is a growing manufacturer of subassembled components used in a variety of home appliances. Because sales have doubled in the past three years, management has decided to convert its manual system of information gathering and processing that has evolved during the company's first ten years in business to a more efficient and effective system based on a planned integrated approach. AndreCo's chief financial officer, Robert Ganning, has been asked to present a plan for the development and implementation of the new system. Peter Martin, an internal auditor for AndreCo, has been asked to review the plan to ensure its validity.

"I think it would be better if we worked together throughout the process," Martin told

Ganning. "I see three distinct review phases that should be handled as consecutive elements in the process of developing the new system: specification, design, and system. Each phase should be completed and reviewed before the next phase is begun."

Martin defined the three phases as follows:

- *Specification review.* A review of the system definition to determine if the system provides for the internal control objectives of authorization, recording, safeguarding assets, and substantiation.
- *Design review.* A review of the detailed design to ensure that the system procedures and controls will accomplish the requirements established and approved in the specification review.
- *System review.* A trial run of the actual system during implementation to ascertain the presence of the original objective. Errors or omissions in translation of the designed system to an actual, implemented system would be detected.

Ganning and Martin agreed that a three-phase review approach would be both effective and efficient, and they proceeded on that basis.

Required:
a. Identify and discuss the considerations that should be part of the specification review process.
b. Recommend procedures that would help to validate the system development activities in the
   1. design review.
   2. system review.
c. Formulate an acceptance test as a final verification of the system's adequacy and integrity.

GLOSSARY

The chapter in which the term is first defined is set in parentheses following the definition.

A

Access controls: Controls that ensure that only authorized personnel have access to the firms assets. (3)

Access method: The technique used to locate records and to navigate through the database. (2)

Access tests: Tests that ensure that the application prevents authorized users from unauthorized access to data. (17)

Accounting information systems (AIS): Specialized subset of information system that processes financial transactions. (1)

Accounting record: A document, journal, or ledger used in transaction cycles. (2)

Accounts payable pending file: File containing a copy of the purchase requisition. (5)

Accuracy tests: Tests that ensure that the system processes only data values that conform to specified tolerances. (17)

Activities: Work performed in a firm. (7)

Activity-based costing (ABC): Accounting technique that provides managers with information about activities and cost objects. (7)

Activity driver: Factor that measures the activity consumption by the cost object. (7)

Agents: Individuals and departments that participate in an economic event. (1)

Alphabetic codes: Alphabetic characters assigned sequentially. (8)

Alphanumeric codes: Codes that allow the use of pure alphabetic characters embedded within numeric codes. (8)

American National Standards Institute (ANSI): The most popular EDI standard in the United States. (12)

Archive file: File that contains records of past transactions that are retained for future reference. (2)

Association: The relationship among record types. (9)

Attendance file: File created by the timekeeping department upon receipt of approved time cards. (6)

Attributes: Equivalents to adjectives in the English language that serve to describe the objects. (9)

Audit opinion: Opinion of auditor regarding the presentation of financial statements. (17)

Audit planning: Stage at which the auditor identifies the financially significant applications and attempts to understand the controls over the primary transactions that are processed by these applications. (17)

Audit risk: Probability that the auditor will render unqualified opinions on financial statements that are, in fact, materially misstated. (17)

Audit trail: Accounting records that trace transactions from their source documents to the financial statements. (2)

Auditing: Form of independent attestation performed by an expert who expresses an opinion about the fairness of a company's financial statements. (1)

Authenticity tests: Tests verifying that an individual, a programmed procedure, or a message attempting to access a system is authentic. (17)

Authority: The right to make decisions pertaining to areas of responsibility. (8)

Automated storage and retrieval systems (AS/RS): Computer-controlled conveyor systems that carry raw materials from stores to the shop floor and finished products to the warehouse. (7)

B

Backbone systems: Basic system structure on which to build. (1)

Base case system evaluation (BCSE): Variant of the test data technique, in which comprehensive test data are used. (17)

Batch: A group of similar transactions accumulated over time and then processed together. (2)

Batch control: Effective method of managing high volumes of transaction data through a system. (16)

Batch control totals: Record that accompanies the sales order file through all of the data processing runs. (4)

Batch systems: Systems that assemble transactions into groups for processing. (2)

Benchmarking: Comparison of key activities with similar activities elsewhere in the firm or in other firms. (7)

Big bang: An attempt by organizations to switch operations from their old legacy systems to the new system in a single event that implements the ERP across the entire company. (11)

Bill of lading: Formal contract between the seller and the shipping company that transports the goods to the customer. (4)

Bill of materials: Document that specifies the types and quantities of the raw materials and subassemblies used in producing a single unit of finished product. (7)

Biometric devices: Devices that measure various personal characteristics, such as fingerprints, voice prints, retina prints, or signature characteristics. (15)

Blind copy: A copy of the purchase order that contains no price or quantity information. (5)

Block code: A coding scheme that assigns ranges of values to specific attributes such as account classifications. (8)

Bolt-on software: Software provided by third-party vendors used in conjunction with already-purchased ERP software. (11)

Bus topology: Nodes in the topology that are connected to a common cable. (12)

C

Call-back device: Hardware component that asks the caller to enter a password and then breaks the connection to perform a security check. (16)

Cardinality: The numerical mapping between entity instances. (2)

Carrier sensing: Random access technique that detects collisions when they occur. (12)

Cash prelist: A list of all cash received by the mail room. (4)

Cells: Configuration of several different types of CNC into one complex machine. (7)

Centralized database: Database retained in a central location. (9)

Certification authorities (CAs): Trusted third parties that issue digital certificates. (12)

Chart of accounts: A listing of an organization's accounts showing the account number and name. (8)

Check digit: Method for detecting data coding errors. A control digit is added to the code when it is originally designed to allow the integrity of the code to be established during subsequent processing. (16)

Check register: A record of all cash disbursements. (5)

Client-server model: A form of network topology in which a user's computer or terminal (the client) accesses the ERP programs and data via a host computer called the server.

Client-server topology: Topology involving the distribution of data processing between the user's application—the client—and the server. (12)

Closed database architecture: A database management system used to provide minimal technological advantage over flat file systems. (11)

Cohesion: Number of tasks a module performs. (14)

Cold turkey cutover: Process of converting in which a firm switches to a new system on a particular day and simultaneously terminates the old system. (14)

Compilers: Language translation modules of the operation system. (15)

Completeness tests: Tests identifying missing data within a single record and entire records missing from a batch. (17)

Computer-aided design (CAD): Use of computers to design products to be manufactured. (7)

Computer-aided manufacturing (CAM): Use of computers in factory automation. (7)

Computer-aided software engineering (CASE): Technology that involves the use of computer systems to design and code computer systems. (13)

Computer-integrated manufacturing (CIM): Completely automated environment. (7)

Computer numerical control (CNC): Computer-controlled machines that replace skilled labor. The computer contains programs for all parts being manufactured by the machine. (7)

Conceptual systems design: The production of several alternative designs for the new system. (13)

Conceptual user views: Description of the entire database. (14)

Control activities: Policies and procedures used to ensure that appropriate actions are taken to deal with the organization's risks. (3)

Control environment: The foundation of internal control. (3)

Control objectives: Objectives used by auditors to test the internal control structure. (17)

Control risk: Likelihood that the control structure is flawed because controls are either absent or inadequate to prevent or detect errors in the account. (17)

Conversion cycle: Cycle comprising the production system and the cost accounting system. (2)

Cookies: Files containing user information that are created by the Web server of the site being visited and are then stored on the visitor's own computer hard drive. (12)

Corrective controls: Actions taken to reverse the effects of errors detected in the previous step. (3)

Cost-benefit analysis: Process that helps management determine whether (and by how much) the benefits received from a proposed system will outweigh its costs. (14)

Cost center: Organizational unit with responsibility for cost management within budgetary limits. (8)

Cost driver: Cause of the cost. (7)

Cost objects: Reasons for performing activities. (7)

Coupling: Measure of the degree of interaction between modules. (14)

Credit memo: Document used to authorize the customer to receive credit for the merchandise returned. (4)

Critical success factors: Items of such importance that failure to meet any one of them would cause the firm to fail. (7)

Customer open order file: File containing a copy of the sales order. (4)

Customer order: Document that indicates the type and quantity of merchandise being requested. (4)

Cutover: Process of converting from the old system to the new system. (14)

Cycle billing: Method of spreading the billing process out over the month. (4)

D

Data: Facts, which may or may not be processed (edited, summarized, or refined) and have no direct effect on the user. (1)

Data collision: Event that occurs when two or more signals are transmitted simultaneously. (12)

Data currency: When the firm's data files accurately reflect the effects of its transactions. (9)

Data definition language (DDL): Programming language used to define the database to the database management system. (9)

Data dictionary: Description of every data element in the database. (9)

Data encryption: Technique that uses an algorithm to scramble selected data, making it unreadable to an intruder browsing the database. (15)

Data encryption standard (DES): Approach that uses a single key known to both the sender and the receiver of the message. (12)

Data flow diagram: Diagram that uses a set of symbols to represent the processes, data sources, data flows, and process sequences of a current or proposed system. (2)

Data manipulation language (DML): Language used to insert special database commands into application programs written in conventional languages. (9)

Data mart: A data warehouse organized for a single department or function. (11)

Data modeling: The task of formalizing the data requirements of the business process as a conceptual model. (10)

Data normalization: Process that promotes effective database design. (9)

Data redundancy: The state of data elements being represented in all user files. (9)

Data structures: Techniques for physically arranging records in a database. (2)

Data warehouse: A database constructed for quick searching, retrieval, ad hoc queries, and ease of use. (11)

Database: Physical repository for financial data. (1)

Database administrator: The individual responsible for managing the database resource. (9)

Database approach: A data management approach utilizing databases that users can share. (2)

Database authorization table: Table containing rules that limit the actions a user can take. (15)

Database lockout: Software control that prevents multiple simultaneous access to data. (9)

Database management system (DBMS): Software system that controls access to the data resource. (1)

Deadlock: A "wait" state that occurs between sites when data are locked by multiple sites waiting for the removal of the locks from the other sites. (9)

Deletion anomaly: The unintentional deletion of data from a table. (9)

Depreciation schedule: Record used to initiate depreciation calculations. (6)

Detailed systems design: Design of screen outputs, reports, and operational documents; entity relationship diagrams; normal form designs for database tables; updated data dictionary; designs for all screen inputs and source documents; context diagrams for overall system; low-level data flow diagrams; and structure diagrams for program modules. (14)

Detection risk: Risk that auditors are willing to take that errors not detected or prevented by the control structure will also not be detected by the auditor. (17)

Detective controls: Devices, techniques, and procedures designed to identify and expose undesirable events that elude preventive controls. (3)

Digital certificate: A sender's public key that has been digitally signed by trusted third parties. (12)

Digital envelope: An encryption method where both DES and RSA are used together. (12)

Digital signature: An electronic authentication technique that ensures the transmitted message originated with the authorized sender and that it was not tampered with after the signature was applied. (12)

Direct access files: Files in which each record has a unique location or address. (2)

Disaster recovery plan (DRP): Comprehensive statement of all actions to be taken before, during, and after a disaster, along with documented, tested procedures that will ensure the continuity of operations. (15)

Disk locks: Devices that prevent unauthorized individuals from accessing the floppy disk drive of a computer. (16)

Distributed databases: Databases distributed using either the partitioned or replicated technique. (9)

Document flowchart: Flowchart that shows the relationship among processes and the documents that flow between them. (2)

Documentation: Written description of how the system works. (14)

Drill-down: Operations permitting the disaggregation of data to reveal the underlying details that explain certain phenomena. (11)

E

Echo check: Technique that involves the receiver of the message returning the message to the sender. (16)

Economic order quantity (EOQ) model: Inventory model designed to reduce total inventory costs. (7)

Electronic data interchange (EDI): The intercompany exchange of computer-processible business information in standard format. (4)

Embedded audit module (EAM): Technique in which one or more specially programmed modules embedded in a host application select and record predetermined types of transactions for subsequent analysis. (17)

Employee file: A file used with the attendance file to create an on-line payroll register. (6)

Employee fraud: Performance fraud by nonmanagement employees generally designed to directly convert cash or other assets to the employees' personal benefit. (3)

Empty shell: Arrangement that involves two or more user organizations that buy or lease a building and remodel it into a computer site, but without the computer and peripheral equipment. (15)

Encryption: Technique that uses a computer program to transform a standard message being transmitted into a coded (ciphertext) form. (16)

End users: Users for whom the system is built. (1)

Enterprise resource planning (ERP): A system assembled of prefabricated software components. (11)

Entity: A resource, event, or agent. (2)

Entity relationship (ER) diagram: Documentation technique used to represent the relationship among activities and users in a system. (2)

Ethics: Principles of conduct that individuals use in making choices in guiding their behavior in situations that involve the concepts of right and wrong. (3)

Events: Phenomena that affect changes in resources. (1)

Expenditure cycle: Acquisition of materials, property, and labor in exchange for cash. (2)

Exposure: Absence or weakness of a control. (3)

F

Financial transaction: An economic event that affects the assets and equities of the organization, is measured in financial terms, and is reflected in the accounts of the firm. (1)

Firewall: Software and hardware that provide a focal point for security by channeling all network connections through a control gateway. (12)

Flat file approach: An organizational environment in which users own their data exclusively. (2)

Formalization of tasks: When organizational areas are subdivided into tasks that represent full-time job positions. (8)

G

Gantt chart: Horizontal bar chart that presents time on a horizontal plane and activities on a vertical plane. (14)

General ledger change report: Report that presents the effects of journal voucher transactions on the general ledger accounts. (8)

General ledger history file: File that presents comparative financial reports on a historic basis. (8)

Generalized audit software (GAS): Software that allows auditors to access electronically coded data files and perform various operations on their contents. (17)

Goal congruence: The merging of goals within an organization. (8)

Grandparent-parent-child technique: Backup technique used in sequential batch systems. (15)

Group codes: Codes used to represent complex items or events involving two or more pieces of related data. (8)

H

Hash total: Control technique that uses nonfinancial data to keep track of the records in a batch. (16)

Hashing structure: Structure employing an algorithm that converts the primary key of a record directly into a storage address. (2)

Hierarchical data model: A database model that represents data in a hierarchical structure and permits only a single parent record for each child. (9)

Hierarchical topology: Topology where a host computer is connected to several levels of subordinate smaller computers in a master-slave relationship. (12)

I

Independence: The separation of the record keeping function of accounting from the functional areas that have custody of physical resources. (1)

Independent verification: Independent check of the accounting system to identify errors and misrepresentations. (3)

Indexed random file: Randomly organized file that is accessed via an index. (2)

Indexed sequential file: Sequential file structure that is accessed via an index. (9)

Indexed structure: A class of file structure that use indexes for its primary access method. (2)

Inference controls: Controls that prevent users from inferring specific data values through normal query features. (15)

Information: Facts that cause the user to take an action that he or she otherwise could not, or would not, have taken. (1)

Information overload: When a manager receives more information than can be assimilated. (8)

Inherent risk: Risk that is associated with the unique characteristics of the business or industry of the client. (17)

Inheritance: Each object instance inherits the attributes and operations of the class to which it belongs. (13)

Insertion anomaly: The unintentional insertion of data into a table. (9)

Instance: Single occurrence of an object within a class. (13)

Integrated test facility (ITF): Automated technique that enables the auditor to test an application's logic and controls during its normal operation. (17)

Intelligent forms: Forms that help the user complete the form and that make calculations automatically. (14)

Internal control system: Policies a firm employs to safeguard the firm's assets, ensure accurate and reliable accounting records and information, promote efficiency, and measure compliance with established policies. (3)

Internal view: The physical arrangement of records in the database. (9)

Interpreters: Language translation modules of the operation system that convert one line of logic at a time. (15)

Inverted list: A cross reference created from multiple indexes. (9)

Investment center: Organizational unit that has the objective of maximizing the return on investment assets. (8)

IP spoofing: A form of masquerading to gain unauthorized access to a Web server and/or to perpetrate an unlawful act without revealing one's identity. (12)

Islands of technology: An environment where modern automation exists in the form of islands that stand alone within the traditional setting. (7)

J

Journal voucher: Document sent to the general ledger for posting. (4)

Journal voucher listing: Listing that provides relevant details about each journal voucher received by the GL/FRS. (8)

Just-in-time (JIT): Philosophy that attacks manufacturing problems through process simplification. (7)

K

Kiting: Method of inflating assets to hide the theft of an asset. (3)

L

Labor distribution summary: A summarization of labor costs in work-in-process accounts. (6)

Lapping: Use of customer checks, received in payment of their accounts, to conceal cash previously stolen by an employee. (3)

Local area network: Network generally confined to a close geographical area. (12)

Logic bomb: Destructive program, such as a virus, that is triggered by some predetermined event. (15)

Logical key pointer: A pointer containing the primary key of the related record. (2)

M

Maintenance: Process that involves changing systems to accommodate changes in user needs. (12)

Management by exception: The concept that managers should limit their attention to potential problem areas rather than being involved with every activity or decision. (8)

Management control decisions: Technique for motivating managers in all functional areas to use resources as productively as possible. (8)

Management fraud: Performance fraud that often uses deceptive practices to inflate earnings or to forestall the recognition of either insolvency or a decline in earnings. (3)

Management information system (MIS): System that processes nonfinancial transactions that are not normally processed by traditional accounting information systems. (1)

Management reporting system (MRS): System that provides the internal financial information needed to manage a business. (1)

Manufacturing resources planning II (MRP II): System that incorporates techniques to execute the production plan, provide feedback, and control the process. (7)

Master file File containing account data. (2)

Material return ticket: Documentation that accompanies materials being returned to the storeroom. (7)

Materials requirements planning (MRP): System used to plan inventory requirements in response to production work orders. (7)

Materials requisition: Document that authorizes the storekeeper to release materials to individuals or work centers in the production process. (7)

Mnemonic codes: Alphabetic characters in the form of acronyms that convey meaning. (8)

Monitoring: The process by which the quality of internal control design and operation can be assessed. (3)

Move ticket: Document that records work done in each work center and authorizes the movement of the job or batch from one work center to the next. (7)

Mutual aid pact: Agreement between two or more organizations (with comparable computer facilities) to aid each other with their data processing needs in the event of a disaster. (15)

N

Navigational model: Model that possesses explicit links or paths among data elements. (9)

Network model: Variation of the hierarchical model. (9)

Network topology: Physical arrangement of the components. (12)

New systems development: Process that involves five steps: identifying the problem, understanding what needs to be done, considering alternative solutions, selecting the best solution, and implementing the solution. (13)

O

Object class: Logical grouping of individual objects that share the same attributes and operations. (13)

Object-oriented design: Building information systems from reusable standard components or modules. (13)

Object-oriented programming (OOP): Programming objects represented in the ER diagram, along with their attributes and operations, into modules. (13)

Object-oriented programming (OOP) language: Programming language containing the attributes and operations that constitute the object modules represented in the ER diagram at the implementation phase of the SDLC. (14)

Objects: Equivalent to nouns in the English language. (13)

On-demand reports: Reports triggered by events. (8)

On-line analytical processing (OLAP): An enterprise resource planning tool used to supply management with real-time information and also permits timely decisions that are needed to improve performance and achieve competitive advantage. (11)

On-line transaction processing (OLTP): Events consisting of large numbers of relatively simple transactions such as updating accounting records that are stored in several related tables. (11)

One-time password: A network password that constantly changes. (16)

Operational control decisions: Technique that ensures that the firm operates in accordance with preestablished criteria. (8)

Operations: Equivalent to verbs and show actions that are performed on objects and that may change their attributes. (13)

P

Packet switching: Messages that are divided into small packets for transmission. (12)

Packing slip: Document that travels with the goods to the customer to describe the contents of the order. (4)

Parallel operation cutover: Process of converting in which the old system and the new system are run simultaneously for a period of time. (14)

Parallel simulation: Technique that requires the auditor to write a program that simulates key features of processes of the application under review. (17)

Parity check: Technique that incorporates an extra bit into the structure of a bit string when it is created or transmitted. (16)

Partitioned databases: Database approach that splits the central database into segments or partitions that are distributed to their primary users. (9)

Password: Secret code entered by the user to gain access to the data files. (15)

Payroll imprest account: An account into which a single check for the entire amount of the payroll is deposited. (6)

Payroll register: Document showing gross pay, deductions, overtime pay, and net pay. (6)

Personnel action form: Document identifying employees authorized to receive a paycheck; is used to reflect changes in pay rates, payroll deductions, and job classification. (6)

PERT chart: Chart that reflects the relationship among the many activities that constitute the implementation process. (14)

Phased cutover: Process of converting to the new system in modules. (14)

Point-of-sale (POS) system: A revenue system in which no customer accounts receivable are maintained and inventory is kept on the store's shelves, not in a separate warehouse. (4)

Pointer structure: A structure in which the address (pointer) of one record is stored in the field on a related record. (2)

Polling: Popular technique for establishing communication session in WANs. (12)

Post-implementation review: Step in implementation phase that measures the success of the system. (8)

Preventive controls: Passive techniques designed to reduce the frequency of occurrence of undesirable events. (3)

Primary key: Characteristics that uniquely identify each record in the tables. (1)

Proactive management: Management that stays alert to subtle signs of problems and aggressively looks for ways to improve the organization's systems. (13)

Product documents: Documents that result from transaction processing. (2)

Production schedule: Formal plan and authorization to begin production. (7)

Profit center: Organizational unit with responsibility for both cost control and revenue generation. (8)

Program flowchart: Diagram that provides a detailed description of the sequential and logical operations of the program. (2)

Programmed reports: Reports that provide information to solve problems that users have anticipated. (8)

Project feasibility: Analysis that determines how best to proceed with a project. (13)

Project planning: Allocation of resources to individual applications within the framework of the strategic plan. (13)

Project schedule: Document that formally presents management's commitment to the project. (13)

Protocols: Rules and standards governing the design of hardware and software that permit network users to communicate and share data. (12)

Prototyping: Technique for providing users a preliminary working version of the system. (13)

Pseudocode: English-like code that describes the logic of a program without specific language systems. (14)

Public key encryption: Technique that uses two keys: one for encoding the message, the other for decoding it. (12)

Purchase order: A document based on a purchase requisition that specifies items ordered from a vendor or supplier. (5)

Purchase requisition: A document that authorizes a purchase transaction. (5)

R

REA (resources, events, and agents) model: An alternative accounting framework for modeling an organization's critical resources, events, and agents and the relationships between them. (10)

Reactive management: Management that responds to problems only when they reach a crisis state and can no longer be ignored. (13)

Real-time systems: Systems that process transactions individually at the moment the economic event occurs. (2)

Receiving report: Report that lists quantity and condition of the inventories. (5)

Recovery operations center (ROC): Arrangement involving two or more user organizations that buy or lease a building and remodel it into a completely equipped computer site. (15)

Redundancy tests: Tests that determine that an application processes each record only once. (17)

Reengineering: The identification and elimination of nonvalue-added tasks by replacing traditional procedures with those that are innovative and different. (4)

Reference file: File that stores data that are used as standards for processing transactions. (2)

Relational database management systems (RDBMS): A database management system that presents data to users as tables and supports the relational algebra functions of restrict, project, and join without requiring any definitions of access paths to support these operations. (9)

Remittance advice: Source document that contains key information required to service the customers account. (4)

Reorder point: Lead time times daily demand. (7)

Replicated database: Database approach in which the central database is replicated at each site. (9)

Request-response technique: Technique in which a control message from the sender and a response from the sender are sent at periodic synchronized intervals. (16)

Resources: Assets of an organization. (10)

Responsibility: An individual's obligation to achieve desired results. (8)

Responsibility accounting: Concept that implies that every economic event affecting the organization is the responsibility of and can be traced to an individual manager. (8)

Responsibility center: Organization of business entities into areas involving cost, profit, and investment. (8)

Responsibility reports: Reports containing performance measures at each operational segment in the firm, which flow upward to senior levels of management. (8)

Reusable password: A network password that can be used more than one time. (16)

Revenue cycle: Cycle comprising of sales order processing and cash receipts. (2)

Ring topology: Topology that eliminates the central site. All nodes in this configuration are of equal status. (12)

Risk assessment: The identification, analysis, and management of risks relevant to financial reporting. (3)

Robotics: CNC machine used in hazardous environments or to perform dangerous and monotonous tasks that are accident prone. (7)

Rounding error tests: Tests that verify the correctness of rounding procedures. (17)

Route sheet: Document that shows the production path a particular batch of product follows during manufacturing. (7)

Run: Each program in a batch system. (2)

Run-to-run controls: Controls that use batch figures to monitor the batch as it moves from one programmed procedure to another. (16)

S

Safety stock: Additional inventories added to the re-order point to avoid unanticipated stockout conditions. (7)

Salami fraud: Fraud in which each victim is unaware of being defrauded. (17)

Sales order: Source document that captures such vital information as the name and address of the customer making the purchase; the customer's account number; the name, number, and description of product; quantities and unit price of items sold; and other financial information. (4)

Scalability: The system's ability to grow smoothly and economically as user requirements increase. (11)

Scheduled reports: Reports produced according to an established time frame. (8)

Schema: Description of the entire database. (9)

Screening router: A firewall that examines the source and destination addresses that are attached to incoming message packets. (16)

Segregation of duties: Separation of employee duties to minimize incompatible functions. (3)

Sequential codes: Codes that represent items in some sequential order. (8)

Sequential files: Files that are structured sequentially and must be accessed sequentially. (2)

Sequential structure: A data structure in which all records in the file lie in contiguous storage spaces in a specified sequence arranged by their primary key. (2)

Servers: Special-purpose computers that manage common resources, such as programs, data, and printers of the LAN. (12)

Shipping notice: Document that informs the billing department that the customer's order has been filled and shipped. (4)

Slicing and dicing: Operations enabling the user to examine data from different viewpoints. (11)

Source documents: Documents that capture and formalize transaction data needed for processing by their respective transaction cycles. (2)

Span of control: Number of subordinates directly under a manager's control. (8)

Spooling: When applications are designed to direct their output to a magnetic disk file rather than to the printer directly. (16)

Stakeholders: Entities either inside or outside an organization that have direct or indirect interest in the firm. (1)

Star topology: A network of IPUs with a large central computer at the hub, which has direct connections to a periphery of smaller computers. (12)

Steering committee: An organizational committee consisting of senior-level management responsible for systems planning. (13)

Stock release: Document that identifies which items of inventory must be located and picked from the warehouse shelves. (4)

Strategic planning decisions: Planning with a long-term time frame and that is associated with a high degree of uncertainty. (8)

Structure diagram: Diagram that divides processes into input, process, and output functions. (14)

Structured design: Disciplined way of designing systems from the top down. (13)

Structured problem: Problem in which data, procedures, and objectives are known with certainty. (8)

Substantive tests: Tests that determine whether database contents fairly reflect the organization's transactions. (17)

Subsystem: A system viewed in relation to the larger system of which it is a part. (1)

Supervision: A control activity involving the critical oversight of employees. (3)

Supplier's invoice: The bill sent from the seller to the buyer showing unit costs, taxes, freight, and other charges. (5)

Supply chain management (SCM): A class of application software that supports the set of activities associated with moving goods from the raw materials stage through to the consumer. (11)

System: Group of two or more interrelated components or subsystems that serve a common purpose. (1)

System development life cycle: The formal process by which in-house development is accomplished. (1)

System flowcharts: Flowcharts used to show the relationship between the key elements—input sources, programs, and output products—of computer systems. (2)

System survey: Determination of what elements, if any, of the current system should be preserved as part of the new system. (13)

Systems analysis: Two-step process that involves a survey of the current system and then an analysis of the user's needs. (13)

Systems development life cycle (SDLC): Formal process consisting of two major phases: new systems development and maintenance. (13)

Systems planning: Linking of individual system projects or applications to the strategic objectives of the firm. (13)

T

Tactical planning decisions: Planning performed by the middle-level manager to achieve the strategic plans of the organization. (8)

Test data method: Technique used to establish application integrity by processing specially prepared sets of input data through production applications that are under review. (17)

Tests of controls: Tests that establish whether internal controls are functioning properly. (17)

Third normal form (3NF): The normalization that occurs by dividing an unnormalized database into smaller tables until all attributes in the resulting tables are uniquely and wholly dependent on (explained by) the primary key. (9)

Third-generation languages: Procedural languages in which the programmer must specify the sequence of events used in an operation. (14)

Three-tier model: A model where the database and application functions are separated. (11)

Token passing: Transmission of a special signal (token) around the network from node to node in a specific sequence. (12)

Tracing: Test data technique that performs an electronic walkthrough of the application's internal logic. (17)

Trading partners: Category of external user, including customer sales and billing information, purchase information for suppliers, and inventory receipts information. (1)

Transaction: An event that affects an organization and that is processed by its information system as a unit of work. (1)

Transaction authorization: Procedure to ensure that employees process only valid transactions within the scope of their authority. (3)

Transaction file: Temporary file that holds transaction records that will be used to change or update data in a master file. (2)

Transaction processing system (TPS): Activity comprising three major subsystems—the revenue cycle, the expenditure cycle, and the conversion cycle. (1)

Transcription error: Type of error that can corrupt a data code and cause processing errors. (16)

Transfer Control Protocol/Internet Protocol (TCP/IP): The basic protocol that permits communication between Internet nodes. (12)

Transposition error: Error that occurs when digits are transposed. (16)

Trojan horse: Program that attaches to another legitimate program but does not replicate itself like a virus. (15)

Turnaround documents: Product documents of one system that become source documents for another system. (2)

Turnkey systems: Completely finished and tested systems that are ready for implementation. (1)

Two-tier model: A model where the server handles both application and database duties. (11)

U

Universal product code (UPC): A label containing price information (and other data) that is attached to items purchased in a point-of-sale system. (4)

Unstructured problem: Problem for which there are no precise solution techniques. (8)

Update anomaly: The unintentional updating of data in a table, resulting from data redundancy. (9)

URL (Uniform Resource Locator): The address that defines the path to a facility or file on the Web. (12)

User view: The set of data that a particular user needs to achieve his or her assigned tasks. (9)

V

Valid vendor file: A file containing vendor mailing information. (5)

Validation controls: Controls intended to detect errors in transaction data before the data are processed. (16)

Value-added banks (VAB): Banks that can accept electronic disbursements and remittance advices from its clients in any format. (12)

Value-added network (VAN): Network that provides service by managing the distribution of the messages between trading partners. (12)

Vendor-supported systems: Custom systems that organizations purchase from commercial vendors. (1)

Virtual table: A table derived from the base tables that is a partial representation of the actual physical base tables. (9)

Virus: Program that attaches itself to a legitimate program to penetrate the operating system. (15)

Voucher register: A register reflecting a firm's accounts payable liability. (5)

W

Walkthrough: Analysis of system design to ensure the design is free from conceptual errors that could become programmed into the final system. (14)

Wide area network: Network that exceeds the geographic limitations of a local area network. (12)

Work order: Document that draws from bills of materials and route sheets to specify the materials and production for each batch. (7)

Worm: Software program that "burrows" into the computer's memory and replicates itself into areas of idle memory. (15)

INDEX

A

Access control list, defined, 758

Access controls: audit procedures for testing, 869; in CBIS environment, 765–69; in computer-based systems, 209, 753, 816–17; in conversion cycle, 351; defined, 150, 765; direct access, 255; in ERP system, 570; in expenditure cycle, 255, 303; in GL/FRS, 406; indirect access, 255; in microcomputer-based systems, 212; in revenue cycle, 190

Access method, defined, 79, 458

Access tests, defined, 881

Access time, 98

Access token, defined, 758

Accountants: and conceptual systems design, 677–78; data normalization and, 481–82; distributed databases and, 488–89; documentation for, 723–24; fraud and, 124–37; as system auditors, 39–40; as system designers, 38; and system implementation, 727; and systems development life cycle, 646, 665, 670; and systems evaluation and selection, 704; as users, 37–38

Accounting: changes in, due to world-class environment, 365–73; responsibility, 427–30

Accounting function, 22–23

Accounting independence, 23

Accounting information, changing role of, 10–11

Accounting information systems (AIS): and data collection, 13–14; and data processing, 14; and data sources, 13–14; database management, 14–16; defined, 2; and end users, 13;

and feedback, 16–17; general model for, 12–17; and information environment, 4–18; and information generation, 16; objectives of, 17; subsystems of, 9–10, 11–12; and world-class manufacturing environment, 365–73

Accounting records, 52–62; and the audit trail, 59–60; in computer-based systems, 210, 752; in conversion cycle, 352; defined, 149; documents, 52–53; in ERP system, 570; in expenditure cycle, 255, 303; in GL/FRS, 406; journals, 53–56; ledgers, 56–59; in manual systems, 52–59; in microcomputer-based systems, 212; in revenue cycle, 189–90

Accounts payable department, expenditure cycle activities, 247–48, 250, 297

Accounts payable pending file, defined, 241

Accounts receivable, defined, 178

Accounts receivable department, revenue cycle activities, 178, 179, 186

Accounts receivable subsidiary ledger, defined, 178

Accuracy, defined, 137

Activities, defined, 368

Activity-based costing (ABC), defined, 368

Activity management, 369–73

Actual cost inventory ledgers, defined, 246

Ad hoc reports, defined, 426

Agents, defined, 34, 515

AICPA/CICA SysTrust, 626

AICPA/CICA WebTrust, 626

Alphabetic codes, 398–99; defined, 398

Alphanumeric codes, defined, 398

American National Standards Institute (ANSI), defined, 598

Analytical review, defined, 572

Anomalies, defined, 477

Application controls, defined, 146; input controls in CBIS environment, 822–35; output controls in CBIS environment, 838–43; processing controls in CBIS environment, 836–38

Application development software, defined, 457

Application layer, defined, 610

Application-level firewalls, defined, 625, 806

Archive file, defined, 61

Assets: acquisition of, 308, 311–12; disposal of, 311, 314; fixed, 307; inspection of, 254–55; maintenance of, 308–10, 314; misappropriation of, 132–37; theft of, 255

Association: defined, 463; many-to-many, 464; one-to-many, 464; one-to-one, 464

Assurance, electronic commerce and, 625–26

Assurance services: attest services versus, 854–60; defined, 39, 854

Attendance file, defined, 305

Attest function, defined, 39

Attest services, defined, 854; versus assurance services, 854–60

Attributes, defined, 463, 533

Audit objectives, defined, 858

Audit objects, and procedures based on management assertions, illustrated, 859

Audit opinion, defined, 858

Audit planning, defined, 859

Audit procedures: audit objectives and, based on management assertions, illustrated, 859; defined, 858